Objective Questions in
PHYSICS
for JEE Main and Advanced

Pratyush Kumar Singh
B.Tech. (Civil Engineering)

Universities Press

OBJECTIVE QUESTIONS IN
PHYSICS FOR JEE MAIN AND ADVANCED

UNIVERSITIES PRESS (INDIA) PRIVATE LIMITED

Registered office
3-6-747/1/A & 3-6-754/1, Himayatnagar, Hyderabad 500 029, Telangana, India
info@universitiespress.com; www.universitiespress.com

Distributed by
Orient Blackswan Private Limited

Registered office
3-6-752 Himayatnagar, Hyderabad 500 029, Telangana, India

Other offices
Bengaluru / Chennai / Guwahati / Hyderabad / Kolkata
Mumbai / New Delhi / Noida / Patna / Visakhapatnam

ISBN: 978-93-89211-85-6

501766

Typeset in Times Ten LT Std 10/12 *by*
SRS Publishing Services, Puducherry

Printed in India by
Navya Printers, Hyderabad 500 013

Published by
Universities Press (India) Private Limited
3-6-747/1/A & 3-6-754/1, Himayatnagar, Hyderabad 500 029, Telangana, India

Preface

The aim of this book is to give students *intensive* as well as *extensive* practice on every topic covered in the JEE syllabus. The questions have been arranged in order of increasing difficulty.

The number of questions in each chapter has been very rigorously determined such that they are *necessary* and *sufficient.* These problems will help students in testing their comprehension of each topic in depth, and also impart breadth to their numerical problem-solving skills. In preparing this book, I have relied heavily on questions asked in the JEE (Main and Advanced) examinations in the past four decades.

Every chapter begins with a list of key concepts, to give the students perspective and act as a guidepost for the chapter. The key concepts are a summary of the important principles and the key equations in that chapter.

Many students experience difficulty when it comes to solving numerical problems. The only way to overcome this is by having a very clear understanding of the associated concepts. I, therefore, strongly urge the students to read the key concepts before solving the questions.

To get the most out of this book, students should attempt all the questions, without skipping any. Every question tests a different aspect of the topic. Care has been taken so as to not repeat any type of question.

I have taken immense efforts to make the subject as interesting as possible, while also ensuring that students are adequately prepared for their exams. This book is the result of my several decades of experience of classroom teaching. I wish all my readers success in their endeavours.

Pratyush Kumar Singh

Acknowledgements

I would like to thank the reviewers of this text, whose detailed line-by-line comments were of fundamental help to me in preparing this book. It is always a joy and a privilege to express gratitude to my family, my teachers and my students for their support during the writing of this book.

I express my deep gratitude to my student, Srikant Singh, for the assistance and attention that he rendered during the computerisation of this book.

I have spent a lot of time and effort in creating the best problem book I could write, and I hope it will help students learn and improve their problem-solving skills. In turn, please help me by letting me know what still needs to be improved.

I welcome communication from students and teachers, especially concerning any errors or deficiencies that you may find in this book. Please feel free to contact me at pratyushkr123@gmail.com.

Pratyush Kumar Singh

Contents

Part IV: Optics and Modern Physics

Truth Alone Triumphs
—Mundaka Upanishad

To
The Almighty
and
My Parents,
Smt. Sharmishtha Sinha
Dr Shashi Kr. Singh

PART I

MECHANICS

CHAPTER

1

Physical Quantities and Measurement

- **The Physical World:** Physics deals with the study of nature. The laws of nature are universal. There are four fundamental forces: gravitational force, electromagnetic force, strong nuclear force and weak nuclear force. Every microscopic as well as macroscopic phenomenon observed in nature is controlled by these four fundamental forces.
- **Units and Dimensions:** Physics is a quantitative science based on the measurement of physical quantities. Seven physical quantities have been chosen as fundamental or base quantities: mass, length, time, electric current, temperature, amount of substance and luminous intensity. The corresponding basic units for measuring these base quantities are kilogram (kg), metre (m), second (s), ampere (A), Kelvin (K), mole (mol) and candela (cd). The units for measuring other physical quantities can be expressed as a combination of the basic units, and these are called derived units. The set of basic units and derived units is collectively called the system of units.

  The dimensions of a physical quantity are the powers to which the base quantities are raised to represent that quantity. Dimensional analysis can be used to check the consistency of equations. A dimensionally consistent equation need not be a correct equation, but a dimensionally inconsistent equation is an incorrect equation.
- **Errors in Measurement:** The smallest quantity that can be measured by an instrument is called its least count. The maximum possible error in the measurement of a physical quantity is equal to the least count of the measuring instrument. If the measured value of a physical quantity is A and the least count of the measuring instrument is ΔA, the value of that quantity is expressed as $A \pm \Delta A$.
  - **Relative Error:** The quantity ΔA is called the absolute error, and the quantity $\frac{\Delta A}{A}$ is called the relative error. Relative errors are always multiplied by 100 and expressed in per cent. Relative errors are the true indicators of the accuracy of a measurement. Smaller relative error means greater accuracy. This can be achieved by measuring large values of any quantity (A), and using instruments with smaller least count (ΔA).
  - **Rules for Calculating Errors:**

    1. If a quantity Z is defined as $Z = kA$, where k is some constant, then the absolute error in the value of Z is
    $$\Delta(kA) = k\Delta A \quad \text{[Constant Rule]}$$
    2. If a quantity Z is defined as $Z = A + B$, then the absolute error in the value of Z is
    $$\Delta(A+B) = \Delta A + \Delta B \quad \text{[Sum Rule]}$$
    3. If a quantity Z is defined as $Z = AB$, then the absolute error in the value of Z is
    $$\Delta(AB) = B\Delta A + A\Delta B \quad \text{[Product Rule]}$$

    If a quantity Z is defined as $Z = A^n$ (n is a rational number), then the absolute error in the value of Z is
    $$\Delta\left(A^n\right) = nA^{n-1}\Delta A$$
    and the relative error in the value of Z is
    $$\frac{\Delta\left(A^n\right)}{A^n} = n\frac{\Delta A}{A}$$
    Using the above rules, we can show that if a quantity Z is defined as $Z = kA^p B^q$, where k is some constant, then the absolute error in the value of Z is

$$\Delta Z = k\Delta\left(A^p B^q\right) = k\left[B^q \Delta\left(A^p\right) + A^p \Delta\left(B^q\right)\right]$$
$$= k\left[B^q p A^{p-1}\Delta(A) + A^p q B^{q-1}\Delta(B)\right]$$

and the relative error in the value of Z is

$$\frac{\Delta Z}{Z} = p\frac{\Delta A}{A} + q\frac{\Delta B}{B}$$

To find the maximum value of the error, you must ensure that all terms have positive values.

- **Vernier Callipers:** It is a length measuring instrument invented by Pierre Vernier. With the Vernier callipers ordinarily available in laboratories, we can measure lengths from 0.01 cm. It consists of a main scale along which an auxiliary scale slides, called the Vernier scale.
  - **Least Count:** If n Vernier scale divisions (VSD) coincide with $n-1$ main scale divisions (MSD), then
  $$1\text{ VSD} = \left(\frac{n-1}{n}\right)\text{MSD}$$
  In the case of Vernier callipers, its least count is given by
  $$1\text{ MSD} - 1\text{ VSD} = \left(\frac{1}{n}\right)\text{MSD}$$
  - **Total Reading:** If N is the main scale division on the left of the zero on the Vernier scale, and n is the Vernier scale division which just coincides with any of the main scale divisions, then
  $$\text{Observed Reading} = N + n \times \text{Least Count}$$
  - **Zero Error:** If the zeros of the Vernier and the main scale do not coincide when the two jaws touch each other, then the instrument has an error called the zero error. The zero error is positive if the Vernier scale zero lies to the right of the main scale zero when the two jaws are in contact. The zero error is negative if the Vernier scale zero lies to the left of the main scale zero when the two jaws are in contact. To obtain the final reading, the zero error must be subtracted from the observed reading:
  $$\text{Final Reading} = \text{Observed Reading} - \text{Zero Error}$$
- **Screw Gauge:** This is another length measuring instrument. With the screw gauge, we can measure lengths from 0.001 cm. It consists of a threaded screw which can move forward or back as it is rotated in a closely fitted nut. Divisions are marked on a circular cap attached to one end of the screw, and it is called the circular scale. A line drawn along the axis of the screw, called the reference line, is also marked with divisions, and it is called the linear scale or the main scale. The linear distance moved by the screw as it rotates can be measured on the linear scale.
  - **Least Count:** The linear distance moved by the screw when it is given one complete rotation is called the pitch of the screw. In the case of a screw gauge, its least count is given by
  $$\text{Least Count} = \frac{\text{Pitch}}{\text{Number of Circular Scale Divisions}}$$
  - **Total Reading:** If N is the linear scale division on the left of the circular cap, and n is the circular scale division which just coincides with the linear scale axis, then
  $$\text{Observed Reading} = N + n \times \text{Least Count}$$
  - **Zero Error:** When the screw face touches the fixed face, the circular cap edge must coincide with the zero of the linear scale, and the zero of the circular scale must coincide with the reference line. Otherwise, the instrument has an error called the zero error. In such a situation, we have a positive zero error if the circular scale zero stays behind the reference line, and a negative zero error if the circular scale zero advances beyond the reference line. To obtain the final reading, the zero error must be subtracted from the observed reading:
  $$\text{Final Reading} = \text{Observed Reading} - \text{Zero Error}$$

  Due to wear and tear, the screw and the nut can become loose. In such cases, if the screw is rotated in one direction and then rotated back, the screw may not move appreciably along the axis. The error arising due to this is called backlash error. To reduce this, the screw must be rotated in the same direction for a particular set of observations.

EXERCISES

1. A new unit of length is chosen such that the speed of light in vacuum is unity. If light takes 8 min and 20 s to cover the distance between the Sun and the Earth, then in terms of the new units, this distance is:

(a) 5 units (b) 50 units
(c) 500 units (d) 5000 units

2. In a particular system, the units of mass, length and time are chosen to be 10 g, 10 cm and 0.1 s, respectively. Then the unit of force in Newton will be:

(a) 0.1 N (b) 1 N
(c) 10 N (d) 100 N

3. If velocity (v), acceleration (a) and force (F) were chosen as base quantities, the dimension of energy would be:

(a) $\left[v^{-1}a^{2}F^{1}\right]$ (b) $\left[v^{-1}a^{-1}F^{2}\right]$
(c) $\left[v^{2}a^{-1}F^{1}\right]$ (d) $\left[v^{2}a^{-1}F^{-1}\right]$

4. A calorie is a unit of heat (energy in transit) and equals about 4.2 J, where $1\text{ J} = 1\text{ kg m}^2\text{ s}^{-2}$. Suppose we employ a system of units in which the unit of mass equals α kg, the unit of length equals β m and the unit of time equals γ s, then the value of calorie in the new system of units is:

(a) $4.2\,\alpha^{1}\beta^{2}\gamma^{-2}$ (b) $4.2\,\alpha^{-2}\beta^{-1}\gamma^{1}$
(c) $4.2\,\alpha^{2}\beta^{-1}\gamma^{-1}$ (d) $4.2\,\alpha^{-1}\beta^{-2}\gamma^{2}$

5. If 1 min is the unit of time, 0.1 kg is the unit of mass and 0.1 m/s^2 is the unit of acceleration, then the unit of work in Joules will be:

(a) 0.036 J (b) 0.36 J
(c) 3.6 J (d) 36 J

6. If the force F acting on a particle is given as $F = A\sin(Bt) + C\cos(Dx)$, where x and t, respectively, represent position and time, and A, B, C and D are constants, then the quantity $\dfrac{A^2B}{CD}$ has the dimension:

(a) $\left[M^{-1}L^{-2}T^{2}\right]$ (b) $\left[M^{1}L^{2}T^{-3}\right]$
(c) $\left[M^{1}L^{-1}T^{-2}\right]$ (d) $\left[M^{-2}L^{1}T^{-1}\right]$

7. If position x of a moving particle is given as $x = \dfrac{A}{B}e^{-At}$, where t represents time and A, B are constants, then the quantity $\dfrac{A^3}{B}$ has the dimension:

(a) $\left[L^{-1}T^{1}\right]$ (b) $\left[L^{1}T^{-2}\right]$
(c) $\left[L^{-2}T^{2}\right]$ (d) $\left[L^{2}T^{-2}\right]$

8. A physical quantity P is related to four other physical quantities a, b, c, d as $P = \dfrac{\pi a^3 b^2}{c\sqrt{d}}$. The percentage errors in the measurement of a, b, c, d are 1%, 1%, 1%, 2%, respectively. The maximum percentage error in the value of P is:

(a) 7% (b) 5%
(c) 3% (d) 2%

9. The measures of length and breadth of a rectangle are $a = (30 \pm 2\%)$ cm and $b = (20 \pm 1\%)$ cm. The maximum relative error in the perimeter is:

(a) 3% (b) 2%
(c) 1.6% (d) 1%

10. A solid metal object hung from a spring balance weighs $m_1 = (5 \pm 0.01)$ kg. When the object is immersed in water, it weighs $m_2 = (4 \pm 0.01)$ kg. The relative density of the metal is calculated using the formula $d = \dfrac{m_1}{m_1 - m_2}$. Then the value of d is:

(a) 5 ± 0.02 (b) 5 ± 0.06
(c) 5 ± 0.11 (d) 5 ± 0.22

11. The main scale attached to a microscope has 20 equal divisions in 1 cm. The Vernier scale has 50 divisions and they coincide with 49 divisions of the main scale. The least count of the microscope is:

(a) 0.1 cm (b) 0.01 cm
(c) 0.001 cm (d) 0.0001 cm

12. A screw gauge that advances by 1 mm for 2 complete rotations has 50 divisions on the circular scale. When the screw face is in contact with the fixed face, the circular scale advances beyond the reference line by 3 divisions. When the diameter of a spherical metal ball is measured, the reading on the linear scale is 2.4 mm and that on the circular scale is 30. The diameter of the ball is:

(a) 2.67 mm (b) 2.73 mm
(c) 2.64 mm (d) 2.76 mm

13. The diameter of a spherical metal ball is measured with a screw gauge whose pitch is 1 mm and there are 100 divisions on the circular scale. The reading on the linear scale is 2.4 mm and that on the circular scale is 30. If the measured mass of the ball has a relative error of 1%, then the relative error in the density of the metal ball is:

(a) 2.1% (b) 1.8%
(c) 1.2% (d) 0.8%

14. The length of a simple pendulum is measured with a metre scale of least count 1 mm, and the value is 20.0 cm. The time for 100 oscillations is measured by a stop-watch of least count 1 s, and the value is 90.0 s. The acceleration due to Earth's gravity (g) can be calculated using the formula $g = \frac{4\pi^2 L}{T^2}$, where L and T, respectively, are the length and the time period of the simple pendulum. The relative error in the value of g is:

(a) 1.24% (b) 1.84%
(c) 2.32% (d) 2.72%

15. When two resistances R_1, R_1 are connected in parallel, the equivalent resistance R of the combination is given by $\frac{1}{R} = \frac{1}{R_1} + \frac{1}{R_2}$. If $R_1 = (100 \pm 2)\ \Omega$ and $R_2 = (200 \pm 3)\ \Omega$, then the value of R is:

(a) $(66.7 \pm 1.2)\ \Omega$ (b) $(66.7 \pm 1.5)\ \Omega$
(c) $(66.7 \pm 1.8)\ \Omega$ (d) $(66.7 \pm 2.0)\ \Omega$

16. When two resistances R_1, R_1 are connected in series, the equivalent resistance R of the combination is given by $R = R_1 + R_2$. When current I flows through resistance R, the electrical power (SI unit is watts, denoted by W) required is given by $P = I^2 R$. If $R_1 = (100 \pm 2)$, $R_2 = (400 \pm 3)$ and $I = (1.00 \pm 0.01)\,\text{mA}$, then the percentage error in the calculation of P is:

(a) $(500 \pm 30)\,\mu\text{W}$ (b) $(500 \pm 25)\,\mu\text{W}$
(c) $(500 \pm 20)\,\mu\text{W}$ (d) $(500 \pm 15)\,\mu\text{W}$

ANSWER KEYS

1. (c)	**2.** (a)	**3.** (c)	**4.** (d)	**5.** (c)	**6.** (b)	**7.** (b)	**8.** (a)	**9.** (c)	**10.** (c)
11. (c)	**12.** (b)	**13.** (a)	**14.** (d)	**15.** (a)	**16.** (d)				

SOLUTIONS

1. (c) The speed of light is $v = 1$ length/s and the time taken by light to travel from the Sun to the Earth is $t = 500$ s.

Hence, the distance between the Sun and the Earth is given by

$$s = vt = (1\ \text{length/s})(500\ \text{s}) = 500\ \text{lengths}$$

2. (a) In the new system of units, we have

$$1\ \text{mass} = 10\ \text{g} \Rightarrow 1\ \text{g} = 0.1\ \text{mass}$$
$$1\ \text{length} = 10\ \text{cm} \Rightarrow 1\ \text{cm} = 0.1\ \text{length}$$
$$1\ \text{time} = 0.1\ \text{s} \Rightarrow 1\text{s} = 10\ \text{time}$$

Now, we have

$$1\ \text{N} = 1\ \text{kg ms}^{-2}$$
$$\Rightarrow \quad 1\ \text{N} = \frac{(1000\ \text{g})(100\ \text{cm})}{(1\ \text{s})^2}$$
$$\Rightarrow \quad 1\ \text{N} = \frac{(1000 \times 0.1\ \text{mass})(100 \times 0.1\ \text{length})}{(10\ \text{time})^2} = 10\ \text{force}$$
$$\Rightarrow \quad 1\ \text{force} = 0.1\ \text{N}$$

3. (c) The dimensions of velocity, acceleration and force in terms of mass, length and time are

$$[v] = [LT^{-1}],\ [a] = [LT^{-2}] \text{ and } [F] = [MLT^{-2}].$$

From the above equations, we have

$$[M] = \left[\frac{F}{a}\right], [L] = \left[\frac{v^2}{a}\right] \text{ and } [T] = \left[\frac{V}{a}\right]$$

Thus, the dimension of energy is

$$[E] = [ML^2T^{-2}] = \left[\left(\frac{F}{a}\right)\left(\frac{v^2}{a}\right)^2\left(\frac{v}{a}\right)^{-2}\right] = [v^2 a^{-1} F^1]$$

4. (d) In the new system of units, we have

$$1\ \text{mass} = \alpha\ \text{kg} \Rightarrow 1\ \text{kg} = \alpha^{-1}\ \text{mass}$$
$$1\ \text{length} = \beta\ \text{m} \Rightarrow 1\ \text{m} = \beta^{-1}\ \text{length}$$
$$1\ \text{time} = \gamma\text{s} \Rightarrow 1\ \text{s} = \gamma^{-1}\ \text{time}$$

Now, we have

$$1\ \text{calorie} = 4.2\ \text{kg m}^2\ \text{s}^{-2}$$
$$\Rightarrow 1\ \text{calorie} = 4.2\,(\alpha^{-1}\ \text{mass})(\beta^{-1}\ \text{length})^2(\gamma^{-1}\ \text{time})^{-2}$$
$$\Rightarrow 1\ \text{calorie} = 4.2\alpha^{-1}\ \beta^{-2}\gamma^2\ \text{energy}$$

5. (c) In the new system of units, we have

$$1 \text{ time} = 1 \text{ min} = 60 \text{ s} \Rightarrow 1 \text{ s} = \frac{1}{60}\text{time}$$

$$1 \text{ mass} = 0.1 \text{ kg} \Rightarrow 1 \text{ kg} = 10 \text{ mass}$$

$$1 \text{ acceleration} = 0.1 \text{ ms}^{-2} \Rightarrow 1 \text{ m} = 10 \text{ acceleration} \cdot \text{s}^2$$

$$\Rightarrow \quad 1 \text{ m} = \frac{10}{3600} \text{acceleration} \cdot \text{time}^2$$

Now, we have

$$1 \text{ Joule} = 1 \text{ kg m}^2 \text{ s}^{-2}$$

$$\Rightarrow \quad 1 \text{ Joule} = 1 \text{ kg m}^2\text{s}^{-2} = (10 \text{ mass})$$

$$\left(\frac{10}{3600}\text{acceleration} \cdot \text{time}^2\right)^2 \left(\frac{1}{60}\text{time}\right)^{-2}$$

$$\Rightarrow \quad 1 \text{ Joule} = \frac{10}{36} \text{energy}$$

$$\Rightarrow \quad 1 \text{ energy} = 3.6 \text{ J}$$

6. (b) The arguments of the sine and cosine functions must be dimensionless. Therefore, we have

$$[B] = [T^{-1}] \text{ and } [D] = [L^{-1}]$$

The quantities A and C must have the dimension of force. That is

$$[A] = [mlt^{-2}] = [C]$$

Hence, we have

$$\left[\frac{A^2B}{CD}\right] = \left[\frac{(MLT^{-2})^2(T^{-1})}{(MLT^{-2})(L^{-1})}\right] = [M^1L^2T^{-3}]$$

7. (b) The argument of the exponential function must be dimensionless, and $\frac{A}{B}$ must have the dimension of length. Thus, we have

$$[A] = [T^{-1}] \text{ and } \left[\frac{A}{B}\right] = [L^1]$$

$$\Rightarrow \quad [B] = [L^{-1}A] = [L^{-1}T^{-1}]$$

Hence, we have

$$\left[\frac{A^3}{B}\right] = \left[\frac{T^{-3}}{L^{-1}T^{-1}}\right] = [L^1T^{-2}]$$

8. (a) We have $P = \pi a^{3b2}c^{-1}d^{-1/2}$. Hence, the maximum relative error in P is given by

$$\frac{\Delta P}{P} = 3\frac{\Delta a}{a} + 2\frac{\Delta b}{b} + \frac{\Delta c}{c} + \frac{1}{2}\frac{\Delta d}{d}$$

$$\Rightarrow \quad \frac{\Delta P}{P} = 3(1\%) + 2(1\%) + (1\%) + \frac{1}{2}(2\%) = 7\%$$

9. (c) The perimeter p of the rectangle is given by $p = 2\,(a + b) = 2(30 \text{ cm} + 20 \text{ cm}) = 100 \text{ cm}$.

The maximum absolute error in p is

$$\Delta p = 2\,(\Delta a + \Delta b) = 2\,[2\%\,(30 \text{ cm}) + 1\,\%\,(20 \text{ cm})] = 1.6 \text{ cm}.$$

Hence, the maximum relative error in p is

$$\frac{\Delta p}{p} = \frac{1.6 \text{ cm}}{100 \text{ cm}} = 1.6\%$$

10. (d) The relative density of the metal is

$$d = \frac{m_1}{m_1 - m_2} = \frac{5 \text{ kg}}{5 \text{ kg} - 4 \text{ kg}} = 5$$

To calculate the maximum relative error, let us write d as $d = m_1{}_{(m1-m2)}{}^{-1}$. Now, using the rules for calculating errors, we have

$$\frac{\Delta d}{d} = \frac{\Delta m_1}{m_1} + \frac{\Delta(m_1 - m_2)}{m_1 - m_2} \quad \text{[Using product rule]}$$

$$\Rightarrow \quad \frac{\Delta d}{d} = \frac{\Delta m_1}{m_1} + \frac{\Delta m_1 + \Delta m_2}{m_1 - m_2} \quad \text{[Using sum rule]}$$

$$\Rightarrow \quad \frac{\Delta d}{d} = \frac{0.01}{5} + \frac{0.01 + 0.01}{5 - 4} = \frac{11}{500} = 0.22$$

11. (c) We have

$$1 \text{ MSD} = \frac{1 \text{ cm}}{20} = 0.05 \text{ cm and}$$

$$59 \text{ VSD} = 49 \text{ MSD} \Rightarrow 1 \text{ VSD} = \frac{49}{50}\text{MSD}$$

Hence, the least count of the microscope is

$$\text{LC} = 1 \text{ MSD} - \frac{49}{50}\text{MSD} = \frac{1}{50}\text{MSD}$$

$$= \frac{1}{50}(0.05 \text{ cm}) = 0.001 \text{ cm}$$

12. (b) The pitch is

$$p = \frac{1 \text{ mm}}{2 \text{ rotations}} = 0.5 \text{ mm/rotation}$$

The least count of the screw gauge is

$$\text{LC} = \frac{\text{Pitch}}{\text{Divisions on the circular scale}}$$

$$= \frac{0.5 \text{ mm}}{50 \text{ div}} = 0.01 \text{ mm}$$

The main scale reading is $N = 2.4$ mm, and the circular scale reading is $n = 30$. Then, we have

$$\text{Observed Reading} = N + n \times \text{LC}$$
$$= 2.4 \text{ mm} + 30\ (0.01 \text{ mm})$$
$$= 2.7 \text{ mm}.$$

However, the instrument has a negative zero error of 3 least counts, that is

$$\text{Zero Error} = -3 \times 0.01 \text{ mm} = -0.03 \text{ mm}.$$

The correct reading is obtained by subtracting the zero error from the observed reading.

$$\text{Correct Reading} = 2.7\text{ mm} - (-0.03\text{ mm}) = 2.73\text{ mm.}$$

13. (a) The least count is

$$LC = \frac{1\text{ mm}}{100} = 0.01\text{ mm}$$

The main scale reading is N = 2.4 mm, and the circular scale reading is n = 30. The observed reading is

$$\text{Observed Reading} = N + n \times LC = 2.4\text{ mm} + 30\ (0.01\text{ mm}) = 2.7\text{ mm.}$$

Thus, the diameter of the ball is $d = (2.7 \pm 0.01)$ mm.

The density of the metal ball is given by

$$\rho = \frac{m}{\frac{1}{6}\pi d^3} = \frac{6}{\pi} m d^{-3}$$

Hence, the maximum relative error in ρ is

$$\frac{\Delta\rho}{\rho} = \frac{\Delta m}{m} + 3\frac{\Delta d}{d}$$

$$\Rightarrow \frac{\Delta\rho}{\rho} = 1\% + 3(\frac{0.01}{27}) = 1\% + \frac{10}{9}\% = 2.1\%$$

14. (d) The length of the pendulum is given as $L = 20.0$ cm, with an absolute error of $\Delta L = 1$ mm = 0.01 cm. For 100 oscillations, the measured time is $T = (90.0 \pm 1)$ s. The time period of oscillation is given by

$$T = \frac{T}{100} = \frac{90.0\text{ s}}{100} = 0.90$$

The absolute error in the value of T is

$$\Delta T = \frac{\Delta T}{100} = \frac{1\text{ s}}{100} = 0.01\text{ s}$$

Writing the formula for acceleration due to gravity as $g = 4\pi^2 L T^{-2}$, the maximum relative error in g is

$$\frac{\Delta g}{g} = \frac{\Delta L}{L} + 2\frac{\Delta T}{T}$$

$$\Rightarrow \frac{\Delta g}{g} = \frac{0.1}{20} + 2\left(\frac{0.01}{0.90}\right) = \left(\frac{1}{2} + \frac{20}{9}\right)\% = 2.72\%$$

15. (a) The equivalent resistance of the parallel combination is

$$\frac{1}{R} = \frac{1}{R_1} + \frac{1}{R_2}$$

$$\Rightarrow \frac{1}{R} = \frac{1}{100\ \Omega} + \frac{1}{200\ \Omega} = \frac{3}{200\ \Omega}$$

$$\Rightarrow R = \frac{200}{3}\Omega$$

To calculate the error, let us write R as

$$R^{-1} = R_1^{-1} + R_2^{-1}$$

Now using rules for calculating errors, we have

$$\Delta\left(R^{-1}\right) = \Delta\left(R_1^{-1}\right) + \Delta\left(R_2^{-1}\right)$$

$$\Rightarrow -R^{-2}\Delta R = -R_1^{-2}\Delta R_1 + -R_2^{-2}\Delta R_2$$

$$\Rightarrow \frac{\Delta R}{R^2} = \frac{\Delta R_1}{R_1^2} + \frac{\Delta R_2}{R_2^2}$$

$$\Rightarrow \Delta R = \left[\frac{\Delta R_1}{R_1^2} + \frac{\Delta R_2}{R_2^2}\right] R^2$$

Thus, the maximum error is

$$\Delta R = \left[\frac{2}{100^2} + \frac{3}{200^2}\right]\left(\frac{200}{3}\right)^2 \Omega = \frac{11}{9}\Omega = 1.2\ \Omega$$

Hence, $R = (66.7 \pm 1.2)\ \Omega$.

16. (d) The value of electrical power is

$$P = I^2 R = I^2 (R_1 + R_2)$$

$$\Rightarrow P = (1\ mA)^2 (100\ \Omega + 400\ \Omega) = 500\ \mu W$$

Now, using rules for calculating errors, we have

$$\frac{\Delta P}{P} = 2\frac{\Delta I}{I} + \frac{\Delta R}{R}$$

$$\Rightarrow \frac{\Delta P}{P} = 2\frac{\Delta I}{I} + \frac{\Delta(R_1 + R_2)}{R_1 + R_2}$$

$$\Rightarrow \frac{\Delta P}{P} = 2\frac{\Delta I}{I} + \frac{\Delta(R_1) + \Delta(R_2)}{R_1 + R_2}$$

Thus, the maximum error is

$$\frac{\Delta P}{P} = 2\left(\frac{0.01}{1}\right) + \frac{2+3}{100+400}$$

$$\Rightarrow \frac{\Delta P}{P} = \frac{2}{100} + \frac{1}{100} = 3\%$$

The error in the value of P is

$$\Delta P = 3\% P = \frac{3}{100}(500\ \mu W) = 15\ \mu W$$

Hence, $P = (500 \pm 15)\ \mu W$.

CHAPTER

2 Kinematics

- **Straight Line Motion**

Average and instantaneous velocity:

$$v_{av} = \frac{x_2 - x_1}{t_2 - t_1} = \frac{\Delta x}{\Delta t} \text{ and } v = \lim_{\Delta t \to 0} \frac{\Delta x}{\Delta t} = \frac{dx}{dt}$$

Average and instantaneous acceleration:

$$a_{av} = \frac{v_2 - v_1}{t_2 - t_1} = \frac{\Delta v}{\Delta t} \text{ and } a = \lim_{\Delta t \to 0} \frac{\Delta v}{\Delta t} = \frac{dv}{dt} \text{ or } v\frac{dv}{dx}$$

The displacement Δx and distance Δs within a given time interval can be found if velocity v is known as a function of time:

$$\Delta x = \int_{t_1}^{t_2} v\,dt \text{ and } \Delta s = \int_{t_1}^{t_2} |v|\,dt$$

If velocity v_0 and position x_0 are known at any one time, say at time $t = 0$, then velocity v and position x at any later time t can be found if acceleration a is known as a function of time:

$$v = v_0 + \int_0^t a\,dt \text{ and } x = x_0 + \int_0^t v\,dt$$

Straight line motion with constant acceleration:

$$v = v_0 + at,\ x = x_0 + v_0 t + \frac{1}{2}at^2,\ v^2 = v_0^2 + 2a(x - x_0) \text{ and } x = x_0 + \left(\frac{v + v_0}{2}\right)t$$

- **Motion in Three Dimensions**

Average and instantaneous velocity:

$$\mathbf{v}_{av} = \frac{\mathbf{r}_2 - \mathbf{r}_1}{t_2 - t_1} = \frac{\Delta \mathbf{r}}{\Delta t} \text{ and } \mathbf{v} = \lim_{\Delta t \to 0} \frac{\Delta \mathbf{r}}{\Delta t} = \frac{d\mathbf{r}}{dt}$$

Average and instantaneous acceleration:

$$\mathbf{a}_{av} = \lim_{\Delta t \to 0} \frac{\mathbf{v}_2 - \mathbf{v}_1}{t_2 - t_1} = \frac{d\mathbf{v}}{dt} \text{ and } \mathbf{a} = \lim_{\Delta t \to 0} \frac{\Delta \mathbf{v}}{\Delta t} = \frac{d\mathbf{v}}{dt}$$

Displacement and change in velocity within a given time interval:

$$\mathbf{r}_2 - \mathbf{r}_1 = \int_{t_1}^{t_2} \mathbf{v}(t)\,dt \text{ and } \mathbf{v}_2 - \mathbf{v}_1 = \int_{t_1}^{t_2} \mathbf{a}(t)\,dt$$

- **Projectile Motion**

Acceleration: $a_x = 0, a_y = -g$

Velocity: $v_x = v_0 \cos\theta_0,\ v_y = v_0 \sin\theta_0 - gt$

Position: $x = (v_0 \cos\theta_0)t,\ y = (v_0 \sin\theta_0)t - \frac{1}{2}gt^2$

Time of flight, maximum height and range: $T = \dfrac{2v_0 \sin\theta_0}{g}$, $H = \dfrac{(v_0 \sin\theta_0)^2}{2g}$, $R = \dfrac{v_0^2 \sin(2\theta_0)}{g}$

Trajectory: $y = x\tan\theta_0 - \dfrac{g}{2v_0^2 \cos^2\theta_0}x^2$ or $y = x\tan\theta_0\left(1 - \dfrac{x}{R}\right)$

The acceleration of a particle is expressed as components parallel and perpendicular to the direction of the instantaneous velocity vector. These components are called the tangential (a_t) and normal (a_n) components, respectively:

$$a_t = \frac{dv}{dt} \text{ and } a_n = \frac{v^2}{r},$$

where v is the instantaneous speed and r is the radius of curvature of the trajectory.

- **Rotation of a Body about a Fixed Axis**

Average and instantaneous angular velocity:

$$\omega_{av} = \frac{\theta_2 - \theta_1}{t_2 - t_1} = \frac{\Delta\theta}{\Delta t} \text{ and } \omega = \lim_{\Delta t \to 0} \frac{\Delta\theta}{\Delta t} = \frac{d\theta}{dt}$$

Average and instantaneous acceleration:

$$\alpha_{av} = \frac{\omega_2 - \omega_1}{t_2 - t_1} = \frac{\Delta\omega}{\Delta t} \text{ and } \alpha = \lim_{\Delta t \to 0} \frac{\Delta\omega}{\Delta t} = \frac{d\omega}{dt}$$

If angular velocity ω_0 and angular position x_0 are known at any one time, say at time $t = 0$, then angular velocity ω and angular position θ at any later time t can be found if acceleration α is known as a function of time:

$$\omega = \omega_0 + \int_0^t \alpha\, dt \text{ and } \theta = \theta_0 + \int_0^t \omega\, dt$$

Rotational motion with constant angular acceleration:

$$\omega = \omega_0 + at,\ \theta = \theta_0 + v_0 t + \frac{1}{2}\alpha t^2,\ \omega^2 = \omega_0^2 + 2\alpha(\theta - \theta_0) \text{ and } \theta = \theta_0 + \left(\frac{\omega + \omega_0}{2}\right)t$$

The relation between the linear and angular quantities of a particle moving with angular speed ω and angular acceleration α in a circular path of radius r:

$$v = \omega r,\ a_t = \alpha r \text{ and } a_n = \omega^2 \alpha r$$

As seen from a reference frame S, if the velocities of particles A and B are $\mathbf{v}_{AS}$ and $\mathbf{v}_{BS}$, respectively, then the velocity of B relative to A is given by

$$\mathbf{v}_{BA} = \mathbf{v}_{BS} - \mathbf{v}_{AS}$$

The same result holds true for relative acceleration.

EXERCISES

1. The position $x(m)$ of a particle moving in a straight line as a function of time $t(s)$ is given as $x = t(1-t)$. The distance and displacement in the first two seconds are, respectively:
(a) 2.5 m, – 2.0 m (b) 2.0 m, – 2.0 m
(c) 2.5 m, 2.5 m (d) 2.0 m, 2.0 m

2. A body moving with uniform acceleration covers 200 m in the first 2 s and 220 m in the next 4 s. The velocity of the body at the end of the seventh second is:
(a) 5 m/s (b) 10 m/s
(c) 15 m/s (d) 20 m/s

3. A particle moving along the x-axis has velocity v_0 at the origin. Thereafter, it moves with deceleration of magnitude proportional to $\sqrt{v}$ (v is its instantaneous speed), and then eventually comes to rest after moving a certain distance. Its average velocity over this distance is:
(a) $v_0/3$ (b) $v_0/4$
(c) $2v_0/3$ (d) $3v_0/4$

4. The figure shows the graph of the square of speed (v^2) versus position (x) of a particle moving in a straight line.

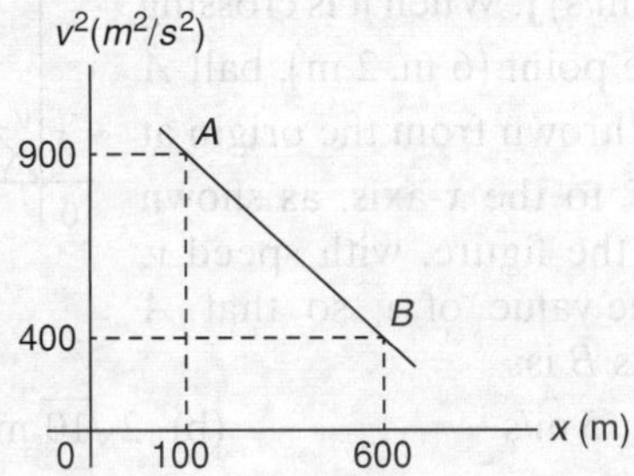

If the motion is in one direction, then the displacement in the last two seconds before arriving at B is:
(a) 41 m (b) 40 m
(c) 39 m (d) 38 m

5. A particle starts moving in a straight line with uniform acceleration. After time t_0, the acceleration changes sign, remaining the same in magnitude. The time from the beginning of motion in which the particle returns to the initial position is:
(a) $2t_0$ (b) $\left(2+\sqrt{2}\right)t_0$
(c) $2\sqrt{2}t_0$ (d) $\left(2+\sqrt{3}\right)t_0$

6. The figure shows the position (x) versus time (t) graph for two particles A and B moving along the same straight line.

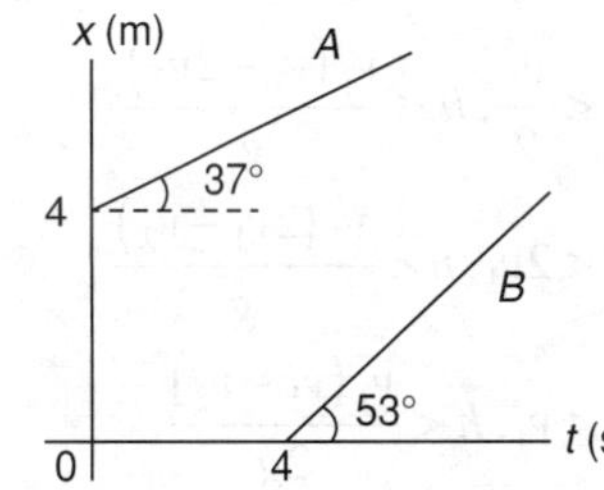

The time after which B catches up with A is:
(a) 8 s (b) 12 s
(c) 16 s (d) 20 s

7. The velocity $v(m/s)$ of a particle moving in a straight line as a function of time $t(s)$ is given by $v = |t-2|-1$. The distance travelled by the particle in the time interval $t = 0$ s to $t = 4$ s is:
(a) 0 (b) 1 m
(c) 2 m (d) 4 m

8. The figure shows the velocity (v) versus position (x) graph of a particle moving in a straight line. From a point P, a line PQ is drawn perpendicular to the x-axis and a line PR is drawn normal to the curve.

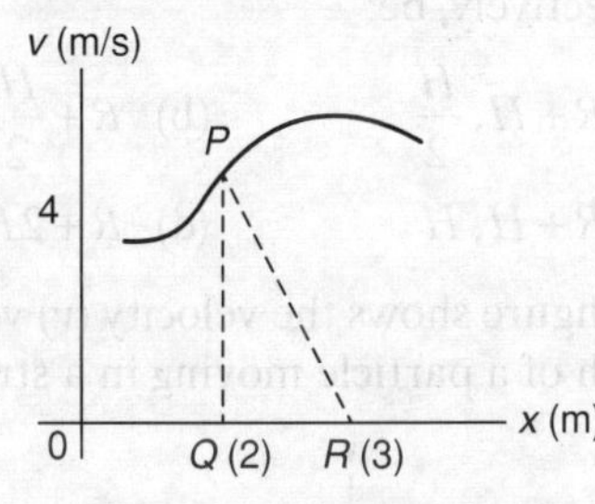

The instantaneous acceleration of the particle at P is:
(a) 3 m/s^2 (b) 2.5 m/s^2
(c) 2 m/s^2 (d) 1 m/s^2

9. A person measures the depth of a well by measuring the time interval between dropping a stone and receiving the sound of impact with the bottom of the well. The acceleration due to gravity is 10 m/s^2 and the velocity of sound is 300 m/s. The depth of the well is calculated as $h = 20$ m. If the error in the measurement of time is 0.01 s, the fractional error $\Delta h/h$ is:
(a) 0.2% (b) 1%
(c) 2% (d) 2.5%

10. Two balls are simultaneously thrown in the vertically upward direction. Ball A is thrown from the ground with speed v_1 and ball B is thrown from a height h vertically above A with speed v_2. The condition for a mid-air collision is:

(a) $v_2 < v_1, h < \dfrac{2v_1(v_1 - v_2)}{g}$

(b) $v_2 < \dfrac{v_1}{2}, h < \dfrac{v_1(v_1 - 2v_2)}{g}$

(c) $v_2 < 2v_1, h < \dfrac{v_1(2v_1 - v_2)}{g}$

(d) $v_2 < v_1, h < \dfrac{v_1(v_1 - v_2)}{2g}$

11. A car is travelling on a straight road. The car can attain a maximum speed of 24 m/s. The maximum acceleration and deceleration it can attain are $1\ m/s^2$ and $4\dfrac{m}{s^2}$, respectively. The shortest time (to the nearest integer) that the car takes to travel a distance of 320 m from rest to rest is:

(a) 32 s (b) 30 s
(c) 28 s (d) 26 s

12. The horizontal range and maximum height attained by a projectile are R and H, respectively. If a constant horizontal acceleration $a = g/4$ is imparted to the projectile due to wind, then its horizontal range and maximum height will, respectively, be:

(a) $R + H, \dfrac{H}{2}$ (b) $R + \dfrac{H}{2}, H$

(c) $R + H, H$ (d) $R + 2H, H$

13. The figure shows the velocity (v) versus position (x) graph of a particle moving in a straight line.

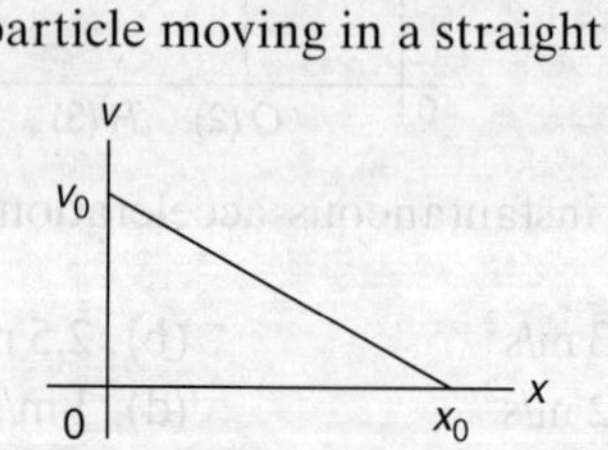

The most appropriate acceleration (a) versus position (x) graph is:

(a)
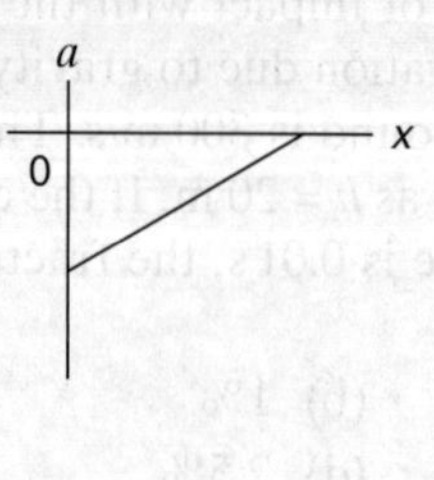

(b)
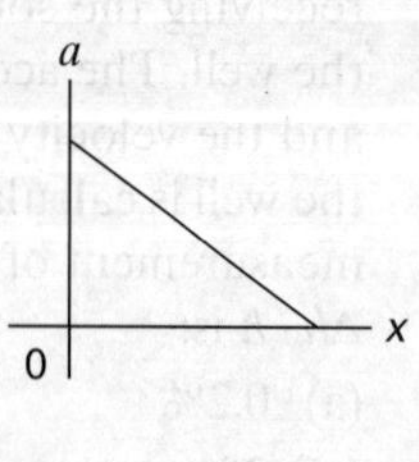

(c)
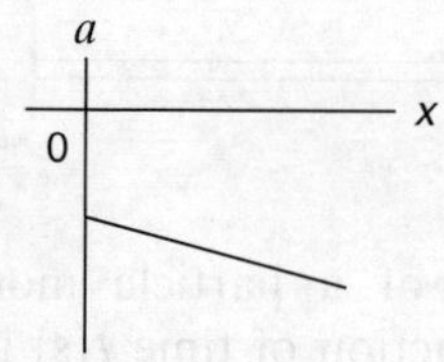

(d)
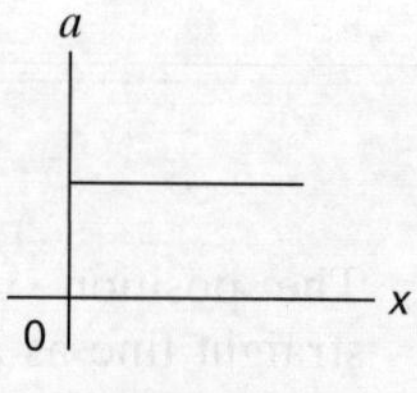

14. A long railroad car is moving along a horizontal road with constant acceleration a. A boy standing on the car throws a ball vertically upward with velocity 9.8 m/s. If the ball lands on the car at a distance of 2 m from the boy, then the value of a is (take $g = 9.8\ m/s^2$):

(a) $1.2\ m/s^2$ (b) $1.0\ m/s^2$
(c) $0.8\ m/s^2$ (d) $0.5\ m/s^2$

15. Two projectiles are thrown simultaneously from two different points. The projectile thrown from the origin has initial velocity $(3\ m/s)\mathbf{i} + (3\ m/s)\mathbf{j}$. The other projectile is thrown from the point (10 m, 2 m) with initial velocity $a\mathbf{i} + b\mathbf{j}$. If the projectiles collide after 2 s, then:

(a) $a = 2$ m/s, $b = -1$ m/s
(b) $a = -1$ m/s, $b = 1$ m/s
(c) $a = -2$ m/s, $b = 1$ m/s
(d) $a = -2$ m/s, $b = 2$ m/s

16. Ball B is moving in the xy plane with uniform velocity $(3\ m/s)\mathbf{j}$. When it is crossing the point (6 m, 2 m), ball A is thrown from the origin at 53° to the x-axis, as shown in the figure, with speed v. The value of v so that A hits B is:

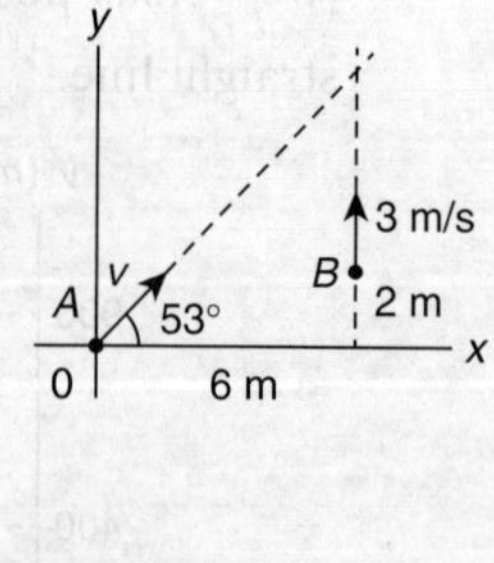

(a) 5 m/s (b) $2\sqrt{10}$ m/s
(c) 6 m/s (d) $6\sqrt{2}$ m/s

17. Consider two vertical poles of heights ηh and h, with a horizontal spacing of $2h$. Balls A and B are projected simultaneously from the top of these vertical poles with the same speed, as shown in the figure.

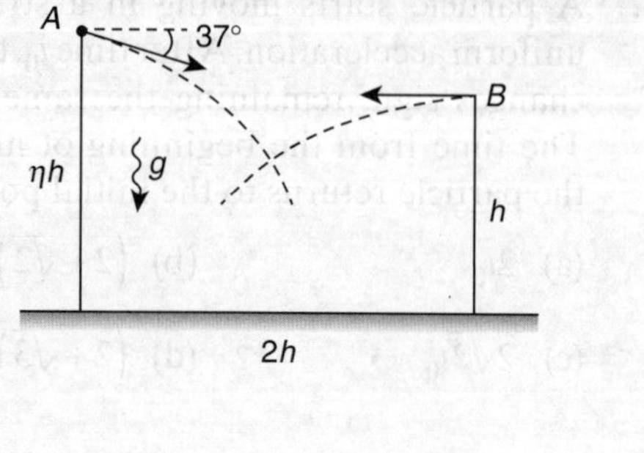

The value of η so that the balls collide is:

(a) $4/3$ (b) $3/2$
(c) $5/3$ (d) 2

18. A particle moves in the xy plane along the path $y = x^2$, with constant acceleration 0.5 m/s^2 directed along the positive y-axis. The velocity of the particle at the origin is:

(a) 0.5 m/s (b) 0.25 m/s
(c) 0.1 m/s (d) 0

19. A balloon rises from the Earth's surface with a constant ascension rate of 2 m/s. Due to wind, the balloon gathers a horizontal velocity component $v_x = 2y$, where y is the height of ascent. The balloon's horizontal drift (x) and tangential acceleration (a_t) as functions of y are:

(a) $x = 2y^2, a_t = \dfrac{2y}{\sqrt{1+y^2}}$

(b) $x = \dfrac{1}{2}y^2, a_t = \dfrac{4y}{\sqrt{1+y^2}}$

(c) $x = \dfrac{1}{2}y^2, a_t = \dfrac{2\sqrt{1+y^2}}{y}$

(d) $x = 2y^2, a_t = \dfrac{4\sqrt{1+y^2}}{y}$

20. A ball is thrown from the ground to clear a wall 3 m high at a distance of 6 m from the point of projection. The ball falls at a distance of 18 m away from the wall. The angle of projection of the ball is:

(a) $\tan^{-1}\left(\dfrac{1}{2}\right)$ (b) $\tan^{-1}\left(\dfrac{2}{3}\right)$

(c) $\tan^{-1}\left(\dfrac{3}{2}\right)$ (d) $\tan^{-1}\left(\dfrac{3}{4}\right)$

21. A particle is projected from the bottom of an inclined plane of inclination 37° with speed 16 m/s at angle 60° with the horizontal. At a point where its velocity is parallel to the inclined plane, the radius of curvature of the trajectory is (take $g = 10 \text{ m/s}^2$):

(a) $20\sqrt{2}$ m (b) $10\sqrt{5}$ m
(c) 15 m (d) 12.5 m

22. Two particles are projected horizontally in opposite directions from the edge of a cliff, with speeds $10\sqrt{2}$ m/s and $20\sqrt{2}$ m/s. The time after which their velocities are mutually perpendicular is (take $g = 10 \text{ m/s}^2$):

(a) 2 s (b) $\sqrt{3}$ s
(c) $\sqrt{2}$ s (d) 1 s

23. The figure shows four points A, B, C, D on the path of a projectile. The lines AD and BC are horizontal and the vertical distance between these lines is h.

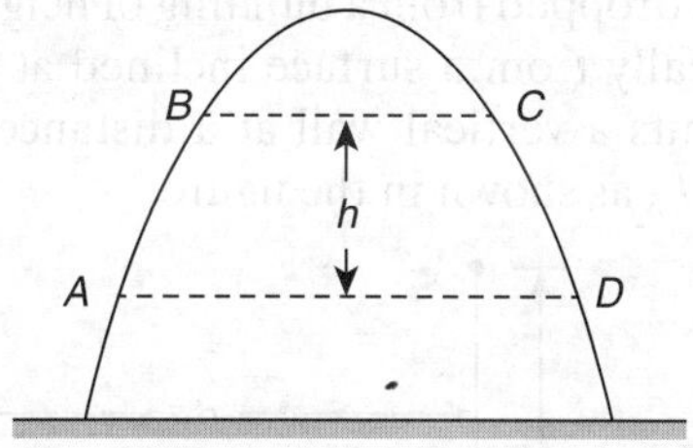

If T_1 is the time taken by the projectile in moving from A to D and T_2 is the time taken by the projectile in moving from B to C, then the acceleration g due to Earth's gravity equals:

(a) $g = \dfrac{8h}{T_1^2 + T_2^2}$ (b) $g = \dfrac{4h}{(T_1 - T_2)^2}$

(c) $g = \dfrac{8h}{T_1^2 - T_2^2}$ (d) $g = \dfrac{4h}{(T_1 + T_2)^2}$

24. If the maximum height attained by a projectile is altered by 5% by changing the angle of projection, the time of flight changes by:

(a) 2.5% (b) 5%
(c) 7.5% (d) 10%

25. Two bodies are projected with the same initial velocities but different angles of projection over the same range R. The product of the times of flight taken by the two bodies is proportional to:

(a) R^{-1} (b) $R^{1/2}$
(c) R (d) R^2

26. A particle projected from A at angle α to the horizontal lands at B. Let P be any point on its trajectory. If lines PA and PB make angles θ_1 and θ_2 with the horizontal, then $\tan\theta_1 + \tan\theta_2$ equals:

(a) $2\tan\alpha$ (b) $\tan\alpha$
(c) $\tan(\alpha/2)$ (d) $\tan(2\alpha)$

27. An elevator ascends from the ground at uniform speed. After time $t_1 = 4$ s, a person inside the elevator drops a ball through a hole in the elevator's floor. The ball falls with uniform acceleration $g = 10 \text{ m/s}^2$ and strikes the floor $t_2 = 4$ s later. The height of the elevator at time t_1 is:

(a) 40 m (b) 50 m
(c) 60 m (d) 80 m

28. One second from its launch, a projectile is moving at 45° to the horizontal, and one second later, it is moving horizontally. Its projection speed is (take $g = 10 \text{ m/s}^2$):

(a) $10\sqrt{2}$ m/s (b) $10\sqrt{3}$ m/s
(c) $5\sqrt{10}$ m/s (d) $10\sqrt{5}$ m/s

29. A ball dropped from a building of height h bounces elastically from a surface inclined at angle α and then hits a vertical wall at a distance d from the point P, as shown in the figure.

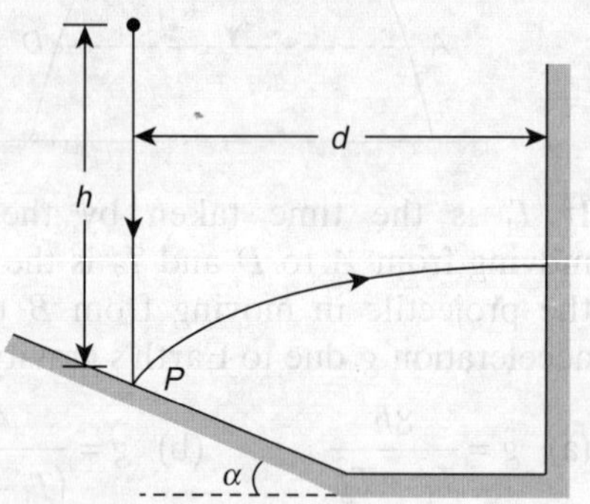

If the velocity of the ball when it hits the wall is horizontal, then:

(a) $\alpha = \frac{1}{4}\sin^{-1}\left(\frac{d}{h}\right)$ (b) $\alpha = \frac{1}{2}\sin^{-1}\left(\frac{d}{h}\right)$
(c) $\alpha = \frac{1}{2}\sin^{-1}\left(\frac{2d}{h}\right)$ (d) $\alpha = \frac{1}{2}\sin^{-1}\left(\frac{4d}{h}\right)$

30. A projectile is projected horizontally with speed u from the top of a plane inclined at angle $\theta = 53°$ to the horizontal. The projectile strikes the plane at a distance $d = 9$ m from the point of projection. The value of u is (take $g = 10 \text{ m/s}^2$):

(a) 3 m/s (b) 3.5 m/s
(c) 4.5 m/s (d) 5 m/s

31. A projectile is projected with speed $u = 15$ m/s and projection angle $\alpha = 60°$ from the bottom of a plane inclined at angle $\theta = 30°$ to the horizontal. Measured from the point of projection, the projectile strikes the plane at a distance d equal to (take $g = 10 \text{ m/s}^2$):

(a) 9 m (b) 10 m
(c) 12 m (d) 15 m

32. A man crosses a river in a boat. If he crosses the river in minimum time, he takes 10 min with a drift of 120 m. If he crosses the river taking the shortest path, he takes 12.5 min. The width of the river is:

(a) 215 m (b) 200 m
(c) 150 m (d) 100 m

33. A gun mounted on a trolley can fire shells at any desired angle with respect to the horizontal. When the trolley is at rest, the gun can fire to a maximum horizontal range of 40 m. When the trolley is moving at a speed of 20 m/s along a horizontal surface, the maximum horizontal range is (take $g = 10 \text{ m/s}^2$):

(a) $40\left(\sqrt{2}+1\right)$m (b) $60\sqrt{3}$ m
(c) 80 m (d) $80\sqrt{2}$ m

34. When a man moves at a speed of 5 m/s along a horizontal plane, he finds the rain falling vertically. When he moves at the same speed in the opposite direction, he finds the rain falling at 45° with the horizontal. The speed of the rain is:

(a) 5 m/s (b) $5\sqrt{5}$ m/s
(c) $5\sqrt{3}$ m/s (d) $5\sqrt{2}$ m/s

35. When a man moves at a speed of 5 m/s down an inclined plane which makes angle of 37° with the horizontal, he finds the rain falling vertically downward. When he moves up the same inclined plane at the same speed, he finds the rain makes angle $\theta = \tan^{-1}(7/8)$ with the horizontal. The speed of rain is:

(a) 5 m/s (b) $4\sqrt{2}$ m/s
(c) $4\sqrt{3}$ m/s (d) $2\sqrt{5}$ m/s

36. A rocket in free space is moving in a straight path with acceleration 2 m/s^2. Two men inside the rocket simultaneously throw a ball towards each other with velocities 0.3 m/s and 0.2 m/s relative to the rocket. If the distance between the two men is 4 m, the balls will collide after time:

(a) 10 s (b) 8 s
(c) 5 s (d) 1 s

37. Two persons A and B start running towards each other with constant velocities v_1 and v_2 from points P and Q, respectively. After crossing each other, A takes time t_1 to reach Q and B takes time t_2 to reach P. Then the ratio v_1/v_2 equals:

(a) $\frac{t_2}{t_1}$ (b) $\frac{t_2^2}{t_1^2}$
(c) $\sqrt{\frac{t_2}{t_1}}$ (d) $\frac{t_1 t_2}{t_1^2+t_2^2}$

38. Two particles A and B are approaching each other with constant velocities at angle 30°, as shown in the figure. Particle A is moving at speed $100\sqrt{3}$ m/s. The velocity of B as seen from A is perpendicular to the velocity of A.

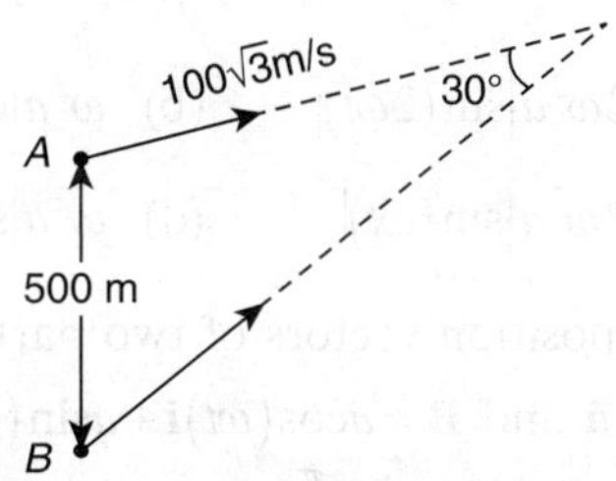

If the distance between them is 500 m, they will collide after:

(a) 5 s (b) 10 s
(c) 15 s (d) 20 s

39. From the edge of a high cliff, ball A is dropped at $t = 0$. Later, at $t = 1$ s, another ball B is thrown upward with velocity 10 m/s. The time when the distance between the balls is 15 m is (take $g = 10\text{ m/s}^2$):

(a) $t = 1.2$ s (b) $t = 1.5$ s
(c) $t = 1.8$ s (d) $t = 2.0$ s

40. Two cars A and B are travelling along a straight road in the same direction with velocities 20 km/h and 40 km/h, respectively; car A is ahead of car B. If the length of each car is 5 m, then the minimum length of the road required for car B to overtake car A is:

(a) 15 m (b) 20 m
(c) 25 m (d) 30 m

41. The ends of a rigid rod slide along mutually perpendicular rails, as shown in the figure. At some instant, the velocity of end A is u and the rod makes angle θ with the horizontal.

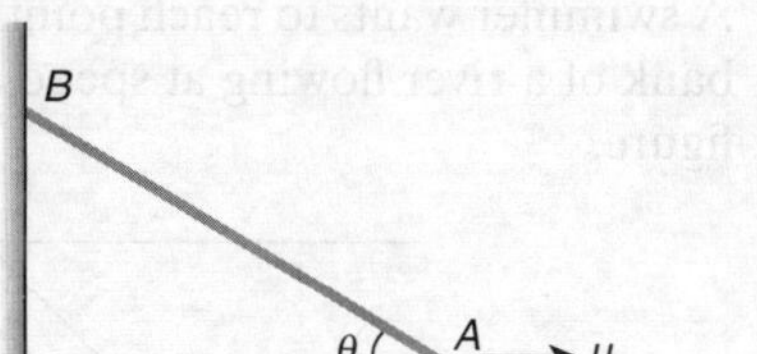

The velocity of end B and the angular velocity of the rod at this instant are, respectively:

(a) $u(1+\cot\theta), \dfrac{u}{l(1+\cot\theta)}$ (b) $u\sec\theta, \dfrac{u\sin\theta}{l}$

(c) $u\cot\theta, \dfrac{u}{l\sin\theta}$ (d) $u\tan\theta, \dfrac{u}{l(1+\tan\theta)}$

42. A rigid body starts rotating from rest at $t = 0$ with constant angular acceleration α. If θ_n denotes the angular displacement of the body in the nth second, the correct statements among the following are:

(a) $\theta_n = \left(n + \dfrac{1}{2}\right)\alpha$ (b) $\theta_3 < \theta_1 + \theta_2$
(c) $\theta_3 = \theta_1 + \theta_2$ (d) $\theta_1 : \theta_2 : \theta_3 = 1:3:5$

43. A radar observes an airplane moving horizontally with velocity v at height h above the ground, as shown in the figure.

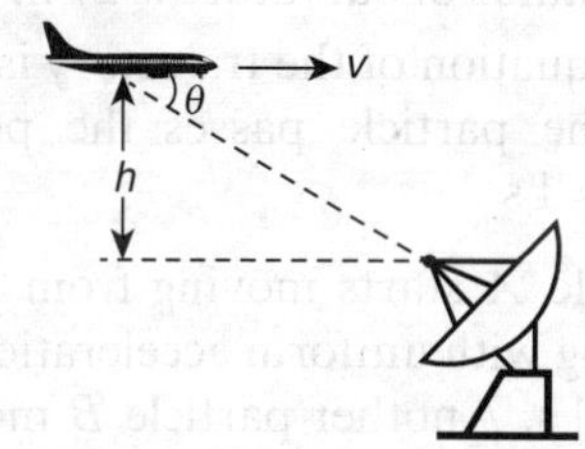

The ratio of angular acceleration to angular velocity of the airplane with respect to the radar is:

(a) $\dfrac{v}{h}\sin^2\theta$ (b) $\dfrac{v}{h}\sin(2\theta)$

(c) $\dfrac{v}{h}\cos^2\theta$ (d) $\dfrac{v}{h}\cos(2\theta)$

44. If the angular position θ of a particle moving in a circular path is related to time t as $2\theta^2 - 3\theta = t$, then the relation between its angular velocity ω and its angular acceleration α is:

(a) $\alpha = 4\omega^{-2}$ (b) $\alpha = -3\omega^2$
(c) $\alpha = 3\omega^{-1}$ (d) $\alpha = -4\omega^3$

45. A particle is moving at uniform speed v in a circular path of radus r. The magnitude of its average acceleration as it moves over one quarter of the circular path is:

(a) $\dfrac{v^2}{\sqrt{2}r}$ (b) $\dfrac{2\sqrt{2}v^2}{\pi r}$

(c) $\dfrac{\sqrt{2}v^2}{r}$ (d) $\dfrac{\sqrt{2}v^2}{\pi r}$

46. A particle is moving in the xy plane along the circular path $x^2 + y^2 = 1$ m, at continuously increasing speed in the anti-clockwise sense. At point $P\left(\dfrac{4}{5}\text{m}, \dfrac{3}{5}\text{m}\right)$, the particle is moving at speed 2 m/s. Let $\mathbf{a}_P$ denote the acceleration vector of the particle at point P. If $|\mathbf{a}_P| = 5\text{ m/s}^2$, then $\mathbf{a}_P$ equals:

(a) $(-5\text{ m/s}^2)\mathbf{i}$

(b) $(-4\text{ m/s}^2)\mathbf{i} + (3\text{ m/s}^2)\mathbf{j}$

(c) $(-\sqrt{5}\text{ m/s}^2)\mathbf{i} + (2\sqrt{5}\text{ m/s}^2)\mathbf{j}$

(d) $(-1\text{ m/s}^2)\mathbf{i} + (2\sqrt{6}\text{ m/s}^2)\mathbf{j}$

47. A particle is moving in the xy plane with acceleration $\mathbf{a} = (1\ \text{m/s}^2)\mathbf{i}$. At $t = 0$, the particle is at the origin and its velocity is $\mathbf{u} = (1\ \text{m/s})\mathbf{j}$. Choose the correct statements from the following:
(a) Tangential acceleration equals normal acceleration at $t = 1$ s
(b) Radius of curvature is 27 m at $t = 2\sqrt{2}$ s
(c) Equation of the trajectory is $y = 2x^2$
(d) The particle passes the point $(2\ \text{m}, 1\ \text{m})$ at $t = 1$ s

48. Particle A starts moving from $x = 0$ at $t = 0$ and, moving with uniform acceleration, reaches $x = 1$ m at $t = 1$ s. Another particle B moves with uniform velocity from $x = 1$ m at $t = 0$ and reaches $x = 2$ m at $t = 1$ s. From a reference frame attached to A, the distance covered by B in this time interval is:
(a) 2 m (b) 1.5 m
(c) 1 m (d) 0.5 m

49. Two projectiles are thrown simultaneously from two different points. The projectile thrown from the origin has initial velocity $(\sqrt{2}\ \text{m/s})\mathbf{i} + (\sqrt{2}\ \text{m/s})\mathbf{j}$. The other projectile is thrown from the point $(60\ \text{m}, 0\ \text{m})$ with initial velocity $(-7\sqrt{2}\ \text{m/s})\mathbf{i} + (7\sqrt{2}\ \text{m/s})\mathbf{j}$. The minimum separation between the projectiles is:
(a) 42 m (b) 36 m
(c) 32 m (d) 24 m

50. Particles A and B move in opposite directions around a circle, with uniform angular speed ω, as shown in the figure. At $t = 0$, both particles are at $\mathbf{r} = a\mathbf{j}$, where a is the radius of the circle.

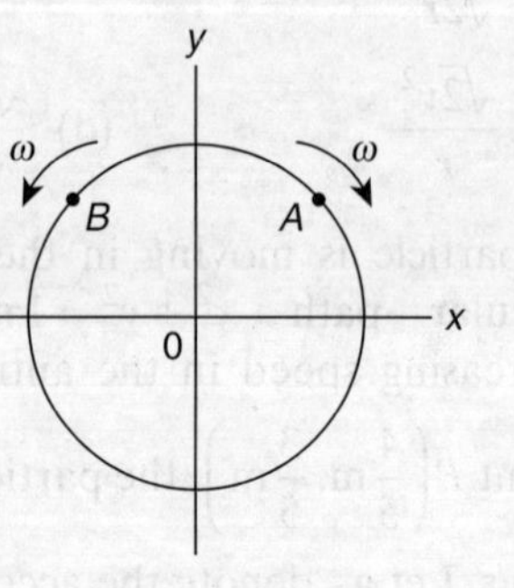

The magnitude of their relative acceleration as a function of time t is:
(a) $2\omega^2 a|\sin(2\omega t)|$ (b) $\omega^2 a|\cos(\omega t)|$
(c) $2\omega^2 a|\sin(\omega t)|$ (d) $\omega^2 a|\sin(2\omega t)|$

51. The position vectors of two particles are given by $\mathbf{A} = a\mathbf{i}$ and $\mathbf{B} = a\cos(\omega t)\mathbf{i} + a\sin(\omega t)\mathbf{j}$, where a is a constant and $\omega = \frac{\pi}{6}$ rad/s. If $|\mathbf{A}+\mathbf{B}| = \sqrt{3}|\mathbf{A}-\mathbf{B}|$ for the first time at $t = \tau$, then the value of τ is:
(a) 0.5 s (b) 1.0 s
(c) 1.5 s (d) 2.0 s

52. Two balls A and B are simultaneously thrown in the vertically upward direction from the edge of a 240-m-high cliff, with velocities 10 m/s and $40\ \frac{\text{m}}{\text{s}}$, respectively. The most appropriate graph representing the separation (s) between the balls versus time (t) is:

(a)
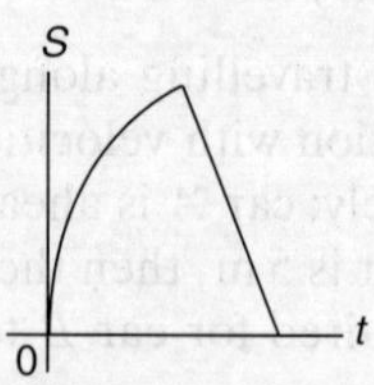

(b)
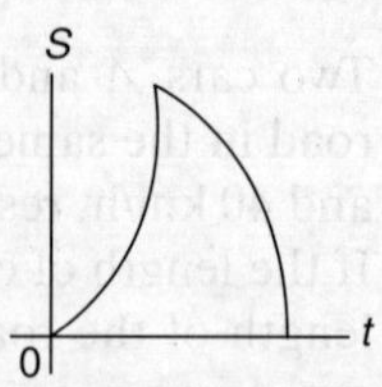

(c)
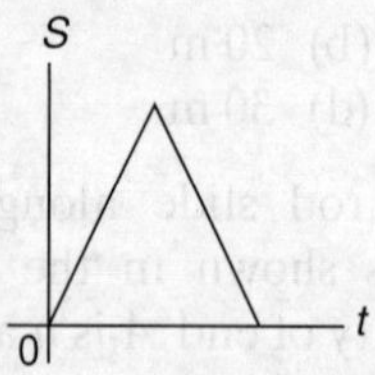

(d)
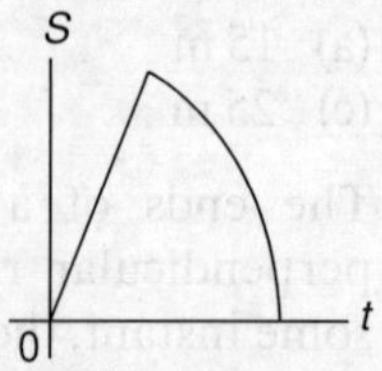

53. A swimmer wants to reach point B on the opposite bank of a river flowing at speed u, as shown in the figure.

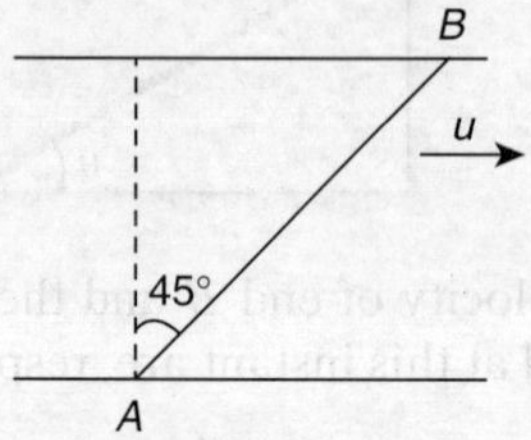

The minimum speed relative to the river that the swimmer should have is:
(a) $\sqrt{2}u$ (b) $u/\sqrt{2}$
(c) $2u$ (d) $u/2$

ANSWER KEYS

1. (a)	**2.** (b)	**3.** (a)	**4.** (a)	**5.** (b)	**6.** (c)	**7.** (c)	**8.** (d)	**9.** (b)	**10.** (a)
11. (c)	**12.** (c)	**13.** (a)	**14.** (b)	**15.** (d)	**16.** (a)	**17.** (c)	**18.** (a)	**19.** (b)	**20.** (b)
21. (d)	**22.** (a)	**23.** (c)	**24.** (a)	**25.** (c)	**26.** (b)	**27.** (a)	**28.** (d)	**29.** (a)	**30.** (c)
31. (d)	**32.** (b)	**33.** (b)	**34.** (b)	**35.** (b)	**36.** (b)	**37.** (c)	**38.** (a)	**39.** (b)	**40.** (c)
41. (c)	**42.** (d)	**43.** (b)	**44.** (d)	**45.** (b)	**46.** (a)	**47.** (a),(b)	**48.** (d)	**49.** (b)	**40.** (c)
51. (d)	**52.** (d)	**53.** (b)							

SOLUTIONS

1. (a) The displacement of the particle is

$$\Delta x = x(2) - x(0) = -2 \text{ m}$$

The velocity of the particle is given by the function $v = 1 - 2t$. The distance travelled by the particle is

$$s = \int_0^2 |v|\,dt = \int_0^{1/2} (1-2t)dt + \int_{1/2}^{2} (2t-1)dt$$

$$= |t - t^2|_0^{1/2} + |t^2 - t|_{1/2}^{2} = 2.5 \text{ m}$$

2. (b) The motion is depicted in the figure below.

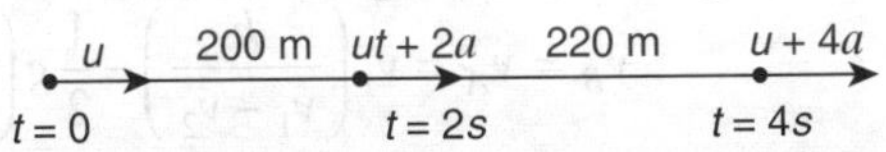

Let u be the initial velocity and a be the acceleration. Then, we have

$$\left(\frac{2u+2a}{2}\right)2 = 200 \Rightarrow u + a = 100 \quad \ldots(1)$$

$$\left(\frac{2u+8a}{2}\right)4 = 200 \Rightarrow u + 4a = 55 \quad \ldots(2)$$

Solving gives $u = 115$ m/s and $a = -15$ m/s^2.
Hence, the velocity at the end of 7 s equals $u + 7a$ = 10 m/s.

3. (a) If we take dv/dt for acceleration, then we have

$$\frac{dv}{dt} = -k\sqrt{v}, \text{ where } k \text{ is some positive constant.}$$

$$\Rightarrow \int \frac{dv}{\sqrt{v}} = -k\int dt$$

$$\Rightarrow 2\sqrt{v} = -kt + 2\sqrt{v_0} \quad [\text{Given } v = v_0 \text{ at } t = 0]$$

Hence, v becomes zero after time $t = \frac{2\sqrt{v_o}}{k}$.

If we take $v\,dv/dx$ for acceleration, then we have

$$v\frac{dv}{dx} = -k\sqrt{v}$$

$$\Rightarrow \int \sqrt{v}dv = -k\int dx$$

$$\Rightarrow \frac{2}{3}v^{3/2} = -kx + \frac{2}{3}v_0^{3/2} \quad [\text{Given } v = v_0 \text{ at } x = 0]$$

Hence, v becomes zero after displacement

$$x = \frac{2v_0^{3/2}}{k}.$$

Now $v_{av} = \frac{x}{t} = \frac{v_0}{3}$.

4. (a) The equation representing the given line is

$$\frac{v^2 - 900}{x - 100} = \frac{400 - 900}{600 - 100}$$

$$\Rightarrow v^2 - 900 = -(x - 100)$$

$$\Rightarrow v^2 = 1000 - x$$

The equation represents uniform acceleration. Comparing with equation $v^2 = u^2 + 2ax$, we have

$$2a = -1 \text{ m/s}^2 \Rightarrow a = -0.5 \text{ m/s}^2$$

Velocity of the particle at position B is $\sqrt{400 \text{ m}^2/\text{s}^2} = 20$ m/s. Two seconds before reaching B, the velocity is 20 m/s + (0.5 m/s^2)(2 s) = 21 m/s.
Hence, displacement in the last 2 s is

$$v_{av}\,t = \left(\frac{20 \text{ m/s} + 21 \text{ m/s}}{2}\right)(2 \text{ s}) = 41 \text{ m}$$

5. (b) Let a be the magnitude of the acceleration. Between the time $t = 0$ and $t = t_0$, the particle will have moved a distance of $\frac{1}{2}at_0^2$. Now, the acceleration reverses its magnitude, still being a. The particle's speed will now start decreasing. Since the magnitude of the deceleration is the same, the particle speed will reduce to zero after travelling the same distance $\frac{1}{2}at_0^2$ and it will take the same amount of time t_0.

At this moment, the particle is at a distance $s = at_0^2$ from its initial point and has already moved for time $2t_0$. Now, it will start moving back towards its initial point with acceleration a. The time t required to cover this distance is given by

$$at_0^2 = \frac{1}{2}at^2 \left[s = ut + \frac{1}{2}at^2, u = 0 \text{ and } s = at_0^2 \right]$$

$$\Rightarrow \quad t = \sqrt{2}t_0$$

Hence, the total time of motion equals $2t_0 + \sqrt{2}t_0$.

6. (c) For particle A

$$x = 4 + \frac{3}{4}t, t \geq 0$$

For particle B

$$x = \frac{4}{3}(t-4), t \geq 4$$

Solving the two equations simultaneously

$$4 + \frac{3}{4}t = \frac{4}{3}(t-4) \text{ gives } t = 16 \text{ s}$$

7. (c) The v–t graph for the given function is shown below.

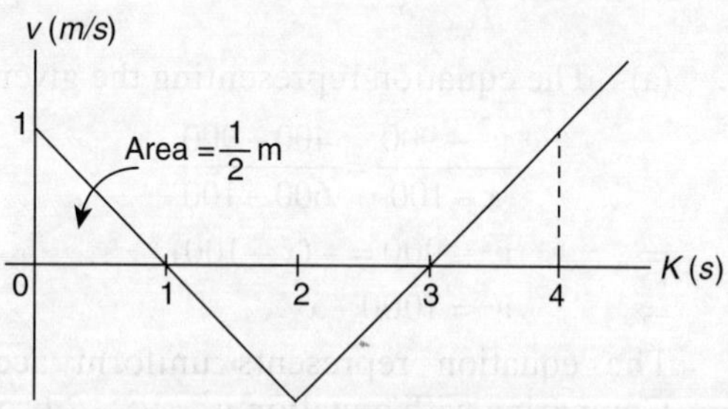

The distance travelled in 4 s equals $4 \times \frac{1}{2}\text{m} = 2$ m

Alternatively

$$S = \int_0^4 |v|\, dt$$

$$= \int_0^1 (1-t)dt + \int_1^2 (t-1)dt + \int_2^3 (3-t)dt + \int_3^4 (t-3)dt$$

8. (d) Instantaneous acceleration equals $v\frac{dv}{dx}$. In the v–x graph, v is the height of the graph and dv/dx is the slope of the tangent. At point P, slope of the normal is $-\frac{PQ}{QR}$. Hence, the slope of the tangent at P is $\frac{QR}{PQ}$. Hence, acceleration

$$a = v\frac{dv}{dx} = PQ \times \frac{QR}{PQ} = QR = 1 \text{ m/s}^2$$

9. (b) The stone falls in time $t_1 = \sqrt{\frac{2h}{g}} = \frac{\sqrt{h}}{\sqrt{5}}$ and sound takes time $t_2 = \frac{h}{300}$.

Hence, total time $T = \frac{\sqrt{h}}{\sqrt{5}} + \frac{h}{300}$. Then

$$T = \left(\frac{1}{2\sqrt{5}\sqrt{h}} + \frac{1}{300} \right) h.$$

Putting $h = 20$ m and $\Delta T = 0.01$ s gives $\Delta h = \frac{3}{16}$ m.

Hence $\frac{\Delta h}{h} = \frac{3}{20 \times 16} = \frac{3 \times 100}{20 \times 16}\% \approx 1\%$

10. (a) Choosing the upward direction as +ve and the initial position of A as the origin, the y-coordinates of balls A and B as functions of time are given by

$$y_A = v_1 t - \frac{1}{2}gt^2 \text{ and } y_B = h + v_2 t - \frac{1}{2}gt^2$$

Collision will take place when $yA = yB$, that is

$$v_1 t - \frac{1}{2}gt^2 = h + v_2 t - \frac{1}{2}gt^2$$

$$\Rightarrow \quad t = \frac{h}{v_1 - v_2}$$

The y-coordinate at this time will be

$$y_B = y_A = v_1\left(\frac{h}{v_1 - v_2}\right) - \frac{1}{2}g\left(\frac{h}{v_1 - v_2}\right)^2$$

$$= \frac{h}{v_1 - v_2}\left(v_1 - \frac{gh}{2(v_1 - v_2)}\right)$$

Both t and the y-coordinate must be +ve quantities, that is

$$\frac{h}{v_1 - v_2} > 0 \Rightarrow v_1 > v_2$$

and $\frac{h}{v_1 - v_2}(v_1 - \frac{gh}{2(v_1 - v_2)}) > 0$

$$\Rightarrow \frac{gh}{2(v_1 - v_2)} < v_1 \Rightarrow h < \frac{2v_1(v_1 - v_2)}{g}$$

11. (c)

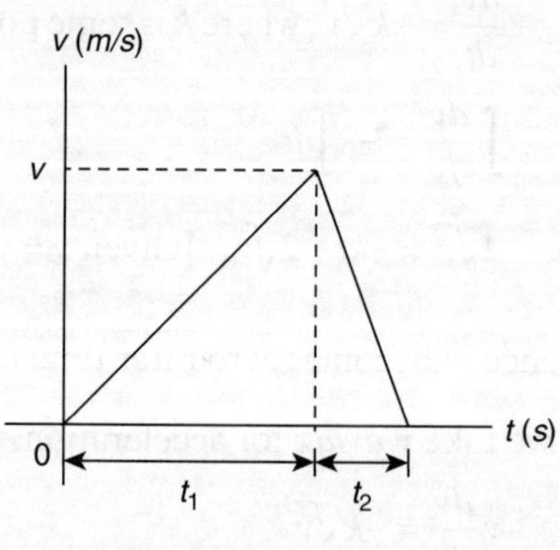

If the car accelerates to a maximum speed of 24 m/s and then retards to rest, the total distance travelled will be

$$\frac{(24\text{ m/s})^2}{2(1\text{ m/s}^2)}+\frac{(24\text{ m/s})^2}{2(4\text{ m/s}^2)}=360\text{ m}>320\text{ m}$$

This means the car should accelerate to maximum speed, say $v(v < 24$ m/s). The v–t graph is shown above. The value of v is given by

$$\frac{v^2}{2(1\text{ m/s}^2)}+\frac{v^2}{2(4\text{ m/s}^2)}=320\text{ m}\Rightarrow v=16\sqrt{2}\text{ m/s}$$

Hence, the total time of motion is

$$\frac{16\sqrt{2}\text{ m/s}}{1\text{ m/s}^2}+\frac{16\sqrt{2}\text{ m/s}}{4\text{ m/s}^2}=20\sqrt{2}\text{ s}\simeq 28\text{ s}$$

12. (c) In the absence of wind, we have

$$H=\frac{u_y^2}{2g}, T=\frac{2u_y}{g}, R=u_xT$$

With wind, the total time of flight and the maximum height attained by the projectile remains the same, but the range changes.

$$R'=u_xT+\frac{1}{2}aT^2$$

$$=R+\frac{1}{2}\left(\frac{g}{4}\right)\left(\frac{4u_y^2}{g^2}\right)=R+\frac{u_y^2}{2g}=R+H$$

13. (a) The equation representing the v–x graph is

$$v=v_o-(\frac{v_o}{x_0})x$$

Acceleration is given by

$$a=v\frac{dv}{dx}=\left(v_0-\frac{v_0x}{x_0}\right)\times\frac{-v_0}{x_0}=\frac{v_{o^2}}{x_{o^2}}x-\frac{v_{o^2}}{x_o}$$

This is a straight line with positive slope and negative y intercept.

14. (b) Let us solve the problem from a reference frame attached to the railroad car. Relative to the railroad car, the ball has an initial velocity of 9.8 m/s in the vertically upward direction. Thereafter, the ball moves with acceleration g along the vertically downward direction and acceleration a along the horizontal direction.

The time of flight of the ball is

$$T=\frac{2(9.8\text{ m/s})}{9.8\text{ m/s}^2}=2\text{ s}$$

Horizontal displacement of the ball is given to be 20 m. Hence, we have

$$\frac{1}{2}a(2s)^2=2\text{ m}$$

$$\Rightarrow\quad a=1\text{ m/s}^2$$

15. (d) The x- and y-coordinates of projectiles A and B as functions of time are

$$x_A=3t, y_A=3t-\frac{1}{2}gt^2$$

and $$x_B=10+at, y_B=2+bt-\frac{1}{2}gt^2$$

Equating $xA = xB$ at $t = 2$ s gives $a = -2$.
Equating $yA = yB$ at $t = 2$ s gives $b = 2$.

16. (a) The x- and y-coordinates of particles A and B as functions of time are

$xA = v \cos 53°t$, $yA = v \sin53°t$ and
$xB = 6$, $yB = 2 + 3t$

For collision, $xA = xB$ and $yA = yB$ at the same time. Hence

$$\frac{3}{5}vt=6\text{ and }\frac{4}{5}vt=2+3t$$

Solving the two equations gives $v = 5$ m/s.

17. (c) Let us choose the foot of the left pole as the origin, the right horizontal direction as the $+x$-axis and the vertically upward direction as the $+y$-axis. Then, the x and y coordinates of particles A and B as functions of time are

$$x_A=\frac{4}{5}vt, y_A=\eta h-\frac{3}{5}vt-\frac{1}{2}gt^2$$

and $$x_B=2h-vt,\quad y_B=h-\frac{1}{2}gt^2$$

For collision, $xA = xB$ and $yA = yB$ at the same time. Hence

$$\frac{9}{5}vt=2h\text{ and }\frac{3}{5}vt=(n-1)h$$

Dividing the two equations, we have

$$3=\frac{2}{n-1}\Rightarrow\eta=\frac{5}{3}$$

18. (a) The particle is moving along $y = x^2$. Differentiating with respect to time, we get

$$\dot{y}=2x\dot{x}\text{ and }y=2\dot{x}^2+2x\ddot{x}$$

It is given that $\ddot{x}$ and $\ddot{y} = 0.5$ m/s^2. Putting in the second equation gives $\dot{x}=\frac{1}{2}$ m/s (constant for all positions of the particle).

Putting $x = 0$ in the first equation gives the value of $\dot{y}$ at origin, equal to 0.

Hence, the magnitude of the velocity at the origin equals $\sqrt{x^2+y^2} = \frac{1}{2}$ m/s.

19. (b) Let us choose the point of projection as the origin, the x-axis along the horizontal and the y-axis along the vertically upward direction. Then, we have

$$\frac{dy}{dt} = 2 \text{ and } \frac{dx}{dt} = 2y$$

Solving the above differential equations, we get $y = 2t$ and $x = 2t^2$ [Given $x = 0, y = 0$ at $t = 0$]

Eliminating t gives the equation of the trajectory,

$$x = \frac{1}{2}y^2$$

The velocity of the particle at time t is

$$v = \sqrt{\dot{x}^2+\dot{y}^2} = 2\sqrt{1+y^2}$$

The tangential acceleration at time t is

$$a_t = \frac{dv}{dt} = 2\times\frac{2y}{2\sqrt{1+y^2}}\times\frac{dy}{dt} = \frac{4y}{\sqrt{1+y^2}}$$

20. (b) Let α be the angle of projection. The equation of the trajectory is

$$y = x\tan\alpha\left(1-\frac{x}{R}\right) = x\tan\alpha\left(1-\frac{x}{24}\right) [R = 24, \text{ given}]$$

The ball passes through the point (6 m, 3 m). Putting the values in the above equation, we get

$$3 = 6\tan\alpha\left(1-\frac{6}{24}\right) \Rightarrow \tan\alpha = \frac{2}{3}$$

21. (d)

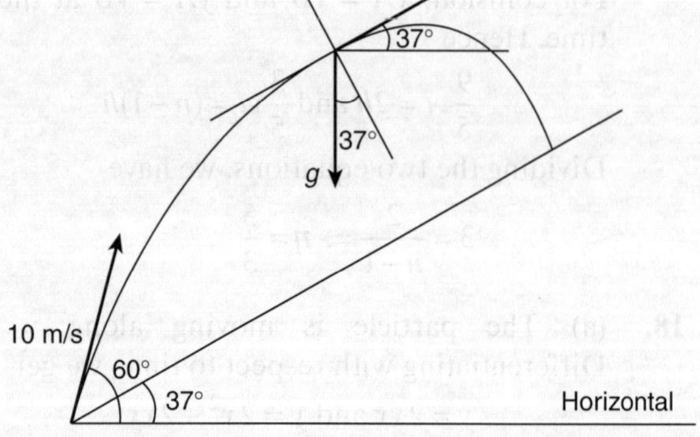

The above figure depicts the motion. The velocity vector along the horizontal remains unchanged. Hence, if v is the speed when the velocity becomes parallel to the incline, then

$$v\cos 37° = 10 \text{ m/s}$$
$$\cos 60° \Rightarrow v = 10 \text{ m/s}$$

The normal component of the acceleration is

$$a_n = g\cos 37° = (10 \text{ m/s}^2)(4/5) = 8 \text{ m/s}^2$$

Hence, the radius of curvature is

$$r = \frac{v^2}{a_n} = \frac{(10 \text{ m/s})^2}{8 \text{ m/s}} = 12.5 \text{ m}$$

22. (a)

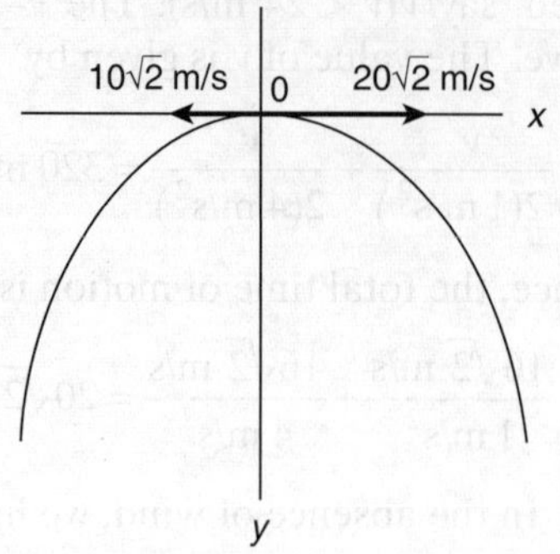

The velocity vectors as functions of time are

$$\vec{v}_1 = 20\sqrt{2}\hat{i} + gt\hat{j} \text{ and } \vec{v}_2 = -10\sqrt{2}\hat{i} + qt\hat{j}$$

The velocities will be perpendicular when

$$\vec{v}_1\cdot\vec{v}_2 = 0$$

$$\Rightarrow \quad -400 + g^2t^2 = 0 \Rightarrow t = \frac{\sqrt{400}}{100} = 2 \text{ s}$$

23. (c)

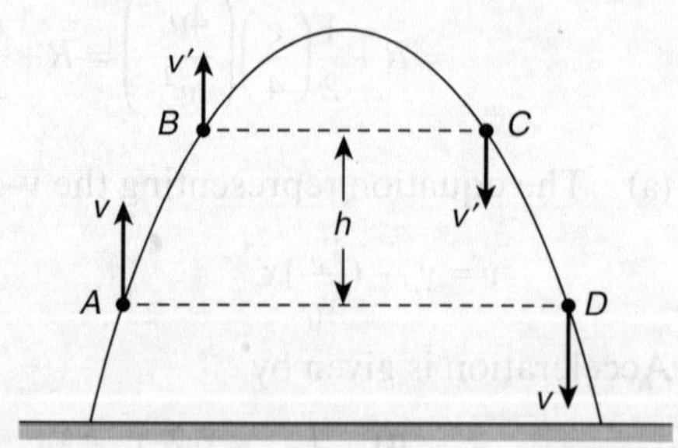

Let v and v' be the vertical velocity components at A and B, respectively. Then

$$T_1 = \frac{2v}{g} \text{ and } T_2 = \frac{2v'}{g}$$

Also $v^2 - v'^2 = 2gh$. Hence, we have

$$\frac{1}{4}g^2(T_1^2 - T_2^2) = 2gh$$

$$\Rightarrow \quad g = \frac{8h}{T_1^2 - T_2^2}$$

24. (a) The total time of flight T and the maximum height attained H for a particle are given by

$$T = \frac{2u\sin\theta}{g} \text{ and } H = \frac{u^2\sin^2\theta}{2g}$$

Eliminating $u \sin \theta$ from the two equations, we get

$$T^2 = \frac{8H}{g} \Rightarrow T \alpha \sqrt{H}$$

Hence $\frac{\Delta T}{T} = \frac{1}{2}\frac{\Delta H}{H} = \frac{1}{2} \times 5\% = 2.5\%$

25. (c) If the range is the same for two angles of projection, then the two angles must be complementary angles; that is, if one of them is α, the other must be $90° - \alpha$.
The product of the two times of flight are

$$T_1 T_2 = \frac{2u \sin\alpha}{g} \times \frac{2u \cos\alpha}{g} = \frac{2u^2 \sin(2\alpha)}{g^2} = \frac{2R}{g}$$

$$\Rightarrow \quad T_1 T_2 \alpha R$$

26. (b)

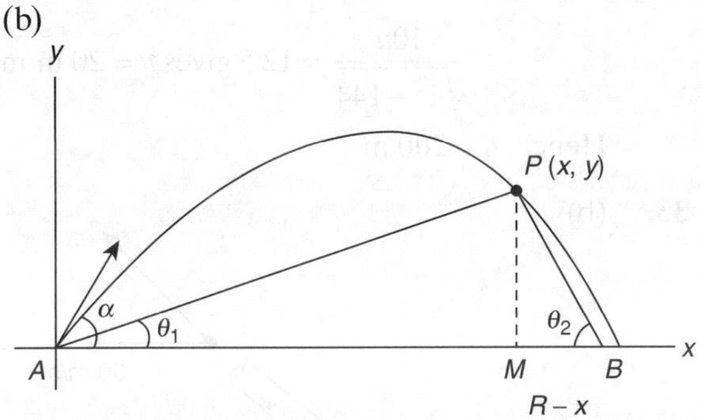

The figure depicts the trajectory; $P(x, y)$ is some arbitrary point on the trajectory. Let R be the range of the particle.
From the figure, we have

$$\tan\theta_1 + \tan\theta_2 = \frac{y}{x} + \frac{y}{R-x} = \frac{Ry}{x(R-x)}$$

The equation of the trajectory is

$$y = x\left(1 - \frac{x}{R}\right)\tan\alpha \Rightarrow \frac{Ry}{x(R-x)} = \tan\alpha$$

Hence, $\tan\theta_1 + \tan\theta_2 = \tan\alpha$.

27. (a) Let u be the uniform speed of the elevator and h be its height at time t_1. Then, we have $h = ut_1$.
When the ball is dropped, it has an initial velocity u in the upward direction and then falls freely with acceleration g to the ground in time t_2. Hence, we have

$$h = -ut_2 + \frac{1}{2}gt_2^2$$

Eliminating u, we have

$$h = -\left(\frac{h}{t_1}\right)t_2 + \frac{1}{2}gt_2^2$$

$$\Rightarrow \quad h = \frac{\frac{1}{2}gt_2^2}{1 + t_2/t_1} = \frac{\frac{1}{2}(10 \text{ m/s}^2)(4 \text{ s})^2}{1 + (4 \text{ s}/4 \text{ s})^2} = 40 \text{ m}$$

28. (d) Let the velocity of the projection be $\vec{u} = (u_x)\hat{i} + (u_y)\hat{j}$.
Then, one second later from the time of projection, its velocity will be $\vec{v}_1 = (u_x)\hat{i} + (u_y - g)\hat{j}$, and two seconds later from the time of projection, it will be $\vec{v}_2 = (u_x)\hat{i} + (u_y - 2g)\hat{j}$. According to the given condition, we have

$$\frac{u_y - g}{u_y} = \tan 45° \text{ and } u_y - 2g = 0$$

Solving the above equations, we get

$$u_x = 10 \text{ m/s and } u_y = 20 \text{ m/s}$$

Hence, the projection speed is $\sqrt{u_x^2 + u_y^2} = 10\sqrt{5}$ m/s.

29. (a) The ball strikes the surface with speed $v = \sqrt{2gh}$ at angle a with the normal to the surface. The ball then rebounds at the same speed at angle $2a$ with the vertical; that is, at angle $\theta = 90° - 2a$ with the horizontal. Now the ball moves in a parabolic trajectory of range $2d$. Hence

$$\frac{v^2 \sin(2\theta)}{g} = 2d$$

$$\Rightarrow \quad \frac{2gh \sin(180° - 4\alpha)}{g} = 2d$$

$$\Rightarrow \quad \sin(4\alpha) = \frac{d}{h}$$

$$\Rightarrow \quad \alpha = \frac{1}{4}\sin^{-1}\left(\frac{d}{h}\right)$$

30. (c) Let us choose our x-axis along the horizontal and the y-axis along the vertically downward direction (see figure).

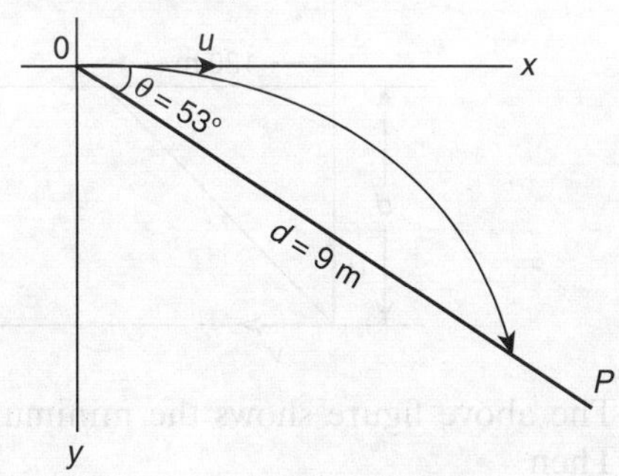

The projectile's position coordinates as a function of time are given by $x = ut$ and $y = \frac{1}{2}gt^2$.

Eliminating t, we get the equation of the projectile's trajectory as $y = \frac{g}{2u^2}x^2 = \frac{5}{u^2}x^2$.

The coordinates of point P are

$$(d\cos(53^\circ), d\sin(53^\circ)) = \left(\frac{27}{5}\text{m}, \frac{36}{5}\text{m}\right)$$

The coordinates of P must satisfy the equation of the projectile's trajectory. Hence, we have

$$\frac{36}{5} = \frac{5}{u^2}\left(\frac{27}{5}\right)^2 \Rightarrow u = \frac{9}{2}\text{m/s}$$

31. (d) Let us choose our reference frame, as shown in the figure.

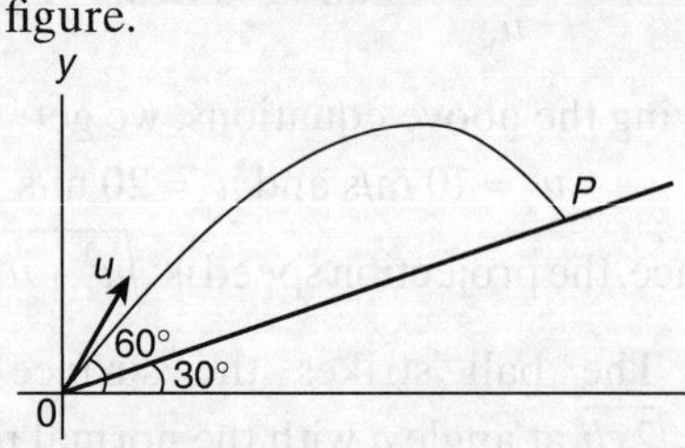

The equation of the projectile's trajectory is

$$y = x\tan(60^\circ) - \frac{gx^2}{2u^2\cos^2(60^\circ)} \Rightarrow y = \sqrt{3}x - \frac{4}{45}x^2$$

The equation of the inclined plane is

$$y = x\tan(30^\circ) \Rightarrow y = \frac{1}{\sqrt{3}}x$$

Solving the two equations simultaneously, we obtain the coordinates of the intersection point P as $\left(\frac{15\sqrt{3}}{2}, \frac{15}{2}\right)$. Hence, the distance OP is

$$d = \sqrt{\left(\frac{15\sqrt{3}}{2}\right)^2 + \left(\frac{15}{2}\right)^2} = \frac{15}{2}\sqrt{3+1} = 15\text{ m}$$

32. (b)

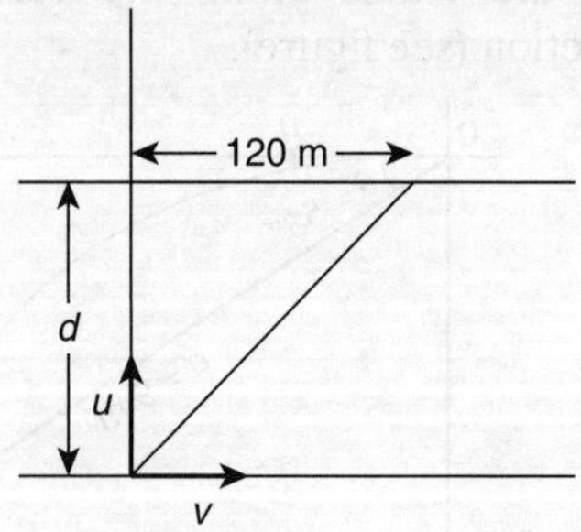

The above figure shows the minimum time path. Then

$$\frac{d}{u} = \frac{120\text{ m}}{v} = 10\text{ min}$$

$\Rightarrow$ $v = 12$ m/min and $d = 10u$

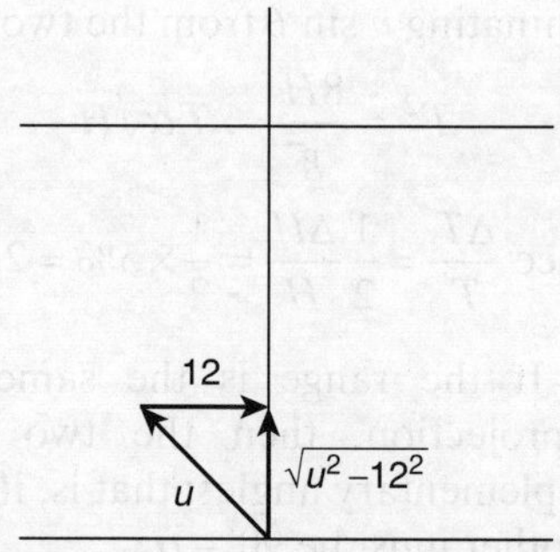

The above figure shows the minimum distance path. Then

$$\frac{d}{\sqrt{u^2 - 12^2}} = 12.5\text{ min}$$

Putting $d = 10u$, we have

$$\frac{10u}{\sqrt{u^2 - 144}} = 12.5 \text{ gives } u = 20\text{ m/min}$$

Hence, $d = 200$ m.

33. (b)

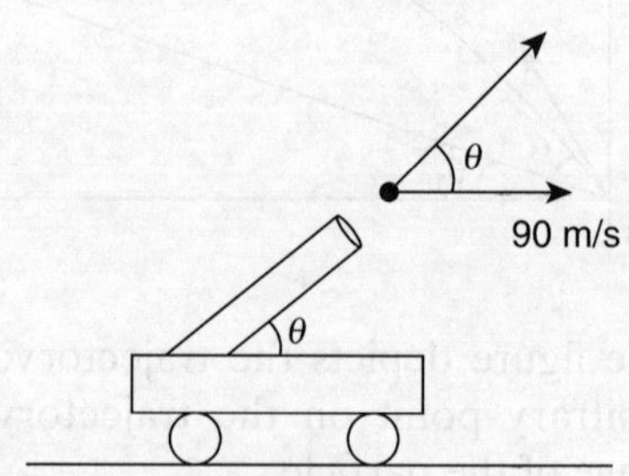

Maximum range is 20 m. Hence

$$\frac{u^2}{g} = 20\text{ m gives } u = 20\text{ m/s}$$

If the shell is fired at angle θ, its absolute velocity is u_x = 20 m/s + 20 m/s cos θ along the horizontal and u_y = 20 m/s sin θ along the vertical. Hence, the range is

$$R(\theta) = \frac{2u_y u_x}{g}$$

$$= \frac{2(20\text{ m/s}\sin\theta)}{10\text{ m/s}^2}(20\text{ m/s} + 20\text{ m/s}\cos\theta)$$

$$= 80\text{ m}\sin\theta(1 + \cos\theta)$$

The maximum of R occurs at angle θ, given by $dR/d\theta = 0$

$\Rightarrow$ $\cos\theta(1 + \cos\theta) - \sin^2\theta = 0$

$\Rightarrow$ $2\cos^2\theta + \cos\theta - 1 = 0$

$\Rightarrow$ $\cos\theta = ½$ given $\theta = 60^\circ$

Hence

$$R_{\max} = \frac{\sqrt{3}}{2}\left(1 + \frac{1}{2}\right)80\text{ m} = 60\sqrt{3}\text{ m}$$

34. (b)

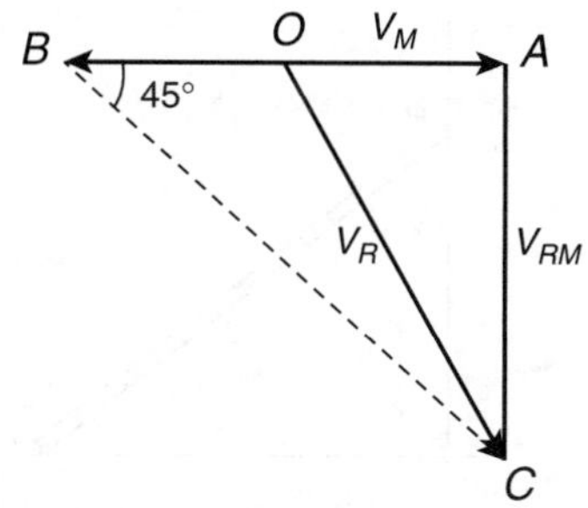

The velocity vector diagram for both the cases is shown above. In the first case, when the man is moving towards the right, $\overrightarrow{OA}$ represents the velocity of the man $(\vec{v}_M)$, $\overrightarrow{OC}$ represents the velocity of the rain $(\vec{v}_R)$ and $\overrightarrow{AC}$ represents the velocity of the rain relative to the man $(\vec{v}_{RM} = \vec{v}_R - \vec{v}_M)$. Similarly, when the man is moving towards the left, $\overrightarrow{OB} = (\vec{v}_M), \overrightarrow{OC} = (\vec{v}_R)$ and $\overrightarrow{BC} = (\vec{v}_{RM})$.
From the figure, $OA = OB = 5$. Hence

$$\tan 45° = \frac{AC}{\Delta R} = \frac{AC}{10} \Rightarrow AC = 10$$

In ΔOAC, $\angle OAC = 90°$. Hence, the length of OC, which is the rain speed, equals

$$v_R = \sqrt{5^2 + 10^2} \text{ m/s} = 5\sqrt{5} \text{ m/s}$$

35. (b)

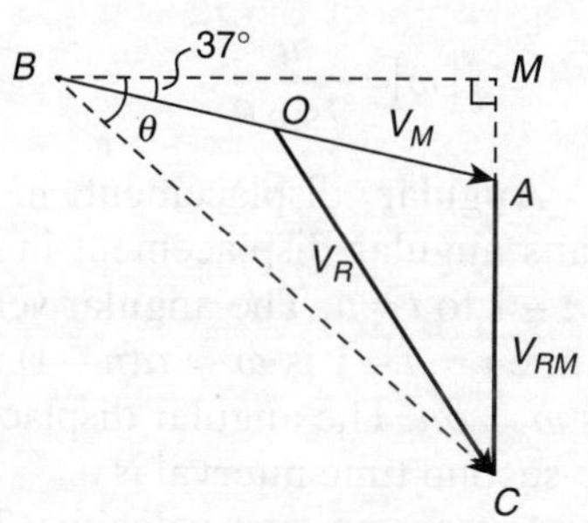

The velocity vector diagram for both the cases is shown above. In the first case, when the man is moving down the incline, $\overrightarrow{OA}$ represents the velocity of the man $(\vec{v}_M)$, $\overrightarrow{OC}$ represents the velocity of the rain $(\vec{v}_R)$ and $\overrightarrow{AC}$ represents the velocity of the rain relative to the man $(\vec{v}_{RM} = \vec{v}_R - \vec{v}_M)$. Similarly, when the man is moving up, $\overrightarrow{OB} = \vec{v}_M, \overrightarrow{OC} = \vec{v}_R$ and $\overrightarrow{BC} = \vec{v}_{RM}$.
In the above figure, $OA = OB = 5$ and $\tan\theta = 7/8$.
Now

$$BM = AB\cos 37° = 10\cos 37° = 8$$

and $\quad AM = AB\sin 37° = 10\sin 37° = 6$

Now, using $\tan\theta = \dfrac{CM}{BM} = \dfrac{AC + AM}{BM}$, we have

$$\frac{7}{8} = \frac{AC+6}{8} \text{ gives } AC = 1$$

In ΔOAC, $OA = 5$, $AC = 1$ and $\angle OAC = 90° + 37°$. Hence, the length of OC, which is the rain speed, equals

$$v_R = \sqrt{5^2 + 1^2 - 2\times 5\times 1\cos(90° + 37°)} \text{ m/s} = 4\sqrt{2} \text{ m/s}$$

36. (b) The two balls approach each other with uniform relative velocity

$$v_{rel} = 0.3 \text{ m/s} + 0.2 \text{ m/s} = 0.5 \text{ m/s}$$

Hence, they will collide after time $T = \dfrac{5 \text{ m}}{0.5 \text{ m/s}} = 8$ s

37. (c)

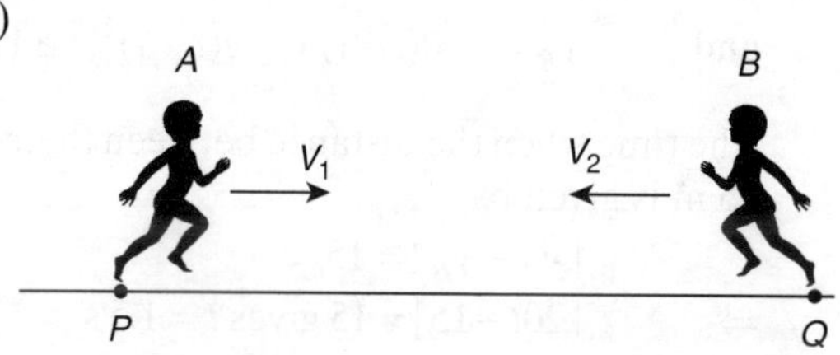

The above figure depicts the motion. Let $PQ = l$. They will cross each other at some point R after time

$$T = \frac{l}{v_1 + v_2}$$

Now, a man A covers the remaining distance $l - v_1 T$ in time t_1

$$\Rightarrow \quad v_1 t_1 = l - v_1 T \Rightarrow v_1 t_1 = \left(\frac{v_1}{v_1 + v_2}\right) l$$

Man B covers the remaining distance $l - v_2 T$ in time t_2

$$\Rightarrow \quad v_2 t_2 = l - v_2 T \Rightarrow v_2 t_2 = \left(\frac{v_1}{v_1 + v_2}\right) l$$

Eliminating l from the two equations, we have

$$\frac{v_1 t_1}{v_2 t_2} = \frac{v_2}{v_1} \Rightarrow \frac{v_1}{v_2} = \sqrt{\frac{t_2}{t_1}}$$

38. (a)

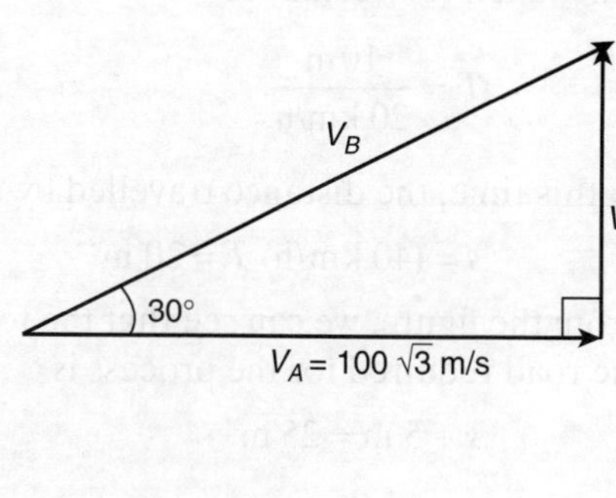

According to the question, VBA is perpendicular to VA. From the velocity diagram shown above, we have

$$VBA = VA \tan 30°$$
$$= 100 \text{ m/s}$$

Hence, they will collide after time

$$= \frac{500 \text{ m}}{100 \text{ m/s}} = 5 \text{ s}$$

39. (b) If we choose the vertically downward direction as positive, then the position coordinates of the two balls as functions of time are

$$y_A = \frac{1}{2}gt^2, t \geq 0$$

and $$y_B = -10(t-1) + \frac{1}{2}g(t-1)^2, t \geq 1$$

The time when the distance between them becomes 15 m is given by

$$|y_A - y_B| = 15$$
$$\Rightarrow |20t - 15| = 15 \text{ gives } t = 1.5 \text{ s}$$

40. (c)

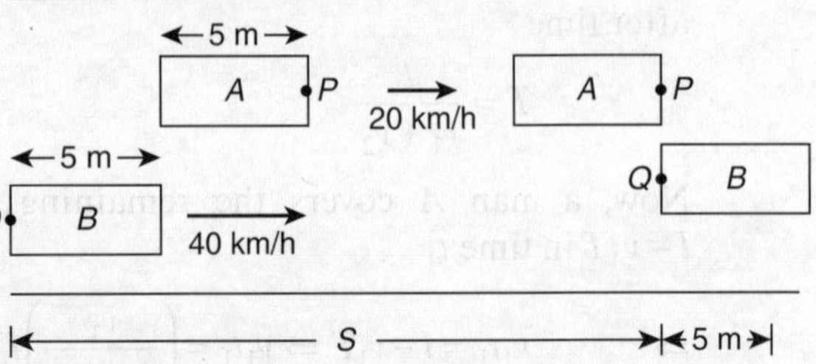

The left portion of the figure shows the situation when the process of overtaking has just begun. At this moment, the front P of car A and the rear Q of car B are separated by a distance of 5 m + 5 m =10 m.

The right portion of the figure shows the situation when the process of overtaking has just been completed. The points P and Q are now placed alongside. Q has moved with velocity 40 km/h – 20 km/h = 20 km/h relative to point P. Hence, the time taken to overtake is

$$T = \frac{10 \text{ m}}{20 \text{ km/h}}$$

In this time, the distance travelled by point Q is

$$s = (40 \text{ km/h})\, T = 20 \text{ m}$$

From the figure, we can see that the total length of the road required for the process is

$$s + 5 \text{ m} = 25 \text{ m}$$

41. (c)

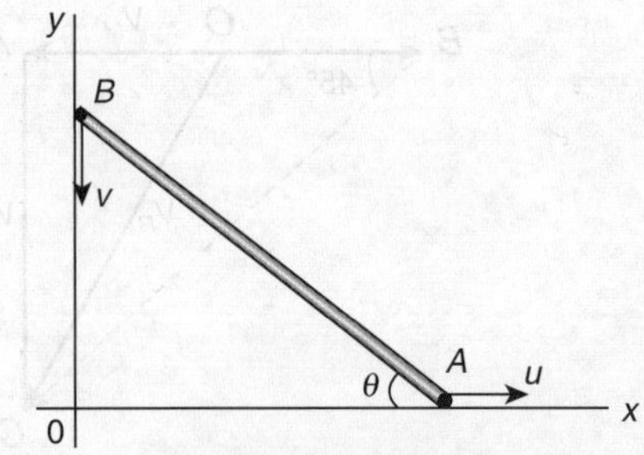

Let us choose our reference frame as shown in the figure. Let x and y be the position coordinates of A and B, respectively, at any time t. Then

$$x^2 + y^2 = l^2$$

Here, x and y are variables whereas l is a constant. Now, differentiating throughout with respect to time, we have

$$x\frac{dx}{dt} + y\frac{dy}{dt} = 0$$
$$\Rightarrow xu - yv = 0$$
$$\Rightarrow v = u\frac{x}{y} = u \cot \theta$$

From the figure, we see that $x = l \cos \theta$. Differentiating with respect to time, we have

$$\frac{dx}{dt} = -l \sin \theta \frac{d\theta}{dt}$$
$$\Rightarrow u = -l \sin \theta\, \omega$$
$$\Rightarrow |\omega| = \frac{u}{l \sin \theta}$$

42. (d) Angular displacement in the nth second means angular displacement in the time interval $t = n - 1$ to $t = n$. The angular velocity of the body at time $t = n - 1$ is $\omega_1 = \alpha(n - 1)$ and at time $t = n$, it is $\omega_2 = \alpha n$. The angular displacement within this one-second time interval is

θn = Average angular velocity × Time interval

$$= \left(\frac{\omega_1 + \omega_2}{2}\right) \times 1s = \frac{\alpha(n-1) + \alpha n}{2}$$
$$= \left(n - \frac{1}{2}\right)\alpha$$

Now, using the above result, we have

$$\theta_1 = \frac{1}{2}\alpha, \theta_2 = \frac{3}{2}\alpha$$
$$\text{and } \theta_3 = \frac{5}{2}\alpha.$$

Hence $\theta_1 : \theta_2 : \theta_3 = 1:3:5$

43. (b) At any instance, let x be the horizontal distance of the plane from the radar. Then

$$x \tan \theta = h$$

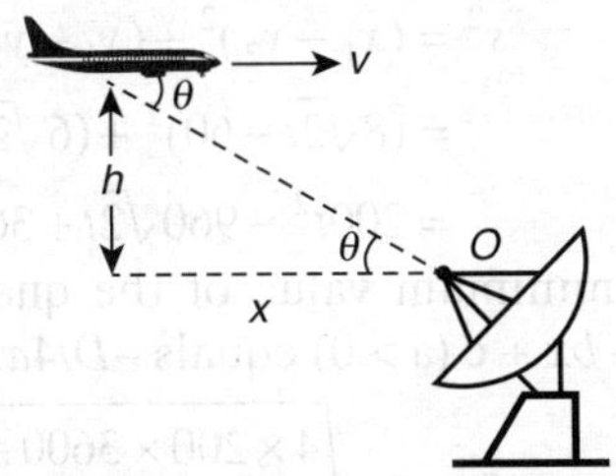

Differentiating throughout with respect to time, we have

$$x\tan\theta + x\sec^2\theta\theta = 0$$

$$\Rightarrow \quad \dot{\theta} = -\frac{\dot{x}\tan\theta}{x\sec^2\theta}$$

Putting $\dot{x} = -v$ and $x = \dfrac{h}{\tan\theta}$, we have

$$\omega = \frac{v}{h}\sin^2\theta$$

Now $\alpha = \omega\dfrac{d\omega}{d\theta}$. Hence

$$\frac{a}{\omega} = \frac{d\varpi}{d\theta}$$

$$= \frac{v}{h}\sin(2\theta)$$

Alternatively

$$\omega = \frac{v\sin\theta}{OP}$$

$$= \frac{v\sin\theta}{h\operatorname{cosec}\theta}$$

$$= \frac{v}{h}\sin^2\theta$$

44. (d) Differentiating the relation $2\theta^2 - 3\theta = t$ twice with respect to time, we have

$$(4\theta - 3)\omega = 1 \quad \ldots(1)$$

$$4\omega^2 + (4\theta - 3)\alpha = 0 \quad \ldots(2)$$

From (1), we get $4\theta - 3 = \dfrac{1}{\omega}$. Putting in (2) gives

$$4\omega^2 + \frac{\alpha}{\omega} = 0$$

$$\Rightarrow \quad \alpha = -4\omega^3$$

45. (b) Over one quarter circle

$$|\Delta\vec{v}| = \sqrt{2}v$$

and $\quad \Delta t = \dfrac{\pi r}{2v}$

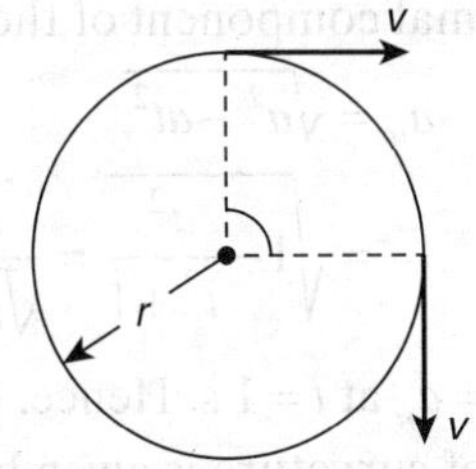

Hence

$$|\overline{a_{aw}}| = \frac{|\Delta\vec{v}|}{\Delta t}$$

$$= \frac{2\sqrt{2}v^2}{\pi r}$$

46. (a)

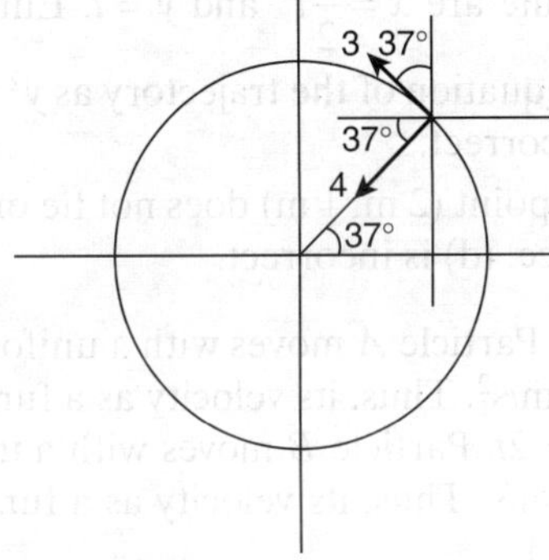

$$a_n = \frac{v^2}{r}$$

$$= \frac{(2\text{ m/s})^2}{1\text{ m}} = 4\text{ m/s}^2$$

Therefore $a_n = \sqrt{(5\text{ m/s})^2 - (4\text{ m/s})^2}$

$$= 3\text{ m/s}^2$$

$$a_x = -(3\sin 37° + 4\cos 37°)$$

$$= -5$$

$$a_y = (3\cos 37° - 4\sin 37°) = 0$$

Hence $\overrightarrow{a_n} = -5\hat{i}$

47. (a), (b) The velocity of the particle as a function of time is

$$\vec{v} = \vec{u} + \vec{a}t$$

$$= (1\text{ m/s}^2)t\hat{i} + (1\text{ m/s})\hat{j}$$

The tangential component of the acceleration is

$$a_t = \frac{\vec{a}\cdot\vec{v}}{v}$$

$$= \frac{t}{\sqrt{t^2+1}}$$

The normal component of the acceleration is

$$a_n = \sqrt{a^2 - at^2}$$

$$= \sqrt{1 - \frac{t^2}{t^2+1}} = \frac{1}{\sqrt{t^2+1}}$$

Now, $a_t = a_n$ at $t = 1$ s. Hence, (a) is correct.

Radius of curvature is given by

$$r = \frac{v^2}{a_n} = \frac{t^2+1}{1/\sqrt{t^2+1}}$$

$$= (t^2+1)^{3/2}$$

Now, $r = 27$ m at $t = 2\sqrt{2}$ s. Hence, (b) is correct.

The x and y coordinates of the particle as functions of time are $x = \frac{1}{2}t^2$ and $y = t$. Eliminating t gives the equation of the trajectory as $y^2 = 2x$. Hence, (c) is incorrect.

The point (2 m, 1 m) does not lie on the trajectory. Hence, (d) is incorrect.

48. (d) Particle A moves with a uniform acceleration of 2 m/s^2. Thus, its velocity as a function of time is $VA = 2t$. Particle B moves with a uniform velocity of 1 m/s. Thus, its velocity as a function of time is $vB = 1$.

Now, the velocity of B as seen from A is $vBA = vB - yA = 1 - 2t$. Hence, the distance travelled by B as seen from A is

$$\Delta s = \int_0^1 |1-2t|\,dt$$

$$= \int_0^{1/2} (1-2t)dt + \int_{1/2}^{1} (2t-1)dt$$

$$= |t - t^2|_0^{1/2} + |t^2 - t|_{1/2}^{1}$$

$$= \left(\frac{1}{4}\text{ m}\right) - \left(\frac{-1}{4}\text{ m}\right) = 0.5\text{ m}$$

49. (b) The x and y coordinates of the projectiles as functions of time are

$$x_1 = \sqrt{2}t, y_1$$

$$= \sqrt{2}t - \frac{1}{2}gt^2$$

and $$x_2 = 60 - 7\sqrt{2}t, y_2$$

$$= 7\sqrt{2}t - \frac{1}{2}gt^2$$

The separation s between the projectiles is given by

$$s^2 = (x_1 - x_2)^2 + (y_1 - y_2)^2$$

$$= (8\sqrt{2}t - 60)^2 + (6\sqrt{2}t)^2$$

$$= 200t^2 - 960\sqrt{2}t + 3600$$

The minimum value of the quadratic expression $ax^2 + bx + c$ (a > 0) equals $-D/4a$. Hence, we have

$$s_{\min} = \sqrt{\frac{4\times 200\times 3600 - (960\sqrt{2})^2}{4\times 200}}$$

$$= 36\text{ m}$$

50. (c)

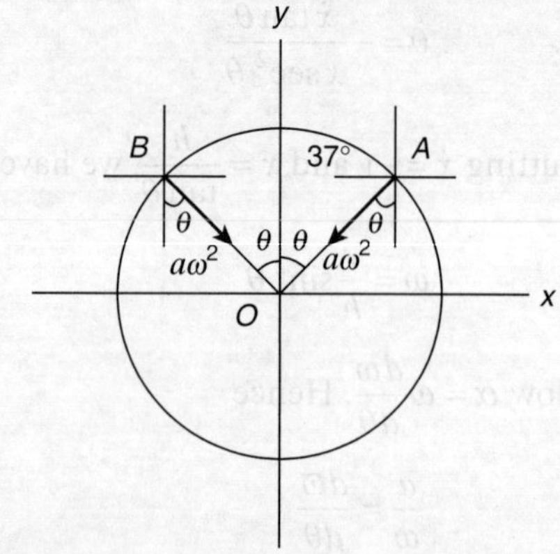

The figure shows the particles at time t, the angle $\theta = \omega t$. Therefore, the respective acceleration vectors are

$$\overrightarrow{w_A} = a\omega^2(-\sin\theta\hat{i} - \cos\theta\hat{j})$$

and $$\overrightarrow{w_B} = a\omega^2(\sin\theta\hat{i} - \cos\theta\hat{j})$$

Hence, the relative acceleration is

$$\overrightarrow{w_R} - \overrightarrow{w_n} = 2a\omega^2 \sin(\omega t)i,$$

whose magnitude is $2a\omega^2 \,|\sin(\omega t)$

51. (d) Vector $\bar{A}$ is a constant vector of magnitude a directed along the x-axis, whereas vector $\bar{B}$ has constant magnitude a but is rotating with a uniform angular speed ω. At any instant t, the angle between the two vectors is $\omega\tau$ (see figure).

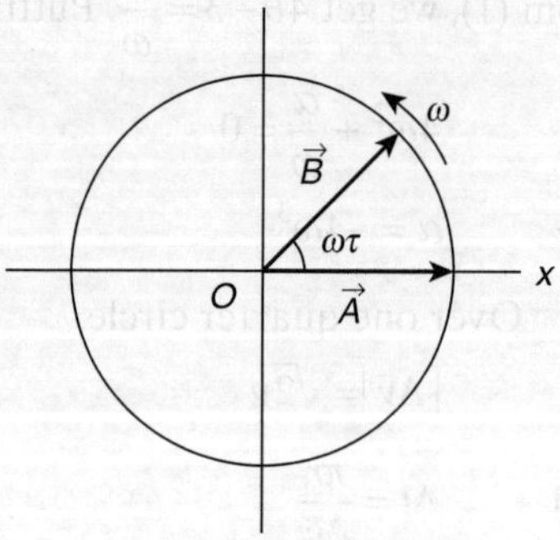

The time τ when $|\vec{A}+\vec{B}| = \sqrt{3}|\vec{A}-\vec{B}|$ is given by

$$a^2 + a^2 + 2a^2\cos(\omega\tau) = 3\{a^2 + a^2 - 2a^2\cos(\omega\tau)\}$$

$\Rightarrow \quad \cos(\omega\tau) = ½$

$\Rightarrow \quad \omega\tau = \pi/3$

Putting $\omega = \pi/6$ rad/s gives the required time $\tau = 2.0$ s.

52. (d) Let us choose the point of projection as the origin and the vertically upward direction as the positive y-axis. Ball A reaches the bottom of the cliff at the time given by

$$-240 = 10t - \frac{1}{2}gt^2$$

$$\Rightarrow \quad t = 8 \text{ s}$$

Ball B reaches the bottom of the cliff at the time given by

$$-240 = 40t - \frac{1}{2}gt^2$$

$$\Rightarrow \quad t = 12 \text{ s}$$

The position of ball A as a function of time is

$$y_A = \begin{cases} 10t - \frac{1}{2}gt^2, 0 \le t \le 8 \text{ s} \\ -240, t \ge 8 \text{ s} \end{cases}$$

The position of ball B as a function of time is

$$y_B = \begin{cases} 40t - \frac{1}{2}gt^2, 0 \le t \le 12 \text{ s} \\ -240, t \ge 12 \text{ s} \end{cases}$$

Separation between the balls as a function of time is $s = |y_A - y_B|$

$$= \begin{cases} 30t, 0 \le t \le 8 \text{ s} \\ 240 + 40t - \frac{1}{2}gt^2, 8 \text{ s} \le t \le 12 \text{ s} \end{cases}$$

The graph will be a straight line for the first 8 s; thereafter, it will be a concave downward parabola.

53. (b) Let us choose the direction of flow of the river as our +ve x direction and the direction right across the river as the +ve y direction. If the swimmer swims at speed v relative to the river, at angle θ to the x-axis, then the absolute velocity of the swimmer is $(v\cos\theta + u)i + (v\sin\theta)j$. According to the required condition, we have

$$\frac{v\sin\theta}{v\cos\theta + u} = \tan(45°)$$

$$\Rightarrow \quad v = \frac{u}{\sin\theta - \cos\theta}$$

$$= \frac{u}{\sqrt{2}\sin(\theta - \frac{\pi}{4})}$$

$$\Rightarrow \quad v_{\min} = \frac{u}{\sqrt{2}} \text{ at } \theta = \frac{3\pi}{4}$$

CHAPTER

3 Force and Motion

- Force, a vector quantity, is a quantitative measure of the interaction between two bodies. When several forces act on a body, the effect on its motion is the same as when a single force, equal to the vector sum (resultant) of the forces, acts on the body.

  The fundamental forces of nature are the gravitational force, electro-magnetic force and the strong nuclear force.

- Newton's first law states that when the resultant of all the forces acting on a body is zero, the body is in equilibrium. This law is valid only in inertial frames of reference.

- Newton's second law states that the acceleration **a** of a body is directly proportional to the resultant **F** of all the forces acting on a body and is inversely proportional to the mass m of the body:

  $$\mathbf{F} = m\mathbf{a}$$

  Like the first law, this law is also valid only in inertial frames of reference. In a non-inertial reference frame moving with acceleration $\mathbf{a}_0$, the equation of dynamics is

  $$\mathbf{F} - m\mathbf{a}_0 = m\mathbf{a}$$

  Here F is the sum of all real forces acting on the body and $-m\mathbf{a}_0$ is a pseudo (imaginary) force that has to be introduced to find the acceleration of the body in the non-inertial frame.

- Newton's third law states that "action equals reaction". When two bodies interact, they exert forces on each other that are equal in magnitude and opposite in direction. Each force in an action–reaction pair acts on only one of the two bodies; the action and reaction forces never act on the same body.

- The contact force between two solid surfaces can always be expressed in terms of a normal force (N) perpendicular to the interaction surface and a frictional force (f) parallel to the interaction surface.

  When sliding occurs, f is proportional to N and the proportionality constant (μ_k) is called the coefficient of kinetic friction:

  $$f = \mu_k N$$

  When there is no relative motion, f may take any value between zero and a limiting value proportional to N, and the proportionality constant (μ_s) is called the coefficient of static friction:

  $$0 \le f \le \mu_s N$$

EXERCISES

1. The figure shows the top view of a crate placed on a smooth horizontal surface.

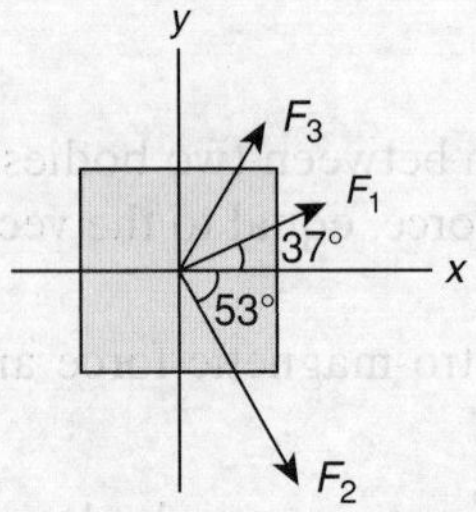

The mass of the crate is $M = 188\,\text{kg}$ and it is to be pushed by three persons with acceleration $0.5\,\text{m/s}^2$ along the x-axis. If two persons exert forces $F_1 = 50\,\text{N}$ and $F_2 = 60\,\text{N}$, as shown, then the magnitude of the force F_3 exerted by the third person is:

(a) $16\sqrt{2}$ N (b) 18N
(c) $18\sqrt{2}$ N (d) Data insufficient

2. A uniform rope of mass m and length l with a block of mass $2m$ attached to its one end is pulled along a smooth inclined plane of inclination θ by a force F parallel to the incline.

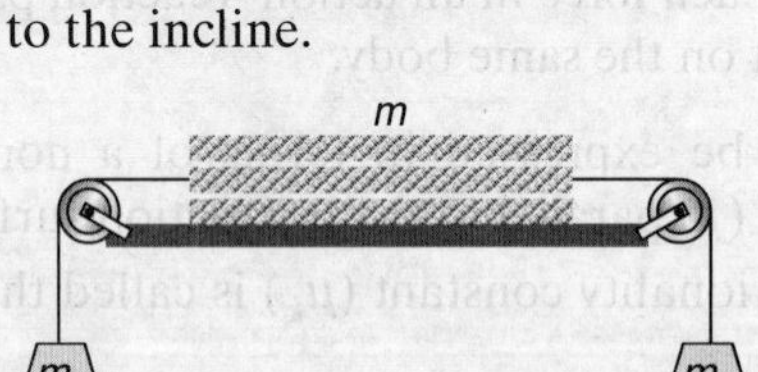

The tension in the middle of the rope is:

(a) F (b) $\frac{2}{3}F$

(c) $\frac{3}{5}F$ (d) $\frac{5}{6}F$

3. Two particles of mass m each are tied at the ends of a light string of length $2a$. The whole system is kept on a smooth horizontal surface with the string held taut. Now the mid-point of the string is pulled vertically upwards with a constant force F. As a result, the particles move towards each other on the horizontal surface, as shown in the figure.

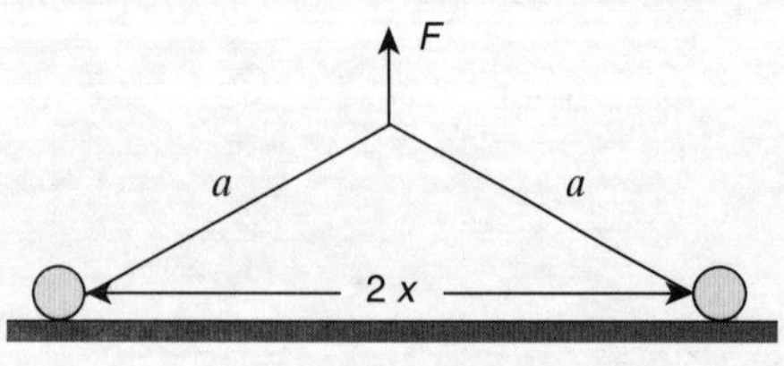

When separation is $2x$, the relative acceleration between the particles is:

(a) $\frac{a}{\sqrt{a^2-x^2}}\cdot\frac{F}{m}$ (b) $\frac{x}{\sqrt{a^2-x^2}}\cdot\frac{F}{m}$

(c) $\frac{x}{a}\frac{F}{m}$ (d) $\frac{\sqrt{a^2-x^2}}{x}\frac{F}{m}$

4. An air car moves up with acceleration a along a cable inclined at angle α to the horizontal, as shown in the figure.

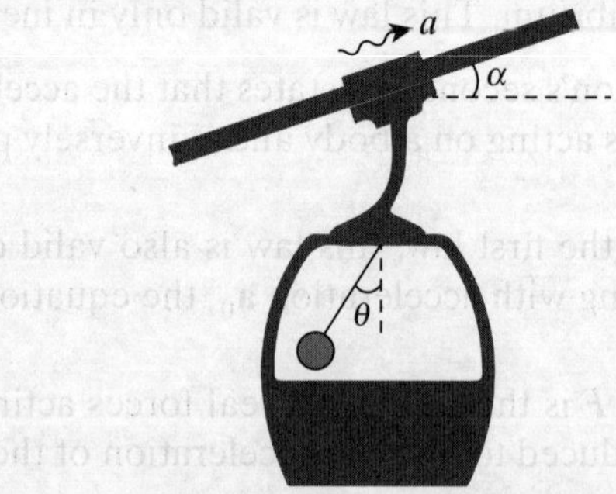

A pendulum hanging in equilibrium inside the cable car makes angle θ with the vertical. The value of $\tan\theta$ is:

(a) $\frac{a\cos\alpha}{g+a\sin\alpha}$ (b) $\frac{a}{g}$

(c) $\frac{a\sin\alpha}{g-a\sin\alpha}$ (d) $\frac{a\cos\alpha}{g-a\sin\alpha}$

5. The figure shows a cart moving up with acceleration a along an incline of inclination α.

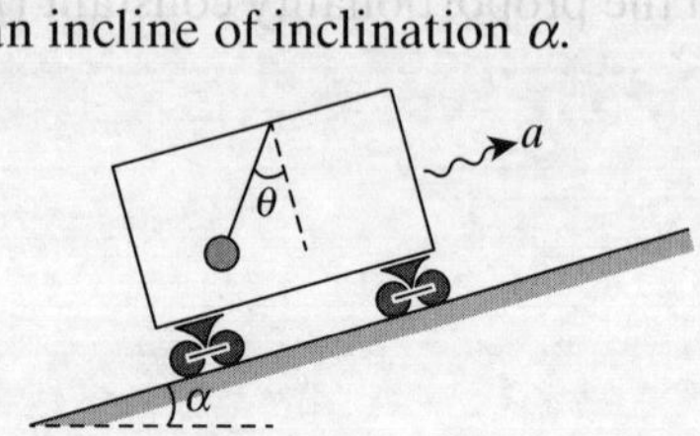

A pendulum hanging in equilibrium inside the cart makes angle θ with the normal to the incline. The value of $\tan\theta$ is:

(a) $\frac{g\sin\alpha+a}{g\cos\alpha}$ (b) $\frac{g\sin\alpha}{a}$

(c) $\frac{g\cos\alpha-a}{g\sin\alpha}$ (d) $\frac{a}{g\cos\alpha}$

6. Two blocks of mass 10 kg each are placed on a smooth horizontal surface, as shown in the figure.

The coefficient of friction between the blocks is 0.2. Initially the blocks are at rest. A time varying horizontal force $F = (20\,\text{N/s})t$ is applied on the upper block.

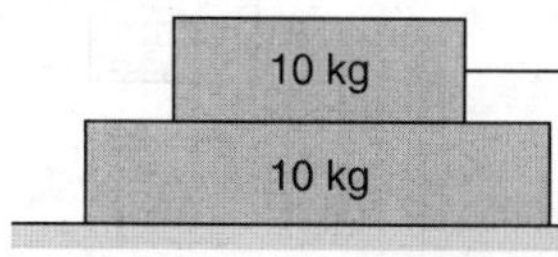

The time when relative motion between the blocks begins is (take $g = 10\ \text{m/s}^2$):

(a) 1 s (b) 2 s
(c) 3 s (d) 4 s

7. A block of mass m is kept on a rough plane inclined at angle θ to the horizontal. The coefficient of friction between the block and the plane is μ ($\mu < \tan\theta$). The block is held stationary by applying a force P parallel to the incline. The direction of the forces pointing up the plane is taken as positive. As P is increased from $P_1 = mg(\sin\theta - \mu\cos\theta)$ to $P_2 = mg(\sin\theta + \mu\cos\theta)$, the friction force f varies with P as:

(a)
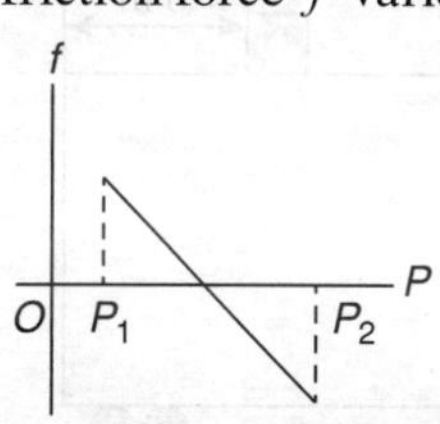

(b)
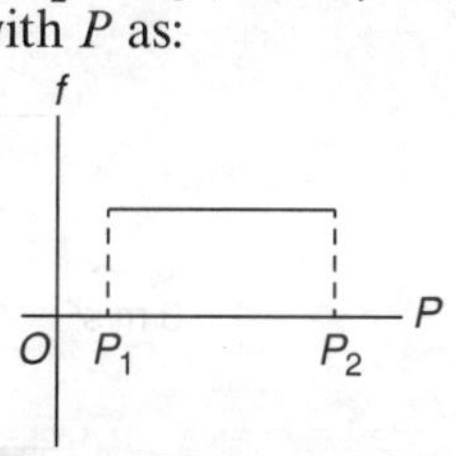

(c)
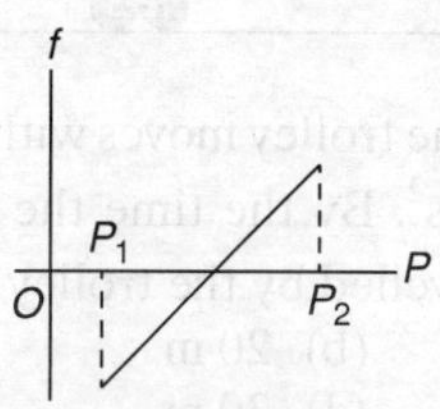

(d)
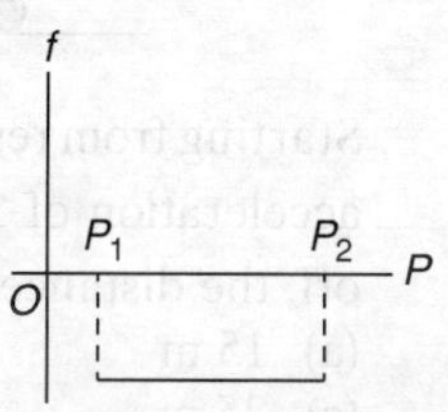

8. The pulley and the string shown in the figure are light. The table surface is horizontal and smooth. There is no slippage between blocks A and B.

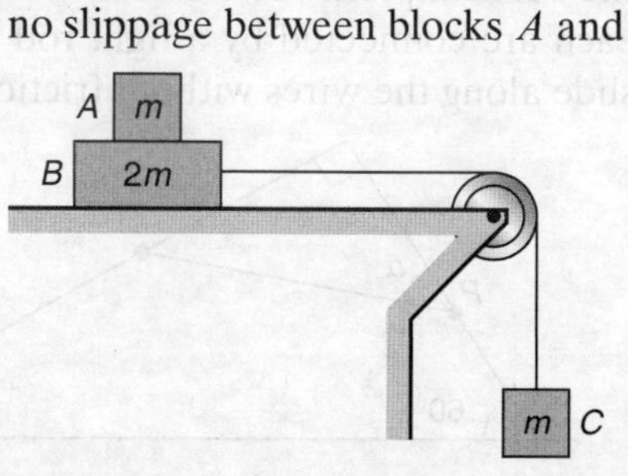

If μ is the coefficient of friction between blocks A and B, and R is the force exerted by the pulley on the table, then:

(a) $R = \dfrac{2}{\sqrt{3}}mg, \mu \geq \dfrac{1}{3}$ (b) $R = \dfrac{2}{\sqrt{3}}mg, \mu \geq \dfrac{1}{4}$

(c) $R = \dfrac{3}{2\sqrt{2}}mg, \mu \geq \dfrac{1}{3}$ (d) $R = \dfrac{3}{2\sqrt{2}}mg, \mu \geq \dfrac{1}{4}$

9. A block of weight W is to be pulled up a rough inclined plane set at angle α with the horizontal. If the coefficient of friction is μ, then the minimum required force is:

(a) $(\sin\alpha + \mu\cos\alpha)W$ (b) $(\sin\alpha - \mu\cos\alpha)W$

(c) $\dfrac{(\sin\alpha + \mu\cos\alpha)W}{\sqrt{1+\mu^2}}$ (d) $\dfrac{(\sin\alpha - \mu\cos\alpha)W}{\sqrt{1+\mu^2}}$

10. In the arrangement shown in the figure, the wedge is fixed. The string is light and the pulley is smooth. Both blocks have the same mass of 2 kg. The coefficient of friction between the wedge and block A is 0.5.

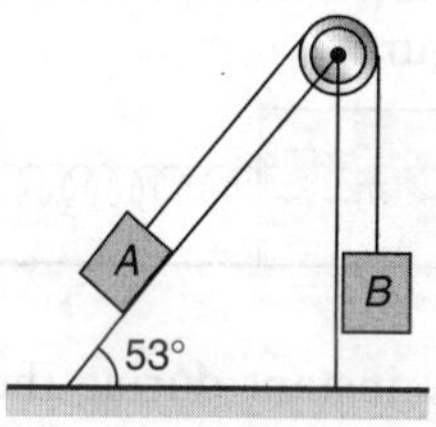

If the system is released from rest, the correct statements from among the following are (take $g = 10\ \text{m/s}^2$):

(a) Tension in the string = 20 N
(b) Contact force between block A and the wedge $= 4\sqrt{10}$ N
(c) Friction force between block A and the wedge = 4 N
(d) None of these

11. An elastic spring has a length l_1 when it is stretched with a force 2 N and a length l_2 when it is stretched by a force 3 N. The length of the spring when it is stretched by a force 5 N is:

(a) $l_1 + l_2$ (b) $\dfrac{1}{2}(l_1 + l_2)$

(c) $3l_2 - 2l_1$ (d) $3l_1 - 2l_2$

12. Three blocks A(5 kg), B(3 kg) and C(2 kg) are placed close together on a rough horizontal surface having coefficient of friction $\mu = 0.1$. A horizontal force F is pushing the blocks, as shown in the figure.

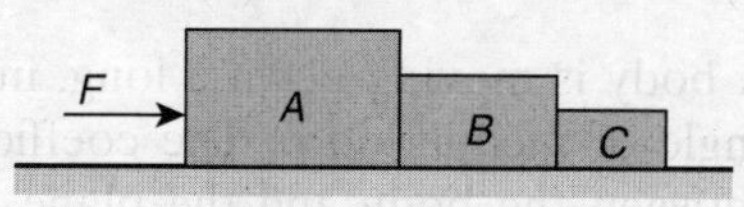

Let N_1 and N_2 be the contact forces between blocks A, B and B, C, respectively. Then:

(a) $N_1 = 10\,\text{N}, N_2 = 4\,\text{N}$ if $F = 20\,\text{N}$
(b) $N_1 = 4\,\text{N}, N_2 = 1\,\text{N}$ if $F = 9\,\text{N}$
(c) $N_1 = 2\,\text{N}, N_2 = 0\,\text{N}$ if $F = 7\,\text{N}$
(d) None of these

13. A small body was launched up along a rough inclined plane set at angle α with the horizontal. If the time of descent of the body is η times greater than the time of ascent, then the coefficient of friction μ is:

(a) $\mu = \dfrac{\eta^2 - 1}{\eta^2 + 1}\tan\alpha$ (b) $\mu = \dfrac{\eta^2 + 1}{\eta^2 - 1}\cot\alpha$

(c) $\mu = \sqrt{\dfrac{\eta^2 + 1}{\eta^2 - 1}}\tan\alpha$ (d) $\mu = \sqrt{\dfrac{\eta^2 + 1}{\eta^2 + 1}}\cot\alpha$

14. Two blocks of mass M and m connected by a light spring are placed on a smooth horizontal surface. Mass M is pulled by a horizontal force F, as shown in the figure.

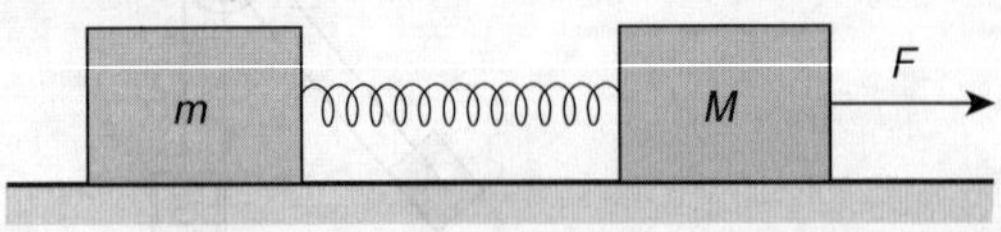

If at any instant during the motion, acceleration of m is a opposite to the direction of F, then acceleration of M at this instant is:

(a) $\dfrac{F - ma}{M}$ (b) $\dfrac{F + ma}{M}$

(c) $\dfrac{F - ma}{M + m}$ (d) $\dfrac{F + ma}{M + m}$

15. Two blocks of mass 5 kg and 3 kg are placed on a horizontal surface, as shown in the figure. The coefficient of friction between the blocks is 0.5 and that between the 5-kg block and the ground is 0.7.

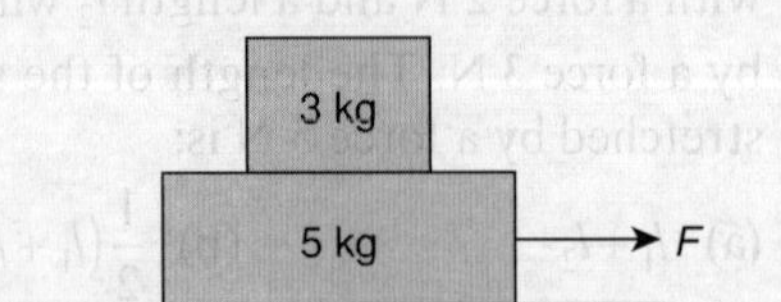

The maximum horizontal force F that can be applied on the 5-kg block so that the two blocks can move without slipping is:

(a) 20 N (b) 36 N
(c) 80 N (d) 96 N

16. A body is moving down a long, inclined plane of angle of inclination θ. The coefficient of friction between the body and the plane varies with the distance travelled as $\mu = 0.5\,s$. The body has maximum velocity at s equal to:

(a) $2\tan\theta$ (b) $2\cot\theta$

(c) $\sqrt{2}\tan\theta$ (d) $\sqrt{2}\cot\theta$

17. The spring and the string shown in the figure have negligible mass.

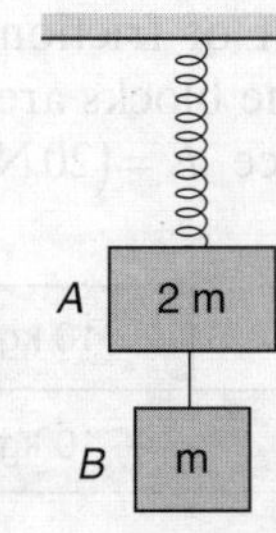

If the string is suddenly cut, the blocks A and B will move with accelerations:

(a) g, g (b) $g, \dfrac{1}{2}g$

(c) $\dfrac{1}{2}g, g$ (d) $\dfrac{1}{2}g, \dfrac{1}{2}g$

18. A small block of mass 10 kg is placed at a distance of 5 m from the rear end of a long trolley, as shown in the figure. The coefficient of friction between the block and the trolley is 0.2.

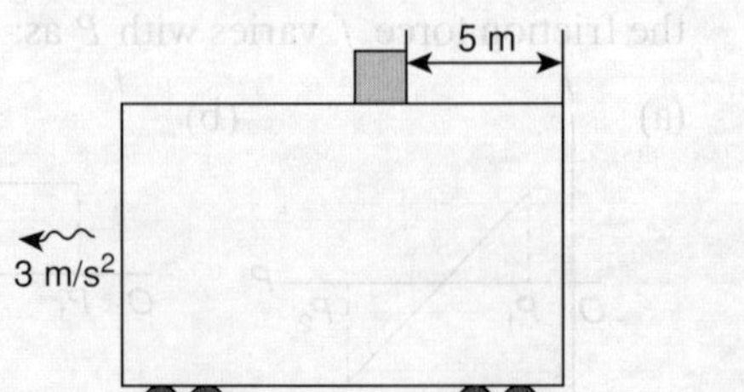

Starting from rest, the trolley moves with a uniform acceleration of 3 m/s^2. By the time the block falls off, the distance travelled by the trolley is:

(a) 15 m (b) 20 m
(c) 25 m (d) 30 m

19. The figure shows a triangular wire frame, fixed in the vertical plane. Two beads A and B of mass m each are connected by a light rod and are free to slide along the wires without friction.

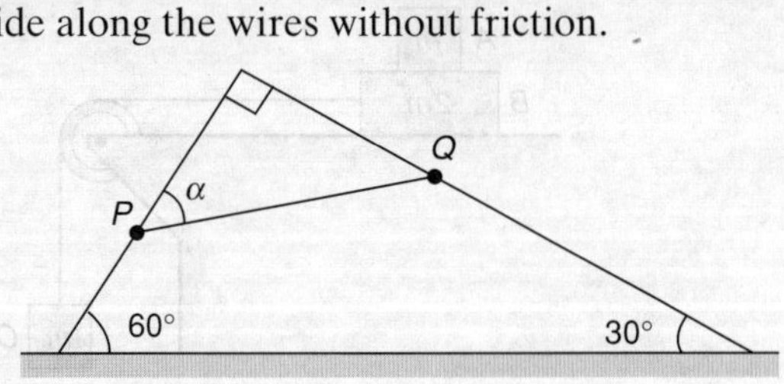

At equilibrium, the correct options are:

(a) Tension in the rod = mg
(b) Angle $\alpha = 30°$
(c) Reaction on bead $P = \sqrt{3}mg$
(d) Reaction on bead $Q = mg$

20. The figure shows a cart that can slide freely along an incline whose inclination angle is α.

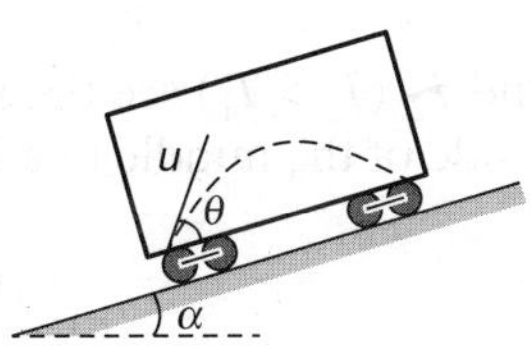

A man inside the cart throws a ball with speed u at angle θ to the incline. The range of the ball as measured by the man inside the cart is:

(a) $\dfrac{u^2 \tan\theta}{g}$ (b) $\dfrac{u^2 \sin 2\theta}{g \cos\alpha}$

(c) $\dfrac{u^2}{g\cos\alpha}$ (d) $\dfrac{u^2 \sin\alpha}{g\cos\theta}$

21. For the arrangement shown in the figure, the pulleys are light and smooth and the strings are ideal. When the system is released from rest, the 10-kg and 5-kg blocks are found to remain at rest. This is possible:

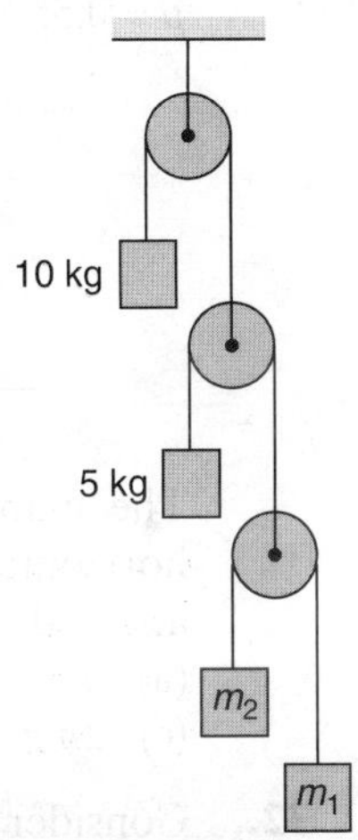

(a) If $m_1 = m_2 = 2.5$ kg
(b) For many values of m_1 and m_2
(c) If the arithmetic mean of $m_1, m_2 = 2.5$ kg
(d) If the harmonic mean of $m_1, m_2 = 2.5$ kg

22. The blocks A and B shown in the figure have masses m and $2m$, respectively. The string is ideal, and the pulleys are light and smooth. The string is pulled by a horizontal force F.

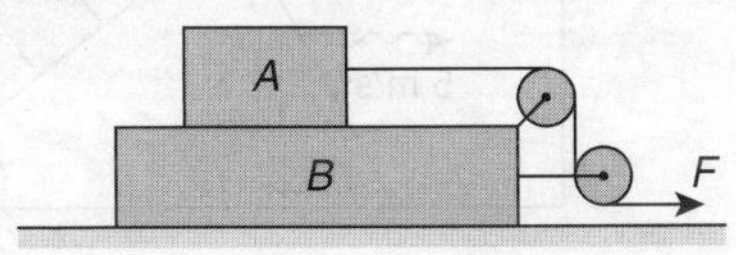

If the ground is smooth and the coefficient of friction between the blocks is $\mu = F/5mg$, then relative acceleration between the blocks is:

(a) $11F/15m$ (b) 0
(c) $3F/10m$ (d) $7F/10m$

23. A rough surface whose vertical cross-section is given by $x^2 = 3y$ is moving with a uniform acceleration $g/8$ along the horizontal; here, the x and y axes are along the Earth's horizontal and vertically upward directions, respectively. A small block placed on the surface remains in equilibrium at a maximum height of $1/12$ m. The coefficient of friction between the block and the surface is:

(a) $1/5$ (b) $1/4$
(c) $1/3$ (d) $1/2$

24. The wedge shown in the figure is pushed by a man with uniform acceleration $a = g/2$. along the horizontal.

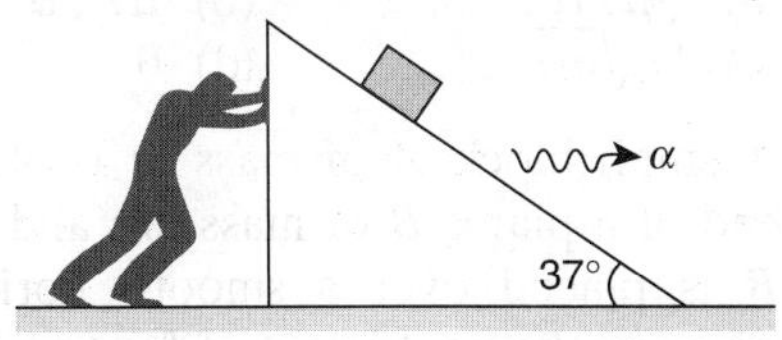

If the wedge surface is smooth, the absolute acceleration of the block kept on the wedge is (take $g = 10\text{ m/s}^2$):

(a) 5 m/s^2 (b) $3\sqrt{5}\text{ m/s}^2$
(c) 3 m/s^2 (d) $2\sqrt{5}\text{ m/s}^2$

25. A body of mass 1 kg moving with an initial speed of $v_0 = 9$ m/s starts experiencing a variable resistive force directed opposite its velocity. Let v denote the speed of the body at time t, and F be the magnitude of the resistive force. If F varies with speed as $F = 2\sqrt{v}$, then variation of F with time is given by:

(a) $F = 2(3-t)^2$ (b) $F = 2(3-t)^{3/2}$

(c) $F = 2\sqrt{3-t}$ (d) $F = 2(3-t)$

26. In the arrangement shown in the figure, the wedge is fixed. The string is light and the pulley is smooth. The blocks have masses m and $2m$. The coefficient of friction between m and the wedge is $2/3$, and that between $2m$ and the wedge is $1/3$.

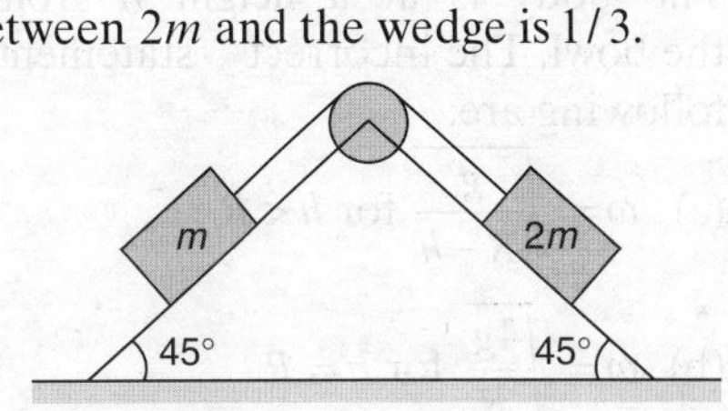

The system is released from rest. The correct statements from the following are:

(a) Friction force between block $2m$ and the wedge $= \dfrac{2\sqrt{2}}{3}mg$
(b) Friction force between block m and the wedge $= \dfrac{1}{3\sqrt{2}}mg$
(c) Tension in the string $= \dfrac{2\sqrt{2}}{3}mg$
(d) None of these

27. A long rod has a sleeve which can slide along its length. The rod is set in angular motion in a horizontal plane about an axis through one end of the rod with uniform angular acceleration α. If gravity is neglected and the friction coefficient between the bead and the rod is μ, then the time after which the sleeve starts slipping is:

(a) $\sqrt{\mu / \alpha}$ (b) $\mu / \sqrt{\alpha}$

(c) $1 / \sqrt{\mu \alpha}$ (d) 0

28. A small block A of mass m is placed at the left end of a plank B of mass $2m$ and length l. Plank B is placed over a smooth horizontal surface, whereas the coefficient of friction between A and B is $\mu = 0.5$. Block A is given a horizontal velocity $u = 3$ m/s towards the right. The minimum value of l so that block A does not fall from plank B is (take $g = 10$ m/s^2):

(a) 0.6 m (b) 0.75 m

(c) 1.0 m (d) 1.25 m

29. A smooth hemispherical bowl of radius R is rotating with a uniform angular speed ω, as shown in the figure. A small body rests on the inner side of the bowl in equilibrium with respect to the bowl.

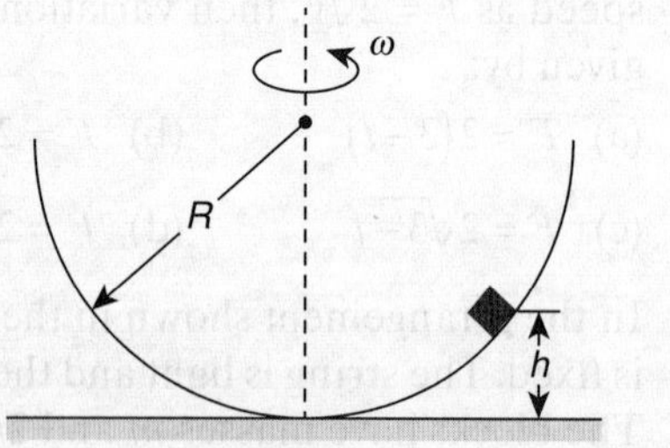

The body is at a height h from the base of the bowl. The incorrect statements from the following are:

(a) $\omega = \sqrt{\dfrac{g}{R-h}}$ for $h < R$

(b) $\omega = \sqrt{\dfrac{4g}{R}}$ for $h = R$

(c) $\omega = \sqrt{\dfrac{2g}{R}}$ for $h = R/2$

(d) $\omega > \sqrt{\dfrac{g}{R}}$ for non-zero h

30. A uniform rod AB of mass m has two small beads, each of mass m attached to it, one at end B and the other in the middle of the rod (see figure). The rod is rotating in a horizontal plane with uniform angular speed about a vertical axis passing through end A.

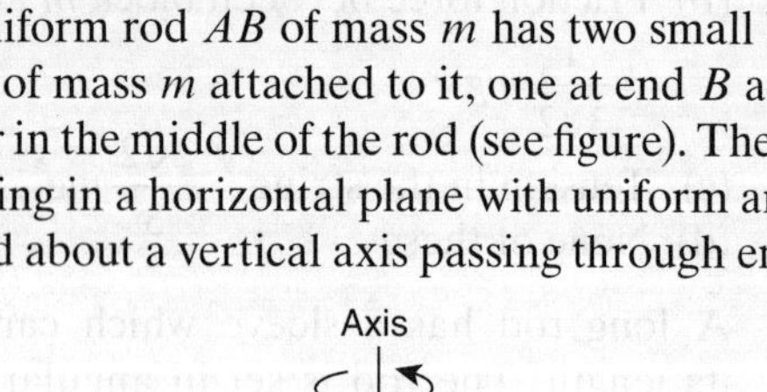

If T_1 and T_2 ($T_2 > T_1$) are the tensions in the rod on either side of the middle bead, then the ratio T_2 / T_1 is:

(a) $\dfrac{15}{11}$ (b) $\dfrac{15}{8}$

(c) $\dfrac{11}{8}$ (d) $\dfrac{3}{2}$

31. In the arrangement shown in the figure, the pulleys are light and smooth and the string is ideal. The mass of block A is $4m$ and that of blocks B and C are m each. The coefficient of friction between A and B and that between A and C is the same, $\mu = 0.5$.

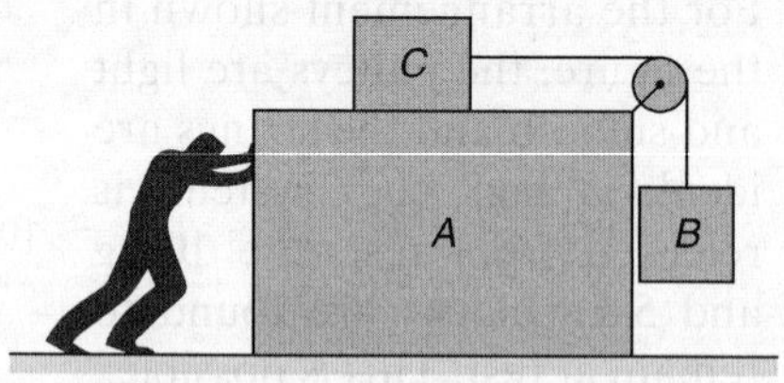

The man is pushing the wedge with a constant horizontal force F. The value of F so that blocks B and C do not move relative to block A is:

(a) $mg < F < 8mg$ (b) $4mg < F < 20mg$

(c) $2mg < F < 18mg$ (d) $mg < F < 20mg$

32. Consider the arrangement shown in the figure. Consider all the surfaces to be smooth.

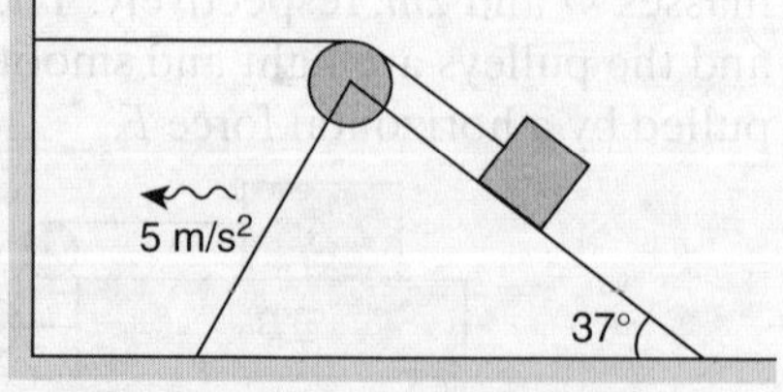

If the wedge is moving with acceleration 5 m/s^2 to the left, then match the given columns regarding the block:

(a) Acceleration relative to the wedge	(p) $\sqrt{10}$ m/s^2
(b) Absolute acceleration	(q) 5 m/s^2
(c) Horizontal component of absolute acceleration	(r) 3 m/s^2
(d) Vertical component of absolute acceleration	(s) 1 m/s^2

33. Consider the arrangement shown in the figure. The mass of the body is 4 kg. The tension in the upper cord is 65 N. The system is rotating about a vertical axis with uniform speed ω.

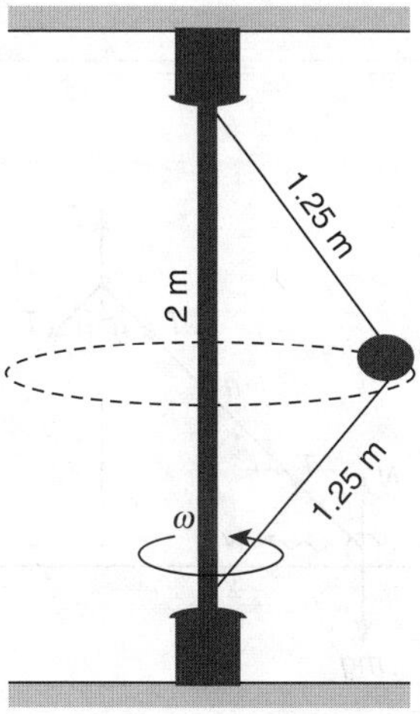

Match the given columns (take $g = 10\ m/s^2$):

(a) Tension in the lower cord	(p) 15 N
(b) Angular speed	(q) 48 N
(c) Net force on the block	(r) 4 rad/s
(d) Centripetal force on the block	(s) 5 rad/s

34. The trolley shown in the figure moves on a horizontal road starting from rest with acceleration 2 m/s^2 for 2 s and then decelerates with 3 m/s^2, finally coming to rest. The coefficient of friction between the trolley and the block P placed on it is 0.1. Initially, block P is also at rest.

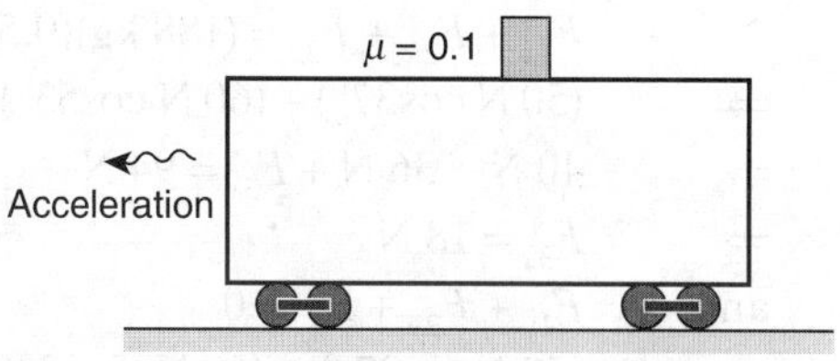

Match the given columns (take $g = 10\ m/s^2$):

(a) Total time of motion of P	(p) 2.5 s
(b) Time when P's velocity is maximum	(q) 5 s
(c) Absolute displacement of P	(r) $\frac{5}{12}$ m
(d) Displacement of P relative to the trolley	(s) 6.25 m

ANSWER KEYS

1. (c)	**2.** (d)	**3.** (b)	**4.** (a)	**5.** (a)	**6.** (b)	**7.** (a)	**8.** (d)
9. (c)	**10.** (a),(b),(c)	**11.** (c)	**12.** (a),(b),(c)	**13.** (a)	**14.** (b)	**15.** (d)	**16.** (a)
17. (c)	**18.** (a)	**19.** (a),(b)	**20.** (b)	**21.** (a),(b),(d)	**22.** (d)	**23.** (a)	**24.** (b)
25. (d)	**26.** (b),(c)	**27.** (a)	**28.** (a)	**29.** (b)	**30.** (a)	**31.** (c)	

32. (a)-(q), (b)-(p), (c)-(s), (d)-(r) **33.** (a)-(p), (b)-(r), (c)-(q), (d)-(q) **34.** (a)-(q), (b)-(p), (c)-(s), (d)-(r)

SOLUTIONS

1. (c) Let F_{3x} and F_{3y} be the components of the force F_3. Then

$$F_{1x} + F_{2x} + F_{3x} = (188 \text{ kg})(0.5 \text{ m/s}^2)$$
$$\Rightarrow \quad (50 \text{ N} \cos 37°) + (60 \text{ N} \cos 53°) + F_3 x = 94 \text{ N}$$
$$\Rightarrow \quad 40 \text{ N} + 36 \text{ N} + F_{3x} = 94 \text{ N}$$
$$\Rightarrow \quad F_{3x} = 18 \text{ N}$$
and
$$F_{1y} + F_{2y} + F_{3y} = 0$$
$$\Rightarrow \quad (50 \text{ N} \sin 37°) + (60 \text{ N} \sin 53°) + F_3 y = 0$$
$$\Rightarrow \quad 30 \text{ N} - 48 \text{ N} + F_{3y} = 0$$
$$\Rightarrow \quad F_{3y} = 18 \text{ N}$$

Hence $F_3 = \sqrt{(18 \text{ N})^2 + (18 \text{ N})^2} = 18\sqrt{2} \text{ N}$

2. (d)

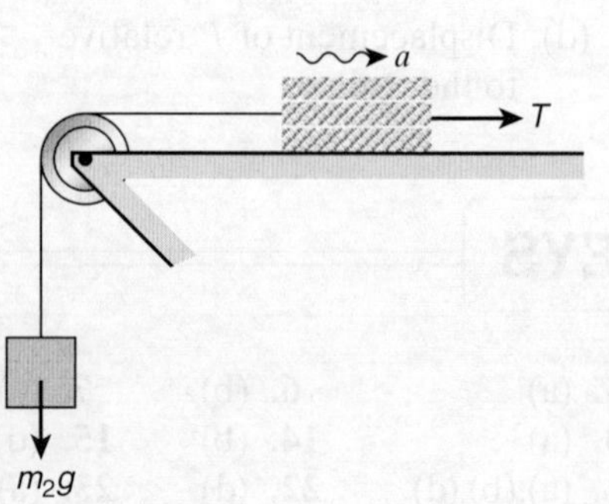

The system moves with acceleration

$$a = \frac{(m_1 - m_2)g}{m_1 + m_2 + m} = \frac{g}{2}$$

Let us cut the rope 10 cm from its left end. If we consider block m_2 and the cut portion of the rope as our system, the forces acting are shown in the figure. The mass of the cut portion of the rope is $\frac{m}{3} = 1 \text{ kg}$. Using dynamics, we have

$$T - m_2 g = \left(m_2 + \frac{m}{3}\right)a$$
$$\Rightarrow \quad T - 1g = 2\left(\frac{g}{2}\right)$$
$$\Rightarrow \quad T = 2g = 20 \text{ N}$$

3. (b) Let T be the tension in the string and W be the acceleration of each particle. The figure shows the forces on a small portion of the thread at the highest point and the two bodies.

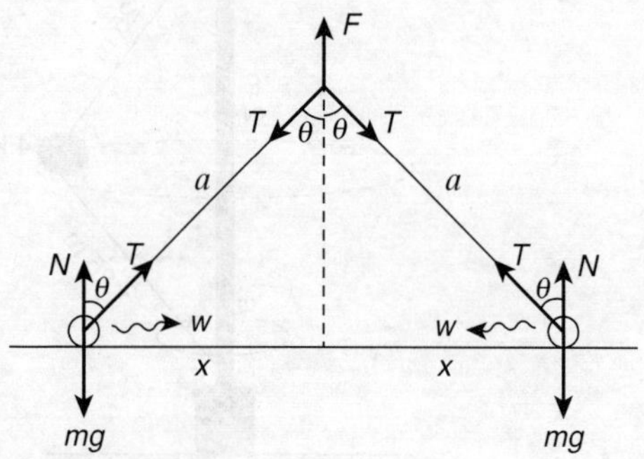

For the small portion of the thread, we have

$$2T\cos\theta = F \qquad \ldots(1)$$

For any one of the particles, we have

$$T\sin\theta = mw \qquad \ldots(2)$$
$$T\cos\theta + N = mg \qquad \ldots(3)$$

Eliminating T from (1) and (2), we have

$$w = \frac{F}{2m}\cot\theta = \frac{F}{2m} \cdot \frac{x}{\sqrt{l^2 - x^2}}$$

The relative acceleration between the particles is

$$2w = \frac{F}{m} \cdot \frac{x}{\sqrt{l^2 - x^2}}$$

4. (a)

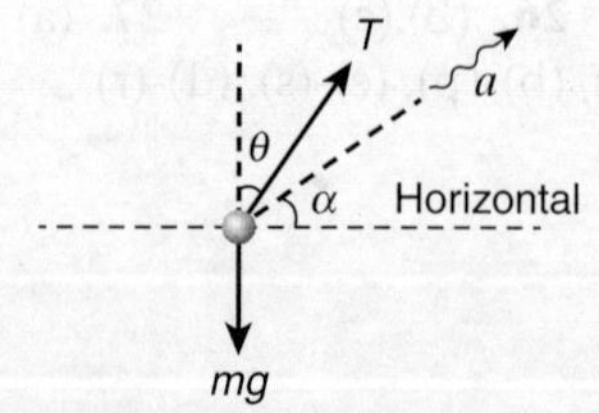

The figure shows the forces acting on the pendulum. Using dynamics along the horizontal and the vertical, we have

$$T\sin\theta = m\,(a\cos\alpha) \qquad \ldots(1)$$
and
$$T\cos\theta - mg = m(a\sin\alpha) \qquad \ldots(2)$$

Eliminating T, we have

$$\tan\theta = \frac{a\cos\alpha}{a + a\sin\alpha}$$

5. (a)

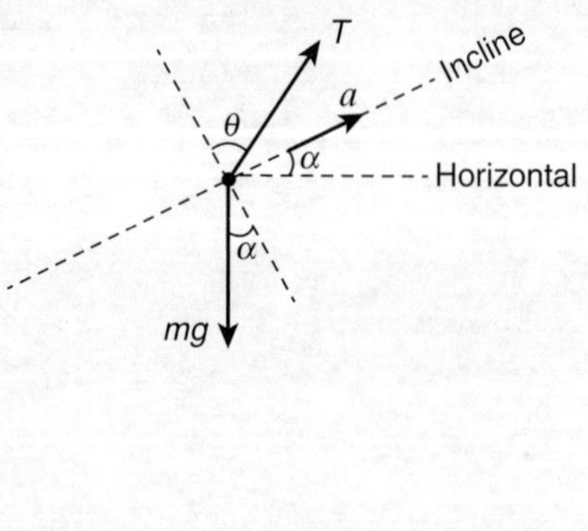

The figure shows the forces acting on the pendulum. Using dynamics along the incline and perpendicular to the incline, we have

$$T\sin\theta - mg\sin\alpha = ma \quad ...(1)$$

and $$T\cos\theta = mg\cos\alpha \quad ...(2)$$

Eliminating T, we have

$$\tan\theta = \frac{g\sin\alpha + a}{g\cos\alpha}$$

6. (b) The limiting friction force between the blocks is f = 0.2(10g) = 20 N. The maximum possible acceleration for the lower block is

$$a = \frac{f}{10\text{ kg}} = \frac{20\text{ N}}{10\text{ kg}} = 2\text{ m/s}^2$$

The blocks will move without slipping till acceleration of the upper block reaches the value a = 2 m/s². This happens at time t given by

$$20t - 20\text{ N} = (10\text{ kg})(2\text{ m/s}^2) \text{ gives } t = 2\text{ s}$$

7. (a) The force trying to pull the block down the incline is $mg\sin\theta$. Initially, the applied force $P_1 = mg(\sin\theta - \mu\cos\theta)$ is less than $mg\sin\theta$, so the block will have a tendency to slip down and, therefore, friction will act up along the incline (see figure).

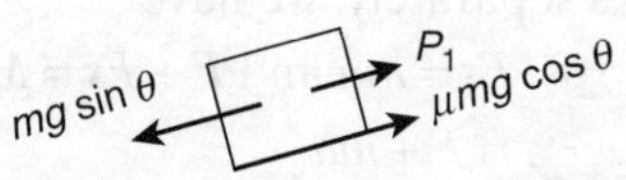

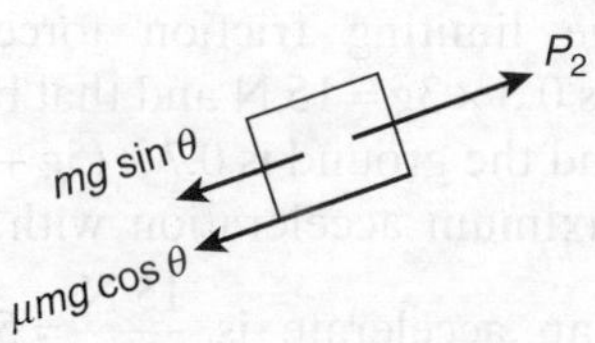

The value of friction force will be

$$f_1 = mg\sin\theta - P_1 = \mu mg\cos\theta$$

As the applied force P increases to a value equal to $mg\sin\theta$, the friction force vanishes, as there is no tendency to slip.

Finally, the applied force $P_2 = mg(\sin\theta + \mu\cos\theta)$ is greater than $mg\sin\theta$, so the block will have a tendency to slip and, therefore, friction will act down along the incline (see figure). The value of friction force will be

$$f_2 = P_2 - mg\sin\theta = \mu mg\cos\theta$$

8. (d) If we consider the three blocks and the connecting string as our system, then the only force along the string is mg in the downward direction. The system, therefore, accelerates with acceleration

$$a = \frac{mg}{4m} = g/4$$

To find the tension in the string, let us consider only block C as our system. Applying dynamics, we have

$$mg - T = ma \Rightarrow T = \frac{3}{4}mg$$

To find the friction force between blocks A and B, let us consider only block A as our system. Applying dynamics, we have

$$f = ma = \frac{1}{4}mg$$

The normal contact force between blocks A and B is $N = mg$. The coefficient of friction is given by

$$\mu \geq \frac{f}{N} = \frac{mg/4}{mq} = 1/4$$

The figure shows the forces acting on the pulley. The force R exerted by the table is

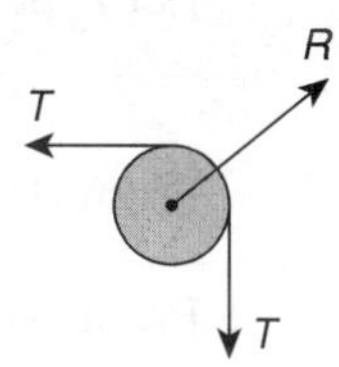

$$R = \sqrt{2}T = \frac{3mg}{2\sqrt{2}}$$

9. (c)

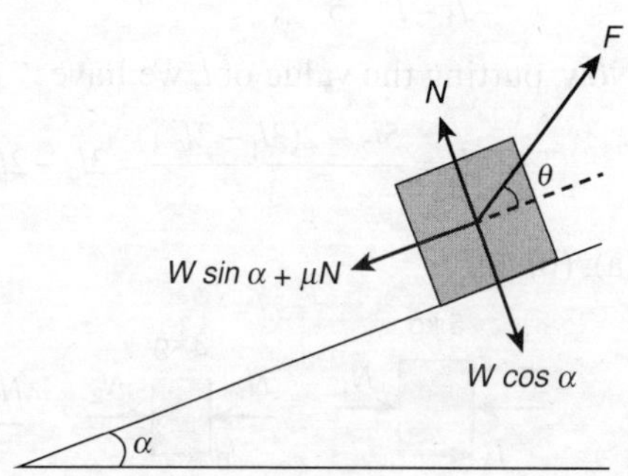

Let force F be applied at angle θ to the inclined plane. Then

$$N + F\sin\theta = W\cos\alpha \quad ...(1)$$

and $$F\cos\theta = W\sin\alpha + \mu N \quad ...(2)$$

Eliminating N from (1) and (2), we have

$$F\cos\theta = W\sin\alpha + \mu(W\cos\alpha - F\sin\theta)$$

$$\Rightarrow \quad F = \frac{(\sin\alpha + \mu\cos\alpha)W}{\cos A + \mu cin\theta}$$

We see that the value of F depends upon the angle θ. The force F is minimum when $\cos\theta + \mu\sin\theta$ is maximum, which is $\sqrt{1+\mu^2}$. Hence

$$F_{\min} = \frac{(\sin\alpha + \mu\cos\alpha)W}{\sqrt{1+\mu^2}}$$

10. (a), (b), (c) Gravitational force on B in the vertically downward direction is 20 N and that on A along the incline is 20 N sin53° = 16 N. Hence, the system will have a tendency to move such that B falls down. In that case, friction on A will act along the downward direction. The limiting friction force on A is 0.5 (20 N cos 53°) = 6 N. We can see that the system will not move since the net pulling force on the system is 20 N – 16 N = 4 N, which is less than the limiting friction force 6 N. Acceleration $a = 0$ and tension in the string = 20 N.
Friction force on block A = 20 N – 16 N = 4 N and contact force between block A and the wedge = $\sqrt{(20\text{ N}\cos 53°)+(4\text{ N})^2} = 4\sqrt{10}$ N

11. (c) Let k be the spring contact and l be its natural length. Then, we have

$$k(l_1 - l) = 2 \quad \text{...[1]}$$

$$k(l_2 - l_1) = 3 \quad \text{...[2]}$$

Let l_3 be the required length. Then we have

$$k(l_3 - l) = 5 \quad \text{...[3]}$$

From (1) and (2), $\dfrac{l_1 - l}{l_2 - l} = \dfrac{2}{3} \Rightarrow l = 3l_1 - 2l_2$

From (2) and (3),

$$\frac{l_2 - l}{l_3 - l} = \frac{3}{5} \Rightarrow l_3 = \frac{5l_2 - 2l}{3}$$

Now, putting the value of l, we have

$$l_3 = \frac{5l_2 - 2(3l_1 - 2l_2)}{3} = 3l_2 - 2l_1$$

12. (a), (b), (c)

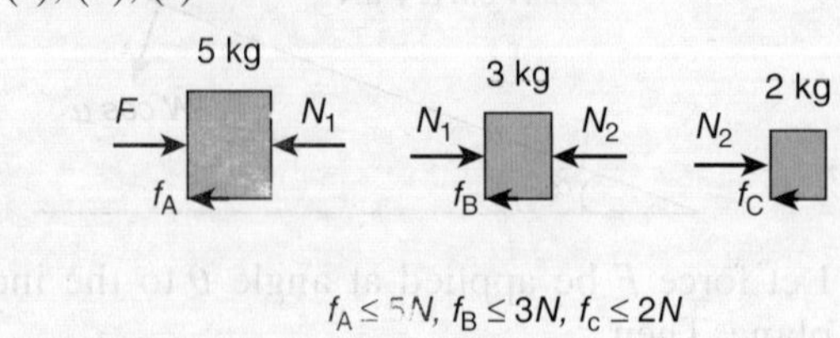

<u>F = 20 N</u>
System will acceler.

$$a = \frac{20\text{ N} - (5\text{ N} + \text{ N} + 2\text{ N})}{5\text{ kg} + 3\text{ kg} + 2\text{ kg}} = 1\text{ m/s}^2$$

$$20\text{ N} - 5\text{ N} - N_1 = (5\text{ kg})(1\text{ m/s}^2) \Rightarrow N_1 = 10\text{ N}$$

$$N_2 - 5\text{ N} = (2\text{ kg})(1\text{ m/s}^2) \Rightarrow N_2 = 4\text{ N}$$

<u>F = 9 N</u>
System will not accelerate

$$N_1 = 9\text{ N} - 5\text{ N} = 4\text{ N},\ N_2 = N_1 - 3\text{N} = 1\text{ N}$$

<u>F = 7 N</u>
System will not accelerate

$$N_1 = 7\text{ N} - 5\text{ N} = 2\text{ N},\ N_2 = 0\ (\text{Since } N_1 < f_{\text{Bmin}})$$

13. (a) During ascent, the ball experiences an acceleration aN = (sin α + μ cos α)g in the downward direction. It travels a distance $S = \dfrac{u^2}{2a_1}$ and takes time $t_1 = \dfrac{u}{a_1}$.

During descent, the ball experiences an acceleration $a_2 = (\sin\alpha - \mu\cos\alpha)\, g$ in the downward direction and takes time $t_2 = \sqrt{\dfrac{2S}{a_2}} = \dfrac{u}{\sqrt{a_1 a_2}}$.

$$\text{Hence } \eta = \frac{t_2}{t_1} = \sqrt{\frac{a_1}{a_2}} = \sqrt{\frac{\sin\alpha + \mu\cos\alpha}{\sin\alpha - \mu\cos\alpha}}$$

$$\Rightarrow \mu = \frac{n^2 - 1}{n^2 + 1}\tan\alpha$$

14. (b)

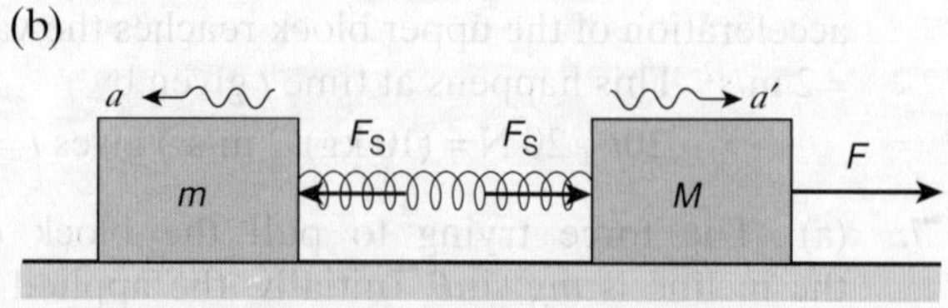

The figure shows the forces acting on both the blocks. The force exerted by the spring at this instant is shown as F_s. Using dynamics for both the blocks separately, we have

$$Fs = ma \text{ and } F + Fs = Ma'$$

$$\text{Hence } a' = \frac{F + ma}{M}$$

15. (d) The limiting friction forces between the blocks is 0.5 × 3g = 15 N and that between the 5-kg block and the ground is 0.7 × (5g + 3g) = 56 N. The maximum acceleration with which the 3-kg block can accelerate is $\dfrac{15\text{ N}}{3\text{ kg}} = 5\text{ m/s}^2$ (it is the friction force between the blocks that accelerates the 3-kg block). Hence, the entire system can move as one single block with a maximum acceleration of 5 m/s².

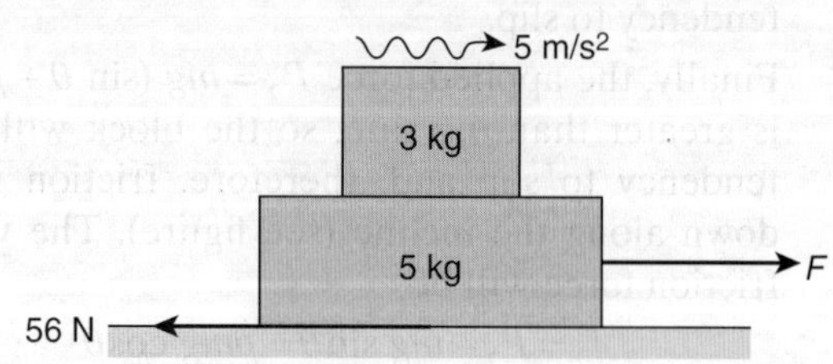

Now, for the two-block system, the forces acting on it are shown in the figure. Using dynamics, we have

$$F - 56\text{ N} = 8\text{ kg} \times 5\text{ m/s}^2 \Rightarrow F = 96\text{ N}$$

16. (a) Net force acting on the body along the incline is $F = mg\sin\theta - \mu mg\cos\theta = mg(\sin\theta - 0.5\,s\cos\theta)$
The value of F reduces to zero at s given by

$$\sin\theta - 0.5\,s\cos\theta = 0\ s = 2\tan\theta$$

Till this point, velocity increases. Beyond this point, the direction of F reverses and velocity starts decreasing. Hence, this is the position where the velocity is maximum.

17. (c) The string is pulling block B upward and block A downward with mg. When the string is at equilibrium, the force of both blocks is distributed. A experiences a net upward force mg and B experiences a net downward force mg. Hence, A accelerates upward with acceleration $\frac{mg}{2m} = \frac{g}{2}$ and

B accelerates downward with acceleration $\frac{mg}{m} = g$

18. (a)

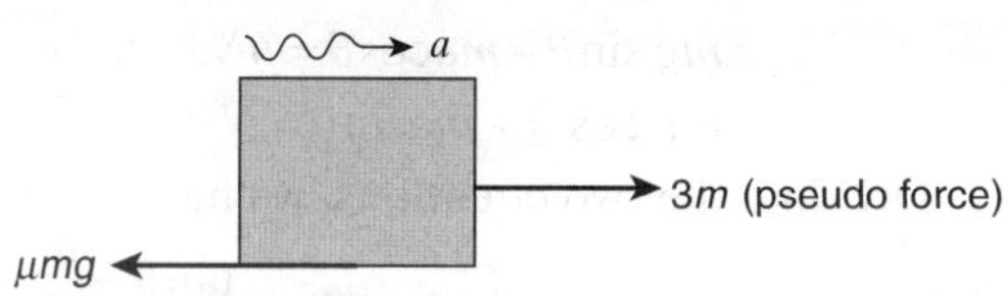

The figure shows the force acting on the block from a reference frame attached to the trolley. The block accelerates towards the right with acceleration

$$a = \frac{3m - \mu mg}{m} = 1\ \text{m/s}^2$$

The time in which the block will fall is given by

$$5m = \frac{1}{2}(1\ \text{m/s}^2)t^2 \Rightarrow t = \sqrt{10}\ \text{s}$$

Distance travelled by the trolley in this time is $\frac{1}{2}(3\ \text{m/s}^2)t^2$

19. (a), (b)

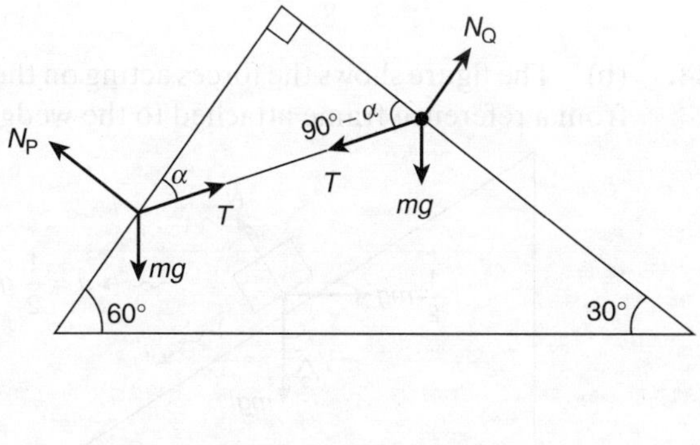

For bead P

$$T\cos\alpha = mg\sin 60° \quad \text{...[1]}$$
$$T\sin\alpha + mg\cos 60° = N_P \quad \text{...[2]}$$

For bead Q

$$T\sin\alpha = mg\sin 30° \quad \text{...[3]}$$
$$T\cos\alpha + mg\cos 30° = N_Q \quad \text{...[4]}$$

Dividing Equations (1) and (3) gives

$$\tan\alpha = \tan 30° \Rightarrow a = 30° \Rightarrow T = mg$$

Putting in Equations (2) and (4) gives $N_P = mg$ and $N_Q = \sqrt{3}\,mg$

20. (b) The cart has an acceleration of $g\sin\alpha$ down the incline. From a surface frame attached to the cart, the ball experiences a pseudo force $mg\sin\alpha$ up the incline and the gravitational force mg vertically downward (see figure).

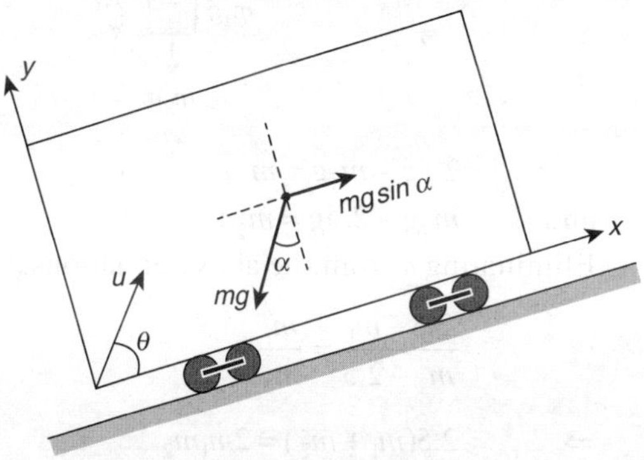

The net force is $mg\cos\alpha$ along the –ve y-axis. Hence, the ball has an acceleration of $g\cos\alpha$ along the –ve y-axis. The total time of flight of the ball is

$$T = \frac{2u\sin\theta}{q\cos\alpha}$$

And its range is

$$R = (u\cos\theta)T = \frac{u^2\sin 2\theta}{g\cos\alpha}$$

21. (a), (b), (d) Tension in the thread over the top-most pulley is 10g. Tension in the thread over the middle pulley is 5 g. Tension in the thread over the bottom-most pulley is 2.5 g.
The question does not state whether the two blocks m_1, m_2 are at rest. So, let their acceleration be a (see figure). Thus, we have

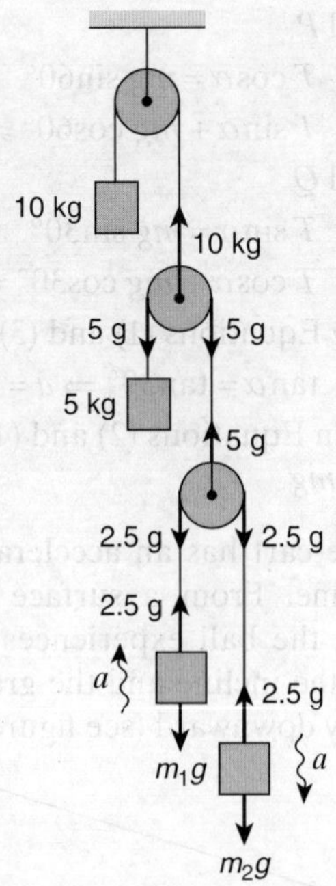

$$2.5g - m_1g = m_1a \quad ...[1]$$

and $$m_2g - 2.5g = m_2a \quad ...[2]$$

Eliminating a from the above equations, we have

$$\frac{2.5 - m_1}{m_2 - 2.5} = \frac{m_1}{m_2}$$

$$\Rightarrow \quad 2.5(m_1 + m_2) = 2m_1m_2$$

$$\Rightarrow \quad \frac{1}{m_1} + \frac{1}{m_2} = \frac{2}{2.5}$$

$\Rightarrow$ HM of m_1, m_2 equals 2.5

Hence, there can be many possible values for m_1, m_2 that will satisfy the above equation.

22. (d)

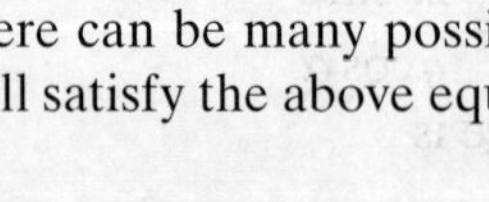

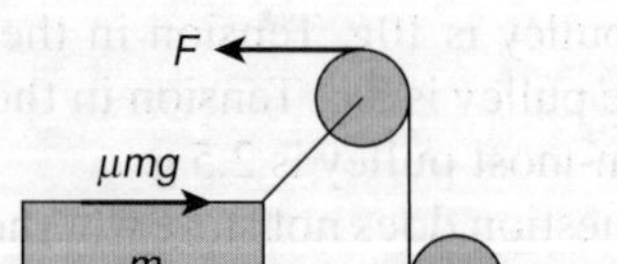

The figure shows the forces acting on the two blocks separately. Using dynamics, we have

$$a_A = \frac{F - \mu mg}{m} = \frac{4F}{5m} \quad \left[\text{Putting } \mu = \frac{F}{5mg}\right]$$

and $$a_B = \frac{\mu mg}{2\text{ m}} = \frac{F}{10\text{ m}}$$

Hence, relative acceleration $= |a_A - a_B| = \dfrac{7F}{10m}$

23. (a) The figure shows the forces acting on the block from a reference frame attached to accelerating surface.

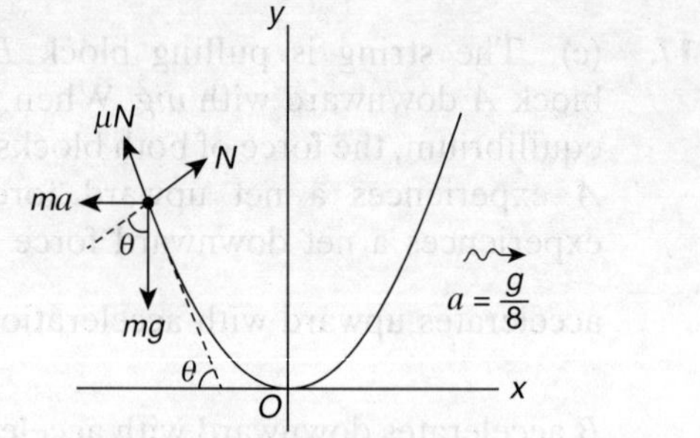

Using dynamics along the tangential and the normal directions, we have

$$mg\sin\theta - ma\cos\theta = \mu N \quad ...[1]$$

$$mg\cos\theta + ma\sin\theta = N \quad ...[2]$$

Dividing the two equations, we have

$$\mu = \frac{g\sin\theta - a\cos\theta}{g\cos\theta + a\sin\theta} = \frac{\tan\theta - \dfrac{a}{g}}{1 + \dfrac{a}{g}\tan\theta}$$

From the figure, we can see that $\tan\theta$ is the slope of the tangent to the curve. Differentiating $y = \frac{1}{3}x^2$, we have

$$y' = \frac{2}{3}x = \frac{2}{3}\sqrt{3y}$$

At $y = \frac{1}{12}$, $y' = \frac{1}{3}$. Hence

$$\mu = \frac{\dfrac{1}{3} - \dfrac{1}{8}}{1 + \dfrac{1}{3} \times \dfrac{1}{8}} = \frac{5}{25} = \frac{1}{5}$$

24. (b) The figure shows the forces acting on the block from a reference frame attached to the wedge.

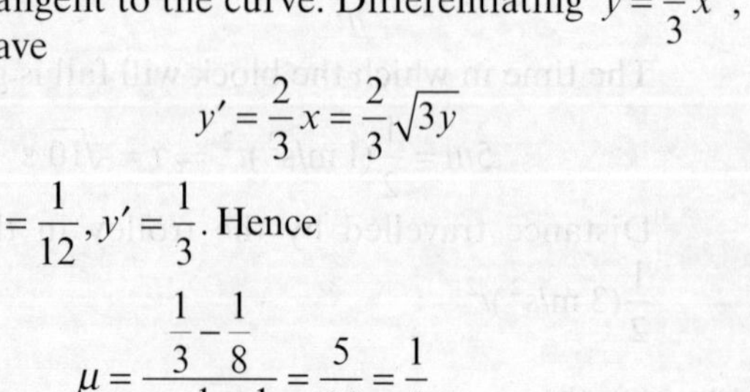

Acceleration of the block relative to the wedge is

$$a' = \frac{mg\sin 37^\circ - \frac{1}{2}mg\cos 37^\circ}{m} = \frac{1}{5}g$$

The absolute acceleration of the block is the vector sum of a' and a, that is

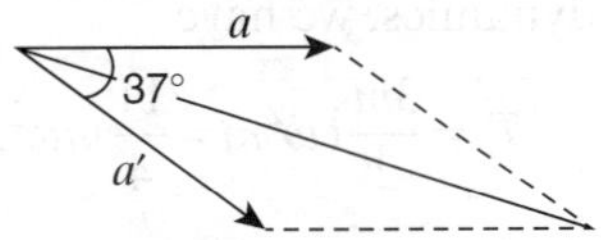

$$\sqrt{a'^2 + a^2 + 2aa'\cos 37^\circ} = \frac{3\sqrt{5}}{10}g$$

25. (d) The 1-kg body experiences an acceleration $a = \frac{-F}{1\text{ kg}} = -2\sqrt{v}$ due to the resistive force. Writing $v\frac{dv}{dx}$ in place of a, we have

$$v\frac{dv}{dx} = -2\sqrt{v}$$

$$\Rightarrow \quad \int \sqrt{v}\,dv = -2\int dx$$

$$\Rightarrow \quad v^{3/2} = -3x + \text{const}^{27} \quad [v = 9 \text{ m/s at } x = 0]$$

$$\Rightarrow \quad v = (3x - 27)^{2/3}$$

$$\Rightarrow \quad \int \frac{dx}{(3x-27)^{2/3}} = \int dt \quad \left[\text{Writing } v = \frac{dx}{dt}\right]$$

$$\Rightarrow \quad (3x-27)^{1/3} = t + \text{const}^{-3} \; [x = 0 \text{ at } t = 0]$$

$$\Rightarrow \quad x = 9 + \frac{1}{3}(t-3)^3$$

Now differentiating twice with respect to time, we have

$$a = 2(t-3)$$

$$\Rightarrow \quad F = -(1\text{ kg})a = 2(3-t)$$

26. (b), (c) The gravitational forces on the two blocks along the incline are $2mg$ cos 45° and mg cos45°. We can see that $2m$ will have a tendency of motion along the downward direction and m along the upward direction. The limiting friction forces on the two blocks are $\frac{1}{3}(2mg\cos 45^\circ) = \frac{\sqrt{2}}{3}mg$ and $\frac{2}{3}(mg\cos 45^\circ) = \frac{\sqrt{2}}{3}m.$

The pulling force along the string in the $2m$ end is $2\,mg\sin 45^\circ = \sqrt{2}\,33\,mg$ and the net opposing force is $mg\sin 45^\circ + \frac{\sqrt{2}}{3}mg + \frac{\sqrt{2}}{3}mg = \frac{7}{3\sqrt{2}}mg$, which is greater than the pulling force $\sqrt{2}\,mg$. Hence, the system will not move.

Consider the forces acting on block $2m$ along the incline. The gravitational force is $2mg$ sin45° = $\sqrt{2}mg$.

The friction force is limiting

$$= \frac{1}{3}(2mg\cos 45^\circ) = \frac{\sqrt{2}}{3}mg$$

The tension in the string $= \sqrt{2}mg - \frac{\sqrt{2}}{3}mg = \frac{2\sqrt{2}}{3}mg$

Now, consider the forces acting on block m. The tension is $\frac{2\sqrt{2}}{3}mg$. The gravitational force along the incline is $mg\sin 45^\circ = \frac{1}{\sqrt{2}}mg$.

The friction force is $= \frac{2\sqrt{2}}{3}mg - \frac{1}{\sqrt{2}}mg = \frac{1}{3\sqrt{2}}mg$

27. (a) The figure shows the forces acting on the bead. Using dynamics, we have

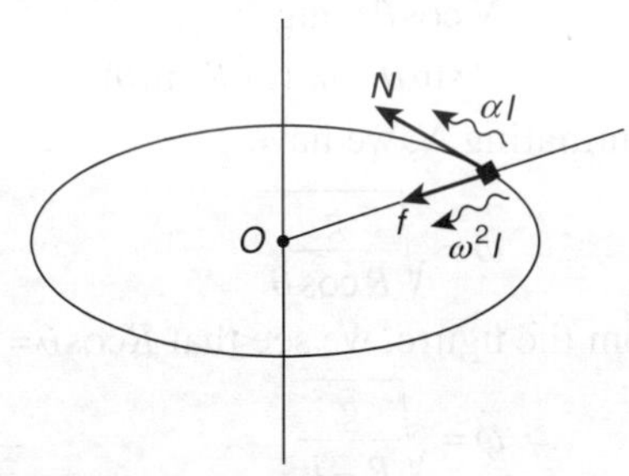

$$N = m(\alpha l) \text{ and } f = m(\omega^2 l)$$

Since $f < \mu N$, we have

$$m(\omega^2 l) < \mu m(\alpha l) \Rightarrow \omega < \sqrt{\mu\alpha}$$

This is the maximum angular velocity with which the bead can rotate. The time in which the rod will acquire this much angular velocity is $\frac{\omega}{\alpha} = \sqrt{\frac{\mu}{\alpha}}$.

28. (a) The figure shows the forces acting on the ball and plank.

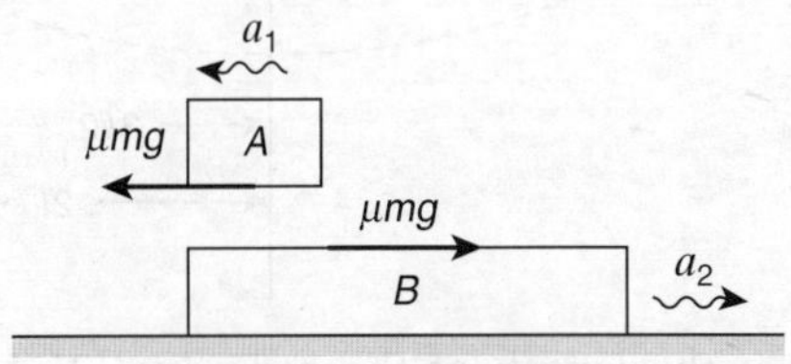

Using dynamics, the absolute acceleration of the block A and plank B are, respectively

$$a_1 = \frac{\mu mg}{m} = \mu g \text{ towards the left}$$

and $a_2 = \dfrac{\mu mg}{2m} = \dfrac{1}{2}\mu g$ towards the right

Relative to the plank, the block can accelerate $= a_1 + a_2 = \dfrac{3}{2}\mu g$ towards the left

The length of the plank should satisfy

$$l \geq \frac{u^2}{2a} = \frac{u^2}{3\mu g} = \frac{(3\ \text{m/s}^2)}{3\times(0.5)(10\ \text{m/s}^2)} = \frac{3}{5}\text{m} = 0.6\ \text{m}$$

29. (b) The figure shows the forces acting on the block and the plank.

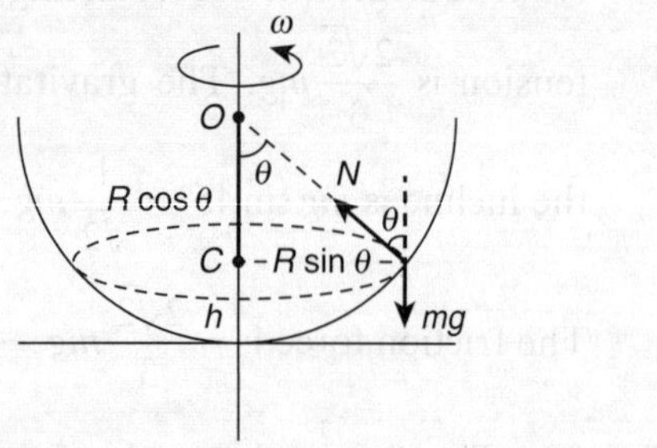

Using dynamics, we have

$$N\cos\theta = mg \qquad \text{...[1]}$$

and $$N\sin\theta = m(\omega^2 R\sin\theta) \qquad \text{...[2]}$$

Eliminating N, we have

$$\omega = \sqrt{\frac{g}{R\cos\theta}}$$

From the figure, we see that $R\cos\theta = R - h$. Hence

$$\omega = \sqrt{\frac{g}{R-h}}$$

The other options follow from this result.

30. (a)

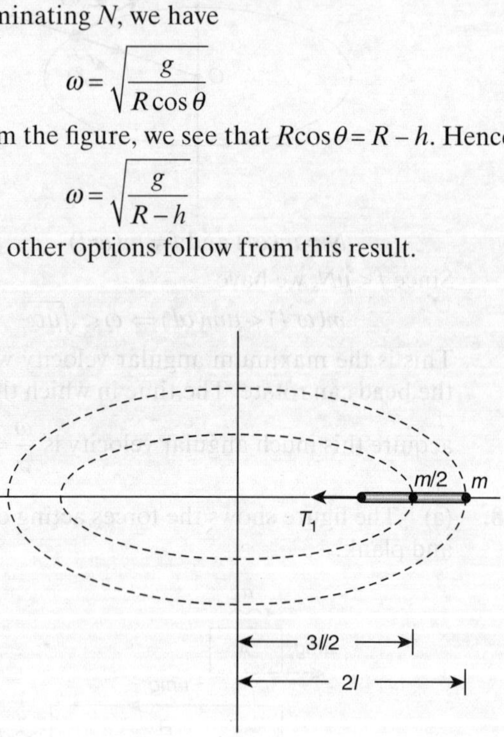

Let the length of the rod equal $2l$. Let ω be the angular speed. The above figure shows the forces acting on the portion of the rod cut just at the right side of the middle bead. The centre of mass of this half of the rod is at a distance of $3l/2$ from the axis, and the centre of mass of the bead attached at its extreme end is at distance $2l$ from the axis. The combined centre of mass is at distance

$$r = \frac{(m/2)(3l/2) + m(2l)}{3m/2} = \frac{11l}{6}$$

Using dynamics, we have

$$T_1 = \frac{3m}{2}(\omega^2 r) = \frac{11}{4}m\omega^2 l$$

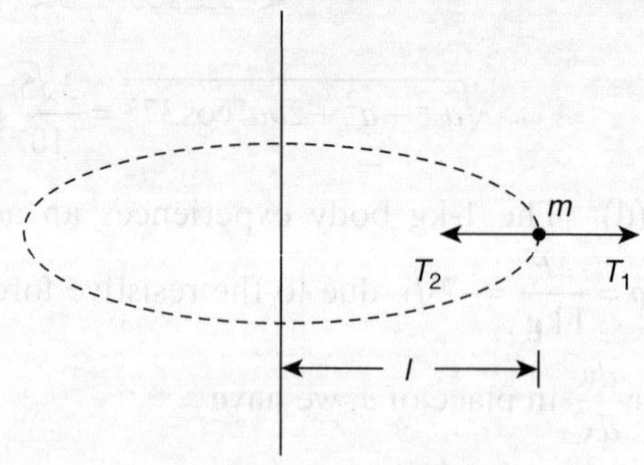

The above figure shows the forces acting on the middle bead. Using dynamics, we have

$$T_2 - T_1 = m\omega^2 l$$

$$\Rightarrow \quad T_2 = \frac{11}{4}m\omega^2 l + m\omega^2 l = \frac{15}{4}m\omega^2 l$$

Hence $\dfrac{T_2}{T_1} = \dfrac{15}{11}$

31. (c) Consider the situation when the force applied is minimum. The figure shows forces on the block B + block C system, as seen from a reference frame attached to block A.

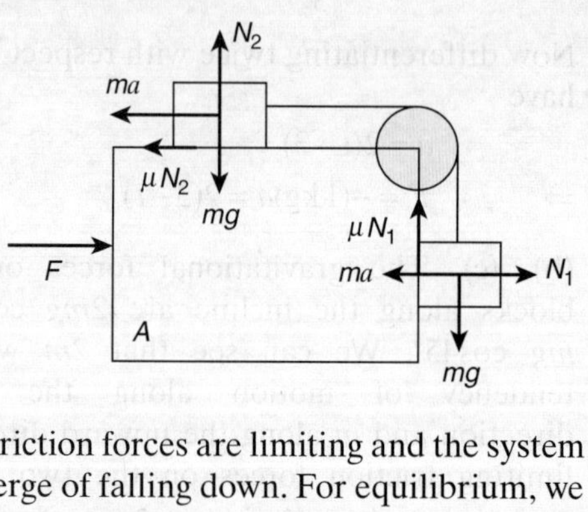

The friction forces are limiting and the system is on the verge of falling down. For equilibrium, we have

$$ma + \mu N_2 + \mu N_1 = mg$$

$$\Rightarrow \quad ma + \mu mg + \mu ma = mg$$

$$\Rightarrow \quad a = \left(\frac{1-\mu}{1\ to\ \mu}\right)g = \left(\frac{1-0.5}{1\ to\ 0.5}\right) = \frac{1}{3}g$$

The required force is $F = 6ma = 2g$.

Now, if the force F is increased, the pseudo force ma on block C will increase and ball B will have a tendency to move up. The friction forces will reverse and the maximum acceleration should be $a = \left(\frac{1+\mu}{1-\mu}\right)g = 3g$. Hence, the result is $2mg < F < 18mg$.

32. (a)-(q), (b)-(p), (c)-(s), (d)-(r)
When the wedge moves left by x, the string between the wall and the wedge shortens in length by x. Now, since the string is inextensible, the block must move down the incline by the same amount x. Thus, we conclude that the acceleration of the block relative to the wedge is the same as the absolute acceleration of the wedge, that is, 5 m/s^2.

Absolute acceleration of the block is the vector sum of the acceleration of the block relative to the wedge, and that of the wedge relative to ground. That is

$$a_{block} = \sqrt{5^2 + 5^2 + 2.5.5\cos(80° \pm 37°)} \text{ m/s}^2$$
$$= \sqrt{10} \text{ m/s}^2$$

Horizontal component of the absolute acceleration = 5 m/s^2 – 5 m/s^2 cos37° = 1 m/s^2

Vertical component of the absolute acceleration = 5 m/s^2 sin37° = 3 m/s^2

33. (a)-(p), (b)-(r), (c)-(q), (d)-(q)
The block is moving in a circle of radius $r = \sqrt{(1.25\text{ m})^2 + (1\text{ m})^2} = \frac{3}{4}$ m.

Also, we have cos θ = 1/1.25 = 4/5, and hence, sinθ = 3/5.

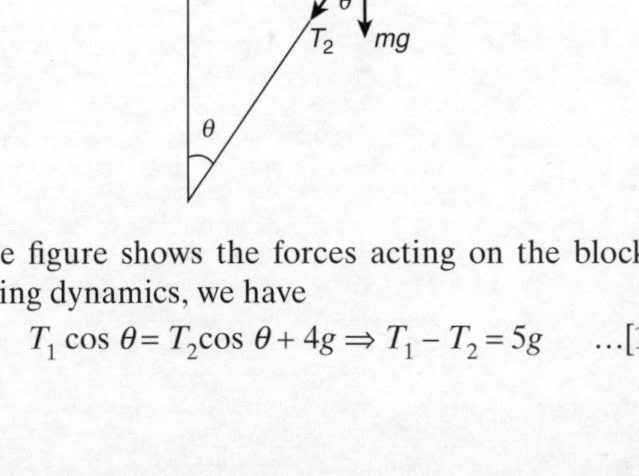

The figure shows the forces acting on the block. Using dynamics, we have

$$T_1 \cos\theta = T_2\cos\theta + 4g \Rightarrow T_1 - T_2 = 5g \quad ...[1]$$

and $T_1\sin\theta + T_2\sin\theta = 4(\omega^2 r) \Rightarrow T_1 + T_2 = 5\omega^2$ ...[2]

Now, putting $T_1 = 65$ N, we have $T_2 = 15$ N and $\omega = 4$ rad/s.

The net force equals the centripetal force $4(\omega^2 r)$ = 48 N.

34. (a)-(q), (b)-(p), (c)-(s), (d)-(r)
When two bodies in contact move relative to each other, the friction force between them acts opposite to their respective velocity directions. The one moving left experiences friction force towards the right and vice-versa.

At $t = 0$, the trolley starts moving to the left. Friction on the trolley acts to the right and friction on the block acts to the left, producing an acceleration μg = 1 m/s^2 in the block.

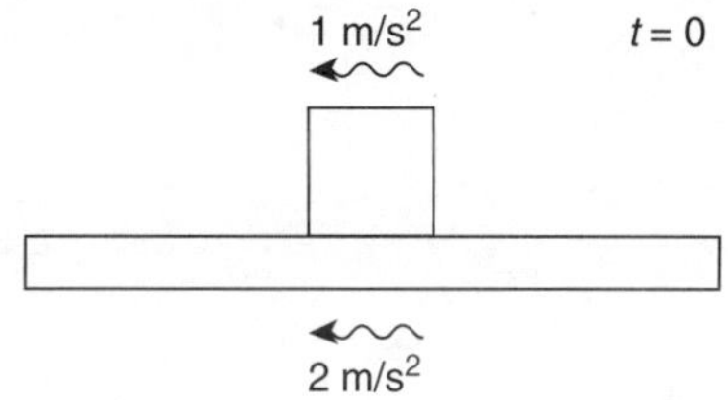

After 2 s, the trolley is moving with velocity 2 m/s^2 × 2 s = 4 m/s and the block is moving with velocity 1 m/s^2 × 2 s = 2 m/s. The trolley now decelerates with magnitude 3 m/s^2. However, the block continues to accelerate towards the left. Hence, the friction on the block is still towards the left. Friction will reverse direction when their velocities become equal. This happens after the time t given by $4 - 3\xi = 2 + 1\xi \Rightarrow \xi = 1/2$ s and velocity = 2.5 m/s.

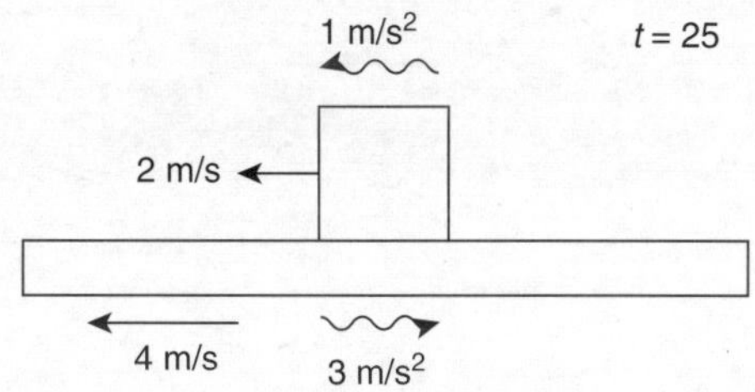

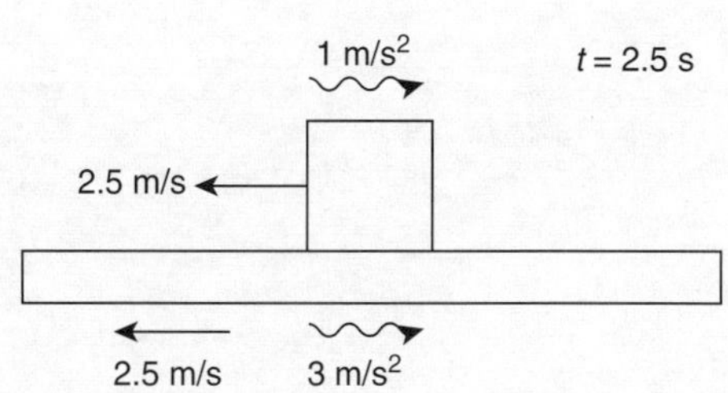

From this time onwards, the block will also decelerate with magnitude 1 m/s^2 till its velocity reduces to zero, that is, for another 2.5 m/s / 1 m/s^2 = 2.5 s.

Hence, the maximum velocity of the block is 2.5 m/s, the total time of motion is 2.5 s + 2.5 s = 5 s

and the displacement is $2\times\frac{(2.5\text{ m/s})^2}{2\times 1\text{ m/s}^2}=\frac{25}{4}\text{ m}$

The trolley displacement is

$$\frac{1}{2}\times(2\text{ m/s}^2)(2\text{ s})^2+\frac{(4\text{ m/s})^2}{2\times 3\text{ m/s}^2}=\frac{20}{3}\text{ m}$$

Hence, the relative displacement of the block is

$$\frac{25}{4}\text{ m}-\frac{20}{3}\text{ m}=-\frac{5}{12}\text{ m}$$

CHAPTER

4 Work–Energy

- When a force **F** acts on a particle that undergoes displacement, the work W done by the force is defined as
$$W = \int \mathbf{F} \cdot d\mathbf{r}$$
If the force is constant throughout the motion, then
$$W = \mathbf{F} \cdot \Delta\mathbf{r}$$
- The kinetic energy K of a particle equals the amount of work required to accelerate the particle from rest to speed v:
$$K = \frac{1}{2}mv^2$$
The gravitational potential energy U_{gr} of a body relative to a horizontal surface equals the amount of work required to raise the centre of mass of the body from that surface to position y:
$$U_{gr} = mgy$$
The spring potential energy U_{sp} of a spring equals the amount of work required to deform (elongate or compress) the spring from its natural length by an amount x:
$$U_{sp} = \frac{1}{2}kx^2$$
- If the work done by a force is independent of the path, the force is called conservative; otherwise, it is called non-conservative. Gravity and spring force are examples of conservative forces. Friction is a non-conservative force. The work done by a conservative force can always be expressed as the negative of the change in a potential energy function:
$$W_{gravity} = -(mgy_2 - mgy_1) = -\Delta U_{gr} \text{ and } W_{spring} = -\left(\frac{1}{2}kx_2^2 - \frac{1}{2}kx_1^2\right) = -\Delta U_{sp}$$
- Work–Energy Theorem states that the work done by all forces (external as well as internal) on a body equals the sum of the changes in its kinetic and potential energies:
$$W_{nc} + W_{other} = \Delta K + \Delta U_{gr} + \Delta U_{sp}$$
The sum $K + U = E$ is called mechanical energy. If $W_{nc} + W_{other} = 0$, the mechanical energy remains conserved:
$$K_2 + U_2 = K_1 + U_1$$
- The work done by non-conservative forces manifests itself as changes in the internal energies of the bodies. The sum of the kinetic, potential and internal energy is always conserved:
$$\Delta K + \Delta U + \Delta U_{int} = 0$$
- Average and instantaneous power:
$$P_{av} = \frac{\Delta W}{\Delta t} \text{ and } P = \lim_{\Delta t \to 0} \frac{\Delta W}{\Delta t} = \frac{dW}{dt}$$
When a force **F** acts on a particle moving with velocity **v**, the instantaneous power is given by
$$P = \mathbf{F} \cdot \mathbf{v}$$
- For one-dimensional motion, a conservative force $F_x(x)$ and its associated potential energy function $U(x)$ are related as
$$F_x = -\frac{dU}{dx}$$
In three-dimensional motion, a conservative force **F** and its associated potential energy function $U(x, y, z)$ are related as
$$\mathbf{F} = -\left(\frac{\partial U}{\partial x}\mathbf{i} + \frac{\partial U}{\partial y}\mathbf{j} + \frac{\partial U}{\partial z}\mathbf{k}\right)$$

EXERCISES

1. A particle moves from position $\mathbf{r}_1 = (3\text{ m})\mathbf{i} + (2\text{ m})\mathbf{j} - (6\text{ m})\mathbf{k}$ to position $\mathbf{r}_2 = (14\text{ m})\mathbf{i} + (13\text{ m})\mathbf{j} + (9\text{ m})\mathbf{k}$ under the influence of a force $\mathbf{F} = (4\text{ N})\mathbf{i} + (1\text{ N})\mathbf{j} + (3\text{ N})\mathbf{k}$. Work done by the force is:
(a) 70 J (b) 100 J
(c) 90 J (d) 110 J

2. A force $\mathbf{F} = -c(y\boldsymbol{i} + x\boldsymbol{j})$ acts on a particle moving in the *xy* plane. Starting from the origin, the particle is taken along the positive *x*-axis to the point $(a, 0)$ and then parallel to the *y*-axis to the point (a, a). Work done by the force is:
(a) $-2ca^2$ (b) ca^2
(c) $2ca^2$ (d) $-ca^2$

3. If the kinetic energy of a body moving along the *x*-axis is proportional to *x*, then the force acting on the body is proportional to:
(a) $x^{1/2}$ (b) $x^{-1/2}$
(c) $x^{3/2}$ (d) Independent of *x*

4. A body of mass *m* accelerates uniformly from rest to velocity v_0 in time t_0. Instantaneous power delivered to the body as a function of time *t* is:
(a) $\left(\dfrac{mv_0}{t_0}\right)t$ (b) $\left(\dfrac{mv_0^2}{t_0^2}\right)t$
(c) $\left(\dfrac{mv_0^2}{t_0^2}\right)t^2$ (d) $\left(\dfrac{mv_0}{t_0}\right)t^2$

5. The kinetic energy acquired by a body of mass *m* in moving a certain distance, starting from rest, under the action of a certain force, is proportional to:
(a) $m^{1/2}$ (b) $m^{3/2}$
(c) $m^{-1/2}$ (d) Independent of *m*

6. A body of mass 200 g is thrown from the Earth's surface with kinetic energy 24 J, at an angle of 60° to the horizontal. Neglecting air drag, the height to which the body rises is (take $g = 10\text{ m/s}^2$):
(a) 9 m (b) 8 m
(c) 7 m (d) 6 m

7. A particle of mass 0.1 kg is subjected to a force which varies with distance, as shown in the figure.

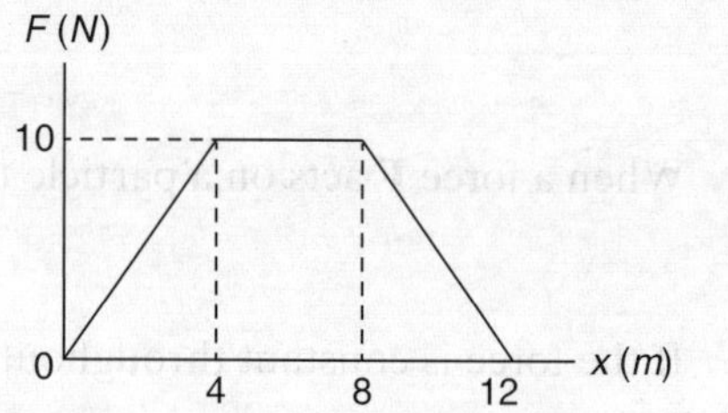

If it starts its journey with initial velocity $u = 20$ m/s at $x = 0$, its velocity at $x = 12$ m is:
(a) 0 (b) $20\sqrt{2}$ m/s
(c) $20\sqrt{3}$ m/s (d) $20\sqrt{5}$ m/s

8. A stone tied to one end of a light string of length 0.7 m is moving in a circle in the vertical plane. If the maximum and minimum tensions in the thread are in the ratio 4 : 1, then the maximum speed of the stone is (take $g = 10\text{ m/s}^2$):
(a) 7 m/s (b) 6 m/s
(c) 5 m/s (d) 4 m/s

9. A body thrown vertically upwards attains maximum height *h*. At what height will its kinetic energy be 75% of its initial value?
(a) $h/3$ (b) $h/4$
(c) $h/5$ (d) $3h/4$

10. A bullet loses $1/10^{\text{th}}$ of its velocity in passing through a wooden plank. The least number of such planks required to stop the bullet is:
(a) 5 (b) 6
(c) 7 (d) 8

11. A uniform chain of mass *m* and length *l* lies on a rough horizontal table with length *x* hanging over the edge. The chain just slips when $x = l/3$. The chain is initially hanging with $x = l/3$; if *W* is the work required to drag the chain up the table, then $\dfrac{36W}{mgl}$ equals:
(a) 1 (b) 4
(c) 7 (d) 8

12. A uniform chain of length *l* lies on a smooth horizontal table with one-third of its length hanging over the edge. The chain is now released and it starts sliding. If g is the acceleration due to the Earth's gravity, then the chain's velocity when it just slips off the table is:

(a) $\sqrt{\frac{4gl}{3}}$ (b) $\sqrt{\frac{2gl}{9}}$

(c) $\sqrt{\frac{3gl}{8}}$ (d) $\sqrt{\frac{8gl}{9}}$

13. Two identical cylindrical vessels have the same cross-section area A with their base at the same level, and each contains a liquid of the same density ρ. The height of the liquid in one vessel is h_1 and that in the other vessel is h_2. The work done by gravity in equalling the liquid level when the vessels are interconnected is:

(a) $\rho Ag(h_1+h_2)^2$ (b) $\rho Ag(h_1-h_2)^2$

(c) $\frac{1}{4}\rho Ag(h_1+h_2)^2$ (d) $\frac{1}{4}\rho Ag(h_1-h_2)^2$

14. An electric pump on the ground floor of a building takes 10 min to fill a tank of volume 30 m^3 with water. If the tank is 60 m above the ground and the efficiency of the pump is 30%, the electric power consumption of the pump is (take $g = 10$ m/s^2, density of water = 1000 kg/m^3):

(a) 100 kW (b) 150 kW

(c) 200 kW (d) 250 kW

15. An engine pulls a block of mass 1500 kg on a rough inclined road of gradient 1/10 at a constant speed of 5 m/s. If the friction force is 1500 N, the power generated by the engine is (take $g = 10$ m/s^2):

(a) 5 kW (b) 10 kW

(c) 15 kW (d) 20 kW

16. A small block of mass m starts from rest and slides along a smooth loop-the-loop of radius R, as shown in the figure.

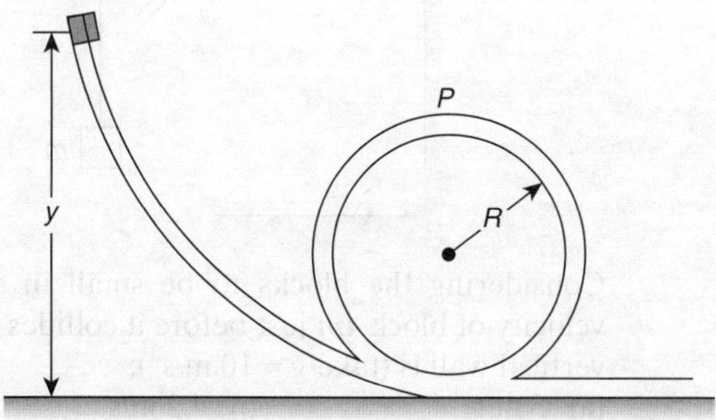

If the block presses against the top of the track (at P) with a force equal to its weight, then the height y from where it was released is:

(a) $2R$ (b) $2.5R$

(c) $3R$ (d) $3.5R$

17. A bullet loses 25% of its speed over a distance of 3.5 cm as it penetrates a wooden plank. The bullet will eventually stop after travelling a total distance equal to:

(a) 8 cm (b) 10 cm

(c) 12 cm (d) 14 cm

18. A horizontal velocity u is imparted to the small body hanging vertically from a light inextensible string of length l, as shown in the figure.

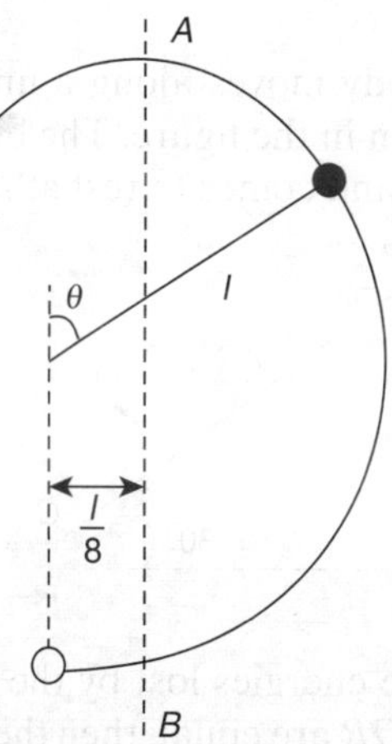

The string becomes slack at some angle θ to the vertical and the body now moves in a parabolic trajectory. If its velocity becomes horizontal when it crosses the line AB, then u^2/gl equals:

(a) $\frac{2\sqrt{3}+3}{2}$ (b) $\frac{4\sqrt{3}+1}{2}$

(c) $\frac{2\sqrt{3}+4}{2}$ (d) $\frac{3\sqrt{3}+4}{2}$

19. Consider the force $\mathbf{F} = (-\alpha x^2)\mathbf{i}$. Then:

(a) **F** is conservative and $\Delta U = \frac{\alpha}{3}\Delta(x^3)$

(b) **F** is conservative and $\Delta U = \frac{\alpha}{2}\Delta(x^2)$

(c) **F** is conservative and $\Delta U = \alpha\Delta x$

(d) **F** is non-conservative

20. A block moving with some initial speed on a rough horizontal surface comes to rest due to friction force. The loss in mechanical energy is ΔE. The same block is now projected with the same initial speed on the same surface, this time inclined at some angle to the horizontal. The block comes to rest after moving a certain distance. If loss in mechanical energy is $\Delta E'$, then:

(a) $\Delta E' = \Delta E$ (b) $\Delta E' > \Delta E$
(c) $\Delta E' < \Delta E$ (d) Insufficient data

21. Constant power is delivered to a particle moving in a straight line. If the initial position and velocity of the particle are zero, then its position x as a function of time t is proportional to:

(a) $t^{1/2}$ (b) $t^{-1/2}$
(c) $t^{3/2}$ (d) Independent of t

22. A body moves along a uniformly rough track, as shown in the figure. The body is released from rest at P and comes to rest at R.

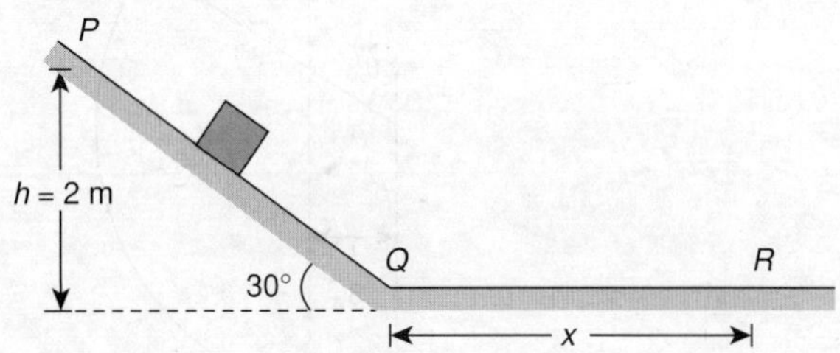

If the energies lost by the body over the parts PQ and QR are equal, then the values of the coefficient of friction μ and the distance x are, respectively:

(a) 0.2 and 6.5 m (b) 0.29 and 6.5 m
(c) 0.2 and 3.5 m (d) 0.29 and 3.5 m

23. A force $\mathbf{F} = \dfrac{-c}{\sqrt{x^2+y^2}}(x\mathbf{i}+y\mathbf{j})$ acts on a particle moving in the xy plane. Work done by the force on a particle as it moves along a circular path of radius a centred at the origin, from a point $A(a,0)$ to the point $B(0,a)$ is:

(a) $-ca$ (b) $\sqrt{2}ca$
(c) $\dfrac{-1}{\sqrt{2}}ca$ (d) 0

24. In the arrangement shown in the figure, both blocks have the same mass m, the spring has spring constant k, and the table surface is smooth. The system is released from rest with the spring in its natural state.

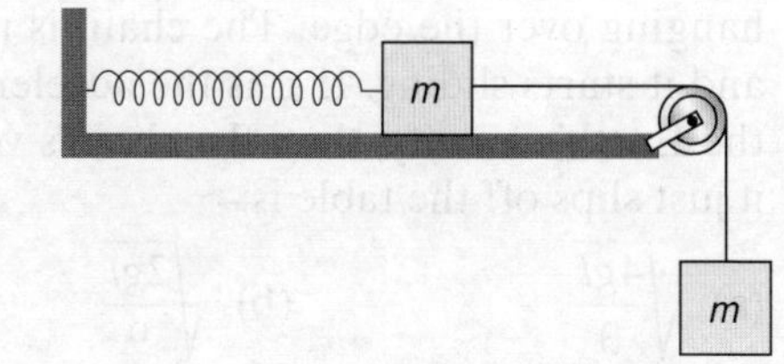

The maximum speed v of the blocks is:

(a) $\sqrt{\dfrac{2mg^2}{k}}$ (b) $\sqrt{\dfrac{3mg^2}{2k}}$
(c) $\sqrt{\dfrac{mg^2}{k}}$ (d) $\sqrt{\dfrac{mg^2}{2k}}$

25. A block slides on a uniformly rough track, starting from rest from point A and finally coming to rest at point B on the horizontal surface, as shown in the figure. The vertical and horizontal displacements of the block are h and s, respectively.

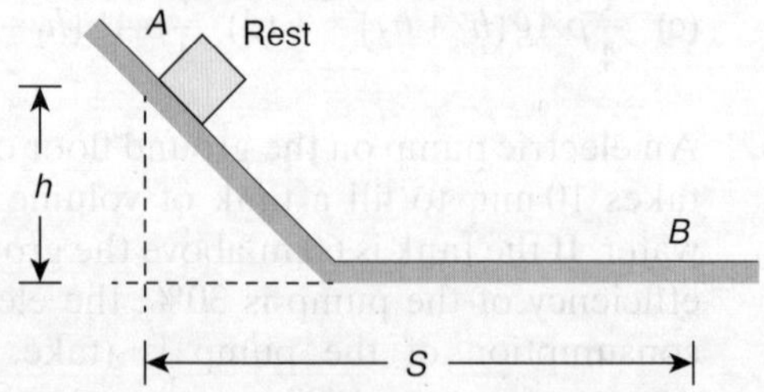

The coefficient of friction between the block and the surface is:

(a) h/s (b) $\dfrac{h}{\sqrt{s^2-h^2}}$
(c) s/h (d) Insufficient data

26. Consider the arrangement shown in the figure. When the system is released from rest, block $4m$ moves in a circular path and block m moves vertically upward.

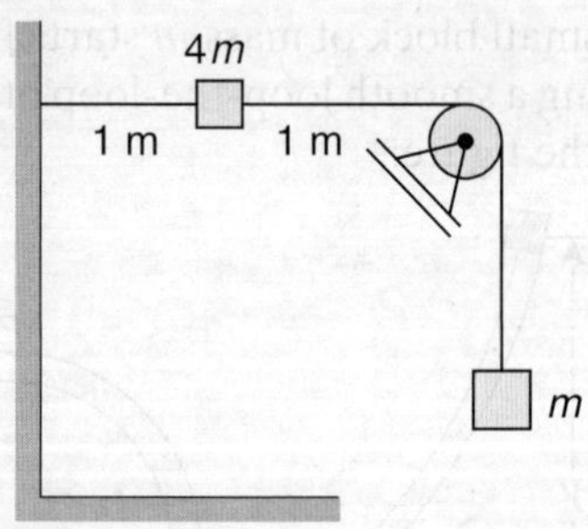

Considering the blocks to be small in size, the velocity of block $4m$ just before it collides with the vertical wall is (take $g = 10\text{ m/s}^2$):

(a) 5 m/s (b) 4.2 m/s
(c) 4 m/s (d) 3.4 m/s

27. A block of mass m is released from rest from a height h above a fixed vertical spring, as shown in the figure. The spring constant is $k = \frac{5mg}{h}$. The block momentarily comes to rest after compressing the spring by a certain amount.

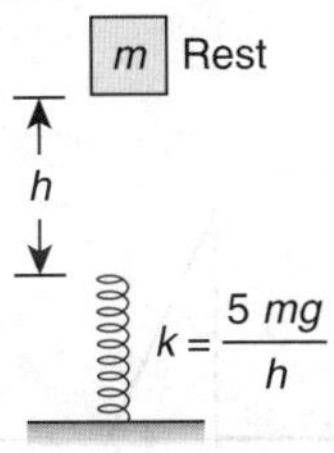

Between these two positions of rest, the maximum velocity of the block is:

(a) $\sqrt{\frac{2gh}{5}}$ (b) $\sqrt{\frac{6gh}{5}}$

(c) $\sqrt{\frac{7gh}{5}}$ (d) $\sqrt{\frac{11gh}{5}}$

28. A bead which is free to slide along a smooth vertical ring of radius R initially rests at the topmost point of the ring. The bead is given a slight push so that it starts sliding along the ring. If θ denotes its angular position measured from its initial vertical position, then the correct statements among the following are:

(a) Acceleration of the bead is vertical at $\theta = \cos^{-1}(1/3)$
(b) Acceleration of the bead is vertical at $\theta = \pi/2$
(c) Acceleration of the bead is horizontal at $\theta = \cos^{-1}(1/3)$
(d) Acceleration of the bead is horizontal at $\theta = \pi - \cos^{-1}(1/3)$

29. In the arrangement shown in the figure, the mass of the block is $m = 0.20$ kg and the force constant of the spring is $k = 4$ N/m. The coefficient of friction between the block and the floor is $\mu = 0.1$. Initially, the block is at rest, and the spring is in its natural state. A constant horizontal force $F = 0.3$ N starts pushing the block towards the wall. The block slides a certain distance before it comes to rest for the first time; it first accelerates to attain peak velocity, and then decelerates to zero velocity.

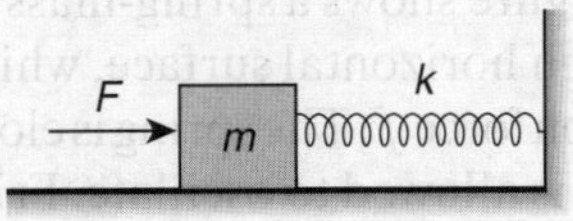

The correct statements from the following are (take $g = 10\ \text{m/s}^2$):

(a) Maximum spring compression = 5 cm
(b) Peak velocity = $5\sqrt{5}$ cm/s
(c) Peak acceleration = 1 m/s^2
(d) None of these

30. A small block of mass m starts from rest and slides along a smooth loop-the-loop of radius R, as shown in the figure.

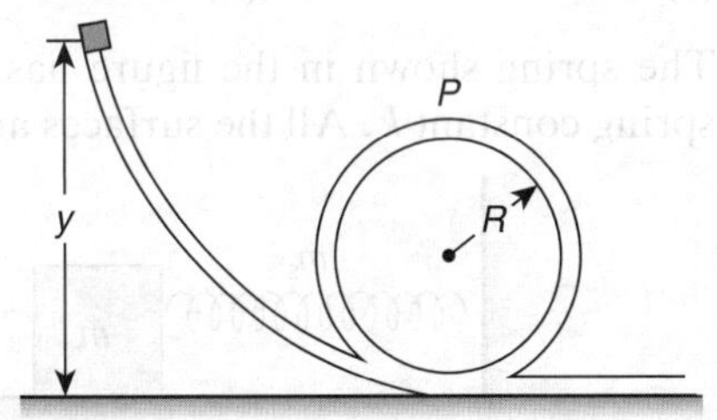

For the block to complete the loop without losing contact, the minimum height y from where it must be released is:

(a) $3R$ (b) $2.5R$
(c) $2.25R$ (d) $2R$

31. The figure shows a track $ABCD$; portions AB and CD are smooth while the horizontal portion BC is rough. One end of a spring of force constant $k = 200$ N/m is fixed at end A of the track, while its other end is free. A block of mass $m = 0.18$ kg is pressed against the free end of the spring, compressing it by $x = 3$ cm and it is then released. At the time of release, the height of the block is $h = 7$ cm above the horizontal. The coefficient of friction between the block and the rough track is $\mu = 0.2$.

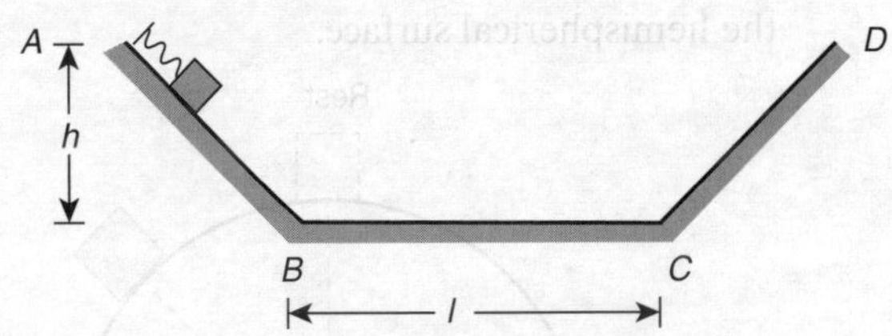

If the length of the rough track BC is $l = 25$ cm, the distance from B where the block finally comes to rest is (take $g = 10\ \text{m/s}^2$):

(a) 0.05 m (b) 0.10 m
(c) 0.15 m (d) 0.20 m

32. The figure shows a smooth surface inclined at angle $\theta = 37°$ to the horizontal. The block of mass m is released from rest, from a distance l with the spring fixed at the bottom of the incline. If the spring constant is $k = \frac{24mg}{l}$, the block compresses the spring by:

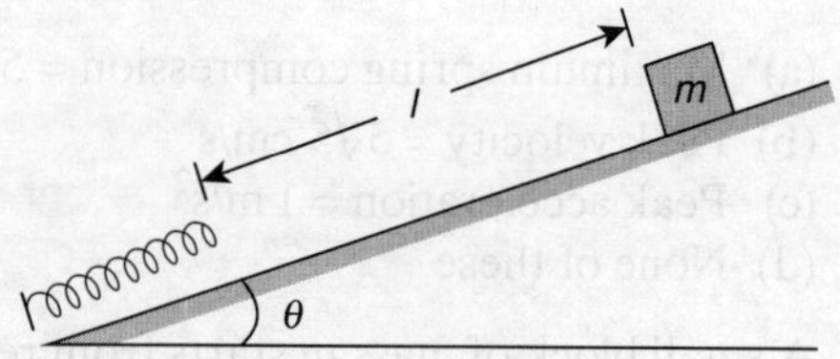

(a) $l/4$ (b) $l/5$
(c) $l/6$ (d) $2l/5$

33. The spring shown in the figure has mass m_s and spring constant k. All the surfaces are smooth.

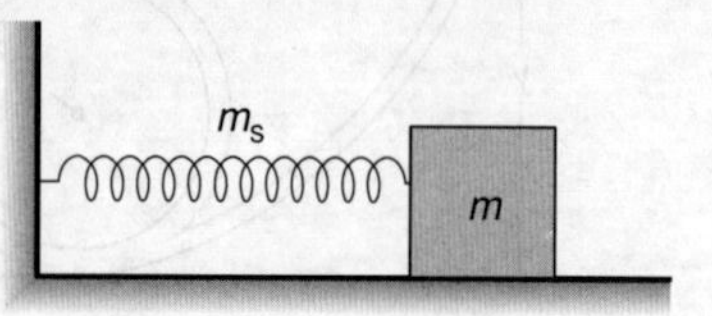

The block m is compressed against the spring by distance x_0 and released from rest. The speed when it leaves the spring is:

(a) $\sqrt{\dfrac{kx_0^2}{m+\dfrac{m_s}{8}}}$ (b) $\sqrt{\dfrac{kx_0^2}{m+\dfrac{m_s}{6}}}$

(c) $\sqrt{\dfrac{kx_0^2}{m+\dfrac{m_s}{5}}}$ (d) $\sqrt{\dfrac{kx_0^2}{m+\dfrac{m_s}{3}}}$

34. A small block starts from rest and slides along a smooth hemispherical surface, as shown in the figure. Let θ denote the block's angular position measured from the vertical position and N denote the normal contact force between the block and the hemispherical surface.

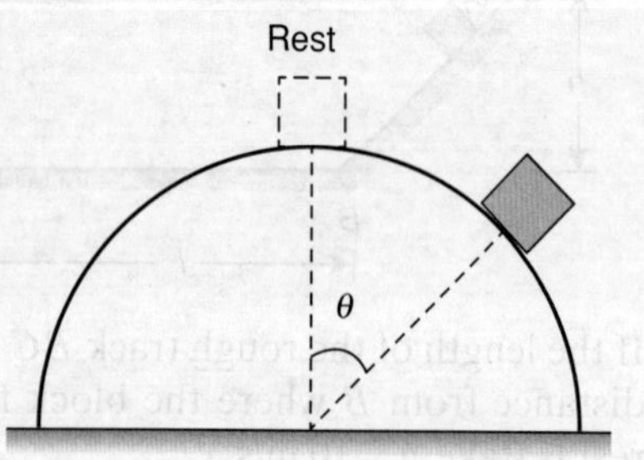

The graph of N versus $\cos\theta$ is:

(a)

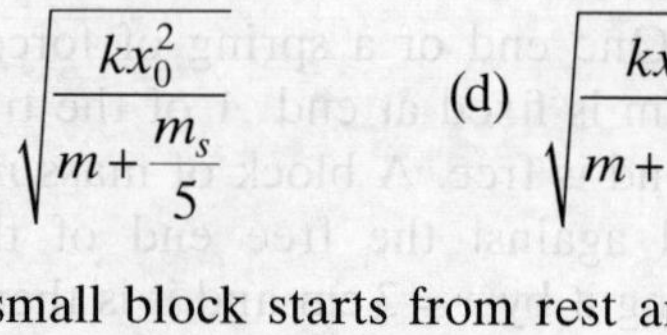

(b)

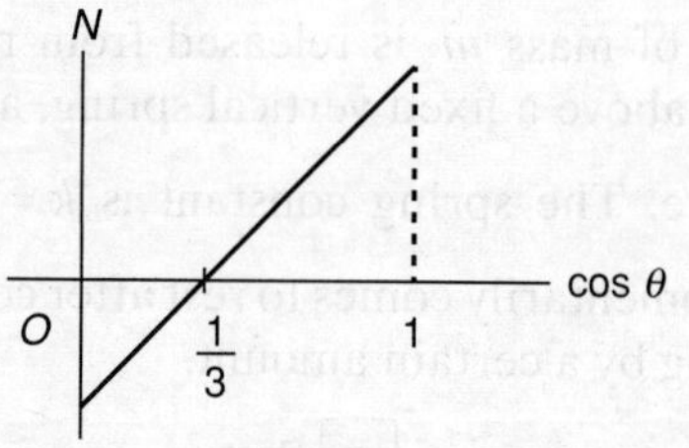

(c)

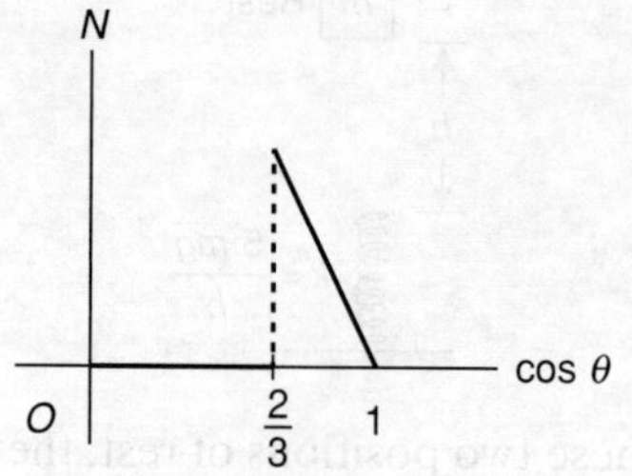

(d)

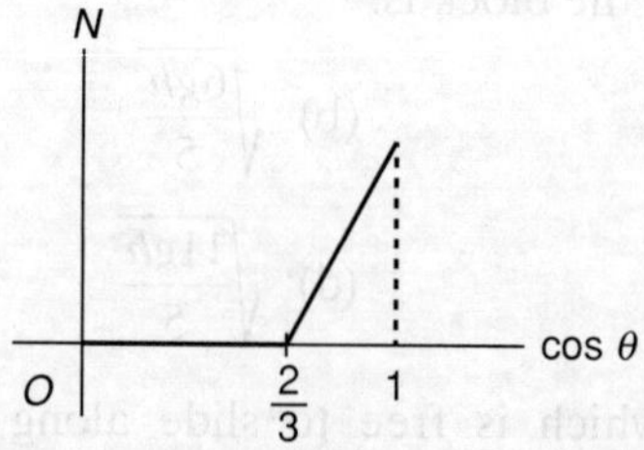

35. A hollow circular tube of mass M is placed vertically on a horizontal surface. Two small smooth spherical balls, each of mass m, are held inside the tube at its top-most point, as shown in the figure. The balls are released simultaneously.

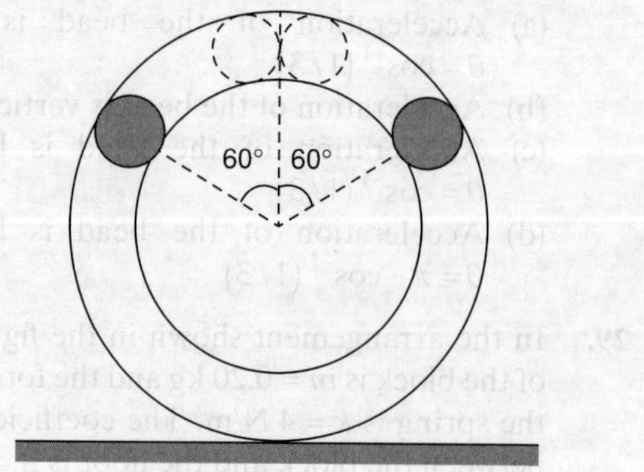

If the tube loses contact with the surface when the balls have fallen through an angle of 60°, then the ratio m/M equals:

(a) 4 (b) 3
(c) 2 (d) 1

36. The figure shows a spring-mass oscillator placed on a rough horizontal surface, which exerts a constant friction force f. The spring is elongated by x_0 and the block is allowed to oscillate. Friction causes energy dissipation and the block eventually comes to rest after a few oscillations.

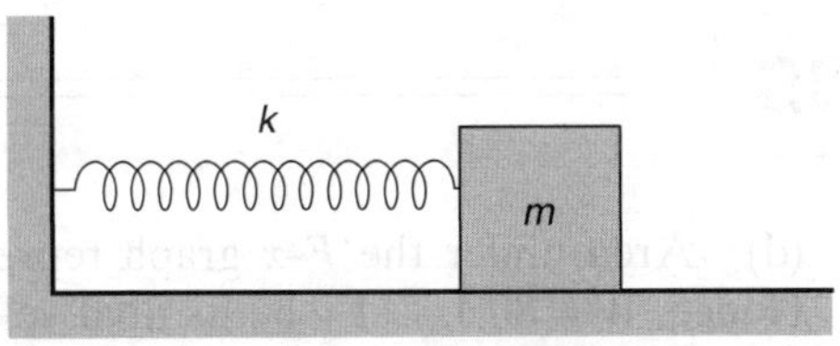

If the spring constant is k, then elongation in the spring after one complete oscillation is:

(a) $x_0 - \frac{4f}{k}$ (b) $x_0 - \frac{2f}{k}$

(c) $x_0 - \frac{4f}{3k}$ (d) $x_0 - \frac{3f}{4k}$

37. The figure shows two identical blocks A and B, each of mass $m = 2$ kg, connected to the ends of a light spring having force constant $k = 1000$ N/m, placed on a rough horizontal surface. The coefficient of friction between the blocks and the floor is $\mu = 0.5$.

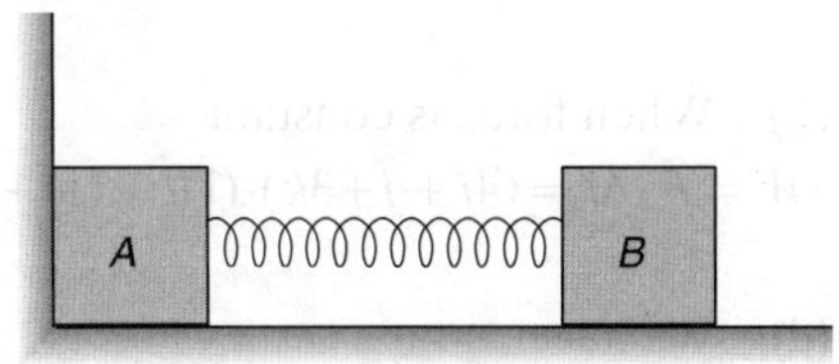

Initially, the spring is compressed by $x_0 = 0.09$ m, and block B is released from rest. The velocity of the centre of mass of the system when block A just leaves contact with the wall is (take $g = 10$ m/s^2):

(a) $3\sqrt{2}$ m/s (b) $2\sqrt{3}$ m/s

(c) $\frac{\sqrt{5}}{2}$ m/s (d) $\frac{\sqrt{3}}{2}$ m/s

ANSWER KEYS

1. (b)	**2.** (d)	**3.** (d)	**4.** (b)	**5.** (d)	**6.** (a)	**7.** (d)	**8.** (a)	**9.** (b)	**10.** (c)
11. (b)	**12.** (d)	**13.** (d)	**14.** (a)	**15.** (c)	**16.** (c)	**17.** (a)	**18.** (d)	**19.** (a)	**20.** (c)
21. (c)	**22.** (d)	**23.** (d)	**24.** (d)	**25.** (a)	**26.** (d)	**27.** (d)	**28.** (d)	**29.** (a), (b)	**30.** (b)
31. (b)	**32.** (a)	**33.** (d)	**34.** (d)	**35.** (c)	**36.** (a)	**37.** (d)			

SOLUTIONS

1. (b) When force is constant

$$W = \vec{F}\cdot\Delta\vec{r} = (4\hat{i}+\hat{j}+3\hat{k})\cdot(11\hat{i}+11\hat{j}+15\hat{k}) = 100\text{ J}$$

2. (d) We have

$$W = \int \vec{F}\cdot d\vec{r}$$

$$= -c\int (y\hat{i}+x\hat{j})\cdot(dx\hat{i}+dy\hat{j})$$

$$= -c\int (ydx + xdy)$$

From (0, 0) to (*a*, 0) along the +ve *x*-axis, $y = 0$, $dy = 0$. Thus, $W_1 = 0$.

From (*a*, 0) to (*a*, *a*) along the +ve *y*-axis, $x = a$, $dx = 0$. Thus, $W_2 = -c\int_0^a a\,dy = -ca^2$

Hence, total work equals $W_1 + W_2 = -ca^2$

3. (d) $F = \dfrac{dK}{dx}$

$\Rightarrow\quad F = \dfrac{d(cx)}{dx}$ [Given $K \propto x$]

$\Rightarrow\quad F = c$

4. (b) Uniform acceleration equals v_o/t_o. The velocity and force at time *t* are

$$v = \left(\frac{v_o}{t_o}\right)t \text{ and } F = m\left(\frac{v_o}{t_o}\right)$$

Hence, instantaneous power $P = \vec{F}\cdot\vec{v} = \left(\dfrac{mv_o^2}{t_o^2}\right)t$

5. (d) When a body is pushed by a certain force *F* over a certain distance *s*, it acquires kinetic energy *Fs*, which is independent of its mass.

6. (a) Let *v* be the velocity of projection. The velocity at the highest point will be $v\cos 60° = v/2$. If *h* is the maximum height, then

$$mgh = \frac{1}{2}mv^2 - \frac{1}{2}m\left(\frac{v}{2}\right)^2 = \frac{3}{4}\left(\frac{1}{2}mv^2\right)$$

$$= \frac{3}{4}\times 24\text{ J} = 18\text{ J}$$

$$\Rightarrow\quad h = \frac{18\text{ J}}{0.2ka\times 10\text{ m/s}^2} = 9\text{ m}$$

7. (d) Area under the *F*–*x* graph represents work. Hence, $W = 80$ J. Let *v* be its final velocity. Then, using the Work–Energy Theorem, we have

$$\frac{1}{2}mv^2 - \frac{1}{2}mu^2 = 80$$

$$\Rightarrow\quad v = \sqrt{u^2 + \frac{160}{m}}$$

$$\Rightarrow\quad v = \sqrt{400 + \frac{160}{0.1}} = 20\sqrt{5}\text{ m/s}$$

8. (a) Let *u* and *v* be the speeds at the lowest and highest points, respectively. Then

$$v^2 = u^2 - 4gl \qquad \text{...(1)}$$

The tension is minimum at the highest point and maximum at the lowest point. They are

$$T_{\min} = m\left(\frac{v^2}{1} - g\right) \text{ and } T_{\max} = m\left(\frac{u^2}{1} + g\right)$$

According to the given condition, we have

$$\frac{u^2}{1} + g = 4\left(\frac{v^2}{1} - g\right) \qquad \text{...(2)}$$

From the above equations, we have

$$\frac{u^2}{l} + g = 4\left(\frac{u^2}{l} - 5g\right) \Rightarrow u = \sqrt{7gl} = 7\text{ m/s}$$

9. (b) The mechanical energy *mgh* of the body remains conserved. When kinetic energy is 3 *mgh*/4, the gravitational potential energy is *mgh*/4, which means the particle is at height *h*/4 from the ground.

10. (b) If the bullet enters with velocity, say *v*, it emerges with velocity 9*v*/ 10, which means a loss in kinetic energy of

$$\Delta K = \frac{1}{2}mv^2\left(1 - \frac{81}{100}\right) = \frac{19}{100}K$$

$$\Rightarrow\quad \frac{\Delta K}{K} = 19\%$$

As the bullet passes through the plank, negative work done by the friction force on the bullet causes the bullet to lose its kinetic energy. Since the planks are identical, the work done by the friction force on the bullet, as it passes through the planks, is the same for each plank. The bullet will, therefore, lose the same amount (19%) of its kinetic energy while passing through each plank. Thus, it will lose 95% of its kinetic energy after passing through 5 planks. Hence, it will need at least 6 such planks to be stopped.

Note: The percentage velocity loss is not 10% in all planks; it increases with successive planks. However, the percentage kinetic energy loss is the same (19%) in all the planks.

11. (c)

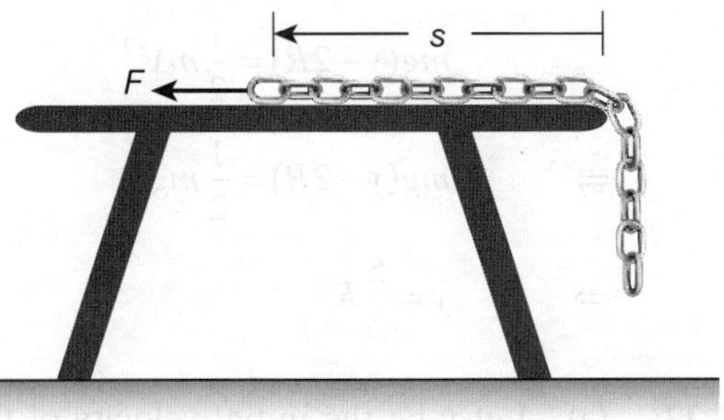

It is given that the chain just slips when its length $l/3$ hangs over the table and length $2l/3$ lies on the table. This means that the weight of the hanging chain is just balanced by the friction force between the chain and the table. Thus, if μ be the friction coefficient between the chain and the table, then we have

$$\mu\left(\frac{2}{3}mg\right) = \frac{2}{3}mg \Rightarrow \mu = 1/2$$

Now let us pull the chain slowly, by applying a force along the chain (see figure). Let s denote the instantaneous length of the chain lying on the table. The friction force between the chain and the table at this instant is $f = \mu\left(\frac{mg}{l}s\right) = \frac{mgs}{2l}$ and the weight of the hanging part of the chain is $w = \frac{mg}{l}(l-s)$. The amount of force required to slowly pull the chain equals the sum of the friction force and the weight of the hanging part of the chain. Thus, we have

$$F(s) = \frac{mgs}{2l} + \frac{mg}{l}(l-s) = mg\left[1 - \frac{s}{2l}\right]$$

Thus, the total work done by F in pulling the chain from $S = 2l/3$ to $s = l$ is

$$W = \int_{2l/3}^{l} mg\left[1-\frac{s}{2l}\right]ds = mg\left|s - \frac{s^2}{2}\right|_{2l/3}^{l} = \frac{7}{36}mgl$$

Hence, we have $\frac{36W}{mgl} = 7$

Alternative: Using the Work–Energy Theorem, we have

$$W_{\text{force}} + W_{fr} = \Delta K^0 + \Delta U_{gr}$$

$$\Rightarrow W_{\text{force}} = -W_{fr} + \Delta U_{gr}$$

To calculate $\Delta P.E_{gr}$, let us consider the surface of the table as our zero-potential surface. Then

$$U_i = \left(\frac{mg}{3}\right)\left(\frac{-l}{6}\right) = \frac{1}{18}mgl \text{ and } U_f = 0$$

$$\Rightarrow \Delta U_{fr} = U_f - U_i = \frac{1}{18}mgl$$

To calculate W_{fr}, let s denote the instantaneous length of the chain lying on the table. The friction force at this instant is $f = \mu\left(\frac{8}{l}mg\right)$ As the chain moves from position s to $s + ds$, the work done by friction is $dW_{fr} = \mu\left(\frac{8}{l}mg\right)ds$. Thus

$$W_{fr} = -\int_{2l/3}^{l}\frac{\mu mgs}{l}ds = -\frac{mg}{2l}\left|\frac{s^2}{2}\right|_{2l/3}^{l} = -\frac{5}{36}mgl$$

Hence, we have,

$$W_{\text{force}} = \frac{5}{36}mgl + \frac{2}{36}mgl = \frac{7}{36}mgl \Rightarrow \frac{36W}{mal} = 7$$

12. (d) If we choose the surface of the table as the zero potential energy level, the initial potential energy of the chain is $U_i = -\frac{m}{3}g\frac{1}{6} = -\frac{1}{18}mgl$ and the final potential energy is $U_f = -mg\frac{l}{2}$. If v is the required velocity, then using the energy conservation principle, we have

$$K_2 + U_2 = K_1 + U_1$$

$$\Rightarrow \quad \frac{1}{2}mv^2 - \frac{1}{2}mgl = -\frac{1}{18}mgl$$

$$\Rightarrow \quad v = \sqrt{\frac{8gl}{9}}$$

13. (d) If we choose the base of the vessels as the zero potential energy level, the initial potential energy of the entire liquid mass is

$$U_i = (\rho A h_1) g \frac{h_1}{2} + (\rho A h_2) g \frac{h_2}{2} = \frac{1}{2}\rho A g (h_1^2 + h_2^2)$$

Finally, the liquid level is the same in both vessels

$$h = \frac{h_1 + h_2}{2}$$

The final potential energy is

$$U_f = 2(\rho A h) g \frac{h}{2} = \rho A g h^2 = \frac{1}{4}\rho A g (h_1 + h_2)^2$$

Work done by gravity is

$$W_{gr} = -\Delta U = \frac{1}{2}\rho A g [2(h_1^2 + h_2^2) - (h_1 + h_2)^2]$$

$$= \frac{1}{1}\rho A g (h_1 - h_2)^2$$

14. (a) Work done by the pump in lifting m mass of water over a height h equals mgh. If this work is done in time T, then the power delivered by the pump is

$$\text{Power} = \frac{mgh}{T}$$

$$= \frac{(30\ \text{m}^3 \times 1000\ \text{kg/m}^3)(10\ \text{m/s}^2)(60\ \text{m})}{600\ \text{s}}$$

$$= 30\ \text{kW}$$

If P is the electrical power, then $0.3P = 30$ kW $\Rightarrow P = 100$ kW

15. (c) The force required is

$$F = mg\sin\theta + f = (15000\ \text{N})\frac{1}{10} + 1500\ \text{N} = 3000\ \text{N}$$

Hence, the power of the engine is

$$P = \vec{F}\cdot\vec{v} = 3000\ \text{N} \times 5\ \text{m/s} = 15\ \text{kW}$$

16. (b) The contact force between the block and the surface of the loop continuously decreases as it moves up the loop; it is minimum when the block is at the highest point P of the loop. The forces acting on the block are its weight mg and the normal contact force N, both acting downward towards the centre of the loop. If v is the velocity of the block at point P, then using dynamics, we have

$$N + mg = m\left(\frac{v^2}{R}\right)$$

$$\Rightarrow \quad N = m\left(\frac{v^2}{R} - g\right)$$

For the block to complete the loop, its contact force with the loop should not vanish. That means the above value of N, which is the minimum contact force, should be greater than or equal to zero. This gives $v \geq \sqrt{gR}$. So, to complete the loop, the block must have a minimum velocity of $\sqrt{gR}$ at point P.

Now, using the energy conservation principle, we have

$$mg(y - 2R) = \frac{1}{2}mV^2$$

$$\Rightarrow \quad mg(y - 2R) = \frac{1}{2}mgR$$

$$\Rightarrow \quad y = \frac{5}{2}R$$

17. (a) Let v be the initial velocity of the bullet. Its velocity reduces to 3 v/4 v over a distance of 3.5 cm. The fractional loss in kinetic energy is

$$\Delta K = \frac{1}{2}mv^2 - \frac{1}{2}m\left(\frac{3}{4}v\right)^2 = \left(1 - \frac{9}{16}\right)K = \frac{7}{16}K$$

If f is the shear force on the bullet, then

$$f(3.5\ \text{cm}) = \frac{7}{16}K \qquad \text{...(1)}$$

Let s be the total distance over which the bullet loses its entire kinetic energy. Then

$$f_s = K \qquad \text{...(2)}$$

From the above equations, we have $s = 8$ cm.

18. (d) Let v be the velocity when the string just becomes slack. Using dynamics along the radial direction, we have

$$mg\cos\theta = \frac{mv^2}{l} \Rightarrow v^2 = g/\cos\theta \qquad \text{...(1)}$$

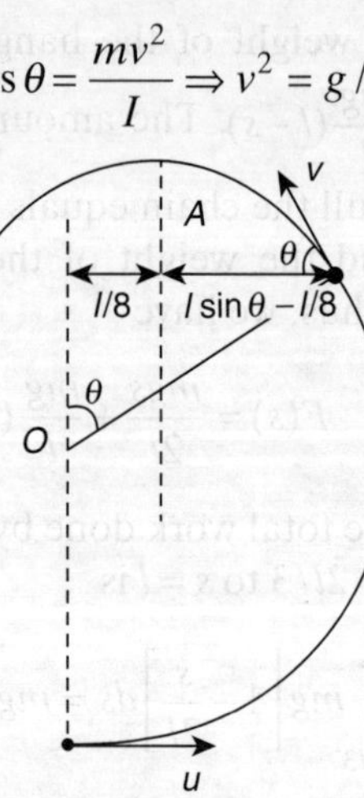

Using the energy conservation principle, we have

$$\frac{1}{2}m(u^2-v^2)=mgl(1+\cos\theta)$$

$$\Rightarrow\quad u^2-v^2=2gl(1+\cos\theta)\qquad ...(2)$$

From the above equations, we have

$$\cos\theta=\frac{v^2}{gl}=\frac{u^2-2gl}{3gl}$$

After the string becomes slack, the body moves in a parabolic path with initial velocity v and angle of projection θ. Its velocity becomes horizontal after a horizontal displacement of $\frac{v^2\sin(2\theta)}{2g}$. Equating it with $l\left(\sin\theta-\frac{1}{8}\right)$, we have

$$\frac{v^2\sin(2\theta)}{2g}=l\left(\sin\theta-\frac{1}{8}\right)$$

$$\Rightarrow\quad \cos^2\theta\sin\theta=\sin\theta-\frac{1}{8}\ [\text{Putting } v^2=g/\cos\theta]$$

$$\Rightarrow\quad \sin\theta-\sin^3\theta=\sin\theta-\frac{1}{8}$$

$$\Rightarrow\quad \sin^3\theta=\frac{1}{8}\Rightarrow\sin\theta=1/2\Rightarrow\cos\theta=\sqrt{3}/2$$

$$\Rightarrow\quad \frac{u^2-2gl}{3gl}=\frac{\sqrt{3}}{2}\Rightarrow\frac{u^2}{gl}=\frac{3\sqrt{3}+4}{2}$$

19. (a) Consider the closed path $OABC$ shown in the figure.

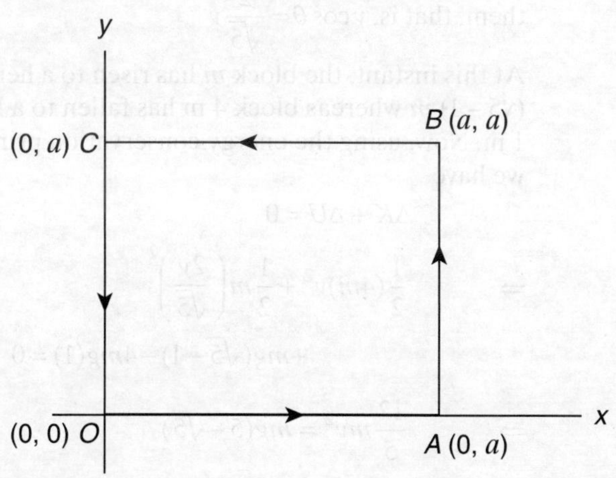

Work done by the force over this closed path is

$$W=\int\vec{F}\cdot d\vec{r}=\int F_x dx+F_y dy$$

$$=\int_{OABC}-\alpha x^2dx\ [\text{Since } F_y=0]$$

$$=\int_{OA}-\alpha x^2dx+\int_{BC}-\alpha x^2dx$$

[Since $dx=0$ along AB, CO]

$$=\int_0^a-\alpha x^2dx+\int_0^0-\alpha x^2dx=0$$

This proves that the force field is conservative. Now, between any two arbitrary points $P(x_1, y_1)$ and $Q(x_2, y_2)$, we have

$$\Delta U=-\int_P^Q\vec{F}\cdot d\vec{r}=-\int F_x dx+F_y dy$$

$$=\int_{x_1}^{x_2}\alpha x^2dx\ [\text{since } F_y=0]$$

$$=\frac{\alpha}{3}(x_2^3-x_1^3)=\frac{a}{3}\Delta(x^3)$$

20. (c) When the block moves up the incline and stops, it still possesses some mechanical energy in the form of gravitational potential energy, so all is not lost. When it had moved along the horizontal and stopped, it had lost all its mechanical energy. Hence, $\Delta E'<\Delta E$.

21. (c) We have

$$P=\frac{dK}{dt}=\frac{1}{2}m\frac{d(v^2)}{dt}$$

$$\Rightarrow\quad \int d(v^2)=\frac{2P}{m}\int dt$$

$$\Rightarrow\quad v^2=\frac{2P}{m}t+\cancel{\text{const}}^{0}$$

[At $t=0$, $v=0\Rightarrow$ const $=0$]

$$\Rightarrow\quad v=\sqrt{\frac{2Pt}{m}}$$

Now $\frac{dx}{dt} = \sqrt{\frac{2P}{m}t}$

$$\Rightarrow \int dx = \sqrt{\frac{2P}{m}}\int \sqrt{t}dt$$

$$\Rightarrow x = \sqrt{\frac{2P}{m}}\frac{t^{3/2}}{3/2} + \cancel{\text{const}}^0$$

[At $t = 0, x = 0 \Rightarrow \text{const} = 0$]

Hence, $x \propto t^{3/2}$

22. (d) Energy is lost due to negative work done by friction. According to the given condition, work done by friction is the same over the inclined and the horizontal parts of the track. Thus, we have

$$(\mu mg\cos 30°)\left(\frac{h}{\sin 30°}\right) = \mu mgx$$

$$\Rightarrow x = \sqrt{3}h = 2\sqrt{3}m$$

From the Work–Energy Theorem, between the initial and final points, we have

$$W_{fr} = Ugr$$

$$\Rightarrow -2\mu mgx = -mgh$$

$$\Rightarrow \mu = \frac{h}{2x} = \frac{1}{2\sqrt{3}} = 0.29$$

23. (d) We have

$$W = \int \vec{F}\cdot d\vec{r} = \int F_x dx + F_y dy$$

$$= -c\int \frac{xdx + ydy}{\sqrt{x^2 + y^2}}$$

The particle is moving along the path

$$x^2 + y^2 = a^2 \Rightarrow xdx + ydy = 0$$

Hence, $W = 0$.

24. (d) Let v be the speed of the blocks at an instant when the lower block has fallen a distance x. Using the Work–Energy Theorem, we have

$$\Delta K + \Delta Ugr + \Delta Usp = 0$$

$$\Rightarrow \frac{1}{2}(2m)v^2 - mgx + \frac{1}{2}kx^2 = 0$$

$$\Rightarrow v^2 = gx - \frac{k}{2m}x^2 \quad \ldots(1)$$

The value of v is greatest where dv/dx equals 0. Differentiating both sides with respect to x, we have

$$\Rightarrow 2v\frac{dv}{dx} = g - \frac{k}{m}x$$

Putting $\frac{dv}{dx} = 0$ gives $x = \frac{mg}{k}$. Putting this value in (1), we get the greatest speed as $\sqrt{\frac{mg^2}{2k}}$.

25. (a) Let l_1 = length of incline, l_2 = length of horizontal and θ = inclination of incline. Using the Work–Energy Theorem, we have

$$W_{fr} = K + U$$

$$\Rightarrow -(\mu mg\cos\theta)\, l_1 - \mu mgl_2 = -mgh$$

$$\Rightarrow \mu mg\,(l_1\cos\theta + l_2) = mgh$$

$$\Rightarrow \mu s = h$$

$$\Rightarrow \mu = \frac{h}{s}$$

26. (d)

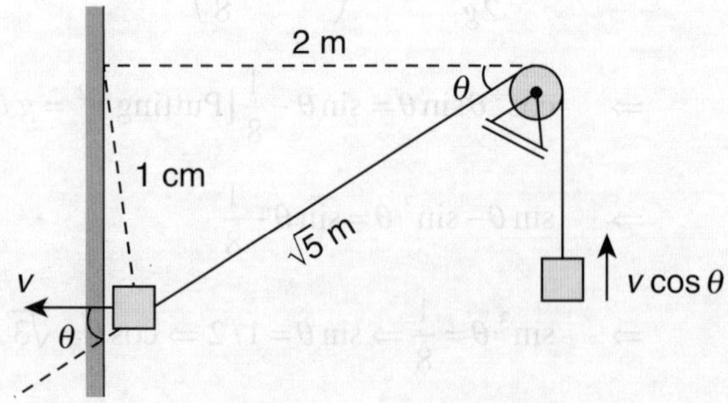

The figure depicts the situation just before the block 4 m collides with the vertical wall. Its velocity v will be perpendicular to the wall. Velocity of block m at this instant will be equal to the velocity component of block 4 m along the thread joining them, that is, $v\cos\theta = \frac{2}{\sqrt{5}}v$

At this instant, the block m has risen to a height of $(\sqrt{5} - 1)\,m$ whereas block 4 m has fallen to a height 1 m. Now, using the energy conservation principle, we have

$$\Delta K + \Delta U = 0$$

$$\Rightarrow \frac{1}{2}(4m)v^2 + \frac{1}{2}m\left(\frac{2v}{\sqrt{5}}\right)^2 + mg(\sqrt{5} - 1) - 4mg(1) = 0$$

$$\Rightarrow \frac{12}{5}mv^2 = mg(5 - \sqrt{5})$$

$$\Rightarrow v = \sqrt{\frac{5(5 - \sqrt{5}) \times 10}{12}} = 3.4 \text{ m/s}$$

27. (d) The velocity of the block will be maximum when the net force (gravity + spring) changes its direction. Initially, the net force is downward till it reduces to zero when the spring is compressed by $x=\dfrac{mg}{K}=\dfrac{h}{5}$. Beyond this point, the net force on the block is upward and its velocity starts decreasing. Let v be the velocity of the block at this position. Using the energy conservation principle, we have

$$\Delta K+\Delta U_{gr}+\Delta U_{sp}=0$$

$$\Rightarrow \quad \frac{1}{2}mv^2-mg(h+x)+\frac{1}{2}kx^2=0$$

$$\Rightarrow \quad \frac{1}{2}mv^2-\frac{6}{5}mgh+\frac{1}{10}mgh=0$$

$$\left[x=h/5,\ k=\frac{5mg}{h}\right]$$

$$\Rightarrow \quad \frac{1}{2}mv^2=\frac{11}{10}mgh$$

$$\Rightarrow \quad v=\sqrt{\frac{11}{5}gh}$$

28. (d) At position θ, let v be its velocity.

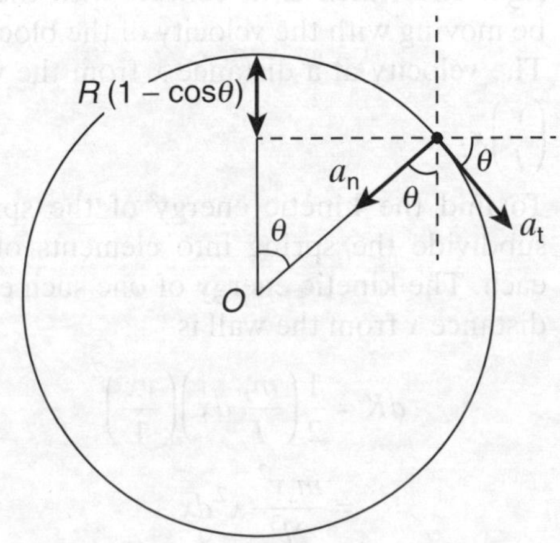

Then, using the energy conservation principle, we have

$$\frac{1}{2}mv^2=mgR(1-\cos\theta)$$

$$\Rightarrow \quad v^2=2gR(1-\cos\theta)$$

The centripetal acceleration is

$$a_n=\frac{v^2}{R}=2g(1-\cos\theta)$$

The tangential acceleration is

$$a_t=\frac{mg\sin\theta}{m}=g\sin\theta$$

The total acceleration will be vertical when the horizontal components add up to zero. This appears when

$$a_n\sin\theta-a_t\cos\theta=0$$

$$\Rightarrow \quad 2g(1-\cos\theta)\sin\theta-g\sin\theta\cos\theta=0$$

$$\Rightarrow \quad 2-3\cos\theta=0$$

$$\Rightarrow \quad \theta=\cos^{-1}(2/3)$$

Similarly, the total acceleration will be horizontal when the vertical components add up to zero. This happens when

$$a_n\cos\theta+a_t\sin\theta=0$$

$$\Rightarrow \quad 2g(1-\cos\theta)\cos\theta+g\sin^2\theta=0$$

$$\Rightarrow \quad 2\cos\theta-2\cos^2\theta+1-\cos^2\theta=0$$

$$\Rightarrow \quad 3\cos^2\theta-2\cos\theta-1=0$$

$$\Rightarrow \quad \cos\theta=1,-1/3$$

$$\Rightarrow \quad \theta=\pi-\cos^{-1}(1/3)$$

At the highest point, there is no acceleration at all, so $\theta=0$ is not an acceptable solution.

29. (a), (b) Let v be the velocity of the block when the spring compression is x. Using the Work–Energy Theorem, we have

$$W_F+W_{friction}=\Delta K+\Delta U_{spring}$$

$$\Rightarrow \quad (F-\mu mg)x=\frac{1}{2}mv^2+\frac{1}{2}kx^2$$

$$\Rightarrow \quad v^2=\frac{2(F-\mu mg)}{m}x-\frac{k}{m}x^2$$

$$=\frac{2(0.3-0.2)}{0.2}x-\frac{4}{0.2}x^2$$

$$\Rightarrow \quad v^2=x-20x^2 \qquad \ldots(1)$$

We see that the velocity is zero when $x=0,\dfrac{1}{20}$ m. Thus, the maximum spring compression $=\dfrac{1}{20}$ m $=5$ cm.

The velocity is maximum when the derivative function vanishes, that is, where $1-40x=0\Rightarrow x=\dfrac{1}{40}$ m.

Putting this value, we obtain the peak velocity as

$$v_{max}=\sqrt{\frac{1}{40}-\frac{20}{40^2}}\ \text{m/s}=\frac{1}{4\sqrt{5}}\ \text{m/s}=5\sqrt{5}\ \text{cm/s}$$

To find the acceleration, let us differentiate equation (1) with respect to x. Thus, we have

$$2v\frac{dv}{dx} = 1 - 40x$$

$$\Rightarrow \quad a = 0.5$$

$$= 20x \qquad \ldots(2)$$

The above function continuously decreases from

$$a(0) = 0.5\text{ m/s}^2 \text{ to } a\left(\frac{1}{20}\right)$$

$$= -0.5\text{ m/s}^2$$

Thus, the magnitude of the peak acceleration is

$$a_{\max} = 0.5\text{ m/s}^2.$$

30. (c) Let v be the velocity of the block at point P. The forces acting on the block are its weight mg and the normal contact force N, both acting downward towards the centre of the loop. Using dynamics, we have

$$N + mg = m\frac{v^2}{R}$$

Putting $N = mg$ gives $v = \sqrt{2gR}$

Now, using the energy conservation principle, we have

$$mg(y - 2R) = \frac{1}{2}mV^2$$

$$\Rightarrow \quad mg(y - 2R) = mgR$$

$$\Rightarrow \quad y = 3R$$

31. (b) Let s be the total distance travelled along the rough track before the block finally comes to rest. Using the Work–Energy Theorem, we have

$$W_{fr} = \Delta U_{gravity} + \Delta U_{spring}$$

$$\Rightarrow \quad -\mu mgs = -mgh - \frac{1}{2}kx^2$$

$$\Rightarrow \quad s = \frac{h}{\mu} + \frac{kx^2}{2\mu mg} = \frac{0.07\text{ m}}{0.2}$$

$$+ \frac{(200\text{ N/m})(0.03\text{ m})^2}{2(0.2)(0.18\text{ kg})(10\text{ m/s}^2)}$$

$$= 0.35\text{ m} + 0.25\text{ m}$$

$$= 0.6\text{ m} = 60\text{ cm}$$

The length of the rough track is 25 cm. This means the block covers distance BC twice completely and then another 10 cm = 0.1 m from end B.

32. (a) Let x be the compression in the string when the block stops at the bottom of the incline. Then

$$\Delta K + U_{sp} + \Delta U_{gr} = 0$$

$$\Rightarrow \quad \frac{1}{2}kx^2 - mg(x+1)\sin 37° = 0$$

$$\Rightarrow \quad \frac{1}{2}\left(\frac{24mg}{1}\right)x^2 - \frac{3}{5}mg(x+1) = 0$$

$$\Rightarrow \quad 20x^2 - lx - l^2 = 0$$

$$\Rightarrow \quad x = \frac{l \pm \sqrt{4l^2}}{4}$$

$$= \frac{1}{4}$$

[Negative x has no physical significance]

33. (d) Let v be the speed of the block when it leaves the spring. At this instant, the spring will be in its natural length, say l. Different portions of the spring will be moving with different velocities; the extreme left end which is in contact with the wall will be at rest, while the extreme right end which is in contact with the block will be moving with the velocity of the block, that is, v. The velocity at a distance x from the wall will be $\left(\frac{v}{l}\right)x$.

To find the kinetic energy of the spring, let us subdivide the spring into elements of length dx each. The kinetic energy of one such element at a distance x from the wall is

$$dK = \frac{1}{2}\left(\frac{m_s}{l}dx\right)\left(\frac{vx}{1}\right)^2$$

$$= \frac{m_s v^2}{2l^3}x^2 dx$$

The kinetic energy of the spring is

$$K_{\text{spring}} = \frac{m_s v^2}{2l^3}\int_0^l x^2 dx$$

$$= \frac{1}{6}m_s v^2$$

The kinetic energy of the block is

$$K_{\text{block}} = \frac{1}{2}mv^2$$

Now, using the mechanical energy conservation principle, we have

$$\frac{1}{2}mv^2 + \frac{1}{6}m_s v^2 = \frac{1}{2}kx_0^2$$

$$\Rightarrow \quad v = \sqrt{\frac{kx_0^2}{m + m_s/3}}$$

34. (d) Let v be the speed at position θ. Then, using the energy conservation principle, we have

$$\frac{1}{0}mv^2 = mgR(1-\cos\theta)$$

Now, using dynamics, we have

$$N = mg\cos\theta - \frac{mv^2}{R}$$
$$= mg\cos\theta - 2mg(1-\cos\theta)$$
$$= 3mg(\cos\theta - 2/3)$$

Hence, the block loses contact at cos 6 = 2/3. N is zero thereafter.

The figure shows the graph of N versus cos θ.

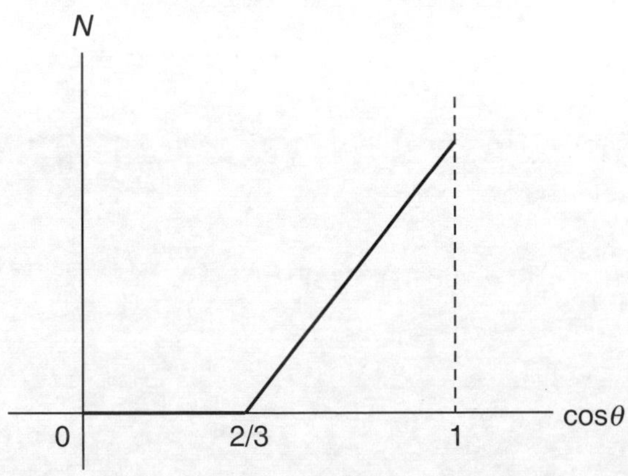

35. (c) Let v be the speed at position 60°. Then, from energy conservation, we have

$$\frac{1}{2}mv^2 = mgR(1-\cos 60°)$$

$$\Rightarrow \quad v^2 = gR$$

The tube loses contact with the ground at position 60°. This means the balls are pressing the outer walls of the tube normally, along the radially outward direction. If N is the normal contact force between each ball and the tube, then

$$2N\cos 60° = Mg$$

$$\Rightarrow \quad N = Mg$$

From dynamics, we have

$$N + mg\cos 60° = \frac{mv^2}{R}$$

$$\Rightarrow \quad N = \frac{1}{2}mg$$

Hence, we have

$$\frac{1}{2}mg = Mg$$

$$\Rightarrow \quad \frac{m}{M} = 2$$

36. (a) Let x be the compression in the string at the end of the first half-cycle. Then

$$W_{fr} = \cancel{\Delta K} + \Delta U_{sp}$$

$$\Rightarrow \quad -f(x_0 + x) = \frac{1}{2}k(x^2 - x_0^2)$$

$$\Rightarrow \quad \frac{2f}{k} = x_0 - x$$

$$\Rightarrow \quad x = x_0 - \frac{2f}{k}$$

Let x' be the elongation in the spring at the end of the first cycle. Then

$$W_{fr} = \cancel{\Delta K} + \Delta U_{sp}$$

$$\Rightarrow \quad -f(x + x') = \frac{1}{2}k(x'^2 - x^2)$$

$$\Rightarrow \quad \frac{2f}{k} = x - x'$$

$$\Rightarrow \quad x' = x - \frac{2f}{k}$$
$$= x_0 - \frac{4f}{k}$$

37. (d) Initial compression in the spring is x_1 – 0.09 m. Block A will lose contact when spring force just equals the limiting friction force.

This happens when the spring elongates by

$$x_2 = \frac{\mu mg}{k}$$
$$= \frac{0.5\times 2 + 10}{1000}\text{ m}$$
$$= 0.01\text{ m}$$

The speed v of block B at this instant is given by

$$W_{fr} = \Delta K + \Delta U_{Sp}$$

$$\Rightarrow \quad -\mu mg(x_1 + x_2) = \frac{1}{2}mv^2 + \frac{1}{2}k(x_2^2 - x_1^2)$$

$$\Rightarrow \quad v^2 = \frac{k}{m}(x_1^2 - x_2^2) - 2\mu g(x_1 + x_2)$$

$$\Rightarrow \quad v = \sqrt{500\left(\frac{81-1}{10^4}\right) - 10\left(\frac{9+1}{100}\right)} \text{ m/s}$$

$$= \sqrt{3} \text{ m/s}$$

Hence, we have

$$v_{cm} = \frac{mv_A + mv_B}{2m}$$

$$= \frac{v}{2}$$

$$= \frac{\sqrt{3}}{2} \text{ m/s}$$

CHAPTER

5

Linear Momentum and Collision

- The momentum $\mathbf{p}$ of a particle with mass m moving with velocity $\mathbf{v}$ is defined as the vector quantity

$$\mathbf{p} = m\mathbf{v}$$

The magnitude of momentum is related to the kinetic energy of the particle as

$$K = \frac{p^2}{2m} \text{ or } p = \sqrt{2mK}$$

Average and instantaneous force:

$$\mathbf{F}_{av} = \frac{\mathbf{p}_2 - \mathbf{p}_1}{t_2 - t_1} = \frac{\Delta \mathbf{p}}{\Delta t} \text{ and } \mathbf{F} = \lim_{\Delta t \to 0} \frac{\Delta \mathbf{p}}{\Delta t} = \frac{d\mathbf{p}}{dt}$$

The impulse $\mathbf{J}$ of a force is defined as

$$\mathbf{J} = \int_{t_1}^{t_2} \mathbf{F}(t)\,dt = \Delta \mathbf{p}$$

- **System of Particles**:

$$\mathbf{r}_{cm} = \frac{\sum m_i \mathbf{r}_i}{M},\ \mathbf{v}_{cm} = \frac{\sum m_i \mathbf{v}_i}{M} \text{ and } \mathbf{a}_{cm} = \frac{\sum m_i \mathbf{a}_i}{M}$$

The total momentum $\mathbf{P}$ of a system of particles equals its total mass M multiplied by the velocity of its centre of mass:

$$\mathbf{P} = \sum m_i \mathbf{v}_i = M\mathbf{v}_{cm}$$

In terms of force and linear momentum, the basic dynamics relation for the translational motion of any system is

$$\mathbf{F}_{ext} = \frac{d\mathbf{P}}{dt}$$

which reduces to $\mathbf{F}_{ext} = M\mathbf{a}_{cm}$ if the mass of the system is constant.

If $\mathbf{F}_{ext} = 0$, the total linear momentum of the system is conserved. The centre of mass velocity $\mathbf{v}_{cm}$ does not change.

If $\mathbf{v}_{cm} = 0$ and $\mathbf{F}_{ext} = 0$, then the centre of mass position $\mathbf{r}_{cm}$ does not change:

$$m_1 \Delta \mathbf{r}_1 + m_2 \Delta \mathbf{r}_2 + m_3 \Delta \mathbf{r}_3 + \ldots = 0$$

- For two colliding rigid bodies, the coefficient of restitution e is defined as

$$e = \frac{\text{Velocity of Separation}}{\text{Velocity of Approach}}\ (0 \le e \le 1)$$

The collision is said to be elastic when $e = 1$ and inelastic when $e < 1$; it is called completely inelastic when $e = 0$. In elastic collisions, both linear momentum and mechanical energy are conserved. In inelastic collisions, only linear momentum is conserved.

EXERCISES

1. A ball of mass m is dropped from a height h on a smooth horizontal floor. If the coefficient of restitution is e, then the total momentum imparted by the ball to the floor, and the total time τ for which the ball is in motion are:

   (a) $\left(\frac{1+e}{1-e}\right)m\sqrt{2gh},\ \tau=\left(\frac{1+e}{1-e}\right)\sqrt{\frac{2h}{g}}$

   (b) $\left(\frac{1+e^2}{1-e^2}\right)m\sqrt{2gh},\ \tau=\left(\frac{1+e}{1-e}\right)\sqrt{\frac{2h}{g}}$

   (c) $\left(\frac{1+e}{1-e}\right)m\sqrt{2gh},\ \tau=\left(\frac{1+e^2}{1-e^2}\right)\sqrt{\frac{2h}{g}}$

   (d) $\left(\frac{1+e^2}{1-e^2}\right)m\sqrt{2gh},\ \tau=\left(\frac{1+e^2}{1-e^2}\right)\sqrt{\frac{2h}{g}}$

2. A car moving with momentum p stops over distance s and time τ, due to friction between the tyres and the road. If the momentum of the car is increased by 20%, the stopping distance and the stopping time will, respectively, increase by:

   (a) 40%, 20% (b) 40%, 40%
   (c) 44%, 20% (d) 20%, 20%

3. A particle of mass $m = 0.1$ kg is moving through a medium which exerts a frictional force of magnitude $f = kv^2$. Its initial speed is $v_0 = 0.5$ m/s. If after 2 s, its kinetic energy is $\frac{1}{8}mv_0^2$, then the value of k is:

   (a) 0.01 (b) 0.1 (c) 1 (d) 10

4. Two boys of mass m and $2m$ are standing at the ends of a wooden plank of length L and mass M floating on water. If they walk along the plank and meet at the ce[illegible], the plank will move by a distance:

   (a) $\left(\frac{2m}{M+3m}\right)L$ (b) $\left(\frac{m}{M+3m}\right)\frac{L}{2}$

   (c) $\left(\frac{M}{M+2m}\right)\frac{L}{2}$ (d) $\left(\frac{2m}{M+2m}\right)\frac{L}{2}$

5. A shell of mass m fired with speed u at angle θ to the horizontal explodes at the highest point of its trajectory into two fragments of mass ratio 1 : 2. If the lighter fragment falls vertically, the distance from the point of projection at which the other fragment falls is:

   (a) $\frac{u^2\sin 2\theta}{g}$ (b) $\frac{2u^2\sin 2\theta}{g}$

   (c) $\frac{3u^2\sin 2\theta}{2g}$ (d) $\frac{5u^2\sin 2\theta}{4g}$

6. An isolated particle of mass m moving in the xy plane along the x-axis suddenly explodes into two fragments of mass ratio 1 : 3. An instant later, the smaller fragment is at $y = -15$ cm. The larger fragment at this instant is at:

   (a) $y = 5$ cm (b) $y = -2$ cm
   (c) $y = -7$ cm (d) $y = 7$ cm

7. In a collinear collision, a particle moving at an initial speed v_0 strikes a stationary particle of the same mass. If the final total kinetic energy is 50% greater than the total kinetic energy before collision, the magnitude of the velocity of separation between the two particles after collision is:

   (a) $2v_0$ (b) $\sqrt{3}v_0$ (c) $\sqrt{2}v_0$ (d) $2\sqrt{2}v_0$

8. The position of a particle moving in the xy plane is given by $\mathbf{r} = a\cos(\omega_1 t)\mathbf{i} + b\sin(\omega_2 t)\mathbf{j}$. The force acting on the particle will be directed towards the origin if and only if:

   (a) $\omega_1 = \omega_2$ and $a = b$ (b) $\omega_1 = \omega_2$
   (c) $a\omega_1^2 = b\omega_2^2$ (d) $a\omega_2^2 = b\omega_1^2$

9. The motion of a ball of mass 0.4 kg is changed by an external impulse, as shown in the figure. If J is the magnitude of the impulse and θ is the angle at which the impulse is applied with respect to the initial direction of motion of the ball, then:

   (a) $J = 4.8$ kg·m/s, $\theta = 37°$
   (b) $J = 8$ kg·m/s, $\theta = 37°$
   (c) $J = 4.8$ kg·m/s, $\theta = 143°$
   (d) $J = 8$ kg·m/s, $\theta = 143°$

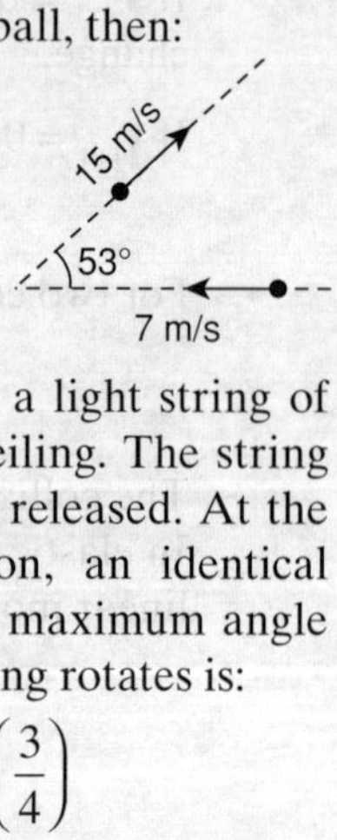

10. A bob of mass m is attached to a light string of length l tied to a point on the ceiling. The string is held horizontal and the bob is released. At the bottom-most point of its motion, an identical mass m is gently stuck to it. The maximum angle from the vertical to which the string rotates is:

    (a) $\cos^{-1}\left(\frac{2}{5}\right)$ (b) $\cos^{-1}\left(\frac{3}{4}\right)$

    (c) $\cos^{-1}\left(\frac{4}{5}\right)$ (d) $\cos^{-1}\left(\frac{3}{5}\right)$

11. A body moving at a certain speed undergoes elastic collision with an identical body at rest. During collision, a fraction of the kinetic energy is stored in the form of elastic potential energy in the deformed surfaces. The maximum value of this fraction is:
(a) 12.5% (b) 25% (c) 33% (d) 50%

12. Three blocks A, B, C are lying on a smooth horizontal surface in a straight line (see figure). A and B have equal masses m, while C has mass M. Now A is given a velocity v towards B, due to which it collides with B perfectly inelastically. The combined mass then collides with C, also perfectly inelastically.

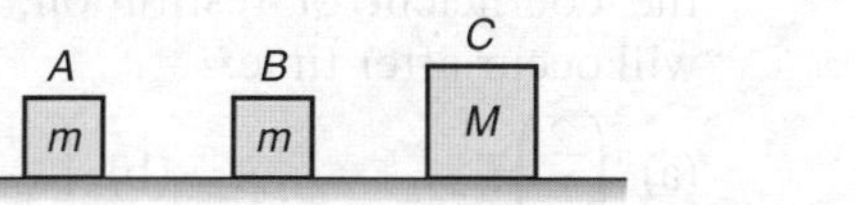

If $\frac{5}{6}$ th of the initial kinetic energy is lost in the entire process, then the value of M/m is:
(a) 5 (b) 4 (c) 3 (d) 2

13. Two boys A and B, both wearing roller skates, are standing on a smooth horizontal surface at a certain distance, facing each other. The mass of each boy is 40 kg. Boy A is holding a 4-kg ball in his hands. He rolls the ball towards B with speed 5 m/s, B picks the ball and then rolls it back towards A with the same speed. They keep doing so as long as they can. At the end of the game, the ball is in A's hands. The total number of trips the ball makes and the final velocity of A are:
(a) 5 trips, 5 m/s (b) 4 trips, 5 m/s
(c) 5 trips, $\frac{50}{11}$ m/s (d) 4 trips, $\frac{50}{11}$ m/s

14. A neutron moving at a certain speed undergoes a head-on elastic collision with a nuclei of mass number A at rest. The fractional loss in kinetic energy of the neutron is maximum for:
(a) $A=1$ (b) $A=\infty$ (c) $A=2$ (d) $A=0$

15. A body P strikes another body Q of mass p times and velocity $1/q$ times that of body P. If body P comes to rest, the coefficient of restitution is:
(a) $\frac{(p-1)(q-1)}{pq-1}$ (b) $\frac{p+q}{q(p-1)}$
(c) $\frac{p+q}{pq-1}$ (d) $\frac{p+q}{p(q-1)}$

16. A particle of mass $m = 0.2$ kg moving in the xy plane with initial momentum $-5\mathbf{i}+8\mathbf{j}$ experiences a variable force $\mathbf{F} = t\mathbf{i} - 1\mathbf{j}$; all quantities are in MKS units. Work done by the force in the next 4 s is:
(a) 80 J (b) 60 J (c) −160 J (d) −20 J

17. A ball collides with a smooth vertical wall at angle θ to its normal. If it rebounds at 90° to its initial direction of motion, then the coefficient of restitution e and the fractional loss η in its kinetic energy are:
(a) $e = \tan\theta, \eta = 1-\sin 2\theta$
(b) $e = \tan^2\theta, \eta = 1-\tan^2\theta$
(c) $e = \cot^2\theta, \eta = 1-\cos 2\theta$
(d) $e = \tan^2\theta, \eta = 1-\cot^2\theta$

18. A wire of uniform linear density is bent into a shape, as shown in the figure.

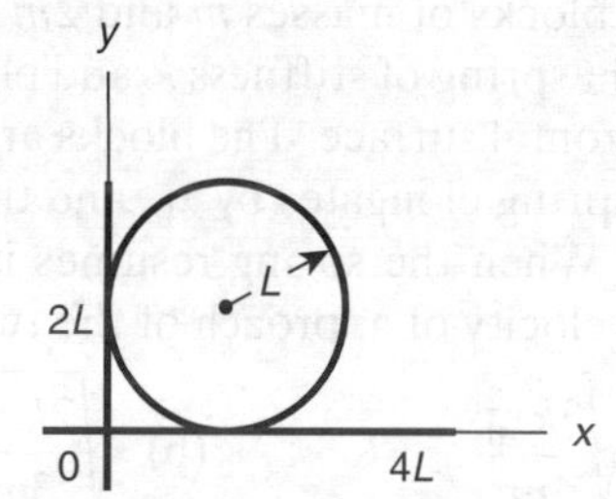

Its centre of mass is located at:
(a) $\left(\frac{2+\pi}{3+\pi}L, \frac{5+\pi}{3+\pi}L\right)$ (b) $\left(L, \frac{1+\pi}{4+\pi}L\right)$
(c) $\left(\frac{4+\pi}{3+\pi}L, \frac{1+\pi}{3+\pi}L\right)$ (d) $\left(\frac{2}{4+\pi}L, \frac{6}{4+\pi}L\right)$

19. Two bodies A and B of masses m and $2m$, respectively, are connected by a light spring of stiffness k and placed on a smooth horizontal surface, as shown in the figure. A third body C of mass m moving with velocity v_0 makes a head-on elastic collision with A.

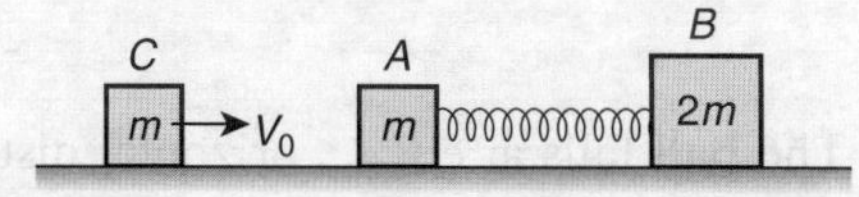

The maximum compression in the spring is:
(a) $\sqrt{\frac{2mv_0^2}{3k}}$ (b) $\sqrt{\frac{mv_0^2}{2k}}$ (c) $\sqrt{\frac{mv_0^2}{k}}$ (d) $\sqrt{\frac{3mv_0^2}{k}}$

20. A rod of length L has a variable linear mass density given by $\lambda(x) = \lambda_0\left(1-\frac{x}{2L}\right)$, where x is measured from one end of the rod and λ_0 is a constant. The centre of mass of the rod is at:
(a) $\frac{2}{5}L$ (b) $\frac{1}{6}L$ (c) $\frac{3}{7}L$ (d) $\frac{4}{9}L$

21. A small body of mass m is placed on a long wooden plank on a smooth horizontal surface, as shown in the figure. The mass m is initially given a velocity v_0. The coefficient of friction between the plank and the body is μ.

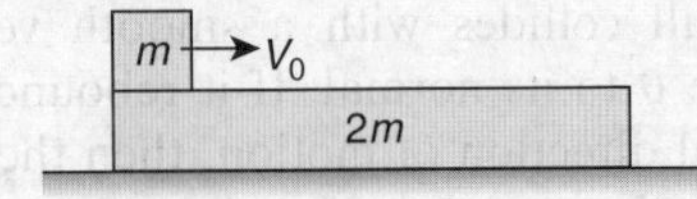

The time τ and distance s travelled by the block over the plank before it stops slipping are:

(a) $\tau = \dfrac{2v_0}{\mu g}, s = \dfrac{v_0^2}{6\mu g}$ (b) $\tau = \dfrac{2v_0}{3\mu g}, s = \dfrac{v_0^2}{3\mu g}$

(c) $\tau = \dfrac{2v_0}{3\mu g}, s = \dfrac{v_0^2}{2\mu g}$ (d) $\tau = \dfrac{3v_0}{2\mu g}, s = \dfrac{v_0^2}{3\mu g}$

22. Two blocks of masses m and $2m$ are connected by a light spring of stiffness k and placed on a smooth horizontal surface. The blocks are pulled apart till the spring elongates by x_0, and then released from rest. When the spring resumes its natural length, the velocity of approach of the two blocks is:

(a) $\sqrt{\dfrac{3kx_0^2}{m}}$ (b) $\sqrt{\dfrac{2kx_0^2}{3m}}$

(c) $\sqrt{\dfrac{kx_0^2}{3m}}$ (d) $\sqrt{\dfrac{3kx_0^2}{2m}}$

23. A small ball is projected from a point P on a staircase of rise h, and the coefficient of restitution is e, as shown in the figure.

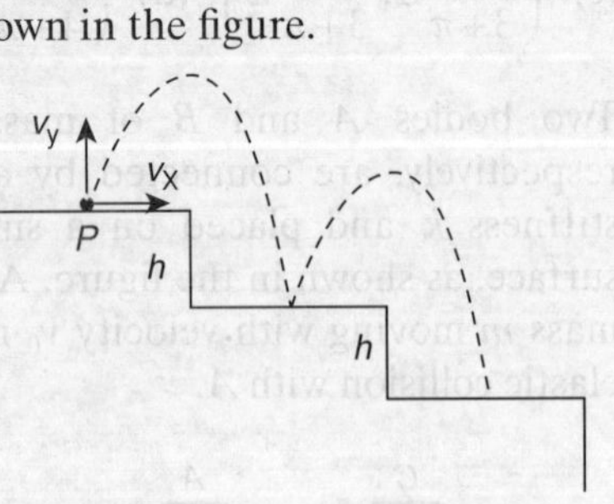

The ball falls at equal horizontal distances. Then the value of v_y is:

(a) $\left(\dfrac{1+e}{1-e}\right)\sqrt{2gh}$ (b) $\left(\dfrac{1+e^2}{1-e^2}\right)\sqrt{2gh}$

(c) $\left(\dfrac{e}{\sqrt{1-e^2}}\right)\sqrt{2gh}$ (d) $\left(\dfrac{e^2}{1-e^2}\right)\sqrt{2gh}$

24. The ball shown in the figure has mass m and is sliding with a uniform speed u on a smooth horizontal surface. It makes an elastic impact with the incline.

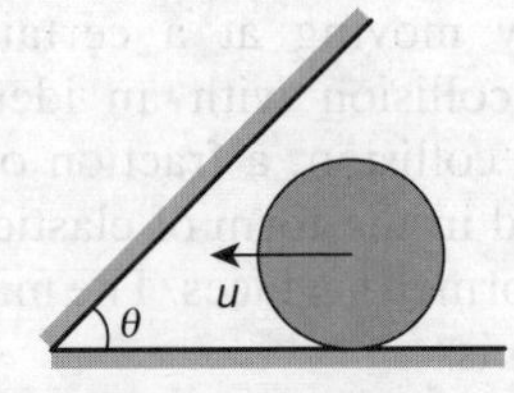

The impulse exerted on the ball by the incline is:

(a) $2mu \sin\theta$ (b) $2mu \operatorname{cosec}\theta$

(c) $mu(1+\cot\theta)$ (d) $mu(1+\tan\theta)$

25. Two equal spheres A and B lie inside a smooth horizontal circular groove at opposite ends of a diameter. Sphere A is projected along the groove and, after time T, it collides with sphere B. If e is the coefficient of restitution, the second impact will occur after time:

(a) $\left(\dfrac{2}{e}\right)T$ (b) $\left(\dfrac{1}{1-e}\right)T$

(c) $\left(\dfrac{1+e}{e}\right)T$ (d) $\left(\dfrac{1+e}{1-e}\right)T$

26. A ball of mass 0.2 kg rests on a vertical post of height 5 m, as shown in the figure. A bullet of mass 0.01 kg, travelling with velocity v along the horizontal direction, hits the centre of the ball. After collision, the bullet and the ball travel independently. The ball hits the ground at a distance of 20 m and the bullet at a distance of 100 m from the foot of the post.

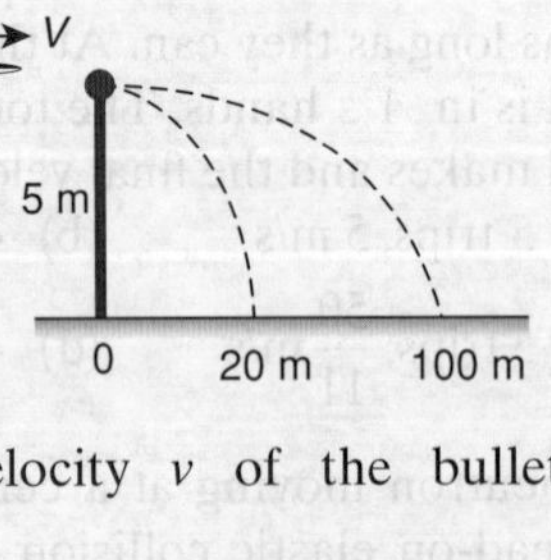

The initial velocity v of the bullet is (take $g = 10\ \text{m/s}^2$):

(a) 250 m/s (b) $250\sqrt{2}$ m/s

(c) 400 m/s (d) 500 m/s

27. A cricket ball moving with speed u collides with a rough vertical wall at angle 37° to the normal and rebounds with speed $u/2$ perpendicular to its initial direction of motion. If the wall exerts force on the ball at angle θ to the normal, then $\tan\theta$ equals:

(a) 1/3 (b) 1/4 (c) 2/5 (d) 2/11

28. The figure shows a bob suspended by a light string of length l from the ceiling of a box. The box is free to slide on the smooth horizontal surface. The mass of the box is η times that of the bob. Initially, the string is taken to the horizontal position and is released from rest. The box executes a periodic motion.

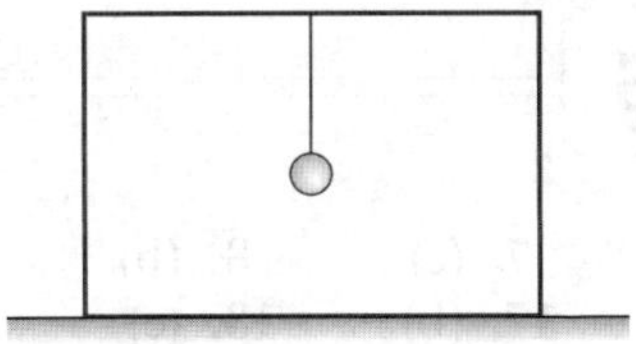

Let v be its maximum velocity and s be the distance between its extreme positions. Then:

(a) $v=\sqrt{\dfrac{2\eta gl}{\eta+1}}, s=\dfrac{2\eta l}{\eta+1}$

(b) $v=\sqrt{\dfrac{2gl}{\eta+1}}, s=\dfrac{2l}{\eta+1}$

(c) $v=\sqrt{\dfrac{2gl}{\eta(\eta+1)}}, s=\dfrac{2l}{\eta(\eta+1)}$

(d) $v=\sqrt{\dfrac{2gl}{\eta(\eta+1)}}, s=\dfrac{2l}{\eta+1}$

29. A small cube of mass m slides down a quarter of a circular path of radius R cut into a large block of mass $4m$, as shown in the figure. Both masses are initially at rest and all surfaces are smooth.

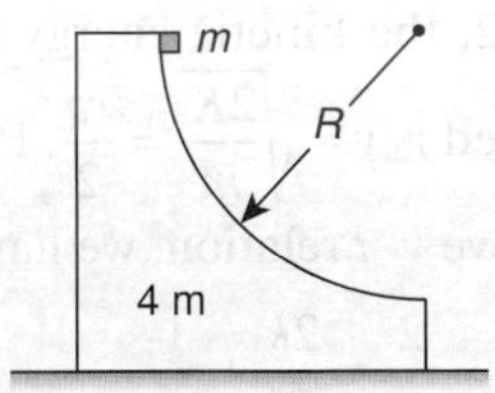

If u is the velocity of the cube as it leaves the block, then $\dfrac{5u^2}{4gR}$ equals:

(a) 7 (b) 6 (c) 2 (d) 9

30. A train of mass M is moving on a circular track with speed v. If the length of the train is equal to the semi-perimeter of the circular track, then the magnitude of the linear momentum of the train is:

(a) $\sqrt{2}\pi Mv$ (b) $\sqrt{5}\pi Mv$

(c) $\dfrac{2Mv}{\pi}$ (d) $\dfrac{3Mv}{2\pi}$

31. Two bodies A and B of masses m and $2m$, respectively, are connected by a light spring of stiffness k and placed on a smooth horizontal surface. The body A is given a velocity u, as shown in the figure.

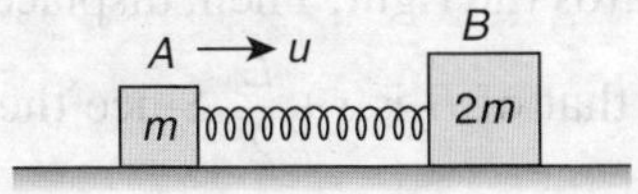

The incorrect statements about the subsequent motion are:

(a) Maximum and minimum kinetic energies of the system are the same in the CM frame and ground frame

(b) Minimum kinetic energy of the system is zero in the CM frame and non-zero in the ground frame

(c) Maximum kinetic energy of the system in the CM frame and in the ground frame are in the ratio 2 : 3

(d) Kinetic energy of the system is maximum in the CM frame and the ground frame, simultaneously

32. A loaded spring gun, initially at rest on a smooth horizontal surface, fires a marble at an angle of elevation of 37°, as shown in the figure. The mass of the gun is M and the mass of the marble is m.

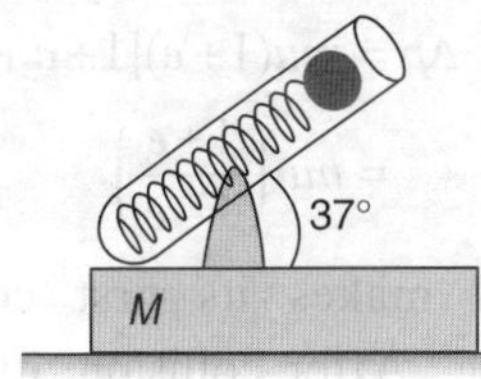

Just when the marble comes out of the gun, its absolute velocity makes an angle of 45° with the horizontal. Then M/m equals:

(a) 1 (b) 2 (c) 3 (d) 4

33. The figure shows an inclined plane ABC, whose inclination changes suddenly from 60° to 30° at B. A small block released from rest from point A suffers a collision at B, as it moves from one slope to another. Consider two cases:
Case I: The collision is completely inelastic, and v_1 is the velocity of the block when it reaches C.
Case II: The collision is elastic, and v_2 is the vertical component of the velocity of the block just after collision at B.

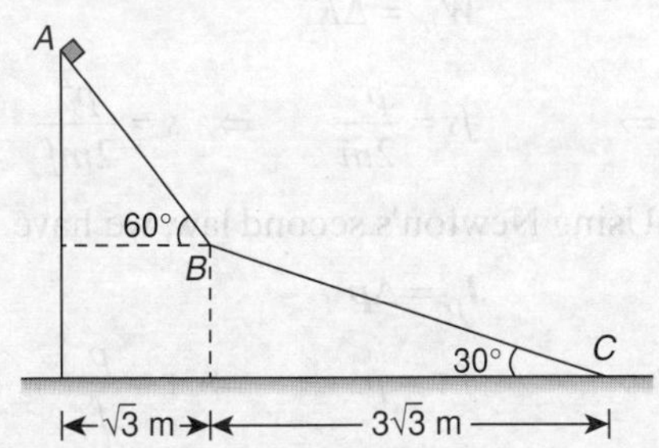

Then the correct statements from the following are: (take $g = 10\text{ m/s}^2$):

(a) $v_1=\sqrt{90}$ m/s (b) $v_1=\sqrt{105}$ m/s

(c) $v_2=\sqrt{3}$ m/s (d) $v_2=0$ m/s

ANSWER KEYS

1. (a)	**2.** (c)	**3.** (b)	**4.** (b)	**5.** (d)	**6.** (a)	**7.** (c)	**8.** (b)	**9.** (d)	**10.** (b)
11. (d)	**12.** (b)	**13.** (c)	**14.** (a)	**15.** (d)	**16.** (c)	**17.** (b)	**18.** (c)	**19.** (a)	**20.** (d)
21. (b)	**22.** (d)	**23.** (c)	**24.** (b)	**25.** (a)	**26.** (d)	**27.** (d)	**28.** (d)	**29.** (c)	**30.** (c)
31. (a)	**32.** (c)	**33.** (b),(d)							

SOLUTIONS

1. (a) In the first collision, initial velocity is $u = \sqrt{2gh}$ and velocity after collision is eu. Momentum change equals $mu(1 + e)$. In the second collision, initial velocity is $\boldsymbol{eu}$ and velocity after collision is $e^2 u$. Momentum change equals $mue(1 + e)$. Hence, the total momentum change

$$\Delta p = mu(1+e)[1+e+e^2+\ldots\ldots\infty \text{ terms}]$$

$$= mu\left(\frac{1+e}{1-e}\right)$$

The ball makes its first collision after time $r = \sqrt{2h/g}$. After collision, its velocity is $\boldsymbol{eu}$ and the ball moves upwards for time $\frac{eu}{g} = e\sqrt{2h/g} = e$.

Then, it falls for time $\boldsymbol{eT}$ and rises for time $\boldsymbol{e^2T}$ and so on.

Hence, the total time for which the ball travels

$$T = T + 2eT + 2e^2T + \ldots\ldots \infty \text{ terms}$$

$$= T + 2eT[1 + e + e^2 + \ldots\ldots\infty]$$

$$= r + \frac{2eT}{1-e} = \left(\frac{1+e}{1-e}\right)$$

2. (c) Let f be the friction force between the tyres and the road. Using the Work–Energy Theorem, we have

$$W_{fr} = \Delta K$$

$$\Rightarrow \quad fs = \frac{p^2}{2m} \quad \Rightarrow \quad s = \frac{p^2}{2mf}$$

Using Newton's second law, we have

$$\boldsymbol{J_{fr} = \Delta p}$$

$$\Rightarrow \quad f\tau = p \quad \Rightarrow \tau = \frac{p}{f}$$

Now, when momentum is $1.20p$ (20% increase), the stopping distance and time are

$$s' = \frac{(1.2p)^2}{2mf} = 1.44s \Rightarrow 44\% \text{ increase}$$

and $\quad \tau' = \frac{1.2p}{f} = 1.20\tau \Rightarrow 20\%$ increase

3. (b) Using Newton's second law $F = m\frac{dv}{dt}$, we have

$$-kv^2 = m\frac{dv}{dt}$$

$$\Rightarrow \quad \int \frac{-1}{v^2}dv = \frac{k}{m}\int dt \Rightarrow \frac{1}{v} = \frac{k}{m}t + C$$

$$\Rightarrow \quad \frac{1}{v} = \frac{k}{m}t + \frac{1}{v_0} \qquad [\text{Given } v = v_0 \text{ at } t = 0]$$

At $t = 2$, the kinetic energy is $K = \frac{1}{8}mv_0^2$. Hence, the speed is $v = \sqrt{\frac{2K}{m}} = \frac{v_0}{2}$. Putting these values in the above v–t relation, we have

$$\frac{2}{v_0} = \frac{2k}{m} + \frac{1}{v_0}$$

$$\Rightarrow \quad \frac{1}{v_n} = \frac{2k}{m} \Rightarrow k = \frac{m}{2v_0} = \frac{0.1}{2(0.5)} = 0.1$$

4. (b)

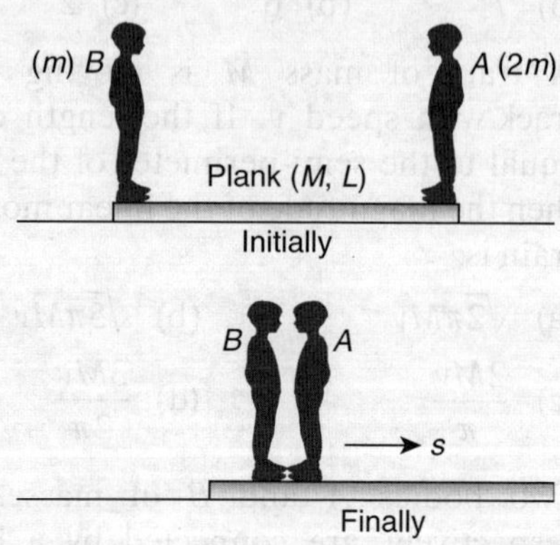

Let us choose the right direction as our +ve direction. Let s be the displacement of the plank towards the right. Then, displacement of A is $s - \frac{L}{2}$ and that of B is $s + \frac{L}{2}$. Since the external force on the system is absent along the horizontal and the CM is initially at rest, there will be no horizontal shift of the CM. Hence, we have

$$m\left(s+\frac{L}{2}\right)+2m\left(s-\frac{L}{2}\right)+Ms=0$$

$$\Rightarrow \quad s=\left(\frac{m}{3m+M}\right)\frac{L}{2}$$

5. (d)

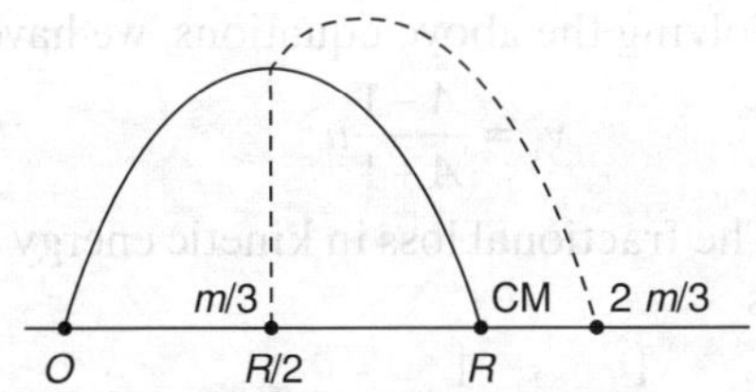

The CM continues to move on the original trajectory and finally coincides with $R=\dfrac{u^2\sin(2\theta)}{g}$. It is given that the lighter fragment of mass $m/3$ falls at $R/2$. Let x be the position where the heavier fragment of mass $2m/3$ falls. Since the CM is at R, we have

$$\left(\frac{m}{3}\right)\left(\frac{R}{2}\right)+\left(\frac{2m}{3}\right)x=mR\Rightarrow x=\frac{5}{4}F$$

6. (a) Since there is no external force acting on the particle, its CM will continue to move along the x-axis. Let y be the y-coordinate of the other fragment. Since the y-coordinate of the CM is zero, we have

$$\frac{m}{4}(-15\text{ cm})+\frac{3m}{4}y=0\Rightarrow y=5\text{ cm}$$

7. (c)

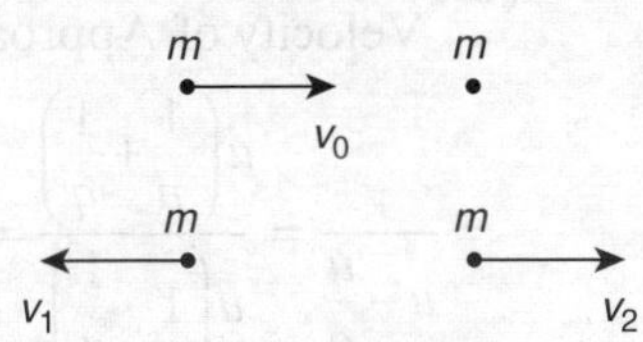

Let the velocities of the particles after collision be as shown in the figure. Then, using momentum conservation and energy condition, we have

$$v_2-v_1=v_0 \qquad \ldots(1)$$

$$v_2^2+v_1^2=\frac{3}{4}v_0^2 \qquad \ldots(2)$$

The velocity of separation, that is, v_1+v_2, can be found from the above equations as follows:

$$(v_2+v_1)^2+(v_2-v_1)^2=2(v_1^2+v_2^2)$$

$$\Rightarrow \quad (v_2+v_1)^2+v_0^2=\frac{3}{2}v_0^2\Rightarrow v_2+v_1=\frac{v_0}{\sqrt{2}}$$

8. (b) The force acting on the particle is

$$\vec{F}=m\frac{d^2\vec{r}}{dt^2}=-m[\omega_1^2 a\cos(\omega_1 t)\hat{i}+\omega_2^2 b\sin(\omega_2 t)\hat{j}]$$

The force will be directed towards the origin if

$\vec{F}=-c\vec{r}=-c[a\cos(\omega_1 t)\hat{i}+b\sin(\omega_2 t)\hat{j}]$ for some positive constant c.

The comparison gives

$$m\omega_1^2=c \text{ and } m\omega_2^2=c$$

$$\Rightarrow \quad \omega_1=\omega_2$$

9. (d)

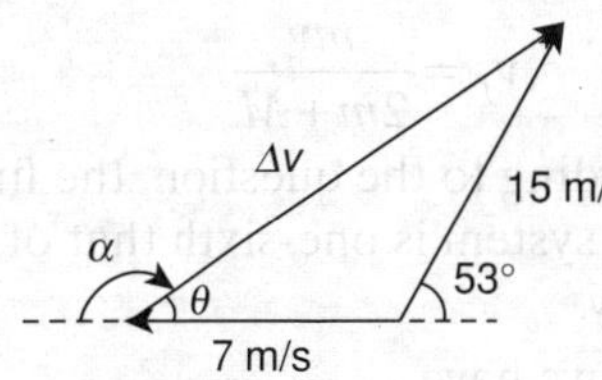

The figure shows the initial velocity (7 m/s), final velocity (15 m/s) and change in velocity (Δv). Magnitude of the impulse is

$$J=\Delta p=m\,\Delta v$$

$$=0.4\sqrt{15^2+7^2+2\times15\times7\cos53^\circ}\text{ kg}\cdot\text{m/s}$$

$$=8\text{ kg m/s}$$

The direction of the impulse should be along the direction of $\Delta\vec{v}$. From the figure, we have

$$\tan\theta=\frac{15\sin53^\circ}{15\cos53^\circ+7}=\frac{3}{4}\Rightarrow\theta=37^\circ$$

With respect to the initial direction of motion, this vector $\Delta\vec{v}$ makes angle $a=180^\circ-\theta=143^\circ$

10. (b) Velocity of the bob at the lowest point is

$$u=\sqrt{2gl}$$

Velocity after an identical mass is stuck

$$v=\frac{u}{2}=\frac{\sqrt{2gl}}{2}$$

The bob will now rise to a height $h=\dfrac{v^2}{2q}=\dfrac{1}{4}$

The angle of deviation of the string is given by

$$l(1-\cos\theta)=h\Rightarrow\cos\theta=3/4\Rightarrow\theta=\cos^{-1}(3/4)$$

11. (d) The elastic potential energy is maximum when the deformation is maximum. At this instant, the relative velocity between the balls is zero. Both balls are moving with the same velocity, given by

$2mv=mu\Rightarrow v=u/2$ [Momentum conservation],

where u is the velocity before collision.

The kinetic energy of the system at this instant is

$$2\left(\frac{1}{2}mv^2\right)=\frac{1}{4}mu^2$$

Energy stored in the form of elastic potential energy is $\frac{1}{2}mu^2 - \frac{1}{4}mu^2 = \frac{1}{4}mu^2$

Hence, the required fraction $= \dfrac{\frac{1}{4}mu^2}{\frac{1}{2}mu^2} = \frac{1}{2}$ or 50%

12. (b) Using linear momentum conservation principle, the final velocity V_f of the combined masses is given by

$$(2m + M)v_f = mv$$

$$\Rightarrow \quad v_f = \frac{mv}{2m+M}$$

According to the question, the final kinetic energy of the system is one-sixth that of the initial kinetic energy.

Thus, we have

$$\frac{1}{2}(2m+M)v_f^2 = \frac{1}{6}\left(\frac{1}{2}mv^2\right)$$

$$\Rightarrow \quad \frac{1}{2}\frac{m^2v^2}{2m+M} = \frac{1}{6}\left(\frac{1}{2}mv^2\right) \Rightarrow \frac{m}{2m+M} = \frac{1}{6}$$

$$\Rightarrow \quad M = 4m$$

13. (c) Every time B holds and then returns the ball, he imparts an impulse equal to 2(4 kg × 5 m/s) = 40 kg m/s to the ball. The same impulse is imparted to B by the ball, causing a change in B's velocity, given by

$$\Delta v = \frac{40 \text{ kg}\cdot\text{m/s}}{40 \text{ kg}} = 1 \text{ m/s}$$

After 5 trips, B's velocity will become 5 m/s, and A will have to hold the ball because if he throws the ball towards B, it will never reach B.

At the end of the game, B is moving with velocity 5 m/s, and A who is holding the ball is moving in the opposite direction with velocity, say v. Now, considering the ball + boy A + boy B as our system. In the absence of external forces along the horizontal, the momentum of the system must be conserved along the horizontal. At the start of the game, the momentum of the system is zero, so it must also be zero at the end of the game. Thus, we have

$$(40 \text{ kg})(5 \text{ m/s}) - (40 \text{ kg} + 4 \text{ kg})\ v = 0\ 50$$

$$\Rightarrow \quad v = \frac{50}{11} \text{ m/s}$$

14. (a)

Let u be the velocity of the neutron before collision. Let v_1 and v_2 be the velocities of the neutron and the nucleus after collision in directions, as shown in the figure. Using momentum conservation, we have

$$Amv_2 - mv_1 = mu$$

$$\Rightarrow \quad Av_2 - v_1 = u \qquad \ldots(1)$$

For elastic collision, the velocities of separation equal the velocities of approach

$$v_2 + v_1 = u \qquad \ldots(2)$$

Solving the above equations, we have

$$v_1 = \frac{A-1}{A+1}u$$

The fractional loss in kinetic energy of the neutron is

$$\eta = \frac{\frac{1}{2}mu^2 - \frac{1}{2}mv_1^2}{\frac{1}{2}mu^2} = 1 - \left(\frac{v_1}{u}\right)^2 = 1 - \left(\frac{A-1}{A+1}\right)^2$$

The value of η will be greatest when $\left(\frac{A-1}{A+1}\right)^2$ is least. This will occur for $A = 1$.

15. (d)

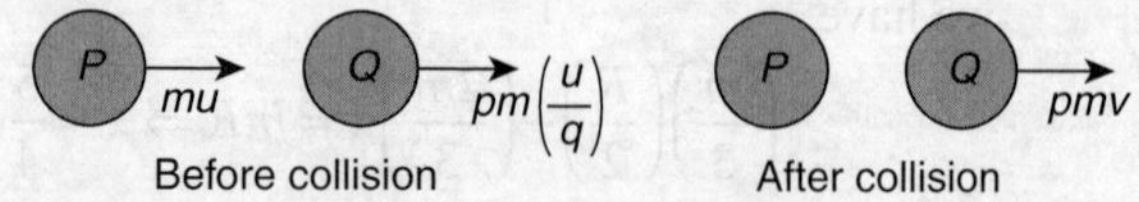

Using momentum conservation, we have

$$pmv = mu + pm\left(\frac{u}{2}\right)$$

$$\Rightarrow \quad v = u\left(\frac{1}{p} + \frac{1}{q}\right)$$

Hence, the coefficient of restitution

$$e = \frac{\text{Velocity of Separation}}{\text{Velocity of Approach}}$$

$$= \frac{v}{u - \frac{u}{q}} = \frac{u\left(\frac{1}{p} + \frac{1}{q}\right)}{u\left(1 - \frac{1}{q}\right)} = \frac{q+p}{p(q-1)}$$

16. (c) The final momentum $\vec{p}$ is given by

$$\vec{p}' = -5\hat{i} + 8\hat{j} + \int_0^4 (t\hat{i} - 1\hat{j})dt = 3\hat{i} + 4\hat{j}$$

Hence $|\vec{p}'| = \sqrt{3^2 + 4^2} = 5$

Magnitude of the initial momentum is

$$|\vec{p}| = \sqrt{5^2 + 8^2} = \sqrt{89}$$

Work done by force is

$$W = K' - K = \frac{p'^2}{2m} - \frac{p^2}{2m} = \frac{25-89}{2\times 0.2}\text{ J} = -160 \text{ J}$$

17. (b)

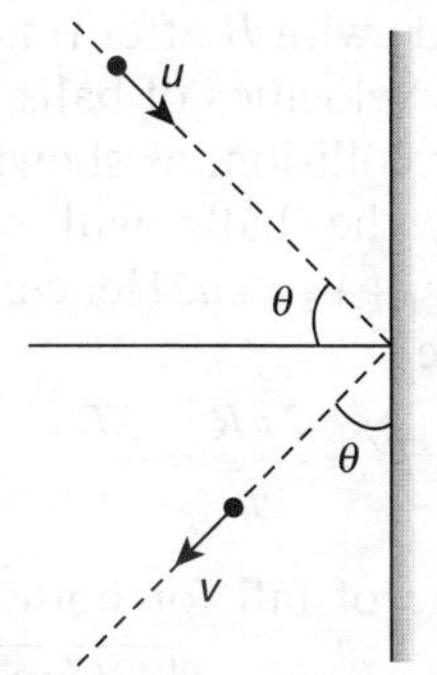

The velocity component parallel to the wall does not change. Hence

$$v \cos \theta = u \sin \theta \qquad \ldots(1)$$

Let e be the coefficient of restitution. Then

$$v \sin \theta = eu \cos \theta \qquad \ldots(2)$$

Dividing the two equations, we have

$$e = \tan^2\theta$$

The fractional loss in kinetic energy is

$$\eta = 1 - \frac{v^2}{u^2} = 1 - \tan^2 \theta$$

18. (c)

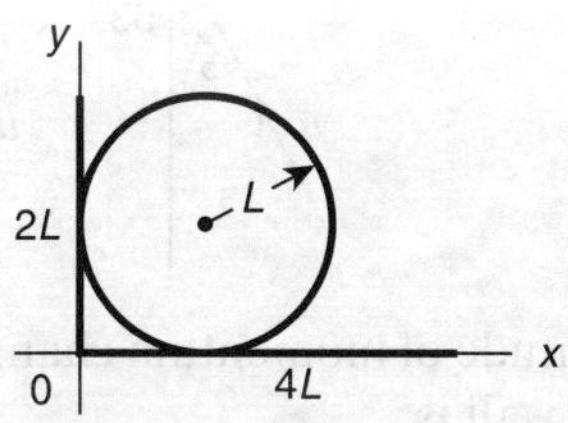

Since the wires are of the same linear mass density, the masses will be in proportion to the lengths. Let the masses of the straight wires be m, $2\,m$ and that of the circular wire be πm. Then

$$x_{cm} = \frac{m(0) + 2m(2L) + \pi m(L)}{(3+\pi)m} = \frac{4+\pi}{3+\pi}L$$

$$y_{cm} = \frac{m(L) + 2m(0) + \pi m(L)}{(3+\pi)m} = \frac{1+\pi}{3+\pi}L$$

19. (a) After collision, C comes to rest and A moves with velocity v_o. The block A + block B system now moves in a combination of oscillation and translation. During the motion, the linear momentum and mechanical energy of the system are conserved. The deformation in the spring is maximum when the relative velocity between the blocks is zero. At this instant, the blocks will be moving with the same velocity v, given by

$$3mv = v_o \Rightarrow v = v_{o/3}$$

Let x be the deformation in the spring at this instant. Then

$$\frac{1}{2}kx^2 + \frac{1}{2}3m\left(\frac{v_0}{3}\right)^2 = \frac{1}{2}mv_0^2 \Rightarrow x = \sqrt{\frac{2mv_0^2}{3k}}$$

20. (d) Let us subdivide the rod into small elements, each of length dx. The mass of one such element situated at position x is

$$dm = \lambda_0\left(1 - \frac{x}{2L}\right)dx$$

Then, we have

$$x_{cm} = \frac{\int x\,dm}{\int dm} = \frac{\int_0^L \lambda_o\left(1 - \frac{x}{2L}\right)x\,dx}{\int_0^L \lambda_o\left(1 - \frac{x}{2L}\right)dx}$$

$$= \frac{\left|\frac{x^2}{2} - \frac{x^3}{6L}\right|_0^L}{\left|x - \frac{x^2}{4L}\right|_0^L} = \frac{\frac{L^2}{2} - \frac{L^2}{6}}{\frac{L}{2} - \frac{L}{4}} = \frac{L/3}{3L/4} = \frac{4}{9}L$$

21. (b) When shipping stops, the system will be moving at velocity v given by (using momentum conservation principle)

$$3mv = mv_o \Rightarrow v = v_o/3$$

The velocity of block m decreases from v_o to $v_o/3$ due to the friction force μmg, which produces a retardation of magnitude $\mu mg/m = \mu g$. The time τ and the distance s_1 are given by

$$\frac{v_o}{3} = v_o - \mu g\tau \Rightarrow \tau = \frac{2v_o}{2mg}$$

and

$$\left(\frac{v_0}{3}\right)^2 = v_0^2 - 2\mu g s_1 \Rightarrow s_1 = \frac{4v_0^2}{9\mu g}$$

The velocity of block $2m$ increases from 0 to $v_o/3$ due to the friction force μmg, which produces an acceleration of magnitude $\mu mg/2m = \mu g/2$. The distance s_2 is given by

$$\left(\frac{v_0}{3}\right)^2 = 2(\mu g/2)s_2 \Rightarrow s_2 = \frac{v_0^2}{9\mu g}$$

Hence, the distance travelled by the block relative to the plank is

$$s = s_1 - s_2 = \frac{4v_0^2}{9\mu g} - \frac{v_0^2}{9\mu g} = \frac{v_0^2}{3\mu g}$$

Alternatively: Using the Work–Energy Theorem for the plank + block system, we have

$$W_{fr} = \Delta K$$

$$\Rightarrow \qquad -\mu mgs = \frac{1}{2}3m\left(\frac{v_o}{3}\right)^2 - \frac{1}{2}mv$$

$$\Rightarrow \qquad s = \frac{v_o^2}{3\mu g}$$

22. (d)

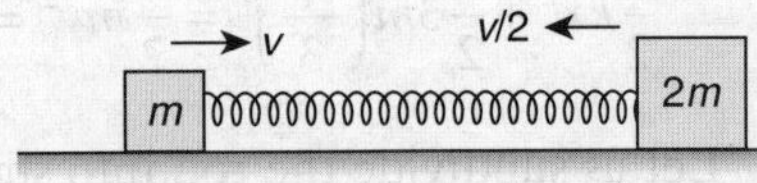

Let us consider the two blocks and the spring as our system. In the absence of external force, the linear momentum of the system will be conserved; it will always be zero. Hence, let us choose the velocities of the blocks, as shown in the figure. Now, using the energy conservation principle, we have

$$\frac{1}{2}mv^2 + \frac{1}{2}(2m)\left(\frac{v}{2}\right)^2 = \frac{1}{2}kx_0^2$$

$$\Rightarrow \quad \frac{3}{4}mv^2 = \frac{1}{2}kx_0^2 \Rightarrow v = \sqrt{\frac{2kx_0^2}{3m}}$$

Now $\quad v_{rel} = \frac{3}{2}v = \sqrt{\frac{3kx_0^2}{2m}}$

23. (c) The ball strikes the staircase with a normal velocity component $\sqrt{v_y^2 + 2gh}$ and rebounds with a normal velocity component $e\sqrt{v_y^2 + 2gh}$. Now this must be equal to v_y; only then will the ball trace a similar trajectory. Thus, we have

$$e\sqrt{v_y^2 + 2gh} = v_y \Rightarrow v_y = \sqrt{\frac{2ghe^2}{1 - e^2}}$$

24. (b)

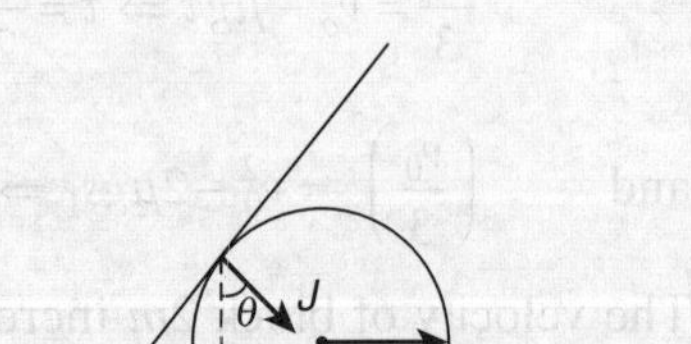

The incline surface being smooth exerts an impulse J on the ball along the normal, as shown in the figure. Since the collision is elastic, the ball's velocity after impact will remain the same, that is, u towards the right. Equating impulse with momentum change along the horizontal direction, we have

$$J \sin\theta = 2mu \Rightarrow J = 2mu \operatorname{cosec}\theta$$

25. (a)

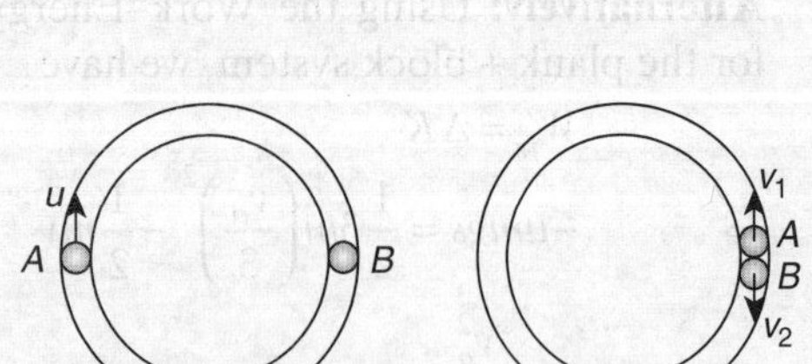

If R is the radius of the circular groove, then A will collide with B after time $T = \pi R/u$. Let v_1 and v_2 be the velocities of balls A and B, respectively, just after collision, as shown in the figures. After collision, the balls will separate with relative velocity $v_1 + v_2 = eu$. Hence, they will collide again after time

$$T' = \frac{2\pi R}{eu} = \frac{2T}{e}$$

26. (d) Time of fall for both ball and bullet is the same, $t = \sqrt{2h/g} = \sqrt{\frac{2(5\text{ m})}{(10\text{ m/s}^2)}} = 1\text{ s}$

Velocities of the ball and bullet after collision are, respectively, $\frac{20\text{ m}}{1\text{ s}} = 20\text{ m/s}$ and $\frac{100\text{ m}}{1\text{ s}} = 100\text{ m/s}$

Using momentum conservation along the horizontal direction, we have

$$(0.01\text{ kg})\, v = (0.2\text{ kg})(20\text{ m/s}) + (0.01\text{ kg})(100\text{ m/s})$$

$$\Rightarrow v = 500\text{ m/s}$$

27. (d)

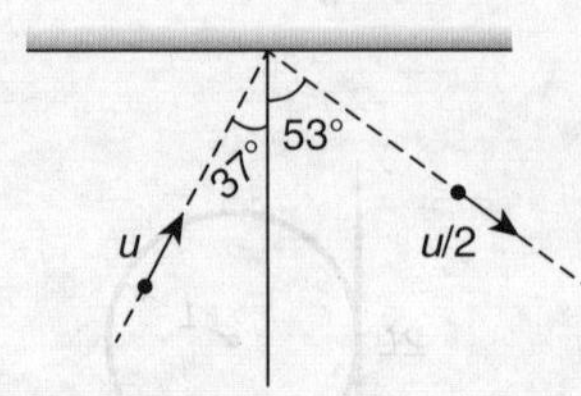

Magnitude of momentum change along the normal to the wall is

$$\Delta p_n = mu\cos 37^\circ + m\frac{u}{2}\cos 53^\circ = \frac{11}{10}mu$$

and that parallel to the wall is

$$\Delta p_t = mu\sin 37^\circ - m\frac{u}{2}\sin 53^\circ = \frac{2}{10}mu$$

The direction of force exerted by the wall is the same as the direction of $\Delta\vec{p}$. The angle made by $\Delta\vec{p}$ with the normal is

$$\theta = \tan^{-1}\left(\frac{\Delta p_t}{\Delta p_n}\right) = \tan^{-1}\left(\frac{2}{11}\right)$$

28. (d) Let the mass of the bob be m and that of the box be ηm. When the bob is at its lowest position, the gravitational potential energy is at its minimum and the kinetic energy is at its maximum. When the bob is at it lowest position, let m be its angular velocity in the clockwise sense, and v be the velocity of the box towards the right. Then, absolute velocity of the bob will be $\omega l - v$ towards the left.

Using momentum conservation principle along the horizontal direction, we have

$$m(\omega l - v) = \eta m v \quad ...(1)$$

Using mechanical energy conservation principle, we have

$$\frac{1}{2}m(\omega l - v)^2 + \frac{1}{2}\eta m v^2 = mgl \quad ...(2)$$

Solving the above equations, we have

$$v = \sqrt{\frac{2gl}{n(n+1)}}$$

The bob will swing further in the clockwise sense until it attains the horizontal position. At this moment, both the box and the bob will come to rest. From here onwards, their motions will change direction. Let s be the displacement of the box towards the right until this instant. Then, the absolute displacement of the bob along the horizontal is $2l - s$ towards the left. In the absence of external force along the horizontal, the CM of the system will not shift. Hence

$$m(2l - s) = \eta m s \Rightarrow s = \frac{2l}{\eta + 1}$$

29. (c)

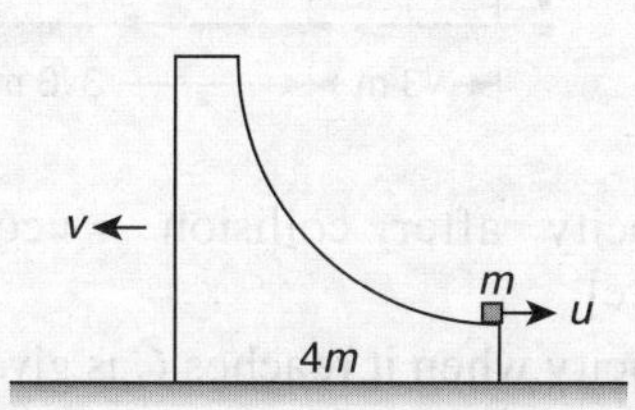

Let the velocities of the cube and the block be as shown in the figure. Using momentum conservation and energy conservation principles, respectively, we have

$$mu = 4mv \Rightarrow u = 4v \quad ...(1)$$

and $$\frac{1}{2}mu^2 + \frac{1}{2}(4m)v^2 = mgR \quad ...(2)$$

Eliminating v from the above equations, we have

$$\frac{1}{2}mu^2 + \frac{1}{2}(4m)\left(\frac{u^2}{16}\right) = mgR$$

$$\Rightarrow \frac{5}{8}mu^2 = mgR \Rightarrow \frac{5mu^2}{4aR} = 2$$

30. (c)

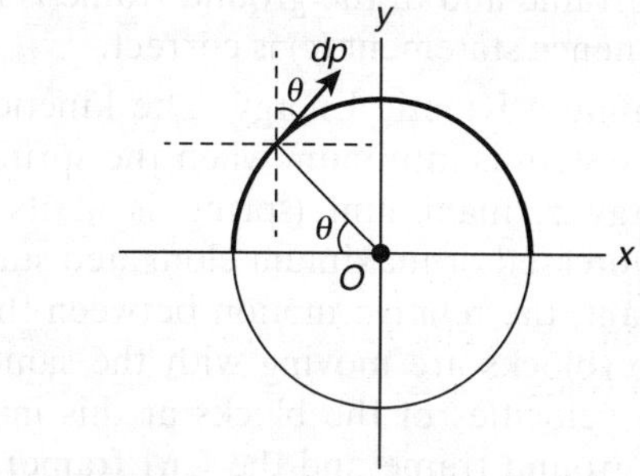

Let us subdivide the length of the train into small elements, each subtending angle $d\theta$ at the centre of the circle. The magnitude of the linear momentum of one such element mass, as shown in the figure, is

$$dp = v\,dm = v\left(\frac{M}{\pi}d\theta\right) = \frac{Mv}{\pi}d\theta$$

The x and y components of linear momentum are

$$P_x = \int_0^{\pi} \frac{Mv}{\pi}\sin\theta\, d\theta = \frac{2Mv}{\pi}$$

$$P_y = \int_0^{\pi} \frac{Mv}{\pi}\cos\theta\, d\theta = 0$$

Hence $P = \dfrac{2Mv}{\pi}$

31. (a) The centre of mass of the two-block system moves with constant velocity $u/3$.

Maximum Kinetic Energy: The kinetic energy of the system is maximum when the spring potential energy is minimum (spring is natural). The velocities of the blocks at this instant (from the ground frame and the CM frame) are shown in the figure.

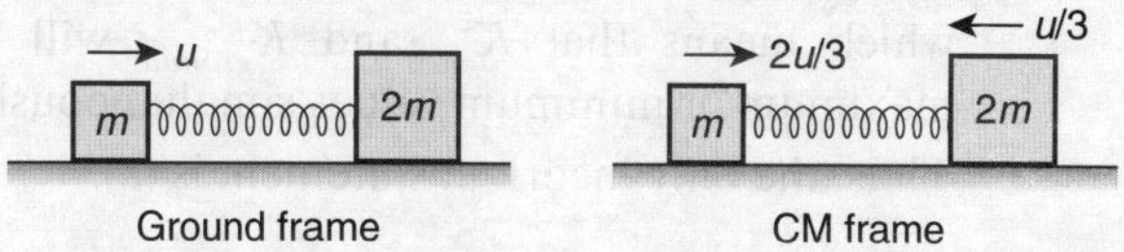

The kinetic energy of the system from the two reference frames are

$$K_{\text{ground}} = \frac{1}{2}mu^2$$

and $$K_{cm} = \frac{1}{2}m\left(\frac{2u}{3}\right)^2 + \frac{1}{2}(2m)\left(\frac{u}{3}\right)^2 = \frac{1}{3}mu^2$$

We see that the maximum kinetic energy in the CM frame and in the ground frame is in the ratio 2:3; hence statement (c) is correct.

Minimum Kinetic Energy: The kinetic energy of the system is minimum when the spring potential energy is maximum (spring is at its maximum compressed or maximum elongated state). At this instant, the relative motion between the blocks is zero (blocks are moving with the same velocity). The velocities of the blocks at this instant (from the ground frame and the CM frame) are shown in the figure.

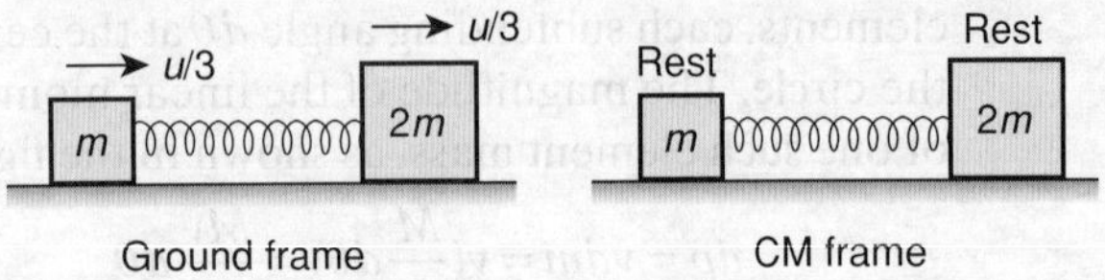

The kinetic energy of the system from the two reference frames are

$$K_{\text{ground}} = \frac{1}{2}(2m)\left(\frac{u}{3}\right)^2 = \frac{1}{6}mu^2$$

and $\quad K_{\text{cm}} = 0$

We see that the minimum kinetic energy of the system is zero in the CM frame and non-zero in the ground frame; hence statement (b) is correct.

We also see that K_{cm} and K_{ground} attain maximum or minimum values simultaneously; hence statement (d) is correct.

To check this statement, we could alternatively have used the relation

$$K_{\text{ground}} = K_{cm} + \frac{1}{2}Mv_{cm}^2$$

$$\Rightarrow \quad K_{\text{ground}} = K_{cm} + \frac{1}{2}(3m)\left(\frac{u}{3}\right)^2 = K_{cm} + \frac{1}{6}mu^2$$

which means that K_{cm} and K_{ground} will attain maximum or minimum values simultaneously.

Thus, the only incorrect statement is (a).

32. (c)

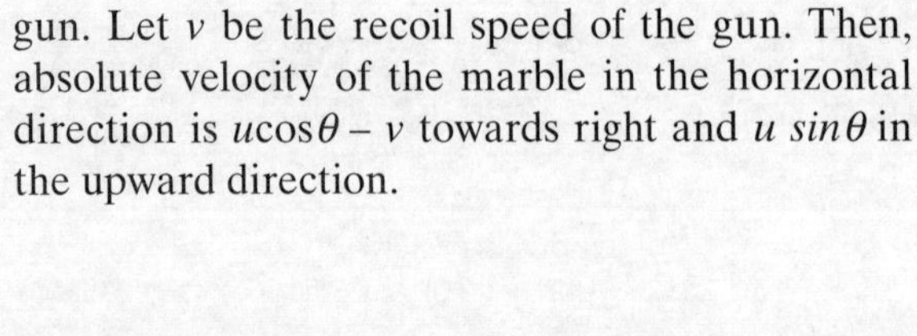

Let u be the velocity of the marble relative to the gun. Let v be the recoil speed of the gun. Then, absolute velocity of the marble in the horizontal direction is $u\cos\theta - v$ towards right and $u \sin\theta$ in the upward direction.

Using momentum conservation principle, we have

$$Mv = m(u\cos\theta - v)$$

$$\Rightarrow \quad v = \left(\frac{m\cos\theta}{M+m}\right)u \quad \text{...(1)}$$

According to the given condition, we have

$$u\cos\theta - v = u\sin\theta$$

$$\Rightarrow \quad v = (\cos\theta - \sin\theta)u \quad \text{...(2)}$$

Dividing the above equations, we have

$$\frac{\cos\theta}{\cos\theta - \sin\theta} = \frac{M+m}{m}$$

$$\Rightarrow \quad \frac{M}{m} = \frac{\sin\theta}{\cos\theta - \sin\theta} = 3$$

33. (b), (d) Velocity before collision at B is given by

$$\frac{1}{2}mv^2 = mg(3m)$$

$$\Rightarrow \quad v^2 = 60 \text{ m}^2/\text{s}^2$$

Case 1: (Completely Inelastic)

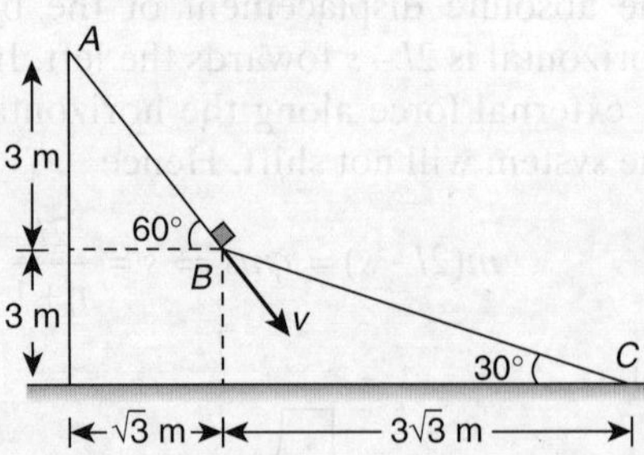

Velocity after collision $= v\cos 30^\circ = \frac{\sqrt{3}}{2}v$ [see figure]

Velocity when it reaches C is given by

$$\frac{1}{2}m(v_1^2 - v^2\cos^2 30^\circ) = mg(3m)$$

$$\Rightarrow \quad v_1^2 = \frac{3}{4}(60 \text{ m}^2/\text{s}^2) + 60 \text{ m}^2/\text{s}^2 = 105 \text{ m}^2/\text{s}^2$$

$$\Rightarrow \quad v_1 = \sqrt{105} \text{ m/s}$$

Case 2: (Elastic Collision)

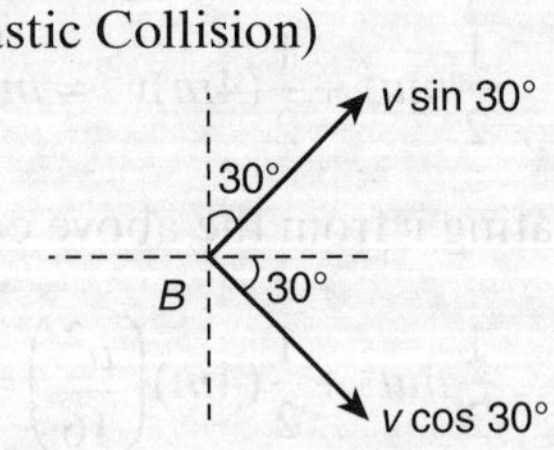

After collision, the normal component just reverses its direction without any change in magnitude, whereas the component along the incline remains as it is (see figure). The velocity along the vertical is $v_2 = (v\sin30^\circ)\cos 30^\circ - (v\cos30^\circ)\sin30^\circ = 0$.

CHAPTER

6 Torque and Angular Momentum

- The torque τ of a force $\mathbf{F}$ with respect to point O is defined as

$$\boldsymbol{\tau} = \mathbf{r} \times \mathbf{F}$$

The moment of inertia I of a body about a given axis is defined as

$$I = \sum m_i r_i^2$$

Parallel Axis Theorem:

$$I = I_{\text{cm}} + md^2$$

Perpendicular Axis Theorem (applicable to a lamina only):

$$I_z = I_x + I_y$$

- When a rigid body is rotating about a fixed axis, its dynamics is given by the equation

$$\tau_{\text{ext}} = I\alpha \text{ (about the axis)}$$

When a rigid body has both translational and rotational motion, its dynamics is given by the equations

$$\mathbf{F}_{\text{ext}} = M\mathbf{a}_{\text{cm}} \text{ and } \tau_{\text{ext}} = I\alpha \text{ (about the CM)}$$

When a rigid body is in equilibrium, that is, $\mathbf{a}_{\text{cm}} = 0$ and $\alpha = 0$ in an inertial frame, then its dynamics is given by the equations

$$\mathbf{F}_{\text{ext}} = 0 \text{ and } \tau_{\text{ext}} = 0 \text{ (about any point)}$$

- When a rigid body is in pure translational motion, its kinetic energy is given by

$$K = \frac{1}{2}Mv_{\text{cm}}^2$$

When a rigid body is rotating about a fixed axis, its kinetic energy is given by

$$K = \frac{1}{2}I\omega^2$$

When a rigid body has both translational and rotational motion, its kinetic energy is given by

$$K = \frac{1}{2}Mv_{\text{cm}}^2 + \frac{1}{2}I_{\text{cm}}\omega^2$$

- When a torque τ acts on a body that undergoes angular displacement, the work W done by the torque is given by

$$W = \int_{\theta_1}^{\theta_1} \tau \cdot d\theta$$

When a torque τ acts on a body rotating with angular velocity ω, the instantaneous power is given by

$$P = \boldsymbol{\tau} \cdot \boldsymbol{\omega}$$

- The angular momentum $\mathbf{L}$ with respect to point O of a particle with mass m moving with velocity $\mathbf{v}$ is defined as

$$\mathbf{L} = \mathbf{r} \times m\mathbf{v} = \mathbf{r} \times \mathbf{p}$$

The total angular momentum $\mathbf{L}$ of a system of particles is given by

$$\mathbf{L} = \sum \mathbf{r}_i \times \mathbf{p}_i$$

- When a rigid body is rotating about a fixed axis, the axial component of its angular momentum with respect to any point O on the axis is given by

$$\mathbf{L} = I\boldsymbol{\omega}$$

The magnitude of the angular momentum is related to the kinetic energy of the rotating body as

$$K = \frac{L^2}{2I} \text{ or } L = \sqrt{2IK}$$

- In terms of torque and angular momentum, the basic dynamics relation for the rotational motion of any system is

$$\tau_{ext} = \frac{d\mathbf{L}}{dt}$$

which reduces to $\tau_{ext} = I\alpha$ if the rotational inertia of the system is constant.

If $\tau_{ext} = 0$, the total angular momentum of the system is conserved.

The angular impulse of a torque is defined as

$$\int_{t_1}^{t_2} \tau(t)\,dt = \Delta\mathbf{L}$$

EXERCISES

1. Seven identical circular discs, each of mass M and radius R, are welded, as shown in the figure.

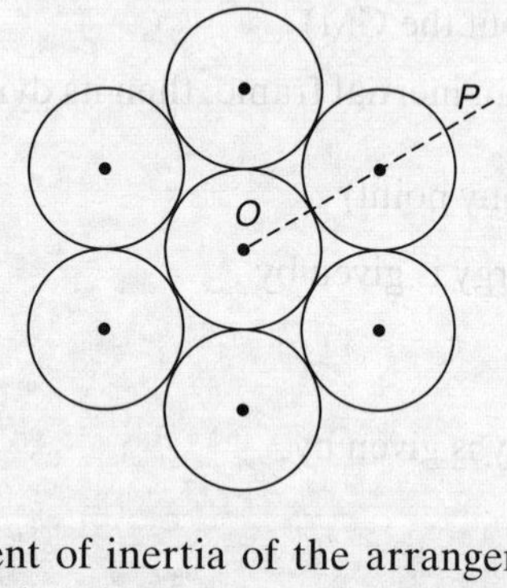

The moment of inertia of the arrangement about an axis passing through P and normal to the plane of the discs is:

(a) $\frac{19}{2}MR^2$ (b) $\frac{55}{2}MR^2$

(c) $\frac{73}{2}MR^2$ (d) $\frac{181}{2}MR^2$

2. The triangular sheet ABC shown in the figure is right-angled at B and $AB = BC = l$ and has mass m.

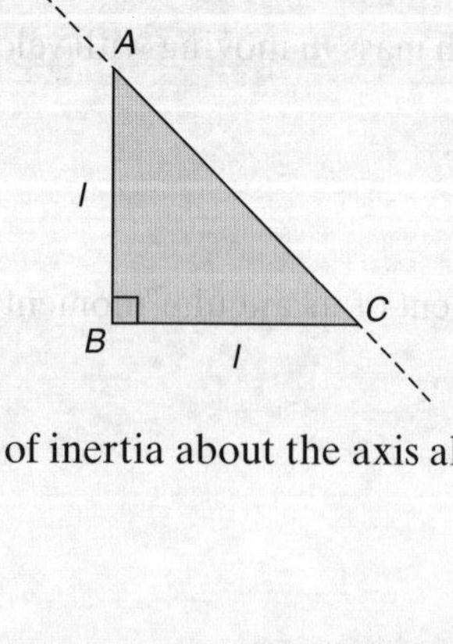

Its moment of inertia about the axis along AC is:

(a) $\frac{1}{12}ml^2$ (b) $\frac{1}{6}ml^2$

(c) $\frac{2}{3}ml^2$ (d) $\frac{1}{3}ml^2$

3. I_1, I_2, I_3 and I_4 are, respectively, the moments of inertia of a thin square plate $ABCD$ about axes 1, 2, 3 and 4, which are in the plane of the sheet, as shown in the figure.

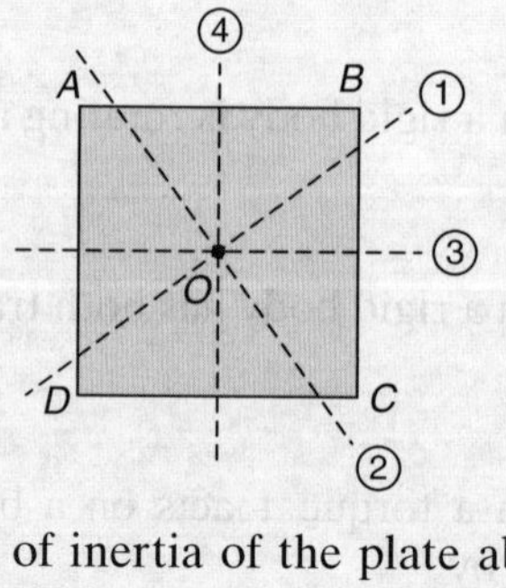

The moment of inertia of the plate about an axis passing through the centre O and perpendicular to the plate is:

(a) $I_1 + I_3$ (b) $I_2 + I_4$

(c) $2I_3$ (d) $3I_4 - I_3$

4. Three metal rods, each of mass m and length l, are welded to form an equilateral triangle. The moment of inertia of the composite structure about an axis passing through the centre of mass of the structure and perpendicular to its plane is:

(a) $\frac{1}{2}ml^2$ (b) $\frac{1}{4}ml^2$

(c) $\frac{1}{8}ml^2$ (d) $\frac{1}{12}ml^2$

5. Two point masses m_1 and m_2 are attached to the ends of a light rigid rod of length l. The system is to be rotated about an axis perpendicular to the rod. The minimum moment of inertia of the system is:

(a) $\left(\dfrac{m_1 m_2}{m_1+m_2}\right)l^2$ (b) $(m_1+m_2)l^2$

(c) $\left(\dfrac{m_1^2+m_2^2}{m_1+m_2}\right)l^2$ (d) $\left(\sqrt{m_1}+\sqrt{m_2}\right)^2 l^2$

6. The figure shows a uniform semi-circular ring of mass m and radius r. Its CM is at C, the distance $OC = \dfrac{2r}{\pi}$.

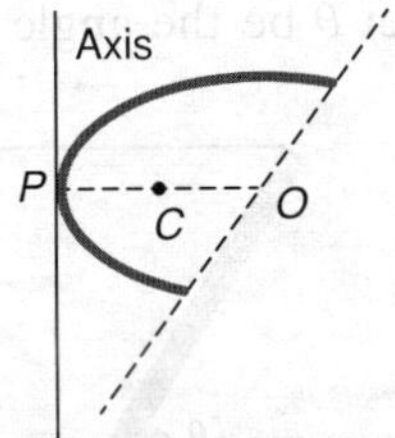

Its moment of inertia about the axis through P and perpendicular to the plane of the ring is:

(a) $\left(2+\dfrac{4}{\pi}\right)mr^2$ (b) $\pi(\pi-2)mr^2$

(c) $\pi(\pi+2)mr^2$ (d) $\left(2-\dfrac{4}{\pi}\right)mr^2$

7. A cube of side l and mass m is placed on a rough horizontal surface and the friction is sufficient to prevent slipping.

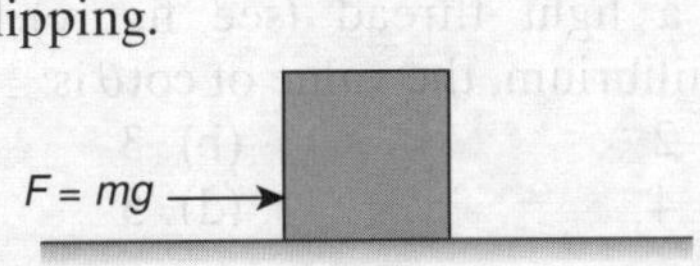

If a force $F = mg$ is applied horizontally, at a height $l/4$ above the surface as shown in the figure, then the moment arm of the normal force from the centre of the cube is:

(a) $l/2$ (b) $l/4$

(c) $l/8$ (d) 0

8. A cube is placed on a rough surface having friction coefficient μ. A horizontal force F is applied on the cube, as shown in the figure. The force is increased until the cube either slips or topples.

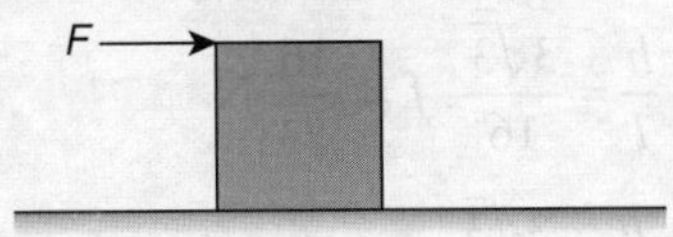

If we want toppling to happen first before slipping, then:

(a) $\mu > 0.25$ (b) $\mu > 0.4$

(c) $\mu > 0.5$ (d) $\mu > 0.75$

9. The height of a solid cylinder is 4 times its radius. It is placed vertically on a conveyor belt which is moving horizontally with velocity $v = \left(2.5\ \text{m/s}^3\right)t^2$. If the cylinder does not slip, it will topple at time (take $g = 10\ \text{m/s}^2$):

(a) 1 s (b) 2 s

(c) 3 s (d) 4 s

10. The figure shows a hollow cylinder of mass m placed on the horizontal surface and a block of same mass m attached through a string tightly wound on the cylinder. The horizontal surface is rough enough to prevent slipping.

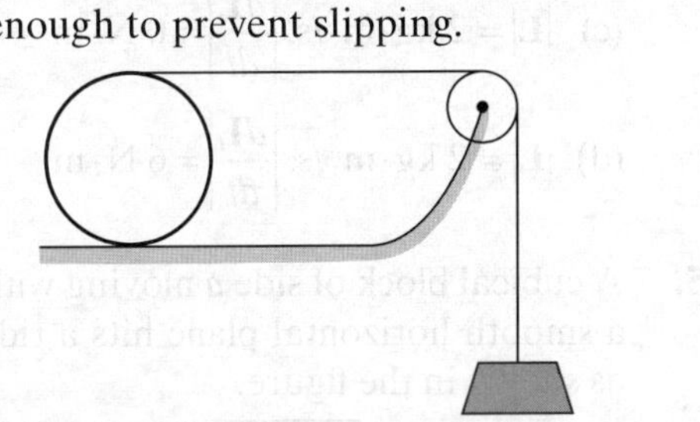

The acceleration a of the cylinder and the minimum coefficient of friction μ required for pure rolling motion are:

(a) $a = 2g/3, \mu = 1/3$ (b) $a = 2g/3, \mu = 1/2$

(c) $a = g/3, \mu = 2/3$ (d) $a = g/3, \mu = 0$

11. A cyclist is riding a bicycle whose wheel base is of length a, and the combined centre of gravity is at height $h = 1.5a$ above the ground. He applies brakes so that the wheels are completely locked. The maximum friction coefficient between the wheels and the ground so that the wheels do not lose contact with the ground is:

(a) $1/3$ (b) $1/6$

(c) $2/3$ (d) $3/4$

12. A uniform rod of mass $4m$ and length l is hanging vertically from a point O on the ceiling. The rod is hinged at O and is free to rotate in the vertical plane. A small bullet of mass m moving horizontally with speed u strikes the lowest end of the rod and gets embedded in it. If the rod just rotates to the horizontal position, then (take acceleration due to gravity = g):

(a) $u = \sqrt{8gl}$ (b) $u = \sqrt{10gl}$

(c) $u = \sqrt{14gl}$ (d) $u = \sqrt{18gl}$

13. A small object of uniform density rolls up a curved surface with an initial velocity v. It reaches a height $h = \dfrac{3v^2}{4g}$. The object is a:

(a) Hollow cylinder (b) Hollow sphere

(c) Solid sphere (d) Solid cylinder

14. A conical pendulum consists of a bob of mass $m = 0.5$ kg suspended by a light thread of length $l = 2$ m, from a point O on the ceiling. The bob is rotating in a horizontal plane with angular speed $\omega = 2.5$ rad/s. If **L** denotes the angular momentum of the bob about O, then (take $g = 10$ m/s^2):

(a) $|\mathbf{L}| = 3\ \text{kg}\cdot\text{m}^2/\text{s}, \left|\frac{d\mathbf{L}}{dt}\right| = 0\ \text{N}\cdot\text{m}$

(b) $|\mathbf{L}| = 3\ \text{kg}\cdot\text{m}^2/\text{s}, \left|\frac{d\mathbf{L}}{dt}\right| = 6\ \text{N}\cdot\text{m}$

(c) $|\mathbf{L}| = 2\ \text{kg}\cdot\text{m}^2/\text{s}, \left|\frac{d\mathbf{L}}{dt}\right| = 0\ \text{N}\cdot\text{m}$

(d) $|\mathbf{L}| = 2\ \text{kg}\cdot\text{m}^2/\text{s}, \left|\frac{d\mathbf{L}}{dt}\right| = 6\ \text{N}\cdot\text{m}$

15. A cubical block of side a moving with velocity v on a smooth horizontal plane hits a ridge at point O, as shown in the figure.

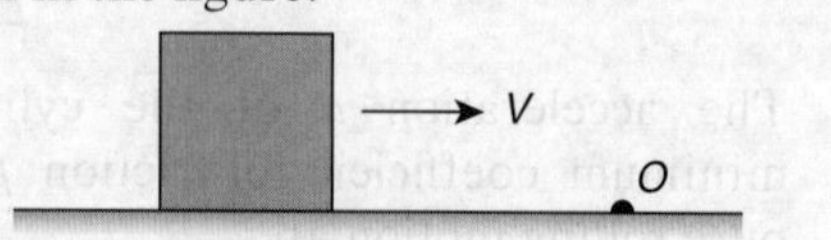

If the cube just manages to topple and fall on the other side of the ridge, then $\frac{v^2}{ag}$ equals:

(a) $\frac{2(\sqrt{2}-1)}{3}$ (b) $\frac{8(\sqrt{2}-1)}{3}$

(c) $\frac{\sqrt{2}+1}{3}$ (d) $\frac{2(\sqrt{2}+1)}{3}$

16. A uniform rod of mass $m = 0.6$ kg and length $l = 0.3$ m is hanging vertically from a point O on the ceiling. The rod is hinged at O and is free to rotate in the vertical plane. A short-duration horizontal impulse J acts on the middle of the rod. If the rod just rotates by angle $\theta = 60°$, then (take $g = 10\ \text{m/s}^2$):

(a) $J = 1.2$ N·s (b) $J = 1.6$ N·s
(c) $J = 2.0$ N·s (d) $J = 3.2$ N·s

17. Consider the Earth to be a uniform sphere rotating about its diameter with time period 24 hours. If its volume decreases by 0.5% due to cooling of its core, its time period will:

(a) Decrease by 8 min (b) Decrease by 4.8 min
(c) Increase by 2 min (d) Increase by 3.6 min

18. A particle in uniform circular motion has angular momentum L with respect to the centre of the circle. If angular speed is doubled and kinetic energy is halved, its angular momentum becomes:

(a) $4L$ (b) $L/2$
(c) $2L$ (d) $L/4$

19. A uniform rod rests in an inclined manner on a smooth vertical wall. The rod makes angle θ with the wall and the bottom of the rod rests on a rough floor. If the magnitude of the reaction force between the rod and the floor is 1.25 times the weight of the rod, then $\tan\theta$ equals:

(a) $\sqrt{2}/3$ (b) $3/2$
(c) $2/\sqrt{3}$ (d) $\sqrt{2}/\sqrt{3}$

20. Two identical rods rest in equilibrium on a rough floor with their top ends tied by a light thread (see figure). Let θ be the angle made by the rods with the floor.

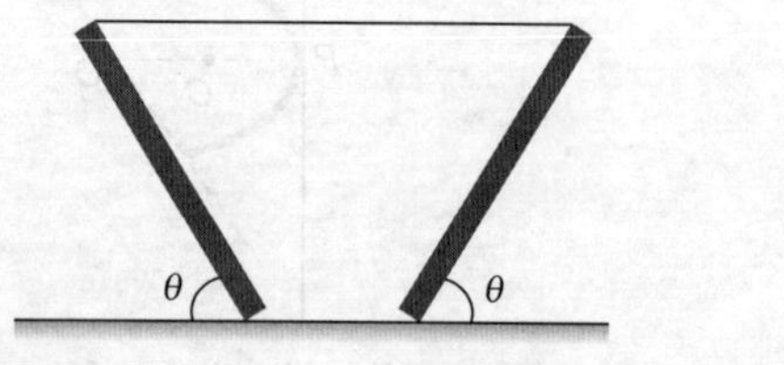

If the coefficient of friction between the rods and the floor is $\mu = 0.5$, then the smallest possible value of θ is:

(a) 30° (b) 37°
(c) 45° (d) 60°

21. Two identical rods are rigidly joined in the shape of an L-frame and the frame is hung from the ceiling by a light thread (see figure). At equilibrium, the value of $\cot\theta$ is:

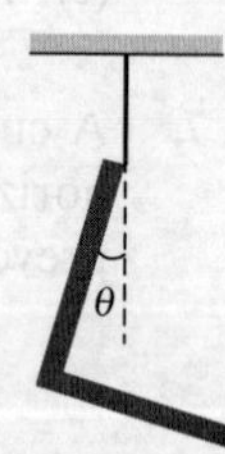

(a) 2 (b) 3
(c) 4 (d) 5

22. A uniform rod of weight 16 N and length l rests in an inclined manner on a smooth vertical wall of height h $(h < l)$ such that a small portion of the rod extends beyond the wall. The rod makes an angle 30° with the wall and the bottom of the rod rests on a rough floor. The magnitude of the reaction force between the rod and the wall is equal to that between the rod and the floor. The ratio h/l and the friction force f between the rod and the floor are:

(a) $\frac{h}{l} = \frac{\sqrt{3}}{16}, f = 16\sqrt{3}$ N

(b) $\frac{h}{l} = \frac{3\sqrt{3}}{16}, f = \frac{16}{\sqrt{3}}$ N

(c) $\frac{h}{l} = \frac{3\sqrt{3}}{8}, f = \frac{8}{\sqrt{3}}$ N

(d) $\frac{h}{l} = \frac{\sqrt{3}}{8}, f = 8\sqrt{3}$ N

23. A uniform rod AB is rotating in a horizontal plane with angular speed ω about a vertical axis passing through its end A. At time $t = 0$, an insect starts crawling along the rod from end A, with uniform speed v relative to the rod. If the torque τ required for the motion is proportional to t^n, then n equals:

(a) $-1/2$ (b) $1/2$
(c) $2/3$ (d) 1

24. An insect of mass m starts crawling along the circumference of a disc of mass $4m$ and radius r. The disc is free to rotate about a vertical axis passing through its centre. By the time the insect reaches the diametrically opposite point, the disc will have turned through angle:

(a) π (b) $\frac{\pi}{2}$
(c) $\frac{\pi}{3}$ (d) $\frac{\pi}{4}$

25. The figure shows a body of mass m, radius r and the moment of inertia I about its natural axis placed on a rough horizontal surface. A horizontal force $\mathbf{F}$ is applied at height h above the centre of mass of the body. The friction force required for pure rolling is:

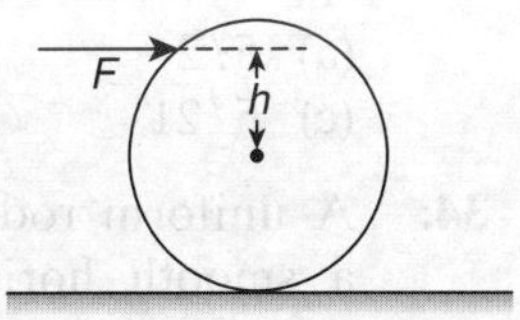

(a) $\mathbf{f} = \left(\dfrac{h/r + I/mr^2}{1 + I/mr^2}\right)\mathbf{F}$

(b) $\mathbf{f} = \left(\dfrac{h/r - I/mr^2}{1 - I/mr^2}\right)\mathbf{F}$

(c) $\mathbf{f} = \left(\dfrac{h/r - I/mr^2}{1 + I/mr^2}\right)\mathbf{F}$

(d) $\mathbf{f} = \left(\dfrac{h/r + I/mr^2}{1 - I/mr^2}\right)\mathbf{F}$

26. A boy is pushing a ring of mass 2 kg and radius 0.5 m with a stick, as shown in the figure. The boy applies a horizontal force of 2 N and the ring rolls without slipping with acceleration 0.3 m/s^2.

If the coefficient of friction between the stick and the ring is $n/10$, then the value of n is:

(a) 2 (b) 3
(c) 4 (d) 5

27. A horizontal circular platform of radius 0.5 m and mass 0.45 kg is free to rotate about a vertical axis. Two light spring toy-guns, each carrying a steel ball of mass 0.05 kg, are attached to the platform at a distance of 0.25 m on diametrically opposite sides of the axis, as shown in the figure. The guns simultaneously fire the balls horizontally with absolute speed 9 m/s in opposite directions.

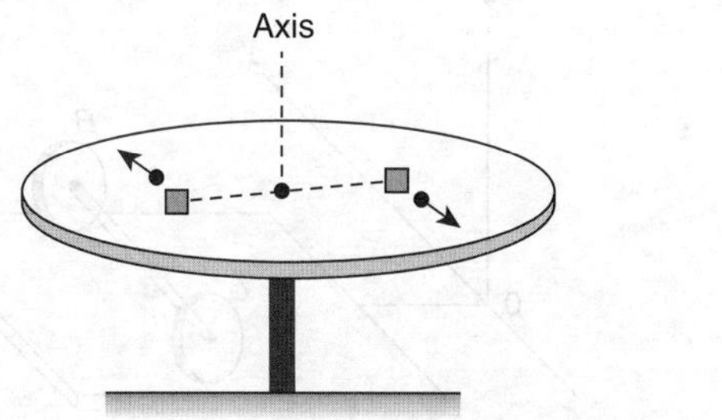

The angular speed of the platform after the balls are fired is:

(a) 2 rad/s (b) 3 rad/s
(c) 4 rad/s (d) 5 rad/s

28. The figure shows the top view of a uniform circular disc of mass 1.5 kg and radius 0.5 m resting on a smooth horizontal surface. Three forces of equal magnitude $F = 0.5$ N are applied simultaneously along the three sides of an equilateral triangle XYZ, as shown in the figure.

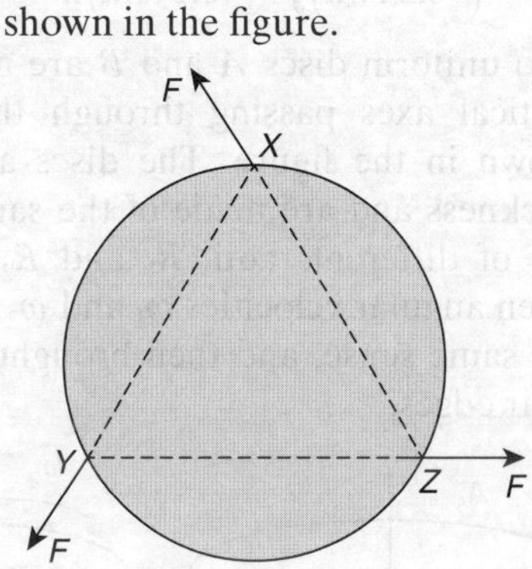

One second after applying the forces, the angular speed of the disc is:

(a) 2 rad/s (b) 3 rad/s
(c) 4 rad/s (d) 5 rad/s

29. A uniform spherical body of radius R is initially imparted a velocity v_0 towards the right and angular velocity ω_0 in the anti-clockwise sense, on a rough horizontal surface. If $\eta = \omega_0 R / v_0$, then the correct statements among the following are:

(a) Sphere comes to a halt if $\eta = 7/5$
(b) Sphere rolls forward if $\eta < 7/5$
(c) Sphere rolls backwards if $\eta > 5/2$
(d) None of these

30. Two uniform discs, each having mass 2 kg and radius 0.5 m, are joined by a light rigid rod of length 2 m, as shown in the figure. The system is placed on a rough horizontal plank such that the rod is parallel to the y-axis and the plank is pulled with a uniform acceleration 0.3 m/s^2 along the x-axis.

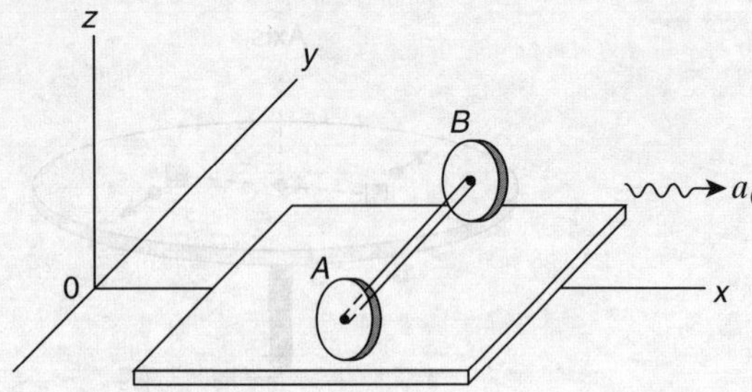

If the friction between the discs and the plank is enough to prevent slipping, then:

(a) Acceleration of the discs $= \left(-0.2\ \text{m/s}^2\right)\mathbf{i}$
(b) Angular acceleration of the discs $= \left(-0.4\ \text{rad/s}^2\right)\mathbf{j}$
(c) Friction force on any one disc $= (0.2\ \text{N})\mathbf{i}$
(d) Torque of the friction force on disc A, about the centre of the rod joining the discs $= (-0.2\ \text{Nm})\mathbf{j} + (-0.1\ \text{Nm})\mathbf{k}$

31. Two uniform discs A and B are mounted on two vertical axes passing through their centres, as shown in the figure. The discs are of the same thickness and are made of the same material but are of different radii, R_1 and R_2. The discs are given angular velocities ω_1 and ω_2, respectively, in the same sense, and then brought into contact at their edges.

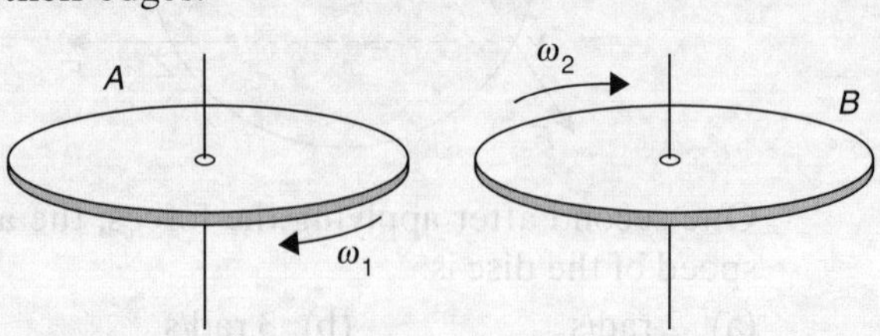

If due to friction the discs eventually come to rest, then the correct relation among the following is:

(a) $\omega_1 R_1^2 = \omega_2 R_2^2$ (b) $\omega_1 R_1^3 = \omega_2 R_2^3$
(c) $\omega_1^2 R_1 = \omega_2^2 R_2$ (d) $\omega_1^2 R_2 = \omega_2^2 R_1$

32. A uniform sphere of mass M is lying at rest on a rough horizontal surface. The sphere is pulled by a horizontal force F which passes through the centre O of the sphere. If the coefficient of friction between the ground and the sphere is μ, the maximum value of F so that the sphere rolls without slipping is:

(a) $\frac{7}{5}\mu Mg$ (b) $\frac{4}{7}\mu Mg$
(c) $\frac{5}{7}\mu Mg$ (d) $\frac{7}{2}\mu Mg$

33. A uniform sphere of mass M is lying at rest on a rough horizontal surface. An impulsive force $2Mg$ acts vertically downward at point P, as shown in the figure. The line joining P and the centre O of the sphere makes angle 60° with the horizontal.

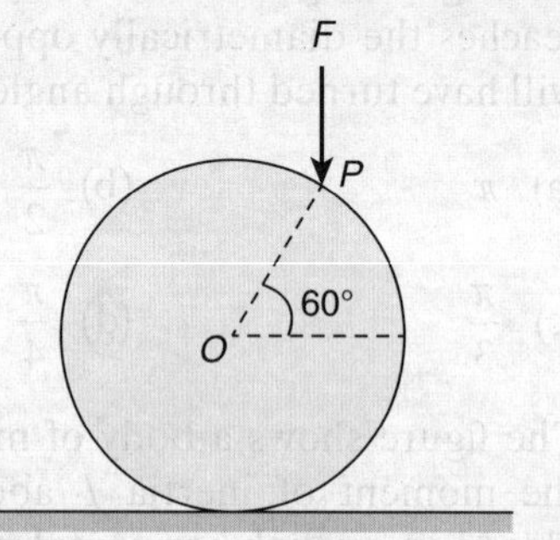

The minimum value of the coefficient of friction μ between the ground and the sphere so that the sphere rolls without slipping is:

(a) 5/2 (b) 5/7
(c) 5/21 (d) 2/5

34. A uniform rod AB of mass M lying at rest on a smooth horizontal surface is struck by two impulsive forces perpendicular to the rod in the horizontal plane, as shown in the figure. Force F_2 passes through the centre O of the rod, and force F_1 passes through a point which is midway between the centre and end B of the rod.

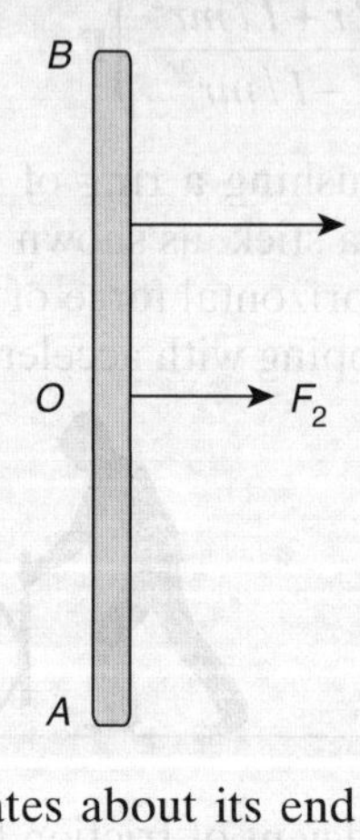

If the rod rotates about its end A, then the ratio F_2/F_1 is:

(a) 1/2 (b) 1/3
(c) 2/3 (d) 3/4

35. The figure shows the top view of a uniform disc placed flat on a smooth horizontal surface. The disc is free to move on the surface. It is struck with an impulse in the horizontal plane at point P, as shown in the figure. The direction of the impulse makes angle 30° with the line joining P and the centre O of the disc.

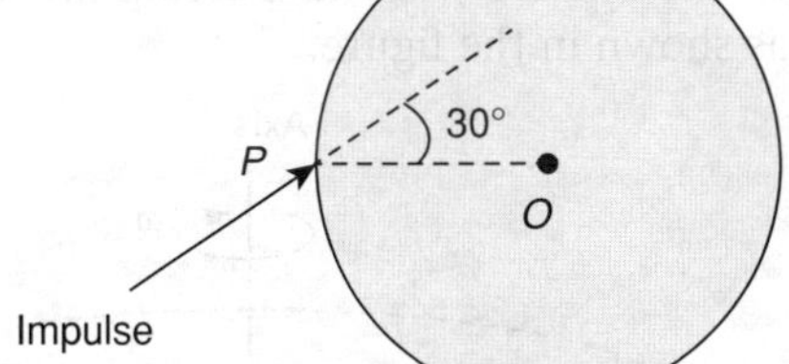

If the velocity of point P immediately after the impulse makes angle θ with line PO, then:

(a) $\theta = 30°$ (b) $\theta = 45°$
(c) $\theta = 53°$ (d) $\theta = 60°$

36. Two uniform cylinders A and B, each of mass 1 kg, are connected by a light spring of force constant 200 N/m at their axles and are placed in equilibrium on a fixed wedge, as shown in the figure. The coefficient of friction between the wedge and the cylinders is 0.2.

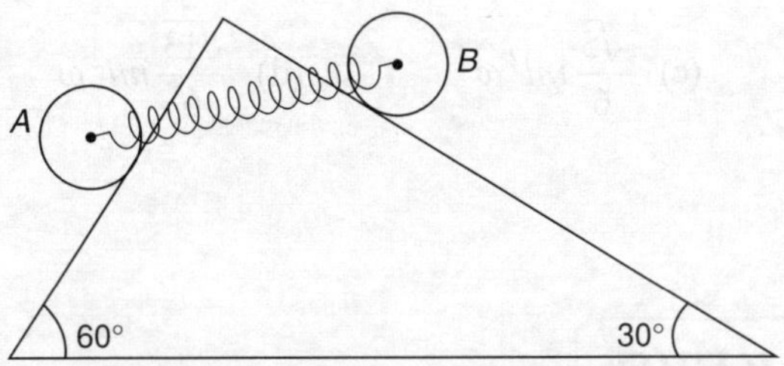

The angle made θ made by the line AB with the horizontal, and the normal contact forces N_A, N_B between the cylinders and the wedge, are:

(a) $\theta = 37°, N_A = mg, N_B = \sqrt{3}mg$
(b) $\theta = 37°, N_A = \sqrt{3}mg, N_B = mg$
(c) $\theta = 30°, N_A = mg, N_B = \sqrt{3}mg$
(d) $\theta = 30°, N_A = \sqrt{3}mg, N_B = mg$

37. A light inextensible string is tightly wound on a hollow cylinder of mass $M = 25$ kg placed on a rough horizontal surface. The outer radius of the hollow cylinder is double the inner radius. The free end P of the string is pulled by a horizontal force $F = 6.5$ N, as shown in the figure. Friction between the cylinder and the ground is sufficient to prevent slipping.

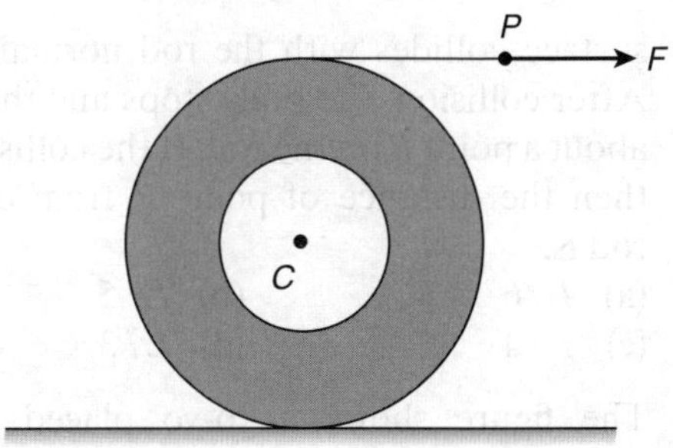

Starting from rest, the velocity of the cylinder when its centre of mass C has moved by a distance $s = 1$ m is:

(a) $\frac{4}{5}$ m/s (b) $\frac{3}{7}$ m/s
(c) $\frac{2}{5}$ m/s (d) $\frac{2}{7}$ m/s

38. A circular portion of diameter R is cut from a circular disc of radius R and mass M, as shown in the figure.

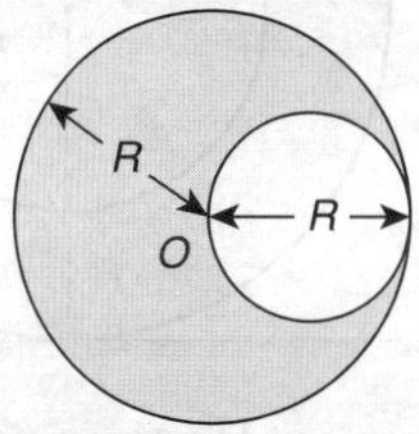

The moment of inertia of the cut disc, about an axis passing through its CM and perpendicular to its plane is:

(a) $\frac{41}{72}MR^2$ (b) $\frac{37}{96}MR^2$
(c) $\frac{15}{36}MR^2$ (d) $\frac{35}{144}MR^2$

39. A mass M whirls on a frictionless table with angular speed ω, held to circular motion by a string which passes through a hole in the table. The string is slowly pulled through the hole so that the radius of the circle changes from R to $R/2$. Work done by the pulling force equals:

(a) $\frac{1}{4}M\omega^2R^2$ (b) $\frac{1}{2}M\omega^2R^2$
(c) $\frac{3}{2}M\omega^2R^2$ (d) $2M\omega^2R^2$

40. A uniform rod AB of length L and mass $4M$ is lying at rest on a smooth horizontal surface. A small body of mass M moving on the same horizontal surface collides with the rod normally at end A. After collision, the body stops and the rod rotates about a point P on the rod. If the collision is elastic, then the distance of point P from end B of the rod is:

(a) $L/6$ (b) $L/5$
(c) $L/4$ (d) $L/3$

41. The figure shows a yo-yo placed on a rough horizontal surface being pulled by a force F at angle θ to the horizontal. The friction is enough to prevent slipping. Rotational inertia of the yo-yo is $\frac{1}{2}MR^2$, where M is its mass and R is its outer radius. Take the right direction in the figure as the positive direction.

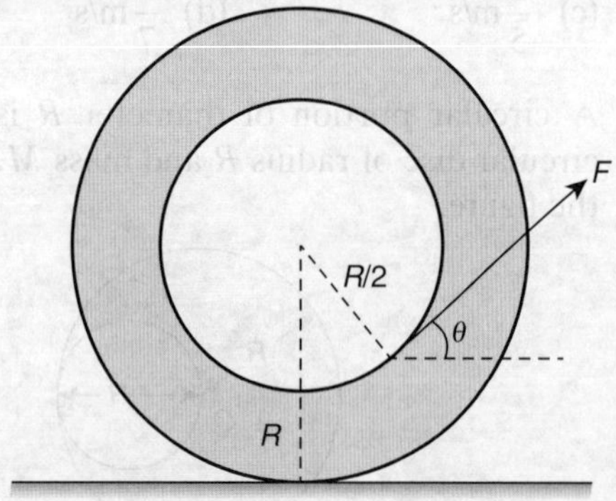

If a is the acceleration of the axis of the yo-yo and f is the friction acting on the yo-yo, then the correct statements from the following are:

(a) $a > 0, f < 0$ for $\theta < 60°$
(b) $a > 0, f > 0$ for $60° < \theta < 90°$
(c) $a < 0, f > 0$ for $\theta = 90°$
(d) $a < 0, f = 0$ for $\theta = 180°$

42. A uniform rod AB of mass m and length l is rotating in a horizontal plane with angular speed ω about a vertical axis passing through its end A, as shown in the figure.

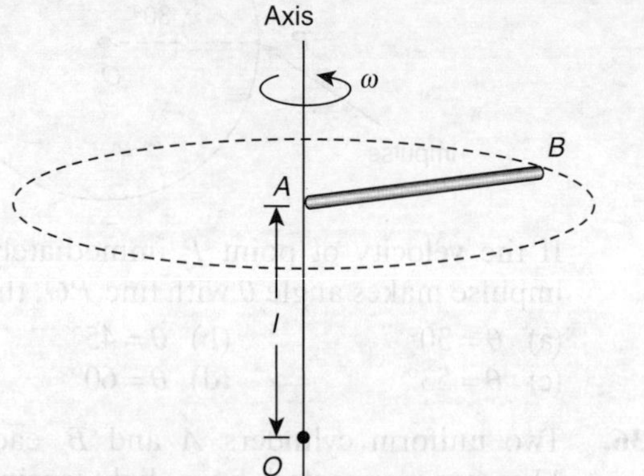

Angular momentum of the rod about O is:

(a) $\frac{\sqrt{2}}{3}ml^2\omega$ (b) $\frac{1}{3}ml^2\omega$
(c) $\frac{\sqrt{5}}{6}ml^2\omega$ (d) $\frac{\sqrt{13}}{6}ml^2\omega$

ANSWER KEYS

1. (d)	**2.** (a)	**3.** (a),(b),(c),(d)	**4.** (a)	**5.** (a)	**6.** (d)	**7.** (b)	**8.** (c)	**9.** (a)
10. (d)	**11.** (a)	**12.** (c)	**13.** (d)	**14.** (b)	**15.** (b)	**16.** (a)	**17.** (b)	**18.** (d)
19. (b)	**20.** (c)	**21.** (b)	**22.** (d)	**23.** (d)	**24.** (c)	**25.** (c)	**26.** (c)	**27.** (c)
28. (a)	**29.** (b),(c)	**30.** (b),(c)	**31.** (b)	**32.** (d)	**33.** (c)	**34.** (a)	**35.** (d)	**36.** (c)
37. (a)	**38.** (b)	**39.** (c)	**40.** (d)	**41.** (a),(d)	**42.** (d)			

SOLUTIONS

1. (d)

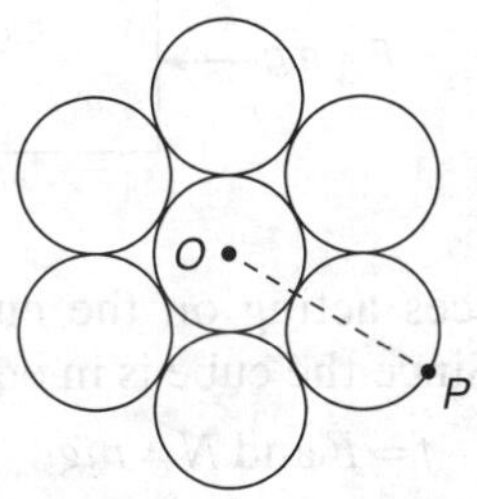

The centre of mass of the arrangement is at O. Its rotational inertia about O is

$$I_O = \frac{1}{2}MR^2 + 6\left[\frac{1}{2}MR^2 + M(2R)^2\right]$$

$$= \frac{1}{2}MR^2 + 27MR^2 = \frac{55}{2}MR^2$$

Now, using the Parallel Axis Theorem, we have

$$l_P = lO + 7M(3R)^2$$

$$= \frac{55}{2}MR^2 + 63MR^2 = \frac{181}{2}MR^2$$

2. (a) To solve the given problem, let us imagine an identical triangle to complete a square of mass $2M$. The moment of inertia of this square about an axis passing through its centre and perpendicular to its plane is $\frac{(2M)l^2}{12} + \frac{(2M)I^2}{12} = \frac{(2M)P^2}{6}$

Now, using the Perpendicular Axis Theorem, the moment of inertia of the square lamina about its diagonal AB will be $\frac{(2M)I^2}{12}$.

The moment of inertia of the triangular lamina equals half of the moment of inertia of the square, that is, $\frac{1}{2} \times \frac{(2M)I^2}{12} = \frac{MI^2}{12}$

3. (a), (b), (c), (d)

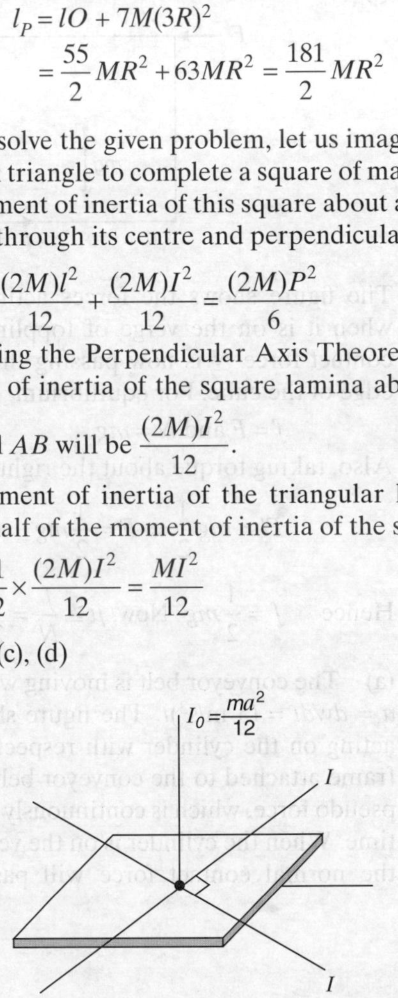

The moment of inertia of a square lamina about an axis passing through its centre and perpendicular to its plane is $I_0 = \frac{ma^2}{12} + \frac{ma^2}{12} = \frac{ma^2}{6}$. Now consider any two mutually perpendicular axes in the plane and passing through the centre of the lamina, as shown in the figure. From symmetry, we can see that the moment of inertia will be the same about both these axes. Let l be the moment of inertia of the lamina about any one of them. Then, from the Perpendicular Axis Theorem

$$I + I = \frac{ma^2}{6} \Rightarrow I = \frac{ma^2}{12}$$

Hence, we have

$$I_1 = I_2 = I_3 = I_4 = \frac{ma^2}{12} = \frac{1}{2}I_0$$

Now, we can see that all the given options are correct.

4. (a)

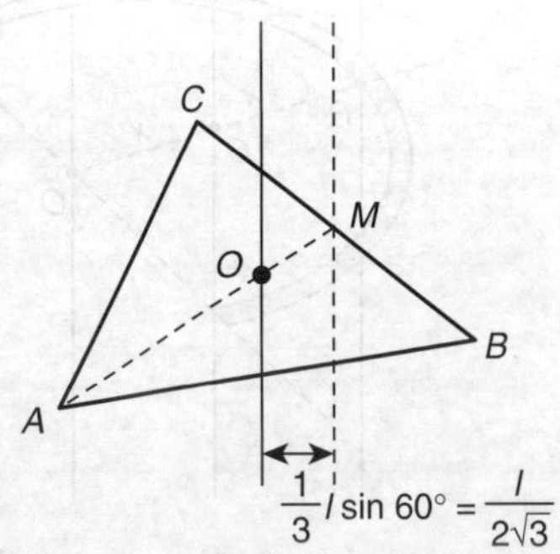

The CM of the triangular structure lies at point O, which is the intersection point of the medians of triangle ABC. We are supposed to find the moment of inertia about the axis passing through O. Consider a parallel axis passing through M, which is the CM of one of the rods. The perpendicular distance between the two parallel axes is $\frac{1}{3}(I \sin 60°) = \frac{l}{2\sqrt{3}}$.

Now, using the Parallel Axis Theorem, the moment of inertia contribution of one rod about the axis through O is $\frac{ml^2}{12} + m(\frac{1}{2\sqrt{3}})^2 = \frac{ml^2}{6}$.

The total moment of inertia due to all the three rods will be $3\left(\frac{ml}{6}\right)^2 = \frac{ml^2}{2}$.

5. (a)

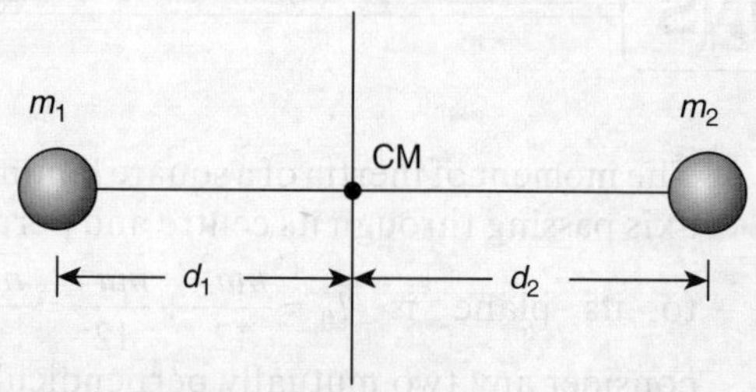

The minimum moment of inertia will be about the axis that passes through the CM, which lies at distance $d_1 = \dfrac{m_2 l}{m_1 + m_2}$ from mass m_1 and distance $d_2 = \dfrac{m_1 l}{m_1 + m_2}$ from mass m_2 (see figure).

The required moment of inertia is

$$I = m_1 d_1^2 + m_2 d_2^2 = \left(\frac{m_1 m_2}{m_1 + m_2}\right) l^2$$

6. (d)

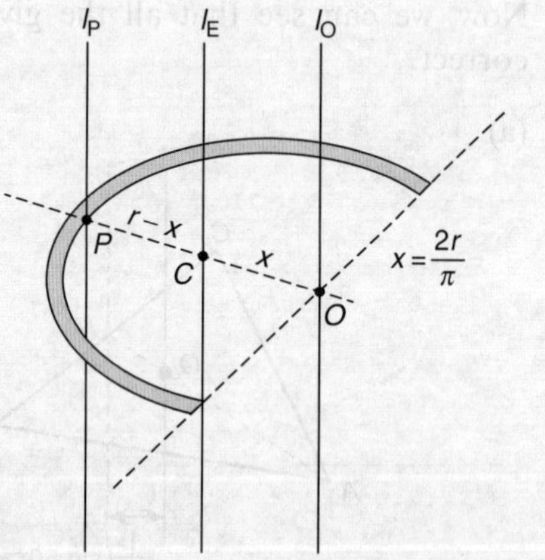

The figure shows three parallel axes drawn through the points P, C and O. Using Parallel Axis Theorem, we have

$$I_P = I_C + m(r - x)^2 \quad \text{...(1)}$$

$$I_O = I_C + mx^2 \quad \text{...(2)}$$

Eliminating I_C from the above equations, we have

$$I_P - I_O = m[(r - x)^2 - x^2] = m(r - 2xr)$$

$$= \left(1 - \frac{4}{\pi}\right) mr^2$$

Now $I_O = mr^2$. Hence

$$I_P = I_O + \left(1 - \frac{4}{\pi}\right) mr^2 = \left(2 - \frac{4}{\pi}\right) mr^2$$

7. (b)

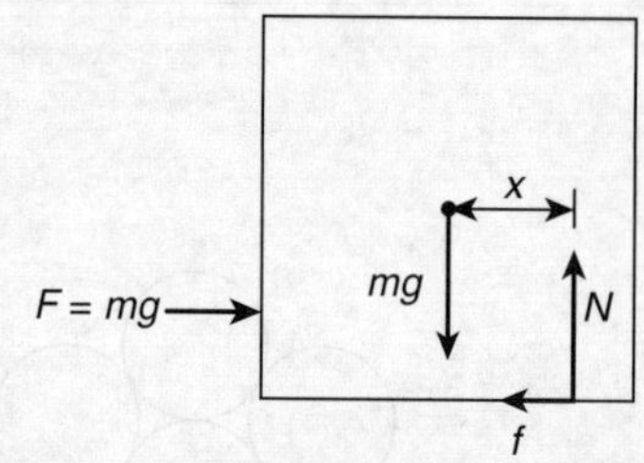

The forces acting on the cube are shown in the figure. Since the cube is in equilibrium

$$f = F \text{ and } N = mg$$

Also, taking torque about the CM, we have

$$Nx + F\frac{1}{4} = f\frac{I}{2}$$

Solving the above equations and putting $F = mg$ (given), we have $x = \dfrac{1}{4}$.

8. (c)

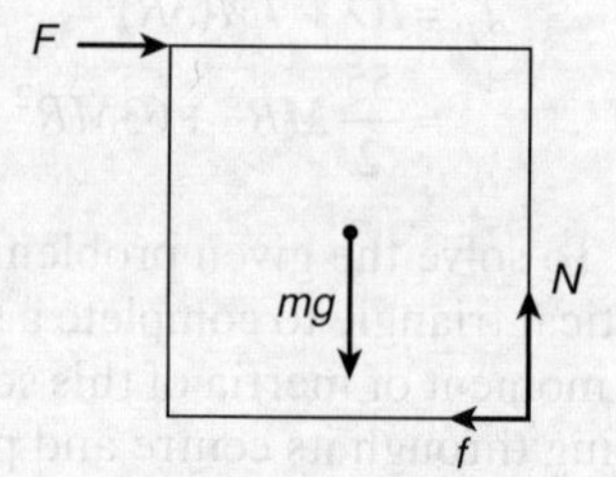

The figure shows the forces acting on the cube when it is on the verge of toppling. The normal contact force N is now passing through the right edge of the cube. For equilibrium

$$f = F \text{ and } N = mg$$

Also, taking torque about the right edge, we have

$$Fl = mg\frac{1}{2} \Rightarrow F = \frac{1}{2}mg$$

Hence $\quad f = \dfrac{1}{2}mg$. Now, $\mu \geq \dfrac{f}{N} = \dfrac{1}{2}$

9. (a) The conveyor belt is moving with acceleration $a = dv/dt = (5 \text{ m/s}^3)t$. The figure shows the forces acting on the cylinder with respect to a reference frame attached to the conveyor belt. Here, ma is a pseudo force, which is continuously increasing with time. When the cylinder is on the verge of toppling, the normal contact force will pass through the extreme left edge of the cylinder. Now, taking torque about the left edge of the cylinder, we have

$ma(2r) = mg(r)$ [Torque of f and N equals zero]

$\Rightarrow \quad a = \frac{1}{2}g = 5 \text{ m/s}^2$

$\Rightarrow \quad (5 \text{ m/s}^3)t = 5 \text{ m/s}^2 \Rightarrow t = 1 \text{ s}$

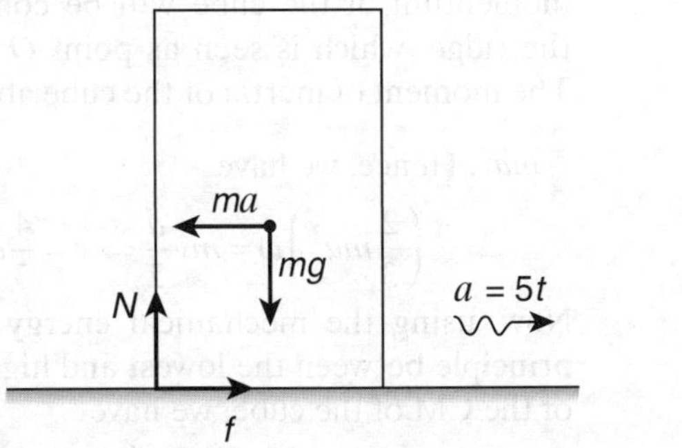

10. (d)

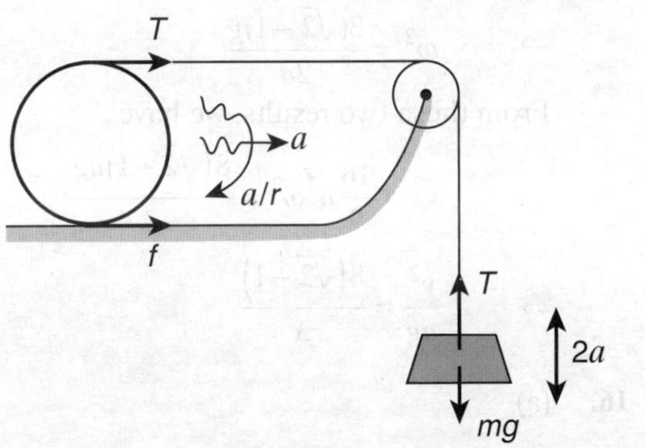

Let a be the acceleration of the axis of the cylinder. If slipping between the cylinder and table is absent, then angular acceleration of the cylinder must be a/r in the clockwise sense, as shown in the figure. Since slipping between the string and cylinder is also absent, the acceleration of the block will be equal to the acceleration of the top-most point on the cylinder, that is, $2a$. Now, using dynamics, we have

$$mg - T = m(2a) \quad \ldots(1)$$

$$T + f = ma \quad \ldots(2)$$

and $\quad (T - f)\, r = mr^2(a/r) \Rightarrow T - f = ma \quad \ldots(3)$

Solving the above equations gives $a = g/3$ and $f = 0$.

11. (a) The figure shows the forces acting on the bicycle when it is just about to topple about the point of contact of its front wheel. Taking torque about the centre of gravity, toppling will be prevented if

$(\mu N)h < N(a/2) \Rightarrow \mu < a/2h = 1/3$ [Putting $h = 1.5a$]

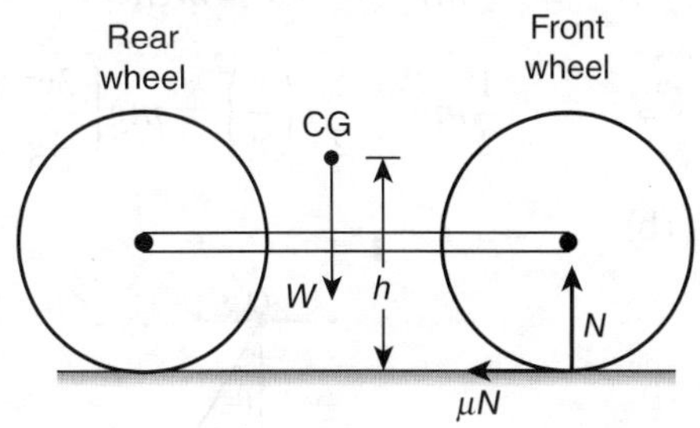

12. (c)

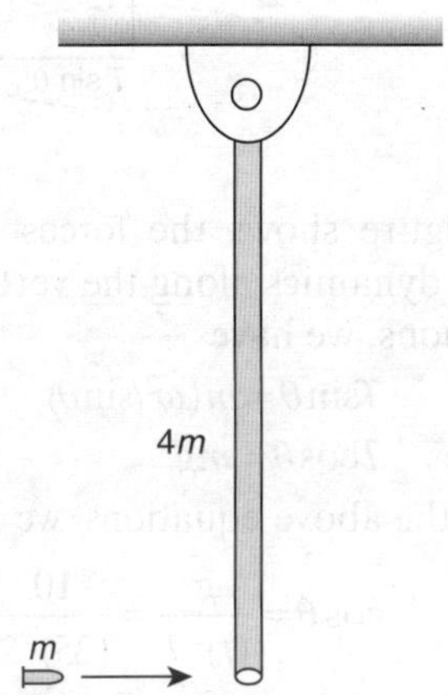

Let us consider the rod + bullet as our system. During collision, the only external impulse on the system is that due to the axis about which the rod is free to rotate. Thus, the angular momentum of the system about this axis will remain conserved during collision. Let w be the angular velocity just after collision. Then, we have

$$mul = \left(ml^2 + \frac{4ml^2}{3}\right)\omega$$

$$\Rightarrow \quad \omega = 3u/7l$$

Now, using mechanical energy conservation between the lowest and highest positions of the rod, we have

$$4mg\left(\frac{1}{2}\right) + mgl = \frac{1}{2}\left(\frac{7}{3}ml^2\right)\omega^2$$

$$\Rightarrow \quad \omega = \sqrt{\frac{18g}{7l}}$$

From the two results, we have $u = \sqrt{14gl}$

13. (d) Let m be the mass, r be the radius and I be the moment of inertia about the natural axis of rotation of the body. Using mechanical energy conservation principle, we have

$$\frac{1}{2}mv^2 + \frac{1}{2}I\omega^2 = mgh$$

$$\Rightarrow \quad \frac{1}{2}mv^2 + \frac{1}{2}I\left(\frac{v}{r}\right)^2 = mg\left(\frac{3v^2}{4g}\right)$$

14. (b)

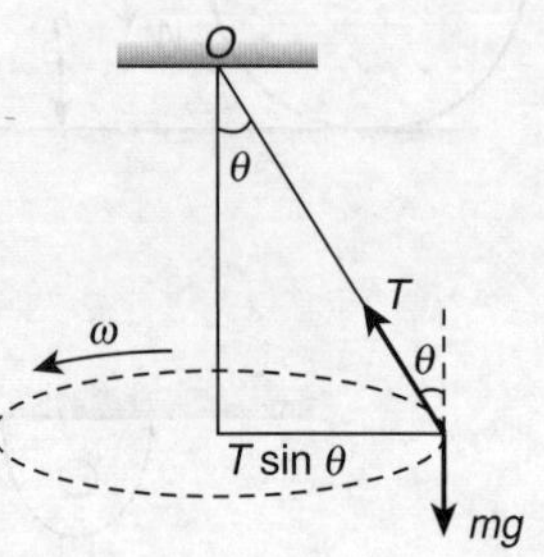

The figure shows the forces acting on the bob. Using dynamics along the vertical and centripetal directions, we have

$$T\sin\theta = m(\omega^2/\sin\theta) \quad \ldots(1)$$

$$T\cos\theta = mg \quad \ldots(2)$$

From the above equations, we have

$$\cos\theta = \frac{g}{(t)^2 I} = \frac{10}{(25)^2 2} = \frac{4}{5}$$

The magnitude of the angular momentum of the bob about point O (see figure) is

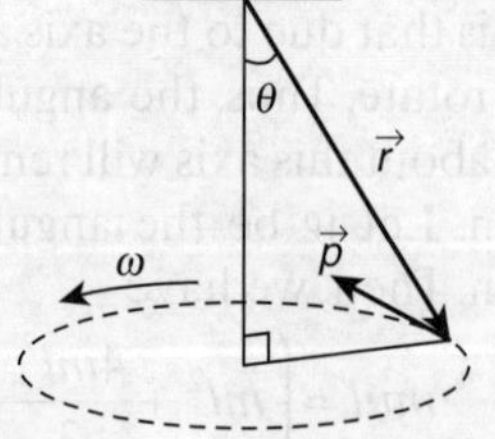

$$|L| = |\vec{r} \times \vec{p}| = |\vec{r}||\vec{p}|\sin 90^\circ$$

$$= l(m\omega/\sin\theta) = m\omega l^2 \sin 90^\circ$$

$$= 0.5 \times 2.5 \times 2^2 \times \frac{3}{5}\,\text{kg}\cdot\text{m}^2/\text{s} = 3\,\text{kg}\cdot\text{m}^2/\text{s}$$

The rate of change of angular momentum equals the torque of all forces (about O) acting on the bob. Hence, we have

$$\left|\frac{d\vec{L}}{dt}\right| = |\vec{T}| = (mg)(l\sin\theta)$$

$$= 0.5 \times 10 \times 2 \times \frac{3}{5}\,\text{N}\cdot\text{m} = 6\,\text{N}\cdot\text{m}$$

$$\Rightarrow \quad \frac{1}{2}mv^2\left(1 + \frac{I}{mr^2}\right) = \frac{3}{4}mv^2$$

$$\Rightarrow \quad \frac{1}{mr^2} = \frac{1}{2}$$

Hence, the body is a solid cylinder.

15. (b) Let ω be the angular speed of the cube just after collision. The ridge will exert a sharp impulse on the cube along the edge of the cube. The angular momentum of the cube will be conserved about the ridge, which is seen as point O in the figure. The moment of inertia of the cube about its edge is $\frac{2}{3}ma^2$. Hence, we have

$$\left(\frac{2}{3}ma^2\right)\omega = mv\frac{a}{2} \Rightarrow v = \frac{4}{3}a\omega$$

Now, using the mechanical energy conservation principle between the lowest and highest positions of the CM of the cube, we have

$$\frac{1}{2}\left(\frac{2}{3}ma^2\right)\omega^2 = mg\left(\frac{a}{\sqrt{2}} - \frac{a}{2}\right)$$

$$\Rightarrow \quad \omega^2 = \frac{3(\sqrt{2}-1)g}{2a}$$

From these two results, we have

$$v^2 = \frac{16}{9}a^2\omega^2 = \frac{8\left(\sqrt{2}-1\right)ag}{3}$$

$$\Rightarrow \quad \frac{v^2}{ag} = \frac{8\left(\sqrt{2}-1\right)}{3}$$

16. (a)

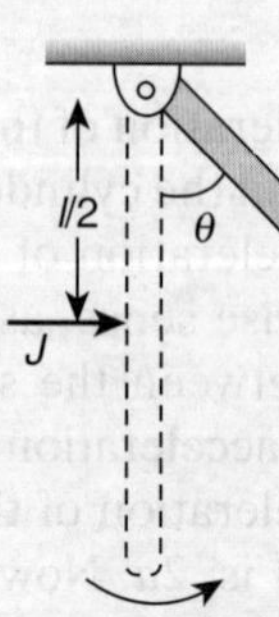

Let ω be the angular speed just after the impulse. Then, angular impulse equals change in angular momentum, and we have

$$J\frac{l}{2} = \left(\frac{1}{3}ml^2\right)\omega \Rightarrow J = \frac{2}{3}ml\omega$$

Now, using mechanical energy conservation

$$\frac{1}{2}\left(\frac{1}{3}ml^2\right)\omega^2 = mg\frac{1}{2}(1-\cos\theta)$$

$$\Rightarrow \quad \omega = \sqrt{\frac{3g}{I}(1-\cos\theta)}$$

From the above equations, we have

$$J=\sqrt{\frac{4}{3}m^2gl(1-\cos\theta)}=1.2\ \text{N}\cdot\text{s}$$

17. (b) In the absence of external torque

$$l\omega=\text{const}$$

$$\Rightarrow\quad R^2/T=\text{const}\ [I\propto R^2\text{ and }\omega\propto 1/T]$$

$$\Rightarrow\quad T\propto V^{2/3}\quad [V\propto R^3\Rightarrow R\propto V^{1/3}]$$

Thus, we have

$$\frac{\Delta T}{T}=\frac{2}{3}\frac{\Delta V}{V}$$

$$=\frac{2}{3}(-0.5$$

$$=-\frac{1}{3}\%$$

$$\Rightarrow\quad \Delta T=\frac{-1}{300}\times 24\ \text{h}=-4.8\ \text{min}$$

18. (d) We have $K=\frac{1}{2}I\omega^2$ and $L=lw$. Eliminating l, we have

$$L=\frac{2K}{\omega}$$

Hence, if K is halved and then doubled, we have

$$L'=\frac{2(K/2)}{2\omega}=\frac{1}{4}\left(\frac{2K}{\omega}\right)=\frac{L}{4}$$

19. (b) The figure shows the forces acting on the rod. For translational equilibrium, we have

$$N=mg\text{ and }f=H$$

For rotational equilibrium, taking torque about the lower end of the rod, we have

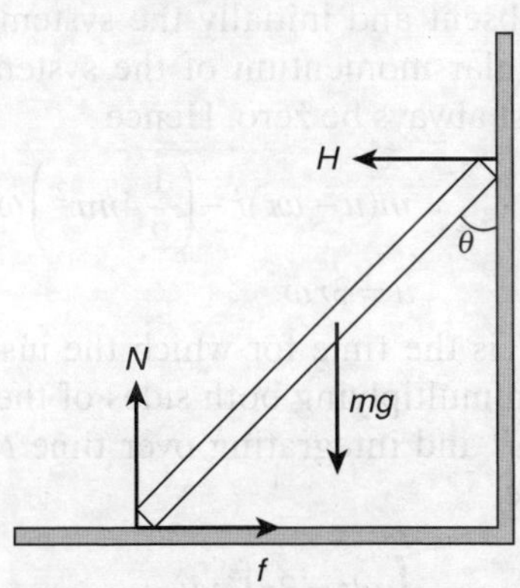

$$H(L\cos\theta)=mg\left(\frac{L}{2}\sin\theta\right)\Rightarrow H=\frac{1}{2}mg\tan\theta$$

The reaction force between the floor and the rod is

$$R=\sqrt{N^2+f^2}=mg\sqrt{1+\frac{1}{4}\tan^2\theta}$$

According to the given condition, we have $R=1.25\ mg$. Hence, we have

$$mg\sqrt{1+\frac{1}{4}\tan^2\theta}=\frac{5}{4}mg\Rightarrow\tan\theta=3/2$$

20. (c) The figure shows the forces acting on one rod. For translational equilibrium, we have

$$N=mg\text{ and }f=T$$

For rotational equilibrium, taking torque about the lower end of the rod, we have

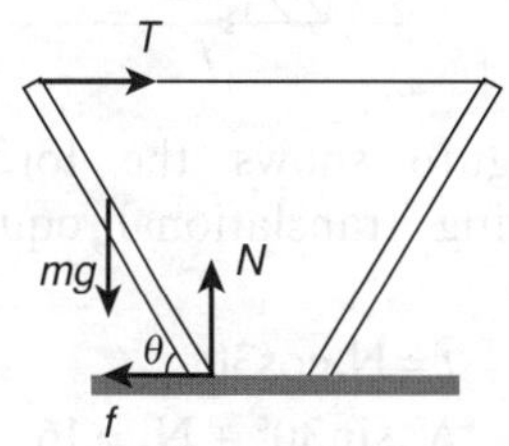

$$T(L\cos\theta)=mg\left(\frac{L}{2}\cos\theta\right)$$

$$\Rightarrow\quad T=\frac{1}{2}mgcor\theta$$

Now, we know that $f<\mu N$. Hence, we have

$$\frac{1}{2}mgcor\theta\le\frac{1}{2}mg$$

$$\Rightarrow\quad \tan\theta\ge 1$$

$$\Rightarrow\quad \theta\ge 45°$$

21. (b) For rotational equilibrium, taking torque about the point of suspension O (see figure), we have

$$(mg)a=(mg)b\ [a\text{ and }b\text{ are the moment arms}]$$

$$\Rightarrow\quad a=b$$

$$\Rightarrow\quad \frac{L}{2}\sin\theta=\frac{L}{2}\cos\theta-L\sin\theta$$

$$\Rightarrow\quad 3\sin\theta=\cos\theta$$

$$\Rightarrow\quad \cot\theta=3$$

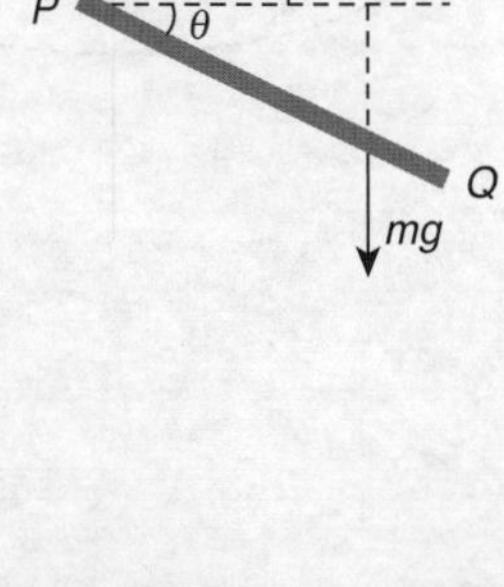

22. (d)

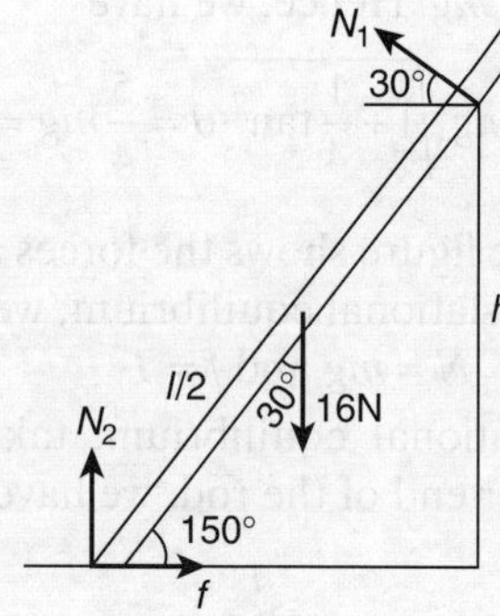

The figure shows the forces acting on the rod. Using translational equilibrium condition, we have

$$f = N_1 \cos 30° \quad ...(1)$$

$$N_1 \sin 30° + N_2 = 16 \quad ...(2)$$

Using rotational equilibrium condition about the point of contact with the ground, we have

$$N_1 (h \sec 30°) = 16\left(\frac{1}{2}\cos 60°\right) \quad ...(3)$$

From the above equations, we have

$$N_1 = 2\sqrt{3}\frac{I}{h},\ N_2 = 16 - \sqrt{3}\frac{I}{h} \text{ and } f = \frac{3l}{h}$$

It is also given that the reaction forces by the ground and the wall are equal in magnitude. Hence

$$N_2^2 + f^2 = N_1^2$$

$$\Rightarrow \quad (16 - \sqrt{3}\frac{1}{h})^2 + \frac{9l^2}{h^2} = \frac{12l^2}{h^2}$$

$$\Rightarrow \quad 16 - \sqrt{3}\frac{1}{h} = \sqrt{3}\frac{I}{h}$$

$$\Rightarrow \quad \frac{1}{h} = \frac{8}{\sqrt{3}} \text{ and hence } f = 8\sqrt{3}N$$

23. (d)

Let M, l be the mass and length of the rod, respectively. Let m be the mass of the insect. The position of the insect at time t is $x = vl$. The angular momentum of the rod + insect system about the axis is

$$L = \left(\frac{ML^2}{2} + mx^2\right)\omega$$

$$= \frac{1}{2}Ml^2\omega + m\omega v^2 t^2$$

We can see that the angular momentum is a function of time. Hence, the torque required for the motion is given by

$$T = \frac{dL}{dr} = (2m\omega v^2)t \Rightarrow T \propto t$$

24. (c)

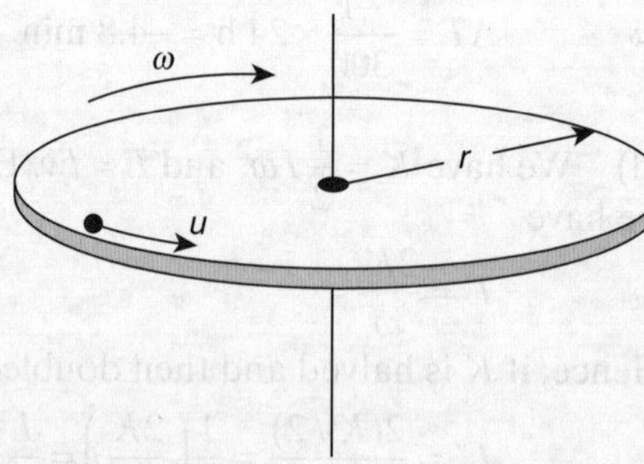

If the insect crawls with speed u (anti-clockwise sense) relative to the disc and the disc rotates with angular speed, say ω (clockwise sense), the absolute speed of the insect will be $u - \omega r$ (anti-clockwise sense). Let us consider the insect + disc as our system. Since external torque about the axis is absent and initially the system was at rest, the angular momentum of the system about the axis must always be zero. Hence

$$m(u - \omega r)r - \left(\frac{1}{2}4mr^2\right)\omega = 0$$

$$\Rightarrow \quad u = 3r\omega$$

If T is the time for which the insect is in motion, then multiplying both sides of the above equation by dt and integrating over time $t = 0$ to $t = T$, we have

$$\int_0^T u\,dt = 3r\int_0^T \omega\,dt$$

The integral on the left side is the distance travelled by the insect relative to the disc, which is πr. The integral on the right side is the angular displacement $\Delta\theta$ of the disc. Thus, we have

$$\pi r = 3r\Delta\theta \text{ gives } \Delta\theta = \pi/3$$

25. (c)

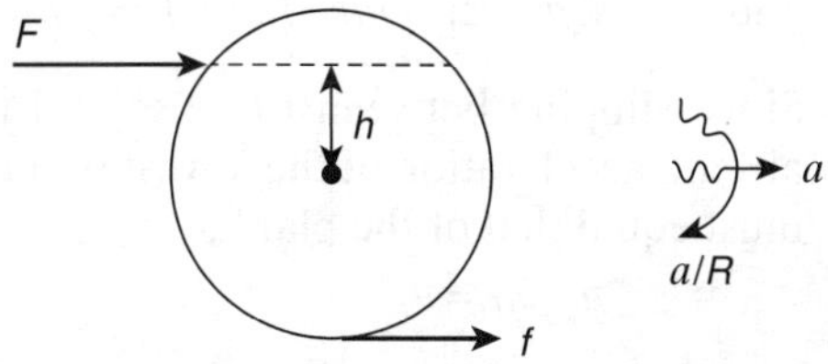

Let a be the acceleration of the centre of mass. Then, a/R will be the angular acceleration, from a no slipping condition. Using dynamics, we have

$$F + f = Ma \qquad ...(1)$$

and $$Fh - fR = I\left(\frac{a}{R}\right) \qquad ...(2)$$

Dividing equation (2) throughout by R and then putting the value of a from equation (1), we have

$$F\frac{h}{R} - f = \frac{I}{MR^2}(F + f)$$

$$\Rightarrow \quad f = \left(\frac{\frac{h}{R} - \frac{I}{MR^2}}{1 + \frac{I}{MR^2}}\right)F$$

26. (c)

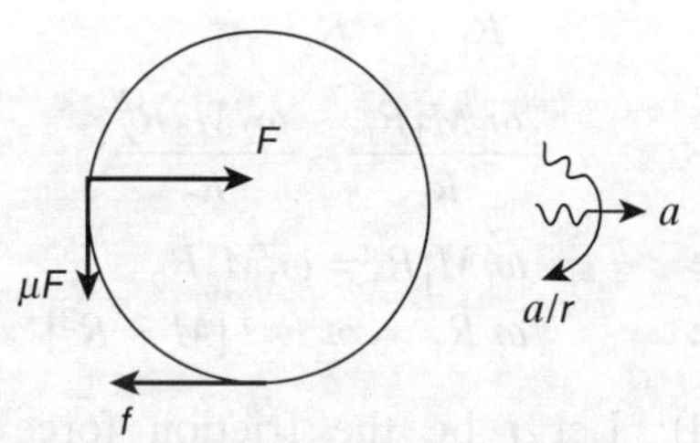

The figure shows the forces acting on the ring. Let a be the acceleration of the centre of the ring. If slipping between the ring and the ground is absent, then angular acceleration of the cylinder must be a/r in the clockwise sense, as shown in the figure.

$$F - f = ma \qquad ...(1)$$

$$(f - \mu F)r = (mr^2)(a/R)$$

$$\Rightarrow \quad f - \mu F = ma \qquad ...(2)$$

Solving the above equations, we have

$$F(1 - \mu) = 2ma$$

$$\Rightarrow \quad \mu = 1 - \frac{2ma}{F} = 1 - \frac{2(2kg)(3m/s^2)}{2N} = \frac{4}{10}$$

Hence $n = 10\mu = 4$

27. (c) Let us consider the platform and the two balls as our system. Using angular momentum conservation principle about the axis of rotation, we have

$$2(mv)a = \frac{1}{2}MR^2\omega$$

$$\Rightarrow \quad \omega = \frac{4mva}{MR^2} = \frac{4 \times 0.5\text{ kg} \times 9\text{ m/s} \times 0.25\text{ m}}{0.45\text{ kg} \times (0.5\text{ m})^2} = 4\text{ rad/s}$$

28. (a)

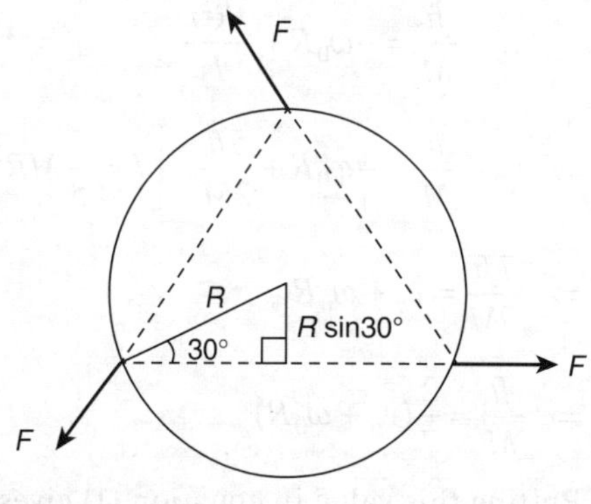

Using angular impulse = change in angular momentum, we have

$$3F(R\sin 30°)I = \frac{1}{2}MR^2\omega$$

$$\Rightarrow \quad \omega = \frac{3F_T}{MR} = \frac{3 \times 0.5\text{ N} \times 1\text{ s}}{1.5\text{ kg} \times 0.5\text{ m}}$$

$$= 2\text{ rad/s}$$

29. (b), (c)

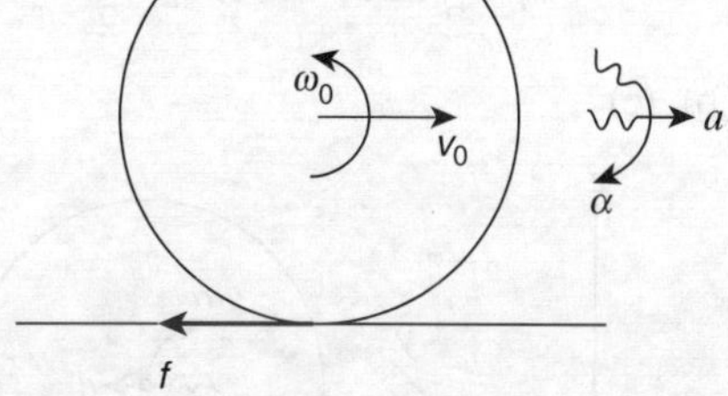

The figure shows the forces acting on the sphere. The point of contact has velocity towards the right; therefore, friction f acts towards the left. The normal contact force and weight have net zero force and net zero torque; therefore, they have not been shown in the figure. Let us choose the right as the positive direction for translational motion, and the clockwise direction as the positive direction for rotational motion. Then, the values of a and α in the directions shown in the figure are

$$a = \frac{f}{M} \text{ and } \alpha = \frac{fR}{I}$$

The velocity v of the centre of mass and the angular velocity ω as functions of time t are

$$v = v_0 - \left(\frac{f}{M}\right)t \quad ...(1)$$

and $$\omega = -\omega_o + \left(\frac{fR}{l}\right)t \quad ...(2)$$

Slipping ceases when $v = \omega R$, that is

$$v_0 - \frac{ft}{M} = -\omega_0 R + \frac{fR^2 t}{J}$$

$$\Rightarrow v_0 - \frac{ft}{M} = -\omega_0 R + \frac{5ft}{2M} \quad \left[I = \frac{2}{5}MR^2\right]$$

$$\Rightarrow \frac{7ft}{\partial M} = v_o + \omega_0 R$$

$$\Rightarrow \frac{ft}{M} = \frac{2}{7}(v_o + \omega_0 R)$$

Putting this value in equation (1) gives the velocity of the sphere when slipping ceases as

$$v = v_0 - \frac{2}{7}(v_0 + \omega_0 R)$$

$$= \frac{5v_0 - 2\omega_0 R}{7}$$

$$= \left(\frac{5-2\eta}{7}\right)v_c$$

Thus, $v = 0$ when $\eta = \frac{5}{2}$, $v > 0$ when

$$\eta < \frac{5}{2} \text{ and } v < 0 \text{ if } \eta > \frac{5}{2}$$

30. (b), (c)

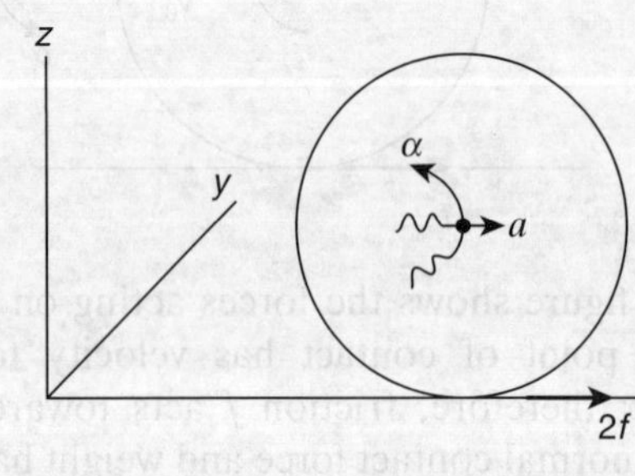

The figure shows the force acting on the system. The weight and normal contact force have not been shown since their net force as well as net torque is zero. Let $a\hat{i}$ be the acceleration of the centre of mass and $-a\hat{j}$ be the angular acceleration of the system. Let the friction force on the cylinder be $f\hat{i}$. Using translational and rotational dynamics, we have

$$2f = 2ma \Rightarrow f = ma \quad ...(1)$$

and $$2fr = 2\left(\frac{1}{2}mr^2\right)a \Rightarrow f = \frac{1}{2}mr\alpha \quad ...(2)$$

Since slipping between the disc and the plank is absent, acceleration of the lowest point of the discs must equal that of the plank.

$$a + ar = a_0 \quad ...(3)$$

Hence, we have $a = \frac{a_0}{3} = 0.1\ \text{m/s}^2$ and

$$\alpha = \frac{2a_0}{3r} = 0.4\ \text{rad/s}^2 \text{ and } f = 0.2\ \text{N}$$

The position vector of the lowest point of disc A with respect to the centre of the rod $\vec{r} = -1m\hat{i} - 0.5m\hat{k}$

The torque of $\vec{r} = \vec{r} \times \vec{f} = (-1m\hat{j} - 0.5m\hat{k}) \times (0.2N\hat{i})$

$= 0.2Nm\hat{k} - 0.1Nm\hat{j}$

31. (b) Let f be the friction force between the discs and let T be the torque in which the disc stops. Then, using angular impulse = change in angular momentum, we have

$(fR_1)\,T = l_1\omega_1$ for disc 1 and $(fR_2)\,T = l_2\omega_2$ for disc 2

Dividing the two equations, we have

$$\frac{\omega_1 I_1}{R_1} = \frac{\omega_2 I_2}{R_2}$$

$$\Rightarrow \frac{\omega_1 M_1 R_1^2}{R_1} = \frac{\omega_2 M_2 R_2^2}{R_2}$$

$$\Rightarrow \omega_1 M_1 R_1 = \omega_2 M_2 R_2$$

$$\Rightarrow \omega_1 R_1^3 = \omega_2 R_2^3 \; [M \propto R^2]$$

32. (d) Let f be the friction force acting in the direction opposite to F. Acceleration of the sphere towards the right is

$$a = \frac{F-f}{M}$$

Angular acceleration of the sphere in the clockwise sense is

$$\alpha = \frac{fR}{\frac{2}{5}MR^2} = \frac{5f}{2MR}$$

For pure rolling motion, $a = aR$. Thus, we have

$$\frac{F-f}{M} = \frac{5f}{2M} \Rightarrow f = \frac{2}{7}F$$

Now $f \le \mu N \Rightarrow \frac{2F}{7} \le \mu Mg \Rightarrow F \le \frac{7}{2}\mu Mg$

33. (c) Let f be the friction force acting towards the right. Acceleration of the CM of the sphere towards the right is

$$a = \frac{f}{M}$$

Angular acceleration in the clockwise sense is

$$\alpha = \frac{F(R\cos 60°) - fR}{\frac{2}{5}MR^2}$$

$$= \frac{2Mg(R\cos 60°) - fR}{\frac{2}{5}MR^2}$$

$$= \frac{5(Mg - f)}{2MR}$$

For pure rolling motion, $a = \alpha R$. Thus, we have

$$\frac{f}{M} = \frac{5(Mg - f)}{\partial M} \Rightarrow f = \frac{5}{7}Mg$$

Now $\quad \mu \geq \frac{f}{N} = \frac{f}{Mq + F}$

$$= \frac{f}{3Mg} = \frac{5}{21}$$

34. (a) Let M be the mass and l be the length of the rod. Acceleration of the CM of the rod towards the right is

$$a = \frac{F_1 + F_2}{m}$$

Angular acceleration of the rod in the clockwise sense is

$$\alpha = \frac{F_2(I/4)}{ml^2/12} = \frac{3F_2}{ml}$$

Acceleration of end A is given to be zero. Hence

$$a - \alpha\left(\frac{1}{2}\right) = 0$$

$$\Rightarrow \quad \frac{F_1 + F_2}{m} = \left(\frac{3F_2}{ml}\right)\frac{1}{2}$$

$$\Rightarrow \quad F_1 + F_2 = \frac{3}{2}F_2$$

$$\Rightarrow \quad F_1/F_2 = 1/2$$

35. (d)

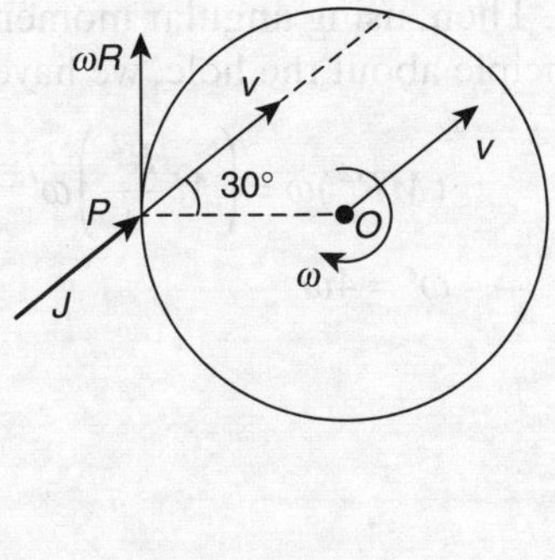

Let J be the impulse. The velocity of the centre of mass and angular velocity of the disc will be in the directions shown in the figure, and their magnitudes will be

$$v = \frac{J}{M} \text{ and}$$

$$\omega = \frac{J(R\sin 30°)}{\frac{1}{2}MR^2}$$

$$= \frac{J}{MR}$$

The velocity of point P is the vector sum of ωR and v (see figure). The angle θ made by the resultant of these two vectors with line PO is given by

$$\tan\theta = \frac{\omega R + v\sin 30°}{v\cos 30°}$$

$$= \frac{\frac{J}{M} + \frac{J}{2M}}{\frac{\sqrt{3}J}{2M}} = \sqrt{3}$$

$$\Rightarrow \quad \theta = 60°$$

36. (c) The figure shows the forces acting on the two cylinders. For rotational equilibrium, the torque of all external forces must be zero. Since weight, normal reaction and spring force all pass through the axis, friction must be zero for torque about the axis to be zero.

Now, balancing the forces along the incline, we have

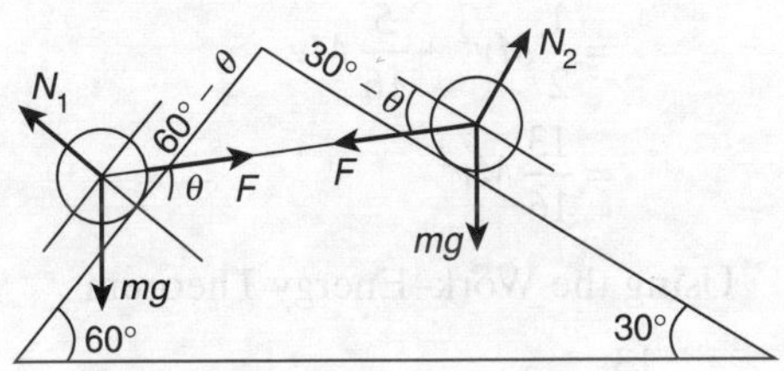

$$F\cos(60° - \theta) = mg\sin 60° \quad \ldots(1)$$

and $\quad F\cos(30° + \theta) = mg\sin 30° \quad \ldots(2)$

Dividing the two equations, we have

$$\frac{\cos(60° - \theta)}{\cos(30° + \theta)} = \frac{\sin 60°}{\sin 30°}$$

$$\Rightarrow \quad \frac{\sin(30° + \theta)}{\cos(30° + \theta)} = \frac{\sin 60°}{\cos 60°}$$

$$\Rightarrow \quad \cot(30° + \theta) = \cot 60°$$

To find the values of N_1 and N_2, let us consider the two cylinders and the spring as one system. Now, balancing the forces along the horizontal and vertical directions, we have

$$N_1 \cos 30° = N_2 \cos 60°$$

$$\Rightarrow \quad \sqrt{3}N_1 = N_2 \qquad \ldots(3)$$

and $$N_1 \sin 30° + N_2 \sin 60° = 2mg$$

$$\Rightarrow \quad N_1 + \sqrt{3}N_2 = 4mg \qquad \ldots(4)$$

Solving the two equations, we have

$$N_1 = mg, N_2 = \sqrt{3}mg$$

37. (a) If v is the velocity of the centre of mass C at any instant, then the angular velocity is $\omega = v/R$ (pure rolling), where R is the outer radius of the cylinder. The velocity of point P is $v + \omega R = 2v$. Hence, when C moves by 1 m, P moves by 2 m. The work done by force F is

$$W = F\,(2\text{ m})$$

$$= (6.5\text{ N})(2\text{ m}) = 13\text{ J}$$

In pure rolling motion, friction does not work. Rotational inertia of the cylinder is

$$I = \int_{R/2}^{R} \Big(\frac{M}{\underbrace{\frac{3}{4}\pi R^2}_{A}} 2\pi x dx\Big)x^2$$

$$= \frac{5}{8}MR^2$$

[Subdividing the cylinder into thin concentric rings and then adding their inertia]

The kinetic energy acquired by the cylinder is

$$K = \frac{1}{2}Mv^2 + \frac{1}{2}I\omega^2$$

$$= \frac{1}{2}Mv^2 + \frac{5}{16}Mv$$

$$= \frac{13}{16}Mv^2$$

Using the Work–Energy Theorem

$$\frac{13}{16}Mv^2 = 9$$

$$\Rightarrow \quad v = \sqrt{\frac{16 \times 13\text{ J}}{13 \times 25\text{ kg}}}$$

$$= \frac{4}{5}\text{ m/s}$$

Alternatively: Let a be the acceleration of the centre of mass and a/R be the angular acceleration of the cylinder. Let the friction force on the cylinder be f along the direction of F. Using translational and rotational dynamics, we have

$$F + f = ma \qquad \ldots(1)$$

and $$(F-2)R = \frac{5}{9}MR^2 \times \frac{a}{n} \Rightarrow F - f = \frac{5}{0}ma \qquad \ldots(2)$$

Solving the above equations gives $a = \dfrac{16F}{13M}$

Hence $v = \sqrt{2as} = \sqrt{\dfrac{32Fs}{13M}}$

38. (b)

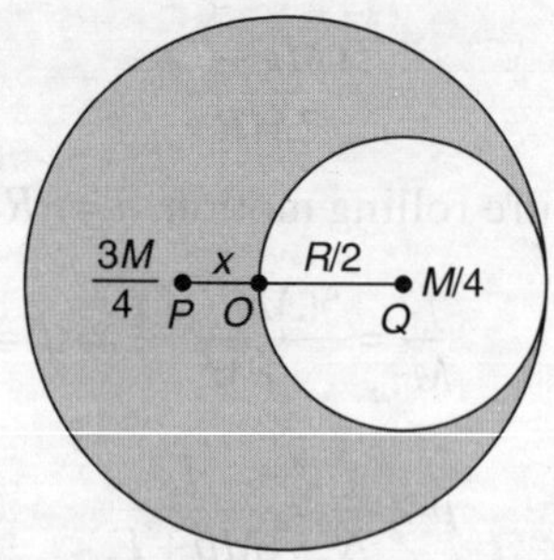

If M is the mass of the entire disc, the mass of the cut portion is $M/4$. Their combined CM is at the centre O of the entire disc. The CM of the remaining portion ($3M/4$) is situated at point P, at a distance say x from O, as shown in the figure. Then

$$\left(\frac{3M}{4}\right)x = \left(\frac{M}{4}\right)\frac{R}{2}$$

$$\Rightarrow \quad x = \frac{R}{6}$$

The required moment of inertia is

$$I_P = I_{\text{entire disc}} - I_{\text{cut portion}}$$

$$= \left[\frac{1}{2}MR^2 + Mx^2\right] - \left[\frac{1}{2}\Big(\frac{M}{4}\Big)\frac{R^2}{4} + \frac{M}{4}\left(\frac{R}{2}+x\right)^2\right]$$

$$= MR^2\left(\frac{1}{2}+\frac{1}{36}\right) - \frac{1}{4}MR^2\left(\frac{1}{8}+\frac{4}{9}\right)$$

$$= \frac{37}{96}MR^2$$

39. (c) Let ω be the angular speed when the radius is $R/2$. Then, using angular momentum conservation principle about the hole, we have

$$(MR^2)\omega = \left(M\frac{R^2}{4}\right)\omega'$$

$$\Rightarrow \quad \omega' = 4\omega$$

Now, using the Work–Energy Theorem, we have

$$W = \Delta K$$
$$= \frac{1}{2}M\left(\omega'\frac{R}{2}\right)^2 - \frac{1}{2}M(\omega R)^2$$
$$= \frac{3}{2}M\omega^2 R^2$$

40. (d)

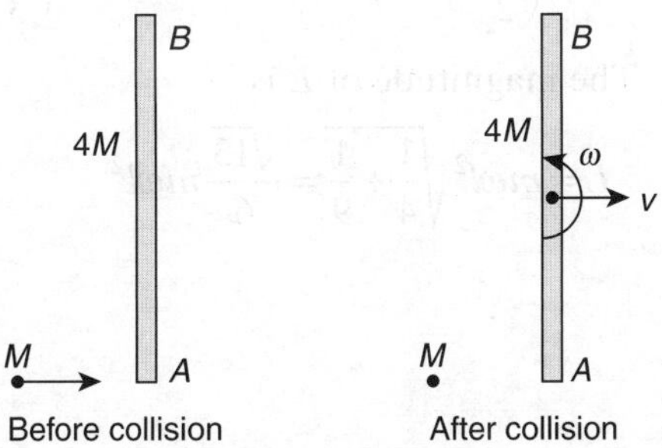

Let v be the velocity of the centre of mass of the rod and ω be its angular velocity, as shown in the figure. Applying momentum conservation, we have

$$(4M)v = Mu \qquad ...(1)$$

Since collision is elastic, the velocity of separation must equal the velocity of approach at the point of collision (B). Hence

$$v + \omega\frac{L}{2} = u \qquad ...(2)$$

From the above equations, we have $v = u/4$ and $\omega = 3u/2L$

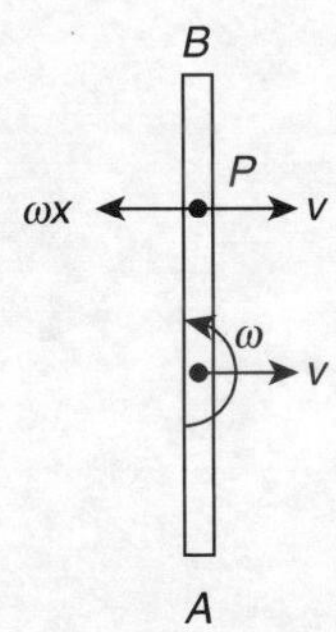

Let the distance of P from the centre be x. If velocity of P is zero, then

$$\omega x = v$$

$$\Rightarrow \quad x = \frac{v}{\omega} = \frac{L}{6}$$

Hence $\quad BP = \frac{L}{2} - \frac{L}{6} = \frac{L}{3}$

41. (a), (d)

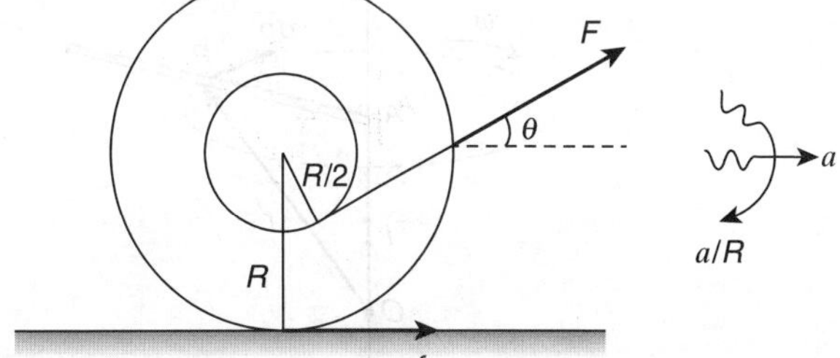

The figure shows the forces acting on the yo-yo. The normal contact force and weight have not been shown in the diagram; they have no consequence on the motion of the yo-yo since the net force as well as net torque is zero. Since the motion is pure rolling, let a be the acceleration of the centre of mass and a/R be the angular acceleration.

Applying translational dynamics, we have

$$F\cos\theta + f = Ma \qquad ...(1)$$

Applying rotational dynamics, we have

$$F\frac{R}{2} + fR = -\left(\frac{1}{2}MR^2\right)\left(\frac{a}{R}\right)$$

$$\Rightarrow \quad \frac{F}{2} + f = -\frac{1}{2}Ma \qquad ...(2)$$

Subtracting, we have

$$F\left(\cos\theta - \frac{1}{2}\right) = \frac{3}{2}Ma$$

$$\Rightarrow \quad a = \frac{2F(\cos\theta - 1/2)}{3M}\begin{cases} > 0 \text{ if } \theta < 60^\circ \\ = 0 \text{ if } \theta = 60^\circ \\ < 0 \text{ if } \theta > 60^\circ \end{cases}$$

And

$$f = Ma - F\cos\theta$$
$$= -\frac{F}{3}(\cos\theta + 1)\begin{cases} = 0 \text{ if } \theta = 180^\circ \\ < 0 \text{ otherwise} \end{cases}$$

42. (d) Let us subdivide the rod into small elements, each of length dx. Momentum of one such element P at distance x from end A is

$$dp = v\,dm = (\omega x)\left(\frac{m}{l}dx\right)$$

along the tangent to the circular path.

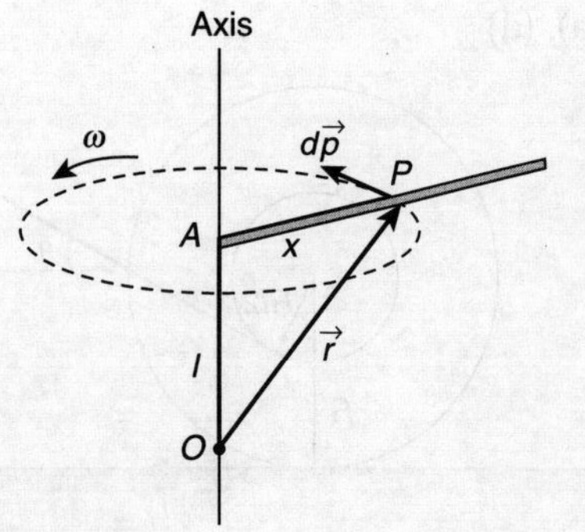

The angular momentum of this element about O is

$$d\vec{i} = \vec{r} \times d\vec{p} = (\overline{OA} + \overline{AP}) \times d\vec{p}$$

$$= \overline{OA} \times d\vec{p} + \overline{AP} \times d\vec{p}$$

$$= 1\left(\frac{m\omega}{1} xdx\right) \text{towards the axis}$$

$$+ x\left(\frac{m\omega}{1} xdx\right) \text{along } \vec{\omega}$$

Hence, total angular momentum is

$$\vec{L} = \left(m\omega \int_0^l xdx\right) \text{towards the axis}$$

$$+ \left(\frac{m\omega}{1} \int_0^l x^2 dx\right) \text{along } \vec{\omega}$$

$$= \left(\frac{1}{2} ml^2 \omega\right) \text{towards the axis} + \left(\frac{1}{3} ml^2\right) \vec{\omega}$$

The magnitude of $\vec{L}$ is

$$L = m\omega l^2 \sqrt{\frac{1}{4} + \frac{1}{9}} = \frac{\sqrt{13}}{6} m\omega l^2$$

CHAPTER

7 Elasticity

- Hooke's law states that in elastic deformation, stress is proportional to strain:

$$\frac{\text{Stress}}{\text{Strain}} = \text{Elastic modulus}$$

Proportionality limit is the maximum stress for which Hooke's law is valid. Elastic limit is the stress beyond which the deformation becomes irreversible. Breaking stress is the stress at which the material breaks.

- Tensile stress is tensile force per unit area, F / A. Tensile strain is the fractional change in length, $\Delta l / l$. Young's modulus Y is the ratio of tensile stress to tensile strain:

$$Y = \frac{F / A}{\Delta l / l} \left(\text{SI unit is N/m}^2\right)$$

Compressive stress and strain are defined the same way as tensile stress and strain. For many materials, Young's modulus has the same value for tension and compression.

- A metal wire of length l, area A and Young's modulus Y behaves like a spring, with spring constant k given by

$$k = \frac{AY}{l} \text{ (SI unit is N/m)}$$

If the wire is stretched by Δl, its elastic potential energy U is given by

$$U = \frac{1}{2} k (\Delta l)^2$$

- Longitudinal strain is the strain along the direction parallel to the force, $\Delta l / l$. Lateral strain is the strain along the direction perpendicular to the force, $\Delta d / d$. Poisson's ratio ε is the negative of the ratio of lateral strain to longitudinal strain:

$$v = -\frac{\Delta d / d}{\Delta l / l}$$

- Bulk stress is pressure change Δp. Bulk strain is fractional change in volume, $\Delta V / V$. Bulk modulus B is the negative of the ratio of bulk stress to bulk strain:

$$B = -\frac{\Delta p}{\Delta V / V}$$

Compressibility k is the reciprocal of bulk modulus: $k = 1 / B$

- Shear stress is force per unit area $\frac{F}{A}$, for a force applied parallel to a surface. Shear strain is angle $\varnothing$ through which the perpendicular to the surface rotates. Shear modulus S is the ratio of shear stress to shear strain:

$$S = \frac{F / A}{\varnothing}$$

- The three quantities Y, B, S are collectively called the elastic constants, and they are related as

$$\frac{3}{Y} = \frac{1}{S} + \frac{1}{3B}.$$

EXERCISES

1. A stone of mass m is attached to the end of a light wire of cross-sectional area A and Young's modulus Y. The stone is rotated in a horizontal circle at a speed such that the wire makes a cone of semi-vertical angle θ. The strain produced in the wire is:

(a) $\frac{mg\cos\theta}{AY}$ (b) $\frac{mg}{AY\cos\theta}$

(c) $\frac{mg\sin\theta}{AY}$ (d) $\frac{mg}{AY\sin\theta}$

2. A wire breaks when subjected to a strain ϵ. If ρ is the density and Y is the Young's modulus of the wire, then the length of the wire so that it breaks by its own weight is:

(a) $\frac{2\epsilon Y}{\rho g}$ (b) $\frac{\epsilon Y}{4\rho g}$

(c) $\frac{\epsilon Y}{2\rho g}$ (d) $\frac{\epsilon Y}{\rho g}$

3. A block of mass M is suspended from a metal wire of the same mass M, length L and area of cross-section A, from a ceiling. The Young's modulus of the wire is Y. Neglecting change in diameter, the elongation in the wire is:

(a) $\frac{MgL}{AY}$ (b) $\frac{MgL}{2AY}$

(c) $\frac{3MgL}{2AY}$ (d) $\frac{2MgL}{AY}$

4. The volume of a wire remains unchanged when it is subjected to a certain tension. The Poisson's ratio of the wire is:

(a) 0.2 (b) 0.3

(c) 0.4 (d) 0.5

5. The figure shows the graph of elongation Δl of a wire of length 1.0 m suspended from a ceiling, and a load W attached at the other end.

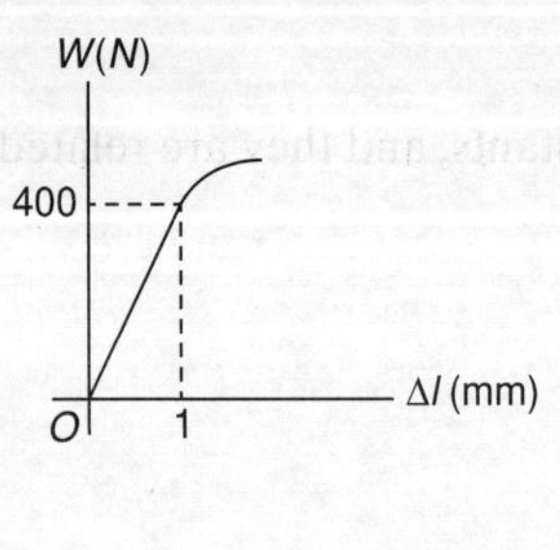

If the cross-section area of the wire is 1.0 mm^2, the Young's modulus of the wire is:

(a) 2.0×10^{11} N/m^2 (b) 2.5×10^{11} N/m^2

(c) 4.0×10^{11} N/m^2 (d) 5.0×10^{11} N/m^2

6. A uniform wire of Young's modulus 2.0×10^{11} N/m^2 is subjected to a longitudinal stress of 5.0×10^{7} N/m^2. If the overall volume change in the wire is 0.02%, the radius decreases by:

(a) 5.0×10^{-5}% (b) 5.0×10^{-4}%

(c) 1.0×10^{-3}% (d) 2.5×10^{-3}%

7. A copper wire of length 1 m and steel wire of length 0.5 m having equal cross-section areas are joined in series. The composite wire is stretched by a certain load which stretches the copper wire by mm. If the Young's modulus of copper and steel are 1.0×10^{11} N/m^2 and 2.0×10^{11} N/m^2, respectively, then the total elongation of the composite wire is:

(a) 1.25 mm (b) 1.50 mm

(c) 1.75 mm (d) 2.00 mm

8. Two rods of different materials having coefficients of linear expansion α_1, α_2 and Young's modulus Y_1, Y_2 are joined in series and fixed between two rigid walls. The rods are heated to some temperature. If the cross-section areas are the same and there is no bending in the rods, then:

(a) $\frac{Y_1}{Y_2}=\frac{\alpha_2}{\alpha_1}$ (b) $\frac{Y_1}{Y_2}=\frac{\alpha_1}{\alpha_2}$

(c) $\frac{Y_1}{Y_2}=\sqrt{\frac{\alpha_1}{\alpha_2}}$ (d) $\frac{Y_1}{Y_2}=\frac{\alpha_1^2}{\alpha_2^2}$

9. A light rod of length L is suspended horizontally from a ceiling by means of two vertical wires P and Q of equal length, as shown in the figure. The cross-section area and Young's modulus of wire Q are double those of wire P. A weight W is hung, as shown in the figure.

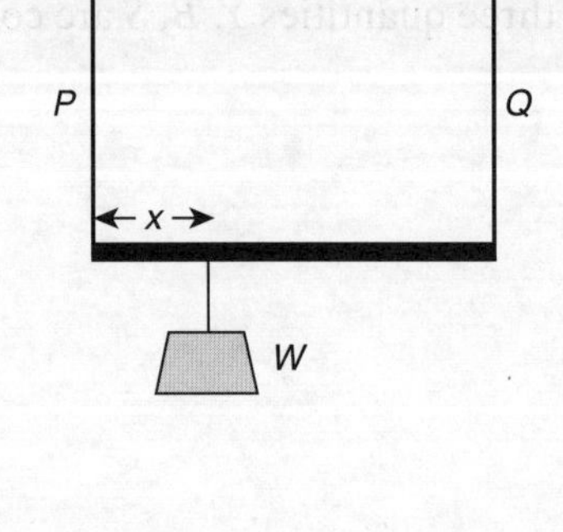

Choose the correct option(s):

(a) For stress to be equal in both wires, $x = \frac{2}{3}L$

(b) For stress to be equal in both wires, $x = \frac{1}{3}L$

(c) For strain to be equal in both wires, $x = \frac{4}{5}L$

(d) For strain to be equal in both wires, $x = \frac{3}{5}L$

10. A wire is suspended vertically from a ceiling and a weight of 80 N is attached to its lower end. The weight stretches the wire by 1 mm. The elastic potential energy stored in the wire is:

(a) 10 mJ (b) 15 mJ
(c) 20 mJ (d) 40 mJ

11. The bulk modulus of water is $B = np_0$, where p_0 is atmospheric pressure. The density of water at the surface of the ocean is ρ. At a depth where the pressure is np_0, the density of ocean water is:

(a) $\left(\frac{n+1}{n}\right)\rho$ (b) $\left(\frac{n+1}{2n}\right)\rho$

(c) $\left(\frac{2n-1}{n}\right)\rho$ (d) $\left(\frac{2n+1}{n+1}\right)\rho$

12. During Searle's experiment, zero of the Vernier scale lies between 3.20×10^{-2} m and 3.25×10^{-2} m of the main scale. The 20th division of the Vernier scale coincides with one of the main scale divisions. When an additional load of 2 kg is applied to the wire, the zero of the Vernier scale still lies between 3.20×10^{-2} m and 3.25×10^{-2} m of the main scale, but now the 45th division of the Vernier scale coincides with one of the main scale divisions. The least count of the Vernier scale is 1.0×10^{-5} m. The natural length of the wire is 2 m and its cross-sectional area is 8.0×10^{-7} m^2. The Young's modulus of the wire is:

(a) 1.0×10^{11} N/m^2 $\pm 8\%$

(b) 2.0×10^{11} N/m^2 $\pm 8\%$

(c) 1.0×10^{11} N/m^2 $\pm 4\%$

(d) 2.0×10^{11} N/m^2 $\pm 4\%$

13. In Searle's experiment, the wire elongates by an amount l_1 when the suspended weight is W_1 and by an amount l_2 when the suspended weight is W_2. If L is the length, A is the cross-section area and Y is the Young's modulus of the wire, then $\frac{AY}{L}$ equals:

(a) $\frac{W_1}{l_1}$ (b) $\frac{W_2}{l_2}$

(c) $\frac{W_2 - W_1}{l_2 - l_1}$ (d) $\frac{W_2 + W_1}{l_2 + l_1}$

14. A pendulum made of uniform wire of cross-section area A has time period T. When an additional mass M is added to its bob, the time period changes to T_M. If Y is the Young's modulus of the wire, then $\frac{Mg}{AY}$ equals:

(a) $\left(\frac{T_M}{T}\right)^2 - 1$ (b) $\left(\frac{T_M}{T}\right)^{3/2} - 1$

(c) $\left(\frac{T_M}{T}\right)^{2/3} - 1$ (d) $\left(\frac{T_M}{T}\right)^{1/2} - 1$

15. A solid sphere made of a material of bulk modulus B is surrounded by a liquid kept in a container. A massive piston of area A floats on the liquid surface. When a weight W is placed above the piston, the fractional decrement in the radius of the sphere is:

(a) $\frac{W}{3BA}$ (b) $\frac{W}{BA}$

(c) $\frac{2W}{3BA}$ (d) $\frac{W}{2BA}$

16. Two wires are made of the same material and have the same volume. The first wire has cross-section area A, and the second wire has cross-section area $3A$. If force F is required to stretch the first wire by an amount Δl, then the force required to stretch the second wire by the same amount is:

(a) F (b) $4F$
(c) $6F$ (d) $9F$

17. A metal ring of radius R is rotated in free space, with a uniform angular speed ω. If ρ is the density and Y is the Young's modulus of elasticity of the metal, then the change in the radius of the ring is:

(a) $\frac{2\rho\omega^2 R^3}{Y}$ (b) $\frac{3\rho\omega^2 R^3}{2Y}$

(c) $\frac{\rho\omega^2 R^3}{2Y}$ (d) $\frac{\rho\omega^2 R^3}{Y}$

18. The figure shows a light metal wire of length $2L$ placed horizontally between two fixed ends, supporting weight W hanging from its middle.

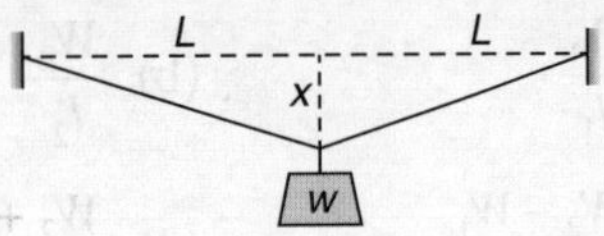

Due to the weight, the middle of the wire dips down by distance $x(x \ll L)$. Then:

(a) $x \propto L^{1/3}$ (b) $x \propto L^{1/2}$

(c) $x \propto L$ (d) $x \propto L^2$

ANSWER KEYS

1. (b)	**2.** (d)	**3.** (c)	**4.** (d)	**5.** (c)	**6.** (d)	**7.** (a)	**8.** (a)
9. (a),(c)	**10.** (d)	**11.** (c)	**12.** (b)	**13.** (a),(b),(c),(d)	**14.** (a)	**15.** (a)	**16.** (d)
17. (d)	**18.** (c)						

SOLUTIONS

1. (b)

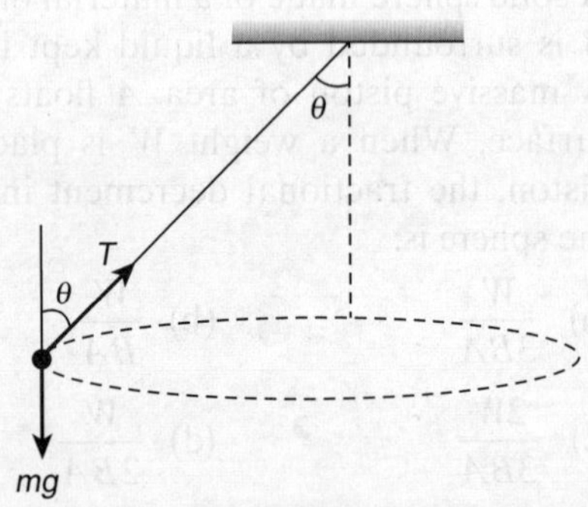

The figure shows the forces acting on the stone. Using dynamics in the vertical direction, we have

$$T\cos\theta = mg \Rightarrow T = \frac{mg}{\cos\theta}$$

The stress in the wire is $\dfrac{T}{A} = \dfrac{mg}{A\cos\theta}$

The strain in the wire is $\dfrac{\text{stress}}{Y} = \dfrac{mg}{YA\cos\theta}$

2. (d) The wire can tolerate a maximum stress of εY. When the wire is hanging from the ceiling, the stress in the wire is maximum near the ceiling since the tension in the wire is maximum at the ceiling. The tension near the ceiling is equal to the entire weight ρALg, where L is the length and A is the cross-section area of the wire. Hence, the maximum length of wire that can hang without breaking is given by

$$\frac{\rho ALg}{A} < \varepsilon Y \Rightarrow L < \frac{\varepsilon Y}{\rho g}$$

3. (c)

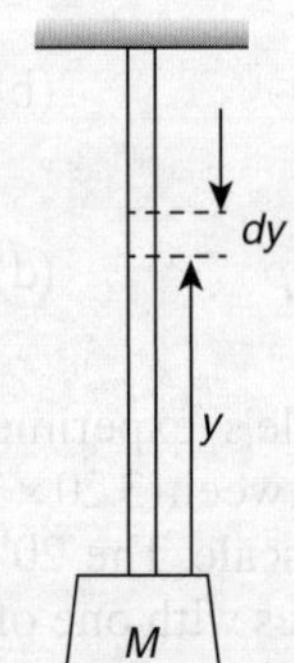

The stress in the wire varies along the length of the wire. At a height y above the lowest end, the tension in the wire equals the weight of the hanging part of the wire plus the weight of the block

$$T = Mg + \frac{Mg}{L}y = Mg\left(1 + \frac{y}{L}\right)$$

The stress at this cross-section is

$$\text{Stress} = T/A = \frac{Mg}{A}\left(1 + \frac{Y}{L}\right)$$

Let us consider a small length dy of the wire. Let de be the elongation in the small portion. Then

$$\text{Strain} = \frac{\text{Stress}}{Y}$$

$$\Rightarrow \quad \frac{de}{dy} = \frac{Mg}{A}\left(1 + \frac{y}{L}\right)$$

$$\Rightarrow \quad de = \frac{Mg}{A}\left(1+\frac{y}{L}\right)dy$$

Now, integrating both sides gives the total elongation in the wire

$$e = \frac{Mg}{AY}\int_0^L \left(1+\frac{y}{L}\right)dy = \frac{3MgL}{2Ay}$$

Alternatively: Since the stress in the wire varies linearly, we can find the average stress by taking the arithmetic mean of the stresses at the lowest end and the uppermost end of the wire. Stress at the lowest end is $\frac{Mg}{AY}$ and stress at the uppermost end is $\frac{2Mg}{AY}$.

$$\text{The average stress} = \frac{1}{2}\left(\frac{Mg}{AY}+\frac{2Mg}{AY}\right)$$

$$= \frac{3Mg}{2AY}.$$

The elongation e in the wire is given by

$$\text{Strain} = \frac{\text{Stress}}{Y}$$

$$\Rightarrow \quad \frac{e}{L} = \frac{3Mg}{2AY}$$

$$\Rightarrow \quad e = \frac{3MgL}{2AY}$$

4. (d) Let l be the length and d be the diameter of the wire. Then $ld^2 = \text{const.}$

$$\Rightarrow \quad l \propto d^{-2}$$

$$\Rightarrow \quad \frac{\Delta l}{l} = -2\frac{\Delta d}{d}$$

Hence, we have

$$\text{Poisson's ratio} = -\frac{\Delta d / d}{\Delta l / l} = 0.5$$

5. (c) $Y = \frac{W/A}{\Delta l / l} = \frac{400\ \text{N}}{10^{-6}\text{m}^2} \times \frac{1\ \text{m}}{10^{-3}\text{m}}$

$$= 4\times 10^{11}\ \text{N/m}^2$$

6. (d) The strain in the wire is

$$\frac{\Delta l}{l} = \frac{\text{Stress}}{Y}$$

$$= \frac{5\times 10^7}{2\times 10^{11}} = 2{,}5\times 10^{-4}$$

$$= 0.025\%$$

If l is the length and r is the radius, the volume of the wire is $V = \pi r^2 l$. For small changes, we have

$$\frac{\Delta V}{V} = 2\frac{\Delta r}{r} + \frac{\Delta l}{l}$$

$$\Rightarrow \quad = \frac{\Delta r}{r} = \frac{1}{2}\left(\frac{\Delta V}{V} - \frac{\Delta l}{l}\right)$$

$$= \frac{1}{2}(0.02\% - 0.025\%) = -0.025\%$$

7. (a) The tension in the two wires must be the same. Hence

$$\frac{A_s Y_s}{l_s}\Delta l_s = \frac{A_c Y_c}{l_c}\Delta l_c$$

$$\Rightarrow \quad \Delta l_s = \frac{l_s Y_c}{l_c Y_s}\Delta l_c \ [A_s = A_c \text{ given}]$$

$$\Rightarrow \quad \Delta l_s = \frac{0.5\ \text{m}}{1.0\ \text{m}} \times \frac{1.0\times 10^{11}\ \text{N/m}^2}{2.0\times 10^{11}\ \text{N/m}^2} \times 1\ \text{mm}$$

$$= 0.25\ \text{mm}$$

Hence, the total elongation of the composite wire equals 1.25 mm.

8. (a) The strain in the two rods will be $a_1\Delta\theta$ and $a_2\Delta\theta$. The stress in the two wires will be $Y_1 a_1\Delta\theta$ and $Y_2 a_2\Delta\theta$, respectively. The tension in the two wires will be $A(Y_1 a_1 \Delta\theta)$ and $A(Y_2 a_2 \Delta\theta)$, respectively. The cross-section area A is given to be the same for the two rods.
In series connection, the tension must be the same in both the rods. Hence

$$A(Y_1 a_1 \Delta\theta) = A(Y_2 a_2 \Delta_\theta)$$

$$\Rightarrow \quad \frac{Y_1}{Y_2} = \frac{\alpha_2}{\alpha_1}$$

9. (a), (c) Let L, A, Y be the length, cross-section area and Young's modulus of elasticity of the wire P and L, $2A$, $2Y$ be those of wire Q. Let T_1 and T_2 be the tensions in the wires P and Q, respectively.
Same stress in both wires means

$$\frac{T_1}{A} = \frac{T_2}{2A}$$

$$\Rightarrow \quad T_2 = 2T_1$$

Now for the rod's equilibrium, balancing the torques about the point of suspension of the weight, we have

$$T_1x = T_2(L-x)$$

$$\Rightarrow \quad T_1x = 2T_1(L-x)$$

$$\Rightarrow \quad x = 2(L-x) \text{ gives } x = \frac{2L}{3}$$

Same strain in both wires means

$$\frac{T_1}{AY} = \frac{T_2}{(2A)(2Y)} \Rightarrow T_2 = 4T_1$$

Now balancing the torques about the point of suspension of the weight, we have

$$T_1x = T_2(L-x)$$

$$\Rightarrow \quad T_1x = 4T_1(L-x)$$

$$\Rightarrow \quad x = 4(L-x) \text{ gives } x = \frac{4L}{5}$$

10. (d) $U = \frac{1}{2} \times \text{Stress} \times \text{Strain} \times \text{Volume}$

$$= \frac{1}{2} \times \frac{W}{A} \times \frac{\Delta l}{l} \times Al$$

$$= \frac{1}{2} W\Delta l$$

$$= \frac{1}{2} \times 80 \text{ N} \times 1 \text{ mm} = 40 \text{ mJ}$$

11. (c) The change in pressure is $(n-1)P_0$. The fractional change in volume is

$$\frac{\Delta V}{V} = \frac{-\Delta P}{B}$$

$$= \frac{-(n-1)P_0}{nP_n} = \frac{-(n-1)}{n}$$

Since mass does not change due to change in pressure, we have $\rho V = \text{const.}$ Hence

$$\frac{\Delta\rho}{\rho} = \frac{-\Delta V}{V}$$

$$= \frac{n-1}{n}$$

Hence, the required density is

$$\rho + \Delta\rho = \left(\frac{2n-1}{n}\right)\rho$$

12. (b) The change in the elongation of the wire due to a change in weight of 20 N is

$\Delta l = (45 - 20)$ division of the Vernier scale $= 25 \times 1.0 \times 10^{-5}$ m

Now, from the relation $W = \frac{AY}{L} l$, we have

$$\Delta W = \frac{AY}{L} \Delta l$$

$$\Rightarrow \quad Y = \frac{\Delta W / A}{\Delta l / L}$$

$$= \frac{20 \text{ N}}{8 \times 10^{-7} \text{ m}^2} \times \frac{2 \text{ m}}{25 \times 10^{-5} \text{ m}}$$

$$= 2 \times 10^{11} \text{ N/m}^2$$

Since $Y \alpha \Delta l^{-1}$

$$\frac{\Delta Y}{Y} = -\frac{\Delta(\Delta l)}{l}$$

$$= \frac{2 \text{ divisions}}{25 \text{ divisions}} = 8\%$$

$$[\Delta l = l_1 - l_2 \Rightarrow \Delta(\Delta l) = \Delta l_1 - \Delta l_2 = 2 \text{ divisions}]$$

13. (a), (b), (c), (d) The weight W and elongation l are directly proportional. Hence

$$\frac{W}{l} = k(\text{say})$$

Hence, we have

$$\frac{W_1}{l_1} = \frac{W_2}{l_2}$$

$$= \frac{W_2 - W_1}{l_2 - l_1}$$

$$= \frac{W_2 + W_1}{l_2 + l_1}$$

14. (a) Let L and L_M be the lengths of the wire in the two cases. Then

$$\frac{L_M}{L} = \frac{T_M^2}{T^2} \left[\text{Since } T \alpha \sqrt{L}\right]$$

Now, we have

$$\frac{Mg}{AY} = \frac{L_M - L}{L}$$

$$= \frac{T_M^2}{T^2} - 1$$

15. (a) The pressure increased by an amount $\Delta P = W/A$. This results in a fractional change in volume

$$\frac{\Delta V}{V} = -\frac{\Delta P}{B} = -\frac{W/A}{B}$$

Now, $V \alpha r^3$. Hence

$$\frac{\Delta V}{V} = 3\frac{\Delta r}{r}$$

$$\Rightarrow \quad \frac{\Delta r}{r} = \frac{W}{3BA}$$

16. (d) Let $3L$ and L be the lengths of the two wires. Their stiffness is

$$k_1 = \frac{AY}{3l}$$

and $$k_2 = \frac{3AY}{1}$$

$\Rightarrow$ $k_2 = 9k_1$

Hence, the force required to stretch the second wire by the same amount equals $9F$.

17. (d) Let us subdivide the ring into small elements, each subtending angle $d\theta$ at the centre. Let A be the cross-section area of the ring. Then, mass of one such element is $dm = \rho(ARd\theta)$. The figure shows the forces acting on one such element, where F is the tension in the ring.

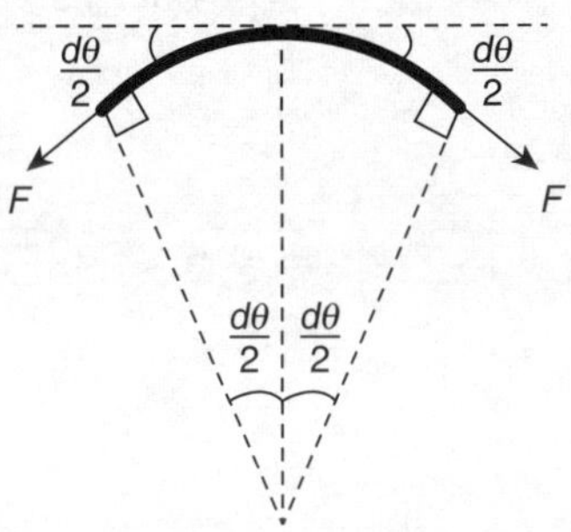

The net force is

$$2F \sin\left(\frac{d\theta}{2}\right) \simeq Fd\theta \text{ directed towards the centre.}$$

The element mass has centripetal acceleration $dm(\omega^2 R) = (\rho\omega^2 R^2 A)\, d\theta$. From dynamics, we have

$$Fd\theta = (\rho\omega^2 R^2 A)d\theta$$

$\Rightarrow F/A = \rho\omega^{2R2}$

Let ΔR be the change in the radius of the ring. Then, the longitudinal strain in the ring is

$$\frac{\Delta L}{L} = \frac{2\pi\Delta R}{2\pi R}$$

$$= \frac{\Delta R}{R}$$

Using the law of elasticity, we have

$$Y\frac{\Delta L}{L} = \frac{F}{A}$$

$$\Rightarrow Y\frac{\Delta R}{R} = \rho\omega^2 R^2$$

$$\Rightarrow \Delta R = \frac{\rho\omega^2 R^3}{Y}$$

18. Let T be the tension in the wire. From the free body diagram shown in the figure, we have

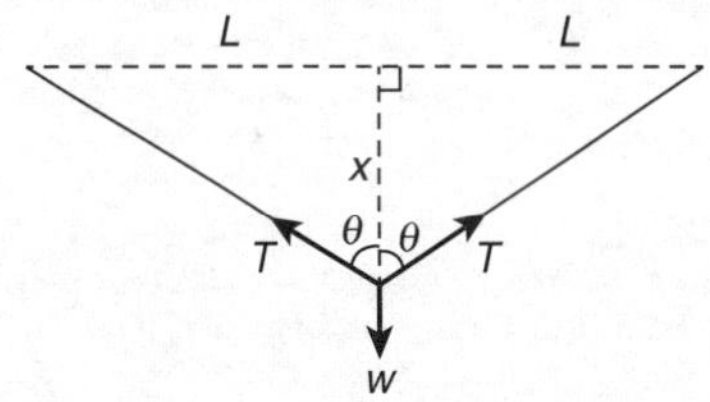

$$2T\cos\theta = W$$

$$\Rightarrow \quad 2T\frac{x}{\sqrt{L^2+x^2}} = W$$

$$\Rightarrow \quad 2T\frac{x}{L} = W \; [X << L]$$

$$\Rightarrow \quad T = \frac{WL}{2x}$$

The elongation in the wire is

$$\Delta L = 2\sqrt{L^2+x^2} - 2L$$

$$\Rightarrow \quad \Delta L = 2L\left[\left(1+\frac{x^2}{L^2}\right)^{1/2} - 1\right]$$

$$\Rightarrow \quad \Delta L = 2L\left[\left(1+\frac{x^2}{2L^2}\right) - 1\right]$$

$$\Rightarrow \quad \Delta L = \frac{x^2}{L^2}$$

Now using Stress = $Y \times$ Strain, we have

$$\frac{T}{A} = Y \times \frac{\Delta L}{2L}$$

$$\Rightarrow \quad \frac{WL}{2Ax} = Y \times \frac{x^2}{2L^2}$$

$$\Rightarrow \quad x^3 = \frac{WL^3}{AY}$$

Hence, $x \propto L$.

CHAPTER

8 Fluid Mechanics

- Pressure is normal force per unit area. Absolute pressure is the total pressure; gauge pressure is the absolute pressure minus atmospheric pressure.

  Pascal's law states that pressure applied to the surface of an enclosed fluid is transmitted undiminished to every portion of the fluid.

- If a static fluid of uniform density ρ (incompressible fluid) is kept in an inertial container, the pressure inside the fluid varies only along the direction of gravity. If we choose the vertically upward direction as the +ve direction of the y-axis, then pressure varies along the y-axis as

$$\Delta P_y = -\rho g \Delta y$$

  The negative sign shows that the pressure increases as we move vertically down along gravity. If the pressure at any point is P_0, the pressure at depth h is

$$P = P_0 + \rho g h$$

  If the container is accelerating with acceleration $\mathbf{a} = a_x\mathbf{i} + a_y\mathbf{j}$, the pressure varies along the vertical as well as the horizontal direction:

$$\Delta P_y = -\rho\left(g - a_y\right)\Delta y \text{ and } \Delta P_x = -\rho a_x \Delta x$$

- Archimedes' principle states that when a body is immersed in a fluid, the fluid exerts an upward buoyant force on the body equal to the weight of the fluid displaced. If a body displaces a volume V of a fluid of density σ, the buoyant force is

$$\mathbf{B} = -\sigma V \mathbf{g}$$

  The above equation is valid only if the liquid is kept in an inertial container. If the container is accelerating with acceleration $\mathbf{a}$, the buoyant force is

$$\mathbf{B} = -\sigma V\left(\mathbf{g} - \mathbf{a}\right)$$

  The force of buoyancy passes through the centre of gravity (CG) of the displaced liquid. Objects floating in liquid will be in stable equilibrium only if the CG of the displaced liquid lies above the CG of the floating object. This concept is of immense importance in the designing of ships.

- The relative density of a material is the ratio of its density to that of water. If an object weighs m_0 in air and m_1 when fully immersed in water, its relative density is given by

$$\text{RD} = \frac{m_0}{m_0 - m_1}$$

  A solid object of material density σ can float in a liquid of density ρ only if $\sigma < \rho$. While floating, the fraction of the object's volume submerged inside the liquid is given by

$$f = \frac{\sigma}{\rho}$$

- Mass continuity equation relates the velocity v and cross-section area A for steady flow in an ideal fluid. At any two cross-sections

$$A_1 v_1 = A_2 v_2$$

- Bernoulli's equation relates the pressure P, velocity v and elevation y for steady flow in an ideal fluid. For any two points lying on the same streamline

$$P_1 + \rho g y_1 + \frac{1}{2}\rho v_1^2 = P_2 + \rho g y_2 + \frac{1}{2}\rho v_2^2$$

EXERCISES

1. The density of air in Earth's atmosphere decreases with height as $\rho = \rho_0 e^{-\alpha y}$, where ρ_0 is the density at sea level and α is a positive constant. Assuming the atmosphere to extend to $y = \infty$, and gravitational intensity to be a constant equal to g, the atmospheric pressure at sea level is:

   (a) $\frac{\rho_0 g}{2\alpha}$ (b) $\frac{\rho_0 g}{\alpha}$

   (c) $\frac{2\rho_0 g}{\alpha}$ (d) $\frac{\sqrt{2}\rho_0 g}{\alpha}$

2. The vessel shown in the figure has volume V and is completely filled with a liquid of density ρ.

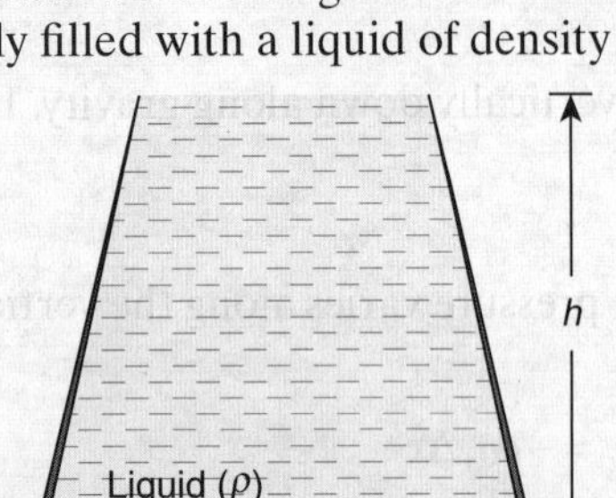

   The cross-section area of the bottom is A and the height of the vessel is h. Force due to liquid on the sides of the vessel is:

   (a) $\frac{1}{3}\rho g(hA+V)$ (b) $\rho g(hA+V)$

   (c) $\frac{1}{3}\rho g(hA-V)$ (d) $\rho g(hA-V)$

3. A cylindrical jar of radius r is filled with liquid to a height h. Let F_{side} be the force exerted by the liquid on one semi-cylindrical half-side of the jar and F_{bottom} be the force on the bottom of the jar. Then $F_{side} = F_{bottom}$ if h/r equals:

   (a) 4π (b) 2π

   (c) π (d) 2

4. A cubical block made of material of density 10^4 kg/m^3 has a cavity inside it. If the block weighs 1 kg in air and 0.8 kg in water, then the volume of the cavity is (density of water = 10^3 kg/m^3):

   (a) 10 cc (b) 50 cc

   (c) 100 cc (d) 200 cc

5. An object weighs m_0 in air, m_1 when fully immersed in water and m_2 when fully immersed in some liquid. The difference in the relative densities of the object and the liquid is:

   (a) $\frac{m_0 - m_1}{m_0 - m_2}$ (b) $\frac{m_0 - m_2}{m_0 - m_1}$

   (c) $\frac{m_1}{m_0 - m_2}$ (d) $\frac{m_2}{m_0 - m_1}$

6. A U-tube contains water and oil separated by mercury. The mercury columns in the two limbs are at the same level, as shown in the figure.

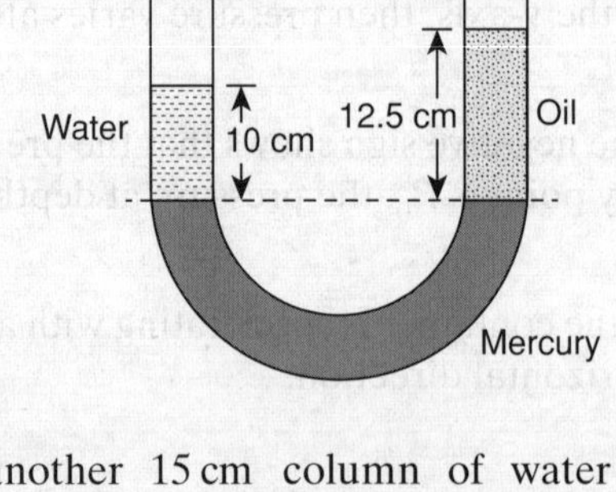

   Now, another 15 cm column of water and oil each are poured in the respective limbs of the U-tube. If the relative density of mercury is k, the difference in the mercury levels in the two limbs will be:

   (a) $\frac{1}{k}$ cm (b) $\frac{2}{k}$ cm

   (c) $\frac{3}{k}$ cm (d) $\frac{4}{k}$ cm

7. A vessel contains oil of density 0.8 g/cm^3 over mercury of density 13.6 g/cm^3. A homogeneous cube of size $a = 20$ cm floats with half volume immersed in mercury and the other half in oil. The amount of work needed to push the cube completely inside mercury is (take $g = 10$ m/s^2):

   (a) 12.8 J (b) 18.4 J

   (c) 25.6 J (d) 32.6 J

8. A spring balance reads 10 kg when a bucket of water is suspended from it. When an iron block of mass 7.2 kg suspended by a string is immersed with half its volume inside the water in the bucket, the spring balance will read (relative density of iron= 7.2):

   (a) 10 kg (b) 10.5 kg

   (c) 13.6 kg (d) 15 kg

9. The figure shows an inverted cylinder of diameter 25 cm and weight 65 N floating in water.

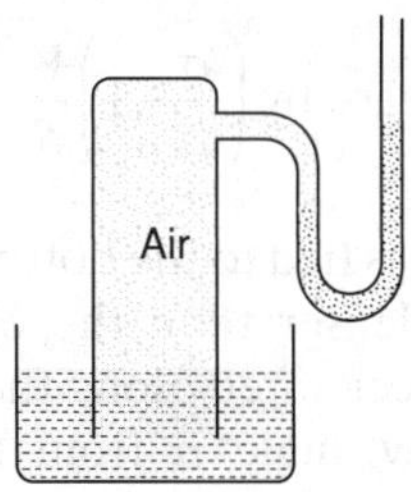

If the density of liquid in the manometer is 2.2 g/cm^3, the difference in height of the liquid columns in its two limbs is:

(a) 6 cm (b) 8 cm
(c) 10 cm (d) 12 cm

10. The figure shows a narrow circular tube kept in the vertical plane, containing two immiscible liquids of densities ρ_1 and ρ_2 $(\rho_1 > \rho_2)$. Each liquid subtends 90° at the centre of the tube.

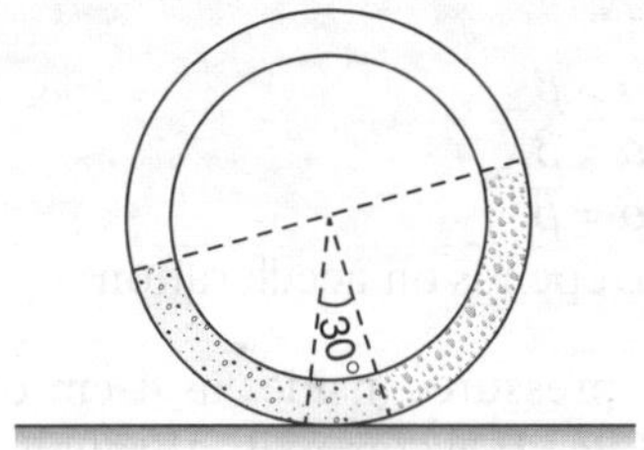

If the radius joining their interfaces makes an angle of 30° with the vertical, then the ratio ρ_1 / ρ_2 equals:

(a) $2\sqrt{3}$ (b) 2
(c) $2+\sqrt{3}$ (d) $\sqrt{3}$

11. The time period of a simple pendulum is T. The pendulum is now oscillated, with its bob immersed in a liquid of density ρ. If the density of the bob is $\sigma (\sigma > \rho)$ and the viscous effect is neglected, the time period of the pendulum will be:

(a) $\sqrt{\dfrac{\rho}{\sigma-\rho}}T$ (b) $\sqrt{\dfrac{\sigma}{\sigma-\rho}}T$

(c) $\sqrt{\dfrac{\sigma}{\sigma+\rho}}T$ (d) $\sqrt{\dfrac{\sigma}{\sigma-\rho}}T$

12. A wooden ball of density σ is released from the bottom of a tank which is filled with a liquid of density $\rho (\rho > \sigma)$ to a height h_1. The ball rises from the liquid and attains a height h_2 in air. The viscous effects are neglected. The ratio of h_2 / h_1 is:

(a) $\dfrac{\sigma}{\rho}-1$ (b) $\dfrac{\rho}{\sigma}-1$

(c) $\dfrac{\sigma}{\rho}$ (d) $\dfrac{\sigma}{\rho}+1$

13. A cube of wood supporting a mass of 200 g first floats in water. When the mass is removed, the cube rises by 2 cm. The size of the cube is (density of water = 1 g/cm^3):

(a) 6 cm (b) 8 cm
(c) 10 cm (d) 12 cm

14. When an air bubble of radius r rises from the bottom to the surface of a lake, its radius becomes $3r/2$. The atmospheric pressure is equal to 8 m height of the water column. Neglecting temperature changes and surface tension, the depth of the lake is:

(a) 19 m (b) 17 m
(c) 9 m (d) 1 m

15. A J-tube, as shown in the figure, contains a volume V of dry air trapped in arm A. The atmospheric pressure is equal to height H of mercury. The difference in mercury levels in arms A and B is H.

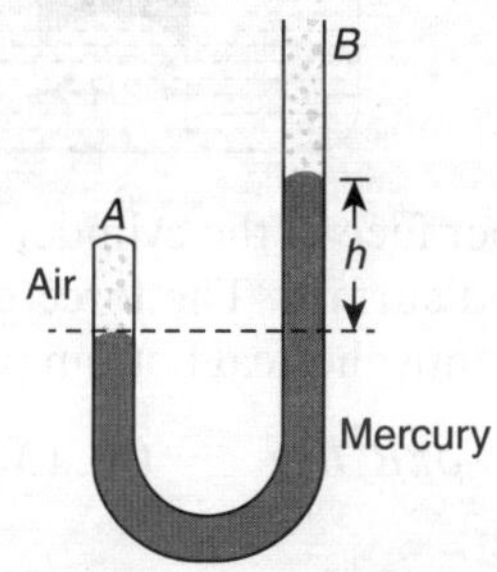

Mercury is now poured in arm B till the volume of the air trapped in arm A reduces to $V/2$. The difference in mercury levels in arms A and B will now be:

(a) H (b) $2H$
(c) $3H$ (d) $4H$

16. A cubical vessel of dimension h is filled with some liquid to a height $9h/10$ and kept on a horizontal surface. The minimum acceleration with which the vessel must be moved so that the liquid spills out is:

(a) $g/4$ (b) $g/5$
(c) $g/8$ (d) $g/10$

17. A rod PQ of length 6 m and relative density 0.5 is hinged at point P, 3 m below the free surface of water, as shown in the figure. The mass of the rod is 12 kg.

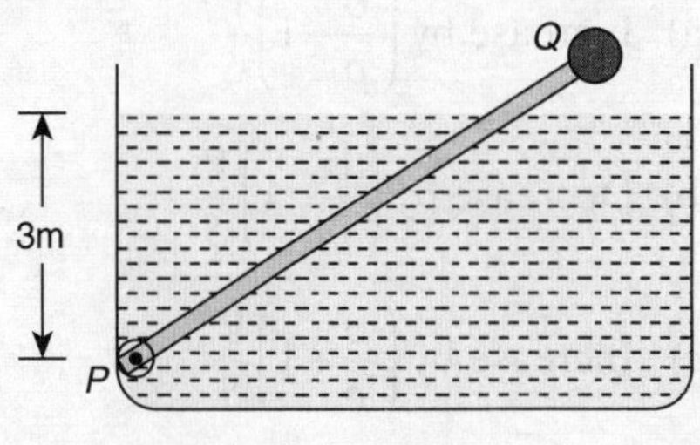

The mass that should be hung at the free end of the rod so that 5 m of the rod is submerged inside the water is:

(a) 2 kg (b) 3 kg

(c) $\frac{7}{3}$ kg (d) $\frac{5}{3}$ kg

18. A hemispherical portion of radius R is removed from the bottom of a cylinder of radius R. The volume of the remaining cylinder is V and its mass is M. It is suspended by a string in a liquid of density ρ, where it stays vertical, as shown in the figure.

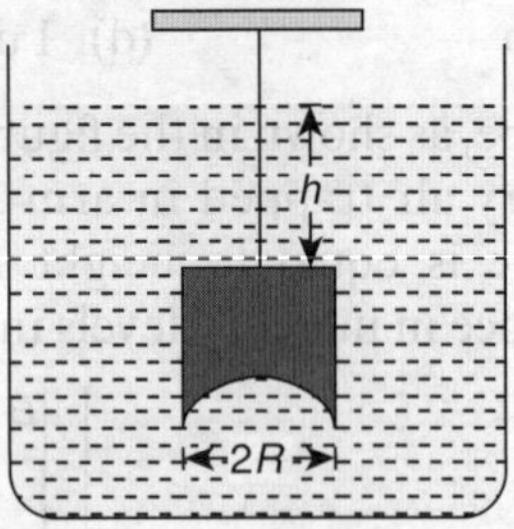

The upper face of the cylinder is at a depth h below the liquid surface. The force exerted by the liquid on the hemispherical bottom part of the cylinder is:

(a) $\left(M-\rho\pi R^2 h\right)g$ (b) $(M-\rho V)g$

(c) $\left(M+\rho\pi R^2 h\right)g$ (d) $\left(V+\pi R^2 h\right)\rho g$

19. A wooden block with a coin of volume V placed on its top floats in a liquid, as shown in the figure. The densities of the coin and the liquid are σ and $\rho\ (\rho<\sigma)$, respectively. The cross-section area of the vessel is S.

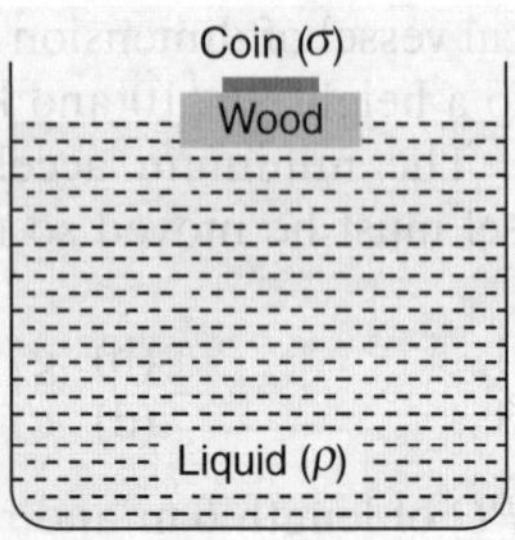

If the coin is dropped inside the liquid, the height of the liquid will:

(a) Increase by $\left(\frac{\sigma}{\rho}-1\right)\frac{V}{S}$

(b) Decrease by $\left(\frac{\sigma}{\rho}-1\right)\frac{V}{S}$

(c) Increase by $\left(\frac{\sigma}{\rho}+1\right)\frac{V}{S}$

(d) Decrease by $\left(\frac{\sigma}{\rho}+1\right)\frac{V}{S}$

20. An object is tied to the bottom of a tank containing a liquid denser than the object. Now, when the tank is accelerated along the horizontal, the chain deflects by angle α from the vertical while the free surface of the liquid tilts by angle β from the horizontal, as shown in the figure.

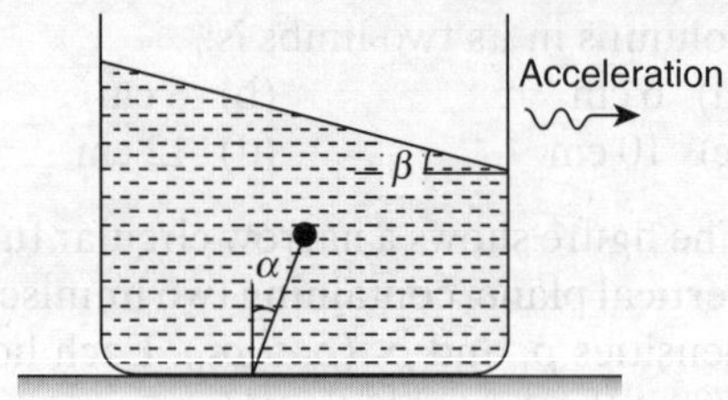

Then:

(a) $\alpha>\beta$

(b) $\alpha<\beta$

(c) $\alpha=\beta$

(d) Depends on acceleration

21. The pressure inside a 4-cm-diameter hose is 400 kPa. If water exits through a 2-cm-diameter nozzle, the maximum height to which it rises is (take $g=10\text{ m/s}^2$, atmospheric pressure = 100 kPa, and density of water = 1 g/cm^3):

(a) 44 m (b) 32 m

(c) 21 m (d) 14 m

22. A cylindrical tank having a small hole at its bottom is filled with liquid to a height h and then the hole is unplugged. If t_1 is the time in which the liquid level falls from h to $h/2$ and t_2 is the time in which the liquid level falls from $h/2$ to 0, then the ratio t_1/t_2 equals:

(a) $\sqrt{2}-1$ (b) $\sqrt{2}$

(c) 2 (d) 1

23. Water from a tap emerges vertically downwards with an initial speed of 1 m/s. The cross-section area of the tap is 1 cm^2. Assuming pressure to be same throughout the stream, the cross-section area of the stream at a point 15 cm below the tap is (take $g=10\text{ m/s}^2$):

(a) 0.5 cm^2 (b) 0.4 cm^2

(c) 0.3 cm^2 (d) 0.2 cm^2

24. A big tank is fitted with a tube bent at right angles, as shown in the figure. The length of the horizontal portion of the tube is l and its inside radius is r.

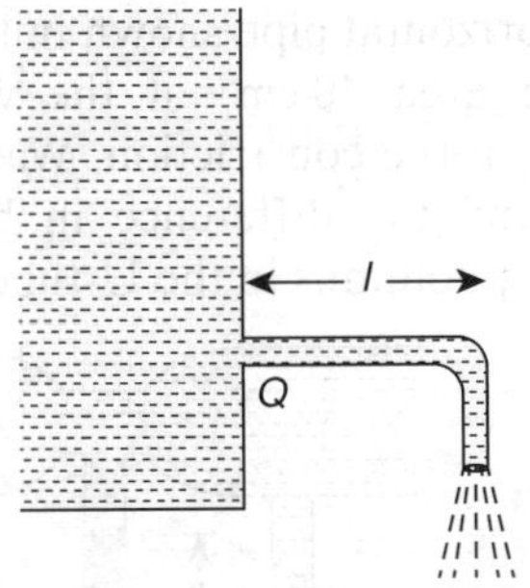

Liquid of density ρ flows out through the tube with a volume flow rate Q. The flowing liquid exerts force on the walls of the tube. The moment of these forces about O is:

(a) $\dfrac{2\rho Q^2 l}{\pi r^2}$ (b) $\dfrac{\rho Q^2 l}{\pi r^2}$

(c) $\dfrac{\sqrt{2}\rho Q^2 l}{\pi r^2}$ (d) $\dfrac{\rho Q^2 l}{\sqrt{2}\pi r^2}$

25. A wide vessel is fitted with a pipe of small cross-section area attached to its side, as shown in the figure. It is filled with a 30-cm-thick layer of water and a 30-cm-thick layer of kerosene. The relative density of kerosene is 0.8.

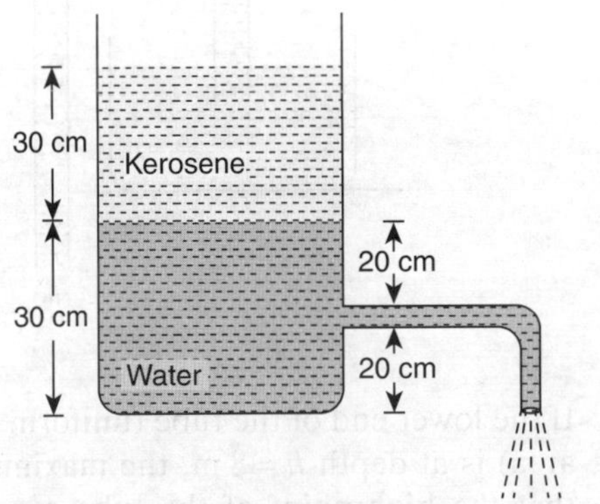

The initial efflux velocity out of the pipe is:

(a) $\dfrac{8}{\sqrt{5}}$ m/s (b) $\dfrac{6}{\sqrt{5}}$ m/s

(c) $4\sqrt{2}$ m/s (d) $\dfrac{5}{\sqrt{2}}$ m/s

26. A wide vessel of negligible mass and uniform cross-section A has a small hole of cross-section a in its side wall near the bottom. The container is placed on a smooth horizontal surface, filled with liquid, and then the hole is unplugged. The acceleration of the container is:

(a) $\dfrac{ag}{A}$ (b) $\dfrac{Ag}{a}$

(c) $\dfrac{2ag}{A}$ (d) $\dfrac{2Ag}{a}$

27. The figure shows a water supply tower of cross-section area S fitted with a freely movable piston of weight W. Water is drained out by a narrow tapering pipe connected to its side wall near the bottom. The cross-section area at the opening A of the pipe is half that of the cross-section area at point B. The height of the liquid is h at any instant, and its density is ρ.

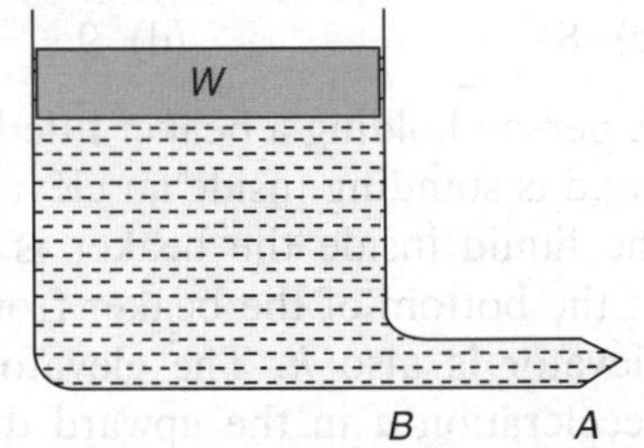

If the atmospheric pressure is p_0, and gravitational intensity is g, the pressure inside the liquid at point B is:

(a) $p_0 + \dfrac{1}{4}\left(\dfrac{W}{S} + \rho gh\right)$ (b) $p_0 + \dfrac{3}{4}\left(\dfrac{W}{S} + \rho gh\right)$

(c) $p_0 + \dfrac{1}{4}\left(\dfrac{2W}{S} + \rho gh\right)$ (d) $p_0 + \dfrac{3}{4}\left(\dfrac{2W}{S} + \rho gh\right)$

28. The figure shows a wide cylindrical container with a hole of radius r which projects into the cylinder to some height. The hole is covered by a wooden block of radius $2r$ and height a. The block just remains in equilibrium when water is filled to a height h above the wooden block.

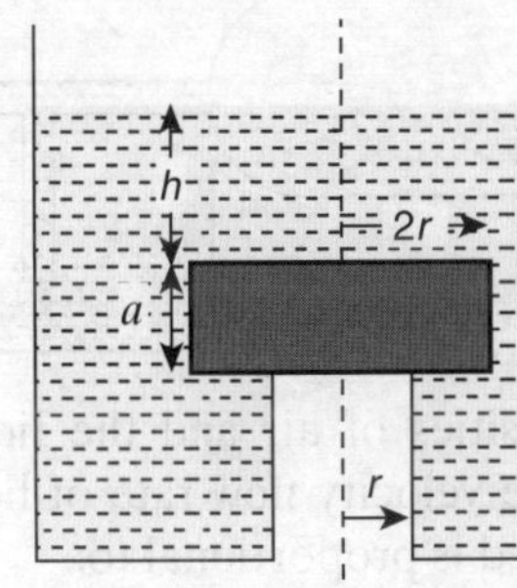

If the relative density of the wood is 1/3, then the correct statements are:

(a) $h = \dfrac{5}{3}a$, block will rise for $h < \dfrac{5}{3}a$

(b) $h = \dfrac{5}{3}a$, block will rise for $h > \dfrac{5}{3}a$

(c) $h = \dfrac{3}{2}a$, block will rise for $h < \dfrac{3}{2}a$

(d) $h = \dfrac{3}{2}a$, block will rise for $h < \dfrac{3}{2}a$

29. A vessel contains oil (specific gravity 0.8) over water. A cube of size a floats with half volume immersed in water and the other half in oil. If g is the gravitational intensity and T is the time period of oscillation for small displacements of the cube, then the value of $\frac{gT^2}{2\pi^2 h}$ is:

(a) 2 (b) 3
(c) 8 (d) 9

30. A person holding a beaker filled with liquid in his hand is standing inside an elevator. The height of the liquid inside the beaker is h and the height of the bottom of the beaker from the floor of the elevator is also h. The elevator is moving with acceleration a in the upward direction. If a tiny hole is punctured on the side wall of the beaker close to its bottom, the horizontal range of the liquid measured from the hole is:

(a) $\left(\frac{a}{g+a}\right)h$ (b) $\left(\frac{g}{g+a}\right)h$
(c) $\left(\frac{a}{g}\right)h$ (d) $2h$

31. The figure shows a spray gun having a movable piston fitted to a very narrow T-shaped nozzle which dips (negligible depth) into an open container filled with liquid. When the piston pushes the air through the nozzle, liquid from the container starts moving up the nozzle.

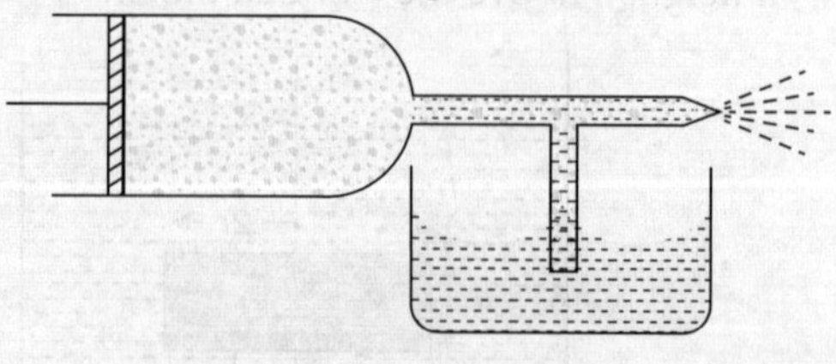

If the densities of air and the liquid are ρ_a and ρ_l, then the velocity flow rate of liquid for a given piston speed is proportional to:

(a) $\frac{\rho_a}{\rho_l}$ (b) $\sqrt{\frac{\rho_a}{\rho_l}}$
(c) $\left(\frac{\rho_a}{\rho_l}\right)^{3/2}$ (d) $\left(\frac{\rho_a}{\rho_l}\right)^2$

32. The horizontal pipe shown in the figure has cross-section area 40 cm^2 at the wider portions and 10 cm^2 at the constriction. Water is flowing in the pipe, and the difference in height between the mercury columns in the U-tube is $h = 9.3$ cm.

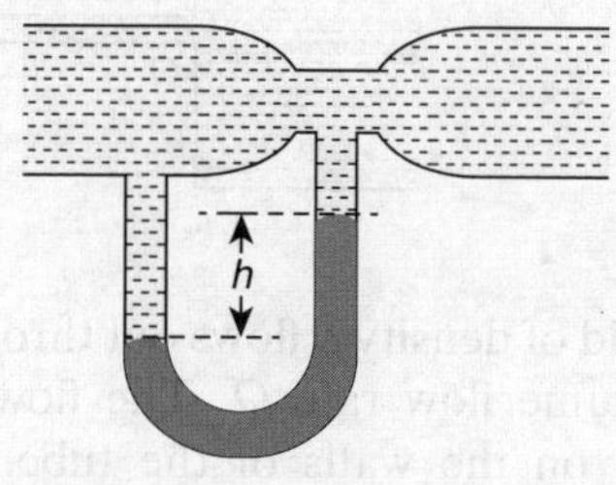

The discharge rate of water is (take $g = 10$ m/s^2 and relative density of mercury = 13.6):

(a) 5×10^{-3} m^3/s (b) 4×10^{-3} m^3/s
(c) 3×10^{-3} m^3/s (d) 2×10^{-3} m^3/s

33. A siphon, as shown in the figure, is a convenient way of removing liquids from containers. To establish the flow, the tube must be initially filled with the liquid.

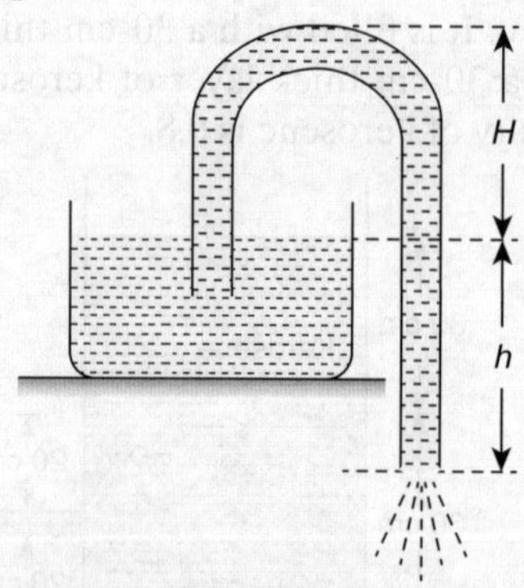

If the lower end of the tube (uniform cross-section area) is at depth $h = 8$ m, the maximum height H that the high point of the tube can have for the siphon to work is (take $g = 10$ m/s^2, atmospheric pressure = 100 kPa, and density of water = 1 g/cm^3):

(a) 1.5 m (b) 2.0 m
(c) 2.5 m (d) 2.8 m

ANSWER KEYS

1. (b)	**2.** (d)	**3.** (c)	**4.** (c)	**5.** (d)	**6.** (c)	**7.** (c)	**8.** (b)	**9.** (a)	**10.** (c)
11. (d)	**12.** (b)	**13.** (c)	**14.** (a)	**15.** (c)	**16.** (b)	**17.** (c)	**18.** (d)	**19.** (b)	**20.** (c)
21. (b)	**22.** (a)	**23.** (a)	**24.** (b)	**25.** (a)	**26.** (c)	**27.** (b)	**28.** (a)	**29.** (d)	**30.** (d)
31. (b)	**32.** (a)	**33.** (b)							

SOLUTIONS

1. (b) The pressure change with y is given by $dp = -\rho g dy$, where ρ is the density of air at height y. The pressure is zero at y = infinity. The pressure, say p_0, at $y = 0$ is given by

$$dp = -\rho g dy = -\rho_0 g e^{-\alpha y} dy$$

$$\Rightarrow \quad \int_0^{p_0} dp = -\rho_0 g \int_{\infty}^{0} e^{-\alpha y} dy$$

$$\Rightarrow \quad p_0 = \frac{\rho_0 g}{\alpha} | e^{-\alpha y} |_{\infty}^{0} = \frac{\rho_0 g}{\alpha}$$

2. (d) $F_{\text{side}} + W = F_{\text{bottom}}$

$F_{\text{side}} = \rho g(hA - V)$

The gauge force is the total force minus the force due to atmosphere. In other words, it is the force only due to the liquid mass. The figure shows the free body diagram of the liquid mass. The values of W and F_{bottom} are known.

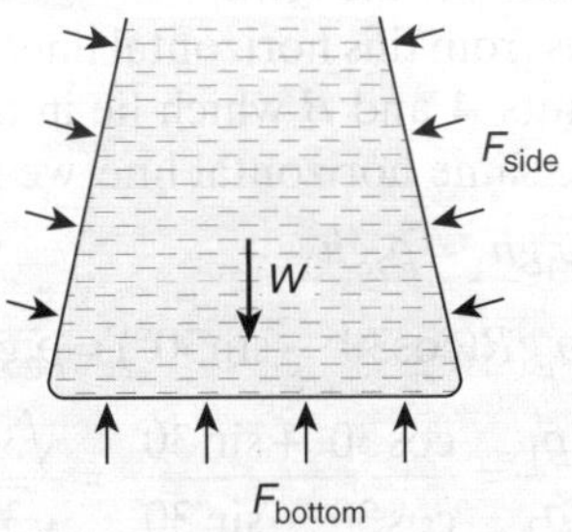

$W = \rho V g$ and $F_{\text{bottom}} = (\rho g h)A$

For equilibrium of the liquid mass, we have

$$F_{side} + W = F_{bottom}$$

$$\Rightarrow \quad F_{\text{side}} = \rho g(hA - V)$$

3. (c) Force on the bottom = $\rho g h(\pi r^2)$

Force on one semi-cylindrical half can be found by multiplying the average pressure over a height h with the projected surface area normal to the force exerted by the liquid (see figure). Thus, we have

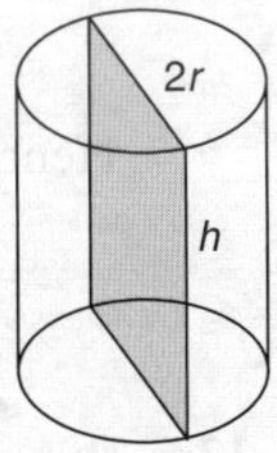

$$\text{Force on one semi-cylindrical half} = \left(\frac{1}{2}\rho g h\right)(2rh)$$

Equating the two, we have $\dfrac{h}{r} = \pi$

4. (c) Let V be the volume of the cavity. Then, total volume of the block $= V + \dfrac{1\text{ kg}}{10^4\text{ kg/m}^3}$

The buoyancy force due to the displaced water $= (10^3\text{ kg/m}^3)\left(V + \dfrac{1\text{ kg}}{10^4\text{ kg/m}^3}\right)g$

The buoyancy force on the block is given to be = (1 kg – 0.8 kg)g = (0.2 kg)g

Equating the two expressions, we have

$$V + 10^{-4}\text{m}^3 = 2 \times 10^{-4}\text{m}^3$$

$$\Rightarrow \quad V = 10^{-4}\text{m}^3 = 100\text{ cm}^3$$

5. (d) Let V be the volume of the object. Let ρ_o, ρ_w, ρ_l be the densities of the object, water and liquid, respectively.

Then, we have the following equations:

$$\rho_o V g = m_0 g \quad \text{...(1)}$$

$$\rho_w V g = (m_0 - m_1)g \quad \text{...(2)}$$

$$\rho_l V g = (m_0 - m_2)g \quad \text{...(3)}$$

From the above equations, we can obtain the relative densities of the object and liquid as

$$\frac{\rho_o}{\rho_w} = \frac{m_0}{m_0 - m_1} \text{ and } \frac{\rho_l}{\rho_w} = \frac{m_0 - m_2}{m_0 - m_1}$$

Hence, the difference between the two relative densities is

$$\frac{\rho_o}{\rho_w} - \frac{\rho_l}{\rho_w} = \frac{m_2}{m_0 - m_1}$$

6. (c) Let d be the relative density of the oil. Equating pressure at the bottom of the water column and at the bottom of the oil column, we have $1g$ (10 cm) = dg (12.5 cm)

$$\Rightarrow \quad d = \frac{10}{12.5} = 0.8$$

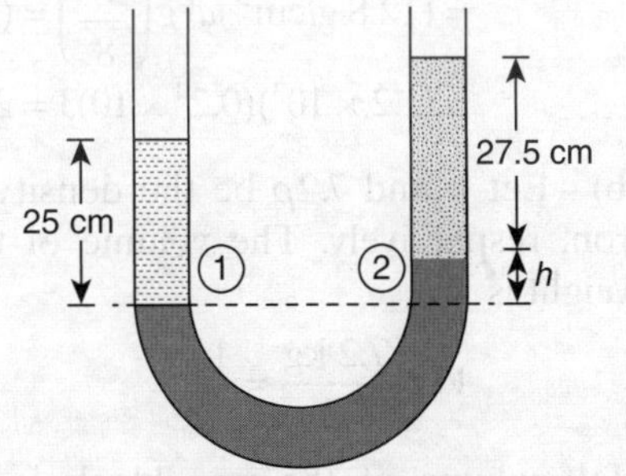

The figure shows the mercury levels after the water and oil columns are both increased by 15 cm. Let us choose two points 1 and 2 at the same horizontal level in the same liquid. Equating the pressures at 1 and 2, we have

$$kh + d\,(27.5 \text{ cm}) = 1(25 \text{ cm})$$

Putting $d = 0.8$ gives $h = \frac{3}{k}$ cm

7. (c) Let ρ be the density of the cube. In equilibrium, the weight of the cube equals the combined weight of the displaced oil and water. Hence, we have

$$\rho a^3 g = 13.6\left(\frac{1}{2}a^3\right)g + 0.8\left(\frac{1}{2}a^3\right)g$$

$\Rightarrow \quad \rho = 7.2$ g/cm^3

At any instant, let y be the displacement of the cube's base in the downward direction (measured from its position of equilibrium). The force of buoyancy on the cube is now greater than its weight, and the cube now experiences a net upward restoring force directed towards its equilibrium position. The force required to hold the cube in this position is (see figure)

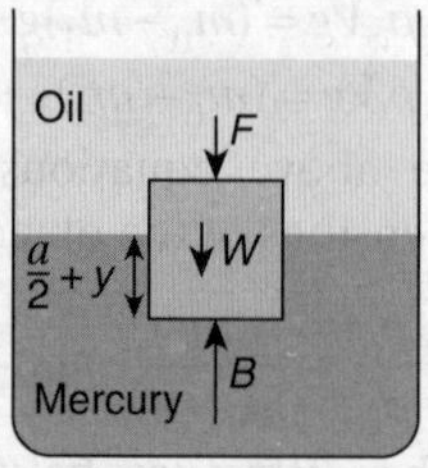

$$F = B - W = \left[13.6\left(\frac{a}{2}+y\right)a^2 g + 0.8\left(\frac{a}{2}-y\right)a^2 g\right]$$

$$-[7.2a^3 g]$$

$\Rightarrow F = (12.8 \text{ g/cm}^3)\, a^2 g y$

Hence, the work needed to push the cube completely inside mercury is

$$\int_0^{a/2} F dy = (12.8 \text{ g/cm}^3) a^2 g \int_0^{a/2} y dy$$

$$= (12.8 \text{ g/cm}^3) a^2 g\left(\frac{a^2}{8}\right) = (1.6 \text{ g/cm}^3) a^4 g$$

$$= (1.2 \times 10^3)(0.2^4 \times 10) \text{J} = 25.6 \text{ J}$$

8. (b) Let ρ and 7.2ρ be the density of water and iron, respectively. The volume of the iron block weight is

$$V = \frac{7.2 \text{ kg}}{7.2\rho} = \frac{1 \text{ kg}}{\rho}$$

Half-volume of the iron block is submerged in water. Then, the buoyant force is

$$B = \frac{1}{2}V\rho g = (0.5 \text{ kg})g$$

Hence, the spring balance will now read the weight of the water + bucket + force by the block on the water, that is 10 kg + 0.5 kg = 10.5 kg

9. (a) The weight of the cylinder is balanced by the upward force exerted by the trapped air. Thus, the gauge pressure of the air trapped inside the cylinder is

$$p_{\text{gauge}} = \frac{65 \text{ N}}{\pi \dfrac{(25\times10^{-2})^2}{4} \text{m}^2} = \frac{260\times10^4}{625\pi} \text{ N/m}^2$$

Equating this with $\rho g h$ gives

$$h = \frac{1}{2.2\times10^3\times10} \times \frac{260\times10^4}{625\pi} \text{ m}$$

$$= \frac{260\times100}{2.2\times625\pi} \text{ cm} = 6 \text{ cm}$$

10. (c) Let us imagine a horizontal line passing through the interface of the two liquids (see figure). Let h_1, h_2 be the heights of the free surfaces of the two liquids from this horizontal line. Equating pressures at points A and B which lie in the same liquid and on the same horizontal line, we have

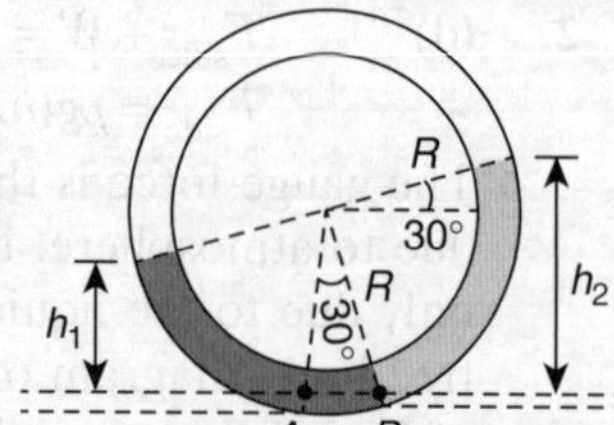

$$\rho_1 g h_1 = \rho_2 g h_2$$

$$\Rightarrow \quad \rho_1 g R(\cos 30° - \sin 30°) = \rho_2 g R(\cos 30° + \sin 30°)$$

$$\Rightarrow \quad \frac{\rho_1}{\rho_2} = \frac{\cos 30° + \sin 30°}{\cos 30° - \sin 30°} = \frac{\sqrt{3}+1}{\sqrt{3}-1} = 2+\sqrt{3}$$

11. (d) The resultant of the gravitational force and the buoyant force is $(\sigma - \rho)Vg$ in the vertically downward direction. The effective gravitational intensity experienced by the pendulum is

$$g_{eff} = \frac{(\sigma-\rho)Vg}{\sigma V} = \frac{(\sigma-\rho)g}{\sigma}$$

Hence, the time period is

$$T' = 2\pi\sqrt{\frac{l}{g_{eff}}} = \sqrt{\frac{\sigma}{\sigma-\rho}}T$$

12. (b) Acceleration of the ball inside water

$$a = \frac{(\rho-\sigma)Vg}{\sigma V} = \left(\frac{\rho}{\sigma}-1\right)$$

Velocity of the ball when it reaches the surface $v = \sqrt{2ah_1}$

The ball now moves with acceleration g in the downward direction. Its velocity reduces from v to zero over distance $h_2 = \frac{v^2}{2g} = \frac{2ah_1}{2g}$

Hence $\frac{h_2}{h_1} = \frac{a}{g} = \frac{\rho}{\sigma} - 1$

13. (c) Let a be the length of one side of the cube. The volume of liquid displaced to support the 200-g weight is (2 cm)a^2. The buoyant force due to this displaced liquid must equal 200 g in weight. Hence, we have

$$(1\ \text{g/cm}^3)\ 2a^2 g = (200\ \text{g})\ g$$

$$\Rightarrow \quad a = 10\ \text{cm}$$

14. (a) Let h be the depth of the lake. The pressure at the bottom is equivalent to h + 8 m height of the water column.
Now, using the ideal gas relation $P_1V_1 = P_2V_2$, we have

$$(h+8\ \text{m})\times\frac{4}{3}\pi r^3 = (8\ \text{m})\times\frac{4}{3}\pi\left(\frac{3r}{2}\right)^3$$

$$\Rightarrow \quad h = 19\ \text{m}$$

15. (c) The pressure of the trapped dry air is $2h$. When its volume is compressed to half of its initial volume, the pressure doubles to $4h$, which is $3h$ above atmospheric pressure. Hence, the difference in the mercury level will now be $3h$.

16. (b) From a reference frame attached to the accelerating container, the effective gravitational field is inclined at angle θ such that $\tan\theta = a/g$. The free surface of the liquid aligns itself perpendicular to the effective gravity, that is, at angle θ to the horizontal.

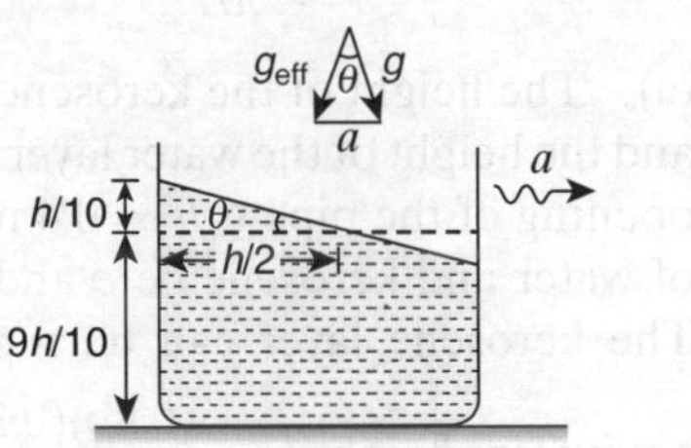

Also, from the figure, we see that $\tan\theta = \frac{h/10}{h/2} = \frac{1}{5}$.

Hence $\frac{a}{g} = \frac{1}{5} \Rightarrow a = \frac{g}{5}$.

17. (c) Let A be the cross-section area of the rod. Mass of the rod is given to be 12 kg. Hence, we have

$$500\ \text{kg/m}^3 \times A \times 6\ \text{m} = 12\ \text{kg}$$

$$\Rightarrow \quad A = \frac{12}{3000}\ \text{m}^2$$

The force of buoyancy is B = 1000 kg/m^3 $\times A \times$ 5 m $\times g = 20g$. The force of buoyancy passes through the centre of gravity (CG) of the displaced liquid, that is, at a distance of 5 m / 2 = 2.5 m from P.

The figure shows the forces acting on the rod and also their moment arms about P. The weight of the rod has been shown as W and W' is the weight of the hanging mass. The reaction force at P produces no torque about P, and hence, has not been shown in the figure.

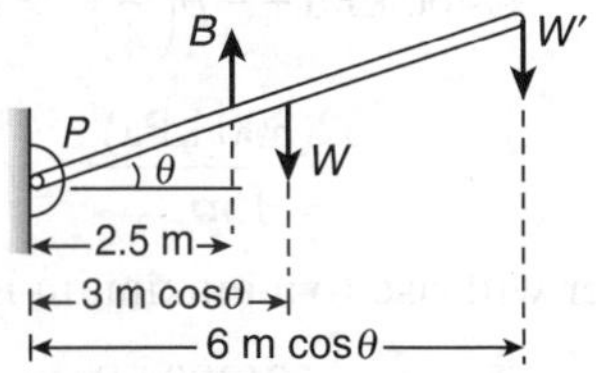

Now, balancing the torques of these forces about P, we have

$$W'(6\ \text{m}\cos\theta) + W(3\ \text{m}\cos\theta) = B\ (2.5\ \text{m}\cos\theta)$$

$$\Rightarrow \quad W' = \frac{2.5B - 3W}{6} = \frac{2.5(20g) - 3(12g)}{6} = \frac{7}{3}g$$

$$W'(6\ \text{m}\cos\theta) + W(3\ \text{m}\cos\theta) = B\ (2.5\ \text{m}\cos\theta)$$

$$\Rightarrow \quad W' = \frac{2.5B - 3W}{6} = \frac{2.5\times 20g - 3\times 12g}{6} = \frac{7}{3}g$$

Hence, the hanging mass equals $\frac{7}{3}$ kg

18. (d) The force exerted by the liquid on the flat part of the cylinder is $(\rho gh)\ \pi R^2$ in the downward direction. The force on the side walls is zero. Let the force on the bottom hemispherical part be F in the upward direction. Then the net force due to the liquid is $F - (\rho gh)\pi R^2$ in the upward direction. According to Archimedes' Principle, the net force exerted by the liquid must equal the weight of liquid displaced, that is, ρVg. Equating, we have

$$F - (\rho gh)\pi R^2 = pVg$$

$$\Rightarrow \quad F = \rho g(V + \pi R^2 h)$$

19. (b) Initially, when the coin is floating, it is displacing liquid equal to its weight. Thus, volume V_1 of the displaced liquid is given by

$$\rho V_1 g = \sigma V g \Rightarrow V_1 = \frac{\sigma V}{\rho}$$

Finally, when it is submerged in the liquid, it displaces liquid by an amount $V_2 = V$. By comparison, $V_2 < V_1$ since $\sigma < p$. Now that the coin is displacing a lesser amount of liquid, the level will fall by a height h, given by

$$h = \frac{V}{S} = \left(\frac{\sigma}{\rho} - 1\right)\frac{V}{S}$$

20. (c) The thread aligns itself along $\vec{g}_{eff}$, that is, along the perpendicular to the free surface of the liquid.

21. (b) Diameter reduces to half ⇒ Area reduces to one-fourth. Hence, if v is the velocity at the outlet, then velocity at the inlet is $v/4$. Applying Bernoulli's Principle between these two points, we have

$$400\text{ kPa} + \frac{1}{2}\rho\left(\frac{v}{4}\right)^2 = 100\text{ kPa} + \frac{1}{2}\rho v^2$$

$$\Rightarrow \quad v^2 = \frac{32(300\text{ kPa})}{15\rho}$$

Water will rise to a maximum height of

$$h = \frac{v^2}{2g} = \frac{32(300\text{ kPa})}{30\rho g} = \frac{32\times 3\times 10^5}{30\times 10^4} = 32\text{ m}$$

22. (a)

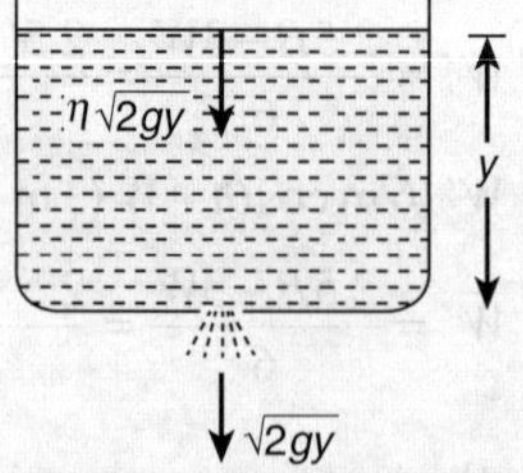

At any instant when the height of the liquid in the beaker is y, the efflux velocity is $\sqrt{2gy}$ and the velocity of the liquid surface is $\eta\sqrt{2gy}$, where η = area of the orifice / area of the container. Hence, we have

$$\frac{dy}{dt} = -c\sqrt{y} \quad [\text{where } c = \eta\sqrt{2g}]$$

The time t_1 in which the liquid level falls from $y = h$ to $y = h/2$ is given by

$$c\int_0^{t_1} dt = -\int_h^{h/2} \frac{dy}{\sqrt{y}}$$

$$\Rightarrow \quad ct_1 = 2\left(\sqrt{h} - \sqrt{h/2}\right) = \left(\sqrt{2}-1\right)\sqrt{2h}$$

Similarly, time t_2 in which the liquid level falls from $y = h$ to $y = 0$ is given by

$$c\int_0^{t_2} dt = -\int_{h/2}^{0} \frac{dy}{\sqrt{y}}$$

$$\Rightarrow \quad ct_2 = 2\sqrt{h/2} = \sqrt{2h}$$

Dividing the two equations, we have

$$\frac{t_1}{t_2} = \sqrt{2} - 1$$

23. (a) Let v be the flow velocity at a depth h. Using Bernoulli's Principle, we have

$$\frac{1}{2}\rho v^2 - \frac{1}{2}\rho(1\text{ m/s})^2 = \rho g h$$

$$\Rightarrow \quad v^2 = (1\text{ m/s})^2 + 2gh$$

Putting $h = 0.15$ m and $g = 10$ m/s² gives $v = 2$ m/s. Now, using the mass continuity equation, the cross-section area will be $\frac{1}{2}\times 1\text{ cm}^2 = 0.5\text{ cm}^2$

24. (b) The flow velocity is $v = \frac{Q}{\pi r^2}$

The momentum flow rate is $p = \rho Q v = \frac{\rho Q^2}{\pi r^2}$.

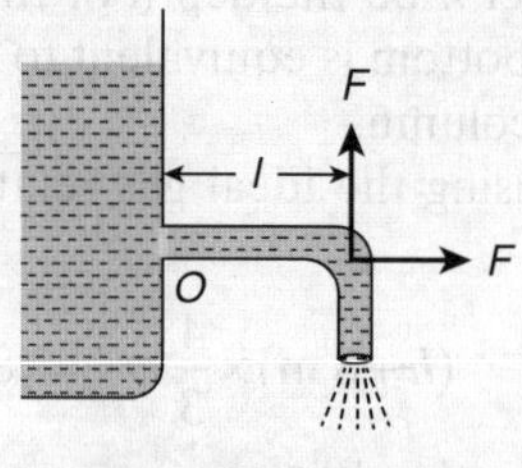

The momentum of the liquid changes its direction at the bend from horizontal to vertical. The tube walls at the bend exert force on the liquid and in reaction the liquid exerts force on the wall, as shown in the figure.

The magnitude of these forces is $F = p = \frac{\rho Q^2}{\pi r^2}$.

The horizontal component exerts no moment about O. Only the vertical component exerts moment about O, that is

$$\tau = Fl = \frac{\rho Q^2 l}{\pi r^2}$$

25. (a) The height of the kerosene layer is $h_1 = 0.3$ m, and the height of the water layer measured from the opening of the pipe is $h_2 = 0.4$ m. Let the densities of water and kerosene be ρ and 0.8ρ, respectively. The kerosene layer can be replaced by water of

$$\text{equivalent height } h_1' = \frac{(0.8\rho)(0.3\text{ m})}{\rho} = 0.24\text{ m}$$

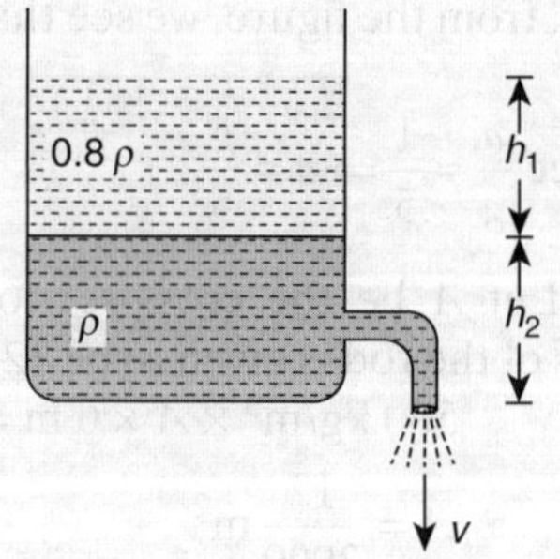

Thus, the vessel can be considered to be filled by only water whose height from the opening of the pipe is

$$h_2 + h_1' = 0.4\text{ m} + 0.24\text{ m} = 0.64\text{ m}$$

Now, by Torricelli's Theorem, the velocity of efflux is

$$v = \sqrt{2g(0.64\text{ m})} = \frac{8}{\sqrt{5}}\text{ m/s}$$

26. (c) The ejecting liquid mass comes out with a momentum flow rate $= v\dfrac{dm}{dt} = v(\rho av) = \rho av^2$, where v is the velocity of the efflux relative to the container. This produces a thrust on the container in the opposite direction; magnitude of thrust equals the momentum flow rate of the liquid.
At an instant when the height of the liquid inside the container is y, the efflux velocity is $v = \sqrt{2gy}$ and hence, thrust $= \rho av^2 = \rho a(2gy)$. At this instant, the mass of the container and its contents is mass $= \rho Ay$ (mass of container is given to be negligible). Dividing thrust by mass gives acceleration $= \dfrac{\rho a(2gy)}{\rho Ay} = \dfrac{2ag}{A}$

27. (b) Let v be the velocity at point A. The velocity at a point just below the piston can be neglected since the cross-section area is large. The pressure at A is P_0, and the pressure just below the piston is $P_0 + \dfrac{W}{S}$. Let us choose a horizontal line passing through A as our zero potential energy level. Now, applying Bernoulli's Principle between point A and a point just below the piston, we have

$$P_0 + \frac{W}{S} + \rho gh = P_0 + \frac{1}{2}\rho v^2$$

$$\Rightarrow \quad v = 2\sqrt{\frac{W}{\rho S} + gh}$$

Now, the velocity at B will be $v/2$ since the cross-section area is double that at A. Let the pressure at B be P. Using Bernoulli's Principle between points A and B, we have

$$P + \frac{1}{2}\rho\frac{v^2}{4} = P_0 + \frac{1}{2}\rho v^2$$

$$\Rightarrow \quad P = P_0 + \frac{3}{8}\rho v^2$$

$$\Rightarrow \quad P = P_0 + \frac{3}{4}\left(\frac{W}{S} + \rho gh\right)$$

28. (a) Let P_0 be the atmospheric pressure. Then, pressure at the points where the block is in contact with the liquid are $P_0 + \rho gh$ (on the upper surface) and $P_0 + \rho g(h + a)$ (on the lower surface).

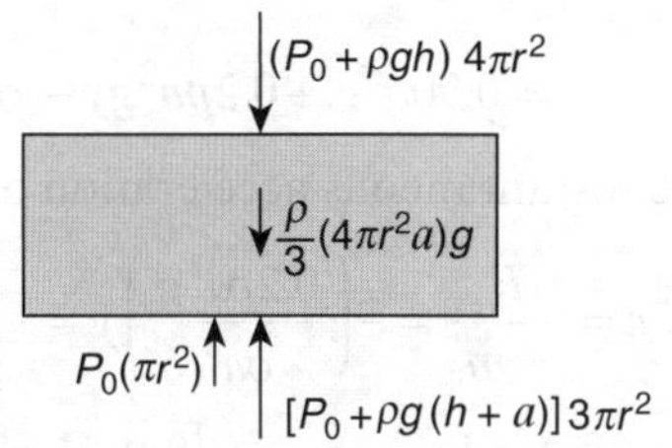

The upper and lower surface areas of the block which are in contact with the liquid are $4\pi r^2$ and $4\pi r^2 - \pi r^2 = 3\pi r^2$, respectively.
The figure shows the forces acting on the block. The net upward force experienced by the block is

$$F_{up} = [P_0 + \rho g(h+a)](3\pi r^2) + P_0(\pi r^2) - \rho gh(4\pi r^2) - \frac{\rho}{3}(4\pi r^2 a)g$$

$$= \rho g\pi r^2\left(\frac{5}{3}a - h\right)$$

Note that the force due to the atmosphere cancels out. Now, we can see that

$$F_{up} = 0 \text{ for } h = \frac{5}{3}a \text{ and } F_{up} > 0 \text{ for } h < \frac{5}{3}a$$

Hence, the block will rise for $h < \dfrac{5}{3}a$.

29. (d) Let ρ and 0.8ρ be the densities of water and oil, respectively. Let σ be the density of the cube. In equilibrium, the weight of the cube equals the combined weight of the displaced oil and water. Hence, we have

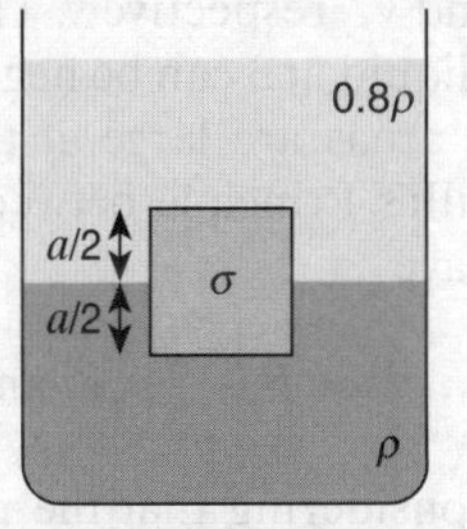

$$\rho\left(\frac{1}{2}a^3\right)g + 0.8\rho\left(\frac{1}{2}a^3\right)g = \sigma a^3 g$$

$$\Rightarrow \quad \sigma = 0.9\rho$$

At any instant, let y be the displacement of the cube's base in the downward direction (measured from its position of equilibrium). The force of buoyancy on the cube is now greater than its weight, and the cube now experiences a net upward restoring force directed towards its equilibrium position. The restoring force is

$$F_{res} = \left[\rho\left(\frac{a}{2}+y\right)a^2 g + 0.8\rho\left(\frac{a}{2}-y\right)a^2 g\right] - [\sigma a^3 g]$$

$$= 0.90a^3 g + 0.2\rho a^2 gy - \sigma a^3 g$$

The instantaneous acceleration of the cube is

$$a = -\frac{F_{res}}{m} = -\left(\frac{0.2\rho a^2 g}{\sigma a^3}\right)y = -\left(\frac{2g}{9a}\right)y$$

Hence, we have $T = 2\pi\sqrt{\frac{9a}{2g}} \Rightarrow \frac{gT^2}{2\pi^2 a} = 9$

30. (d) In a reference frame attached to the elevator, the effective gravity is $g_{eff} = g + a$. The liquid comes out of the beaker with a horizontal velocity $u = \sqrt{2(g+a)h}$. After coming out of the beaker, the liquid moves with acceleration $g_{eff} = g + a$ in the downward direction. It reaches the floor after time $t = \sqrt{\frac{2h}{g+a}}$.

The horizontal range is

$$R = ut = \sqrt{2(g+a)h} \times \sqrt{\frac{2h}{g+a}} = 2h$$

31. (b)

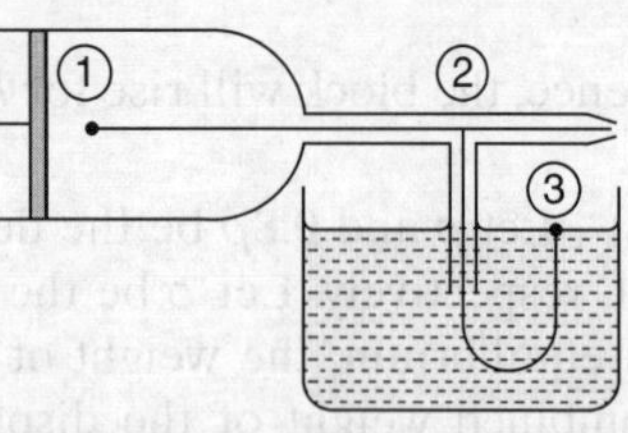

Let the speed of air and liquid at point 2 (see figure) be v_a and v_l, respectively. The velocities of air at 1 and of liquid at 3 can be neglected, since the cross-section areas are large at these points. Applying Bernoulli's Principle between 1, 2 and between 3, 2, we have

$$P_1 = P_2 + \frac{1}{2}\rho_a v_a^2 \text{ and } P_3 = P_2 + \frac{1}{2}\rho_l v_l^2$$

Now, considering that the piston is being pushed slowly, we can take $P_1 = P_{atm}$. Since point 3 is exposed to the atmosphere, $P_3 = P_{atm}$. Thus, equating the two values obtained above, we have

$$v_l = \sqrt{\frac{\rho_a}{\rho_l}}v_a$$

32. (a) Let us choose two points 1 and 2 inside the moving liquid, as shown in the figure. The cross-section areas of the pipe at these two points are in the ratio 4:1. Thus, the velocities at these points will be in the ratio 1:4. Let $v_1 = v$ and $v_2 = 4v$. From Bernoulli's Principle, we have

$$p_1 - p_2 = \frac{1}{2}\rho_w(v_2^2 - v_1^2) = \frac{15}{2}\rho_w v^2$$

Pressure at points 3 and 4 (see figure) are the same since they lie in the same liquid (mercury) on the same horizontal line.

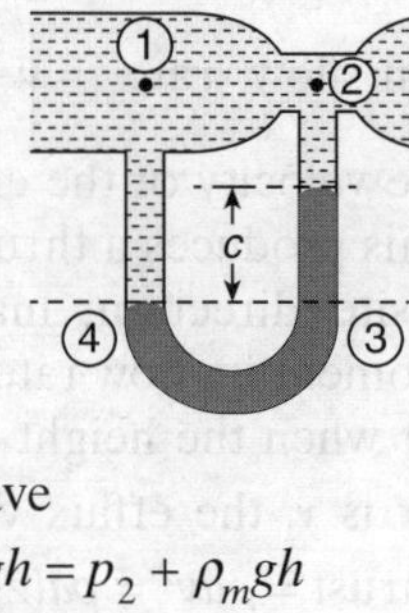

Thus, we have

$$p_1 + \rho_w gh = p_2 + \rho_m gh$$

$$\Rightarrow p_1 - p_2 = (\rho_m - \rho_w)gh$$

From the results above, we have

$$\frac{15}{2}\rho_w v^2 = (\rho_m - \rho_w)gh$$

$$\Rightarrow \; v = \sqrt{\frac{2gh}{15}\left(\frac{\rho_m}{\rho_w} - 1\right)}$$

$$= \sqrt{\frac{20(9.3\times10^{-2})(13.6-1)}{15}}\text{ m/s} = 1.25 \text{ m/s}$$

Hence, discharge rate $Q = v_1 A_1 = (1.25 \text{ m/s})(40 \times 10^{-4}\text{m}^2) = 5 \times 10^{-3} \text{ m}^3/\text{s}$

33. (b) Let 1 and 2 be the highest and exit points of the siphon, respectively (see figure). Point 2 is open to the atmosphere; hence pressure at this point is $P_2 = P_0$. The velocity head is the same at all points inside the siphon, since it has a uniform cross-section area. Hence, pressure inside the siphon varies only due to difference in gravity head. Pressure is the least at point 1 and that is $P_1 = P_0 - \rho g(H + h)$.

For the siphon to work, the pressure should not be negative at any point. That is

$$P_o - \rho g(H+h) > 0$$

$$\Rightarrow \quad H < \frac{P_o}{\rho g} - h = \frac{10^5}{10^4}\text{ m} - 8 \text{ m} = 2 \text{ m}$$

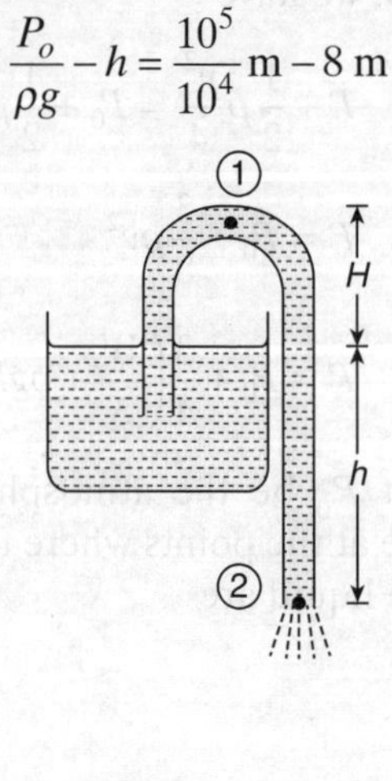

CHAPTER

9

Surface Tension and Viscosity

- Molecules at the surface of a liquid experience a net inward force drawing it into the liquid volume. Thus, the liquid tends to minimise its surface area, just like a stretched membrane. Surface tension S is the force of attraction between the liquid molecules measured per unit length on the liquid surface:
$$S = \frac{F}{l} \text{ (SI unit is N/m)}$$
A liquid surface with area A and surface tension S is said to possess surface energy U, given by
$$U = SA$$
The amount of energy required to increase the surface area of a liquid by ΔA is given by
$$\Delta U = S\Delta A$$
Another unit for surface tension is J/m^2.
- **Pressure Difference in a Soap Bubble:** A soap bubble consists of two spherical surface films with a thin layer of liquid in between. Because of surface tension, the films tend to contract in order to minimise their surface area. This compresses the air inside, causing a rise in its pressure. The pressure p of the air inside above the surrounding air pressure p_a is given by
$$p - p_a = \frac{4S}{r}$$
- **Pressure Difference in a Liquid Drop:** A liquid drop has only one surface film. The pressure p of the liquid inside above the surrounding air pressure p_a is given by
$$p - p_a = \frac{2S}{r}$$
- **Capillarity:** When a gas–liquid interface meets a solid surface, such as the walls of a container, the interface usually curves up or down near the solid surface. The angle θ (measured inside the liquid) at which it meets the solid surface is called the angle of contact.
Surface tension causes elevation or depression of liquid, in a narrow tube. This effect is called capillarity. A liquid with $\theta < 90°$ rises inside the tube until it reaches an equilibrium height h at which the total surface tension force balances the weight of the extra liquid in the tube:
$$h = \frac{2S\cos\theta}{\rho g r}$$
For $\theta > 90°$, we get a negative value for h, which indicates depression.
- Viscosity is the internal friction in a fluid. Viscous forces oppose relative motion between two fluid layers. A moving fluid is in a state of continuously increasing shear strain because different layers of the fluid move with different speeds. If two fluid layers separated by a distance Δl differ in their velocities by Δv, the strain rate is the velocity gradient $\Delta v / \Delta l$. A force F parallel to the liquid surface is required to maintain the motion. Shear stress is force per unit area F / A. Coefficient of viscosity η is the ratio of shear stress to strain rate:
$$\eta = \frac{F/A}{\Delta v / \Delta l} \text{ (SI unit is N}\cdot\text{s/m}^2 \text{ or Pa}\cdot\text{s)}$$
Thus, the viscous force between two fluid layers moving relative to each other is given by
$$F = \eta A \frac{\Delta v}{\Delta l}$$
Another commonly used unit for viscosity is the Poise $(1\,\text{P} = 0.1\,\text{Pa}\cdot\text{s})$. Viscosity of a fluid decreases with increase in temperature.

- **Stokes's Law:** A sphere of radius r moving with speed v through a liquid having viscosity η experiences a viscous force F, given by

$$F = 6\pi\eta r v$$

A sphere of radius r and density ρ, falling through a viscous liquid of density σ and coefficient of viscosity η, acquires a terminal speed v_T, given by

$$v_T = \frac{2(\rho - \sigma) g r^2}{9\eta}$$

- **Laminar and Turbulent Flow:** Fluid flow is said to be laminar when the fluid particles move in well-defined directions without any lateral mixing, and it is said to be turbulent when the velocity of the fluid at any point is continuously changing.

Reynold's number R is a dimensionless number that helps us in predicting whether fluid flow will be laminar or turbulent. It is the ratio of the inertial force $\rho A v^2$ required to maintain the fluid flow to the viscous force $\eta A v/D$ that opposes the fluid flow. Thus

$$R = \frac{\rho v D}{\eta}$$

Here, ρ is the fluid density, η is the fluid viscosity coefficient, v is the fluid velocity and D is the flow width (diameter of a pipe, width of a canal or width of an airplane wing). For $R < 1000$, the flow will be laminar, for $R > 2000$, the flow becomes turbulent. For intermediate values of R, the flow is a mix of both laminar and turbulent.

Fluid flows in nature are mostly turbulent. Even the twinkling of stars is due to the continuously changing refractive index of the turbulent atmosphere. Laminar flow generally occurs at the leading edge of a solid object when it moves through a fluid. Turbulence leads to dissipation of kinetic energy in the form of heat. Racing cars, airplanes, ships and submarines are designed in such a way as to minimise turbulence.

EXERCISES

1. A ring of external and internal radii r_1 and r_2 just touches the horizontal surface of a liquid of surface tension S. The force required to pull the ring away from the liquid surface is:

(a) $2\pi(r_1 + r_2)S$ (b) $2\pi(r_1 - r_2)S$
(c) $4\pi(r_1 + r_2)S$ (d) $4\pi(r_1 - r_2)S$

2. A thin loop of a thread floats on a soap film formed inside a wire frame which is placed horizontally. When the film within the loop is pierced, the wire rearranges itself in the form of a circle of radius r. If S is the surface tension of the soap solution, the tension in the thread will be:

(a) Sr (b) $2Sr$
(c) $4Sr$ (d) $8Sr$

3. A drop of liquid of radius $R = 10^{-2}$ m and surface tension $S = \frac{0.1}{4\pi}$ N/m is divided into n equal drops. The energy required for this process is $E = 10^{-3}$ J. If $n = 10^{\alpha}$, then α equals:

(a) 6 (b) 7
(c) 8 (d) 9

4. If W is the work required to blow a spherical bubble of volume V from a soap solution, then the work required to blow a bubble of volume $2V$ from the soap solution is:

(a) $2W$ (b) $2^{1/4}W$
(c) $2^{1/3}W$ (d) $2^{2/3}W$

5. Two separate air bubbles of radii r_1 and r_2 $(r_2 > r_1)$ formed of the same liquid come together to form a double-bubble. The radius of the film surface common to both bubbles is:

(a) $\frac{r_1 r_2}{r_2 - r_1}$ (b) $\frac{r_1 r_2}{r_2 + r_1}$
(c) $\frac{r_2 + r_1}{2}$ (d) $\frac{r_2 - r_1}{2}$

6. Two spherical soap bubbles formed in vacuum have radii r_1 and r_2. They coalesce to form a single spherical bubble. Assuming no temperature changes, the radius of the bubble so formed is:

(a) $r_1 + r_2$ (b) $\sqrt[3]{r_1^3 + r_2^3}$

(c) $\sqrt{r_1^2 + r_2^2}$ (d) $\left(\sqrt{r_1} + \sqrt{r_2}\right)^2$

7. A needle of length l and density ρ will float on a liquid of surface tension S if its radius r is less than:

(a) $\sqrt{\dfrac{4S}{\pi \rho g}}$ (b) $\sqrt{\dfrac{2S}{\pi \rho g}}$

(c) $\sqrt{\dfrac{S}{4\pi \rho g}}$ (d) $\sqrt{\dfrac{S}{2\pi \rho g}}$

8. A glass tube of radius r is dipped vertically into a container of mercury, with its lower end at a depth h below the mercury surface. A hemispherical bulb is to be blown at the lower end of the tube, as shown in the figure.

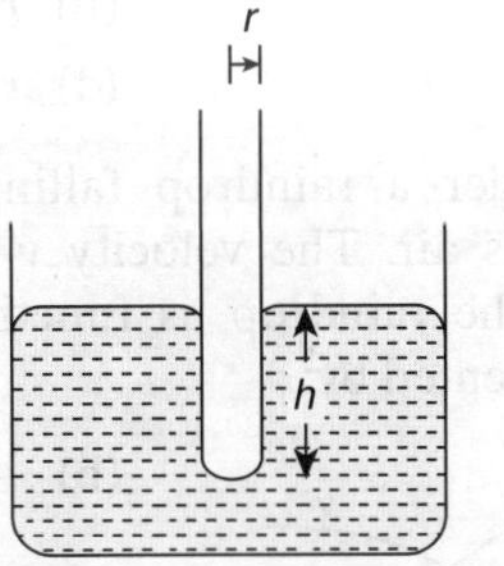

If ρ is the density and S is the surface tension of mercury, the gauge pressure of air in the tube should be:

(a) $\rho gh - \dfrac{2S}{r}$ (b) $\rho gh + \dfrac{2S}{r}$

(c) $\rho gh - \dfrac{4S}{r}$ (d) $\rho gh + \dfrac{4S}{r}$

9. A small drop of water is squeezed between two clean glass plates so that a thin film of thickness d and area A is formed between them. If θ is the angle of contact and S is the surface tension of water, the force required to pull the glass plates apart is:

(a) $\dfrac{AS\cos\theta}{d}$ (b) $\dfrac{2AS\cos\theta}{d}$

(c) $\dfrac{4AS\cos\theta}{d}$ (d) $\dfrac{2AS(1-\cos\theta)}{d}$

10. A capillary tube of radius r is immersed in water and m mass of water rises in the tube. If the radius is doubled, the mass of water that will rise in the tube is:

(a) $\dfrac{1}{2}m$ (b) m

(c) $\dfrac{3}{2}m$ (d) $2m$

11. The height to which a liquid rises in a capillary tube is found to drop by 0.5% when temperature is raised by 1%. Considering all other quantities to be unchanged, the dependence of surface tension S of the liquid on absolute temperature T is:

(a) $S \propto T^{-1}$ (b) $S \propto T^{-1/2}$

(c) $S \propto T^{-3/2}$ (d) $S \propto T^{-2}$

12. A soap film of surface tension S is formed inside a circular wire frame of radius a. Air is now blown at the soap film to form a bubble, as shown in the figure.

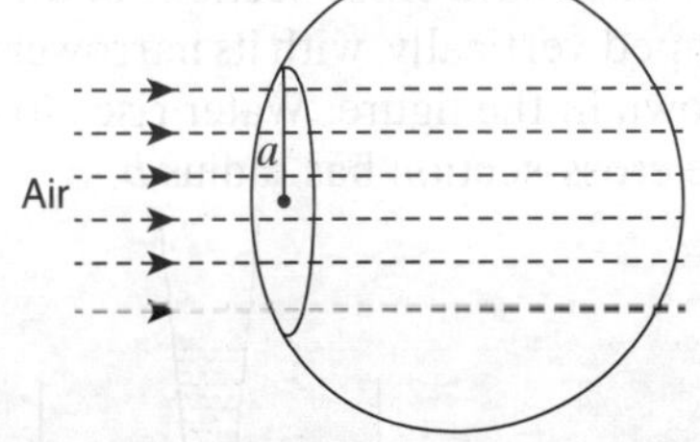

If ρ is the density and v is the velocity of air, then the radius of the largest bubble that can be blown is:

(a) $\dfrac{2S}{\rho v^2}$ (b) $\dfrac{4S}{\rho v^2}$

(c) $\dfrac{S}{2\rho v^2}$ (d) $\dfrac{S}{4\rho v^2}$

13. The figure shows a liquid drop hanging from a dropper of nozzle radius a.

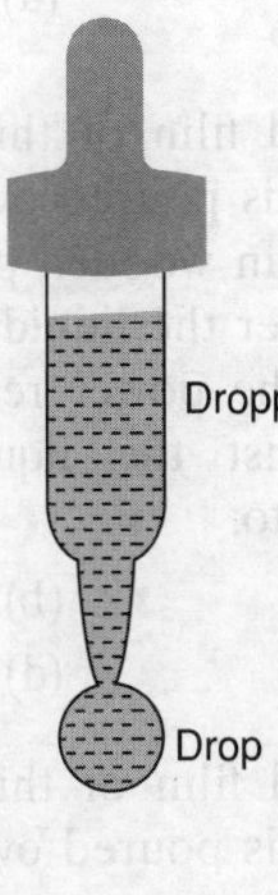

If ρ is the density and S is the surface tension of the liquid, the radius of the largest drop that can hang from the dropper is (take gravitational intensity = g):

(a) $\left(\frac{Sa^2}{2\rho g}\right)^{1/4}$ (b) $\left(\frac{3Sa^2}{4\rho g}\right)^{1/4}$

(c) $\left(\frac{3Sa^2}{2\rho g}\right)^{1/4}$ (d) $\left(\frac{3Sa^2}{\rho g}\right)^{1/4}$

14. Two glass plates held close to each other at distance d are dipped vertically inside a liquid of density ρ and surface tension S. The height to which the liquid rises in between the plates is:

(a) $\frac{4S\cos\theta}{\rho gd}$ (b) $\frac{2S\cos\theta}{\rho gd}$

(c) $\frac{S\cos\theta}{\rho gd}$ (d) $\frac{S\cos\theta}{2\rho gd}$

15. A glass capillary tube is of the shape of a truncated cone with an apex angle α so that its two ends have cross-sections of different radii. It is dipped vertically, with its narrower end in water, as shown in the figure. Water rises to height h, where the cross-section has radius b.

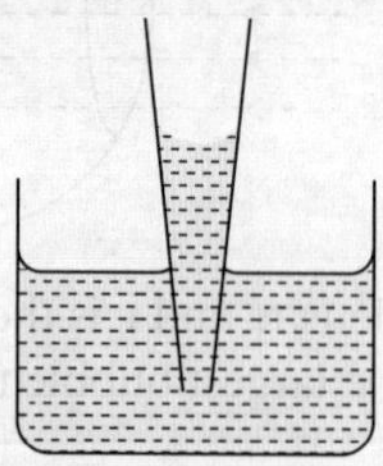

If the surface tension of water is S, its density ρ and its angle of contact θ, then h equals (take acceleration due to gravity = g):

(a) $\frac{2S\cos(\theta-\alpha)}{\rho gb}$ (b) $\frac{2S\cos(\theta+\alpha)}{\rho gb}$

(c) $\frac{2S\cos(\theta-\alpha/2)}{\rho gb}$ (d) $\frac{2S\cos(\theta+\alpha/2)}{\rho gb}$

16. A thin liquid film of thickness h and viscosity coefficient η is poured over a smooth horizontal surface. A thin wooden plank of surface area A is dragged over the liquid surface with a uniform velocity v. The power required to maintain the motion against the liquid's viscous forces is proportional to:

(a) v^1 (b) v^2

(c) v^3 (d) v^4

17. A thin liquid film of thickness h and viscosity coefficient η is poured over a smooth horizontal surface. A thin wooden disc of radius R is placed over the liquid surface and is rotated with a uniform angular velocity ω. The power required to maintain the motion against the liquid's viscous forces is proportional to:

(a) ω^2R^3 (b) ω^2R^2

(c) ω^3R^2 (d) ω^3R^3

18. Consider two small metal spheres P and Q, each of density 8 g/cm^3 and diameters 1.0 cm and 0.5 cm, respectively. Sphere P is dropped into a liquid of density 0.8 g/cm^3 and viscosity 3 P. Sphere Q is dropped into a liquid of density 1.6 g/cm^3 and viscosity 2 P. The ratio of the terminal velocities of P and Q is:

(a) 3 : 1 (b) 3 : 2

(c) 4 : 3 (d) 7 : 5

19. A small sphere of radius r and density ρ falls from rest in a viscous liquid of density σ and coefficient of viscosity η. Due to viscosity, heat is produced. When the sphere has acquired terminal velocity, the rate of heat production is proportional to:

(a) r^2 (b) r^3

(c) r^4 (d) r^5

20. Consider a raindrop falling from rest through viscous air. The velocity v and the acceleration a of the raindrop as functions of time are best represented by:

(a) 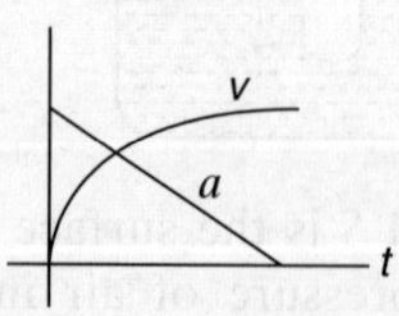

(b) 

(c) 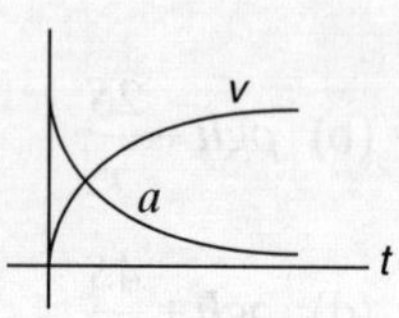

(d) 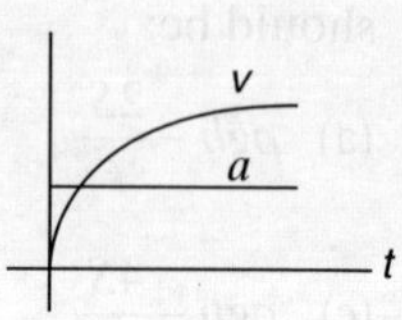

21. Spheres P and Q of equal radii have densities ρ_1 and ρ_2, respectively. They are connected by a light string and placed in liquids L_1 and L_2 (see figure) of densities σ_1 and σ_2, and coefficients of viscosity η_1 and η_2, respectively; they float in equilibrium.

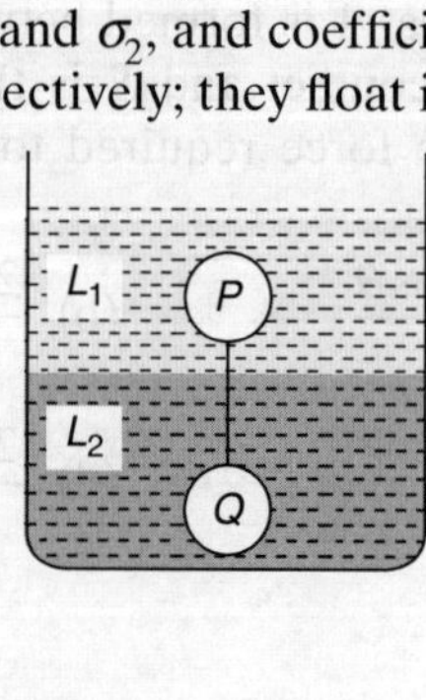

If P alone in L_2 has terminal velocity $\mathbf{v}_P$, and Q alone in L_1 has terminal velocity $\mathbf{v}_Q$, then:

(a) $\frac{|\mathbf{v}_P|}{|\mathbf{v}_Q|} = \frac{\eta_2}{\eta_1}$ (b) $\frac{|\mathbf{v}_P|}{|\mathbf{v}_Q|} = \frac{\eta_1}{\eta_2}$

(c) $\mathbf{v}_P \cdot \mathbf{v}_Q > 0$ (d) $\mathbf{v}_P \cdot \mathbf{v}_Q < 0$

22. A fluid of density $\rho = 900$ kg/m^3 having viscosity coefficient $\eta = 0.04$ Pa·s is flowing through a pipe of diameter $D = 2$ cm. The maximum permissible volume flow rate Q so that the flow remains laminar is (take $R < 1000$ for laminar flow):
(a) 691 cm^3/s (b) 549 cm^3/s
(c) 359 cm^3/s (d) 231 cm^3/s

ANSWER KEYS

1. (a)	**2.** (b)	**3.** (a)	**4.** (d)	**5.** (a)	**6.** (c)	**7.** (b)	**8.** (b)	**9.** (b)	**10.** (d)
11. (b)	**12.** (b)	**13.** (c)	**14.** (b)	**15.** (d)	**16.** (b)	**17.** (a)	**18.** (a)	**19.** (d)	**20.** (c)
21. (b),(d)		**22.** (a)							

SOLUTIONS

1. (a) When the ring is pulled, the liquid surface that clings to the inner part pulls with a force $(2\pi r_1)S$ and the outer part with a force $(2\pi r_2)S$. Hence, a net force of $2\pi(r_1 + r_2)S$ will be required to pull the ring away from the liquid surface.

2. (b)

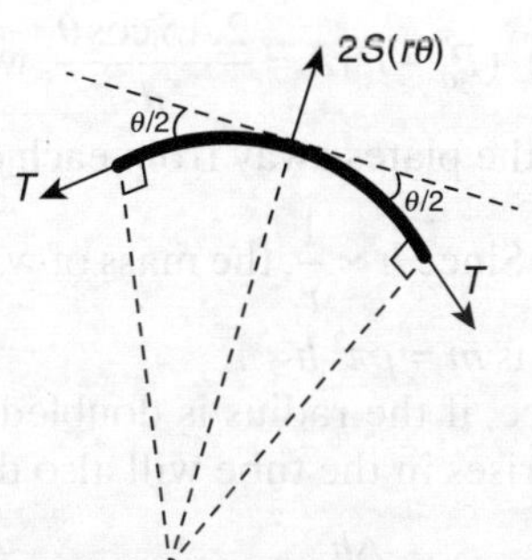

The figure shows the forces acting on a small portion of the string. Let θ be the angle subtended by the arc. The length of the arc equals $r\theta$. The liquid surface exerts a force $2S(r\theta)$ along the radially outward direction. This is balanced by the radial component of the tension

$$2T\cos(90° - \theta/2) = 2T\sin\frac{\theta}{2} = T\theta \text{ for small } \theta$$

Equating the two forces, we have

$$T\theta = 2Sr\theta \Rightarrow T = 2Sr$$

3. (a) Radius of each drop is given by

$$n\left(\frac{4}{3}\pi r^3\right) = \frac{4}{3}\pi R^3 \Rightarrow r = \frac{R}{n^{1/3}}$$

Energy required to create the drops is the product of surface tension and the change in surface area. Thus, we have

$$E = S\,[n(4\,\pi r^2) - 4\pi R^2]$$

$$\Rightarrow \quad \frac{E}{4\pi S} = nr^2 - R^2 = n\left(\frac{R^2}{n^{2/3}}\right) - R^2 = R^2(n^{1/3} - 1)$$

$$\Rightarrow \quad n = \left(\frac{E}{4\pi SR^2} + 1\right)^3 = \left(\frac{10^{-3}}{0.1\times 10^{-4}} + 1\right)^3$$

$$= (101)^3 \simeq 10^6 \Rightarrow \alpha = 6$$

4. (d) Work required to increase the surface of a liquid is directly proportional to the increase in surface area. Thus, we have

$$W = S\Delta A \propto r^2 \propto (r^3)^{2/3} \propto V^{2/3}$$

Hence, work required to blow a bubble of volume $2V$ will be

$$W' = 2^{2/3}W$$

5. (a) If p_0 is the atmospheric pressure, the pressures inside the two bubbles are

$$p_1 = p_o + \frac{4S}{r_1} \text{ and } p_2 = p_o + \frac{4S}{r_2}$$

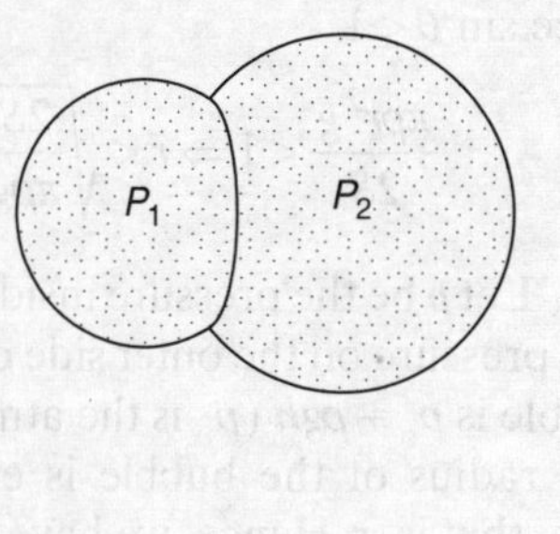

At the boundary of the double-bubble, let r be the curvature. Then

$$P_1 - P_2 = \frac{4S}{r}$$

$$\Rightarrow \quad \frac{4S}{r_1} - \frac{4S}{r_2} = \frac{4S}{r}$$

$$\Rightarrow \quad \frac{1}{r_1} - \frac{1}{r_2} = \frac{1}{r}$$

$$\Rightarrow \quad r = \frac{r_1 r_2}{r_2 - r_1}$$

6. (c) The pressures inside the two bubbles are

$$P_1 = \frac{4S}{r_1} \text{ and } P_2 = \frac{4S}{r_2}$$

If r is the radius of the single bubble, then pressure inside the single bubble will be $4S/r$.

The volumes of the bubbles are

$$V_1 = \frac{4}{3}\pi r_1^3, V_2 = \frac{4}{3}\pi r_2^3 \text{ and } V = \frac{4}{3}\pi r^3$$

If T is the temperature, then the number of moles of air molecules is

$$n_1 = \frac{P_1 V_1}{RT}, n_2 = \frac{P_2 V_2}{RT} \text{ and } n = \frac{PV}{RT}$$

Now, using $n_1 + n_2 = n$, we have

$$PV = P_1 V_1 + P_2 V_2$$

$$\Rightarrow \quad r^2 = r_1^2 + r_2^2$$

$$\Rightarrow \quad r = \sqrt{r_1^2 + r_2^2}$$

7. (b) The figure shows forces acting on a portion of a liquid surface supporting the peddle.

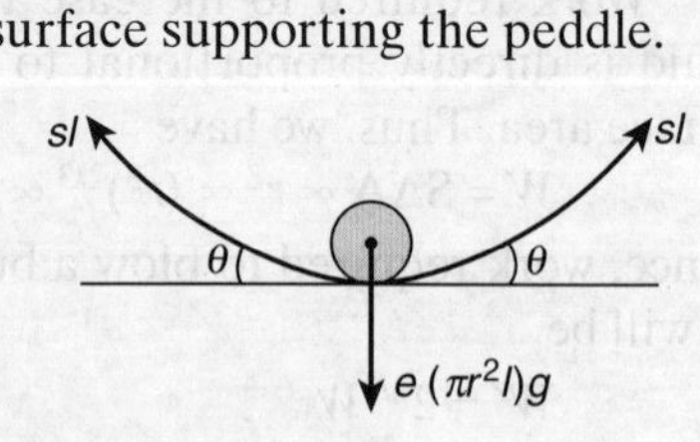

Using dynamics, we have

$$2Sl \sin\theta = \rho(\pi r^2 l)g$$

$$\Rightarrow \quad \sin\theta = \frac{\pi\rho r^2 g}{2S}$$

Since $\sin\theta < 1$

$$\frac{\pi\rho r^2 g}{2S} < 1 \Rightarrow r < \sqrt{\frac{2S}{\pi\rho g}}$$

8. (b) Let p be the pressure inside the capillary tube. The pressure on the outer side of the hemispherical bubble is $p_o + \rho gh$ (p_o is the atmospheric pressure). The radius of the bubble is equal to that of the tube, that is, r. Hence, we have

$$p - (p_o + \rho gh) = \frac{2S}{r}$$

$$\Rightarrow \quad p - p_o = \rho gh + \frac{2S}{r}$$

9. (b) The liquid meniscus has radius r (see figure), given by

$$r\cos\theta = d/2$$

$$\Rightarrow \quad r = \frac{d}{2\cos\theta}$$

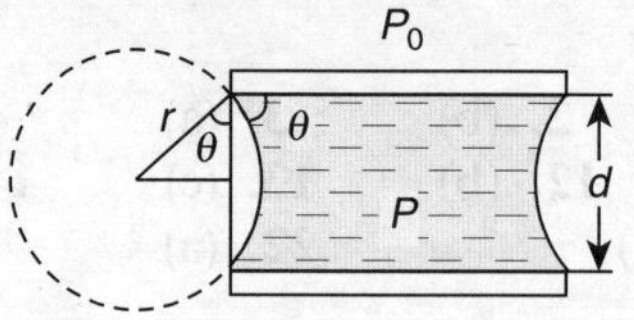

The pressure P of the liquid in between the plates is less than the atmospheric pressure P_o as can be seen from the shape of the meniscus which has caved inward. The meniscus is cylindrical in shape; its radius of curvature is r in one direction and ∞ in the other direction. Thus, we have

$$P_o - P = \frac{S}{r} + \frac{S}{\infty} = \frac{2S\cos\theta}{d}$$

Since the liquid pressure P is less than the atmospheric pressure P_o outside the plates, a net force $(P_o - P)A = \dfrac{2AS\cos\theta}{d}$ will be required to pull the plates away from each other.

10. (d) Since $h \propto \frac{1}{r}$, the mass of water that rises in the tube is $m = \rho\pi r^2 h \propto r$.

Hence, if the radius is doubled, the mass of water that rises in the tube will also double.

11. (b) Given $\frac{\Delta h}{h} = -0.5\%$ when $\frac{\Delta T}{T} = 1\%$

$$\Rightarrow \quad \frac{\Delta h}{h} = -\frac{1}{2}\frac{\Delta T}{T}$$

Also, we have $h \propto S$. Thus, we have

$$\Rightarrow \quad \frac{\Delta S}{S} = \frac{\Delta h}{h} = -\frac{1}{2}\frac{\Delta T}{T}$$

$$\Rightarrow \quad S \propto T^{-1/2}$$

12. (b) The figure shows the forces acting on the soap bubble.

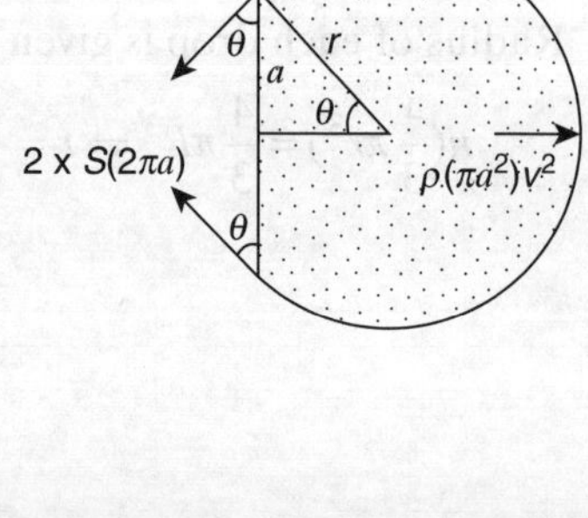

The air molecules are striking the inner side of the bubble with a force equal to the momentum flow rate = $\rho(\pi a^2)v^2$. This force is balanced by the horizontal component of the force due to surface tension. Thus, we have

$$2 \times S(2\pi a)\sin\theta = \rho(\pi a^2)\, v^2$$

$$\Rightarrow \quad 4\pi Sa \times \frac{a}{r} = \rho \pi a^2 v^2$$

$$\Rightarrow \quad r = \frac{4S}{\rho v^2}$$

13. (c) The figure shows the forces acting on the liquid drop. The weight of the liquid drop is balanced by the vertical component of the force due to surface tension.

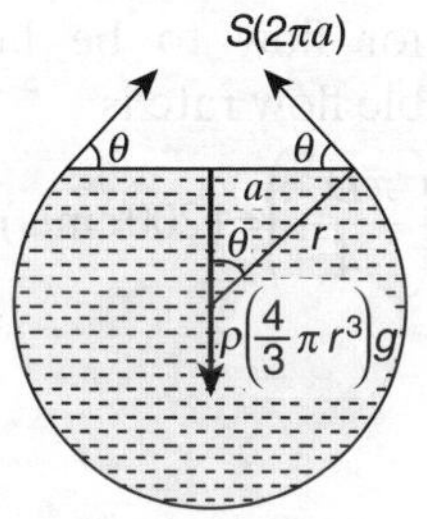

If r is the radius of the drop, then

$$S(2\pi a)\sin\theta = \rho\left(\frac{4}{3}\pi r^3\right)g$$

$$\Rightarrow \quad S(2\pi a) \times \frac{a}{r} = \frac{4}{3}\pi \rho g r^3$$

$$\Rightarrow \quad r = \left(\frac{3Sa^2}{2\rho g}\right)^{1/4}$$

14. (b) The figure shows the forces acting on the portion of the liquid that has risen in between the plates. The weight of the liquid column is balanced by the vertical component of the force due to surface tension.

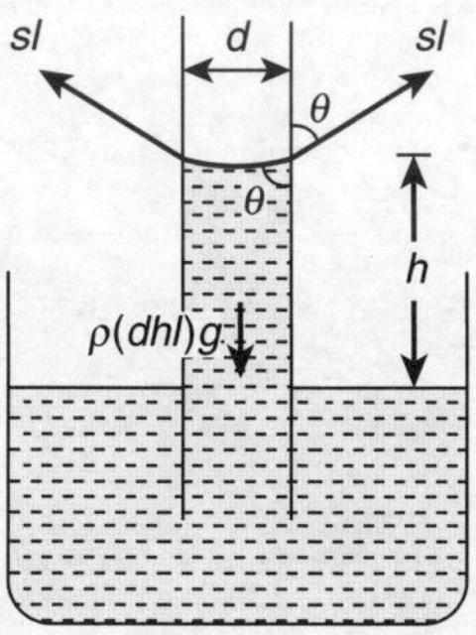

For a transverse length l of the liquid column, we have

$$2(Sl\cos\theta) = \rho(dhl)g$$

$$\Rightarrow \quad h = \frac{2S\cos\theta}{\rho g d}$$

15. (d) The angle between the meniscus surface and the vertical is $\theta + a/2$ (see figure).

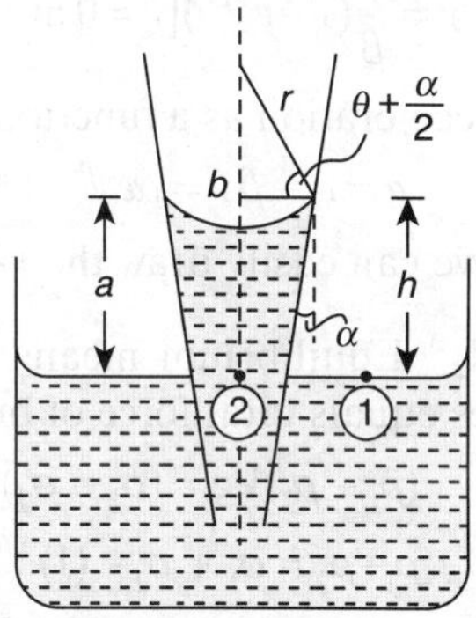

Pressure just below the meniscus is $p_0 - 2S/r$, where the radius r of the meniscus is given by $r\cos(\theta + a/2) = b$. Equating pressures at (1) and (2), we have

$$p_o - \frac{2S}{r} + \rho g h = p_o$$

$$\Rightarrow \quad h = \frac{2S}{\rho g r} = \frac{2S\cos(\theta + \alpha/2)}{\rho g b}$$

16. (b)

17. (a)

18. (a) The terminal velocity is given by

$$v_T = \frac{2(\rho - \sigma)gr^2}{9\eta}$$

Hence, we have

$$\frac{v_P}{v_Q} = \left(\frac{8-0.8}{8-1.6}\right)\left(\frac{1}{0.5}\right)^2\left(\frac{2}{3}\right) = 3$$

19. (d) The viscous force is $F = 6\pi\eta r v$ and hence the rate of heat dissipation is $P = Fv = 6\pi\eta r v^2$. Since $v_T \propto r^2$, when the ball has acquired terminal velocity, $P \propto r^5$.

20. (c) If v is the velocity of the raindrop at any instant, the net force on the raindrop in the downward direction is

$$F = \frac{4}{3}\pi r^3(\rho - \sigma)g - 6\pi n r v,$$

where ρ and σ are the densities of the raindrop and the surrounding air, respectively. The instantaneous acceleration is

$$\frac{dv}{dt} = \alpha - \beta v$$

Solving the above differential equation, we have

$$\frac{d(v - \alpha/\beta)}{dt} = -\beta(v - \alpha/\beta)$$

$\Rightarrow \quad v - \alpha/\beta = Ae^{-\beta t}$

$\Rightarrow \quad v = \frac{a}{\beta}(1 - e^{-\beta t})[v = 0 \text{ at } t = 0 \text{ gives } A = -\alpha/\beta]$

And acceleration as a function of time is

$$a = a - \beta v = \alpha e^{-\beta t}$$

Now, we can easily draw the v–t and a–t graphs.

21. (b), (d) Equilibrium means total weight of the spheres equals total force of buoyancy

$$(\rho_1 + \rho_2)Vg = (\sigma_1 + \sigma_2)Vg$$

$\Rightarrow \quad \rho_1 + \rho_2 = \sigma_1 + \sigma_2 - (1)$

String is taut means buoyancy > weight for ball 1, and weight > buoyancy for ball 2. Thus, we have

$$\sigma_1 < \sigma_1 \text{ and } \sigma_2 < \rho_2$$

Also note that liquid 1 is lighter than liquid 2, that is, $\sigma_1 < \sigma_2$. Thus, we have

$$\rho_1 < \sigma_1 < \sigma_2 < \rho_2$$

Taking the downward direction as +ve, the terminal velocities V_P and V_Q are proportional to

$$v_P \alpha \frac{\rho_1 - \sigma_2}{\eta_2} \text{ and } v_Q \alpha \frac{\rho_2 - \sigma_1}{\eta_1}$$

We can see that $V_P < 0$ and $V_Q > 0$. Hence, we have

$$\vec{v}_p \cdot \vec{v}_q < 0 \text{ and } \frac{|\vec{v}_P|}{|\vec{v}_Q|} = \frac{|\rho_1 - \sigma_2|}{|\rho_2 - \sigma_1|} \times \frac{\eta_1}{\eta_2} = \frac{\eta_1}{\eta_2}$$

22. (a) For laminar flow, $R < 1000$. Thus, we have

$$\frac{\rho v D}{\eta} < 1000$$

$$\Rightarrow v < \frac{1000\eta}{\rho D} = \frac{1000(0.04)}{(900)(0.02)} = 2.2 \text{ m/s.}$$

Hence, for flow to be laminar, the maximum permissible flow rate is

$$Q = v_{\max}\left(\frac{\pi D^2}{4}\right) = (200 \text{ cm/s}) \times \frac{\pi(2 \text{ cm})^2}{4} = 691 \text{ cm}^3/\text{s}$$

CHAPTER

10 Gravitation

- Newton's law of gravitation states that two particles with masses m_1 and m_2, separated by a distance r, attract each other with a force of magnitude

$$F = G\frac{m_1 m_2}{r^2},$$

where $G = 6.67\times10^{-11}\ \text{N}\cdot\text{m}^2/\text{kg}^2$ is called the constant of gravitation.

- A distribution of masses creates a gravitational field in the surrounding space. The gravitational field exerts a force **F** on any other mass m that is present in the field. The field intensity **g** at any field point is the force experienced per unit test mass present at that point:

$$\mathbf{g} = \lim_{m\to 0}\frac{\mathbf{F}}{m}$$

The test mass must be small enough so that it does not disturb the masses that cause the field. The value of g for a few mass distributions is as follows:

1. At distance r from a point mass M:

$$g = \frac{GM}{r^2}$$

2. At distance x from the centre (along the axis) of a uniform ring of mass M and radius R:

$$g = \frac{GMx}{\left(R^2 + x^2\right)^{3/2}} \quad \text{(greatest at } x = R/\sqrt{2}\text{)}$$

3. At distance r from the centre of a uniform spherical shell of mass M and radius R:

$$g = \begin{cases} 0, 0 \le r < R \\ \dfrac{g_0 R^2}{r^2}, r \ge R \end{cases}, \text{ where } g_0 = \frac{GM}{R^2} \text{ (intensity at the surface)}$$

4. At distance r from the centre of a uniform sphere of mass M and radius R:

$$g = \begin{cases} \dfrac{g_0}{R}r, 0 \le r < R \\ \dfrac{g_0 R^2}{r^2}, r \ge R \end{cases}, \text{ where } g_0 = \frac{GM}{R^2} \text{ (intensity at the surface)}$$

At small heights $h\ (h \ll R)$ above the surface of the uniform sphere, $g = g_0\left(1 - \dfrac{2h}{R}\right)$.

At small depths $d\ (d \ll R)$ below the surface of the uniform sphere, $g = g_0\left(1 - \dfrac{d}{R}\right)$.

- The field potential V at any field point is the negative of the work done by the field per unit test mass, as it moves from infinity to that point:

$$V = -\int_{\infty}^{r}\mathbf{g}\cdot d\mathbf{r}$$

The value of V (with respect to infinity) for a few mass distributions:

1. At distance r from a point mass M:

$$V = -\frac{GM}{r}$$

2. At distance x from the centre (along the axis) of a uniform ring of mass M and radius R:

$$V = -\frac{GM}{\left(R^2 + x^2\right)^{1/2}}$$

3. At distance r from the centre of a uniform spherical shell of mass M and radius R:

$$V = \begin{cases} V_0, 0 \le r < R \\ \dfrac{V_0 R}{r}, r \ge R \end{cases}, \text{ where } V_0 = -\frac{GM}{R} \text{ (potential at the surface)}$$

4. At distance r from the centre of a uniform sphere of mass M and radius R:

$$V = \begin{cases} \dfrac{3}{2}V_0\left(1 - \dfrac{r^2}{3R^2}\right), 0 \le r < R \\ \dfrac{V_0 R}{r}, r \ge R \end{cases}, \text{ where } V_0 = -\frac{GM}{R} \text{ (potential at the surface)}$$

- A particle of mass m, present at a field point with intensity **g** and potential V, experiences a force **F** and possesses potential energy U, given by

$$\mathbf{F} = m\mathbf{g} \text{ and } U = mV$$

When the point mass moves from one potential V_1 to another potential V_2, the work done by the gravitational field on the point mass is given by

$$W_{gr} = -\Delta U = -m\left(V_2 - V_1\right)$$

For a system of two particles with masses m_1 and m_2, separated by a distance r, the associated potential energy function is

$$U = -\frac{Gm_1 m_2}{r}$$

When the distance between the particles changes from r_i to r_f, the work done by the mutual gravitational force is given by

$$W_{gr} = -\Delta U = \frac{Gm_1 m_2}{r_i} - \frac{Gm_1 m_2}{r_f}$$

- For a body to escape the Earth's gravitational field, it must be thrown (in any direction) with a speed greater than the escape speed v_e, given by

$$v_e = \sqrt{\frac{2GM_E}{R}} \text{ or } \sqrt{2g_0 R} = 11.2 \text{ km/s}$$

Note that v_e is independent of the mass of the body.

- When a satellite moves around the Earth in a circular orbit, the centripetal acceleration is provide by the Earth's gravity. The speed v, the period T and energy E of a satellite in a circular orbit of radius r are given by

$$v = \sqrt{\frac{GM_E}{r}}, T = \frac{2\pi}{\sqrt{GM_E}} r^{3/2} \text{ and } E = -\frac{GM_E M_s}{2r}$$

The kinetic energy and the potential energy of the satellite are

$$K = -E \text{ and } U = 2E$$

A satellite that appears to be stationary relative to the Earth is called a geo-stationary satellite. The period of such a satellite is 24 hours and its orbit radius is roughly 42000 km.

EXERCISES

1. The acceleration due to gravity on the Earth's surface is g. For a planet whose radius is two-third that of the Earth and with density twice that of Earth, the acceleration due to gravity on its surface is:
(a) $\frac{4}{3}g$ (b) g
(c) $\frac{1}{2}g$ (d) $\frac{1}{4}g$

2. A small planet is revolving around a massive star in a circular orbit of radius R. If the gravitational force between the planet and the star were inversely proportional to R^n, then the angular momentum of the planet about the centre of the star will be proportional to:
(a) $R^{\frac{n-1}{2}}$ (b) $R^{\frac{n+3}{2}}$
(c) $R^{\frac{1+n}{2}}$ (d) $R^{\frac{3-n}{2}}$

3. If g is acceleration due to gravity on the Earth's surface, then the work required to raise an object of mass m from depth $R/2$ to height equal to the Earth's radius R is:
(a) $\frac{1}{4}mgR$ (b) $\frac{7}{8}mgR$
(c) $\frac{3}{4}mgR$ (d) mgR

4. The acceleration due to gravity at the surface of a planet of radius R is g. It decreases by 10% at a certain height above its surface. The gravitational potential at this height is:
(a) $\frac{-1}{\sqrt{10}}gR$ (b) $\frac{-2}{\sqrt{10}}gR$
(c) $\frac{-3}{\sqrt{10}}gR$ (d) $\frac{-4}{\sqrt{10}}gR$

5. Earth's average density is determined using the values of acceleration due to gravity g at the Earth's surface and the radius R of the Earth. If there is an error of ±1% and ±1.5% in the measurement of g and R, respectively, then the maximum error in the calculated average density of the Earth will be:
(a) 4.0% (b) 3.5%
(c) 2.5% (d) 0.5%

6. A geo-stationary satellite is orbiting the Earth at a height of $6R$ above the Earth's surface, where R is the Earth's radius. The period of another satellite at a height $2.5R$ from the Earth's surface is:
(a) $3\sqrt{2}$ h (b) $4\sqrt{2}$ h
(c) $6\sqrt{2}$ h (d) $12\sqrt{2}$ h

7. The masses of the Earth and Moon are M and $M/81$, respectively. The distance between their centres is d. An object of mass m is to be projected from a point where the gravitational intensity due to the Earth and Moon is zero. The minimum kinetic energy required so that the object escapes to infinity is:
(a) $\frac{100GMm}{9d}$ (b) $\frac{100GMm}{81d}$
(c) $\frac{100GMm}{729d}$ (d) $\frac{GMm}{9d}$

8. A particle is moving in a circular path of radius R under the influence of an attractive force field. If potential energy is given by $U = -\frac{k}{2r^2}$ (k is a positive constant), then the total mechanical energy of the particle is:
(a) $-\frac{k}{3r^2}$ (b) $-\frac{k}{4r^2}$
(c) $\frac{k}{5r^2}$ (d) 0

9. An object thrown vertically upwards with velocity v from the Earth's surface reaches its maximum height where the Earth's gravitational intensity is one-fourth that at its surface. The escape velocity from the Earth's surface is:
(a) $\sqrt{2}v$ (b) $\sqrt{3}v$
(c) $2v$ (d) $3v$

10. An object weighs W on Earth. It is suspended by a spring balance from the ceiling of a satellite moving in an elliptical orbit around the Earth. The reading of the spring balance will be:
(a) Less than W but not zero
(b) Greater than W
(c) Depends on the satellite's position
(d) Zero

11. A satellite is revolving in a near-Earth orbit. A stone is to be thrown from inside the satellite so that it escapes the Earth's gravitational field. If v_e is the escape velocity from the Earth's surface, then the minimum velocity with which the stone must be thrown relative to the satellite is:

(a) $\frac{1}{\sqrt{2}} v_e$ (b) $\left(1+\frac{1}{\sqrt{2}}\right) v_e$

(c) $\left(1-\frac{1}{\sqrt{2}}\right) v_e$ (d) $(\sqrt{2}-1) v_e$

12. A particle is projected from the centre of a fixed uniform ring of radius R, with velocity v along its axis. The particle reaches a distance $2\sqrt{2}R$ along the axis. The escape velocity from the centre of the ring is:

(a) $\sqrt{2.4}\ v$ (b) $\sqrt{2}\ v$

(c) $\sqrt{1.8}\ v$ (d) $\sqrt{1.5}\ v$

13. A stone is thrown vertically upward from the Earth's surface with initial speed v. The Earth's radius is R and acceleration due to gravity at its surface is g. Neglecting atmospheric resistance, the maximum height attained by the stone is:

(a) $R\left(\frac{2gR}{v^2}+1\right)^{-1}$ (b) $R\left(1+\frac{v^2}{2gR}\right)^{-1}$

(c) $R\left(\frac{2gR}{v^2}-1\right)^{-1}$ (d) $R\left(1-\frac{v^2}{2gR}\right)^{-1}$

14. If R is the Earth's radius, the minimum energy required to launch a satellite of mass m from the Earth's surface into an orbit of altitude $2R$ is:

(a) $\frac{GMm}{3R}$ (b) $\frac{GMm}{2R}$

(c) $\frac{2GMm}{3R}$ (d) $\frac{5GMm}{6R}$

15. The period of revolution of a satellite in circular orbit is T. The kinetic energy is proportional to:

(a) T^{-1} (b) T^{-2}

(c) T^{-3} (d) $T^{-2/3}$

16. Satellite A is moving in a circular orbit of radius r around the Earth. Satellite B is moving in a radius $1.01r$ around the Earth. The period of revolution of satellite B is longer than that of satellite A by:

(a) 0.5% (b) 1%

(c) 1.5% (d) 2%

17. Two masses m_1 and m_2 initially at rest are an infinite distance apart. They move towards each other under mutual gravitational attraction. When separation between them reduces to r, the relative velocity of approach will be:

(a) $\sqrt{\frac{2G(m_1+m_2)}{r}}$ (b) $\sqrt{\frac{G(m_1+m_2)}{2r}}$

(c) $\sqrt{\frac{Gm_1m_2}{r(m_1+m_2)}}$ (d) $\sqrt{\frac{2Gm_1m_2}{r(m_1+m_2)}}$

18. A uniform sphere of mass M and radius R exerts a force F on a small body of mass m situated at a distance of $2R$ from its centre O. A spherical cavity of diameter R is cut from the sphere, as shown in the figure.

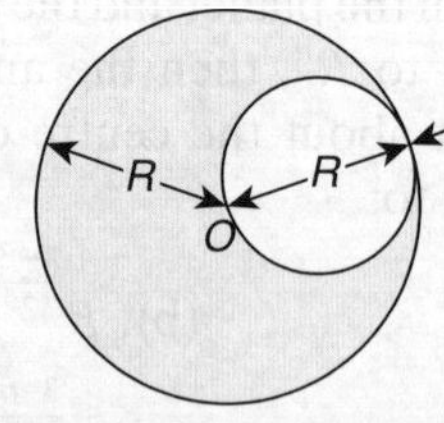

The force of attraction between the remaining portion of the sphere and the mass m is:

(a) $\frac{7}{36}F$ (b) $\frac{2}{3}F$

(c) $\frac{4}{9}F$ (d) $\frac{7}{9}F$

19. The figure shows a uniform sphere of radius 4 units located with its centre at origin O of coordinates. Two spherical cavities of equal radii 1 unit with their centres at $A(2,0,0)$ and $B(-2,0,0)$ are taken out from the solid sphere.

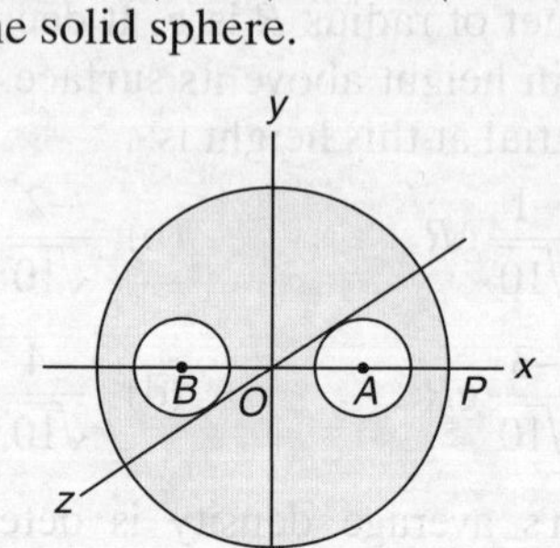

The ratio of the gravitational field intensities at $P(4,0,0)$ and at A equals:

(a) $\frac{536}{279}$ (b) $\frac{134}{31}$

(c) $\frac{172}{81}$ (d) $\frac{64}{31}$

20. A massive spherical planet has radius R, and the gravitational intensity at its surface is g. A long rigid rod of length l, with its length aligned along a line passing through the planet's centre (see figure), is revolving around the planet with angular velocity $\omega = \sqrt{\dfrac{g}{42R}}$.

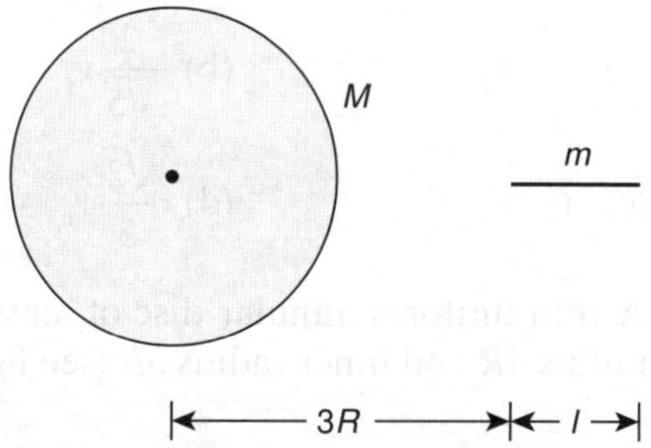

Then the value of l/R is:

(a) $1/5$ (b) $2/5$
(c) $2/3$ (d) 1

21. A binary star system consists of two stars of masses m_1 and m_2 revolving in circular orbits about their common centre of mass. Their kinetic energies are in the ratio:

(a) $\dfrac{m_1}{m_2}$ (b) $\dfrac{m_2}{m_1}$

(c) $\sqrt{\dfrac{m_1}{m_2}}$ (d) $\sqrt{\dfrac{m_2}{m_1}}$

22. A smooth straight tunnel is made through the Earth from one end to the other, passing at a perpendicular distance h from the earth's centre. A body released from one end of the tunnel executes SHM (simple harmonic motion) with time period (Earth's radius = R and intensity at Earth's surface = g):

(a) $2\pi\sqrt{\dfrac{h}{g}}$ (b) $2\pi\sqrt{\dfrac{R^2-h^2}{gR}}$

(c) $2\pi\sqrt{\dfrac{R}{g}}$ (d) $2\pi\sqrt{\dfrac{R^2}{g(R+h)}}$

23. A planet as dense as the Earth has radius $R = \dfrac{1}{10} \times$ Radius of Earth. A hole of depth $R/5$ is dug on the planet and a wire of the same length and linear density 10^{-3} kg/m is hung into the hole. The force required to hold the wire from the top is (take Earth's radius = 6×10^6 m and gravitational intensity at Earth's surface = 10 N/kg):

(a) 150 N (b) 108 N
(c) 120 N (d) 150 N

24. The figure shows a uniform sphere of radius 4 units located with its centre at origin O of coordinates. Two spherical cavities of equal radii 1 unit with their centres at $A(2,0,0)$ and $B(-2,0,0)$ are taken out from the solid sphere.

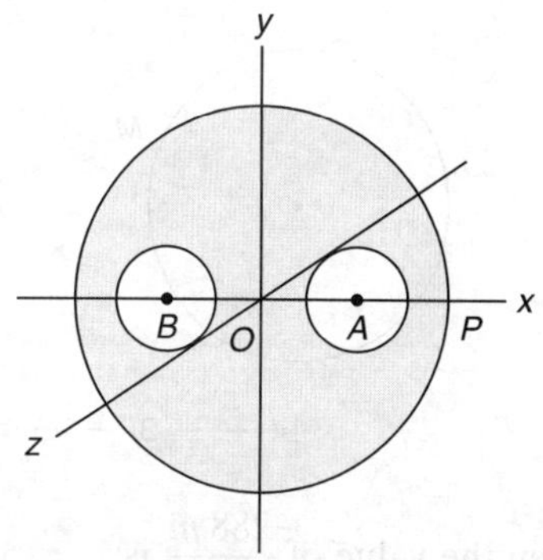

Choose the correct statements from the following:
(a) Gravitational intensity at O is zero
(b) Gravitational intensity at A is zero
(c) Gravitational potential is the same at all points on the circle $y^2 + z^2 = 36$
(d) Gravitational potential is the same at all points on the circle $x^2 + z^2 = 36$

25. Three stars, each of mass M, form an equilateral triangle of side a. If the only force acting on them is their mutual gravitational force, then each one of them must be moving with velocity:

(a) $\sqrt{\dfrac{2GM}{a}}$ (b) $\sqrt{\dfrac{3GM}{a}}$

(c) $\sqrt{\dfrac{GM}{3a}}$ (d) $\sqrt{\dfrac{GM}{a}}$

26. From a uniform sphere of radius R, a spherical cavity of diameter R is removed, as shown in the figure.

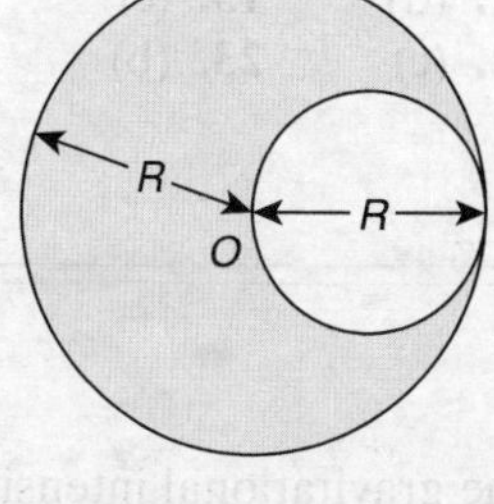

If g is the gravitational intensity at the centre of the cavity, then the gravitational potential at the centre of the cavity is:
(a) $-gR$ (b) $-2gR$
(c) $-3gR$ (d) $-4gR$

27. A large spherical mass M is fixed at one position. A dumb-bell consisting of two point masses m connected by a light rigid rod of length l is free to move along a line passing through the centre of M, as shown in the figure. All three masses interact through their mutual gravitational attraction only. When the distance between M and the nearer point mass is $3l$, tension in the rod equals zero.

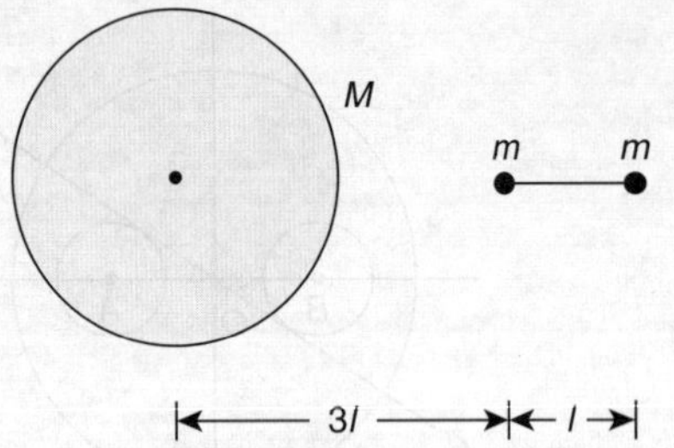

Then the value of $\frac{288\,m}{M}$ is:

(a) 5 (b) 6
(c) 7 (d) 8

28. A liquid drop radius of R in free space is in equilibrium under in its own gravity. If $P(r)$ is the pressure at a distance r $(r \le R)$ from its centre, then $\frac{P(3R/4)}{P(2R/3)}$ equals:

(a) $\frac{7}{18}$ (b) $\frac{63}{80}$
(c) $\frac{16}{21}$ (d) $\frac{20}{27}$

29. A spherical shell of outer radius R and inner radius $R/2$ has a narrow tunnel through which tiny particles can pass. Let v_e be the escape velocity for a particle lying inside the shell. If a particle was shot from the outer surface of the shell with velocity $\frac{4}{3}v_e$, then its velocity at a faraway point will be:

(a) $\frac{2}{\sqrt{3}}v_e$ (b) $\frac{2}{\sqrt{5}}v_e$
(c) v_e (d) $\frac{\sqrt{2}}{3}v_e$

30. A thin uniform annular disc of mass M has outer radius $4R$ and inner radius $3R$ (see figure).

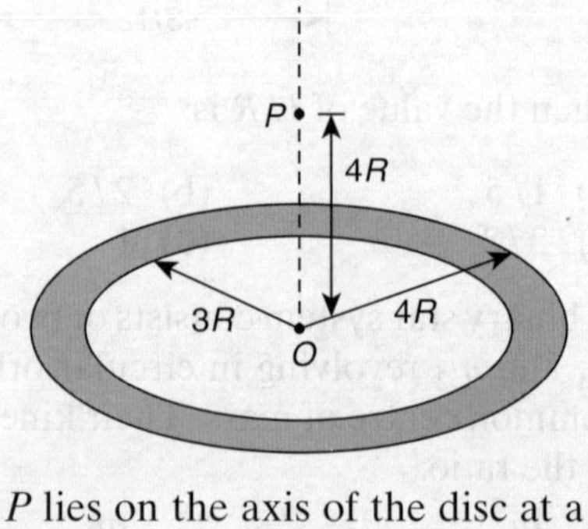

A point P lies on the axis of the disc at a distance $4R$ from its centre. If $W = \alpha\left(\frac{2GM}{7R}\right)$ is the work required to take a unit mass from point P to infinity, then the value of α is:

(a) $2\sqrt{2}+5$ (b) $2\sqrt{2}-5$
(c) $4\sqrt{2}+5$ (d) $4\sqrt{2}-5$

ANSWER KEYS

1. (a)	**2.** (d)	**3.** (b)	**4.** (c)	**5.** (c)	**6.** (c)	**7.** (b)	**8.** (d)	**9.** (a)	**10.** (d)
11. (c)	**12.** (d)	**13.** (c)	**14.** (d)	**15.** (d)	**16.** (c)	**17.** (a)	**18.** (d)	**19.** (a)	**20.** (d)
21. (b)	**22.** (c)	**23.** (b)	**24.** (a),(c)	**25.** (d)	**26.** (b)	**27.** (c)	**28.** (b)	**29.** (c)	**30.** (d)

SOLUTIONS

1. (a) The gravitational intensity at the surface of a spherical body is given by

$$g = \frac{GM}{R^2} \propto \frac{\rho R^3}{R^2} \propto \rho R$$

[ρ is the density and R is the radius]

If g' is the gravitational intensity at the surface of the planet, then

$$\frac{g'}{g} = 2 \times \frac{2}{3} = \frac{4}{3} \Rightarrow g' = \frac{4}{3}g$$

2. (d) If m is the mass of the planet, then its angular velocity w is given by

$$m\omega^2 R = \frac{c}{R^n} \Rightarrow \omega \propto R^{-\left(\frac{n+1}{2}\right)}$$

The angular momentum of the star is

$$L = (mR^2)\omega \propto R^{\frac{3-n}{2}}$$

3. (d) The gravitational potentials of the initial and final positions are, respectively

$$V_i = \frac{-3GM}{2R}\left(1 - \frac{R^2/4}{3R^2}\right) = \frac{-11GM}{8R} \text{ and}$$

$$V_f = \frac{-GM}{2R}$$

Using the Work–Energy Theorem, we have

$$W = m\Delta V = m\left(\frac{-GM}{2R} - \frac{-11GM}{8R}\right) = \frac{7GMm}{8R}$$

$$= \frac{7}{8}mgR \quad [\text{Putting } GM = gR^2]$$

4. (c) Let r be the distance where the field is $9g/10$. Then

$$\frac{9g}{10}r^2 = gR^2 \Rightarrow r = \frac{\sqrt{10}}{3}R$$

Gravitational potential at this position is

$$V = -\frac{GM}{r} = -\frac{3GM}{\sqrt{10}R}$$

$$= -\frac{3}{\sqrt{10}}gR \quad [\text{Putting } GM = gR^2]$$

5. (c) The gravitational intensity at the Earth's surface is given by

$$g = \frac{GM}{R^2} \propto \frac{\rho R^3}{R^2} \propto \rho R \Rightarrow \rho \propto gR^{-1}$$

Now, taking the differential, we have

$$\frac{\Delta\rho}{\rho} = \frac{\Delta g}{q} - \frac{\Delta R}{R}$$

Hence, the maximum error in the determination of ρ is

$$\frac{\Delta\rho}{\rho} = 1\% + 1.5\% = 2.5\%$$

6. (c) Time period of revolution of a geo-stationary satellite is 24 hours. Now, since $T \propto R^{3/2}$, we have

$$\frac{T}{24\text{ h}} = \frac{(3.5R)^{3/2}}{(7R)^{3/2}}$$

$$\Rightarrow \quad T = \frac{24\text{ h}}{2\sqrt{2}} = 6\sqrt{2}\text{ h}$$

7. (b) Let d_1, d_2 be the distances of the neutral point from the Earth and Moon, respectively. Then, we have

$$d_1 + d_2 = d \text{ and } \frac{GM}{d_1^2} = \frac{GM/81}{d_2^2} \Rightarrow \frac{d_1}{9} = \frac{d_2}{1}$$

Solving the two equations, we have $d_1 = 9d/10$ and $d_2 = d/10$

The gravitational potential energy of mass m at this position is

$$U = \frac{-GMm}{9d/10} + \frac{-G(M/81)m}{d/10} = \frac{-100GMm}{81d}$$

The minimum kinetic energy K required to escape from this position is given by

$$K + U = 0 \Rightarrow K = \frac{100GMm}{81d}$$

8. (d) Since $U = -\frac{k}{2r^2} \Rightarrow F = -\frac{dU}{dr} = -\frac{k}{r^3}$

The –ve sign indicates that the force is directed radially inwards. Now, using dynamics along the centripetal direction, we have

$$\frac{k}{r^3} = m(\omega^2 r) \Rightarrow \omega^2 = \frac{k}{mr^4}$$

The kinetic energy is $K = \frac{1}{2}mr^2\omega^2 = \frac{k}{2r^2}$

Hence, the mechanical energy is $E = K + U = 0$.

9. (a) Let R be the Earth's radius and g be the gravitational intensity at the Earth's surface. The gravitational intensity falls to $g/4$ at distance $2R$ from the Earth's centre. According to the question, the object thrown with velocity v rises to this position. If M and m are the respective masses of the Earth and the object, then we have

$$\frac{1}{2}mv^2 - \frac{GMm}{R} = -\frac{GMm}{2R} \Rightarrow v = \sqrt{\frac{GM}{R}}$$

The escape velocity from the Earth's surface is

$$v_e = \sqrt{\frac{2GM}{R}} = \sqrt{2}v$$

10. (d)

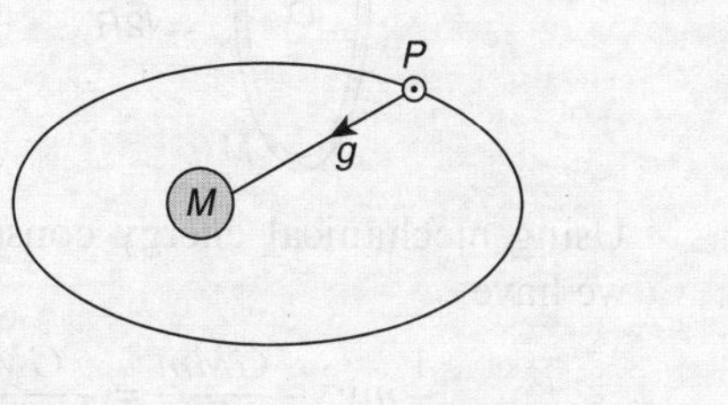

At any position P in its path (see figure), the satellite is moving with acceleration $\vec{a} = \vec{g}$, which is directed towards the central mass, and its magnitude equals the gravitational intensity of M at P.

The effective gravity $\vec{g}_{eff}$ experienced by a person sitting inside the satellite is the vector sum of gravitational intensity $\vec{g}$ due to M and $-\vec{a}$ (due to the pseudo force).

Hence, $\vec{g}_{eff} = \vec{g} - \vec{a} = 0$

11. (c) Let M and R be the Earth's mass and radius, respectively. Escape velocity from the Earth's surface is $v_e = \sqrt{\dfrac{2GM}{R}}$. The satellite is moving in near-Earth orbit, hence its velocity is $v_c = \sqrt{\dfrac{GM}{R}} = v_e/\sqrt{2}$. If the stone is thrown with relative velocity v at angle θ to the velocity of the satellite, then its absolute velocity will be $\sqrt{v^2 + v_c^2 + 2vv_c\cos\theta}$. For the stone to escape, we have

$$\frac{1}{2}m(v^2 + v_c^2 + 2vv_c\cos\theta) = \frac{GMm}{R}$$

$$\Rightarrow \quad v^2 + v_c^2 + 2vv_c\cos\theta = v_e^2$$

For $\theta = 0$ and $\theta = \pi$, we have

$$v = v_e - v_c = \left(1 - \frac{1}{\sqrt{2}}\right)v_e \text{ and}$$

$$v = v_e + v_c = \left(1 + \frac{1}{\sqrt{2}}\right)v_e$$

Note that the velocity v required for escape is least when the stone is thrown along the velocity of the satellite.

12. (d) Let M be the mass of the ring and m be the mass of the particle. When the particle is at distance $\sqrt{2}R$ from the centre of the ring, its distance from all points on the circumference of the ring is $3R$ (see figure).

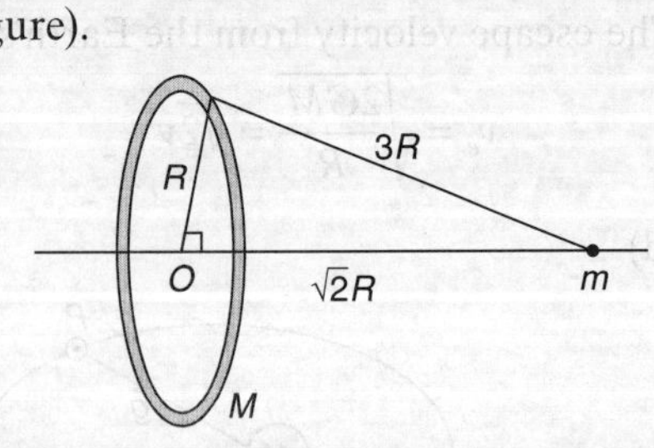

Using mechanical energy conservation principle, we have

$$\frac{1}{2}mv^2 - \frac{GMm}{R} = -\frac{GMm}{3R} \Rightarrow v^2 = \frac{4GM}{3R}$$

If v_e is the escape velocity, then

$$\frac{1}{2}mv_e^2 - \frac{GMm}{R} = 0 \Rightarrow v_e^2 = \frac{2GM}{R}$$

Now, we have

$$\frac{v_e^2}{v^2} = \frac{3}{2} \Rightarrow v_e = \sqrt{1.5}v$$

13. (c) Let h be the maximum height attained by the stone. Using mechanical energy conservation principle, we have

$$-\frac{GMm}{R+h} = -\frac{GMm}{R} + \frac{1}{2}mv^2$$

$$\Rightarrow \quad \frac{1}{R} - \frac{1}{R+h} = \frac{v^2}{2GM}$$

$$\Rightarrow \quad \frac{h}{R(R+h)} = \frac{v^2}{2aR^2} \quad \text{[Putting } GM = gr^2\text{]}$$

$$\Rightarrow \quad \frac{R+h}{h} = \frac{2gR}{v^2}$$

$$\Rightarrow \quad \frac{R}{h} = \frac{2gR}{v^2} - 1$$

$$\Rightarrow \quad h = \left(\frac{2gR}{v^2} - 1\right)^{-1} R$$

14. (d) The mechanical energy of a satellite in orbit of radius $3R$ is $E = -\dfrac{GMm}{2(3R)}$

Potential energy at the Earth's surface is $U = -\dfrac{GMm}{R}$. The required kinetic energy is given by

$$K + U = E \Rightarrow K = E - U$$

$$= \left(\frac{-GMm}{6R}\right) - \left(\frac{-GMm}{R}\right) = \frac{5GMm}{6R}$$

15. (d) For a satellite moving in a circular orbit of radius R, its period of revolution T and kinetic energy K are given by

$$T = \frac{2\pi}{\sqrt{GM}}R^{3/2} \propto R^{3/2} \text{ and } K = \frac{GMm}{2R} \propto \frac{1}{R}$$

Hence, we have $K \propto T^{-2/3}$

16. (c) From Kepler's third law, $T \propto r^{3/2}$. Now, taking the differential, we have

$$\frac{\Delta T}{T} = \frac{3}{2}\frac{\Delta r}{r} = \frac{3}{2} \times 1\% = 1.5\%$$

17. (a)

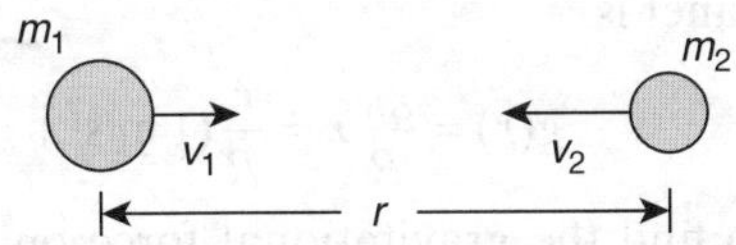

Let the velocities be v_1 and v_2 when the separation between them is r (see figure).

From momentum conservation principle, we have

$$m_1v_1 - m_2v_2 = 0 \text{ [Initial momentum = 0]}$$

$$\Rightarrow \quad \frac{v_1}{m_2} = \frac{v_2}{m_1} \qquad \ldots(1)$$

From mechanical energy conservation principle, we have

$$-\frac{Gm_1m_2}{r} + \frac{1}{2}m_1v_1^2 + \frac{1}{2}m_2v_2^2 = 0$$

[Initial energy = 0]

$$\Rightarrow \quad m_1v_1^2 + m_2v_2^2 = \frac{2Gm_1m_2}{r} \qquad \ldots(2)$$

Solving the two equations, we have

$$v_1 = \sqrt{\frac{2G}{(m_1+m_2)r}}m_2 \text{ and } v_2 = \sqrt{\frac{2G}{(m_1+m_2)r}}m$$

The velocity of approach is

$$v_1 + v_2 = \sqrt{\frac{2G(m_1+m_2)}{r}}$$

18. (d) Before the cavity is taken out, the field at the position of m is $g = \dfrac{GM}{(2R)^2}$. Radius of the cavity is $R/2$. Hence, the mass taken out is $M/8$. After the cavity is taken out, the field at the position of m is

$$g' = g_{\text{entire sphere}} - g_{\text{cut portion}}$$

$$= \frac{GM}{(2R)^2} - \frac{G(M/8)}{(1.5R)^2} = \frac{7GMm}{36R^2}$$

Hence, the ratio of the gravitational force on m in the two situations is

$$\frac{F'}{F} = \frac{g'}{a} = \frac{7}{9} \Rightarrow F' = \frac{7}{9}F$$

19. (a) Let M be the mass of the entire sphere of radius 4 units. Then, the mass of the spherical portions of radius 1 unit will be $M/64$ (mass cube of the radius). The gravitational intensity at P is

$$g_P = g_{\text{entire sphere}} - g_{\text{cut portion}}$$

$$= \frac{GM}{4^2} - \left[\frac{G(M/64)}{2^2} + \frac{G(M/64)}{6^2}\right] = \frac{133GM}{36\times 64}$$

The gravitational intensity at A is

$$g_A = g_{\text{entire sphere}} - g_{\text{cut portion}}$$

$$= \frac{(GM)2}{4^3} - \frac{G(M/64)}{4^2} = \frac{31GM}{16\times 64}$$

$$\text{Hence } \frac{g_P}{g_A} = \frac{134}{36\times 64}\times\frac{16\times 64}{31} = \frac{536}{279}$$

= (GM)2 – G(M/64) = 31 GM

20. (d)

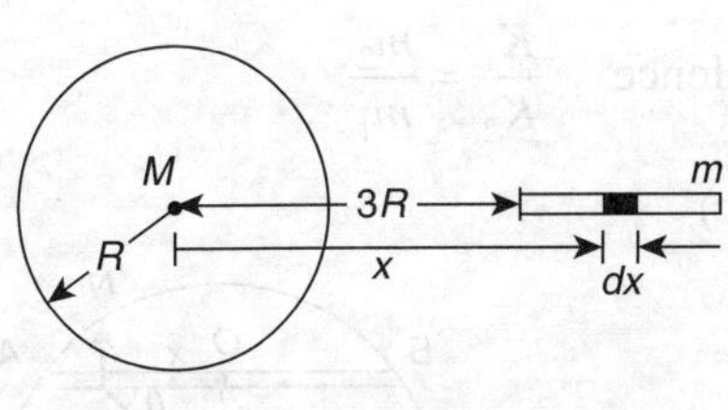

Let us subdivide the rod into elements, each of length dx. The mass of each element is $dm = \dfrac{m}{l}dx$.

The force on one such element at distance x from the planet's centre is

$$dF = \frac{gR^2}{x^2}dm = \frac{mgR^2}{1}\frac{dx}{x^2}$$

The total force on the rod is

$$F = \frac{mgR^2}{I}\int_{3R}^{3R+1}\frac{dx}{x^2}$$

$$= \frac{mgR^2}{I}\left(\frac{1}{3R} - \frac{1}{3R+1}\right) = \frac{mgR}{3(3R+I)}$$

The CM of the rod is moving in a circle of radius 3R +1/2. Hence

$$F = m\omega^2(3R + 1/2)$$

$$\Rightarrow \quad \frac{mgR}{3(3R+I)} = m\left(\frac{g}{42R}\right)\left(3R + \frac{I}{2}\right)$$

$$\Rightarrow \quad l^2 + 9Rl - 10R^2 = 0 \Rightarrow l = R$$

(Neglecting the –ve root)

21. (b)

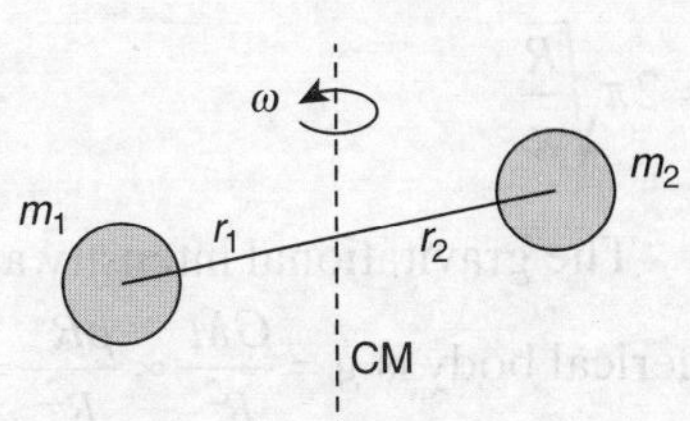

The two stars rotate with the same angular speed ω in circles of different radii r_1 and r_2 (see figure).

The centres of their circular paths coincide with their centre of mass. Hence, we have

$$m_1r_1 = m_2r_2 \Rightarrow \frac{r_1}{m_2} = \frac{r_2}{m_1}$$

Their kinetic energies are

$$K_1 = \frac{1}{2}m_1r_1^2\omega^2 \propto m_1m_2^2 \text{ and}$$

$$K_2 = \frac{1}{2}m_2r_2^2\omega^2 \propto m_1^2m_2$$

Hence $\dfrac{K_1}{K_2} = \dfrac{m_2}{m_1}$

22. (c)

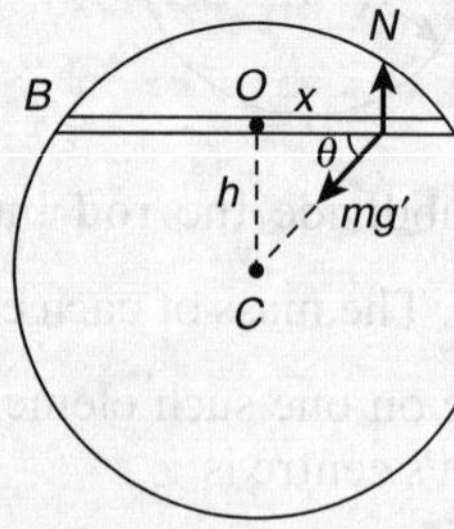

Force on the body is zero in the middle of the tunnel; the Earth's gravitational pull is balanced by the normal contact force. Let us choose our origin O in the middle of the tunnel. The figure shows the forces on the body at some position x from O.

The gravitational intensity at this position is $g' = \dfrac{g\sqrt{x^2+h^2}}{R}$. The net force on the body is directed towards O, and has magnitude

$$F = mg'\cos\theta = mg\frac{\sqrt{x^2+h^2}}{R}\cdot\frac{x}{\sqrt{x^2+h^2}} = \left(\frac{mg}{R}\right)x$$

The instantaneous acceleration of the body is $a = -\dfrac{F}{m} = -\dfrac{g}{R}x$

This shows that the motion is SHM with period

$$T = 2\pi\sqrt{\frac{R}{g}}$$

23. (b) The gravitational intensity at the surface of a spherical body is $g = \dfrac{GM}{R^2} \propto \dfrac{\rho R^3}{R^2} = \rho F$

The planet is as dense as the Earth, but its radius is one-tenth that of the Earth. Hence, the gravitational intensity at the surface of the planet is $g_0 = \dfrac{1}{10}\times 10\text{ m/s}^2 = 1\text{ m/s}^2$. The gravitational intensity as a function of r for points inside the planet is

$$g(r) = \frac{g_o}{R}r = \frac{r}{R}(1\text{ m/s}^2)$$

To find the gravitational force on the wire, let us subdivide the wire into elements, each of length dr. The mass of each element is $dm = (10^{-3}\text{kg/m})dr$. The total weight of the wire is

$$W = \int_{4R/5}^{R} g(r)dm = \frac{10^{-3}}{R}\int_{4R/5}^{R} rdr$$

$$= \frac{9\times 10^{-3}}{50}R = 108\text{ N } [R = 6\times 10^5\text{ m}]$$

24. (a), (c) All answers can be explained from symmetry.

25. (d) The figure shows the forces acting on one of the stars. The net force is

$$F = \left(\frac{GM^2}{a^2}\right)(2\cos 30^\circ) = \frac{\sqrt{3}GM^2}{a^2}$$

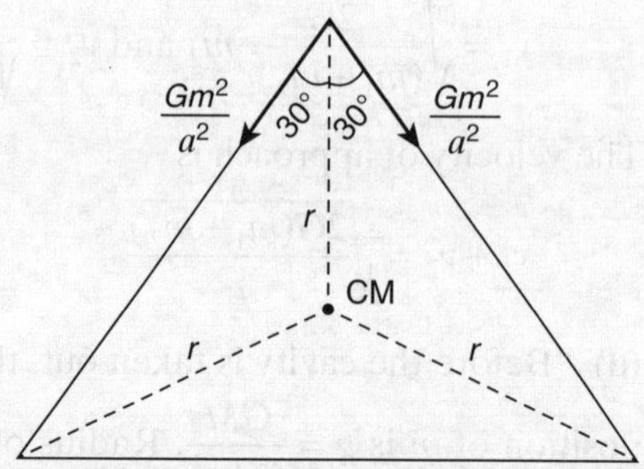

All the stars will move in circular orbits around their common centre of mass (CM).

Radius of the orbit is $r = \dfrac{2}{3}(a\sin 60^\circ) = \dfrac{a}{\sqrt{3}}$

Let v be the orbital velocity of the star. Using dynamics $F = mv^2/r$, we have

$$\frac{\sqrt{3}GM^2}{a^2} = \frac{mv^2}{a/\sqrt{3}} \Rightarrow v = \sqrt{\frac{GM}{a}}$$

26. (b) Let M be the mass of the entire sphere. The potential at the centre of the cavity due to the entire sphere is

$$V_1 = \frac{3GM}{2R}\left(1 - \frac{R^2/4}{3R^2}\right) = -\frac{11GM}{8R}$$

Radius of the cavity is $R/2$. Hence, the mass of the portion inside the cavity will be $M/8$. The potential at the centre of the cavity due to this mass portion is

$$V_2 = -\frac{3G(M/8)}{2(R/2)} = -\frac{3GM}{8R}$$

Hence, the potential at the centre of the cavity due to the remaining mass is

$$V = V_1 - V_2 = \left(\frac{-11GM}{8R}\right) - \left(\frac{-3GM}{8R}\right) = \frac{-GM}{R}$$

Similarly, the gravitational intensity at the centre of the cavity is

$$g = g_{\text{entire sphere}} - g_{\text{cut portion}} = \frac{GM(R/2)}{R^3} - 0 = \frac{GM}{2R^2}$$

Hence, we have $V = -2gR$

27. (c)

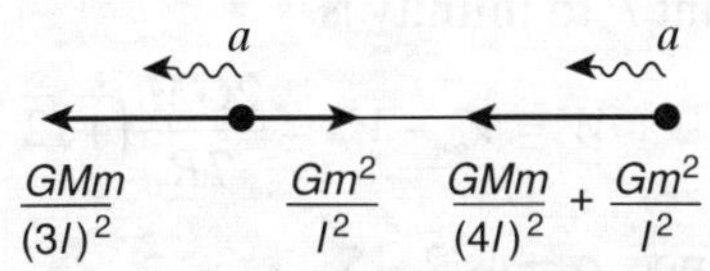

The figure shows the forces acting on the two point masses. Tension in the connecting rod is given to be zero. Let a be their acceleration. Using dynamics, we have

$$\frac{GMm}{(3l)^2} - \frac{Gm^2}{p^2} = ma \qquad \ldots(1)$$

$$\frac{GMm}{(4l)^2} + \frac{Gm^2}{p^2} = ma \qquad \ldots(2)$$

Eliminating a, we have

$$\frac{GMm}{a\,l^2} - \frac{GMm}{16l^2} = \frac{2Gm^2}{p} \Rightarrow \frac{7M}{144} = 2m \Rightarrow \frac{288m}{M} = 7$$

28. (b)

Let p and $p + dp$ be the pressures at distances r and $r + dr$, respectively. If g is the gravitational intensity at distance r, then we have

$$dp = -\rho g dr \qquad [\rho \text{ is the liquid density}]$$

Inside a uniform sphere, $g \propto r$. So let $g = cr$. Thus, we have

$$\int dp = -\rho c \int r dr$$

$$\Rightarrow \qquad p = -\frac{1}{2}\rho c r^2 + C$$

$$\Rightarrow \qquad p = \frac{1}{2}\rho c(R^2 - r^2) \text{ [Since } p = 0 \text{ at } r = R]$$

$$\text{Hence } \frac{p(3R/4)}{p(2R/3)} = \frac{1 - 9/16}{1 - 4/9} = \frac{63}{80}$$

29. (c) We need to first find the gravitational potential at the centre. To do so, let us subdivide the spherical mass into thin concentric shells, each of thickness dx. The mass of one such element of radius x is

$$dm = \frac{M}{\frac{4}{3}\pi(R^3 - R^3/8)} \times 4\pi x^2 dx = \frac{24M}{7R^3} x^2 dx$$

Gravitational potential at the centre due to this element is

$$dV = -\frac{Gdm}{x} = -\frac{24GM}{7R^3} x dx$$

The net value of the potential at the centre is

$$V_0 = -\frac{24GM}{7R^3} \int_{R/2}^{R} x dx = -\frac{9GM}{7R}$$

Hence, the escape velocity ve from the centre is given by

$$\frac{1}{2} m v_e^2 = \frac{9GMm}{7R} \Rightarrow v_e^2 = \frac{18GM}{7R}$$

To find the gravitational potential at the surface, the entire mass can be treated as a point mass concentrated at the centre. Thus, the potential at the centre is $V_s = -\frac{GM}{R}$. Hence, when it is thrown with velocity $\frac{4}{3}ve$ from the surface, its velocity v at a faraway point is given by

$$\frac{1}{2} m v^2 = \frac{1}{2} m \left(\frac{4}{3} v_e\right)^2 - \frac{GMm}{R}$$

$$\Rightarrow \qquad v^2 = \frac{16}{9} v_e^2 - \frac{7}{9} v_e^2 = v_e^2 \Rightarrow v = v_e$$

30. (d) We need to find the gravitational potential due to the disc, at point P. To do so, let us subdivide the disc into thin rings, each of width dx. The figure shows one such element ring of radius x.

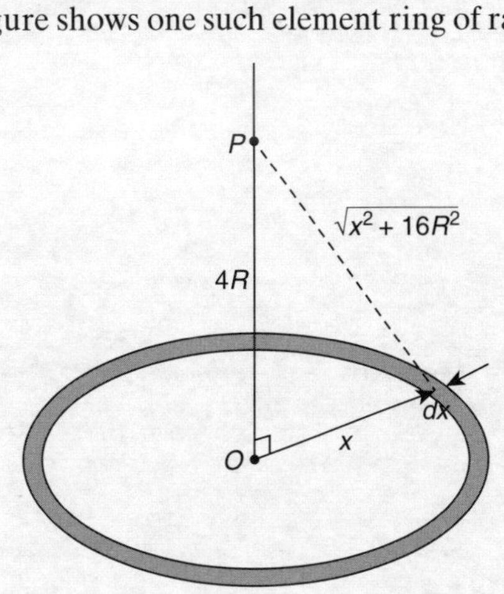

The surface area of the annular disc is $\pi(16R^2 - 9R^2) = 7\pi R^2$ and that of the element ring is $(2\pi x)dx$. Thus, the mass of the element ring is

$$dm = \frac{M}{7\pi R^2} \times (2\pi x)dx = \left(\frac{2M}{7R^2}\right)xdx$$

The gravitational potential at point P due to this element ring is

$$dV = -\frac{Gdm}{\sqrt{x^2+16R^2}}$$

$$= -\left(\frac{2GM}{7R^2}\right)\frac{xdx}{\sqrt{x^2+16R^2}}$$

Thus, the gravitational potential at P due to the entire disk is

$$V_P = -\frac{2GM}{7R^2}\int_{3R}^{4R}\frac{xdx}{\sqrt{x^2+16R^2}}$$

$$= -\frac{GM}{7R^2}\int_{25R^2}^{32R^2}\frac{dt}{\sqrt{t}}$$

[Put $x^2 + 16R^2 = t$ and $2xdx = dt$]

$$= -\frac{GM}{7R^2}\left|2\sqrt{t}\right|_{25R^2}^{35R^2} = -\frac{2GM}{7R}\left(4\sqrt{2}-5\right)$$

Thus, the work required to take a unit mass from point P to infinity is

$$W = V_\infty - V_P = \frac{2GM}{7R}\left(4\sqrt{2}-5\right) \quad [V_\infty = 0]$$

Hence, $\alpha = 4\sqrt{2} - 5$.

CHAPTER

11 Simple Harmonic Motion

- Periodic motion is motion that repeats itself at regular intervals of time. It occurs when a body has a stable equilibrium position, and a restoring force or torque acts when the body is displaced from its equilibrium. Period T is the time for one cycle. Frequency f is the number of cycles per unit time:

$$f = \frac{1}{T}$$

Angular frequency ω is

$$\omega = 2\pi f$$

- If the net restoring force F is directly proportional to the displacement x from the equilibrium, the periodic motion is called linear simple harmonic motion. In that case, $F = -kx$ and acceleration is $a = -\frac{k}{m}x$. If we write $\frac{d^2x}{dt^2}$ in the place of a, we have

$$\frac{d^2x}{dt^2} = -\frac{k}{m}x$$

The solution to the above differential equation is $x = A\cos(\omega t + \phi)$, where $\omega = \sqrt{\frac{k}{m}}$

The angular frequency, frequency and period do not depend on the amplitude. They depend only upon mass m and force constant k:

$$\omega = \sqrt{\frac{k}{m}},\ f = \frac{1}{2\pi}\sqrt{\frac{k}{m}} \text{ and } T = 2\pi\sqrt{\frac{m}{k}}$$

- In undamped (no dissipating force) SHM, the position, velocity and acceleration are all sinusoidal functions of time:

$$x = A\cos(\omega t + \phi)$$

$$v = \omega A\cos\left(\omega t + \phi + \frac{\pi}{2}\right) = \omega\sqrt{A^2 - x^2}$$

$$a = \omega^2 A\cos(\omega t + \phi + \pi) = -\omega^2 x$$

where $\omega = \sqrt{k/m}$. A sinusoidal function can be represented by a phasor that rotates anti-clockwise, with angular velocity ω equal to the angular frequency of the function. Its projection on the horizontal axis at any instant represents the instantaneous value of the function.

The mechanical energy remains conserved:

$$\frac{1}{2}mv^2 + \frac{1}{2}kx^2 = \frac{1}{2}kA^2 \text{ (constant)}$$

If we replace ω with $2\pi f$, the oscillation energy is given by $E = 2\pi^2 mf^2 A^2$. Thus, the oscillation energy is directly proportional to the square of the frequency, and the square of the oscillation amplitude.

- In the case of angular SHM, the net restoring torque τ is directly proportional to the angular displacement θ from the equilibrium. In that case, $\tau = -c\theta$ and angular acceleration is $\alpha = -\frac{c}{I}\theta$. If we write $\frac{d^2\theta}{dt^2}$ in the place of α, we have

$$\frac{d^2\theta}{dt^2} = -\frac{c}{I}\theta$$

The solution to the above differential equation is $\theta = A\cos(\omega t + \phi)$.

The angular frequency, frequency and period do not depend on the angular amplitude. They depend only upon rotational inertia I and torsion constant c:

$$\omega = \sqrt{\frac{c}{I}},\ f = \frac{1}{2\pi}\sqrt{\frac{c}{I}} \text{ and } T = 2\pi\sqrt{\frac{I}{c}}$$

- A spring-mass oscillator consists of a body of mass M connected to one end of a spring of stiffness k. The period T is given by

$$T = 2\pi\sqrt{\frac{M}{k}}$$

If two bodies of masses m_1 and m_2 are connected to the extreme ends of a spring of stiffness k, the period T is given by

$$T = 2\pi\sqrt{\frac{M}{k}},$$

where $M = \frac{m_1 m_2}{m_1 + m_2}$ is called the reduced mass of the system.

A simple pendulum consists of a point mass m suspended by a string of length L. Its motion is approximately SHM for small amplitudes. The period T is given by

$$T = 2\pi\sqrt{\frac{L}{g}}$$

A physical pendulum is a body of mass M suspended from an axis of rotation a distance L above its centre of gravity. Its motion is approximately SHM for small amplitudes. If the moment of inertia about the axis of rotation is I, the period T is given by

$$T = 2\pi\sqrt{\frac{I}{MgL}}$$

- **Combination of Springs**: Two springs of spring constants k_1 and k_2, when connected in parallel, behave like a single spring of spring constant k given by

$$k = k_1 + k_2$$

and when connected in series, they behave like a single spring of spring constant k given by

$$\frac{1}{k} = \frac{1}{k_1} + \frac{1}{k_2}$$

In parallel combination, the deformation is the same for both springs. In series combination, the force is the same for both springs.

EXERCISES

1. In solid state, two silver atoms execute SHM along their bond, with frequency 10^{12} Hz. If the molar mass of silver is 108 g/mol, the force constant of the bond between the two silver atoms is (Avogadro's number $= 6.02 \times 10^{23}$):
(a) 8.42 N/m (b) 3.54 N/m
(c) 5.58 N/m (d) 2.26 N/m

2. Time period of a simple pendulum oscillating in vacuum is T. The pendulum is now completely immersed in a liquid whose density is four-third that of the pendulum mass. Neglecting viscosity, the time period will now be:
(a) $\sqrt{3}T$ (b) $2T$
(c) $\frac{2}{\sqrt{3}}T$ (d) $\frac{4}{3}T$

3. A small spherical ball is placed a little away from the centre of a large hemispherical bowl of radius R, and then released. If there is no friction, the time period of oscillation of the ball is:
(a) $2\pi\sqrt{R/2g}$ (b) $2\pi\sqrt{R/g}$
(c) $2\pi\sqrt{2R/g}$ (d) $2\pi\sqrt{3R/4g}$

4. The total length of the liquid column in the U-tube shown in the figure is L.

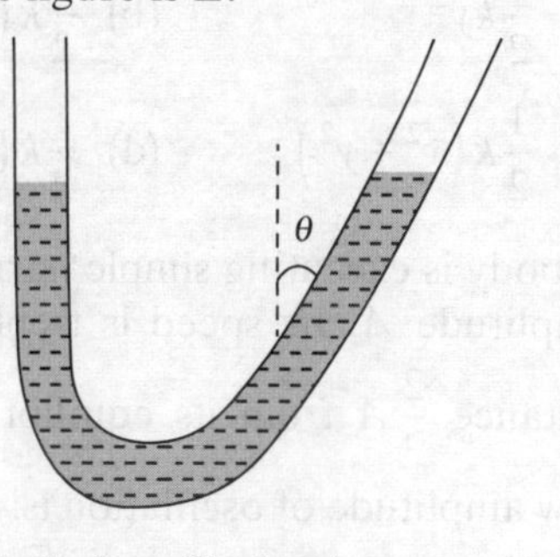

Its time period of oscillation is:
(a) $2\pi\sqrt{\frac{L}{(1+\cos\theta)g}}$ (b) $2\pi\sqrt{\frac{L\cos\theta}{g}}$
(c) $2\pi\sqrt{\frac{(1+\cos\theta)L}{g}}$ (d) $2\pi\sqrt{\frac{L}{g\sin\theta}}$

5. A cylindrical object of specific gravity 0.8, mass $m = 1.6$ kg and length $l = 0.4$ m is hung from the ceiling by a spring of stiffness $k = 110$ N/m, and its lower part is partially submerged in water (see figure).

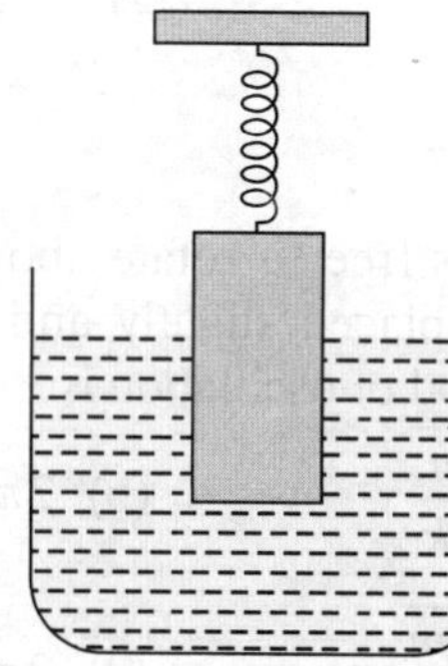

If the cylinder oscillates with amplitude $A = 0.5$ cm, its velocity amplitude is (neglect viscosity, take $g = 10\text{ m/s}^2$):
(a) 3 cm/s (b) 4 cm/s
(c) 5 cm/s (d) 6 cm/s

6. A pendulum clock loses 12 s a day if the temperature is 40°C, and gains 4 s a day if the temperature is 20°C. The temperature at which the clock shows correct time and the coefficient of linear expansion of the metal of the pendulum shaft are, respectively:
(a) 25°C, 2.25×10^{-5}°C^{-1}
(b) 25°C, 1.85×10^{-5}°C^{-1}
(c) 35°C, 2.25×10^{-5}°C^{-1}
(d) 35°C, 1.85×10^{-5}°C^{-1}

7. The figure shows a uniform disc of mass m connected to a spring of stiffness k.

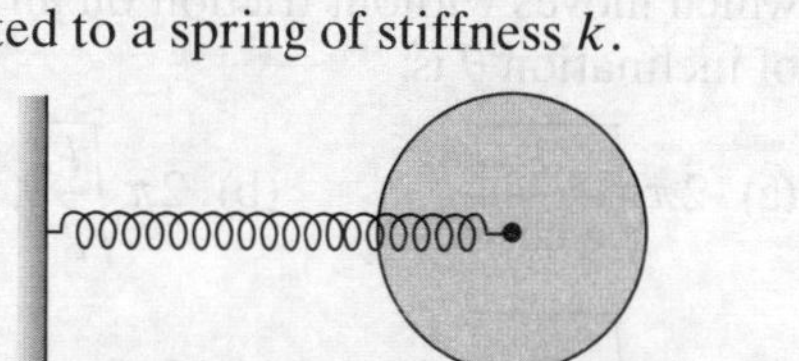

If the horizontal surface has friction coefficient μ, the maximum amplitude for which the disc can execute SHM without slipping is:
(a) $\frac{3\mu mg}{k}$ (b) $\frac{2\mu mg}{k}$
(c) $\frac{2\mu mg}{3k}$ (d) $\frac{3\mu mg}{4k}$

8. The ends of a uniform rod of mass m and length l are attached to two identical springs of stiffness k each, as shown in the figure.

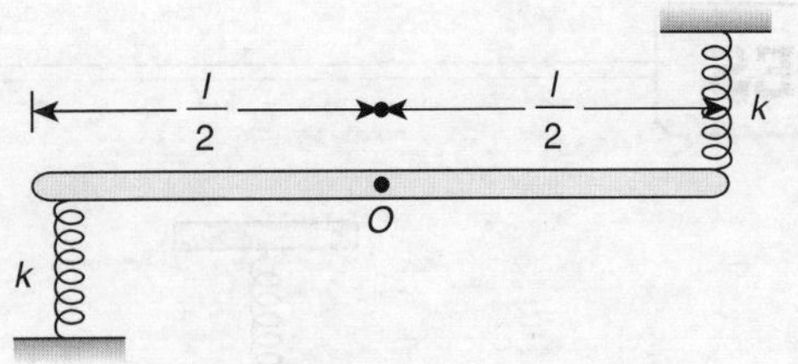

The rod is free to rotate about its centre O. The rod is displaced slightly and then released. The time period of oscillation is:

(a) $2\pi\sqrt{\frac{m}{2k}}$ (b) $2\pi\sqrt{\frac{m}{6k}}$

(c) $2\pi\sqrt{\frac{2m}{3k}}$ (d) $2\pi\sqrt{\frac{3m}{2k}}$

9. A block of mass m is hung vertically from the ceiling by a spring of stiffness k. Initially, the block is at rest. A bullet of mass m moving with velocity $v=\sqrt{\frac{6mg^2}{k}}$ in the vertically upward direction strikes the block from below and gets embedded in the block. The minimum time after which the spring will attain its natural length is:

(a) $\pi\sqrt{\frac{3m}{4k}}$ (b) $\pi\sqrt{\frac{m}{3k}}$

(c) $\pi\sqrt{\frac{2m}{9k}}$ (d) $\pi\sqrt{\frac{2m}{3k}}$

10. The time period of oscillation of a simple pendulum of length l suspended from the roof of a vehicle which moves without friction on an inclined plane of inclination θ is:

(a) $2\pi\sqrt{\frac{l}{g\cos\theta}}$ (b) $2\pi\sqrt{\frac{l}{g}}$

(c) $2\pi\sqrt{\frac{l}{g\sin\theta}}$ (d) Infinity

11. A spring-mass oscillator is hung vertically from the ceiling of a stationary elevator. The mass of the block is $m = 0.2$ kg and the spring constant is $k = 80$ N/m. The elevator starts moving up with acceleration $a = 0.2\ \text{m/s}^2$, and the block starts oscillating. The maximum velocity v_0 of the block relative to the elevator is:

(a) $v_0 = 6$ cm/s (b) $v_0 = 5$ cm/s
(c) $v_0 = 2.5$ cm/s (d) $v_0 = 1.5$ cm/s

12. A block of mass m is connected to a light spring of stiffness k. The spring is compressed by an amount A and the block is released. There is a rigid wall on the other side of the mean position at a distance $A/2$, as shown in the figure.

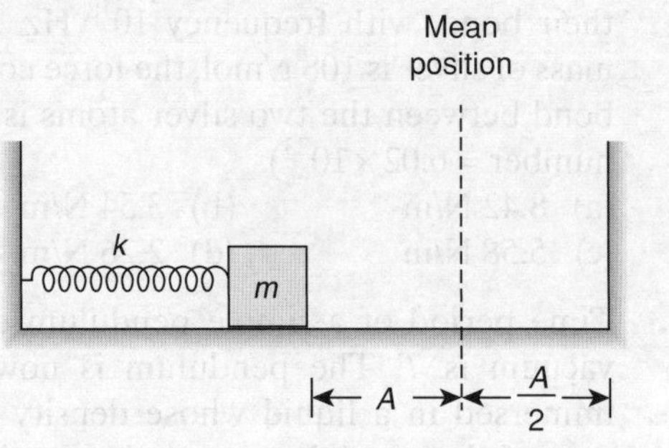

If the collision between the block and the wall is elastic, the period of oscillation is:

(a) $2\pi\sqrt{\frac{2m}{9k}}$ (b) $2\pi\sqrt{\frac{4m}{9k}}$

(c) $2\pi\sqrt{\frac{6m}{9k}}$ (d) $2\pi\sqrt{\frac{8m}{9k}}$

13. A light spring of spring constant k extends by an amount x when a mass m is hung from it. The mass is pulled down by a further distance y and then released. The system begins to execute simple harmonic motion. The maximum kinetic energy during oscillation is:

(a) $\frac{1}{2}ky^2$ (b) $\frac{1}{2}k(x+y)^2$

(c) $\frac{1}{2}k(x^2+y^2)$ (d) $\frac{1}{2}k(x+y)^2-\frac{1}{2}kx^2$

14. A body is executing simple harmonic motion with amplitude A. Its speed is trebled when it is at a distance $\frac{2}{3}A$ from its equilibrium position. The new amplitude of oscillation is:

(a) $3A$ (b) $\sqrt{3}A$

(c) $\frac{7}{3}A$ (d) $\frac{\sqrt{29}}{3}A$

15. The figure shows a smooth horizontal rod AB being rotated with angular speed ω about a vertical axis through end A. A sleeve of mass m, free to slide along the rod, is connected by a light spring of natural length l and stiffness k to end A of the rod. The spring is initially held in its natural state.

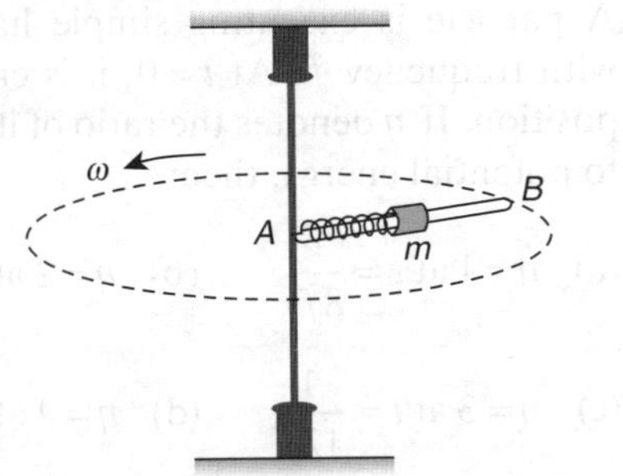

When it is released, the bead starts executing simple harmonic motion along the rod. The amplitude and frequency of oscillation is:

(a) Amplitude $= \left(\dfrac{m\omega^2}{k}\right)l$

(b) Amplitude $= \left(\dfrac{m\omega^2}{k - m\omega^2}\right)l$

(c) Frequency $= \dfrac{1}{2\pi}\sqrt{\dfrac{k}{m}}$

(d) Frequency $= \dfrac{1}{2\pi}\sqrt{\dfrac{k - m\omega^2}{m}}$

16. A simple pendulum oscillates with period T and angular amplitude α. At time $t = 0$, the pendulum is at angular position β, moving away from its mean position. The first time at which the pendulum crosses the same position is:

(a) $\left\{1 - \dfrac{1}{\pi}\cos^{-1}\left(\dfrac{\beta}{\alpha}\right)\right\}T$

(b) $\left\{\dfrac{1}{\pi}\cos^{-1}\left(\dfrac{\beta}{\alpha}\right)\right\}T$

(c) $\left\{2 - \dfrac{1}{\pi}\cos^{-1}\left(\dfrac{\beta}{\alpha}\right)\right\}T$

(d) $\left\{1 - \dfrac{1}{2\pi}\cos^{-1}\left(\dfrac{\beta}{\alpha}\right)\right\}T$

17. A body attached to a spring oscillates with period T_1. When attached to another spring, the same mass oscillates with period T_2. With the two springs connected in parallel, the same mass will oscillate with period:

(a) $T_1 + T_2$ (b) $\sqrt{T_1^2 + T_2^2}$

(c) $\dfrac{T_1 T_2}{T_1 + T_2}$ (d) $\dfrac{T_1 T_2}{\sqrt{T_1^2 + T_2^2}}$

18. Two simple pendulums of length 1 m and 16 m are both given a small push from their equilibrium position, in the same direction at the same time $t = 0$, and left to oscillate. Let $t = t_1$ be the first time when they cross each other, and let $t = t_2$ be the first time when they are in phase with each other. If $t_2 - t_1 = n$ oscillations of the shorter pendulum, then $15n$ equals:

(a) 8 (b) 10

(c) 12 (d) 14

19. Two particles P and Q are oscillating with the same frequency but different amplitudes A and $2A$, respectively. At some instant, P is at $\dfrac{\sqrt{3}}{2}A$ and Q at $-\sqrt{2}A$, both moving towards their respective mean positions. The phase difference between the particles is:

(a) $7\pi/12$ (b) $2\pi/3$

(c) $3\pi/4$ (d) $11\pi/12$

20. Two particles are executing simple harmonic motion of the same amplitude and same frequency along the same straight line and about the same mean position. If the maximum separation between them is $\sqrt{2}$ times the amplitude, the phase difference between them is:

(a) π (b) $\pi/2$

(c) $\pi/3$ (d) $\pi/4$

21. The time period of a particle executing simple harmonic motion is 8 s. At $t = 0$, it is at its mean position. The ratio of the distances travelled by it in the first and second seconds is:

(a) $\dfrac{\sqrt{2}}{\sqrt{2}+1}$ (b) $\dfrac{\sqrt{2}-1}{\sqrt{2}}$

(c) $\sqrt{2}-1$ (d) $\sqrt{2}+1$

22. Consider the arrangement shown in the figure. The ground is smooth but there is friction between the blocks sufficient to prevent slipping. The spring is light and its spring constant is k. The system is made to oscillate with amplitude A.

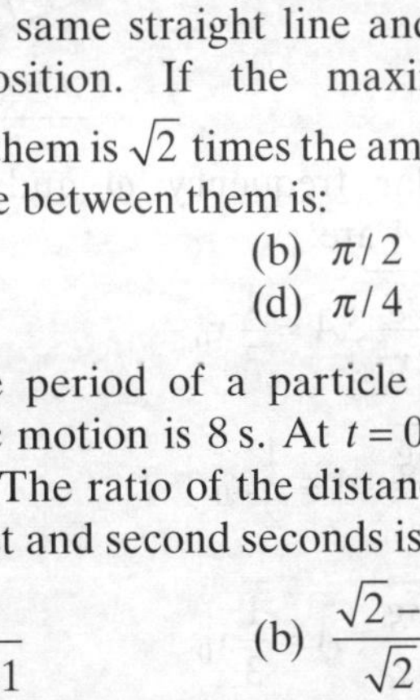

The maximum friction force between the blocks is:

(a) $\left(\dfrac{M}{M+m}\right)kA$ (b) $\left(\dfrac{m}{M+m}\right)kA$

(c) $\left(\dfrac{m}{M}\right)kA$ (d) $\left(\dfrac{M}{m}\right)kA$

23. A horizontal platform with an object placed on it is executing simple harmonic motion in the vertical direction. If the amplitude of oscillation is 2.5 cm, the minimum time period of oscillation so that the object does not lose contact with the platform is (take $g = 10\text{ m/s}^2$):
(a) $\pi/10$ (b) $\pi/5$
(c) π (d) 2π

24. Three blocks each of mass m are connected to a spring, as shown in the figure. The system is in equilibrium and the elongation in the spring is x_0. Now, the lower block is disconnected and the system starts executing simple harmonic motion.

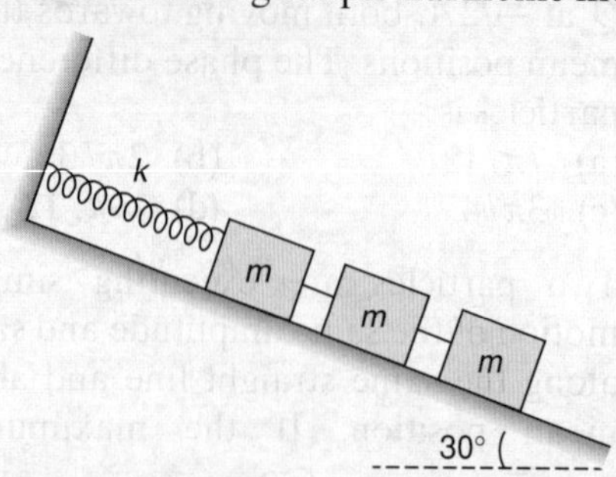

The angular frequency ω and the oscillation amplitude A are:

(a) $\omega = \sqrt{\frac{3g}{2x_0}}, A = \frac{1}{3}x_0$

(b) $\omega = \sqrt{\frac{3g}{x_0}}, A = \frac{1}{2}x_0$

(c) $\omega = \sqrt{\frac{3g}{4x_0}}, A = \frac{1}{3}x_0$

(d) $\omega = \sqrt{\frac{g}{2x_0}}, A = \frac{1}{2}x_0$

25. A spring mass oscillator of mass M is oscillating on a smooth horizontal surface with amplitude A. Consider two cases: (i) when the block is crossing its mean position; and (ii) when the block is at its extreme position. A sticky clay of mass m is dropped from above, which sticks to the block. For the motion of the oscillator after the clay is dropped, the correct statements from the following are:

(a) Amplitude changes by a factor $\sqrt{\frac{M}{M+m}}$ in the first case

(b) Amplitude changes by a factor $\sqrt{\frac{m}{M+m}}$ in the second case

(c) Oscillation energy decreases in both cases

(d) Speed amplitude decreases in both cases

26. A particle is executing simple harmonic motion with frequency f. At $t = 0$, it is crossing its mean position. If η denotes the ratio of its kinetic energy to potential energy, then:

(a) $\eta = 1$ at $t = \frac{1}{8f}$ (b) $\eta = 2$ at $t = \frac{1}{8f}$

(c) $\eta = 3$ at $t = \frac{1}{12f}$ (d) $\eta = 4$ at $t = \frac{1}{12f}$

27. A vertical cylinder fitted with a smooth movable piston is filled with an ideal gas to a height L, and the entire arrangement is kept in vacuum. The adiabatic exponent of the gas is γ. Considering adiabatic changes, for small displacements the piston will oscillate with time period (take acceleration due to gravity = g):

(a) $2\pi\sqrt{\frac{5\gamma L}{2g}}$ (b) $2\pi\sqrt{\frac{3\gamma L}{8g}}$

(c) $2\pi\sqrt{\frac{L}{\gamma g}}$ (d) $2\pi\sqrt{\frac{3L}{2\gamma g}}$

28. The figure shows a block of mass m placed at the centre of a smooth turntable rotating with angular speed ω about a vertical axis. Both springs are in their natural state and are of the same stiffness k. The ends of the springs are attached to two diametrically opposite points A and B.

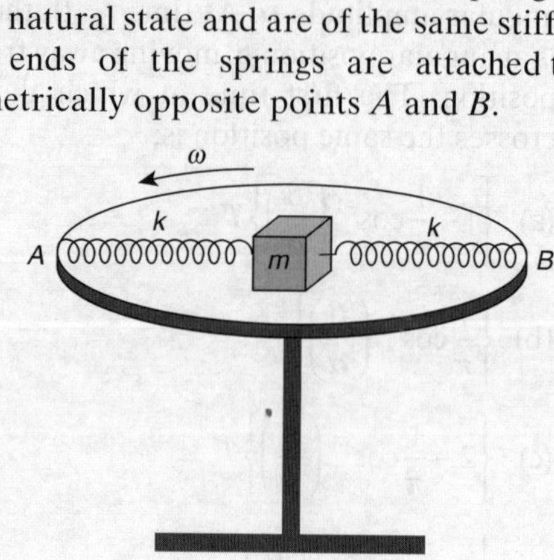

The maximum value of ω for which the block executes SHM for small displacements along the springs is:

(a) $\sqrt{\frac{k}{m}}$ (b) $\sqrt{\frac{2k}{m}}$

(c) $\sqrt{\frac{k}{2m}}$ (d) $\sqrt{\frac{3k}{2m}}$

29. Two particles are executing simple harmonic motion of the same frequency and the same amplitude A along the x-axis. Their mean positions are separated by a distance L. If maximum

separation between them is $L + A$, then the phase difference between their motion is:
(a) $\pi/6$ (b) $\pi/2$
(c) $\pi/3$ (d) $\pi/4$

30. A particle is moving along the x-axis under the influence of a conservative force. Its mechanical energy E is conserved and its potential energy is given by $U(x) = \frac{U_0}{2}\left(1 - \frac{x^2}{a^2}\right)^2$, where $U_0 > 0$. Then the correct statements from the following are:
(a) Force acting on the particle is zero at $x = 0, \pm a$
(b) If $E = \frac{U_0}{4}$, the particle can oscillate about $x = -a$
(c) If $E = \frac{U_0}{2}$, the particle can oscillate about $x = 0$
(d) If $E = \frac{3U_0}{4}$, the particle can oscillate about $x = a$

31. A particle is moving along the x-axis under the influence of a conservative force. Its mechanical energy E is conserved and its potential energy is given by $U(x) = U_0\left(1 - e^{-\frac{x^2}{a^2}}\right)$, where $U_0 > 0$. Then the correct statements from the following are:
(a) Force acting on the particle is zero at $x = 0, \pm a$
(b) For small displacements from $x = 0$, the motion is SHM
(c) The particle can oscillate about $x = 0$ if $E < U_0$
(d) The particle is in stable equilibrium at $x = \pm\infty$

32. In the arrangement shown in the figure, the pulleys are light and smooth and the strings are ideal.

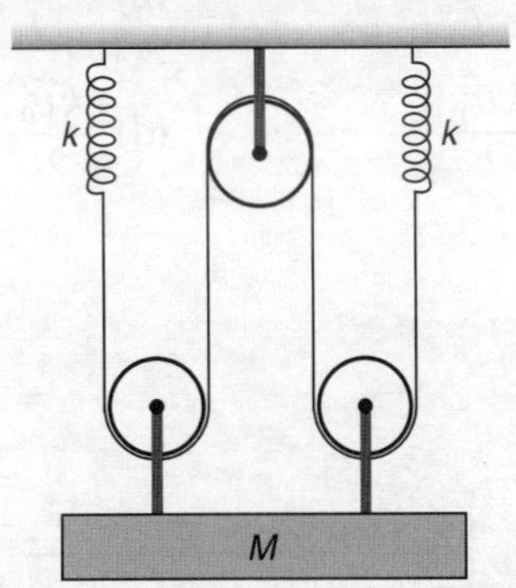

For small vertical displacements, the body oscillates with time period:
(a) $2\pi\sqrt{\frac{M}{8k}}$ (b) $2\pi\sqrt{\frac{M}{6k}}$
(c) $2\pi\sqrt{\frac{M}{4k}}$ (d) $2\pi\sqrt{\frac{M}{2k}}$

33. A simple pendulum of length 1 m is found to make 20 oscillations in 40 s. The least count of the stop watch is 1 s, and that of the measuring scale is 0.5 cm. The maximum possible percentage error in the calculation of acceleration due to gravity is:
(a) 5.5% (b) 4.5%
(c) 3.5% (d) 3.0%

34. A particle is oscillating with amplitude A about its mean position $x = 0$. Its potential energy function is given by $U = k|x^3|$. If the period of oscillation is proportional to A^n, then the value of n is:
(a) 0 (b) $-1/2$
(c) -1 (d) $1/2$

35. The kinetic energy of a body executing SHM is given by $K(x) = a^2 - b^2x^2$. Let F_0 be the maximum restoring force experienced by the body and x_0 be the position of the body where $K(x_0) = 3U(x_0)$, where $U(x)$ denotes potential energy at position x. Then:
(a) $F_0 = 2ab,\ x_0 = \pm\frac{a}{\sqrt{2}b}$
(b) $F_0 = ab,\ x_0 = \pm\frac{a}{\sqrt{2}b}$
(c) $F_0 = 2ab,\ x_0 = \pm\frac{a}{2b}$
(d) $F_0 = \frac{1}{2}ab,\ x_0 = \pm\frac{a}{2b}$

36. The figure shows a spring-mass oscillator placed on a smooth spherical surface of radius R. The angular position of the block with respect to the vertical is denoted by θ. Initially, the block is held at $\theta = 15°$ and the spring is in its natural state. When the block is released, it oscillates along the spherical surface. Its velocity is maximum at $\theta = 30°$.

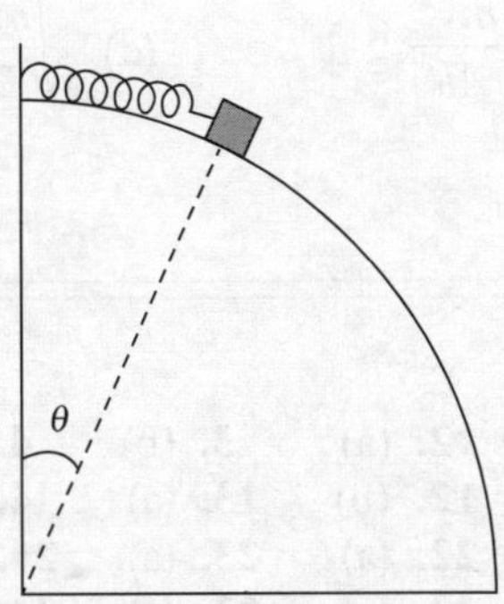

If acceleration due to gravity is g, the maximum velocity is:

(a) $\sqrt{\dfrac{gR}{6\pi}}$ (b) $\sqrt{\dfrac{gR}{12\pi}}$

(c) $\sqrt{\dfrac{\pi gR}{12}}$ (d) $\sqrt{\dfrac{\pi gR}{24}}$

37. Two independent harmonica oscillators of equal mass are executing SHM with angular frequencies ω_1 and ω_2 and energies E_1 and E_2, respectively. The variations of their momentum p with their position x are shown in the figures.

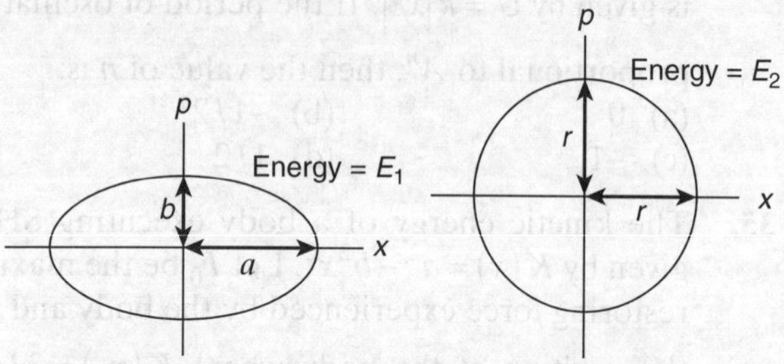

If $a = n^2 b$ and $a = nr$, then the correct relations are:

(a) $E_1\omega_1 = E_2\omega_2$ (b) $\omega_2 = n^2\omega_1$

(c) $\omega_1 = n^2\omega_2$ (d) $E_1\omega_2 = E_2\omega_1$

38. Two identical blocks of mass m each are connected by a light spring of spring constant k and kept on a smooth horizontal surface (see figure).

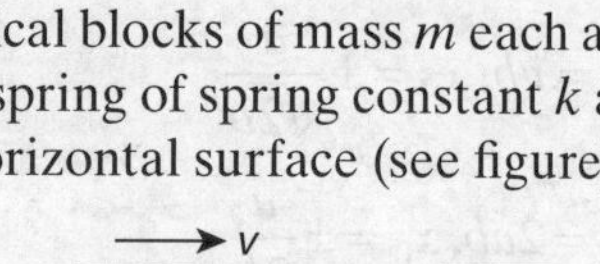

Initially, the system is in equilibrium. The left block is suddenly imparted a velocity v along the length of the spring. The system starts executing a combination of translation plus oscillation. The maximum compression in the spring is:

(a) $\sqrt{\dfrac{2mv^2}{k}}$ (b) $\sqrt{\dfrac{mv^2}{k}}$

(c) $\sqrt{\dfrac{mv^2}{4k}}$ (d) $\sqrt{\dfrac{mv^2}{2k}}$

39. A block of mass $m = 0.1$ kg connected to a spring of stiffness $k = 250$ N/m is oscillating with amplitude $A = 3$ mm on a smooth horizontal surface. When the block is crossing its equilibrium position, a constant horizontal force $F = 1$ N (see figure) starts acting on the block.

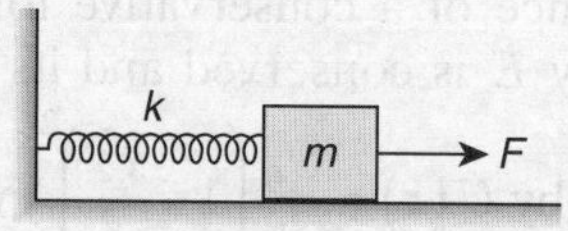

If the force continues to act, then the correct statements from the following are:

(a) Oscillation amplitude of the block = 5 mm

(b) Maximum elongation in the spring = 7 mm

(c) Maximum velocity of the block = 0.25 m/s

(d) Maximum acceleration of the block = 10 m/s^2

40. Two masses m and $m/2$ are connected by a light rigid rod of length i. The system is suspended at its centre of mass by a thin wire of torsional constant k (see figure). Because of torsional constant k, the wire exerts a restoring torque $\tau = k\theta$ for angular displacement θ.

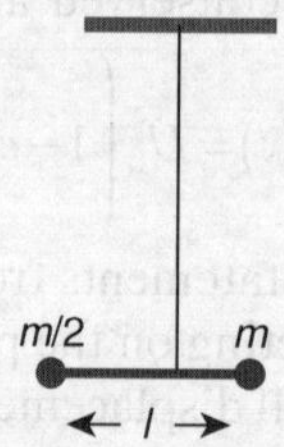

If the rod is rotated by θ_0 and then released, the tension in it when it passes through its mean position is:

(a) $\dfrac{3k\theta_0^2}{l}$ (b) $\dfrac{2k\theta_0^2}{l}$

(c) $\dfrac{k\theta_0^2}{l}$ (d) $\dfrac{k\theta_0^2}{2l}$

ANSWER KEYS

1. (b)	**2.** (a)	**3.** (b)	**4.** (a)	**5.** (c)	**6.** (b)	**7.** (a)	**8.** (b)	**9.** (c)	**10.** (a)
11. (b)	**12.** (b)	**13.** (a)	**14.** (c)	**15.** (b),(d)	**16.** (b)	**17.** (d)	**18.** (d)	**19.** (d)	**20.** (b)
21. (d)	**22.** (a)	**23.** (a)	**24.** (c)	**25.** (a),(d)	**26.** (a),(c)	**27.** (c)	**28.** (b)	**29.** (c)	**30.** (a),(b)
31. (b), (c)	**32.** (a)	**33.** (a)	**34.** (b)	**35.** (c)	**36.** (d)	**37.** (b),(d)	**38.** (d)	**39.** (a),(c)	**40.** (c)

SOLUTIONS

1. (b) For a two-body oscillation connected by a spring, the spring constant is given by $k = \mu\omega^2$, where $\mu = \dfrac{m_1 m_2}{m_1 + m_2}$ is the reduced mass of the two-body system. If m is the mass of each silver atom, then their reduced mass is $\mu = m / 2$. Hence, we have

$$k = \frac{1}{2}m\omega^2 = \frac{1}{2}\left(\frac{108\times10^{-3}}{6.02\times10^{23}}\right)\times(2\pi\times10^{12})^2$$
$$= 3.54 \text{ N/m}$$

2. (a) Let $4\rho/3$ and ρ be the densities of the liquid and the pendulum, respectively. Due to the buoyancy force, the effective gravity experienced by the pendulum is

$$g' = \frac{\frac{4}{3}\rho Vg - \rho Vg}{\rho V} = \frac{1}{3}g$$

Now, since $T \propto \dfrac{1}{\sqrt{g}}$, therefore

$$\frac{T'}{T} = \sqrt{\frac{g}{g'}} \Rightarrow T' = \sqrt{3}T$$

3. (b) At any instant when the ball is displaced by an amount s from its equilibrium, the restoring force acting on the ball is $F_{res} = mg\sin\theta$ (see figure).

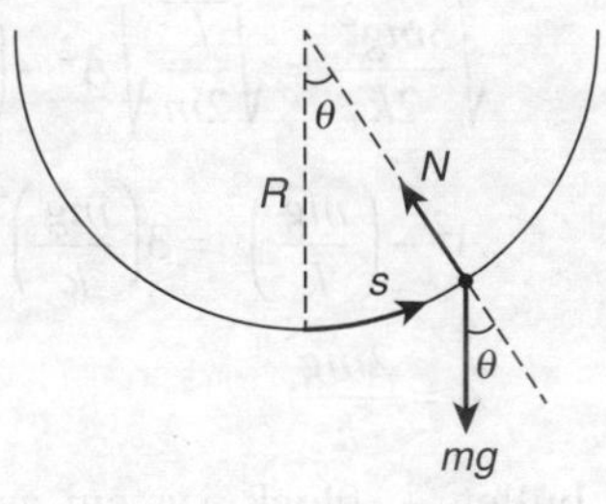

The instantaneous acceleration of the ball, is

$$a = -\frac{F_{res}}{m} = -g\sin\theta$$
$$= -\left(\frac{g}{R}\right)s \quad [\text{For small } \theta, \sin\theta = \theta = s/R]$$

Hence, time-period $T = 2\pi\sqrt{\dfrac{R}{g}}$.

4. (a) The figure shows the liquid mass in a slightly displaced position. The restoring force on the liquid mass is $F_{res} = \rho g x\,(1 + \cos\theta)A$.

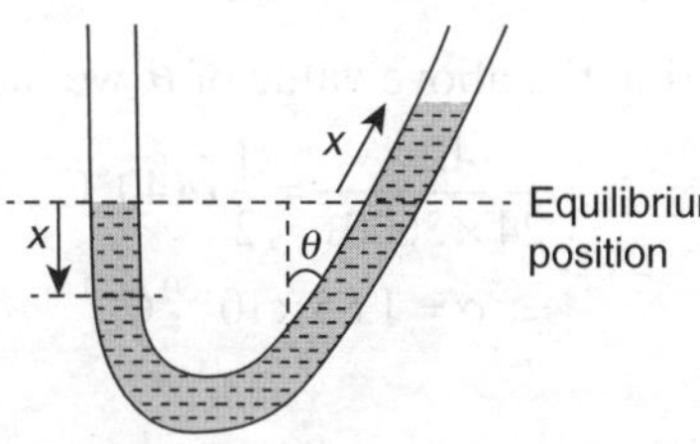

The total mass of the liquid is $m = \rho AL$. The instantaneous acceleration of the liquid mass is

$$a = -\frac{F_{res}}{m} = -\frac{g(1+\cos\theta)}{L}x$$

Hence, time period $T = 2\pi\sqrt{\dfrac{L}{g(1+\cos\theta)}}$.

5. (c) Let the densities of water and the object be ρ and 0.8ρ, respectively. At any instant when the cylinder is displaced by an amount x below its equilibrium, the extra elongation in the spring and the extra amount of displaced liquid together produce a restoring force given by

$$F_{res} = \rho Axg + kx = (\rho Ag + k)x$$

[A is the cross-section area of the cylinder]

Instantaneous acceleration of the cylinder is

$$a = -\left(\frac{\rho Ag + k}{m}\right)x$$

Since $m = 0.8\rho Al \Rightarrow \rho A = \dfrac{5m}{4l}$. Hence

$$a = -\left(\frac{\frac{5mg}{4l} + k}{m}\right)x$$

Putting $m = 1.6$ kg, $l = 0.4$ m and $k = 110$ N/m, we get $a = -100x$. Hence, $\omega = 10$ rad/s and

$$v_{max} = \omega A = (10 \text{ rad/s})(0.5 \text{ cm}) = 5 \text{ cm/s}$$

6. (b) For a simple pendulum, we have

$$T \propto \sqrt{L}$$

$$\Rightarrow \quad \frac{\Delta T}{T} = \frac{1}{2}\frac{\Delta L}{L} = \frac{1}{2}\alpha\Delta\theta$$

Let θ be the temperature at which the clock shows the correct time. Then

$$\frac{12 \text{ s}}{1 \text{ day}} = \frac{1}{2}\alpha(40°\text{C} - \theta) \qquad \ldots(1)$$

$$\frac{4 \text{ s}}{1 \text{ day}} = \frac{1}{2}\alpha(\theta - 20°\text{C}) \qquad \ldots(2)$$

Dividing the two equations, we have

$$\frac{12}{4}=\frac{40°C-\theta}{\theta-20°C} \Rightarrow \theta = 25°C$$

Putting the above value of θ, we have

$$\frac{12s}{24\times 3600s}=\frac{1}{2}\alpha(40°C-25°C)$$

$$\Rightarrow \alpha = 1.85\times 10^{-50}\,C^{-1}$$

7. (a)

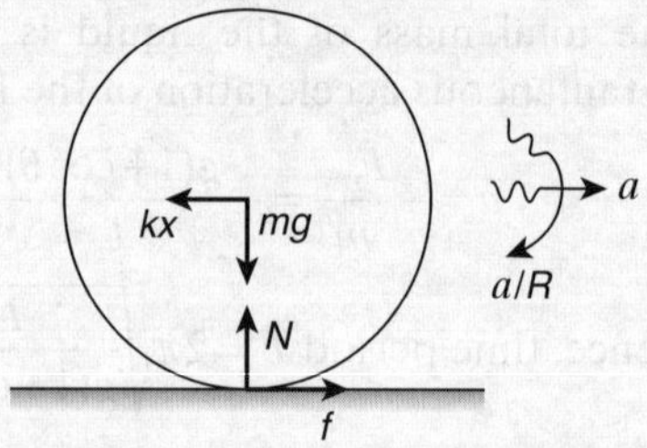

The figure shows the forces acting on the disc at an instant when its CM is displaced by an amount x from its equilibrium position. Let a be the acceleration of the CM. If slipping is absent, then the angular acceleration must be a/R (let R be the radius). Then, using dynamics, we have

$$f-kx=ma \quad ...(1)$$

and $$-fR=\left(\frac{1}{2}mR^2\right)\left(\frac{a}{R}\right)\Rightarrow f=-\frac{1}{2}ma \quad ...(2)$$

From the above equations, we have $f=\frac{1}{3}kx$. Since the friction force is limited ($f\le \mu mg$), we have

$$\frac{1}{3}kx\le \mu mg \Rightarrow x\le \frac{3\mu mg}{k}$$

8. (b) The figure shows the rod in a slightly displaced angular position θ. The elongation in each spring is $\frac{1}{2}l\theta$. The restoring torque on the rod, about the axis of rotation, is $\tau_{res}=2\left(\frac{kl\theta}{2}\times\frac{l}{2}\right)=\frac{1}{2}kl^2\theta$.

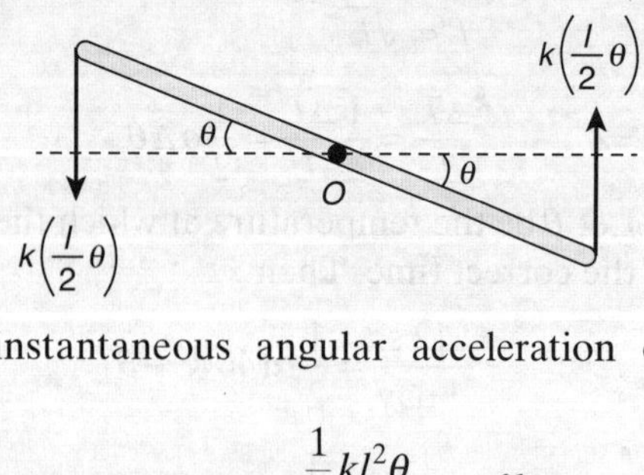

The instantaneous angular acceleration of the rod is

$$\alpha=-\frac{\tau_{res}}{I}=-\frac{\frac{1}{2}kl^2\theta}{\frac{1}{12}ml^2}=-\frac{6k}{m}\theta$$

Hence, time period $T=2\pi\sqrt{\frac{m}{6k}}$.

9. (c) After the bullet gets stuck in the block, the mass of the block + bullet equals $2m$. Immediately after the collision, the block + bullet system has an upward velocity $v/2=\sqrt{\frac{3mg^2}{2k}}$ (from momentum conservation principle). The spring-mass oscillator will oscillate with a natural angular frequency of $\omega=\sqrt{k/2m}$ about its equilibrium position, which is at a distance mg/k below the position of collision. The equilibrium position has shifted lower because of the additional mass of the bullet. Thus, the oscillator is moving with speed $\sqrt{\frac{3mg^2}{2k}}$ when it is at a distance mg/k from its equilibrium position.

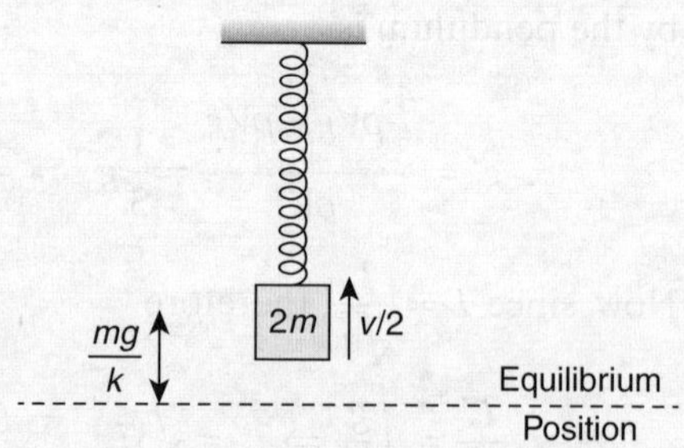

We can now find the oscillation amplitude using the relation $v=\omega\sqrt{A^2-x^2}$ between the speed and position of a body executing SHM. Putting the values, we have

$$\sqrt{\frac{3mg^2}{2k}}=\sqrt{\frac{k}{2m}}\sqrt{A^2-\left(\frac{mg}{k}\right)^2}$$

$$\Rightarrow \quad A^2-\left(\frac{mg}{k}\right)^2=3\left(\frac{mg}{k}\right)^2$$

$$\Rightarrow \quad A=\frac{2mg}{k}$$

The bullet + block system will oscillate with amplitude $A = 2mg/k$. Thus, when the block reaches its uppermost extreme, the spirng will be in its natural state. Now, we have to find the time taken by the oscillator to move from initial position $x_1=\frac{mg}{k}=\frac{1}{2}A$ to the extreme position

$x_2=\frac{2mg}{k}=A$. From the phasor diagram, we can see that the phase difference between these two positions is $\pi/3$, and hence, the time taken is

$$T=\frac{\pi}{3\omega}=\pi\sqrt{\frac{2m}{9k}}$$

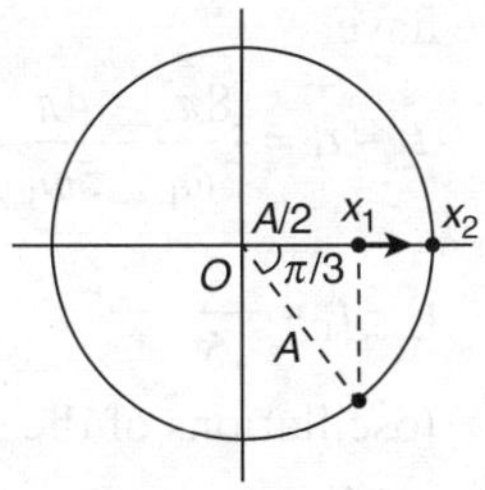

10. (a)

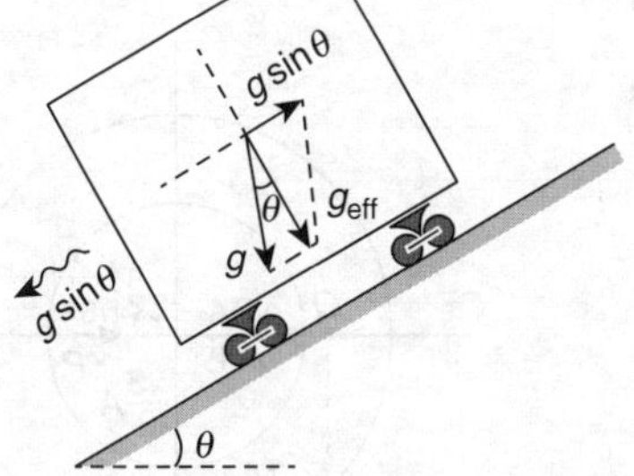

The vehicle has an acceleration $a = g \sin\theta$ down the incline. From a reference frame attached to the vehicle, the effective gravity is $\vec{g}_{eff} = \vec{g} - \vec{a}$, which comes out to be $g\cos\theta$ in a direction perpendicular to the incline (see figure).

Hence, the time period is $T = 2\pi\sqrt{\dfrac{1}{g\cos\theta}}$.

11. (b) Let us attach our reference frame with the elevator. The acceleration introduces a pseudo force = ma in the downward direction, on the block. The equilibrium position shifts lower by distance = ma/k. The block will start oscillating with amplitude $A = ma/k$ (amplitude is the distance between equilibrium position and position of rest). The maximum velocity is given by

$$v_0 = \omega A = \sqrt{\frac{k}{m}}\frac{ma}{k} = \sqrt{\frac{m}{k}}a$$

$$= \sqrt{\frac{0.2\text{ kg}}{80\text{ N/m}}}(1\text{ m/s}^2) = 5\text{ cm/s}$$

12. (b)

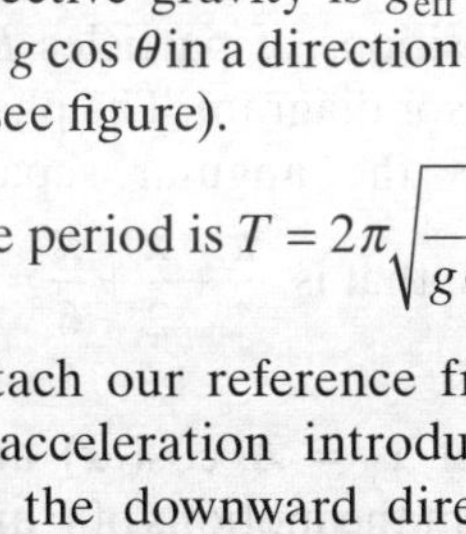

The time T taken by the block to travel from one extreme position A to $-A/2$, which is the same as travelling from $-A$ to $A/2$, can be found from the phasor diagram, as shown in the figure.

The phase angle between the two positions is 120° = $2\pi/3$ rad. Hence, time $r = \dfrac{2\pi/3}{\omega}$, where $\omega = \sqrt{k/m}$.

The time period is $T = 2\times\dfrac{2\pi}{3\omega} = \dfrac{4\pi}{3}\sqrt{\dfrac{m}{k}}$.

13. (a) The mass oscillates with amplitude y. The maximum velocity of the particle is ωy. The maximum kinetic energy is

$$\frac{1}{2}m(\omega y)^2 = \frac{1}{2}m\omega^2 y^2 = \frac{1}{2}ky^2.$$

14. (c) At $x = \dfrac{2}{3}A$, velocity is

$$v = \omega\sqrt{A^2 - \frac{4A^2}{9}} = \frac{\sqrt{5}}{3}\omega A$$

When velocity is trebled, let A' be the new amplitude. Then

$$\sqrt{5}\omega A = \omega\sqrt{A'^2 - \frac{4A^2}{9}}$$

$$\Rightarrow \quad A'^2 = 5A^2 + \frac{4}{9}A^2 = \frac{79}{9}A^2$$

$$\Rightarrow \quad A' = \frac{7}{3}A$$

15. (b), (d) When the bead is released, it is at its extreme position (the extreme position is where the velocity is zero).

Its velocity increases till the bead reaches its equilibrium position. Let A be this distance. Then A is the displacement amplitude. At this position, the net force on the bead is zero, that is

$$kA = m\omega^2(I + A) \Rightarrow A = \left(\frac{m\omega^2}{k - m\omega^2}\right)l$$

For displacement x further away (from the axis) from the equilibrium, elongation in the spring is $A + x$. The spring force is directed towards the equilibrium while the centrifugal force is directed away from the equilibrium. The restoring force is

$$F_{res} = k(A + x) - m\omega^2(l + A + x) = (k - m\omega^2)x$$

We can see that oscillation will be possible if $k - m\omega^2 > 0 \Rightarrow \omega < \sqrt{k/m}$

The instantaneous acceleration is

$$a = -\frac{F_{res}}{m} = -\left(\frac{k - m\omega^2}{m}\right)x$$

Hence, the frequency of oscillation is $f = \dfrac{1}{2\pi}\sqrt{\dfrac{k - m\omega^2}{m}}$.

16. (b) The required time can be found from the phasor diagram. The figure shows the initial ($t = 0$) and final ($t = \tau$) positions of the phasor.

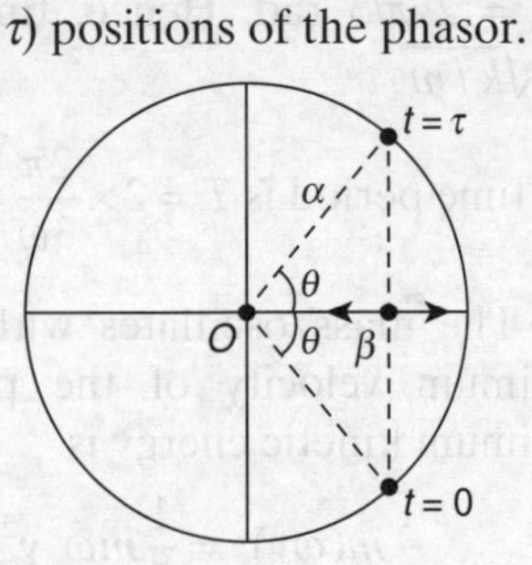

The required time is

$$\tau = \frac{2\theta}{\omega} = \frac{2\theta}{2\pi/T} = \frac{T}{\pi}\theta = \frac{T}{\pi}\cos^{-1}\left(\frac{\beta}{\alpha}\right)$$

17. (d) We have $T_1^2 \propto \frac{1}{k_1}$ and $T_2^2 \propto \frac{1}{k_2}$. When connected in parallel, the effective spring constant k is given by

$$k = k_1 + k_2$$

$$\Rightarrow \quad \frac{1}{T^2} = \frac{1}{T_1^2} + \frac{1}{T_2^2}\left[T^2 \propto \frac{1}{k}\right]$$

$$\Rightarrow \quad T = \frac{T_1 T_2}{\sqrt{T_1^2 + T_2^2}}$$

18. (d) The functions representing the motions of two pendulums are

$A\sin(\omega_1 t)$ and $A\sin(\omega_2 t)$, where

$$\omega_1 = \sqrt{\frac{g}{1\text{ m}}} \text{ and } \omega_2 = \sqrt{\frac{g}{16\text{ m}}} = \frac{1}{4}\omega_1$$

The times when they cross each other are given by

$$\sin(\omega_1 t) = \sin(\omega_2 t)$$

$$\Rightarrow \quad \omega_1 t = m\pi + (-1)^m \omega_2 t, m = 0, 1, 2, \ldots$$

The first time t_1 when they cross each other is found by putting $m = 1$. Thus, we have

$$\Rightarrow \quad \omega_1 t_1 = \pi - \omega_2 t_1$$

$$\Rightarrow \quad t_1 = \frac{\pi}{\omega_1 + \omega_2} = \frac{4\pi}{5\omega_1}\left[\text{Putting } \omega_2 = \frac{1}{4}\omega_1\right]$$

The times when they are in phase with each other are given by

$$|\omega_1 - \omega_2| t = m(2\pi), m = 0, 1, 2, \ldots$$

The first time t_2 when they are in phase with each other is found by putting $m = 1$. Thus, we have

$$\Rightarrow \quad t_2 = \frac{2\pi}{|\omega_1 + \omega_2|} = \frac{8\pi}{3\omega_1}\left[\text{Putting } \omega_2 = \frac{1}{4}\omega_1\right]$$

Thus, we have

$$t_2 - t_1 = \frac{8\pi}{3\omega_1} - \frac{4\pi}{5\omega_1} = \frac{28\pi}{15\omega_1} = \frac{14}{15}\left(\frac{2\pi}{\omega_1}\right)$$

$$\Rightarrow \quad t_2 - t_1 = \frac{14}{15}$$

(oscillations of the shorter pendulum).

Hence, $n = \frac{14}{15} \Rightarrow 15n = 14$.

19. (d)

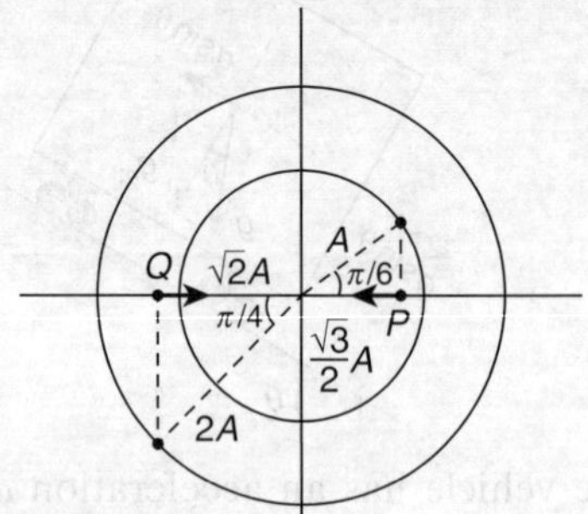

The positions of particles P and Q are shown in the phasor diagram. The phase difference between them is the angular separation between their phasors, that is, $\frac{\pi}{4} + \frac{\pi}{2} + \frac{\pi}{6} = \frac{11\pi}{12}$.

20. (b) Let $x_1 = A\cos(\omega t)$ and $x_2 = A\cos(\omega t + \phi)$ represent the motions of P and Q, respectively. The separation between them at any instant is given by

$$\Delta x = A\,|\cos(\omega t) - \cos(\omega t + \phi)|$$

$$= 2A\sin\left(\frac{\phi}{2}\right)\left|\sin\left(\omega t + \frac{\phi}{2}\right)\right|$$

The maximum value of the function is $2A\sin(\phi/2)$, which is given to be $\sqrt{2}A$. Hence, we have

$$2A\sin\left(\frac{\phi}{2}\right) = \sqrt{2}A \Rightarrow \sin\left(\frac{\phi}{2}\right) = \frac{1}{\sqrt{2}} \Rightarrow \phi = \frac{\pi}{2}$$

21. (d) The function representing the position of the particles is $x = A\sin(\frac{\pi}{4}t)$. Its period is $T = \frac{2\pi}{\pi/4}\text{ s} = 8\text{ s}$. In the first two seconds, it moves from its mean position to its positive extreme position. Its position after 1 s and 2 s are, respectively

$$x_1 = A\sin\left(\frac{\pi}{4}\right) = \frac{A}{\sqrt{2}} \text{ and } x_2 = A\sin\left(\frac{\pi}{2}\right) = A$$

Hence, distance travelled in the first second and second second are given by

$$s_1 = x_1 = \frac{A}{\sqrt{2}} \text{ and } s_2 = x_2 - x_1 = A\left(1 - \frac{1}{\sqrt{2}}\right)$$

Hence, the required ratio is $\dfrac{S_1}{S_2} = \dfrac{1}{\sqrt{2}-1} = \sqrt{2}+1.$

22. (a) The system oscillates with angular frequency $\omega = \sqrt{\dfrac{k}{M+m}}$. The acceleration of block M is provided by the friction force between the two blocks. The maximum acceleration of the block M is $\omega^2 A$, and hence, the maximum required friction force equals $M\omega^2 A = \dfrac{MkA}{M+m}$.

23. (a) The figure shows the forces acting on the block when it is at position x from its equilibrium position.

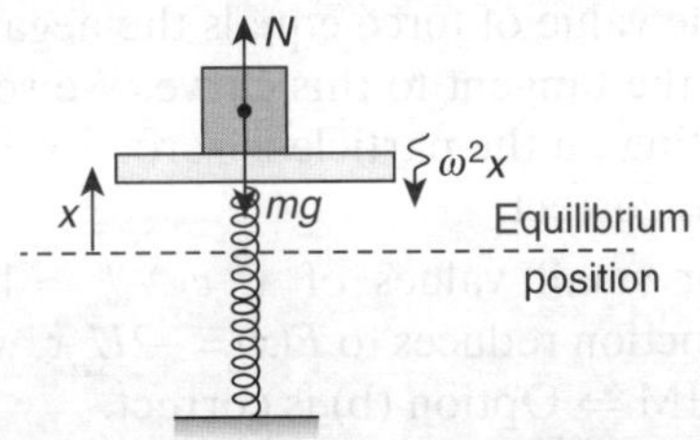

Using dynamics, we have

$$mg - N = m\omega^2 x$$

$$\Rightarrow N = m(g - \omega^2 x)$$

We see that the normal contact force varies between $N_{min} = m(g - \omega^2 A)$ and $N_{max} = m(g + \omega^2 A)$. For the block to remain in contact with the platform, $N > 0$ at all positions.

Hence, we have

$$g - \omega^2 A > 0$$

$$\Rightarrow \quad \omega < \sqrt{\frac{g}{A}}$$

$$\Rightarrow \quad T = \frac{2\pi}{\omega} > 2\pi\sqrt{\frac{A}{g}} = \pi/10$$

24. (c) From equilibrium condition, we have

$$kx_o = 3mg\sin 30° \Rightarrow \frac{k}{m} = \frac{3g}{2x_o}.$$

The system oscillates with angular frequency

$$\omega = \sqrt{\frac{k}{2m}} = \sqrt{\frac{3g}{4x_0}}.$$

Also, the new equilibrium position moves up by distance $\dfrac{mg\sin 30°}{k} = \dfrac{x_o}{3}$, which is the oscillation amplitude A.

25. (a), (d) In the first case, the maximum speed decreases to $\left(\dfrac{M}{M+m}\right)A\omega$, where A is the initial amplitude and $\omega = \sqrt{\dfrac{k}{M}}$ is the initial angular frequency. The new angular frequency is $\omega' = \sqrt{\dfrac{k}{M+m}}$. If A' is the new amplitude, then

$$A'\omega' = \left(\frac{M}{M+m}\right)A\omega \Rightarrow A' = \sqrt{\frac{M+m}{M}}A$$

Hence, (a) is correct.

In the second case, the speed remains zero even after the clay is dropped. So the amplitude remains the same. Hence, (b) is incorrect.

Oscillation energy in the first case is $\frac{1}{2}kA'^2 < \frac{1}{2}kA^2$

$\Rightarrow$ energy decreases. Oscillation energy in the second case is $\frac{1}{2}kA^2$, which is unchanged. Hence, (c) is incorrect.

The maximum speed in the first case is $A'\omega' < A\omega$. The maximum speed in the second case is $A\omega' < A\omega$. Thus, the speed amplitude decreases in both cases. Hence, (d) is correct.

26. (a), (c) The function representing the particle's motion is $x = A\sin(2\pi ft)$. The potential energy and kinetic energy functions are

$$U = \frac{1}{2}kx^2 = \frac{1}{2}kA^2\sin^2(2\pi ft)$$

$$\text{and} \quad K = \frac{1}{2}kA^2 - U = \frac{1}{2}kA^2\cos^2(2\pi ft)$$

The required ratio is

$$\eta = \frac{K}{U} = \cot^2(2\pi ft)$$

At $t = \dfrac{1}{8f}$, $\eta = 1$ and at $t = \dfrac{1}{12f}$, $\eta = 3$.

27. (c) Consider the piston in the slightly displaced position, say x, below its equilibrium position. If A is the cross-section area of the piston, the volume occupied by the gas changes by $\Delta V = -Ax$.

Considering the process to be adiabatic, that is, pV^{γ} = constant, the corresponding pressure change is given by

$$\frac{\Delta P}{P} = -\gamma\frac{\Delta V}{V} \Rightarrow \Delta P = \gamma P_o \frac{Ax}{AL} = \frac{YP_o}{L}x,$$

where P_0 denotes the undisturbed gas pressure. The piston experiences a restoring force

$$F_{\text{res}} = A\Delta p = \frac{\gamma P_o A}{L}x = \frac{\gamma Mg}{L}x,$$

where Mg is the weight of the piston that is balanced by the upward force exerted by the gas. The instantaneous acceleration of the piston is

$$a = -\frac{F_{\text{res}}}{M} = -\frac{\gamma g}{L}x$$

Hence $T = 2\pi\sqrt{\frac{L}{\gamma g}}$.

28. (b) Consider the block in a slightly displaced position, say x, from its equilibrium position. From a reference frame attached to the rotating turntable, the restoring force on the block is

$$F_{res} = 2\,kx - m\omega^2 x = (2k - m\omega^2)x$$

For SHM to be possible, $F_{res} > 0 \Rightarrow \omega < \sqrt{\frac{2k}{m}}$

29. (c) Let $x_1 = A\sin(\omega t)$ and $x_2 = L + A\sin(\omega t + \phi)$ be the functions representing their motions. At any instant, the separation between them is given by

$$|x_2 - x_1| = |L + A[\sin(\omega t + \phi) - \sin(\omega t)]|$$

$$\Rightarrow |x_2 - x_1| = |L + 2A\sin(\phi/2)\cos(\omega t + \phi/2)|$$

We see that

$$|L - 2A\sin(\phi/2)| \le |x_2 - x_1| \le |L + 2A\sin(\phi/2)|.$$

According to the given condition

$$L + 2A\sin(\phi/2) = L + A$$

$$\Rightarrow \sin(\phi/2) = \frac{1}{2} \text{ gives } \phi = \pi/3$$

30. (a), (b) The force acting on the particle is given by the function

$$F = \frac{dU}{dx} = \frac{2U_0}{a^2}x\left(1 - \frac{x^2}{a^2}\right) = -\frac{2U_0}{a^2}x(x-a)(x+a)$$

The figure shows the graph of U versus x.

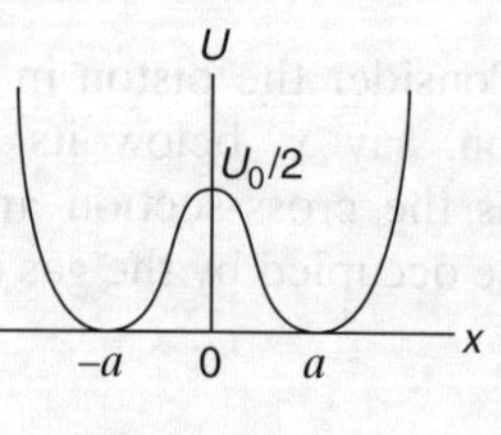

The value of force equals the negative of the slope of the tangent to this curve. We see that the force acting on the particle is zero at $x = 0, \pm a$. But the particle cannot oscillate about $x = 0$ since it is a position of unstable equilibrium. It can oscillate about points $x = \pm a$ and that too only if its mechanical energy is less than $U_0/2$; if the energy is greater than $U_0/2$, the particle will cross over the potential well.

31. (a) Force acting on the particle is given by the function

$$F(x) = -\frac{dU}{dx} = -2U_o\left(xe^{-x^2/a^2}\right)$$

The figure shows the graph of U versus x.

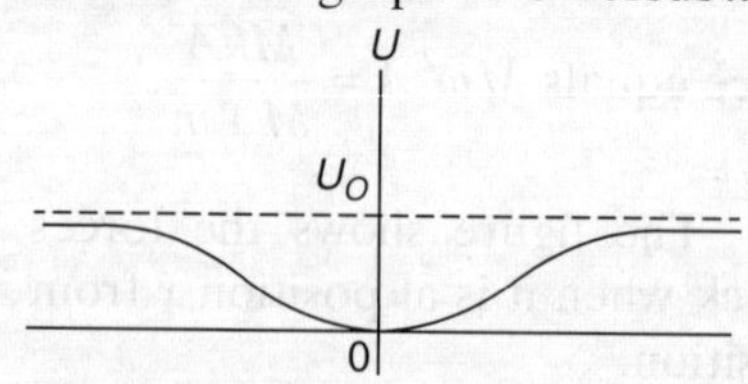

The value of force equals the negative of the slope of the tangent to this curve. We see that the force acting on the particle is zero at $x = 0 \Rightarrow$ Option (a) is incorrect.

For small values of x, $e^{-x^2/a^2} \approx 1$ and the force function reduces to $F(x) = -2U_o x$, which represents SHM $\Rightarrow$ Option (b) is correct.

The particle can oscillate about $x = 0$ if its energy E is less than U_o. For $E > U_o$, the particle will cross over the potential well $\Rightarrow$ Option (c) is correct.

When the particle is at $x = \pm\infty$, the force on the particle is almost zero, but not zero. Even slight displacement towards the origin side and the particle will be pulled towards the origin $\Rightarrow$ Option (d) is incorrect.

32. (a)

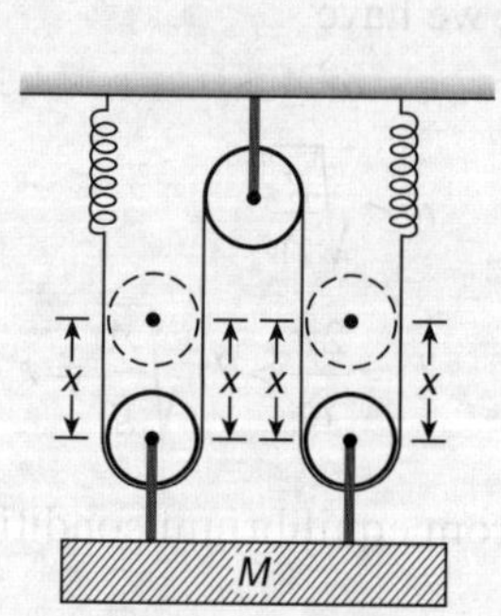

Imagine that the body is displaced by an amount x in the downward direction. In this position, both the lower pulleys have also moved down by x. This should cause an increase in length of $4x$ in the strings (see figure). Since the strings are inextensible, each spring must elongate by $2x$ to compensate for the increased $4x$ length. So, the tension in the string, which is equal to the tension in the spring, is $T = k(2x)$. The restoring force on the body is $F_{res} = 4T = 8kx$. The instantaneous acceleration of the body is $a = -\frac{8k}{M}x$.

Hence, the time period is $T = 2\pi\sqrt{\frac{M}{8k}}$.

33. (a) We have $T = 2\pi\sqrt{L/g} \Rightarrow g\alpha LT^{-2}$. Hence

$$\frac{\Delta g}{q} = \frac{\Delta l}{l} - 2\frac{\Delta T}{T}$$

Let T denote the total time and n denote the number of oscillations. Then $T = T/n$.

Thus

$$\frac{\Delta T}{T} = \frac{\Delta T}{T} = \frac{\pm 1 \text{ s}}{40 \text{ s}} = \pm 2.5\%$$

and $\frac{\Delta l}{l} = \frac{\pm 0.5 \text{ cm}}{100 \text{ cm}} = \pm 0.5\%$

Hence, maximum error in the measurement of g is

$$\frac{\Delta g}{a} = 0.5\% + 2(2.5\%) = 5.5\%$$

34. (b) Time period T will depend upon the elasticity k, inertia m and, in this question, also on amplitude A. Let $T \propto k^a m^b A^c$. Here, k has the units J/m^3 (given). Dimensionally, we have

$$T^1 = (ML^{-1}T^{-2})^a M^b L^c$$

Comparing the exponents, we have

$$a + b = 0, -a + c = 0 \text{ and } -2a = 1$$

$\Rightarrow$ $a = -1/2$, $b = 1/2$ and $c = -1/2$

35. (c) From the given function $K(x) = a^2 - b^2x^2$, we see that the potential energy function is $U(X) = b^2X^2$.

Then, force as a function of x is

$$F = -\frac{dU}{dx} = -2b^2x$$

The kinetic energy is zero at the extreme position, say $x = A$. This gives

$$a^2 - b^2A^2 = 0 \Rightarrow A = a/b.$$

Using the other relation $K(x_0) = 3\,U(x_0)$, we have

$$a^2 - b^2x^2 = 3b^2x^0 \Rightarrow x_o = \pm a/2b$$

36. (d) The velocity is maximum when force on the block is zero. Elongation in the spring at this instant is $R(\frac{\pi}{6} - \frac{\pi}{12}) = \frac{\pi R}{12}$. The spring force is $k\left(\frac{\pi R}{12}\right)$. The gravitational force along the surface is $mg\sin\left(\frac{\pi}{6}\right) = \frac{1}{2}mg$. Equating the two, we have

$$k\left(\frac{\pi R}{12}\right) = \frac{1}{2}mg \Rightarrow \frac{k}{m} = \frac{6g}{\pi R}$$

The angular frequency is $\omega = \sqrt{k/m}$ and the displacement amplitude is $A = \frac{\pi R}{12}$. Hence, maximum velocity is

$$V_{\max} = \omega A = \sqrt{\frac{k}{m}}\left(\frac{\pi R}{12}\right) = \sqrt{\frac{6g}{\pi R}} \cdot \frac{\pi R}{12} = \sqrt{\frac{\pi g R}{24}}$$

37. (b), (d) From the given figure, we can see that the displacement amplitudes of particles 1 and 2 are, respectively, a and r. We can also see that the maximum magnitudes of their momentum are b and r. The energy of oscillation equals the maximum kinetic energy, or the maximum potential energy. Hence, we have

$$E_1 = \frac{b^2}{2m} = \frac{1}{2}m\omega_1^2a^2 \text{ and } E_2 = \frac{r^2}{2m} = \frac{1}{2}m\omega_2^2r^2$$

Dividing the above equations, we have

$$\frac{b^2}{r^2} = \frac{a^2\omega_1^2}{r^2\omega_2^2} \Rightarrow \frac{\omega_1}{\omega_2} = \frac{b}{a} = \frac{1}{n^2} \Rightarrow \omega_2 = n^2\omega_1$$

and $\frac{E_1}{E_2} = \frac{b^2}{r^2} = \frac{a^2/n^4}{a^2/n^2} = \frac{1}{n^2} = \frac{\omega_1}{\omega_2} \Rightarrow E_1\omega_2 = E_2\omega_1$

38. (d) If we consider the two blocks plus the spring as our system, we can see that there is no external force on this system. So the center of mass of this system will move with a constant velocity

$$v_{cm} = \frac{mv}{m+m} = v/2 \text{ towards right.}$$

From a reference frame attached to the center of mass, the motion of the blocks will only be simple harmonic. From this reference frame, the initial velocities of the blocks are towards each other having same magnitude $v/2$. At this moment, the spring is in natural state. The blocks will move closer and will eventually stop together.

The kinetic energy of the two blocks is converted into spring potential energy. If A be the maximum compression in the spring, then we have

$$\frac{1}{2}m\left(\frac{v}{2}\right)^2 + \frac{1}{2}m\left(\frac{v}{2}\right)^2 = \frac{1}{2}kA^2$$

$$\Rightarrow \quad \frac{1}{4}mv^2 = \frac{1}{2}kA^2$$

$$\Rightarrow \quad A = \sqrt{\frac{mv^2}{2k}}.$$

39. (a), (c) Let the initial equilibrium position be chosen as $x = 0$. The new equilibrium position will shift to the right by an amount

$$\frac{F}{k} = \frac{1\text{ N}}{250\text{ N/m}} = 4\text{ mm}$$

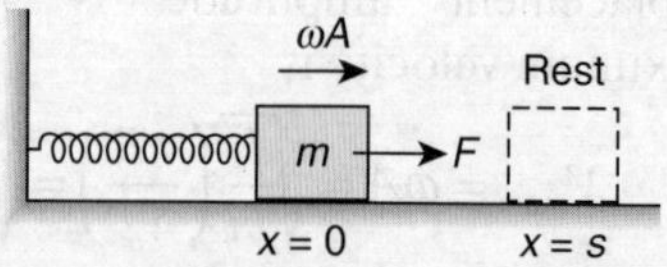

When F begins to act, the block is moving with velocity ωA, where A = 3 mm (given). Let $x = s$ be the position where the block's velocity is zero. Then, using the Work–Energy Theorem between these two states, we have

$$W = \Delta U_{sp} + \Delta K$$

$$\Rightarrow \quad Fs = \frac{1}{2}ks^2 - \frac{1}{2}m(\omega A)^2$$

$$\Rightarrow \quad Fs = \frac{1}{2}ks^2 - \frac{1}{2}kA^2$$

$$\Rightarrow \quad s^2 - \frac{2F}{k}s - A^2 = 0$$

$$\Rightarrow \quad s^2 - 8s - 9 = 0 \Rightarrow s = 4\text{ mm} \pm 5\text{ mm}$$

So, there are two positions where the velocity becomes zero, namely, 4 mm – 5 mm and 4 mm + 5 mm. Thus, the block oscillates about $x = 4$ mm with amplitude $A' = 5$mm. The maximum elongation in the spring is 4 mm + 5 mm = 9 mm ⇒ (a) is right but (b) is incorrect.

Maximum velocity

$$= \omega A' = \sqrt{\frac{k}{m}}A' = \sqrt{\frac{250\text{ N/m}}{0.1\text{ kg}}}(5\text{ mm}) = 0.25\text{ m/s}$$

⇒ (c) is correct

Maximum acceleration

$$= \omega^2 A' = \left(\frac{250\text{ N/m}}{0.1\text{ kg}}\right)(5\text{ mm}) = 12.5\text{ m/s}^2$$

⇒ (d) is incorrect

40. (c) The masses are in the ratio 1:2, so the CM will divide the length in the ratio 2:1. The CM is at a distance of 1/3 from mass m and 21/3 from mass $m/2$. The rotational inertia of the system about an axis perpendicular to the rod and passing through its CM is $I = m\left(\frac{1}{3}\right)^2 + \frac{m}{2}\left(\frac{21}{3}\right)^2 = \frac{1}{3}ml^2$.

When the rod is at angular position θ, it experiences a restoring torque $T = k\theta$. Thus, its angular acceleration is

$$\alpha = \frac{-k\theta}{I} = -\frac{3k}{ml^2}\theta$$

We see that the system performs angular SHM with angular frequency $\omega = \sqrt{\frac{3k}{ml^2}}$.

If the angular amplitude of the rod is θ_0, its angular velocity when it passes through its mean position is

$$\omega_0 = \omega\theta_0 = \sqrt{\frac{3k\theta_0^2}{ml^2}}$$

Now, applying dynamics along the centripetal direction on any one of the masses, say m, gives the tension in the rod as

$$T = m\omega_0^2\frac{l}{3} = \frac{ml}{3} \times \frac{3k\theta_0^2}{ml^2} = \frac{k\theta_0^2}{l}$$

CHAPTER

12 Mechanical Waves

- A wave is any disturbance from an equilibrium condition that propagates from one region of space to another. A mechanical wave always travels within some material called the medium. If the displacements of the medium are perpendicular to the direction of wave propagation, it is called a transverse wave. If the displacements of the medium are along the direction of wave propagation, it is called a longitudinal wave.
- A wave function $y(x,t)$ describes the displacement of individual particles of the medium. For a wave travelling with speed v along the $+x$ direction, $y(x,t)=f\left(t-\frac{x}{v}\right)$ or $f(x-vt)$. The velocity v_y and acceleration a_y of a particle of the medium at any point x and any time t can be found from the derivatives of the wave function:
$$v_y=\frac{\partial y(x,t)}{\partial t} \text{ and } a_y=\frac{\partial^2 y(x,t)}{\partial t^2}$$
The wave functions obey a partial differential equation called the wave equation:
$$\frac{\partial^2 y(x,t)}{\partial x^2}=\frac{1}{v^2}\frac{\partial^2 y(x,t)}{\partial t^2}$$
This equation is one of the most important equations in all of physics.
- In a periodic wave, the motion of each point of the medium is periodic. The frequency f of a periodic wave is the number of repetitions per unit time, and the period T is the time for one cycle. The wavelength λ is the distance over which the wave pattern repeats. For any periodic wave, these quantities are related as
$$v=\lambda f$$
- The wave function for a sine wave of amplitude A travelling with speed v along the $+x$ direction:
$$y(x,t)=A\sin\left\{\omega\left(t-\frac{x}{v}\right)+\phi\right\}=A\sin(\omega t-kx+\phi),$$
where ω is called the angular frequency and k is called the wave number. The frequency, wavelength and speed of the wave are
$$f=\frac{\omega}{2\pi},\ \lambda=\frac{2\pi}{k},\text{ and } v=\lambda f=\frac{\omega}{k}$$
The quantity $\omega t-kx+\phi$ is called the phase, and its value for any x, t determines what part of the sinusoidal cycle is occurring at that particular point and time.
- The speed of a transverse wave on a taut string with tension F and mass per unit length μ:
$$v=\sqrt{F/\mu}$$
The speed of a longitudinal wave in a liquid with bulk modulus B and density ρ:
$$v=\sqrt{B/\rho}$$
The speed of a longitudinal wave in a solid rod with Young's modulus Y and density ρ:
$$v=\sqrt{Y/\rho}$$
The speed of a longitudinal wave in an ideal gas with pressure P and density ρ (wave propagation in gases is ordinarily an adiabatic process):
$$v=\sqrt{\gamma P/\rho}=\sqrt{\gamma RT/M}$$

- Longitudinal waves in fluids may also be described in terms of pressure variations at various points:

$$p(x,t) = -B\frac{\partial y(x,t)}{\partial x}$$

For the sinusoidal wave function $y(x,t) = A\sin(\omega t - kx + \phi)$, $p(x,t) = BkA\cos(\omega t - kx + \phi)$

Here $p_{amp} = BkA$ is called the pressure amplitude.

- When a wave travels from one medium to another, its speed and wavelength changes, but the frequency remains the same. If the speed and the wavelength are v_1, λ_1 in one medium and v_2, λ_2 in the other medium, then

$$\frac{v_1}{\lambda_1} = \frac{v_2}{\lambda_2}$$

When a wave travelling in medium 1 enters into another medium 2, partial reflection and partial transmission occur at the boundary separating the two mediums. The transmitted wave is in phase with the incident wave. But the reflected wave undergoes a phase change of π if medium 2 is denser than medium 1, and no phase change if medium 2 is rarer than medium 1.

- Wave motion conveys energy from one region to another. For a sinusoidal wave on a stretched string, the average power is

$$P_{av} = \frac{1}{2}\sqrt{\mu F}\,\omega^2 A^2$$

For a sinusoidal longitudinal wave in a fluid, the average intensity is

$$I_{av} = \frac{1}{2}\sqrt{\rho B}\,\omega^2 A^2$$

and for a solid rod, it is given by

$$I_{av} = \frac{1}{2}\sqrt{\rho Y}\,\omega^2 A^2$$

- Overlapping of two or more waves in the same region of space is called interference. The principle of superposition states that the total displacement at any point where two or more waves interfere is the vector sum of the displacements of the individual waves.

If two sinusoidal waves of amplitudes A_1 and A_2 arrive at a point, with a phase difference of ϕ, then the resultant amplitude A_{res} at that point is

$$A_{res}^2 = A_1^2 + A_2^2 + 2A_1A_2\cos\phi$$

$$\Rightarrow |A_1 - A_2| \le A_{res} \le A_1 + A_2$$

When $\phi = 0$, the resultant amplitude equals $A_1 + A_2$, and the interference is called constructive. When $\phi = \pi$, the resultant amplitude equals $|A_1 - A_2|$, and the interference is called destructive. Note that the amplitudes add like vectors. This observation will be useful when finding the resultant amplitude of more than two waves.

- Beats occur when two waves of different frequencies interfere. If the individual functions representing the two waves arriving at a point are $y_1 = A\sin(\omega_1 t)$ and $y_2 = A\sin(\omega_2 t)$, then the resultant wave function obtained by adding the two functions is

$$y(t) = 2A\cos\left\{\left(\frac{\omega_1 - \omega_2}{2}\right)t\right\}\sin\left\{\left(\frac{\omega_1 + \omega_2}{2}\right)t\right\}$$

The resultant wave oscillates with frequency $\dfrac{\left|\dfrac{\omega_1+\omega_2}{2}\right|}{2\pi}=\dfrac{f_1+f_2}{2}$, called the oscillation frequency. The resultant amplitude $A_{res}=2A\left|\cos\left\{\left(\dfrac{\omega_1-\omega_2}{2}\right)t\right\}\right|$ varies periodically with time. It repeats with frequency $2\times\dfrac{\left|\dfrac{\omega_1-\omega_2}{2}\right|}{2\pi}=|f_1-f_2|$, called the beat frequency.

- Standing waves are formed when two sinusoidal waves of the same frequency, same amplitude, but travelling in opposite directions, interfere. Consider a string stretched along the positive half of the x-axis, with its fixed end at the origin. A wave $y_1=A\sin(\omega t+kx)$ travelling towards the $-x$ direction reaches the fixed point. A reflected wave $y_2=A\sin(\omega t-kx+\pi)=-A\sin(\omega t-kx)$, which is completely out of phase with the incident wave, travels towards the $+x$ direction. The resultant wave function obtained by adding the two functions is

$$y(x,t)=2A\sin(kx)\cos(\omega t)$$

The resultant amplitude $A_{res}=2A|\sin(kx)|$ repeats periodically with position. Points not moving at all $(\text{where }\sin(kx)=0)$ are called nodes, and those oscillating with greatest amplitude $(\text{where }\sin(kx)=\pm1)$ are called antinodes. The distance between two successive nodes/antinodes is $\lambda/2$.

- **Normal Modes of Vibration in a String and in an Organ Pipe:** When both ends of a taut string are fixed, standing waves can occur only when its length l is an integral multiple of $\lambda/2$. The corresponding possible frequencies are:

$$f_n=n\left(\frac{v}{2l}\right),\ \text{where } n=1,2,3,\ldots$$

If one end of the string is fixed and the other end is free, standing waves can occur only when its length l is an odd integral multiple of $\lambda/4$. The corresponding possible frequencies are:

$$f_n=n\left(\frac{v}{4l}\right),\ \text{where } n=1,3,5,\ldots$$

The same results hold true for an organ pipe of length l. The lowest possible frequency is called the fundamental frequency and all other possible frequencies are called harmonics (2nd harmonic, 3rd harmonic, and so on). The effective length of the organ pipe is taken as $l+\Delta l$ for a closed pipe (one opening) and $l+2\Delta l$ for an open pipe (two openings), where $\Delta l=0.6r$, r is the radius of the pipe. The length Δl is called the end correction.

- The Doppler effect for sound is the frequency shift that occurs when there is motion of the sound source or the observer or both, relative to the medium. The source and observer frequencies f_S and f_O are related to the source and observer velocities v_S and v_O relative to the medium as

$$f_O=\left(\frac{v\pm v_O}{v\pm v_S}\right)f_S,$$

where v is the speed of sound relative to the medium. The choice of sign has to be made keeping in mind that the observed frequency increases when they are approaching and decreases when they are receding. While choosing the sign in the numerator, only the observer's motion must be taken into account, and while choosing the sign in the denominator, only the source's motion must be taken into account.

The speed of moving objects can be measured by using the Doppler effect. A wave of frequency f fired from a Doppler gun towards a moving object, say a car, is reflected with a changed frequency $f+\Delta f$. The change in frequency Δf is positive when the car is approaching, and negative when it is receding. If v is the velocity of the wave and v_C is the velocity of the car, then

$$\frac{\Delta f}{f}=\frac{2v_C}{v}(\text{for } v_C\ll v)$$

EXERCISES

1. Transverse waves are generated at the end $(x = 0)$ of a long string by a tuning fork of frequency 500 Hz. At a certain instant of time, the displacement of particle $A(x = 1.0\text{ m})$ is -0.05 cm and of particle $B(x = 2.0\text{ m})$ is $+0.05$ cm, with both particles moving towards their mean position. In between A and B, there is no other particle in phase with either of them. Time taken by the wave to travel from A to B is:

(a) 5 ms (b) 2 ms
(c) 1 ms (d) 0.1 ms

2. The speed of longitudinal waves through brass is ten times the speed of transverse waves in a taut wire of brass. Then the strain in the wire is:

(a) 0.2% (b) 0.5%
(c) 0.7% (d) 1.0%

3. The figure shows the shape of a string at $t = 0$. The wave is travelling along the +ve x direction with velocity $v = 80$ m/s. P is a point on the string at $x = 2$ m.

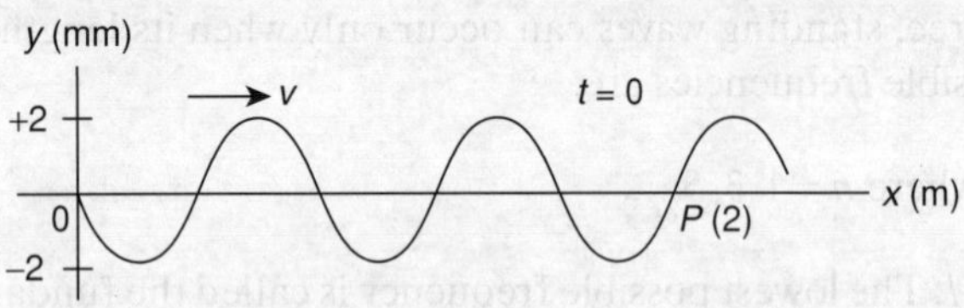

If $y_P(t)$ and $v_P(t)$ represent its displacement and velocity at time t, then:

(a) $y_P(t) = 2\text{ mm}\sin\{(200\pi\text{s}^{-1})t\}$

(b) $y_P(t) = -2\text{ mm}\sin\{(200\pi\text{ s}^{-1})t\}$

(c) $v_P(0) = -0.4\pi$ m/s

(d) $v_P(0) = 0.4\pi$ m/s

4. Equations of a travelling and a stationary wave are, respectively, $y = A\sin(\omega t - kx)$ and $y = B\sin(kx)\cos(\omega t)$. Phase difference between two points $x_1 = \dfrac{\pi}{3k}$ and $x_2 = \dfrac{3\pi}{2k}$, is φ_1 and φ_2, respectively, for the two waves. Then $\dfrac{\varphi_2}{\varphi_1}$ equals:

(a) $1/2$ (b) $6/7$
(c) $3/4$ (d) $6/5$

5. The figure shows two snapshots of a transverse wave travelling along a string, at times $t = 0$ and $t = 0.05$ s; in this time interval, the shape has not repeated.

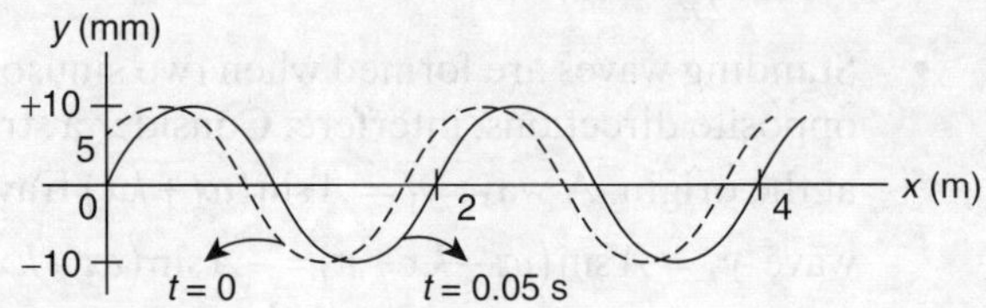

The function representing the wave motion is:

(a) $y(x,t) = 10\text{ mm}\cos\left(\dfrac{20\pi}{3}t - \pi x + \dfrac{\pi}{3}\right)$

(b) $y(x,t) = 10\text{ mm}\cos\left(\dfrac{10\pi}{3}t - \pi x + \dfrac{\pi}{6}\right)$

(c) $y(x,t) = 10\text{ mm}\cos\left(\dfrac{20\pi}{3}t - \pi x + \dfrac{\pi}{6}\right)$

(d) $y(x,t) = 10\text{ mm}\cos\left(\dfrac{10\pi}{3}t - \pi x + \dfrac{\pi}{3}\right)$

6. A transverse wave has amplitude $A = \sqrt{3}$ mm and frequency $f = 4$ Hz. Two particles P and Q are separated by a distance $\Delta x = 47$ cm, and the wave is travelling with velocity $v = 48$ cm/s from P to Q. At some instant when P is crossing its mean position and moving upward, the velocity of Q will be:

(a) 8πmm/s downward
(b) 8π mm/s upward
(c) 12π mm/s downward
(d) 12π mm/s upward

7. A tuning fork of frequency 244 Hz is used in a resonance column experiment. If the minimum height at which resonance occurs is (0.350 ± 0.005) m, the gas in the tube is (take $\sqrt{167RT} = 640\text{ J}^{1/2}\text{mole}^{-1/2}$ $\sqrt{140RT} = 590\text{ J}^{1/2}\text{mole}^{-1/2}$; the values of $\sqrt{10/M}$ where M is molar mass in gram/mole are also given for each gas):

(a) Neon $\left(\sqrt{\dfrac{10}{M}} = \dfrac{7}{10}\right)$

(b) Nitrogen $\left(\sqrt{\dfrac{10}{M}} = \dfrac{3}{5}\right)$

(c) Oxygen $\left(\sqrt{\frac{10}{M}}=\frac{9}{10}\right)$

(d) Argon $\left(\sqrt{\frac{10}{M}}=\frac{17}{32}\right)$

8. Two parts of a sonometer wire divided by a moveable knife edge differ in length by 1 cm and produce 1 beat / s when sounded together in their fundamental modes. If the total length of the wire is 100 cm, the fundamental frequencies of these two parts of the wire are:
(a) 51.5 Hz, 50.5 Hz (b) 50.5 Hz, 49.5 Hz
(c) 49.5 Hz, 48.5 Hz (d) 49 Hz, 48 Hz

9. A tuning fork of frequency 340 Hz is vibrated above a cylindrical tube 1 m high. Water is slowly poured into the tube. If the speed of sound is 340 m/s, the water levels at which resonance occurs are:
(a) 25 cm, 75 cm (b) 20 cm, 80 cm
(c) 15 cm, 85 cm (d) 17 cm, 83 cm

10. A sonometer wire 65 cm long is in resonance with a tuning fork. If the length of the wire is decreased by 1 cm and is vibrated in the same mode with the same tuning fork, 8 beats are heard per second. Frequency of the tuning fork is:
(a) 256 Hz (b) 384 Hz
(c) 480 Hz (d) 512 Hz

11. A metal wire is held on two knife edges. The tension in the wire is 100 N. The wire vibrating in its fundamental mode with a tuning fork produces 5 beats/s. The tension in the wire is then reduced to 81 N. When the two are excited, beats are heard at the same rate. The frequency of the tuning fork is:
(a) 90 Hz (b) 95 Hz
(c) 100 Hz (d) 105 Hz

12. Two longitudinal waves of wavelength 1 m and 1.01 m interfere to produce 10 beats in 3 seconds. Velocity of the waves is:
(a) 333.33 m/s (b) 336.67 m/s
(c) 636.67 m/s (d) 833.33 m/s

13. Two identical flutes are in unison when they are at the same temperature 27°C. When the temperature of air in one flute is increased to 31°C, 2 beats are heard per second. Frequency of the note when the flutes were in unison is:
(a) 250 Hz (b) 300 Hz
(c) 350 Hz (d) 400 Hz

14. A wave is propagating along the x-axis. At $t = 0$, the displacement of the particles of the medium along the x-axis is given by the function $y = A\exp\{-(x+2)^2\}$; all quantities are in SI units. At $t = 1$ ms, the same wave disturbance is given by $y = A\exp\{-(2-x)^2\}$. Then the wave velocity is:
(a) 2000 m/s along +ve x-axis
(b) 2000 m/s along −ve x-axis
(c) 4000 m/s along +ve x-axis
(d) 4000 m/s along −ve x-axis

15. An aluminium wire of length 60 cm and cross-sectional area 3 mm^2 is joined to a steel wire of length 80 cm and cross-sectional area 1 mm^2. The composite wire is held between two fixed supports, under a tension of 40 N. The minimum frequency of the tuning fork which can produce standing waves with the joint as a node is (take $\rho_{Al} = 2.6$ g/cc and $\rho_{st} = 7.8$ g/cc):
(a) 150 Hz (b) 179 Hz
(c) 250 Hz (d) 289 Hz

16. An organ pipe A open at both ends and containing a mono-atomic gas is vibrating in its second harmonic. Another organ pipe B open at one end and containing a di-atomic gas is vibrating in its third harmonic. The pipes are in resonance with a given tuning fork. If the temperature and length of the pipes are the same, the ratio M_A / M_B of the molar mass of the gases is:
(a) $\frac{96}{75}$ (b) $\frac{112}{27}$
(c) $\frac{100}{63}$ (d) $\frac{400}{189}$

17. A taut metal wire at temperature 30°C vibrates with its fundamental frequency of 1 kHz. The same wire with the same tension but at temperature 10°C vibrates with a fundamental frequency of 1.01 kHz. Coefficient of linear expansion of the wire is:
(a) $2.0\times10^{-3}\,°C^{-1}$ (b) $1.5\times10^{-3}\,°C^{-1}$
(c) $1.0\times10^{-3}\,°C^{-1}$ (d) $0.5\times10^{-3}\,°C^{-1}$

18. A knife edge divides a sonometer wire into two parts having fundamental frequencies f_1 and f_2. The fundamental frequency of the sonometer wire when the knife edge is removed will be:

(a) $f_1 + f_2$ (b) $\frac{1}{2}(f_1 + f_2)$

(c) $\sqrt{f_1 + f_2}$ (d) $\frac{f_1 f_2}{f_1 + f_2}$

19. A metal rod of length 1 m is clamped at its middle point and set into longitudinal vibrations in such a manner that there are two nodes on either side of the mid-point. Density of the rod is 8×10^3 kg/m^3 and its Young's modulus is 2×10^{11} Pa. If the amplitude of the antinode is $2\sqrt{2}$ μm, the motion of a point 1 cm from its mid-point may be represented by the equation:

(a) $1\ \mu\text{m} \sin\{(25000\pi\,\text{s}^{-1})t\}$

(b) $2\ \mu\text{m} \sin\{(25000\pi\,\text{s}^{-1})t\}$

(c) $1\ \mu\text{m} \sin\{(12500\pi\,\text{s}^{-1})t\}$

(d) $2\ \mu\text{m} \sin\{(12500\pi\,\text{s}^{-1})t\}$

20. In the resonance experiment for determining the speed of sound using a tuning fork of frequency 480 Hz, the first resonance was observed at 17.7 cm of the air column and the second at 53.1 cm. If the least count of the metre scale is 0.1 cm, the maximum possible error in the speed of sound in air is:

(a) 1.92 m/s (b) 0.96 m/s

(c) 0.64 m/s (d) 0.48 m/s

21. Four harmonic waves of equal frequency and intensity I_0 have initial phase angles $0, \frac{\pi}{3}, \frac{2\pi}{3}, \pi$. When they are superposed, the intensity is nI_0. The value of n is:

(a) 2 (b) 3

(c) 4 (d) 5

22. A detector receives two EM waves of the same amplitude A but different frequencies; $\Delta f = 1000$ Hz. If the detector detects amplitudes $\geq A$, the time interval for which the detector remains idle in each beat cycle is:

(a) 0.10 ms (b) 0.20 ms

(c) 0.25 ms (d) 0.33 ms

23. A source emitting sound waves and a detector are stationed at the same position. If an object approaches the source, the sound waves reflected from the object's surface will be received by the detector. If the received frequency is found to be 1.5 times the emitted frequency and the speed of the sound and is 360 m/s, then the speed of the approaching object is:

(a) 20 m/s (b) 40 m/s

(c) 60 m/s (d) 72 m/s

24. The correct statements among the following are:

(a) When ultrasonic wave travels from air into water, the speed of the wave increases and it bends towards the normal.

(b) The decrease in the speed of sound at high altitudes is due to the fall in pressure.

(c) Thermal radiations from the Sun are transverse waves.

(d) If the apparent frequency is f_1 when the source approaches the observer, and f_2 when the observer approaches the source with the same velocity, then $f_2 < f_1$.

25. Beats are produced by superposition of two waves represented by $y_1 = 0.001\cos(0.5\pi x - 100\pi t)$ and $y_2 = 0.001\cos(0.46\pi x - 92\pi t)$; all quantities are in MKS units. The number of oscillations made by a particle in one beat cycle is:

(a) 14 (b) 12

(c) 10 (d) 18

26. The vibrations of a string of length 60 cm fixed at both ends are represented by the equation $y = 0.4\sin(\pi x/15)\cos(96\pi t)$; all quantities are in CGS units. The harmonic mode in which the string is vibrating is:

(a) Fundamental (b) Third

(c) Fourth (d) Fifth

27. A train blows a whistle as it passes through a station at a constant speed. A stationary observer at the station platform measures the frequency of the whistle as 484 Hz when the train is approaching the station, and 442 Hz when the train is leaving the station. If the speed of sound in air is 330 m/s, then the train's speed is:

(a) 72 km/h (b) 60 km/h

(c) 56 km/h (d) 54 km/h

28. From the following pairs of progressive waves, those which will combine to produce a stationary wave with a node at $x = 0$ are:

(a) $y_1 = A\sin(\omega t - kx)$ and $y_2 = A\sin\left(\omega t + kx + \frac{\pi}{2}\right)$

(b) $y_1 = A\sin(\omega t - kx)$ and $y_2 = A\sin(\omega t + kx) + \pi$

(c) $y_1 = A\cos(\omega t - kx)$ and $y_2 = A\cos\left(\omega t + kx + \frac{\pi}{2}\right)$

(d) $y_1 = A\cos(\omega t - kx)$ and $y_2 = A\cos(\omega t + kx) + \pi$

29. One end of a taut string of length 3 m along the x-axis is fixed at $x = 0$. The speed of the wave is 100 m/s. Stationary waves are set in the string such that its other end $x = 3$ m vibrates freely along the y direction. The possible functions of these stationary waves are:

(a) $y = A\sin\left(\frac{\pi x}{6}\right)\cos\left(\frac{50\pi t}{3}\right)$

(b) $y = A\sin\left(\frac{\pi x}{3}\right)\cos\left(\frac{100\pi t}{3}\right)$

(c) $y = A\sin\left(\frac{5\pi x}{6}\right)\cos\left(\frac{250\pi t}{3}\right)$

(d) $y = A\sin\left(\frac{5\pi x}{2}\right)\cos(250\pi t)$

30. The air column in a pipe closed at one end is vibrating in its second overtone. The end correction may be neglected. Let P_0 denote the pressure amplitude at the positions of the displacement nodes. Then the pressure amplitude at the middle of the air column is:

(a) 0 (b) P_0

(c) $P_0/2$ (d) $P_0/\sqrt{2}$

31. The figure shows two sources A and B emitting longitudinal waves uniformly in all directions. The amplitude of the waves from source A is 4 mm, and that from source B is 3 mm. Both sources are vibrating in phase at a frequency of 172 Hz.

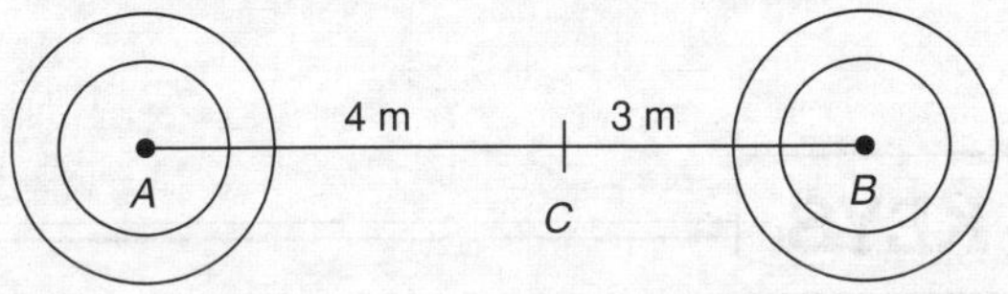

If the velocity of wave propagation is 344 m/s, then the amplitude of the resultant wave at point C is:

(a) 1 mm (b) 4 mm

(c) 5 mm (d) 7 mm

32. A bird in air and a fish in water are moving along the vertical direction away from each other, with velocities $v/3$ and $v/4$, respectively. The bird is producing a sound of wavelength λ in air. If sound travels with velocity v in air and $9v/4$ in water, then the wavelength of the wave received by the fish is:

(a) 3λ (b) 4λ

(c) $\frac{27}{8}\lambda$ (d) $\frac{81}{64}\lambda$

33. Two loudspeakers A and B are located 20 m apart and emit sound of frequencies 118 Hz and 121 Hz, respectively. A car moves along the perpendicular bisector PQR of line AB, where Q is the mid-point of AB. Points P and R lie on opposite sides of Q at a distance of 1800 m from Q. The car starts from point P, crosses Q and then reaches R. Let $f(t)$ represent the beat frequency measured by a person sitting in the car. If the car moves with a uniform speed 60 km/h and the speed of sound is 330 m/s, then the correct statements from the following are:

(a) Rate of change of f is greatest when the car crosses Q

(b) Rate of change of f is least when the car crosses Q

(c) $f_p + f_R$ equals four times f_Q

(d) $f_P - f_R$ approximately equals one-tenth of f_Q

34. The figure shows the displacement y as a function of x for $t = 0$. The wave is travelling along the +ve x direction with velocity 100 m/s.

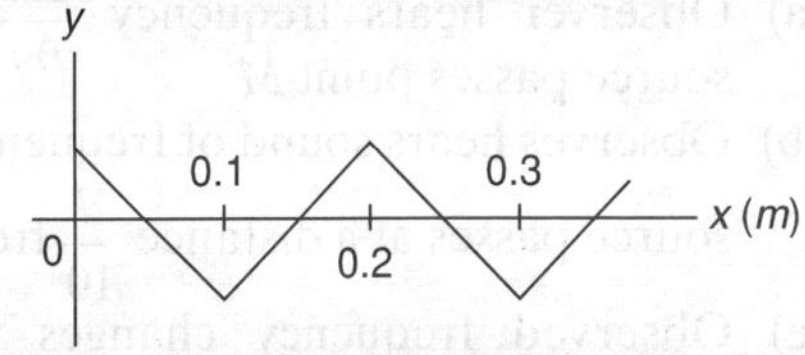

The graph showing the displacement as a function of t for the particle located at $x = 0.05$ m is:

(a)

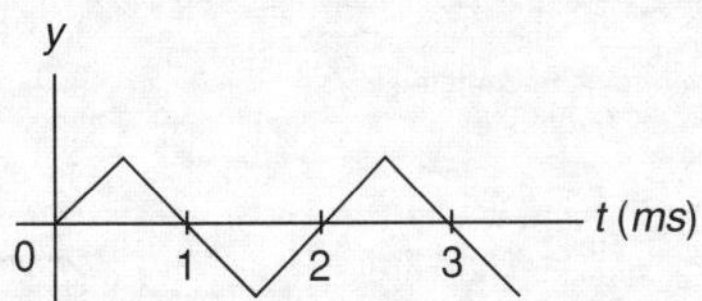

(b)

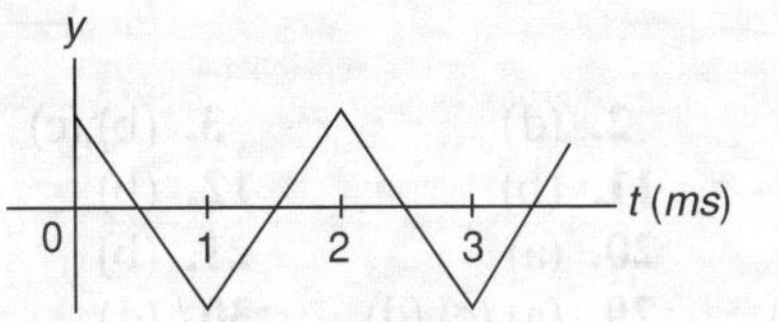

(c)

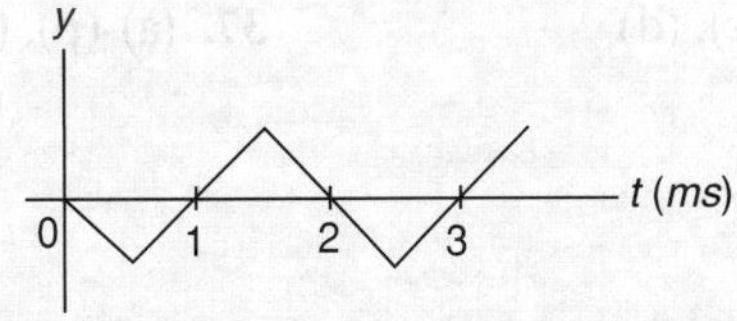

(d)

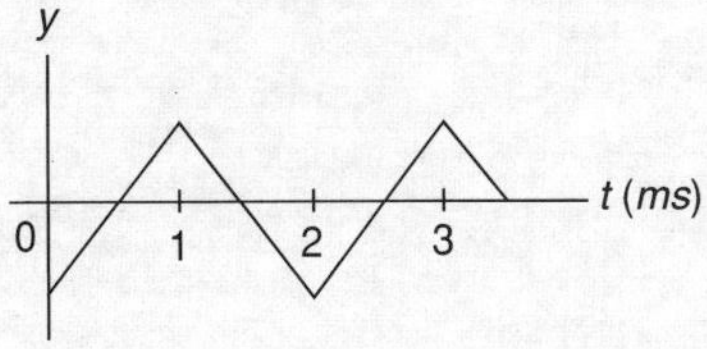

35. An aluminium rod of length 1 m is clamped at two points, 5 cm from the left end and 15 cm from the right end. The density of aluminium is 2500 kg/m^3 and its Young's modulus is 1.6×10^{11} Pa. The fundamental and the first overtone frequencies of the natural longitudinal oscillations are:
(a) 40 kHz, 80 kHz (b) 40 kHz, 120 kHz
(c) 60 kHz, 120 kHz (d) 60 kHz, 180 kHz

36. A source S emitting sound of frequency f, moving along a straight track, approaches an observer O standing at a perpendicular distance d from the track (see figure).

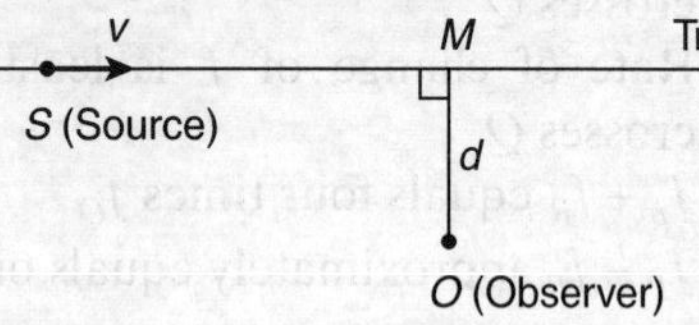

If the velocity of the source is v and the velocity of sound is $10v$, then the correct statements from the following are:
(a) Observer hears frequency $\frac{100}{99}f$ when the source passes point M
(b) Observes hears sound of frequency f when the source passes at a distance $\frac{d}{10}$ from point M
(c) Observed frequency changes most rapidly when the source passes point M
(d) Observed frequency varies over a range of $\frac{20}{99}f$

37. A pulse is travelling with speed v along a taut string of length L. One end of the string is fixed and one end free. The figure shows the shape of the string at time $t = 0$. Consider the length of the pulse to be negligibly small in comparison to the length of the string.

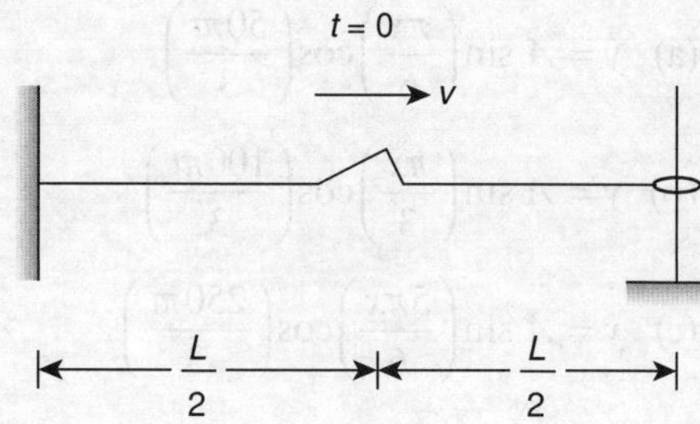

Match the shape of the string with time in the two columns:

(a) $t = L/v$ (p) 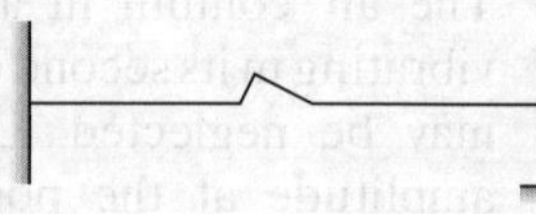

(b) $t = 2L/v$ (q) 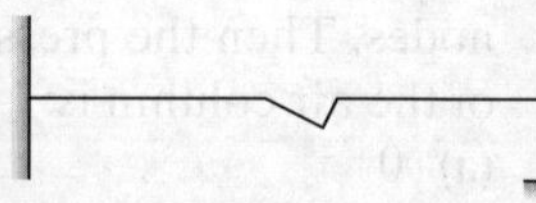

(c) $t = 3L/v$ (r) 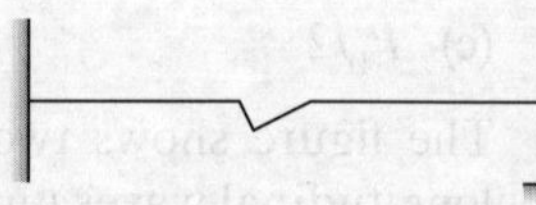

(d) $t = 4L/v$ (s) 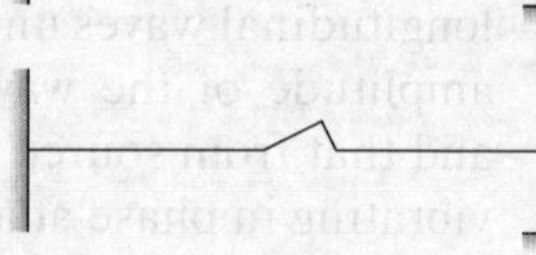

ANSWER KEYS

1. (c)	**2.** (d)	**3.** (b),(c)	**4.** (d)	**5.** (d)	**6.** (d)	**7.** (d)	**8.** (b)	**9.** (a)
10. (d)	**11.** (b)	**12.** (b)	**13.** (b)	**14.** (c)	**15.** (b)	**16.** (d)	**17.** (c)	**18.** (d)
19. (b)	**20.** (a)	**21.** (b)	**22.** (d)	**23.** (d)	**24.** (c),(d)	**25.** (b)	**26.** (c)	**27.** (d)
28. (b), (d)	**29.** (a),(c),(d)	**30.** (d)	**31.** (a)	**32.** (c)	**33.** (a),(d)	**34.** (a)	**35.** (b)	

36. (a), (b), (c), (d) **37.** (a)-(p), (b)-(r), (c)-(q), (d)-(s)

SOLUTIONS

1. (c) The phase difference between the two particles is $\Delta\theta = \pi$ rad (see figure) and the angular velocity of the phasor is $\omega = 2\pi f = 1000\,\pi$ rad/s.

Hence the required time $\Delta t = \dfrac{\Delta\theta}{\omega} = \dfrac{1}{1000}\text{ s} = 1\text{ ms}$

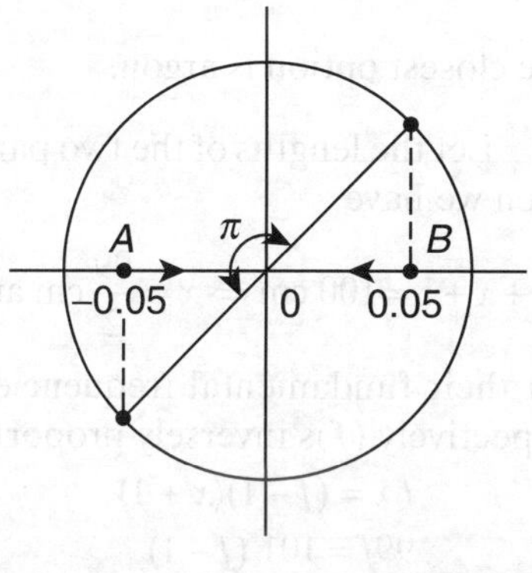

2. (d) Let Y and ρ be the Young's modulus of elasticity and the density of brass, respectively. The speed of longitudinal waves though brass equals $\sqrt{\dfrac{Y}{\rho}}$. If a wire of cross-section area A is made of brass, its linear density will be $\mu = \rho A$. If F is the tension in the wire, then the speed of the transverse waves in the wire equals $\sqrt{\dfrac{F}{\rho A}}$.

According to the question, we have

$$\sqrt{\frac{Y}{\rho}} = 10\sqrt{\frac{F}{\rho A}}$$

$$\Rightarrow \quad \frac{F/A}{Y} = \frac{1}{100}$$

$\Rightarrow$ Strain in the wire = 1%

3. (b), (c) From the graph, we see that

$$2.5\lambda = 2\text{ m} \Rightarrow \lambda = 0.8\text{ m}$$

Hence $k = \dfrac{2\pi}{\lambda} = 2.5\pi\,\text{m}^{-1}$

The wave pattern at time $t = 0$ is given by

$$y(x, 0) = -2\text{ mm}\sin(2.5\pi x)$$

The wave velocity is given to be $v = 80$ m/s. Hence, the wave pattern at time $t = t$ is given by

$$y(x, t) = -2\text{ mm}\sin\{2.5\pi(x - 80t)\}$$
$$= -2\text{ mm}\sin(2.5\pi x - 200t)$$

For particle P, we insert $x = 2m$. Hence, we have

$$y_P(t) = -2\text{ mm}\sin(5\pi - 200t)$$
$$= -2\text{ mm}\sin(200t)$$

$\Rightarrow \quad v_P(t) = -0.4\,\pi\text{ m/s}\cos(200t)$

Hence $\quad v_P(0) = -0.4\,\pi$ m/s

4. (d) For the travelling wave, the phase difference between the two points is given by

$$\varphi_1 = k\,|x_2 - x_1| = k\left|\frac{3\pi}{2k} - \frac{\pi}{3k}\right| = \frac{7\pi}{6} = \frac{5\pi}{6}$$

The phase difference is always a number lying between 0 and π. It is always chosen as the smallest angular separation between the phasors.

For the stationary wave, the equation of motion for the two points x_1 and x_2 are, respectively

$$y_1 = B\sin\left(\frac{\pi}{3}\right)\cos(\omega t) = \frac{\sqrt{3}}{2}B\cos(\omega t)$$

and $$y_2 = B\sin\left(\frac{3\pi}{2}\right)\cos(\omega t) = -B\cos(\omega t)$$
$$= B\cos(\omega t + \pi)$$

Thus, the phase difference between the two points in the case of stationary waves is $\phi_2 = \pi$.

Hence $\dfrac{\varphi_2}{\varphi_1} = \dfrac{6}{5}$.

5. (d)

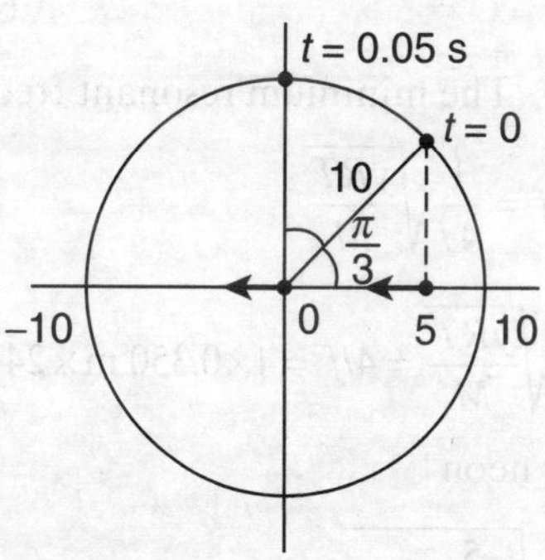

From the graph, we see that

$$\lambda = 2\text{ m} \Rightarrow k = \frac{2\pi}{\lambda} = \pi\,\text{m}^{-1}$$

From the phasor diagram (see figure) of the particle, we see that the phase angle changes from $\pi/3$ to $\pi/2$ in time 0.05 s. Thus, we have

$$\omega = \frac{\frac{\pi}{2} - \frac{\pi}{3}}{0.05} \text{ rad/s} = \frac{10\pi}{3} \text{ rad/s}$$

The function representing the motion of the particle located at $x = 0$ is

$$y(0, t) = 10 \text{ mm} \cos\left(\omega t + \frac{\pi}{3}\right)$$

[$\pi/3$ is the initial phase angle]

Hence, the wave function is

$$y(x,t) = 10 \text{ mm} \cos\left(\omega t - \pi x + \frac{\pi}{3}\right)$$

6. (d) The angular frequency is $\omega = 2\pi f = 8\pi$ rad/s. Motion of P can be represented by the function

$$y_P(t) = \sqrt{3} \text{ mm} \sin(8\pi t)$$

The particle Q lags in phase with respect to P by

$$\varphi = k\Delta x = \frac{8\pi \text{ rad/s}}{48 \text{ cm/s}} \times 47 \text{ cm} = \frac{47\pi}{6} = 8\pi + \frac{-\pi}{6}$$

Thus, the motion of Q can be represented by the function

$$y_Q(t) = \sqrt{3} \text{ mm} \sin\left(8\pi t + \frac{\pi}{6}\right)$$

The velocity of Q is given by the function

$$v_Q(t) = 8\pi\sqrt{3} \text{ mm}/s \cos\left(8\pi t + \frac{\pi}{6}\right)$$

Thus, the velocity of Q at $t = 0$ is

$$v_Q(0) = 8\pi\sqrt{3} \text{ mm/s} \cos\left(\frac{\pi}{6}\right) = 12 \text{ mm/s.}$$

7. (d) The minimum resonant frequency is given by

$$f = \frac{1}{4l}\sqrt{\frac{yRT}{M}}$$

$$\Rightarrow \sqrt{\frac{yRT}{M}} = 4lf = 4 \times 0.350 \text{ m} \times 244 \text{ Hz} = 341.6 \text{ m/s}$$

For neon

$$\sqrt{\frac{\frac{5}{3}RT}{M \times 10^{-3}}} = \sqrt{\frac{10}{M} \times 167RT} = \frac{7}{10} \times 640 = 168 \text{ m/s}$$

For nitrogen

$$\sqrt{\frac{\frac{7}{5}RT}{M \times 10^{-3}}} = \sqrt{\frac{10}{M} \times 140RT} = \frac{3}{5} \times 590 = 354 \text{ m/s}$$

For oxygen

$$\sqrt{\frac{\frac{7}{5}RT}{M \times 10^{-3}}} = \sqrt{\frac{10}{M} \times 140RT} = \frac{9}{16} \times 590 = 332 \text{ m/s}$$

For argon

$$\sqrt{\frac{\frac{5}{3}RT}{M \times 10^{-3}}} = \sqrt{\frac{10}{M} \times 167RT} = \frac{17}{32} \times 640 = 340 \text{ m/s}$$

The closest option is argon.

8. (b) Let the lengths of the two parts be x and $x + 1$. Then we have

$$x + x + 1 = 100 \text{ cm} \Rightarrow x = \frac{99}{2} \text{ cm and } x + 1 = \frac{101}{2} \text{ cm}$$

Let their fundamental frequencies be f and $f - 1$, respectively (f is inversely proportional to l).

$$f x = (f - 1)(x + 1)$$

$$\Rightarrow \quad 99f = 101\,(f - 1)$$

$$\Rightarrow \quad f = 50.5 \text{ Hz and } f - 1 = 49.5 \text{ Hz}$$

9. (a) The length l of air column at which resonance occurs is given by

$$340 \text{ Hz} = (2n - 1)\frac{340 \text{ m/s}}{4l} (n = 1, 2, \ldots)$$

$$\Rightarrow \quad l = \frac{2n - 1}{4} \text{ m} = \frac{1}{4} \text{ m}, \frac{3}{4} \text{ m}, \ldots$$

The corresponding water levels are

$$1 \text{ m} - l = \frac{3}{4} \text{ m}, \frac{1}{4} \text{ m}$$

10. (d) Let f be the frequency of the tuning fork and that of the sonometer wire when its length is 65 cm. According to the question, the frequency of the wire increases to $f + 8$ when its length is reduced to 64 cm. Since frequency is inversely proportional to length, we have

$$f \times 65 \text{ cm} = (f + 8) \times 64 \text{ cm}$$

$$\Rightarrow \quad f = 512 \text{ Hz}$$

11. (b) Let f be the frequency of the tuning fork. Then, the frequency of the sonometer wire is $f + 5$ when tension is 100 N and $f - 5$ when tension is 81 N.

Since f is directly proportional to $\sqrt{F}$, we have

$$\frac{f + 5}{f - 5} = \frac{\sqrt{100}}{\sqrt{81}} = 95 \text{ Hz}$$

12. (b) Let v be the velocity of the waves. Then

$$\frac{v}{1m} - \frac{v}{1.01m} = \frac{10}{3}\,\text{s}^{-1}$$

$$\Rightarrow \quad v = 336.67 \text{ m/s}$$

13. (b) The temperature has changed from 300 K to 304 K, that is, $\frac{\Delta T}{T} = \frac{4}{300}$.

Since $f \propto \sqrt{T}$

$$\frac{\Delta f}{f} = \frac{1}{2}\frac{\Delta T}{T}$$

$$\Rightarrow \quad f = \frac{2\Delta f}{\Delta T/T} = \frac{2 \times 2 \text{ Hz}}{4/300} = 300 \text{ Hz}$$

14. (c) From the given functions

$$y(0) = Ae^{-(x+2)^2} \text{ and } y(1\text{ ms}) = Ae^{-(x-2)^2}$$

$$= Ae^{-(x-4+2)^2}$$

we see that in the wave function at $t = 1$ ms, x has been replaced by $x - 4$. This means the disturbance has moved 4 m along the +ve direction of x-axis. Hence, wave velocity $= \frac{4 \text{ m}}{1 \text{ ms}} = 4000$ m/s (along the $+x$-axis).

15. (b) The natural frequencies of a wire having nodes at both ends are given by

$$f = \frac{n}{2l}\sqrt{\frac{F}{\mu}} = \frac{n}{2l}\sqrt{\frac{F}{\rho A}} \quad (n = 1, 2, \ldots)$$

For standing waves to be formed, both the wires must be vibrating with the same natural frequency. That is

$$\frac{n_1}{2l_1}\sqrt{\frac{F}{\rho_1 A_1}} = \frac{n_2}{2l_2}\sqrt{\frac{F}{\rho_2 A_2}}$$

$$\Rightarrow \quad \frac{n_1}{n_2} = \frac{l_1}{l_2}\sqrt{\frac{\rho_1 A_1}{\rho_2 A_2}} = \frac{60}{80}\sqrt{\frac{2.6 \times 3}{7.8 \times 1}} = \frac{3}{4}$$

$$\Rightarrow \quad \frac{n_1}{3} = \frac{n_2}{4}$$

Hence, the minimum frequency for which standing waves are formed in the composite wire with the joint as a node is

$$f = \frac{3}{2l_1}\sqrt{\frac{F}{\rho_1 A_1}}$$

$$\Rightarrow \quad f = \frac{3}{2(0.6 \text{ m})}\sqrt{\frac{40 \text{ N}}{(2.6 \times 10^3 \text{ kg/m}^3)(3 \times 10^{-6} \text{ m}^2)}}$$

$$= 179 \text{ Hz.}$$

16. (d) Let l be the length of the pipes. Let v_A and v_B be the velocities of wave propagation in pipes A and B, respectively. Then, according to the question

$$2\left(\frac{v_A}{2l}\right) = 3\left(\frac{v_B}{4l}\right)$$

$$\Rightarrow \quad \frac{v_A}{v_A} = \frac{3}{4}$$

$$\Rightarrow \quad \sqrt{\frac{Y_A M_B}{Y_B M_A}} = \frac{3}{4}$$

$$\Rightarrow \quad \frac{M_A}{M_B} = \frac{16}{9} \times \frac{Y_A}{Y_B} = \frac{16}{9} \times \frac{5/3}{7/5} = \frac{400}{189}$$

17. (c) The fundamental frequency of a wire fixed at both ends is

$$f = \frac{1}{2l}\sqrt{\frac{F}{\mu}} = \frac{1}{2l}\sqrt{\frac{Fl}{m}}$$

We see that $f \propto \frac{1}{\sqrt{l}}$. Hence, we have

$$\Rightarrow \quad \frac{\Delta f}{f} = -\frac{1}{2}\frac{\Delta l}{l} = -\frac{1}{2}(\alpha \Delta T)$$

(α is the coefficient of linear expansion)

$$\Rightarrow \quad \frac{0.01}{1} = -\frac{1}{2}a(-20°\text{C})$$

$$\Rightarrow \quad \alpha = 10^{-3}\,°\text{C}^{-1}$$

18. (d) We know that f is inversely proportional to l.

So, let $f_1 = \frac{c}{l_1}$ and $f_2 = \frac{c}{l_2}$.

Then, the required frequency f is given by

$$f = \frac{c}{l_1 + l_2} = \frac{c}{\frac{c}{f_1} + \frac{c}{f_2}} = \frac{f_1 f_2}{f_1 + f_2}$$

19. (b) The edges of the rod must be the positions of the antinodes. Two nodes on either side of the mid-point means five complete loops (see figure).

Hence, we have

$$\frac{5\lambda}{2} = 1m \Rightarrow \lambda = \frac{2}{5}m$$

The velocity of wave propagation is

$$v = \sqrt{\frac{Y}{\rho}} = \sqrt{\frac{2\times 10^{11}\,\text{N/m}^2}{8\times 10^3\,\text{kg/m}^3}} = 5000\text{ m/s}$$

The angular frequency and the wave number are, respectively

$$\omega = 2\pi\frac{v}{\lambda} = 25000\pi\text{ rad/s and } k = \frac{2\pi}{\lambda} = 5\pi\text{ m}^{-1}$$

If we choose the mid-point as origin, then

$$A(x) = 2\sqrt{2}\mu m\,|\sin(5\pi x)|$$

At a distance 5 cm from the mid-point, the amplitude is

$$A(5cm) = 2\sqrt{2}\mu m\left|\sin\left(5\pi\frac{5}{100}\right)\right| = 2\mu m$$

Hence, the equation of motion at this point will be of type $y(t) = 2\ \mu m\ \sin(25000\ \mu t + \varphi)$ hence, (b) is a possible option.

20. (a) In this experiment, $\frac{\lambda}{2} = l_2 - l_1$.

The error in determination of wavelength is given by

$$\Delta\lambda = 2\,(\Delta l_1 + \Delta l_2) = 0.4\text{ cm}$$

Hence, the error in determination of v is given by

$$\Delta v = f\Delta\lambda = 0.4\times 480\text{ Hz} = 192\text{ cm/s or } 1\ 92\text{ m/s}$$

21. (b) Let A be the amplitude of each wave. We know that amplitudes add like vectors. Hence, the resultant amplitude (see figure) is

$$A_{\text{res}} = 2A\sin 60° = \sqrt{3}A$$

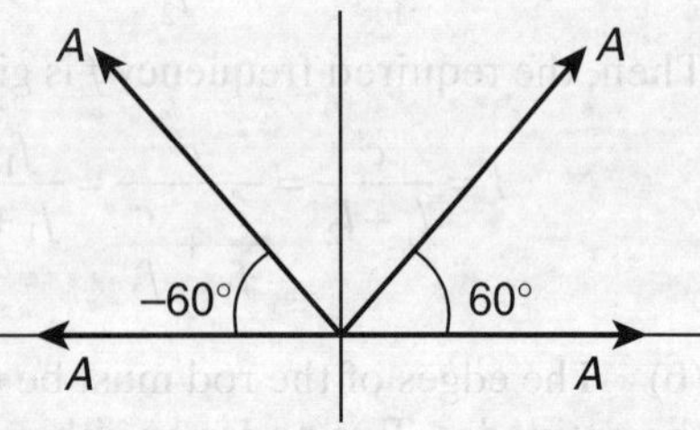

The resultant intensity

$$I_{\text{res}} \propto A_{\text{res}}^2 = 3A^2 = 3I_0 \Rightarrow n = 3$$

22. (d) The resultant amplitude is given by

$$A_{\text{res}}(t) = 2A\left|\cos\left(\frac{\Delta\omega}{2}t\right)\right| = 2A\,|\cos(1000\pi t)|$$

The figure shows the graph of A_{res} versus time t. The times when $A_{\text{res}} = A$ are given by

$$2A\cos(1000\ \pi t) = \pm A$$

$$\Rightarrow \quad \cos(1000\pi t) = \pm\frac{1}{2}$$

$$\Rightarrow \quad 1000\pi t = \frac{\pi}{3}, \frac{2\pi}{3}, \frac{4\pi}{3}, \frac{5\pi}{3}, \ldots$$

$$\Rightarrow \quad t = \frac{1}{3}\text{ ms}, \frac{2}{3}\text{ ms}, \frac{4}{3}\text{ ms}, \ldots$$

Hence, the time for which the detector remains idle in each beat cycle (see figure) $= \frac{2}{3}\text{ ms} - \frac{1}{3}\text{ ms} = 0.33\text{ ms}$.

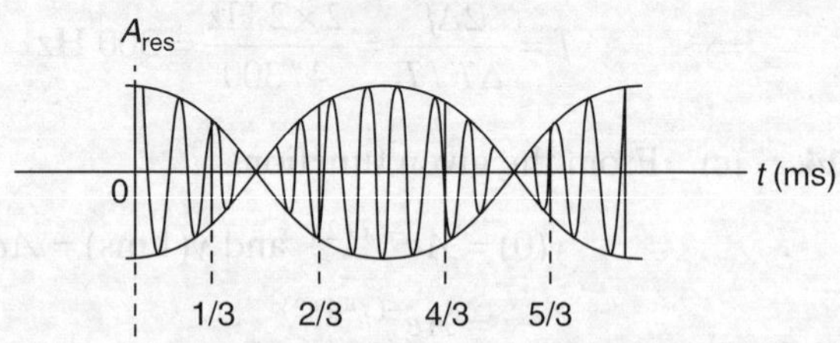

23. (d) The source S is stationary and the object is approaching the source at speed, say u. With respect to the object, the source S, the detector D and the image S' will have velocities as shown in the figure. The frequency received by the detector after reflection from the object can be found by treating S' as the source.

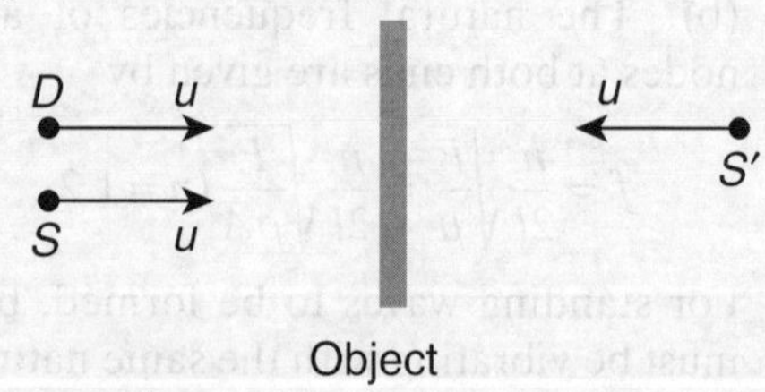

Thus, we have

$$f' = \left(\frac{v+u}{v-u}\right)f$$

It is given that $f' - 1.5f$. Hence

$$\frac{v+u}{v-u} = 1.5 \Rightarrow u = \frac{v}{5} = \frac{360\text{ m/s}}{5} = 72\text{ m/s}$$

24. (c), (d) Sound waves travel faster in water than in air, and hence, bend away from the normal. So (a) is incorrect.

At high altitudes, sound waves travel slower because of the drop in temperature. So (b) is incorrect.

Electromagnetic waves are transverse waves. So (c) is correct.

If v is the speed of the sound wave and u is the speed of the source or the observer, then

$$f_1 = \left(\frac{v}{v-u}\right)f \text{ and } f_2 = \left(\frac{v+u}{v}\right)f$$

Then $f_1 - f_2 = \dfrac{u^2 f}{v(v-u)} > 0 \Rightarrow f_1 > f.$

So (d) is correct.

25. (b) The frequencies of the two waves are

$$f_1 = \frac{100\pi}{2\pi} = 50 \text{ Hz and } f_2 = \frac{92\pi}{2\pi} = 46 \text{ Hz}$$

The beat frequency is $\Delta f = 50 \text{ Hz} - 46 \text{ Hz} = 4$ beats/second and oscillation frequency is

$$\frac{f_1 + f_2}{2} = \frac{50 \text{ Hz} + 46 \text{ Hz}}{2} = 48 \text{ Hz}$$

In a 4-beat cycle, the particle completes 48 oscillation cycles. Hence, in a 1-beat cycle, the particle will complete $\dfrac{48}{4} = 12$ oscillation cycles.

26. (c) The wave number is $k = \dfrac{\pi}{15}$. The wavelength is $\lambda = \dfrac{2\pi}{k} = 30$ cm.

The length of one loop is $\dfrac{\lambda}{2} = 15$ cm.

So, there are $\dfrac{60 \text{ cm}}{15 \text{ cm}} = 4$ loops, which means the fourth harmonic.

27. (d) Let u be the velocity of the train and f be the frequency of the whistle. Then

$$\left(\frac{330}{330-u}\right)f = 484 \quad \ldots(1)$$

and

$$\left(\frac{330}{330+u}\right)f = 442 \quad \ldots(2)$$

Dividing (1) by (2) gives

$$\frac{330+u}{330-u} = \frac{484}{442}$$

$$\Rightarrow \quad u = 15 \text{ m/s} = 54 \text{ km/h}$$

28. (d), (b) Putting $x = 0$ in the two equations and adding, we have

(a) $y(0,t) = A\sin(\omega t) + A\sin\left(\omega t + \dfrac{\pi}{2}\right) = A\sin(\omega t) + A\cos(\omega t) = \sqrt{2}A\cos\left(\omega t + \dfrac{\pi}{4}\right)$

The particle oscillates with amplitude $\sqrt{2}A$, so it not a node.

(b) $y(0,t) = A\sin(\omega t) + A\sin(\omega t + \pi) = A\sin(\omega t) - A\sin(\omega t) = 0$

The particle does not oscillate at all, so it a node.

(c) $y(0,t) = A\cos(\omega t) + A\cos\left(\omega t + \dfrac{\pi}{2}\right) = A\cos(\omega t) - A\sin(\omega t) = \sqrt{2}A\cos\left(\omega t + \dfrac{\pi}{4}\right)$

The particle oscillates with amplitude $\sqrt{2}A$, so it not a node.

(d) $y(0,t) = A\cos(\omega t) + A\cos(\omega t + \pi) = A\cos(\omega t) - A\cos(\omega t) = 0$

The particle does not oscillate at all, so it a node.

29. (a), (c, (d) One end of the string is a node and the other end is an antinode. These boundary conditions will be satisfied if

$$(2n-1)\frac{\lambda}{4} = 3 \text{ m} \Rightarrow \lambda = \frac{12}{2n-1} \text{ m}$$

Hence

$$k = \frac{2\pi}{\lambda} = (2n-1)\frac{\pi}{6} \text{ and}$$

$$\omega = vk = (2n-1)\frac{\pi}{6} \times 100 \text{ m/s} = (2n-1)\frac{50\pi}{3} \text{ rad/s}$$

$$\text{In}(a) k = \frac{\pi}{6} \text{ and } \omega = \frac{50\pi}{3} \Rightarrow \text{correct}$$

$$\text{In}(b) k = 2\left(\frac{\pi}{6}\right) \text{ and } \omega = 2\left(\frac{50\pi}{3}\right) \Rightarrow \text{incorrect}$$

$$\text{In}(c) k = 5\left(\frac{\pi}{6}\right) \text{ and } \omega = 5\left(\frac{50\pi}{3}\right) \Rightarrow \text{correct}$$

$$\text{In}(d) k = 15\left(\frac{\pi}{6}\right) \text{ and } \omega = 15\left(\frac{50\pi}{3}\right) \Rightarrow \text{correct}$$

30. (d) The figure shows the pressure standing wave pattern. The closed end is a position of pressure antinode and the free end is a position of pressure node. The air column is vibrating in its second overtone (5th harmonic), hence there are two and a half loops. If l is the length of the tube, then

$$\frac{5\lambda}{4} = l \Rightarrow \lambda = \frac{4l}{5}$$

Hence $k = \frac{2\pi}{\lambda} = \frac{5\pi}{21}$

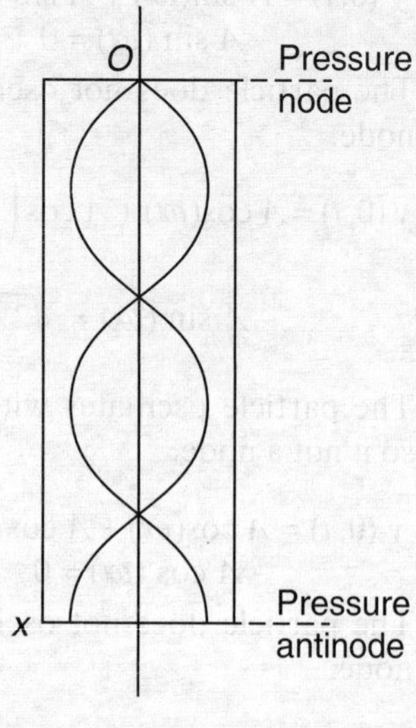

If we choose the x-axis and the origin, as shown in the figure, then the pressure amplitude as a function of x will be

$$P(x) = P_0\,|\sin(kx)| = P_0\left|\sin\left(\frac{5\pi}{21}x\right)\right|$$

At the middle of the tube ($x = l/2$), the pressure amplitude is $P_0\left|\sin\left(\frac{5\pi}{4}\right)\right| = \frac{P_0}{\sqrt{2}}$.

31. (a) Wavelength $\lambda = \frac{v}{f} = \frac{344\text{ m/s}}{172\text{ Hz}} = 2\text{ m}$

Path difference between the two waves arriving at C is $= 4\text{ m} - 3\text{ m} = 1\text{ m}$.

Hence, the phase difference between the two waves arriving at C is

$$\phi = \left(\frac{2\pi}{\lambda}\right)x = \left(\frac{2\pi}{2\text{ m}}\right)1\text{ m} = \pi$$

Thus, the resultant amplitude is

$$A = \sqrt{A_1^2 + A_2^2 + 2A_1A_2\cos\phi}$$
$$= |A_1 - A_2| \text{ for } \phi = \pi = |4\text{ mm} - 3\text{ mm}| = 1\text{ mm}$$

32. (c) Let f be the frequency of the sound emitted by the bird. Then, $f = 0/\lambda$.

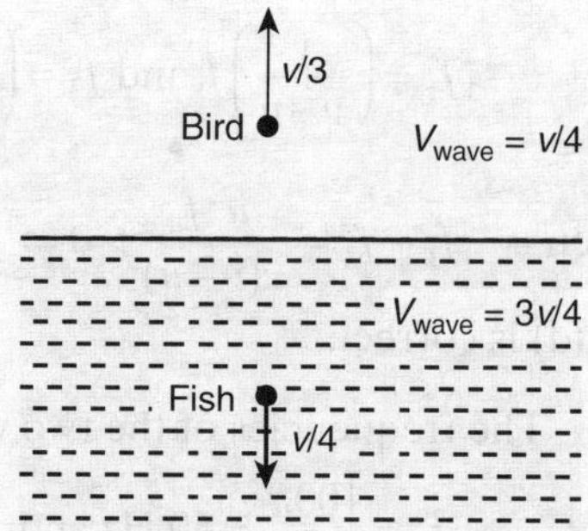

Frequency of the wave arriving at the surface of the water is

$$f' = \frac{v}{v + v/3}f = \frac{3}{4}f$$

Frequency of the wave received by the fish is

$$f' = \frac{9v/4 - v/4}{9v/4}f' = \frac{8}{9}\left(\frac{3}{4}f\right) = \frac{2f}{3}$$

Hence, the wavelength of the wave received by the fish is $\frac{9v/4}{f'} = \frac{27v}{8f} = \frac{27}{8}\lambda$.

33. (a), (d)

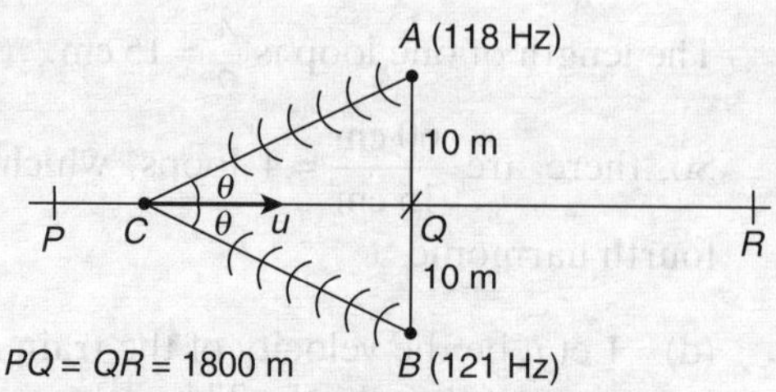

Let C denote the portion of the car at any instance and let θ denote the angle shown in the figure. At this position, the frequencies heard from the sources A and B are, respectively

$$f_A = \left(\frac{v + u\cos\theta}{v}\right)118\text{ Hz and}$$

$$f_A = \left(\frac{v + u\cos\theta}{v}\right)121\text{ Hz}$$

And the beat frequency is

$$f_{beat} = f_B - f_A = \left(\frac{v + u\cos\theta}{v}\right)3\text{ Hz}$$

At P, $\theta \simeq 0$. Thus, the beat frequency at P is

$$f_P = \left(\frac{v+u}{v}\right)3\text{ Hz} = \left(\frac{104}{99}\right)3\text{ Hz}$$

At Q, $\theta \simeq \pi/2$. Thus, the beat frequency at Q is

$$f_Q = 3\text{ Hz}$$

At R, $\theta \simeq \pi$. Thus, the beat frequency at R is

$$f_R = \left(\frac{v-u}{v}\right) 3\text{ Hz} = \left(\frac{94}{99}\right) 3\text{ Hz}$$

The value of $\cos\theta$ changes most rapidly as θ approaches $90^\circ \Rightarrow$ (a) is correct.

Now $f_p + f_R = 6\text{ Hz} = 2f_Q \Rightarrow$ (c) is incorrect.

and $f_p - f_R = \left(\frac{10}{99}\right) 3\text{ Hz} = \frac{1}{10} f_Q \Rightarrow$ (d) is correct.

34. (a) The figure shows the wave pattern after a little while, when $t = \Delta t$. The pattern has shifted by a small amount $\Delta x = v\Delta t$ to the right.

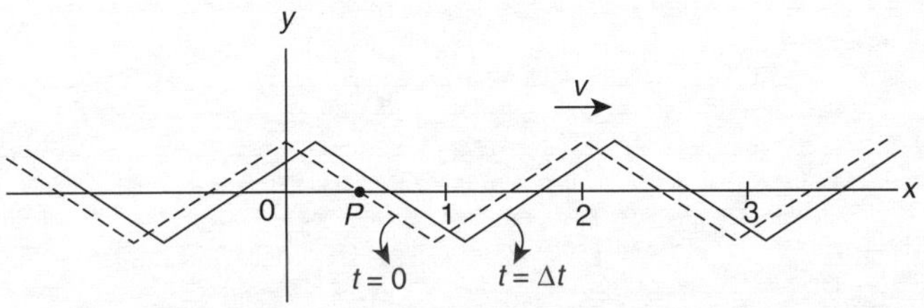

We see that the particle located at position P has moved along the +ve y-direction, starting from $y = 0$ at $t = 0$.

Hence (a) is the correct option.

35. (b) The velocity of wave propagation is

$$v = \sqrt{\frac{Y}{\rho}} = \sqrt{\frac{1.6\times10^{11}}{2500}}\text{ m/s} = 8000\text{ m/s}$$

The portion of the rod (80 cm) between the clamps will have nodes at both ends. The left (5 cm) and the right (15 cm) portions of the rod will have a node at one end and an antinode at the other end. At resonance frequency f, we have

$$f = \frac{n_1 v}{4(0.05\text{ m})} = \frac{n_2 v}{2(0.80\text{ m})} = \frac{n_3 v}{4(0.15\text{ m})}$$

For fundamental frequency, we take $n_1 = 1$, and for the first overtone, we take $n_1 = 3$. Thus, we have

$$f_1 = \frac{8000\text{ m/s}}{4(0.05\text{ m})} = 40\text{ kHz and } f_3 = 3f_1 = 120\text{ kHz}$$

36. (a), (b), (c), (d)

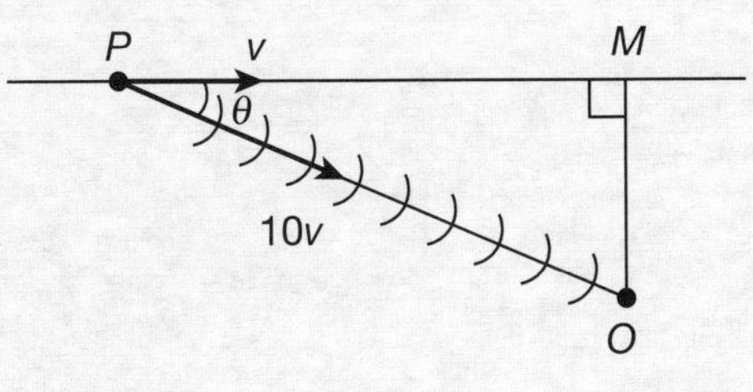

(a) When the observer O sees the source at M, the sound he hears was emitted by the source earlier when it was at some position, say P (see figure). So that time taken by the source to travel from P to M equals the time taken by sound to travel from P to O. Thus, we have

$$\frac{PM}{v} = \frac{PO}{10v} \Rightarrow \frac{PM}{PO} = \frac{1}{10} \Rightarrow \cos\theta = \frac{1}{10}$$

Using Doppler's formula, we have

$$f' = \left(\frac{10v}{10v - v\cos\theta}\right) f = \left(\frac{10}{10 - \frac{1}{10}}\right) f = \frac{100}{99} f$$

(b) When the source is passing point M, its velocity component towards O is zero. Therefore, the sound emitted at point M will be heard by the observer in its original frequency f. But this sound takes time $\frac{d}{10v}$ to reach O. In this time, the train moves a distance $v\left(\frac{d}{10v}\right) = \frac{d}{10}$ from M.

(c) Frequency heard by O as S moves along the track is represented in the figure. As the source moves from far left to far right, the angle θ changes from 0° to 180°. The value of $\cos\theta$ changes most rapidly as θ approaches 90°. Thus, the frequency changes most rapidly as the sources crosses M.

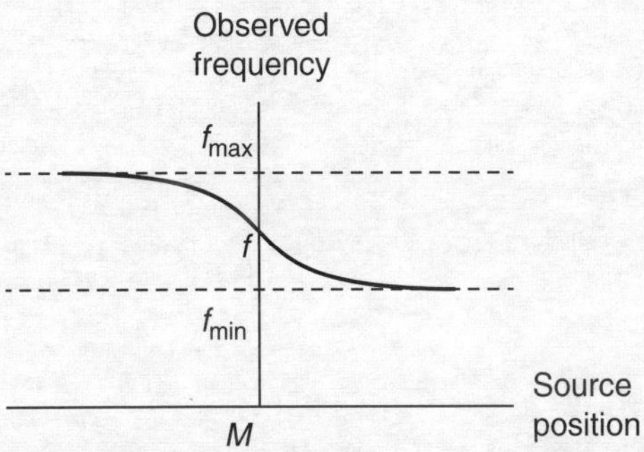

(d) The observed frequency is greatest when the source is far away and approaching, and it is lowest when the source is far away and receding. The greatest and the least values of the observed frequencies can be found by putting $\cos\theta = 1$ and -1, respectively. Thus, we have

$$f_{max} = \left(\frac{10v}{10v - v}\right) f = \frac{10}{9} f \text{ and}$$

$$f_{max} = \left(\frac{10v}{10v + v}\right) f = \frac{10}{11} f$$

Thus, the observed frequency is

$$\Delta f = f_{max} - f_{min} = \frac{10}{9} f - \frac{10}{11} f = \frac{20}{99} f$$

37. (a)-(p), (b)-(r), (c)-(q), (d)-(s)
At the free end, the pulse is reflected back without inversion. At the fixed end, an inverted pulse is reflected back.

PART II

THERMODYNAMICS

CHAPTER

13 Calorimetry, Thermal Expansion and Heat Transfer

- A thermometer measures temperature. When two bodies at different temperatures are brought in contact, flow of energy occurs from the hotter body to the colder body, until equilibrium is reached. Two bodies in thermal equilibrium must have the same temperature.
  The zeroth law of thermodynamics states that if body A is in thermal equilibrium with body B, and body B is in thermal equilibrium with body C, then bodies A and C will be in thermal equilibrium with each other.
- The Celsius and Fahrenheit temperature scales are based on the freezing temperature $(0°C = 32°F)$ and boiling temperature $(100°C = 212°F)$ of water. They are related by
$$T_F = \frac{9}{5}T_C + 32 \text{ or } T_c = \frac{5}{9}(T_F - 32), \text{ and } 1°C = 1.8°F$$
- The Kelvin scale has its zero at the extrapolated zero-pressure temperature for a constant volume gas thermometer, which is –273.15°C. Thus, 0 K = –273.15°C and $T_K = T_C + 273.15$.
  In the constant volume gas thermometer, the temperature T (in Kelvin) is proportional to the gas pressure p:
$$\frac{T_2}{T_1} = \frac{p_2}{p_1}$$
  The triple-point temperature (when all phases co-exist in equilibrium) of water is 0.01°C = 273.16 K.
- Under a temperature change ΔT, any linear dimension L_0 of a solid body changes by an amount $\Delta L = \alpha L_0 \, \Delta T$. Its changed length L is given by
$$L = L_0 (1 + \alpha \Delta T),$$
  where α is called the coefficient of linear expansion.
  Under a temperature change ΔT, volume V_0 of any solid or liquid body changes by an amount $\Delta V = \gamma V_0 \Delta T$. Its changed volume V is given by
$$V = V_0 (1 + \gamma \Delta T),$$
  where γ is the coefficient of volume expansion. For solids $\gamma = 3\alpha$, the density also changes from ρ_0 to ρ, given by
$$\rho = \frac{\rho_0}{1 + \gamma\Delta T} \approx \rho_0 (1 - \gamma \Delta T)$$
- When a body is heated and held so that it cannot expand, the compressive stress F / A is given by
$$\frac{F}{A} = Y(\alpha \Delta T)$$
  A tensile stress develops in the body if it is cooled and held so that it cannot contract.
- Heat is energy in transmitted from one body to another as a result of temperature difference. The quantity of heat Q required to raise the temperature of a mass m of a material by an amount ΔT is
$$Q = ms \, \Delta T,$$
  where s is called the specific heat capacity of that material. When the quantity of the material is given by the number of moles n, the corresponding relation is
$$Q = nc \, \Delta T,$$
  where $c = Ms$ is called the molar heat capacity (M is the molar mass). The number of moles n and the mass of the material are related by $m = nM$. For many solid elements, the value of molar heat capacity is a constant $c = 25$ J/mol·K; this is the law of Dulong and Petit.

- To change the phase (solid ↔ liquid or liquid ↔ gas) of a mass m of a material, the quantity of heat Q required is
$$Q = \pm mL,$$
where L is called the latent heat of fusion for solid ↔ liquid phase change and is called the latent heat of vaporisation for liquid ↔ gas phase change.

- When heat is added to a system, Q is taken as positive; when it is removed from a system, Q is taken as negative. The basic principle of calorimetry comes from the principle of conservation of energy. In an isolated system whose parts interact by heat exchange, the algebraic sum of Qs for all parts of the system must be zero.

- The three mechanisms of heat transfer are conduction, convection and radiation. Conduction is transfer of energy by molecular motion within materials without bulk motion of the materials. Convection involves mass motion of the material from one region to another. Radiation is energy transfer through electromagnetic waves.

- The heat current $H = dQ/dt$ (time rate of flow of energy) for conduction depends on the area A through which the heat flows, the length L of the heat path, the temperature difference $\Delta T = T_H - T_C$ and the thermal conductivity k (SI unit is $\mathrm{W/m\cdot K}$) of the material:
$$H = \frac{\Delta T}{R} \text{ (SI unit is J/s or W)},$$
where $R = \frac{L}{kA}$ (SI unit is K/W) is called the thermal resistance. When several resistances $R_1, R_2, R_3, \ldots$ are connected in series, the equivalent resistance is given by
$$R_{eq} = R_1 + R_2 + R_3 + \ldots \text{ (resistors in series)}.$$
The same heat current flows through all the resistors in a series connection. When several resistors are connected in parallel, the equivalent resistance is given by
$$\frac{1}{R_{eq}} = \frac{1}{R_1} + \frac{1}{R_2} + \frac{1}{R_3} + \ldots \text{ (resistors in parallel)}.$$
All resistors connected in parallel have the same temperature difference across them.

- The heat current H from the body for radiation is
$$H = e\sigma A T^4 \text{ (Stefan's law)},$$
where e is the emissivity of the surface, A is the surface area, T is the absolute temperature of the surface and $\sigma = 5.67\times10^{-8}\ \mathrm{W/m^2\cdot K^4}$ is the Stefan constant. For a black body, $e = 1$; for any other body, $0 \le e < 1$.

  When a body at temperature T is kept in surroundings at temperature T_S, the net heat current coming from the body to its surroundings is
$$H_{net} = e\sigma A\left(T^4 - T_S^4\right)$$

- Line spectra are emitted by matter in gaseous state when each atom behaves as an isolated system. Matter in condensed state (solid or liquid) emits radiation with a continuous distribution of wavelengths. However, the intensity of all wavelengths is not uniform; the most intense wavelength λ_m is inversely proportional to the absolute temperature T of the body:
$$\lambda_m T = 2.90\times10^{-3}\ \mathrm{m\cdot K} \text{ (Wien's displacement law)}$$

- Newton's law of cooling states that if the temperature difference $\Delta T = T - T_S$ is much smaller in comparison to the surrounding temperature T_S, the rate of cooling of the body is directly proportional to ΔT:
$$\left|\frac{dT}{dt}\right| = \frac{4e\sigma A T_S^3}{ms}\Delta T \text{ (for } \Delta T \ll T_S),$$
where m is the mass of the body and s is its specific heat capacity.

EXERCISES

1. Steam at 100°C is passed into 1.1 kg of water contained in a container of water equivalent 0.02 kg at 15°C till the temperature of the container rises to 80°C. The mass of steam condensed is (specific heat capacity of water = 1 kcal/kg·°C, latent heat of steam = 540 kcal/kg):
   (a) 0.123 kg (b) 0.065 kg
   (c) 0.260 kg (d) 0.130 kg

2. A 0.1-kg aluminium plate at 95°C is immersed in 0.5 kg of water at 20°C kept in a vessel of negligible heat capacity, and then removed. If the temperature of water is 23°C, then the temperature of the plate is (specific heat capacities of water and aluminium are 4200 J/kg·°C and 900 $\frac{J}{kg}$·°C, respectively):
   (a) 18°C (b) 25°C
   (c) 40°C (d) 64°C

3. A water cooler of storage capacity 120 litres can cool water at the rate of P watts. In a closed circulation system, as shown in the figure, the water from the cooler is used to cool an electric generator which produces heat at the rate of 3 kW. The temperature of water fed into the generator should not exceed 30°C.

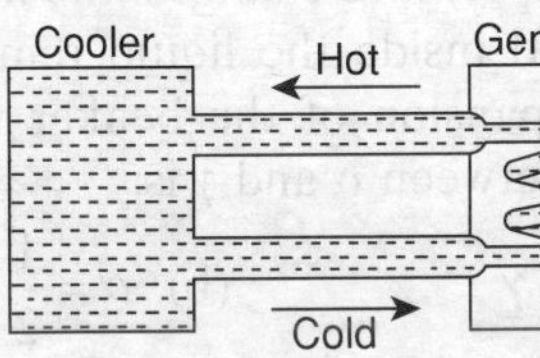

   If the initial temperature of water in the cooler is 10°C, then the minimum value of P so that the generator can be operated for 3 hours is (specific heat capacity of water= 4200 J/kg·°C and density of water = 1 kg/litre):
   (a) 1600 (b) 2067
   (c) 2533 (d) 3933

4. A 1-kW electric kettle contains 2 kg of water at 27°C. The kettle is operated for 10 minutes. If heat is lost to the surroundings at a constant rate of 160 J/s, the temperature attained by water in 10 minutes will be (specific heat capacity of water = 4.2 kJ/kg·°C):
   (a) 57°C (b) 67°C
   (c) 77°C (d) 87°C

5. In an industrial process, 10 kg of water per hour is to be heated from 20°C to 80°C. To do this, steam at 150°C is passed from a copper coil immersed in water. The steam condenses in the coil and is returned to the boiler water at 90°C. The amount of steam required per hour is (specific heat capacities of steam and water are the same = 1kcal/kg·°C, latent heat of steam = 540 kcal/kg):
   (a) 1 kg (b) 2 kg
   (c) 3 kg (d) 4 kg

6. A calorimeter of mass m contains an equal mass of water at temperature $\beta < 0$°C. A block of ice of mass and temperature is dropped into the calorimeter. Let s_1, s_2, s_3 be the specific heats of calorimeter, water and ice, respectively, and L be the latent heat of ice. Then the correct statements from the following are:
   (a) All water will turn into ice if $\alpha s_1 + \alpha s_2 + L + \beta s_3 < 0$
   (b) All water will turn into ice if $\alpha s_1 + \alpha s_2 + L - \beta s_3 < 0$
   (c) All ice will turn into water if $\alpha s_1 + \alpha s_2 - L + \beta s_3 < 0$
   (d) All ice will turn into water if $\alpha s_1 + \alpha s_2 - L - \beta s_3 < 0$

7. 400 g of ice at 253 K is mixed with 50 g of steam at 160°C in an insulated vessel of negligible heat capacity. When equilibrium is attained, the mass of water in the vessel is (specific heat capacities of steam and water are the same = 1 cal/g·°C, specific capacity of ice = 0.5 cal/g·°C, latent heat of steam = 540 cal/g and latent heat of ice = 80 cal/g):
   (a) 437.5 g (b) 357.5 g
   (c) 325 g (d) 300 g

8. A certain mass of ice is supplied heat at a constant rate. Its temperature rises for the first 1 minute and remains constant for the next 4 minutes before it starts rising again. The initial temperature of ice is (latent heat of ice = 80 cal/g and specific heat of ice = 0.5 cal/g·°C):
   (a) −40°C (b) −25°C
   (c) −20°C (d) −10°C

9. The coefficient of linear expansion of a crystal in one dimension is 2.0×10^{-6} K^{-1} and in the other two perpendicular directions it is 1.0×10^{-6} K^{-1}. The coefficient of cubical expansion of the crystal is:
   (a) 1.6×10^{-6} K^{-1} (b) 1.8×10^{-6} K^{-1}
   (c) 2.0×10^{-6} K^{-1} (d) 4.0×10^{-6} K^{-1}

10. A metal ball immersed in alcohol weighs W_1 at 0°C and W_2 at 52°C. If the coefficient of cubical expansion of metal is less than that of alcohol, then:

(a) $W_1 > W_2$ (b) $W_1 = W_2$

(c) $W_1 < W_2$ (d) $W_1 = 2W_2$

11. Two rods of lengths l_1 and l_2 are welded together to make a composite rod of length $l_1 + l_2$. If the coefficients of linear expansion of the rods are α_1 and α_2, respectively, the coefficient of linear expansion of the composite rod is:

(a) $\frac{1}{2}(\alpha_1 + \alpha_2)$ (b) $\sqrt{\alpha_1 \alpha_2}$

(c) $\frac{l_1\alpha_1 + l_2\alpha_2}{l_1 + l_2}$ (d) $\sqrt{\frac{l_1 l_2 \alpha_1 \alpha_2}{l_1 + l_2}}$

12. The coefficient of linear expansion of a non-homogeneous rod varies linearly from α_1 to α_2 from one end to the other end of the rod. The effective coefficient of linear expansion of the rod is:

(a) $\alpha_1 + \alpha_2$ (b) $\frac{1}{2}(\alpha_1 + \alpha_2)$

(c) $\sqrt{\alpha_1 \alpha_2}$ (d) $\frac{2}{3}(\alpha_1 + \alpha_2)$

13. A cylindrical block of wood floats vertically with 80% of its volume submerged in a liquid at 0°C. When the temperature of the liquid is raised to 100°C, the block just sinks in the liquid. If cubical expansion of wood is 1.2×10^{-3} K^{-1}, the cubical expansion of liquid is:

(a) 2.00×10^{-3} K^{-1} (b) 2.50×10^{-3} K^{-1}

(c) 3.00×10^{-3} K^{-1} (d) 4.00×10^{-3} K^{-1}

14. The coefficient of apparent expansion of a liquid when determined using two different vessels A and B are γ_1 and γ_2, respectively. If the coefficient of linear expansion of vessel A is α, the coefficient of linear expansion of vessel B is:

(a) $\frac{\alpha\gamma_1\gamma_2}{\gamma_1 + \gamma_2}$ (b) $\frac{\alpha\gamma_1\gamma_2}{\gamma_1 - \gamma_2}$

(c) $\gamma_1 - \gamma_2 + \frac{1}{3}\alpha$ (d) $\alpha + \frac{1}{3}(\gamma_1 - \gamma_2)$

15. A closed vessel of volume V contains some liquid. It is found that for small changes in temperature, the volume of air inside the vessel remains the same. If γ_1 and γ_2 are coefficients of the cubical expansion of the vessel and the liquid, respectively, then the volume of liquid in the vessel is:

(a) $\left(\frac{\gamma_1}{\gamma_2}\right)V$ (b) $\left(\frac{\gamma_2}{\gamma_1}\right)V$

(c) $\left(1 - \frac{\gamma_1}{\gamma_2}\right)V$ (d) $\left(1 - \frac{\gamma_2}{\gamma_1}\right)V$

16. A uniform metallic circular disc mounted on frictionless bearings is rotating at angular frequency ω about a vertical axis passing through its centre and perpendicular to its plane. The coefficient of linear expansion of the metal is α. If the temperature changes by ΔT, the angular frequency will change by:

(a) $2\alpha\omega\,\Delta T$ (b) $-\frac{1}{2}\alpha\omega\Delta T$

(c) $\frac{1}{2}\alpha\omega\,\Delta T$ (d) $-2\alpha\omega\Delta T$

17. A vertical glass tube closed at the bottom contains a mercury column. If γ_m and γ_g are coefficients of cubical expansion of mercury and glass, respectively, then the coefficient of linear expansion of the mercury column is:

(a) $\gamma_m + \gamma_g$ (b) $\gamma_m + \gamma_g$

(c) $\gamma_m + \frac{2}{3}\gamma_g$ (d) $\gamma_m - \frac{2}{3}\gamma_g$

18. A solid cube of coefficient of linear expansion α is floating in a liquid of volume expansion γ. For small temperature changes, the height of the cube submerged inside the liquid remains unchanged. If the expansion of the beaker is neglected, the relation between α and γ is:

(a) $\alpha = \frac{1}{3}\gamma$ (b) $\alpha = \frac{1}{2}\gamma$

(c) $\alpha = \frac{2}{3}\gamma$ (d) $\alpha = 3\gamma$

19. Heat energy Q is supplied to a metal block of specific heat capacity s, density ρ and coefficient of volume expansion γ. If the atmospheric pressure is P_0, work done by the block on the surroundings is:

(a) $\frac{P_0 Q}{\gamma\rho s}$ (b) $\frac{\gamma P_0 Q}{(1-\gamma)\rho s}$

(c) $\frac{\gamma P_0 Q}{\rho s}$ (d) $\frac{\gamma P_0 Q}{(1+\gamma)\rho s}$

20. The figure shows a rigid framework of three metal rods. The lengths are $PQ = PR = a$ and $QR = b$. The coefficients of linear expansion of rods PQ and PR are the same and equal to α and that of the rod QR is β.

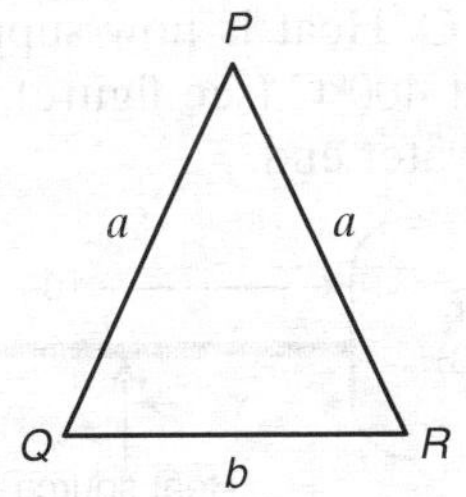

If the perpendicular distance of P from QR does not change for small temperature changes, then the ratio b/a is:

(a) $\sqrt{\frac{4\alpha}{\beta}}$ (b) $\sqrt{\frac{2\alpha}{\beta}}$

(c) $\sqrt{\frac{\beta}{4\alpha}}$ (d) $\sqrt{\frac{3\beta}{4\alpha}}$

21. The temperature of a metal rod is raised by 50°C, but it is constrained to elongate only by 99.5% of its change in length. If $Y = 2.0 \times 10^{11}$ N/m^2 and $\alpha = 10^{-4}$ K^{-1}, stress in the rod is:

(a) 2.5×10^6 N/m^2 (b) 5.0×10^6 N/m^2

(c) 7.5×10^6 N/m^2 (d) 8.0×10^6 N/m^2

22. Two metal wires A and B of the same length l and same cross-section area S are joined in series and their ends connected to two rigid walls separated by a distance $2l$ so that there is no tension in the wires. Their coefficient of linear expansion and Young's modulus of elasticity are α_1, Y_1 and α_2, Y_2, respectively. If the temperature is now reduced by ΔT, the tension in the composite wire will be:

(a) $(Y_1\alpha_1 + Y_2\alpha_2)S\Delta T$ (b) $\frac{(Y_1+Y_2)\alpha_1\alpha_2 S\Delta T}{\alpha_1+\alpha_2}$

(c) $\frac{(Y_1+Y_2)\alpha_1\alpha_2 S\Delta T}{\alpha_1+\alpha_2}$ (d) $\frac{Y_1Y_2(\alpha_1+\alpha_2)S\Delta T}{Y_1+Y_2}$

23. Two slabs A and B of thermal conductivities k_1 and k_2, respectively, are connected in series. Their cross-section areas are the same but their lengths are l_1 and l_2, respectively. The effective thermal conductivity of the composite slab is:

(a) $\frac{k_1l_2 + k_2l_1}{l_1+l_2}$ (b) $\frac{k_1k_2}{k_1+k_2}$

(c) $\frac{k_1k_2(l_1+l_2)}{k_1l_1+k_2l_2}$ (d) $\frac{k_1k_2(l_1+l_2)}{k_1l_2+k_2l_1}$

24. A solid cylindrical rod of radius R made of material of thermal conductivity k_1 is surrounded by another cylindrical shell of inner radius R and outer radius $2R$ made of a material of thermal conductivity k_2. Considering heat flow along the length of the cylinders, the effective thermal conductivity of the system is:

(a) $k_1 + \frac{1}{4}k_2$ (b) $\frac{3}{4}k_1 + \frac{1}{4}k_2$

(c) $\frac{1}{4}k_1 + \frac{3}{4}k_2$ (d) $\frac{3}{4}k_1 + k_2$

25. Two identical rods of conductivities k and $2k$ transfer a given amount of heat in 12 s when they are joined end to end (parallel). When they are joined length-wise (series), they will transfer the same amount of heat in:

(a) 3 s (b) 24 s

(c) 45 s (d) 54 s

26. Two identical rods AB and CD made of the same material are joined, as shown in the figure. Point B is the mid-point of CD. Ends A, C and D are maintained at temperatures 25°C, 100°C and 0°C, respectively.

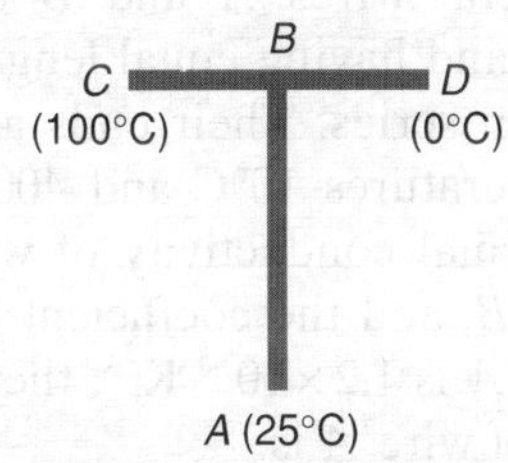

The temperature at B is:

(a) 30°C (b) 35°C

(c) 45°C (d) 55°C

27. Three rods of the same cross-section area and made from the same metal form the sides of an isosceles triangle ABC, right-angled at B. The points A and B are maintained at temperatures T and $\sqrt{2}\,T$ in a steady state. Temperature at point C is:

(a) $\frac{2T}{\sqrt{2}+1}$ (b) $\frac{3T}{\sqrt{2}+1}$

(c) $\frac{7T}{2\sqrt{2}+1}$ (d) $\frac{3T}{2\sqrt{2}-1}$

28. The rods shown in the figure are made of the same material and have the same cross-section area.

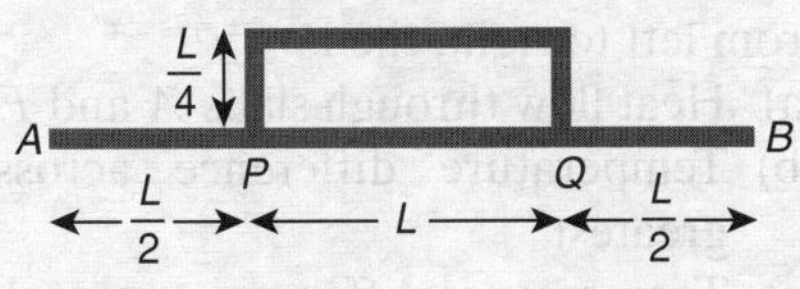

If the ends A and B are maintained at a temperature difference of 120°C, then the temperature difference between points P and Q is:

(a) 30°C (b) 45°C

(c) 60°C (d) 75°C

29. The rods shown in the figure are of the same dimensions, but have different thermal conductivities (given in terms of k). Points A and E are maintained at temperatures θ_1 and θ_2, respectively.

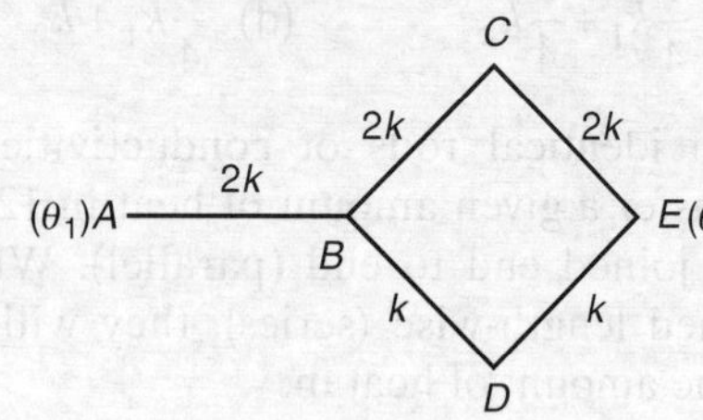

Temperature at point C is:

(a) $\frac{5\theta_1 + 2\theta_2}{7}$ (b) $\frac{2\theta_1 + 5\theta_2}{7}$

(c) $\frac{\theta_1 + 6\theta_2}{7}$ (d) $\frac{4\theta_1 + 3\theta_2}{7}$

30. Two metal wires A and B of the same cross-section and having equal lengths 1 m at 10°C are joined in series. Their ends are now maintained at temperatures 10°C and 400°C, respectively. If the thermal conductivity of wire A is twice that of wire B, and the coefficient of linear expansion of wire A is $1.2 \times 10^{-5}\ \text{K}^{-1}$, then the change in the length of wire A is:

(a) 0.78 mm (b) 0.90 mm

(c) 1.56 mm (d) 2.34 mm

31. A composite block is made of slabs A, B, C, D and E of different thermal conductivities (given in terms of k) and sizes (given in terms of l), as shown in the figure.

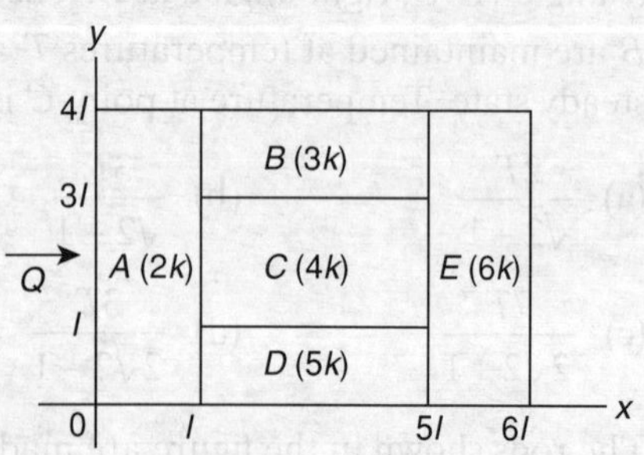

All slabs are of the same width. If heat Q flows from left to right, then:

(a) Heat flow through slabs A and E is the same

(b) Temperature difference across slab A is greatest

(c) Temperature difference across slab E is least

(d) Heat flow through C = Heat flow through B + Heat flow through D

32. A uniform rod of length $10l$ has its one end inserted into hot water at 100°C and the other end into cold ice at 0°C. Heat is now supplied to the rod by a source at 400°C (see figure), at a distance x from the hot water end.

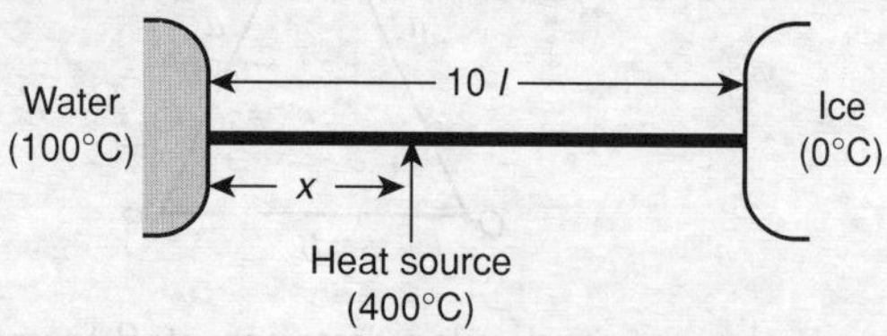

If the rate at which ice melts equals the rate at which water evaporates, then the value of x is (latent heat of ice = 80 cal/g and latent heat of steam = 540 cal/g):

(a) l (b) $3l$

(c) $6l$ (d) $9l$

33. The ends of a metal rod are maintained at steady temperatures T_H (hot) and T_C (cold).

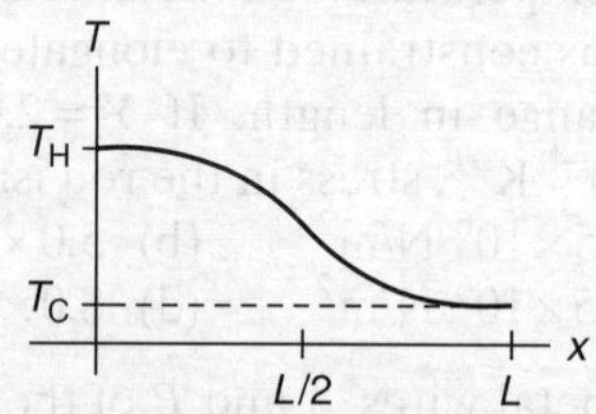

If the temperature (T) varies along the length (x) of the rod, as shown in the figure, then the cross-section area of the rod:

(a) Continuously decreases

(b) First decreases and then increases

(c) Continuously increases

(d) First increases and then decreases

34. The figure shows three large identical metal plates at temperatures T_1, T_2 and T_3.

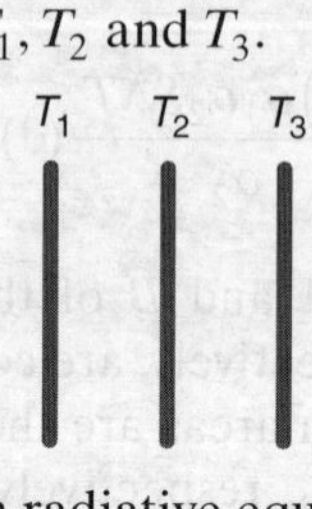

If the plates are in radiative equilibrium, then:

(a) $2T_1^4 - T_2^4 + 2T_3^4 = 0$ (b) $3T_1^4 - 2T_2^4 + 3T_3^4 = 0$

(c) $T_1^4 - 2T_2^4 + T_3^4 = 0$ (d) $T_1^4 - T_2^4 + T_3^4 = 0$

35. Two spheres A and B are made of the same material and have identical surface finish. The mass of A is three times the mass of B. Both the spheres are heated to the same temperature and placed in the same room having lower temperature. The ratio of initial rate of cooling of A to that of B is:

(a) 3^{-1} (b) $3^{2/3}$

(c) $3^{1/2}$ (d) $3^{-1/3}$

36. A body cools from 90°C to 50°C in 5 s in surroundings of temperature 30°C. The time taken by the body to cool from 50°C to 40°C is:
(a) 2.5 s (b) 3.3 s
(c) 5.0 s (d) 7.5 s

37. A copper ball starts cooling from an initial temperature of 62°C. In the first 10 min, it cools down to 50°C. In the next 10 min, it cools down to 42°C. After another 10 min, its temperature to the nearest integer will be (assume Newton's law of cooling to be valid):
(a) 40°C (b) 39°C
(c) 38°C (d) 37°C

38. A metal is heated in a furnace which is fitted with a sensor above the metal surface to read the power P radiated by the metal. The sensor is calibrated to display $\log_2(P/P_0)$, where P_0 is a constant. When the metal surface is at temperature 487°C, the sensor shows a value 1. When the temperature of the metal surface is raised to 2767°C, the value shown by the sensor is:
(a) 3 (b) 5
(c) 7 (d) 9

39. A human body has a surface area of approximately $A = 1\text{ m}^2$. The normal body temperature is 10 K above the surrounding temperature $T_0 = 300$ K. If $\epsilon\sigma T_0^4 = 460\text{ W/m}^2$ (ϵ is the emissivity of the human body and σ is Stefan's constant), the correct statements from the following are:
(a) Energy radiated by the body in 1 s is close to 60 J
(b) If the surrounding temperature reduces by 1%, then to maintain the same body temperature, the body must radiate $\Delta E = 18.4$ J more energy per unit time
(c) Reducing the exposed surface area of the body allows humans to maintain the same body temperature while reducing energy lost by radiation
(d) If the body temperature rises, then the peak in the radiation spectrum emitted by the body shifts to a longer wavelength

40. Assuming Newton's law of cooling to be valid, the time taken by a body to cool from a temperature T_1 to a temperature T_2 in a room where the temperature is T_0, proportional to ($T_0 < T_2 < T_1$), is:
(a) $\ln\left(\frac{T_1 - T_0}{T_2 - T_0}\right)$ (b) $\ln\left(\frac{T_1}{T_2}\right)$
(c) $\ln\left(\frac{T_1 - T_2}{T_0}\right)$ (d) None of these

41. The Earth is in a continuous state of absorbing the Sun's radiation, and also emitting radiation from its surface. The most intense wavelength radiated from the Earth is 20 times longer than that radiated from the Sun. Considering the Earth to be in radiative equilibrium and the Sun to be a black body, if R_S is the radius of the Sun, then the distance of the Earth from the Sun is:
(a) $100\sqrt{53}R_S$ (b) $200R_S$
(c) $100\sqrt{3}R_S$ (d) $100\sqrt{2}R_S$

ANSWER KEYS

1. (d)	**2.** (b)	**3.** (b)	**4.** (d)	**5.** (a)	**6.** (a),(c)	**7.** (a)	**8.** (a)	**9.** (d)
10. (c)	**11.** (c)	**12.** (b)	**13.** (d)	**14.** (d)	**15.** (a)	**16.** (d)	**17.** (d)	**18.** (b)
19. (c)	**20.** (a)	**21.** (b)	**22.** (d)	**23.** (d)	**24.** (c)	**25.** (d)	**26.** (c)	**27.** (b)
28. (b)	**29.** (b)	**30.** (a)	**31.** (a),(c),(d)	**32.** (a)	**33.** (b)	**34.** (c)	**35.** (d)	**36.** (b)
37. (d)	**38.** (d)	**39.** (a),(b),(c)	**40.** (a)	**41.** (b)				

SOLUTIONS

1. (d) Let m be the mass of steam that condenses into water and further cools down to 80°C. The amount of energy released by steam is

$$mL_{seam} + ms_{water}\ (100°C - 80°C)$$

The amount of energy absorbed by the water and the container is

$$(1.12\ kg)s_{water}\ (80°C - 15°C)$$

Equating the two, we have

$$m(L_{steam} + 20s_{water}) = 12 \times 65 \times s_{water}$$

$$\Rightarrow \quad m = \frac{1.12 \times 65}{540 + 20} kg = 0.13\ kg$$

2. (b) Let T be the temperature of the aluminium plate. Then, we have

$$Q_{absorbed\ by\ water} = Q_{released\ by\ aluminium}$$

$$(0.5\ kg)(4200\ J/kg°C)(23°C - 20°C)$$
$$= (0.1\ kg)(900\ J/kg°C)(95°C - T)$$

$$\Rightarrow \quad T = 95°C - \frac{5 \times 42 \times 3}{9}°C = 25°C$$

3. (b) Mass of water = 120 litres × 1 kg/litre = 120 kg. Heat is being supplied at the rate of 3 kW and is being taken out at the rate of P watts. Total amount of heat absorbed by water in 3 hours is (3 kW – P)(3 h).

The water heats up from 10°C to 30°C in this time. Thus, we have

$$(3\ kW - P)(3\ h) = (120\ kg)(4.2 \times 103\ J/kg\ °C)(30°C - 10°C)$$

$$\Rightarrow \quad P = 3000\ W - \frac{120 \times 4.2 \times 10^3 \times 20}{3 \times 3600} W = 2067\ W$$

4. (d) Total energy absorbed by water in 10 minutes, Q = (1000 J/s – 160 J/s) × 600 s = 504 kJ. The temperature rise will be

$$\Delta T = \frac{Q}{ms_{water}} = \frac{504\ kJ}{(2\ kg)(4.2\ kJ/kg \cdot °C)} = 60°C$$

Hence, the final temperature is 27°C + 60°C = 87°C.

5. (a) Energy is required at the rate of

$$\frac{dQ}{dt} = \frac{dm}{dt} s_{water} \Delta T$$
$$= (10\ kg/h)(1\ kcal/kg°C)(80°C - 20°C)$$
$$= 600\ kcal/h$$

Let x kg/h be the rate at which steam condenses from 150°C and further cools down to 90°C. Then, the rate at which energy is released by steam

$$\frac{dQ}{dt} = \frac{dm}{dt}(L_{steam} + s_{water}\Delta T)$$
$$= (x\ kg/h)\ [540\ kcal/h + (1\ kcal/kg°C)(150°C - 90°C)]$$
$$= 600x\ kcal/h$$

Equating the two, we have

$$600x\ kcal/h = 600\ kcal/h \Rightarrow x = 1$$

6. (a), (c) Energy released if all the water turns into ice at 0°C = $m\alpha s_1 + m\alpha s_2 + mL$

Energy required to heat ice from β to 0°C = $-m\beta s_3$

Hence, all the water will turn into ice if

$$m\alpha s_1 + m\alpha s_2 + mL < -m\beta s_3$$
$$\Rightarrow \quad \alpha s_1 + \alpha s_2 + L + \beta s_3 < 0$$

Energy released if water cools down from α to 0°C = $m\alpha s_1 + m\alpha s_2$

Energy required to melt all the ice into water = $-m\beta s_3 + mL$

Hence, all the ice will melt into water if

$$m\alpha s_1 + m\alpha s_2 > -m\beta s_3 + mL$$
$$\Rightarrow \quad \alpha s_1 + \alpha s_2 - L + \beta s_3 > 0$$

7. (a) Energy required to melt ice at 0°C

$$Q_1 = 400\ g\ [0.5\ cal/g°C \times 20°C + 80\ cal/g]$$
$$= 36000\ cal$$

Energy released if the steam condenses to water at 0°C

$$Q_2 = 50\ g\ [1\ cal/g°C \times 160°C + 540\ cal/g]$$
$$= 35000\ cal$$

Since $Q_2 < Q_1$, some ice will remain unmelted, and the final composition of the mixture will be ice + water at 0°C.

Mass of unmelted ice

$$= \frac{36000\ cal - 35000\ cal}{80\ cal/am} = 12.5\ g$$

Hence, mass of water = 400 g + (50 g – 12.5 g) = 437.5 g.

8. (a) Let the initial temperature of ice be θ and the mass be m. The rate of heat supply in the first minute is $\frac{m(0.5\ cal/g \cdot °C)(0°C - \theta)}{1\ min}$ and the rate of heat supply in the next four minutes is $\frac{m(80\ cal/g)}{4\ min}$

Equating the two, we have

$$\frac{-(0.5\ cal/g \cdot °C)\theta}{1\ min} = \frac{(80\ cal/g)}{4\ min} \Rightarrow \theta = -40°C$$

9. (d) Let a, b, c be the lengths of the sides of the crystal. Then its volume is $V = abc$.
For small changes, we have

$$\frac{\Delta V}{V} = \frac{\Delta a}{a} + \frac{\Delta b}{b} + \frac{\Delta c}{c}$$

Dividing throughout by ΔT, we have

$$\frac{1}{V}\frac{\Delta V}{\Delta T} = \frac{1}{a}\frac{\Delta a}{\Delta T} + \frac{1}{b}\frac{\Delta b}{\Delta T} + \frac{1}{c}\frac{\Delta c}{\Delta T}$$

$$\Rightarrow \quad \gamma = \alpha_a + \alpha_b + \alpha_c = 4 \times 10^{-6}\text{K}^{-1}$$

10. (c) Let ρ be the density of the liquid and V be the volume of the immersed metal ball at 0°C. The force of buoyancy on the ball is $F_1 = \rho Vg$. When the temperature is increased to 52°C, the force of buoyancy becomes

$$F_2 = \frac{\rho}{1+50\gamma_l} \times V(1+50\gamma_s) \times g = \left(\frac{1+50\gamma_s}{1+50y_l}\right)F$$

Since $\gamma_S > \gamma_l$, we conclude that force of buoyancy decreases, which means the ball will weigh more. Hence $W_2 > W_1$.

11. (c) The total length of the rod is $l = l_1 + l_2$. For a temperature change of ΔT, the length of the rod changes by $\Delta l = \Delta l_1 + \Delta l_2 = (l_1\alpha_1 + l_2\alpha_2)\,\Delta T$. Dividing throughout by $l\Delta T$, we have

$$\frac{\Delta l}{l\Delta T} = \frac{l_1\alpha_1 + l_2\alpha_2}{l_1 + l_2}$$

This is the required coefficient of linear expansion of the composite rod.

12. (b) Let l be the length of the rod. Let us choose our x-axis along the length of the rod. The end where the coefficient of linear expansion is α_1 will be the origin. The coefficient of linear expansion as a function of x is

$$\alpha(x) = a_1 + \lambda x, \text{ where } \lambda = \frac{a_2 - a_1}{1}$$

Now, let us subdivide the rod into small elements of length dx. When temperature increases by ΔT, the element dx situated at position x elongates by an amount $dl = \alpha(x)dx\Delta T = \Delta T(\alpha_1 + \lambda x)dx$. Total elongation in the rod is

$$\Delta I = \Delta T\int_0^l(\alpha_1 + \lambda x)dx = \Delta T\left(a_1\, l + \frac{1}{2}\lambda l^2\right)$$

Putting $\lambda = \dfrac{\alpha_2 - \alpha_1}{I}$, we have $\Delta l = l\Delta T\left(\dfrac{\alpha_2 + \alpha_1}{2}\right)$

Hence, coefficient of linear expansion of the rod is

$$\frac{\Delta l}{l\Delta T} = \frac{\alpha_2 + \alpha_1}{2}.$$

13. (d) Let σ be the density of wood and ρ be the density of the liquid at 0°C. The fraction of wood that is submerged in the liquid equals σ/p. According to the question

$$\frac{\sigma}{\rho} = 80\% = \frac{4}{5} \qquad \ldots(1)$$

At 100°C, the density of liquid becomes equal to that of wood. Hence

$$\frac{\sigma}{1+100\gamma_w} = \frac{\rho}{1+100\gamma_1} \qquad \ldots(2)$$

From the above equations, we have

$$\frac{4}{1+100\gamma_w} = \frac{5}{1+100\gamma_l}$$

$$\Rightarrow \quad 5 + 500\gamma_W = 4 + 400\gamma_L$$

$$\Rightarrow \quad \gamma_L = \frac{1}{400} + \frac{5}{4}\gamma_W = (2.5\times10^{-3} + 1.5\times10^{-3})\text{K}^{-1}$$

$$= 4.0\times10^{-3}\,\text{K}^{-1}$$

14. (d) Let γ be the coefficient of cubical expansion of the liquid and a_2 be the coefficient of linear expansion of vessel B. The coefficient of apparent expansion of a liquid is its actual coefficient of volume expansion minus the coefficient of volume expansion of the container. Thus, we have

$$\gamma - 3\alpha_1 = \gamma_1 \text{ and } \gamma - 3\alpha_2 = \gamma_2$$

Subtracting the two equations, we have

$$3a_2 - 3a_1 = \gamma_1 - \gamma_2 \Rightarrow a_2 = a_1 + \frac{1}{3}(\gamma_1 - \gamma_2)$$

15. (a) Let V' be the volume of liquid. The volume of air is $V_{air} = V - V'$. For small changes, $\Delta V - \Delta V'$. Since volume of air remains unchanged

$$\Delta V - \Delta V' = 0$$

$$\Rightarrow \quad \gamma_1 V\Delta T = \gamma_2 V'\Delta T$$

$$\Rightarrow \quad V' = \left(\frac{\gamma_1}{\gamma_2}\right)V$$

16. (d) In the absence of external torque, the angular momentum $L = I\omega \propto r^2\omega$ remains unchanged. Thus for small changes, we have

$$2\frac{\Delta r}{r} + \frac{\Delta\omega}{\omega} = 0$$

$$\Rightarrow \quad 2\alpha\Delta T + \frac{\Delta\omega}{\omega} = 0 \Rightarrow \Delta\omega = -2\alpha\omega\Delta T$$

17. (d) Let V be the volume of mercury in the glass tube and A be the cross-section area of the glass tube. The height of the mercury column is $h = V/A$. For small changes, we have

$$\frac{\Delta h}{h} = \frac{\Delta V}{V} - \frac{\Delta A}{A} = \gamma_m \Delta T - \frac{2}{3} Y_g \Delta T$$

$$\Rightarrow \quad \frac{\Delta h}{h \wedge T} = \gamma_m - \frac{2}{3}\gamma_g$$

This is the required coefficient of linear expansion of the mercury column.

18. (b) Let ρ be the density of the liquid. Let a be the side of the cube and h be the submerged height of the cube. For a floating object, the weight of the liquid displaced equals the weight of the object, that is, $\rho a^2 hg = W$ (weight of the cube). Since weight of the cube is constant and according to the question, h is constant $\Rightarrow \rho a^2 = c$ (constant). Hence, for small changes, we have

$$\frac{\Delta\rho}{\rho} + 2\frac{\Delta a}{a} = 0$$

$$\Rightarrow \quad -\gamma\Delta T + 2\alpha\Delta T = 0 \Rightarrow \alpha = \frac{1}{2}\gamma$$

19. (c) Rise in temperature $\Delta T = Q/ms$.

Change in volume $\Delta V = \gamma V \Delta T = \frac{\gamma VQ}{ms} = \frac{\gamma Q}{\rho s}$.

Work done by the expanding block on the surrounding, $W = P_0 \Delta V = \frac{\gamma P_0 Q}{\rho s}$.

20. (a) The perpendicular distance of P from base QR is $\sqrt{a^2 - \frac{b^2}{4}}$, which is given to be a constant. Thus, we have $4a^2 - b^2$ = constant. For small changes, we have

$$4\Delta(a^2) - \Delta(b^2) = 0$$

$$\Rightarrow \quad 4a\Delta a = b\Delta b$$

$$\Rightarrow \quad 4a(a\alpha\Delta T) = b(b\beta\Delta T)$$

$$\Rightarrow \quad 4a^2\alpha = b^2\beta$$

$$\Rightarrow \quad \frac{b}{a} = \sqrt{\frac{4a}{\beta}}$$

21. (b) Fractional change in length due to temperature change $\frac{\Delta l}{l} = \alpha\Delta T$.

Strain produced due to constraining

$$= (0.5\%)\alpha\Delta T = \frac{5\times 10^{-4}\times 50}{10^3} = 2.5\times 10^{-5}.$$

Stress inside the wire = $Y \times$ Strain = $(2\times 10^{11}\ \text{N/m}^2)(2.5\times 10^{-5}) = 5\times 10^6\ \text{N/m}^2$.

22. (d) At reduced temperature, the natural lengths of the wires A and B are, respectively, $l_1 = l - \alpha_1 l\Delta T$ and $l_2 = l - \alpha_2 l\Delta T$. In this question, the combined length of the wires must remain 21. Let us assume that the length of A reduces to $l - x$, while that of B increases to $l + x$. Both wires are in a state of tension. The tensile strain in the two wires are, respectively

$$\eta_1 = \frac{(l-x)-l_1}{l} = \frac{\alpha_1 / \Delta T - x}{l} \text{ and}$$

$$\eta_2 = \frac{(l+x)-l_2}{l} = \frac{\alpha_2 l\Delta T + x}{l}$$

The tension, say F, is the same in both the wires. Hence, $F = SY_1\eta_1 = SY_2\eta_2$. Solving the equation, we have

$$Y_1\left(\frac{\alpha_1 / \Delta T - x}{I}\right) = Y_2\left(\frac{\alpha_2 I\Delta T + x}{I}\right)$$

$$\Rightarrow x = \left(\frac{Y_1\alpha_1 - Y_2\alpha_2}{Y_1 + Y_2}\right) I\Delta T$$

Putting the value of x gives

$$F = \frac{Y_1 Y_2(\alpha_1 + \alpha_2)S\Delta T}{Y_1 + Y_2}.$$

23. (d) Let A be the cross-section area. The thermal resistance of the composite slab is $\frac{l_1}{k_1 A} + \frac{l_2}{k_2 A}$. If we consider one slab of length $l_1 + l_2$, cross-section area A and thermal conductivity k, having resistance equal that of the composite slab, then

$$\frac{l_1 + l_2}{kA} = \frac{l_1}{k_1 A} + \frac{l_2}{k_2 A} \Rightarrow k = \frac{k_1 k_2(l_1 + l_2)}{k_1 l_2 + k_2 l_1}$$

24. (c) Let L be the length of the cylinders. The thermal resistance of the inner and outer conductors are, respectively

$$R_1 = \frac{L}{k_1(\pi R^2)} \text{ and } R_2 = \frac{L}{k_2(3\pi R^2)}$$

If we consider one single cylindrical conductor of length L, cross-section area $4\pi R^2$ and conductivity k whose resistance $R_3 = \frac{L}{k(4\pi R^2)}$ equals the combined resistance of the given conductors, then

$$\frac{1}{R_3} = \frac{1}{R_1} + \frac{1}{R_2}$$

$$\Rightarrow \quad \frac{k(4\pi R^2)}{L} = \frac{k_1(\pi R^2)}{L} + \frac{k_2(3\pi R^2)}{L}$$

$$\Rightarrow \quad k = \frac{1}{4}k_1 + \frac{3}{4}k_2$$

25. (d) Let R and $2R$ be the resistances of the two rods. In parallel combination, the resistance is $\frac{2R}{3}$, and in series combination, the resistance is $3R$. If the same temperature difference is applied, the time taken for the same amount of energy transfer is proportional to the resistance.

$$\left[\frac{\Delta Q}{\Delta t}=\frac{\Delta\theta}{R}\Rightarrow \Delta t\propto R\right]$$

Hence, the time during series connection

$$=\frac{3R}{2R/3}\times 12\text{ s}=54\text{ s}$$

26. (c)

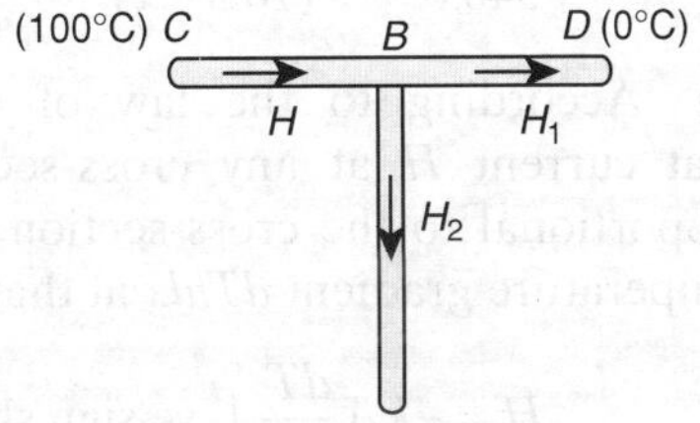

Let lengths $CB = CD = L$ and $AB = 2L$. Let k be the thermal conductivity and S be the cross-section area which is the same for all the rods. Let T be the temperature at B. If we choose the heat currents as shown in the figure, then we have

$$H=H_1+H_2$$

$$\Rightarrow \quad kS\left(\frac{100°\text{C}-T}{L}\right)=kS\left(\frac{T-0°\text{C}}{L}\right)+kS\left(\frac{T-25°\text{C}}{2L}\right)$$

$$\Rightarrow \quad 100°\text{C}-T=T+\frac{1}{2}(T-25°\text{C})\Rightarrow T=45°\text{C}$$

27. (b) Heat flows from B to A through two parallel paths, as shown in the figure. Let lengths $AB = BC = l$ and then $AC=\sqrt{2}l$. Let k be the thermal conductivity and S be the cross-section area for all the rods. Let T' be the temperature at C. The heat current through BC equals that through CA.

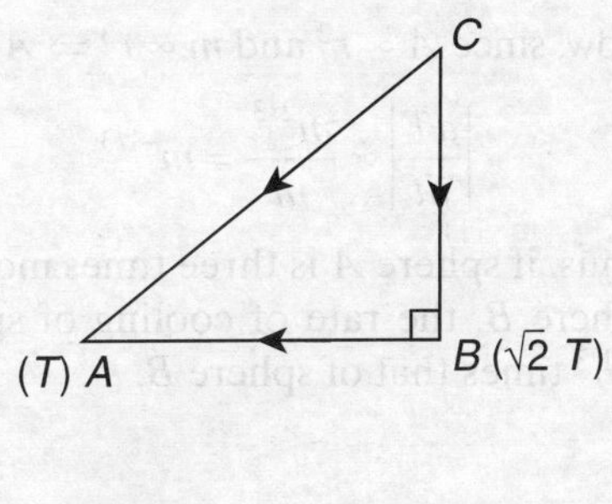

Hence

$$kS\left(\frac{\sqrt{2}T-T'}{l}\right)=kS\left(\frac{T'-T}{\sqrt{2}l}\right)\Rightarrow T'=\frac{3T}{\sqrt{2}+1}$$

28. (b) Since the thermal resistance of a rod is proportional to its length, the thermal resistances of the different portions can be chosen as shown in the figure.

The thermal resistance between points P and Q is

$$R_{PQ}=\frac{(2R)(3R)}{2R+3R}=\frac{6}{5}R$$

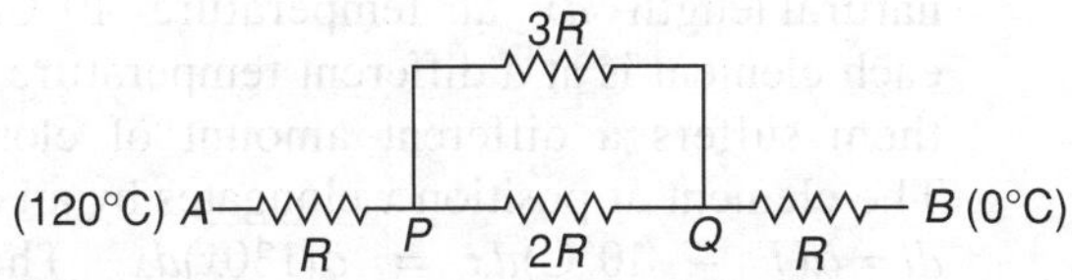

The thermal resistance between points A and B is

$$R_{AB}=R+\frac{6}{5}R+R=\frac{16}{5}R$$

Hence, the temperature difference between points P and Q is

$$\Delta T_{PQ}=\frac{\frac{6R}{5}}{\frac{16R}{5}}\times 120°\text{C}=45°\text{C}$$

29. (b)

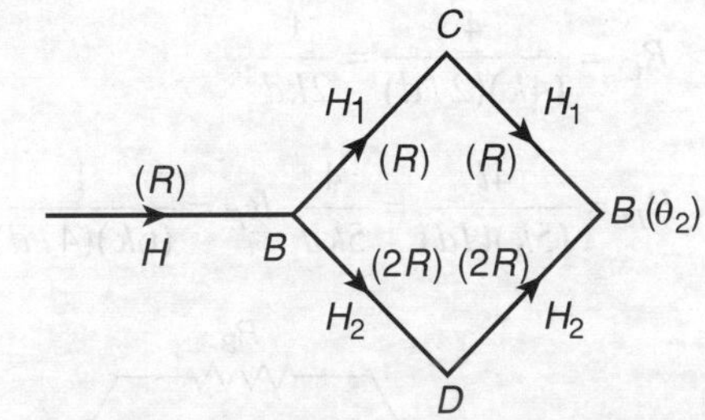

All rods have the same dimensions. In this case, their resistance will be in inverse proportion to their conductivity. Let us choose their resistance, as shown in the figure. The resistance of path BCE is $2R$ and that of BDE is $4R$. Let the temperature of B be θ_B. Then, we have

$$H=H_1+H_2$$

$$\Rightarrow \quad \frac{\theta_1-\theta_B}{R}=\frac{\theta_B-\theta_2}{2R}+\frac{\theta_B-\theta_2}{4R}\Rightarrow \theta_B=\frac{4\theta_1+3\theta_2}{7}$$

Let the temperature of C be θ_C. Equating the heat current through BC and CD, we have

$$\frac{\theta_B-\theta_C}{R}=\frac{\theta_C-\theta_2}{R}\Rightarrow \theta_C=\frac{\theta_B+\theta_2}{2}=\frac{2\theta_1+5\theta_2}{7}$$

30. (a) Let T_0 be the junction temperature. Then, we have

$$\frac{T_0 - 10°C}{R} = \frac{400°C - T_0}{2R} \Rightarrow T_0 = 140°C$$

Let us choose our x-axis along AB with origin at end A. The temperature T along rod A, as a function of position x, is given by

$$\frac{T - 10°C}{x} = \frac{140°C - 10°C}{1\text{ m}} \Rightarrow T = 10°C + (130°C/m)x$$

Let us subdivide rod A into elements, each of natural length dx at temperature 10°C. Since each element is at a different temperature T, each them suffers a different amount of elongation. The element at position x elongates by an amount $dl = \alpha(T - 10°C)dx = \alpha(130x)dx$. The total elongation in rod A is

$$\Delta l = 130\alpha \int_0^{1\text{ m}} x dx = 65(1.2 \times 10^{-5})\text{m} = 0.78\text{ mm}$$

31. (a), (c), (d)
Let the width of each slab be d. The given composite block can be represented as shown in the figure, where

$$R_A = \frac{1}{(2k)(4/d)} = \frac{1}{8kd}, R_B = \frac{4l}{(3k)(Id)} = \frac{4}{3kd},$$

$$R_C = \frac{4}{(4k)(2/d)} = \frac{1}{2kd},$$

$$R_D = \frac{4l}{(5k)(Id)} = \frac{4}{5kd}, R_E = \frac{1}{(6k)(4/d)} = \frac{1}{24kd}$$

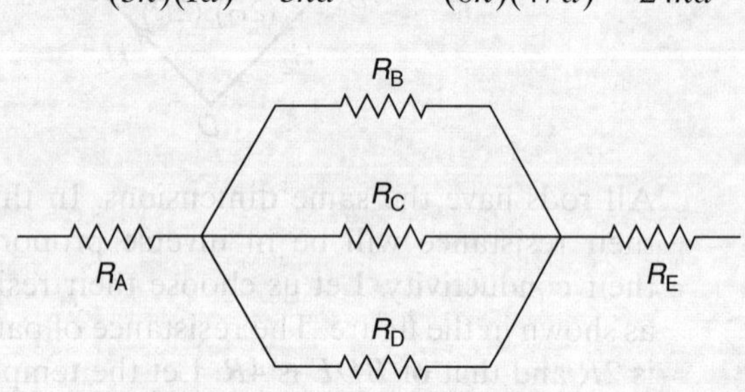

Slabs A and E are in series, so heat flow through them will be the same ⇒ (a) is correct.

The resistances of B, C, D combined is $R = \frac{1}{2kd}$.
Now $R > R_A > R_E \Rightarrow \Delta\theta > \Delta\theta_A > \Delta\theta_E$ ($\Delta\theta/R$ is the same for resistances in series) ⇒ (b) is incorrect but (c) is correct.
The combined resistance of B and D equals that of $C \Rightarrow$ (d) is correct.

32. (a) Let H_1 and H_2 be the heat currents towards the boiling water and ice containers, respectively. The water evaporation rate and ice melting rate are given to be equal. Thus, we have

$$\frac{H_1}{540\text{ cal/g}} = \frac{H_2}{80\text{ cal/g}}$$

If k is the thermal conductivity and A is the cross-section area of the rod, then

$$H_1 = kA\left(\frac{300}{x}\right) \text{ and } H_2 = kA\left(\frac{400}{10L - x}\right)$$

Putting these values in the above equation, we have

$$\frac{300}{540x} = \frac{400}{80(10L - x)} \Rightarrow x = L$$

33. (b) According to the law of conduction, the heat current H at any cross-section is directly proportional to the cross-section area A and the temperature gradient dT/dx at that cross-section:

$$H = -kA\frac{dT}{dx} \text{ [–ve sign shows that } H \text{ flows along decreasing } T]$$

At steady state, the value of H is the same at all cross-sections. This means that the product of A and $|dT/dx|$ must be the same throughout the rod. Hence, for the given graph, the cross-section area first decreases and then increases, since the steepness of the tangent first increases and then decreases.

34. (c) Let A be the surface area of one side of the plate. The middle plate is absorbing energy in proportion to AT_1^4 and AT_3^4 on its left and right surfaces, respectively. At the same time, it is emitting energy from both its surfaces in proportion to $2AT_2^4$. At equilibrium, the absorption rate must equal the emission rate. Hence $T_1^4 + T_3^4 = 2T_2^4$.

35. (d) The rate of cooling of a body is given by

$$\left|\frac{dT}{dt}\right| = \frac{4\varepsilon\sigma AT_S^3}{ms}\Delta T$$

Now, since $A \propto r^2$ and $m \propto r^3 \Rightarrow A \propto m^{2/3}$

$$\left|\frac{dT}{dt}\right| \propto \frac{m^{2/3}}{m} = m^{-1/3}$$

Thus, if sphere A is three times more massive than sphere B, the rate of cooling of sphere A will be $3^{-1/3}$ times that of sphere B.

36. (b) In the first 5 seconds, the average rate of cooling is $\frac{90°C - 50°C}{5\text{ s}} = 8°C/s$ and the average temperature difference between the body and the surrounding is $\frac{90°C + 50°C}{2} - 30°C = 40°C$. Let T be the time taken by the body to cool from 50°C to 40°C. Then, during this time interval, the average rate of cooling is $\frac{50°C - 40°C}{T} = \frac{10°C}{T}$ and the average temperature difference between the body and the surrounding is $\frac{50°C + 40°C}{2} - 30°C = 15°C$. Using Newton's law of cooling, we have

$$\frac{8°C/s}{10°C/r} = \frac{40°C}{15°C} \Rightarrow T = 3.3\text{ s}$$

37. (d) Let θ_s be the surrounding temperature, and let θ be the temperature at the end of the 30th minute.
In the first 10 minutes, the average cooling rate is $\frac{62°C - 50°C}{10\text{ min}} = 1.2°C/\text{min}$, and the average temperature difference between the body and the surroundings is $\frac{62°C + 50°C}{2} - \theta_s = 56°C - \theta_s$
In the next 10 minutes, the average cooling rate is $\frac{50°C - 42°C}{10\text{ min}} = 0.8°C/\text{min}$, and the average temperature difference between the body and the surrounding is $\frac{50°C + 42°C}{2} - \theta_S = 46°C - \theta_s$
In the last 10 minutes, the average cooling rate is $\frac{42°C - \theta}{10\text{ min}}$, and the average temperature difference between the body and the surrounding is $\frac{42°C + \theta}{2} - \theta_S$
From Newton's law of cooling, we have

$$\frac{56°C - \theta_s}{1.2°C/\text{min}} = \frac{46°C - \theta_s}{0.8°C/\text{min}} = \frac{\frac{42°C + \theta}{2} - \theta_S}{\frac{42°C - \theta}{10\text{ min}}}$$

Solving the first equation gives $\theta_s = 26°C$. Then, putting this value and solving the second equation gives $\theta = 37°C$.

38. (d) The initial and final temperatures are, respectively, $T_1 = 487°C + 273°C = 760$ K and $T_2 = 276°C + 273°C = 3040$ K.

$$\text{Now } \frac{T_2}{T_1} = \frac{3040\text{ K}}{760\text{ K}} = 4 \Rightarrow \frac{P_2}{P_1} = \frac{T_2^4}{T_1^4} = 2^8$$

$$\text{Now } \log_2\left(\frac{P_1}{P_0}\right) = 1 \Rightarrow P_1 = 2P_0$$

$$\text{Hence } P_2 = 2^8(2P_0) = 2^9 P_0 \Rightarrow \log_2\left(\frac{P_2}{P_0}\right) = 9$$

39. (a), (b), (c) The net rate of energy radiation from the body surface is $H_{net} = \varepsilon_0\sigma A\,[(300\text{ K} + 10\text{ K})^4 - 300\text{ K}^4]$

$$= \varepsilon_0\sigma A(300\text{ K})^4\left[\left(1+\frac{10}{300}\right)^4 - 1\right]$$

$$= (460\text{ W/m}^2 \times 1\text{ m}^2)\left(\frac{40}{300}\right) = 60\text{ W} \Rightarrow \text{(a) is correct}$$

For surrounding temperature T_o and body temperature 310 K, the net rate of energy radiation from the body surface is $H_{net} = \varepsilon_0\sigma A[310^4 - T_0^4]$. For small changes in T_o, we have

$$\Delta H_{net} = -\varepsilon_o\sigma A(4T_o^3\Delta T_o) = -4(\varepsilon_0\sigma A T_o^4)\frac{\Delta T_o}{T_o}$$

If surrounding temperature $T_o = 300$ K is reduced by 1%, then

$$\Delta H_{net} = -4(460\text{ W})\left(\frac{-1}{100}\right) = 18.4\text{ W} \Rightarrow \text{(b) is correct}$$

Reducing surface area A reduces H_{net} ⇒ (c) is correct.
Increase in temperature causes a shift towards the shorter wavelength ⇒ (d) is incorrect.

40. (a) From Newton's law of cooling, we have

$$\frac{dT}{dt} = -c(T - T_0)$$

If T is the time in which the body cools from T_1 to T_2, then we have

$$c\int_0^T dt = -\int_{T1}^{T2}\frac{dT}{T - T_0}$$

$$\Rightarrow \quad CT = \ln\left(\frac{T_1 - T_0}{T_2 - T_0}\right)$$

41. (b) Let T_E, T_S be the temperatures of the Earth's and Sun's surfaces, respectively. Given $\lambda_E = 20\lambda_S$. Then, by Wien's law

$$T_S = 20T_E \qquad \text{...(1)}$$

Energy radiated per second from the Sun's surface

$$= \sigma(4\pi R_S^2)T_S^4$$

Energy received per second by the Earth

$$= \left(\frac{\pi R_E^2}{4\pi d^2}\right)\sigma(4\pi R_S^2)T_S^4$$

Energy radiated per second from the Earth's surface $= \sigma(4\pi R_E^2)T_E^4$

At equilibrium, the absorption rate must equal the emission rate. Therefore

$$\left(\frac{\pi R_E^2}{4\pi d^2}\right)\sigma(4\pi R_S^2)T_S^4 = \sigma(4\pi R_E^2)T_E^4$$

$$\Rightarrow d = \frac{T_S^2}{2T_E^2}R_S \quad \ldots(2)$$

From the above equations, we have $d = 200R_S$

CHAPTER 14

Gas Laws and First Law of Thermodynamics

- The pressure P, volume V and absolute temperature T of a given quantity of a substance are called the state variables; a relation between them is called an equation of state. For μ moles of an ideal gas (gas at low pressures and high temperatures), the state variables are related by the following laws:

  (Boyle's law) $V \propto 1/P$ at constant μ, T

  (Charles's law) $V \propto T$ at constant μ, P

  (Avogadro's law) $V \propto \mu$ at constant P, V

  All the above laws can be combined into one equation of state. For μ moles of an ideal gas, the equation of state, known as the ideal gas equation, is

  $$PV = \mu RT,$$

  where $R = 8.314$ J/mol·K is the universal gas constant. The ideal gas equation can also be written in terms of the total number of molecules N as

  $$pV = NkT,$$

  where $k = 1.38 \times 10^{-23}$ J/K is the Boltzmann constant. The number of moles μ and the number of molecules N of the gas are related by Avogadro's number $N_A = 6.022 \times 10^{23}$ as $\mu = N/N_A$. The gas constant R and the Boltzmann constant k are also related as $k = R/N_A$. The ideal gas equation can also be written in terms of the gas density ρ and the molar mass M (mass of one mole) of the gas as

  $$P = \frac{\rho RT}{M}$$

- The kinetic molecular model represents molecules of an ideal gas as tiny particles of negligible size in constant motion, exerting no force on each other except during collisions; all collisions being elastic. The molecules of the gas move with variable speeds distributed over a range. The most probable speed v_{mp}, the average speed v_{av} and the RMS (root mean square) speed v_{rms} of molecules in an ideal gas are

  $$v_{mp} = \sqrt{\frac{2RT}{M}}, \; v_{av} = \sqrt{\frac{8RT}{\pi M}} \text{ and } v_{rms} = \sqrt{\frac{3RT}{M}}$$

- A number of velocity components are required to describe the motion of a molecule completely. The equipartition of energy states that the energy of a molecule is equally distributed amongst its degrees of freedom. At absolute temperature T, the kinetic energy per molecule per degree of freedom equals $\frac{1}{2}kT$.

  A monoatomic molecule has three (translational), a diatomic molecule has five (3 translational + 2 rotational) and a polyatomic molecule has six (3 translational + 3 rotational) degrees of freedom. Thus, the average kinetic energy per molecule for a monoatomic, diatomic and polyatomic molecule is, respectively, $\frac{3}{2}kT$ (monoatomic), $\frac{5}{2}kT$ (diatomic) and $3kT$ (polyatomic).

- The internal energy U of an ideal gas, which is the total kinetic energy of its molecules (measured relative to the container), depends on the absolute temperature of the gas as

  $$U = \mu c_v T,$$

  where c_v (SI unit is J/mol·K) is the molar heat capacity for a constant volume process.

  For a gas with f degrees of freedom, $c_v = f\left(\frac{1}{2}R\right)$; its values for an ideal monoatomic, diatomic and polyatomic gas are $\frac{3}{2}R$ (monoatomic), $\frac{5}{2}R$ (diatomic) and $3R$ (polyatomic).

When the temperature of an ideal gas changes by an amount ΔT, the change in internal energy of the gas is given by

$$\Delta U = \mu c_v \Delta T$$

The value of ΔU can be positive, negative or zero depending upon the value of ΔT.

For the process PV^n = constant $\Rightarrow TV^{n-1}$ = constant, we have $\frac{\Delta T}{T} = (1-n)\frac{\Delta V}{V}$. Thus, during expansion, $(\Delta V > 0)$, ΔU is positive, negative or zero depending upon whether n is less than, greater than or equal to 1. During compression, it is vice-versa.

- A thermodynamic system can exchange energy with its surroundings in two ways; heat (Q) transfer and mechanical work (W). A system does work on the surroundings when its volume changes. When a system at pressure P changes volume from V_1 to V_2, the amount of work done by the system on the surroundings is given by

$$W = \int_{V_1}^{V_2} P dV$$

Work done by the system is positive when the system expands, and negative if the system is compressed. The value of W can be determined only if the pressure is known throughout the process. For the process PV^n = constant, the work done by an ideal gas is

$$W = \begin{cases} \dfrac{\Delta(PV)}{1-n} \text{ or } \dfrac{\mu R \Delta T}{1-n}, \text{ if } n \neq 1 \\ \mu RT \ln\left(\dfrac{V_2}{V_1}\right), \text{ if } n = 1 \text{ (isothermal process)} \end{cases}$$

- The first law of thermodynamics states that when heat Q is added to a system while it does work W, the internal energy of the system changes by an amount ΔU given by

$$Q = \Delta U + W$$

When heat flows into the system, Q is positive; Q is negative when heat flows out of the system. If the system is an ideal gas, the first law reduces to

$$Q = \mu c_v \Delta T + \int_{V_1}^{V_2} P dV$$

- The molar heat capacity c of a gas is the amount of heat required per mole per unit change in temperature:

$$c = \frac{1}{\mu}\frac{dQ}{dT} = c_v + \frac{P}{n}\frac{dV}{dT}$$

The value of c depends on the process. For the process PV^n= constant, the molar heat capacity of an ideal gas is

$$c = c_v + \frac{R}{1-n} = c_v + \frac{R}{1-n}$$

For a constant pressure process (n = 0), the molar heat capacity c_p of an ideal gas is

$$c_p = c_v + R$$

The ratio c_p / c_v of heat capacities, denoted by γ, is called the adiabatic exponent of the gas:

$$\gamma = c_p / c_v$$

In terms of γ, the values of the heat capacities c_p and c_v are

$$c_v = \frac{R}{\gamma - 1} \text{ and } c_p = \frac{\gamma R}{\gamma - 1}$$

For a mixture of two gases in the mole ratio $n_1 : n_2$, the values of c_v, c_p and γ are

$$c_v = \frac{n_1 c_{v1} + n_2 c_{v2}}{n_1 + n_2},\ c_p = \frac{n_1 c_{p1} + n_2 c_{p2}}{n_1 + n_2} \text{ and } \gamma = \frac{n_1 c_{p1} + n_2 c_{p2}}{n_1 c_{v1} + n_2 c_{v2}}$$

- If c is known for any process (PV^n = constant), then the heat required for the process is given by $Q = \mu c \Delta T$. For the process PV^n = constant, the heat required is

$$Q = \begin{cases} \dfrac{\mu R \Delta T}{\gamma - 1} + \dfrac{\mu R \Delta T}{1 - n} \text{ or } \dfrac{\Delta(PV)}{\gamma - 1} + \dfrac{\Delta(PV)}{1 - n}, \text{ if } n \neq 1 \\ \mu RT \ln\left(\dfrac{V_2}{V_1}\right), \text{ if } n = 1 \text{ (isothermal process)} \end{cases}$$

During expansion, Q is positive, negative or zero depending upon whether n is less than, greater than or equal to γ. During compression, it is vice-versa.

- An isochoric process is one in which V = constant. For such a process, $W = 0$.

  An isobaric process is one in which P = constant. For such a process, $W = P\Delta V = \mu R \Delta T$.

  An isothermal process is one in which T = constant. For such a process, $W = \mu RT \ln\left(\dfrac{V_2}{V_1}\right)$.

  An adiabatic process is one in which $Q = 0$. For such a process, PV^γ = constant and $W = \dfrac{\Delta(PV)}{1-\gamma}$ or $\dfrac{\mu R \Delta T}{1-\gamma}$.

EXERCISES

1. A vessel contains a mixture of 7 g of nitrogen and 11 g of carbon dioxide at temperature $T = 290$ K and pressure $P = 1$ atm. The density of the mixture is (molar masses of nitrogen and carbon dioxide are 28 g/mol and $44\frac{\text{g}}{\text{mol}}$, respectively, and $R = 0.082\ \text{l·atm/mol·K}$):

(a) 0.5 g/l (b) 1.0 g/l
(c) 1.5 g/l (d) 2.0 g/l

2. A vessel of volume $V = 20$ l contains a mixture of hydrogen and helium at temperature $T = 293$ K and pressure $P = 2$ atm. The mass of the mixture is 5 g. The ratio of mass of hydrogen to that of helium is (molar masses of hydrogen and helium are 2 g and 4 g, respectively, and $R = 0.082\ \text{l·atm/mol·K}$):

(a) 0.1 (b) 0.2
(c) 0.4 (d) 0.5

3. A vessel of volume $V = 30$ l contains ideal gas at temperature 0°C. After a certain amount of gas is let out, the pressure inside the vessel drops by $\Delta P = 0.78$ atm with negligible change in temperature. If the density of the gas at normal conditions (0°C and 1 atm) is $\rho_0 = 1.3$ g/l, the mass of gas released is:

(a) 10 g (b) 20 g
(c) 30 g (d) 50 g

4. n_1 moles of a monoatomic gas at temperature T_1 and n_2 moles of a diatomic gas at temperature T_2 are mixed. Assuming no loss of energy in this process, the equilibrium temperature of the mixture will be:

(a) $T_1 + \left(\frac{5n_2}{3n_1}\right)T_2$

(b) $T_2 + \left(\frac{3n_1}{5n_2}\right)T_1$

(c) $\frac{n_1T_1 + n_2T_2}{n_1 + n_2}$

(d) $\frac{3n_1T_1 + 5n_2T_2}{3n_1 + 5n_2}$

5. The figure shows a smooth vertical tube having two different sections open from both ends and equipped with freely movable pistons. The cross-section area of the upper piston is ΔS greater than that of the lower one. The combined weight of the pistons is W and the outside air pressure is P_0. The pistons are tied with an inextensible thread and the volume between them is filled with 1 mole of ideal gas.

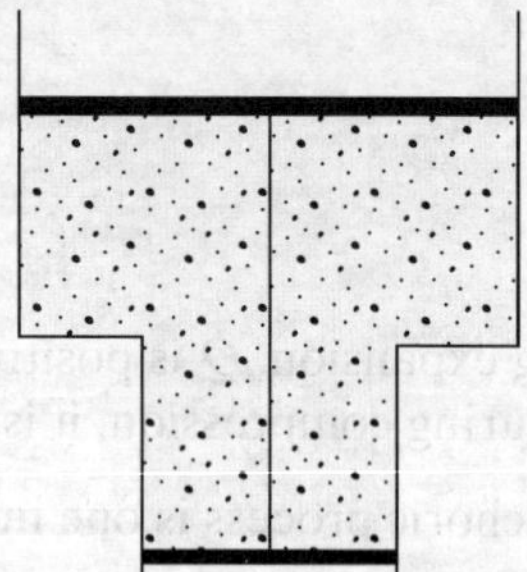

If the temperature of the gas is raised by ΔT, the pistons move up by:

(a) $\frac{2R\Delta T}{P_0\Delta S + 2W}$ (b) $\frac{R\Delta T}{P_0\Delta S + W}$

(c) $\frac{2R\Delta T}{2P_0\Delta S + W}$ (d) $\frac{R\Delta T}{2P_0\Delta S + W}$

6. An insulated box containing a diatomic gas of molar mass M is moving with velocity v. If the box is suddenly stopped, and assuming that the lost kinetic energy of the gas molecules completely changes into its internal energy, the temperature of the gas rises by:

(a) $\frac{Mv^2}{5R}$ (b) $\frac{2Mv^2}{3R}$

(c) $\frac{Mv^2}{2R}$ (d) $\frac{2Mv^2}{5R}$

7. A container contains 0.5 moles of a gaseous mixture at temperature 27°C. If the adiabatic exponent of the mixture is 1.50, the amount of heat energy to be supplied to the mixture to double the root mean square (RMS) speed of its molecules is:

(a) 450 R (b) 900 R
(c) 1000 R (d) 1125 R

8. Hydrogen molecules strike a 2 cm^2 wall with velocity 10^3 m/s at angle 45° and rebound elastically. The mass of a hydrogen molecule is 3.32×10^{-27} kg. If the number of hydrogen molecules striking the

wall per second equals 10^{23}, then the pressure on the wall is:
(a) 3.70×10^2 N/m^2
(b) 3.70×10^3 N/m^2
(c) 2.35×10^2 N/m^2
(d) 2.35×10^3 N/m^2

9. A container at 400 K contains 2 moles of an ideal gas whose molecules possess f degrees of freedom. If its volume is decreased by 1% adiabatically, the increase in the rotational kinetic energy of the molecules is:

(a) $\left(\frac{f-3}{3}\right)2R$

(b) $\left(\frac{f}{3}\right)4R$

(c) $\left(\frac{f-3}{f}\right)8R$

(d) $\left(\frac{f-3}{2}\right)3R$

10. An ideal gas initially having pressure $P_1 = 10^5$ Pa and volume $V_1 = 10^{-3}$ m^3 is adiabatically expanded to a final volume $V_2 = 8\times10^{-3}$ m^3. The thermodynamic process is represented by the equation $P^3V^5 =$ constant. Consider another thermodynamic process that takes the gas from the same initial state to the same final state in two steps: isobaric expansion followed by isochoric cooling. The amount of heat supplied to the gas in the second process is nearly:
(a) 112 J (b) 294 J
(c) 588 J (d) 813 J

11. A mixture of n_1 moles of a monoatomic gas and n_2 moles of a diatomic gas is heated at constant pressure. The fraction of heat energy converted into mechanical work is:

(a) $\frac{5n_1+7n_2}{n_1+n_2}$ (b) $\frac{n_1+7n_2}{5n_1+n_2}$

(c) $\frac{2n_1+2n_2}{5n_1+7n_2}$ (d) $\frac{n_1+5n_2}{n_1+7n_2}$

12. A flat plate is pulled normal to its plane through a gas by a constant force F. The speed v of the plate is much less than the average speed u of the gas molecules. The correct statements from the following are:
(a) Pressure difference between the faces of the plate is proportional to uv
(b) Resistive force experienced by the plate is proportional to v
(c) The plate will move with ever increasing velocity
(d) The plate will eventually move with uniform velocity

13. Two cylinders A and B fitted with pistons contain equal amounts of an ideal diatomic gas at 300 K. The piston of cylinder A is free to move, while that of B is held fixed. The same amount of heat is given to the gas in each cylinder. If the temperature of cylinder A rises by 30 K, then the rise in temperature of cylinder B will be:
(a) 38 K (b) 42 K
(c) 48 K (d) 50 K

14. A diatomic gas does 4.2 J of work during adiabatic expansion. If its temperature falls by 2 K, then the amount of gas in the container is ($R = 8.3$ J/mol·K):
(a) 0.1 moles (b) 0.2 moles
(c) 0.3 moles (d) 0.4 moles

15. C_P and C_V are specific heats at constant pressure and constant volume, respectively. If $C_P - C_V$ equals a for hydrogen gas (2 g/mol), and b for nitrogen gas (28 g/mol), then:
(a) $b = 7a$ (b) $b = 14a$
(c) $a = 7b$ (d) $a = 14b$

16. An ideal gas is isobarically heated. The quantity $\delta = \frac{1}{V}\left(\frac{\Delta V}{\Delta T}\right)$, called the coefficient of volume expansion, varies with temperature T as:

(a) 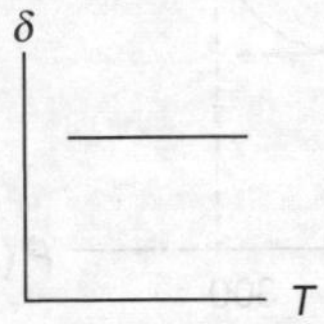

(b) 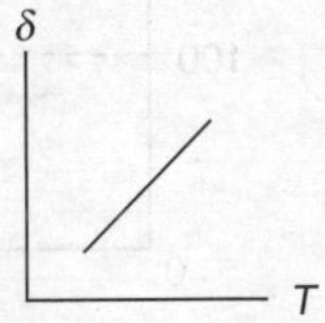

(c) 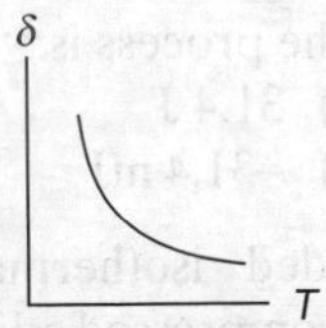

(d) 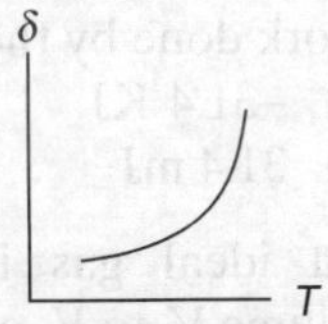

17. The pressure P versus volume V plots for two gases during adiabatic process are shown in the figure.

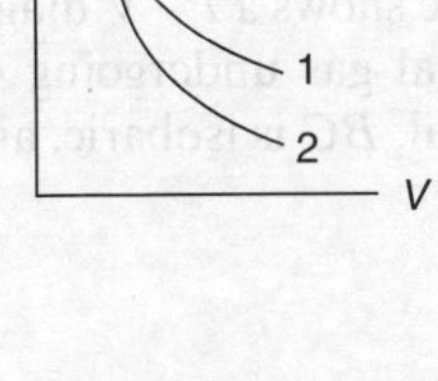

Plots 1 and 2 should correspond, respectively, to:
(a) He and O_2 (b) O_2 and He
(c) He and Ar (d) O_2 and N_2

18. The figure shows a closed insulated cylinder of length $2L$ kept horizontally and filled with gas at 27°C. It also contains a freely moving non-conducting piston, initially in the middle. The gas in the left chamber is now heated to 127°C using an internally fitted heater, while the temperature in the other chamber remains unchanged at 27°C.

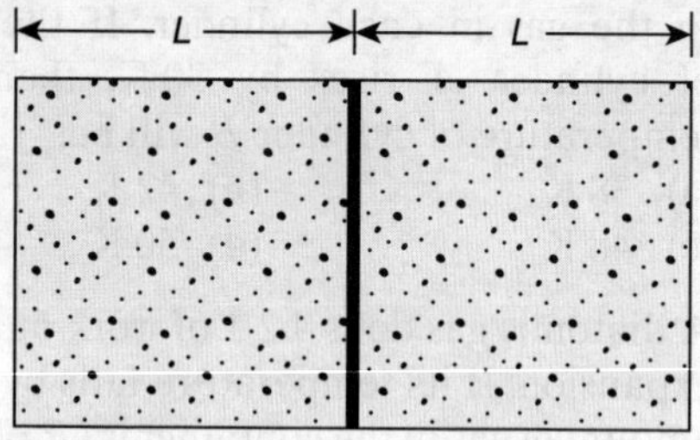

If the piston moves through a distance x, then the fraction x/L is:
(a) $1/4$ (b) $1/5$
(c) $1/6$ (d) $1/7$

19. An ideal gas is taken through a circular path, as shown in the figure.

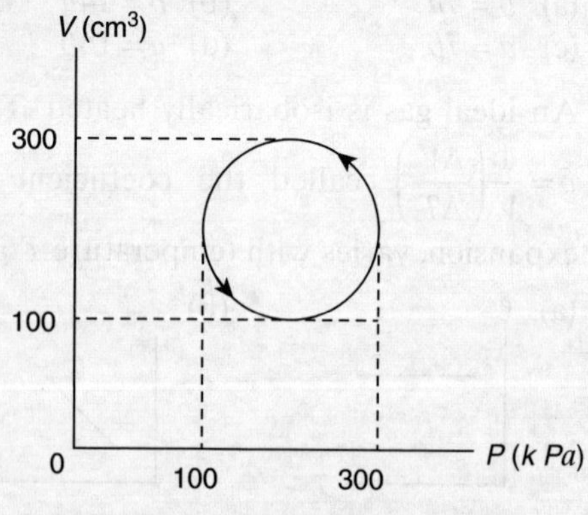

Work done by the gas in the process is:
(a) –31.4 KJ (b) 31.4 J
(c) 31.4 mJ (d) –31.4 mJ

20. An ideal gas is expanded isothermally from volume V_1 to V_2 and then compressed adiabatically to original volume V_1. The initial pressure is P and the final pressure is P' and the net work done by the gas is W. Then:
(a) $P' > P, W > 0$ (b) $P' < P, W < 0$
(c) $P' > P, W < 0$ (d) $P' = P, W = 0$

21. The figure shows a $P-V$ diagram for a mixed mass of an ideal gas undergoing cyclic process. AB is isothermal, BC is isobaric, and CA is adiabatic.

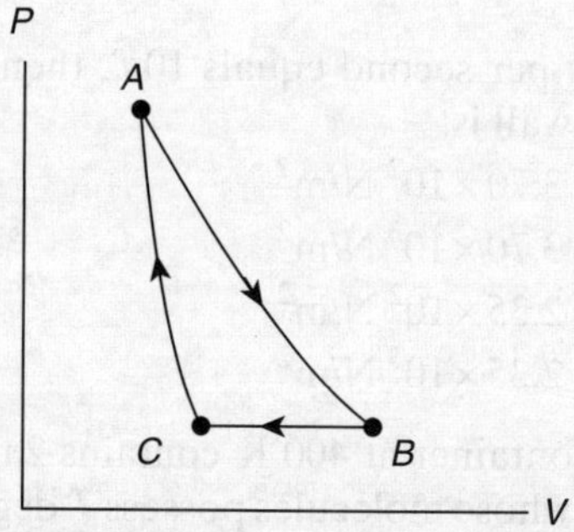

The $P-T$ diagram for the same process is:

(a)
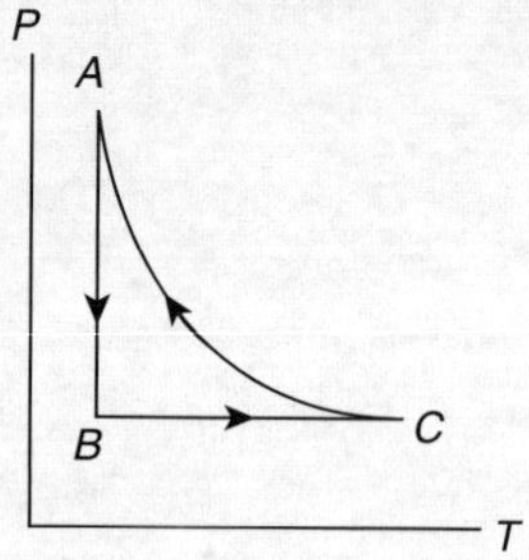

(b)
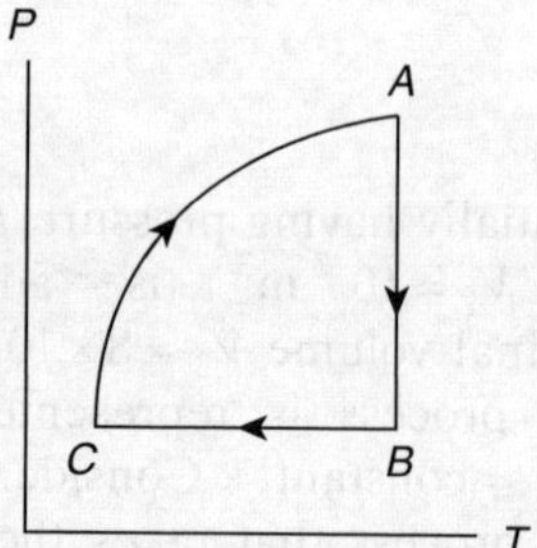

(c)
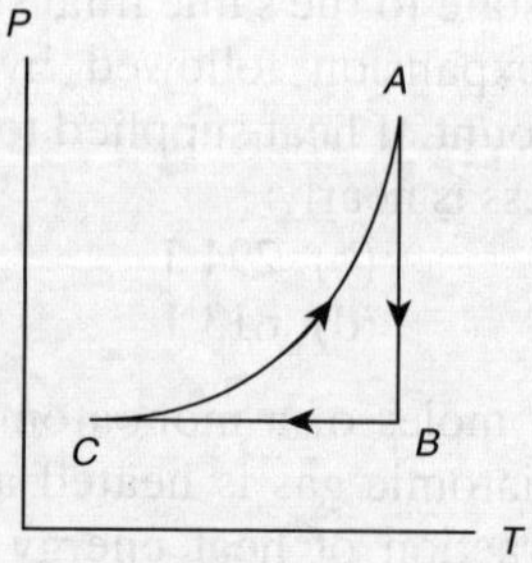

(d)
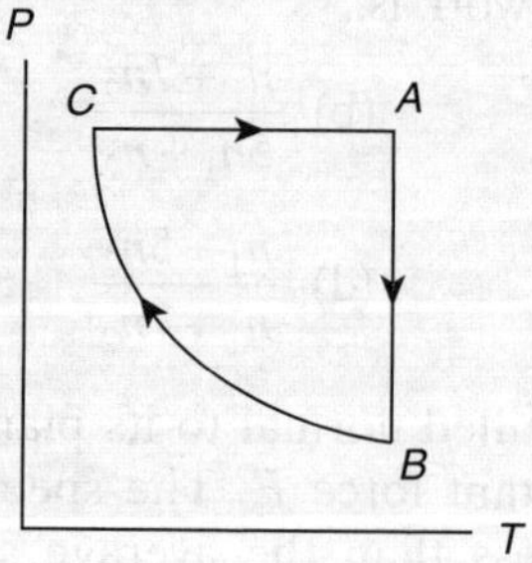

22. Two different adiabatic paths for the same gas intersect two isothermals T_1 and T_2, as shown in the $P-V$ diagram.

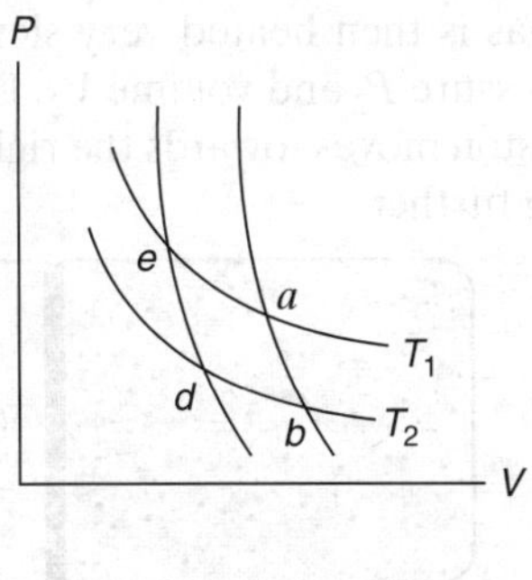

Then:

(a) $\frac{V_a}{V_b} = \frac{V_c}{V_d}$ (b) $\frac{V_a}{V_b} = \frac{T_1}{T_2}$

(c) $\frac{V_a}{V_d} = \frac{V_b}{V_c}$ (d) $\frac{V_a V_c}{V_b V_d} = \frac{T_1}{T_2}$

23. Three moles of an ideal gas are taken through a cyclic process $ABCA$, as shown in the $T-V$ diagram. The gas loses 2510 J of heat in the complete cycle.

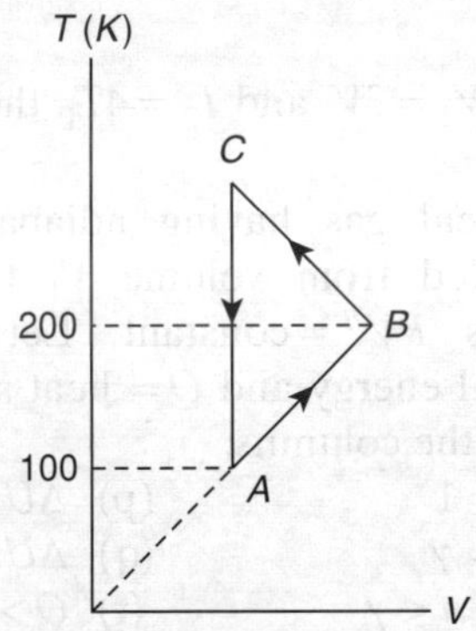

The work done by the gas during the process BC is ($R = 8.3$ J/mol·K):

(a) 5000 J (b) –5000 J
(c) 4000 J (d) –2500 J

24. The figure shows the $P-V$ diagram for 2 moles of an ideal gas undergoing the process AB.

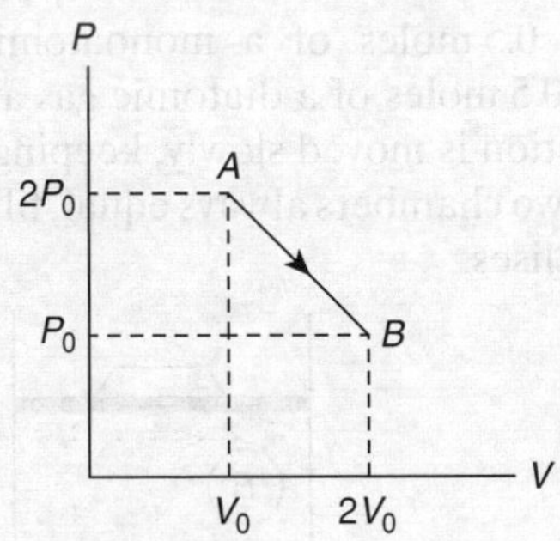

The maximum temperature of the gas during the process is:

(a) $\frac{3P_0V_0}{4R}$ (b) $\frac{3P_0V_0}{2R}$

(c) $\frac{9P_0V_0}{4R}$ (d) $\frac{9P_0V_0}{8R}$

25. A vertical cylinder fitted with a movable piston contains a certain amount of air. The cylinder is slowly heated such that P^3V^2 = constant during the process. The molar heat capacity of air for the process is:

(a) $\frac{13}{6}R$ (b) $\frac{11}{2}R$

(c) $3R$ (d) $\frac{17}{3}R$

26. A vertical cylinder fitted with a movable piston contains a certain amount of air at pressure P_0 and volume V_0. The cylinder is slowly heated till the pressure becomes $\frac{3}{2}P_0$ and volume becomes $2V_0$, such that pressure and volume are linearly dependent during the process. The molar heat capacity of air for the process is:

(a) $\frac{13}{6}R$ (b) $\frac{17}{6}R$

(c) $3R$ (d) $\frac{25}{8}R$

27. Two moles of helium gas are taken over the cycle $ABCDA$, as shown in the $P-T$ diagram.

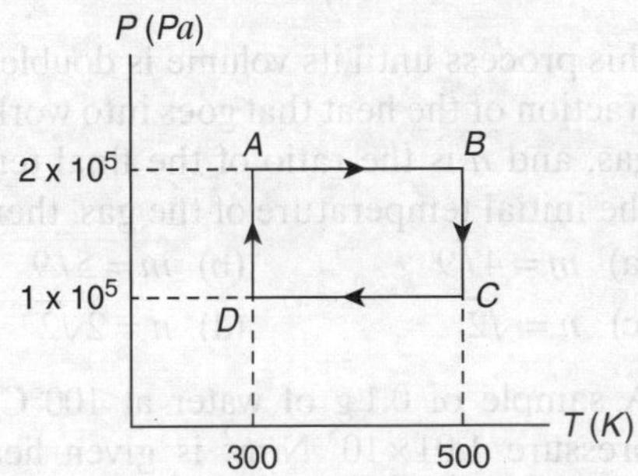

The net work done by the gas in the cycle is (take ln2 = 0.69):

(a) 1904 R (b) 1076 R
(c) 276 R (d) 0

28. The figure shows a thermally insulated, smooth horizontal tube, open at one end and equipped with a piston. The cross-section area of the piston is $S = 10^{-4}$ m^2. Initially the spring is in its natural state and the piston is at distance $x_0 = 0.1$ m from the closed end of the tube. The spring constant is k = 100 N/m and outside air pressure is $P_0 = 10^5$ N/m^2.

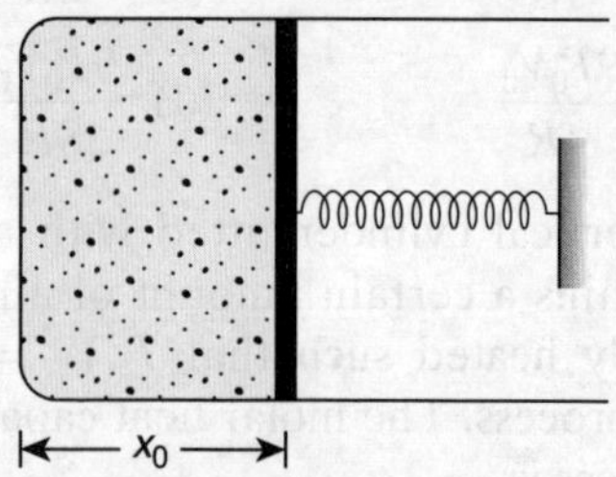

The ideal monoatomic gas is heated until the piston moves further by x_0. The amount of heat required is:

(a) 2.5 J (b) 3.5 J
(c) 5 J (d) 6 J

29. Consider a spherical shell of radius R at temperature T. The black body radiation inside the shell can be considered as an ideal gas of photons with internal energy per unit volume $\frac{U}{V} \propto T^4$ and pressure $P = \frac{U}{3V}$. If the shell now undergoes an adiabatic expansion, the relation between T and R is:

(a) $T \propto e^{-R}$ (b) $T \propto e^{-2R}$
(c) $T \propto \frac{1}{R}$ (d) $T \propto \frac{1}{R^2}$

30. The molar heat capacity of a diatomic gas for some process is $\frac{9}{2}R$. The gas is heated through this process until its volume is doubled. If m is the fraction of the heat that goes into work done by the gas, and n is the ratio of the final temperature to the initial temperature of the gas, then:

(a) $m = 4/9$ (b) $m = 5/9$
(c) $n = \sqrt{2}$ (d) $n = 2\sqrt{2}$

31. A sample of 0.1 g of water at 100°C and normal pressure 1.01×10^5 N/m^2 is given heat energy to convert it into steam at 100°C. If the volume of the steam produced is 166 cc, the change in its internal energy is (latent heat of steam = 540 cal/g, 1 cal = 4.18 J):

(a) 46 cal (b) 48 cal
(c) 50 cal (d) 52 cal

32. The figure shows a thermally insulated, smooth horizontal tube, closed at both ends and equipped with a spring-loaded piston. The region to the left of the piston contains an ideal monoatomic gas, while the region to its right is vacuum. Initially, the gas is at temperature T_1, pressure P_1 and volume V_1. The gas is then heated very slowly to temperature T_2, pressure P_2 and volume V_2. During this process, the piston moves towards the right, compressing the spring further.

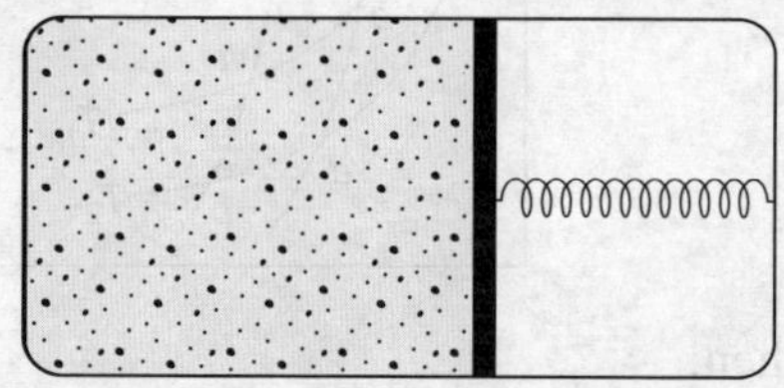

If W and Q, respectively, denote the work done by the gas and heat supplied to the gas, then the correct statements from the following are:

(a) If $V_2 = 2V_1$ and $T_2 = 3T_1$, then $W = \frac{1}{4}P_1V_1$

(b) If $V_2 = 2V_1$ and $T_2 = 3T_1$, then $Q = \frac{17}{4}P_1V_1$

(c) If $V_2 = 3V_1$ and $T_2 = 4T_1$, then $W = \frac{7}{3}P_1V_1$

(d) If $V_2 = 3V_1$ and $T_2 = 4T_1$, then $Q = \frac{31}{6}P_1V_1$

33. An ideal gas having adiabatic exponent γ is expanded from volume V_1 to V_2 through the process PV^n = constant. Let ΔU = change in internal energy and Q = heat supplied to the gas. Match the columns:

(a) $n = 1$ (p) $\Delta U > 0$
(b) $n = \gamma$ (q) $\Delta U < 0$
(c) $1 < n < \gamma$ (r) $Q > 0$
(d) $n > \gamma$ (s) $Q < 0$

34. The figure shows a vertical cylinder fitted with a piston and a partition, both of which are free to slide. The walls of the container and the piston are insulated, but the partition allows slow transfer of heat. Initially, the partition is held stationary and chambers A and B are, respectively, filled with 0.5 moles of a monoatomic gas at 700 K, and 0.5 moles of a diatomic gas at 400 K. Now the partition is moved slowly, keeping the pressures in the two chambers always equal, till the temperature equalises.

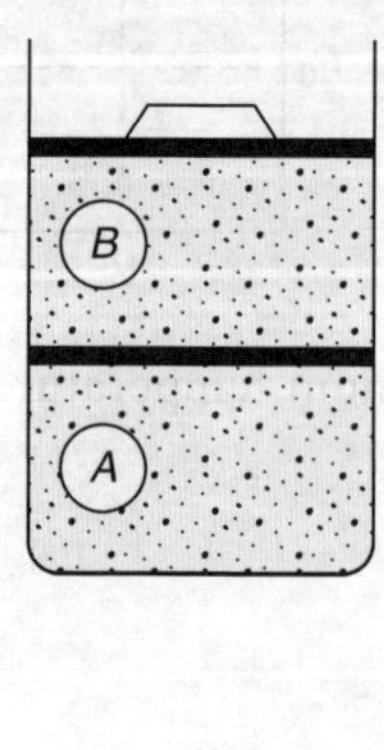

Match the columns: (all quantities are in MKS units and $R = 8.3$ J/mol·K)

(a) Equilibrium temperature in Kelvin — (p) 519

(b) Magnitude of work done in Joules by gas in A — (q) 525

(c) Magnitude of work done in Joules by gas in B — (r) 726

(d) Heat flow in Joules through the partition — (s) 1816

35. The figure shows a cyclic process $ABCDA$ in the $P-V$ diagram. Let W = work done by gas and Q = heat supplied to the gas.

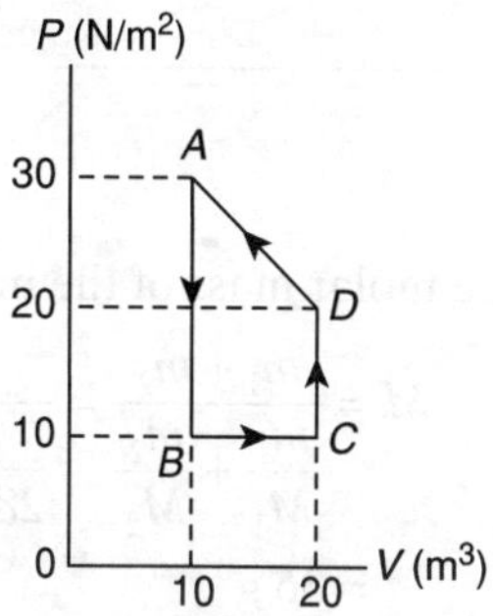

Match the columns:

(a) Path AB — (p) $W > 0$

(b) Path BC — (q) $Q > 0$

(c) Path CD — (r) $W < 0$

(d) Path DA — (s) $Q < 0$

ANSWER KEYS

1. (c) **2.** (d) **3.** (c) **4.** (d) **5.** (b) **6.** (a) **7.** (b) **8.** (d) **9.** (c)
10. (c) **11.** (c) **12.** (a),(b),(d) **13.** (b) **14.** (a) **15.** (d) **16.** (c) **17.** (b) **18.** (d)
19. (b) **20.** (c) **21.** (c) **22.** (a) **23.** (b) **24.** (d) **25.** (b) **26.** (d) **27.** (c)
28. (d) **29.** (c) **30.** (a),(c) **31.** (c) **32.** (b),(c) **33.** (a)-(r), (b)-(q), (c)-(q,r), (d)-(q,s)
34.(a)-(q), (b)-(r), (c)-(p), (d)-(s) **35.** (a)-(s), (b)-(p,q), (c)-(q), (d)-(r,s)

SOLUTIONS

1. (c) The molar mass of the mixture is

$$M = \frac{m_1 + m_2}{\dfrac{m_1}{M_1} + \dfrac{m_2}{M_2}} = \frac{7\text{ g} + 11\text{ g}}{\dfrac{7\text{ g}}{28\text{ g/mol}} + \dfrac{11\text{ g}}{44\text{ g/mol}}}$$

$$= 36\text{ g}$$

The density of the mixture is

$$\rho = \frac{PM}{RT} = \frac{(1\text{ atm})(36\text{ g})}{(0.082\,1\cdot\text{atm/mol}\cdot\text{K})(290\text{ K})}$$

$$= 1.5\text{ g/l}$$

2. (d) The total number of moles is

$$n = \frac{PV}{RT} = \frac{(2\text{ atm})(20\text{ l})}{(0.082\,1\times\text{atm/mol}\times\text{K})(293\text{ K})} = \frac{5}{3}$$

Let m_1 and m_2 be the masses of hydrogen and helium, respectively. Then, we have

$$m_1 + m_2 = 5\text{ g} \quad \ldots(1)$$

and $$\frac{m_1}{2\text{ g/mol}} + \frac{m_2}{4\text{ g/mol}} = \frac{5}{3} \quad \ldots(2)$$

Solving the two equations, we have

$$m_1 = \frac{5}{3}\text{g and } m_2 = \frac{10}{3}\text{ g. Hence } \frac{m_1}{m_2} = 0.5$$

3. (c) The mass m of gas inside the vessel is given by

$$PV = \frac{mRT}{M} \Rightarrow m = \frac{PVM}{RT}$$

Thus, we have

$$\Delta m = \frac{VM}{RT}\Delta P$$ [Since all other quantities are constant]

Also, we have

$$P_0 = \frac{\rho_0 RT_0}{M} \Rightarrow M = \frac{\rho_0 RT_0}{P_0}$$

$[P_0 = 1\text{ atm and } T_0 = 273\text{ K}]$

Thus, we have

$$\Delta m = \frac{V\Delta P}{T} \times \frac{\rho_0 T_0}{P_0}$$

$$= \frac{(30\text{ l})(0.78\text{ atm})}{273\text{ K}} \times \frac{(1.3\text{ g/l})(273\text{ K})}{1\text{ atm}} = 30\text{ g}$$

4. (d) Internal energy lost by one gas equals energy absorbed by the other. Let T be the equilibrium temperature. Then

$$n_1 \frac{3}{2}R(T_1 - T) = n_2 \frac{5}{2}R(T - T_2)$$

$$\Rightarrow \quad T = \frac{3n_1T_1 + 5n_2T_2}{3n_1 + 5n_2}$$

5. (b)

6. (a) If n is the number of moles, then mass of the gas inside the box equals nM. The loss in energy due to stopping of the box $= \frac{1}{2}(nM)v^2$. Let ΔT be the rise in the temperature of the gas. Then, we have

$$n\left(\frac{5}{2}R\right)\Delta T = \frac{1}{2}(nM)v^2 \Rightarrow \Delta T = \frac{Mv^2}{5R}$$

7. (b) To double the RMS speed, the temperature must be quadrupled, since $v_{rms}\,\alpha\sqrt{T}$. The initial temperature of 300 K must be increased to 1200 K $\Rightarrow \Delta T$ = 1200 K – 300 K = 900 K. The energy required is

$$\Delta U = nc_V\,T = n\left(\frac{R}{y-1}\right)T$$

$$= \frac{0.5R(900\text{ K})}{1.50-1} = 900R$$

8. (d) Change in momentum of one hydrogen molecule during collision = $2mv\cos45°$. Force on the wall equals total momentum change per second = $(2mv\cos45°)n$, where n is the total number of hydrogen molecules colliding per second. The pressure on the walls is

$$P = \frac{(2mv\cos 45^\circ)n}{A}$$

$$= \frac{\sqrt{2}(3.37\times10^{-27}\text{ kg})(10^3\text{ m/s})(10^{23}\text{ s}^{-1})}{2\times10^{-4}\text{ m}^2}$$

$$= 2.35\times10^3\text{ N/m}^2$$

9. (c) For an adiabatic process, $TV\gamma^{-1}$ = constant. For small changes

$$\frac{\Delta T}{T} = -(\gamma-1)\frac{\Delta V}{V}$$

Putting $\frac{\Delta V}{V} = -1\%$ and $T = 400$ K, we have

$$\Delta T = (y-1)\frac{400\text{ K}}{100} = 4(\gamma-1)$$

The increase in internal energy is

$$\Delta U = n\left(\frac{R}{\gamma-1}\right)\Delta T = 2\left(\frac{R}{\gamma-1}\right)4(\gamma-1) = 8R$$

This energy is distributed into translational and rotational kinetic energy in the ratio $3: f-3$. Hence, increase in rotational kinetic energy is $\left(\frac{f-3}{f}\right)8R$

10. (c) Final pressure is $P_2 = P_1\left(\frac{V_1}{V_2}\right)^{5/3} = \frac{1}{32}\times10^5$ Pa.

The adiabatic exponent of the gas is $\gamma = 5/3$. Since initial and final temperatures are the same in both processes, ΔU is the same for both processes. Hence

$$\Delta U = \mu c_v \Delta T = \frac{\mu R\Delta T}{\gamma-1} = \frac{P_2V_2 - P_1V_1}{\gamma-1}$$

$$= \frac{\left(\frac{1}{4}-1\right)10^2\ \text{J}}{5/3-1} = -112.5\ \text{J}$$

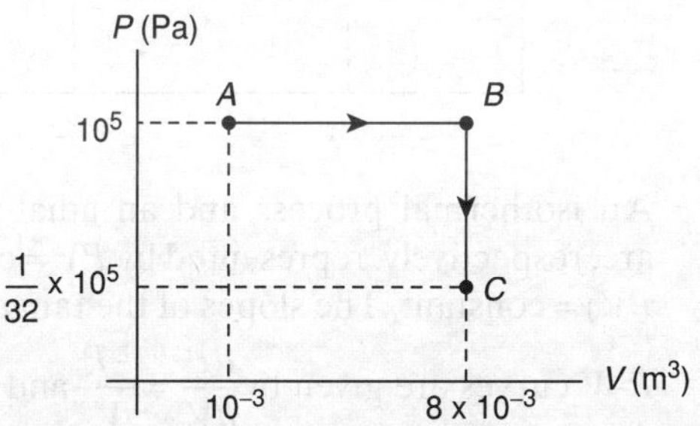

The figure shows the P–V diagram representing the second process. The work done in this process is $W = P_1(V_2 - V_1) = 700$ J. Hence

$$Q = \Delta U + W = 587.5\ \text{J}$$

11. (c) Let ΔT be the temperature change during the constant pressure process. For an isobaric process, $Q = nc_p\,\Delta T$ and $W = P\Delta V = nR\Delta T$. Thus, we have

$$Q = n_1\left(\frac{5}{2}R\right)\Delta T + n_2\left(\frac{7}{2}R\right)\Delta T \text{ and}$$

$$W = (n_1 + n_2)R\Delta T$$

Hence, the required fraction $\frac{W}{Q} = \frac{2(n_1+n_2)}{5n_1+7n_2}$.

12. (a), (b), (d) Measured with respect to the plate, the velocity of the molecules are $u - v$ and $u + v$ on the two sides of the plate (see figure). The pressure exerted on the plate by the colliding molecules is directly proportional to the square of their speeds relative to the plate.

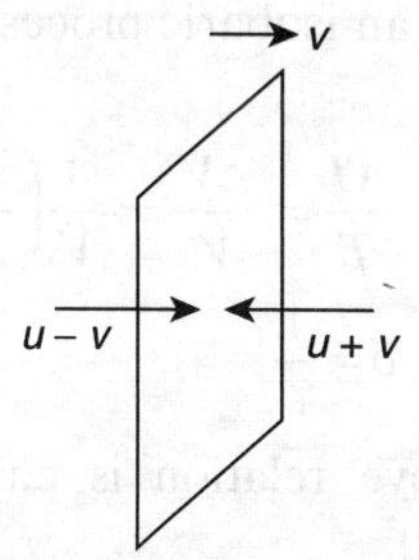

Hence, the pressure difference on the two sides of the plate is

$$\Delta p \propto [(u+v)^2 - (u-v)^2] \propto uv \Rightarrow \text{(a) is correct.}$$

The resistive force due to the pressure difference is

$$F_{res} = A\Delta P \propto v \Rightarrow \text{(b) is correct.}$$

The instantaneous acceleration of the plate is

$$a = \frac{F - F_{\text{res}}}{m} = \frac{F - cV}{m}$$

When the resistive force cv becomes equal to the applied force F, the plate will move with zero acceleration $\Rightarrow$ Uniform velocity

$\Rightarrow$ (d) is correct and (c) is incorrect.

13. (b) The gas in cylinder A undergoes isobaric process, whereas that in cylinder B undergoes isochoric process. Let ΔT be the temperature change in B. The heat supplied is given to be the same. Hence

$$nc_p\,(30\ \text{K}) = nc_v\,\Delta T$$

$$\Rightarrow \quad n\left(\frac{7}{2}R\right)(30\ \text{K}) = n\left(\frac{5}{2}R\right)\Delta T$$

$$\Rightarrow \quad \Delta T = 42\ \text{K}$$

14. (a) Let n be the number of moles. For an adiabatic process, $W = -\,nc_v\,\Delta T$. Thus, we have

$$4.2\ \text{J} = -n\left(\frac{5}{2}\times 8.3\ \text{J/mol}\cdot\text{K}\right)(-2\ \text{K})$$

$$\Rightarrow \quad n = \frac{4.2}{5\times 8.314}\ \text{mol} \approx 0.1\ \text{mol}$$

15. (d) Specific heat capacity C is the energy required per kg per Kelvin change in temperature, whereas molar heat capacity c is the energy required per mole per Kelvin change in temperature. The relation between them is $C = \frac{c}{M}$ (M is the molar mass). Thus, we have

$$C_P - C_V = \frac{c_p - c_V}{M} = \frac{R}{M}$$

(R is the universal gas constant)

For hydrogen gas and nitrogen gas, we have

$$a = \frac{R}{2\ \text{g/mol}} \text{ and } b = \frac{R}{28\ \text{g/mol}}$$

16. (c) For an isobaric process, $T \propto V$, and for small changes

$$\frac{\Delta T}{T} = \frac{\Delta V}{V} \Rightarrow \frac{1}{V}\left(\frac{\Delta V}{\Delta T}\right) = \frac{1}{T}$$

$$\Rightarrow \quad \delta = \frac{1}{T}$$

The above relation is correctly represented in option (c).

17. (b) For an adiabatic process, the relation between pressure P and volume V is $PV\gamma$= constant. On the P–V curve representing an adiabatic process, the slope of the tangent is given by

$$V^{\gamma}dP + P(\gamma V^{V-1}dV) = 0$$

$$\Rightarrow \quad \frac{dP}{dV} = -\frac{\gamma P}{V}$$

From the above expression for slope, we conclude that at the intersection point, the graph that falls more steeply has a greater γ.

Since monoatomic gases have a greater γ than diatomic gases, plot 2 corresponds to He and plot 1 corresponds to O_2.

18. (d) The amount of gas is the same in both the chambers since initially they are at the same P, V, T state. At equilibrium, the pressure is the same in both the chambers. Thus, v/t is the same in both chambers. Hence

$$\frac{L+x}{400\text{ K}} = \frac{L-x}{300\text{ K}}$$

$$\Rightarrow \quad x = L/7$$

19. (b)

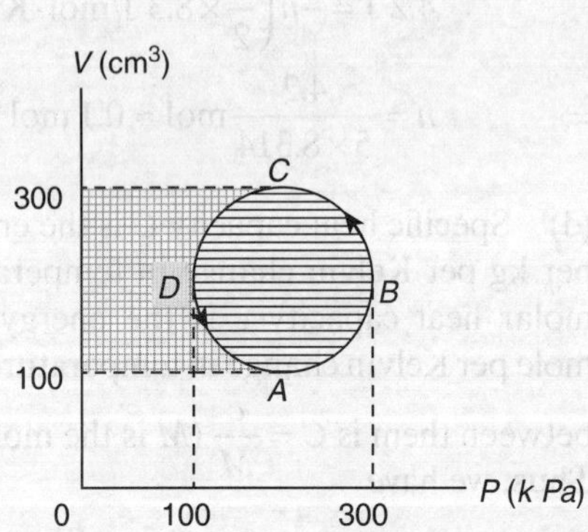

Work done by the gas in a cyclic process equals area enclosed within the cyclic path. Work done by the gas along the path ABC equals area of the region shaded by horizontal lines (see figure), and it is positive since the gas has expanded. Work done by the gas along the path CDA equals the area of the region shaded by horizontal and vertical lines, and it is negative since the gas has compressed. Since the positive work is more than the negative work, the total work done by the gas will have a positive sign. Hence

$$W_{\text{cycle}} = \text{Area of the circle}$$
$$= \frac{\pi}{4}(200)^2\,\text{kPa}\cdot\text{cm}^3$$
$$= (\pi\times10^4)(10^3\text{ Pa})(10^{-6}\text{ m}^3) = 31.4\text{ J}$$

20. (c)

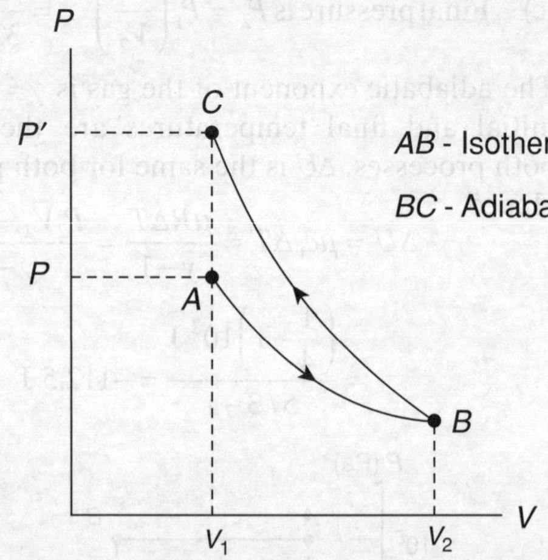

An isothermal process and an adiabatic process are, respectively, represented by PV= constant and $PV\gamma$= constant. The slopes of the tangents on their P–V curves are given by $\frac{dP}{dV} = \frac{-P}{V}$ and $\frac{dP}{dV} = \frac{-\gamma P}{V}$.

Since γ is greater than 1, it means that at intersection points, an adiabatic curve has a steeper slope in magnitude than an isothermal curve.

The P–V diagram representing the given process is shown in the figure. Note the slopes of the two curves at their intersection point. From the diagram, we see that $P' > P$. We also see that area under the adiabatic compression curve is more than the isothermal expansion curve. Thus, work done by the gas is more negative than positive. Hence $W_{ABC} < 0$.

21. (c) Along path AB, which is isothermal expansion, T remains constant and P drops.

Along path BC, which is isobaric compression, P remains constant and T drops.

Along path CA, which is adiabatic compression, both P and T increase, and the curve will be increasing and concave upwards, since for an adiabatic process

$$P \propto T^{\frac{\gamma}{\gamma-1}}, \text{ where } \frac{\gamma}{\gamma-1} > 1$$

22. (a) Since points a and b lie on the same adiabat, we have

$$T_1V_a^{\gamma-1} = T_2V_b^{\gamma-1} \Rightarrow \frac{V_a}{V_b} = \left(\frac{T_2}{T_1}\right)^{\gamma-1}$$

Since points c and d lie on the same adiabat, we have

$$T_1V_c^{V-1} = T_2V_d^{\gamma-1} \Rightarrow \frac{V_c}{V_d} = \left(\frac{T_2}{T_1}\right)^{\gamma-1}$$

Hence $\dfrac{V_a}{V_b} = \dfrac{V_c}{V_d}$

23. (b) Path AB is a straight line passing through the origin $\Rightarrow T \propto V \Rightarrow$ An isobaric process.
Hence, work done by the gas along path AB is

$$W_{AB} = P\Delta V = nR\Delta T = (3 \text{ mol})\ (8.3 \text{ J/mol K})\ (200 \text{ K} - 100 \text{ K}) = 2490 \text{ J}$$

Path CA is an isochoric process. Hence, work done by the gas along path CA is $W_{CA} = 0$. Let work done by the gas along path BC be W_{BC}. For a cyclic process

$W_{\text{cycle}} = Q_{\text{cycle}}$. Hence $W_{AB} + W_{BC} + W_{CA} = Q_{\text{cycle}}$
$\Rightarrow 2490 \text{ J} + W_{BC} = -2510 \text{ J} = W_{BC} = -5000 \text{ J}$

24. (d) The path AB is represented by the equation

$$P - 2P_0 = -\frac{P_0}{V_0}(V - V_0)$$

$$\Rightarrow \quad P = \frac{-P_0}{V_0}V + 3P_0$$

The temperature as a function of volume is given by

$$T = \frac{PV}{nR} = \frac{-P_0}{2RV_0}V^2 + \frac{3P_0}{2R}V$$

The derivative function is

$$\frac{dT}{dV} = \frac{-P_0}{RV_0}V + \frac{3P_0}{2R}$$

Maxima occurs when $\dfrac{dT}{dV} = 0$, that is, at $V = \dfrac{3}{2}V_0$.

Hence, the maximum temperature is

$$T_{\max} = \frac{-P_0}{2RV_0}\left(\frac{3V_0}{2}\right)^2 + \frac{3P_0}{2R}\left(\frac{3V_0}{2}\right) = \frac{9P_0V_0}{8R}$$

25. (b) The relation PT^2 = constant can be written as $P(PV)^2$ = constant $\Rightarrow P^3V^2$ = constant.
The molar heat capacity for the process PV^n = constant is given by

$$c = c_v + \frac{R}{1-n}$$

For the given process, $PV^{2/3}$ = constant $\Rightarrow n = 2/3$, the molar heat capacity is $c = \dfrac{5}{2}R + 3R = \dfrac{11}{2}R$

26. (d)

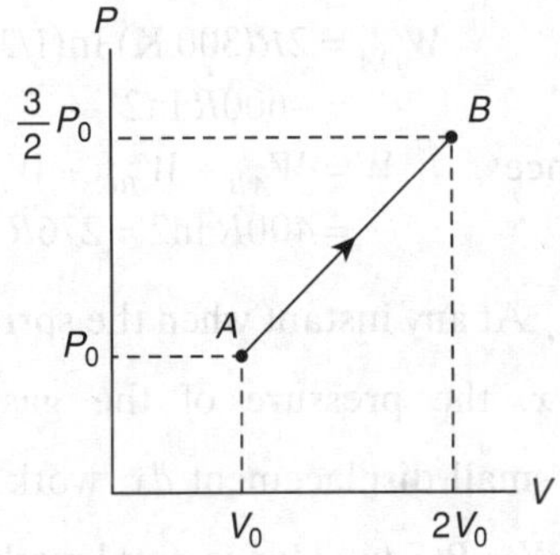

The P–V diagram representing the given process is shown in the figure. If n is the number of moles, then the initial and final temperatures are, respectively

$$T_1 = \frac{P_0V_0}{nR} \text{ and}$$

$$T_2 = \frac{(3P_0/2)(2V_0)}{nR} = \frac{3P_0V_0}{nR}$$

Then $\quad \Delta U = nc_v\Delta T$

$$= n\left(\frac{5}{2}R\right)\left(\frac{2P_0V_0}{nR}\right) = 5P_0V_0$$

Work done by the gas is area under the P–V diagram. Hence $W = \dfrac{5}{4}P_0V_0$.

Then $Q = \Delta U + W = \dfrac{25}{4}P_0V_0$. Hence, the molar heat capacity for the process is

$$C_{\text{process}} = \frac{Q}{n\Delta T} = \frac{\frac{25}{4}P_0V_0}{n\left(\frac{2P_0V_0}{nR}\right)} = \frac{25}{8}R$$

27. (c) For an isobaric process, $W = P\Delta V$ or $nR\Delta T$. For an isothermal process,

$$W = nRT\ln\left(\frac{V_2}{V_1}\right) \text{ or } nRT\ln\left(\frac{P_1}{P_2}\right).$$

Hence
$$W_{AB} = 2R(500\text{ K} - 300\text{ K})$$
$$= 400R$$
$$W_{BC} = 2R(500\text{ K})\ln 2$$
$$= 1000R\ln 2$$
$$W_{CD} = 2R(300\text{ K} - 500\text{ K})$$
$$= -400R$$
$$W_{DA} = 2R(300\text{ K})\ln(1/2)$$
$$= -600R\ln 2$$

Hence $W = W_{AB} + W_{BC} + W_{CD} + W_{DA}$
$$= 400R\ln 2 = 276R$$

28. (d) At any instant when the spring is compressed by x, the pressure of the gas is $P = P_o + \dfrac{kx}{S}$. For small displacement dx, work done by the gas is $dW = P(Sdx)$. Hence, total work done by the gas is

$$W = \int_0^{x_0}\left(P_0 + \frac{kx}{s}\right)Sdx$$
$$= P_0(Sx_0) + \frac{1}{2}kx_0^2$$
$$= (10^5\text{ N/m}^2)(10^{-5}\text{ m}^3) + \frac{1}{2}(100\text{ N/m})(0.1\text{ m})^2$$
$$= 1.5\text{ J}$$

The change in internal energy is given by

$$\Delta U = \mu\left(\frac{3}{2}R\right)(T_2 - T_1)$$
$$= \frac{3}{2}(\mu RT_2 - \mu RT_1)$$
$$= \frac{3}{2}(P_2V_2 - P_1V_1)$$

The initial pressure and volume is $P_1 = P_0 = 10^5$ N/m^2 and $V_1 = Sx_o = 10^{-5}$ m^3

The final pressure and volume is

$$P_2 = P_0 + \frac{kx_0}{s}$$
$$= 2\times10^{-5}\text{ N/m}^2 \text{ and}$$
$$V_2 = S(2x_0)$$
$$= 2\times10^{-5}\text{ m}^3.$$

Hence $\Delta U = \dfrac{3}{2}(4\text{ J} - 1\text{ J}) = 4.5$ J. The amount of heat required for the process is

$$Q = \Delta U + W$$
$$= 4.5\text{ J} + 1.5\text{ J} = 6\text{ J}.$$

29. (c) Eliminating U from the given relations $\dfrac{U}{V} \propto T^4$ and $P = \dfrac{U}{3V}$, we have

$$P \propto T^4$$
$$\Rightarrow \quad \frac{T}{V} \propto T^4 \left[\text{Using } P = \frac{nRT}{V}\right]$$
$$\Rightarrow \quad T^3 \propto \frac{1}{V}$$
$$\Rightarrow \quad T^3 \propto \frac{1}{R^3}\left[\text{Using } V = \frac{4}{3}\pi R^3\right]$$
$$\Rightarrow \quad T \propto \frac{1}{R}$$

30. (a), (c) Let the process be PV^n = constant. The molar heat capacity is given by

$$c = c_v + \frac{R}{1-n}$$
$$\Rightarrow \quad \frac{9}{2}R = \frac{5}{2}R + \frac{R}{1-n}$$
$$\Rightarrow \quad n = 1/2$$

Hence, the process is $P\sqrt{V}$ = constant

$$\Rightarrow \quad \frac{T}{\sqrt{V}} = \text{constant}$$

Hence, if $V_2 = 2V_1$ then $T_2 = \sqrt{2}T_1 \Rightarrow m_2 = \sqrt{2}$

Now $\quad Q = \mu c\Delta T = \mu\left(\dfrac{9}{2}R\right)\Delta T$

and $\quad \Delta U = \mu\left(\dfrac{5}{2}R\right)\Delta T$

$$\Rightarrow \quad W = Q - \Delta U = 2\mu R\Delta T$$

Hence, $\quad m_1 = W/Q = 4/9$

31. (c) Heat given to water sample

$$Q = 540\text{ cal/g}\times 0.1\text{ g} = 54\text{ cal}$$

Work done by steam during expansion

$$W = (1.01\times10^5\text{ N/m}^2)(1.67\times10^{-6}\text{ m}^3)$$
$$= 16.8\text{ J} = 4\text{ cal}$$

Hence, $\Delta U = Q - W = 54\text{ cal} - 4\text{ cal} = 50\text{ cal}$

32. (b), (c) Work done by the gas equals change in spring potential energy. Hence

$$W = \frac{1}{2}k(x_2^2 - x_1^2)$$
$$= \frac{1}{2}(kx_2 + kx_1)(x_2 - x_1)$$
$$= \frac{1}{2}(P_2A + P_1A)(x_2 - x_1)$$
$$= \frac{1}{2}(P_2 + P_1)\Delta V$$

Change in the internal energy of the gas is given by

$$\Delta U = \mu\left(\frac{3}{2}R\right)\Delta T$$
$$= \frac{3}{2}\Delta(PV)$$

When $V_2 = 2V_1$ and $T_2 = 3T_1$, $P_2 = \frac{3}{2}P_1$, then

$$W = \frac{5}{4}P_1V_1,$$

$$\Delta U = 3P_1V_1$$

and $Q = \frac{17}{4}P_1V_1.$

Hence (b) is correct.

When $V_2 = 3V_1$ and $T_2 = 4T_1$, $P_2 = \frac{4}{3}P_1$, then

$$W = \frac{7}{3}P_1V_1, \Delta U = \frac{9}{2}P_1V_1$$

and $Q = \frac{41}{6}P_1V_1.$

Hence (c) is correct.

33. (a)-(r), (b)-(q), (c)-(q,r), (d)-(q,s)

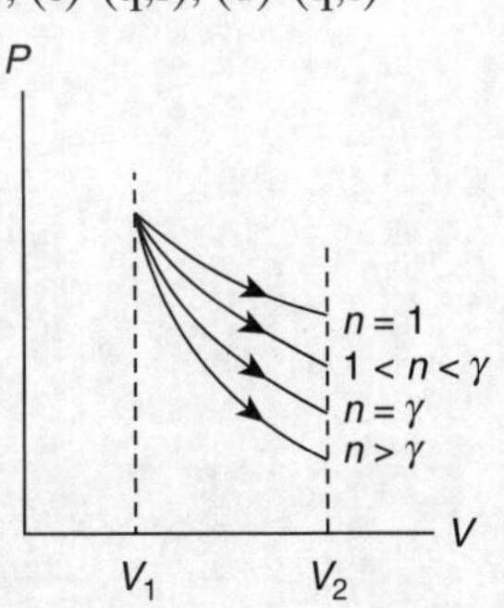

The process PV^n = constant = TV^{n-1} = constant

$$\Rightarrow \quad T = \frac{\text{constant}}{V^{n-1}}$$

For $n = 1$, T is constant = $\Delta U = 0$, and $W > 0$ since the gas is expanding

$$\Rightarrow \quad Q = \Delta U + W > 0$$

For all the other processes ($n > 1$), T decreases as V increases $\Rightarrow \Delta U < 0$ and

$$Q = \frac{\mu R\Delta T}{y-1} + \frac{\mu R\Delta T}{1-n}$$
$$= \frac{\mu R\Delta T}{y-1}\left(\frac{n-y}{n-1}\right)$$
$$= \left(\frac{n-y}{n-1}\right)\Delta U,$$

where $\Delta U < 0$

$$\Rightarrow \quad Q = 0 \text{ for } n = \gamma,$$
$$Q > 0 \text{ for } 1 < n < \gamma,$$
$$Q < 0 \text{ for } n > \gamma$$

34. (a)-(q), (b)-(r), (c)-(p), (d)-(s)

Since the piston is free to slide, the gas in chamber B undergoes isobaric changes. Also, since the pressure in the two chambers is always the same, we conclude that the gas in chamber A also undergoes isobaric changes.

If we consider the gas in the two chambers as our system, then no heat has flowed into the system. The hotter chamber A releases heat and it is absorbed by the colder chamber B. Thus, $Q_A + Q_B = 0$. If T is the final temperature in both the chambers, then

$$(nc_p\Delta T)_A + (nc_p\Delta T)_B = 0$$

$$\Rightarrow \quad 0.5\left(\frac{5}{2}R\right)(T - 700\text{ K}) + 0.5\left(\frac{7}{2}R\right)(T - 400\text{ K}) = 0$$

$\Rightarrow \quad T = 525$ K

For an isobaric process, work done by the gas is given by $W = P\Delta V$ or $nR\Delta T$. Hence $W_A = 0.5R(525\text{ K} - 700\text{ K}) = -726$ J and WB = $0.5R(525\text{ K} - 400\text{ K}) = 519$ J.

Heat flow through partition is

$$|Q_A| \text{ or } |Q_B| = 0.5\left(\frac{7}{2}R\right)(525\text{ K} - 400\text{ K})$$
$$= 1816\text{ J}$$

35. (a)-(s), (b)-(p,q), (c)-(q), (d)-(r,s)

If n is the number of moles of the gas, using the relation $T = \frac{PV}{nR}$, the temperatures at points A, B, C, and D are, respectively

$$T_A = \frac{300\text{ J}}{nR},$$

$$T_B = \frac{100\text{ J}}{nR},$$

$$T_C = \frac{200\text{ J}}{nR} \text{ and}$$

$$T_D = \frac{400\text{ J}}{nR}$$

Along path AB: $W = 0$ and $\Delta T < 0$

$\Rightarrow$ $\Delta U < 0$. Hence $Q < 0$.

Along path BC: $W > 0$ and $\Delta T > 0$

$\Rightarrow$ $\Delta U > 0$. Hence $Q > 0$.

Along path CD: $W = 0$ and $\Delta T > 0$

$\Rightarrow$ $\Delta U > 0$. Hence $Q > 0$.

Along path DA: $W < 0$ and $\Delta T < 0$

$\Rightarrow$ $\Delta U < 0$. Hence $Q < 0$.

PART III

ELECTRICITY AND MAGNETISM

CHAPTER

15 Electrostatic Field and Potential

- The fundamental entity in electrostatics is charge. Charge exists as an integral multiple of the number $e = 1.6 \times 10^{-19}$ C. There are two types of charges: positive and negative. All ordinary matter is made up of electrons, protons and neutrons. The charge on an electron is $-e$ and that on a proton is $+e$, whereas a neutron has no charge. A body is said to be neutral when the number of electrons equals the number of protons; positively charged when there are surplus protons; and negatively charged when there are surplus electrons.

  Charge is conserved. In any isolated system, charge may flow from one part of the system to another, but the net charge is constant.

  Coulomb's law is the basic law for interaction of point charges. For two point charges q_1 and q_2, separated by a distance r, the magnitude of the force on either charge is

$$F = \frac{1}{4\pi\epsilon_0}\frac{|q_1 q_2|}{r^2} \text{ (free space)}$$

  The force is attractive when the charges are alike, and repulsive when the charges are different. The constant ϵ_0 is called the electric permittivity of free space; it can be considered as the resistance of free space to the formation of electric field. In SI units, $\epsilon_0 = 8.854 \times 10^{-12}\ \mathrm{C^2/N \cdot m^2}$.

  If the charges are kept in any medium other than free space, then ϵ_0 is replaced by the electric permittivity ϵ of that medium. The value of ϵ for any medium is always greater than ϵ_0. The ratio $k = \epsilon/\epsilon_0$ is called the relative electric permittivity or the dielectric constant of that medium. The dielectric constant for free space is 1, and for any other medium, it is greater than 1.

  In general, Coulomb's force law is written as

$$F = \frac{1}{4\pi(k\epsilon_0)}\frac{|q_1 q_2|}{r^2} \text{ (medium of dielectric constant } k\text{)}$$

  Thus, if F is the force between a given pair of charges kept in free space, then it reduces to F/k when the charges are surrounded by a medium of dielectric constant k.

- A distribution of electric charges at rest creates an electric field in the surrounding space. The electric field exerts a force **F** on any other charge q present in the field. The field intensity **E** at any field point is the force experienced per unit positive test charge present at that point:

$$\mathbf{E} = \lim_{q \to 0} \frac{\mathbf{F}}{q} \text{ (SI unit is N/C or V/m)}$$

  The value of E for a few charge distributions is as follows:

  1. At distance r from a point charge Q:

$$E = \frac{1}{4\pi\epsilon_0}\frac{Q}{r^2}$$

  2. At distance x (along the axis) from the centre of a uniform ring of charge Q and radius R:

$$E = \frac{1}{4\pi\epsilon_0}\frac{Qx}{\left(R^2 + x^2\right)^{3/2}} \text{ (greatest at } x = R/\sqrt{2}\text{)}$$

  3. At distance r from the centre of a uniform spherical shell of charge Q and radius R:

$$E = \begin{cases} 0, & 0 \le r < R \\ \dfrac{E_0 R^2}{r^2}, & r \ge R \end{cases}, \text{ where } E_0 = \frac{1}{4\pi\epsilon_0}\frac{Q}{R^2} \text{ (intensity at the surface)}$$

4. At distance r from the centre of a uniform sphere of charge Q and radius R:

$$E = \begin{cases} \dfrac{E_0}{R}r, 0 \le r < R \\ \dfrac{E_0 R^2}{r^2}, r \ge R \end{cases}, \text{ where } E_0 = \frac{1}{4\pi\epsilon_0}\frac{Q}{R^2} \text{ (intensity at the surface)}$$

5. At distance r from an infinitely long line charge of uniform linear charge density λ:

$$E = \frac{\lambda}{2\pi\epsilon_0 r}$$

6. At distance r from an infinitely long hollow cylinder of uniform linear charge density λ:

$$E = \begin{cases} 0, 0 \le r < R \\ \dfrac{E_0 R}{r}, r \ge R \end{cases}, \text{ where } E_0 = \frac{\lambda}{2\pi\epsilon_0 R} \text{ (intensity at the surface)}$$

7. At distance r from an infinitely long uniform cylinder of linear charge density λ:

$$E = \begin{cases} \dfrac{E_0}{R}r, 0 \le r \le R \\ \dfrac{E_0 R}{r}, r \ge R \end{cases}, \text{ where } E_0 = \frac{\lambda}{2\pi\epsilon_0 R} \text{ (intensity at the surface)}$$

8. At distance r from a infinitely large sheet of uniform surface charge density σ:

$$E = \frac{\sigma}{2\epsilon_0} \text{ (field is uniform)}$$

- The field potential V at any field point is the negative of the work done by the field per unit positive test charge, as it moves from infinity to that point:

$$V = -\int_{\infty}^{r} \mathbf{E} \cdot d\mathbf{r} \text{ (SI unit is J/C or V)}$$

If V_1 and V_2 are the field potentials of points 1 and 2, then the difference in their potentials is given by

$$V_2 - V_1 = -\int_1^2 \mathbf{E} \cdot d\mathbf{r}$$

The value of V (with respect to infinity) for a few charge distributions is listed below:

1. At distance r from a point charge Q:

$$V = \frac{1}{4\pi\epsilon_0}\frac{Q}{r}$$

2. At distance x (along the axis) from the centre of a uniform ring of charge Q and radius R:

$$V = \frac{1}{4\pi\epsilon_0}\frac{Q}{\left(R^2 + x^2\right)^{1/2}}$$

3. At distance r from the centre of a uniform spherical shell of charge Q and radius R:

$$V = \begin{cases} V_0, 0 \le r \le R \\ \dfrac{V_0 R}{r}, r \ge R \end{cases}, \text{ where } V_0 = \frac{1}{4\pi\epsilon_0}\frac{Q}{R} \text{ (potential at the surface)}$$

4. At distance r from the centre of a uniform sphere of charge Q and radius R:

$$V = \begin{cases} \dfrac{3}{2}V_0\left(1 - \dfrac{r^2}{3R^2}\right), 0 \le r \le R \\ \dfrac{V_0 R}{r}, r \ge R \end{cases}, \text{ where } V_0 = \frac{1}{4\pi\epsilon_0}\frac{Q}{R} \text{ (potential at the surface)}$$

- A particle of charge q, present at a field point of intensity **E** and potential V, experiences a force **F** and possesses potential energy U, given by
$$\mathbf{F} = q\mathbf{E} \text{ and } U = qV$$
When the point charge moves from one potential V_1 to another potential V_2, the work done by the electric field on the point charge equals the negative of the change in the potential energy
$$W_{\text{elec}} = -\Delta U = -q(V_2 - V_1)$$
For a system of two particles with charges q_1 and q_2, separated by a distance r, the associated potential energy function is
$$U = \frac{1}{4\pi\epsilon_0}\frac{q_1 q_2}{r}$$
For a uniform spherical shell of charge Q and radius R, the associated potential energy function is
$$U = \frac{Q^2}{8\pi\epsilon_0 R}$$
When a system of charges moves from one potential energy state U_i to another potential energy state U_f, the work done by the electric field can be found using $W_{\text{elec}} = -\Delta U$

- A pair of equal charges q but opposite signs, separated by a distance d, is called an electric dipole having dipole moment
$$\mathbf{p} = qd \text{ directed from } -\text{ve toward } +\text{ve charge}$$
The magnitude of the electric field due to a dipole at a distance $r(r \gg d)$ varies with angle θ from the dipole axis as
$$E(r,\theta) = \frac{1}{4\pi\epsilon_0}\frac{p}{r^3}\sqrt{1+3\cos^2\theta}$$
At points along the dipole axis, the electric field magnitude is $E(r, \theta) = \frac{1}{4\pi\epsilon_0}\frac{2p}{r^3}$, and at points along the perpendicular to the dipole axis, the electric field magnitude is $E(r, \pi/2) = \frac{1}{4\pi\epsilon_0}\frac{p}{r^3}$.
The potential due to a dipole at a distance $r(r \gg d)$ varies with angle θ from the dipole axis as
$$V(r, \theta) = \frac{1}{4\pi\epsilon_0}\frac{p\cos\theta}{r^2}$$
At points along the dipole axis, the field potential is $V(r, \theta) = \frac{1}{4\pi\epsilon_0}\frac{p}{r^2}$, and at points along the perpendicular to the dipole axis, the field potential is $V(r, \pi/2) = 0$.
An electric dipole **p** kept in a uniform electric field **E** experiences no net force but experiences a torque and possesses potential energy given by
$$\tau = \mathbf{p} \times \mathbf{E} \text{ and } \mathbf{U} = -\mathbf{p} \cdot \mathbf{E}$$

- Electric flux is a measure of the "flow" of electric field through a surface. It equals the product of area and the component of electric field along the normal to the area:
$$\phi_E = \int \mathbf{E} \cdot ds$$
Gauss's law states that the total electric flux through a closed surface is proportional to the net charge enclosed by that surface:
$$\oint \mathbf{E} \cdot d\mathbf{s} = \frac{Q_{\text{encl}}}{\epsilon_0}$$
Logically Gauss's law is the same as Coulomb's law, but it is very useful in finding the magnitude of an electric field involving symmetrical charge distributions.

- Conductors are materials that permit electric charge to move freely within them. This is due to the abundance of freely moving electrons, even at room temperature. Insulators permit charges to move much less readily. Most metals are good conductors; most non-metals are insulators.
When surplus charge is added to a conductor, it resides entirely on the surface; the charge density σ at different

points on the surface of the conductor is inversely proportional to the radius of curvature r of the surface at that point. The field is zero everywhere in the material of the conductor; at the surface, the field is normal to the surface everywhere, having magnitude $\frac{\sigma}{\epsilon_0}$, where σ is the charge density at that point on the surface.

When a conductor is placed in an external field, induced charges appear on the surface arranged in a way such that the net field in the material of the conductor is zero, and the field at the surface everywhere is normal to the surface.

- If the potential is known as a function of the position coordinate (r), the electric field at that point is given by

$$\mathbf{E} = -\frac{dV}{dr}\mathbf{e}_r \; (\mathbf{e}_r \text{ is a unit vector along } \mathbf{r})$$

In other words, the electric field at any point equals the negative of the potential gradient at that point; the negative sign shows that the electric field is directed towards decreasing potential.

EXERCISES

1. Four point charges, each equal to Q, are placed at the corners of a square and a charge q is placed at its centre. The system will be in equilibrium if q equals:

(a) $-\left(\frac{1+2\sqrt{2}}{4}\right)Q$ (b) $-\left(\frac{1+\sqrt{2}}{2}\right)Q$

(c) $-\left(\frac{\sqrt{2}+2}{4}\right)Q$ (d) $-\left(\frac{1+\sqrt{2}}{2\sqrt{2}}\right)Q$

2. Three charges q_1, q_2 and $4q_1$ are placed in a straight line, in that order, at certain distances from each other. If there is no force other than the mutual Coulomb force, then the three-charge system will remain in equilibrium if $\frac{q_2}{q_1}$ equals:

(a) $-4/9$ (b) $-2/3$

(c) $-5/4$ (d) $-7/4$

3. A metal sphere A of radius a carrying charge $-Q$ and another metal sphere B of radius $2a$ carrying charge $2Q$ are placed at a large distance $d(d \gg a)$ from each other. The Coulomb force between them has magnitude F. The spheres are brought in contact with each other, and are kept at a distance $d/3$. The force of repulsion between them now is:

(a) $\frac{1}{4}F$ (b) $\frac{2}{3}F$

(c) F (d) $\frac{3}{8}F$

4. A quantity x is given by $x = \epsilon_0 L\frac{\Delta V}{\Delta t}$, where ϵ_0 is the permittivity of free space, L is the length, ΔV is the electric potential difference and Δt is the time interval. The dimensional formula for x is the same as:

(a) Resistance (b) Charge

(c) Current (d) Voltage

5. Two small, equally charged spheres, each of mass m, are suspended from a common point by silk threads, each of length l. At equilibrium, the separation between them is $x(x \ll l)$. Now, charge starts leaking from both the spheres at the same rate. If the spheres move towards each other with approach velocity $a/\sqrt{x}$ (a is a constant), the rate at which the charge leaks is:

(a) $\frac{3}{4}a\sqrt{\frac{\pi\varepsilon_0 mg}{l}}$ (b) $\frac{1}{2}a\sqrt{\frac{6\pi\varepsilon_0 mg}{l}}$

(c) $\frac{3}{2}a\sqrt{\frac{2\pi\varepsilon_0 mg}{l}}$ (d) $\frac{2}{3}a\sqrt{\frac{\pi\varepsilon_0 mg}{l}}$

6. Positive and negative charges are distributed along the circumference of a circle, as shown in the figure.

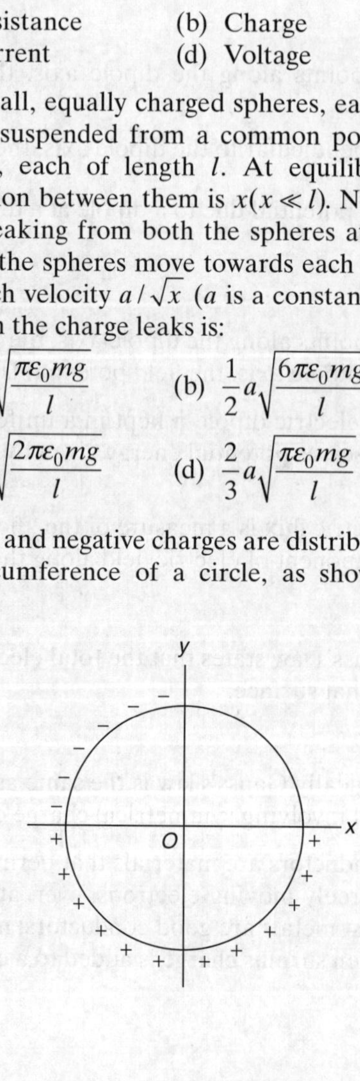

If the density of charge distribution has uniform magnitude, the angle made by the electric field at O with the $+x$-axis is:

(a) $\tan^{-1}(3)$ (b) $\frac{\pi}{2}+\tan^{-1}\left(\frac{1}{3}\right)$

(c) $\frac{\pi}{2}+\tan^{-1}(3)$ (d) $\pi-\tan^{-1}\left(\frac{1}{3}\right)$

7. A solid conducting sphere having charge Q is surrounded by an uncharged conducting spherical shell. The potential difference between the solid sphere and the spherical shell is V. If the shell is given a charge $-3Q$, the new potential difference between the conductors is:

(a) $-2V$ (b) $2V$
(c) V (d) $-3V$

8. Two long, hollow metal cylinders A and B of radii R and $2R$, respectively, are coaxially placed. If the line charge density is λ and -2λ, respectively, for the two cylinders, the potential difference between them is:

(a) $\frac{2\lambda \ln 2}{\pi\epsilon_0}$ (b) $\frac{\lambda \ln 2}{\pi\epsilon_0}$

(c) $\frac{3\lambda \ln 2}{2\pi\epsilon_0}$ (d) $\frac{\lambda \ln 2}{2\pi\epsilon_0}$

9. A simple pendulum consists of a small sphere of mass m suspended by a thread of length l. The sphere carries a positive charge q. The pendulum is placed in a uniform electric field of strength E directed vertically upward. The period of oscillation of the pendulum is:

(a) $2\pi\sqrt{\frac{l}{g}}$ (b) $2\pi\sqrt{\frac{ml}{mg-qE}}$

(c) $2\pi\sqrt{\frac{ml}{mg+qE}}$ (d) $2\pi\sqrt{\frac{ml}{qE}}$

10. Two hollow metal spheres of radii R and $2R$ are placed concentrically. The spheres carry charge such that the inner sphere has a uniform potential V_0 whereas the outer sphere is earthed. The electric field E at a point midway between the spheres is:

(a) $E=\frac{8V_0}{9R}$ (b) $E=\frac{3V_0}{5R}$

(c) $E=\frac{4V_0}{9R}$ (d) $E=\frac{5V_0}{6R}$

11. An infinitely long positively charged straight wire has a linear charge density λ. An electron is in uniform circular motion around the wire in a plane perpendicular to the wire. Quantities associated with the electron's motion, which are independent of the radius of the circular path, are:

(a) Kinetic energy
(b) Frequency of circular motion
(c) Linear momentum
(d) Angular momentum about the wire

12. Three particles H^+, He^+ and Li^{++} are allowed to move from rest through the same potential difference. If v_A, v_B and v_C are the velocities acquired as they emerge from the field region, then $v_A : v_B : v_C$ equals:

(a) $2\sqrt{3}:\sqrt{3}:2$ (b) $\sqrt{6}:\sqrt{3}:\sqrt{2}$
(c) $2\sqrt{2}:\sqrt{3}:1$ (d) $\sqrt{3}:\sqrt{2}:1$

13. The figure shows a few equipotential lines drawn in the xy plane.

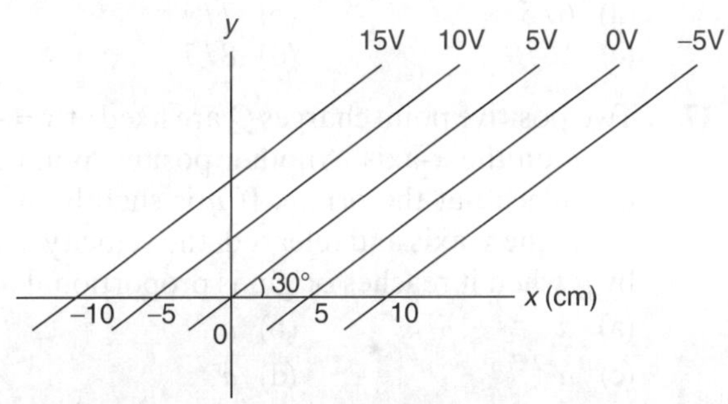

The electric field $\mathbf{E}$ in this region is:

(a) $-\left(\sqrt{3}\,\text{V/cm}\right)\mathbf{i}+(1\,\text{V/cm})\mathbf{j}$

(b) $(1\,\text{V/cm})\mathbf{i}-\left(\sqrt{3}\,\text{V/cm}\right)\mathbf{j}$

(c) $-(1\,\text{V/cm})\mathbf{i}+\left(\sqrt{3}\,\text{V/cm}\right)\mathbf{j}$

(d) $\left(\sqrt{3}\,\text{V/cm}\right)\mathbf{i}-(1\,\text{V/cm})\mathbf{j}$

14. Two non-conducting spheres A and B, each of radii R, are placed a distance $3R$ apart (centre-to-centre distance). Each sphere carries charge Q distributed uniformly on their surfaces. A particle having charge $-q$ is projected from the surface of sphere A towards sphere B along the line joining their centres. The minimum kinetic energy with which the particle must be projected so that it reaches the surface of the sphere is:

(a) $\frac{3Qq}{8\pi\epsilon_0 R}$ (b) $\frac{Qq}{24\pi\epsilon_0 R}$

(c) $\frac{Qq}{12\pi\epsilon_0 R}$ (d) $\frac{3Qq}{4\pi\epsilon_0 R}$

15. A non-conducting ring of radius 0.5m carries a total charge of 1.11×10^{-10} C distributed non-uniformly along its circumference. If O is the centre of the ring, then the value of $-\int_{\infty}^{O}\mathbf{E}\cdot d\mathbf{r}$ is $\left(\frac{1}{4\pi\varepsilon_0}=9\times10^9\ \text{N}\cdot\text{m}^2/\text{C}^2\right)$:

(a) −1 V (b) 2 V
(c) −3 V (d) 4 V

16. A charged particle is shot from a distance a towards a fixed charged particle, with a certain velocity directed at angle 30° to the line joining the two particles. The minimum approach distance between the two particles is $2a/3$. If K and U, respectively, represent the initial kinetic and potential energies of the two particle system, then the ratio K/U equals:

(a) 6/5 (b) 7/4
(c) 16/9 (d) 8/7

17. Two positive point charges Q are fixed at $x=-a$ and $x=a$ on the x-axis. Another positive point charge q is placed at the origin. If q is slightly displaced along the x-axis and released, the velocity acquired by q when it reaches origin is proportional to:

(a) $a^{-3/2}$ (b) a^{-3}
(c) $a^{-2/3}$ (d) a^{-2}

18. Two particles, each of mass m, are attached to the ends of a light rigid rod of length l. The particles are given charges $-q$ and $+q$ and placed in a uniform electric field of strength E. If the rod is slightly displaced from its stable position, it performs angular SHM of angular frequency:

(a) $\sqrt{\frac{2qE}{ml}}$ (b) $\sqrt{\frac{4qE}{ml}}$

(c) $\sqrt{\frac{qE}{ml}}$ (d) $\sqrt{\frac{qE}{2ml}}$

19. Let $E_1(r)$, $E_2(r)$ and $E_3(r)$ be the respective electric fields at a distance r from a point charge Q, an infinitely long wire with uniform linear charge density λ, and an infinite plane with uniform charge density σ. If $E_1(r_0)=E_2(r_0)=E_3(r_0)$ at some distance r_0, then:

(a) $Q=4\pi r_0^2\sigma$
(b) $\lambda=2\pi r_0\sigma$
(c) $E_1(r_0/2)=2E_2(r_0/2)$
(d) $E_2(r_0/2)=4E_3(r_0/2)$

20. A uniform electric field of intensity 2 V/m exists parallel to the xy plane at angle 60° to the x-axis. A particle carrying charge 0.5 mC is moving in the field region. If its kinetic energy while passing through point $A(1\text{m}, 2\text{m}, 3\text{m})$ is 5 mJ, then its kinetic energy while passing through point $B(-3\text{m}, 2\text{m}, 1\text{m})$ will be:

(a) 3 mJ (b) 5 mJ
(c) 7 mJ (d) None of these

21. The figure shows a point charge $+Q$ placed off-centre in the cavity of a spherical conducting shell.

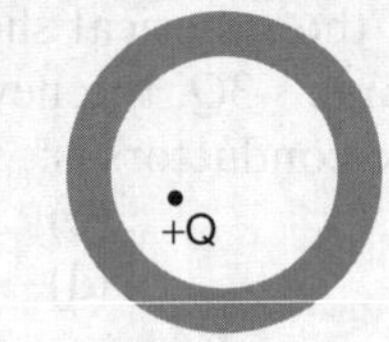

If σ_1 is the surface charge density on the inner surface and σ_2 is the surface charge density on the outer surface, then the correct statements from the following are:

(a) σ_1, σ_2 are uniform
(b) σ_1, σ_2 are non-uniform
(c) σ_1 is uniform and σ_2 is non-uniform
(d) σ_1 is non-uniform and σ_2 is uniform

22. The figure shows a point charge Q_1 placed off-centre in the cavity of a spherical conducting shell, and point charge Q_2 placed outside the shell.

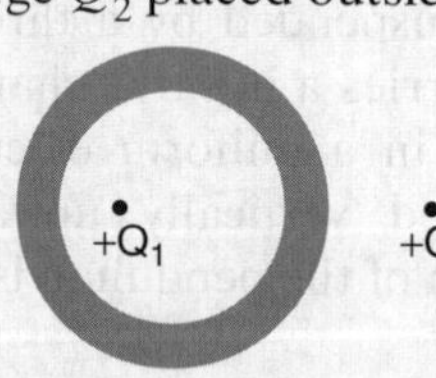

If σ_1, σ_2 are the surface charge densities on the inner and outer surfaces, respectively, and F_1, F_2 are the forces experienced by Q_1 and Q_2, respectively, then the incorrect statements from the following are:

(a) The position of Q_1 affects σ_1 only
(b) The position of Q_2 affects σ_2 only
(c) $F_1=0, F_2=0$
(d) $F_1=0, F_2\neq0$

23. Three hollow metal spheres A, B and C of radii R, $2R$ and $3R$, respectively are placed concentrically. Spheres A and C are given charge q and $3q$, respectively, whereas sphere B is earthed without giving any surplus charge. The potential difference V_C-V_A equals:

(a) $\frac{-q}{6\pi\varepsilon_0 R}$ (b) $\frac{-q}{24\pi\varepsilon_0 R}$

(c) $\frac{q}{18\pi\varepsilon_0 R}$ (d) $\frac{q}{12\pi\varepsilon_0 R}$

24. Three identical metal plates A, B and C carrying charges 10 nC, – 40 nC and 20 nC, respectively, are kept 1 cm apart parallel to each other such that plate B lies in the middle. If the area of each plate is 400 sq. cm, the potential difference $V_C - V_A$ equals ($\epsilon_0 = 8.85 \times 10^{-12}$ C^2/N·m^2):
(a) –480 V (b) 420 V
(c) –340 V (d) 280 V

25. A uniformly charged solid sphere of radius R has potential V_0 on its surface. For this sphere, the equipotential surfaces with potentials $\frac{3V_0}{2}, \frac{5V_0}{4}, \frac{3V_0}{4}$ and $\frac{V_0}{4}$ have radii R_1, R_2, R_3 and R_4, respectively. Then:
(a) $R_1 \neq 0$ and $R_4 > 2R$
(b) $R_1 = 0$ and $R_4 < 2R$
(c) $R_2 > R_4 - R_3$
(d) $R_2 - R_1 < R_4 - R_3$

26. A uniform electric field region of strength E exists between two parallel metal plates. A beam of particles, each carrying charge $-e$, enters the region at a point midway between the plates, with velocity parallel to the plates, as shown in the figure.

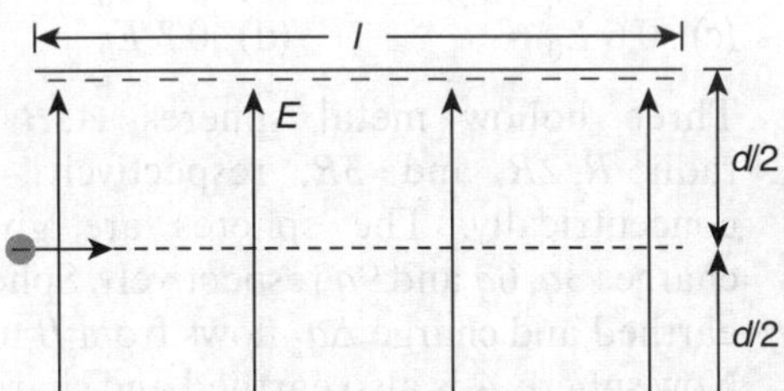

If the length of the plates is l and the distance between them is d, the minimum kinetic energy K of the particles which emerge from the field region is:
(a) $\frac{2l^2eE}{d}$ (b) $\frac{l^2eE}{d}$
(c) $\frac{l^2eE}{2d}$ (d) $\frac{l^2eE}{4d}$

27. Three identical metal plates A, B and C, each of area 400 sq. cm, are kept parallel to each other such that plate B lies in the middle. The separation between plates A and B is 1 cm and that between plates B and C is 2 cm. If plates A and C are earthed and plate B is given a surplus charge of –15 nC, the potential difference $V_A - V_B$ equals ($\epsilon_0 = 8.85 \times 10^{-12}$ C^2/N·m^2):
(a) –480 V (b) 420 V
(c) –340 V (d) 280 V

28. Two identical metal plates A, B of area S are kept parallel to each other in a uniform electric field E perpendicular to the plates along the direction $\overline{AB}$. If surplus charge Q is given to plate A, then the correct statements from the following are:
(a) Charge on the inner side of plate $A = \epsilon_0 SE - \frac{Q}{2}$
(b) Charge on the inner side of plate $B = -\epsilon_0 SE - \frac{Q}{2}$
(c) Charge on the outer side of plate $A = \epsilon_0 SE + \frac{Q}{2}$
(d) Charge on the outer side of plate $B = -\epsilon_0 SE + \frac{Q}{2}$

29. The field potential V inside a charged ball depends only on the radial distance r, as $V(r) = ar^2 + b$, where a and b are constants. If the space charge density ρ inside the ball is proportional to r^n, then n equals:
(a) –1 (b) 0
(c) 1/2 (d) 1

30. The region between two concentric spheres of radii a and $b (b > a)$ is filled with charge such that the charge density depends only on the radial distance r, as $\rho(r) = \frac{c}{r}$. Also, there is a point charge Q placed at the centre of the spheres. If the field in the region $a < r < b$ is constant in magnitude, then c equals:
(a) $\frac{Q}{2\pi a^2}$ (b) $\frac{Q}{2\pi(b^2 - a^2)}$
(c) $\frac{Q}{2\pi b^2}$ (d) $\frac{Q}{2\pi ab}$

31. A spherical region of radius R is filled with charge such that the charge density depends only on the radial distance r, as $\rho(r) = \rho_0\left(\frac{5}{4} - \frac{r}{R}\right)$. The field at a distance $r (r \leq R)$ from the origin is given by:
(a) $\frac{4\rho_0 r}{3\epsilon_0}\left(\frac{5}{3} - \frac{r}{R}\right)$ (b) $\frac{\rho_0 r}{4\epsilon_0}\left(\frac{5}{3} - \frac{r}{R}\right)$
(c) $\frac{4\rho_0 r}{3\epsilon_0}\left(\frac{5}{4} - \frac{r}{R}\right)$ (d) $\frac{\rho_0 r}{3\epsilon_0}\left(\frac{5}{4} - \frac{r}{R}\right)$

32. A non-conducting rod of uniform mass M and length L is suspended vertically at its one end. The rod can swing freely in the vertical plane without any friction. The rod is uniformly charged with linear density λ, and a uniform horizontal electric field E_0 is switched on in the region. The rod's angular velocity first increases to a peak value ω_0, then decreases to zero, and then it swings back. If the rod just manages to swing to the horizontal position, then:

(a) $E_0 = \frac{3Mg}{4\lambda L}, \frac{\omega_0^2 L}{g} = 2\left(\sqrt{3}-1\right)$

(b) $E_0 = \frac{Mg}{\lambda L}, \frac{\omega_0^2 L}{g} = 2\left(\sqrt{3}-1\right)$

(c) $E_0 = \frac{3Mg}{4\lambda L}, \frac{\omega_0^2 L}{g} = 3\left(\sqrt{2}-1\right)$

(d) $E_0 = \frac{Mg}{\lambda L}, \frac{\omega_0^2 L}{g} = 3\left(\sqrt{2}-1\right)$

33. Positive charge is distributed along the x-axis from $x = 0$ to $x = L$ such that the charge density varies with x, as $\lambda(x) = 4\pi x$. A point charge q is projected from infinity with kinetic energy K. If the particle is confined to move along the y-axis and it just manages to reach origin, then $\frac{2\epsilon_0 K}{qL}$ equals:

(a) 1 (b) 2
(c) 3 (d) 4

34. Two tiny dipoles A and B are placed along the x-axis at distance r from each other. If the magnitude of the force between them is proportional to r^{-n}, then n equals:

(a) 1 (b) 2
(c) 3 (d) 4

35. Positive charge is uniformly distributed all along the x-axis, with linear charge density λ. Consider a plane square surface S of side $2a$, at distance a from the xy plane, having its centre on the z-axis and sides parallel to the x and y axes (see figure).

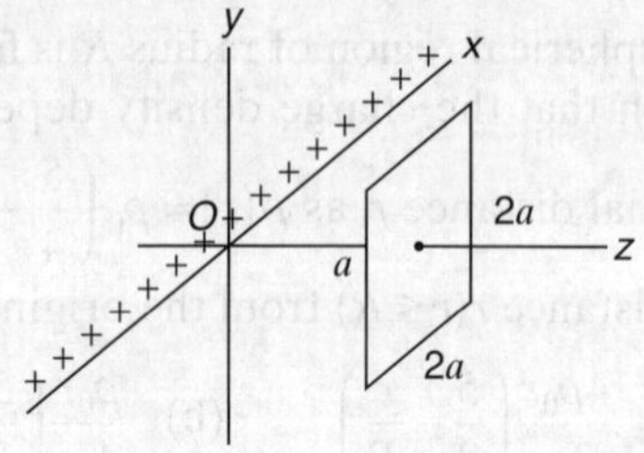

If ϕ is the electric flux through S, then $\frac{2\epsilon_0 \phi}{\lambda a}$ equals:

(a) 1 (b) 2
(c) 3 (d) 4

36. Charge is distributed in space such that the charge density ρ varies with position x, as $\rho \propto x^2$. At points close to the x-axis, the electric field has an x component only. If the magnitude E of the electric field varies with position x, as $E \propto x^n$, then n equals:

(a) −2 (b) −1
(c) 1 (d) 3

37. A particle of mass $m = 10^{-3}$ kg and charge $q = 1$ C is initially at rest. At time $t = 0$, the particle starts experiencing an electric field $\mathbf{E} = E_0 \sin(\omega t)\mathbf{i}$, where $E_0 = 1$ N/C and $\omega = 10^3$ rad/s. The maximum speed attained by the particle is:

(a) 2.0 m/s (b) 1.5 m/s
(c) 1.0 m/s (d) 0.5 m/s

38. Three concentric metal spherical shells A, B and C of radii a, b and c have surface charge densities of $+\sigma, -\sigma$ and $+\sigma$, respectively. The potential of shell B is:

(a) $\frac{\sigma}{\epsilon_0}\left(a - \frac{c^2 - b^2}{c}\right)$ (b) $\frac{\sigma}{\epsilon_0}\left(a - \frac{c^2 - b^2}{b}\right)$

(c) $\frac{\sigma}{\epsilon_0}\left(c - \frac{b^2 - a^2}{b}\right)$ (d) $\frac{\sigma}{\epsilon_0}\left(c - \frac{b^2 - a^2}{a}\right)$

39. Consider a uniformly charged disc of radius R. If the field at the centre of the disc is E_0, then the field along the axis at a distance R from the centre is nearly:

(a) 0.8 E_0 (b) 0.7 E_0
(c) 0.6 E_0 (d) 0.3 E_0

40. Three hollow metal spheres A, B and C of radii $R, 2R$ and $3R$, respectively, are placed concentrically. The spheres are given surplus charges $3q$, $6q$ and $9q$ respectively. Sphere B is now earthed and charge Δq_1 flows from B to the Earth. Now sphere A is also earthed and charge Δq_2 flows from A to the Earth. The ratio $\frac{|\Delta q_1|}{|\Delta q_2|}$ equals:

(a) 1 (b) 3
(c) 5 (d) 9

41. Electric field in a region varies with the x-coordinate as $\mathbf{E} = (ax + b)\mathbf{i} + c\mathbf{j}$, where $a = 0.1$ V/m^2, $b = c = 0.2$ V/m. In this region, a hypothetical closed volume is taken, as shown in the figure.

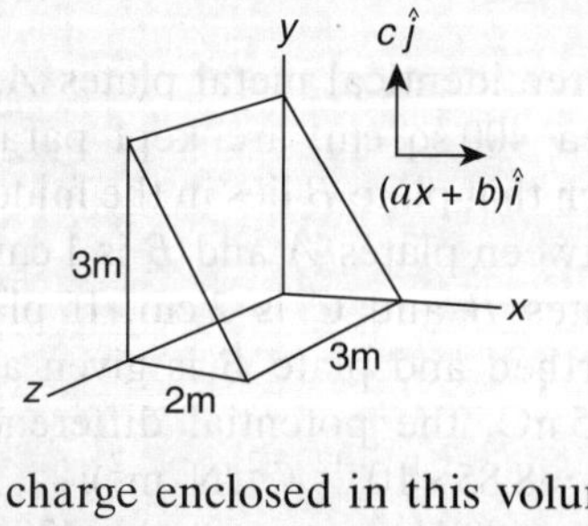

If the total charge enclosed in this volume is $k\epsilon_0$, then the value of k is:

(a) Equal to 0.9 (b) Independent of a
(c) Independent of b (d) Independent of c

ANSWER KEYS

1. (a)	**2.** (a)	**3.** (c)	**4.** (c)	**5.** (c)	**6.** (b)	**7.** (c)	**8.** (d)	**9.** (b)	**10.** (a)
11. (a),(c)	**12.** (a)	**13.** (b)	**14.** (b)	**15.** (b)	**16.** (d)	**17.** (a)	**18.** (a)	**19.** (c)	**20.** (a)
21. (d)	**22.** (c)	**23.** (b)	**24.** (d)	**25.** (d)	**26.** (c)	**27.** (d)	**28.** (b)	**29.** (b)	**30.** (a)
31. (b)	**32.** (d)	**33.** (b)	**34.** (d)	**35.** (a)	**36.** (d)	**37.** (a)	**38.** (c)	**39.** (d)	**40.** (c)
41. (a),(c),(d)									

SOLUTIONS

1. (a)

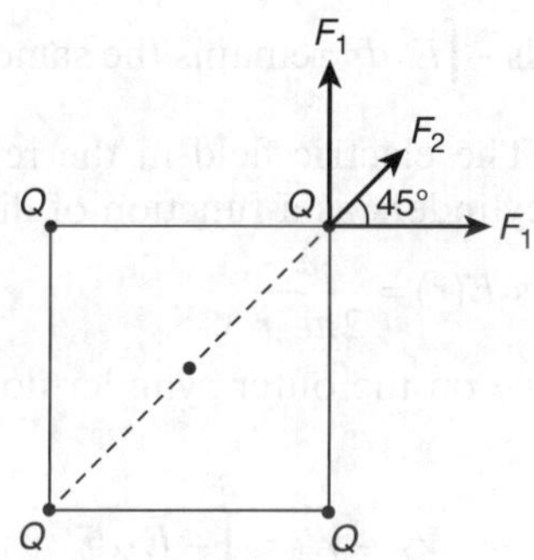

The figure shows forces acting on any one charge due to the other three corner charges.

Here, $F_1 = \dfrac{KQ^2}{a^2}$ and $F_2 = \dfrac{KQ^2}{(\sqrt{2}a)^2}$

The net force is along F_2 and its magnitude is

$$F = 2F_1 \cos 45^\circ + F_2 = \frac{KQ^2}{a^2}\left(\sqrt{2} + \frac{1}{2}\right)$$

If a charge q is placed at the centre of the square to keep the system in equilibrium, the force due to q must be equal to F and opposite in direction. Thus, q must be opposite in sign to Q, and its magnitude is given by

$$\frac{KQ|q|}{\left(\frac{a}{\sqrt{2}}\right)^2} = \frac{KQ^2}{2a^2}\left(\sqrt{2} + \frac{1}{2}\right)$$

$$\Rightarrow \quad |q| = Q\left(\frac{2\sqrt{2}+1}{4}\right)$$

Hence, $q = -Q\left(\dfrac{2\sqrt{2}+1}{4}\right)$

2. (a) Let separation between the charges be as shown in the figure.

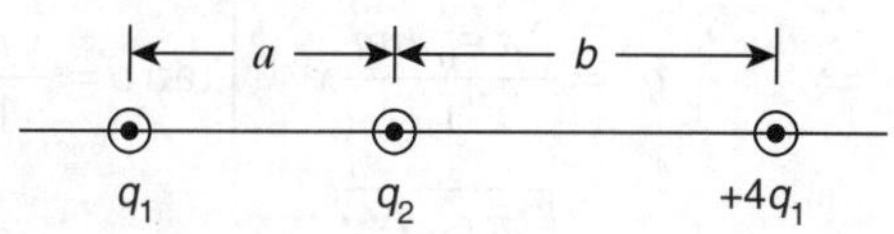

For q_2 to be in equilibrium, the field at its position must be zero

$$\frac{q_1}{a^2} = \frac{4q_1}{b^2} \Rightarrow b = 2a$$

For q_1 to be in equilibrium, the field at its position must be zero

$$\frac{q_2}{a^2} + \frac{4q_1}{(a+b)^2} = 0$$

$$\Rightarrow \quad \frac{q_2}{a^2} + \frac{4q_1}{(3a)^2} = 0 \quad \text{[Putting } b = 2a\text{]}$$

$$\Rightarrow \quad \frac{q_2}{q_1} = -4/9$$

3. (c) Initially $F = \dfrac{K2Q^2}{d^2}$. After A and B are bought in contact, the total charge $-Q + 2Q = Q$ distributes on A and B in proportion to their radii, that is, $\dfrac{Q}{3}$ and $\dfrac{2Q}{3}$, respectively.

Now $\quad F' = \dfrac{K\dfrac{2Q^2}{9}}{\dfrac{d^2}{9}} = \dfrac{K2Q^2}{d^2} = F$

4. (c) The SI unit for x is

$$\frac{c^2}{\text{N}\cdot\text{m}^2} \times \text{m} \times \frac{\text{J/C}}{\text{s}} = \frac{\text{C}}{\text{s}} \quad [\text{J} = \text{N}\cdot\text{m}]$$

which is the same as that for current.

5. (c)

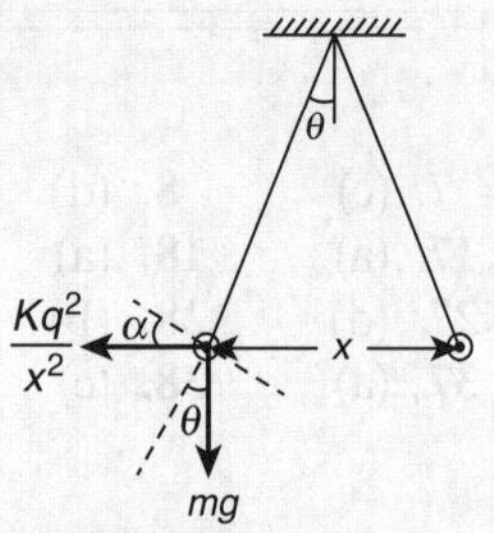

For equilibrium, we have

$$\frac{Kq^2}{x^2}\cos\theta = mg\sin\theta$$

[Balancing forces along the tangential direction]

$$\Rightarrow \quad q^2 = 4\pi\epsilon_0 mgx^2\tan\theta$$

$$\Rightarrow \quad q^2 = \frac{2\pi\epsilon_0\, mg}{1} \cdot x^3 \quad \left[\tan\theta = \frac{x/2}{1}\right]$$

$$\Rightarrow \quad q = \sqrt{\frac{2\pi\epsilon_0\, mg}{l}}\, x^{3/2}$$

Differentiating both sides with respect to t, we have

$$\Rightarrow \quad \frac{dq}{dt} = \sqrt{\frac{2\pi\epsilon_o\, mg}{I}} \times \frac{3}{2} x^{1/2} \frac{dx}{dt}$$

$$\Rightarrow \quad \frac{dq}{dt} = \sqrt{\frac{2\pi\varepsilon_o mg}{I}} \times \frac{3}{2} x^{1/2} \frac{dx}{dt}$$

$$\Rightarrow \quad \frac{dq}{dt} = -\frac{3}{2} a \sqrt{\frac{2\pi\epsilon_o\, mg}{1}} \quad \left[\frac{dx}{dt} = -\frac{a}{\sqrt{x}}, \text{ given}\right]$$

Negative sign shows that charge is leaking from the spheres.

6. (b)

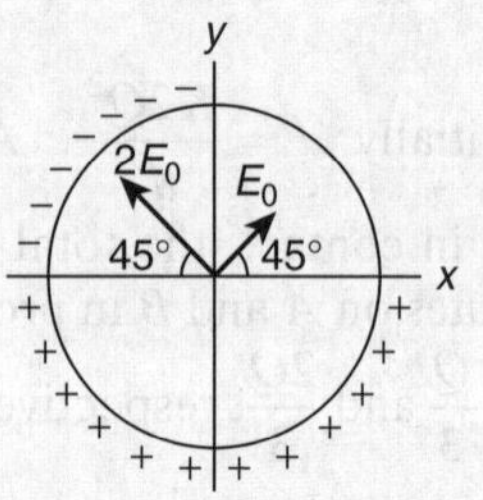

Let E_0 be the magnitude of the electric field at the centre, due to charge in one quadrant. From symmetry, we can see that their directions will be along the angular bisectors of the coordinate axes (see figure).

The resultant electric field (see figure) at the centre is

$$\vec{E} = (-E_0\cos 45^\circ)\hat{i} + (3E_0\sin 45^\circ)\hat{j} = \frac{-E_0}{\sqrt{2}}\hat{i} + \frac{3E_0}{\sqrt{2}}\hat{j}$$

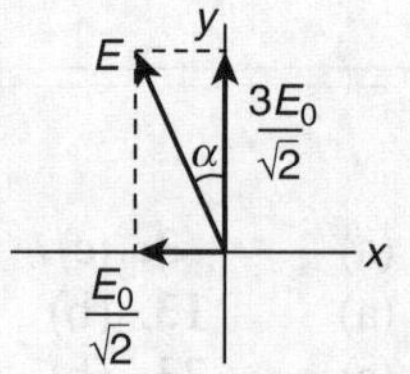

$\vec{E}$ makes angle $\alpha = \tan^{-1}\left(\frac{1}{3}\right)$ with the +ve y-axis.

Hence, the angle with the +ve x-axis

$$\frac{\pi}{2} = \alpha = \frac{\pi}{2} + \tan^{-1}\left(\frac{1}{3}\right)$$

7. (c) The electric field in the region between the two conductors remains unaffected by the charge on the shell. Hence, the potential difference which equals $-\int \vec{E}\cdot d\vec{r}$ remains the same.

8. (d) The electric field in the region between the two cylinders as a function of distance r from the axis is $E(r) = \frac{\lambda}{2\pi\varepsilon_o r}$.

Charge on the outer cylinder does not contribute. Now

$$V_B - V_A = \int_{A}^{B} -\vec{E}\cdot d\vec{r}$$

$$\Rightarrow \quad V_B - V_A = -\int_{R}^{2R} \frac{\lambda}{2\pi\varepsilon_o r} dr = \frac{-\lambda \ln 2}{2\pi\varepsilon_o}$$

The negative sign shows that B is at a lower potential than A. The potential difference is simply

$$|V_B - V_A| = \frac{\lambda \ln 2}{2\pi\varepsilon_0}$$

9. (b) Force acting on the sphere equals the vertically downward direction. The presence of the electric field has reduced the effect of gravity, whose value can now be taken as

$$g' = \frac{mg - qE}{m} = g - \frac{qE}{m}$$

The period of oscillation of the simple pendulum is

$$T = T = 2\pi\sqrt{\frac{I}{g'}} = 2\pi\sqrt{\frac{ml}{mg - qE}}$$

10. (a)

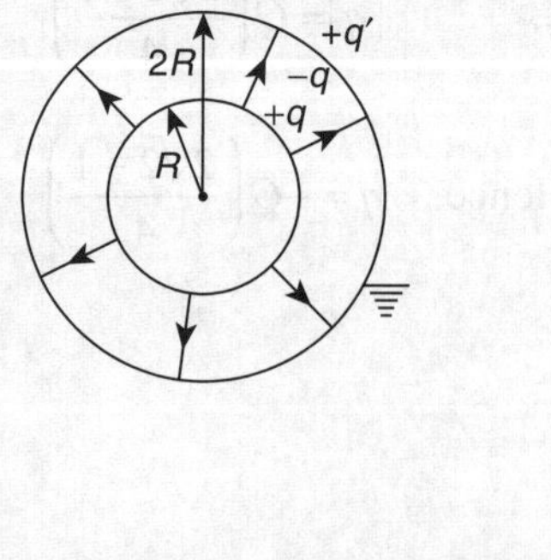

Let the charge on the two spheres be as shown in the figure. Since the outer sphere is earthed, its potential is zero. Hence

$$\frac{Kq'}{2R} = 0 \Rightarrow q' = 0$$

Potential of the inner sphere is V_o. Hence

$$\frac{Kq}{R} - \frac{Kq}{2R} = V_0 \Rightarrow Kq = 2RV_o$$

Now, we have

$$E(r) = E(r) = \frac{Kq}{r^2} = \frac{2RV_0}{r^2}, \quad R \le r \le 2R$$

Putting $r = \frac{3R}{2}$ gives the electric field in the middle

$$E = \frac{8V_o}{9R}$$

11. (a), (c) Coulomb force provides the necessary centripetal force for the circular motion of the particle. Thus

$$\frac{\lambda e}{2\pi\varepsilon_0 r} = m\frac{v^2}{r}$$

$$\Rightarrow \quad v = \sqrt{\frac{\lambda e}{2\pi\varepsilon_0 m}} \Rightarrow v \text{ is independent of } r$$

Frequency of revolution $= \frac{v}{2\pi r}$ depends on r

Kinetic energy $= \frac{1}{2}mv^2$ independent of r

Linear momentum $= mv$ independent of r

Angular momentum about the wire $= mvr$ depends on r

12. (a) A particle of mass m and charge q moving through a potential difference V acquires a velocity v given by

$$\frac{1}{2}mv^2 = qV$$

$$\Rightarrow \quad v \propto \sqrt{\frac{q}{m}} \text{ if } V \text{ is the same}$$

For the particles ${}^{1}_{+1}H$, ${}^{4}_{+1}He$, ${}^{6}_{+2}L$, the ratio q/m is in the ratio $1 : \frac{1}{4} : \frac{1}{3}$. Hence, we have

$$v_A : v_B : v_C = 1 : \frac{1}{2} : \frac{1}{\sqrt{3}} = 2\sqrt{3} : \sqrt{3} : 2$$

13. (b) Magnitude of the electric field is

$$E = \frac{5 \text{ V}}{5 \text{ cm} \sin 30^\circ} = 2 \text{ V/cm}$$

The direction of the electric field is towards decreasing potential. In this case, it is inclined at angle 60° to the $+x$-axis in the clockwise sense. Hence

$$\vec{E} = 2 \text{ V/cm}(\cos 60^\circ \hat{j} - \sin 60^\circ \hat{j})$$

$$\Rightarrow \quad \vec{E} = 1 \text{ V/cm } \hat{i} - \sqrt{3} \text{ V/cm } \hat{j}$$

14. (b) The particle is projected from point E towards point F (see figure). Initially the particle experiences a net force towards the centre of sphere A, causing retardation in its motion. Once it crosses the mid-point of EF (say G), it experiences a net force towards the centre of sphere B, causing acceleration in its motion. Hence, if the particle is given just enough kinetic energy to reach G (mid-point of EF), it will automatically be sucked in towards F thereafter.

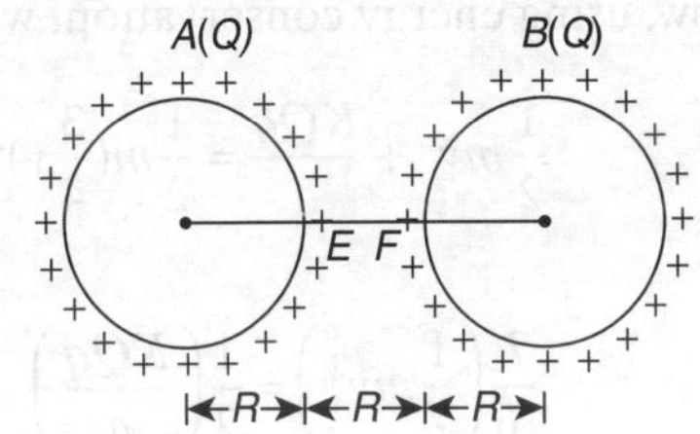

Potential at points E and G are

$$V_E = \frac{Q}{4\pi\varepsilon_0 R} + \frac{Q}{4\pi\varepsilon_0(2R)} = \frac{3Q}{8\pi\varepsilon_0 R}$$

and $$V_G = \frac{Q}{4\pi\varepsilon_0(3R/2)} + \frac{Q}{4\pi\varepsilon_0(3R/2)} = \frac{Q}{3\pi\varepsilon_0 R}$$

Let K be the kinetic energy of the particle at E so that it just reaches G. Then, using mechanical energy conservation principle, we have

$$K_1 + U_1 = K_2 + U_2$$

$$\Rightarrow \quad K - qV_E = -qV_G$$

$$\Rightarrow \quad K = q(V_E - V_G) = \frac{Qq}{24\pi\varepsilon_0 R}$$

15. (b) In this, we are required to find the potential at the centre O of the ring. Let us subdivide the ring into a large number of point charges. If dq represents any one element charge, the potential to this dq at O is $\frac{Kdq}{R}$. Integrating all along the ring, we obtain the potential due to all charges

$$V_O = \frac{K}{R}\oint_{\text{ring}} dq = \frac{Q}{4\pi\varepsilon_O R}$$

Putting the values, we have

$$V_0 = \frac{(9\times10^9)(1.11\times10^{-10})}{0.5} \text{V} = 2 \text{ V}$$

16. (d) Let Q and q be the charges on the fixed and moving particles, respectively. Let v be the initial velocity and v' be the velocity at closest approach.

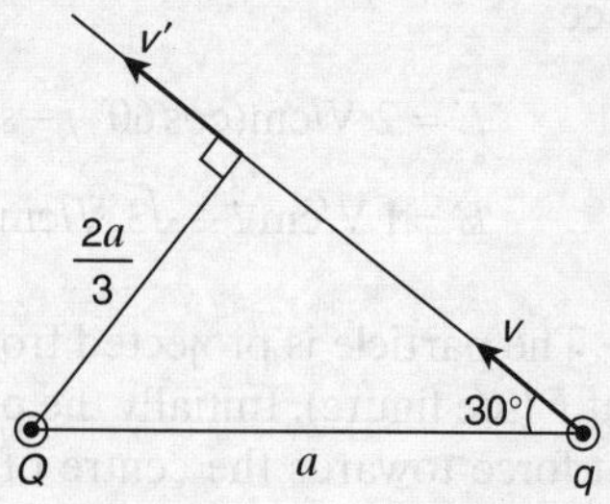

Angular momentum of q relative to Q will be conserved since the force on q is always directed towards Q; its torque relative to Q is zero. Hence

$$(mv\sin 30^\circ)a = mv'\frac{2a}{3} \Rightarrow v' = \frac{3}{4}v$$

Now, using energy conservation, we have

$$\frac{1}{2}mv^2 + \frac{KQq}{a} = \frac{1}{2}m\left(\frac{3}{4}v\right)^2 + \frac{KQq}{\frac{2a}{3}}$$

$$\Rightarrow \quad \frac{7}{16}\left(\frac{1}{2}mv^2\right) = \frac{1}{2}\left(\frac{KQq}{a}\right)$$

$$\Rightarrow \quad \frac{\frac{1}{2}mv^2}{\frac{KQq}{a}} = \frac{8}{7}$$

17. (a) The potential due to the two-charge system at any point x from the origin is

$$V(x) = \frac{KQ}{a+x} + \frac{KQ}{a-x} = \frac{2KQa}{a^2 - x^2}$$

Potential at origin is

$$V(o) = \frac{2KQ}{a}$$

If v is the velocity required by q when it reaches origin, using $\Delta K + \Delta U = 0$, we have

$$\frac{1}{2}mv^2 + q\left(\frac{2KQ}{a} - \frac{2KQa}{a^2 - x^2}\right) = 0$$

$$\Rightarrow \quad \frac{1}{2}mv^2 - \frac{2KQqx^2}{a(a^2 - x^2)} = 0$$

$$\Rightarrow \quad \frac{1}{2}mv^2 = \frac{2KQqx^2}{a^3} \text{(for } x \ll a)$$

Hence, $v \propto a^{-3/2}$

18. (a) The system is a dipole of strength $p = ql$. When it is at angle θ from its stable position, it experiences a restoring torque

$$T_{res} = pE\sin\theta = qlE\theta \text{ (for small } \theta)$$

The instantaneous angular acceleration is

$$\alpha = \frac{-T_{res}}{I} = \frac{-qlE}{2m\left(\frac{1}{2}\right)^2}\theta = \frac{-2qE}{ml}\theta$$

Hence, the dipole perform angular SHM with angular frequency

$$\omega = \sqrt{\frac{2qE}{ml}}$$

19. (c) We have

$$\frac{Q}{4\pi\varepsilon_O r^2} = \frac{\lambda}{2\pi\varepsilon_O r_o} = \frac{\sigma}{2\varepsilon_O}$$

$$\Rightarrow \quad Q = 2\pi r_o^2\sigma \text{ and } \lambda = \pi r_o\sigma$$

Thus, (a) and (b) are incorrect.

Let $E_1(r_o) = E_2(r_o) = E_3(r_o) == E_0$ (say). Then

$$E_1\left(\frac{r_o}{2}\right) = 4E_0, E_2\left(\frac{r_o}{2}\right) = 2E_0, E_3\left(\frac{r_o}{2}\right) = E_0$$

Thus we see that

$$\frac{E_1\left(\frac{r_o}{2}\right)}{E_2\left(\frac{r_o}{2}\right)} = 2 \Rightarrow \text{(c) is correct}$$

And $$\frac{E_2\left(\frac{r_o}{2}\right)}{E_3\left(\frac{r_0}{2}\right)} = 2 \Rightarrow \text{(d) is incorrect}$$

20. (a) The given electric field in vector form is

$$\bar{E} = 2\text{ V/m}\cos 60^\circ i + 2\text{ V/m}\sin 60^\circ j$$

$$= 1\text{ V/m}\hat{i} + \sqrt{3}\text{ V/m}\hat{j} + 0\hat{k}$$

The line joining A to B in vector form is

$$\Delta r = -4m\,\text{i} + 0\,j - 2mk$$

The potential difference between points A and B is

$$V_B - V_A = \int_A^B -\bar{E}\cdot d\bar{r} = -E\cdot\Delta\bar{r} = 4V$$

Now, using $\Delta K + \Delta U = 0$, we have

$$\Delta K + (0.5\text{ mC})(4\text{ V}) = 0$$

$$\Rightarrow \quad \Delta K = -2\text{ mJ}$$

Hence, the kinetic energy at position B equals 5 mJ – 2 mJ = 3 mJ.

21. (d) Since the field inside the conductor must be zero, it can be easily shown by using Gauss's theorem that $-Q$ charge will be induced on the inner surface. These induced charges distribute themselves in such a way (see figure) that the net field due to the induced charges and the charge inside the cavity is zero inside the conductor's body. Hence, σ_1 is non-uniform. Since the conductor is neutral, from charge conservation we conclude that $+Q$ charge will appear on the outer surface, and it distributes itself in such a way (see figure) that the field due to it is zero inside the conductor's body. The surface being spherical, it therefore distributes uniformly. Hence, σ_2 is non-uniform.

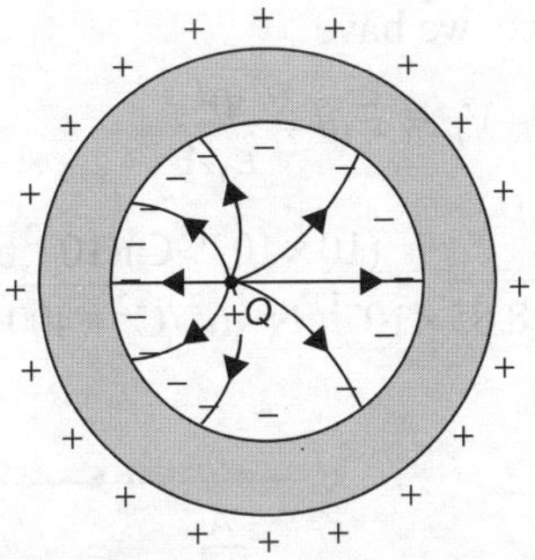

22. (c) Since the field inside the conductor must be zero, it can be easily shown by using Gauss's theorem that $-Q_1$ charge will be induced on the inner surface. These induced charges distribute themselves in such a way (see figure) that the net field due to the induced charges and the charge inside the cavity, is zero inside the conductor's body. Since the conductor is neutral, from charge conservation we conclude that $+Q_1$ charge will appear on the outer surface, and it distributes itself in such a way (see figure) that the field due to it and $+Q_2$ is zero inside the conductor's body.

Thus, the position of Q_1 only affects the charge distribution on the inner surface, while the position of Q_2 only affects the charge distribution on the outer surface.

Charge Q_1 experiences a net zero field and hence $F_1 = 0$, whereas charge Q_2 experiences a non-zero field and hence $F_2 = 0$. In other words, everything surrounded by the conductor is shielded from the fields of outside charges, but vice-versa is not true.

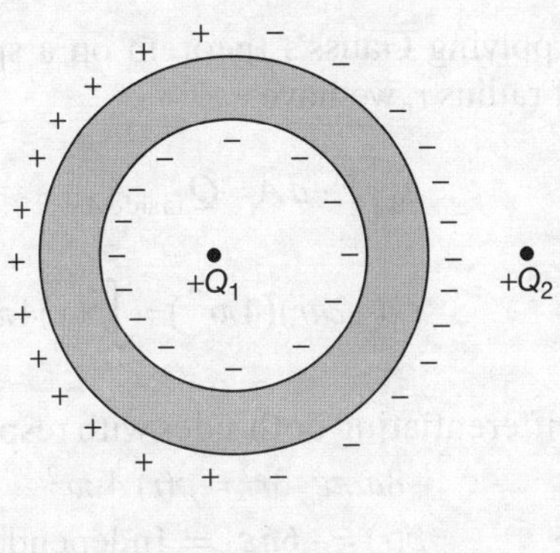

23. (b)

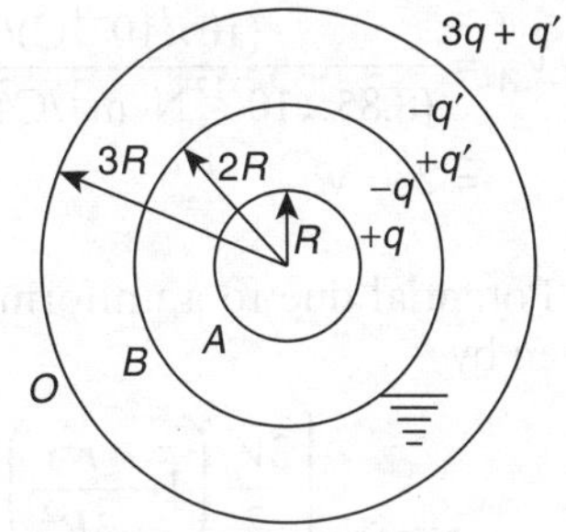

The figure shows the charge distribution at steady state on the conductors.

Using the condition $V_B = 0$, we have

$$\frac{Kq'}{2R} + \frac{K(3q)}{3R} = 0$$

$$\Rightarrow \quad q' = -2q$$

Taking the radially outward direction as positive, the electric field in the region between A and B is given by $E(r) = \dfrac{Kq}{r^2}$ and that between B and C is given by $E(r) = \dfrac{Kq'}{r^2} = \dfrac{-2Kq}{r^2}$. Thus, we have

$$V_C - V_A = \int_A^B -\vec{E}\cdot d\vec{r} + \int_B^C -\vec{E}\cdot d\vec{r}$$

$$= \int_R^{2R} \frac{-Kq}{r^2}dr + \int_{2R}^{3R} \frac{2Kq}{r^2}dr$$

$$= \frac{-Kq}{2R} + \frac{Kq}{3R} = \frac{-q}{24\pi\varepsilon_0 R}$$

24. (d)

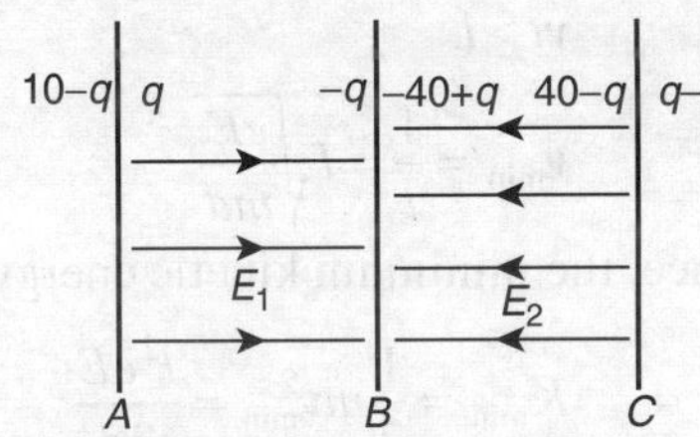

The figure shows the charge distribution on the plates. At steady state, charge on the outermost surfaces must be equal. Thus, we have

$$10 - q = q - 20$$

$$\Rightarrow \quad q = 15 \text{ nC}$$

The electric fields in the two regions are

$$E_1 = \frac{q}{\varepsilon_o A} \text{ and } E_2 = \frac{40-q}{\varepsilon_o A}$$

The required potential difference is

$$V_C - V_A = -E_1 d + E_2 d = \frac{(40-2q)d}{\varepsilon_0 A}$$

Putting the values, we have

$$V_C - V_A = \frac{(10\times10^{-9}\,\text{C})(10^{-2}\,\text{m})}{(8.85\times10^{-12}\,\text{N}\cdot\text{m}^2/\text{C}^2)(400\times10^{-4}\,\text{m}^2)}$$
$$= 280\ \text{V}$$

25. (d) Potential due to a uniformly charged sphere is given by

$$V(r) = \begin{cases} \dfrac{3V_o}{2}\left(1-\dfrac{r^2}{3R^2}\right), 0 \le r \le R \\ \dfrac{V_o R}{r}, r \ge R \end{cases}$$

Thus, we have

$$R_1 = 0, R_2 = \frac{R}{\sqrt{2}}, R_3 = \frac{4}{3}R \text{ and } R_4 = 4R$$

Now, $R_2 - R_1 = \dfrac{R}{\sqrt{2}}$ and $R_4 - R_3 = \dfrac{8}{3}R$

We see that $R_2 - R_1 < R_4 - R_3$.

26. (c) The particles move with uniform acceleration $a = \dfrac{eE}{m}$ directed towards the lower plate. The time in which these particles will fall down by distance $d/2$ is given by

$$\frac{d}{2} = \frac{1}{2}at^2$$

$$\Rightarrow \quad t = \sqrt{\frac{d}{a}} = \sqrt{\frac{md}{eE}}$$

The horizontal distance travelled by the particles in this time is vt. The particles will emerge from the field region if

$$vt > l$$

$$\Rightarrow \quad v_{\min} = \frac{1}{t} = l\sqrt{\frac{eE}{md}}$$

Hence, the minimum kinetic energy should be

$$K_{\min} = \frac{1}{2}mv_{\min}^2 = \frac{l^2 eE}{2d}$$

27. (d)

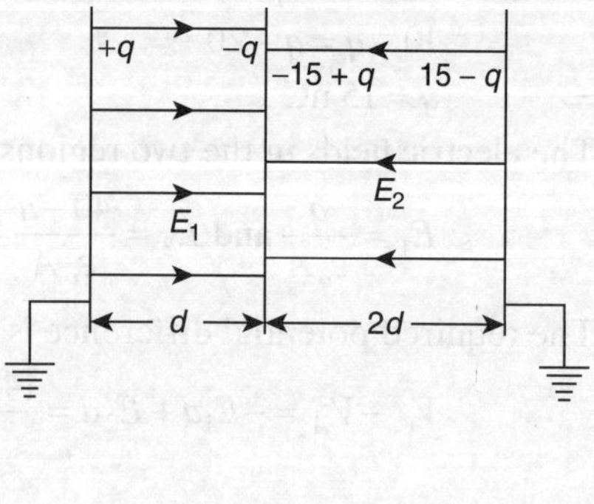

The figure shows the charge distribution on the plates. The electric fields in the two regions are

$$E_1 = \frac{q}{\varepsilon_o A} \text{ and } E_2 = \frac{15-q}{\varepsilon_o A}$$

The potential difference between plates A and C is zero. Hence

$$-E_1 d + E_2(2d) = 0$$
$$\Rightarrow \quad -q + 2(15-q) = 0 \Rightarrow q = 10\ \text{nC}$$

Hence, we have

$$V_A - V_B = E_1 d = \frac{qd}{\varepsilon_0 A}$$

$$= \frac{(10\times10^{-19}\,\text{C})(10^{-2}\,\text{m})}{(8.85\times10^{-12}\,\text{N}\cdot\text{m}^2/\text{C}^2)(400\times10^{-4}\,\text{m}^2)} = 280\ \text{V}$$

28. (b)

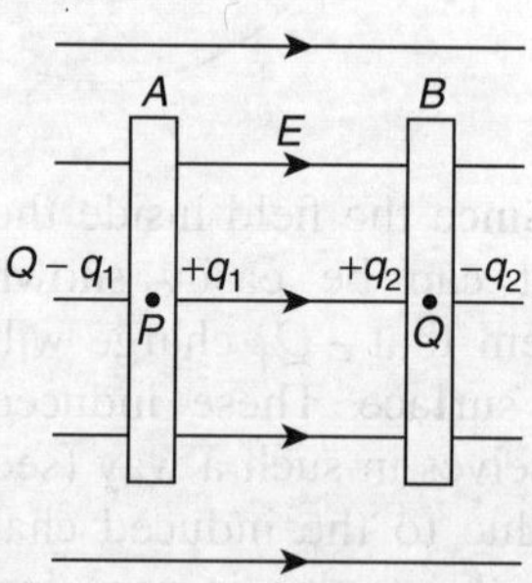

The figure shows the charge distribution on the plates. P and Q are two field points inside plates A and B, respectively. The electric field at these points must be zero. Hence

$$\frac{Q-q_1}{2\varepsilon_o S} + E = \frac{q_1}{2\varepsilon_o S} \Rightarrow q_1 = \varepsilon_0 SE + \frac{Q}{2}$$

and $$\frac{q_2}{\varepsilon_o S} + \frac{Q}{2\varepsilon_0 S} + E = 0 \Rightarrow q_2 = -\varepsilon_0 SE - \frac{Q}{2}$$

Then $Q - q_1 = \dfrac{Q}{2} - \varepsilon_o SE$ and $q_2 = \dfrac{Q}{2} + E_0 SE$

29. (b) The electric field is given by

$$E(r) = \frac{-dV}{dr} = -2ar$$

Applying Gauss's theorem on a spherical surface of radius r, we have

$$\varepsilon_0 \oint \vec{E}\cdot d\vec{A} = Q_{\text{inside}\,A}$$

$$\Rightarrow \quad \varepsilon_0(-2ar)(4\pi r^2) = \int_0^r \rho(x) 4\pi x^2 dx$$

Differentiating both sides with respect to r, we have

$$-8a\,\pi\varepsilon_o\,3r^2 = \rho(r)\,4\,\pi r^2$$

$$\Rightarrow \quad \rho(r) = -6\dot{a}\varepsilon_o \Rightarrow \text{Independent of } r \Rightarrow n = 0.$$

30. (a)

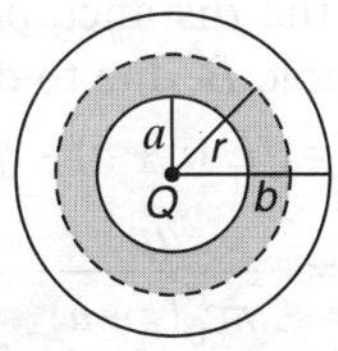

The charge in the shaded region (see figure) is

$$q = \int_a^r \frac{c}{x}(4\pi x^2 dx) = 2\pi c(r^2 - a^2)$$

Field at distance r is

$$E(r) = \frac{K(Q+q)}{r^2} = K\left(\frac{Q + 2\pi c(r^2 - a^2)}{r^2}\right)$$

$$= K(Q - 2\pi a^2 c)\frac{1}{r^2} + K(2\pi c)$$

The above function will be independent of r if

$$Q - 2\pi a^2 c = 0 \Rightarrow c = \frac{Q}{2\pi a^2}$$

31. (b) To find the field at distance r ($r < R$), let us imagine a spherical boundary of radius r (see figure). The charge in the shaded region is

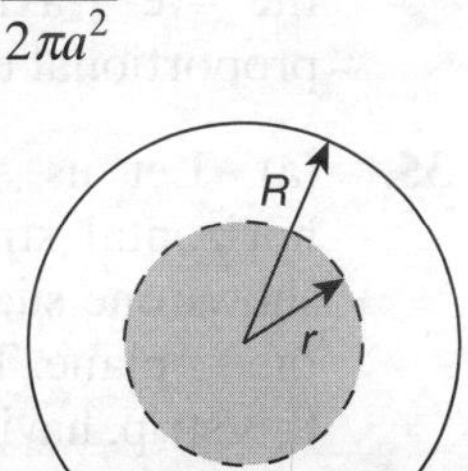

$$q = \int_a^r \rho_0\left(\frac{5}{4} - \frac{x}{R}\right)(4\pi x^2 dx)$$

$$= 4\pi\rho_0 \int_a^r \left(\frac{5x^2}{4} - \frac{x^3}{R}\right)dx = 4\pi\rho_0\left(\frac{5r^3}{12} - \frac{r^4}{4R}\right)$$

Now, field at distance r is

$$E(r) = \frac{1}{4\pi\varepsilon_0}\frac{q}{2} = \frac{1}{4\pi\varepsilon_0}\frac{4\pi\rho_0}{r^2}\left(\frac{5r^3}{12} - \frac{r^4}{4R}\right)$$

$$= \frac{\rho_0 r}{4\varepsilon_0}\left(\frac{5}{3} - \frac{r}{R}\right)$$

32. (d) The work done by the electric force on the charge is transformed into the gravitational potential energy of the rod. To find the work done by the electric field, we can imagine the entire charge λL on the rod to be concentrated as a point charge at its centre (see figure). The point charge experiences a constant electric force $(\lambda L)E_0$ as the rod swings in the vertical plane. The displacement of the point charge along the direction of this force is $L/2$. So the work done by the electric field on the charge is

$$W_{elec} = (\lambda L)E_0 \times \frac{L}{2} = \frac{1}{2}\lambda L^2 E_0$$

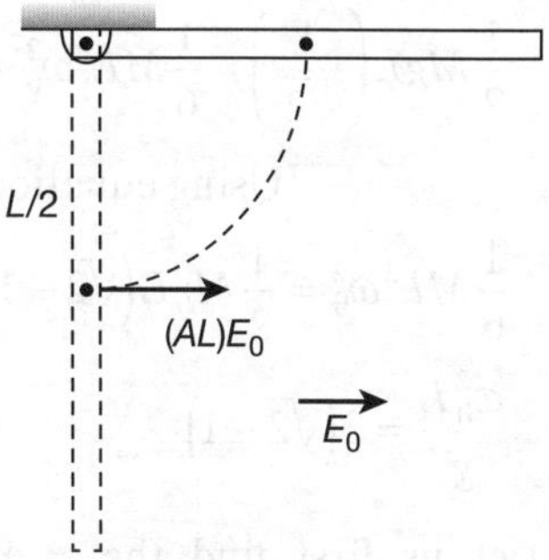

The change in the gravitational potential energy of the rod is

$$U_{gr} = (Mg)\frac{L}{2} = \frac{1}{2}MgL$$

Equating the two, we have

$$\frac{1}{2}\lambda L^2 E_0 = \frac{1}{2}MgL \qquad \text{...(1)}$$

$$\Rightarrow E_0 = \frac{Mg}{\lambda L}$$

The rod experiences a torque due to two forces, the electric force and the gravitational force. Initially the net torque points out of the figure causing an increase in the angular velocity of the rod. At one particular angle, say θ_0 (from the vertical), the torque becomes zero, and thereafter it changes its direction and the angular velocity starts decreasing. To find the maximum angular velocity, we first need to find θ_0. Equating the torques (about the point of suspension), we have

$$(Mg)\left(\frac{L}{2}\sin\theta_0\right) = (\lambda L E_0)\left(\frac{L}{2}\cos\theta_0\right)$$

$$\Rightarrow \quad \tan\theta_0 = 1 \qquad \text{[Using equation (1)]}$$

$$\Rightarrow \quad \theta_0 = \pi/4$$

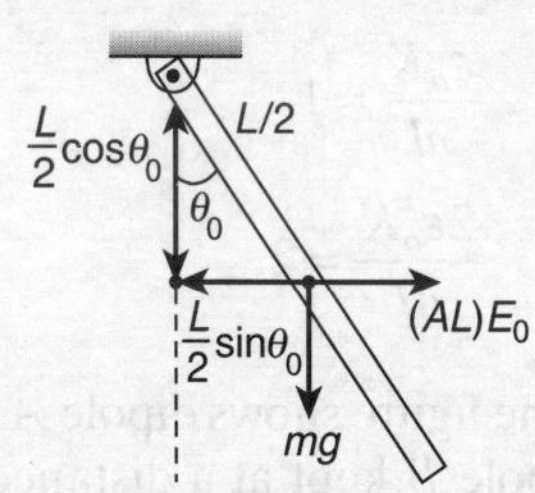

Now, using the Work–Energy Theorem between $\theta = 0$ and $\theta = \theta_0$ positions of the rod, we have

$$W_{elect} = \Delta KE + \Delta PE_{gr}$$

$$\Rightarrow \quad (\lambda L E_0)\left(\frac{L}{2}\sin\theta_0\right) = \frac{1}{2}\left(\frac{ML^2}{3}\right)\omega_0^2 + Mg\left(\frac{L}{2} - \frac{L}{2}\cos\theta_0\right)$$

$$\Rightarrow \quad \frac{1}{2}MgL\left(\frac{1}{\sqrt{2}}\right) = \frac{1}{6}ML^2\omega_0^2 + \frac{1}{2}MgL\left(1 - \frac{1}{\sqrt{2}}\right)$$

[Using equation (1) and $\theta_0 = \pi/4$]

$$\Rightarrow \quad \frac{1}{6}ML^2\omega_0^2 = \frac{1}{2}MgL\left(\sqrt{2} - 1\right)$$

$$\Rightarrow \quad \frac{\omega_0^2 L}{g} = 3\left(\sqrt{2} - 1\right)$$

33. (b) Let us first find the electric potential at points along the y-axis. Consider an arbitrary point $P(0, y)$ on the y-axis (see figure). To find the potential at this point, let us sub-divide the line charge distribution into elements of length dx.

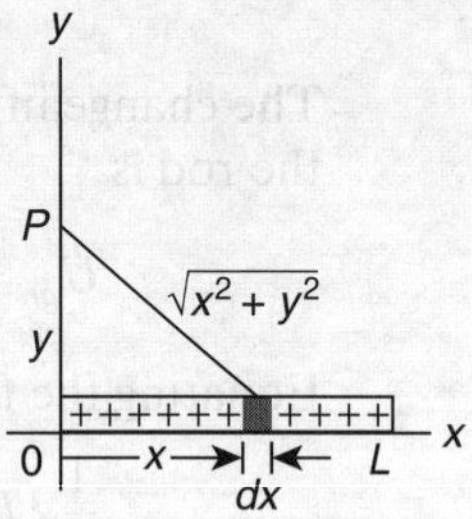

The figure shows one such element at position x. This element contains charge $dq = \lambda(x)\,dx = (4\pi x)\,dx$. The electric potential at P due to this element is $dV = \dfrac{1}{4\pi\varepsilon_o}\dfrac{(4\pi x)dx}{\sqrt{x^2 + y^2}}$ Thus, the potential at P due to the entire line charge is

$$V(y) = \frac{1}{4\pi\varepsilon_0}\int_0^l \frac{4\pi x dx}{\sqrt{x^2 + y^2}}$$

$$= \frac{1}{\varepsilon_0}\left|\sqrt{x^2 + y^2}\right|_0^l = \frac{1}{\varepsilon_0}\left(\sqrt{l^2 + y^2} - y\right)$$

Now, using the energy conservation principle, we have

$$K_1 + qV_1 = K_2 + qV_2$$

$$\Rightarrow \quad K + 0 = 0 + \frac{ql}{\varepsilon_0} \quad [V_\infty = 0, V_O = l/\varepsilon_o]$$

$$\Rightarrow \quad \frac{\varepsilon_o K}{al} = 1$$

Hence, $\dfrac{2\varepsilon_o K}{ql} = 2.$

34. (d) The figure shows dipole A placed at the origin and dipole B kept at a distance r from the origin. If p is the dipole moment of dipole A, the electric field due to dipole A at points along the x-axis is

$$E(x) = \frac{p}{2\pi\varepsilon_0 x^3}$$

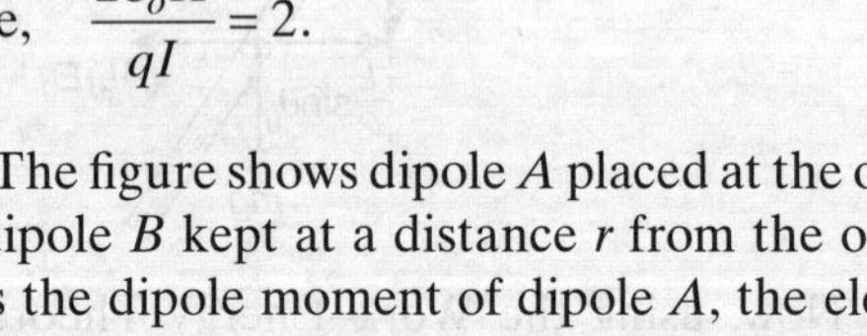

Let $-q$ and $+q$ be the charges on dipole B and $2a$ ($a \ll r$) be the distance between them. Then, the force on dipole B, due to dipole A, is

$$F = qE\,(r + a) - qE\,(r - a)$$

$$= \frac{qp}{2\pi\varepsilon_0(r+a)^3} - \frac{qp}{2\pi\varepsilon_0(r-a)^3}$$

$$= \frac{qp}{2\pi\varepsilon_0}\left[\frac{1}{(r+a)^3} - \frac{1}{(r-a)^3}\right]$$

$$= \frac{qp}{2\pi\varepsilon_0} \times \frac{-(6r^2a + 2a^3)}{(r^2 - a^2)^3}$$

$$= \frac{qp}{2\pi\varepsilon_n} \times \frac{-6r^2 a}{r^6} \quad [a \ll r]$$

$$= \frac{-3aqp}{\pi\varepsilon_0 r^4}$$

The negative sign shows that the force is along the –ve x-axis. The magnitude of the force is proportional to r^{-4}. Hence $n = 4$.

35. (a) Let us subdivide the surface S into thin horizontal strips, each of width dy. The figure shows one such element strip at distance y above the xz plane. The electric field is uniform all along this strip, having magnitude

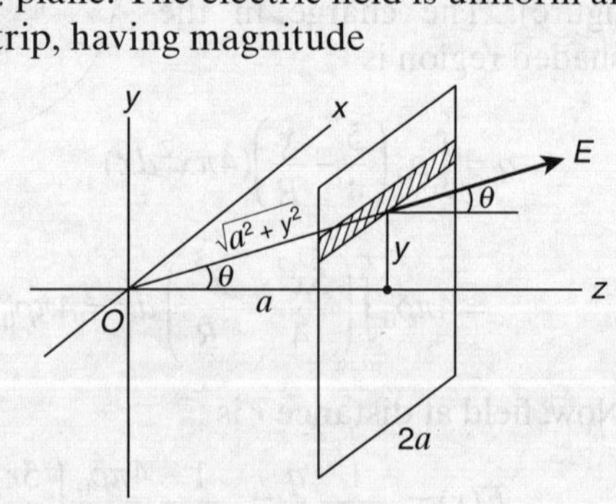

$$E = \frac{\lambda}{2\pi\varepsilon_0\sqrt{a^2 + y^2}}$$

The flux cutting this element strip is

$$d\phi = (E\cos\theta)(2a\,dy)$$

$$= \frac{1}{2\pi\varepsilon_0\sqrt{a^2 + y^2}} \times \frac{a}{\sqrt{a^2 + y^2}} \times 2ady$$

$$= \frac{\lambda a^2}{\pi\varepsilon_0} \times \frac{dy}{a^2 + y^2}$$

Hence, total flux is

$$\phi = \frac{\lambda a^2}{\pi\varepsilon_0}\int_{-a}^{a} \frac{dy}{a^2 + y^2} = \frac{2\lambda a^2}{\pi\varepsilon_0}\left|\frac{1}{a}\tan^{-1}\left(\frac{y}{a}\right)\right|_0^a = \frac{\lambda a}{2\varepsilon_0}$$

Hence $\dfrac{2\varepsilon_0\phi}{\lambda a} = 1$

Alternatively: Imagine a cube of side $2a$, symmetrically wrapped around the x-axis (see figure). The total charge inside this cube is $\lambda(2a)$.

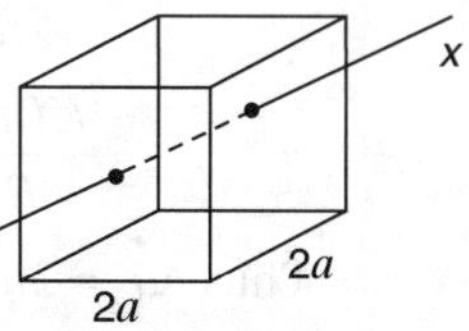

By Gauss's theorem, the total flux cutting the cube is $\dfrac{2a\lambda}{\varepsilon_0}$. This flux is equally distributed on the four surfaces that are parallel to the x-axis (from symmetry), and there is no flux cutting the two surfaces that are perpendicular to the x-axis (field lines are parallel to these surfaces).

Thus, the required flux is $\phi = \dfrac{1}{4}\left(\dfrac{2a\lambda}{\varepsilon_0}\right) = \dfrac{a\lambda}{2\varepsilon_0}$.

Hence $\dfrac{2\varepsilon_0\phi}{\lambda a} = 1$.

36. (d) Consider the closed box shown in the figure. Two surfaces of the box, each having area A, are parallel to the yz plane and located at positions x and $x + dx$. Let E and $E + dE$ be the electric fields at positions x and $x + dx$ directed along the +ve x-axis. The volume of this box is Adx. The charge inside the box is $Q = \rho(x)Adx = (cx^2)(Adx)$, where c is a constant of proportionality. The electric flux cutting the box is $\varphi = (E + dE)A - EA = AdE$.

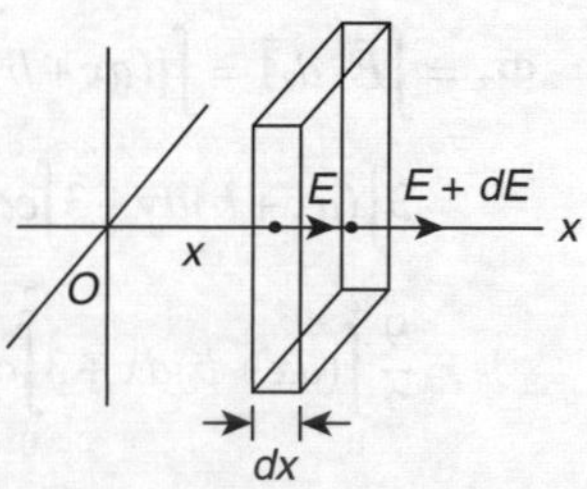

Now using Gauss's theorem, we have

$$\varepsilon_o AdE = (cx^2)(Adx)$$

$$\Rightarrow \quad dE = \frac{c}{\varepsilon_0}x^2dx$$

$$\Rightarrow \quad E = \frac{c}{\varepsilon_0}\int x^2dx = \frac{c}{3\varepsilon_0}x^3 + D$$

Since charge distribution is symmetrical about $x = 0$, the electric field must also be symmetrical about $x = 0$. Hence, the arbitrary constant of integration D must be zero. Hence, $E \propto x^3$.

37. (a) The instantaneous acceleration of the particle is $a(t) = \dfrac{qE_0}{m}\sin(\omega t)$. The instantaneous velocity is given by

$$v(t) = v(0) + \int_0^t a(t)dt$$

$$\Rightarrow \quad v(t) = \frac{qE_0}{m}\int_0^t \sin(\omega t)dt \quad [v(0) = 0, \text{given}]$$

$$\Rightarrow \quad v(t) = \frac{qE_0}{m\omega}[1 - \cos(\omega t)]$$

The greatest speed is

$$v_{\max} = \frac{2qE_0}{m\omega} = \frac{2(1\,\text{C})(1\,\text{N/C})}{(10^{-3}\,\text{kg})(10^3\,\text{rad/s})} = 2\ \text{m/s}$$

38. (c)

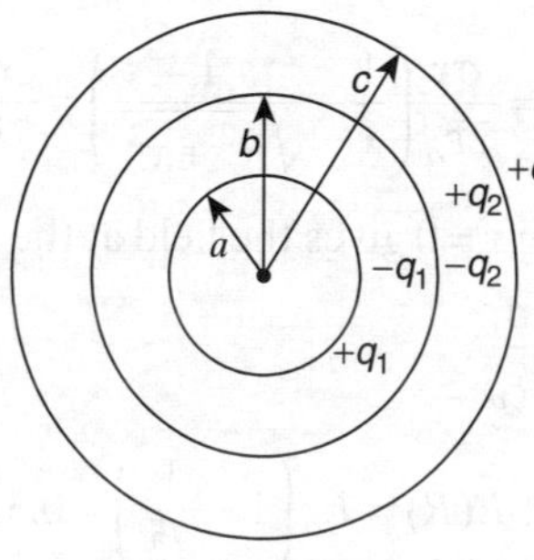

Let charge distribution on the surfaces of the shells be as shown in the figure. Then

$$\frac{q_1}{4\pi a^2} = \sigma \qquad \ldots(1)$$

$$\frac{-q_1 - q_2}{4\pi b^2} = -\sigma \qquad \ldots(2)$$

$$\frac{q_2 + q_3}{4\pi c^2} = \sigma \qquad \ldots(3)$$

$$\Rightarrow \quad q_1 = \sigma(4\pi a^2),\ q_2 = \sigma 4\pi(b^2 - a^2),$$
$$q_3 = \sigma 4\pi(c^2 - b^2 + a^2)$$

Hence, we have

$$V_B = \frac{-Kq_2}{b} + \frac{K(q_3 - q_2)}{c}$$

$$= \sigma 4\pi K\left(\frac{-b^2 - a^2}{b} + \frac{c^2}{c}\right)$$

$$= \frac{\sigma}{\varepsilon_0}\left(c - \frac{b^2 - a^2}{b}\right)$$

39. (d)

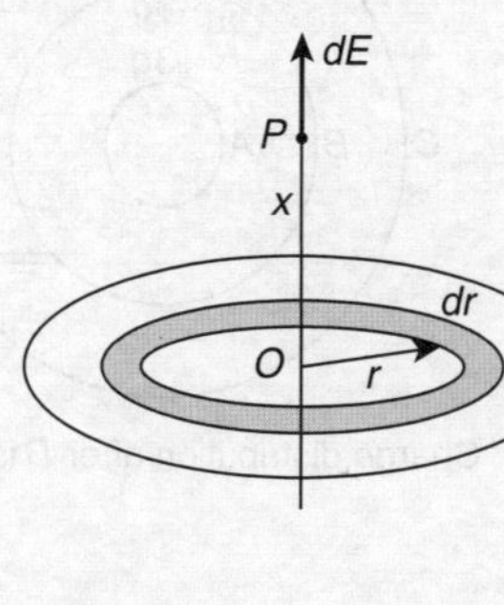

Let us subdivide the disc into thin concentric rings of width dr each. Charge on one such element ring of radius r is $dq = \sigma(2\pi r dr)$.

Field at P due to this element ring is

$$dE = \frac{1}{4\pi\varepsilon_0}\frac{x\,dq}{(x^2+r^2)^{\frac{3}{2}}} = \frac{\sigma x}{2\varepsilon_o}\frac{r\,dr}{(x^2+r^2)^{\frac{3}{2}}}$$

$$\Rightarrow \quad E = \frac{\sigma x}{2\varepsilon_0}\int_0^R \frac{r\,dr}{(x^2+r^2)^{\frac{3}{2}}}$$

$$= \frac{\sigma x}{4\varepsilon_o}\left|\frac{-2}{\sqrt{x^2+r^2}}\right|_0^R \quad [\text{Putting } x^2+r^2=t^2]$$

$$= \frac{\sigma x}{2\varepsilon_o}\left(\frac{1}{x}-\frac{1}{\sqrt{R^2+x^2}}\right) = \frac{\sigma}{2\varepsilon_o}\left(1-\frac{x}{\sqrt{R^2+x^2}}\right)$$

Putting $x = 0$ gives the field at the centre of the disc,

$$E_o = \frac{\sigma}{2\varepsilon_o}.$$

Hence, $E(R) = E_o\left(1-\dfrac{1}{\sqrt{2}}\right) = 0.3E_o$

40. (c) The figure shows the charge distribution on the conductors, before earthing.

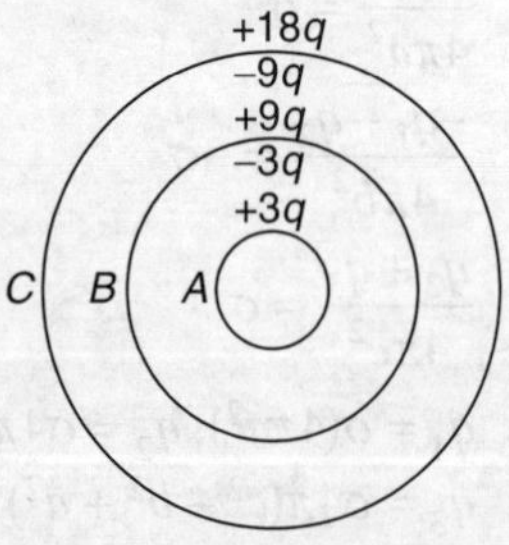

Charge distribution before earthing

After B is earthed, $V_B = 0$. Hence

$$\frac{K(q_1)}{\partial R} + \frac{K(9q)}{3R} = 0 \Rightarrow q_1 = -6q$$

Thus, $\Delta q_1 = 9q - q_1 = 15q$

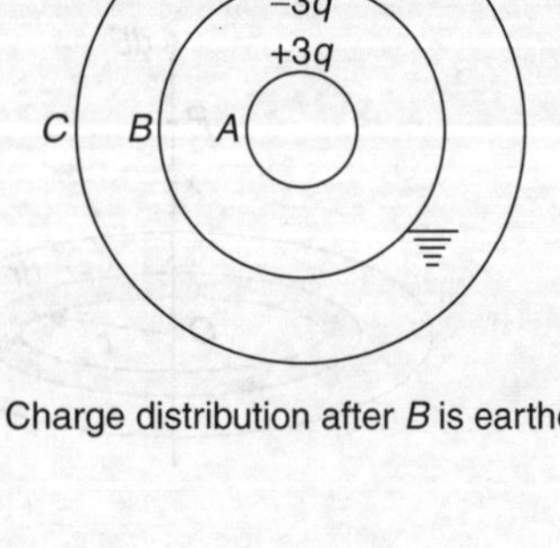

Charge distribution after B is earthed

After A is also earthed, $V_B = 0 = V_A$. Hence

$$\frac{K(q_3)}{2R} + \frac{K(9q)}{3R} = 0 \Rightarrow q_3 = -6q$$

$$\frac{K(q_2)}{R} + \frac{K(q_3-q_2)}{2R} + \frac{K(9q)}{3R} = 0 \Rightarrow q_2 = 0$$

Thus $\Delta q_2 = 3q - q_2 = 3q$

Hence $\dfrac{|\Delta q_1|}{|\Delta q_2|} = 5$

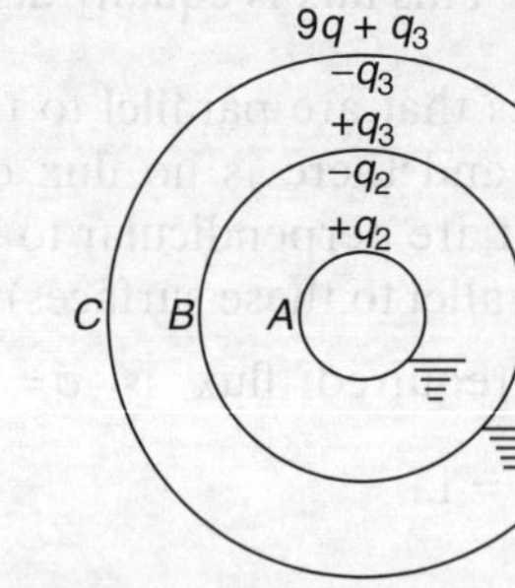

Charge distribution after A is also earthed

41. (d), (c), (a) Flux cutting surface $OPQR$ is

$$f = \int \vec{E}\cdot d\vec{A} = (bi)\cdot(-9i) = -9b$$

Flux cutting surface $ORST$ is

$$\Phi_2 = \int \vec{E}\cdot d\vec{A} = (cj)\cdot(-6j) = -6c$$

Flux cutting surface $PQST$ is

$$\Phi_3 = \int \vec{E}\cdot d\vec{A} = \int\{(ax+b)i+c]\}\cdot\{3dyi+3dxj\}$$

$$= 3\int(ax+b)dy + 3\int c\,dx$$

$$= \frac{9}{2}\int_0^2(ax+b)dx + 3\int_0^2 c\,dx\left[\text{since } \frac{dy}{dx} = \frac{3}{2}\right]$$

$$= \frac{9}{2}(2a+2b) + 6c = 9a + 9b + 6c$$

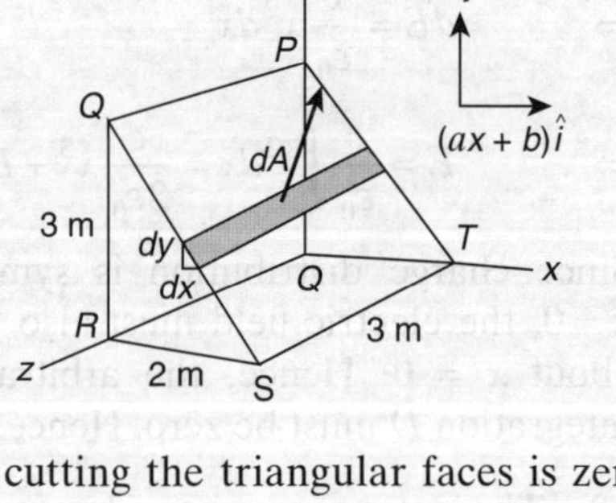

The flux cutting the triangular faces is zero. The total flux is $\Phi = 9a$. Hence, by Gauss's theorem, total charge inside the volume is $Q = \varepsilon_0(9a)$. Hence, $k = 9a = 0.9$ and its value is independent of the constants b and c.

CHAPTER

16 Current Electricity

- Current is the amount of charge flowing through a specified area, per unit time. Current is conventionally described as flow of positive charge, even though the actual charge carriers are negative or both. If the charge carriers in a material have concentration n, charge of magnitude q and drift velocity v, the current through area A is
$$I = \frac{dQ}{dt} = nqvA$$
Current density j is current per unit area:
$$j = I / A = nqv$$
- Electric field E is required to establish a current density j inside the conductor. In some materials, especially metals, j is directly proportional to E. Such materials are said to obey Ohm's law. The resistivity ρ of a material is the ratio of the magnitude of the electric field and the current density
$$\rho = E / j$$
The greater the resistivity, the greater the field needed to establish a given current density. The reciprocal of resistivity is conductivity.
The resistivity of a metal nearly always increases with temperature. Over a small temperature range (up to 100°C or so), resistivity can be represented by the equation
$$\rho = \rho_0 (1 + \alpha T),$$
where ρ_0 is the resistivity at 0°C and α is called the temperature coefficient of resistivity.
- For conductors that obey Ohm's law, we have $E = \rho j$. If the conductor is of length L and cross-section area A, the above relation can be expressed in terms of potential difference V across the conductor and the current I flowing inside the conductor as
$$V = IR, \text{ where } R = \frac{\rho L}{A}$$
This shows that I is proportional to V. The quantity R, which is the ratio of V to I, is called the resistance of the conductor. This equation is also known as the Ohm's law.
- Kirchhoff's junction rule states that the algebraic sum of the currents into any junction is zero. This rule is based on conservation of charge.
- Kirchhoff's loop rule states that the algebraic sum of potential differences around any loop is zero. This rule is based on the conservative nature of electrostatic fields.
- When several resistances $R_1, R_2, R_3, \ldots$ are connected in series, the equivalent resistance is given by
$$R_{eq} = R_1 + R_2 + R_3 + \ldots \text{ (resistors in series)}$$
The same current flows through all the resistors in a series connection. When several resistors are connected in parallel, the equivalent resistance is given by
$$\frac{1}{R_{eq}} = \frac{1}{R_1} + \frac{1}{R_2} + \frac{1}{R_3} + \ldots \text{ (resistors in parallel)}$$
All resistors connected in parallel have the same potential difference across them.
- A complete circuit is a conducting loop that provides a continuous current carrying path. A complete circuit carrying a current must contain a source of electromotive force (emf) ξ. An ideal source of emf maintains a constant potential difference, independent of current. But every real source has an internal resistance r. The terminal potential difference then depends on the current I:
$$V_{ter} = \xi - Ir$$

- A circuit element with potential difference V and current I puts energy into the circuit if the direction of current is from lower to higher potential, and takes energy out of the circuit if the direction of current is from higher to lower potential. The power P (rate of energy transfer) is given by
$$P = VI$$
A resistor R always takes electrical energy out of a circuit, converting it to thermal energy at a rate given by
$$P = VI = I^2R = V^2/R$$
- Electric appliances are designed to operate at a particular voltage V, and when connected to that voltage, they consume electrical energy at a specified rate P. If several electrical appliances with operating voltage V and power ratings $P_1, P_2, P_3,\ldots$ are joined in series and connected to a voltage source of emf V, the total power consumption P is given by
$$\frac{1}{P} = \frac{1}{P_1} + \frac{1}{P_2} + \frac{1}{P_3} + \ldots \text{ (appliances in series)}$$
and when they are all joined in parallel and connected to a voltage source of emf V, the total power consumption P is given by
$$P = P_1 + P_2 + P_3 + \ldots \text{ (appliances in parallel)}$$
- In a D'Arsonval galvanometer, the deflection is proportional to the current. It is designed to measure feeble currents. For a larger current range, a shunt resistance is added in parallel, so some of the current bypasses the meter coil. Such an instrument is called an ammeter. If a resistor is added in series, the galvanometer can also be calibrated to read potential difference. The instrument is then called a voltmeter. A good ammeter has very low resistance and a good voltmeter has very high resistance.

EXERCISES

1. Each resistor in the network has a resistance R. Find the resistance between the points A and B and match with the column on the right:

(a) 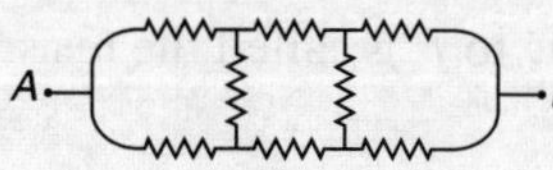 (p) $3R$

(b) 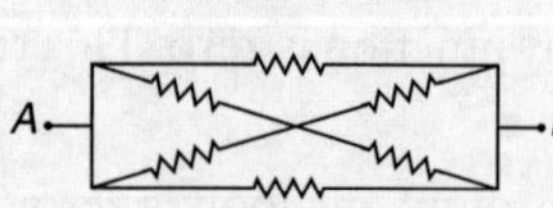 (q) $\frac{3}{2}R$

(c) 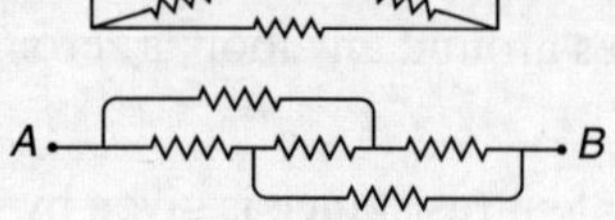 (r) R

(d) 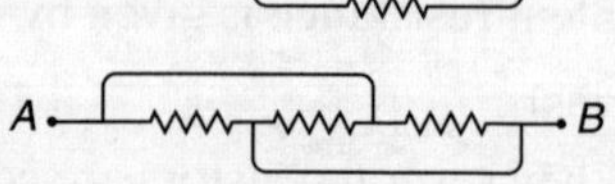 (s) $\frac{1}{3}R$

2. In an aluminium bar of square cross-section, a square hole is drilled and filled with iron, as shown in the figure. The electrical resistivity of Al and Fe are 2.7×10^{-8} Ωm and 1.0×10^{-7} Ωm, respectively.

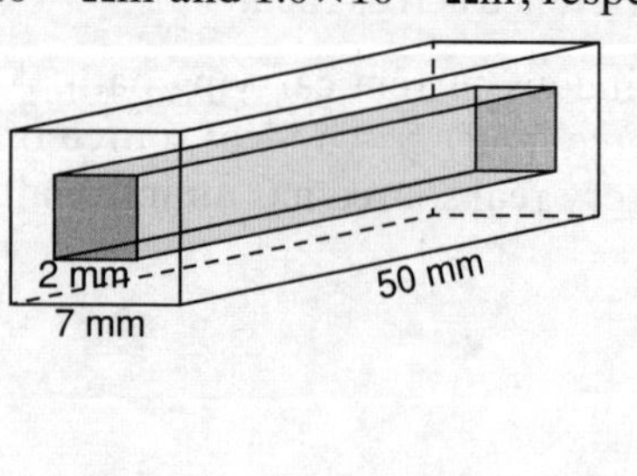

The electrical resistance of the composite bar is:

(a) $\frac{2475}{64}\ \mu\Omega$ (b) $\frac{1875}{64}\ \mu\Omega$

(c) $\frac{1875}{49}\ \mu\Omega$ (d) $\frac{2475}{132}\ \mu\Omega$

3. The figure shows a conductor of length l having a circular cross-section. The radius of the cross-section varies linearly from a to b $(b > a)$.

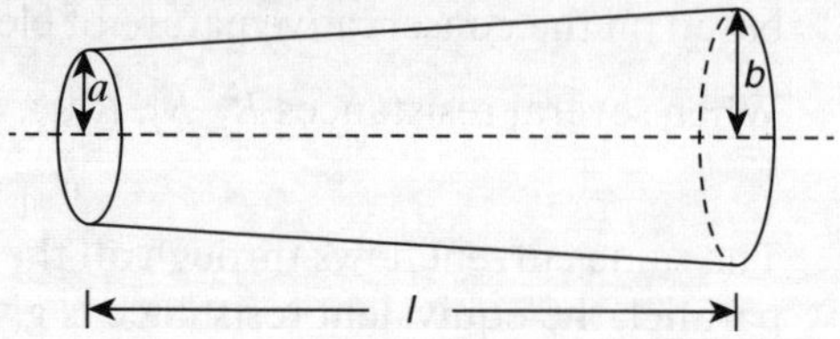

If the resistivity of the conductor is ρ, its electrical resistance is:

(a) $\frac{\rho l}{\pi(b-a)^2}$ (b) $\frac{\rho l}{\pi(a+b)^2}$

(c) $\frac{\rho l}{\pi(b^2-a^2)}$ (d) $\frac{\rho l}{\pi ab}$

4. Of the following circuits, the one having the greatest resistance across the terminals A and B is:

(a)
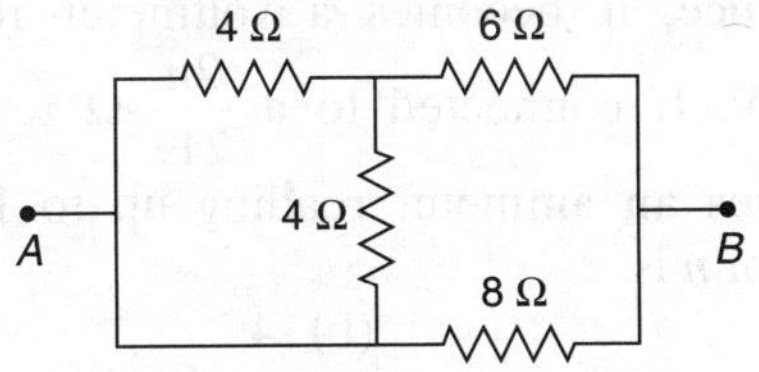

(b)
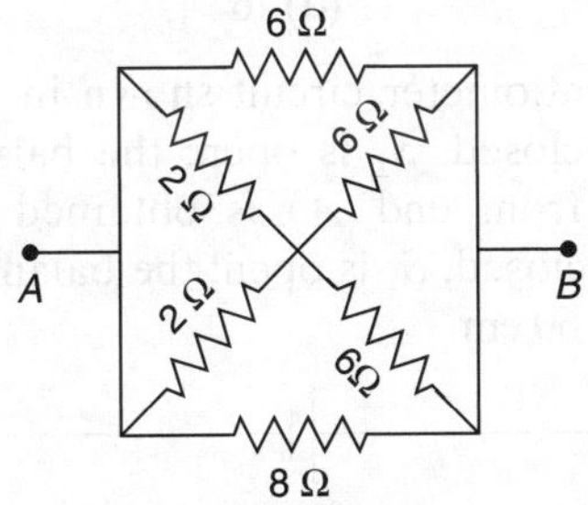

(c)
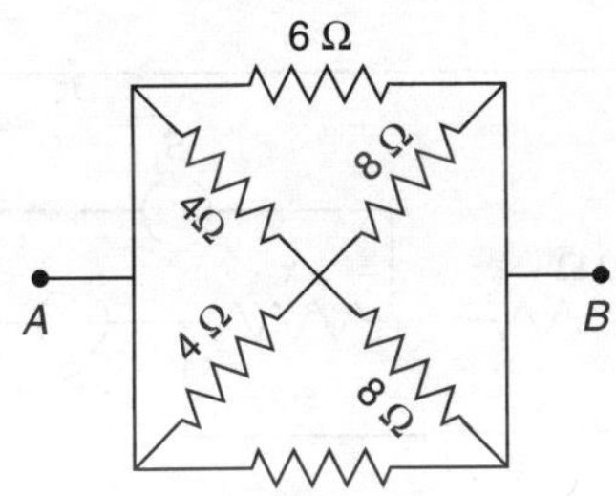

(d)
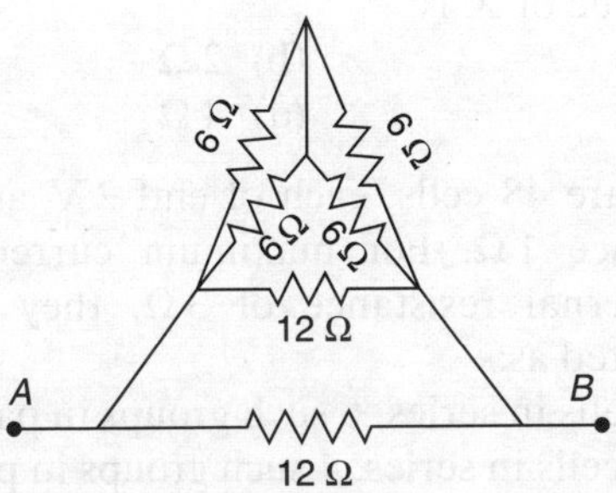

5. In the circuit shown in the figure, current in R_3 is zero when:

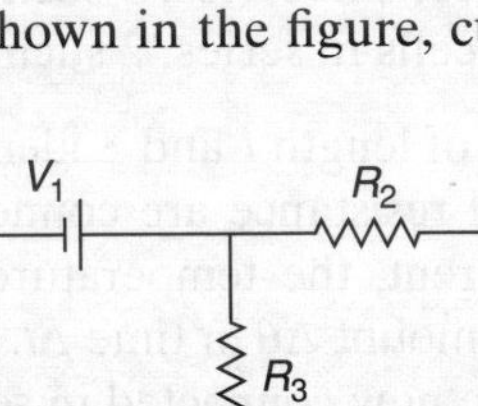

(a) $V_1 = V_2, R_1 = R_3 = R_2$
(b) $V_1 = 2V_2, 2R_1 = 2R_3 = R_2$
(c) $2V_1 = 3V_2, R_1 = R_3 = 1.5R_2$
(d) $2V_1 = V_2, R_1 = R_3 = 2R_2$

6. A uniform copper wire of length 1 m and area of cross-section $5\times10^{-7}\ m^2$ carries a current of 1 A. Assuming that there are 8×10^{28} free electrons / m^3 in copper, the time taken by an electron to drift from one end of the wire to the other is (take $e = 1.6\times10^{-19}$ C):

(a) 0.8×10^3 s (b) 1.6×10^3 s
(c) 3.2×10^3s (d) 6.4×10^3 s

7. A voltmeter having a resistance of 1800 Ω is employed to measure the potential difference across a 200-Ω resistor, which is connected to the terminals of a cell having an electromotive force (emf) of 50 V and internal resistance of 20 Ω. The percentage decrease in the potential difference across the 200-Ω resistor as a result of connecting the voltmeter is:

(a) 1% (b) 2%
(c) 3% (d) 4%

8. In the circuit shown in the figure, the reading of the ammeter is:

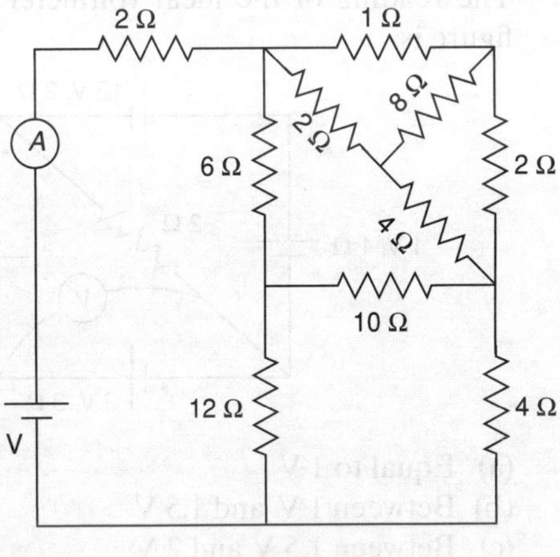

(a) 0.25 A (b) 0.5 A
(c) 0.75 A (d) 1.0 A

9. In the circuit shown in the figure, the reading of the ammeter is:

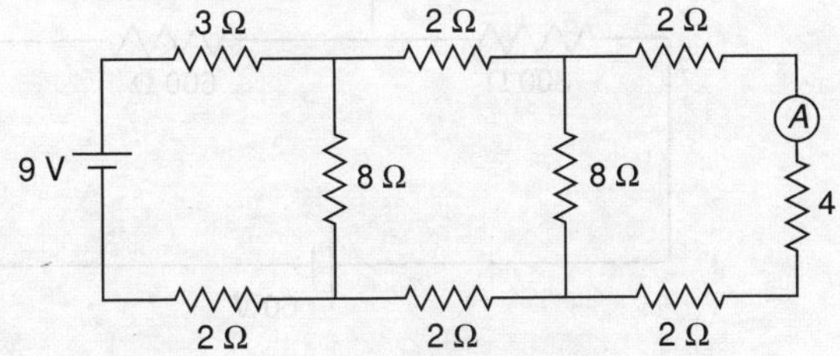

(a) 1.00 A (b) 0.75 A
(c) 0.50 A (d) 0.25 A

10. In the circuit shown in the figure, the reading of the ammeter is:

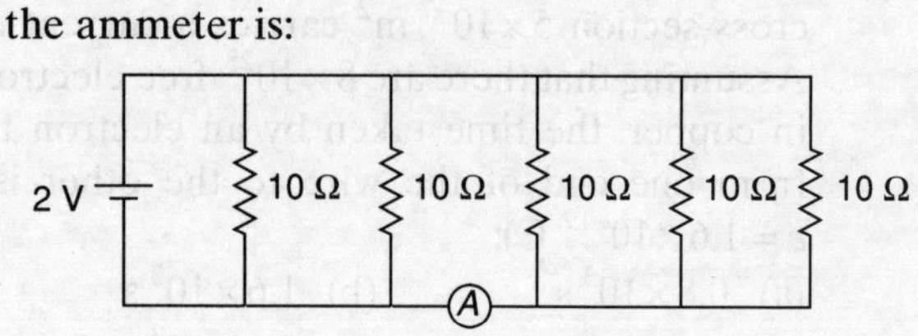

(a) 1/5 A (b) 2/5 A
(c) 3/5 A (d) 4/5 A

11. In the circuit shown in the figure, the potential difference between the points X and Y equals:

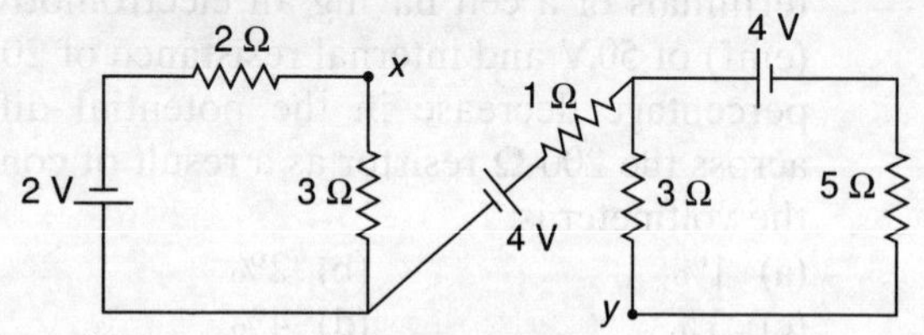

(a) 5.2 V (b) 4.8 V
(c) 4.2 V (d) 3.7 V

12. The reading of the ideal voltmeter shown in the figure is:

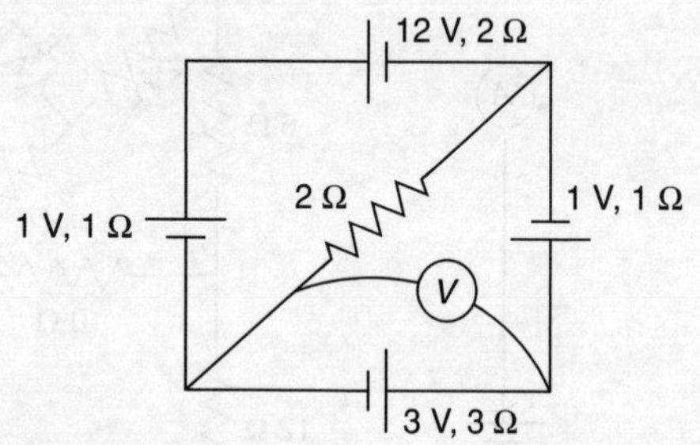

(a) Equal to 1 V
(b) Between 1 V and 1.5 V
(c) Between 1.5 V and 2 V
(d) More than 2 V

13. The voltmeter shown in the figure reads 36 V.

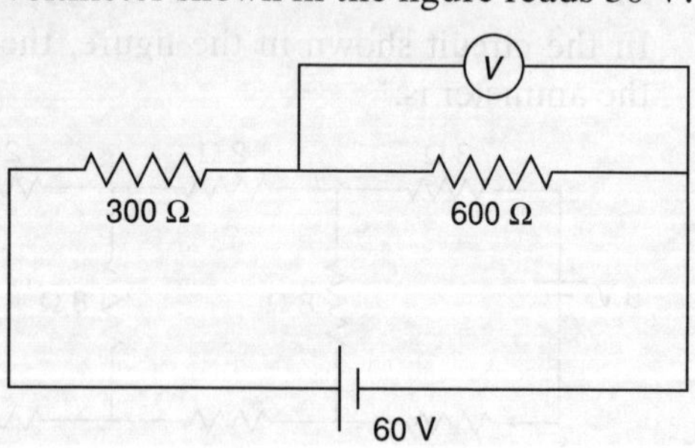

Its internal resistance is:
(a) 1200 Ω (b) 1400 Ω
(c) 1600 Ω (d) 1800 Ω

14. A galvanometer gives full-scale deflection with 6-mA current. By connecting it to a 4990-Ω resistance, it becomes a voltmeter reading up to 30 V. If connected to a $\frac{2n}{249}$-Ω resistance, it becomes an ammeter reading up to 15 A. The value of n is:
(a) 3 (b) 4
(c) 5 (d) 6

15. In the potentiometer circuit shown in the figure, when S_1 is closed, S_2 is open; the balance point (measured from end A) is obtained at 50 cm. When S_2 is closed, S_1 is open; the balance point is obtained at 60 cm.

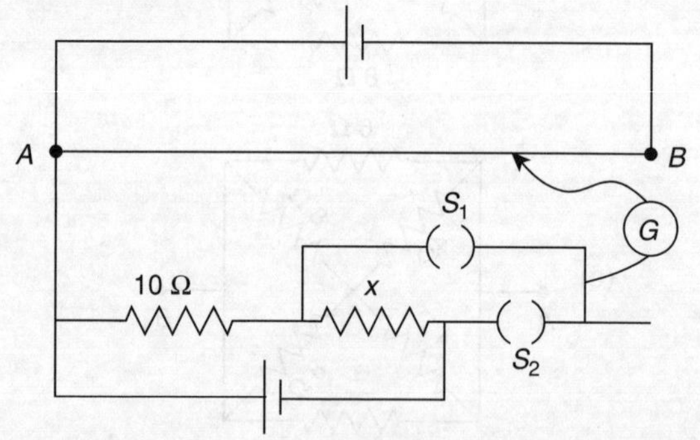

The value of X is:
(a) 1 Ω (b) 2 Ω
(c) 3 Ω (d) 4 Ω

16. There are 48 cells, each of emf 2 V and internal resistance 1 Ω. For maximum current through an external resistance of 3 Ω, they should be connected as:
(a) 8 cells in series, 6 such groups in parallel
(b) 12 cells in series, 4 such groups in parallel
(c) 16 cells in series, 3 such groups in parallel
(d) 24 cells in series, 2 such groups in parallel

17. A wire of length l and 3 identical cells of negligible internal resistance are connected in series. Due to the current, the temperature of the wire is raised by an amount $\Delta\theta$ in time Δt. A number n of similar cells are now connected in series with a wire of the same material and cross-section, but length $2l$. If the temperature of the wire is raised by the same amount $\Delta\theta$ in the same time Δt, then the value of n is:
(a) 4 (b) 5
(c) 6 (d) 7

18. A 100-W, 250-V bulb B_1 and two 60-W, 250-V bulbs B_2 and B_3 are connected to a 250-V source, as shown in the figure.

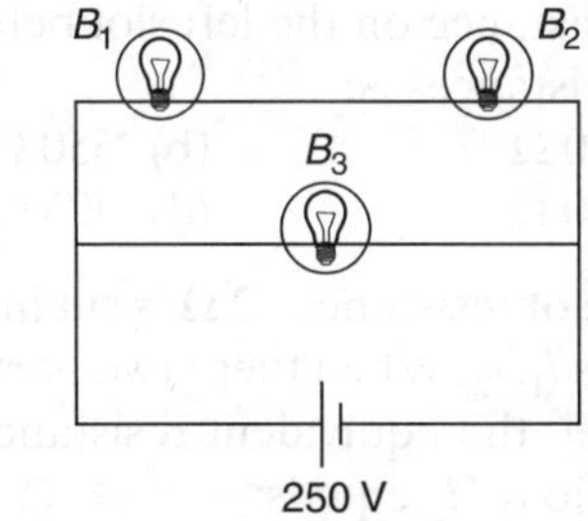

If W_1, W_2 and W_3 are the output powers of the bulbs B_1, B_2 and B_3, respectively, then:
(a) $W_1 > W_2 = W_3$ (b) $W_1 > W_2 > W_3$
(c) $W_1 < W_2 = W_3$ (d) $W_1 < W_2 < W_3$

19. Two bulbs A and B of ratings 40 W, 200 V and 100 W, 200 V are connected in series to a 400-V supply. Then:
(a) Both bulbs will fuse
(b) Bulb A will fuse but bulb B will not
(c) Bulb B will fuse but bulb A will not
(d) None of the bulbs will fuse

20. The power rating of a heater is 100 W, 100 V. It is connected as shown in the figure.

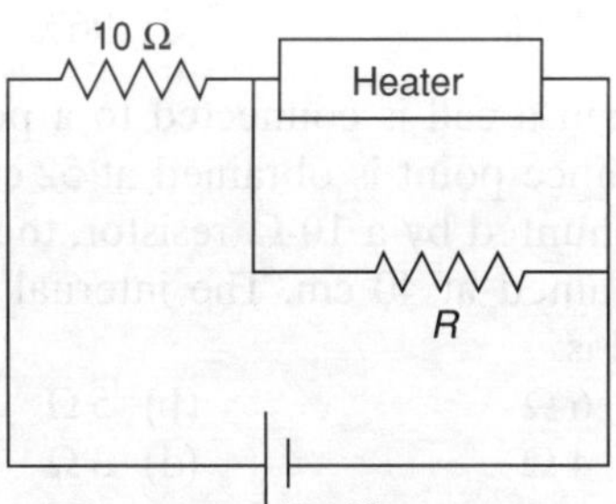

The value of R so that the heater consumes 62.5 W is nearly:
(a) 15 Ω (b) 25 Ω
(c) 35 Ω (d) 60 Ω

21. An electric heater made of a wire of length l and diameter d takes 4 s to boil a certain amount of water over a certain temperature. If two wires of the same material of length l and diameter $d/2$ each are joined in parallel, the electric heater thus formed will boil the same amount of water over the same temperature in time:
(a) 2 s (b) 4 s
(c) 8 s (d) 16 s

22. Consider two identical galvanometers with internal resistance r and two identical resistors of resistance R. If $r < R/2$, then the correct statements from the following are:
(a) For maximum voltage range, all components must be connected in series
(b) For maximum voltage range, the two galvanometers must be connected in parallel, and then in series with the two resistors
(c) For maximum current range, all components must be connected in parallel
(d) For maximum current range, the two galvanometers must be connected in series, and then in parallel with the two resistors

23. A 25-kW DC generator produces a potential difference of 250 V. If the resistance of the transmission line is 1 Ω, the percentage of original power lost during transmission is:
(a) 10% (b) 20%
(c) 30% (d) 40%

24. A heater boils a certain quantity of water in time t_1. Another heater boils the same quantity of water in time t_2. If the two heaters are connected in parallel across the same source, the combination will boil the same quantity of water in time:
(a) $\frac{t_1 + t_2}{2}$ (b) $\frac{t_1 t_2}{t_1 + t_2}$
(c) $t_1 + t_2$ (d) $\sqrt{t_1 t_2}$

25. Two identical cells, each of emf 1 V and internal resistance 1 Ω, are connected to an external load once in series and once in parallel. The power dissipated across the load is H_1 and H_2, respectively. If $H_1 = 2.25 H_2$, the load resistance is:
(a) 1 Ω (b) 2 Ω
(c) 3 Ω (d) 4 Ω

26. In the circuit shown in the figure, the potential difference between points A and B is:

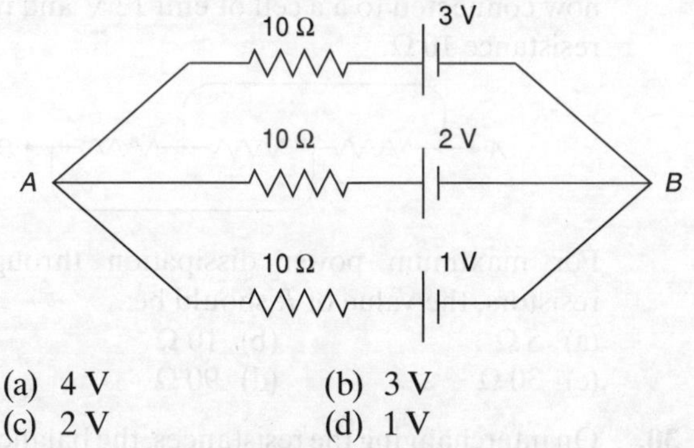

(a) 4 V (b) 3 V
(c) 2 V (d) 1 V

27. In the circuit shown in the figure, the ideal ammeters A_1 and A_2 draw currents 3 A and 4 A, respectively. Even after the left and the middle resistors are interchanged, the readings of the ammeter do not change.

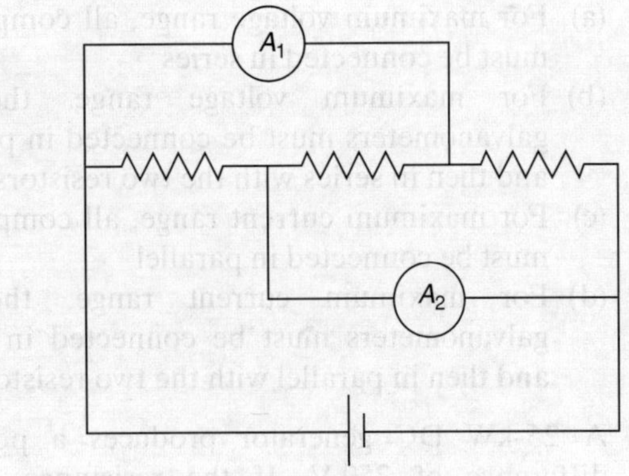

Then the current flow through the cell is:
(a) 2 A (b) 3 A
(c) 4 A (d) 5 A

28. A storage battery whose emf is 200 V is connected across a 220-V DC supply through a 1 Ω resistor (see figure). A resistor of resistance R is also connected across the terminals of the storage battery.

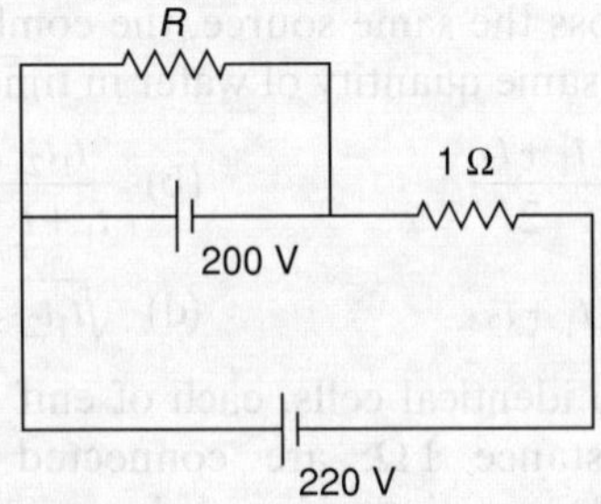

The minimum value of R so that the storage battery starts getting charged is:
(a) 7 Ω (b) 9 Ω
(c) 10 Ω (d) 11 Ω

29. Three resistors, each of resistance R, are connected as shown in the figure. The network is now connected to a a cell of emf 12 V and internal resistance 10 Ω.

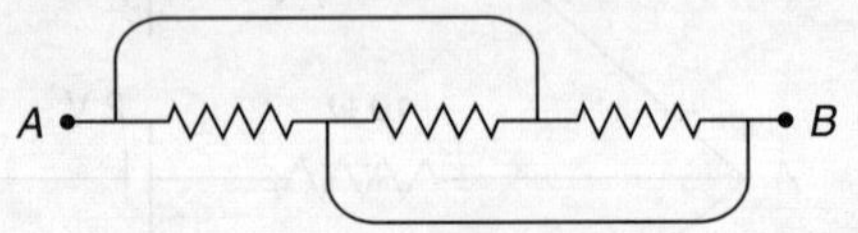

For maximum power dissipation through the resistors, the value of R should be:
(a) 5 Ω (b) 10 Ω
(c) 30 Ω (d) 90 Ω

30. On interchanging the resistances, the balance point of a meter-bridge shifts to the left by 10 cm. If the resistance of their series combination is 1 kΩ, then the resistance on the left slot before interchanging the resistances is:
(a) 990 Ω (b) 550 Ω
(c) 810 Ω (d) 425 Ω

31. A wire of resistance 12 Ω is cut into two portions of lengths l_1, l_2. When these two portions are joined in parallel, the equivalent resistance is $8/3$ Ω. Then the ratio l_1/l_2 equals:
(a) 5 (b) 4
(c) 3 (d) 2

32. Consider the network shown in the figure.

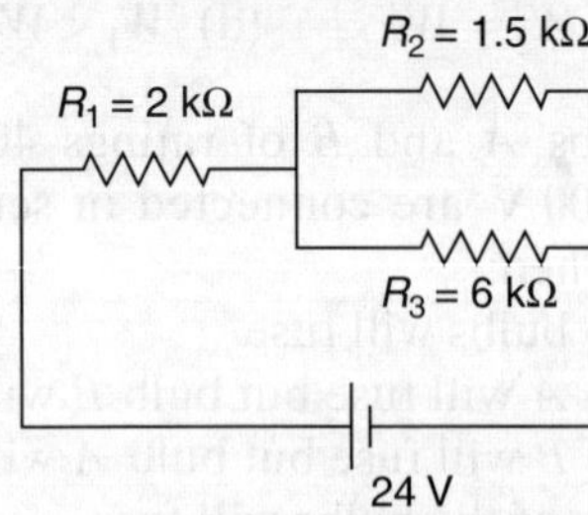

If the resistances R_1 and R_3 are interchanged, the power consumption of R_1 decreases by:
(a) 4% (b) 10%
(c) 40% (d) 96%

33. When a cell is connected to a potentiometer, the balance point is obtained at 52 cm. When the cell is shunted by a 10-Ω resistor, the balance point is obtained at 40 cm. The internal resistance of the cell is:
(a) 6 Ω (b) 5 Ω
(c) 4 Ω (d) 3 Ω

34. In the circuit shown in the figure, the potentials of points P and Q are:

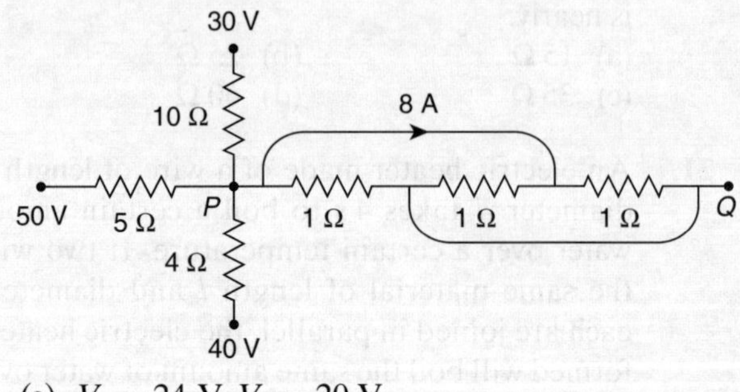

(a) $V_P = 24$ V, $V_Q = 20$ V
(b) $V_P = 20$ V, $V_Q = 16$ V
(c) $V_P = 30$ V, $V_Q = 22$ V
(d) $V_P = 22$ V, $V_Q = 14$ V

35. In the circuit shown in the figure, all resistors have the same resistance $R = 5\ \Omega$, and the emf of the cell is $\xi = 20$ V.

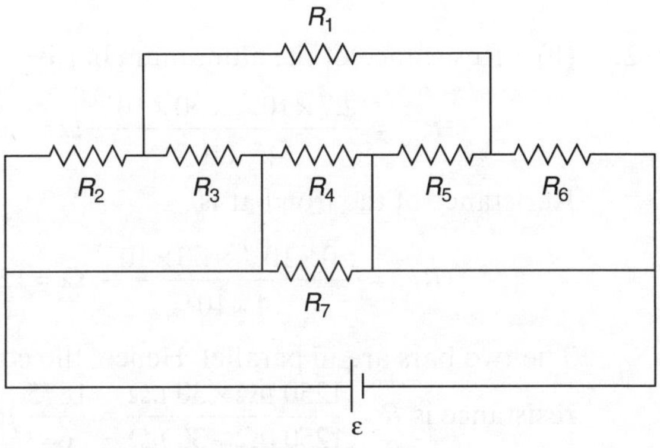

The correct options from the following are:
(a) PD across $R_1 = 10$ V
(b) Current along $R_3 = 2$ A
(c) Current along $R_4 = 4$ A
(d) Power consumption = 80 W

36. In the circuit shown in the figure, the potential difference between points A and B is:

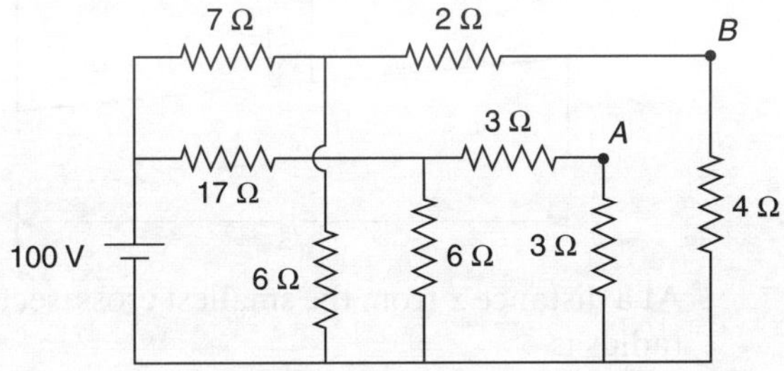

(a) 2.5 V
(b) 12.5 V
(c) 22.5 V
(d) 32.5 V

37. Model a torch battery of length l to be made up of a cylindrical bar of radius α and a co-axial cylindrical shell of radius b, filled in between with an electrolyte of resistivity ρ (see figure). If the battery is connected to a load of resistance R, the maximum joule heating in the load will take place for:

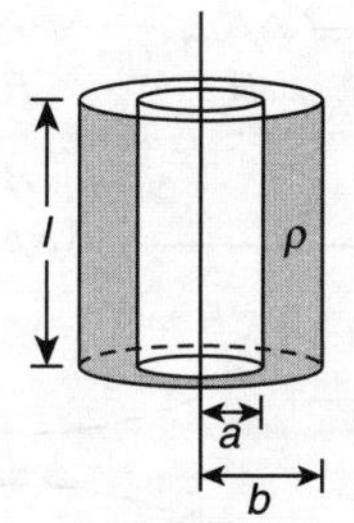

(a) $R = \dfrac{2\rho}{\pi l}\ln\left(\dfrac{b}{a}\right)$
(b) $R = \dfrac{\rho}{2\pi l}\ln\left(\dfrac{b}{a}\right)$
(c) $R = \dfrac{3\rho}{4\pi l}\ln\left(\dfrac{b}{a}\right)$
(d) $R = \dfrac{3\rho}{2\pi l}\ln\left(\dfrac{b}{a}\right)$

ANSWER KEYS

1. (a)–(q), (b)–(s), (c)–(r), (d)–(s)		**2.** (b)	**3.** (d)	**4.** (a)	**5.** (a),(c)	**6.** (d)	**7.** (a)	**8.** (d)
9. (d)	**10.** (c)	**11.** (d)	**12.** (c)	**13.** (d)	**14.** (c)	**15.** (b)	**16.** (b)	**17.** (c)	**18.** (d)
19. (b)	**20.** (d)	**21.** (c)	**22.** (b),(c)	**23.** (d)	**24.** (b)	**25.** (d)	**26.** (c)	**27.** (d)	**28.** (d)
29. (c)	**30.** (b)	**31.** (d)	**32.** (d)	**33.** (d)	**34.** (b)	**35.** (a),(c)	**36.** (d)	**37.** (b)	

SOLUTIONS

1. (a)–(q), (b)–(s), (c)–(r), (d)–(s)

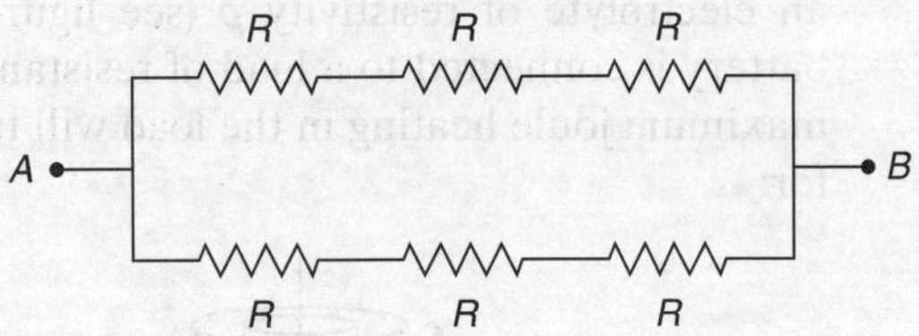

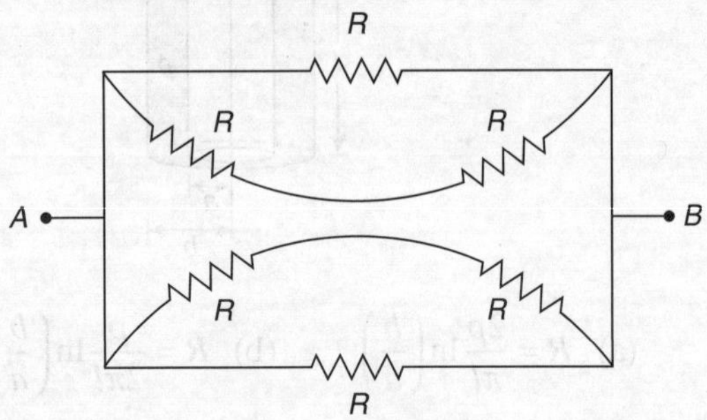

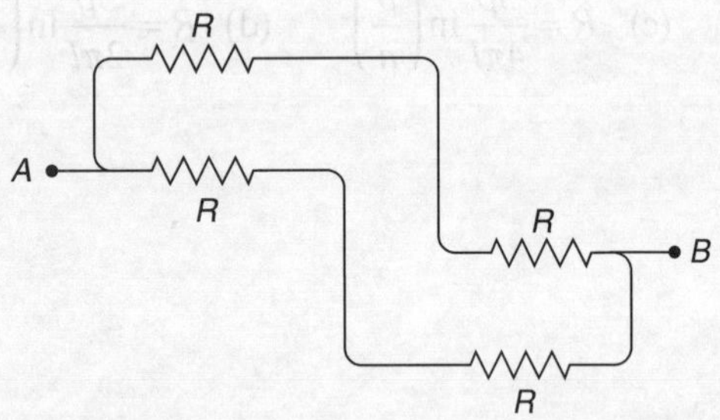

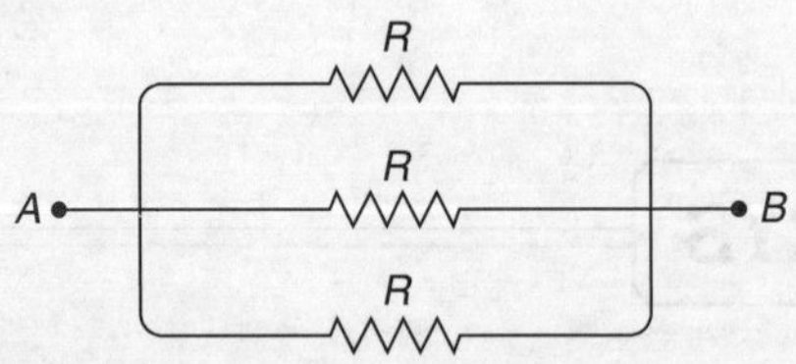

In option (a), the arrangement is a Wheatstone's network. No current flows through the bridges since the ratio of the resistances in the upper and lower branches is equal. The circuit reduces to two parallel branches. Hence $R_{AB} = 3R/2$.

In option (b), from symmetry, we can see that the circuit reduces to four parallel branches. Hence $R_{AB} = R/3$.

In option (c), the arrangement is a Wheatstone's network. No current flows through the bridge since the ratio of the resistances in the upper and lower branches is equal. The circuit reduces to two parallel branches. Hence $R_{AB} = R$.

In option (d), the circuit is a standard parallel connection. Hence $R_{AB} = R/3$.

2. (b) Resistance of the aluminium bar is

$$R_{Al} = \frac{2.7\times10^{-8}\times50\times10^{-3}}{45\times10^{-6}}\Omega = 30\ \mu\Omega$$

Resistance of the iron bar is

$$R_{Fe} = \frac{1.0\times10^{-7}\times50\times10^{-3}}{4\times10^{6}}\Omega = 1250\ \mu\Omega$$

The two bars are in parallel. Hence, the combined resistance is $R = \frac{1250\ \mu\Omega\times30\ \mu\Omega}{1250\ \mu\Omega+30\ \mu\Omega} = \frac{1875}{64}\ \mu\Omega$.

3. (d) Let us subdivide the conductor into thin element discs, each of width dx (see figure).

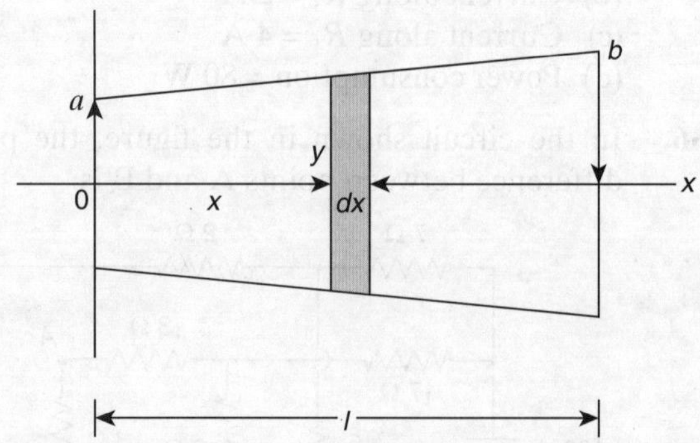

At a distance x from the smallest cross-section, the radius is

$$y = a + mx, \text{ where } m = \frac{b-a}{1}$$

(Slope of the slant surface)

Electrical resistance of this element disc is

$$dR = \frac{\rho dx}{\pi y^2} = \frac{\rho dx}{\pi(a+mx)^2}$$

Since all the elements are in series, the total electrical resistance is

$$R = \frac{\rho}{\pi}\int_0^l \frac{dx}{(a+mx)^2} = \frac{\rho}{\pi}\left|\frac{-1}{m(a+mx)}\right|_0^l$$

$$= \frac{\rho}{m\pi}\left(\frac{1}{a} - \frac{1}{a+ml}\right)$$

Now, putting the value of m, we have

$$R = \frac{\rho l}{\pi(b-a)}\left(\frac{1}{a} - \frac{1}{b}\right) = \frac{\rho l}{\pi ab}$$

4. (a)
The circuit in (a) reduces to

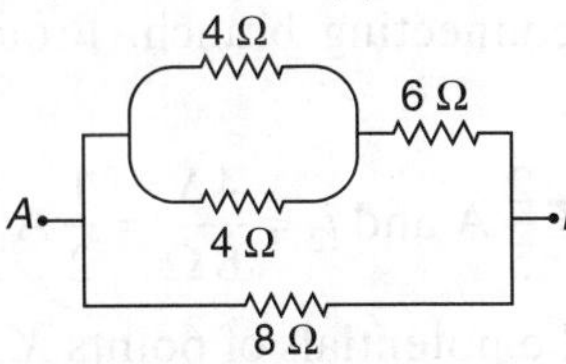

$\Rightarrow R_{AB} = 4\ \Omega$

The circuit in (b) reduces to

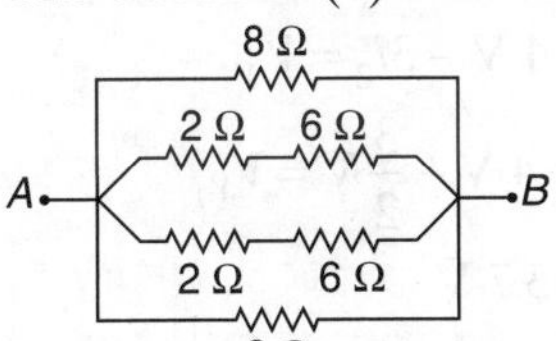

$\Rightarrow R_{AB} = 2\ \Omega$

The circuit in (c) reduces to

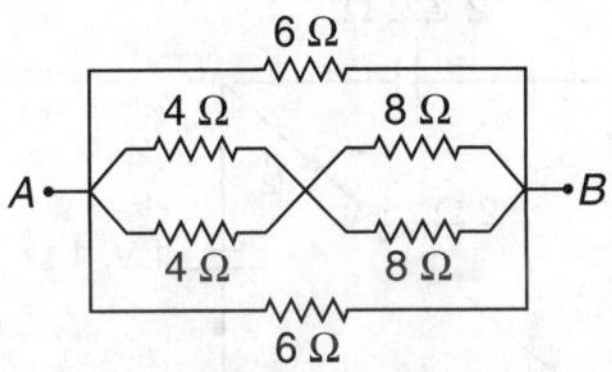

$\Rightarrow R_{AB} = 2\ \Omega$

The circuit in (d) reduces to

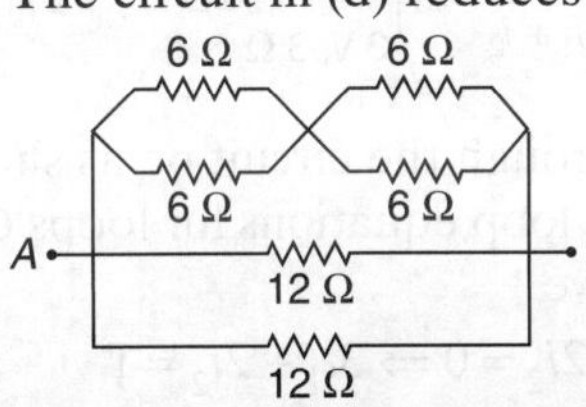

$\Rightarrow R_{AB} = 3\ \Omega$

Hence, the circuit in (a) has the greatest resistance.

5. (a), (c) Let I be the current in the circuit in the clockwise sense. Writing loop equations for the left and right loops, we have

$$V_1 = IR_1 \text{ and } V_2 = IR_2$$

Dividing the two equations, we have

$$\frac{V_1}{V_2} = \frac{R_1}{R_2}$$

The above condition is satisfied in options (a) and (c).

6. (d) The drift velocity of the electrons is given by

$$v_d = \frac{I}{neA} = \frac{1A}{(8\times10^{28}\ \text{m}^{-3})(1.6\times10^{-19}\ \text{C})(5\times10^{-7}\ \text{m}^2)}$$

$$= \frac{1}{6.4\times10^3}\ \text{m/s}$$

The time taken to drift a distance of 1 m is

$$T = \frac{1\ \text{m}}{v_d} = 6.4\times10^3\ \text{s}$$

7. (a)

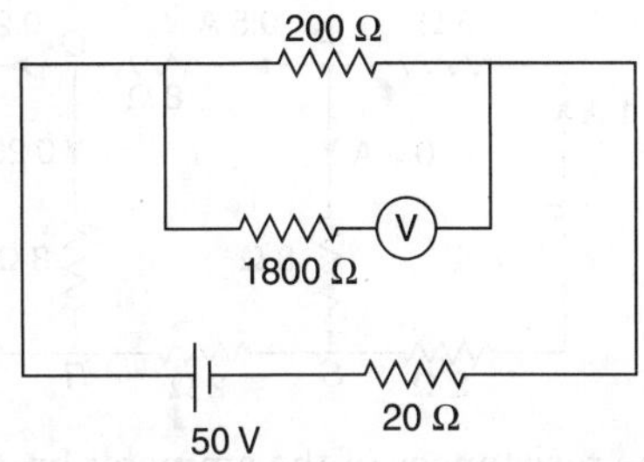

Before the voltmeter is connected, the PD across 200 Ω is

$$V_1 = \frac{200\ \Omega}{200\ \Omega + 20\ \Omega}\times 50\ \text{V} = \frac{10}{11}(50\ \text{V})$$

After the voltmeter is connected, the combined resistance of 200 Ω and 1800 Ω equals $\frac{200\times1800}{200+1800}\ \Omega = 180\ \Omega$. Now the PD across 200 Ω is

$$V_2 = \frac{180\ \Omega}{180\ \Omega + 20\ \Omega}\times 50\ \text{V} = \frac{9}{10}(50\ \text{V})$$

$$\text{Hence } \frac{V_2 - V_1}{V_1} = \frac{\frac{9}{10} - \frac{10}{11}}{\frac{10}{11}} = \frac{-1}{100} \Rightarrow 1\%$$

$\Rightarrow$ 1% decrease in the PD across 200 Ω.

8. (d)

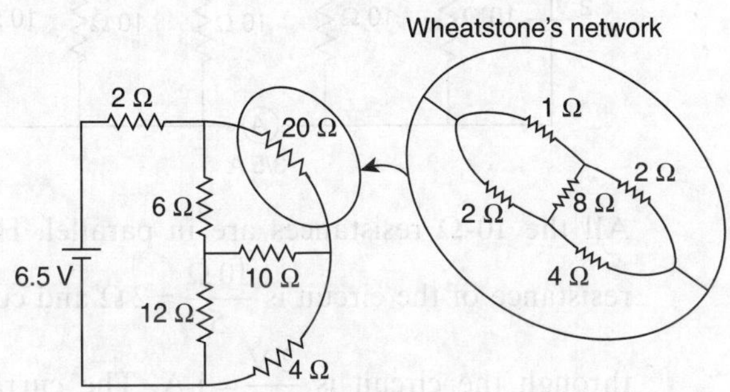

The upper right triangular part of the circuit (see figure) is a Wheatstone's network. It reduces to two parallel branches with resistances 3 Ω and 6 Ω, whose equivalent resistance is $\frac{3\ \Omega\times6\ \Omega}{3\ \Omega+6\ \Omega} = 2\ \Omega$. Now the circuit reduces to another Wheatstone's network. It reduces to two parallel branches with resistances 6 Ω and 18 Ω, whose equivalent resistance is $\frac{6\ \Omega\times18\ \Omega}{6\ \Omega+18\ \Omega} = 4.5\ \Omega$. Now the circuit reduces to two resistances 2 Ω and 4.5 Ω in series.

$$\text{Hence } I = \frac{6.5\ \text{V}}{2\ \Omega + 4.5\ \Omega} = 1\ \text{A}.$$

9. (d)

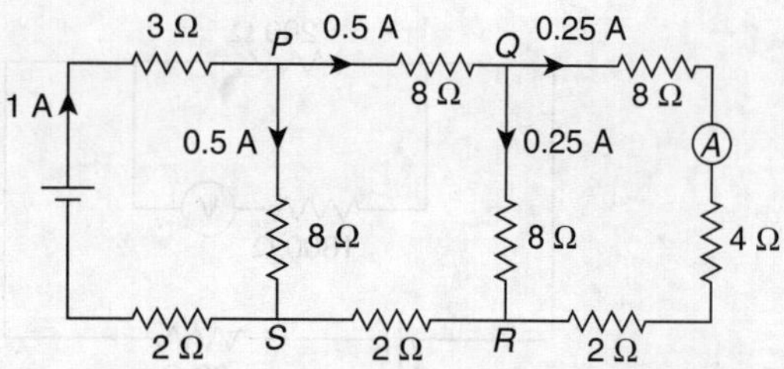

The resistences of the ammeter branch (see figure) are 2 Ω + 4 Ω + 2 Ω = 8 Ω. Now 8 Ω and 8 Ω in parallel add up to 4 Ω. Then 4 Ω + 2 Ω + 2 Ω = 8 Ω. Again 8 Ω and 8 Ω in parallel add up to 4 Ω. Finally, 3 Ω + 4 Ω + 2 Ω = 9 Ω is the resistance of the circuit. Hence, the current through the cell is $\frac{9\text{ V}}{9\,\Omega} = 1\text{ A}$.

The current distributes into two equal halves of 0.5 A each at junction P since the two parallel paths joining P to S have equal resistances of 8 Ω each. Similarly, the current distributes into two equal halves of 0.25 A each at junction Q since the two parallel paths joining Q to R have equal resistances of 8 Ω each.

10. (c)

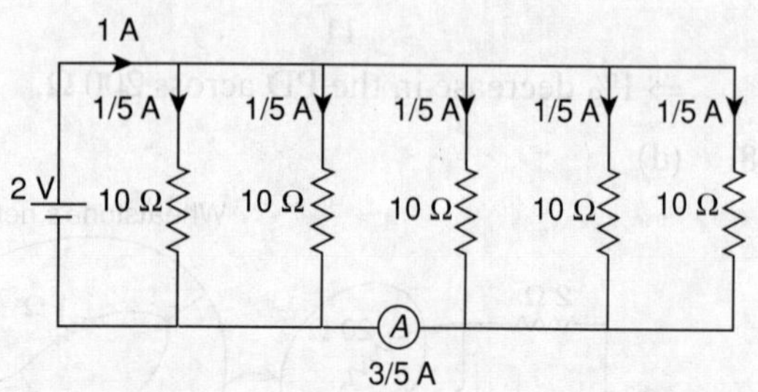

All the 10-Ω resistances are in parallel. Hence, resistance of the circuit is $\frac{10\,\Omega}{5} = 2\,\Omega$ and current through the circuit is $\frac{2\text{ V}}{2\,\Omega} = 1\text{ A}$. The current is distributed equally in the five parallel branches since their resistances are equal (see figure). Current through the ammeter equals the sum of the currents arriving from the three branches to the right of the ammeter. Hence, the reading of the ammeter is $\frac{3}{5}$ A.

11. (d)

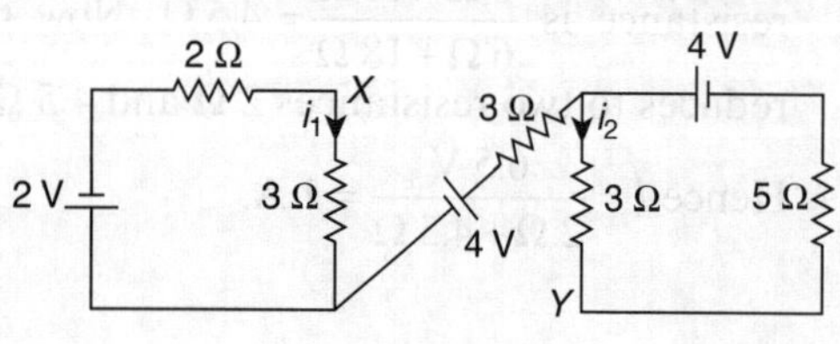

Let i_1 and i_2 be the currents in the left and right loops, respectively. There will be no current flow through the connecting branch. From loop equations, we have

$$i_1 = \frac{2\text{ V}}{5\,\Omega} = \frac{2}{5}\text{ A and } i_2 = \frac{4\text{ V}}{8\,\Omega} = \frac{1}{2}\text{ A}$$

Let V_x and V_Y be the potentials of points X and Y. Then, we have

$$V_x + 3i_1 + 4\text{ V} - 3i_2 = V_Y$$

$$\Rightarrow \quad V_x + \frac{6}{5}\text{V} + 4\text{ V} - \frac{3}{2}\text{V} = V_Y$$

$$\Rightarrow \quad V_Y - V_x = 3.7\text{ V}$$

12. (c)

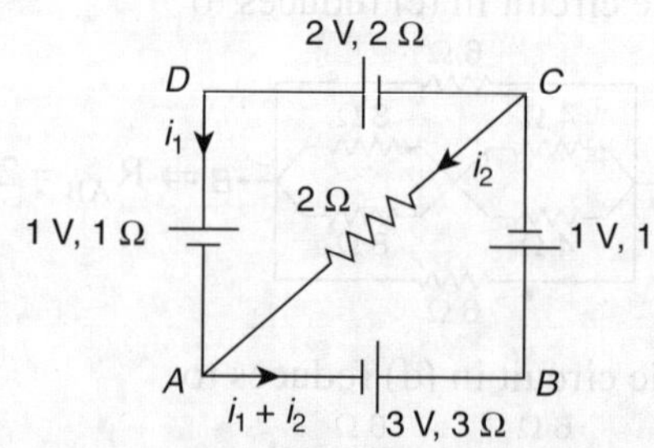

Let the current through the circuit be as shown in the figure. Writing loop equations for loops $CDAC$ and $CBAC$, we have

$$1 - 3i_1 + 2i_2 = 0 \Rightarrow 3i_1 + 2i_2 = 1 \quad \ldots(1)$$

$$2 - 4(i_1 + i_2) - 2i_2 = 0 \Rightarrow 2i_1 + 3i_2 = 1 \ldots(2)$$

Solving the two equations, gives $i_1 = \frac{5}{13}$ A and $i_2 = \frac{1}{13}$ A. The voltmeter reads the PD across points A and B, which is

$$V_{AB} = 3 - 3(i_1 + i_2) = \frac{21}{13}\text{ V}.$$

13. (d) Let x be the internal resistance of the voltmeter. Then 600 Ω and x in parallel connection add up to $R = \frac{(600\,\Omega)x}{600\,\Omega + x}$. The PD across R is given to be 36 V. Hence, the PD across 300 Ω will be 60 V − 36 V = 24 V. Since the current is the same in the two resistors, we have

$$\frac{36\text{ V}}{R} = \frac{24\text{ V}}{3\text{ nn}} \Rightarrow R = 450\,\Omega$$

$$\Rightarrow \quad \frac{(600\,\Omega)x}{600\,\Omega + x} = 450\,\Omega \Rightarrow x = 1800\,\Omega$$

14. (c) Let R be the internal resistance of the galvanometer. To convert it into a voltmeter, the

4990-Ω resistance must be connected in series. Thus, we have $(R+4990\,\Omega)6\text{ mA}=30\text{ V}\Rightarrow R=10\,\Omega$. For converting it into an ammeter, the resistance $\frac{2n}{249}\Omega$, say x, must be connected in parallel so that at full-scale deflection, only 6 mA current flows through the galvanometer and the remaining 1.5 A – 0.006 A = 1.494 A current flows through x. Thus, we have

$$(1.494\text{ A})x=(0.006\text{ A})R$$

$$\Rightarrow \quad x=\frac{10}{249}\Omega$$

Hence $n=5$.

15. (b) Let λ be the resistance per unit length of the wire and l1, l2 be the respective currents (at balance) in the primary and secondary circuits.
When S_1 is closed and S_2 is open, the PD across the 50-cm length of wire equals the PD across the 10-Ω resistor

$\Rightarrow l_1(\lambda 50\text{ cm})=l_2(10\,\Omega)$ ...(1)

When S_2 is closed and S_1 is open, the PD across the 60-cm length of wire equals the PD across the X + 10-Ω resistor

$\Rightarrow \quad l_1(\lambda 60\text{ cm})=l_2(X+10\,\Omega)$ ...(2)

Dividing the two equations, we have

$$\frac{10\,\Omega}{50\text{ cm}}=\frac{X+10\,\Omega}{60\text{ cm}}\Rightarrow X=2\,\Omega$$

16. (b) Let us connect m cells in series and n such groups in parallel, where $mn=48$.
Equivalent emf will be $m(2\text{ V})$ and internal resistance will be $\frac{m(1\,\Omega)}{n}$. Current flow through the circuit will be

$$i=\frac{2m}{3+m/n}=\frac{2m}{3+m^2/48}$$

$$=\frac{96m}{m^2+144}\text{ [Putting } n=48/m]$$

The maxima occurs when $di/dm=0$, that is

$$\frac{96[(m^2+144)-2m^2]}{(m^2+144)^2}=0\Rightarrow m=12\text{ and hence } n=4$$

17. (c) Let m, s and R denote the mass, specific heat capacity and resistance of the wire, and V denote the supply voltage. Then, the rate $\frac{\Delta\theta}{\Delta t}$ at which the temperature rises is given by

$$ms\frac{\Delta\theta}{\Delta t}=\frac{V^2}{R}\Rightarrow V\propto\sqrt{mR}$$

(If other things are the same)

Now, $R\propto l$ and $m\propto l$ if the cross-section area is the same. Thus, $V\propto\sqrt{l^2}=1$. Hence, doubling the length of the wire will require double the voltage supply, that is, $n=6$.

18. (d) The output power of bulb B_3 is $W_3=60$ W, since it is receiving 250 V equal to its operating voltage.
The output power of bulb B_2 is $W_2<60$ W, since it is receiving voltage less than 250 V, which is its operating voltage.
Comparing bulbs B_1 and B_2, the output power of B_1 will be less than that of B_2, since the same current flows through both but the resistance of B_1, that is, $\frac{(250\text{ V})^2}{100\text{ W}}$, is less than that of B_2, that is, $\frac{(250\text{ V})^2}{60\text{ W}}$.
Hence $W_1<W_2<W_3$.

19. (b) Resistance of bulb A, that is, $\frac{(200\text{ V})^2}{40\text{ W}}$, is greater than the resistance of bulb B, that is, $\frac{(200\text{ V})^2}{100\text{ W}}$. Therefore, when connected to a 400-V supply, bulb A will experience a voltage drop greater than 200 V, while bulb B will experience a voltage drop of less than 200 V. Hence, bulb A will fuse while bulb B will not fuse.

20. (d) Resistance of the heater is $\frac{(100\text{ V})^2}{100\text{ W}}=100\,\Omega$.
According to the required condition, the voltage drop V across the heater should be such that

$$\frac{V^2}{100\,\Omega}=62.5\text{ W}\Rightarrow V\approx 79\text{ V}$$

In that case, voltage drop across the 10 Ω resistor would be 100 V – 79 V = 21 V.
Resistance R and 100 Ω add up to $R'=\frac{(100\,\Omega)R}{100\,\Omega+R}$ since the current through the R' and 10-Ω resistors is the same. Hence, we have

$$\frac{79V}{\frac{(100\,\Omega)R}{1000+R}}=\frac{21\text{ V}}{10\,\Omega}$$

$$\Rightarrow \quad \frac{(100\,\Omega)R}{100\,\Omega+R}=37.6\,\Omega\Rightarrow R\approx 60\,\Omega$$

21. (c) If R denotes the resistance of the wire, V denotes the supply voltage and Q denotes the heat supplied in time Δt, then

$$Q = \left(\frac{V^2}{R}\right)\Delta t \Rightarrow \Delta t \propto R$$

(If other things are the same)

Let R be the resistance of the wire of length l and diameter d. Then, resistance of a wire of the same length l and diameter $d/2$ will be $4R$, since the cross-section area has reduced to 1/4th and resistance is inversely proportional to the cross-section area. Two such wires in parallel will have resistance $2R$.

Since resistance has doubled, the time taken will also double, that is, 2×4 s = 8 s.

22. (b), (c)

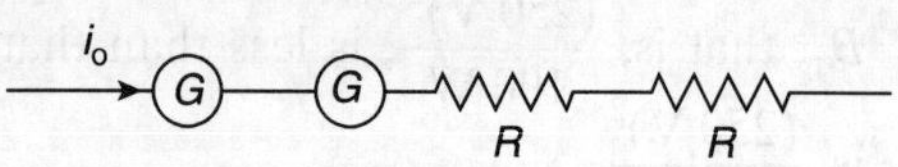

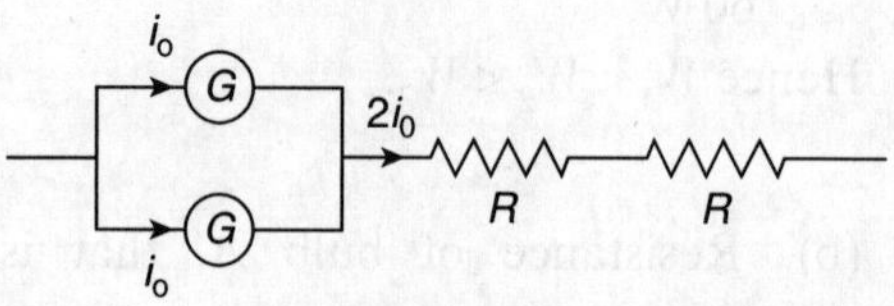

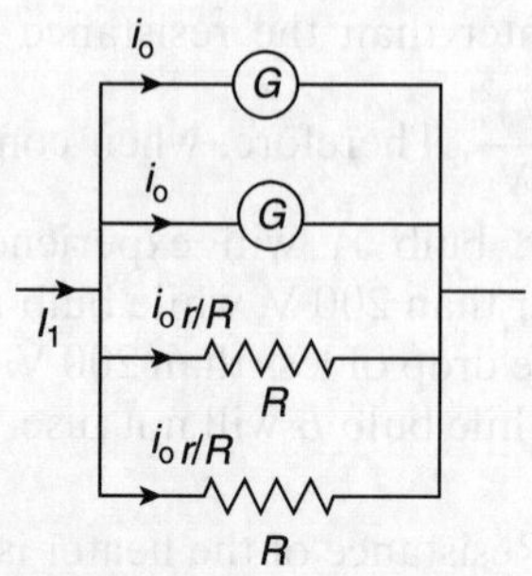

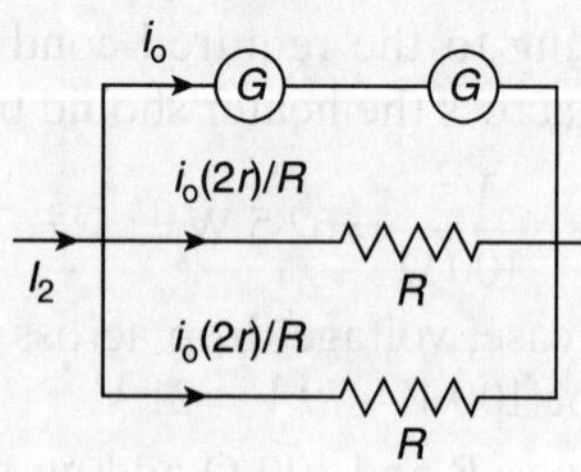

Let i_0 be the full-scale deflection current through the galvanometer. In option (a), the maximum voltage that can be measured is

$$V_1 = i_0(2r + 2R)$$

In option (b), the maximum voltage that can be measured is

$$V_2 = i_0 r + (2i_0)(2R) = i_0(r + 4R)$$

Now, $V_2 - V_1 = i_0(2R - r) > 0$ since $R > 2r$ (given).

$\Rightarrow$ Option (b) will give greater voltage range.

In option (c), the maximum current that can be measured is

$$I_1 = i_0(2 + 2r/R)$$

In option (d), the maximum current that can be measured is

$$I_2 = i_0(1 + 4r/R)$$

Now, $I_2 - I_1 = i_0(2r/R - 1) < 0$ since $R > 2r$ (given).

$\Rightarrow$ Option (c) will give greater current range.

23. (d) The current flowing through the transmission line is

$$I = \frac{P}{V} = \frac{25\text{ kW}}{250\text{ V}} = 100\text{ A}$$

The power loss in the transmission line is

$$P_{loss} = I^2R = (100\text{A})^2 \times 1\ \Omega = 10\text{ kW}$$

The fractional loss equals $\dfrac{10\text{ kW}}{25\text{ kW}} = 0.4$ or 40%

24. (b) Let P_1 and P_2 be the output powers of the two heaters. If Q is the energy required to boil the given quantity of water, then $P_1t_1 = P_2t_2 = Q$. When connected in parallel, the equivalent power output is $P = P_1 + P_2$. Hence the required time t is given by

$$\frac{Q}{t} = \frac{Q}{t_1} + \frac{Q}{t_2} \Rightarrow t = \frac{t_1t_2}{t_1 + t_2}$$

25. (d) Let load resistance be x. When the cells are connected in series, the equivalent emf is 2 V and the internal resistance is 2 Ω. Current through the load is $\dfrac{2\text{ V}}{2\ \Omega + x}$ and power dissipation is

$$H_1 = \left(\frac{2\text{ V}}{2\ \Omega + x}\right)^2 x.$$

When the cells are connected in parallel, the equivalent emf is 1 V and the internal resistance is 0.5 Ω. Current through the load is $\dfrac{1\text{ V}}{0.5\ \Omega + x}$ and power dissipation is $H_2 = \left(\dfrac{1\,E}{0.5\ \Omega + x}\right)^2 x.$

It is given that $H_1 = 2.25H_2$ Hence

$$\left(\frac{2\text{ V}}{2\ \Omega + x}\right)^2 x = \frac{9}{4}\left(\frac{1\text{ V}}{0.5\ \Omega + x}\right)^2 x$$

$\Rightarrow$ $16(x + 0.5\ \Omega)^2 = 9(x + 2\ \Omega)^2$

$\Rightarrow$ $4(x + 0.5\ \Omega) = \pm 3(x + 2\ \Omega) \Rightarrow x = 4\ \Omega$

[Neglecting the negative solution]

26. (c)

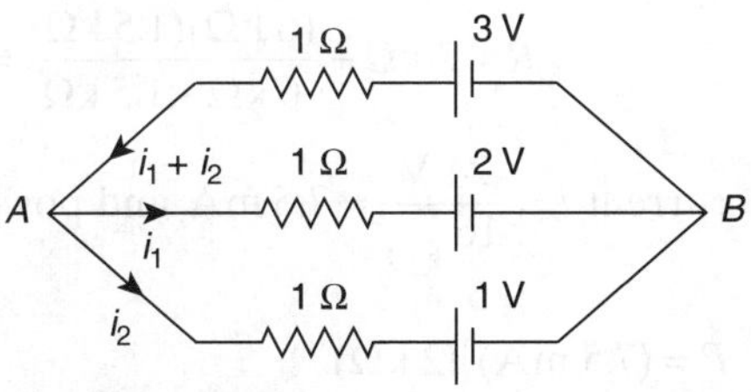

Let current flow through the circuit be as shown in the figure. Equating PD across the three parallel branches, we have

$$1\text{ V} + i_2(1\,\Omega) = 2\text{ V} + i_1\,(1\,\Omega) = 3\text{ V} - (i_1 + i_2)(1\,\Omega)$$

$\Rightarrow\ i_2 - i_1 = 1\text{ A}$ ...(1)

and $i_2 + 2i_1 = 1\text{ A}$ ...(2)

Solving the two equations gives $i_1 = 0$ and $i_2 = 1$ A. Hence $V_{AB} = 2$ V.

27. (d)

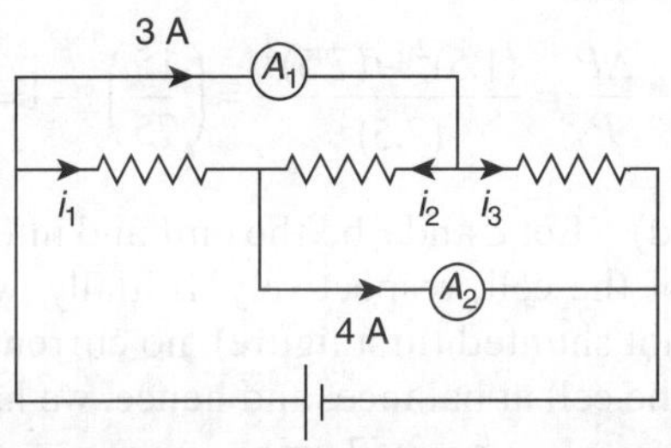

The three resistors are connected in parallel. Let current flow through the circuit be as shown in the figure. No change in the reading of the ammeter, even after the middle and left resistances are interchanged, is possible only if they are equal.

In that case, $i_1 = i_2 = \dfrac{1}{2}(4\text{ A}) = 2\text{ A}$ and $i_3 = 3\text{ A} - i_2 = 1\text{ A}$. Hence, current flow through the cell is $i_3 + 4\text{ A} = 5\text{ A}$.

28. (d)

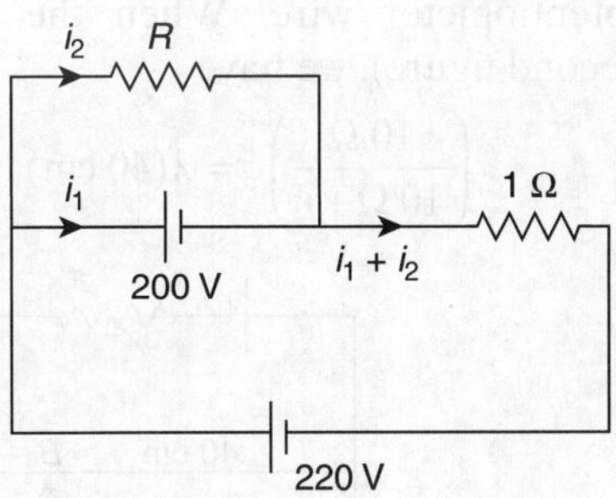

Let current flow in the circuit be as shown in the figure. From loop equations, we have

$$(i_1 + i_2)\,1\,\Omega = 220\text{ V} - 200\text{ V}$$

$\Rightarrow\quad i_1 + i_2 = 20\text{ A}$ ...(1)

and $\quad i_2R = 200\text{ V}$ ...(2)

Solving the above equations, we have $i_1 = 20\text{ A} - \dfrac{200\text{ V}}{R}$. The storage battery will get charged only if current flows opposite to its sense of emf, that is, only if $i_1 > 0$.

Hence, we have

$$20\text{ A} - \frac{200\text{ V}}{R} > 0 \Rightarrow R > 10\,\Omega$$

29. (c) The figure shows a cell of emf ξ and internal resistance r connected to a load of resistance x. The current through the circuit is $i = \dfrac{\xi}{r+x}$ and the power dissipation across the load is

$$P = i^2x = \frac{\xi^2 x}{(R+x)^2}$$

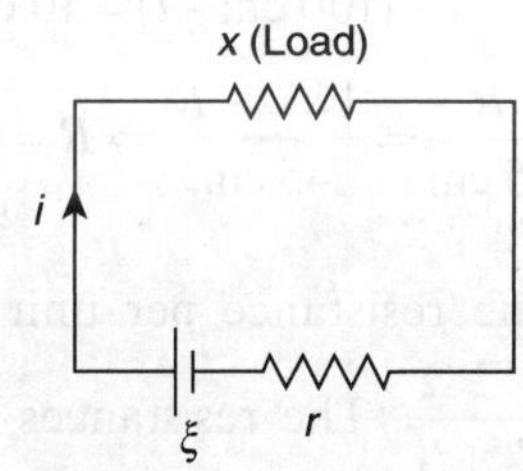

The power dissipation is maximum when $\dfrac{dP}{dx} = 0$. That is, when

$$\frac{\xi^2[(R+x)^2 - 2(R+x)x]}{(R+x)^4} = 0$$

$$\Rightarrow\quad \frac{\xi^2(R-x)}{(R+x)^3} = 0$$

$$\Rightarrow\quad x = R$$

Thus, we see that for maximum power dissipation, load resistance must equal internal resistance of the cell.

Note. This is an important result, worth remembering.

In this question, the resistors in the given network are connected in parallel. Thus, the load resistance is $R/3$. For maximum power dissipation, we have

$$\frac{R}{3} = 10\,\Omega \text{ gives } R = 30\,\Omega.$$

30. (b)

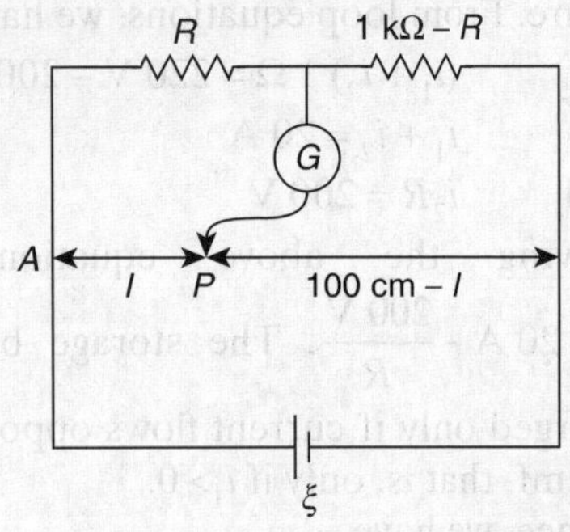

The series combination of the resistors in the two slots is given to be 1 kΩ. So, let R and $1\ \text{k}\Omega - R$ be the resistances in the left and right slots, respectively, before interchanging the resistors. Let the lengths of the two parts of the potentiometer wire be $PA = l$ and $PB = 100\ \text{cm} - l$. When the resistances are interchanged, $100\ \text{cm} - l$ and $PB' = l$. It is given that the balance point P shifts towards A by 10 cm. Hence, we have

$$PA - PA' = 10\ \text{cm}$$

$$\Rightarrow \quad l - (100\ \text{cm} - l) = 10\ \text{cm} \Rightarrow l = 55\ \text{cm}$$

Now $\dfrac{R}{55\ \text{cm}} = \dfrac{1\ \text{k}\Omega - R}{45\ \text{cm}} \Rightarrow R = 550\ \Omega$

31. (d) The resistance per unit length of the wire is $\lambda = \dfrac{12\ \Omega}{l_1 + l_2}$. The resistances of the two portions of length l_1 and l_2 are, respectively, λl_1 and λl_2. According to the given condition, we have

$$\frac{1}{\lambda l_1} + \frac{1}{\lambda l_2} = \frac{3}{8\ \Omega}$$

$$\Rightarrow \quad \frac{l_1 + l_2}{(12\ \Omega) l_1} + \frac{l_1 + l_2}{(12\ \Omega) l_2} = \frac{3}{8\ \Omega}$$

$$\Rightarrow \quad 1 + \frac{l_2}{l_1} + 1 + \frac{l_1}{l_2} = \frac{9}{2}$$

$$\Rightarrow \quad x + \frac{1}{x} = \frac{5}{2} \quad \left[\text{let } \frac{l_2}{l_1} = x\right]$$

$$\Rightarrow \quad 2x^2 - 5x + 2 = 0 \Rightarrow x = \tfrac{1}{2}, 2$$

32. (d)

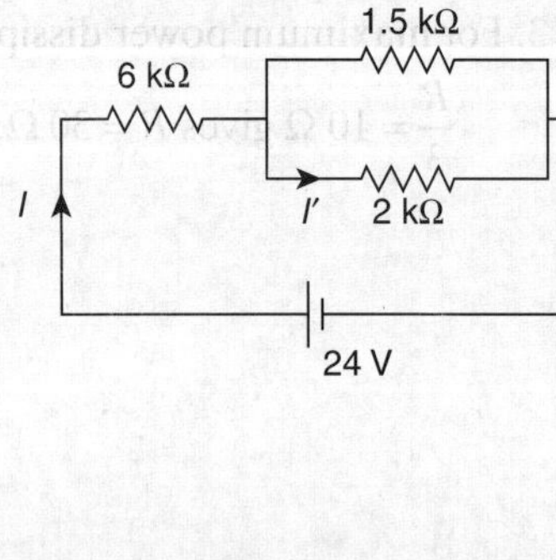

In the first case, equivalent resistance

$$R = 2\ \text{k}\Omega + \frac{(6\ \text{k}\Omega)(1.5\ \text{k}\Omega)}{6\ \text{k}\Omega + 1.5\ \text{k}\Omega} = \frac{16}{5}\ \text{k}\Omega,$$

current $I = \dfrac{24\ \text{V}}{\frac{16}{5}\ \text{k}\Omega} = 7.5\ \text{mA}$ and power dissipation

$P = (7.5\ \text{mA})^2(2\ \text{k}\Omega)$.

In the second case (see figure), equivalent resistance $R = 6\ \text{k}\Omega + \dfrac{(2\ \text{k}\Omega)(1.5\ \text{k}\Omega)}{2\ \text{k}\Omega + 15\ \text{k}\Omega} = \dfrac{48}{7}\ \text{k}\Omega$,

current $I = \dfrac{24\ \text{V}}{\frac{48}{7}\ \text{k}\Omega} = 3.5\ \text{mA}$, current through 2 kΩ is $I' = \left(\dfrac{1.5\ \text{k}\Omega}{2\ \text{k}\Omega + 1.5\ \text{k}\Omega}\right) I = 1.5\ \text{mA}$ and power dissipation $P' = (1.5\ \text{mA})^2(2\ \text{k}\Omega)$.

Hence

$$\frac{\Delta P}{P} = \frac{(1.5)^2 - (7.5)^2}{(7.5)^2} = \left(\frac{15}{75}\right)^2 - 1 = -\frac{24}{25} \text{ or } -96\%$$

33. (d) Let ξ and r be the emf and internal resistance of the cell, respectively. Initially, when the cell is not shunted (first figure), no current flows through the cell at balance, and hence, we have

$$\xi = \lambda(52\ \text{cm}) \qquad \text{...(1)}$$

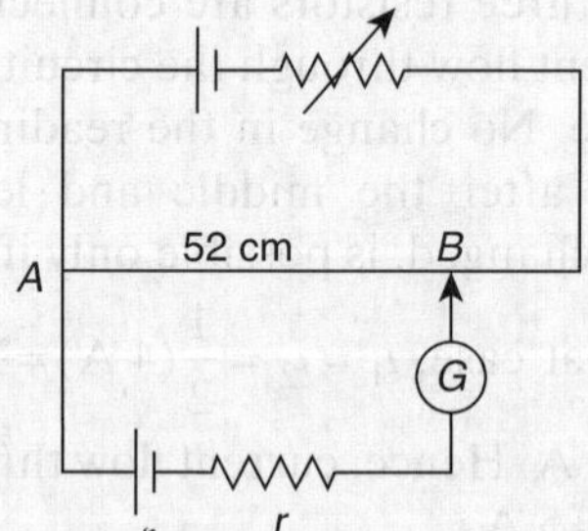

Here, λ is the potential gradient along the potentiometer wire. When the cell is shunted (second figure), we have

$$\left(\frac{10\ \Omega}{10\ \Omega + r}\right)\xi = \lambda(40\ \text{cm}) \qquad \text{...(2)}$$

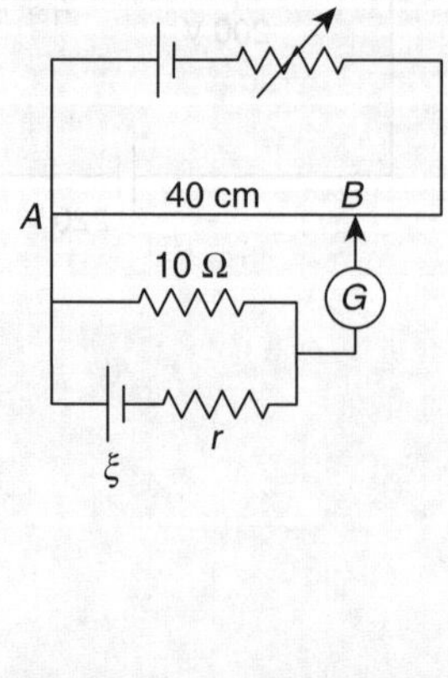

Dividing the two equations, we have

$$\frac{10\ \Omega}{10\ \Omega + r} = \frac{40}{52} \Rightarrow r = 3\ \Omega$$

34. (b)

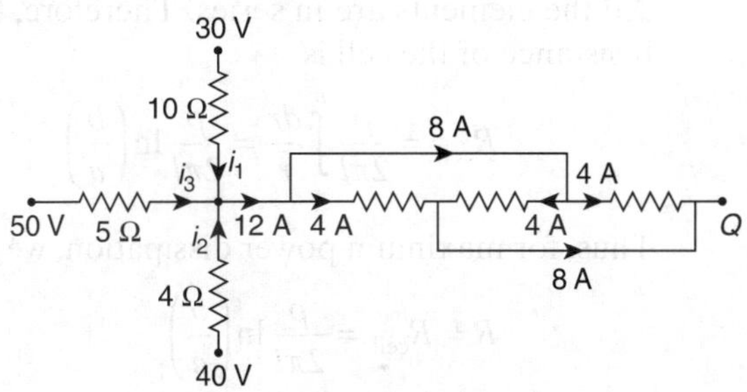

The right-hand portion of the circuit is actually three 1-Ω resistors in parallel, with 4-A current flowing through each resistor. Now, applying Kirchhoff's junction law at *P*, we have

$$I_1 + I_2 + I_3 = 12\ \text{A}$$

$$\Rightarrow \quad \frac{30\ \text{V} - V_P}{10\ \Omega} + \frac{40\ \text{V} - V_P}{4\ \Omega} + \frac{50\ \text{V} - V_P}{5\ \Omega} = 12\ \text{A}$$

$$\Rightarrow \quad V_P = 20\ \text{V}$$

The potential of *Q* is given by

$$v_Q = v_P - (4\ \text{A})\ (1\ \Omega) = 16\ \text{V}$$

35. (a), (c) Let us name the junctions as shown in figure. Note that the junctions *a*, *c* are equipotential, as are junctions *d*, *f*. The circuit can be redrawn as shown in the subsequent figures.

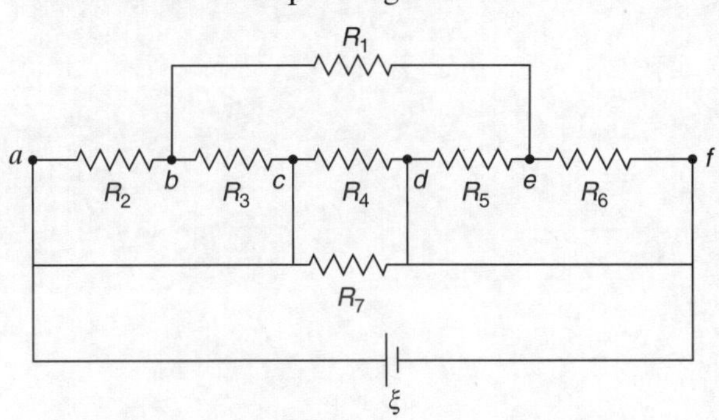

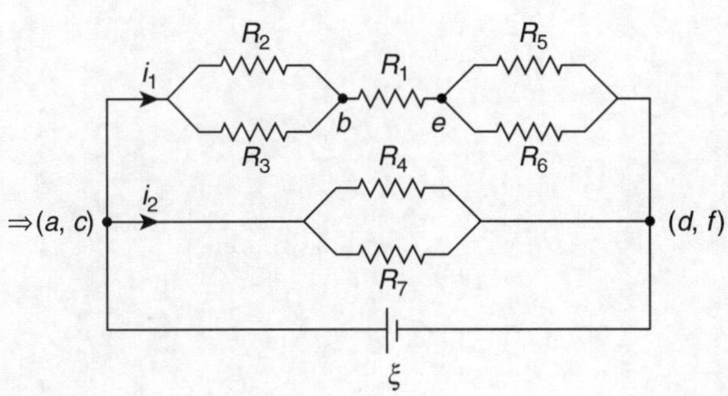

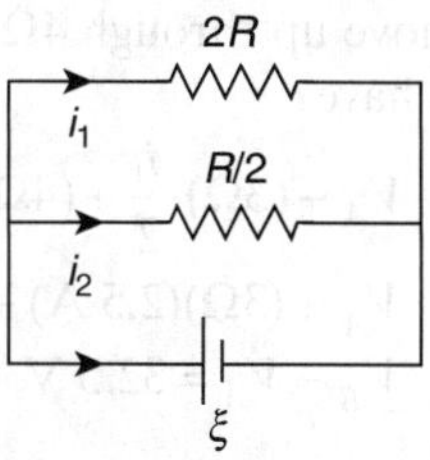

The equivalent resistance of the circuit is $R_{eq} = \frac{2R}{5} = 2\ \Omega$. The currents through the two parallel branches are

$$i_1 = \frac{\xi}{2R} = \frac{20\ \text{V}}{10\ \Omega} = 2\ \text{A and } i_2 = \frac{\xi}{R/2} = \frac{20\ \text{V}}{2.5\ \Omega} = 8\ \text{A}$$

Hence, we have

PD across $R_1 = i_1 R = 10$ V

Current along $R_3 = \frac{1}{2} i_1 = 1$ A

Current along $R_4 = \frac{1}{2} i_2 = 4$ A

Power consumption $= \frac{\xi^2}{R_{eq}} = 80$ W

36. (d)

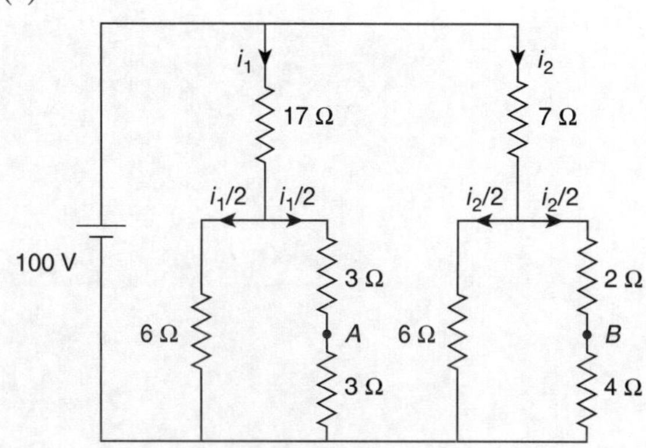

The circuit can be drawn as shown in the figure. There are two parallel branches connected across the cell. The resistances of the left and the right branches are 17Ω + 3Ω = 20Ω and 7Ω + 3Ω = 10Ω7Ω + 3Ω = 10Ω, respectively. The respective currents in these two branches are

$$i_1 = \frac{100\ \text{V}}{20\ \Omega} = 5\ \text{A and } i_2 = \frac{100\ \text{V}}{10\ \Omega} = 10\ \text{A}$$

Let V_A and V_B be the potentials of points *A* and *B*, respectively. Now starting from point *A*, let us move down through 3Ω, then turn right, and finally move up through 4Ω to reach *B*. Along this path, we have

$$V_A - (3\Omega)\frac{i_1}{2} + (4\Omega)\frac{i_2}{2} = V_B$$

$$\Rightarrow \quad V_A - (3\Omega)(2.5\text{ A}) + (4\Omega)(10\text{ A}) = V_B$$

$$\Rightarrow \quad V_B - V_A = 32.5\text{ V}$$

37. (b) We know that for maximum power dissipation, load resistance must equal internal resistance of the cell. In this question, we therefore only need to find the internal resistance of the cell. Let us subdivide the cell into thin co-axial cylindrical shells, each of thickness *dr*.

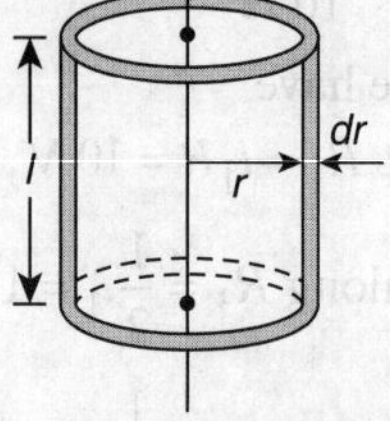

The figure shows one such element cylindrical shell of radius *r*. Resistance of this element is

$$dR_{\text{cell}} = \frac{\rho dr}{l(2\pi r)}$$

All the elements are in series. Therefore, the total resistance of the cell is

$$R_{\text{cell}} = \frac{\rho}{2\pi l}\int_a^b \frac{dr}{r} = \frac{\rho}{2\pi l}\ln\left(\frac{b}{a}\right)$$

Thus, for maximum power dissipation, we have

$$R = R_{\text{cell}} = \frac{\rho}{2\pi l}\ln\left(\frac{b}{a}\right)$$

CHAPTER

17 Capacitors

- A capacitor is any pair of conductors separated by a dielectric (insulator). When charges of opposite signs but having equal magnitude Q appear on the two conductors, we say that the capacitor is charged. The potential V of the positively charged conductor with respect to the negatively charged conductor is proportional to Q. The capacitance C of the capacitor is defined as

$$C = \frac{Q}{V}$$

- A parallel plate capacitor composed of two parallel conducting plates, each with area A, placed at a distance d and separated by vacuum has capacitance

$$C = \frac{\epsilon_0 A}{d}$$

- When the space between the conductors is filled by a dielectric material, the capacitance increases by a factor k, called the dielectric constant of the material. For a parallel plate capacitor with such a dielectric material filling the space between them, the capacitance is

$$C = k\frac{\epsilon_0 A}{d}$$

- When a dielectric is inserted between the plates while the charge is kept constant, the electric field inside the dielectric material decreases by the factor k. If E_{pres} is the electric field in the presence of the dielectric, and E_{abs} is the field in the absence of the dielectric, then

$$E_{pres} = \frac{E_{abs}}{k}$$

  When a dielectric is inserted between the plates, induced charges of opposite signs appear on both faces of the dielectric; the induced charges appear as a result of redistribution of charges within the dielectric material, a phenomenon called polarisation. The magnitude of the surface charge density σ on the capacitor plates is related to the magnitude of the induced charge density σ_P appearing on the dielectric as

$$\sigma_P = \sigma\left(1 - \frac{1}{k}\right)$$

- When several capacitors with capacitances $C_1, C_2, C_3, \ldots$ are connected in series, the equivalent capacitance is given by

$$\frac{1}{C_{eq}} = \frac{1}{C_1} + \frac{1}{C_2} + \frac{1}{C_3} + \ldots \text{ (capacitors in series)}$$

  The same charge appears on all capacitors in a series connection. When several capacitors are connected in parallel, the equivalent capacitance is given by

$$C_{eq} = C_1 + C_2 + C_3 + \ldots \text{ (capacitors in parallel)}$$

  All capacitors connected in parallel have the same potential difference across them.

- The energy U required to charge a capacitor C to a potential V and charge Q is equal to the energy stored in the capacitor and is given by

$$U = \frac{1}{2}QV = \frac{1}{2}CV^2 = \frac{Q^2}{2C}$$

The energy can be thought of as residing in the electric field between the conductors; the energy density u (energy per unit volume) is given by

$$u = \frac{1}{2}\epsilon_0 E^2$$

- When a capacitor C is connected in series with a resistor R, and a battery of emf ξ, the charge on the capacitor approaches its final value $C\xi$ exponentially:

$$Q = C\xi\left(1 - e^{-t/\tau}\right) \text{ and } I = \frac{\xi}{R}e^{-t/\tau},$$

where $\tau = RC$ is called the time constant of the circuit. After this much time, the capacitor is charged to 63% of its final value, and the current is at 37% of its initial value.
When a capacitor having charge Q_0 is discharged by connecting it to a resistor R, the charge and the current are given as functions of time by

$$Q = Q_0 e^{-t/\tau} \text{ and } I = \frac{Q_0}{CR}e^{-t/\tau}$$

EXERCISES

1. Metal plates are arranged as shown in the figures. The area of each plate is A and the separation between the plates is d. Find the capacitance between the points A and B and match with the column on the right:

(a) 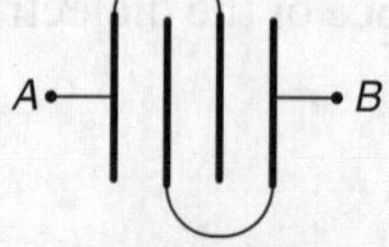

(p) $\frac{3\epsilon_0 A}{d}$

(b) 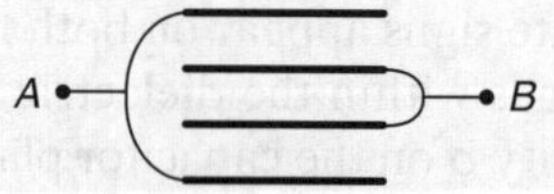

(q) $\frac{2\epsilon_0 A}{d}$

(c) 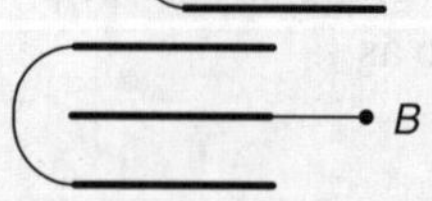

(r) $\frac{2\epsilon_0 A}{3d}$

(d) 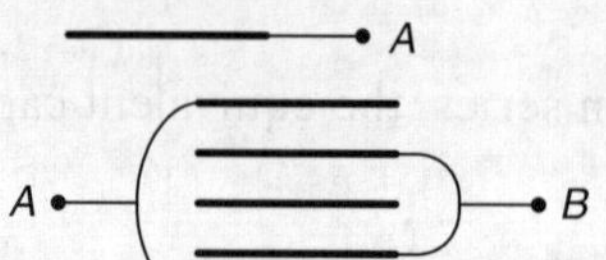

(s) $\frac{\epsilon_0 A}{3d}$

2. Find the capacitance between points A and B and match with the column on the right:

(a) 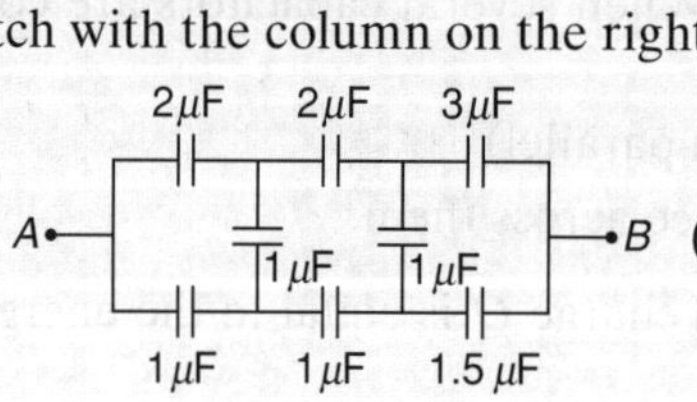

(p) 4 μF

(b) 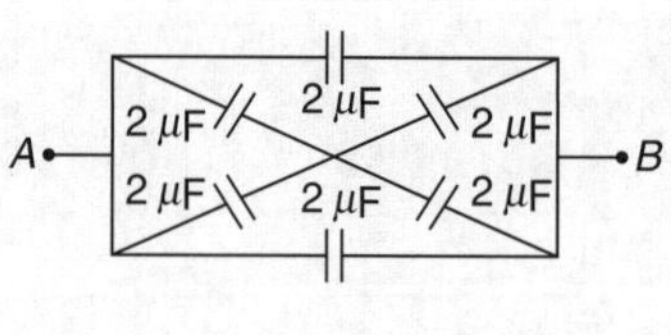

(q) 5 μF

(c) 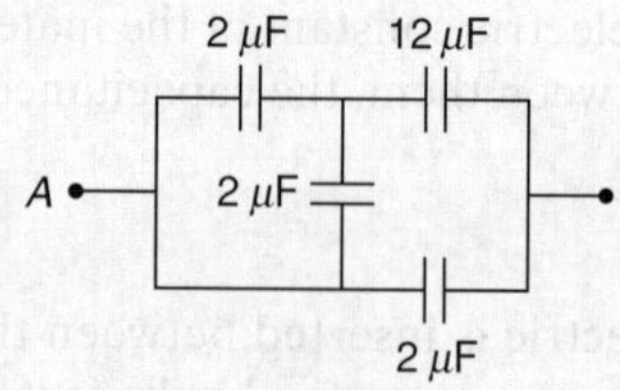

(r) 6 μF

(d) 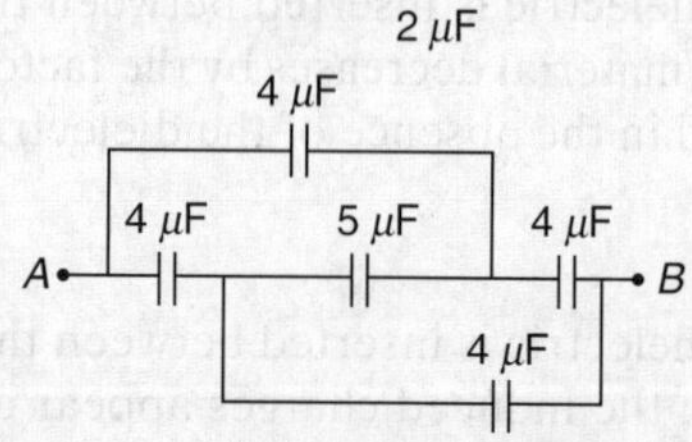

(s) $\frac{9}{8}$ μF

3. Capacitors, each of capacitance $C = 1\,\mu$F, are connected in an infinite network, as shown in the figure.

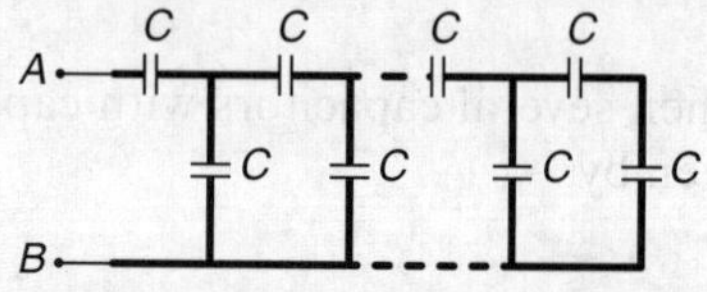

The equivalent capacitance between points A and B is:

(a) $\left(\sqrt{5}+1\right)\mu$F
(b) $\left(\frac{\sqrt{5}+1}{2}\right)\mu$F
(c) $\left(\sqrt{5}-1\right)\mu$F
(d) $\left(\frac{\sqrt{5}-1}{2}\right)\mu$F

4. The introduction of a metal plate between the plates of a parallel plate capacitor increases its capacitance by 45 times. If d is the separation between the capacitor plates, the thickness of the metal plate is:

(a) $\frac{1}{3}d$ (b) $\frac{5}{9}d$

(c) $\frac{7}{9}d$ (d) d

5. Consider the capacitor shown in the figure.

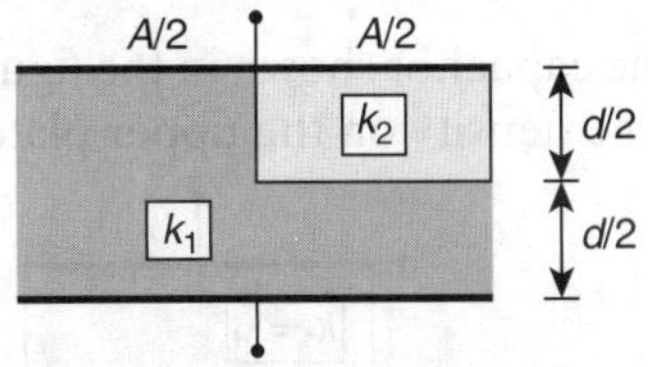

If the region between the plates were to be replaced by one single material of dielectric constant k, then:

(a) $k = \frac{2k_1(k_1+k_2)}{3k_1+k_2}$ (b) $k = \frac{k_1(k_1+3k_2)}{2(k_1+k_2)}$

(c) $k = \frac{2k_1(k_1+k_2)}{k_1+3k_2}$ (d) $k = \frac{k_1(3k_1+k_2)}{2(k_1+k_2)}$

6. The charge on the 2-μF capacitor shown in the figure is:

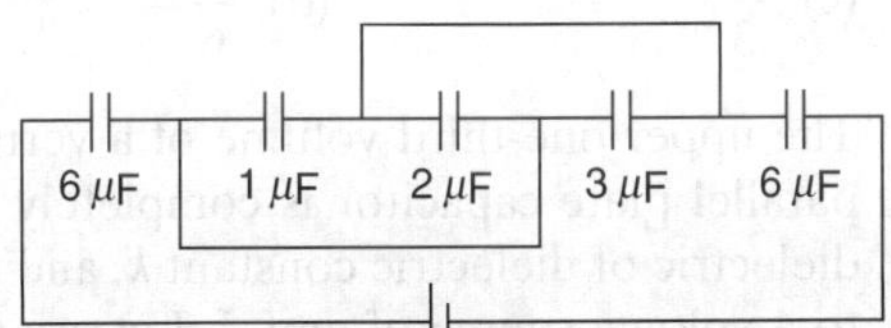

(a) 12 μC (b) 10 μC
(c) 8 μC (d) 6 μC

7. The charge on the 2-μF capacitor shown in the figure is:

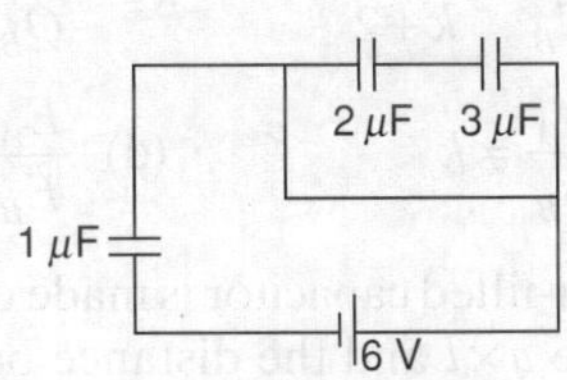

(a) 0 (b) 1 μC
(c) 2 μC (d) 3 μC

8. Two air-filled parallel plate capacitors C_1 and C_2 of equal capacitance are connected in series to a cell. When steady state is reached, capacitor C_1 is completely filled with a slab of dielectric constant k. If E_i and E_f, respectively, denote the electric fields in capacitor C_1 before and after the dielectric is introduced, then the ratio E_f / E_i is:

(a) $\frac{1}{k}$ (b) $\frac{2}{k+1}$

(c) $\frac{k-1}{k+1}$ (d) $\frac{k}{k+1}$

9. In the circuit shown in the figure, the potential difference between points A and B is $\frac{200}{m}$ V, and charge on the capacitor is $\frac{50}{n}$ mC at steady state.

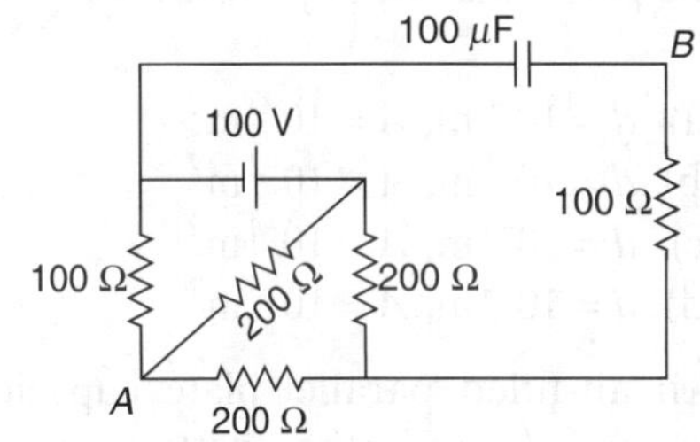

Then the values of m and n are:

(a) $m = 3, n = 7$ (b) $m = 7, n = 7$
(c) $m = 7, n = 5$ (d) $m = 3, n = 5$

10. The figure shows two capacitors of capacitances $C_1 = 2$ pF and $C_2 = 3$ pF. Both capacitors are charged to potential differences $V_1 = 30$ V and $V_2 = 20$ V, respectively.

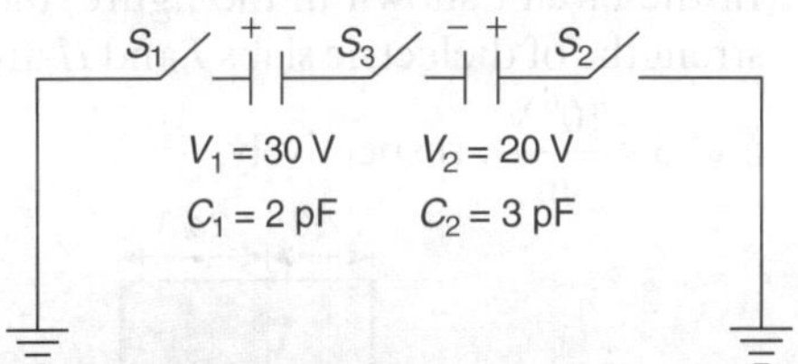

Choose the correct statements from the following:

(a) With S_1 closed, $V_1 = 15$ V, $V_2 = 20$ V
(b) With S_3 closed, $V_1 = V_2 = 25$ V
(c) With S_1 and S_2 closed, $V_1 = 30$ V, $V_2 = 20$ V
(d) With S_1, S_2 and S_3 closed, $V_1 = V_2 = 24$ V

11. An air-filled parallel plate capacitor is charged using a battery of 10 V and the battery is then removed. The separation between the plates is 5 cm. If a dielectric slab of dielectric constant 4 and thickness 1 cm is inserted between the plates, the potential difference will be:

(a) 7.5 V (b) 8 V
(c) 8.5 V (d) 9 V

12. A capacitor of capacitance $C_1 = 1\,\mu$F can withstand a maximum voltage $V_1 = 6$ kV. Another capacitor of capacitance $C_2 = 2\,\mu$F can withstand a maximum voltage $V_1 = 4$ kV. If the capacitors are connected in series, the combination can withstand a maximum voltage of

(a) 6 kV (b) 7 kV
(c) 8 kV (d) 9 kV

13. A parallel plate capacitor of value 1.77 μF is to be designed using a dielectric whose dielectric constant is 200 and breakdown strength is

3×10^6 V/m. In order to make such a capacitor which can withstand a potential difference of 20 V, the separation d between the plates and area A of the plates may be $\left(\epsilon_0 = 8.85 \times \frac{10^{-12}\,C^2}{N} \cdot m^2\right)$:

(a) $d = 10^{-6}$ m, $A = 10^{-3}$ m^2
(b) $d = 10^{-5}$ m, $A = 10^{-2}$ m^2
(c) $d = 10^{-4}$ m, $A = 10^{-4}$ m^2
(d) $d = 10^{-4}$ m, $A = 10^{-5}$ m^2

14. An air-filled parallel plate capacitor is charged to 100 V and the battery is disconnected. A 2-mm-thick dielectric is now inserted between the plates and the distance between the plates is increased by 1.6 mm. If the potential difference between the plates remains unchanged, the dielectric constant of the dielectric is:

(a) 5 (b) 4
(c) 2.5 (d) 1.5

15. In the circuit shown in the figure, the breakdown strengths of dielectric slabs I and II are 9×10^6 V/m and $3 \times \frac{10^6\,V}{m}$, respectively.

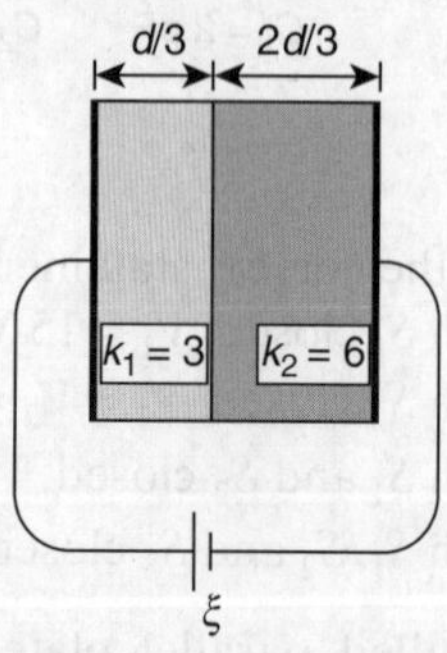

If plate separation $d = 1\,\mu$m, then the maximum permissible emf ξ of the DC voltage source is:

(a) 4 V (b) 6 V
(c) 8 V (d) 10 V

16. In a series C–R circuit, the capacitor is charged to 10 V in two different ways. Case I: Charged by a 10-V battery. Case II: Charged first by a 5-V battery and then further by a 10-V battery. Let H_1 and H_2 denote the heat generated in the resistor in the first and second cases, respectively. Then H_1/H_2 equals:

(a) 1 (b) 2
(c) 1/2 (d) 1/3

17. Two parallel plate capacitors of capacitances C and $2C$ are connected in parallel and charged to a potential difference V by a battery. The battery is then disconnected and the space between the plates of capacitor C is completely filled with a slab of dielectric constant k. The potential difference across the capacitors now becomes:

(a) $\frac{V}{k+1}$ (b) $\frac{2V}{k+2}$
(c) $\frac{3V}{k+2}$ (d) $\frac{3V}{k+3}$

18. In the capacitor shown in the figure, σ is the surface charge density on the upper plate.

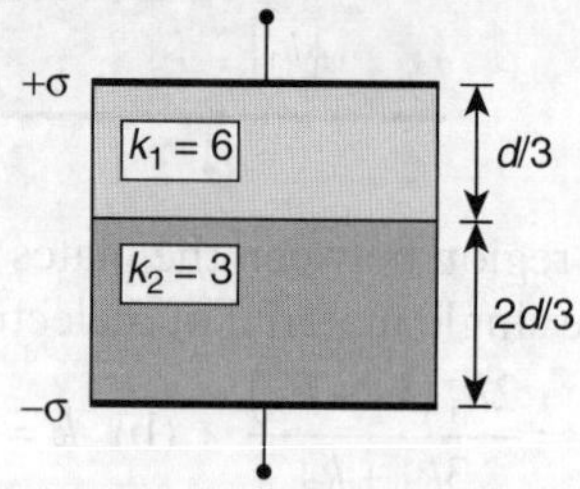

The charge density at the boundary of the dielectrics is:

(a) $\frac{\sigma}{2}$ (b) $\frac{2\sigma}{3}$
(c) $\frac{\sigma}{3}$ (d) $\frac{\sigma}{6}$

19. The upper one-third volume of a vertically placed parallel plate capacitor is completely filled with a dielectric of dielectric constant k, and is connected to a voltage source of emf ξ. Let A and B denote the upper and lower parts of the capacitor. If C, Q, σ and E denote capacitance, charge, charge density and electric field, respectively, then the correct statements among the following are:

(a) $\frac{C_A}{C_B} = \frac{k}{k+2}$ (b) $\frac{Q_A}{Q_B} = \frac{k}{2}$
(c) $\frac{\sigma_A}{\sigma_B} = k$ (d) $\frac{E_A}{E_B} = \frac{2}{k}$

20. An air-filled capacitor is made of rectangular plates of size $a \times l$ and the distance between the plates is d. It is connected to a cell of emf ξ. A rectangular dielectric slab of size $a \times 2l/3$, thickness d and dielectric constant k is now $(t = 0)$ inserted between the plates of the capacitor, at a uniform speed v. Let $I(t)$ denote instantaneous current in the circuit, chosen positive along the sense of emf of the cell. The correct options are:

(a) $I(l/3v) = \frac{\epsilon_0 (k-1) a v \xi}{d}$
(b) $I(4l/3v) = -\frac{\epsilon_0 (k-1) a v \xi}{d}$
(c) $I(3l/4v) = 0$
(d) None of these

21. A 200-μF capacitor charged to 200 V is allowed to discharge once through a series combination and once through a parallel combination of a 10-Ω and a 30-Ω resistor. If H_1 and H_2 denote the heat generated in the 10-Ω resistor in the first and the second case, respectively, then:

(a) $H_1 = 3$ J, $H_2 = 1$ J
(b) $H_1 = 1$ J, $H_2 = 3$ J
(c) $H_1 = 1.5$ J, $H_2 = 2.5$ J
(d) $H_1 = 2.5$ J, $H_2 = 1.5$ J

22. A parallel plate capacitor of capacitance C is charged to a potential difference V and another capacitor of capacitance $2C$ is charged to a potential difference $2V$. The charging batteries are disconnected and the capacitors are connected in parallel in such a way that the positive terminal of one is connected to the negative terminal of the other. The amount of heat generated in the wires is:

(a) $\frac{1}{2}CV^2$ (b) $\frac{5}{2}CV^2$
(c) $2CV^2$ (d) $3CV^2$

23. Initially, capacitors C_1 and C_2 carry a charge of 300 μC and 360 μC, respectively, with polarities as shown in the figure, while capacitor C_3 is uncharged.

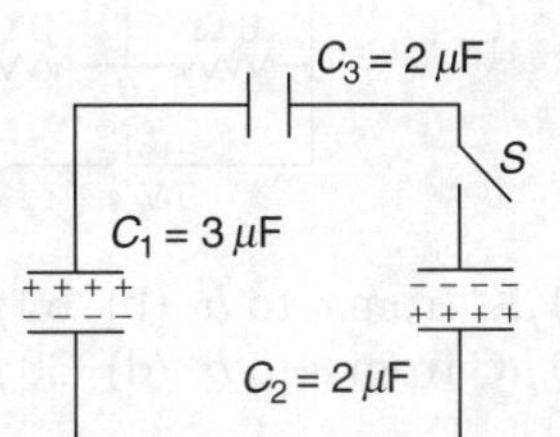

After switch S is closed, steady state charge on C_3 is:

(a) 100 μC (b) 120 μC
(c) 180 μC (d) 210 μC

24. An air-filled parallel plate capacitor of plate area A and separation between the plates d is charged by a battery of voltage V. Neglecting heat dissipation in the wires, the work required to pull the plates to separation $2d$ with the battery connected during the process is:

(a) $\frac{2\epsilon_0 AV^2}{3d}$ (b) $\frac{3\epsilon_0 AV^2}{2d}$
(c) $\frac{\epsilon_0 AV^2}{4d}$ (d) $\frac{\epsilon_0 AV^2}{2d}$

25. In the circuit shown in the figure, $C_1 = C$ and $C_2 = 2C$.

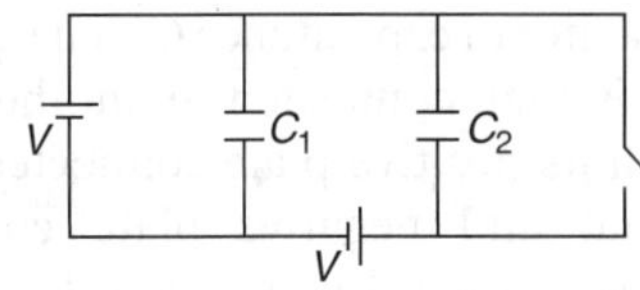

The amount of heat generated in the wires after closing the switch is:

(a) 0 (b) $\frac{1}{3}CV^2$
(c) $\frac{1}{2}CV^2$ (d) CV^2

26. The circuit shown in the figure is in steady state. One-third of the distance between the capacitor plates is now filled with a dielectric of dielectric constant 2.

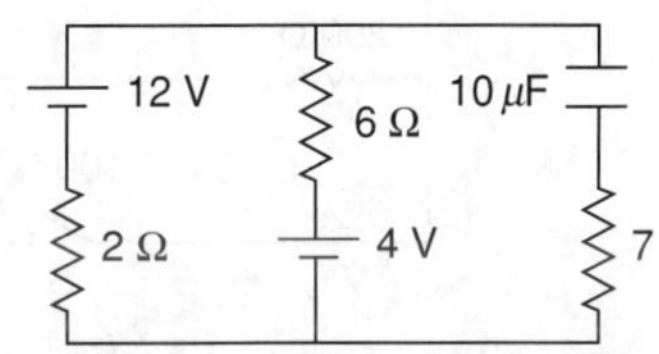

The charge on the capacitor changes by:

(a) –10 μC (b) –20 μC
(c) +20 μC (d) +30 μC

27. In the circuit shown in the figure, polarity of the cell is reversed and the circuit is allowed to reach steady state.

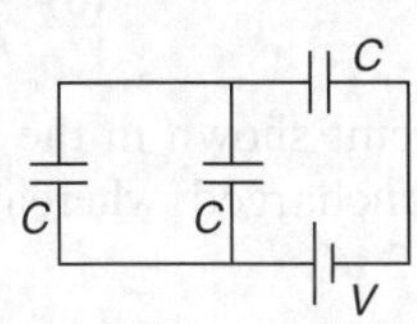

The amount of heat generated in the wires is:

(a) $\frac{1}{3}CV^2$ (b) $\frac{2}{3}CV^2$
(c) $\frac{4}{3}CV^2$ (d) 0

28. A leaky parallel plate capacitor is completely filled with a slab of dielectric constant k and conductivity σ. The surface area of each plate is A, and the distance between them is d. A charge $2Q$ is given to one plate and $-Q$ to the other plate. The dielectric slab gets heated as charge flows through it. The total amount of heat H generated in the dielectric and the time constant τ of the circuit are:

(a) $H = \frac{4Q^2 d}{k\epsilon_0 A}$, $\tau = \frac{\sigma}{k\epsilon_0}$ (b) $H = \frac{9Q^2 d}{8k\epsilon_0 A}$, $\tau = \frac{k\epsilon_0}{\sigma}$
(c) $H = \frac{2Q^2 d}{k\epsilon_0 A}$, $\tau = \frac{k\sigma}{\epsilon_0}$ (d) $H = \frac{3Q^2 d}{4k\epsilon_0 A}$, $\tau = \frac{\epsilon_0}{k\sigma}$

29. A capacitor of capacitance C is charged to a potential $2V$. It is then connected to another cell of voltage V, with its positive plate connected to the positive terminal and negative plate connected to the negative terminal of the cell. By the time steady state is attained, the amount of heat generated in the wires is:

(a) $\frac{1}{3}CV^2$ (b) $\frac{2}{3}CV^2$

(c) $\frac{4}{3}CV^2$ (d) $\frac{1}{2}CV^2$

30. In the circuit shown in the figure, the capacitor is charged up to maximum charge by closing switch S.

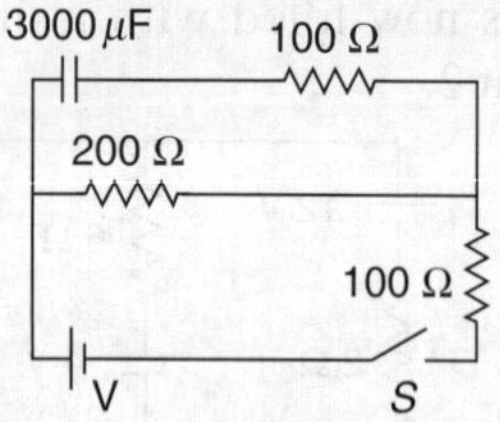

If the capacitor were to be charged at a constant rate, equal to the initial charging rate in the given circuit, then the time required for charging the capacitor up to the maximum charge would be:

(a) $\frac{1}{4}$ s (b) $\frac{1}{2}$ s

(c) $\frac{2}{3}$ s (d) $\frac{3}{4}$ s

31. In the circuit shown in the figure, capacitor C_2 is initially uncharged whereas capacitor C_1 has a charge of 2 μC.

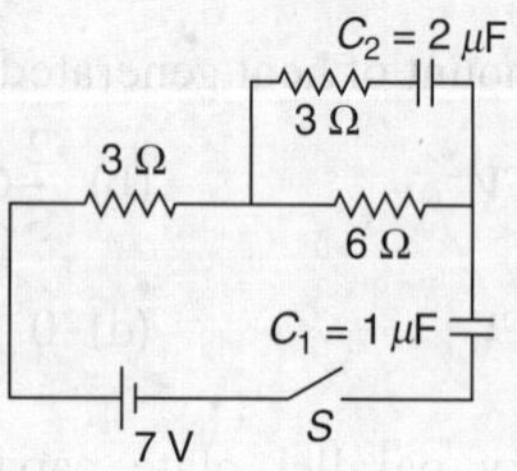

Immediately after the switch is closed, the current flow through the cell is:

(a) 0 (b) 1 A

(c) 1.4 A (d) 1.8 A

32. In the circuit shown in the figure, $C_1 = C_2 = C, C_3 = 2C$. A steady current I enters at junction a.

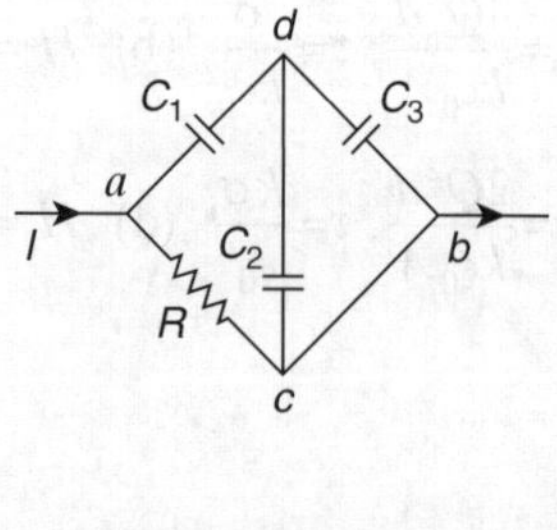

If charge on capacitor C_3 is ICR/n, then the value of n is:

(a) 1 (b) 2

(c) 6 (d) 9

33. The PD across a capacitor $C = 2$ μF varies with time, as shown in the figure.

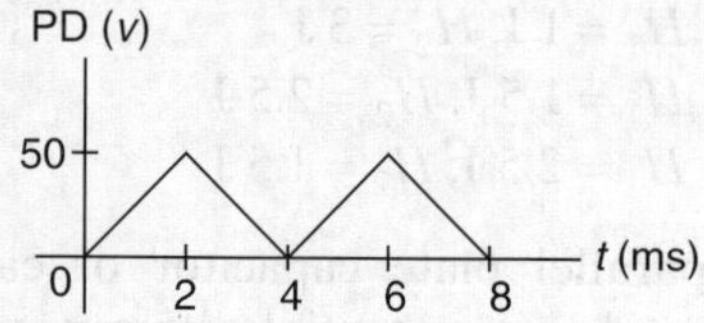

The maximum power P_0 and the maximum current I_0 are:

(a) $P_0 = 2.5$ W, $I_0 = 10$ mA

(b) $P_0 = 2.5$ W, $I_0 = 50$ mA

(c) $P_0 = 2.0$ W, $I_0 = 10$ mA

(d) $P_0 = 2.0$ W, $I_0 = 50$ mA

34. In the circuit shown in the figure, when the switch S is closed, the total amount of charge that flows through the switch equals:

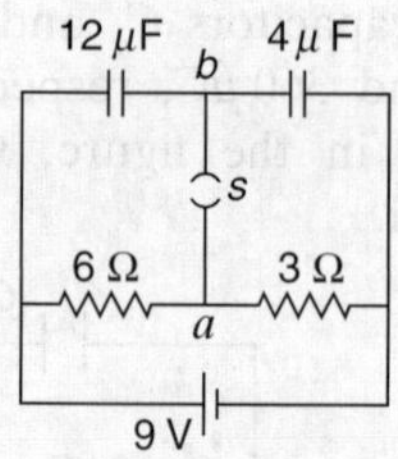

(a) 60 μC from a to b (b) 60 μC from b to a

(c) 30 μC from a to b (d) 30 μC from b to a

35. In the circuit shown in the figure, $C = 1$ μF and $R = \frac{4\times10^6}{\ln 3}$ Ω. Before switch S is closed, plate A of the capacitor carries charge $q_0 = -1$ mC whereas plate B has no net charge. The switch is closed at $t = 0$.

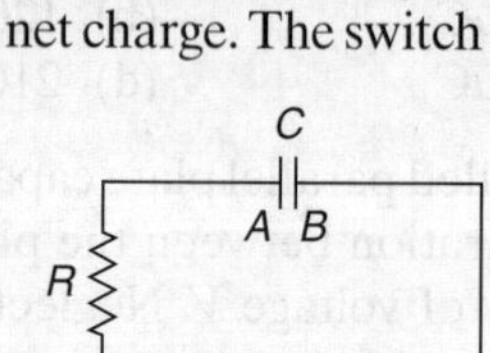

The time after which the net charge on plate A becomes zero is:

(a) 9 s (b) 6 s

(c) 5 s (d) 4 s

36. The figure shows the circuit of a flashing lamp. The fluorescent lamp L having negligible resistance is connected in parallel to the capacitor of a C-R circuit. Current flows through the lamp only when the potential difference across it reaches a

breakdown voltage V_L. In this event, the capacitor discharges completely and the lamp flashes briefly.

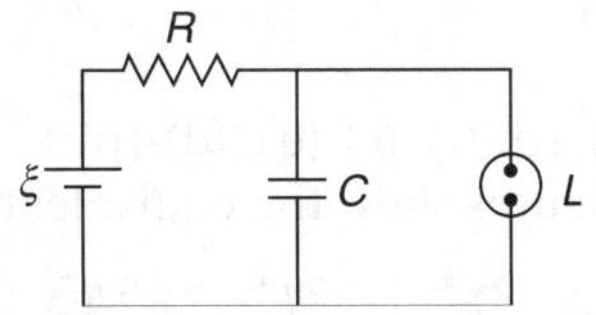

Neglecting discharging time, the time interval between two flashes is:

(a) $CR\ln\left(\frac{\xi}{\xi-V_L}\right)$ (b) $CR\ln\left(\frac{\xi}{V_L}\right)$

(c) $CR\left[1-\ln\left(\frac{\xi}{V_L}\right)\right]$ (d) $CR\left[1-\ln\left(\frac{\xi}{\xi-V_L}\right)\right]$

37. At $t=0$, terminals A and B are connected and a current $I(t)=I_0\cos(\omega t)$, where $I_0=1$ A and $\omega=500$ rad/s starts flowing in the direction shown in the figure. At $t=\frac{7\pi}{6\omega}$, the key is switched from B to D and left connected thereafter.

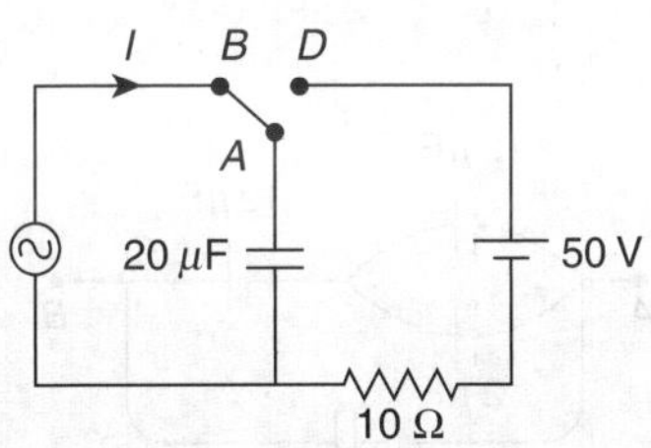

Then the correct statements are:

(a) Maximum charge on the capacitor before $t=\frac{7\pi}{6\omega}$ is 1 mC

(b) Current in the left part of the circuit just before $t=\frac{7\pi}{6\omega}$ is clockwise

(c) Current in the right part of the circuit just after $t=\frac{7\pi}{6\omega}$ is 10 A

(d) Total charge flow through the cell after $t=\frac{7\pi}{6\omega}$ until steady state is 2 mC

38. The figure shows an evacuated cylindrical chamber of height h, having conducting plates at the ends and an insulating curved surface. A number of spherical balls made of light and soft material and coated with a conducting material are placed on the bottom plate. The balls have radius $r (r \ll h)$. Now, a high voltage V is applied across the plates. The balls get charged, become equipotential with the plate and are repelled by it. The charged balls now reach the other plate and the process repeats.

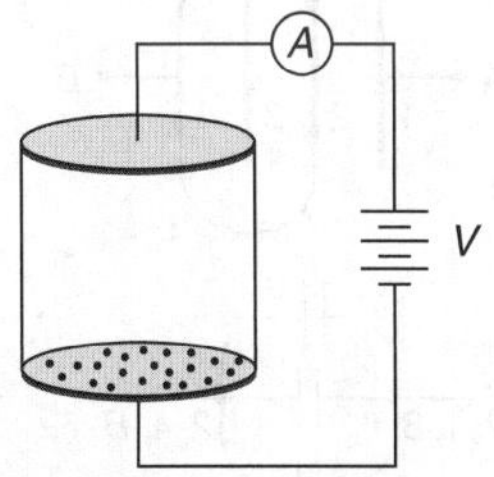

If the average current registered by the ammeter in the circuit is proportional to V^n, then n equals:

(a) 0 (b) 2

(c) 1 (d) 1/2

39. In the circuit shown in the figure, consider the voltmeter and the ammeter to be ideal.

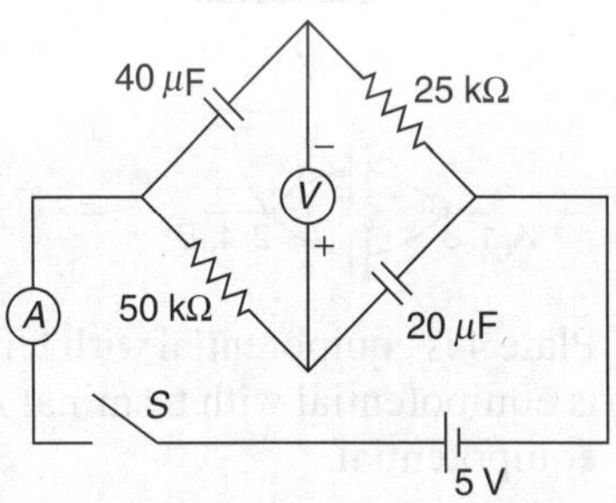

If the switch S is closed at $t=0$, then the correct statements from the following are:

(a) At $t=0$, voltmeter reads –5 V and ammeter reads 0.3 mA

(b) At $t=\ln 2$ s, voltmeter reads 0 V and ammeter reads 0.15 mA

(c) After a long time, voltmeter reads 5 V and ammeter reads 0 mA

(d) At $t=1$ s, ammeter reads $1/e$ of its initial reading

ANSWER KEYS

1. (a)-(p), (b)-(q), (c)-(r), (d)-(q)			**2.** (a)-(s), (b)-(r), (c)-(q), (d)-(p)			**3.** (d)	**4.** (c)	**5.** (b)
6. (c)	**7.** (a)	**8.** (b)	**9.** (b)	**10.** (c),(d)	**11.** (c)	**12.** (d)	**13.** (b)	**14.** (a)
15. (a)	**16.** (b)	**17.** (c)	**18.** (d)	**19.** (b),(c)	**20.** (a),(b),(c)	**21.** (b)	**22.** (d)	**23.** (d)
24. (c)	**25.** (a)	**26.** (c)	**27.** (c)	**28.** (b)	**29.** (d)	**30.** (b)	**31.** (b),(d)	**32.** (b)
33. (b)	**34.** (a)	**35.** (d)	**36.** (a)	**37.** (c),(d)	**38.** (b)	**39.** (a),(b),(c),(d)		

SOLUTIONS

1. (a)-(p), (b)-(q), (c)-(r), (d)-(q)

The figures show the equivalent circuits:

(a) Plates 1, 3 are equipotential with terminal A. Plates 2, 4 are equipotential with terminal B.

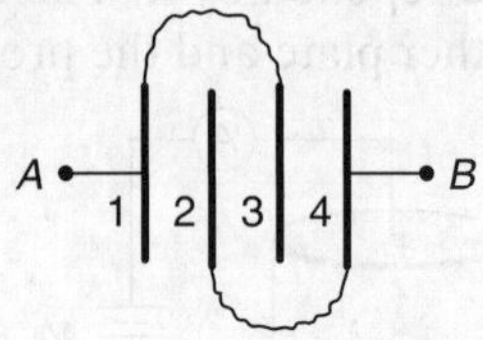

⇒ 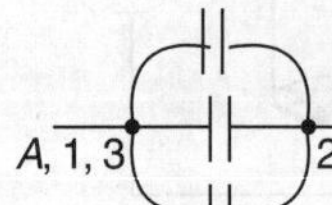

$\Rightarrow C_{AB} = \frac{3\epsilon_0 A}{d}$

(b) Plates 1, 4 are equipotential with terminal A. Plates 2, 3 are equipotential with terminal B.

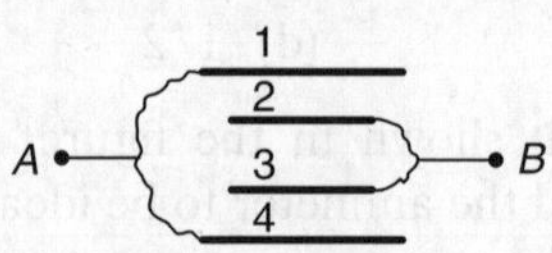

⇒ 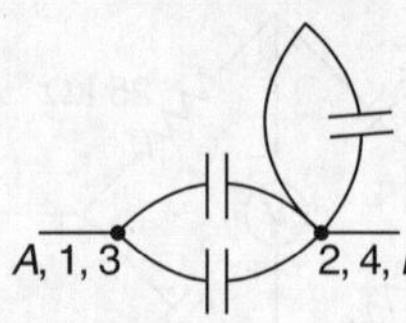

$\Rightarrow C_{AB} = \frac{2\epsilon_0 A}{d}$

(c) Plate 4 is equipotential with terminal A. Plate 2 is equipotential with terminal B. Plates 1, 3 are equipotential.

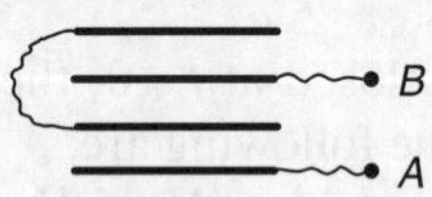

⇒ 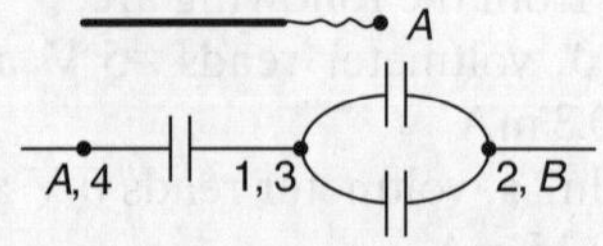

$\Rightarrow C_{AB} = \frac{2\epsilon_0 A}{3d}$

(d) Plates 1, 5 are equipotential with terminal A. Plates 2, 4 are equipotential with terminal B.

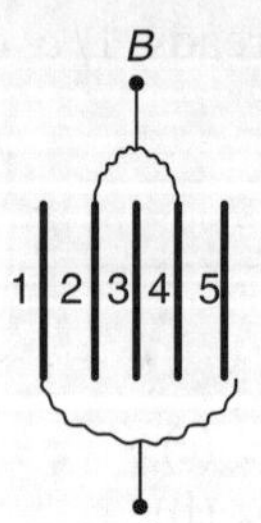

⇒ 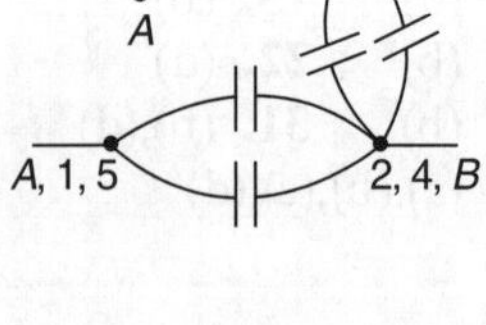

$\Rightarrow C_{AB} = \frac{\epsilon_0 A}{3d}$

2. (a)-(s), (b)-(r), (c)-(q), (d)-(p)

The figures show the equivalent circuits:

(a) 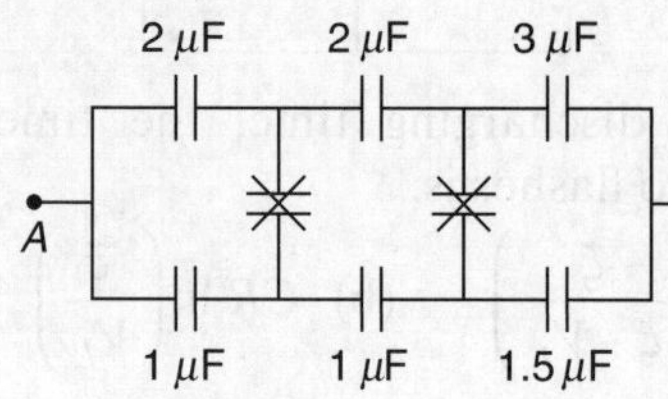

$\Rightarrow C_{AB} = \frac{9}{8}\,\mu F$

(b) 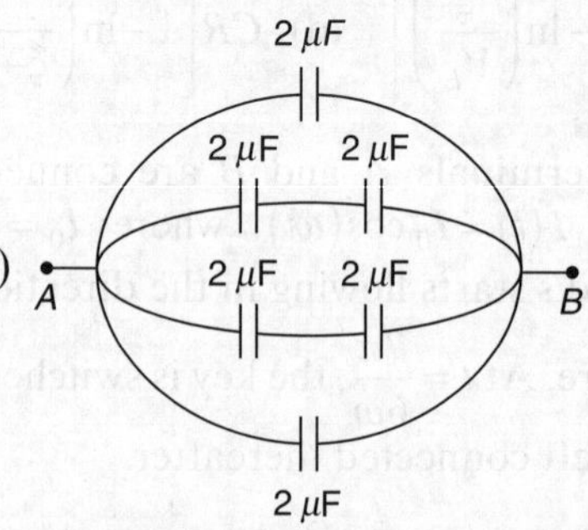

$\Rightarrow C_{AB} = 6\,\mu F$

(c) 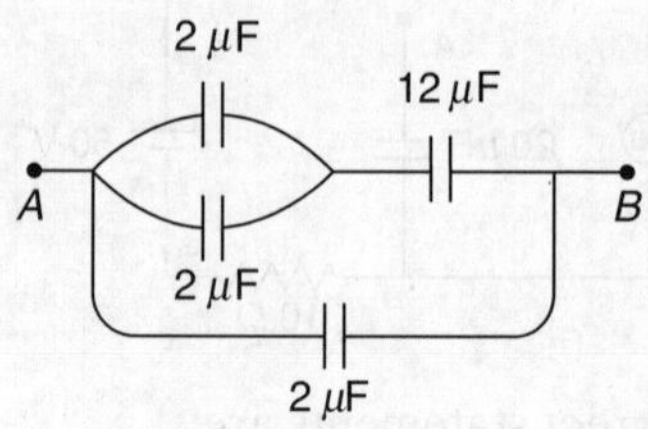

$\Rightarrow C_{AB} = 5\,\mu F$

(d) 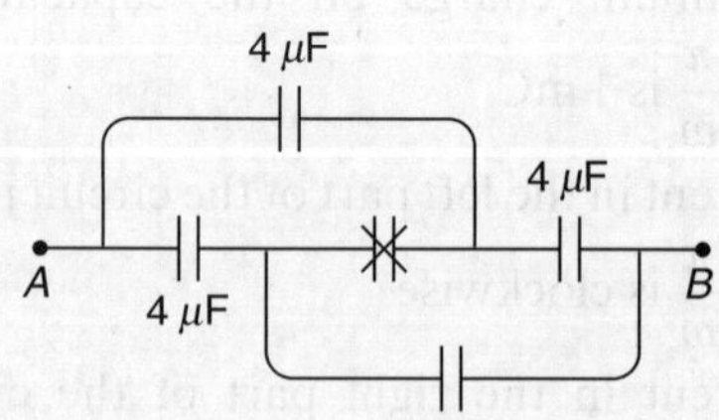

$\Rightarrow C_{AB} = 4\,\mu F$

3. (d) Let x be the equivalent capacitance. The given circuit is made by connecting a large number of identical units. Since it is an infinite network, adding one such unit will not change the equivalent capacitance of the circuit.

The equivalent capacitance (see figure) is still equal to x.

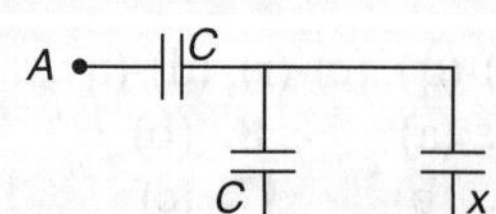

Hence, we have

$$\frac{(c+x)c}{2c+x}=x$$

$$\Rightarrow \quad x^2+Cx-C^2=0$$

Putting $C = 1\ \mu F$ and taking the positive root, we have $x=\frac{\sqrt{5}-1}{2}\mu F$.

4. (c) Let t be the thickness of the metal plate. Before introducing the metal plate, the capacitance is $c=\frac{\varepsilon_0 A}{d}$.

After introducing the metal plate, the capacitance is $C'=\frac{\varepsilon_0 A}{d-t}$

It is given that $C' = 4.5C$. Hence, we have

$$\frac{\varepsilon_0 A}{d-t}=4.5\frac{\varepsilon_0 A}{d}$$

$$\Rightarrow \quad 9(d-t)=2d \Rightarrow t=\frac{7}{9}d$$

5. (b) The given capacitor can be considered to be a combination of three capacitors C_1. C_2 in series and then in parallel to C_3, where

$$C_1=\frac{k_1\varepsilon_0(A/2)}{(d/2)}=k_1C_0, C_2=\frac{k_2\varepsilon_0(A/2)}{(d/2)}=k_2C_0,$$

$$C_3=\frac{k_1\varepsilon_0(A/2)}{d}=\frac{k_1}{2}C_0.$$

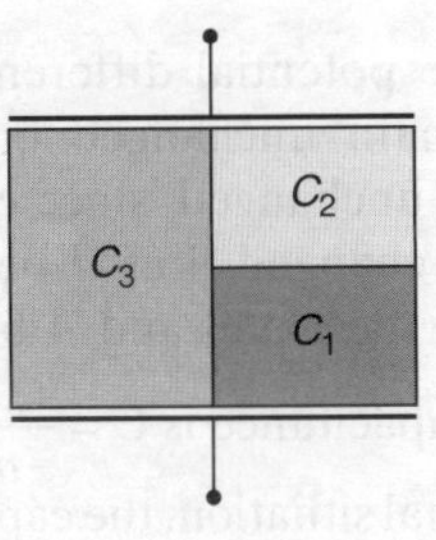

The equivalent capacitance is

$$\frac{C_1C_2}{C_1+C_2}+C_3=\frac{k_1k_2}{k_1+k_2}C_0+\frac{k_1}{2}C_0=\frac{k_1(k_1+3k_2)}{2(k_1+k_2)}C_0$$

Thus, the region between the capacitor plates can be replaced by one single dielectric of dielectric constant

$$k=\frac{k_1(k_1+3k_2)}{2(k_1+k_2)}$$

6. (c) The 1-μF, 2-μF, 3-μF capacitors are in parallel, which add up to 6 μF. Now, there are three 6-μF capacitors in series which add up to 2 μF.

Hence, charge flow through the cell is

$$2\ \mu F \times 12\ V = 24\ \mu C$$

Charge flow through the 2-μF capacitor will be

$$\left(\frac{2\ \mu F}{1\ \mu F+2\ \mu F+3\ \mu F}\right)24\ \mu C=8\ \mu C$$

7. (a) Let the charge distribution on the capacitors be as shown in the figure.

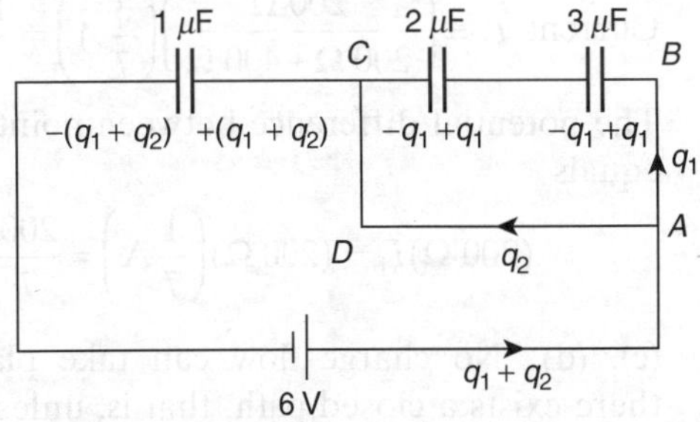

Writing the loop equation for $ABCDA$, we have

$$\frac{q_1}{2\ \mu F}+\frac{q_1}{3\ \mu F}=0 \Rightarrow q_1=0$$

8. (b) Let V be the voltage of the cell and C be the capacitance of the two capacitors before introducing the dielectric.

After introducing the dielectric, the capacitance of C_1 changes to kC whereas that of C_2 still remains C. Before introducing the dielectric, the potential difference across C_1 is $V_i=\frac{1}{2}V$. After the dielectric is introduced, the potential difference across C_1 is $V_f=\left(\frac{C}{kC+C}\right)V=\frac{1}{k+1}V$

Since the distance between the plates is the same in both situations, the ratio of electric fields equals the ratio of potential differences. Hence we have

$$\frac{E_f}{E_i}=\frac{V_f}{V_i}=\frac{2}{k+1}$$

9. (b) At steady state, there is no current flow in the outer branch that contains the capacitor.

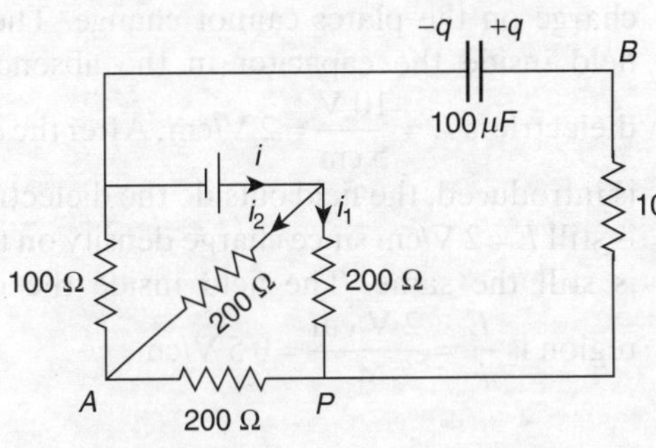

The inner part of the circuit has equivalent resistance $\frac{700}{3}\Omega$. Hence, current flow through the cell is $I = \frac{100\text{ V}}{\frac{700}{3}\Omega} = \frac{3}{7}\text{A}$.

Current I is distributed into two parallel branches, as shown in the figure.

Current $I_1 = \left(\frac{200\ \Omega}{200\ \Omega + 400\ \Omega}\right)\left(\frac{3}{7}A\right) = \frac{1}{7}A$

The potential difference between points A and B equals

$$(200\ \Omega)I_1 = (200\ \Omega)\left(\frac{1}{7}\text{A}\right) = \frac{200}{7}\text{V} \Rightarrow n = 7$$

10. (c), (d) No charge flow can take place unless there exists a closed path, that is, unless all three switches are closed. Hence, (c) is correct since the circuit is open and the PDs are the same. With all switches closed, the circuit reduces to the amount shown in the figure.

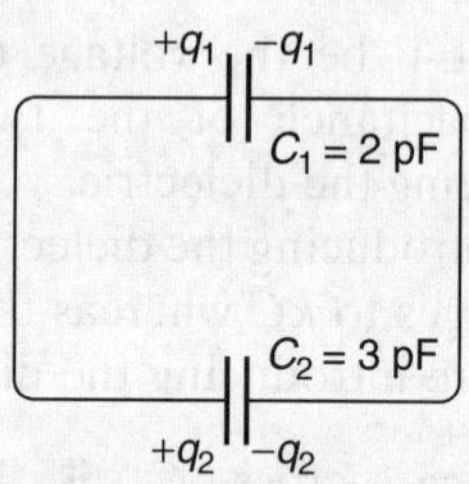

Initially, the charge on each capacitor is 60 pC. After redistribution, let q_1 and q_2 be the charges on the capacitors, as shown in the figure. Then

$$q_1 + q_2 = 120\text{ pC and } \frac{q_1}{2\text{ pF}} = \frac{q_2}{3\text{ nF}}$$

Solving the two equations gives $q_1 = 48$ pC and $q_2 =$ 72 pC.

Hence $V_1 = V_2 = \frac{48\text{ pc}}{2\text{ pF}} = 24$ V.

11. (c) Once it is disconnected from the battery, the charge on the plates cannot change. The electric field inside the capacitor in the absence of the dielectric is $E = \frac{10\text{ V}}{5\text{ cm}} = 2$ V/cm. After the dielectric is introduced, the field outside the dielectric region is still $E = 2$ V/cm since charge density on the plates is still the same. The field inside the dielectric region is $\frac{E}{k} = \frac{2\text{ V/cm}}{4} = 0.5$ V/cm.

Hence, the potential difference between the capacitor plates is

$$V = (2\text{ V/cm} \times 4\text{ cm}) + (0.5\text{ V/cm} \times 1\text{ cm}) = 8.5\text{ V.}$$

12. (d) Let ξ be the applied voltage. The potential drop across the capacitors $C_1 = 1\ \mu$F and $C_2 = 2\ \mu$F will be $\frac{2}{3}\xi$ and $\frac{1}{3}\xi$.

These values must be less than their respective breakdown voltages $V_1 = 6$ kV and $V_2 = 4$ kV. Thus $\frac{2}{3}\xi < 6\text{ kV} \Rightarrow \xi < 9\text{ kV}$ and $\frac{1}{3}\xi < 4\text{ kV} \Rightarrow \xi < 12$ k

Hence, the maximum value of ξ is 9 kV.

13. (b) When connected to 20 V, the field between the plates is $\frac{20V}{d}$, which should be less than the breakdown strength 3 × 106 V/m. Thus

$$\frac{20\text{ V}}{d} < 3\times10^6\text{ V/m}$$

$$\Rightarrow \quad d > 6.67 \times 10^{-6}\text{ m}$$

Also, the capacitance should be equal to 1.77 μF. Thus

$$\frac{k\varepsilon_0 A}{d} = 1.77\ \mu\text{F}$$

$$\Rightarrow \quad A = \frac{(1.77\times10^{-6})d}{200(8.85\times10^{-12})} = 1000d$$

In options (b), (c) and (d), the values of d are all greater than 6.67 × 10^{-6} m, but only option (b) satisfies the other condition, A = 1000d.

14. (a) The potential difference between the plates will remain unchanged only if the capacitance remains unchanged, since charge on the capacitor has not changed. Let d be the initial separation between the plates and A be the plate area. Then, initial capacitance is $C = \frac{\varepsilon_0 A}{d}$.

In the final situation, the capacitor can be treated as a combination of two series capacitors: an air-filled capacitor having plate separation d + 1.6 mm − 2 mm = d − 0.4 mm and a dielectric-filled capacitor having plate separation 2 mm whose respective capacitances are

$$C_1 = \frac{\varepsilon_0 A}{d - 0.4\text{ mm}} \text{ and } C_2 = \frac{k\varepsilon_0 A}{2\text{ mm}}$$

The combination of C_1 and C_2 must equal C. Thus, we have

$$\frac{1}{C} = \frac{1}{C_1} + \frac{1}{C_2}$$

$$\Rightarrow \quad \frac{d}{\varepsilon_0 A} = \frac{d - 0.4\text{ mm}}{\varepsilon_0 A} + \frac{2\text{ mm}}{k\varepsilon_0 A}$$

$$\Rightarrow \quad d = d - 0.4\text{ mm} + \frac{2\text{ mm}}{k}$$

$$\Rightarrow \quad k = 5$$

15. (a) The arrangement can be treated as a combination of two capacitors in series, having capacitances

$$C_1 = 3\left(\frac{\varepsilon_0 S}{d/3}\right) \text{ and } C_2 = 6\left(\frac{\varepsilon_0 S}{2d/3}\right)$$

$$\Rightarrow \quad C_1 = C_2$$

If ξ is the cell emf, then PD across each capacitor will be equal to $\xi/2$. The electric field in the two dielectric regions will be

$$E_1 = \frac{\xi/2}{d/3} = \frac{3\xi}{2d} \text{ and } E_2 = \frac{\xi/2}{2d/3} = \frac{3\xi}{4d}$$

These values must be less than their respective breakdown strengths. Thus, we have

$$\frac{3\xi}{2(1\,\mu m)} < 9\times10^6 \text{ V/m} \Rightarrow \xi < 6 \text{ V}$$

and $$\frac{3\xi}{4(1\,\mu m)} < 3\times10^6 \text{ V/m} \Rightarrow \xi < 4 \text{ V}$$

Hence, the maximum permissible value of ξ is 4 V.

16. (b) Let C be the capacitance of the capacitor.

Case I: Charge flow through battery = $10C$. Work done by the battery $=10(10C)=100C$.

Energy stored in the capacitor $= \dfrac{(10C)^2}{2C} = 50C$.

Total heat generated in the wires $H_1 = 100C - 50C = 50C$.

Case II: Connected to 5-V battery: Charge flow through the battery $= 5C$. Work done by the battery $= 5(5C) = 25C$.

Energy stored in the capacitor $= \dfrac{(5C)^2}{2C} = \dfrac{25}{2}C$.

Heat generated in the wires $= 25C - \dfrac{25}{2}C = \dfrac{25}{2}C$.

Connected to 10-V battery: Charge flow through the battery = $10C - 5C = 5C$. Work done by the battery $= 10(5C) = 50C$.

Energy stored in the capacitor

$$= \frac{(10C)^2 - (5C)^2}{2C} = \frac{75}{2}C.$$

Heat generated in the wires $= 50C - \dfrac{75}{2}C = \dfrac{25}{2}C$.

Total heat generated in the wires

$$H_2 = \frac{25}{2}C + \frac{25}{2}C = 25C.$$

Hence $\dfrac{H_1}{H_2} = 2$.

17. (c) Before the dielectric is inserted, the charge on the capacitors C and $2C$ are CV and $2CV$, respectively. When the capacitor is filled with the dielectric slab, its capacitance changes and redistribution of charge takes place, as shown in the figure.

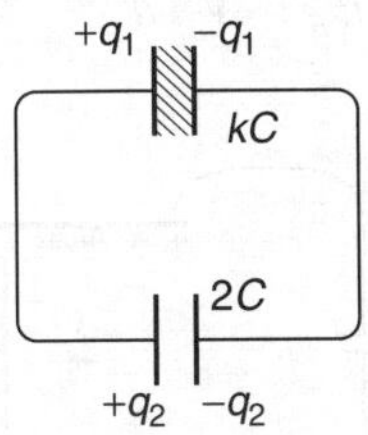

From charge conservation, we have

$$q_1 + q_2 = CV + 2CV = 3CV \qquad \ldots(1)$$

From loop equation, we have

$$\frac{q_1}{kc} = \frac{q_2}{2c} \qquad \ldots(2)$$

Solving the two equations gives

$$q_1 = \left(\frac{k}{k+2}\right)3CV \text{ and } q_2 = \left(\frac{2}{k+2}\right)3CV.$$

The potential difference across the capacitors is

$$\frac{q_2}{2c} = \frac{3V}{k+2}$$

18. (d) The charge density in the upper dielectric is $\sigma_1 = \sigma(1 - \frac{1}{k_1}) = \frac{5}{6}\sigma$ and that in the lower dielectric is $\sigma_2 = \sigma\left(1 - \frac{1}{k_2}\right) = \frac{2}{3}\sigma$

The charge density at the boundary of the dielectrics is $\sigma_{\text{boundary}} = \sigma_1 - \sigma_2 = \dfrac{\sigma}{6}$.

19. (b), (c) The upper and lower parts can be treated as two capacitors in parallel, with plate areas $A/3$ and $2A/3$, respectively. Their individual capacitances are, respectively

$$C_A = k\frac{\varepsilon_0(A/3)}{d} \text{ and } C_B = \frac{\varepsilon_0(2A/3)}{d}$$

$$\Rightarrow \quad \frac{C_A}{C_B} = \frac{k}{2} \Rightarrow \text{Option (a) is correct}$$

Since they are in parallel

$$\frac{Q_A}{Q_B} = \frac{C_A}{C_B} = \frac{\varepsilon}{2}$$

The ratio of charge densities

$$\frac{\sigma_A}{\sigma_B} = \frac{Q_A/(A/3)}{Q_B/(2A/3)} = 2\frac{Q_A}{Q_B} = k$$

$\Rightarrow$ Option (c) is correct

The potential difference V and the separation d between the plates is the same. Thus

$$\frac{E_A}{E_B} = \frac{V/d}{V/d} = 1 \Rightarrow \text{Option (d) is correct}$$

20. (a), (b), (c)

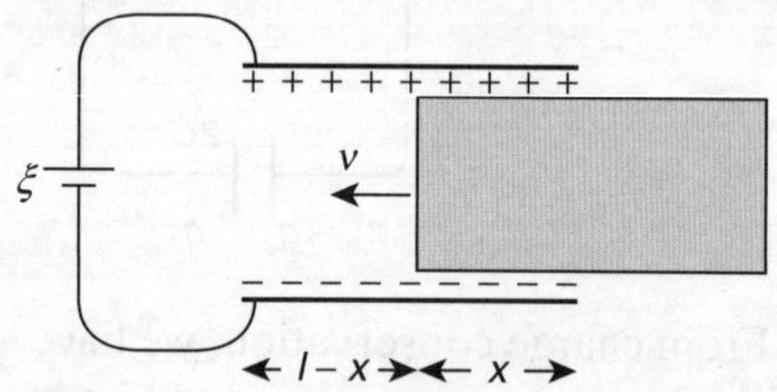

Consider a situation where the length x of the dielectric is inside the capacitor (see figure). The arrangement can be treated as a combination of two parallel capacitors. The equivalent capacitance at this instant is

$$C(x) = \frac{k\varepsilon_0 ax}{d} + \frac{\varepsilon_0 a(l-x)}{d} = \frac{\varepsilon_0 a}{d}[(k-1)x+1]$$

The charge on the capacitor at this instant is $q(x) = \xi C(x)$. The instantaneous current is given by

$$I = \frac{dq}{dt} = \xi\frac{dC}{dt} = \frac{\xi\varepsilon_0(k-1)a}{d}\frac{dx}{dt} = \frac{\xi\varepsilon_0(k-1)av}{d}$$

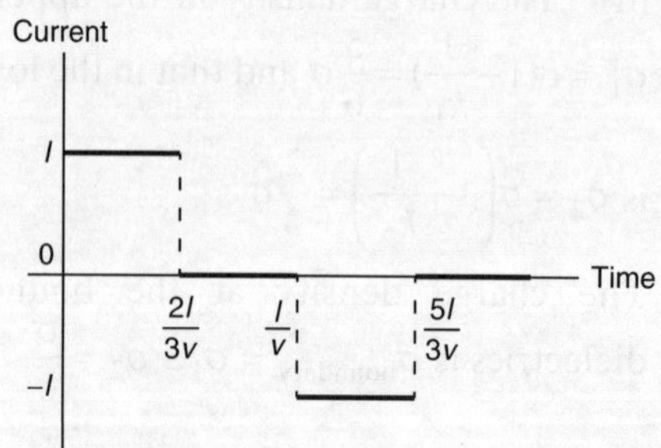

Current flows only as long as the capacitance changes. Once the slab is completely inside the capacitor, the capacitance does not change even as the slab moves, and hence, there is no current during this time interval. Current flows in the opposite direction when the slab comes out from the other side of the capacitor. The figure shows the current versus time plot.

21. (b) Potential energy of the capacitor $U = \frac{1}{2}(200\ \mu\text{F})(200\ \text{V})^2 = 4$ J. The total heat dissipated in the resistors equals U.

Case I (Series Connection): Heat dissipated in the two resistors is given by

$$H_1 = \int_0^\infty I^2(100\ \Omega)dt \text{ and } H_1' = \int_0^\infty I^2(30\ \Omega)dt$$

[I is the same in series connection]

$$\Rightarrow \frac{H_1}{10} = \frac{H_1'}{30} \Rightarrow H_1 = \frac{1}{4}U = 1\ \text{J}$$

Case II (Parallel Connection): Heat dissipated in the two resistors is given by

$$H_2 = \int_0^\infty \frac{V^2}{10\ \Omega}dt \text{ and } H_2' = \int_0^\infty \frac{V^2}{30\ \Omega}dt$$

[V is the same in parallel connection]

$$\Rightarrow \quad 10H_2 = 30H_2' \Rightarrow \frac{H_2}{30} = \frac{H_2'}{10} \Rightarrow H_2 = \frac{3}{4}U = 3J$$

22. (d) Initially, the charge on the capacitors C and $2C$, are CV and $4CV$, respectively. After being connected, let charge distribution be as shown in the figure.

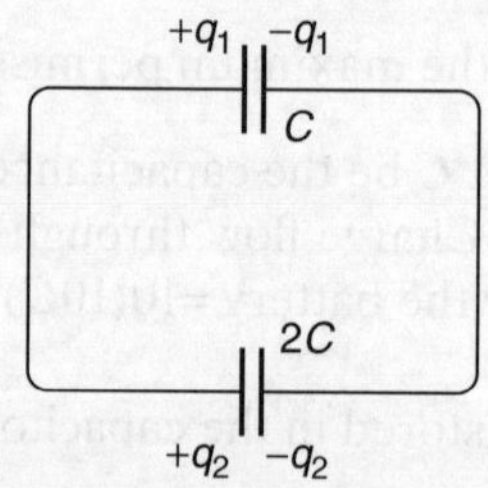

From charge conservation, we have

$$q_1 + q_2 = 4CV - CV = 3CV \quad \text{...(1)}$$

From loop equation, we have

$$\frac{q_1}{c} = \frac{q_2}{2c} \quad \text{...(2)}$$

Solving the two equations gives $q_1 = CV$ and $q_2 = 2CV$

The initial potential energy is

$$U_i = \frac{1}{2}CV^2 + \frac{1}{2}(2C)(2V)^2 = \frac{9}{2}CV^2$$

The final potential energy is

$$U_f = \frac{1}{2}(C+2C)V^2 = \frac{3}{2}CV^2$$

[PD across both capacitors is V]

The lost potential energy is converted into heat in the wires. Hence, heat generated is $U_i - U_f = 3CV^2$

23. (d) The initial charges on the two capacitors are $q_1 = 300\ \mu$C and $q_2 = 360\ \mu$C.
Let steady state charge distribution be as shown in the figure.

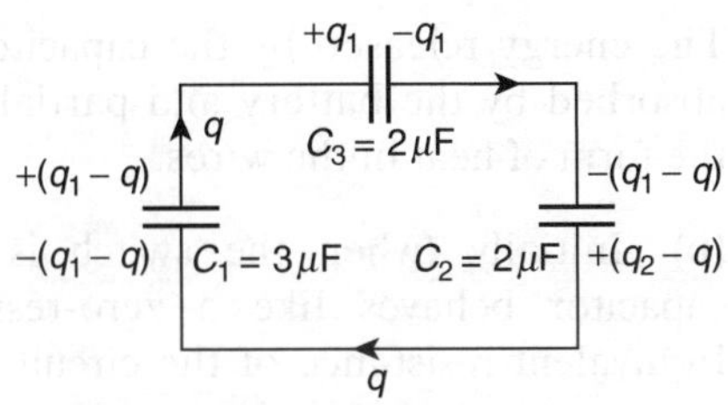

Writing loop equations, we have

$$\frac{q_1 - q}{3} - \frac{q}{2} + \frac{q_2 - q}{2} = 0$$

$$\Rightarrow \quad 2(q_1 - q) - 3q + 3(q_2 - q) = 0$$

$$\Rightarrow \quad q = \frac{2q_1 + 3q_2}{8} = 210\ \mu\text{C}$$

24. (c) When the plates are pulled apart, the capacitance changes by an amount

$$\Delta C = \frac{\varepsilon_0 A}{2d} - \frac{\varepsilon_0 A}{d} = -\frac{\varepsilon_0 A}{2d}$$

The PD across the capacitor remains the same and equal to V. So, charge flows through the cell by an amount $\Delta q = V\Delta C$.
Let W be the mechanical work required to pull the plates, W_{batt} be the work done by the battery during this period and ΔU be the change in potential energy of the capacitor. Now, using the Work–Energy Theorem $W + W_{batt} = \Delta U$, we have

$$W + V\Delta q = \frac{1}{2}V^2\Delta C$$

$$\Rightarrow \quad W + V^2\Delta C = \frac{1}{2}V^2\Delta C$$

$$\Rightarrow \quad W = -\frac{1}{2}V^2\Delta C = \frac{\varepsilon_0 A V^2}{4d}$$

25. (a) Let the charge distribution be as shown in the figure. Writing loop equations along loops *ABEFA* and *ABCDEFA*, we have

$$\frac{q_1}{c_1} = V \Rightarrow q_1 = CV \text{ and } \frac{q_2}{C_2} = 0 \Rightarrow q_2 = 0$$

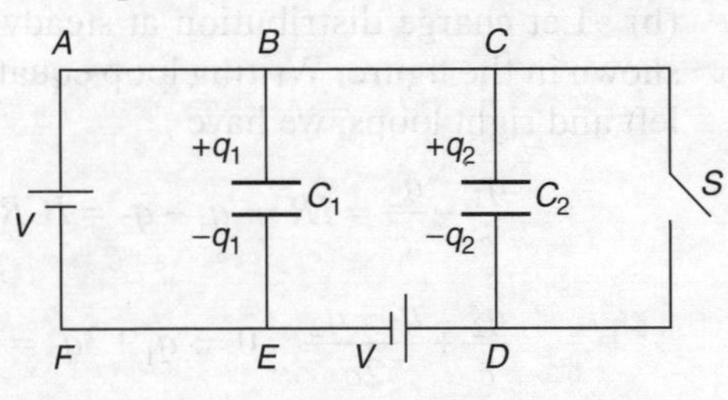

When the switch is closed, capacitor C_2 is short-circuited, but the charge on it is already zero, so nothing changes. The charge on C_1 still remains q_1 and no charge flows through the cells.
The change in potential energy $\Delta U = 0$, and work done by the battery $W = 0$. Now, using the Work–Energy Theorem $W = \Delta U + H$, the heat H generated in the wires is

$$H = W - \Delta U = 0$$

26. (c) At steady state, current through the capacitor branch is zero. Current in the left part of the circuit is $\dfrac{12\text{ V} - 6\text{ V}}{2\ \Omega + 4\ \Omega} = 1$ A. The potential difference across the capacitor plates is 4 V + (6 Ω)(1 A) = 10 V. Before the dielectric is introduced, charge on the capacitor is (10 V)(10 μF) = 100 μC.
After the dielectric is introduced, capacitance changes. It is now a combination of two parallel capacitors. If d is the separation between the plates and A is the plate area, then $\dfrac{\varepsilon_0 A}{d} = 10\mu$F. The new capacitance C is given by

$$\frac{1}{C} = \frac{2d/3}{\varepsilon_0 A} + \frac{d/3}{2\varepsilon_0 A} = \frac{5d}{6\varepsilon_0 A}$$

$$\Rightarrow \quad C = \frac{6\varepsilon_0 A}{5d} = \frac{6}{5}(10\ \mu\text{F}) = 12\ \mu\text{F}$$

Now, charge on the capacitor will be (10 V) (12 μF)= 120 μC.
Hence change in the amount of charge on the capacitor is 120 μC –100 μC = 20 μC.

27. (c)

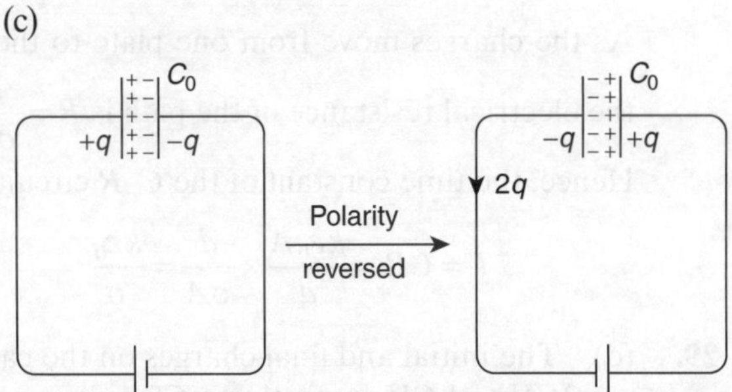

The equivalent capacitance of the circuit is $c_0 = \dfrac{2}{3}c$. Charge flow through the cell is $q = \dfrac{2}{3}CV$. When the polarity of the cell is reversed, the same amount of charge (see figure) appears on the capacitors but with the polarity reversed.
A total charge $2q$ flows through the cell, so the battery does work $W = \left(\dfrac{4}{3}CV\right)V$. However, there is no change in the potential energies of the

capacitors $\Rightarrow \Delta U = 0$. Now, using the Work–Energy Theorem, $W = \Delta U + H$, the heat H generated in the wires is

$$H = W - \Delta U = \frac{4}{3}CV^2$$

Work done by the cell has been entirely converted into heat in the wires.

28. (b) The figure shows the initial charge distribution on the capacitor plates, where $2Q - q = -Q + q$.

$$\Rightarrow q = \frac{3}{2}Q$$

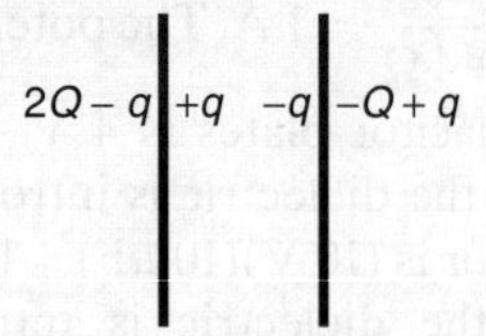

When the plates are connected by a wire, positive charge flows from the left plate to the right plate until the plates become equipotential. Eventually, no charge remains on the inner side of the plates, whereas the charge on the outer side of the plates remains as it is.

The initial and final potential energies of the capacitor are $U_i = \dfrac{q^2}{2C}$ and $U_f = 0$. The heat generated in the wires equals the loss in the potential energy. Thus, we have

$$H = \frac{q^2}{2C} = \frac{9Q^2 d}{8k\varepsilon_0 A}$$

As the charges move from one plate to the other, the electrical resistance of the path is $R = \dfrac{d}{\sigma A}$.

Hence, the time constant of the C–R circuit is

$$T = CR = \frac{k\varepsilon_0 A}{d} \times \frac{d}{\sigma A} = \frac{k\varepsilon_0}{\sigma}$$

29. (d) The initial and final charges on the capacitor are $2CV$ and CV, respectively. Change in potential energy of the capacitor is

$$\Delta U = \frac{1}{2}CV^2 - \frac{1}{2}C(2V)^2 = -\frac{3}{2}CV^2$$

The negative sign indicates loss in potential energy. During this process of discharge, charge CV has flow through the cell opposite to its sense of emf. Work done by the cell is $W = -(CV)V = -CV^2$

The negative sign indicates that the cell has absorbed energy.

Now, using the Work–Energy Theorem $W = \Delta U + H$, the heat H generated in the wires is

$$H = W - \Delta U = \frac{1}{2}CV^2$$

The energy released by the capacitor is partially absorbed by the battery and partially appears in the form of heat in the wires.

30. (b) Initially (when the switch is closed), the capacitor behaves like a zero-resistance path. Equivalent resistance of the circuit just after the switch is closed is $\dfrac{500}{3}\,\Omega$. Current flow through the cell is $\dfrac{1\text{ V}}{\dfrac{500}{3}\,\Omega} = \dfrac{3}{500}$ A. Initial charging rate of the capacitor equals the current through that branch

$$I = \frac{2}{3}\left(\frac{3}{500}\text{ A}\right) = \frac{2}{500}\text{ A.}$$

At steady state, the capacitor behaves like an infinite resistance path. No current flows through the capacitor branch. The PD across the capacitor branch is $\dfrac{2}{3}(1\text{ V}) = \dfrac{2}{3}$ V. The steady state charge in the capacitor is $q_0 = \left(\dfrac{2}{3}\text{ V}\right)(3000\,\mu\text{F}) = 2$ mC. If the capacitor were to be charged at a constant rate I, the time required to charge it till q_0 would be $T = \dfrac{q_0}{I} = \dfrac{2\text{ mC}}{\dfrac{2}{500}\text{ A}} = 500\text{ ms} = \dfrac{1}{2}$ s.

31. (b), (d) Initially (when the switch is closed), the capacitor C_2 behaves like a zero-resistance path. Equivalent resistance just after closing the switch is 5 Ω.

Capacitor C_1 behaves like a cell of emf $\dfrac{2\,\mu\text{C}}{1\,\mu\text{F}} = 2$ V.

Since the polarity of C_1 is not given, the current through the circuit may be $\dfrac{7\text{ V} + 2\text{ V}}{5\,\Omega} = 1.8$ A or $\dfrac{7\text{ V} - 2\text{ V}}{5\,\Omega} = 1$ A depending on the polarity of C_1.

32. (b) Let charge distribution at steady state be as shown in the figure. Writing loop equations for the left and right loops, we have

$$\frac{q_1}{c} - \frac{q_2}{c} = IR \Rightarrow q_1 - q_2 = ICR \quad \ldots(1)$$

$$\frac{q_2}{c} + \frac{q_1 + q_2}{2c} = 0 \Rightarrow q_1 + 3q_2 = 0 \quad \ldots(2)$$

Solving the two equations gives

$$q_1 = \frac{3}{4}ICR \text{ and } q_2 = -\frac{1}{4}ICR.$$

Thus, charge on C_3 is $q_1 + q_2 = \frac{1}{2}ICR$. Hence $n = 2$.

33. (b) At any instant, charge on the capacitor is $q = CV$ and the current is $I = \frac{dq}{dt} = C\frac{dV}{dt}$. From the V–t graph, we see that at all instants, the slope has the same magnitude $\left|\frac{dV}{dt}\right| = \frac{50 \text{ V}}{2 \text{ ms}} = 25000$ V/s.

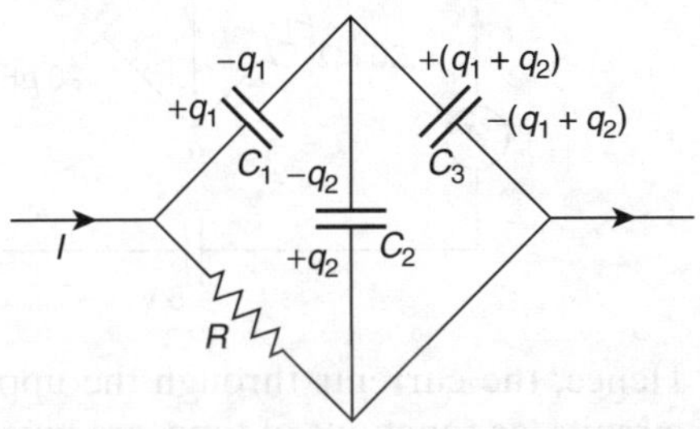

Hence, the current has a constant value $I_0 = (2\ \mu\text{F})(25000 \text{ V/s}) = 50$ mA. The direction of the current, however, changes at regular intervals of 2 ms.
The instantaneous power is $P = VI$. Since the current has a constant value, P is maximum when V is maximum. Hence, $P_0 = (50 \text{ V})(50 \text{ mA}) = 2.5$ W.

34. (b) At steady state, PD across 12-μF capacitor = PD across the 6-Ω resistor $= \left(\frac{6}{9}\right) 9 \text{ V} = 6$ V.

Hence, the charge on it = (12 μF) (6 V) = 72 μC.
The PD across the 4-μF capacitor = PD across the 3-Ω resistor $= \left(\frac{6}{9}\right) 9 \text{ V} = 3$ V.

Hence, the charge on it= (4 μF)(3 V)= 12 μC.
Hence, charge flow through the switch = 72 μC – 12 μC = 60 μC from b to a.

35. (d)

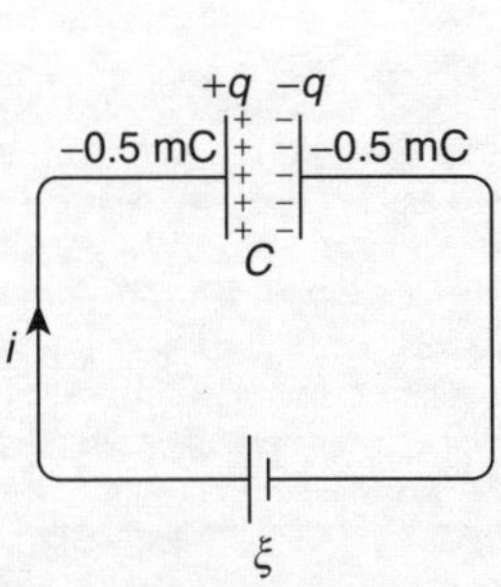

Initially, the charge on the outer side of each plate is $\frac{q_0}{2} = -0.5$ mC whereas for the inner side of the plates A and B, the respective charges are –0.5 mC and +0.5 mC. At any time t after closing the switch, let the charge on the inner side of the plates be $+q$ and $-q$, as shown in the figure. Initially, the value of q is –0.5 mC. The charge on the outer side of the plates does not change during charging. The rate of charging of the capacitor at time t is given by

$$\frac{dq}{dt} = \frac{\xi - \frac{q}{C}}{R} = \frac{C\xi - q}{CR} = \frac{1 \text{ mC} - q}{\frac{4 \text{ s}}{\ln 3}}$$

For net charge on plate A to become zero, the value of q must become +0.5 mC. Let T be the time in which this happens. Then we have

$$\int_0^T dt = \frac{4 \text{ s}}{\ln 3} \int_{-0.5mC}^{+0.5mC} \frac{dq}{1 \text{ mC} - q}$$

$$\Rightarrow \quad T = \frac{4 \text{ s}}{\ln 3} \left| \ln(1 \text{ mc} - q) \right|_{+0.5 \text{ mC}}^{-0.5 \text{ mC}}$$

$$= \frac{4 \text{ s}}{\ln 3} \ln\left(\frac{1 \text{ mC} + 0.5 \text{ mC}}{1 \text{ mC} - 0.5 \text{ mC}}\right) = 4 \text{ s}$$

36. (a) Let us choose $t = 0$ as the time when the capacitor has just discharged completely. The potential difference across the capacitor as a function of time is given by

$$V = \xi(1 - e^{-t/CR})$$

The lamp flashes when the value of V reaches the breakdown voltage V_L.
The time T when this happens is given by

$$V_L = \xi(1 - e^{-T/CR})$$

$$\Rightarrow \quad e^{-T/CR} = 1 - \frac{V_L}{\xi}$$

$$\Rightarrow \quad e^{T/CR} = \frac{\xi}{\xi - V_L}$$

$$\Rightarrow \quad T = CR \ln\left(\frac{\xi}{\xi - V_L}\right)$$

37. (c), (d) Charge on the upper plate of the capacitor as a function of time is given by

$$q(t) = \int I_0 \cos(\omega t) dt = \frac{I_0}{\omega} \sin(\omega t)$$

The constant of integration is zero since the initial value of q is zero.
In the time interval $t = 0$ to $t = \frac{7\pi}{6\omega}$, the charge is maximum at $t = \frac{\pi}{2\omega}$ and it is equal to $\frac{I_0}{\omega} = \frac{1 \text{ A}}{500 \text{ rad/s}} = 2$ mC. Hence (a) is incorrect.

The value of I just before $t = \frac{7\pi}{6\omega}$ is $I_0 \cos(\frac{7\pi}{6})$, which is negative. Therefore, current is anti-clockwise. Hence (b) is incorrect.

At $t = \frac{7\pi}{6\omega}$, the value of q is $\frac{1\text{ A}}{500\text{ rad/s}} \sin\left(\frac{7\pi}{6}\right) = -1$ mC. The PD across the capacitor plates is $\frac{1\text{ mC}}{20\text{ uF}} = 50$ V in the same sense as the 50-V cell. Therefore, the current in the right part of the circuit at this instant is $\frac{50\text{ V} + 50\text{ V}}{10\ \Omega} = 10$ A. Hence (c) is correct.

At steady state, charge on the upper plate of the capacitor will be (50 V) (20 μF) = 1 mC. Initially, charge on this plate was –1 mC. Therefore, a total charge of 2 mC will flow through the cell before steady state is reached. Hence (d) is correct.

38. (b) Let r be the radius of each sphere. Then, the charge on each sphere will be $q = (4\ \pi\varepsilon 0 r)V$.

The electric field between the plates is $E = \frac{V}{h}$. The spheres will move between the plates with acceleration $a = \frac{qE}{m} = \frac{qV}{mh}$. The time required to cover the distance h between the plates is $T = \sqrt{\frac{2h}{a}} = \sqrt{\frac{2mh^2}{qV}}$. If n is the total number of spheres, the average current is

$$I = \frac{nq}{T} = nq\sqrt{\frac{qV}{2mh^2}} \propto q^{3/2}V^{1/2}$$

Now, putting $q = (4\pi\varepsilon_0 r)$V, we have $I \propto V^{3/2}V^{1/2} = V^2$

39. (a), (b), (c), (d) There will be no current through the voltmeter, since an ideal voltmeter means infinite resistance. The given circuit is simply two C–R circuits connected in parallel to the same source of emf, 50 V. The time constant $T = CR = 1$ s is the same for both the circuits. The initial currents through the upper and lower circuits are $\frac{5\text{ V}}{25\text{ k}\Omega} = \frac{1}{5}$ mA and $\frac{5\text{ V}}{50\text{ k}\Omega} = \frac{1}{10}$ mA, respectively.

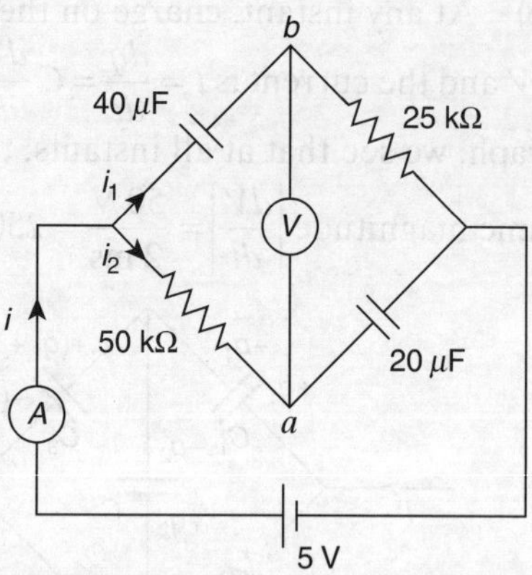

Hence, the currents through the upper and lower circuits, as functions of time, are given by

$$i_1 = \frac{1}{5}\text{mA}e^{-t} \text{ and } i_2 = \frac{1}{10}\text{mA}e^{-t}$$

The current flow through the ammeter is given by

$$i = i_1 + i_2 = \frac{3}{10}\text{mA}e^{-t}$$

Now, moving from a to b through the 50-kΩ resistor, the cell and then the 25-kΩ resistor, we have

$$V_a + i_2(50\text{ k}\Omega) - 5\text{ V} + i_1(25\text{ k}\Omega) = V_b$$

$$\Rightarrow V_a - V_b = 5V - 10Ve^{-t}$$

Here, $V_a - V_b$ is the voltmeter reading.

At $t = 0$, $V_a - V_b = -5V$, $i = 0.3$ mA.

At $t = \ln 2$, $V_a - V_b = 0$, $i = 0.15$ mA.

At $t = \infty$, $V_a - V_b = 5$ V, $i = 0$.

At $t = 1$, $i = (0.3/e)$ mA = $1/e$ of its initial reading.

CHAPTER

18 Magnetism

- Magnetic interactions are fundamentally interactions between moving charged particles. A moving charge or a current creates a magnetic field **B** in the surrounding space (in addition to its electric field). The magnetic field exerts a force **F** on any other moving charge or current that is present in the field.

  A magnet derives its magnetism from the coordinated motion of its atomic electrons; in non-magnetic substances, these motions are not coordinated. When a magnet is hung by a thread from a ceiling, one end of the magnet points towards the Earth's north pole and the other end towards the south pole; this indicates that the Earth is also a magnet. The two ends of the magnet are called the north and the south poles of the magnet, respectively.

  Magnetic poles always occur in pairs. Magnetic field lines drawn using another test magnet are always closed. Therefore, the magnetic flux through a closed surface is always zero:

  $$\oint \mathbf{B}\cdot d\mathbf{s}=0$$

  This equation is called Gauss's law for magnetism. The SI unit for magnetic flow is Weber (Wb). The magnetic field is generally referred to as magnetic flux density and its SI unit is Wb/m^2 or Tesla (T).

- A particle with charge q moving with velocity $\mathbf{v}$ in a magnetic field $\mathbf{B}$ experiences a force given by

  $$\mathbf{F}=q(\mathbf{v}\times\mathbf{B})$$

  A particle with charge of magnitude q, moving with a speed v perpendicular to a uniform magnetic field of magnitude B, moves in a circular path with radius R, and time-period T given by

  $$R=\frac{mv}{qB} \text{ and } T=\frac{2\pi m}{qB}$$

  A particle with charge of magnitude q, moving with a speed v at angle θ to a uniform magnetic field of magnitude B, moves in a helical path with radius R, time-period T and pitch p given by

  $$R=\frac{mv\sin\theta}{qB}, T=\frac{2\pi m}{qB} \text{ and } p=(v\cos\theta)T$$

- Cyclotrons are particle accelerators composed of two semi-circular portions called "dees" because of their D-shape; charged particles move in circular paths with increasing radii. The energy of the particle keeps on increasing but the frequency remains unchanged. An alternating voltage is maintained across the two Ds. The voltage alternates with the same frequency as the particle frequency (number of revolutions per unit time). This frequency is, therefore, called the cyclotron frequency:

  $$f=\frac{qB}{2\pi m}$$

  If the radius of the cyclotron is R, the particle finally emerges out of the cyclotron with velocity $v=qBR/m$. Energy of the particle is

  $$E=\frac{q^2B^2R^2}{2m}$$

- When a charged particle moves in a region of space where both electric and magnetic fields are present, the total force **F** on the particle is the vector sum of the electric and magnetic forces:

  $$\mathbf{F}=q(\mathbf{E}+\mathbf{v}\times\mathbf{B})$$

In a region of perpendicular **E** and **B** fields, a charged particle moving perpendicular to the plane containing the field vectors (along $\mathbf{E}\times\mathbf{B}$) will continue undeviated if its speed is $v=\dfrac{E}{B}$.

- Current carrying wires contain moving charged particles; so they experience force when present in a magnetic field region. The force on a current carrying wire kept in a magnetic field region is given by

$$\mathbf{F}=I\int d\mathbf{l}\times\mathbf{B}$$

If the magnetic field **B** is uniform, then the above equation reduces to $\mathbf{F}=I(\Delta\mathbf{l}\times\mathbf{B})$.

- A closed current loop with area A and current I is called a magnetic dipole having dipole moment

$$\mu = I\mathbf{A}\ (\text{SI unit A}\cdot\text{m}^2)$$

The direction of the area vector A is to be chosen along the direction of the thumb, when the right-hand fingers are curled along the flow of the current in the loop.
A particle with charge q moving in a circular path of radius R, with angular speed ω, has an associated angular momentum $\mathbf{l}=mR^2\omega$ and magnetic moment $\mu=\dfrac{1}{2}qR^2\omega$. They are related as

$$\mu=\frac{q}{2m}\mathbf{l}$$

When the magnetic dipole is kept in a uniform magnetic field B, the dipole experiences no net force but experiences a torque and possesses potential energy given by

$$\tau=\mu\times\mathbf{B} \text{ and } \mathbf{U}=-\mu\cdot\mathbf{B}$$

A magnetic dipole is similar to an electric dipole. In many situations, it is convenient to replace the magnetic dipole with a pair of imaginary magnetic poles of strengths $-m$ and $+m$ separated by a distance l such that $\mu=ml$. The force on the magnetic poles can be taken as $\mathbf{F}=m\mathbf{B}$.

- The magnetic field due to a current element is given by the law of Biot and Savart:

$$d\mathbf{B}=\frac{\mu_0}{4\pi}\frac{I(d\mathbf{l}\times\mathbf{r})}{r^3},$$

where $d\mathbf{l}$ is a vector of length dl chosen along the direction of the current in the conductor. The constant μ_0 is called the magnetic permeability of free space; it can be considered as the ability of free space to allow the formation of magnetic field. In SI units, $\mu_0=4\pi\times10^{-7}$ N/A^2.

The value of B for a few current carrying conductors is as follows:

1. Field of a finite straight current carrying wire:

$$B=\frac{\mu_0 I}{4\pi d}(\cos\theta_1-\cos\theta_2)$$

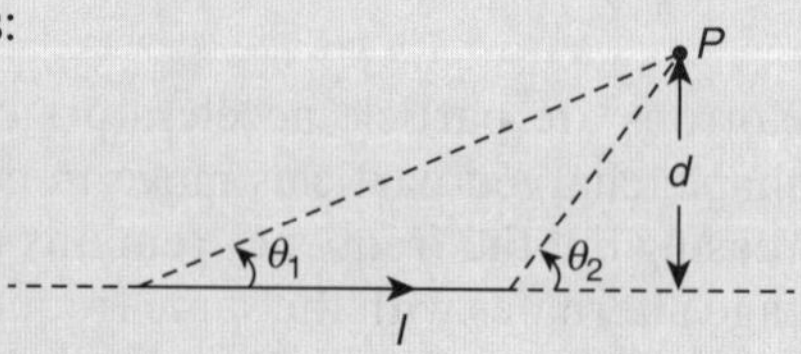

2. At distance x (along the axis) from the centre of a circular current carrying wire of radius R:

$$B=\frac{\mu_0 IR^2}{2\left(R^2+x^2\right)^{3/2}} \text{ (greatest at centre)}$$

3. At distance r from an infinitely long straight current carrying wire:

$$B=\frac{\mu_0 I}{2\pi r}$$

4. At distance r from an infinitely long hollow cylindrical current carrying conductor of radius R:

$$E=\begin{cases}0, 0\le r<R\\ \dfrac{B_0R}{r}, r\ge R\end{cases}, \text{ where } B_0=\frac{\mu_0 I}{2\pi R} \text{ (field at the surface)}$$

5. At distance r from an infinitely long solid cylindrical current carrying conductor of radius R:

$$E = \begin{cases} \dfrac{B_0}{R} r, 0 \le r < R \\ \dfrac{B_0 R}{r}, r \ge R \end{cases}, \text{ where } B_0 = \frac{\mu_0 I}{2\pi R} \text{ (field at the surface)}$$

6. Inside a long solenoid of length l and N number of turns:

$$B = \frac{\mu_0 N I}{l}$$

The same formula holds for a field inside a toroidal solenoid. No field exists outside the toroid tube, whereas in the solenoid, a weak field exists outside the solenoid tube.

- Ampere's law states that the line integral of **B** around a closed path is proportional to the algebraic sum of the currents enclosed by the integration path; the positive sign for the currents is to be chosen along the direction of the thumb when the right-hand fingers are curled along the direction of the integration path:

$$\oint \mathbf{B} \cdot d\mathbf{l} = \mu_0 I_{\text{encl}}$$

Ampere's law is very useful in finding the magnetic field involving symmetrical current distributions.

- The magnitude of the force per unit length between two parallel wires carrying currents I_1 and I_2, separated by a distance r, is

$$\frac{F}{l} = \frac{\mu_0 I_1 I_2}{2\pi r}$$

The force is attractive when the currents are in the same direction, and repulsive when the currents are in opposite directions.

- Magnetic materials are magnetised in the presence of external magnetic fields due to the alignment of the magnetic dipoles inside the material. This causes an additional contribution to the field inside the material. If $\mathbf{B_0}$ is the magnetic flux density caused by the current in the conductor, and $\mathbf{B_m}$ is the magnetic flux density caused by magnetisation of the material, then the net magnetic flux density **B** inside the material is $\mathbf{B} = \mathbf{B_0} + \mathbf{B_m}$.

For convenience, we define quantities magnetic field intensity $\mathbf{H} = \dfrac{\mathbf{B_0}}{\mu_0}$ and magnetisation $\mathbf{M} = \dfrac{\mathbf{B_m}}{\mu_0}$ so that the above equation can be written as

$$\mathbf{B} = \mu_0 (\mathbf{H} + \mathbf{M})$$

Both H and M have the same SI unit A/m. The internal magnetisation **M** equals the net magnetic moment per unit volume and is proportional to the external field **H**; the proportionality constant χ_m is called the magnetic susceptibility of the material. The above equation now reduces to

$$\mathbf{B} = (\chi_m + 1)\mathbf{B_0} = \mu_r \mathbf{B_0}$$

The ratio B/B_0, denoted by symbol $\mu_r = \chi_m + 1$, is called the relative magnetic permeability of the material. For diamagnetic materials, χ_m has a small negative value; for a perfect diamagnetic material, $\chi_m = -1$. For paramagnetic materials, χ_m has a small positive value less than unity and it decreases with increasing temperature. For ferromagnetic materials, χ_m is much larger than unity and when heated above Curie temperature, they become paramagnetic. Diamagnetic materials are weakly repelled by magnets, while paramagnetic materials are weakly attracted by magnets and ferromagnetic materials are very strongly attracted by magnets.

- The magnetic behaviours of substances can be explained by considering the circular motion of electrons. The electrons in an atom move in circular orbits around the nucleus which is equivalent to a circular coil carrying current. The orbital motion of electrons gives rise to orbital magnetic moment. In addition, the electron spins about its own axis, constituting a spin magnetic moment. The resultant magnetic moment of an atom is the vector sum of the orbital and the spin magnetic moments.

In diamagnetic materials, each atom has zero magnetic moment. In the presence of an external magnetic field, the speed of electrons moving in one direction increases and those revolving in the opposite direction decreases. The substance as a whole acquires a net magnetic moment in a direction opposite to the applied field. Examples are copper, silver and gold.

In paramagnetic materials, each atom has a non-zero magnetic moment. In the absence of an external field, these atomic magnets are randomly oriented, so the net magnetic moment is zero. In the presence of an external magnetic field, each atomic magnet tends to align along the external field. The substance as a whole acquires a small net magnetic moment in the direction of the applied field. When the external field is removed, the alignment is disturbed by thermal vibrations and the substance is demagnetised. This is why paramagnetic substances cannot be used as permanent magnets. Examples are aluminium, platinum and tungsten.

A ferromagnetic material is divided into a large number of small regions, called domains. Each domain contains a large number of atomic magnets aligned in the same direction. Each domain has a resultant magnetic moment. In the absence of an external field, these domains are randomly oriented, so the net magnetic moment is zero. In the presence of an external magnetic field, these domains tend to align along the external field. The substance as a whole acquires a large net magnetic moment in the direction of the applied field. Even when the external field is removed, some alignment remains inside the substance. This is why ferromagnetic substances are used as permanent magnets. Examples are iron, cobalt and nickel.

- Magnetic hysteresis occurs when an external magnetic field is applied to a ferromagnet such as iron. The atomic dipoles align themselves with the external field. Even when the external field is removed, part of the alignment is retained and the material is magnetised indefinitely. This property of the magnetic material is known as its retentivity; the remnant internal magnetisation (M) is the measure of retentivity. This is the effect that provides memory in a hard disk drive. To demagnetise, we have to heat or apply an external magnetic field in the opposite direction. The magnetic field (H) required to demagnetise the material completely is known as its coercivity.

EXERCISES

1. Two particles X and Y having equal charge, after being accelerated through the same potential difference, enter a region of uniform magnetic field and describe circular paths of radii r_1 and r_2, respectively. The ratio of mass of the X to that of Y is:

(a) $\frac{r_1}{r_2}$ (b) $\left(\frac{r_1}{r_2}\right)^2$

(c) $\left(\frac{r_1}{r_2}\right)^{1/2}$ (d) $\left(\frac{r_1}{r_2}\right)^{-1/2}$

2. An α particle moving with velocity v in a uniform magnetic field is moving in a circular path at frequency f, called the cyclotron frequency. The cyclotron frequency of a proton moving with speed $2v$ in the same magnetic field will be:

(a) $f/4$ (b) $f/2$

(c) f (d) $2f$

3. An electron is accelerated to high speed down a cathode ray tube by applying a potential difference of V volts between the cathode and the anode. The particle then passes through a uniform transverse magnetic field in which it moves with acceleration a. If the potential difference is increased to $2V$, the electron will move with acceleration:

(a) a (b) $\sqrt{2}a$

(c) $a/\sqrt{2}$ (d) $2a$

4. An electron moves in a circular orbit of radius r around a nucleus. The magnetic field due to the orbital motion of the electron at the site of the nucleus is B. The angular velocity of the electron is:

(a) $\frac{2\mu_0 eB}{\pi r}$ (b) $\frac{4\pi rB}{\mu_0 e}$

(c) $\frac{2\pi eB}{\mu_0 r}$ (d) $\frac{\mu_0 er}{4\pi B}$

5. An electron projected parallel to the plates of a parallel plate capacitor with velocity 2×10^6 m/s moves undeflected between the plates. The separation between the plates is 3 mm and there exists a potential difference of 600 V across the plates. If there is a cross-magnetic field between the plates, its magnitude is:

(a) 0.1 T (b) 0.2 T

(c) 0.3 T (d) 0.4 T

6. A uniform magnetic field $B\mathbf{k}$ extends only in the first quadrant of the xy plane. A particle with charge q enters the field with momentum $p\mathbf{i}$ at point $P_1(0, a, 0)$ and emerges at $P_2(2a, 0, 0)$. The value of $\frac{5qaB}{p}$ equals:

(a) 2 (b) –4

(c) 7 (d) –5

7. A uniform magnetic field $B\mathbf{k}$ extends between $x=0$ to $x=3a/2$. A particle with charge $+q$ enters the field with momentum $p\mathbf{i}$ at point $P_1(0,a,0)$, as shown in the figure; O is the origin and $P_2=(3a/2,0,0)$.

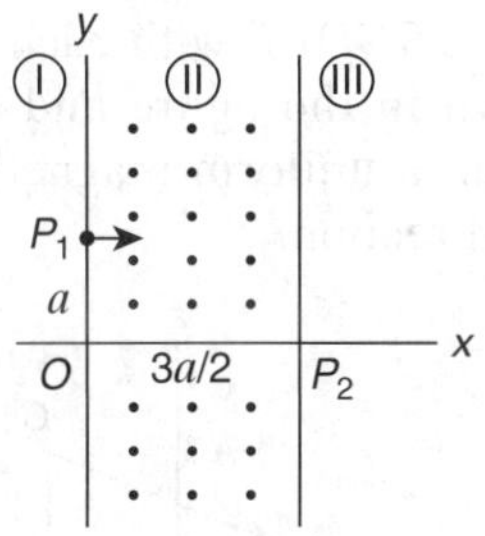

The correct options are:

(a) For $B=\dfrac{3p}{5qa}$, the particle re-enters region I

(b) For $B=\dfrac{p}{2qa}$, the particle enters region III at a point above P_2

(c) For $B=\dfrac{13p}{20qa}$, the particle enters region III at a point below P_2

(d) For $B=\dfrac{2p}{3qa}$, the particle re-enters region I at point $(0,-2a,0)$

8. A particle of mass m carrying charge q and moving with velocity $v_0\mathbf{i}$ enters a magnetic field region given by $B_0(\mathbf{i}+\mathbf{j}+\mathbf{k})$. Since velocity is not perpendicular to the magnetic field, the particle describes a helix whose radius r and pitch p are:

(a) $r=\dfrac{mv_0}{qB_0}, p=\dfrac{2\pi mv_0}{qB_0}$

(b) $r=\dfrac{mv_0}{\sqrt{3}qB_0}, p=\dfrac{2\pi mv_0}{\sqrt{3}qB_0}$

(c) $r=\dfrac{\sqrt{2}mv_0}{\sqrt{3}qB_0}, p=\dfrac{2\pi mv_0}{\sqrt{3}qB_0}$

(d) $r=\dfrac{\sqrt{2}mv_0}{3qB_0}, p=\dfrac{2\pi mv_0}{3qB_0}$

9. An ionised gas contains both positive and negative ions. If it is subjected simultaneously to an electric field along the $+x$ direction and a magnetic field along the $+z$ direction, then:

(a) Positive ions deflect along the $+y$ direction and negative ions along the $-y$ direction

(b) All ions deflect towards the $+y$ direction

(c) All ions deflect towards the $-y$ direction

(d) Positive ions deflect along the $-y$ direction and negative ions along the $+y$ direction

10. An electron moving along the $+x$-axis suddenly deflects towards the $+y$-axis in a non-circular trajectory due to the presence of an electric and/or magnetic field. A possible combination from the following is:

(a) $\mathbf{E}=0, \mathbf{B}=b\mathbf{i}+c\mathbf{k}$ (b) $\mathbf{E}=a\mathbf{i}, \mathbf{B}=b\mathbf{j}+c\mathbf{k}$

(c) $\mathbf{E}=0, \mathbf{B}=b\mathbf{j}+c\mathbf{k}$ (d) $\mathbf{E}=a\mathbf{i}, \mathbf{B}=b\mathbf{i}+c\mathbf{k}$

11. A proton having velocity $v=5\sqrt{2}$ m/s enters a magnetic field of intensity $\mathbf{B}=(0.1\text{ T})\mathbf{k}$, as shown in the figure. The geometric figure drawn using dashed lines is a cube whose three edges lie along the coordinate axes.

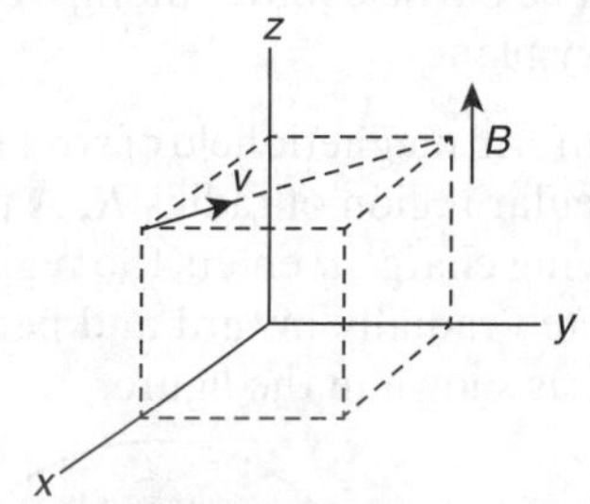

The acceleration produced in the proton is (charge to mass ratio of proton $=0.96\times10^8$ C/kg):

(a) $-4.8\times10^7\text{ m/s}^2(\mathbf{i}-\mathbf{j})$

(b) $4.8\times10^7\text{ m/s}^2(\mathbf{i}+\mathbf{j})$

(c) $-2.8\times10^7\text{ m/s}^2(\mathbf{i}-\mathbf{j})$

(d) $2.8\times10^7\text{ m/s}^2(\mathbf{i}+\mathbf{j})$

12. A uniform magnetic field $B_0\mathbf{k}$ extends between $x=0$ to $x=a$. A charged particle enters the field with velocity $v_0\mathbf{i}$ at the origin, and is deflected by 30° when it emerges from the field. If it is required that the particle be deflected by 180°, the field should be extended at least to:

(a) $x=\sqrt{2}a$ (b) $x=\sqrt{3}a$

(c) $x=1.8a$ (d) $x=2.1a$

13. A particle carrying charge q is released from the origin with momentum $\mathbf{p}=a\mathbf{i}+a\mathbf{j}$ in a uniform magnitude field $\mathbf{B}=b\mathbf{k}$ that extends in the region $x\ge0$. If q, a, b are positive quantities, the particle will cross the y-axis at a point whose y-coordinate is:

(a) $\dfrac{a}{qb}$ (b) $\dfrac{2a}{qb}$

(c) $-\dfrac{a}{qb}$ (d) $-\dfrac{2a}{qb}$

14. A particle of mass m carrying charge q enters a region of uniform electric and magnetic fields directed along $+x$-axis and $+z$-axis, respectively. The particle enters the region at point $P(0,a,0)$

with velocity $v\mathbf{i}$ and comes out of the region at point $Q(2a,0,0)$ with velocity $-2v\mathbf{j}$. The correct statements from the following are:

(a) Strength of the electric field $= \dfrac{3mv^2}{4qa}$

(b) Power of the electric plus magnetic force at $P = \dfrac{3mv^3}{4a}$

(c) Power of the electric plus magnetic force at $Q = \dfrac{mv^3}{4a}$

(d) The particle moves along a circular path in the xy plane

15. A uniform magnetic field of strength B extends over a circular region of radius R. A particle of mass m carrying charge q enters the region with velocity v directed radially inward and perpendicular to the field, as shown in the figure.

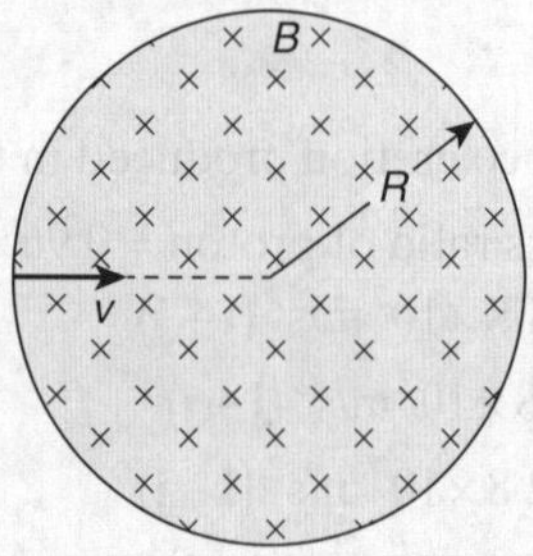

The particle emerges from the region after time:

(a) $\dfrac{2m}{qB}\tan^{-1}\left(\dfrac{qBR}{mv}\right)$ (b) $\dfrac{m}{qB}\tan^{-1}\left(\dfrac{mv}{qBR}\right)$

(c) $\dfrac{m}{qB}\tan^{-1}\left(\dfrac{qBR}{mv}\right)$ (d) $\dfrac{2m}{qB}\tan^{-1}\left(\dfrac{mv}{qBR}\right)$

16. A particle having specific charge q/m enters a magnetic field of strength B, with velocity v. It enters at angle 53° and emerges at angle 60° to the magnetic field boundary (see figure). The width d of the magnetic field region is:

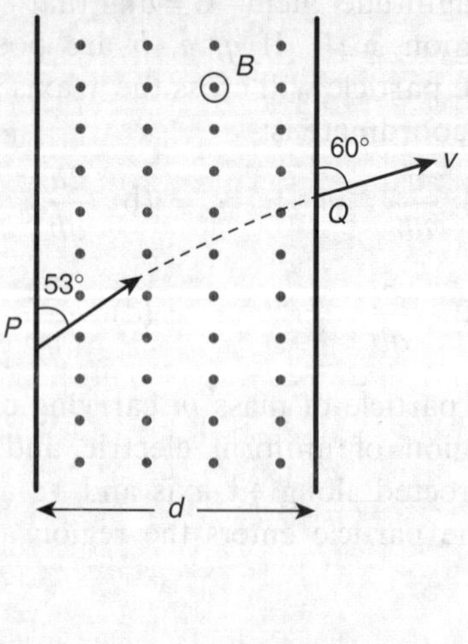

(a) $\dfrac{3mv}{5qB}$ (b) $\dfrac{mv}{2qB}$

(c) $\dfrac{2mv}{5qB}$ (d) $\dfrac{mv}{10qB}$

17. A wire $ABCDEF$ with each side of length a bent as shown in the figure and carrying current I is placed in a uniform magnetic field B_0 parallel to the $+y$ direction.

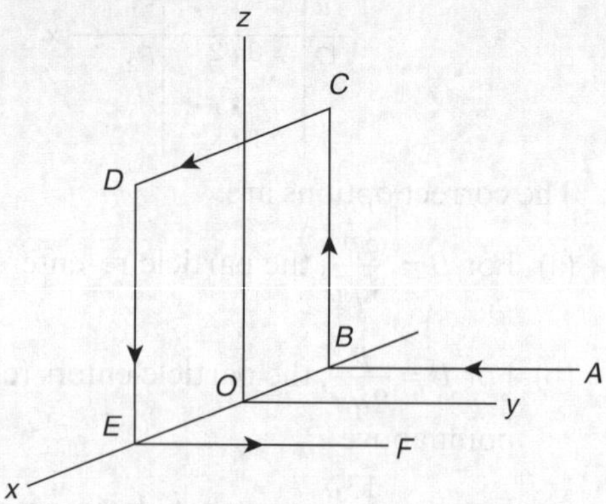

The force experienced by the wire is:

(a) IaB_0 along the $+z$ direction

(b) IaB_0 along the $-z$ direction

(c) $2IaB_0$ along the angular bisector of the $+y$ and $+z$ directions

(d) IaB_0 along the angular bisector of the $+y$ and $+z$ directions

18. The left column shows current carrying wires. The right column shows the Ampere force experienced by these wires when they are kept in a uniform magnetic field of strength B perpendicular to the plane of the figure. Match the columns:

(a) 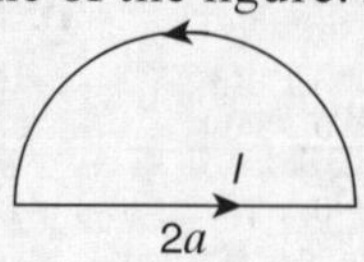

(p) 0

(b) 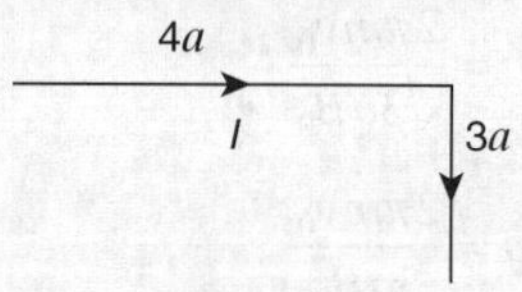

(q) $3IaB$

(c) 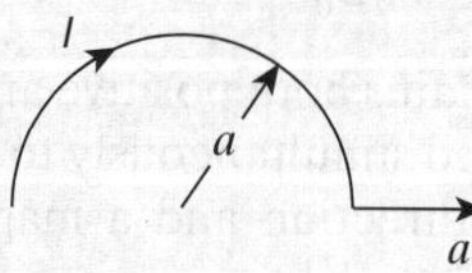

(r) $5IaB$

(d) 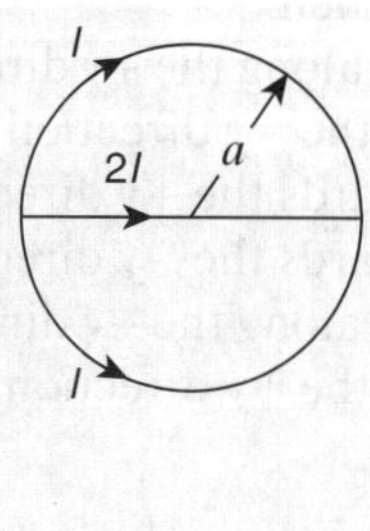

(s) $8IaB$

19. A circular wire of radius a carrying current I is placed in a uniform magnetic field B perpendicular to the plane of the wire. Due to Ampere force, the wire becomes taut. The tension in the wire is:
(a) IaB (b) $2IaB$
(c) $4IaB$ (d) 0

20. Consider the arrangement shown in the figure. The metal rod having mass m and horizontal length l is hung from the ceiling by two threads, not shown in the figure. The two lower ends of the rod are dipped to a depth a inside a metal trough containing mercury and there is a uniform magnetic field of strength B in the plane of the figure.

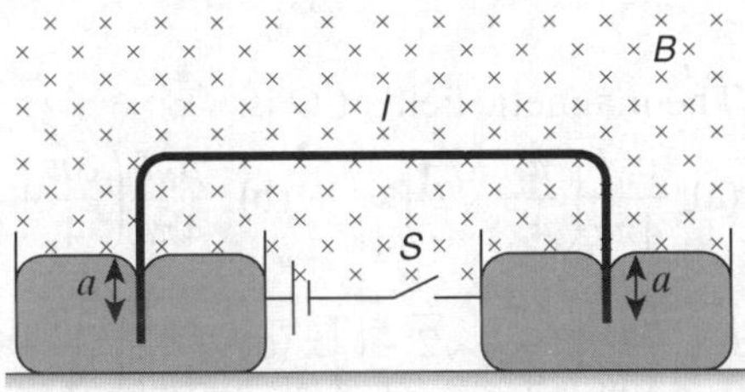

When switch S is closed, a current I flows through the rod and the wire jumps to a height h equal to:
(a) $\frac{4IlBa}{mg}$ (b) $\frac{2IlBa}{mg}$
(c) $\frac{IlBa}{2mg}$ (d) $\frac{IlBa}{mg}$

21. Two long and straight conductors carrying currents of the same magnitude are kept in a plane at a distance d apart. A point charge is moving between the wires parallel to them, at a distance $d/3$ from one of the wires. When the currents in the wires are in the same direction, the charge moves in a circle of radius r_1, and when the currents in the wires are in opposite directions, the charge moves in a circle of radius r_2. The value of $\frac{r_1}{r_2}$ is:
(a) 3 (b) 4
(c) 5 (d) 6

22. A metal disc of radius R carries a net charge Q uniformly spread over its surface. If the disc is rotated with angular speed ω about an axis through its centre and perpendicular to its plane, the magnetic moment of the disc is:
(a) ωQR^2 (b) $\frac{1}{2}\omega QR^2$
(c) $\frac{1}{3}\omega QR^2$ (d) $\frac{1}{4}\omega QR^2$

23. The figure shows a rigid frame of three metal rods, each of mass m and length l, which is free to swing about a horizontal metal bar. A uniform magnetic field of strength B exists in the vertically upward direction. If a current I starts flowing in the rods, the frame experiences a torque and swings in the vertical plane.

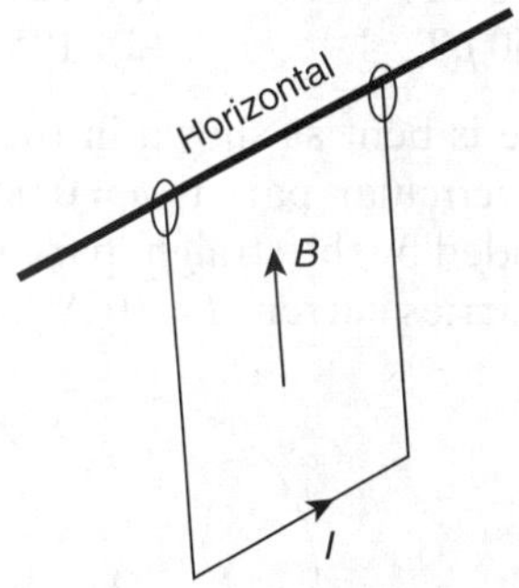

If g is the acceleration due to the Earth's gravity, the maximum angular deflection of the swing is:
(a) $2\tan^{-1}\left(\frac{\mu B}{2mgl}\right)$ (b) $2\tan^{-1}\left(\frac{mgl}{2\mu B}\right)$
(c) $\tan^{-1}\left(\frac{2mgl}{\mu B}\right)$ (d) $\tan^{-1}\left(\frac{mgl}{\mu B}\right)$

24. A magnetic dipole is acted upon by two uniform magnetic fields inclined to each other at an angle of 75°. One of the fields has a magnitude of $\sqrt{2}\times 10^{-2}$ T. The dipole attains stable equilibrium at an angle of 30° with this field. The magnitude of the other field is:
(a) 0.04 T (b) 0.03 T
(c) 0.02 T (d) 0.01 T

25. Two long and straight conductors AOB and COD are perpendicular to each other and carrying currents I_1 and I_2, respectively. The magnitude of the magnetic field at a point P at a distance d from point O in a direction perpendicular to the plane $ABCD$ is:
(a) $\frac{\mu_0(I_1+I_2)}{2\pi d}$ (b) $\frac{\mu_0\left(\sqrt{I_1}+\sqrt{I_2}\right)^2}{2\pi d}$
(c) $\frac{\mu_0\sqrt{I_1^2+I_2^2}}{2\pi d}$ (d) $\frac{\mu_0 I_1 I_2}{2\pi d(I_1+I_2)}$

26. A long current carrying wire is bent into a circular loop of one turn and the magnetic field at the centre of the loop is B. If the wire is now bent into a circular coil of n turns, the magnetic field at the centre will be:
(a) nB (b) n^2B
(c) $2nB$ (d) $2n^2B$

27. The magnetic field due to a current carrying circular loop of radius 3 cm at a point on its axis at a distance of 4 cm from the centre of the loop is 54 μT. The magnetic field at the centre of the loop is:

(a) 250 μT (b) 172 μT
(c) 150 μT (d) 125 μT

28. A wire is bent as shown in the figure. The radius of the circular part is $a = 0.02$ m, and the angle subtended by the straight part at O is $\theta = \pi/2$. The wire carries current $I = 10$ A.

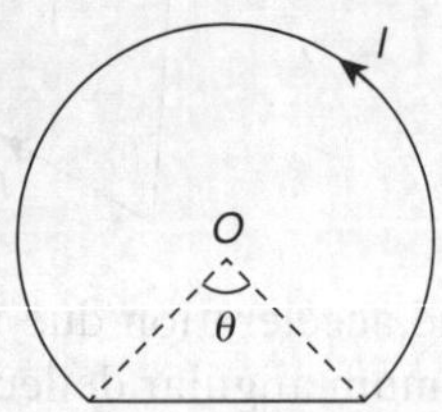

The magnetic field at O is $\left(\dfrac{\mu_0}{4\pi} = 10^{-7}\ \text{Wb/A}\cdot\text{m}\right)$:

(a) 7.1×10^{-4} T (b) 5.7×10^{-4} T
(c) 3.4×10^{-4} T (d) 1.2×10^{-4} T

29. The magnetic field due to a square loop of side $2a$ carrying current I at a point P vertically above its centre and at a distance a from the centre is:

(a) $\dfrac{\mu_0 I}{\sqrt{3}\pi a}$ (b) $\dfrac{\sqrt{2}\mu_0 I}{\sqrt{3}\pi a}$
(c) $\dfrac{\mu_0 I}{4\sqrt{3}\pi a}$ (d) $\dfrac{\mu_0 I}{2\sqrt{3}\pi a}$

30. Two long parallel wires distance $2a$ apart carry equal currents I each. The magnetic field at a distance a above the plane of the wires equidistant from both wires is:

(a) $\dfrac{\mu_0 I}{\sqrt{2}\pi a}$ (b) $\dfrac{\mu_0 I}{2\pi a}$
(c) $\dfrac{\mu_0 I}{2\sqrt{2}\pi a}$ (d) $\dfrac{\sqrt{2}\mu_0 I}{\pi a}$

31. An infinitely long wire carrying current I is placed along the z-axis. The magnetic field at a point $P(x, y, 0)$ is:

(a) $\dfrac{\mu_0 I}{2\pi\left(x^2+y^2\right)}(-y\mathbf{i}+x\mathbf{j})$

(b) $\dfrac{\mu_0 I}{2\pi\left(x^2+y^2\right)}(y\mathbf{i}+x\mathbf{j})$

(c) $\dfrac{\mu_0 I}{2\pi\left(x^2+y^2\right)}(-x\mathbf{i}+y\mathbf{j})$

(d) $\dfrac{\mu_0 I}{2\pi\left(x^2+y^2\right)}(x\mathbf{i}+y\mathbf{j})$

32. An infinitely long wire, bent and placed in the xy plane as shown in the figure, carries current I. The radius of the circular part is a.

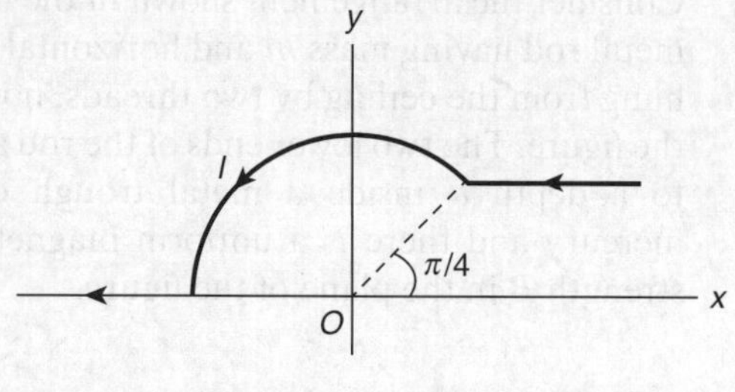

The magnetic field at O is:

(a) $\dfrac{\mu_0 I}{4\pi a}\left(\dfrac{\pi}{4}+\sqrt{2}\right)\mathbf{k}$ (b) $\dfrac{\mu_0 I}{4\pi a}\left(\dfrac{3\pi}{4}+\sqrt{2}\right)\mathbf{k}$

(c) $\dfrac{\mu_0 I}{4\pi a}\left(\dfrac{3\pi}{4}+\sqrt{2}-1\right)\mathbf{k}$ (d) $\dfrac{\mu_0 I}{4\pi a}\left(\dfrac{3\pi}{4}+1-\dfrac{1}{\sqrt{2}}\right)\mathbf{k}$

33. Two long parallel wires distance $2a$ apart carry equal currents flowing out of the plane of the paper, as shown in the figure. The variation of the magnetic field along the line XX' is correctly represented by:

(a) 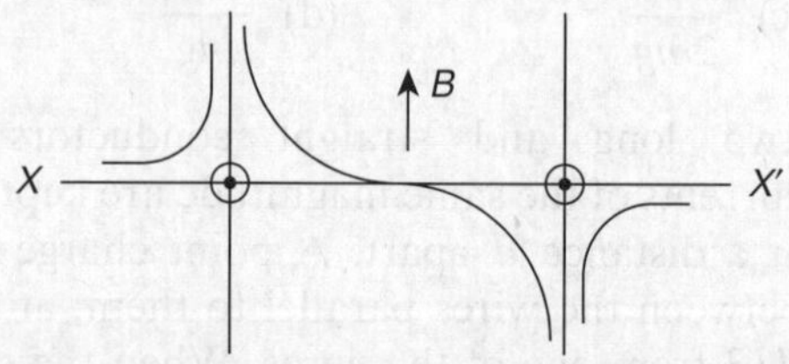

(b) 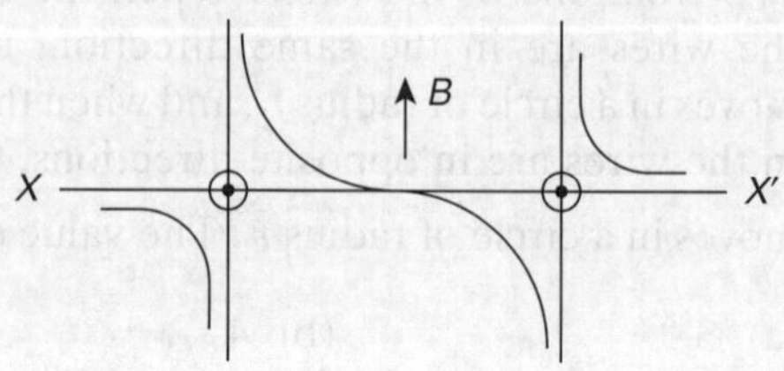

(c) 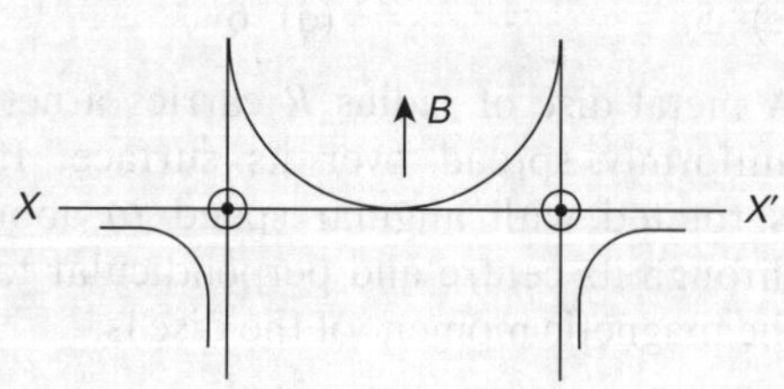

(d) 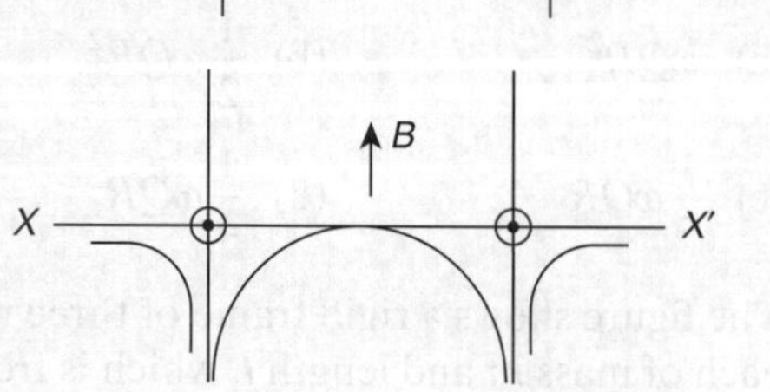

34. Consider the wire arrangement shown in the figure. The two straight wires are semi-infinite in length and the circular wire has radius a. The current in the straight wires is I. The current in the two branches of the circular wire distribute in accordance to the resistances of the two branches.

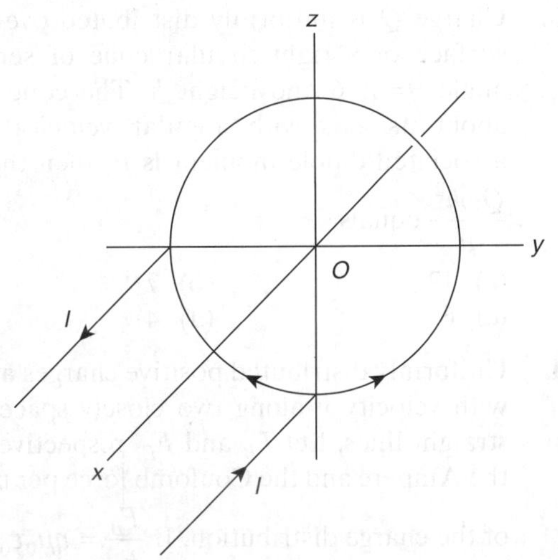

The magnetic field at O is:

(a) $\frac{\mu_0 I}{4\pi a}(\mathbf{j}+\mathbf{k})$ (b) $\frac{\mu_0 I}{4\pi a}(2\pi\mathbf{i}+\mathbf{j}+\mathbf{k})$

(c) $\frac{\mu_0 I}{4\pi a}(\pi\mathbf{i}+\mathbf{j}+\mathbf{k})$ (d) $\frac{\mu_0 I}{4\pi a}(\pi\mathbf{i}+\mathbf{j}-\mathbf{k})$

35. Three infinitely long straight wires P, Q and R carrying current in the same direction are kept parallel to each other in the same plane. The wire Q is kept in the middle and the other two wires at distance a on either side of wire Q. Another finite current carrying wire S is placed parallel to the wires in the same plane at a distance x from the middle wire. If S remains in equilibrium, then:

(a) $x=0$ (b) $x=a/\sqrt{3}$

(c) $x=a/\sqrt{2}$ (d) $x=a/2$

36. A long insulated copper wire is closely wound as a spiral of N turns, as shown in the figure. The spiral has inner radius a and outer radius b.

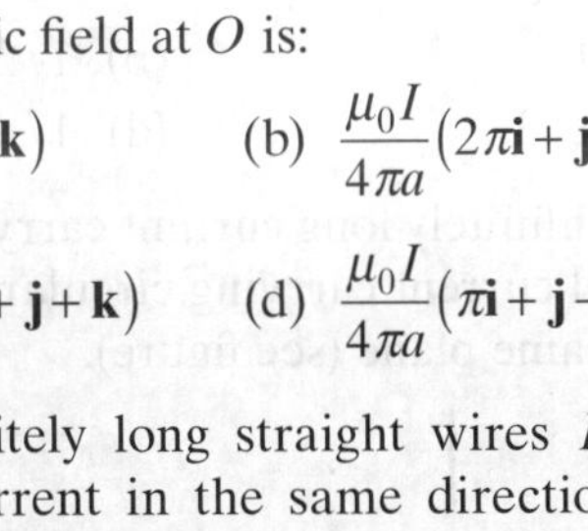

If a steady current I flows through the spiral, then the magnetic field at its centre is:

(a) $\frac{\mu_0 NI}{2(b-a)}\ln\left(\frac{b}{a}\right)$ (b) $\frac{\mu_0 NI}{2(b-a)}\ln\left(\frac{b+a}{b-a}\right)$

(c) $\frac{\mu_0 NI}{2b}\ln\left(\frac{b}{b}\right)$ (d) $\frac{\mu_0 NI}{2b}\ln\left(\frac{b+a}{b-a}\right)$

37. Consider a straight wire of length L, carrying current I. If it is bent into an equilateral triangle, the magnetic field at the centroid is B_1. If it is bent into a square, the magnetic field at the centroid is B_2. The ratio B_1/B_2 equals:

(a) $\frac{27\sqrt{2}}{32}$ (b) $\frac{9\sqrt{2}}{8}$

(c) $\frac{8\sqrt{3}}{9}$ (d) $\frac{16\sqrt{3}}{27}$

38. A semi-circular wire of radius R, lying in the xy plane with its centre at the origin, carries current I flowing in the clockwise sense. If a uniform magnetic field $B\mathbf{i}$ is switched on, the torque on the wire about the y-axis has magnitude:

(a) $\frac{1}{2}\pi R^2 IB$ (b) $\frac{1}{3}R^2 IB$

(c) $R^2 IB$ (d) 0

39. The arrangement in the figure consists of two straight wires of linear mass density λ, each hung by a pair of threads from a horizontal bar. The length of each thread is l. When current I flows, the wires are deflected away due to Ampere force and remain in equilibrium at angle θ from the vertical.

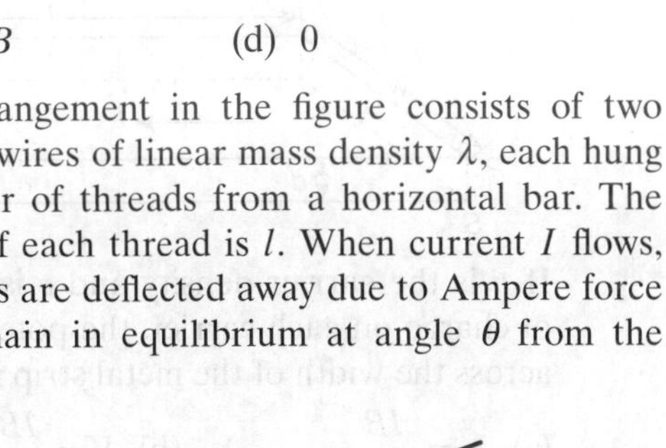

If acceleration due to the Earth's gravity is g, then the universal constant $\frac{\mu_0}{4\pi}$ equals:

(a) $\frac{\lambda gl\cot^2\theta}{I^2}$ (b) $\frac{\lambda gl\sin^2\theta}{I^2\cos\theta}$

(c) $\frac{\lambda gl\sin\theta}{I^2\cos^2\theta}$ (d) $\frac{\lambda gl\tan^2\theta}{I^2}$

40. Two infinitely long straight wires P, Q carrying current I in the same direction, are kept parallel to each other at a distance $2a$ from each other and are rigidly fixed. A finite wire R of linear mass density λ and carrying same current I in the same direction is placed midway and parallel to the wires P, Q in the same plane. If wire R is slightly displaced perpendicular to this plane, it oscillates with a frequency:

(a) $\frac{1}{2\pi}\sqrt{\frac{2\mu_0 I^2}{\lambda\pi a^2}}$ (b) $\frac{1}{2\pi}\sqrt{\frac{\mu_0 I^2}{2\lambda\pi a^2}}$

(c) $\frac{1}{2\pi}\sqrt{\frac{\mu_0 I^2}{\lambda\pi a^2}}$ (d) $\frac{1}{2\pi}\sqrt{\frac{3\mu_0 I^2}{4\lambda\pi a^2}}$

41. The figure shows a metal strip of length l, width w and thickness d carrying current I along the +ve x direction. A uniform magnetic field B is applied along the +ve y direction, which exerts a force on the charge carriers. This results in accumulation of +ve charges on surface $PQRS$ and equal amount of –ve charges on its opposite surface. A potential difference is created along the z direction. Accumulation continues until the magnetic force is balanced by the electric force.

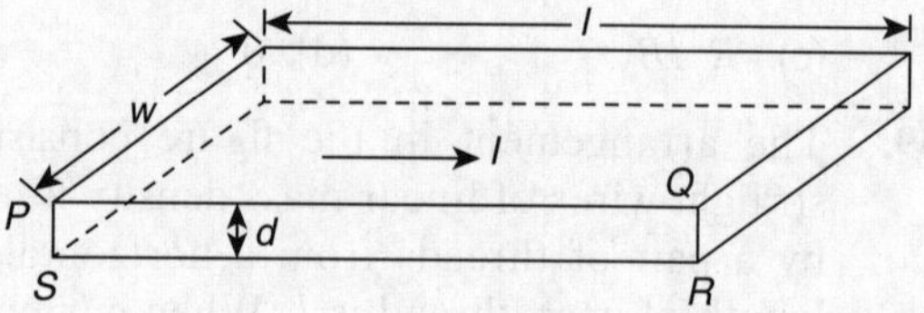

If n is the carrier density and e is the magnitude of charge on each carrier, the potential difference across the width of the metal strip is:

(a) $V = \frac{IB}{new}$ (b) $V = \frac{IBw}{ned^2}$

(c) $V = \frac{IB}{ned}$ (d) $V = \frac{IBd}{new^2}$

42. A charged particle of specific charge (charge/mass) α is released from origin at time $t = 0$ with velocity $\mathbf{v} = v_0(\mathbf{i}+\mathbf{j})$ in a uniform magnetic field $\mathbf{B} = B_0\mathbf{i}$. Coordinates of the particle at time $t = \frac{\pi}{\alpha B_0}$ are:

(a) $\left(\frac{\pi v_0}{\alpha B_0}, \frac{v_0}{\alpha B_0}, \frac{-2v_0}{\alpha B_0}\right)$ (b) $\left(\frac{\pi v_0}{\alpha B_0}, 0, \frac{-\pi v_0}{\alpha B_0}\right)$

(c) $\left(\frac{\pi v_0}{\alpha B_0}, \frac{v_0}{\alpha B_0}, \frac{-v_0}{\alpha B_0}\right)$ (d) $\left(\frac{\pi v_0}{\alpha B_0}, 0, \frac{-2v_0}{\alpha B_0}\right)$

43. Charge Q is uniformly distributed over the slant surface of a right-circular cone of semi-vertical angle $\theta = \pi/6$ and height h. The cone is rotated about its axis with angular velocity ω. If the associated dipole moment is μ, then the value of $\frac{Q\omega h^2}{\mu}$ equals:

(a) 12 (b) 7
(c) 6 (d) 4

44. Uniformly distributed positive charges are moving with velocity v along two closely spaced parallel straight lines. Let F_B and F_E, respectively, denote the Ampere and the Coulomb force per unit length of the charge distribution. If $\frac{F_B}{F_E} = \eta\mu_0\varepsilon_0 v^2$, then η equals:

(a) 1 (b) 1/2
(c) 1/3 (d) 1/4

45. An infinitely long current carrying wire and a very small current carrying circular loop, are placed in the same plane (see figure).

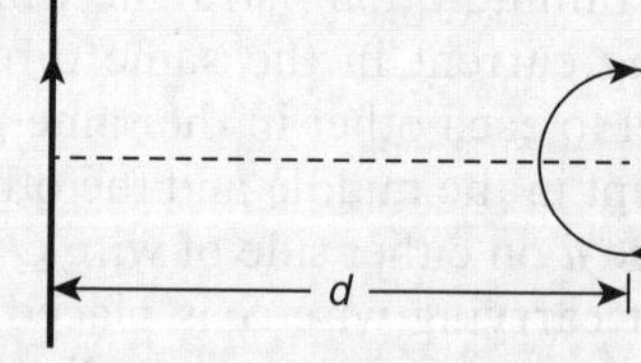

The radius of the loop is a and its distance from the wire is $d (d \gg a)$. The force between the wire and the loop is:

(a) $F = 0$ (b) $F \propto \left(\frac{a}{d}\right)^{-1}$

(c) $F \propto \left(\frac{a}{d}\right)^{-2}$ (d) $F \propto \left(\frac{a}{d}\right)^{2}$

ANSWER KEYS

1. (b)	**2.** (d)	**3.** (b)	**4.** (b)	**5.** (a)	**6.** (a)	**7.** (b),(c),(d)	**8.** (d)
9. (c)	**10.** (d)	**11.** (b)	**12.** (d)	**13.** (d)	**14.** (a),(b)	**15.** (a)	**16.** (d)
17. (a)	**18.** (a)-(p), (b)-(r), (c)-(q), (d)-(s)			**19.** (a)	**20.** (d)	**21.** (a)	**22.** (d)
23. (a)	**24.** (d)	**25.** (c)	**26.** (b)	**27.** (a)	**28.** (c)	**29.** (a)	**30.** (b)
31. (a)	**32.** (c)	**33.** (b)	**34.** (a)	**35.** (a),(b)	**36.** (a)	**37.** (a)	**38.** (a)
39. (b)	**40.** (c)	**41.** (c)	**42.** (d)	**43.** (a)	**44.** (a)	**45.** (d)	

SOLUTIONS

1. (b) The kinetic energy K acquired by both particles is the same and equal to qV, where q is their charge and V is the potential through which the particles have been accelerated. The radius of the circular path is given by

$$r = \frac{mv}{qB} = \frac{\sqrt{2mK}}{qB}$$

We see that $r \propto \sqrt{m}$ if all other quantities are the same. Hence, we have

$$\frac{r_1^2}{r_2^2} = \frac{m_1}{m_2}$$

2. (d) The frequency f is given by

$$f = \frac{qB}{2\pi m} \propto \frac{q}{m}$$

For an alpha particle, the charge to mass ratio is 2e/4m = e/2m and for a proton, the ratio is e/m, which is double that of an alpha particle.
Hence, the cyclotron frequency for a proton will be 2f.

3. (b) The electron requires kinetic energy $K = eV$, where V is the accelerating potential. While moving through the magnetic field, it experiences a force $F = evB$ and hence moves with acceleration

$$a = \frac{evB}{m} = \frac{e(mv)B}{m^2} = \frac{eB\sqrt{2mK}}{m^2} = \frac{eB\sqrt{2\,meV}}{m^2}$$

We see that $a \propto \sqrt{V}$ if all other quantities remain the same. Hence, doubling the accelerating potential will increase the acceleration to $\sqrt{2}a$.

4. (b) Let ω be the angular velocity of the electron. Then, it can be considered to constitute a current

$$I = \frac{e}{2\pi/\omega} = \frac{e\omega}{2\pi}$$

The field at the centre is given by

$$B = \frac{\mu_0 I}{2r} = \frac{\mu_0 e\omega}{4\pi r}$$

$$\Rightarrow \quad \omega = \frac{4\pi r B}{\mu_0 e}$$

5. (a) The electric field between the plates is

$$E = \frac{600 \text{ V}}{3 \text{ mm}} = 2\times10^5 \text{ V/m}$$

The electron will go undefeated only if the electric force eE and magnetic force evB balance each other. Thus, we have

$$evB = eE$$

$$\Rightarrow \quad B = \frac{E}{V} = \frac{2\times10^5 \text{ V/m}}{2\times10^6 \text{ m/s}} = 0.1 \text{ T}$$

6. (a) The particle moves in a circular path as long as it is moving in the magnetic field region. Once it is outside the magnetic field region, it moves in a straight line. Let the radius of the circular path be r. Then, the centre of the circular path lies at a distance $r - a$ below the origin (see figure).

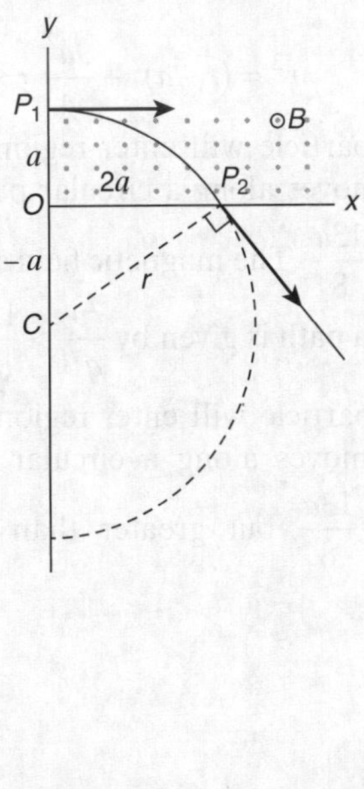

The radius r is given by

$$(r-a)^2 + 4a^2 = r^2 \Rightarrow r = \frac{5}{2}a$$

Now, using the relation $r = \dfrac{p}{qB}$, we have

$$\frac{5a}{2} = \frac{p}{qB} \Rightarrow \frac{5qaB}{p} = 2$$

From the path, we can see that the charge is positive.

7. (b), (c), (d)

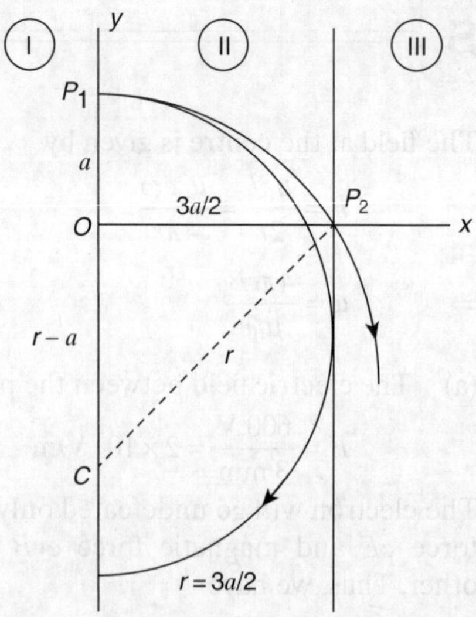

The particle will re-enter region *I* if it moves along a circular path of radius less than $\dfrac{3a}{2}$. The magnetic field strength required for such a path is given by

$$\frac{p}{qB} < \frac{3a}{2} \Rightarrow B > \frac{2p}{3qa}$$

The particle will enter region III at point P_2 if it moves along a circular path of radius given by (see figure)

$$r^2 = (r-a)^2 + \frac{9a^2}{4} \Rightarrow r = \frac{13a}{8}$$

The particle will enter region III above point P_2 if it moves along a circular path of radius greater than $\dfrac{13a}{8}$. The magnetic field strength required for such a path is given by $\dfrac{p}{qB} > \dfrac{13a}{8} \Rightarrow B < \dfrac{8p}{13qa}$.

The particle will enter region III below point P_2 if it moves along a circular path of radius less than $\dfrac{13a}{8}$ but greater than $\dfrac{3a}{2}$. The magnetic field strength required for such a path is given by $\dfrac{8p}{13qa} < B < \dfrac{2p}{3qa}$.

8. (d) The velocity component along the magnetic field is

$$v_1 = \frac{\vec{v}\cdot\vec{B}}{B} = \frac{v_0 B_0}{\sqrt{3}B_0} = \frac{v_0}{\sqrt{3}}$$

The component perpendicular to the field is

$$v_2 = \sqrt{v_0^2 - \frac{v_0^2}{3}} = \frac{\sqrt{2}v_0}{\sqrt{3}}$$

Hence $r = \dfrac{mv_2}{qB} = \dfrac{\sqrt{2}mv_0}{3qB_0}$ and $p = \dfrac{2\pi m v_1}{qB} = \dfrac{2\pi m v_0}{3qB_0}$.

9. (c) Due to the electric field, the positive ions will initially acquire a velocity along the i direction and the negative ions along the $-i$ direction. The positive ions will experience magnetic force along $\vec{v}\times\vec{B}$, that is, along $i \times k = -j$ direction.

The negative ions will experience magnetic force along $-(\vec{v}\times\vec{B})$, that is, along $-(i \times k) = -j$ direction. Hence, both the ions will be deflected along $-y$ direction.

10. (d) The net force on the electron is given by $\vec{F} = -e[\vec{E} + \vec{v}\times\vec{B}]$. According to the question, the particle that is moving along the +x-axis is suddenly deflected towards the +y-axis. This means that the force acting on the electron should have a y component. It may or may not have an x component. Inserting the values of the given $\vec{E}$ and $\vec{B}$ in the expression for the force $\vec{F}$, we see that only option (d) satisfies the above conditions:

$$\vec{F} = -e\left[a\hat{i} + v\hat{i}\times\left(b\hat{i} + c\hat{k}\right)\right] = -e\left[a\hat{i} - vc\hat{j}\right]$$

11. (b) In vector form, the velocity of the particle is

$$\vec{v} = 5\sqrt{2}\ \text{m/s}\left(\cos 45^\circ\,(-\hat{i}) + \cos 45^\circ\,(\hat{j})\right)$$

$$= 5\ \text{m/s}\left(-\hat{i} + \hat{j}\right)$$

Force on the proton is $\vec{F} = e(\vec{v}\times\vec{B})$. Acceleration of the proton is given by

$$\vec{a} = \frac{\vec{F}}{m} = \frac{e}{m}(\vec{v}\times\vec{B}) = (0.96\times10^8\ \text{C/kg})(5\ \text{m/s})$$

$$(0.1\ \text{T})[(-\hat{i}+\hat{j})\times\hat{k}]$$

$$= 4.8\times10^7\ \text{m/s}^2(\hat{i}+\hat{j})$$

12. (d) If r is the radius of the circular path, then (see figure)

$$r\sin(30^\circ) = a \Rightarrow r = 2a$$

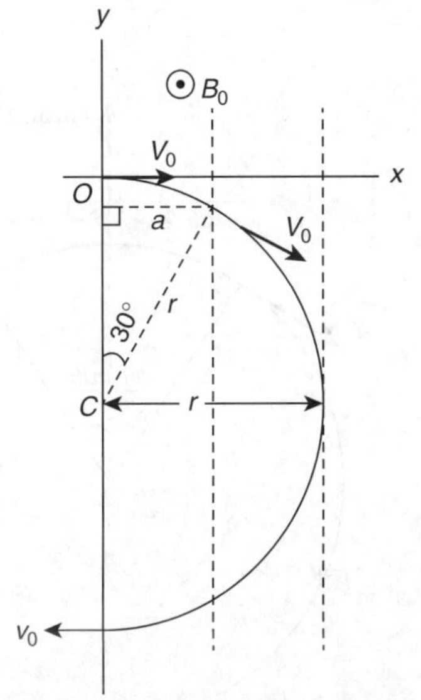

For the particle to be deflected by 180°, the particle will have to complete the semicircle. In that case, the field must extend to at least $x = r = 2a$.

13. (d) Since q, a and b are positive quantities, the path of the charged particle will be as shown in the figure.

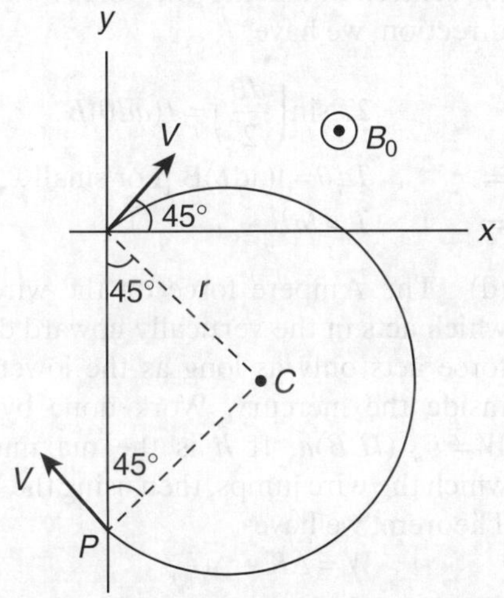

The radius of the circular path is

$$r = \frac{p}{qB} = \frac{\sqrt{2}a}{qb}$$

It emerges at point P on the y-axis whose y-coordinate is

$$y = -2r\cos(45^\circ) = -\frac{2a}{qb}$$

14. (a), (b)

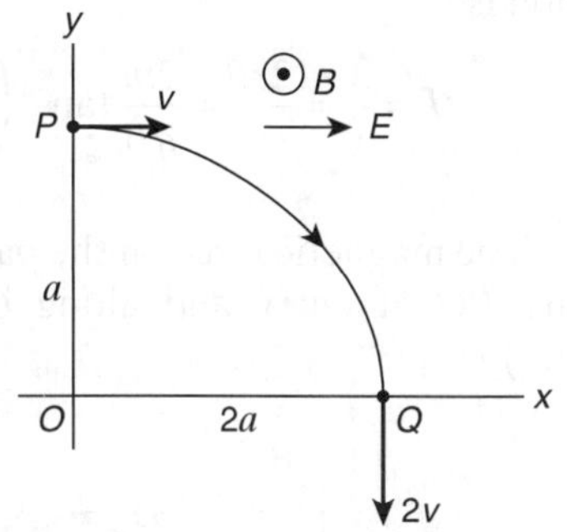

The kinetic energy changes due to the work done by the electric field; the magnetic field does no work since magnetic force is always perpendicular to the particle's velocity. Thus, using the Work–Energy Theorem $W_{electric} = \Delta K$, we have

$$(qE)2a = \frac{1}{2}m(4v^2 - v^2) \Rightarrow E = \frac{3mv^2}{4qa}$$

$\Rightarrow$ (a) is correct

Power due to magnetic force is always zero since it acts perpendicular to the velocity. The power is only due to the electric force. Hence, power at P is

$$(qE)v = \frac{3mv^3}{4a} \Rightarrow (b) \text{ is correct}$$

At Q, the electric force is perpendicular to velocity. Hence, power at Q is zero. $\Rightarrow$ (c) is incorrect.

The particle does not move in a circular trajectory $\Rightarrow$ (d) is incorrect.

15. (a)

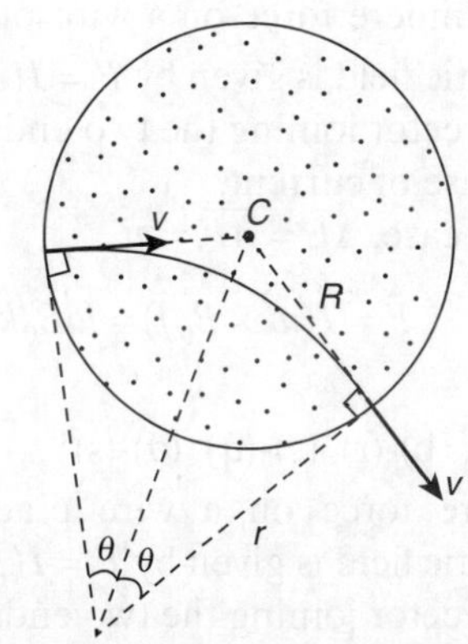

The particle moves in a circle of radius $r = \dfrac{mv}{qB}$.

The length of the arc is

$$s = r(2\theta), \text{ where } \theta = \tan^{-1}\left(\frac{R}{r}\right) = \tan^{-1}\left(\frac{qBR}{mv}\right)$$

The time for which the particle stays inside the region is

$$T = \frac{s}{v} = \frac{2r\theta}{v} = \frac{2m}{qB}\tan^{-1}\left(\frac{qBR}{mv}\right)$$

16. (d) The magnetic force on the particle is directed along PO at entry and along QO at exit (see figure).

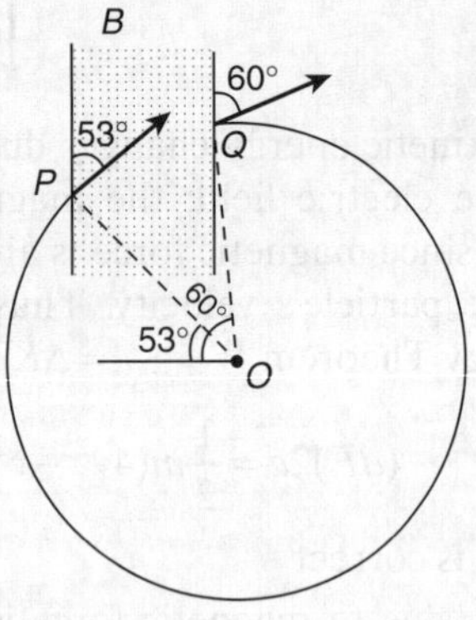

Here, O is the centre of the circular path along which the particle moves. The radius of the circular path is $r = \frac{mv}{qB}$.

From the figure, we can see that the width of the magnetic field region is

$$d = r\cos(53^\circ) - r\cos(60^\circ) = \frac{3r}{5} - \frac{r}{2} = \frac{r}{10} = \frac{mv}{10qB}$$

17. (a) Ampere force on a wire placed in a uniform magnetic field is given by $\vec{F} = I(\Delta\vec{L} \times \vec{B})$, where $\Delta\vec{L}$ is the vector joining the two ends of the wire along the sense of current.

In this case, $\Delta\vec{L} = \overline{AF} = a\hat{i}$.

Hence $\quad \vec{F} = I(a\hat{i} \times B_0\hat{j}) = laB_0\hat{k}$

18. (a)-(p), (b)-(r), (c)-(q), (d)-(s)

Ampere force on a wire placed in a uniform magnetic field is given by $\vec{F} = I(\Delta\vec{L} \times \vec{B})$, where $\Delta\vec{L}$ is the vector joining the two ends of the wire along the sense of current.

In option (a), the wire is closed; therefore $\Delta L = 0$. Hence $F = 0$.

In option (b), $\Delta L = \sqrt{(3a)^2 + (4a)^2} = 5a$. Hence $F = l(5a)B = 5laB$.

In option (c), $\Delta L = 3a$. Hence $F = l(3a)B = 3laB$.

In option (d), there are three wires, each having $\Delta L = 2a$, with two of them carrying currents l and the third one carrying current $2l$. Hence $F = 4l(2a)B = 8laB$.

19. (a)

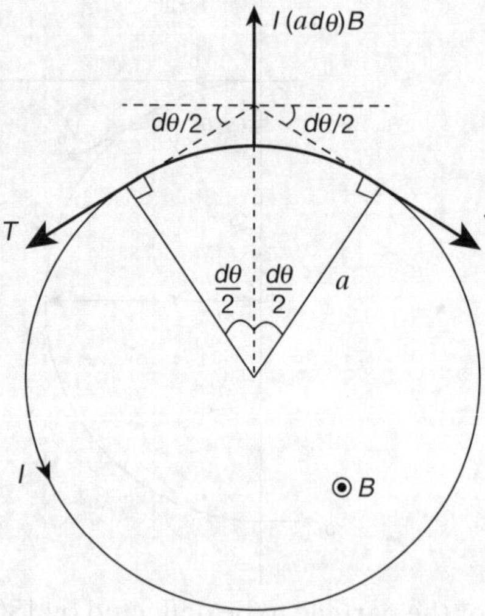

The figure shows the forces acting on a small portion of the wire. The tension on either side is T and the ampere force which is along the radially outward direction is $l(ad\theta)B$. Here, $d\theta$ is the angle subtended by the element portion of the wire at its centre. Balancing the forces along the radial direction, we have

$$2T\sin\left(\frac{d\theta}{2}\right) = I(ad\theta)B$$

$\Rightarrow \quad Td\theta = \text{l}(\text{a}d\theta)\text{B}$ [For small x, $\sin x \sim x$]

$\Rightarrow \quad T = laB$

20. (d) The Ampere force on the wire is $F = ILB$, which acts in the vertically upward direction. This force acts only as long as the lower end remains inside the mercury. Work done by this force is $W = F_a\ (ILB)a$. If h is the maximum height to which the wire jumps, then using the Work–Energy Theorem, we have

$$W = \Delta K + \Delta U_{gr}$$

$\Rightarrow \quad (ILB)a = 0 + \text{mgh}$

$\Rightarrow \quad h = \frac{ILBa}{mg}$

21. (a) The magnetic field experienced by the charge will be different in the two cases.

Since $r \propto \frac{1}{B}$

$$\frac{r_1}{r_2} = \frac{B_2}{B_1} = \frac{\frac{\mu_0 I}{2\pi}\left(\frac{1}{d/3} + \frac{1}{2d/3}\right)}{\frac{\mu_0 I}{2\pi}\left(\frac{1}{d/3} - \frac{1}{2d/3}\right)} = 3$$

22. (d) Let us subdivide the disc into thin concentric rings, each of thickness dx. Consider one such element ring of radius x. The charge contained in this element ring is

$$dq = \frac{Q}{\pi R^2} \times 2\pi x dx = \frac{2Q}{R^2} x dx$$

The current constituted due to the rotation of this element ring is

$$dI = \frac{dq}{2\pi/\omega} = \frac{\omega Q}{\pi R^2} x dx$$

The magnetic moment due to this element ring is

$$d\mu = (\pi x^2) dI = \frac{\omega Q}{R^2} x^3 dx$$

Hence, the net magnetic moment is

$$\mu = \frac{\omega Q}{R^2}\int_0^R x^3 dx = \frac{1}{4}\omega Q R^2$$

23. (a)

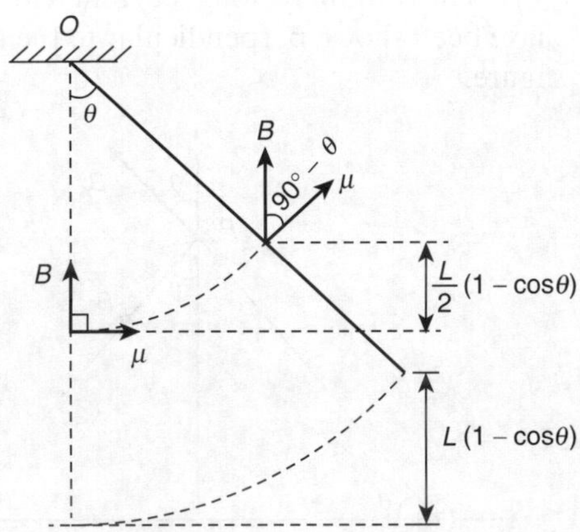

The figure shows the side view of the swing. The horizontal bar passes through O perpendicular to the plane of the figure. The motion of the swing is like a magnetic dipole of magnetic moment $\mu = IL^2$ rotating in a uniform magnetic field B. Initially, the angle between $\vec{\mu}$ and $\vec{B}$ is 90° and at maximum angular deflection, say θ, the angle between $\vec{\mu}$ and $\vec{B}$ is 90°– 0.The magnetic potential energy changes by

$$\Delta U_{mag} = -\mu B\cos(90° - \theta) = -\mu B\sin\theta$$

The gravitational potential energy changes by

$$\Delta U_{gr} = 2\text{ mg}\frac{L}{2}(1-\cos\theta) + \text{mgL}(1-\cos\theta)$$
$$= 2\text{ mgL}(1-\cos\theta)$$

Using the Work–Energy Theorem, we have

$$\Delta U_{mag} + \Delta U_{gr} = 0$$

$$\Rightarrow \quad -\mu B\sin\theta + 2mgL(1-\cos\theta) = 0$$

$$\Rightarrow \quad \frac{1-\cos\theta}{\sin\theta} = \frac{\mu B}{2mgL}$$

$$\Rightarrow \quad \tan\left(\frac{\theta}{2}\right) = \frac{\mu B}{2mgL}$$

$$\Rightarrow \quad \theta = 2\tan^{-1}\left(\frac{\mu B}{2mgL}\right)$$

24. (d) A magnetic dipole is in stable equilibrium when it is aligned along the magnetic field. Thus, the resultant of the two magnetic fields should be along $\vec{\mu}$ (see figure).

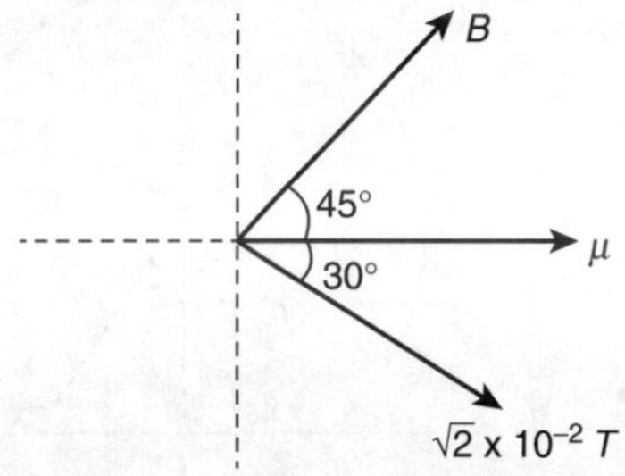

In other words, the magnetic field components along the perpendicular to $\vec{\mu}$ must add up to zero. Hence, we have

$$B\sin 45° = \sqrt{2}\times 10^{-2}\,T\sin 30° \Rightarrow B = 10^{-2}\,T$$

25. (c) The magnetic field at P due to the two wires is $\frac{\mu_0 I_1}{2\pi d}$ and $\frac{\mu_0 I_2}{2\pi d}$ and they are mutually perpendicular. Hence, the resultant field at P is

$$B = \frac{\mu_0}{2\pi d}\sqrt{I_1^2 + I_2^2}$$

26. (b) Let L be the length of the wire. If it is bent into a circular loop, its radius will be $r = \frac{L}{2\pi}$. The magnetic field at its centre will be $B = \frac{\mu_0 I}{2r} = \frac{\pi\mu_0 I}{L}$.

When the wire is bent into a circular coil of n turns,

its radius will be $r' = \frac{L}{2\pi n}$. The magnetic field at its centre will be $B' = n\left(\frac{\mu_0 I}{2r'}\right) = n^2\left(\frac{\pi\mu_0 I}{L}\right) = n^2 B.$

27. (a) Let I be the current in the wire and B be the magnetic field at the centre of the loop. Then, we have

$$54\mu T = \frac{\mu_0 I a^2}{2(a^2 + x^2)^{3/2}} \text{ and } B = \frac{\mu_0 I}{2a}$$

Dividing the two equations, we have

$$\frac{54\mu T}{B} = \frac{a^3}{(a^2 + x^2)^{3/2}} = \frac{3^3}{5^3}$$

[Given $a = 3$ cm, $x = 4$ cm]

$$\Rightarrow \quad B = \frac{125}{27} \times 54\ \mu T = 250\ \mu T$$

28. (c)

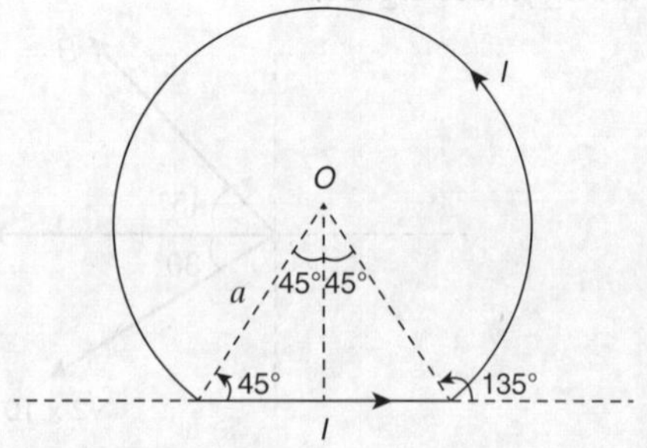

The magnetic field at O is

$$B = \left(\frac{2\pi - \pi/2}{2\pi}\right)\frac{\mu_0 I}{2a} + \frac{\mu_0 I}{4\pi(a/\sqrt{2})}(\cos 45^\circ - \cos 135^\circ)$$

$$= \left(\frac{3\pi}{8} + \frac{1}{2}\right)\frac{\mu_0}{\pi a} = 1.7\left(\frac{4 \times 10^{-7} \times 40}{0.02}\right)\text{T}$$

$$= 3.4 \times 10^{-4}\ \text{T}$$

29. (a)

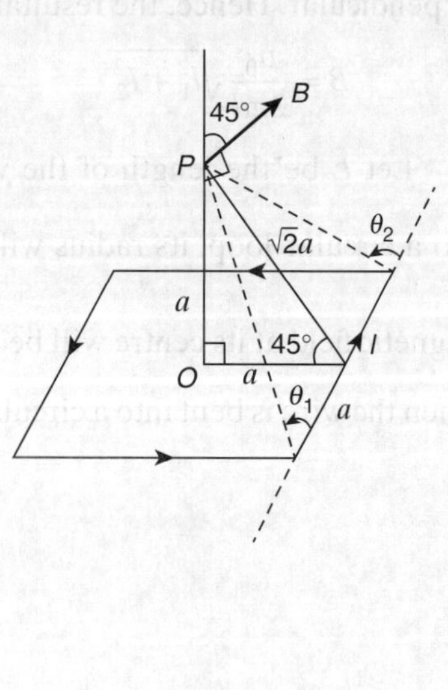

The perpendicular distance of P is $\sqrt{2}a$ from each side of the square. The magnetic field at P is the same due to each branch of the square loop.

The field at P due to one branch is

$$B = \frac{\mu_0 I}{4\pi(\sqrt{2}a)}(\cos\theta_1 - \cos\theta_2)$$

From the figure, we see that

$$\tan\theta_1 = \frac{\sqrt{2}a}{a} = \sqrt{2} \Rightarrow \cos\theta_1 = \frac{1}{\sqrt{3}}$$

and $\quad \theta_2 = \pi - \theta_1 \Rightarrow \cos\theta_2 = -\frac{1}{\sqrt{3}}$

Hence $\quad B = \frac{\mu_0 I}{4\pi(\sqrt{2}a)}\left(\frac{1}{\sqrt{3}} - \frac{-1}{\sqrt{3}}\right) = \frac{\mu_0 I}{2\sqrt{6}\pi a}$

The resultant magnetic field at P is upwards and its magnitude is

$$B_{res} = 4(B\cos 45^\circ) = \frac{\mu_0 I}{\sqrt{3}\pi a}$$

30. (b) The infinitely long current carrying wires have been shown perpendicular to the plane of the figure.

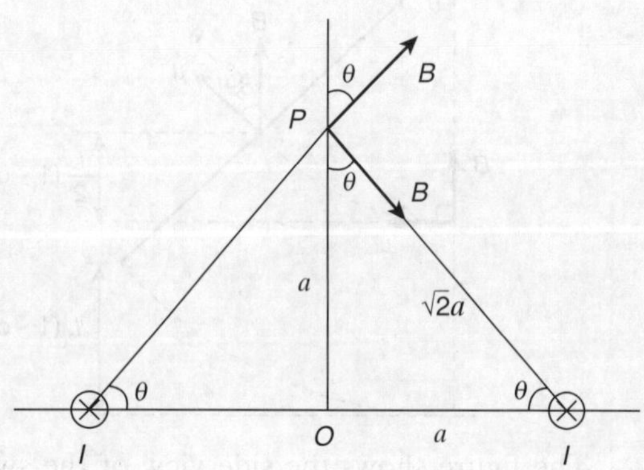

The magnetic field at P due to each one of them has magnitude $B = \frac{\mu_0 I}{2\pi(\sqrt{2}a)}$.

The resultant magnetic field at P is directed towards the right and its magnitude is

$$B_{res} = 2(B\sin\theta) = \frac{\mu_0 I}{2\pi a} \quad [\sin\theta = 1/\sqrt{2}]$$

31. (a)

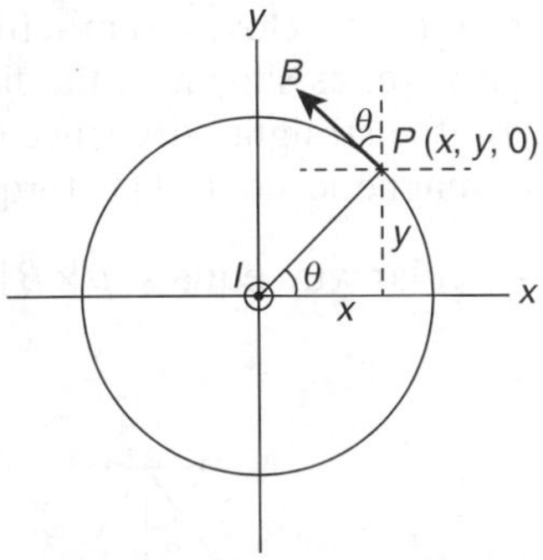

The point $P(x, y, 0)$ lies in the xy plane. The magnitude of the magnetic field at P is $B = \frac{\mu_0 I}{2\pi\sqrt{x^2+y^2}}$. In vector form, the magnetic field is $\vec{B} = B(-\sin\theta\hat{i} + \cos\theta\hat{j})$

$$= \frac{\mu_0 I}{2\pi\sqrt{x^2+y^2}}\left(\frac{-y}{\sqrt{x^2+y^2}}\hat{i} + \frac{x}{\sqrt{x^2+y^2}}\hat{j}\right)$$

$$= \frac{\mu_0 I}{2\pi(x^2+y^2)}(-y\hat{i} + x\hat{j})$$

32. (c) The field at O due to the straight part of the wire placed along the –ve x-axis is zero. The field at O due to the circular part of the wire is directed out of the plane of the figure, and its magnitude is

$$B_1 = \frac{3\pi/4}{2\pi} \times \frac{\mu_0 I}{2a} = \frac{3\mu_0 I}{16a}$$

The field at O due to the straight wire placed in the first quadrant is directed out of the plane of the figure, and its magnitude is

$$B_2 = \frac{\mu_0 I}{4\pi a\cos(\pi/4)}[\cos 0 - \cos(\pi/4)]$$

$$= \frac{\mu_0 I}{4\pi a}(\sqrt{2}-1)$$

Thus, the resultant magnetic field at O is directed out of the plane of the figure, and its magnitude is

$$B = B_1 + B_2 = \frac{\mu_0 I}{4\pi a}\left(\frac{3\pi}{4} + \sqrt{2} - 1\right)$$

33. (b) In the extreme left region, the field due to both wires is downwards, whereas in the extreme right region, the field due to both wires is upwards. In the region between the wires, the field is upwards due to the left wire and downwards due to the right wire. Hence, the net field is zero in the middle, upwards as we move towards the left wire and downwards as we move towards the right wire.

34. (a) The resistances of the major and the minor portions of the circular wire are in the ratio 3:1. The current I therefore distributes in the ratio 1:3. The current in the major portion is $I_1 = 14\ I$ and that in the minor portion is $I_2 = 34\ I$.

The magnetic field at O due to I_1 is directed along $\hat{i}$ and has magnitude $\frac{3}{4}\left(\frac{\mu_0 I_1}{2a}\right) = \frac{3\mu_0 I}{32a}$, and that due to I_2 is directed along the $-\hat{i}$ and has magnitude $\frac{1}{4}\left(\frac{\mu_0 I_2}{2a}\right) = \frac{3\mu_0 I}{32a}$. We see that they cancel each other. Hence, the magnetic field at O is only due to the two semi–infinite wires and that is $\vec{B} = \frac{\mu_0 I}{4\pi a}(\hat{j} + \hat{k})$

35. (a), (b)

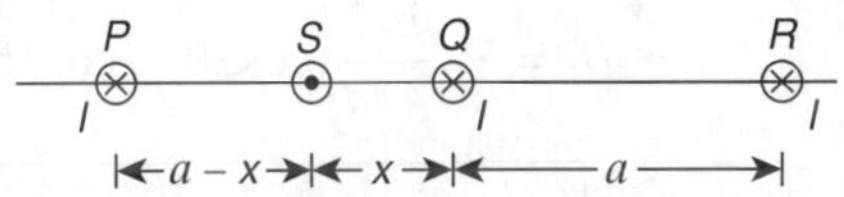

The wire S will remain in equilibrium at a position where the field is zero. Thus, we have (see figure)

$$\frac{\mu_0 I}{2\pi(a-x)} = \frac{\mu_0 I}{2\pi x} + \frac{\mu_0 I}{2\pi(a+x)}$$

$$\Rightarrow \quad \frac{1}{a-x} - \frac{1}{a+x} = \frac{1}{x}$$

$$\Rightarrow \quad 2x^2 = a^2 - x^2$$

$$\Rightarrow \quad x = \pm\frac{a}{\sqrt{3}}$$

The field will also be zero all along the wire Q. Hence, $x = 0$ is also the correct answer.

36. (a) Let us subdivide the spiral into thin concentric rings of width dx. The number of wires contained in each such element ring is $dN = \left(\frac{N}{b-a}\right)dx$. The magnetic field at the centre due to an element ring of radius x is

$$dB = dN\left(\frac{\mu_0 I}{2x}\right) = \left(\frac{N}{b-a}dx\right)\left(\frac{\mu_0 I}{2x}\right)$$

Hence, the net magnetic field at the centre is

$$B = \frac{\mu_0 NI}{2(b-a)}\int_a^b \frac{dx}{x} = \frac{\mu_0 NI}{2(b-a)}\ln\left(\frac{b}{a}\right)$$

37. (a)

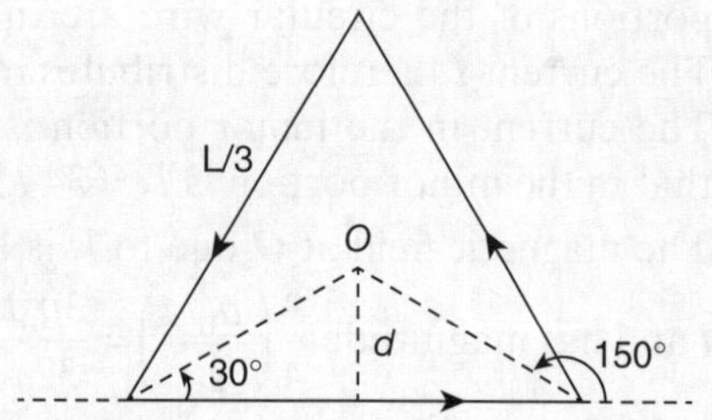

The length of each side of the equilateral triangle is $L/3$. The distance of the centroid from each side of the triangle is

$$d = \frac{1}{3}\left(\frac{L}{3}\sin 60^\circ\right) = \frac{L}{6\sqrt{3}}$$

The magnetic field at the centroid of the equilateral triangle is

$$B_1 = 3\times\frac{\mu_0 I}{4\pi d}(\cos 30^\circ - \cos 150^\circ) = \frac{27\mu_0}{2\pi L}$$

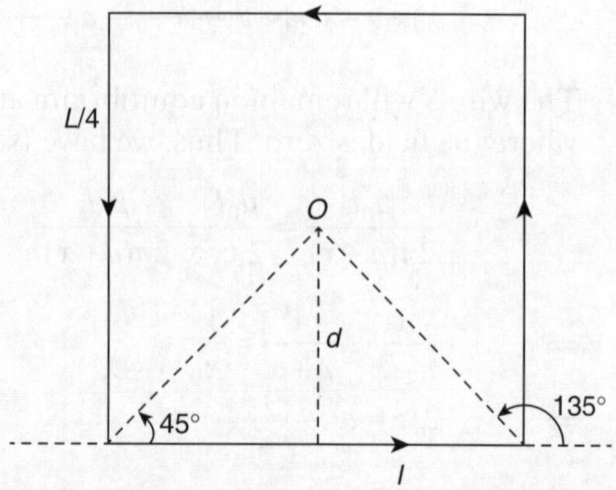

The length of each side of the equilateral triangle is $L/3$. The distance of the centroid from each side of the triangle is $d = L/8$. The magnetic field at the centroid of the square is

$$B_2 = 4\times\frac{\mu_0 I}{4\pi d}(\cos 45^\circ - \cos 135^\circ) = \frac{8\sqrt{2}\mu_0 I}{\pi L}$$

Hence $\dfrac{B_1}{B_2} = \dfrac{27}{16\sqrt{2}} = \dfrac{27\sqrt{2}}{32}$

38. (a)

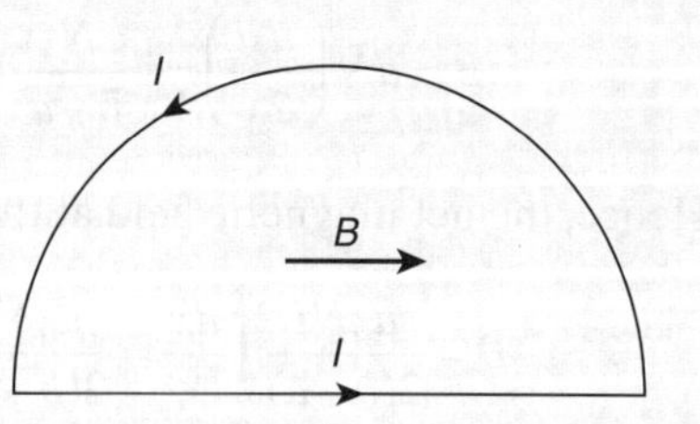

The given arrangement can be considered as a combination of closed semi-circular wire and a straight wire, as shown in the figure. There is no force on the straight wire since current is parallel to the magnetic field. The torque on the closed semi-circular wire equals $|\vec{\mu}\times\vec{B}| = I\left(\frac{1}{2}\pi R^2\right)B$.

39. (b)

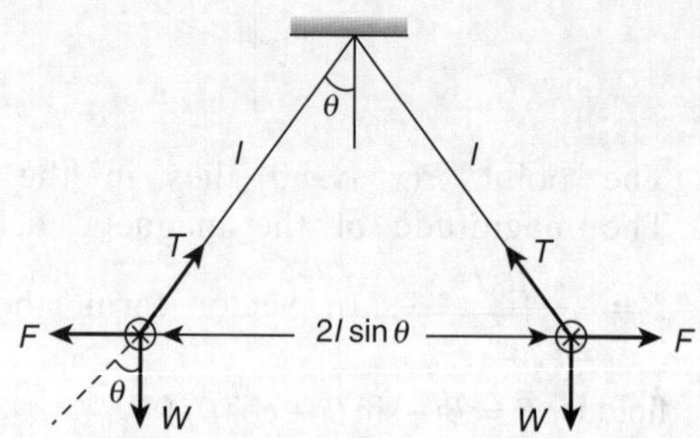

The figure shows the forces acting on the wire. The Ampere force per unit length is

$$F = \frac{\mu_0 I^2}{2\pi(2l/\sin\theta)}$$

The weight per unit length is

$W = \lambda g$

For equilibrium, we have

$F\cos\theta = W\sin\theta$ [Components $\perp$ to the thread]

$$\Rightarrow \quad \frac{\mu_0 I^2\cos\theta}{4\pi l/\sin\theta} = \lambda g\sin\theta$$

$$\Rightarrow \quad \frac{\mu_0}{4\pi} = \frac{\lambda\, \mathrm{lg}\sin^2\theta}{P^2\cos\theta}$$

40. (c)

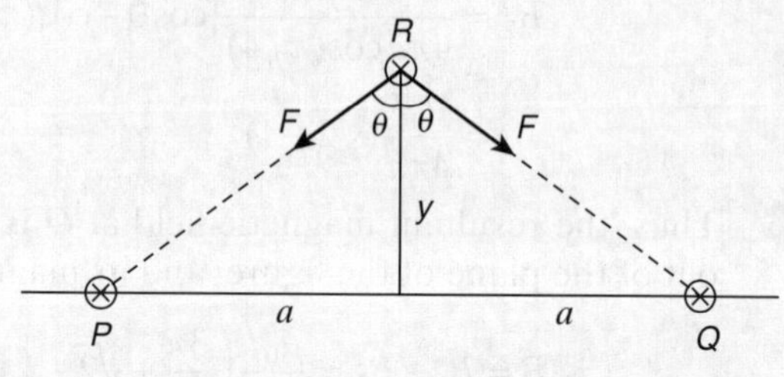

The figure shows the Ampere force F acting per unit length of wire R when it is slightly displaced from its equilibrium position. The net restoring force per unit length of wire R is

$$F_{res} = 2(F\cos\theta) = 2\left(\frac{\mu_0 I^2}{2\pi\sqrt{a^2+y^2}}\times\frac{y}{\sqrt{a^2+y^2}}\right)$$

$$= \frac{\mu_0 I^2}{\pi}\times\frac{y}{a^2+y^2} = \frac{\mu_0 I^2}{\pi a^2}y \text{ [for small } y]$$

The instantaneous acceleration of wire R is

$$\ddot{y} = -\frac{F_{res}}{\Lambda} = -\frac{\mu_0 I^2}{\lambda \pi a^2} y$$

Hence, the wire R will execute SHM with frequency

$$f = \frac{1}{2\pi}\sqrt{\frac{\mu_0 I^2}{\lambda \pi a^2}}$$

41. (c) The drift velocity of the current carriers is given by

$$v = \frac{j}{ne} = \frac{1/wd}{ne}$$

At steady state

$$eE = evB$$

$$\Rightarrow \quad E = vB = \frac{IB}{newd}$$

Hence, the PD across the width of the metal strip is

$$V = Ew = \frac{IB}{ned}$$

42. (d) The particle has a velocity component v_0 along the magnetic field and a component v_0 perpendicular the field. Hence, the particle will move in a helical path. The plane of revolution moves along the magnetic field (+x-axis) with velocity v_0 as shown in the figure. So the x-coordinate at time $T = \dfrac{\pi}{\alpha B_0}$ will be $x = v_0 T$.

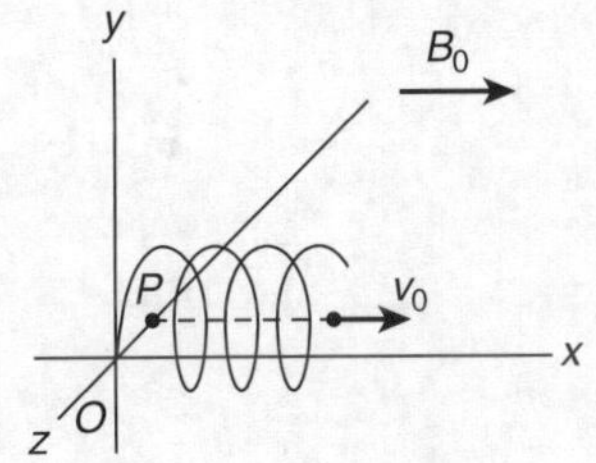

To find the y and z coordinates, let us view the particle's motion from the +x direction. The particle will appear to be moving in the yz plane in a circle of radius $r = \dfrac{mv_0}{qB_0} = \dfrac{v_0}{\alpha B_0}$, centred at point $P(0, 0, -r)$ and angular velocity $\omega = \dfrac{v_0}{r} = \alpha B_0$. In time $T = \dfrac{\pi}{\alpha B_n}$, the particle will rotate by angle $\theta = \omega T = \pi$. The particle will appear to be at a point diametrically opposite to O, that is, $y = 0$, $z = -2r$.

Hence, the required coordinates are $(v_0 T, 0, -2r) = \left(\dfrac{\pi v_0}{\alpha B_0}, 0, \dfrac{-2v_0}{\alpha B_0}\right)$.

43. (a) The surface charge density is

$$\frac{Q}{\pi(h\tan\theta)(h\sec\theta)} = \frac{Q\cos^2\theta}{\pi h^2 \sin\theta}$$

Let us subdivide the slant surface into element rings of width dx. The charge present on the element ring, as shown in the figure, is

$$dq = \frac{Q\cos^2\theta}{\pi h^2\sin\theta} \times (2\pi x\sin\theta)dx = \frac{2Q\cos^2\theta}{h^2} x\,dx$$

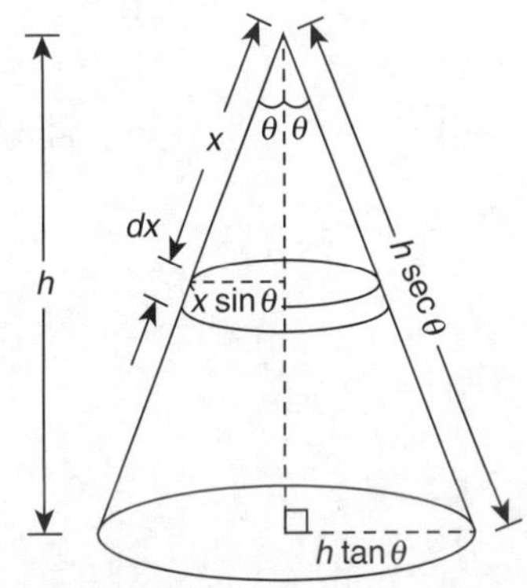

The associated dipole moment is

$$d\mu = \pi(x\sin\theta)^2 \frac{dq}{2\pi/\omega} = \frac{\omega Q\sin^2\theta\cos^2\theta}{h^2} x^3 dx$$

The net dipole moment is

$$\mu = \frac{\omega Q\sin^2\theta\cos^2\theta}{h^2}\int_0^{h\sec\theta} x^3 dx = \frac{1}{4}\omega Q h^2 \tan^2\theta$$

Now, inserting $\theta = \pi/6$, we have

$$\frac{Q\omega h^2}{\mu} = 12$$

44. (a) Let λ be the line charge density and d be the space between the two lines. The Coulomb force per unit length is

$$F_E = \frac{\lambda^2}{2\pi\varepsilon_0 d}$$

The moving charges constitute an electric current $I = \lambda v$. The Ampere force per unit length is

$$F_B = \frac{\mu_0 I^2}{2\pi d} = \frac{\mu_0 \lambda^2 v^2}{2\pi d}$$

Hence, we have

$$\frac{F_B}{F_E} = \mu_0\varepsilon_0 v^2 \Rightarrow \eta = 1$$

45. (d) Let I_1 and I_2 be the currents flowing through the infinite wire and the circular loop, respectively. The circular loop is a magnetic dipole directed into the plane of the figure. Let us replace the circular loop with two magnetic poles of strength $-m$ and $+m$ separated by a distance $2l$ such that $m(2l) = l_2(\pi a^2)$.

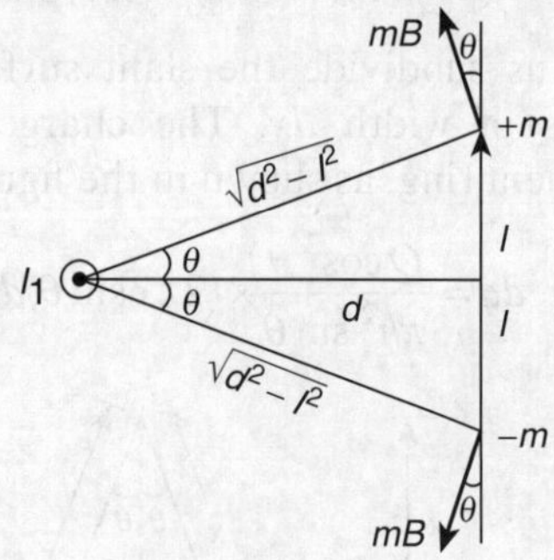

From the top view (see figure), we see that the force on each magnetic pole has magnitude mB, where

$$B = \frac{\mu_0 I_1}{2\pi\sqrt{d^2 + l^2}}.$$

The net force is attractive in nature and has magnitude

$$F = 2mB\sin\theta.$$

$$\Rightarrow \quad F = \frac{I_2(\pi a^2)}{I} \times \frac{\mu_0 I_1}{2\pi\sqrt{d^2 + 1^2}} \times \frac{I}{\sqrt{d^2 + 1^2}}$$

$$\Rightarrow \quad F = \frac{\mu_0 I_1 I_2 a^2}{2(d^2 + I^2)} = \frac{\mu_0 I_1 I_2 a^2}{2d^2} [I >> d]$$

CHAPTER

19 Electromagnetic Induction

- Magnetic flux is the product of area and the component of magnetic field along the normal to the area:

$$\phi_B = \int \mathbf{B} \cdot d\mathbf{s}$$

Faraday's law states that the induced emf in a closed loop equals the negative of the time rate of change of magnetic flux through the loop

$$\xi = -\frac{d\phi_B}{dt}$$

Lenz's law states that an induced emf always tends to oppose or cancel out the change that caused it.

- When a conductor moves in a steady (not varying with time) magnetic field **B**, the emf induced across its ends is given by

$$\xi = \int (\mathbf{v} \times \mathbf{B}) \cdot d\mathbf{l}$$

If $\mathbf{v} \times \mathbf{B}$ is uniform all along the length of the conductor, the above equation reduces to

$$\xi = (\mathbf{v} \times \mathbf{B}) \cdot \Delta \mathbf{l}$$

- When an emf is induced by a changing magnetic flux in a stationary closed path, there is an induced electric field **E** of non-electrostatic origin such that

$$\oint \mathbf{E} \cdot d\mathbf{l} = -\frac{d\phi_B}{dt}$$

This electric field is non-conservative and cannot be associated with a potential. They are closed and they perform non-zero work on charged particles, moving along these closed paths.

- When two coils are kept close, a current i_1 in one coil produces magnetic flux ϕ_{B2} in a second coil, and a current i_2 in the second coil produces magnetic flux ϕ_{B1} in the first coil. The magnetic flux in one coil is proportional to the current in the other coil. The proportionality constant is called the mutual inductance M for that pair of coils:

$$M = \frac{\phi_{B2}}{i_1} = \frac{\phi_{B1}}{i_2}$$

The value of M depends on the geometry and relative placing of the two coils. For a Tesla coil, which consists of a long solenoid of length l and area A, wound by N_1 turns of one coil and wound by N_2 number of another coil over the first one, the value of M is

$$M = \frac{\mu_0 N_1 N_2 A}{l}$$

A current i_1 in one coil produces magnetic flux $\phi_{B2} = Mi_1$ in the second coil. If i_1 changes, it induces an emf ξ_2 in the second coil; likewise a changing current i_2 in the second coil induces an emf ξ_1 in the first coil:

$$\xi_2 = -M\frac{di_1}{dt} \text{ and } \xi_1 = -M\frac{di_2}{dt}$$

- Current i flowing through a coil produces a magnetic flux ϕ_B in itself, which is proportional to the current. The proportionality constant is called the self-inductance L of the coil:

$$L = \frac{\phi_B}{i}$$

The value of L depends on the geometry of the coil. For a long solenoid of length l, area A and N number of turns, the value of L is

$$L = \frac{\mu_0 N^2 A}{l}$$

A current i through the coil produces magnetic flux $\phi_B = Li$ in the coil. If i changes, it induces an emf ξ (in the direction of current) given by

$$\xi = -L\frac{di}{dt}$$

Such a coil is called an inductor, and the purpose of its presence in a circuit is to oppose changes in current.

- The energy U required to build up a current I in an inductor L is equal to the energy stored in the inductor and is given by

$$U = \frac{1}{2}LI^2$$

The energy can be thought of as residing in the magnetic field inside the coil; the energy density u (energy per unit volume) is given by

$$u = \frac{B^2}{2\mu_0}$$

- When an inductor L is connected in series with a resistor R and a battery of emf ξ, the current approaches its final value ξ / R exponentially:

$$I = \frac{\xi}{R}\left(1 - e^{-t/\tau}\right),$$

where $\tau = L/R$ is called the time constant of the circuit. After this much time, the current has grown to 63% of its final value.

When an inductor with initial current I_0 is connected in series to a resistor R, the current decays exponentially:

$$I = I_0 e^{-t/\tau}$$

- An L–C circuit without any electrical resistance, undergoes electrical oscillations with angular frequency ω:

$$\omega = \frac{1}{\sqrt{LC}}$$

An L–C circuit without any electrical resistance is a conservative system. The magnetic-field energy $Li^2/2$ and the electric-field energy $q^2/2C$ correspond to the kinetic and potential energy, respectively, of a mechanical oscillator. The sum of these energies is a constant:

$$\frac{1}{2}Li^2 + \frac{q^2}{2C} = \frac{Q^2}{2C},$$

where Q is the maximum charge on the capacitor. When charge on the capacitor is q, the current i in the circuit is

$$i = \omega\sqrt{Q^2 - q^2}$$

EXERCISES

1. A rectangular loop of sides 8 cm and 2 cm having resistance of 1.6 Ω is placed in a magnetic field of 0.3 T directed normal to the loop. The magnetic field is gradually reduced at the rate of 0.02 T/s. The power dissipated in the loop as heat is:
(a) 1.6×10^{-10} W (b) 3.2×10^{-10} W
(c) 6.4×10^{-10} W (d) 12.8×10^{-10} W

2. An ideal solenoid of cross-section area 10^{-4} m^2 has 500 turns/m. Near the centre of the solenoid, another coil of 100 turns is wrapped closely around it. If the current in the solenoid changes from 0 to 2 A in 3.14 ms, the emf developed in the other coil is $\left(\frac{\mu_0}{4\pi} = 10^{-7} \text{ Wb/A}\cdot\text{m}\right)$:
(a) 1 mV (b) 2 mV
(c) 3 mV (d) 4 mV

3. In an AC generator, the number of turns in the coil is 2000 and the area of the coil is 0.1 m^2. The coil is rotated at an angular frequency of 200 rad/s in a magnetic field of 0.2 T. The induced emf when the plane of the coil makes an angle of 60° with the field is:
(a) 1000 V (b) 2000 V
(c) 4000 V (d) 8000 V

4. A circular loop is placed in a time varying magnetic field. Electrical power is dissipated due to the current induced in the coil. If the number of turns was to be quadrupled and the loop radius halved, the electrical power dissipated will be:
(a) Halved (b) The same
(c) Doubled (d) Quadrupled

5. A uniform metal rod of length l is moving with a uniform velocity v parallel to a long straight wire carrying a steady current I, as shown in the figure.

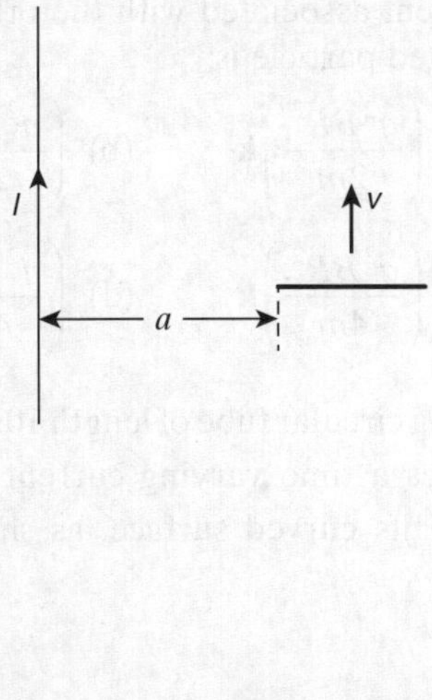

The emf induced in the rod is:
(a) 0 (b) $\frac{\mu_0 I v}{2\pi} \ln\left(\frac{l+a}{a}\right)$
(c) $\frac{\mu_0 I v}{2\pi} \ln\left(\frac{l-a}{a}\right)$ (d) $\frac{\mu_0 I v}{2\pi} \ln\left(\frac{l}{a}\right)$

6. A metallic wheel with 8 metal spokes, each of length r, is rotating with angular speed ω in a plane perpendicular to a magnetic field B. The magnitude of the induced emf between the axle and the rim of the wheel is:
(a) $\frac{1}{2}\omega r^2 B$ (b) $\frac{1}{4}\omega r^2 B$
(c) $2\omega r^2 B$ (d) $4\omega r^2 B$

7. The figure shows two coaxial conducting loops P and Q separated by some distance. When switch S is closed, a current I flows in P and an induced current I_1 flows in Q. The switch remains closed for a long time. When S is opened, a current I_2 flows in Q.

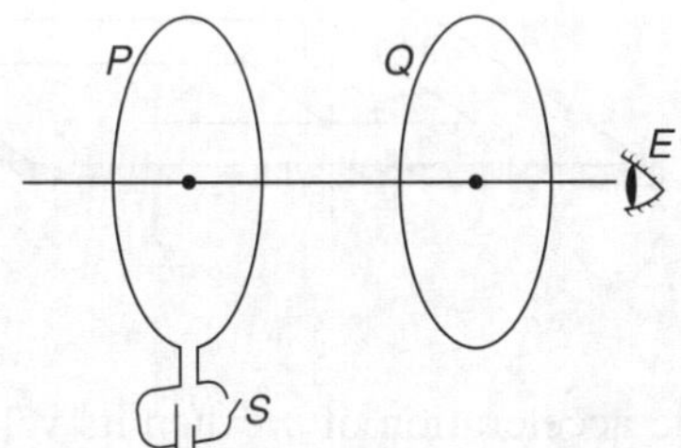

The directions of I_1 and I_2 (as seen by the eye E) are:
(a) Respectively clockwise and anti-clockwise
(b) Both clockwise
(c) Respectively anti-clockwise and clockwise
(d) Both anti-clockwise

8. A small square loop of side l is placed inside a large square loop of side L ($L >> l$). The loops are coplanar and their centres coincide. The number of turns for both loops is N. The mutual inductance of the pair of coils is:
(a) $\frac{\mu_0 N^2 l^2}{\sqrt{2}\pi L}$ (b) $\frac{2\sqrt{2}\mu_0 N^2 l^2}{\pi L}$
(c) $\frac{\mu_0 N^2 l^2}{2\sqrt{2}\pi L}$ (d) $\frac{\mu_0 N^2 l^2}{2\pi L}$

9. In a uniform magnetic field B, a closed semi-circular wire of radius r rotates about its diameter with angular velocity ω. The axis of rotation is perpendicular to the field. If the resistance of the wire is R, the mean power generated per cycle of rotation is:

(a) 0 (b) $\dfrac{(\pi r^2 \omega B)^2}{2R}$

(c) $\dfrac{(\pi r^2 \omega B)^2}{4R}$ (d) $\dfrac{(\pi r^2 \omega B)^2}{8R}$

10. A pair of parallel horizontal conducting rails of negligible resistance shorted at one end is fixed on a horizontal table, as shown in the figure. The distance between the rails is l. A light conducting rod of resistance R can slide on the rails without friction. The rod is tied to a mass m by a light string, which passes over a smooth pulley. A uniform magnetic field B exists perpendicular to the table. When the system is released from rest, the mass m falls with acceleration but eventually acquires a terminal velocity.

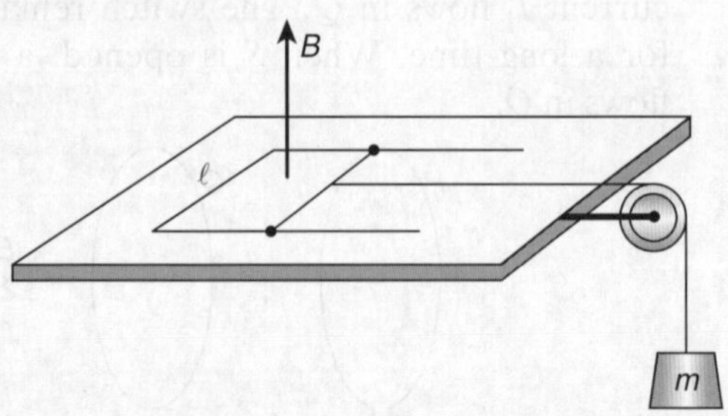

The acceleration of m when its velocity is half the terminal velocity is:

(a) g (b) $g/4$

(c) $g/3$ (d) $g/2$

11. The figure shows an infinitely long straight wire carrying current I and a semi-circular wire of radius r lying in the same plane. The centre of the semi-circular wire is at a distance d from the infinite wire, and its diameter PQ is inclined at angle θ to the infinite wire.

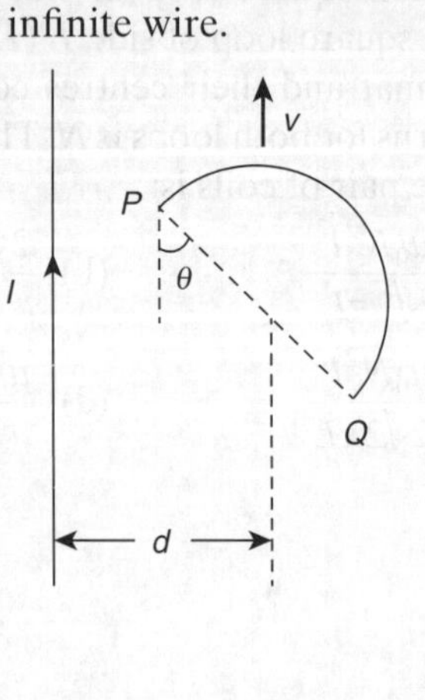

If the semi-circular wire is pulled with a uniform velocity v parallel to the infinite wire, the potential difference between points P and Q is:

(a) $\dfrac{\mu_0 I v}{2\pi}\ln\left(\dfrac{d+2r\sin\theta}{d-2r\sin\theta}\right)$

(b) $\dfrac{\mu_0 I v}{4\pi}\ln\left(\dfrac{d+2r\sin\theta}{d-2r\sin\theta}\right)$

(c) $\dfrac{\mu_0 I v}{2\pi}\ln\left(\dfrac{d+r\sin\theta}{d-r\sin\theta}\right)$

(d) $\dfrac{\mu_0 I v}{4\pi}\ln\left(\dfrac{d+r\sin\theta}{d-r\sin\theta}\right)$

12. The figure shows a metal wheel of radius R in pure rolling motion in a uniform magnetic field B perpendicular to the plane of the figure. The velocity of the centre of the wheel is v.

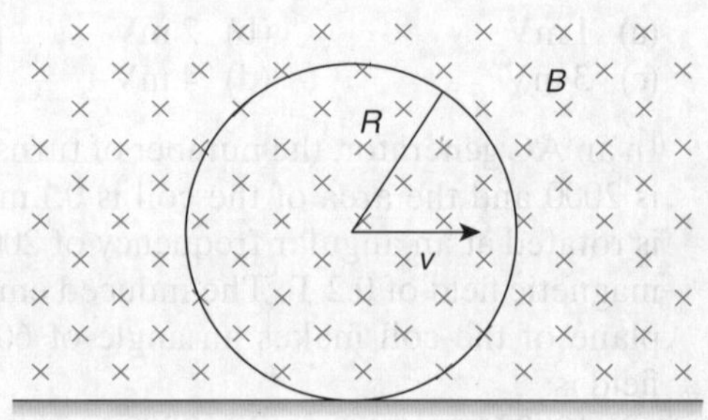

The potential difference between the lowest and highest points on the wheel is:

(a) 0 (b) $2vBR$

(c) $\dfrac{1}{2}vBR$ (d) $\sqrt{2}vBR$

13. A particle of mass m and carrying charge q is confined to move in a circular path of radius R in the xy plane. Initially, it is moving with some angular velocity. A magnetic field is now switched on along the $+z$-axis, which increases at a uniform rate from 0 to B in 1 s. The change in the magnetic moment associated with the orbital motion of the charged particle is:

(a) $-\left(\dfrac{q^2BR^2}{2m}\right)\mathbf{k}$ (b) $\left(\dfrac{q^2BR^2}{2m}\right)\mathbf{k}$

(c) $-\left(\dfrac{q^2BR^2}{4m}\right)\mathbf{k}$ (d) $\left(\dfrac{q^2BR^2}{4m}\right)\mathbf{k}$

14. A long circular tube of length 10 m and radius 0.3 m carries a time varying current $I(t) = I_0 \cos(300t)$ along its curved surface, as shown in the figure.

A wire loop of resistance 5 mΩ and radius 0.1 m is placed co-axially inside the tube.

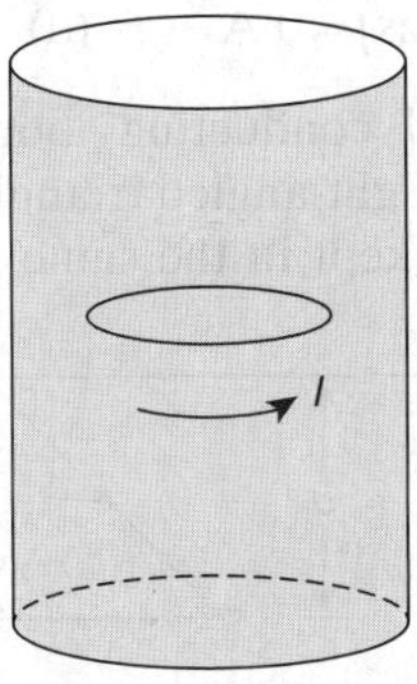

If the magnetic moment of the loop is given by $N\mu_0 I_0 \sin(300t)$, then N equals:
(a) 6 (b) 5
(c) 3 (d) 0

15. A solenoid of inductance L and resistance R is connected to a battery at time $t = 0$. The time when the energy dissipation rate across the resistor equals the energy accumulation rate in the solenoid is:
(a) $\frac{L}{R}$ (b) $\frac{L}{R}\ln 2$
(c) $\frac{L}{2R}$ (d) $\frac{L}{R}\ln 4$

16. A circuit having self-inductance of 1 H carries a current of 2 A. To prevent sparking when the circuit is broken, a capacitor which can withstand 400 V is used. The least capacitance of the capacitor that must be connected across the switch is:
(a) 125 μF (b) 100 μF
(c) 50 μF (d) 25 μF

17. A capacitor of capacitance 2 μF is charged to a potential difference of 12 V. The charging battery is then removed and the capacitor is connected across an inductor of self-inductance 0.6 mH. Let I and dI/dt denote the current and magnitude of the rate of change of current, respectively. At a time when the potential difference across the capacitor is 6 V, we have:

(a) $I = 0.6$ A, $\frac{dI}{dt} = 10^3$ A/s

(b) $I = 0.6$ A, $\frac{dI}{dt} = 10^4$ A/s

(c) $I = 0.9$ A, $\frac{dI}{dt} = 10^3$ A/s

(d) $I = 0.9$ A, $\frac{dI}{dt} = 10^4$ A/s

18. Two ideal inductors of inductances $L_1 = 0.1$ mH and $L_2 = 0.5$ mH are joined in parallel, and then connected (at $t = 0$) to a DC voltage source of emf 6 V and internal resistance 10 Ω. If V and I, respectively, denote the voltage and current for the inductors, the correct statements from the following are:
(a) At $t = 0$, $V_1 = 6$ V, $I_1 = 0$ A
(b) At $t = \infty$, $V_1 = 0$ V, $I_1 = 0.5$ A
(c) At all times $I_1 / I_2 = 5$
(d) At all times $V_1 / V_2 = 5$

19. In the network shown in the figure, the current varies with time as $I(t) = 5\text{ A} - (10^3\text{ A/s})t$. At $t = 0$, the potential difference between the extreme ends is:

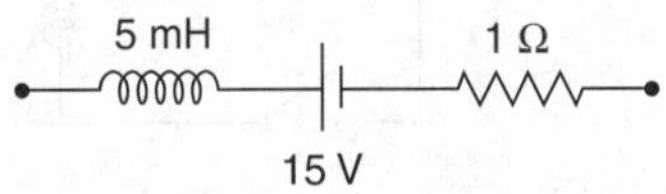

(a) 5 V (b) 10 V
(c) 15 V (d) 25 V

20. A capacitor of capacitance 2 μF is charged to a potential difference of 12 V. The charging battery is then removed and the capacitor is connected across an inductor of self-inductance 0.6 mH. The potential energy of the capacitor changes periodically from a maximum value to zero value and then again to a maximum value with a frequency of:
(a) $\frac{25}{\pi\sqrt{3}}$ kHz (b) $\frac{50}{\pi\sqrt{3}}$ kHz
(c) 25π kHz (d) $\frac{25\sqrt{3}}{\pi}$ kHz

21. In a car spark coil, an emf of 40,000 V is induced in its secondary when the current in its primary changes from 4 A to zero in 10 μs. The mutual inductance between the primary and the secondary windings of the spark coil is:
(a) 0.1 H (b) 0.2 H
(c) 0.2 H (d) 0.4 H

22. In the network shown in the figure, the switch is closed at $t = 0$.

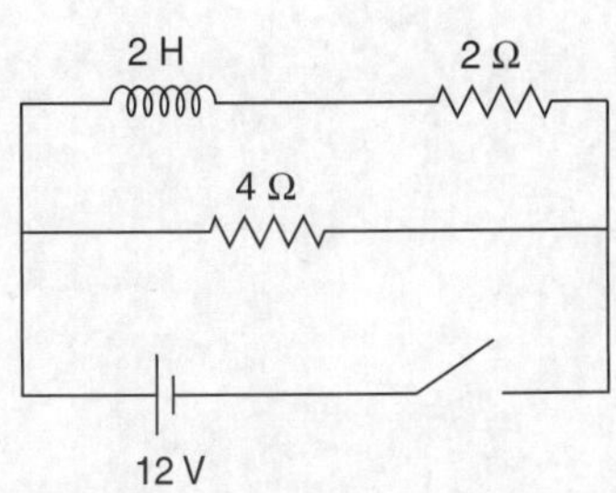

At time $t = \ln 2$ s, the incorrect statements from the following are:

(a) Current through 4-Ω resistor = 3 A
(b) Current through 2-Ω resistor = 3 A
(c) Power delivered by the cell = 36 W
(d) Potential difference across the inductor = 6 V

23. In the network shown in the figure, the switch is closed at $t = 0$. Once steady state is reached, the switch is opened.

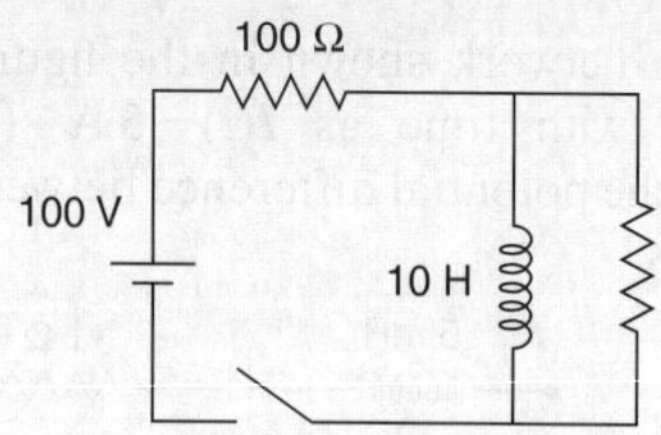

From this moment on till the current in the circuit falls to zero, the heat generated in the 10-Ω resistor is:

(a) 5 J (b) 4 J
(c) 3 J (d) 2 J

24. The PD across an inductor ($L = 3$ mH), measured along the direction of current flow, varies with time as $V(t) = \begin{cases} -15\text{ V}, 0 \le t \le 2\text{ ms} \\ 0\text{ V}, 2\text{ ms} < t < 4\text{ ms} \\ 30\text{ V}, 4\text{ ms} \le t \le 6\text{ ms} \end{cases}$

If current $I = 0$ at time $t = 0$, then:

(a) $I(2\text{ ms}) = 5$ A (b) $I(3\text{ ms}) = 10$ A
(c) $I(5\text{ ms}) = 0$ A (d) None of these

25. A closed conducting loop of the shape of an isoceles right-angled triangle and an infinitely long wire are kept in the same plane, as shown in the figure.

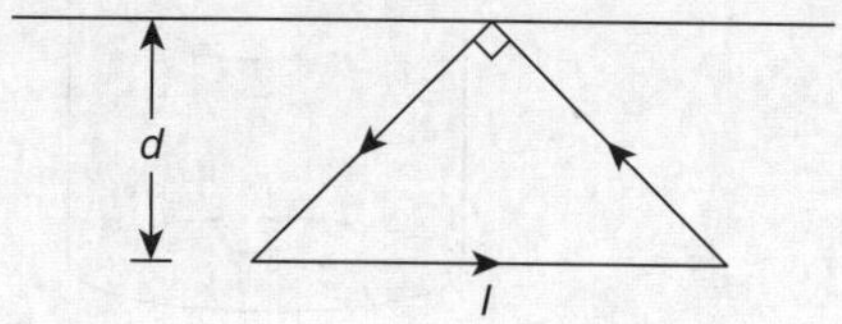

The wire and the loop are electrically insulated from each other. The hypotenuse of the triangle is parallel to the wire, at a distance $d = 10$ cm from the wire. If a counter-clockwise current I flows through the loop and it increases at a steady rate of 10 A/s, then the correct statements from the following are:

(a) An emf of $\frac{\mu_0}{\pi}$ V is induced in the wire
(b) The induced current in the wire is in opposite direction to the current along the hypotenuse
(c) There is a repulsive force between the wire and the loop
(d) If the loop is rotated about the wire with some constant angular speed, an additional emf of $\frac{\mu_0}{\pi}$ V is induced in the wire

ANSWER KEYS

1. (c)	**2.** (d)	**3.** (c)	**4.** (a)	**5.** (b)	**6.** (a)	**7.** (c)	**8.** (b)	**9.** (d)	**10.** (d)
11. (c)	**12.** (b)	**13.** (c)	**14.** (a)	**15.** (b)	**16.** (d)	**17.** (b)	**18.** (a),(b),(c)	**19.** (c)	
20. (b)	**21.** (a)	**22.** (c)	**23.** (a)	**24.** (b),(c)	**25.** (a),(c)				

SOLUTIONS

1. (c) The induced emf is given by

$$\xi = \left|\frac{d\phi}{dt}\right| = A\left|\frac{dB}{dt}\right| = (16\times10^{-4}\ \text{m}^2)(0.02\ \text{T/s})$$
$$= 3.2\times10^{-5}\ \text{V}$$

Power dissipated is given by

$$P = \frac{\xi^2}{R} = \frac{(3.2\times10^{-5}\ \text{V})^2}{1.6\ \Omega} = 6.4\times10^{-10}\ \text{W}$$

2. (c) When current is I, the magnetic field inside the solenoid is $B = 500\ \mu_0 I$.
The emf induced is given by

$$\xi = NA\left|\frac{dB}{dt}\right| = (100\times10^{-4}\ \text{m}^2)\left(500\mu_0\frac{dI}{dt}\right)$$
$$= 5(4\pi\times10^{-7})\left(\frac{2}{3.14\times10^{-3}}\right)\text{V} = 4\ \text{mV}$$

3. (c) Magnetic flux when the normal to the plane of the coil makes angle θ with the field is

$$\phi = NAB\cos\theta$$

Induced emf is given by

$$\xi = -\frac{d\phi}{dt} = NAB\omega\sin\theta$$

When the plane of the coil makes angle 60° with the field, the normal to the plane of the coil makes angle $\theta = 30°$ with the field. The induced emf at this instant is $\xi = 2000 \times 0.1\ \text{m}^2 \times 0.2\ \text{T} \times 200\ \text{rad/s} \times \sin 30° = 4000\ \text{V}$.

4. (a) Let N be the number of turns and r be the radius of one loop. The emf induced is

$$\xi = N(\pi r^2)\frac{dB}{dt} \propto Nr^2$$

If λ is the resistance / length, the resistance of the wire is

$$R = \lambda N(2\pi r) \propto Nr$$

Power dissipated is given by

$$P = \frac{\xi^2}{R} \propto \frac{N^2 r^4}{Nr} = Nr^3$$

Hence, if N is quadrupled and r is halved, P is halved.

5. (b) Let us subdivide the moving rod into small elements, each of length dx. If x is the distance of one such element from the current carrying wire, then emf induced in this element is given by

$$d\xi = vB(x)dx = v\left(\frac{\mu_0 I}{2\pi x}\right)dx$$

Hence, total emf induced is

$$\xi = \frac{\mu_0 I v}{2\pi}\int_a^{l+a}\frac{dx}{x} = \frac{\mu_0 I v}{2\pi}\ln\left(\frac{l+a}{a}\right)$$

6. (a) The emf induced across each spoke is $\frac{1}{2}\omega r^2 B$. Since all the spokes are parallel, the net emf between the axle and the rim equals emf across any one spoke, that is, $\frac{1}{2}\omega r^2 B$.

7. (c) When S is closed, magnetic field lines through Q are directed to the left and are increasing. Induced emf will be in the anti-clockwise sense so that it opposes the increasing magnetic field.
When S is opened, the situation reverses. Magnetic field lines start decreasing. Induced emf in Q is now in the clockwise sense so that it opposes the decreasing magnetic field.

8. (b) If current I flows in the larger square loop, the magnetic field at its centre is

$$B = 4N\times\frac{\mu_0 I}{4\pi(L/2)}(\cos 45° - \cos 135°)$$
$$= \frac{2\sqrt{2}\mu_0 NI}{\pi L}$$

The magnetic flux linking the smaller square loop kept at its centre is

$$\phi = N(Bl^2) = \left(\frac{2\sqrt{2}\mu_0 N^2 l^2}{\pi L}\right)I$$

Hence, mutual inductance is

$$M = \frac{\phi}{I} = \frac{2\sqrt{2}\mu_0 N^2 l^2}{\pi L}$$

9. (d) When the normal to the plane of the coil makes angle θ with the field, the magnetic flux is given by

$$\phi = \frac{1}{2}(\pi r^2)B\cos\theta$$

Induced emf is given by

$$\xi = -\frac{d\phi}{dt} = \frac{1}{2}\pi r^2 B\omega\sin\theta$$

Instantaneous power is given by

$$P = \frac{\xi^2}{R} = \frac{(\pi r^2 B\omega)^2 \sin^2\theta}{4R}$$

The mean value over one cycle is

$$P_{\text{mean}} = \frac{(\pi r^2 B\omega)^2}{8R} \text{ [Mean value of } \sin\theta = 1/2]$$

10. (d) At any instant when the rod is moving with velocity v, the emf induced across the rod is $\xi = v/B$.

The current in the rod is $I = \frac{v/B}{R}$.

There are two forces acting on the (rod + block) system, along the direction of motion.

The ampere force $ILB = \frac{vL^2B^2}{R}$ opposite the velocity, and the gravitational force mg along the velocity of the rod.

The block attains terminal velocity, say v_T, when gravitational force is balanced by ampere force. Thus, we have

$$\frac{v_T L^2 B^2}{R} = mg \Rightarrow v_T = \frac{mgR}{L^2B^2}$$

When the velocity of the block is $\frac{1}{2}V_T$, ampere force is $\frac{1}{2}mg$ and its acceleration is

$$a = \frac{mg - \frac{1}{2}mg}{m} = \frac{g}{2}$$

11. (c)

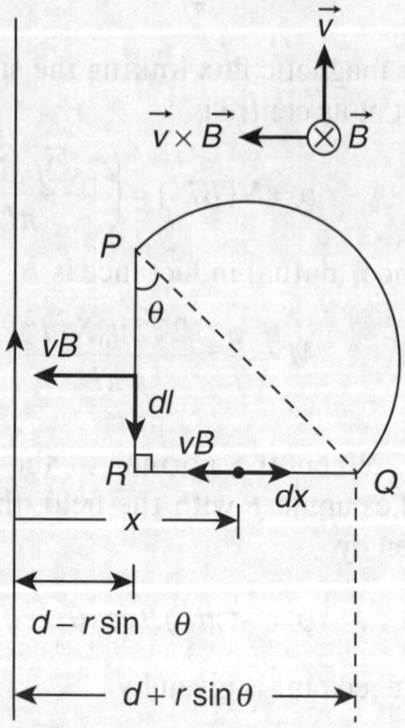

Suppose we join the ends P, Q of the semi-circular wire by two straight wires PR and RQ (see figure) so as to form a closed loop. We can see that the magnetic flux through the loop does not change as it moves parallel to the infinite wire. This means there will be no emf induced in the loop. This is because the semi-circular part and the straight part PRQ of the loop behave as identical seats of emf, thereby cancelling each other. Thus, we conclude that finding emf across the semi-circular part is the same as finding emf across the straight wires PQ and QR.

The magnetic field in this region is directed inward, so $v \times B = vB$ directed towards the infinite wire. To find emf across PR, let us subdivide the wire into small elements, each of length dl (see figure). The induced emf across this element is $d\xi = v \times B \cdot dl = 0$.

So emf across PR is zero. To find emf across RQ, let us subdivide the wire into small elements, each of length dx. The figure shows one such element at distance x from the infinite wire. The induced emf across this element is

$$d\xi = v \times B \cdot dl = -vBdx = -\frac{\mu_0 I v}{2\pi x}dx$$

The total emf across RQ is

$$\xi = -\frac{\mu_0 I v}{2\pi}\int_{d-r\sin\theta}^{d+r\sin\theta}\frac{1}{x}dx = -\frac{\mu_0 I v}{2\pi}\ln\left(\frac{d+r\sin\theta}{d-r\sin\theta}\right)$$

The negative sign shows that potential drops along the direction of increasing x, which means Q is at a lower potential than R. Hence, the potential difference between points P and Q = sum of the emfs across PR and RQ

$$= \frac{\mu_0 I v}{2\pi}\ln\left(\frac{d+r\sin\theta}{d-r\sin\theta}\right)$$

12. (b)

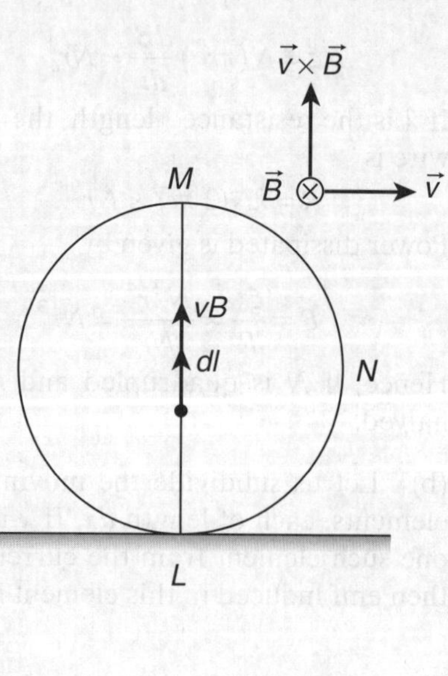

Suppose, we join the lowest and the highest points of the wheel by a straight wire LM (see figure). The wire is to be attached such that it always remains vertical even as the wheel rolls. Now, if we consider the semi-circular loop LMN, we can see that the magnetic flux through the loop does not change as it moves along. This means there will be no emf induced in the loop. This is because the semi-circular part and the straight part of the loop behave as identical seats of emf in the same sense, thereby cancelling each other. Thus, we conclude that finding emf across the semi-circular part is the same as finding emf across the straight wire. The straight wire LM is moving with velocity v towards the right and the magnetic field is directed inward, so $v \times B = vB$ directed upwards.

To find emf across LM, let us subdivide the wire into small elements, each of length dl (see figure). The induced emf across this element is $d\xi = v \times B \cdot dl = vBdl$. The total emf across LM is

$$\xi = vB\int dl = vB(2R)$$

Point M is at a higher potential than point L.

13. (c) The time varying magnetic field produces circular electric fields. The magnetic field is increasing along $\hat{k}$. The electric field over a circle of radius R is given by

$$\oint \vec{E} \cdot d\vec{l} = -\frac{d\phi}{dt}$$

$$\Rightarrow \quad E(2\pi R) = -\pi R^2 \frac{dB}{dt}$$

$$\Rightarrow \quad E = -\frac{1}{2}R\frac{dB}{dt} = -\frac{1}{2}R\frac{B}{1\text{ s}} = -\frac{1}{2}RB$$

The negative sign shows that the electric field is in the clockwise sense as seen from the $+z$ direction. The charge experiences force qE and hence a torque about its axis of rotation, given by

$$\vec{\tau} = -(qER)\hat{k} = -\left(\frac{1}{2}qBR^2\right)\hat{k}$$

In 1 s time, the angular momentum changes by

$$\Delta\vec{L} = \vec{\tau} \times 1\text{ s} = -\left(\frac{1}{2}qBR^2\right)\hat{k}$$

The magnetic moment $\vec{\mu}$ and the angular momentum $\vec{L}$ are related as $\vec{\mu} = \frac{q}{2m}\vec{L}$.

Hence, we have

$$\Delta\vec{\mu} = \frac{q}{2m}\Delta\vec{L} = -\left(\frac{q^2BR^2}{4m}\right)\hat{k}$$

14. (a) The tube behaves like a solenoid. The magnetic field inside the tube is along its axis, having magnitude $B = \frac{\mu_0 I}{L} = \frac{\mu_0 I_0}{L}\cos(300t)$.

Since B is time varying, an emf is induced in the circular wire placed inside the tube. The induced emf is given by

$$\xi = -\pi r^2 \frac{dB}{dt} = 300\pi r^2 \frac{\mu_0 I_0}{L}\sin(300t)$$

Current ξ/R flows in the wire. The associated magnetic moment is

$$\mu = \left(\frac{\xi}{R}\right)(\pi r^2) = \frac{300(\pi r^2)^2}{LR}\mu_0 I_0 \sin(300t)$$

$$\text{Hence} \quad N = \frac{300(\pi r^2)^2}{LR} = \frac{300 \times (\pi \times 10^{-2})^2}{10(5 \times 10^{-3})} = 6$$

15. (b) Electrical power across any circuit element equals VI. Since the solenoid and the resistor are connected in series, the same current flows through them. Hence, energy dissipation rate across the resistor and energy accumulation rate in the solenoid will be equal when $V_R = V_L = \xi/2$, where ξ is the emf of the battery. Hence, we have

$$\xi[1 - e^{-t/T}] = \frac{1}{2}\xi$$

$$\Rightarrow \quad e^{t/T} = 2$$

$$\Rightarrow \quad t = r\ln 2 = \frac{L}{R}\ln 2$$

16. (d) When the circuit is broken, the energy in the inductor is transferred to the capacitor. Hence, we have

$$\frac{1}{2}CV^2 = \frac{1}{2}LI^2$$

$$\Rightarrow \quad C = \frac{LI^2}{V^2} = \frac{(1\text{ H})(2\text{ A})^2}{(400\text{ V})^2} = 25\ \mu\text{F}$$

17. (b) Let I be the current in the circuit. Using energy conservation principle, we have

$$\frac{1}{2}LI^2 = \frac{1}{2}C(12\text{ V})^2 - \frac{1}{2}C(6\text{ V})^2$$

$$\Rightarrow \quad I = \sqrt{\frac{2 \times 10^{-6}\text{ F}}{0.6 \times 10^{-3}\text{ H}} \times (108\text{ V})^2} = 0.6\text{ A}$$

The voltage drop across the inductor is always equal to that across the capacitor. Hence, we have

$$L\left|\frac{dI}{dt}\right| = 6\text{ V}$$

$$\Rightarrow \quad \left|\frac{dI}{dt}\right| = \frac{6\text{ V}}{0.6\times 10^{-3}\text{ H}} = 10^4\text{ A/s}$$

18. (a), (b), (c)

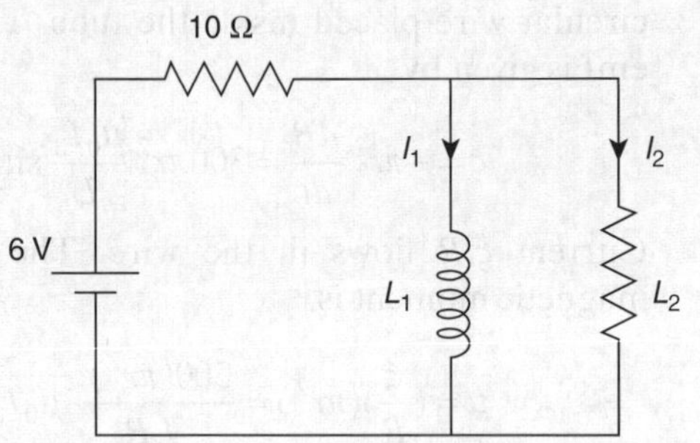

At all times, $V_1 = V_2$ since the inductors are connected in parallel. Hence

$$L_1\frac{dI_1}{dt} = L_2\frac{dI_2}{dt}$$

$$\Rightarrow \quad L_1I_1 = L_2I_2 \text{ [Since } I_1 = I_2 = 0 \text{ at } t = 0]$$

$$\Rightarrow \quad \frac{I_1}{I_2} = \frac{L_2}{L_1} = 5 \Rightarrow \text{(c) is correct}$$

At t = 0, the inductor behaves like an infinite resistance path. Hence $I_1 = I_2 = 0$.

In the absence of current, the PD across the internal resistance is zero. Hence $V_1 = V_2 = 6$ V $\Rightarrow$ (a) is correct.

At $t = \infty$, the inductor behaves like a zero-resistance path. Current flow becomes steady and hence $V_1 = V_2 = 0$. A steady current 6 V/10 = 0.6 A flows through the circuit, and it distributes in the two inductors in inverse proportion to their inductances. Hence

$$I_1 = \left(\frac{L_2}{L_1 + L_2}\right)0.6\text{ A} = 0.5\text{ A} \Rightarrow \text{(b)}$$

19. (c) At t = 0, I = 5 A and $\frac{dI}{dt} = -10^3$ A/s. The direction of current is not given. However, the magnitude of the PD between the extreme ends is the same whether the current flows towards left or right. It is given by

$$V = \left|L\frac{dI}{dt} - 15\text{ V} + IR\right|$$

$$= |(5\text{ mH})(-10^3\text{ A/s}) - 15\text{ V} + (5\text{ A})(1\,\Omega)|$$

$$= 15\text{ V}$$

20. (b) The oscillation frequency is

$$f = \frac{1}{2\pi\sqrt{LC}} = \frac{1}{2\pi\sqrt{(0.6\times 10^{-3}\text{ H})(2\times 10^{-6}\text{ F})}}$$

$$= \frac{25}{\pi\sqrt{3}}\text{ kHz}$$

The frequency of the energy cycle is $2f = \frac{50}{\pi\sqrt{3}}$ kHz.

21. (a) If I is the current in primary, flux induced in secondary is $\phi = MI$, where M is the mutual inductance. The induced emf is

$$\xi = M\left|\frac{dI}{dt}\right|$$

$$\Rightarrow \quad M = \frac{\xi}{|dI/dt|} = \frac{40000\text{ V}}{4\text{ A}/10\,\mu s} = 0.1\text{ H}$$

22. (c) Current through the 4-Ω resistor is always equal to 12 V/ 4 Ω = 3 A. Hence (a) is correct. Current through the inductor varies with time from 0 to 12 V/ 2 Ω = 6 A as

$$I(t) = 6A[1 - e^{-t/1s}]$$

[Time constant = $L/R = 2\,H/2\,\Omega = 1$ s]

At t = ln2 s, I = 3 A. Hence (b) is correct.

At t = ln2 s, the total current through the cell is 3 A + 3 A = 6 A. Therefore, the power delivered by the cell is P = (12 V)(6 A) = 72 W. Hence (c) is incorrect.

Voltage across the inductor varies with time from 12 V to 0 as $V(t) = 12\text{V}e^{-t/1\text{s}}$.

At t = ln2 s, V = 6 V. Hence (d) is correct.

23. (a) At steady state, the inductor behaves like a zero-resistance path. So, between the two parallel branches, all current flows through the inductor, and no current flows through the 10-Ω resistor. The current flows through the 100-Ω resistor and the inductor and its value is

$$I = \frac{100\text{ V}}{100\,\Omega} = 1\text{ A}.$$

Now, when the switch is opened, current flows through the inductor and the 10-Ω resistor. The value of the current exponentially drops to zero, and all energy stored in the inductor is dissipated in form of heat across the 10-Ω resistor. That is

$$H = \frac{1}{2}LI^2 = \frac{1}{2}(19\text{ F})(1\text{ A})^2 = 5\text{ J}$$

24. (b), (c) The PD across an inductor, measured along the direction of current flow, is

$$V = -L\frac{dI}{dt} = -(3\text{ mH})\frac{dI}{dt}.$$

Thus, we have

For $0 < t \leq 2$ ms

$$-(3\text{ mH})\frac{dI}{dt} = -15\text{ V}$$

$\Rightarrow \quad \frac{dI}{dt} = 5000$ A/s

$\Rightarrow \quad I(t) = (5000\text{ A/s})t$ [Using $I = 0$ at $t = 0$]

In this time interval, the current grows linearly from 0 to $I(2\text{ ms}) = (5000\text{ A/s})(2\text{ ms}) = 10$ A.

For 2 ms $< t <$ 4 ms

$$-(3\text{ mH})\frac{dI}{dt} = 0$$

$\Rightarrow \quad \frac{dI}{dt} = 0$

$\Rightarrow \quad I(t) = 10$ A [Using $I = 10$ A at $t = 2$ ms]

In this time interval, the current remains constant equal to $I(2\text{ ms}) = 10$ A. Thus $I(3\text{ ms}) = 10$ A.

For 4 ms $\leq t \leq$ 6 ms

$$-(3\text{ mH})\frac{dI}{dt} = 30\text{ V}$$

$\Rightarrow \quad \frac{dI}{dt} = -10000$ A/s

$\Rightarrow \quad I(t) = 50\text{ A} - (10000\text{ A/s})t$

[Using $I = 10$ A at $t = 4$ ms]

In this time interval, the current decreases linearly from 10 A to – 10 A. Thus $I(5\text{ ms}) = 0$.

25. (a), (c) The infinite wire is also part of a large closed circuit. So what we have is a pair of closed coils kept close to each other. A current I in any one coil produces the same magnetic flux in the other coil. So instead of finding magnetic flux through the larger circuit due to current in the triangular loop, let us choose current I flowing in the larger circuit, as shown in the figure, and find magnetic flux through the triangular loop.

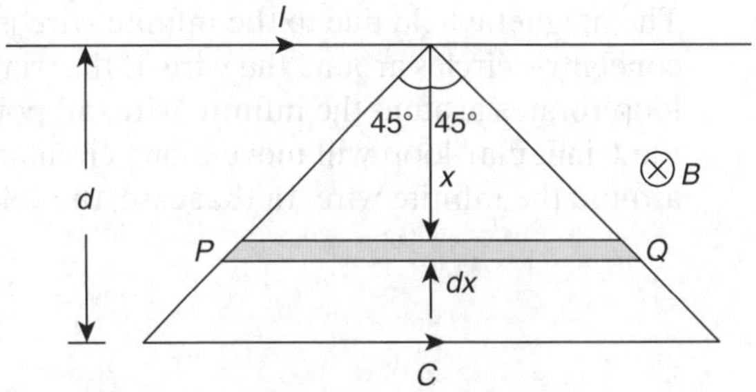

Let us choose the positive sense of the triangular loop C in the counter-clockwise sense (see figure). The area vector of the triangular loop then points out of the plane of the figure. The magnetic field points into the plane of the figure and it varies with distance x from the infinite wire as $B = \frac{\mu_0 I}{2\pi x}$. To find the magnetic flux through the triangular loop, let us sub-divide it into thin strips, each of width dx, as shown in the figure. One such element strip PQ is at a distance x from the infinite wire. Its length is $2x$ and the magnetic flux through this element strip is $d\phi = \mathbf{B} \cdot d\mathbf{A} = -\left(\frac{\mu_0 I}{2\pi x}\right)(2x\,dx) = -\frac{\mu_0 I}{\pi}dx$. The total magnetic flux through the triangular loop is

$$\phi = \frac{\mu_0 I}{\pi}\int_0^d dx = -\frac{\mu_0 dI}{\pi}$$

Now if the current I changes with time, the emf induced in the triangular loop is

$$\xi = -\frac{d\phi}{dt} = \frac{\mu_0 d}{\pi}\frac{dI}{dt} = \frac{\mu_0}{\pi}(0.1\text{m})(10\text{ A/s}) = \frac{\mu_0}{\pi}\text{V}$$

The positive value of ξ shows that the direction of the induced current in the triangular loop is along the direction of C. Thus, we conclude that a time varying counter-clockwise current in the triangular loop will induce emf of $\frac{\mu_0}{\pi}$V in the infinite wire towards the right ⇒ (a) is correct but (b) is incorrect.

Currents flowing in the same direction attract, while currents flowing in opposite directions repel. The hypotenuse side experiences attraction while the other two sides experience repulsion. The repulsion is stronger than the attraction because the hypotenuse is farther away than the other two sides, from the infinite wire ⇒ (c) is correct.

The magnetic field due to the infinite wire is along concentric circles around the wire. If the triangular loop rotates around the infinite wire, all points on the triangular loop will move along circular paths around the infinite wire. In that case, the velocities will be parallel to the magnetic field $\Rightarrow \mathbf{v} \times \mathbf{B} = 0$ at every point on the triangular loop. So no additional emf will be induced due to the rotation of the triangular loop $\Rightarrow$ (d) is incorrect.

CHAPTER

20

AC Circuits and EM Waves

- An alternator or an AC source produces an emf $V = V_0 \cos(\omega t)$ that varies sinusoidally with time. A sinusoidal voltage or current can be represented by a phasor that rotates anti-clockwise, with angular velocity ω equal to the angular frequency of the function. Its projection on the horizontal axis at any instant represents the instantaneous value of that quantity.
- If a voltage $V = V_0 \cos(\omega t)$ is applied to a circuit, then the current I through the circuit is

$$I = I_0 \cos(\omega t + \phi),$$

where ϕ is the phase angle of the current with respect to the voltage. The current and voltage amplitudes are related by $I_0 = V_0 / Z$, where Z is the impedance of the circuit.

For a pure resistor R: $I = \dfrac{V_0}{R} \cos(\omega t)$.

For a pure capacitor C: $I = \dfrac{V_0}{X_C} \cos\left(\omega t + \dfrac{\pi}{2}\right)$, where $X_C = 1/\omega C$ is the capacitive reactance.

For a pure inductor L: $I = \dfrac{V_0}{X_L} \cos\left(\omega t - \dfrac{\pi}{2}\right)$, where $X_L = \omega L$ is the inductive reactance.

For a series L-C-R circuit: $I = \dfrac{V_0}{Z} \cos(\omega t + \phi)$, where $Z = \sqrt{(X_C - X_L)^2 + R^2}$, $\tan\phi = \dfrac{X_C - X_L}{R}$.

- For sinusoidal quantities, the RMS (root mean square) values are related to the peak values as:

$$V_{\text{rms}} = \frac{V_0}{\sqrt{2}} \text{ and } I_{\text{rms}} = \frac{I_0}{\sqrt{2}}$$

The RMS voltage and RMS current are related as

$$V_{\text{rms}} = Z I_{\text{rms}}$$

The average power input P_{av} to an AC circuit is

$$P_{\text{av}} = V_{\text{rms}} I_{\text{rms}} \cos\phi = I_{\text{rms}}^2 Z \cos\phi = \frac{V_{\text{rms}}^2}{Z} \cos\phi$$

The quantity $\cos\phi = R/Z$ is called the power factor; the power factor for a resistive circuit is 1, and it is 0 for a capacitive or an inductive circuit. This indicates that in AC circuits, no power is consumed by the capacitors or the inductors.

- In a series L-C-R circuit connected to a voltage source $V = V_0 \cos(\omega t)$, the voltage drops across the three circuit elements are, respectively,

$$V_L = \frac{X_L V_0}{Z} \cos\left(\omega t + \phi + \frac{\pi}{2}\right), V_C = \frac{X_C V_0}{Z} \cos\left(\omega t + \phi - \frac{\pi}{2}\right), V_R = \frac{R V_0}{Z} \cos(\omega t + \phi)$$

The peak voltages are related as

$$\left(V_{C\text{peak}} - V_{L\text{peak}}\right)^2 + V_{R\text{peak}}^2 = V_0^2$$

The same relation holds for the RMS voltages.

- In a series L-C-R circuit, the current amplitude V_0 / Z is maximum when the impedance Z is minimum; this occurs when $X_C - X_L = 0$. The angular frequency of the source for which this happens is called the resonance angular frequency of the circuit:

$$\omega_{\text{res}} = \frac{1}{\sqrt{LC}}$$

The resonance frequency is $f_{\text{res}} = \omega_{\text{res}} / 2\pi$.

- A transformer is used to transform the voltage and current levels in an AC circuit. The winding to which power is supplied is called the primary; the winding from which power is delivered is called the secondary. In an ideal transformer with no energy losses, if the primary has N_1 turns and the secondary N_2, the amplitudes (or RMS values) of the two voltages are related by

$$\frac{V_2}{V_1} = \frac{N_2}{N_1}$$

The amplitudes (or RMS values) of the primary and secondary voltages and currents are related by

$$V_2 I_2 = V_1 I_1$$

- The relationships between the electric and magnetic fields and their sources can be stated compactly in four equations called Maxwell's equations:

$$\oint \mathbf{E} \cdot d\mathbf{s} = \frac{Q_{\text{encl}}}{\epsilon_0}$$

$$\oint \mathbf{B} \cdot d\mathbf{s} = 0$$

$$\oint \mathbf{B} \cdot d\mathbf{l} = \mu_0 \left(I_c + I_d\right), \text{ where } I_d = \epsilon_0 \frac{d\phi_E}{dt}$$

$$\oint \mathbf{E} \cdot d\mathbf{l} = -\frac{d\phi_B}{dt}$$

This first equation is Gauss's law for electrostatics; the second is Gauss's law for magnetism, stating the non-existence of magnetic monopoles. The third is Ampere's law generalised by Maxwell to include displacement current I_d along with the conduction current I_c; and the fourth is Faraday's law. These equations apply to electric and magnetic fields in vacuum. If a material is present, the permittivity ϵ_0 and permeability μ_0 of free space are replaced by the permittivity ϵ and permeability μ of the material.

- **Electromagnetic Waves (Energy and Momentum):** According to Maxwell's equations, a point charge at rest produces a static **E** field and no **B** field; a point charge moving with uniform velocity produces both **E** and **B** fields. An accelerating charged particle produces electromagnetic waves consisting of time varying **E** and **B** fields that can propagate in space even when there is no matter; the **E** and **B** fields oscillate perpendicular to each other and perpendicular to the direction of propagation.
For a sinusoidal EM wave propagating along the z-axis, the electric field E_x oscillates along the x-axis and the magnetic field B_y oscillates along the y-axis. They can be written as

$$E_x = E_0 \sin\left(\omega t - kz\right) \text{ and } B_y = B_0 \sin\left(\omega t - kz\right)$$

The speed with which electromagnetic waves propagate depends upon the medium. In vacuum, their speed is

$$c = \frac{1}{\sqrt{\mu_0 \epsilon_0}}$$

At any instant, the direction of $\mathbf{E} \times \mathbf{B}$ is along the direction of propagation, and the magnitudes of the **E** and **B** fields are related as

$$E = cB$$

Electromagnetic waves carry energy as they propagate. The magnitude and the direction of energy flow rate per unit area (intensity) is represented by the Poynting vector **S** given by

$$\mathbf{S} = \frac{1}{\mu_0}(\mathbf{E} \times \mathbf{B})$$

The instantaneous energy flow rate per unit area of the electromagnetic wave is the magnitude of the Poynting vector **S**:

$$I = \frac{EB}{\mu_0}$$

The average energy flow rate is the average of the Poynting vector magnitude over a full cycle. For a sinusoidal electromagnetic wave

$$I_{av} = \frac{E_0 B_0}{2\mu_0} = \left(\frac{1}{2}\epsilon_0 E_0^2\right)c \text{ or } \left(\frac{B_0^2}{2\mu_0}\right)c,$$

where E_0 and B_0 are the peak values of the oscillating electric and magnetic fields, respectively.
Electromagnetic waves also possess momentum. This momentum is a property of the field; it is not associated with mass. This momentum is responsible for the phenomenon of radiation pressure. The instantaneous radiation pressure P_{rad} equals the instantaneous momentum flow rate per unit area:

$$P_{rad} = \frac{1}{A}\frac{dp}{dt} = \frac{I}{c}$$

Thus, we have

$$P_{rad} = \begin{cases} \dfrac{I}{c}, \text{ wave totally absorbed} \\ \dfrac{2I}{c}, \text{ wave totally reflected} \end{cases}$$

The average value of the radiation pressure is found by substituting I_{av} for I.
All the above equations apply to electromagnetic waves travelling through free space. If a material is present, the permittivity ϵ_0 and permeability μ_0 of free space are replaced by the permittivity ϵ and permeability μ of the material.

EXERCISES

1. When an AC source of emf $V(t) = V_0 \sin(100t)$ is applied across a circuit, the current I in the circuit is observed to be $\pi/4$ out of phase with voltage V, as shown in the figure.

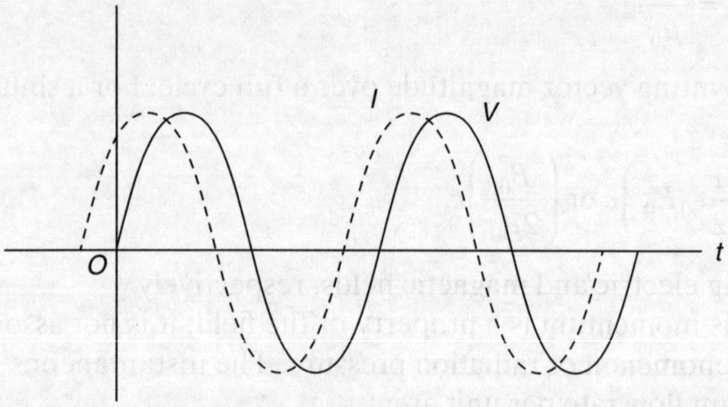

If the circuit consists of only two of the three circuit elements L, C and R connected in series, then the correct combination is:
(a) $R = 1\ \text{k}\Omega, C = 5\ \mu\text{F}, L = 10\ \text{H}$
(b) $R = 1\ \text{k}\Omega, C = 2\ \mu\text{F}, L = 5\ \text{H}$
(c) $R = 1\ \text{k}\Omega, C = 5\ \mu\text{F}, L = 5\ \text{H}$
(d) $R = 1\ \text{k}\Omega, C = 2\ \mu\text{F}, L = 10\ \text{H}$

2. An electric circuit is connected to a 100-V (RMS), 60-Hz supply. If the current through the circuit leads voltage by $\pi/3$ and the impedance of the circuit is 1 kΩ, then the average value of power dissipation is:
(a) 10 W (b) $5\sqrt{2}$ W
(c) 5 W (d) 2.5 W

3. An arc lamp (purely resistive) requires 80 V, 10 A to function. If it is connected to a 220-V (RMS), 50 Hz supply, the series inductor needed for the lamp to function is:
(a) 25 mH (b) 65 mH
(c) 70 mH (d) 80 mH

4. An alternating voltage $V(t) = 200\sqrt{2}\ \text{V} \sin(100t)$ is connected to an L-R series circuit having $L = 100$ mH and resistance $R = 10\ \Omega$. The current in the circuit is given by:
(a) $20\sqrt{2}\ \text{A} \cos(100t)$
(b) $20\ \text{A} \sin(100t + \pi/4)$
(c) $20\ \text{A} \sin(100t - \pi/4)$
(d) $20\sqrt{2}\ \text{A} \sin(100t)$

5. The energy of an inductor changes from its maximum value to zero value in 5 ms. The frequency of the alternating source is:
(a) 50 Hz (b) 100 Hz
(c) 200 Hz (d) 400 Hz

6. An alternating voltage $V(t)$ of angular frequency $\omega < \frac{1}{\sqrt{LC}}$ is connected to a series L-C-R circuit. Let $V_C(t), V_L(t)$ denote the instantaneous voltages across the capacitor and the inductor, respectively. Let δ denote the phase difference between voltages. The correct statements from the following are:
(a) V_C lags V by $0 < \delta < \pi/2$
(b) V_C leads V by $\pi/2 < \delta < \pi$
(c) V_L lags V by $0 < \delta < \pi/2$
(d) V_L leads V by $\pi/2 < \delta < \pi$

7. A radio tuner has a frequency range from 500 kHz to 5 MHz. If its L-C-R circuit has an inductance of 400 μH, the range of its variable capacitor is:
(a) 2.5 pF to 250 pF
(b) 5 pF to 500 pF
(c) 7.5 pF to 750 pF
(d) 10 pF to 100 pF

8. A series L-C-R circuit having $L = 5$ H, $C = 80\ \mu$F and $R = 40\ \Omega$ is connected to a 200-V (RMS) AC source. The RMS potential drop across the inductor at resonance is:
(a) 200 V (b) 500 V
(c) 750 V (d) 1250 V

9. In the circuit shown in the figure, the 20-V (RMS) AC source has $\omega = 100$ rad/s.

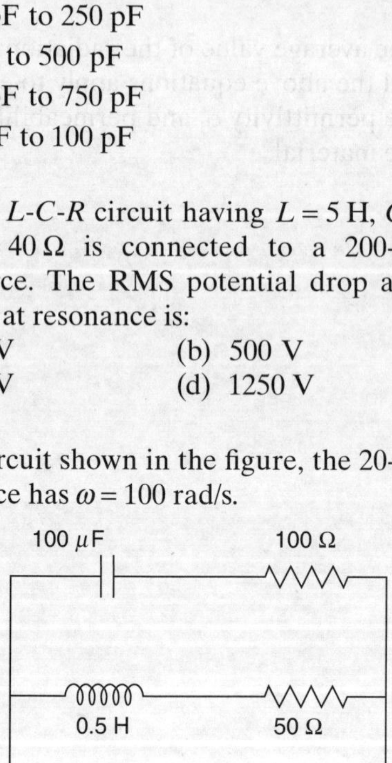

If I_{rms} is the RMS current through the circuit and V_{rms} is the RMS voltage across the 100-Ω resistor, then:

(a) $I_{rms} = 0.3$ A, $V_{rms} = 10\sqrt{2}$ V
(b) $I_{rms} = 0.3\sqrt{2}$ A, $V_{rms} = 10$ V
(c) $I_{rms} = 0.3$ A, $V_{rms} = 10$ V
(d) $I_{rms} = 0.3\sqrt{2}$ A, $V_{rms} = 10\sqrt{2}$ V

10. A series L-C-R circuit having $L = 20$ mH, $C = 100\ \mu$F, $R = 50\ \Omega$ is connected to an AC source of emf $V = 10\text{ V}\sin(314t)$. The power loss in the circuit is:

(a) 0.42 W (b) 0.79 W
(c) 2.71 W (d) 2.71 W

11. An ideal coil of self inductance $L = 5$ mH is connected to an AC source of emf V = 10 V sin(314t). The coil absorbs and releases energy at regular intervals of time. If T_0 represents the time during which the coil absorbs energy from zero value to peak value and E_0 represents the peak energy in the coil, then:

(a) $T_0 = 10$ ms, $E_0 = 0.1$ J
(b) $T_0 = 10$ ms, $E_0 = 0.2$ J
(c) $T_0 = 5$ ms, $E_0 = 0.1$ J
(d) $T_0 = 5$ ms, $E_0 = 0.2$ J

12. A series L-C-R circuit having $R = 100\ \Omega$ is connected to a 200-V AC source. The RMS potential drops across the capacitor and the inductor are 300 V and 300 V, respectively. Let X_C, X_L denote the reactances of the capacitor and inductor, respectively, and let P be the power consumed by the circuit. Then:

(a) $X_C = X_L = 400\sqrt{2}\ \Omega$, $P = 400$ W
(b) $X_C = X_L = 400\sqrt{2}\ \Omega$, $P = 300$ W
(c) $X_C = X_L = 150\ \Omega$, $P = 400$ W
(d) $X_C = X_L = 150\ \Omega$, $P = 300$ W

13. A parallel plate capacitor with circular plates of radius $a = 1$ m has capacitance $C = 1$ nF. At $t = 0$, it is connected for charging in series with resistance $R = 1\text{ M}\Omega$ across a battery of emf $\xi = 2$ V. Consider a point P halfway between the centre and the periphery of the circular plates. The magnetic field at P at $t = 1$ ms is:

(a) 2.4×10^{-14} T (b) 1.2×10^{-14} T
(c) 7.4×10^{-14} T (d) 3.7×10^{-14} T

14. For a sinusoidal EM wave propagating with speed $c = 3\times10^8$ m/s along the z-axis, the oscillating electric and magnetic fields are given as $\mathbf{E} = E_0\sin(\omega t - kz)\mathbf{i}$ and $\mathbf{B} = B_0\sin(\omega t - kz)\mathbf{j}$. If $E_0 = 3$ V/m and $\omega = 1.5\times10^{10}\text{ s}^{-1}$, then the values of B_0 and k are:

(a) $B_0 = 10^{-6}$ T, $k = 500\text{ m}^{-1}$
(b) $B_0 = 10^{-6}$ T, $k = 50\text{ m}^{-1}$
(c) $B_0 = 10^{-8}$ T, $k = 500\text{ m}^{-1}$
(d) $B_0 = 10^{-8}$ T, $k = 50\text{ m}^{-1}$

15. A 100-W electric bulb is emitting light with efficiency 2.7%. The RMS value of the electric field at a distance of 3 m from the bulb is:

(a) $E_{\text{rms}} = 1$ V/m (b) $E_{\text{rms}} = 0.1$ V/m
(c) $E_{\text{rms}} = 3$ V/m (d) $E_{\text{rms}} = 0.3$ V/m

16. A series resonant RLC circuit consists of $R = 30\ \Omega$, $L = 20$ mH and $C = 2\ \mu$F. The quality factor and the band-width of the circuit are:

(a) $Q = 2.00$, $\Delta f = 300$ Hz
(b) $Q = 2.50$, $\Delta f = 288$ Hz
(c) $Q = 3.33$, $\Delta f = 238$ Hz
(d) $Q = 4.00$, $\Delta f = 200$ Hz

ANSWER KEYS

1. (a)	**2.** (c)	**3.** (b)	**4.** (c)	**5.** (a)	**6.** (a),(d)	**7.** (a)	**8.** (d)	**9.** (a)	**10.** (b)
11. (c)	**12.** (c)	**13.** (d)	**14.** (d)	**15.** (c)	**16.** (c)				

SOLUTIONS

1. (a) From the given figure, we see that I leads V, which means the circuit is capacitive. The phase difference is $\pi/4$, which means

$$\tan(\pi/4) = \frac{X_C - X_L}{R}$$

$$\Rightarrow \quad \frac{1}{\omega C} - \omega L = R$$

This is true in option (a) only.

2. (c) The average power dissipation is

$$P = \frac{V_{rms}^2}{Z}\cos\phi = \frac{(100\text{ V})^2}{10^3\,\Omega}\cos\left(\frac{\pi}{3}\right) = 5\text{ W}$$

3. (b)

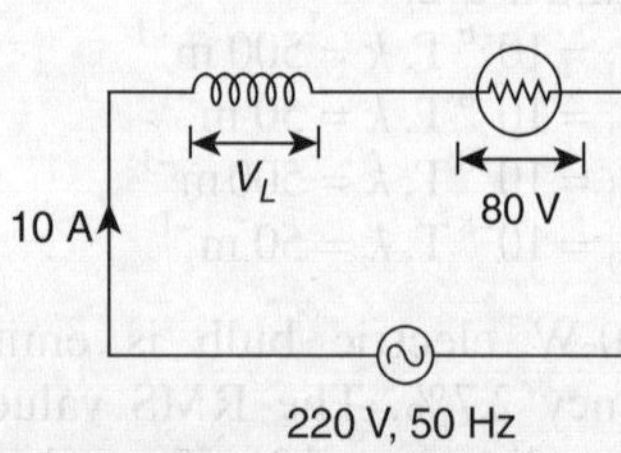

Let V_L be the RMS voltage drop across the inductor when the voltage drop across the lamp is 80 V (see figure). Then

$$V_L^2 + (80)^2 = (220)^2$$

$$\Rightarrow \quad V_L = \sqrt{42000}\text{v} = 205\text{ V}$$

Now if L is the inductance, then

$$V_L = (10\text{ A})(\omega L)$$

$$\Rightarrow \quad 205\text{ V} = (10\text{ A})(100\,\pi L)$$

$$\Rightarrow \quad L = \frac{205}{\pi}\text{ mH} = 65\text{ mH}$$

4. (c) The inductive reactance is

$$X_L = \omega L = 100\text{ rad/s} \times 100\text{ mH} = 10\,\Omega$$

The circuit impedance is

$$Z = \sqrt{X_L^2 + R^2} = \sqrt{(10\,\Omega)^2 + (10\,\Omega)^2} = 10\sqrt{2}\,\Omega$$

The current I will lag the voltage V by a phase angle

$$\phi = \tan^{-1}\left(\frac{X_L}{R}\right) = \tan^{-1}\left(\frac{10\,\Omega}{10\,\Omega}\right) = \frac{\pi}{4}$$

Hence, the instantaneous current is

$$I = \frac{200\sqrt{2}V}{Z}\sin(100t - \phi) = 20A\sin(100t - \pi/4)$$

5. (a) The energy cycle takes 2×5 ms = 10 ms. Then the oscillating cycle will take 2×10 ms = 20 ms. Hence, oscillation frequency is

$$f = \frac{1}{20 \times 10^{-3}\text{ s}} = 50\text{ Hz}$$

6. (a), (d) Consider an L-C-R series circuit connected to a voltage source $V(t) = V_0\cos(\omega t)$. Then $I = I_0\cos(\omega t + \phi)$b, where $I_0 = V_0/Z$. It is given that

$$\omega < \frac{1}{\sqrt{LC}} \Rightarrow \frac{1}{\omega C} > \omega L \Rightarrow X_C > X_L$$

This means that the circuit is more capacitive than inductive, and hence, $0 < \phi < \pi/2$ (current leads voltage).

Now, voltage across the capacitor is

$$V_C = X_C I_0\cos(\omega t + \phi - \pi/2)$$

$$= X_C I_0\cos(\omega t - \delta),\text{ where } \delta = \pi/2 - \phi$$

$\Rightarrow$ V_C lags V by δ, where $0 < \delta < \pi/2$

and voltage across the inductor is

$$V_L = X_L I_0\cos(\omega t + \phi + \pi/2)$$

$$= X_L I_0\cos(\omega t + \delta),\text{ where } \delta = \pi/2 + \phi$$

$\Rightarrow$ V_L leads V by δ, where $\pi/2 < \delta < \pi$

7. (a) The resonance frequency of an L-C-R circuit is given by

$$f = \frac{1}{2\pi\sqrt{LC}} \Rightarrow C = \frac{1}{4\pi^2 f^2 L}$$

When f – 500 KHz, the required capacitance is

$$C = \frac{1}{4\pi^2(5\times10^5\text{ Hz})^2(400\times10^{-6}\text{ H})} = 250\text{ pF}$$

When f – 5 MHz, the required capacitance is

$$C = \frac{1}{4\pi^2(5\times10^6\text{ Hz})^2(400\times10^{-6}\text{ H})} = 2.5\text{ pF}$$

8. (d) The resonance angular frequency is

$$\omega = \frac{1}{\sqrt{LC}} = \frac{1}{\sqrt{5\text{ H}\times80\times10^{-6}\text{ F}}} = 50\text{ rad/s}$$

At resonance impedance, $Z = R = 50\,\Omega$ and hence RMS current

$$I_{rms} = \frac{V_{rms}}{Z} = \frac{200\text{ V}}{50\,\Omega} = 5\text{ A}$$

The RMS potential drop across the inductor is

$$V_L = I_{rms}(\omega L) = 5\text{ A}(50\text{ rad/s} \times 5\text{ H}) = 1250\text{ V}$$

9. (a) We have

$$X_L = \omega L = 100\text{ rad/s} \times 0.5\text{ A} = 50\ \Omega$$

and $$X_C = \frac{1}{\omega C} = \frac{1}{100\text{ rad/s} \times 10^{-6}\text{ F}} = 100\ \Omega$$

The impedances of the upper and lower branches are, respectively

$$Z_1 = \sqrt{X_C^2 + (100\ \Omega)^2} = 100\sqrt{2}\ \Omega \text{ and}$$

$$Z_2 = \sqrt{X_L^2 + (50\ \Omega)^2} = 50\sqrt{2}\ \Omega$$

The phase difference between current and voltage (measured with respect to voltage) in the two branches are, respectively

$$\phi_1 = \tan^{-1}\left(\frac{X_C}{R}\right) = \frac{\pi}{4} \text{ and}$$

$$\phi_2 = \tan^{-1}\left(\frac{-X_L}{R}\right) = -\frac{\pi}{4}$$

The source voltage is given by $V(t) = 20\sqrt{2}V\cos(\omega t)$. Current flow through the two branches is

$$I_1 = \frac{20\sqrt{2}V}{Z_1}\cos(\omega t + \pi/4) = \frac{1}{5}A\cos(\omega t + \pi/4)$$

$$I_2 = \frac{20\sqrt{2}V}{Z_2}\cos(\omega t - \pi/4) = \frac{2}{5}A\cos(\omega t - \pi/4)$$

The instantaneous current through the circuit is

$$I = I_1 + I_2 = \frac{1}{5\sqrt{2}}A(3\cos\omega t + 1\sin\omega t)$$

$$= \frac{1}{\sqrt{5}}A\cos(\omega t - \phi)$$

$$\phi = \tan^{-1}(1/3). \text{ Hence } I_{rms} = \frac{1}{\sqrt{2}\sqrt{5}}A$$

$$= \frac{1}{\sqrt{10}}A = 0.3A$$

The RMS current through the upper branch is A. Hence, the RMS voltage across the 100-Ω resistor is

$$V_{rms} = \frac{1}{5\sqrt{2}} \times 100\ \Omega = 10\sqrt{2}\text{ V}.$$

10. (b) Source voltage is $V(t) = 10\text{ V}\sin(100\,\pi t)$ [$314 = 100\pi$].

Now, we have

$$X_C = \frac{1}{\omega C} = \frac{1}{100\pi \times 100 \times 10^{-6}}\Omega = 10\,\pi\Omega$$

$$X_L = \omega L = 100\pi \times 20 \times 10^{-3}\Omega = 2\,\pi\Omega.$$

Hence $Z = \sqrt{50^2 + (10\pi - 2\pi)^2}\ \Omega = \sqrt{3140}\ \Omega$

The RMS voltage across the circuit is

$$V_{rms} = \frac{10\text{ V}}{\sqrt{2}} = 5\sqrt{2}\text{ V}$$

The RMS current through the circuit is

$$I_{rms} = \frac{V_{rms}}{7} = \frac{5\sqrt{2}\text{ V}}{7}$$

Power is consumed only by the resistor. Hence, average power dissipation is

$$P = I_{rms}^2\text{ R} = \frac{50\text{ R}}{Z^2} = \frac{50 \times 50}{3140}\text{ W} = 0.79\text{ W}$$

11. (c) The energy in the coil is zero when the current is zero, and the energy is at its peak when the current is at its peak. The current cycle takes time $\frac{2\pi}{\omega} = \frac{2\pi}{100\pi}\text{s} = 20\text{ ms}$. The current rises from zero to peak in one-fourth of 20 ms. Hence, $T_0 = 5$ ms. The peak energy in the coil is

$$E_0 = \frac{1}{2}LI_0^2 = \frac{1}{2}L\left(\frac{V_0}{\omega L}\right)^2 = \frac{V_0^2}{2\omega^2 L}$$

$$= \frac{10^2}{2(100\pi)^2(5 \times 10^{-3})}\text{J} = 0.1\text{ J}$$

12. (c)

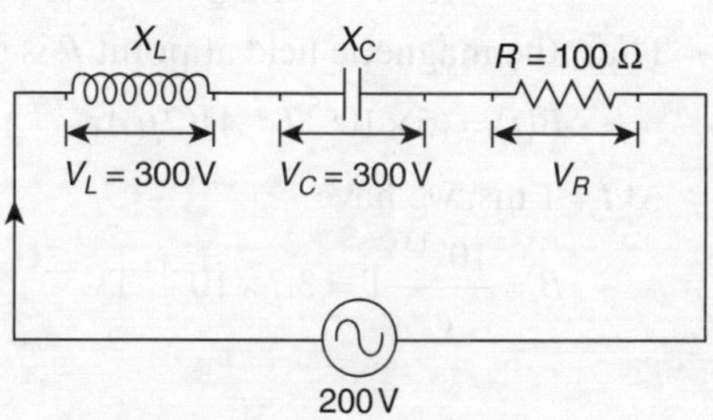

Using relation $V^2 = V_R^2 + (V_L - V_C)^2$, we have

$$(200\text{ V})^2 = V_R^2 + (300\text{ V} - 300\text{ V})^2 \Rightarrow V_R = 200\text{ V}$$

In series circuit, the RMS current I is the same through all circuit elements. Hence, we have

$$I = \frac{200\text{ V}}{R} = \frac{300\text{ V}}{X_C} = \frac{300\text{ V}}{X_L}, \text{ where } R = 100\ \Omega$$

$$\Rightarrow I = 2\text{A}, X_C = X_L = 150\ \Omega$$

Power is consumed only by the resistor. The average power consumption is

$$P = V_R I = 200\text{ V} \times 2\text{A} = 400\text{ W}$$

13. (d) At any instant when charge on the capacitor is Q, the electric field between the plates is $E = \frac{Q}{\varepsilon_0(\pi a^2)}$. Consider a circular loop of radius $a/2$ passing through point P, and coaxial to the circular plates. The electric flux through this loop is $\phi_E = E\left(\frac{1}{4}\pi a^2\right) = \frac{Q}{4\varepsilon_n}$.

As Q changes with time, so does the electric flux. Magnetic field is produced in concentric circles coaxial to the circular plates. The magnitude B of the magnetic field along the loop through P is given by

$$B(2\pi a) = \mu_0 \varepsilon_0 \frac{d\phi_E}{dt}$$

$$\Rightarrow B(2\pi a) = \frac{1}{4}\mu_0 \frac{dQ}{dt} = \frac{1}{4}\mu_0 I$$

$$\Rightarrow B = \left(\frac{\mu_0}{8\pi a}\right) I = \left(\frac{4\pi \times 10^{-7}\,\text{Wb/A}\cdot\text{m}}{8\pi(1\,\text{m})}\right) I$$

$$= (5\times 10^{-8}\,\text{T/A}) I$$

The time constant of the circuit is $T = CR = (1\,n\text{F})(1\,\text{M}\Omega) = 1$ ms. The current through the circuit is given by

$$I(t) = \frac{\xi}{R} e^{-t/T} = \frac{2V}{1M\Omega} e^{-t/T} = 2\mu A e^{-t/T}$$

Thus, the magnetic field at point P is given by

$$B(t) = (5\times 10^{-8} T/A)(2\mu A e^{-t/T}) = 10^{-13} T e^{-t/T}$$

At $t = 1$ ms, we have

$$B = \frac{10^{-13}}{e}\,\text{T} = 3.7\times 10^{-14}\,\text{T}$$

14. (d) The required values are

$$B_0 = \frac{E_0}{c} = \frac{3\,\text{V/m}}{3\times 10^8\,\text{m/s}} = 10^{-8}\,\text{T}$$

and $$k = \frac{\omega}{c} = \frac{1.5\times 10^{10}\,\text{s}^{-1}}{3\times 10^8\,\text{m/s}} = 50\,\text{m}^{-1}$$

15. (c) At a distance of 3 m, the intensity of light is

$$I = \frac{2.7\%(100\,\text{W})}{4\pi(3\,\text{m})^2} = 0.024\,\text{W}$$

Now, using the relation between light intensity I and the RMS value of the electric field E_{rms}, we have

$$I = \left(\frac{1}{2}\varepsilon_0 E_0^2\right)c = (\varepsilon_0 E_{rms}^2)c$$

$$\Rightarrow E_{rms} = \sqrt{\frac{I}{c\varepsilon_0}} = \sqrt{\frac{0.024}{(3\times 10^8)(8.85\times 10^{-12})}}\,\text{V/m}$$

$$= 3\,\text{V/m}$$

16. (c) The quality factor is given by

$$Q = \frac{\omega_{res} L}{R} = \frac{1}{\sqrt{LC}} \times \frac{L}{R} = \frac{1}{R}\sqrt{\frac{L}{C}}$$

$$= \frac{1}{30}\sqrt{\frac{20\times 10^{-3}}{2\times 10^{-6}}} = 3.33$$

The band-width is given by

$$\Delta f = \frac{f_{res}}{Q} = \frac{f_{res}}{X_L / R} = \frac{f_{res} R}{2\pi f_{res} L} = \frac{R}{2\pi L}$$

$$= \frac{30}{2\pi(20\times 10^{-3})} = 238.7\,\text{Hz}$$

PART IV

OPTICS AND MODERN PHYSICS

CHAPTER

21 Geometrical Optics

- Light is an electromagnetic wave. When emitted or absorbed by matter, it also shows particle properties. It is emitted by accelerated charges that have been given excess energy by heat or by electric discharge. The speed of light is a fundamental physical constant.
  When light is transmitted from one material to another, its frequency does not change, but its speed and wavelength may change. The refractive index μ of a material is the ratio of speed of light in vacuum c to the speed v in that material:
  $$\mu = \frac{c}{v}(\mu \geq 1)$$
  If c is the speed and λ is the wavelength of light in vacuum, the same light moves with speed c/μ and has wavelength λ/μ in a material with refractive index μ.

- A wave front is a surface of constant phase. A ray is a line along the direction perpendicular to the wave front. Wave fronts move along these rays with speed equal to the propagation speed of the wave.
  Huygens' principle states that if the position of a wave front is known at one instant, its position at a later time can be constructed by imagining each point on the wave front as a source of secondary wavelets. This principle can be used to derive the laws of reflection and refraction.

- At a smooth interface between two optical materials, the incident ray, reflected ray, refracted ray and the normal to the interface all lie in the same plane, called the plane of incidence.
  The law of reflection states that the angle of incidence equals the angle of reflection. The law of refraction is
  $$\mu_1 \sin\theta_1 = \mu_2 \sin\theta_2$$
  When light travels from a material of greater refractive index (μ_1) to a material of smaller refractive index (μ_2), total internal reflection occurs at the interface when the angle of incidence exceeds a critical angle C, given by
  $$\sin C = \frac{\mu_2}{\mu_1}$$

- When light enters at an angle of incidence i and emerges at an angle of emergence e, through a prism of refracting angle A, the total deviation angle δ is given by
  $$\delta = i + e - A$$
  The sum of the angles r_1 and r_2 made by the ray inside the prism always equals the refracting angle A:
  $$r_1 + r_2 = A$$
  Minimum deviation δ_m occurs when $i = e = \dfrac{\delta_m + A}{2}$ and $r_1 = r_2 = \dfrac{A}{2}$. The refractive index of the prism relative to the surrounding is given by
  $$\mu = \frac{\sin\left(\dfrac{\delta_m + A}{2}\right)}{\sin\left(\dfrac{A}{2}\right)}$$

- For a small angled (A) prism with refractive index μ relative to the surrounding, the total deviation angle δ for near normal incidence is given by
  $$\delta = A(\mu - 1)$$

When light passes through a parallel-faced slab ($A = 0$), there is no deviation; the rays emerge parallel to the incident ray. However, if the light coming from a point object passes through a slab of thickness t, and refractive index μ relative to the surroundings, the object appears to be shifted from its position by an amount given by

$$\text{Shift} = t\left(1 - \frac{1}{\mu}\right)$$

- The variation of refractive index μ of a material with wavelength λ of light causes dispersion. The value of μ decreases with increasing λ. When white light passes through a small angled prism, the angular separation $\delta_v - \delta_r$ between the violet and the red is called the angle of dispersion:

$$\delta_v - \delta_r = A(\mu_v - \mu_r)$$

The ratio of angle of dispersion $\delta_v - \delta_r$ to the deviation δ_y of the yellow light is called the dispersive power ω of the prism:

$$\omega = \frac{\delta_v - \delta_r}{\delta_y} = \frac{\mu_v - \mu_r}{\mu_y - 1}$$

- Reflection formula:

$$\frac{1}{v} + \frac{1}{u} = \frac{1}{f}, \text{ where } \frac{1}{f} = \frac{2}{R} \text{ and } \frac{y_2}{y_1} = -\frac{v}{u}$$

- Refraction formula:

$$\frac{\mu_2}{v} - \frac{\mu_1}{u} = \frac{\mu_2 - \mu_1}{R} \text{ and } \frac{y_2}{y_1} = \frac{\mu_1 v}{\mu_2 u}$$

- Lens formula:

$$\frac{1}{v} - \frac{1}{u} = \frac{1}{f}, \text{ where } \frac{1}{f} = (\mu - 1)\left(\frac{1}{R_1} - \frac{1}{R_2}\right) \text{ and } \frac{y_2}{y_1} = \frac{v}{u}$$

[Here, μ is the refractive index of the lens relative to the surrounding.]

In the displacement method (used for determining the focal length of a converging lens), the object is kept at a fixed distance, say D, from a screen and the lens is moved between them. If $D > 4f$, a sharp image is obtained on the screen for two positions of the lens, say x_1 and x_2 (measured from the object), where $x_1 + x_2 = D$ and $x_1 x_2 = Df$. The focal length of the lens is given by

$$f = \frac{D^2 - (\Delta x)^2}{4D}, \text{ where } \Delta x = |x_2 - x_1|$$

Also, if h is the object size and h_1, h_2 are the two image sizes, then

$$\frac{h_1}{h} = \frac{x_2}{x_1} \text{ and } \frac{h_2}{h} = \frac{x_1}{x_2} \Rightarrow h = \sqrt{h_1 h_2}$$

- Two lenses kept close behave like a single lens. The relation between u and v is given by

$$\frac{1}{v} - \frac{1}{u} = \frac{1}{f}, \text{ where } \frac{1}{f} = \frac{1}{f_1} + \frac{1}{f_2}$$

A lens and a mirror kept close behave like a single mirror. The relation between u and v is given by

$$\frac{1}{v} + \frac{1}{u} = \frac{1}{f}, \text{ where } \frac{1}{f} = \frac{1}{f_{\text{mirror}}} - \frac{2}{f_{\text{lens}}}$$

- **Compound Microscope**: The object is placed just outside the first focal point of the objective. The objective first forms a real image just inside the first focal point of the eyepiece, and then the eyepiece forms a final image (inverted) at infinity. The overall angular magnification is the product of the lateral magnification at the objective and the angular magnification at the eyepiece. If l is the distance between the lenses and the near point is at 25 cm, the overall angular magnification (for image at infinity) is given by

$$M = \frac{s(25\text{ cm})}{f_o f_e}, \text{ where } s \approx l - (f_o + f_e)$$

- **Telescope**: The object is at infinity. The objective first forms a real image at the second focal point of the objective which coincides with the first focal point of the eyepiece, and then the eyepiece forms a final image (inverted) at infinity; the distance between the lenses equals $f_o + f_e$. The angular magnification is given by

$$M = \frac{f_o}{f_e}$$

- A myopic or nearsighted eye can clearly see objects that are close to the eyes. Images of far objects are formed in front of the retina. A diverging lens is used for correction.

  A hyperopic or farsighted eye can clearly see objects that are far from the eyes. Images of near objects are formed behind the retina. A converging lens is used for correction.

EXERCISES

1. A point source S is located on a horizontal ground. A plane mirror kept parallel to the ground is moving with velocity v parallel to the ground. If the length of the mirror is l, then the bright patch formed on the ground by reflected light:
(a) Moves with velocity v and has length $2l$
(b) Moves with velocity v and has length l
(c) Moves with velocity $2v$ and has length $2l$
(d) Moves with velocity $2v$ and has length l

2. A 50-cm-long plane mirror is hung on a vertical wall, with its lower edge 50 cm above the ground. A man stands in front of the mirror at a distance of 2 m from it. If his eyes are at a height of 1.8 m, the length of his image that he can see in the mirror is:
(a) 120 cm (b) 80 cm
(c) 60 cm (d) 20 cm

3. A short linear object of length b lies along the axis of a concave mirror of focal length f at a distance $a(b \ll a)$ from the pole. The length of the image will be:
(a) $\left(\frac{f}{a-f}\right)b$ (b) $\left(\frac{a-f}{f}\right)b$
(c) $\left(\frac{f}{a-f}\right)^2 b$ (d) $\left(\frac{a-f}{f}\right)^2 b$

4. A car is fitted with a convex mirror of focal length 20 cm. A truck 2.8 m behind the car is overtaking at a relative speed of 15 m/s. The speed of the image of the truck as seen in the mirror of the car is:
(a) $\frac{1}{5}$ m/s (b) $\frac{1}{10}$ m/s
(c) $\frac{1}{15}$ m/s (d) $\frac{1}{20}$ m/s

5. A concave mirror has aperture diameter $d = 4$ cm and the depth at its pole is $t = 1$ mm. A square wire frame of side 3 cm is placed perpendicular to the axis, at 25 cm from the mirror. The area enclosed by the image of the wire is:
(a) 4 cm^2 (b) 2 cm^2
(c) 1 cm^2 (d) 0.25 cm^2

6. In the arrangement shown in the figure, the concave mirror is of focal length 10 cm and the glass ($\mu_{\text{glass}} = 3/2$) slab has thickness 3 cm. A point source S is kept at a distance x from the slab.

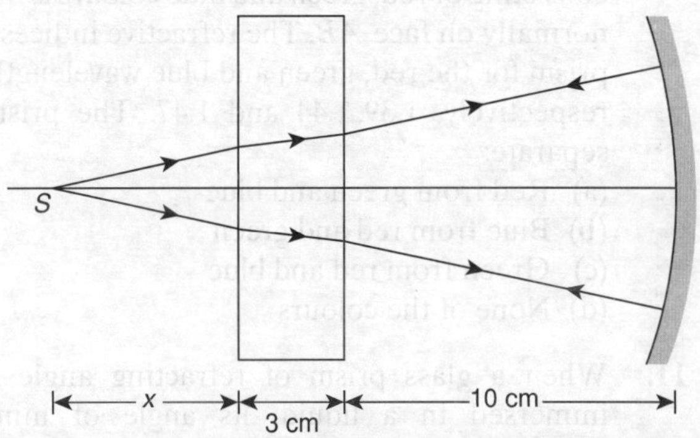

If the final image coincides with the source itself, then the value of x equals:
(a) 5 cm (b) 6 cm
(c) 7 cm (d) 8 cm

7. A tiny air bubble in a glass slab ($\mu = 1.5$) is 5-cm deep when viewed through one face and 2-cm deep when viewed through the opposite face. The thickness of the slab is:
(a) 6.5 cm (b) 7.5 cm
(c) 8.5 cm (d) 10.5 cm

8. A fish F inside a lake is moving towards the surface of the lake with velocity v_1 along the vertically upward direction. A bird B in air is moving towards the surface of the lake with velocity v_2 along the vertically downward direction. Both are moving along the same line. The velocity of the bird as seen by the fish is $(\mu_{water} = 4/3)$:
(a) $v_1 + \frac{4}{3}v_2$ (b) $\frac{3}{4}(v_1 + v_2)$
(c) $\frac{3}{4}v_1 + v_2$ (d) $\frac{4}{3}(v_1 + v_2)$

9. For an isosceles prism of angle A and refractive index μ, the angle of minimum deviation is $\delta_m = A$. If i_1 and r_1 denote the incident angle and the corresponding refracting angle, then the correct options are:
(a) For $i_1 = A$, the ray inside the prism is parallel to its base
(b) The refractive index and the prism angle are related as $A = \frac{1}{2}\cos^{-1}\left(\frac{\mu}{2}\right)$
(c) At minimum deviation, $i_1 = 2r_1$
(d) The ray emerges tangent to the prism surface if $\sin i_1 = \sin A\sqrt{4\cos^2\frac{A}{2} - 1} - \cos A$

10. The principal section of a glass prism is an isosceles triangle ABC right-angled at B. A beam of light consisting of red, green and blue colours is incident normally on face AB. The refractive indices of the prism for the red, green and blue wavelengths are, respectively, 1.39, 1.44 and 1.47. The prism will separate:
(a) Red from green and blue
(b) Blue from red and green
(c) Green from red and blue
(d) None of the colours

11. When a glass prism of refracting angle 60° is immersed in a liquid, its angle of minimum deviation is 30°. The critical angle for glass with respect to the liquid medium is:
(a) 37° (b) 45°
(c) 53° (d) 60°

12. If the minimum deviation angle of a prism is equal to its refracting angle, the refractive index μ of the prism lies between:
(a) $\sqrt{2} \le \mu < 2$ (b) $1 \le \mu < \sqrt{2}$
(c) $\sqrt{2} \le \mu < \sqrt{3}$ (d) $\sqrt{3} \le \mu < 2$

13. An equilateral prism deviates a ray through 45° for two angles of incidence differing by 20°. The angles of incidence are:
(a) 40° and 60° (b) 50° and 70°
(c) 40° 30′ and 60° 30′ (d) 42° 30′ and 62° 30′

14. A right-angled prism is to be made of refractive index μ and angles A and $B (B \le A)$, as shown in the figure. It is desired that a ray of light incident normally on face AB emerges parallel to the incident direction after two internal reflections.

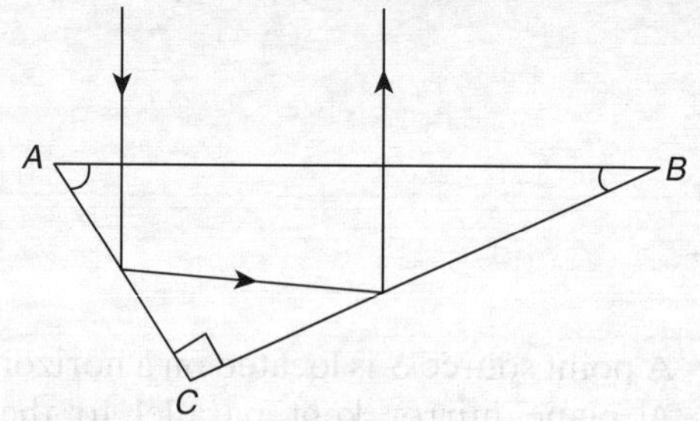

The minimum value of μ should be:
(a) cosec$A$ (b) cosec$B$
(c) $\sin A \cdot \text{cosec}B$ (d) $\sqrt{\sin A \cdot \sin B}$

15. Light is incident at angle α on one planar end of a transparent cylindrical rod of refractive index μ. If light entering the rod does not emerge from the curved surface of the rod for any value of α, then the least value of μ is:
(a) $\sqrt{2}$ (b) 1.5
(c) $\sqrt{3}$ (d) $2\sqrt{3}$

16. A concave mirror of focal length f is placed on a horizontal table with its axis directed vertically upwards. The mirror is now filled with some liquid to a height h. The image of an object placed at a distance x above the liquid surface coincides with the object itself. The refractive index of the liquid is:
(a) $\frac{2x-h}{f}$ (b) $\frac{2f-h}{x}$
(c) $\frac{x-h}{f}$ (d) $\frac{2f-x}{h}$

17. A spherical air bubble of radius 2 cm is formed inside a lake. Light coming from a distant object passes through the bubble and is seen by a fish on the other side of the bubble. If the refractive index of water is 4/3, the distance of the image from the centre of the bubble is:
(a) 3 cm (b) 4 cm
(c) 5 cm (d) 6 cm

18. A beaker contains water ($\mu_{water} = 4/3$) filled to a height of 32 cm. A concave mirror is fixed 6 cm above the surface of the water, as shown in the figure. An object O is placed at the bottom of the beaker and its image I is formed 12 cm below the surface of the water.

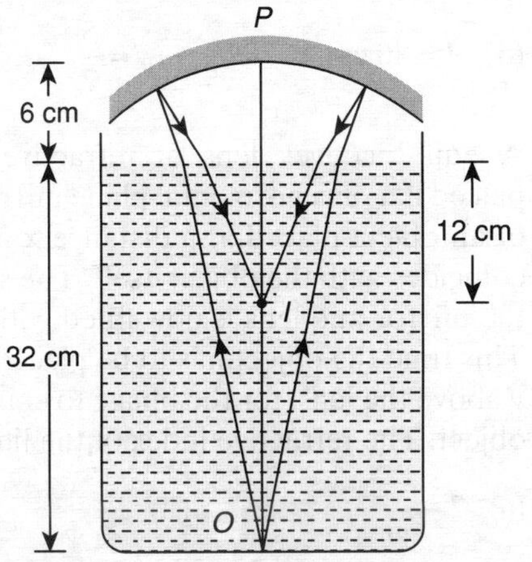

The focal length of the mirror is:
(a) 7.5 cm (b) 10 cm
(c) 10.5 cm (d) 12 cm

19. A spherical mirror is placed 10 cm below the level of water ($\mu_{water} = 4/3$). A point object is placed in air 30 cm above the water surface, on the axis of the mirror. If the image formed by partial reflection at the water surface coincides with the image formed by emerging light after reflection from the mirror, then the focal length of the mirror is:
(a) 80 cm (b) 75 cm
(c) 60 cm (d) 50 cm

20. A beaker contains water ($\mu_{water} = 4/3$) filled to a height of 18 cm. A thin oil film ($\mu_{oil} = 7/4$) having a curved upper surface is formed on the water surface, as shown in the figure. Light from a point source S kept 24 cm above the water surface converges into a point image I inside the water at 2 cm from the bottom of the container.

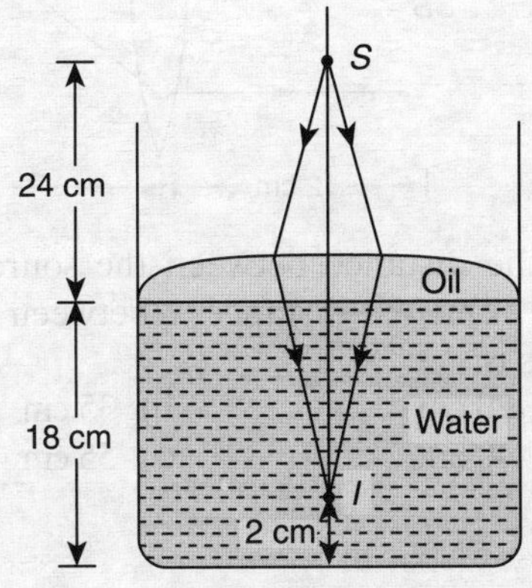

The radius of curvature of the oil film is:
(a) 3 cm (b) 4 cm
(c) 5 cm (d) 6 cm

21. The two surfaces of the lens, as shown in the figure, have the same radius of curvature.

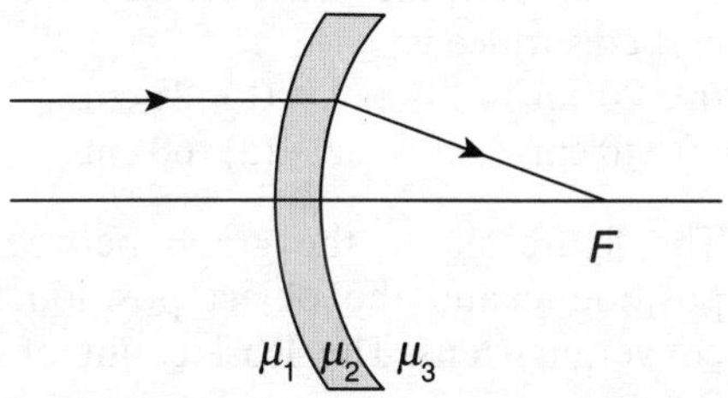

The lens will behave like a converging lens if:
(a) $\mu_3 + \mu_1 > \mu_2$ (b) $\mu_2 < \sqrt{\mu_1\mu_3}$
(c) $\mu_3 + \mu_1 < 2\mu_2$ (d) $\mu_3 > \mu_1$

22. A pin is placed in front of a converging lens of focal length 20 cm. The surface of the lens farther away from the pin is silvered and has a radius of curvature of 22 cm. If the image is real and 1.1 times the size of the object, then the distance of the object from the lens is:
(a) 11 cm (b) 10 cm
(c) 20 cm (d) 22 cm

23. A converging lens kept 10 cm from a light source forms a sharp image on a screen placed 10 cm from the lens. Now a glass slab ($\mu = 1.5$) of thickness 1.5 cm is inserted in contact with the light source. To obtain a sharp image again, the screen has to be shifted by:
(a) 1.1 cm away from the lens
(b) 1.1 cm towards the lens
(c) 0.55 cm away from the lens
(d) 0.55 cm towards the lens

24. The size of the image of an object, which is at infinity as formed by a converging lens of focal length 30 cm, is 1.6 cm. If a diverging lens of focal length 20 cm is placed between the converging lens and the image at a distance of 26 cm from the converging lens, the size of the final image will be:
(a) 0.8 cm (b) 1.2 cm
(c) 2.0 cm (d) 2.4 cm

25. A plano-convex lens has a thickness of 4 cm. When placed on a horizontal table with the curved surface in contact with it, the thickness of the lens appears to be 3 cm. If the lens is inverted such that the plane face is in contact with the table, the thickness of the lens appears to be 25/8 cm. The radius of the curved surface of the lens is:
(a) 25 cm (b) 50 cm
(c) 75 cm (d) 100 cm

26. A plano-convex lens has a thickness of 4 cm. When parallel rays are incident on its plane surface, they are brought into focus at 75 cm from the curved surface. When parallel rays are incident on its curved surface, they are brought into focus at 72 cm from the plane surface. The radius of its curved surface is:

(a) 20 cm (b) 25 cm
(c) 40 cm (d) 60 cm

27. The figure shows the graph between the image position v and the object position u for a thin converging lens. The least count of the graph is 0.1 cm.

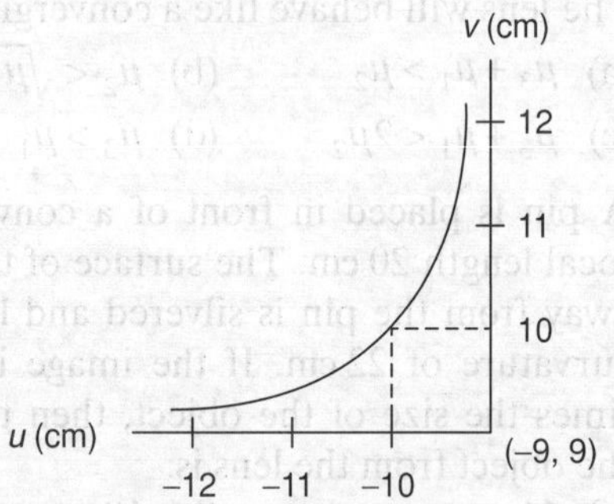

The focal length of the lens is:

(a) 5.00 cm ± 0.05 cm (b) 5.00 cm ± 0.10 cm
(c) 10.00 cm ± 0.05 cm (d) 10.00 cm ± 0.10 cm

28. The image of the Sun is formed by a converging lens of focal length f. The image is a circular patch and is formed in the focal plane of the lens. Choose the correct statements from the following:

(a) The area of the image is proportional to f
(b) The area of the image is proportional to f^2
(c) The intensity of the image increases if f is increased
(d) If the lower half of the lens is covered, the area of the image becomes half

29. A thin rod AB of length $f/3$ is placed along the axis of a concave mirror of focal length f such that its image $A'B'$, which is real and elongated, just touches the rod. The magnification produced is

(a) 1 (b) 3/2
(c) 4/3 (d) 2

30. An object and a screen are placed at a distance $D = 100$ cm. A converging lens of focal length $f = 21$ cm is placed between them. A real image of the object is formed on the screen for two positions A and B of the lens separated by a distance d. The respective linear magnifications for positions A and B are m_A and m_B. Then:

(a) $d = 38$ cm, $m_A = \frac{5}{3}, m_B = \frac{3}{5}$

(b) $d = 38$ cm, $m_A = \frac{7}{3}, m_B = \frac{5}{7}$

(c) $d = 40$ cm, $m_A = \frac{7}{3}, m_B = \frac{3}{7}$

(d) $d = 40$ cm, $m_A = \frac{7}{5}, m_B = \frac{5}{7}$

31. A equi-biconvex lens of refractive index 1.5 is placed flat on a horizontal plane mirror. The image of an object placed at a distance x above the lens coincides with the object itself. The space between the mirror and lens is now filled with some liquid. This time the object has to be placed at a distance y above the lens, for the image to coincide with the object. The refractive index of the liquid is:

(a) $2 - \frac{x}{y}$ (b) $1 + \frac{x}{y}$

(c) $1 + \frac{y}{2x}$ (d) $\frac{y}{x}$

32. A plano-convex lens acts like a concave mirror of 28-cm focal length when its plane surface is silvered and like a concave mirror of 10-cm focal length when its curved surface is silvered. The refractive index of the material of the lens is:

(a) 1.50 (b) 1.55
(c) 1.60 (d) 1.65

33. Light rays from a point source S first pass through a converging lens of focal length 15 cm, are then reflected by a converging mirror of focal length 20 cm, and then finally emerge parallel after passing through the lens, as shown in the figure.

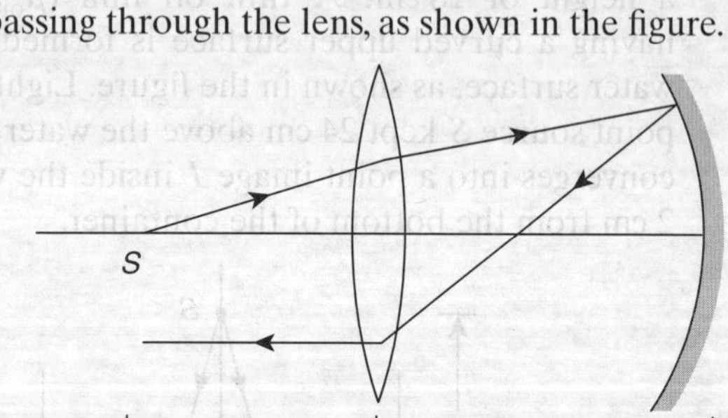

If the distance between the source and the lens is 12 cm, the distance x between the mirror and lens is:

(a) 20 cm (b) 35 cm
(c) 40 cm (d) 55 cm

34. A thin concavo-convex lens with its convex side silvered is placed on a horizontal table with its concave side facing upward and is filled with water, as shown in the figure. The radii of the two surfaces of the lens are also shown in the figure. A point source of light is placed on the axis at a distance x from the lens.

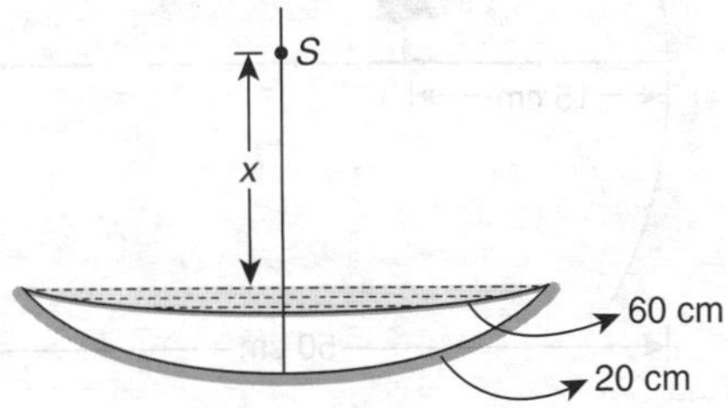

If the final image coincides with the source, then x equals:

(a) 8 cm (b) 9 cm
(c) 10 cm (d) 14 cm

35. A converging lens of focal length 10 cm forms a real image I of a point object O placed on the axis at a distance of 15 cm from the lens, as shown in the figure. A convex mirror is then inserted between the lens and I, and its position adjusted until the final image now coincides with O.

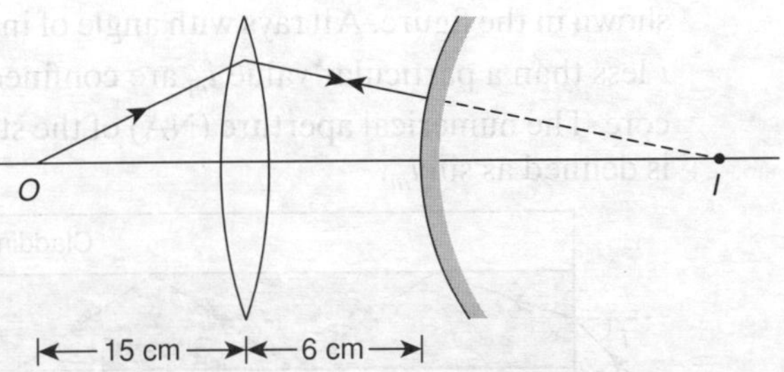

If this happens when the mirror is at a distance of 6 cm from the lens, then the focal length of the mirror is:

(a) 14 cm (b) 12 cm
(c) 10 cm (d) 6 cm

36. A converging lens of focal length 10 cm forms a real image I of a point object O placed on the axis at a distance of 15 cm from the lens, as shown in the figure. When a diverging lens is inserted between the lens and I, the image shifts by 4 cm.

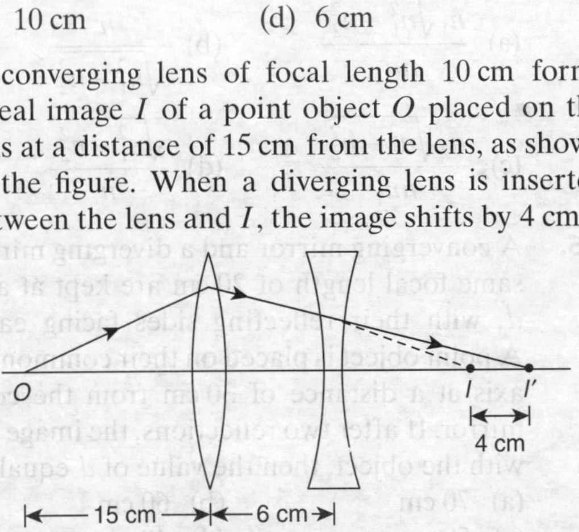

The focal length of the diverging lens is:

(a) 128 cm (b) 156 cm
(c) 168 cm (d) 256 cm

37. A point source S is kept on the axis of a converging lens of focal length f, at a distance a $(a > f)$ from the lens. The lens is now split into two halves along a plane containing the axis of the lens, and the two halves are separated by a distance $2b$ symmetrically above and below the axis, as shown in the figure. Now two image points S_1 and S_2 are formed.

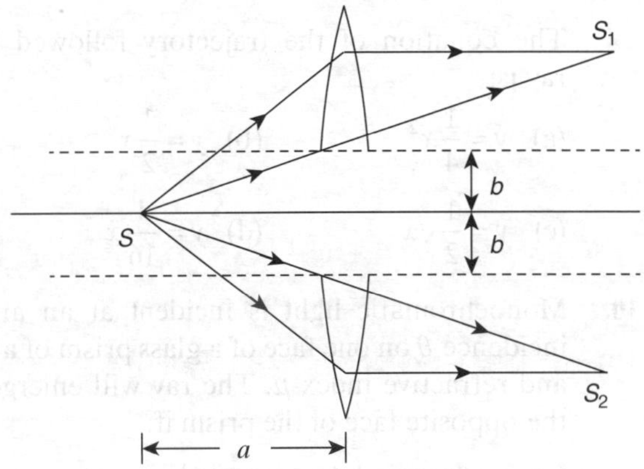

The distance between the two images is:

(a) $\dfrac{2ab}{a-f}$ (b) $\dfrac{ab}{2a-f}$

(c) $\dfrac{2ab}{ab-f^2}$ (d) $\dfrac{2a^2b}{a^2-f^2}$

38. The xy-plane is the boundary separating two transparent media. Medium 1 $(z>0)$ has a refracting index $\sqrt{2}$ and medium 2 $(z<0)$ has a refracting index $\sqrt{3}$. A ray of light in medium 1 along the vector $\mathbf{A} = 6\sqrt{3}\mathbf{i} + 8\sqrt{3}\mathbf{j} - 10\mathbf{k}$ is incident on the plane of separation. The vector representing the refracted ray is:

(a) $6\sqrt{3}\mathbf{i}+8\sqrt{3}\mathbf{j}-10\sqrt{2}\mathbf{k}$

(b) $3\sqrt{3}\mathbf{i}+4\sqrt{3}\mathbf{j}+10\mathbf{k}$

(c) $8\sqrt{3}\mathbf{i}+6\sqrt{3}\mathbf{j}-10\sqrt{3}\mathbf{k}$

(d) $6\sqrt{3}\mathbf{i}+8\sqrt{3}\mathbf{j}-10\sqrt{3}\mathbf{k}$

39. A ray of light travelling in air is incident at grazing angle (incident angle = 90°) on a long rectangular slab of a transparent medium, as shown in the figure. The point of incidence is the origin $A(0,0)$. The medium has a variable refractive index given by $\mu(y) = \sqrt{y+1}$. The refractive index of air is 1.

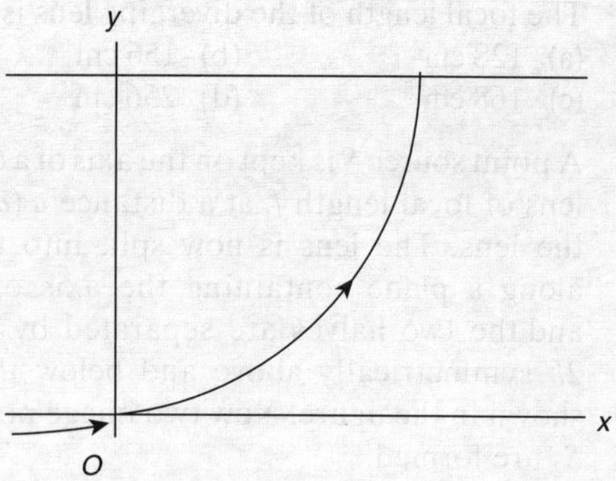

The equation of the trajectory followed by the ray is:

(a) $y=\frac{1}{4}x^2$ (b) $y=\frac{1}{2}x^4$

(c) $y=\frac{1}{2}\sqrt{x}$ (d) $y=\frac{1}{16}x$

40. Monochromatic light is incident at an angle of incidence θ on one face of a glass prism of angle A and refractive index μ. The ray will emerge from the opposite face of the prism if:

(a) $\sin\theta > \mu \sin\left(A - \text{cosec}^{-1}\mu\right)$

(b) $\sin\theta < \mu \sin\left(A - \sin^{-1}\mu\right)$

(c) $\cos\theta > \mu \sin\left(A - \text{cosec}^{-1}\mu\right)$

(d) $\cos\theta < \mu \sin\left(A - \sin^{-1}\mu\right)$

41. An object and a screen are placed at a distance D. A converging lens is placed between them. A real image of the object is formed on the screen for two positions A and B of the lens separated by a distance $d = 10$ cm. If the linear magnifications for positions A and B are in the ratio $9:4$, then the focal length of the lens is:

(a) 12.5 cm (b) 12 cm

(c) 11 cm (d) 10.5 cm

42. A monochromatic beam of light is incident at 60° on one face of an equilateral prism of refractive index n. The ray emerges from the opposite face at angle $\theta(n)$ with the normal. For $n=\sqrt{3}$, the value of $\frac{d\theta}{dn}$ is:

(a) 1 (b) 2

(c) 3 (d) 4

43. The figure shows a concave mirror and a convex lens (refractive index = 1.5) of focal length 10 cm, each separated by a distance of 50 cm in air. An object is placed at a distance of 15 cm from the mirror. The erect image formed by this combination has magnification m_1.

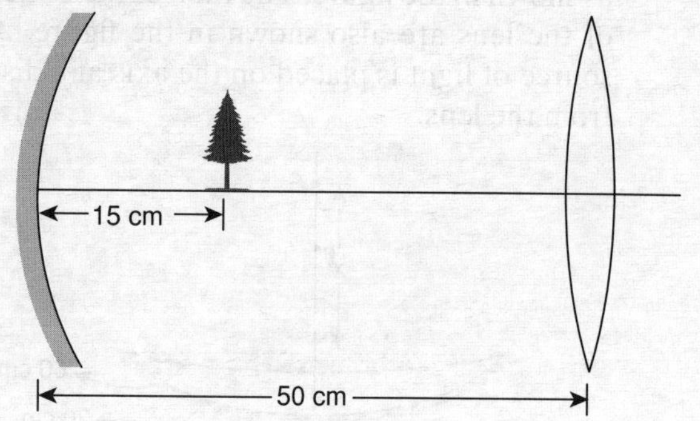

When the set-up is immersed in a medium of refractive index $7/6$, the magnification becomes m_2. The ratio $\frac{m_2}{m_1}$ is:

(a) 4 (b) 5

(c) 6 (d) 7

44. An optical fibre consists of a solid glass cylinder of refractive n_1 surrounded by a medium of lower refractive index n_2. Light guidance in the structure takes place due to successive total internal reflections at the interface of the two media, as shown in the figure. All rays with angle of incidence i less than a particular value i_m are confined to the core. The numerical aperture (NA) of the structure is defined as $\sin i_m$.

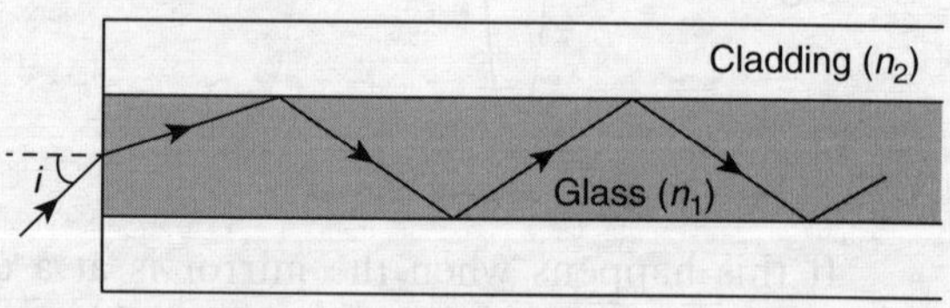

If the structure is immersed in a medium of refractive index n, its NA is:

(a) $\frac{n_1\sqrt{n_1^2-n_2^2}}{nn_2}$ (b) $\frac{n}{\sqrt{n_1^2-n_2^2}}$

(c) $\frac{n_2\sqrt{n_1^2-n_2^2}}{nn_1}$ (d) $\frac{\sqrt{n_1^2-n_2^2}}{n}$

45. A converging mirror and a diverging mirror of the same focal length of 20 cm are kept at a distance d, with their reflecting sides facing each other. A point object is placed on their common principal axis at a distance of 30 cm from the converging mirror. If after two reflections, the image coincides with the object, then the value of d equals:

(a) 70 cm (b) 60 cm

(c) 50 cm (d) 40 cm

46. An object is placed 30 cm from the curved surface of a plano-convex lens. An image double the size of the object is formed. Due to reflection from the convex surface of the lens, a faint image is also observed at a distance of 10 cm from the lens. The correct statements from the following are:
(a) Refractive index of the lens material is 2.5
(b) Radius of curvature of the curved surface is 45 cm
(c) The faint image is erect and real
(d) Focal length of the lens is 20 cm

47. For a converging lens, the relation between the image distance v and the magnification m is given by $\frac{m}{a}+\frac{v}{b}=1$. The correct statements are:
(a) Focal length of lens = a
(b) $m=2$ for object distance = $b/2$
(c) Focal length of lens = b
(d) $m=-1$ for object distance = b

48. The figure shows a glass container (refractive index 1.5) with a thick base, containing liquid of refractive index μ.

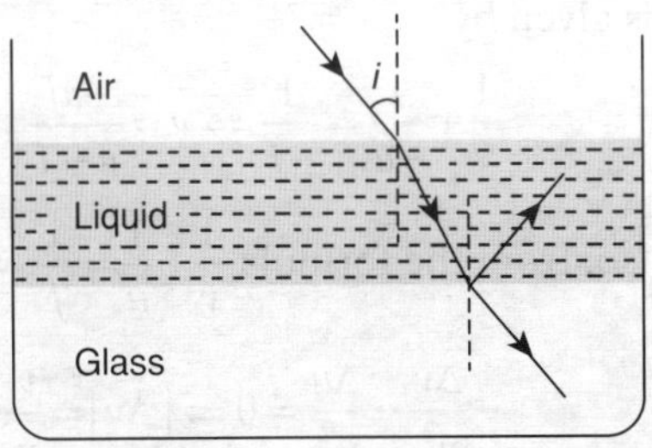

If for any value of the angle of incidence i, light rays reflected at the liquid–glass interface undergoes maximum polarisation, then the greatest value of μ is:
(a) $\sqrt{5}/2$ (b) $\sqrt{3}/2$
(c) $3/\sqrt{2}$ (d) $3/\sqrt{5}$

49. Sunlight of intensity I_0 is incident normally on a thin convex lens of focal length 20 cm. The intensity of light at a distance of 22 cm from the lens on its other side is:
(a) $4I_0$ (b) $9I_0$
(c) $16I_0$ (d) $100I_0$

50. The far point of a myopic person is 80 cm from the eye. The power of the lens required to enable her to see very distant objects clearly is:
(a) –0.80 dioptres (b) +0.50 dioptres
(c) –1.25 dioptres (d) +1.50 dioptres

51. The near point of a hyperopic person is 50 cm from the eye. The power of the lens required to enable him to read books held 25 cm from the eye is:
(a) –0.80 dioptres (b) +1.50 dioptres
(c) –1.25 dioptres (d) +2.00 dioptres

52. A telescope has objective of focal length $f_o = 90.0$ cm and eyepiece of focal length $f_e = 30.0$ cm. If the telescope is used to view a 80.0-m-tall building that is 2.00 km away, the angular size of the final image is:
(a) 0.120 rad (b) 0.240 rad
(c) 0.360 rad (d) 0.480 rad

53. A compound microscope has objective of focal length $f_o = 1.0$ cm, eyepiece of focal length $f_e = 2.0$ cm and a tube of length $l = 23$ cm. If the unaided eye can distinguish two points at its near point, that is, 25 cm, if they are about 0.10 mm apart, the minimum distance that can be resolved using the microscope is:
(a) 0.1 μm (b) 0.2 μm
(c) 0.3 μm (d) 0.4 μm

ANSWER KEYS

1. (c)	**2.** (d)	**3.** (c)	**4.** (c)	**5.** (a)	**6.** (d)	**7.** (d)	**8.** (a)	**9.** (a),(c),(d)
10. (b)	**11.** (a),(b),(c)	**12.** (a)	**13.** (d)	**14.** (b)	**15.** (a)	**16.** (b)	**17.** (a)	**18.** (b)
19. (b)	**20.** (d)	**21.** (d)	**22.** (b)	**23.** (c)	**24.** (c)	**25.** (a)	**26.** (b)	**27.** (a)
28. (b)	**29.** (b)	**30.** (c)	**31.** (a)	**32.** (b)	**33.** (c)	**34.** (d)	**35.** (b)	**36.** (c)
37. (a)	**38.** (d)	**39.** (a)	**40.** (a)	**41.** (b)	**42.** (b)	**43.** (d)	**44.** (d)	**45.** (c)
46. (a),(d)	**47.** (b),(c)	**48.** (d)	**49.** (d)	**50.** (c)	**51.** (d)	**52.** (a)	**53.** (d)	

SOLUTIONS

1. (c)

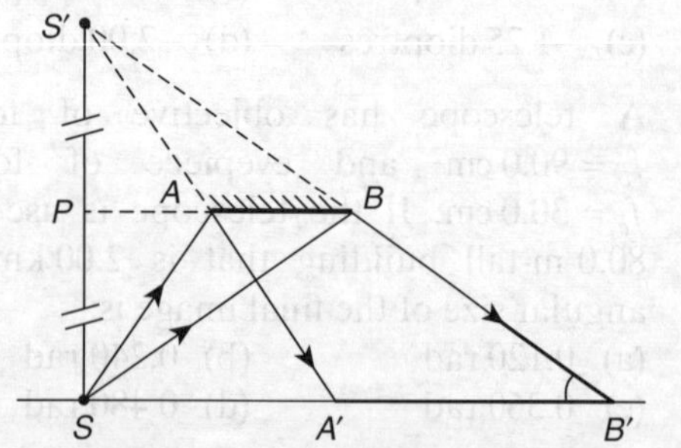

S is the source point and AB is the mirror. S' is the image point and $A'B'$ is the bright patch formed on the ground (see figure).

The triangles $\Delta S'PA$ and $\Delta S'SA'$ are similar to $S'P = SP$. Thus, $SA' = 2(PA)$ and $SB' = 2(PB)$. Hence, the length of the bright patch is

$$A'B' = SB' - SA' = 2(PB - PA) = 2AB = 2l.$$

The speed with which A is moving is given to be v, that is, $\frac{d(PA)}{dt} = v$. The speed with which A' moves is given by

$$\frac{d(SA')}{dt} = \frac{d(2PA)}{dt} = 2\frac{d(PA)}{dt} = 2v$$

2. (d)

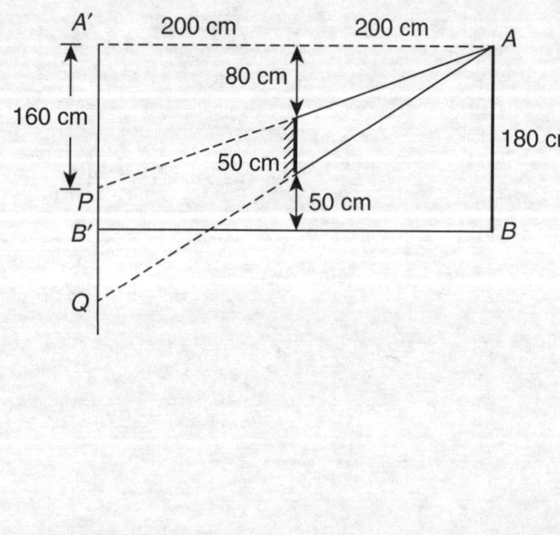

A is the eye and B is the foot of the man, and $A'B'$ is the image (see figure). Rays that can reach A (eye) are only from points lying between P and Q. From similar triangles, we can see that $A'P = 2 \times 80$ cm $= 160$ cm. Hence, the man can see portion $B'P = 180$ cm $- A'P = 20$ cm.

3. (c) From the mirror formula, the image position v is given by

$$\frac{1}{v} + \frac{1}{-a} = \frac{1}{-f} \Rightarrow v = \frac{-af}{a-f}$$

Also, from the formula $\frac{1}{v} + \frac{1}{u} = \frac{1}{f}$, we have

$$-\frac{\Delta v}{v^2} - \frac{\Delta u}{u^2} = 0 \Rightarrow |\Delta v| = \frac{v^2}{u^2}|\Delta u|$$

For the small object length $|\Delta u| = b$, the above relation gives the length $|\Delta v|$ of the image as

$$|\Delta v| = \left(\frac{f}{a-f}\right)^2 b$$

4. (c) The image of the truck is given by

$$\frac{1}{v} + \frac{1}{-2.8 \text{ m}} = \frac{1}{+0.2 \text{ m}} \Rightarrow v = \frac{0.56}{3} \text{ m}$$

Also, from the formula $\frac{1}{v} + \frac{1}{u} = \frac{1}{f}$, we have

$$-\frac{1}{v^2}\frac{dv}{dt} - \frac{1}{u^2}\frac{du}{dt} = 0$$

$$\Rightarrow \quad \frac{dv}{dt} = -\frac{v^2}{u^2}\frac{du}{dt} = -\left(\frac{0.56 \text{ m}}{3 \times 2.8 \text{ m}}\right)^2 (15 \text{ m/s})$$

$$= -\frac{1}{15} \text{ m/s}$$

5. (a)

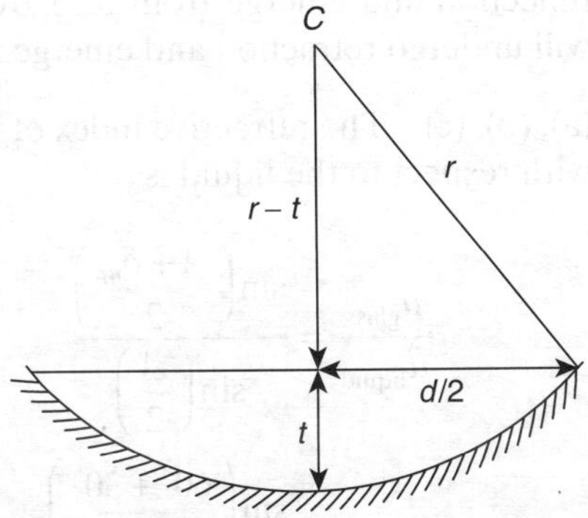

Let r be the radius of curvature of the concave mirror. Then, from the figure, we see that

$$(r-t)^2 + \left(\frac{d}{2}\right)^2 = r^2$$

$$\Rightarrow \quad 2rt = \frac{d^2}{4} + t^2 \simeq \frac{d^2}{4} \quad [t << d]$$

$$\Rightarrow \quad r = \frac{d^2}{8t} = \frac{(4\text{ cm})^2}{8(0.1\text{ cm})} = 20\text{ cm}$$

Hence focal length $= \frac{r}{2} = 10$ cm. Now, the position of the image square is given by

$$\frac{1}{v} + \frac{1}{-25\text{ cm}} = \frac{1}{-10\text{ cm}} \Rightarrow v = -\frac{50}{3}\text{cm}$$

Let a be the length of the image square. Then, we have

$$\frac{a}{3\text{ cm}} = \frac{50/3}{25} \Rightarrow a = 2\text{ cm}$$

Hence, area of the image square equals $(2\text{ cm})^2$.

6. (d)

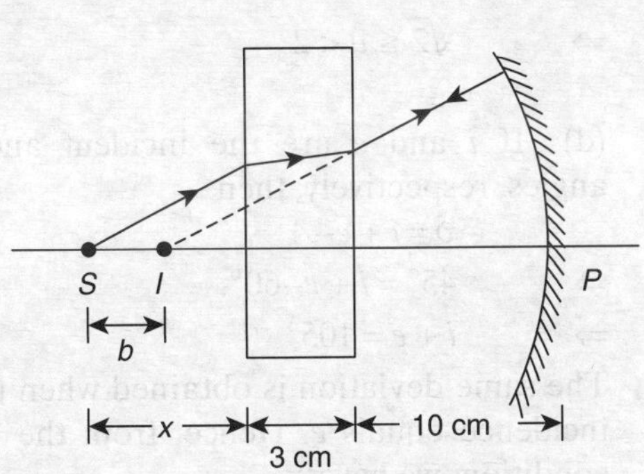

After refraction from the slab, the image is formed at I (see figure). The shift is given by

$$SI = t\left(1 - \frac{1}{\mu}\right) = 3\text{ cm}\left(1 - \frac{2}{3}\right) = 1\text{ cm}$$

The final image will coincide with S itself only if the rays fall normally on the mirror and retrace their path. This is possible only if I coincides with the centre of curvature of the mirror. The radius of the mirror is 2(10 cm) = 20 cm. Hence, we have

$$PI = 20\text{ cm}$$

$$\Rightarrow \quad (x - 1\text{ cm}) + 13\text{ cm} = 20\text{ cm gives } x = 8\text{ cm}$$

7. (d) Let t_1 and t_2 be the actual depths of the air bubbles from the two faces of the slab. Then, we have

$$\frac{t_1}{\mu} = 5\text{ cm and } \frac{t_2}{\mu} = 2\text{ cm}$$

Adding the above equations, we get the slab thickness

$$t_1 + t_2 = \mu(7\text{ cm}) = 10.5\text{ cm.}$$

8. (a)

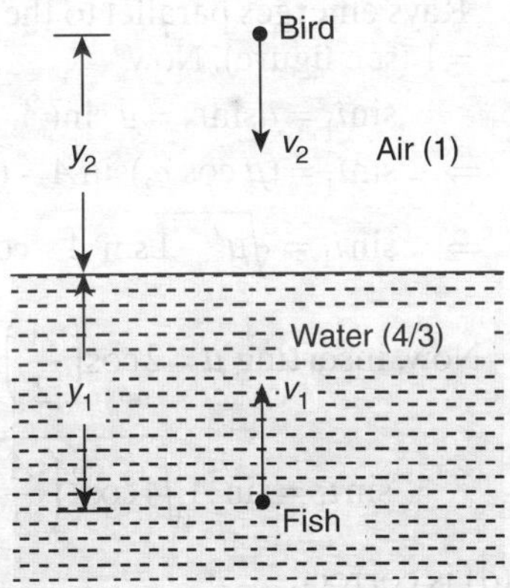

Let y_1 and y_2 be the respective distances of the fish F and bird B, measured from the water surface (see figure). The distance of the bird as seen from the fish is $s = y_1 + \frac{4}{3}y_2$.

Differentiating with respect to time, we have

$$\frac{ds}{dt} = \frac{dy_1}{dt} + \frac{4}{3}\frac{dy_2}{dt} = -\left(v_1 + \frac{4}{3}v_2\right)$$

The fish and bird are both approaching the water surface, hence the negative sign.

9. (a), (c), (d)

(a) At minimum deviation

$$i_1 = i_2 = \frac{\delta_m + A}{2} = \frac{A + A}{2} = A.$$

Also $r_1 = r_2 = \frac{A}{2}$ and since the prism is isosceles, the ray moves parallel to the base

$\Rightarrow$ (a) is correct.

(b) $\mu = \dfrac{\sin\left(\dfrac{A+\delta_m}{2}\right)}{\sin\left(\dfrac{A}{2}\right)} = \dfrac{\sin A}{\sin\left(\dfrac{A}{2}\right)} = 2\cos\left(\dfrac{A}{2}\right)$

$\Rightarrow \quad A = 2\cos^{-1}\left(\dfrac{\mu}{2}\right) \Rightarrow$ (b) is incorrect.

(c) At minimum deviation, $i_1 = A$ and $r_1 = A/2$. Hence $i_1 = 2r_1 \Rightarrow$ (c) is correct.

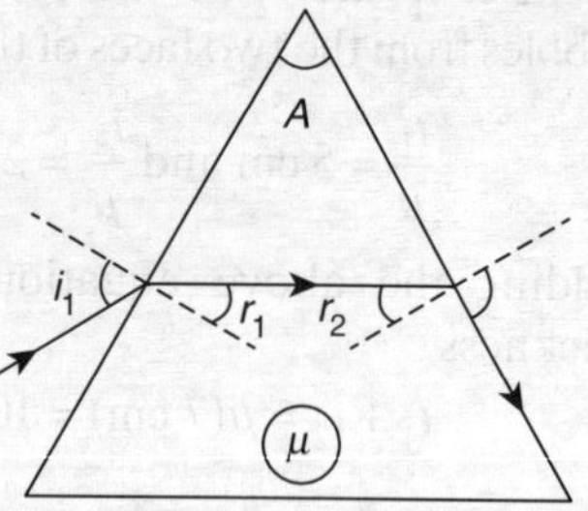

(d) Rays emerges parallel to the surface $\Rightarrow \mu\sin r_2 = 1$ (see figure). Now

$$\sin i_1 = \mu\sin r_1 = \mu\sin(A - r_2)$$

$$\Rightarrow \quad \sin i_1 = (\mu\cos r_2)\sin A - (\mu\sin r_2)\cos A$$

$$\Rightarrow \quad \sin i_1 = \sqrt{\mu^2 - 1}\,\sin A - \cos A$$

Now, inserting $\mu = 2\cos\left(\dfrac{A}{2}\right)$, we have

$$\sin i_1 = \sin A\sqrt{4\cos^2\left(\frac{A}{2}\right) - 1} - \cos A$$

$\Rightarrow$ (d) is correct.

10. (b)

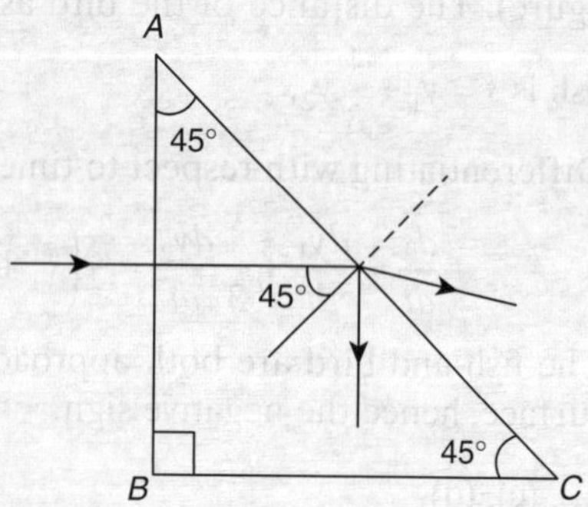

The rays whose critical angle C is less than or equal to 45° will undergo total internal reflection. That is, $\sin C \le 1/\sqrt{2}$

$$\Rightarrow \quad \frac{1}{\mu} \le \frac{1}{\sqrt{2}} \Rightarrow \mu \ge 1.414$$

Hence, blue and green will undergo total internal reflection and emerge from face BC, whereas red will undergo refraction and emerge from face AC.

11. (a), (b), (c) The refractive index of the glass prism with respect to the liquid is

$$\frac{\mu_{\text{glass}}}{\mu_{\text{liquid}}} = \frac{\sin\left(\dfrac{A+\delta_m}{2}\right)}{\sin\left(\dfrac{A}{2}\right)}$$

$$= \frac{\sin\left(\dfrac{60^\circ + 30^\circ}{2}\right)}{\sin\left(\dfrac{60^\circ}{2}\right)} = \sqrt{2}$$

The critical angle for the glass–liquid boundary is

$$C = \sin^{-1}\left(\frac{\mu_{\text{glass}}}{\mu_{\text{liquid}}}\right) = \sin^{-1}\left(\frac{1}{\sqrt{2}}\right) = 45^\circ$$

12. (a) Given $\delta_{\min} = A$. When deviation is minimum

$$i = \frac{\delta_{\min} + A}{2} = A \text{ and } r = A/2$$

Hence $\quad \mu = \dfrac{\sin A}{\sin(A/2)} = 2\cos(A/2)$

Now, since $0 \le i < 90^\circ$

$\Rightarrow \quad 0 \le A < 90^\circ$

$\Rightarrow \quad 0 \le A/2 < 45^\circ$

$\Rightarrow \quad \dfrac{1}{\sqrt{2}} \le \cos(A/2) < 1$

$\Rightarrow \quad \sqrt{2} \le 2\cos(A/2) < 2$

$\Rightarrow \quad \sqrt{2} \le \mu < 2$

13. (d) If i and e are the incident and emergent angles, respectively, then

$$\delta = i + e - A$$

$\Rightarrow \quad 45^\circ = i + e - 60^\circ$

$\Rightarrow \quad i + e = 105^\circ \qquad \ldots(1)$

The same deviation is obtained when the angle of incidence equals e. Hence, from the other given condition, we have

$$i - e = 20^\circ \qquad \ldots(2)$$

Solving the two equations, we get the two angles of incidence as 62°30′ and 42°30′.

14. (b)

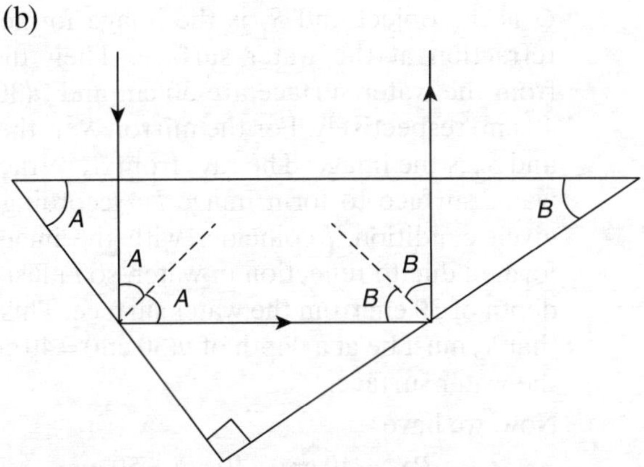

The angles of incidence at the two faces inside the prism are A and B. For total internal refraction at both faces, $A \geq \theta_{critical}$ and $B \geq \theta_{critical}$. Since $A > B$, both these inequalities will be satisfied if

$$B \geq \theta_{critical}$$

$$\Rightarrow \quad \sin B \geq \sin \theta critical = 1/\mu$$

$$\Rightarrow \quad \mu \geq \text{cosec } B$$

15. (a)

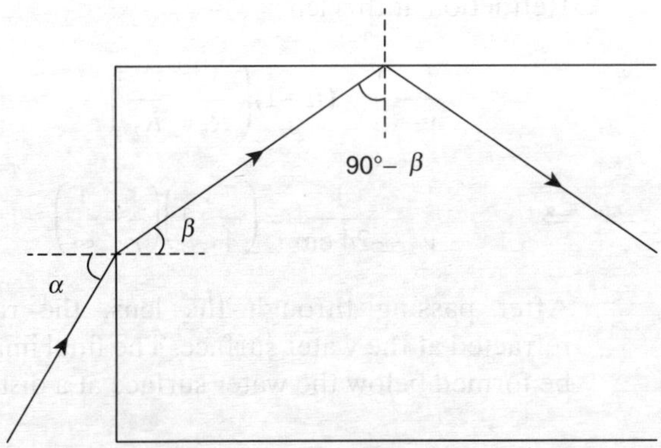

For total internal reflection (see figure), we have

$$90° - \beta > C$$

$$\Rightarrow \quad \cos\beta > \sin C$$

From Snell's law, we have

$$\mu \sin\beta = \sin\alpha \Rightarrow \cos\beta = \sqrt{1 - \frac{\sin^2\alpha}{\mu^2}}$$

The above inequality then reduces to

$$\sqrt{1 - \frac{\sin^2\alpha}{\mu^2}} > \frac{1}{\mu} \Rightarrow \mu^2 - \sin^2\alpha > 1$$

$$\Rightarrow \quad \mu > \sqrt{1 + \sin^2\alpha}$$

The maximum value of $\sin\alpha$ is 1. Hence, μ should be $\sqrt{2}$.

16. (b)

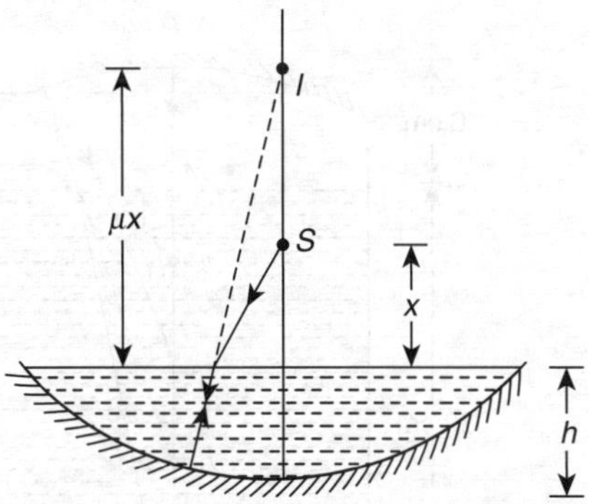

The figure shows a point object S kept at a distance x above the liquid surface. The final image will coincide with object S itself only if the rays fall normally on the mirror and hence retrace their path. Let μ be the refractive index of the liquid. After refraction at the liquid surface, the image I is formed at a distance μx above the liquid surface. Now I serves as the object point for the mirror. According to the required condition, the rays must fall normally on the mirror and retrace their path. In that case, I must coincide with the centre of curvature of the mirror.

Hence, we have

$$\mu x + h = r = 2f \Rightarrow \mu = \frac{2f - h}{x}$$

17. (a)

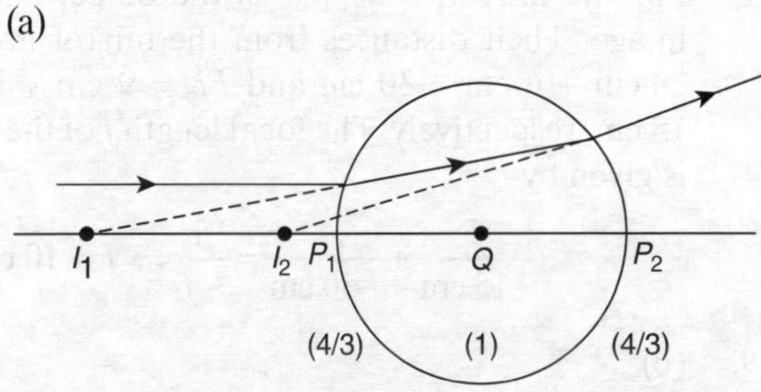

First refraction: Image position v_1 is given by

$$\frac{1}{v_1} - \frac{4/3}{\infty} = \frac{1 - 4/3}{+2 \text{ cm}}$$

$$\Rightarrow \quad v_1 = -6 \text{ cm} \Rightarrow P_1 I_1 = 6 \text{ cm}$$

Second refraction: I_1 serves as the object and P_2 is the new origin. The object distance is $P_2 I_1 = 6$ cm + 4 cm = 10 cm. Image position v_2 is given by

$$\frac{4/3}{v_2} - \frac{1}{-10} = \frac{4/3 - 1}{-2 \text{ cm}}$$

$$\Rightarrow \quad v_2 = -5 \text{ cm} \Rightarrow P_2 I_2 = 5 \text{ cm}$$

Distance of the image from the centre of the bubble is $CI_2 = 5$ cm – 2 cm = 3 cm.

18. (b)

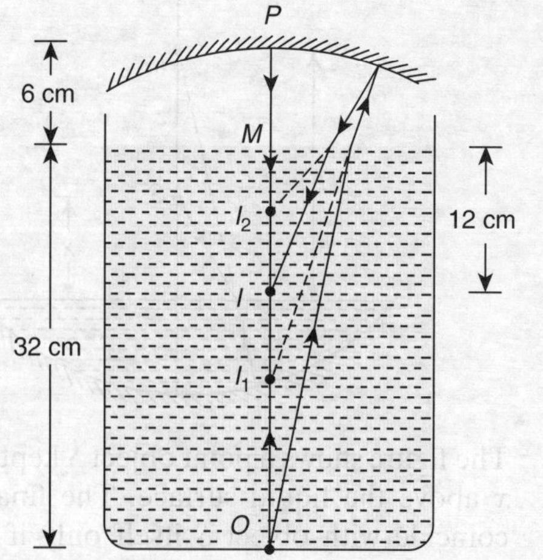

When rays from O refract at the water surface, the image I_1 is formed at a distance $\frac{32\text{ cm}}{4/3} = 24$ cm below the water surface. After reflection from the mirror, the rays refract again and finally meet at I, which is given to be 12 cm below the water surface. In the absence of water, those rays would have converged at some point, say I_2, at a distance $\frac{12\text{ cm}}{4/3} = 9$ cm below the water surface.

For the mirror, I_1 serves as the object and I_2 its image. Their distances from the mirror are $PI_1 =$ 24 cm + 6 cm = 30 cm and PI_2 = 9 cm + 6 cm = 15 cm, respectively. The focal length f of the mirror is given by

$$\frac{1}{-15\text{ cm}} + \frac{1}{-30\text{ cm}} = \frac{1}{-f} \Rightarrow f = 10\text{ cm}$$

19. (b)

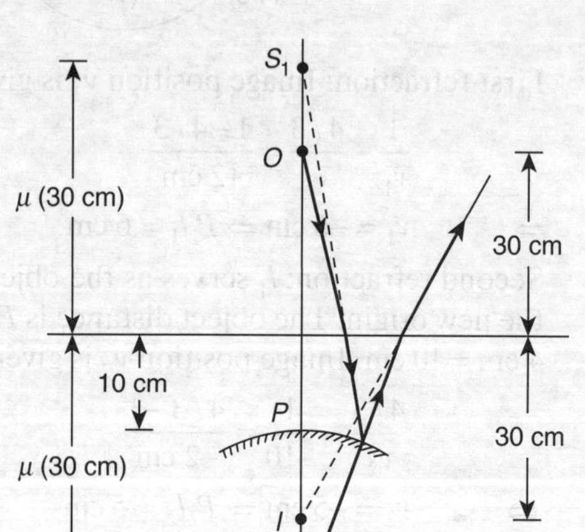

O is the object and S_1 is the image formed after refraction at the water surface. Their distances from the water surface are 30 cm and μ(30 cm) = 40 cm, respectively. For the mirror, S_1 is the object and S_2 is the image. The rays from S_2 refract at the water surface to form image I. According to the given condition, I coincides with the image of O formed due to reflection in water, so I must be at a depth of 30 cm from the water surface. This means that S_2 must be at a depth of μ(30 cm) = 40 cm from the water surface.

Now, we have

$$PS_1 = 40\text{ cm} + 10\text{ cm} = 50\text{ cm}$$

and $$PS_2 = 40\text{ cm} - 10\text{ cm} = 30\text{ cm}$$

Using the mirror formula, we have

$$\frac{1}{f} = \frac{1}{+30\text{ cm}} + \frac{1}{-50\text{ cm}} \Rightarrow f = -75\text{ cm}$$

20. (d) Let r be the radius of curvature of the upper surface of the oil film. The oil film behaves like a thin lens.

Refraction at this lens:

$$\frac{1}{v} - \frac{1}{u} = (\mu - 1)\left(\frac{1}{R_1} - \frac{1}{R_2}\right)$$

$$\Rightarrow \quad \frac{1}{v} - \frac{1}{-24\text{ cm}} = \left(\frac{7}{4} - 1\right)\left(\frac{1}{r} - \frac{1}{\infty}\right) \quad \text{...(1)}$$

After passing through the lens, the rays are refracted at the water surface. The final image will be formed below the water surface at a distance

$$v' = \frac{4}{3}v \quad \text{...(2)}$$

Inserting the value of v' = 18 cm – 2 cm = 16 cm in equation (2) gives v = 12 cm.

Now, inserting the value of v in equation (1) gives r = 6 cm.

21. (d) Refraction at the first surface:

$$\frac{\mu_2}{v} - \frac{\mu_1}{\infty} = \frac{\mu_2 - \mu_1}{R} \quad \text{...(1)}$$

Refraction at the second surface:

Now, the object position is v and f is the image position. Then, we have

$$\frac{\mu_3}{f} - \frac{\mu_2}{V} = \frac{\mu_3 - \mu_2}{R} \quad \text{...(2)}$$

Eliminating v by adding the two equations, we have

$$\frac{\mu_3}{f} = \frac{\mu_3 - \mu_1}{R} \Rightarrow f = \frac{\mu_3 R}{\mu_3 - \mu_1}$$

The lens will be converging if $f > 0 \Rightarrow \mu_3 > \mu_1$.

22. (b)

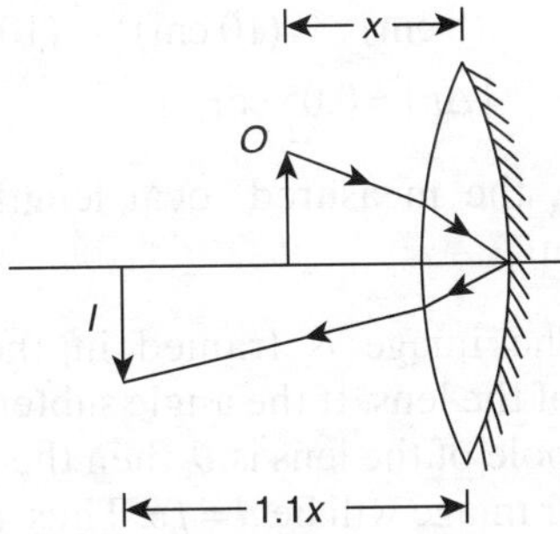

The silvered lens behaves like a mirror of focal length f given by

$$\frac{1}{f} = \frac{1}{f_m} - \frac{2}{f_l} = \frac{2}{-22 \text{ cm}} - \frac{2}{20 \text{ cm}}$$

$$\Rightarrow \quad \frac{1}{f} = \frac{-21}{110 \text{ cm}}$$

Let the object distance be x. Then image distance is $1.1x$. Now, using the mirror formula, we have

$$\frac{1}{v} + \frac{1}{u} = \frac{1}{f}$$

$$\Rightarrow \quad \frac{1}{1.1x} + \frac{1}{-x} = \frac{-21}{110 \text{ cm}} \Rightarrow x = 10 \text{ cm}$$

23. (c) The focal length of the lens is given by

$$\frac{1}{f} = \frac{1}{+10 \text{ cm}} - \frac{1}{-10 \text{ cm}} = \frac{1}{5 \text{ cm}} \Rightarrow f = 5 \text{ cm}$$

The glass slab shifts the object position closer to the lens by

$$s = \left(1 - \frac{1}{\mu}\right)t = \left(1 - \frac{1}{1.5}\right)1.5 \text{ cm} = 0.5 \text{ cm}$$

The new object distance is 10 cm – 0.5 cm = 9.5 cm. The new image position is given by

$$\frac{1}{v} - \frac{1}{-9.5 \text{ cm}} = \frac{1}{5 \text{ cm}} \Rightarrow v = 10.55 \text{ cm}$$

Hence, the screen has to be moved farther away from the lens by 10.55 cm – 10 cm = 0.55 cm.

24. (c)

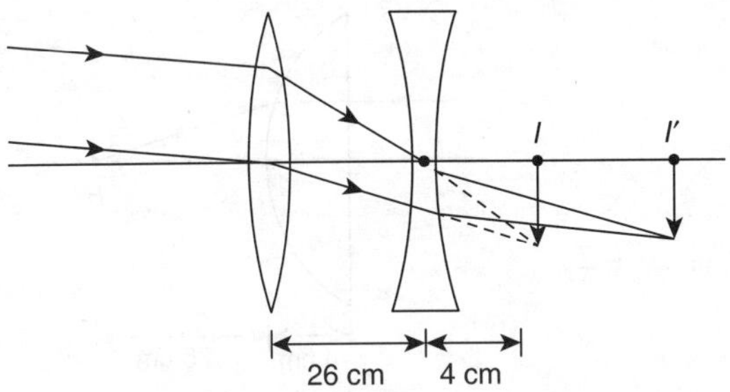

The image I is at a distance of 30 cm from the converging lens. Therefore, its distance from the diverging lens is 4 cm. I serves as a virtual object for refraction at the diverging lens. The position of image I' is given by

$$\frac{1}{v} - \frac{1}{4 \text{ cm}} = \frac{1}{-20 \text{ cm}} \Rightarrow v = 5 \text{ cm}$$

The magnification produced is $\frac{v}{u} = \frac{5}{4}$.

Hence, image size is $\frac{5}{4}(1.6 \text{ cm}) = 2.0 \text{ cm}$

25. (a)

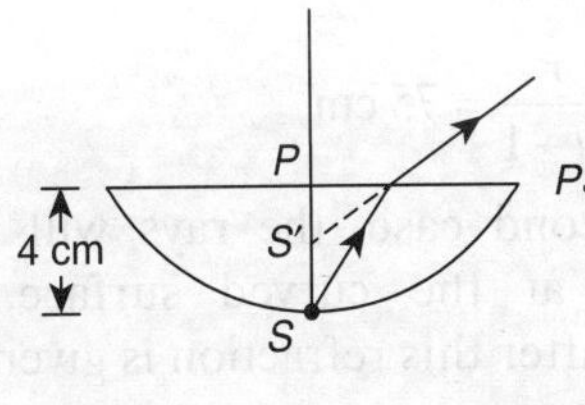

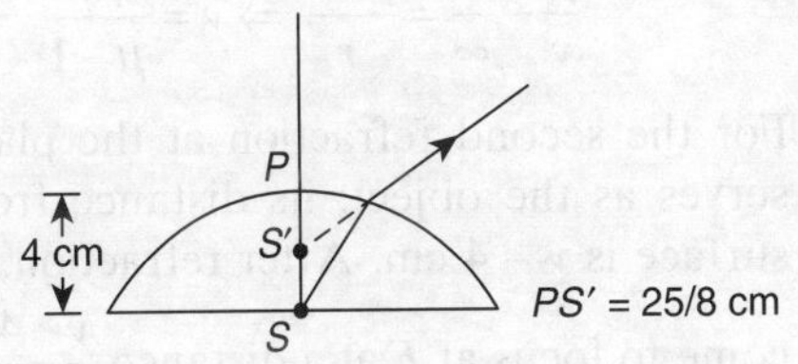

Let μ be the refractive index and r be the radius of the curved surface of the lens. In the first case, the distances of the object point S and the image point S' (measured from the plane surface) are 4 cm and 3 cm, respectively. Hence $\mu = 4/3$. In the second case, the distances of S and S' (measured from the pole of the curved surface) are 4 cm and 25/8 cm, respectively.

Hence, using refraction formula, we have

$$\frac{1}{-25/8} - \frac{\mu}{-4 \text{ cm}} = \frac{1 - \mu}{-r}$$

Inserting the value of μ gives $r = 25$ cm.

26. (b)

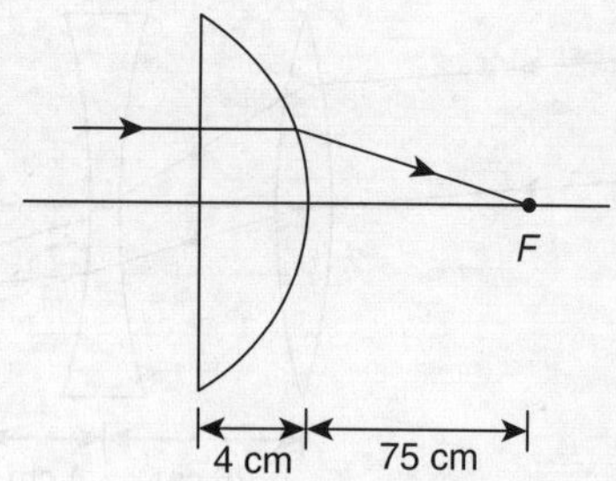

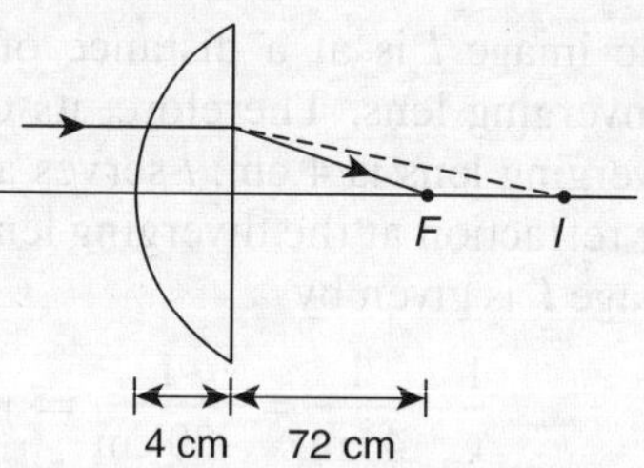

Let μ be the refractive index and r be the radius of the curved surface of the lens. In the first case, the rays undergo refraction only at the curved surface. Using the refraction formula, we have

$$\frac{1}{75\text{ cm}} - \frac{\mu}{\infty} = \frac{1-\mu}{-r}$$

$$\Rightarrow \quad \frac{r}{\mu - 1} = 75\text{ cm} \qquad (1)$$

In the second case, the rays will first undergo refraction at the curved surface. The image position I after this refraction is given by

$$\frac{\mu}{v} - \frac{1}{\infty} = \frac{\mu-1}{r} \Rightarrow v = \frac{\mu r}{\mu - 1}$$

For the second refraction at the plane surface, I serves as the object; its distance from the plane surface is v – 4 cm. After refraction, the rays will come to focus at F at a distance $\frac{v-4\text{ cm}}{\mu}$, which is given to be 72 cm. Equating, we have

$$\frac{r}{\mu-1} - \frac{4\text{ cm}}{\mu} = 72\text{ cm} \qquad (2)$$

Solving the two equations gives μ = 4/3 and r = 25 cm.

27. (a) When u = –10 cm, v = 10 cm (from the graph). This gives the focal length of the lens as

$$\frac{1}{f} = \frac{1}{v} - \frac{1}{u} = \frac{1}{10\text{ cm}} - \frac{1}{-10\text{ cm}} \Rightarrow f = 5\text{ cm}$$

There are 10 divisions between each 1-cm division. Hence, the least count of the scale is 1 mm. From the lens formula, we have

$$\frac{|\Delta f|}{f^2} = \frac{|\Delta v|}{v^2} + \frac{|\Delta u|}{u^2}$$

$$\Rightarrow \quad \frac{|\Delta f|}{(5\text{ cm})^2} = \frac{1\text{ mm}}{(10\text{ cm})^2} + \frac{1\text{ mm}}{(10\text{ cm})^2}$$

$$\Rightarrow \quad |\Delta f| = 0.05\text{ cm}$$

Hence, the measured focal length is 5.00 cm ± 0.05 cm.

28. (b) The image is framed in the second focal plane of the lens. If the angle subtended by the Sun at the pole of the lens is θ, then the diameter of the circular image will be $d = f\theta$. Thus, $d \propto f \Rightarrow$ Area of the circular image $\propto f^2$.
The intensity depends on the lens aperture, not on its focal length. Covering the lower half of the lens reduces the amount of light entering the lens, and hence, reduces the image intensity but not its size.

29. (b)

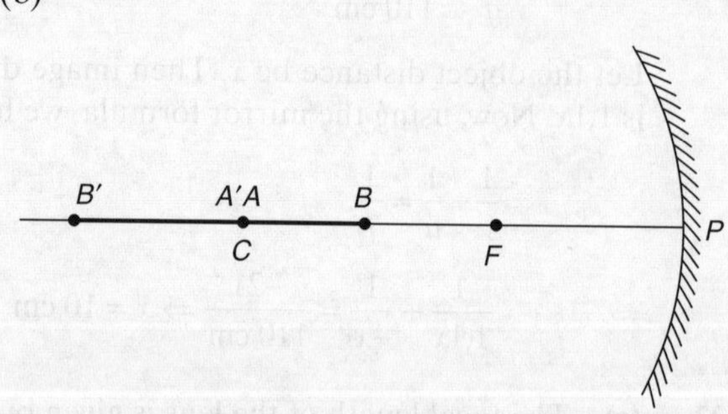

One end A of the rod and its image A' lie at the centre C of the mirror. Since the image of AB is elongated, it means that the other end B lies between centre C and focus F of the mirror; its distance from the pole P (see figure) is $2f - \frac{f}{3} = \frac{5}{3}f$.

The image position B' is given by

$$\frac{1}{v} + \frac{1}{-5f/3} = \frac{1}{-f} \Rightarrow v = -5f/2$$

The length $A'B'$= 5f/2 – 2f = f/2. Hence, magnification equals $\frac{f/2}{f/3} = \frac{3}{2}$.

30. (c)

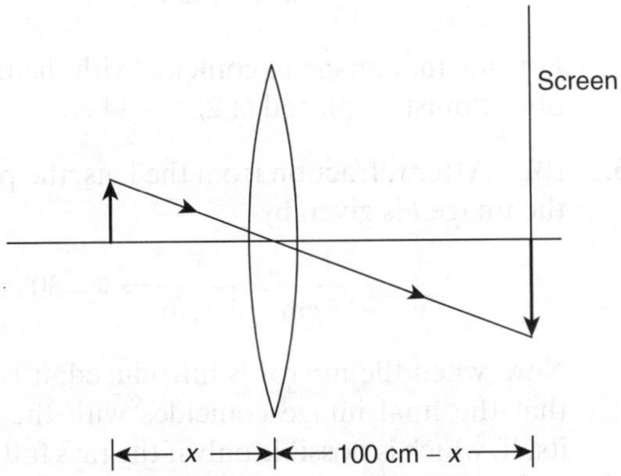

The figure shows the lens position when a red image is obtained on the screen. Using the lens formula, we have

$$\frac{1}{100-x}-\frac{1}{-x}=\frac{1}{21\text{ cm}}$$

$$\Rightarrow \quad \frac{100}{x(100-x)}=\frac{1}{21}$$

$$\Rightarrow \quad x^2-100x+2100=0 \Rightarrow x=30\text{ cm, }70\text{ cm}$$

Thus, there are two positions of the lens. The distance between these positions is d = 70 cm − 30 cm = 40 cm. The magnification is given by $\frac{100\text{ cm}-x}{x}$, which equals 7/3 and 3/7 for the two positions.

31. (a) If R is the radius of the surfaces of the equi-biconvex lens, then its focal length is given by

$$\frac{1}{f_1}=(1.5-1)\frac{2}{R}\Rightarrow f_1=R$$

In the absence of liquid, the object distance must equal f_1 (see figure).

$$\Rightarrow \quad x=R \qquad \ldots(1)$$

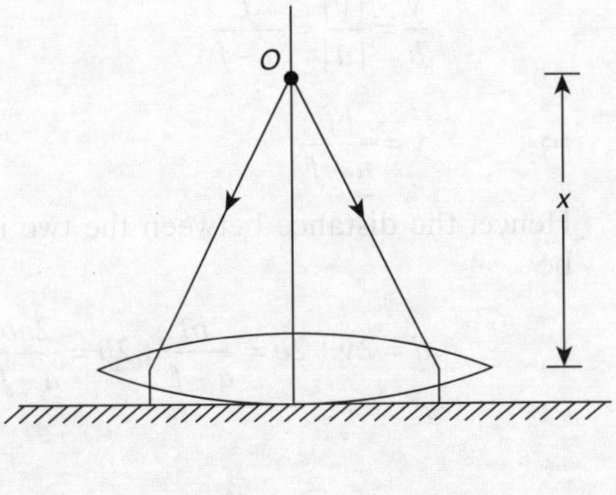

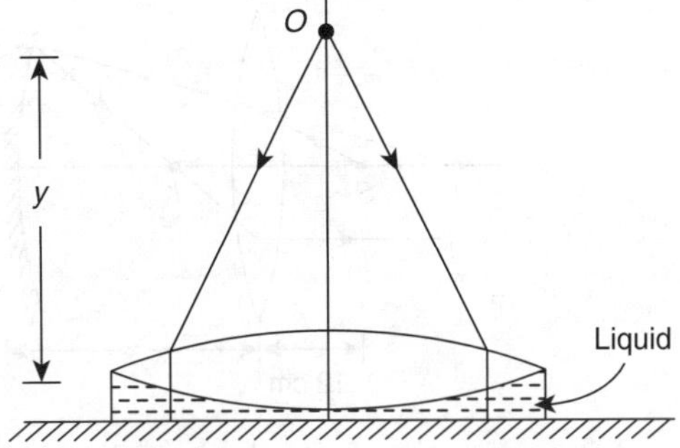

The region filled with liquid behaves like a plano-concave lens (see figure) of focal length f_2 given by

$$\frac{1}{f_2}=(\mu-1)\left(\frac{1}{-R}\right)=\frac{1-\mu}{R}$$

The combined focal length f is given by

$$\frac{1}{f}=\frac{1}{f_1}+\frac{1}{f_2}=\frac{1}{R}+\frac{1-\mu}{R}=\frac{2-\mu}{R}\Rightarrow f=\frac{R}{2-\mu}$$

In the presence of liquid, the object distance equals f

$$\Rightarrow \quad y=\frac{R}{2-\mu} \qquad \ldots(2)$$

Eliminating R from equations (1) and (2), we have

$$\frac{x}{y}=2-\mu\Rightarrow \mu=2-\frac{x}{y}$$

32. (b) Let μ be the refractive index and r be the radius of the curved surface of the lens. If the focal lengths of the lens and the mirrored surface are f_l and f_m, respectively, then the combination behaves as a mirror of focal length f given by

$$\frac{1}{f}=\frac{1}{f_m}-\frac{2}{f_l}\text{, where }\frac{1}{f_l}=\frac{\mu-1}{r}$$

When the plane surface is silvered, $\frac{1}{f_m}=0$ and when the curved surface is silvered, $\frac{1}{f_m}=\frac{2}{-r}$

Thus, we have

$$\frac{1}{-28\text{ cm}}=0-\frac{2(\mu-1)}{r}\Rightarrow\frac{r}{\mu-1}=56\text{ cm} \qquad \ldots(1)$$

$$\frac{1}{-10\text{ cm}}=\frac{2}{-r}-\frac{2(\mu-1)}{r}\Rightarrow\frac{r}{\mu}=20\text{ cm} \qquad \ldots(2)$$

Solving the two equations gives $\mu = 14/9 = 1.55$.

33. (c)

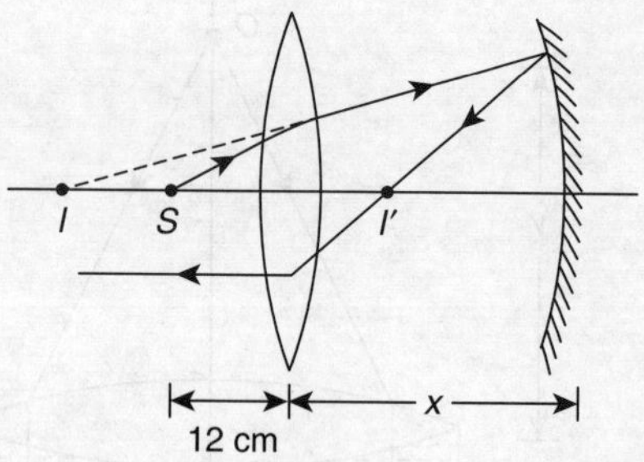

After refraction from the lens, the position I (see figure) of the image is given by

$$\frac{1}{v}-\frac{1}{-12\text{ cm}}=\frac{1}{15\text{ cm}}\Rightarrow v=-60\text{ cm}$$

Now, I behaves as the object for the mirror and I' is its image. The position of I' coincides with the focus of the lens since it is given that the rays finally emerge parallel from the lens. The distances of I and I' from the mirror are $x + 60$ cm and $x - 15$ cm, respectively.

Now, using the mirror formula, we have

$$\frac{1}{-(x+15\text{ cm})}+\frac{1}{-(x+60\text{ cm})}=\frac{1}{-20\text{ cm}}$$

$$\Rightarrow \quad x^2+5x-1800=0$$

$$\Rightarrow \quad x=-45\text{ cm}, 40\text{ cm}$$

Since x cannot be negative, $x = 40$ cm.

34. (d) Let f_1, f_2, and f_m be the focal lengths of the water lens, glass lens and mirror, respectively. Then

$$\frac{1}{f_1}=\left(\frac{4}{3}-1\right)\left(\frac{1}{60\text{ cm}}-\frac{1}{\infty}\right)=\frac{1}{180\text{ cm}}$$

$$\frac{1}{f_2}=\left(\frac{3}{2}-1\right)\left(\frac{1}{-60\text{ cm}}-\frac{1}{-20\text{ cm}}\right)=\frac{1}{60\text{ cm}}$$

$$\frac{1}{f_m}=\frac{2}{-20\text{ cm}}=\frac{-1}{10\text{ cm}}$$

The combination behaves like a mirror of focal length f given by

$$\frac{1}{f}=\frac{1}{f_m}-2\left(\frac{1}{f_1}+\frac{1}{f_2}\right)$$

$$\Rightarrow \quad \frac{1}{f}=\frac{-1}{10\text{ cm}}-2\left(\frac{1}{180\text{ cm}}+\frac{1}{60\text{ cm}}\right)=\frac{-13}{90\text{ cm}}$$

$$\Rightarrow \quad f=\frac{-90}{13}\text{ cm}\simeq -7\text{ cm}$$

For the final image to coincide with the object, the object must be placed at $2f \simeq -14$ cm.

35. (b) After refraction from the lens, the position of the image I is given by

$$\frac{1}{v}-\frac{1}{-15\text{ cm}}=\frac{1}{10\text{ cm}}\Rightarrow v=30\text{ cm}$$

Now, when the mirror is introduced, it is required that the final image coincides with the object O itself, which is possible only if the rays fall normally on the mirror and retrace their path. For this to happen, the position of I must coincide with the centre of the mirror. Thus, the radius of the mirror is 30 cm – 6 cm = 24 cm and hence its focal length is 24 cm/2 = 12 cm.

36. (c) After refraction from the converging lens, the position I of the image is given by

$$\frac{1}{v}-\frac{1}{-15\text{ cm}}=\frac{1}{18\text{ cm}}\Rightarrow v=30\text{ cm}$$

Now I serves as a virtual object for refraction at the diverging lens and I' is the image. The distances of I and I' from the diverging lens are 30 cm – 6 cm = 24 cm and 24 cm + 4 cm = 28 cm, respectively. The focal length f of the diverging lens is given by

$$\frac{1}{28\text{ cm}}-\frac{1}{24\text{ cm}}=\frac{1}{-f}\Rightarrow f=168\text{ cm}$$

37. (a) The image position is given by

$$\frac{1}{v}-\frac{1}{-a}=\frac{1}{f}\Rightarrow v=\frac{af}{a-f}$$

The object S is at a distance b from the principal axis. The distance y of the images S_1 or S_2 from their respective principal axes is given by

$$\frac{y}{b}=\frac{|v|}{|u|}=\frac{f}{a-f}$$

$$\Rightarrow \quad y=\frac{bf}{a-f}$$

Hence, the distance between the two images will be

$$d=2y+2b=\frac{2bf}{a-f}+2b=\frac{2ab}{a-f}$$

38. (d)

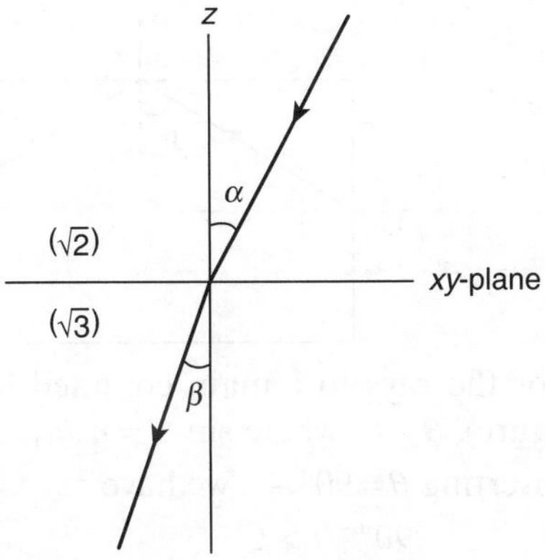

The acute angle α made by the incident ray (see figure) is given by

$$\cos\alpha = \left|\frac{\vec{A}\cdot\hat{k}}{A}\right| = \frac{10}{\sqrt{(6\sqrt{3})^2 + (8\sqrt{3})^2 + 10^2}}$$

$$= \frac{1}{2} \Rightarrow \sin\alpha = \sqrt{3}/2$$

Using Snell's law, we have

$$\sqrt{3}\sin\beta = \sqrt{2}\sin\alpha$$

$$\Rightarrow \quad \sin\beta = 1/\sqrt{2} \Rightarrow \cos\beta = 1/\sqrt{2}$$

If the ray is refracted along vector $\vec{B}$, then the angle it makes with the $+z$-axis is $\pi - \beta$, and it must be coplanar with vector $\vec{A}$ and the z-axis.

$$\Rightarrow \quad \frac{\vec{B}\cdot\hat{k}}{B} = \cos(\pi - \beta) = -1/\sqrt{2} \text{ and } \vec{A}\times\vec{B}\cdot\hat{k} = 0$$

Both these conditions are satisfied only by the vector in option (d).

39. (a)

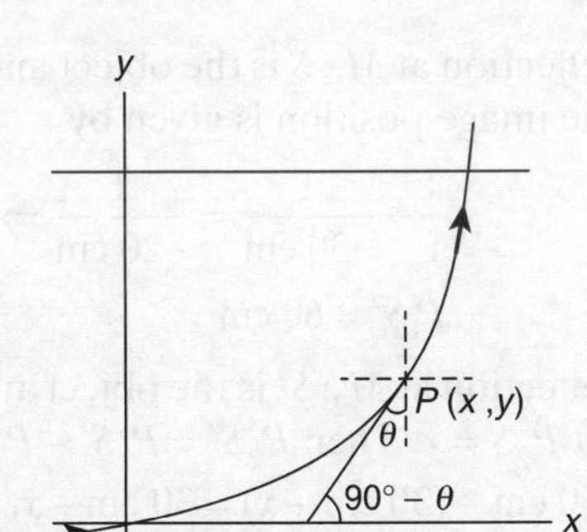

The figure shows some arbitrary point P on the trajectory. Consider a line through P parallel to the x-axis; this line serves as a boundary separating two different media. For a ray arriving at P, if the angle of incidence at this point is θ, then

$$\mu\sin\theta = 1\sin 90° \Rightarrow \sin\theta = 1/\mu$$

Slope of the tangent at this point is $\tan(90° - \theta) = \cot\theta$. Hence

$$\frac{dy}{dx} = \cot\theta = \sqrt{\mu^2 - 1} = \sqrt{y}$$

Solving the above differential equation, we have

$$\int\frac{dy}{\sqrt{y}} = \int dx$$

$$\Rightarrow \quad \sqrt{y} = x + C$$

Since the ray passes through the origin, $C = 0$.

Hence, the equation of the trajectory is $y = \frac{1}{4}x^2$.

40. (a)

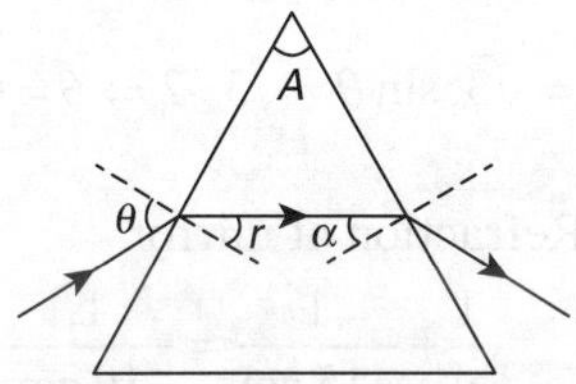

For emergence from the opposite face

$$\alpha < C$$

$$\Rightarrow \quad A - r < C$$

$$\Rightarrow \quad r > A - C$$

$$\Rightarrow \quad \mu\sin r > \mu\sin(A - C)$$

$$\Rightarrow \quad \sin\theta > \mu\sin(A - \text{cosec}^{-1}\mu)$$

[Inserting $C = \sin^{-1}(1/\mu) = \text{cosec}^{-1}\mu$]

41. (b) Let x_1 and x_2 be the two positions of the lens. Then, the magnifications are x_2/x_1 and x_1/x_2, respectively.

Given $\frac{x_2/x_1}{x_1/x_2} = \frac{9}{4} \Rightarrow \frac{x_2}{x_1} = \frac{3}{2}$.

Also given $x_2 - x_1 = 10$ cm. Hence $x_1 = 20$ cm and $x_2 = 30$ cm.

Thus, the distance between the object and the screen is $D = x_1 + x_2 = 20$ cm + 30 cm = 50 cm.

Now, the focal length of the lens is

$$f = \frac{D^2 - (\Delta x)^2}{4D} = \frac{50^2 - 10^2}{4\times 50} = 12 \text{ cm.}$$

42. (b)

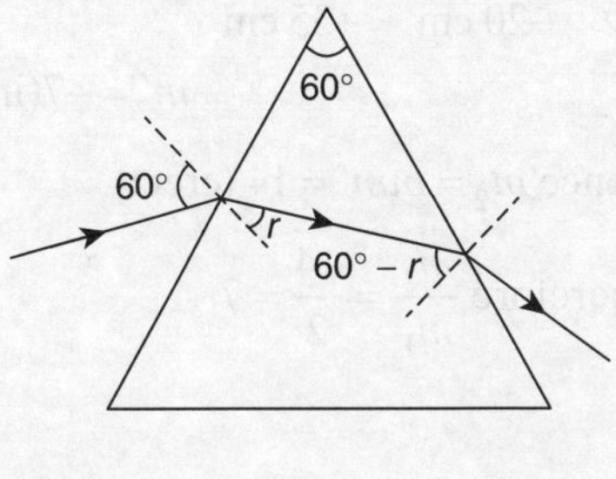

Using Snell's law for refraction at both faces of the prism, we have

$N \sin r = \sin 60° = \sqrt{3}/2$ and $\sin \theta = n \sin (60° - r)$

Eliminating r from the above equations, we have

$$\sin\theta = \frac{\sqrt{3}}{2} n\cos r - \frac{1}{2} n \sin r$$
$$= \frac{\sqrt{3}}{2}\sqrt{n^2 - \frac{3}{4}} - \frac{\sqrt{3}}{4}$$

Now, differentiating both sides with respect to n, we have

$$\cos\theta \frac{d\theta}{dn} = \frac{\sqrt{3}}{2} \cdot \frac{n}{\sqrt{n^2 - 3/4}}$$

For $n = \sqrt{3}$, $\sin\theta = \sqrt{3}/2 \Rightarrow \theta = 60^\circ$ and $\dfrac{d\theta}{dn} = 2$

43. (d) Refraction at mirror:

$$\frac{1}{v} + \frac{1}{-15\text{ cm}} = \frac{1}{-10\text{ cm}} \Rightarrow v = -30\text{ cm and}$$
$$m = -2(\text{inverted})$$

Refraction at the lens: The image from the mirror serves as the object for the lens; its distance from the lens is 50 cm – 30 cm = 20 cm.

$$\frac{1}{v} - \frac{1}{-20\text{ cm}} = \frac{1}{10\text{ cm}} \Rightarrow v = 20\text{ cm and}$$
$$m' = -1(\text{inverted})$$

Hence $m_1 = mm' = 2$ (erect).
In the second case, the focal length of the lens changes to f, given by

$$\frac{1}{f} = \left(\frac{1.5}{7/6} - 1\right)\left(\frac{1}{R_1} - \frac{1}{R_2}\right), \text{ where}$$
$$\frac{1}{10\text{ cm}} = (1.5-1)\left(\frac{1}{R_1} - \frac{1}{R_2}\right)$$
$$\Rightarrow \quad \frac{f}{10} = \frac{1.5-1}{\frac{1.5}{7/6}-1} = \frac{1/2}{2/7} \Rightarrow f = \frac{35}{2}\text{ cm}$$

Refraction at the lens:

$$\frac{1}{v} - \frac{1}{-20\text{ cm}} = \frac{2}{+35\text{ cm}} \Rightarrow v = 140\text{ cm and}$$
$$m' = -7(\text{inverted})$$

Hence $m_2 = mm' = 14$ (erect).

Therefore $\dfrac{m_2}{m_1} = \dfrac{14}{2} = 7$.

44. (d)

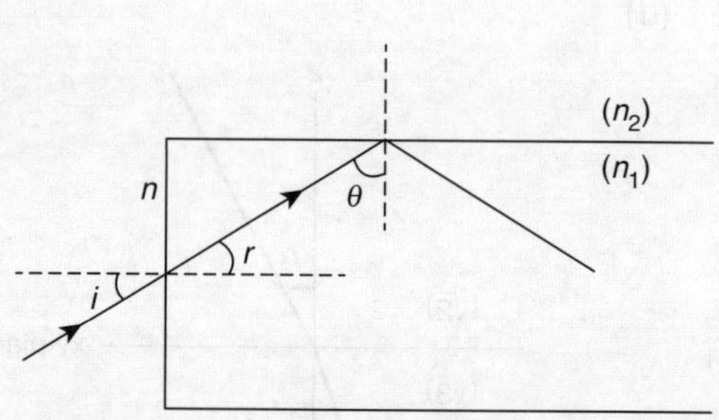

For the rays to remain confined in the core (see figure), $\theta > C$, where $\sin C = n_2/n_1$.
Inserting $\theta = 90° - r$, we have

$$90° - r > C$$
$$\Rightarrow \quad r < 90° - C$$
$$\Rightarrow \quad \sin r < \cos C$$
$$\Rightarrow \quad \frac{n \sin i}{n_1} < \sqrt{1 - \frac{n_2^2}{n_1^2}} \quad [\text{Since } n_1 \sin r = n \sin i]$$
$$\Rightarrow \quad \sin i < \frac{\sqrt{n_1^2 - n_2^2}}{n}$$

Hence $NA = \dfrac{\sqrt{n_1^2 - n_2^2}}{n}$

45. (c)

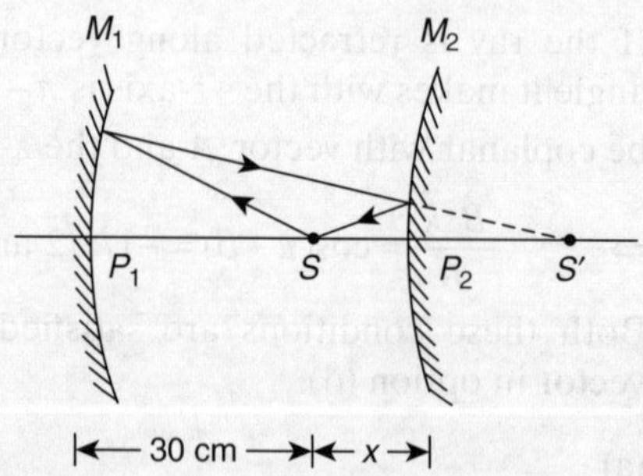

Reflection at M_1: S is the object and S' is the image. The image position is given by

$$\frac{1}{v} + \frac{1}{-30\text{ cm}} = \frac{1}{-20\text{ cm}} \Rightarrow v = -60\text{ cm}$$
$$\Rightarrow \quad P_1S' = 60\text{ cm}$$

Reflection at M_2: S' is the object and S is the image. Let $P_2S = x$. Then $P_2S' = P_1S' - P_1P_2$ = 60 cm – (30 cm + x) = 30 cm – x. Then, we have

$$\frac{1}{30\text{ cm} - x} + \frac{1}{-x} = \frac{1}{20\text{ cm}}$$
$$\Rightarrow \quad x^2 + 10x - 600 = 0$$
$$\Rightarrow \quad x = 20\text{ cm (Neglecting the –ve value)}$$

Hence, the distance between the mirrors is 30 cm + 20 cm = 50 cm.

46. (a), (d) Double image size ⇒ Image distance = 2×30 cm = 60 cm. Hence, the focal length f of the lens is given by

$$\frac{1}{f} = \frac{1}{+60 \text{ cm}} - \frac{1}{-30 \text{ cm}} \Rightarrow f = 20 \text{ cm}$$

The reflected image formed from the convex surface will be erect and virtual. Hence, the radius of curvature R of the convex surface is given by

$$\frac{2}{R} = \frac{1}{10 \text{ cm}} + \frac{1}{-30 \text{ cm}} \Rightarrow R = 30 \text{ cm}$$

Now, we have

$$\frac{1}{f} = (\mu - 1)\frac{1}{R}$$

$$\Rightarrow \quad \mu = \frac{R}{f} + 1 = 2.5$$

47. (b), (c) For a converging lens of focal length f, we have

$$\frac{1}{v} - \frac{1}{u} = \frac{1}{f} \text{ and } \frac{v}{u} = m$$

Eliminating u, we have $m + \frac{v}{f} = 1$

Comparing with the given relation $\frac{m}{a} + \frac{m}{b} = 1$, we have $a = 1$ and $f = b$ (b must be +ve since the lens is converging)

For $m = 2$, $v = -b$ and $u = -b/2 \Rightarrow |u| = b/2$

For $m = 1$, $v = 2b$ and $u = -2b \Rightarrow |u| = 2b$

48. (d) Using Snell's law at the air–liquid interface, we have sin $i = \mu$ sin r. The reflected ray at the liquid–glass interface will undergo maximum polarisation if the angle r (see figure) satisfies $\tan r = \frac{1.5}{\mu}$.

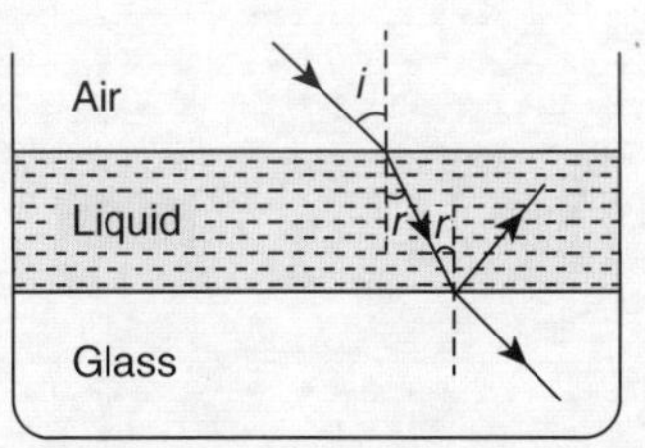

Eliminating r, we have $\sin i = \frac{1.5\mu}{\sqrt{1.5^2 + \mu^2}}$. Now, since sin $i \le 1$, we have

$$(1.5\mu)^2 \le 1.5^2 + \mu^2$$

$$\Rightarrow \quad 1.25\,\mu^2 \le 2.25$$

$$\Rightarrow \quad \mu \le 3/\sqrt{5}$$

49. (d) Let R be the radius of the lens aperture. Let r be the radius of the light patch at a distance of 22 cm from the lens (see figure). Then

$$\frac{r}{2 \text{ cm}} = \frac{R}{20 \text{ cm}} \Rightarrow r = \frac{1}{10}R$$

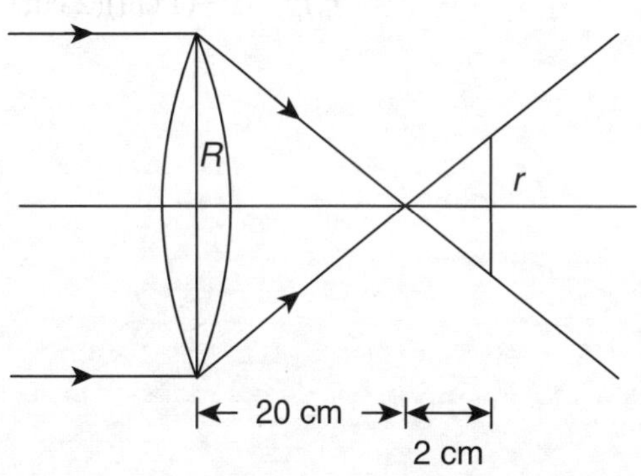

The light energy that is spread over the lens aperture area πR^2 is now concentrated over a circular patch of area $\pi r^2 = \frac{1}{100}\pi R^2$, which is one-hundredth the aperture area. Thus, the light will be hundred times more intense, that is, $100 I_0$.

50. (c) If an object is far away from the eye, the lens must produce a virtual image at the far point 80 cm, which then can be focused by the eye. If f is the focal length of the lens, then

$$\frac{1}{f} = \frac{1}{v} - \frac{1}{u} = \frac{1}{-80 \text{ cm}} - \frac{1}{\infty} = -1.25 \text{ dioptres}$$

51. (d) When the object is at a distance of 25 cm, the lens must form a virtual image at the near point 50 cm, which then can be focussed by the eye. If f is the focal length of the lens, then

$$\frac{1}{f} = \frac{1}{v} - \frac{1}{u} = \frac{1}{-50 \text{ cm}} - \frac{1}{-25 \text{ cm}} = +2.00 \text{ dioptres}$$

52. (a) The angular magnification produced by the telescope is

$$m = \frac{f_0}{f_e} = \frac{90 \text{ cm}}{30 \text{ cm}} = 3$$

The angle subtended by the building without the telescope is

$$\theta = \frac{80 \text{ m}}{2 \text{ km}} = 0.04$$

With the telescope, the angle subtended will be

$$\theta' = m\theta = 3(0.04 \text{ rad}) = 0.120 \text{ rad}$$

53. (d) Distance between the second focal point of the objective and the first focal point of the eyepiece is $s = l - (f_o + f_e) = 23\text{ cm} - 3\text{ cm} = 20\text{ cm}$. The magnification produced by the microscope is

$$m = \frac{s(25\text{ cm})}{f_o f_e} = \frac{(20\text{ cm})(25\text{ cm})}{(1\text{ cm})(2\text{ cm})} = 250$$

If two points separated by distance d are viewed through the microscope, the separation between them is magnified to $250d$. If the magnified separation is 0.10 mm, the eye will be able to distinguish the two points. Thus, we have $250d = 0.10\text{ mm} \Rightarrow d = 0.4\ \mu\text{m}$.

CHAPTER

22

Atomic Physics

- Phenomena like interference, diffraction and polarisation demonstrate the wave nature of electromagnetic radiation. However, phenomena like line spectra, photoelectric effect and production of X-rays demonstrate its particle-like behaviour. We find that the energy of electromagnetic radiation is emitted and absorbed in quanta.

  Planck's Theory of Electromagnetic Radiation states that the energy in an electromagnetic wave is carried in packets called photons or quanta. The energy E of a single photon is proportional to the frequency f of the radiation:

$$E = hf = \frac{hc}{\lambda},$$

  where $h = 6.63\times10^{-34}$ J·s is called Planck's constant, $c = 2.99\times10^8$ m/s is the speed of light in vacuum and $hc = 1240$ eV·nm.

  These photons also carry momentum:

$$p = \frac{h}{\lambda} = \frac{E}{c}$$

- In the photoelectric effect, a metal surface can absorb a photon and emit an electron if the photon energy hf is greater than or equal to the work function $\varnothing$ of that metal.

  The stopping potential V_s for the emitted electrons is given by

$$eV_s = hf - \varnothing = \frac{hc}{\lambda} - \phi$$

  Increasing the frequency of the incident light will require greater stopping potential. Increasing the intensity of the incident light implies an increase in the number of photons striking the metal surface per second per unit area; this causes an increase in the saturation current due to increased emission of electrons per second.

  The frequency f, intensity I and number n of photons striking the metal surface per second per unit area are related as

$$I = n(hf)$$

- **Bohr's Atomic Model for H-like Atoms:** Bohr postulated that the electron moves around the nucleus in certain stable circular orbits, without emitting radiation. The Coulomb force between the protons and the electrons provides the required centripetal force for the circular motion.
  Every physical quantity inside the atom is quantised; they are functions of a natural number n $(n = 1,2,3,\ldots)$, called the principal quantum number corresponding to the orbit in which the electron is moving.

  Angular momentum (L) and magnetic moment (μ):

$$L = n\frac{h}{2\pi} \text{ and}$$

$$\mu = \left(\frac{e}{2m}\right)L = n\mu_0,$$

  where $\mu_0 = \dfrac{eh}{4\pi m} = 9.27\times10^{-24}$ J/T (Bohr magneton).

Radius (r), velocity (v) and energy (E):

$$r = n^2 \frac{r_0}{Z},$$

where $r_0 = \dfrac{\epsilon_0 h^2}{\pi m e^2} = 0.529 \times 10^{-10}$ m

$$v = \frac{Z v_0}{n},$$

where $v_0 = \dfrac{e^2}{2\epsilon_0 h} = 2.19 \times 10^6$ m/s

$$E = -\frac{Z^2 E_0}{n^2},$$

where $E_0 = \dfrac{me^4}{8\epsilon_0^2 h^2} = 13.60$ eV

Kinetic energy $K = -E$ and potential energy $U = 2E$.

- When an atom de-excites from a higher energy state n_i to a lower energy state n_f, a photon is emitted with energy equal to the energy difference between $|\Delta E| = Z^2 E_0 \left(\dfrac{1}{n_f^2} - \dfrac{1}{n_i^2} \right)$ the two states. Its wavelength $\lambda = |\Delta E| / hc$ is given by

$$\frac{1}{\lambda} = RZ^2 \left(\frac{1}{n_f^2} - \frac{1}{n_i^2} \right),$$

where $R = \dfrac{E_0}{hc} = \dfrac{me^4}{8\epsilon_0^2 ch^3} = 1.097 \times 10^7\ \text{m}^{-1}$; here, m is the electron's mass.

The spectral series for the hydrogen atom is named after its discoverers, as

Lyman series: $\dfrac{1}{\lambda} = RZ^2 \left(\dfrac{1}{1^2} - \dfrac{1}{n^2} \right)$, $n = 2, 3, \ldots$ (ultra-violet range)

Balmer series: $\dfrac{1}{\lambda} = RZ^2 \left(\dfrac{1}{2^2} - \dfrac{1}{n^2} \right)$, $n = 3, 4, \ldots$ (visible range)

Paschen series: $\dfrac{1}{\lambda} = RZ^2 \left(\dfrac{1}{3^2} - \dfrac{1}{n^2} \right)$, $n = 4, 5, \ldots$ (infra-red range)

Brackett series: $\dfrac{1}{\lambda} = RZ^2 \left(\dfrac{1}{4^2} - \dfrac{1}{n^2} \right)$, $n = 5, 6, \ldots$ (infra-red range)

Pfund series: $\dfrac{1}{\lambda} = RZ^2 \left(\dfrac{1}{5^2} - \dfrac{1}{n^2} \right)$, $n = 6, 7, \ldots$ (infra-red range)

Energy ΔE is required to excite an atom from a lower energy state n_i to a higher energy state n_f. The energy required to take the lone electron completely out of the atom is called its ionisation energy:

$$\text{IE} = (13.60\ \text{eV}) Z^2$$

- X-rays are electromagnetic radiations of wavelength ranging between 0.001 nm and 1 nm. Such short wavelength radiations are produced when electrons accelerated to a potential difference of the order of 10^3 V to 10^6 V strike a metal target.

  The X-ray spectra is continuous, with a minimum wavelength determined by the accelerating voltage V:

$$\lambda_{min} = \frac{hc}{eV}$$

  The X-ray spectra has two peaks which are characteristic of the metal target. One of these peaks, which is the most intense wavelength in the spectra, corresponds to the K_α $(n = 2 \rightarrow n = 1)$ transition.

  For a metal target with atomic number Z, the wavelength of this line is given by

$$\lambda_{K_\alpha} = \frac{4}{3R(Z-1)^2}$$

  Moseley expressed the above relationship in terms of frequency:

$$\sqrt{f_{K_\alpha}} = \sqrt{\frac{3cR}{4}}(Z-1)$$

  In words, Moseley's law states that the square root of the frequency of the K_α line is directly proportional to $Z-1$.

- **Wave–Particle Duality:** The wave description and particle description are complementary. That is, we need both descriptions to complete our model of nature. However, we will never need to use both descriptions at the same time to describe a phenomenon.

  Considering the dual behaviour of light, de Broglie proclaimed a similar dualistic behaviour for particles. He postulated that a free particle moving with momentum p should have a related wavelength

$$\lambda = h/p$$

  The frequency f, according to de Broglie, is related to the particle's energy E as

$$f = E/h$$

  The waves associated with moving particles are called matter waves. The velocity of a matter wave has no physical significance. The product λf represents nothing in case of matter waves.

  The de Broglie wavelength associated with the electron in an H-like atom in its nth state is given by

$$\lambda_n = n\frac{\lambda_0}{Z},$$

$$\text{where } \lambda_0 = 2\pi r_0 = 3.322 \times 10^{-10} \text{ m}$$

  Electron diffraction experiments in which accelerated electrons striking the surface of a nickel crystal were found to be scattered in a particular direction confirms the wave nature of particles. Scattering in a particular direction is due to the constructive interference of electrons scattered from different layers of the regularly spaced atoms of the crystal; this experiment was conducted by Davisson and Germer, and by Thomson.

EXERCISES

1. When a point source of light is at a distance of 50 cm from a photoelectric cell, the cut-off voltage and the saturation current are found to be V_0 and I_0, respectively. If the same source is placed at a distance of 1 m from the cell, these values will be:
(a) $V_0/4, I_0$ (b) $V_0, I_0/4$
(c) $V_0/2, I_0/4$ (d) V_0, I_0

2. A 1.5-mW source emitting light of wavelength 400 nm is directed at a photoelectric cell. If 0.10% of the incident photons produces photoelectrons, the current in the cell is (take $hc = 1240$ eV·nm):
(a) 2.0 μA (b) 1.5 μA
(c) 0.5 μA (d) 0.1 μA

3. A silver ball (work function of silver = 4.7 eV) of radius 1 cm is suspended by a string in a vacuum chamber and is illuminated with ultraviolet light of wavelength 200 nm. The total number of photoelectrons emitted from the ball is of the order (take $hc = 1240$ eV·nm and $\frac{1}{4\pi\varepsilon_0} = 9\times10^9\ \text{N}\cdot\text{m}^2/\text{C}^2$):
(a) 10^{10} (b) 10^9
(c) 10^8 (d) 10^7

4. A metal surface is illuminated by light of two different wavelengths, 248 nm and 310 nm. The maximum speed of the photoelectrons corresponding to these wavelengths are v_1 and v_2, respectively. If the ratio $v_1 : v_2 = 2:1$ and $hc = 1240$ eV·nm, the work function of the metal is nearly equal to:
(a) 3.7 eV (b) 3.2 eV
(c) 2.8 eV (d) 2.5 eV

5. Radiation of wavelength λ is incident on a photocell. The fastest emitted electron has speed v. When the wavelength is changed to $3\lambda/4$, the speed of the fastest emitted electron is v'. Then the correct statement from the following is:
(a) $v' = \sqrt{\frac{4}{3}}v$
(b) $v' = \sqrt{\frac{8}{3}}v$
(c) $v' < \sqrt{\frac{4}{3}}v$
(d) $v' > \sqrt{\frac{4}{3}}v$

6. In an experiment to determine Planck's constant, a metal surface was irradiated by light of two different wavelengths, 0.3 μm and 0.4 μm. The corresponding stopping potentials were measured as 2.0 V and 1.0 V. The value of Planck's constant determined from this experiment is ($c = 3\times10^8$ m/s and $e = 1.6\times10^{-19}$ C):
(a) 6.2×10^{-34} Js
(b) 6.4×10^{-34} Js
(c) 6.6×10^{-34} Js
(d) 6.8×10^{-34} Js

7. The wavelength of K_α line of an element of atomic number 41 is λ. Then the wavelength of K_α line of an element of atomic number 21 is:
(a) 4λ (b) $\lambda/4$
(c) 3λ (d) $2\lambda/3$

8. The de Broglie wavelength of a neutron at 927°C is λ. Its wavelength at 27°C will be:
(a) $\lambda/2$ (b) λ
(c) 2λ (d) 4λ

9. A proton when accelerated through a potential difference of V has wavelength λ associated with it. If an α particle is to have the same wavelength, it must be accelerated through a potential difference:
(a) $V/8$ (b) $V/4$
(c) $4V$ (d) $8V$

10. The potential energy U of a moving particle of mass m varies with x, as shown in the figure. The de Broglie wavelength of the particle in the regions $0 \le x \le 1$ and $x > 1$ are λ_1 and λ_2, respectively.

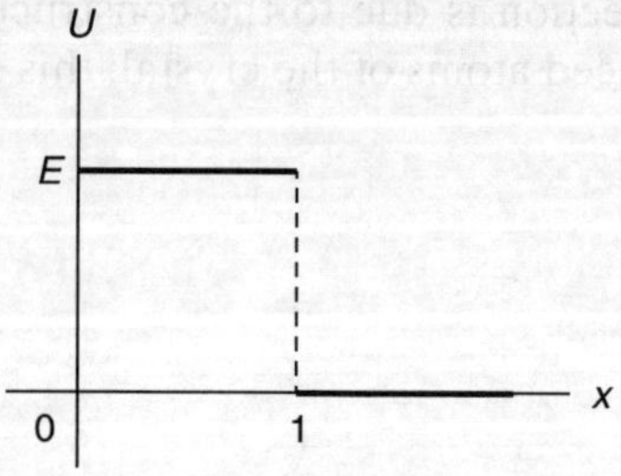

If the total energy of the particle is cE ($c > 1$), the ratio λ_1 / λ_2 is:

(a) $\frac{\sqrt{c-1}}{\sqrt{c+1}}$

(b) $\sqrt{\frac{c}{c-1}}$

(c) $\frac{\sqrt{c-1}}{\sqrt{c}}$

(d) $\frac{\sqrt{c}}{\sqrt{c-1}}$

11. A hydrogen atom in the ground state is irradiated by light of wavelength 970 Å. Taking $hc = 1237$ eV·nm and ground state energy of the hydrogen atom as −13.6 eV, the number of lines present in the emission spectrum is:
(a) 1 (b) 3
(c) 6 (d) 10

12. A triply ionised beryllium (Be^{+++}) atom has the same orbital radius as that of the ground state of a hydrogen (H) atom. If E_1 and E_2 denote the energies of the Be^{+++} and H atoms, respectively, then the ratio E_1 / E_2 equals:
(a) 1 (b) 2
(c) 3 (d) 4

13. The energy of a hydrogen atom in its ground state is −13.6 eV. The kinetic energy and the potential energy of the electron in the first excited state of a singly ionised helium (He^+) atom are, respectively:
(a) 6.8 eV, −20.4 eV
(b) 13.6 eV, −27.2 eV
(c) 13.6 eV, −40.8 eV
(d) 27.2 eV, −54.4 eV

14. When a hydrogen atom is in energy state E, λ is the de Broglie wavelength and B is the magnetic field at the centre of the atom associated with the orbital motion of the electron. If the atom is excited to energy state $E/4$, the respective values of de Broglie wavelength and magnetic field are:
(a) $\lambda/4, 8B$ (b) $2\lambda, B/16$
(c) $\lambda/4, 16B$ (d) $2\lambda, B/8$

15. The electron in a hydrogen atom moves from state n_1 to n_2. The time period of the electron in the initial state is 8 times that in the final state. The possible values of n_1 and n_2 are:
(a) $n_1 = 4, n_2 = 8$ (b) $n_1 = 8, n_2 = 2$
(c) $n_1 = 8, n_2 = 1$ (d) $n_1 = 6, n_2 = 3$

16. Energy levels A and C have energies in increasing order. If λ_1, λ_2 and λ_3 are the wavelengths of radiations corresponding to transitions $C-B$, $B-A$ and $C-A$, respectively, then the correct relation from the following is:
(a) $\lambda_3 = \lambda_1 + \lambda_2$
(b) $\lambda_3 = \sqrt{\lambda_1 \lambda_2}$
(c) $\frac{1}{\lambda_3} = \frac{1}{\lambda_1} + \frac{1}{\lambda_2}$
(d) None of these

17. Energy of 24.6 eV is required to remove one of the electrons from a neutral helium atom. The energy required to remove both the electrons from a neutral helium atom is (ionisation energy for hydrogen atom = 13.6 eV):
(a) 38.2 eV (b) 49.2 eV
(c) 51.8 eV (d) 79.0 eV

18. Imagine an atom made up of a proton and a particle of double the mass of the electron, but having the same charge as the electron. If we consider all possible de-excitations of this atom to the first excited level ($n = 2$), the longest wavelength that will be emitted is (in terms of R for the normal hydrogen atom):
(a) $\frac{4}{5R}$ (b) $\frac{12}{5R}$
(c) $\frac{18}{5R}$ (d) $\frac{36}{5R}$

19. A photoelectric material having work function ϕ is illuminated by light of wavelength λ ($\lambda < hc/\phi$). The fastest emitted electron has a de Broglie wavelength λ_d. A change $\Delta\lambda$ in wavelength of the incident light results in a change $\Delta\lambda_d$ of the de Broglie wavelength. The ratio $\Delta\lambda_d / \Delta\lambda$ is proportional to:
(a) λ_d / λ (b) λ_d^2 / λ^2
(c) λ_d^3 / λ^2 (d) λ_d^2 / λ

20. Let λ_n be the de Broglie wavelength of the electron in a hydrogen atom in its nth state. If λ is the wavelength of the emitted photon in the transition of the atom from the nth state to the ground state, then for large n (A and B are positive constants):

(a) $\lambda = A + \frac{B}{\lambda_n^2}$

(b) $\lambda = A + B\lambda_n^2$

(c) $\lambda^2 = A + \frac{B}{\lambda_n^2}$

(d) $\lambda^2 = A + B\lambda_n^2$

21. Electron transfer takes place from one neutral atom to another placed distance d apart. If the electric potential energy loss results in the emission of a photon, its wavelength is:

(a) $\frac{4\pi\varepsilon_0 chd}{e^2}$

(b) $\frac{4\pi\varepsilon_0 d}{e^2 ch}$

(c) $\frac{chd}{4\pi\varepsilon_0 e^2}$

(d) $\frac{e^2 chd}{4\pi\varepsilon_0}$

22. A hydrogen atom makes a completely inelastic collision with another stationary hydrogen atom. The minimum kinetic energy of the moving hydrogen atom so that a photon is emitted in the process is (energy of hydrogen atom in ground state = −13.6 eV):

(a) 54.4 eV (b) 30.6 eV
(c) 27.2 eV (d) 20.4 eV

23. Consider a singly ionised helium atom (He^+) with its lone electron in its nth orbital. An electromagnetic radiation of wavelength 90 nm is used to doubly ionise the atom. If the kinetic energy of the ejected electron is 10.4eV, then the value of n is (take $hc = 1240$ eV·nm):

(a) 2 (b) 3
(c) 4 (d) 5

24. An electron in an excited state of Li^{++} ion has angular momentum $3h/2\pi$. If the de Broglie wavelength in this excited state is $m\pi r_0$, where r_0 is the Bohr radius, then the value of m is:

(a) 2 (b) 3
(c) 4 (d) 5

25. An electron is confined to move in a straight line in between the walls of a closed cubical box of side a. Consider the electron to behave like a wave, forming a standing wave pattern similar to that in a taut string fixed at both ends. In that case, the kinetic energy that the electron can have is quantised. If the electron is irradiated with light, the minimum frequency that the electron will absorb if it is in ground state is (mass of electron = m and Planck's constant = h):

(a) $\frac{3h}{\pi^2 ma^2}$

(b) $\frac{3h}{8ma^2}$

(c) $\frac{5h}{16ma^2}$

(d) $\frac{3\pi^2 h}{2ma^2}$

26. The highlight of Bohr's theory is the quantisation of angular momentum. If we apply the same rule to the rotational motion of a CO molecule, we can obtain permissible values for its rotational kinetic energy. If f is the minimum frequency of light required to excite the molecule from its ground state, the rotational inertia of the molecule about an axis passing through its centre of mass and perpendicular to its bond axis is (Planck's constant = h):

(a) $\frac{3\pi^2 h}{4f}$

(b) $\frac{3\pi^2 h}{16f}$

(c) $\frac{5h}{16\pi^2 f}$

(d) $\frac{3h}{8\pi^2 f}$

27. When voltage applied to an X-ray tube is increased from $V_1 = 10$ kV to $V_2 = 20$ kV, the wavelength interval between the K_α line and the short-wave cut-off of the continuous X-ray spectrum increases by a factor of $n = 3$ (take $chR = 13.6$ eV):

(a) 29 (b) 32
(c) 40 (d) 52

28. In a standard Young's double-slit arrangement, fast moving electrons are allowed to enter the two slits instead of light. Fringes are observed on the screen, thus confirming the wave nature of particles and de Broglie's hypothesis. The distance between the slits is $d = 10^{-4}$ m, and distance of the screen from the plane of the slits is $D = 1.0$ m. Before entering the slits, if the electrons are accelerated through potential $V = 15$ kV from negligible initial kinetic energy, then the fringe width will be (take $h^2/2m = 1.5\ \text{eV}\cdot(\text{nm})^2$ where m is mass of electron and h is Planck's constant):

(a) 10 nm (b) 50 nm
(c) 100 nm (d) 150 nm

29. For a K_α X-ray photon to be emitted from molybdenum $(Z = 42)$, the required accelerating potential (the nearest integer) in kV is (take $chR = 13.6$ eV):

(a) 7 kV (b) 10 kV
(c) 15 kV (d) 17 kV

ANSWER KEYS

1. (b)	**2.** (c)	**3.** (d)	**4.** (a)	**5.** (d)	**6.** (b)	**7.** (a)	**8.** (c)	**9.** (a)	**10.** (b)
11. (c)	**12.** (d)	**13.** (b)	**14.** (d)	**15.** (d)	**16.** (c)	**17.** (d)	**18.** (c)	**19.** (c)	**20.** (a)
21. (a)	**22.** (d)	**23.** (c)	**24.** (a)	**25.** (b)	**26.** (d)	**27.** (a)	**28.** (c)	**29.** (d)	

SOLUTIONS

1. (b) Intensity I is proportional to $1/r^2$, where r is the distance from the point source. When r is doubled, I is reduced to one-fourth. Hence, the current reduces to $I_0/4$ since the number of photoelectrons emitted per second is directly proportional to the intensity of light. However, the cut-off voltage remains V_0 since the cut-off voltage depends upon the frequency and not on the intensity of the light.

2. (c) Energy of each incident photon

$$E = \frac{hc}{\lambda}$$

$$= \frac{1240\ \text{eV}\cdot\text{nm}}{4\ \text{nm}} = 3.1\ \text{eV}$$

Number of photons incident per sec

$$N = \frac{1.5\ \text{mW}}{3.1\ \text{eV}}$$

$$\approx 0.5\ \text{mA/e}$$

Number of electrons emitted per sec $N_e = 0.1\ \%\ N \approx 0.5\ \mu\text{A/e}$

Current I is the charge flow per sec. Hence, $I = eN_e \approx 0.5\ \mu\text{A}$

3. (d) Energy of each incident photon

$$= \frac{hc}{\lambda} = \frac{1240\ \text{eV}\cdot\text{nm}}{200\ \text{nm}}$$

$$= 6.2\ \text{eV}$$

Maximum kinetic energy of the emitted electrons $= 6.2\ \text{eV} - 4.7\ \text{eV} = 1.5\ \text{eV} = 1.5$ eV. As electrons are emitted from the silver ball, it acquires a positive potential. If V is the potential, then electron emission will take place as long as $KE_{\text{max}} > eV$. Electron emission will stop when the potential of the silver ball reaches

$$V = \frac{K.E_{\text{max}}}{e} = \frac{1.5\ \text{eV}}{e}$$

$$= 1.5\ \text{V}$$

If n is the number of electrons emitted from the ball, then

$$\frac{ne}{4\pi\varepsilon_0 r} = 1.5V$$

$$\Rightarrow \quad n = \frac{(1.5\ \text{V})(10^{-2}\ \text{m})}{(9\times10^9\ \text{N}\cdot\text{m}^2/\text{C}^2)(1.6\times10^{-19}\ \text{C})}$$

$$= \frac{150}{144}\times10^7$$

4. (a) Let ϕ be the work function of the metal. If the maximum speeds are in the ratio 2:1, the maximum kinetic energies will be in the ratio 4:1. Then, we have

$$\frac{\dfrac{hc}{\lambda_1} - \phi}{\dfrac{hc}{\lambda_2} - \phi} = \frac{4}{1}$$

$$\Rightarrow \quad \frac{\frac{1240}{248}\text{eV}-\phi}{\frac{1240}{310}\text{eV}-\phi}=4$$

$$\Rightarrow \quad 5eV-\phi=4(4eV-\phi)$$

$$\Rightarrow \quad \phi=3.7\text{ eV}$$

5. (d) Let ϕ be the work function of the metal. Then, we have

$$\frac{1}{2}mv^2=\frac{hc}{\lambda}-\phi \qquad \ldots(1)$$

and $$\frac{1}{2}mv'^2=\frac{4hc}{3\lambda}-\phi \qquad \ldots(2)$$

Subtracting the two equations, we have

$$v'^2=v^2+\frac{2hc}{3m\lambda}$$

Now, since $\frac{hc}{\lambda}>\frac{1}{2}mv^2$, the above equation reduces to

$$v'^2>v^2+\frac{1}{3}v^2=\frac{4}{3}v^2$$

$$\Rightarrow \quad v'>\sqrt{\frac{4}{3}}v$$

6. (b) We have

$$eV_1=\frac{hc}{\lambda_1}-\phi \text{ and } eV_2=\frac{hc}{\lambda_2}-\phi$$

Subtracting the two equations, we have

$$e\Delta V=\Delta hc\left(\frac{1}{\lambda}\right)$$

$$\Rightarrow \quad e(1V)=hc\left(\frac{1}{0.3\ \mu m}-\frac{1}{0.4\ \mu m}\right)$$

$$=\frac{hc}{1.2\ \mu m}$$

$$\Rightarrow \quad h=\frac{(1.2\ \mu\text{m})(1.6\times10^{-19}\text{ C})(1\text{ V})}{(3\times10^8\text{ m/s})}$$

$$=6.4\times10^{-34}\text{ Js}$$

7. (a) From Moseley's law, we have

$$f_{K_\alpha}\propto(Z-1)^2$$

$$\Rightarrow \quad \lambda_{K_\alpha}\propto\frac{1}{(Z-1)^2}$$

Let λ' be the wavelength of the K_α line of the element whose atomic number is 21. Then, we have

$$\frac{\lambda'}{\lambda}=\frac{(41-1)^2}{(21-1)^2}=4$$

$$\Rightarrow \quad \lambda'=4\lambda$$

8. (c) The mean speed v of the neutrons is proportional to $\sqrt{T}$. The de Broglie wavelength λ is given by

$$\lambda=\frac{h}{mv}\propto\frac{1}{\sqrt{T}}$$

If λ' is the de Broglie wavelength at 27°C, we have

$$\frac{\lambda'}{\lambda}=\frac{\sqrt{273+927}}{\sqrt{273+27}}=2$$

$$\Rightarrow \quad \lambda'=2\lambda$$

9. (a) For a particle of mass m and charge q, accelerated though potential V, the corresponding de Broglie wavelength λ is given by

$$\lambda=\frac{h}{\sqrt{2mK}}=\frac{h}{\sqrt{2mqV}}$$

For the same wavelength, we see that mqV is a constant $\Rightarrow V\propto\frac{1}{qm}$

The product of charge number and mass number of a proton and an α particle are 1 and 8, respectively. If V' is the accelerating potential required for the α particle, then

$$\frac{V'}{V}=\frac{1}{8}$$

$$\Rightarrow \quad V'=\frac{1}{8}V$$

10. (b) The respective kinetic energies in the regions $0<x<1$ and $x>1$ are $K_1=(c-1)E$ and $K_2=cE$. The corresponding de Broglie wavelengths are

$$\lambda_1=\frac{h}{\sqrt{2mK_1}} \text{ and}$$

$$\lambda_2=\frac{h}{\sqrt{2mK_2}}$$

Hence, we have $\frac{\lambda_1}{\lambda_2}=\sqrt{\frac{K_2}{K_1}}=\sqrt{\frac{c}{c-1}}$

11. (c) Energy of incident wavelength

$$=\frac{hc}{\lambda}=\frac{1237}{97}\text{eV}=12.75\text{ eV}$$

Energy of the atom after absorption of light = –13.6 eV + 12.75 eV = –0.84 eV

Energy to excite it to $n = 4$ state (–0. 85 eV)

Hence number of lines in emission spectrum $= {}^4_2C = 6$.

12. (d) The permissible orbit radii and energy levels for a Be^{+++} atom are, respectively

$$r = \frac{n^2}{4} r_0 \text{ and}$$

$$E = \frac{4^2}{n^2} E_0,$$

where r_0 and E_0 are the radius and energy, respectively, of the H atom in ground state.

Now, $r = r_0$ when $n = 2$. Hence

$$\frac{E_1}{E_2} = \frac{\left(\frac{4^2}{2^2}\right) E_0}{E_0} = 4$$

13. (b) Permissible energies of the He^+ atom are given by

$$E = \frac{2^2}{n^2}(-13.6 \text{ eV})$$

In the first excited state, that is, $n = 2$, the energy of the atom is

$$E = \frac{2^2}{2^2}(-13.6 \text{ eV})$$
$$= -13.6 \text{ eV}$$

The values of kinetic energy and potential energy are, respectively,

$$K = |E| = 13.6 \text{ eV and } U = 2E = -27.2 \text{ eV}.$$

14. (d) The permissible energies, de Broglie wavelengths and magnetic fields at the centre of an H atom are, respectively, given by

$$E \propto \frac{1}{n^2},$$

$$\lambda = \frac{h}{mv} \propto n,$$

$$B = \frac{\mu_0 I}{2r}$$

$$= \frac{\mu_0}{2r}\frac{ev}{2\pi r} \propto \frac{v}{r^2} \propto \frac{1}{n^3}.$$

Since $E \propto 1/n^2$, therefore if n_1 and n_2 are quantum members corresponding to energy states E and $E/4$, then

$$\frac{n_2}{n_1} = \frac{\sqrt{E_1}}{\sqrt{E_2}} = 2$$

Since $\lambda \propto n$, therefore de Broglie wavelength becomes 2λ.

Since $B \propto 1/n^3$, therefore magnetic field at the centre becomes $B/2^3 = B/32$.

15. (d) The time period of revolution for the nth orbit is given by

$$T = \frac{2\pi r}{v} \propto \frac{n^2}{1/n} = n^3$$

Since T has reduced to one-eighth, the value of n must have reduced to half. Only (d) is correct.

16. (c) Let ΔE_1, ΔE_2, ΔE_3 be the energy differences between $C - B$, $B - A$ and $C - A$, respectively. Then $\Delta E_3 = \Delta E_1 + \Delta E_2$

$$\Rightarrow \quad \frac{hc}{\lambda_3} = \frac{hc}{\lambda_1} + \frac{hc}{\lambda_2}$$

$$\Rightarrow \quad \frac{1}{\lambda_3} = \frac{1}{\lambda_1} + \frac{1}{\lambda_2}$$

17. (d) After the first electron is removed, the He^+ ion is reduced to a H-like atom. Ionisation energy for the He^+ atom can now be determined using

$$I.E. = Z^2 (13.6 \text{ eV})$$
$$= 2^2 (13.6 \text{ eV}) = 54.4 \text{ eV}$$

Hence, the total energy required to remove both electrons is 54.4 eV + 24.6 eV = 79.0 eV.

18. (c) The Rydberg's constant $R = \dfrac{me^4}{8\varepsilon_0^2 ch^3}$ is proportional to m (mass of electron). The Rydberg's constant for the given atom will be $2R$. The longest wavelength for the given electron corresponds to $n = 3 \rightarrow n = 2$ de-excitation. This wavelength λ is given by

$$\frac{1}{\lambda} = 2R\left(\frac{1}{2^2} - \frac{1}{3^2}\right) = \frac{5R}{18}$$

$$\Rightarrow \quad \lambda = \frac{18}{5R}$$

19. (c) The maximum kinetic energy of the emitted photoelectron is

$$K = \frac{hc}{\lambda} - \phi \qquad \text{...(1)}$$

The corresponding de Broglie wavelength is given by

$$\lambda_d = \frac{h}{p} = \frac{h}{\sqrt{2mK}}$$

$$\Rightarrow \quad K = \frac{h^2}{2m\lambda_d^2} \quad \text{...(2)}$$

From the above equations, we have

$$\frac{h^2}{2m\lambda_d^2} = \frac{hc}{\lambda} - \phi$$

Now, taking the differential, we have

$$\frac{-h^2}{m\lambda_d^3}\Delta\lambda_d = \frac{-hc}{\lambda^2}\Delta\lambda$$

$$\Rightarrow \quad \frac{\Delta\lambda_d}{\Delta\lambda} \propto \frac{\lambda_d^3}{\lambda^2}$$

20. (a) For an H atom, the de Broglie wavelength corresponding to the nth state is $\lambda_n = n\lambda_0$. Wavelength of the emitted photon during de-excitation from the nth state to the ground state is given by

$$\frac{1}{\lambda} = R\left(\frac{1}{1^2} - \frac{1}{n^2}\right)$$

$$\Rightarrow \quad \lambda = \frac{1}{R}\left(1 - \frac{1}{n^2}\right)^{-1}$$

$$\Rightarrow \quad \lambda = \frac{1}{R}\left(1 + \frac{1}{n^2}\right) \quad \text{[For large } n\text{]}$$

$$\Rightarrow \quad \lambda = \frac{1}{R}\left(1 + \frac{\lambda_0^2}{\lambda_n^2}\right)$$

$$\Rightarrow \quad \lambda = A + \frac{B}{\lambda_n^2}$$

21. (a) Initially the two atoms are neutral, and in the final state, one of them has charge $+e$ and the other has charge $-e$. Thus, the electrostatic potential energy changes from 0 to $\frac{-e^2}{4\pi\varepsilon_n d}$. The potential energy loss is $\frac{e^2}{4\pi\varepsilon_0 d}$. The wavelength λ of the emitted photon is given by

$$\frac{hc}{\lambda} = \frac{e^2}{4\pi\varepsilon_0 d}$$

$$\Rightarrow \quad \lambda = \frac{4\pi\varepsilon_0 dch}{e^2}$$

22. (d) Let v be the velocity of the moving H atom. Then velocity of the combined atoms after collision will be $v/2$. If m is the mass of the hydrogen atoms, then loss in kinetic energy is

$$\Delta K = \frac{1}{2}mv^2 - \frac{1}{2}(2m)\left(\frac{v}{2}\right)^2$$

$$= \frac{1}{4}mv^2 = \frac{1}{2}K$$

For photon emission, the loss in kinetic energy must equal the first excitation energy of the H atom, which is $13.6\text{ eV}\left(\frac{1}{1^2} - \frac{1}{2^2}\right) = 10.2\text{ eV}$. Hence, we have $\frac{1}{2}K = 10.2\text{ eV}$

$$\Rightarrow \quad K = 20.4\text{ eV}$$

23. (c) Energy required to ionise the He atom, which is already in its nth energy state is $\frac{2^2(13.6\text{ eV})}{n^2}$.

Energy of the incident photon is

$$\frac{1240\text{ eV}\cdot\text{nm}}{90\text{ nm}} = 13.8\text{ eV}.$$

Hence, we have

$$13.8\text{ eV} - 10.4\text{ eV} = \frac{13.6\text{ eV}\times 4}{n^2}$$

$$\Rightarrow \quad n = 4$$

24. (a) Angular momentum is given to be $3h/2\pi$, which means the electron is in the third orbit. When the electron is in its nth orbit, the corresponding de Broglie wavelength is

$$\lambda = \frac{2\pi r}{n}$$

$$= \frac{2\pi}{n}\left(\frac{n^2 r_0}{Z}\right)$$

$$= \frac{n}{Z}(2\pi r_0)$$

Putting $Z = 3$ and $n = 3$, we have $\lambda = 2\pi r_0$

$$\Rightarrow \quad m = 2.$$

25. (b) For standing waves, the length of the box must contain integral multiples of $\lambda/2$.

Thus, we have

$$a = n\left(\frac{\lambda}{2}\right)$$
$$= n\left(\frac{h}{2p}\right) \quad n = 1,2,\ldots$$

$$\Rightarrow \quad p = n\left(\frac{h}{2a}\right) \quad n = 1,2,\ldots$$

$$\Rightarrow \quad K = \frac{p^2}{2m}$$
$$= n^2\left(\frac{h^2}{8ma^2}\right) \quad n = 1,2,\ldots$$

The minimum energy required for excitation from the ground state is

$$E = \frac{h^2}{8ma^2}(2^2 - 1^2)$$
$$= \frac{3h^2}{8ma^2}$$

Thus, the minimum frequency required for excitation is

$$f = \frac{E}{h} = \frac{3h^2}{8ma^2}$$

26. (d) Angular momentum must equal integral multiples of $\frac{h}{2\pi}$, that is,

$$L = n\left(\frac{h}{2\pi}\right)$$

The rotational kinetic energies will be

$$K = \frac{L^2}{2I}$$
$$= n^2\left(\frac{h^2}{8\pi^2 I^2}\right) \quad n = 1,2,\ldots$$

The minimum energy required for excitation from the ground state is

$$E = \frac{h^2}{8\pi^2 I^2}(2^2 - 1^2)$$
$$= \frac{3h^2}{8\pi^2 I^2}$$

Equating with the minimum frequency f, we have

$$hf = \frac{3h^2}{8\pi^2 p^2}$$

$$\Rightarrow \quad I = \frac{3h}{8\pi^2 f}$$

27. (a) The difference between the K_α photon wavelength and the minimum wavelength is

$$\lambda_{K_\alpha} - \lambda_{\min} = \frac{4}{3R(Z-1)^2} - \frac{hc}{eV}$$

According to the given condition, we have

$$\frac{4}{3R(Z-1)^2} - \frac{hc}{eV_2} = 3\left(\frac{4}{3R(Z-1)^2} - \frac{hc}{eV_1}\right)$$

$$\Rightarrow \quad \frac{8}{3R(Z-1)^2} = \frac{hc}{e}\left(\frac{3}{V_1} - \frac{1}{V_2}\right)$$

$$\Rightarrow \quad \frac{1}{(Z-1)^2} = \frac{3chR}{8e}\left(\frac{3}{V_2} - \frac{1}{V_2}\right)$$
$$= \frac{3(13.6\,\text{V})}{8}\left(\frac{3}{10\,\text{kV}} - \frac{1}{20\,\text{kV}}\right)$$

$$\Rightarrow \quad \frac{1}{(Z-1)^2} = \frac{204}{16\times 10^4}$$

$$\Rightarrow \quad (Z-1)^2 \approx 784 \text{ gives } Z = 29$$

28. (c) Electrons accelerated through potential V, acquire kinetic energy $K = eV$. Momentum of these electrons is $p = \sqrt{2mK} = \sqrt{2meV}$. The corresponding de Broglie wavelength is

$$\lambda = \frac{h}{p} = \frac{h}{\sqrt{2meV}}$$
$$= \sqrt{\frac{h^2}{2meV}}$$
$$= \sqrt{\frac{1.5\,\text{eV}\cdot\text{nm}^2}{e(15\,\text{kV})}}$$
$$= 10^{-2}\text{ nm.}$$

Hence, fringe width is

$$\beta = \frac{\lambda D}{d}$$
$$= \frac{(10^{-2}\text{ nm})(1.0\text{ m})}{10^{-4}\text{ m}}$$
$$= 100\text{ nm.}$$

29. (d) Frequency of the K_α photon is $f = \frac{3cR}{4}(z-1)^2$. The minimum accelerating potential V required for emission of a K_α photon, is given by

$$eV = hf$$

$$\Rightarrow \quad V = \frac{3chR}{4e}(Z-1)^2$$
$$= \frac{3(13.6\text{ V})}{4}\times 41^2 \approx 17\text{ kV}$$

CHAPTER

23 Nuclear Physics

- Nuclei are composed of protons and neutrons, collectively called nucleons. All nuclei have about the same density, of the order of 10^{17} kg/m^3. The relation of radius R of a nucleus with mass number A (total number of nucleons) is approximately given by

$$R = R_0 A^{1/3},$$

where $R_0 = 1.2\times10^{-15}$ m. Isotopes are nuclides of the same element having different number of neutrons. Nucleons have angular momentum and magnetic moment.

- The mass M of a nucleus ${}^A_Z X$ is always less than the mass of its nucleons:

$$M_X < Z\left(m_p + m_e\right) + Nm_n = ZM_H + Nm_n$$

According to Einstein's Theory of Relativity, mass can be converted into energy, and vice-versa. The mass difference multiplied by c^2 is the binding energy E_B of the nucleus; it is the energy required to disintegrate the nucleus into its constituent particles:

$$E_B = \left(ZM_H + Nm_n - M\right)c^2$$

The binding energy per nucleon of a nucleus is the binding energy divided by the total number of nucleons. It is a measure of the stability of a nuclei; large binding energy per nucleon means greater stability. The maximum binding energy per nucleon occurs at around mass number $A = 50$. The Fe^{56} nuclei is the most stable one, with binding energy per nucleon of 8.8 MeV.

- In every nuclear reaction, the mass of the end products is less than the mass of the reactants. This mass loss is released in the form of energy. The energy Q released in a nuclear reaction

$$X_1 + X_2 + \ldots \rightarrow Y_1 + Y_2 + \ldots + Q$$

equals mass loss multiplied by c^2 or simply change in the binding energy of the nuclei:

$$Q = \left(\Sigma M_X - \Sigma M_Y\right)c^2$$

The reaction energy Q, also known as the Q value of the reaction, appears largely in the form of kinetic energy of the end products. Some energy may also appear in the form of atomic excitation of the end products, and may subsequently be emitted in the form of radiations. In any nuclear reaction, there is a conservation of charge, energy and momentum; mass is not conserved.

- The nuclear force is of short range and exists between $n-n$, $n-p$ and $p-p$ pairs. A nucleus is unstable if the ratio N/Z is wrong. Most odd/odd nuclei are highly unstable whereas even/even nuclei are highly stable due to nuclear pairing effects. Unstable nuclei usually decay into different nuclei by emitting an alpha (α) or beta (β) particle or a gamma (γ) ray photon. There may be a series of decays until a stable structure is reached. The process of decay of unstable nuclei is called radioactivity. The particles emitted during decay are called radioactive particles. Radiation has a variety of effects on living tissue, some beneficial, some harmful. Particles with greater amount of charge are more dangerous because of their greater ionising power. But fortunately, particles with greater ionising power have a low penetrating power because they interact with matter more readily and hence lose their energy quickly. That makes α particles the most dangerous and γ rays the least.

- **Alpha (α) Decay:** An α particle is a ${}^4_2$He nucleus. Two protons and two neutrons from inside the nucleus bind together with zero spin. It generally occurs in large nuclei.

$${}^A_Z X \rightarrow {}^{A-4}_{Z-2}X + {}^4_2\alpha$$

- **Beta-minus (β^-) Decay:** A β^- particle is an electron. A neutron inside the nucleus transforms into a proton, an electron and an anti-neutrino. It generally occurs when N/Z is too large.

$$^{A}_{Z}X \rightarrow {}^{A}_{Z+1}X + {}^{0}_{-1}\beta + \bar{\nu}_e$$

- **Beta-plus (β^+) Decay:** A β^+ particle is a positron. A proton inside the nucleus transforms into a neutron, a positron and a neutrino. It generally occurs when N/Z is too small.

$$^{A}_{Z}X \rightarrow {}^{A}_{Z-1}X + {}^{0}_{+1}\beta + \nu_e$$

- **Gamma (γ) Decay:** A γ particle is a photon. The energy associated with the internal motion of a nucleus is quantised. A nucleus has a set of energy levels with energy gaps of the order of MeV due to the great strength of nuclear interactions. When an excited nucleus decays into a lower energy state, a γ photon is emitted.

$$^{A}_{Z}X \rightarrow {}^{A}_{Z}X + {}^{0}_{0}\gamma$$

- In every decay process, the combined mass of the daughter nuclei and the emitted particles is less than the mother nuclei. The equivalent energy arising due to this mass loss is known as the decay energy. The decay energy, which appears in the form of kinetic energy, is shared between the daughter nuclei and the emitted particles. The emitted particles and the daughter nuclei fly in different directions, obeying the linear momentum conservation principle. The daughter nuclei, which are much more massive than the emitted particles, take away a negligible amount of kinetic energy. The lightest particle takes away the most of the kinetic energy. For example, in β^- decay, the decay energy is largely shared between the emitted electrons and the anti-neutrinos. The emitted electrons have kinetic energies ranging from zero value to a maximum equal to the decay energy, but there is predominance of low-energy electrons; the anti-neutrinos being much lighter take away most of the kinetic energy.

- The rate of decay of an unstable nuclei sample is called the activity of the sample; the activity is proportional to the number of nuclei N:

$$\frac{dN}{dt} = -\lambda N$$

The proportionality constant λ is called the decay constant of that sample. The mean-life T_{mean} and the half-life $T_{1/2}$ are related to the decay constant λ as

$$T_{\text{mean}} = \frac{1}{\lambda} = \frac{T_{1/2}}{\ln 2}$$

If N_0 is the number of nuclei at time $t = 0$, then the number N at time t is given by

$$N = N_0 e^{-\lambda t} \text{ or } N_0 2^{-t/T_{1/2}}$$

The fraction of nuclei that decay in time t is given by

$$\frac{|\Delta N|}{N_0} = 1 - e^{-\lambda \Delta t} \text{ or } 1 - 2^{-\Delta t/T_{1/2}}$$

For $\Delta t \ll T_{1/2}$, the above equation reduces to $\frac{|\Delta N|}{N_0} = \lambda \Delta t$.

The product λN is the activity of the sample. If A_0 is the activity at time $t = 0$, then the activity A at time t is given by

$$A = A_0 e^{-\lambda t} \text{ or } A_0 2^{-t/T_{1/2}}$$

- Nuclear fission is the splitting of a heavy nucleus into two lighter nuclei (always unstable), with the release of energy. Nuclear fusion is the combining of two light nuclei into a heavier nucleus, with the release of energy. In nuclear reactors, the uncommon isotope $^{235}_{92}U$ is bombarded by slow moving neutrons. The neutrons are slowed by allowing them to collide with nuclei in the surrounding material, called a moderator. When $^{235}_{92}U$ absorbs a neutron, the resulting nuclide $^{236}_{92}U^*$ is in a highly excited state and splits into two fragments almost instantaneously. The resulting kinetic energy of the fission fragments is enormous, about 200 MeV. These fission fragments are also unstable and they further release energy, about 15 MeV, by undergoing β^- decays. The two typical fission reactions in a fission reactor are

$$^{236}_{92}U^* \rightarrow {}^{144}_{56}Ba + {}^{89}_{36}Kr + 3{}^{1}_{0}n$$

$$^{236}_{92}U^* \rightarrow {}^{140}_{54}Xe + {}^{94}_{38}Sr + 2{}^{1}_{0}n$$

Both of these reactions occur with equal probability. Hence, we say that an average of 2.5 neutrons are emitted in each reaction.

EXERCISES

1. If Z, A and N denote the atomic number, mass number and neutron number for a given nucleus, choose the incorrect statements:
   (a) $N = Z + A$
   (b) Isobars have the same A but different Z and N
   (c) Isotopes have the same Z but different N and A
   (d) Isotones have the same N but different Z and A

2. If the nucleus of $^{256}_{104}X$ has density ρ and radius r, the density and radius of the $^{4}_{2}He$ nucleus will be:
   (a) $\rho, \frac{r}{4}$ (b) $\rho, \frac{r}{8}$
   (c) $4\rho, \frac{r}{16}$ (d) $8\rho, \frac{r}{16}$

3. The atomic weight of Boron is 10.81 g/mole and it has two isotopes $^{10}_{5}B$ and $^{11}_{5}B$. The ratio of $^{10}_{5}B : ^{11}_{5}B$ in nature is:
   (a) 10:11 (b) 12:13
   (c) 17:51 (d) 19:81

4. The distance of closest approach of an alpha particle fired at a nucleus with momentum p is r_0. The distance of closest approach when the alpha particle is fired at the same nucleus with momentum $2p$ is:
   (a) $2r_0$ (b) r_0
   (c) $\frac{r_0}{2}$ (d) $\frac{r_0}{4}$

5. The binding energies per nucleon of deuteron $^{2}_{1}D$ and alpha particle $^{4}_{2}He$ are 1.15 MeV and 7.1 MeV, respectively. Then the energy released in the reaction $^{2}_{1}D + ^{2}_{1}D \rightarrow ^{4}_{2}He + Q$ is:
   (a) 8.25 MeV (b) 9.4 MeV
   (c) 23.8 MeV (d) 29.55 MeV

6. A star produces energy by the process

$$^{2}_{1}H + ^{2}_{1}H \rightarrow ^{3}_{1}H + ^{1}_{1}p + Q_1$$

$$^{2}_{1}H + ^{3}_{1}H \rightarrow ^{4}_{2}He + ^{1}_{0}n + Q_2$$

   Masses of the nuclei are $m(^{2}_{1}H) = 2.014$ u, $m(p) = 1.007$ u, $m(n) = 1.008$ u and $m(^{4}_{2}He) = 4.001$ u. If $1\text{ u} = 931\text{ MeV}/c^2$, total energy released in the process is:
   (a) 24.2 MeV (b) 28.6 MeV
   (c) 30.6 MeV (d) 38.4 MeV

7. According to Einstein's theory of relativity, mass can be converted into energy and vice-versa. The two lightest elementary particles, electron and positron, each have mass equivalent to 0.51 MeV of energy. Choose the incorrect statements:
   (a) The minimum amount of energy available through conversion of mass into energy is 1.02 MeV
   (b) The least energy of a gamma ray photon that can be converted into mass is 1.02 MeV
   (c) A gamma ray photon of energy 1.80 MeV will produce an electron–positron pair with total kinetic energy 0.78 MeV
   (d) An electron and a positron moving with kinetic energy 1 MeV each will annihilate, emitting two photons, each having energy 0.51 MeV

8. The binding energies per nucleon of $^{12}_{6}C$ and $^{13}_{6}C$ are 7.68 MeV and 7.48 MeV. The energy required to remove the extra neutron from $^{13}_{6}C$ is:
   (a) 0.2 MeV (b) 3.7 MeV
   (c) 5.08 MeV (d) 11.9 MeV

9. Choose the incorrect statements from the following:
   (a) Energy released per unit mass of reactant is much larger in fission than in fusion
   (b) Moderators are used in nuclear reactors to slow down neutrons
   (c) Average number of neutrons released during fission of the uranium atom is 2.5
   (d) The critical mass of a fissionable material can be reduced by surrounding it with a shield that will reflect neutrons

10. A radioactive nuclei $^{200}_{90}X$ decays into $^{168}_{80}Y$. The number of α and β^- particles, respectively, emitted in the process are:
   (a) 8 and 6 (b) 6 and 6
   (c) 4 and 6 (d) 4 and 4

11. A stationary nucleus ruptures into two nuclei which move in opposite directions with velocities in the ratio 8 : 1. The ratio of their radii is:
   (a) $1:2^{1/3}$ (b) $1:3^{1/2}$
   (c) 1:2 (d) 2:1

12. A heavy nuclei at rest disintegrates by emitting an α particle having kinetic energy 48 MeV. If the Q value of the reaction is 50 MeV, the mass number of the mother nuclei is (assume the daughter nuclei to be in ground state):

(a) 100 (b) 148
(c) 182 (d) 208

13. Masses of two isobars ${}^{64}_{29}Cu$ and ${}^{64}_{30}Zn$ are 63.9298 u and 63.9292 u, respectively. It can be concluded from this data that:

(a) Both the isobars are stable
(b) ${}^{64}_{30}Zn$ will decay to ${}^{64}_{29}Cu$ through β^+ decay
(c) ${}^{64}_{29}Cu$ will decay to ${}^{64}_{30}Zn$ through γ decay
(d) ${}^{64}_{29}Cu$ will decay to ${}^{64}_{30}Zn$ through β^- decay

14. Choose the incorrect statements from the following:

(a) In nuclear reactions, there is conservation of energy, charge and momentum
(b) Beta-minus rays are charged particles emitted when a neutron converts into a proton
(c) Beta-minus decay increases the neutron–proton ratio
(d) Mass number of a nucleus is always more than its atomic number, except for hydrogen

15. The ionising power and penetrating range of radioactive radiations increase in the order:

(a) γ, β, α and γ, β, α, respectively
(b) γ, β, α and α, β, γ, respectively
(c) α, β, γ and α, β, γ, respectively
(d) α, β, γ and γ, β, α, respectively

16. The time interval between 32% decay and 83% decay is 69.3 s. The mean life of the sample is:

(a) 1 s (b) 10 s
(c) 50 s (d) 100 s

17. The electrostatic energy of Z protons uniformly distributed throughout a nucleus of radius R is given by $E = \frac{3}{5}\frac{Z(Z-1)e^2}{4\pi\varepsilon_0 R}$. The measured masses of ${}^{1}_{0}n$, ${}^{1}_{1}H$, ${}^{15}_{7}N$ and ${}^{15}_{8}O$ are 1.008665 u, 1.007825 u, 15.000109 u and 15.003065 u, respectively. It is given that the radii of ${}^{15}_{7}N$ and ${}^{15}_{8}O$ nuclei are the same. Assuming that the difference in their binding energies is purely due to the difference in the electrostatic energies of their protons, their nuclei radii is ($1\,u = 931\,MeV/c^2$ and $e^2/4\pi\varepsilon_0 = 1.44\,MeV \cdot fm$):

(a) 2.85 fm (b) 3.01 fm
(c) 3.42 fm (d) 3.80 fm

18. For a certain radioactive substance, it is observed that after 4 hours, only 6.25% of the original sample is left un-decayed. Choose the incorrect statements from the following (take $\ln 2 = 0.693$):

(a) Half-life of the sample is 1 hour
(b) Mean life of the sample is 0.693 hours
(c) Decay constant of the sample is 0.693 hr^{-1}
(d) After another 4 hours, the amount of substance left will be 0.39% of the original amount

19. The half-life of a radioactive sample is 6.93 hours. In a time interval of 15 min, the activity of the sample drops by (take $\ln 2 = 0.693$):

(a) 1.25% (b) 1.5%
(c) 2.25% (d) 2.5%

20. A radioactive sample which emits α particles originally contains 10^{10} nuclei. If the ratio of α particles emitted in the third year to that emitted in the second year is 0.3, then the number of α particles emitted in the first year is:

(a) 5×10^3 (b) 3×10^5
(c) 4×10^7 (d) 7×10^9

21. A small amount of solution containing ${}^{24}_{11}Na$ radioactive isotope having activity 2×10^3 dis./sec was injected in the bloodstream of a man. The activity of 1 cc of the blood sample taken after 5 hours was 16 dis./min. If the half-life of ${}^{24}_{11}Na$ is 15 hours, the volume of the man's blood is

(a) 4500 cc (b) 5500 cc
(c) 6000 cc (d) 6500 cc

22. A radioactive nuclei undergoes alpha decay with average life T_α and beta decay with average life T_β. If both decays occur simultaneously, the average life of the sample will be:

(a) $\frac{T_\alpha + T_\beta}{2}$ (b) $\sqrt{T_\alpha T_\beta}$
(c) $\frac{T_\alpha T_\beta}{T_\alpha + T_\beta}$ (d) $\sqrt{T_\alpha^2 + T_\beta^2}$

23. A radioactive isotope of decay constant $0.5\,s^{-1}$ is being produced at a constant rate of 100 nuclei/second. If the number of nuclei is zero at $t = 0$, then the time at which the number of nuclei becomes 50 is:

(a) $2\ln\left(\frac{3}{2}\right)$ (b) $2\ln\left(\frac{5}{4}\right)$
(c) $2\ln\left(\frac{5}{3}\right)$ (d) $2\ln\left(\frac{4}{3}\right)$

24. If the fission of one $^{235}_{92}U$ releases 200 MeV of energy, then the mass of $^{235}_{92}U$ required each day for a 1000-MW nuclear reactor is nearly equal to ($1\ u = 1.66\times10^{-27}$ kg):
(a) 1 kg (b) 2 kg
(c) 3 kg (d) 4 kg

25. For two protons to fuse together, they must come within the range of nuclear force which is typically of the order of 2 fm. For this, the protons must possess large kinetic energies, which is possible only at high temperatures. If translational kinetic energy of a gas molecule at temperature T is $\frac{1}{2}kT$, then the temperature at which two protons can fuse is:
(a) 1.5×10^7 K (b) 2.0×10^8 K
(c) 2.9×10^9 K (d) 3.5×10^{10} K

26. A fission reaction is given by $^{236}_{92}U \rightarrow {}^{140}_{54}Xe + {}^{94}_{38}Sr + x + y$, where x and y are two particles. Consider $^{236}_{92}U$ to be at rest and the kinetic energies of the products are denoted by $K_{Xe}, K_{Sr}, K_x = K_y = 2$ MeV, respectively. If the binding energies per nucleon of $^{236}_{92}U$, $^{140}_{54}Xe$, $^{94}_{38}Sr$ are 7.5 MeV, 8.5 MeV, 8.5 MeV, respectively, then:
(a) $x = n, y = n, K_{Xe} = 86$ MeV, $K_{Sr} = 129$ MeV
(b) $x = p, y = n, K_{Xe} = 86$ MeV, $K_{Sr} = 129$ MeV
(c) $x = n, y = n, K_{Xe} = 129$ MeV, $K_{Sr} = 86$ MeV
(d) $x = p, y = n, K_{Xe} = 129$ MeV, $K_{Sr} = 129$ MeV

27. A nucleus having energy E_1 decays by β^- emission to a daughter nucleus having energy E_2. The β^- rays are emitted with a continuous energy spectrum ranging from zero value to a maximum value $E_1 - E_2$. The incorrect statements from the following are:
(a) β^- decay involves emission of electrons and anti-neutrinos other than the daughter nuclei
(b) β^- decay generally occurs when N/Z is too large
(c) β^- decay causes an increase in the N/Z ratio
(d) β^- spectrum consists predominantly of low-energy electrons

ANSWER KEYS

1. (a)	**2.** (a)	**3.** (d)	**4.** (d)	**5.** (c)	**6.** (a)	**7.** (d)	**8.** (c)	**9.** (a)	**10.** (a)
11. (c)	**12.** (a)	**13.** (b),(d)	**14.** (c)	**15.** (b)	**16.** (c)	**17.** (c)	**18.** (b)	**19.** (d)	**20.** (d)
21. (c)	**22.** (c)	**23.** (d)	**24.** (a)	**25.** (c)	**26.** (a)	**27.** (c)			

SOLUTIONS

1. (a) The correct statement is $A = Z + N$.
Isotopes have the same number of protons. Isotones have the same number of neutrons. Isobars have the same mass number.

2. (a) Density ρ is the same for all nuclei and hence $r \propto A^{1/3}$. Hence, the radius r' of the ^4_2He nucleus is given by

$$\frac{r'}{r} = \frac{4^{1/3}}{256^{1/3}} \Rightarrow r' = \frac{r}{4}$$

3. (d) Let the ratio be λ: 1. Then, we have

$$\frac{\lambda}{\lambda+1}(10\text{ g/mole}) + \frac{1}{\lambda+1}(11\text{ g/mole})$$
$$= 10.81\text{ g/mole}$$

$$\Rightarrow \quad 10\lambda + 11 = 10.81(\lambda + 1)$$

$$\Rightarrow \quad 0.81\lambda = 0.19 \Rightarrow \lambda = \frac{19}{81}$$

4. (d) The charge on the alpha particle is $+2e$. Let the charge on the nucleus be $+Ze$. If the initial momentum of the alpha particle is p, then the initial kinetic energy is $K = p^2/2m$.
The distance of minimum approach r is given by

$$\frac{(2e)(Ze)}{4\pi\varepsilon_0 r} = K = \frac{p^2}{2m} \Rightarrow r \propto 1/p^2$$

Hence, if momentum is doubled, the distance of minimum approach becomes $r_0/4$.

5. (c) Energy Q released equals change in binding energy

$$Q = (4 \times 7.1 \text{ MeV}) - 2\,(2 \times 1.15 \text{ MeV}) = 23.8 \text{ MeV}$$

6. (a) The net reaction is

$$3{}_1^2\text{H} \rightarrow {}_2^4\text{He} + {}_1^1P + {}_0^1n + Q$$

The energy released Q equals loss of rest mass energy. Hence

$$Q = [(3 \times 2.014 \text{ u}) - (4.001 \text{ u} + 1.007 \text{ u} + 1.002 \text{ u})]c^2$$
$$= 0.026 \times 931 \text{ MeV} = 24.2 \text{ MeV}$$

7. (d) An electron ($-e$) and a positron (e) can combine to give a gamma photon of energy 2(0.51 MeV) = 1.02 MeV and vice-versa. Hence (a) and (b) are both correct. A gamma photon of energy 1.80 MeV will produce an electron–positron pair with kinetic energy 1.80 MeV – 1.02 MeV = 0.72 MeV. Hence (c) is also correct.

Only (d) is incorrect since initial energy 2(1 MeV) does not match with the final energy 4 (0.51 MeV) = 2.04MeV.

8. (c) Energy E required equals initial binding energy minus final binding energy. Hence

$$E = 13(7.48 \text{ MeV}) - 12(7.68 \text{ MeV}) = 5.08 \text{ MeV}$$

9. (a) Only (a) is incorrect.

10. (a) Let x and y be the number of emitted α and β particles. The reaction is

$$\frac{200}{90}X \rightarrow {}_{80}^{168}Y + x{}_2^4\alpha + y{}_{-1}^{\;0}\beta$$

Then, we have

$$2x - y = 90 - 80 = 10 \text{ and } 4x = 200 - 168 = 32$$
$$\Rightarrow \quad x = 8 \text{ and } y = 6$$

11. (c) Since momentum must be conserved, the two nuclei must fly in opposite directions with moment of the same magnitude. Since their velocities are given to be in the ratio 8:1, their masses must be in the ratio 1:8. Since $r \propto A^{1/3}$, their radii will be in the ratio $1:8^{\;1/3} = 1:2$.

12. (a) The value $Q = 50$ MeV is the total energy released (due to mass loss) in the disintegration process. Thus, if the kinetic energy of the α particle is 48 MeV, then that of the daughter nuclei is 2 MeV. The combined momentum of the α particle and the daughter nuclei will be zero since the mother nuclei is intially at rest. This means that the α particle and the daughter nuclei will fly in opposite directions with equal momentum magnitude.

Let X be the mass number of the daughter nuclei. Then equating their momentum magnitude ($p^2 = 2mK$), we have

$$X(2 \text{ MeV}) = 4(48 \text{ MeV}) \Rightarrow X = 96$$

Hence, mass number of the mother nucleus equals 96 + 4 = 100.

13. (b), (d) In β^+(positron) decay, a proton disintegrates into a neutron and a positron. The neutron stays inside and the positron is emitted out of the nucleus. Hence, the atomic number decreases by 1 while the mass number remains unchanged.

14. (c) In β decay, a neutron disintegrates into a proton and an electron; this decreases the N/Z ratio.

15. (b) α particles carry the greatest amount of charge, and hence the greatest ionising power. The greater the ionising power, the lesser the penetrating range because particles with great ionising power interact with matter and lose their energy more readily.

16. (c) Let t_1 and t_2 be the times taken for 32% and 83% decay, respectively. Then

$$0.32 = 1 - e^{-\lambda t_1} \text{ and}$$

$$0.83 = 1 - e^{-\lambda t_2} \quad \left[\text{Using } \frac{\Delta N}{N_0} = 1 - e^{-\lambda t}\right]$$

$$\Rightarrow \quad e^{-\lambda t_1} = 0.68 \text{ and } e^{-\lambda t_2} = 0.17$$

Dividing the two equations, we have

$$e^{\lambda \Delta t} = 4 \Rightarrow \lambda = \frac{2\ln 2}{\Delta t} = \frac{1}{50 \text{ s}}$$

Hence, mean life $= \dfrac{1}{\lambda} = 50$ s

17. (c) The binding energies of oxygen and nitrogen nuclei are, respectively

$$BE_O = (8m_p + 7m_n - m_O)c^2$$
$$\text{and } BE_N = (7m_p + 8m_n - m_N)c^2$$
$$\Rightarrow BE_O - BE_N = (m_p - m_n - m_O + m_N)c^2$$
$$= 0.003796 \times 931.5 \text{ MeV}$$

Also, from the given expression for binding energy, we have

$$BE_O - BE_N = \frac{3}{5}\frac{e^2}{4\pi\varepsilon_0 R}(8 \times 7 - 7 \times 6)$$
$$= \frac{52}{5} \times \frac{1.44 \text{ MeV} \cdot \text{fm}}{R}$$

Equating the two, we have

$$\frac{52}{5} \times \frac{1.44 \text{ MeV} \cdot \text{fm}}{R} = 3.796 \times 10^{-3} \times 931.5 \text{ MeV}$$

$$\Rightarrow \quad R = \frac{52 \times 1.44}{5 \times 3.796} \times \frac{1000}{931.5} \text{ fm} = 3.42 \text{ fm}$$

18. (b) Using the equation $N = N_0 e^{-\lambda t}$, we have

$$\frac{6.25}{100} N_0 = N_0 e^{-\lambda(4hr)}$$

$$\Rightarrow \quad e^{\lambda(4hr)} = 16$$

$$\Rightarrow \quad \lambda = \frac{4\ln 2}{4\text{ h}} = \ln 2\text{ h}^{-1} \Rightarrow \text{(c)}$$

$$\text{Half-life} = \frac{\ln 2}{\lambda} = 1\text{ h} \Rightarrow \text{(a) is correct.}$$

$$\text{Mean life} = \frac{1}{\lambda} = \frac{1}{\ln 2}\text{ h} \Rightarrow \text{(b) is incorrect.}$$

After another 4 hours, the number of nuclei left undecayed is given by

$$N = N_0 2^{\frac{-8\text{ h}}{1\text{ h}}} = \frac{4}{2^{10}} N_0 \approx 0.004 N_0$$

or 0.4% [Since $2^{10} \approx 1000$]

19. (d) The fractional drop in activity is given by

$$\frac{|\Delta A|}{A} = 1 - e^{-\lambda \Delta t}$$

In this question, the time interval $\Delta t = 15$ min is very small in comparison to the half-life of 6.93 h. Hence, the above equation reduces to

$$\frac{|\Delta A|}{A} = \lambda \Delta t = \frac{\ln 2}{T_{1/2}} \times \Delta t$$

$$= \frac{0.693 \times 15\text{ min}}{6.93\text{ hr}} = \frac{1}{40}\text{ or } 2.5\%$$

20. (d) Let λ be the decay constant. Let ΔN_1, ΔN_2 and ΔN_3 denote the number of nuclei decayed in the first, second and third year, respectively. Then we have

$$\Delta N_1 = N_0 - N_0 e^{-\lambda(1\text{ yr})} = N_0 [1 - e^{-\lambda(1\text{ yr})}]$$

$$\Delta N_2 = N_0 e^{-\lambda(1\text{ yr})} - N_0 e^{-\lambda(2\text{ yr})}$$

$$= N_0 e^{-\lambda(1\text{ yr})} [1 - e^{-\lambda(1\text{ yr})}]$$

$$\Delta N_3 = N_0 e^{-\lambda(2\text{ yr})} - N_0 e^{-\lambda(3\text{ yr})}$$

$$= N_0 e^{-\lambda(2\text{ yr})} [1 - e^{-\lambda(1\text{ yr})}]$$

It is given that $\Delta N_3 = 0.3\,\Delta N_2$. Hence, we have

$$e^{-\lambda(2\text{ yr})} = 0.3 e^{-\lambda(1\text{ yr})} \Rightarrow e^{-\lambda(1\text{ yr})} = 0.3$$

Hence $\Delta N_1 = 10^{10}(1 - 0.3) = 7 \times 10^9$

21. (c) Let V be the volume in cc of man's blood. Activity after 5 hours is $\frac{16V}{60}$ dis./sec. Then, we have

$$A_2 = A_1 2^{-\frac{\Delta t}{T_{1/2}}}$$

$$\Rightarrow \quad \frac{16V}{60} = (2 \times 10^3) 2^{\frac{-5\text{ h}}{15\text{ h}}}$$

$$\Rightarrow \quad V = \frac{2 \times 10^3 \times 60}{16 \times 2^{1/3}} = 6000\text{ cc}$$

[Taking $2^{1/3} \approx 1.25 = 5/4$]

22. (c) Let λ_α and λ_β be the decay constants for the α and β decays, respectively. Then, the rate of decay of the sample is given by

$$\frac{dN}{dt} = -(\lambda_\alpha + \lambda_\beta) N$$

Hence, the decay constant A of the sample is

$$\lambda = \lambda_\alpha + \lambda_\beta$$

$$\Rightarrow \quad \frac{1}{T} = \frac{1}{T_f} + \frac{1}{T_R} \quad [T \text{ is the average life}]$$

$$\Rightarrow T = \frac{T_\alpha T_\beta}{T_\alpha + T_\beta}$$

23. (d) Let N denote the number of nuclei at time t. Then, we have

$$\frac{dN}{dt} = 100 - 0.5N$$

$$\Rightarrow \quad \int \frac{dN}{200 - N} = 0.5 \int dt$$

$$\Rightarrow \quad \ln|200 - N| = -0.5t + C$$

$$\Rightarrow \quad \ln|200 - N| = -0.5t + \ln 200$$

$[N = 0 \text{ at } t = 0 \Rightarrow C = \ln 200]$.

$$\Rightarrow \quad \ln\left|\frac{200 - N}{200}\right| = -0.5t$$

Hence, $N = 50$ at time given by

$$\ln\left(\frac{200 - 50}{200}\right) = -0.5t \Rightarrow t = 2\ln(4/3)\text{s}$$

24. (a) The total energy required per day is

$$E = (1000\text{ MW})(24 \times 3600\text{ s}) = 8.64 \times 10^{13}\text{ J}$$

Energy released by fission of one ^{235}U nuclei is 200 MeV. Hence, the total number of ^{235}U nuclei required per day is

$$n = \frac{8.64 \times 10^{13}\text{ J}}{200 \times 10^6 \times 1.6 \times 10^{-19}\text{ J}} = 2.7 \times 10^{24}$$

The mass of this much of ^{235}U is

$$M = (2.7 \times 10^{24})(235 \times 1.66 \times 10^{-27}\text{ kg}) \approx 1\text{ kg}$$

25. (c) For two protons at a distance of 2 fm, the electrostatic potential energy is

$$U = \frac{e^2}{4\pi\varepsilon_0 r} = \frac{(9 \times 10^9\text{ N}\cdot\text{m}^2/\text{C}^2)(1.6 \times 10^{-19}\text{ C})^2}{2 \times 10^{-15}\text{ m}}$$

$$= 1.2 \times 10^{-13}\text{ J}$$

For the protons to approach a distance of 2 fm in a head-on collision, each proton must be moving towards each other with initial kinetic energy $\frac{1}{2}U = 0.6 \times 10^{-13}$ J

Let T be the temperature at which the protons move with this much kinetic energy. Then, we have

$$\frac{3}{2}kT = 0.6 \times 10^{-13} \text{ J}$$

$$\Rightarrow \quad T = \frac{2(0.6 \times 10^{-13} \text{ J})}{3(1.38 \times 10^{-23} \text{ J/K})} = 2.9 \times 10^{9} \text{ K}$$

26. (a) From conservation of the number of neutrons and protons, we have $x = n$, $y = n$.

Energy Q released in the process equals change in the binding energy. Hence, we have

$$Q = (140 + 94) \times 8.5 \text{ MeV} - 236 \times 7.5 \text{ MeV}$$
$$= 219 \text{ MeV}$$

The released energy Q equals the sum of the kinetic energies of all the product particles. Hence, we have

$$K_{Xe} + K_{Sr} = 219 \text{ MeV} - (K_x + K_y)$$
$$= 215 \text{ MeV}$$

Neglecting the momenta of x and y, the momenta of Xe and Sr will be the same in magnitude and opposite in direction. Hence, $p = \sqrt{2mK}$ must be the same for them. Hence, we have

$$140K_{Xe} = 94K_{Sr} \Rightarrow \frac{K_{Xe}}{94} = \frac{K_{Sr}}{140}$$

$$\Rightarrow \quad K_{Xe} = \frac{94}{234}(215 \text{ MeV}) = 86 \text{ MeV and } K_{Sr}$$
$$= \frac{140}{234}(215 \text{ MeV}) = 129 \text{ MeV}$$

27. (c) In a β^- decay, a neutron inside the nucleus transforms into a proton, an electron and an anti-neutrino. This generally occurs when N/Z is too large. The decay decreases the N/Z ratio.

The decay energy $E_1 - E_2$ is shared by the electrons and the anti-neutrinos. The emitted electrons have kinetic energies ranging from zero value to a maximum equal to the decay energy, but there is predominance of low-energy electrons; the anti-neutrinos, being much lighter, take away most of the kinetic energy.

CHAPTER

24 Wave Optics

- Monochromatic light is light with a single frequency. While it is fairly easy to create sound waves of a single frequency, common sources of light do not emit monochromatic light. By far the most nearly monochromatic source is the laser. Coherence is the definite unchanging phase relationship between two wave sources. The overlap of waves from a pair of monochromatic and coherent sources forms a steady interference pattern.
- Consider two coherent sources S_1 and S_2 with zero phase difference, emitting monochromatic light of wavelength λ. When light from the two sources reaches a point P constructive interference occurs when the path difference contains integer number wavelengths

$$|S_1P - S_2P| = n\lambda$$

Destructive interference occurs when the path difference contains a half-integer number of wavelengths

$$|S_1P - S_2P| = \left(n - \frac{1}{2}\right)\lambda$$

The phase difference ϕ is related to the path difference $|S_1P - S_2P|$ as

$$\phi = |S_1P - S_2P|\frac{2\pi}{\lambda}$$

- In Young's double-slit experiment, light from a single source is allowed to pass through a pair of narrow slits a distance d apart. Cylindrical wave fronts spread out from the two slits and form an interference pattern on a screen kept at a large distance $D\,(D \gg d)$ from the plane of the slits. Equally spaced bright and dark lines are observed on the screen.

At point $P(\theta)$ on the screen, the path difference between the two arriving waves is $d\sin\theta$, and the corresponding phase difference is $\phi = \frac{2\pi}{\lambda}(d\sin\theta)$. The angular positions θ of the bright and dark lines, measured with respect to the centre of the two slits, are given by

$$\text{Bright lines: } d\sin\theta = n\lambda\ (n = 0, \pm 1, \pm 2, \ldots),$$

$$\text{Dark lines: } d\sin\theta = \left(n - \frac{1}{2}\right)\lambda\ (n = 0, \pm 1, \pm 2, \ldots)$$

The linear positions y of the bright and dark lines, measured from the centre of the screen, are given by $y = D\theta$ (for small θ):

$$\text{Bright lines: } y = n\beta\ (n = 0, \pm 1, \pm 2, \ldots),$$

$$\text{Dark lines: } y = \left(n - \frac{1}{2}\right)\beta\ (n = 0, \pm 1, \pm 2, \ldots)$$

Here $\beta = \frac{\lambda D}{d}$ is called the fringe width; it is the separation between two successive bright/dark lines. The phase difference ϕ is related to the linear position y as $\phi = \frac{2\pi}{\beta}y$.

- If two sinusoidal waves of intensities I_1 and I_2 arrive at a point with a phase difference of ϕ, then the resultant intensity at that point is

$$I_{res} = I_1 + I_2 + 2\sqrt{I_1 I_2}\cos\phi$$

$$\Rightarrow \left(\sqrt{I_1} - \sqrt{I_2}\right)^2 \le I_{res} \le \left(\sqrt{I_1} + \sqrt{I_2}\right)^2$$

If $I_1 = I_2 = I$, the resultant intensity is $I_{res} = 4I\cos^2\left(\frac{\phi}{2}\right)$

In Young's double-slit experiment, suppose I is the intensity of light arriving from each slit. Then the resultant intensity at point $P(\theta)$ on the screen is given by

$$I_{res} = I_0 \cos^2 \gamma, \text{ where } \gamma = \frac{\pi d \sin\theta}{\lambda} = \frac{\pi y}{\beta}$$

Here, $I_0 = 4I$ is the intensity at the positions of the bright lines. Note that the resultant intensity at the bright positions is four times the intensity due to any one of the slits.

- While calculating the path difference between the two arriving waves, it is the optical path that has to be taken and not the geometrical path. When light travels a certain geometrical path in a medium of refractive index μ, the optical path travelled by the light is given by

  $$\text{Optical path} = \mu \times \text{Geometrical path}$$

  Introducing a thin transparent film of thickness t and refractive index μ in front of a slit has the effect of increasing the path length by an amount $t(\mu-1)$ for light coming from that slit. The central bright line will now form closer to that slit; it will shift on the screen by

  $$\text{Shift} = \frac{t(\mu-1)D}{d}$$

- Spreading of light at the edges of obstacles is called diffraction. A single slit of width a (provided a is comparable to λ) gives a diffraction pattern with a central maxima and the intensity falling to zero at angles

  $$\theta = \pm\frac{\lambda}{a}, \pm\frac{2\lambda}{a}, \ldots \text{ (positions of minima)},$$

  with successively weaker maxima in between.

  For a circular aperture of diameter D (provided D is large compared to λ), the first minima in the diffraction pattern occurs at $\theta = \frac{1.22\,\lambda}{D}$. Diffraction limits the angular resolution of optical instruments. If light coming from two point sources is brought into focus using a lens of diameter D, the minimum angle subtended by the two sources at the pole of the lens is given by

  $$\Delta\theta = \frac{1.22\,\lambda}{D}$$

  If the angular separation between the two point sources is less than this angle, their images are strongly overlapped.

- In unpolarised light, the electric field vector takes all possible directions in the transverse plane. A polarising filter passes components parallel to its polarising axis and blocks components perpendicular to its axis. If I_0 is the intensity of the unpolarised light, intensity of the light passing through the filter is reduced to $I_0/2$. The direction of polarisation of a linearly polarised wave is the direction of its electric field vector **E**.

- **Malus' Law:** When linearly polarised light of intensity I_0 passes through a polarising filter at angle θ to its polarising axis, the intensity I of the transmitted light is given by

  $$I = I_0 \cos^2\theta$$

- **Brewster's Law:** When unpolarised light moving in one material (μ_1) strikes an interface of another material (μ_2), the reflected light is completely polarised perpendicular to the plane of incidence for angle of incidence θ_P given by

  $$\tan\theta_P = \frac{\mu_2}{\mu_1}$$

  Light is scattered by air molecules. Scattered light is partially polarised.

EXERCISES

1. The ratio of the intensities of the maxima and minima in an interference pattern is 49 : 9. The ratio of the intensities of the coherent sources is:
(a) 7 : 3 (b) 49 : 9t
(c) 5 : 2 (d) 25 : 4

2. In a standard Young's double-slit experiment, the intensity of the maxima is I_0. If the width of one slit is quadrupled, the intensity of the maxima will be:
(a) $\frac{5}{4}I_0$ (b) I_0
(c) $2I_0$ (d) $\frac{9}{4}I_0$

3. In a standard Young's double-slit experiment using two coherent sources, the intensity of the maxima is I_0. If the sources become incoherent, the intensity at the centre of the screen becomes:
(a) I_0 (b) $\frac{1}{2}I_0$
(c) $\frac{1}{4}I_0$ (d) 0

4. In a Young's double-slit experiment, the slits are 0.5 mm apart and the screen is 100 cm from the slits. The 9th bright fringe and the 2nd dark fringe are separated by 9 mm. The wavelength of the light used is:
(a) 200 nm (b) 400 nm
(c) 600 nm (d) 800 nm

5. In a Young's double-slit experiment, the wavelength of light used is 600 nm. If the path difference between the waves reaching a point P on the screen is 1.5 μm, then at point P:
(a) 2nd bright fringe occurs
(b) 2nd dark fringe occurs
(c) 3rd bright fringe occurs
(d) 3rd dark fringe occurs

6. There is a difference of one wavelength when light of wavelength 600 nm propagates through air and vacuum columns of the same thickness. If the refractive index of air is 1.0003, the thickness of the air column is:
(a) 1.8 mm (b) 2 mm
(c) 2 cm (d) 2.2 cm

7. In a Young's double-slit experiment, 12 fringes are observed in a certain region of the screen when light of 600 nm is used. If light of 400 nm is used, the number of fringes that will be formed in the same region of the screen is:
(a) 8 (b) 12
(c) 18 (d) 24

8. In a Young's double-slit experiment, when a glass film of refractive index 1.5 is inserted in the path of one of the interfering beams, the intensity at the centre of the screen remains unchanged. If the wavelength of light used is 600 nm, then the minimum thickness of the glass plate is:
(a) 1200 nm (b) 800 nm
(c) 600 nm (d) 400 nm

9. White light is used to illuminate the two slits in a Young's double-slit experiment. The separation between the slits is d and the distance between the screen and the plane of the slits is D $(D \gg d)$. At a point on the screen directly in front of one of the slits, certain wavelengths are missing. The missing wavelengths are:
(a) $\frac{d^2}{(2n-1)D}$
(b) $\frac{D^2}{(2n-1)d}$
(c) $\frac{2D^2}{(2n-1)d}$
(d) $\frac{2d^2}{(2n-1)D}$

10. As shown in the figure, PQ is a plane wave front and AQ and BP are the extreme rays separated by a distance d.

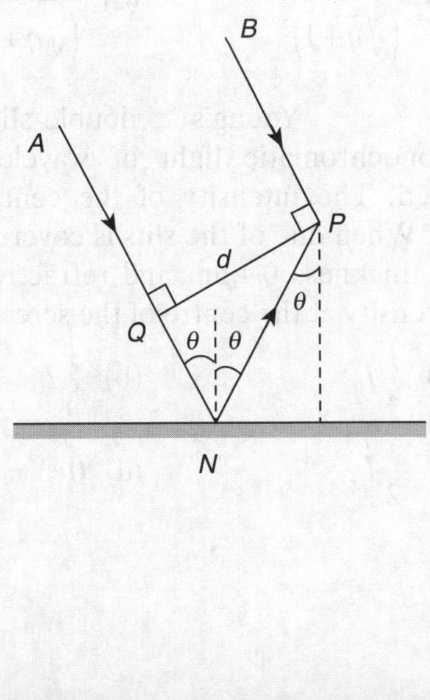

If wavelength of the light used is λ, the maximum value of θ for which the ray BP and the reflected ray NP interfere constructively at P is given by:

(a) $\tan\theta = \frac{3\lambda}{2d}$

(b) $\tan\theta = \frac{2d}{\lambda}$

(c) $\tan\theta = \frac{d}{\lambda}$

(d) $\tan\theta = \frac{\lambda}{2d}$

11. A beam of light consisting of two wavelengths, 650 nm and 520 nm, is used to obtain interference fringes in a Young's double-slit experiment. The separation between the slits is 2.6 mm and the distance between the plane of the slits and the screen is 1.0 m. The least distance from the central maximum, where the bright fringes due to both wavelengths coincide, is:

(a) 1.0 mm (b) 1.5 mm
(c) 2.0 mm (d) 2.5 mm

12. In a Young's double-slit experiment, the angular width of a fringe formed on a distant screen is 0.1°. If the wavelength of light used is 628 nm, the spacing between the slits is:

(a) 0.9×10^{-4} m
(b) 1.8×10^{-4} m
(c) 3.6×10^{-4} m
(d) 7.2×10^{-4} m

13. An interference pattern is obtained by two light sources of intensity ratio η. In the interference pattern, the ratio $\frac{I_{max}-I_{min}}{I_{max}+I_{min}}$ equals:

(a) $\frac{\sqrt{\eta}}{\eta+1}$ (b) $\frac{2\sqrt{\eta}}{\eta+1}$

(c) $\frac{\sqrt{\eta}}{(\sqrt{\eta}+1)^2}$ (d) $\frac{2\sqrt{\eta}}{(\sqrt{\eta}+1)^2}$

14. In a Young's double-slit experiment, monochromatic light of wavelength 600 nm is used. The intensity of the central maximum is I_0. When one of the slits is covered by a glass film of thickness 0.4 μm and refractive index 1.5, the intensity at the centre of the screen will be:

(a) $\frac{1}{4}I_0$ (b) $\frac{1}{3}I_0$

(c) $\frac{1}{2}I_0$ (d) 0

15. A beam of light consisting of two wavelengths, 450 nm and 750 nm, Is used to obtain interference in Young's double-slit experiment. The distance between the slits is 1 mm and the distance between the plane of the slits and the screen is 1.2 m. The distance between the adjacent regions of complete darkness on the screen is:

(a) 5.4 mm (b) 4.5 mm
(c) 2.7 mm (d) 1.2 mm

16. In a Young's double-slit experiment, the intensity at point P is half the maximum intensity in the interference pattern. If the wavelength of light used is λ and d is the distance between the slits, the angular separation between point P and its nearest bright fringe is:

(a) $\frac{\lambda}{d}$ (b) $\frac{\lambda}{2d}$

(c) $\frac{\lambda}{3d}$ (d) $\frac{\lambda}{4d}$

17. A coherent parallel beam of microwaves of wavelength 0.5 mm falls normally on a Young's double-slit experiment apparatus. The separation between the slits is 1 mm and the screen is placed at a distance of 1 m from the slits. The number of minima in the interference pattern observed on the screen is:

(a) 3 (b) 4
(c) 5 (d) Much greater than 5

18. Monochromatic light of wavelength λ emerging from slit S illuminates slits S_1 and S_2 which are placed with respect to S, as shown in the figure. The distance d between the slits is small compared to other distances.

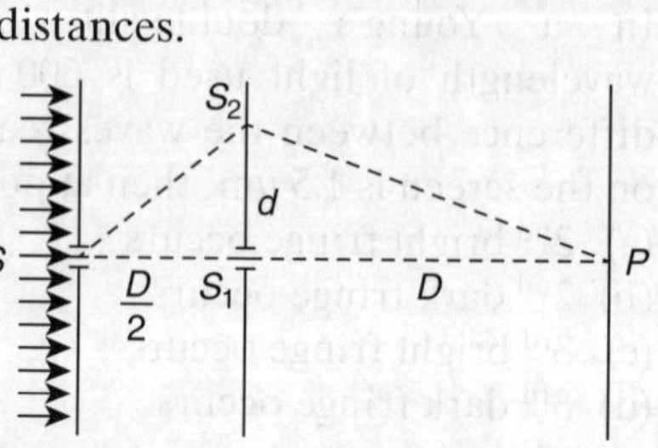

The minimum value of d so that there is a dark line at the centre P of the screen is:

(a) $\sqrt{\frac{\lambda D}{8}}$ (b) $\sqrt{\frac{\lambda D}{6}}$

(c) $\sqrt{\frac{\lambda D}{3}}$ (d) $\sqrt{\frac{2\lambda D}{3}}$

19. Two coherent monochromatic point sources S_1 and S_2 of wavelength $\lambda = 600$ nm are placed symmetrically on either side of the centre of a large circle (see figure) at distance d = 1.8 mm. This arrangement produces alternate bright and dark spots on the circumference of the circle.

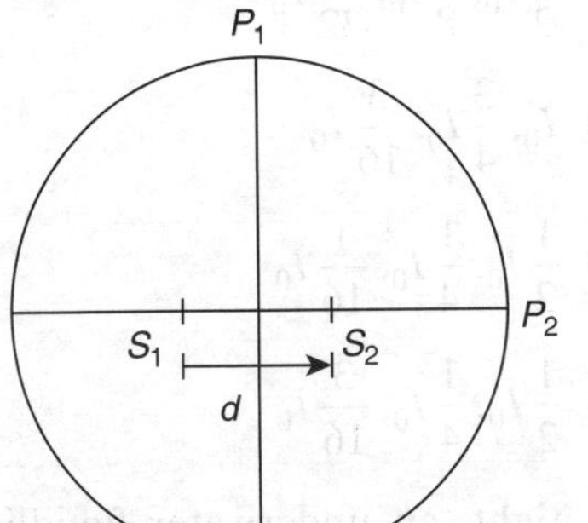

The incorrect statements from the following are:
(a) A dark spot is formed at P_2
(b) Angular separation between two consecutive bright spots decreases as we move from P_1 to P_2 along the first quadrant
(c) Total number of fringes in the first quadrant equals 3000
(d) The order of the fringe is maximum at P_2

20. Column I shows four situations of a standard Young's double-slit arrangement. In each of these cases, $S_1P_0 = S_2P_0$, $S_1P_1 - S_2P_1 = \lambda/4$, and $S_1P_2 - S_2P_2 = \lambda/3$, where λ is the wavelength of the light used. In cases (b), (c) and (d), a transparent sheet of refractive index μ and thickness t is pasted on slit S_2. The thickness is different in different cases. At any point P on the screen, the phase different between the waves is denoted by $\delta(P)$ and intensity by $I(P)$. Match the columns:

(a) 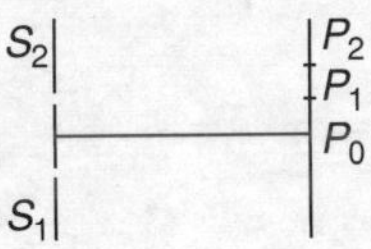 (p) $\delta(P_0)=0$

(b) 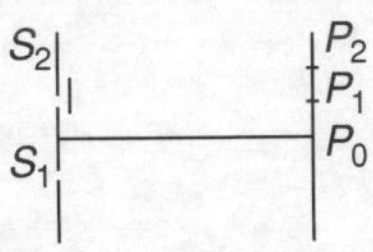 $t(\mu-1)=\dfrac{\lambda}{4}$ (q) $\delta(P_1)=0$

(c) 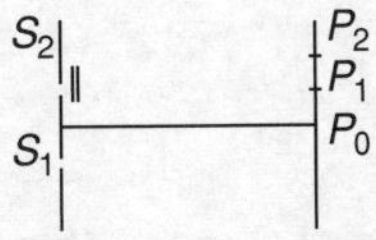 $t(\mu-1)=\dfrac{\lambda}{2}$ (r) $I(P_1)=0$

(d) 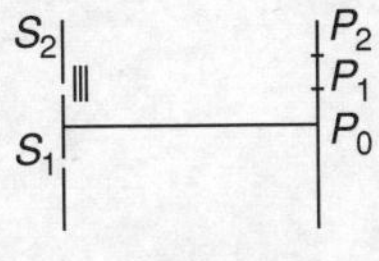 $t(\mu-1)=\dfrac{3\lambda}{4}$ (s) $I(P_1)>I(P_0)$

21. In a Young's double-slit experiment, the 10th bright fringe for light of wavelength λ_1 is at a distance x from the central fringe. If light of wavelength λ_2 is used, the distance of its 5th dark fringe measured from the central fringe will be:
(a) $\dfrac{4\lambda_2 x}{5\lambda_1}$ (b) $\dfrac{\lambda_2 x}{10\lambda_1}$
(c) $\dfrac{3\lambda_2 x}{10\lambda_1}$ (d) $\dfrac{9\lambda_2 x}{20\lambda_1}$

22. In a Young's double-slit experiment using two coherent sources, the intensity of the maxima is I_0 and the fringe width is β. The intensity at a distance $4\beta/3$ from the centre of the screen is:
(a) $\dfrac{1}{2}I_0$ (b) $\dfrac{3}{4}I_0$
(c) $\dfrac{1}{4}I_0$ (d) $\dfrac{9}{16}I_0$

23. Laser light of wavelength $\lambda = 633$ nm is passed through a narrow slit and diffraction pattern is observed on a screen $D = 6.0$ m away. If the width of the central bright band on the screen is $y = 27$ mm, then the width of the slit is:
(a) 0.14 mm (b) 0.28 mm
(c) 0.56 mm (d) 1.12 mm

24. A camera lens with focal length $f = 50$ mm and maximum aperture $f/2$ is used to film an object from a distance $x = 9.0$ m away. If the wavelength of light is $\lambda = 500$ nm, the minimum distance between two points on the object that are barely resolved is:
(a) 0.01 mm (b) 0.02 mm
(c) 0.11 mm (d) 0.22 mm

25. A beam of sodium light consisting of two wavelengths 589 nm and 589.6 nm is used to obtain interference fringes in a Young's double-slit experiment. The separation between the slits is 2.9 mm. The angular position where the visibility of the fringes is minimum is:
(a) 0.05 rad (b) 0.06 rad
(c) 0.08 rad (d) 0.10 rad

26. If a human eye can just distinguish two points separated by a distance $s = 0.25$ mm from a distance of $x = 1.0$ m with light of wavelength $\lambda = 600$ nm, then the effective diameter of the eye to the nearest integer is:
(a) 1 mm (b) 2 mm
(c) 3 mm (d) 4 mm

27. Two satellites at an altitude of $h = 900$ km are separated by a distance $s = 42$ km. If they broadcast microwaves of wavelength $\lambda = 4.0$ cm, the minimum diameter of the receiving dish antenna needed to resolve is:

(a) 0.5 m (b) 1.05 m
(c) 2.05 m (d) 3.05 m

28. The box of a pin-hole camera of length L has a hole of radius a. When the hole is illuminated by light of wavelength λ, the radius b of the spot formed on the screen is found to be greater than a, due to diffraction. The value of b will be minimum when:

(a) $a = \dfrac{0.61\lambda^2}{L}$ and $b_{min} = \dfrac{2.44\lambda^2}{L}$

(b) $a = \dfrac{0.61\lambda^2}{L}$ and $b_{min} = \sqrt{2.44\lambda L}$

(c) $a = \sqrt{0.61\lambda L}$ and $b_{min} = \dfrac{2.44\lambda^2}{L}$

(d) $a = \sqrt{0.61\lambda L}$ and $b_{min} = \sqrt{2.44\lambda L}$

29. Unpolarised light of intensity I_0 passes through three polarisers P_1, P_2 and P_3, arranged in that order. If the angle between the polarising axis of P_1 and P_2 is $\theta = 30°$ while those of P_1 and P_3 are crossed, then the intensity of light emerging from the three polarisers are, respectively:

(a) $\dfrac{1}{2}I_0, \dfrac{3}{8}I_0, \dfrac{3}{32}I_0$

(b) $I_0, \dfrac{3}{4}I_0, \dfrac{3}{16}I_0$

(c) $\dfrac{1}{2}I_0, \dfrac{1}{4}I_0, \dfrac{1}{16}I_0$

(d) $\dfrac{1}{2}I_0, \dfrac{1}{4}I_0, \dfrac{3}{16}I_0$

30. At night, an underwater floodlight is turned on inside a swimming pool. Let θ_1 and θ_2 be the angles of reflection and refraction when the reflected light inside the pool is completely polarised. If $\mu_{water} = 4/3$, then:

(a) $\theta_1 = 37°, \theta_2 = 53°$
(b) $\theta_1 = 30°, \theta_2 = 60°$
(c) $\theta_1 = 53°, \theta_2 = 37°$
(d) $\theta_1 = 45°, \theta_2 = 45°$

ANSWER KEYS

1. (d) **2.** (d) **3.** (b) **4.** (c) **5.** (d) **6.** (b) **7.** (c) **8.** (a) **9.** (a) **10.** (b)
11. (a) **12.** (c) **13.** (b) **14.** (a) **15.** (c) **16.** (d) **17.** (b) **18.** (c) **19.** (a),(b)
20. (a)-(p), (b)-(q),(s), (c)-(s), (d)-(r) **21.** (d) **22.** (c) **23.** (b) **24.** (d) **25.** (d) **26.** (c)
27. (b) **28.** (d) **29.** (a) **30.** (a)

SOLUTIONS

1. (d) We have

$$10\left(\frac{\lambda_1 D}{d}\right) = x \Rightarrow \frac{D}{d} = \frac{X}{10\lambda_1}$$

The 5th dark fringe of λ_2 is at

$$y = \left(5-\frac{1}{2}\right)\frac{\lambda_2 D}{d} = \left(\frac{9}{2}\lambda_2\right)\left(\frac{x}{10\lambda_1}\right)$$

$$= \frac{9\lambda_2 x}{20\lambda_1}$$

2. (d) If the intensity of the maxima is I_0, then the intensity of light from each slit is $I_0/4$. If one slit is quadrupled, the intensity from this slit becomes $4(I_0/4) = I_0$. The resultant intensity of the bright line on the screen will now be $\left(\sqrt{I_0}+\sqrt{I_0/4}\right)^2 = \frac{9I_0}{4}$.

3. (b) The light from the two slits becomes incoherent, no interference pattern is observed on the screen. At every point on the screen, the observed intensity is the average of the minimum and maximum possible intensities, that is, average of 0 and I_0, which is $I_0/2$.

4. (c) Position of the 9th bright fringe is $\frac{9\lambda D}{d}$ and that of the 2nd dark fringe is

$$\left(2-\frac{1}{2}\right)\frac{\lambda D}{d} = \frac{3\lambda D}{2d}$$

Thus, we have

$$\frac{9\lambda D}{d} - \frac{3\lambda D}{\partial d} = 9 \text{ mm}$$

$$\Rightarrow \quad \lambda = \frac{2d(9\text{ mm})}{15D} = \frac{2(0.5\text{ mm})(9\text{ mm})}{15(100\text{ cm})}$$

$$= 600 \text{ nm}$$

5. (d) The number of wavelengths contained in $1.5\ \mu m$ is $\frac{1.5\ \mu m}{600\text{ nm}} = 2.5$

$\Rightarrow$ 3rd dark fringe occurs

6. (b) Let t be the thickness of the air column. Then number of wavelengths contained in the column equals $\frac{t}{\lambda}$ if the column is vacuum and $\frac{t}{\lambda/\mu} = \frac{\mu t}{\lambda}$ if the column is air.

Thus, we have

$$\frac{\mu t}{\lambda} - \frac{t}{\lambda} = 1$$

$$\Rightarrow \quad t = \frac{\lambda}{\mu - 1} = \frac{600\text{ nm}}{1.0003-1}$$

$$= 2 \text{ mm}$$

7. (c) The number of fringes framed over a length, say l, on the screen is given by

$$n = \frac{1}{\lambda D/d} = \frac{1d}{\lambda D} \propto \frac{1}{\lambda}$$

Hence, we have

$$n(400\text{ nm}) = 12(600\text{ nm})$$

$$\Rightarrow \quad n = 18$$

8. (a) Intensity at centre does not change. This implies $(\mu - 1)\,t = n\lambda$

Then, the minimum value of t is

$$t_{\min} = \frac{\lambda}{\mu-1} = \frac{600\text{ nm}}{1.5-1}$$

$$= 1200 \text{ nm}$$

9. (a) At the given point, the lengths of the paths travelled from the two slits are D and $\sqrt{D^2+d^2}$. The path difference is

$$\Delta = \sqrt{D^2+d^2} - D = D\left(1+\frac{d^2}{D^2}\right)^{1/2} - D$$

$$= D\left(1+\frac{d^2}{2D^2}\right) - D = \frac{d^2}{2D}$$

$$[(1+x)^n \approx 1+nx \text{ for small } x]$$

If λ is a missing wavelength, then

$$\frac{d^2}{2D} = \left(n-\frac{1}{2}\right)\lambda$$

$$\Rightarrow \quad \lambda = \frac{d^2}{(2n-1)D}$$

10. (b) The path difference is

$$\Delta = QN + NP = d\cot(2\theta) + d\,\mathrm{cosec}(2\theta)$$

$$= \frac{d(1+\cos 2\theta)}{\sin 2\theta} = d\cot\theta$$

A phase change of π has occurred during reflection at N. Hence, for constructive interference at P, we have

$$d\cot\theta = (2n-1)\frac{\lambda}{2}(n = 1,2,3,...)$$

$$\Rightarrow \quad \tan\theta = \frac{2d}{(2n-1)\lambda}(n = 1,2,3,...)$$

Hence, the maximum value of $\tan\theta$ is $\frac{2d}{\lambda}$.

11. (a) The positions of maxima for the wavelengths $\lambda_1 = 650$ nm and $\lambda_2 = 520$ m coincide where

$$n_1\left(\frac{\lambda_1 D}{d}\right) = n_2\left(\frac{\lambda_2 D}{d}\right)$$

$$\Rightarrow \quad n_1(650 \text{ nm}) = n_2(520 \text{ nm})$$

$$\Rightarrow \quad \frac{n_1}{4} = \frac{n_2}{5}$$

The least values satisfying the above relation are $n_1 = 4$ and $n_2 = 5$. Hence, the nearest such position from the central maxima is at

$$y = 4\left(\frac{\lambda_1 D}{d}\right) = \frac{4(650 \text{ nm})(1.0 \text{ m})}{(2.6 \text{ mm})} = 1 \text{ mm}$$

12. (c) The angular width of a fringe is given by λ/d. Thus, we have

$$\frac{\lambda}{d} = 0.1° \times \frac{\pi}{180°}$$

$$\Rightarrow \quad d = \frac{1800\lambda}{\pi} = \frac{1800(628 \text{ nm})}{3.14} = 3.6\times10^{-4} \text{ m}$$

13. (b) Let I and ηI be the intensities of light from the two sources. Then

$$I_{\max} = (\sqrt{\eta I} + \sqrt{I})^2 = (\eta + 2\sqrt{\eta} + 1)$$

and

$$I_{\max} = (\sqrt{\eta I} - \sqrt{I})^2 = (\eta - 2\sqrt{\eta} + 1)I$$

The required ratio is

$$\frac{I_{\max} - I_{\min}}{I_{\max} + I_{\min}} = \frac{4\sqrt{\eta}I}{2(\eta+1)I} = \frac{2\sqrt{\eta}}{\eta+1}$$

14. (a) Path difference at the centre of the screen is

$$\Delta = (\mu - 1)t = (1.5 - 1)0.4\ \mu\text{m} = 0.2\ \mu\text{m}$$

The corresponding phase difference is

$$\phi = \Delta\left(\frac{2\pi}{\lambda}\right) = (0.2\ \mu\text{m})\left(\frac{2\pi}{600 \text{ nm}}\right) = \frac{2\pi}{3}$$

Hence, intensity at the centre is

$$I = I_0\cos^2\left(\frac{\phi}{2}\right) = I_0\cos^2\left(\frac{\pi}{3}\right) = \frac{I_0}{4}$$

15. (c) The minima positions for the wavelengths $\lambda_1 = 450$ nm and $\lambda_2 = 750$ nm coincide where

$$(2n_1 - 1)\frac{\lambda_1 D}{2d} = (2n_2 - 1)\frac{\lambda_2 D}{2d}$$

$$\Rightarrow \quad (2n_1 - 1)450 \text{ nm} = (2n_2 - 1)750 \text{ nm}$$

$$\Rightarrow \quad \frac{(2n_1 - 1)}{5} = \frac{(2n_2 - 1)}{3} = k(k = 1,3,5,...)$$

Thus, complete darkness occurs at positions given by

$$y = 5k\left(\frac{\lambda_1 D}{2d}\right) \text{ or } 3k\left(\frac{\lambda_2 D}{2d}\right), \text{ where } k = 1,3,5,...$$

Hence, distance between the two successive darkness is

$$\Delta y = 10\left(\frac{\lambda_1 D}{2d}\right) = \frac{5(450 \text{ nm})(1.2 \text{ m})}{1 \text{ mm}} = 2.7 \text{ mm}$$

16. (d) Positions of such points where the intensity is $I_0/2$ are given by

$$I_0\cos^2\left(\frac{\pi y}{\beta}\right) = \frac{1}{2}I_0$$

$$\Rightarrow \quad \cos^2\left(\frac{\pi y}{\beta}\right) = \frac{1}{2}$$

The smallest value of y is given by

$$\Rightarrow \quad \frac{\pi y}{\beta} = \frac{\pi}{4}$$

$$\Rightarrow \quad y = \frac{\lambda D}{4d}$$

The nearest bright fringe from the above point is the central bright fringe (see figure). Hence, the required angular separation is

$$\theta = \frac{y}{D} = \frac{\lambda}{4d}$$

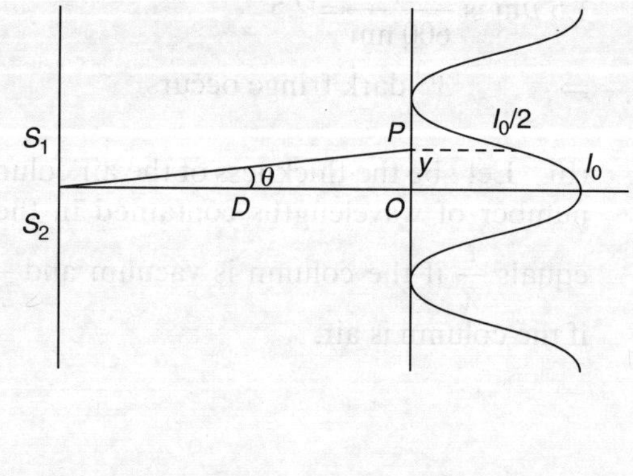

17. (b) Angular positions of minima are given by

$$\sin\theta = \left(n - \frac{1}{2}\right)\frac{\lambda}{d}$$

Since $\sin\theta \le 1$

$$\left(n - \frac{1}{2}\right)\frac{\lambda}{d} \le 1$$

$$\Rightarrow \quad n \le \frac{1}{2} + \frac{1}{d} = \frac{1}{2} + \frac{1\text{ mm}}{0.5\text{ mm}} = 2.5$$

Since n can only take integer values, $n = 1, 2$. Thus, there will be four minima, two on either side of the central maxima.

18. (c) The path difference is

$$\Delta = (SS_1 - SS_2) + (S_2P - S_1P)$$

$$= \left(\sqrt{\frac{D^2}{4} + d^2} - \frac{D}{2}\right) + \left(\sqrt{D^2 + d^2} - D\right)$$

$$= \frac{D}{2}\left(\sqrt{1 + \frac{4d^2}{D^2}} - 1\right) + D\left(\sqrt{1 + \frac{d^2}{D^2}} - 1\right)$$

$$= \frac{D}{2}\left(1 + \frac{2d^2}{D^2} - 1\right) + D\left(1 + \frac{d^2}{2D^2} - 1\right)$$

$$[(1+x)^n \approx 1 + nx \text{ for small } x]$$

$$= \frac{d^2}{D} + \frac{d^2}{2D} = \frac{3d^2}{2D}$$

For darkness at P, the minimum value of Δ is $\lambda/2$. Hence, we have

$$\frac{3d^2}{2D} = \frac{\lambda}{2} \Rightarrow d = \sqrt{\frac{\lambda D}{3}}$$

19. (a), (b)

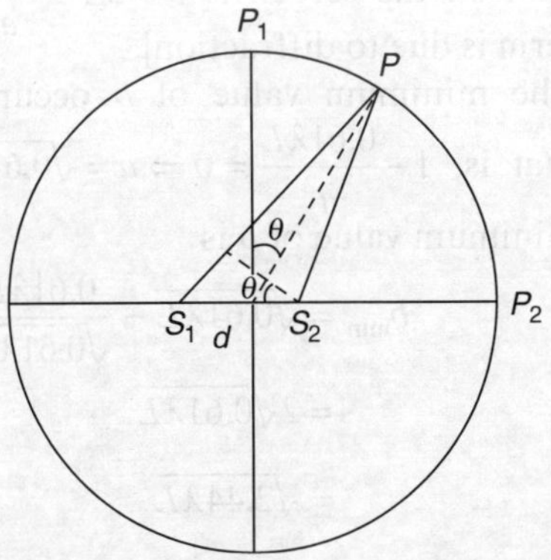

$$\left[\frac{d}{\lambda} = \frac{1.8\text{ mm}}{600\text{ mm}} = 3000\right]$$

Path difference at P_1 is $0 \Rightarrow$ Bright fringe

Path difference at P_2 is $d = 3000\lambda \Rightarrow$ Bright fringe

Thus, P_1 is the position of the central fringe, and P_2 is the position of the 3000th bright fringe.

The figure shows some arbitrary point P on the circle. Let θ be its angular position measured with respect to P_1. Then path difference at P is

$$p = d\sin\theta$$

Taking differential of the above equation, we have

$$dp = (d\cos\theta)d\theta$$

Between two successive bright fringes, $dp = \lambda$. Hence, angular separation between two successive bright fringes is $d\theta = \frac{\lambda}{d\cos\theta}$, which increases with θ.

Hence, the incorrect statements are those in options (a), (b).

20. (a)-(p), (b)-(q),(s), (c)-(s), (d)-(r)

Let $\Delta(P)$ denote path difference at point P.

In case (a), $\Delta(P_0) = 0 \Rightarrow \delta(P_0) = 0$

$\Rightarrow I(P_0)$ is maximum

In case (b), $\Delta(P_1) = 0 \Rightarrow \delta(P_1) = 0$

$\Rightarrow I(P_1)$ is maximum

In case (c), $\Delta(P_0) = \frac{\lambda}{2} \Rightarrow I(P_0) = 0$

In case (d),

$$\Delta(P_1) = \frac{3\lambda}{4} - \frac{\lambda}{4} = \frac{\lambda}{2} \Rightarrow \delta(P_1)$$

$$\Rightarrow \quad I(P_1) = 0$$

21. (d) We have

$$10\left(\frac{\lambda_1 D}{d}\right) = x$$

$$\Rightarrow \quad \frac{D}{d} = \frac{X}{10\lambda_1}$$

The 5th dark fringe of λ_2 is at

$$y = \left(5 - \frac{1}{2}\right)\frac{\lambda_2 D}{d}$$

$$= \left(\frac{9}{2}\lambda_2\right)\left(\frac{x}{10\lambda_1}\right)$$

$$= \frac{9\lambda_2 x}{20\lambda_1}$$

22. (c) The intensity at a distance $y = \frac{4\beta}{3}$ from the centre is given by

$$I = I_0 \cos^2\left(\frac{\pi y}{\beta}\right)$$

$$= I_0 \cos^2\left(\frac{4\pi}{3}\right) = \frac{I_0}{4}$$

23. (b) Width of the central bright band on the screen is given by $y = \frac{2\lambda D}{d}$

$$\Rightarrow \quad d = \frac{2\lambda D}{y} = \frac{2(633\text{ nm})(6.0\text{ m})}{27\text{ mm}}$$

$$= 0.28\text{ mm}$$

24. (d) Let s be the minimum distance between two points that can be barely resolved by the camera. The angle $\Delta\theta$ subtended by the two points at the lens is $\Delta\theta = s/x$. The aperture diameter is $d = f/2 =$ 25 mm. Then we have

$$\Delta\theta = \frac{1.22\lambda}{d}$$

$$\Rightarrow \quad \frac{s}{x} = \frac{1.22\lambda}{d}$$

$$\Rightarrow \quad s = \frac{1.22\lambda x}{d} = \frac{1.22(500\text{ nm})(9\text{ m})}{25\text{ mm}}$$

$$= 0.22\text{ mm}$$

25. (d) Visibility is minimum where the maxima of one wavelength coincides with the minima of the other. That is, where the path difference p contains an integral multiple of one wavelength and a half-integral multiple of the other wavelength

$$\Rightarrow \quad \frac{p}{589\text{ nm}} - \frac{p}{589.6\text{ nm}} = n\left(\frac{1}{2}\right),$$

where $n = 1, 3, 5, \ldots$

$$\Rightarrow \quad p = n\left(\frac{589 \times 589.6}{2 \times 0.6}\text{ nm}\right)$$

$$= n(0.29\text{ mm}),\text{ where } n = 1, 3, 5, \ldots$$

The corresponding annular positions are $\theta = \frac{p}{d} = \frac{n(0.29\text{ mm})}{2.9\text{ mm}} = n(0.10\text{ rad})$, where $n = 1,$ 3, 5, ...

26. (c) The angle $\Delta\theta$ subtended by the two points at the eye is

$$\Delta\theta = \frac{x}{s} = \frac{0.25\text{ mm}}{1\text{ m}}$$

$$= \frac{1}{4000}$$

If d is the diameter of the eye, we have

$$\Delta\theta = \frac{1.22\lambda}{d}$$

$$\Rightarrow \quad d = \frac{1.22\lambda}{\Delta\theta} = \frac{1.22(600\text{ nm})}{1/4000}$$

$$\approx 3\text{ mm}$$

27. (b) The angle $\Delta\theta$ subtended by the two satellites at the antenna is

$$\Delta\theta = \frac{s}{h} = \frac{42\text{ km}}{900\text{ km}}$$

$$= \frac{14}{300}$$

If d is the diameter of the dish antenna, for resolution we have

$$\Delta\theta \ge \frac{1.22\lambda}{d}$$

$$\Rightarrow \quad d \ge \frac{1.22\lambda}{\Delta\theta} = \frac{1.22(4\text{ cm})}{14/300}$$

$$= 1.05\text{ m}$$

28. (d) If the radius of the hole is a, the radius of the spot on the screen is $b = a + \frac{0.61\lambda L}{a}$ [the second term is due to diffraction].

The minimum value of b occurs when $\frac{db}{da} = 0$, that is, $1 - \frac{0.61\lambda L}{a^2} = 0 \Rightarrow a = \sqrt{0.61\lambda L}$. Thus, the minimum value of b is

$$b_{\min} = \sqrt{0.61\lambda L} + \frac{0.61\lambda L}{\sqrt{0.61\lambda L}}$$

$$= 2\sqrt{0.61\lambda L}$$

$$= \sqrt{2.44\lambda L}$$

29. (a) If unpolarised light is incident on an ideal polariser, the intensity of the transmitted linearly polarised light is $I_0/2$.

The second polariser reduces the intensity of this linearly polarised light to $\frac{1}{2}\cos^2 30° = \frac{3}{8}I_0$

The third polariser reduces the intensity to

$$\frac{3}{8}I_0\cos^2(90° - 30°) = \frac{3}{32}I_0$$

30. (a) The angle of reflection is given by

$$\theta_1 = \tan^{-1}\left(\frac{\mu_{air}}{\mu_{water}}\right)$$

$$= \tan^{-1}\left(\frac{3}{4}\right) = 37°$$

The angle of refraction is given by $\theta_2 = 90° - \theta_1 = 53°$

Appendix A: Previous Years' JEE Main Questions and Solutions

Only One Correct Option

- Each question has **FOUR** options. **ONLY ONE** of these four options is the correct answer.
- For each question, choose the option corresponding to the correct answer.
- The answer to each question will be evaluated according to the following marking scheme:

Full Marks: +3	If ONLY the correct option is chosen;
Zero Marks: 0	If none of the options is chosen (i.e. the question is unanswered);
Negative Marks: –1	In all other cases

1. Charges are placed at the corners of a cube, as shown in the figure. The electric field at the centre of the cube is:

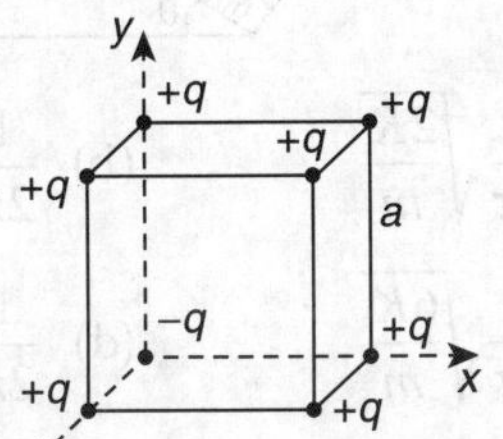

(a) $\frac{-2q}{3\sqrt{3}\pi\epsilon_0 a^2}(\hat{i}+\hat{j}+\hat{k})$

(b) $\frac{q}{3\sqrt{3}\pi\epsilon_0 a^2}(\hat{i}+\hat{j}+\hat{k})$

(c) $\frac{-q}{3\sqrt{3}\pi\epsilon_0 a^2}(\hat{i}+\hat{j}+\hat{k})$

(d) $\frac{2q}{3\sqrt{3}\pi\epsilon_0 a^2}(\hat{i}+\hat{j}+\hat{k})$

2. In a transistor, if increase in emitter current is 4 mA and the corresponding increase in collector current is 3.5 mA, then the value of β is:

(a) 8 (b) 7.5
(c) 7 (d) 5

3. In a Young's double slit experiment, the width of the two slits are w_1, w_2. If $\frac{w_1}{w_2} = \frac{1}{3}$ and it is given that the wave amplitude is proportional to the slit width, then the value of $\frac{I_{max}}{I_{min}}$ is:

(a) 9 : 1 (b) 3 : 1
(c) 4 : 1 (d) 2 : 1

4. A small block of mass m is placed gently on block M when it is passing through its mean position. If block M was initially oscillating with amplitude A, then the new oscillation amplitude is:

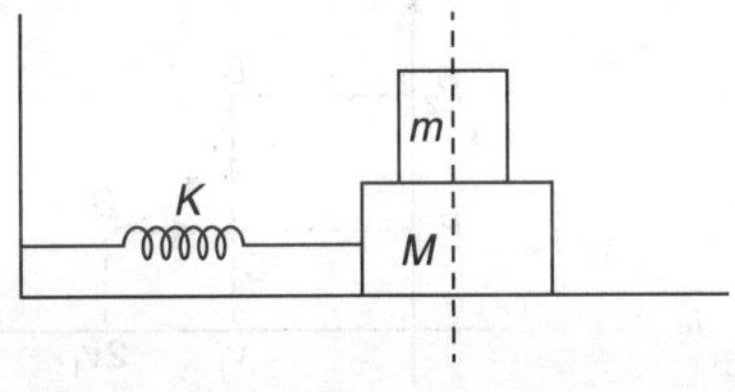

(a) $\sqrt{\frac{M}{M+m}}A$ (b) $\sqrt{\frac{M+m}{M}}A$

(c) $\sqrt{\frac{M+m}{2M}}A$ (d) $\sqrt{\frac{M}{M-m}}A$

5. A double-star system consists of two stars of masses m and $2m$ rotating about their common CM. If d is the separation between the stars, then the period of revolution of the double-star system is:

(a) $2\pi\sqrt{\frac{d^3}{3Gm}}$ (b) $2\pi\sqrt{\frac{d^3}{Gm}}$

(c) $2\pi\sqrt{\frac{d^3}{6Gm}}$ (d) $2\pi\sqrt{\frac{3d^3}{Gm}}$

6. If Y is Young's modulus, K is the bulk modulus, and η is the modulus of rigidity, then the relation between them is:

(a) $K = \frac{\eta Y}{9\eta - 3Y}$ (b) $Y = \frac{\eta K}{9\eta - 3K}$

(c) $K = \frac{\eta Y}{9\eta + 3Y}$ (d) $Y = \frac{\eta K}{9\eta + 3K}$

7. For the circuit shown in the figure, the value of $|V_X - V_Y|$ is:

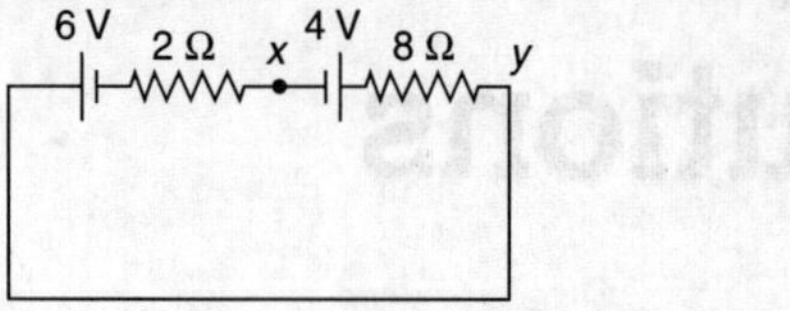

(a) 5.6 V (b) 3.6 V
(c) 2.6 V (d) 1.6 V

8. If Work $= \alpha\beta^2 e^{\frac{-x^2}{\alpha kT}}$, where k = Boltzmann's constant, T = temperature and x = length, then the dimension of β is:
(a) $[M^1L^1T^{-2}]$ (b) $[M^{-1}L^{-1}T^2]$
(c) $[M^1L^2T^{-2}]$ (d) $[M^2L^1T^2]$

9. It is given that AB is an isothermal, BC is an isobaric and CA is an isochoric process. If $P_1V_1 = nRT$, then the total work done by the gas in the cyclic process is:

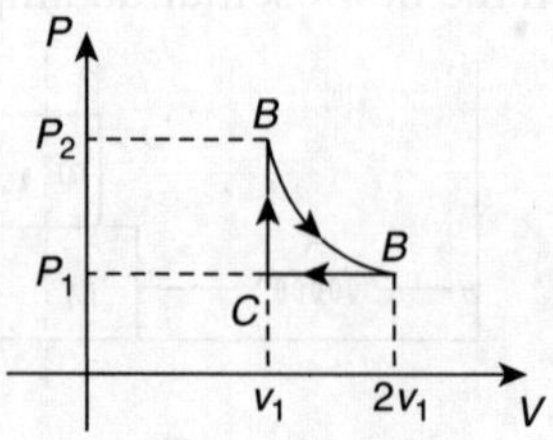

(a) $nRT\,[\ell n2 - 2]$ (b) $2nRT\,[\ell n2 - 1/2]$
(c) $nRT\,[\ell n2 - 1/2]$ (d) $nRT\,[\ell n2 + 2]$

10. A cube of side length a is made from six identical metal sheets whose coefficient of linear expansion is α. If temperature is increased from T to $T + \Delta T$, then the change ΔV in the volume of the cube is:
(a) $3a^3\alpha\Delta T$ (b) $\frac{4}{3}\pi a^3\alpha\Delta T$
(c) $4a^3\alpha\Delta T$ (d) $6a^3\alpha\Delta T$

11. The intensity of light after passing through a polaroid is 100 lumen. If the same polaroid is now rotated by 30° about its axis, then the intensity of light after passing through it is:
(a) 25 lumen (b) 50 lumen
(c) 75 lumen (d) 100 lumen

12. Four particles, each of mass 1 kg and equidistant from each other, move along a circle of radius 1 m under the action of their mutual gravitational attraction. The speed of each particle is:
(a) $\sqrt{G(2\sqrt{2}+1)}$ (b) $\frac{1}{2}\sqrt{G(2\sqrt{2}+1)}$
(c) $\sqrt{G(2\sqrt{2}-1)}$ (d) $\frac{1}{2}\sqrt{G(2\sqrt{2}-1)}$

13. Which of the following is correct for Zener diode:
(a) Lightly doped, depletion layer thickness is less
(b) Heavily doped, depletion layer thickness is less
(c) Lightly doped, depletion layer thickness is more
(d) Heavily doped, depletion layer thickness is more

14. A body is projected from the origin with velocity $v_0\hat{i}$. If a force $F = -\alpha x^2\hat{i}$ (x is the position of the particle) acts on the particle, then the maximum distance that the particle can go from the origin is:
(a) $\left(\frac{3mv_0^2}{2\alpha}\right)^{\frac{1}{3}}$ (b) $\left(\frac{3mv_0^2}{2\alpha}\right)^{\frac{1}{2}}$
(c) $\left(\frac{2mv_0^2}{3\alpha}\right)^{\frac{1}{3}}$ (d) $\left(\frac{2mv_0^2}{3\alpha}\right)^{\frac{1}{2}}$

15. The frequency of oscillation of the spring-block system shown in the figure is:

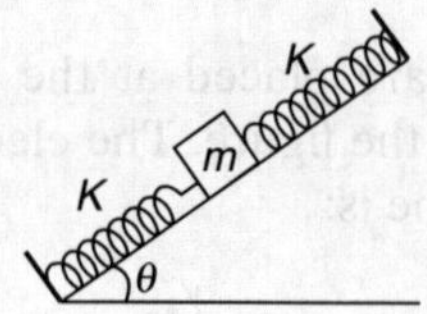

(a) $\frac{1}{2\pi}\sqrt{\frac{2K}{m}}$ (b) $\frac{1}{2\pi}\sqrt{\frac{4K}{m}}$
(c) $\frac{1}{2\pi}\sqrt{\frac{6K}{m}}$ (d) $\frac{1}{2\pi}\sqrt{\frac{K}{m}}$

16. Two electrons are fixed at separation $2d$. In the middle of these two electrons, a proton is free to oscillate along the perpendicular to the line joining the two fixed electrons. Given the mass of proton $= m_p$ and charge of proton $= e$. Now if the proton is slightly displaced, then the angular frequency of oscillation is:
(a) $\sqrt{\frac{e^2}{2\pi \epsilon_0 m_p d^3}}$ (b) $\sqrt{\frac{2e^2}{\pi \epsilon_0 d^2 m_p}}$
(c) $\sqrt{\frac{2e^2 \epsilon_0 m_p}{\pi d^2}}$ (d) $\sqrt{\frac{2\epsilon_0 e^2 m_p}{\pi d^2}}$

17. One mole of an ideal gas undergoes a cyclic thermodynamic process, as shown in the figure. AB is an isothermal process and during AB the temperature is T. BC is an isochoric and CA is an adiabatic process. If the adiabatic exponent of the gas is γ, then the total work done by the gas in the cyclic process is:

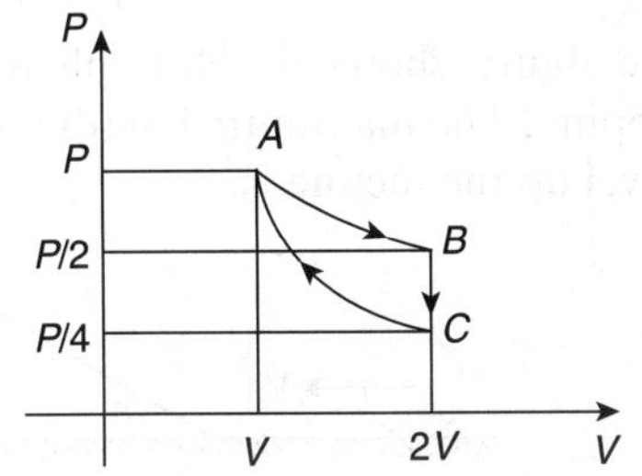

(a) $RT\left[\ln 2 - \frac{1}{2(\gamma-1)}\right]$

(b) $RT \ln 2$

(c) $\frac{RT}{2(\gamma-1)}$

(d) Zero

18. Which of the following curves represents the relation between velocity and displacement of a particle performing SHM:

(a) Ellipse (b) Circle
(c) Hyperbola (d) Straight line

19. Which of the following is most appropriate regarding the Bohr model?

(A) Speed $\propto \frac{Z}{n}$

(B) Frequency of oscillation $\propto \frac{Z^3}{n^3}$

(C) Coulomb force of attraction $\propto \frac{Z^3}{n^4}$

(D) Kinetic energy $\propto \frac{Z^2}{n^2}$

(a) A,C,D (b) A,B,D
(c) B,D (d) A,B

20. A train passes by a pole with uniform acceleration a. When its front end passes the pole, its speed is u, and when its back end passes the pole, its speed is v. The speed of the train when its middle point passes by the pole is:

(a) $\frac{\sqrt{v^2+u^2}}{2}$ (b) $\sqrt{\frac{v^2+u^2}{2}}$

(c) $\frac{\sqrt{v^2-u^2}}{2}$ (d) $\sqrt{\frac{v^2-u^2}{2}}$

21. A screw gauge shows 8 divisions on the circular scale below the reference line, when no object is placed. The number of divisions on the circular scale is 100 and in one complete rotation it advances by 1 mm. When a copper wire is measured with it, it completes one rotation and 72 divisions on the circular scale. The radius of the copper wire is:

(a) 1.80 mm (b) 0.90 mm
(c) 0.82 mm (d) 1.64 mm

22. A particle revolves in a vertical circular motion attached to a light string of length 1 m. Ratio of maximum to minimum tension is given as 5 : 1. The minimum speed of the particle during the motion is:

(a) $\sqrt{\frac{5g\ell}{4}}$ (b) $\sqrt{\frac{5g\ell}{8}}$

(c) $\sqrt{\frac{5g\ell}{2}}$ (d) $\sqrt{\frac{5g\ell}{16}}$

23. In the given L-R circuit (see figure), the currents I at $t = 0$ and at steady state are:

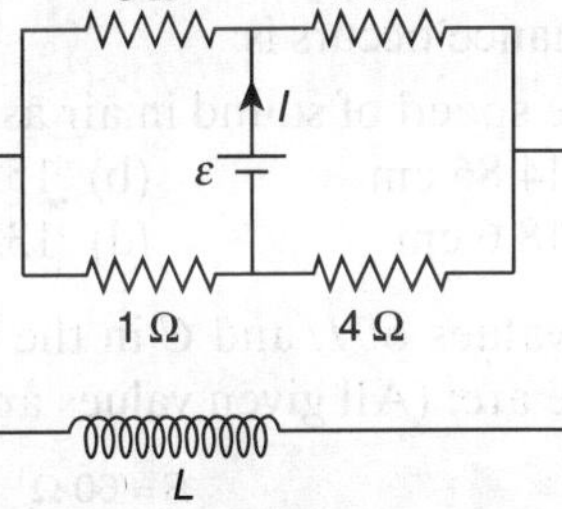

(a) $I(0) = \frac{5\xi}{18}, I(\infty) = \frac{10\xi}{33}$

(b) $I(0) = \frac{10\xi}{33}, I(\infty) = \frac{5\xi}{18}$

(c) $I(0) = \frac{5\xi}{33}, I(\infty) = \frac{5\xi}{9}$

(d) $I(0) = \frac{5\xi}{9}, I(\infty) = \frac{7\xi}{18}$

24. A 5-V cell is placed between the terminals x and y (see figure) with terminal x positive. If the potential barrier across each diode is 0.7 V, then the current through the cell is:

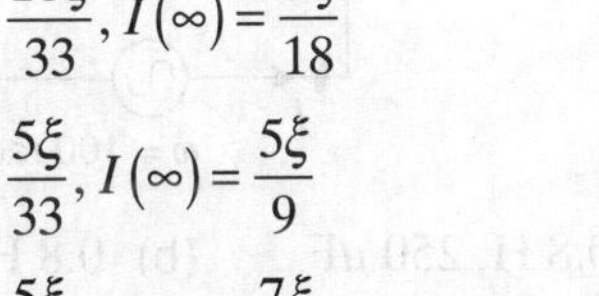

(a) 0.43 A (b) 0.73 A
(c) 1.5 A (d) 0.3 A

25. An ideal gas undergoes an isobaric process. If the adiabatic exponent of the gas is 1.4, then the ratio of $dU : dQ : dW$ is:
(a) $5:7:2$ (b) $7:5:2$
(c) $5:2:7$ (d) $2:5:7$

26. Electric field exists in space as $\vec{E} = \frac{3}{5}E_0\hat{i} + \frac{4}{5}E_0\hat{j}$. Consider two planes P_1 and P_2, one in the xy-plane of area 0.2 m^2, and the other in the xz-plane of area 0.3 m^2. If the ratio of the electric flux through them $\frac{\Phi_{P_1}}{\Phi_{P_2}} = \frac{a}{b}$ (in lowest form), then the value of a is:
(a) 5 (b) 4
(c) 3 (d) 1

27. A tuning fork of frequency 504 Hz is used as a sound source for the resonance column tube experiment. If the tube has a diameter of 6 cm, and the zero of the metre scale coincides with the top of tube, then the reading of the metre scale when the first resonance occurs is:
(Take speed of sound in air as 336 m/sec)
(a) 14.86 cm (b) 15.5 cm
(c) 18.6 cm (d) 13.5 cm

28. The values of L and C in the circuit shown in the figure are: (All given values are RMS)

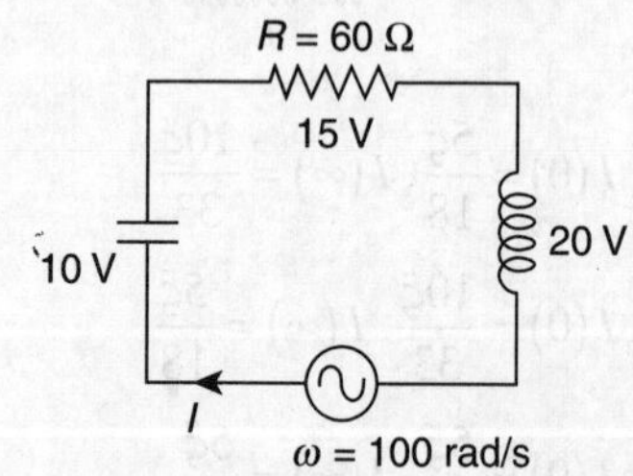

(a) 0.8 H, 250 μF (b) 0.8 H, 500 μF
(c) 0.4 H, 250 μF (d) 1.33 H, 500 μF

29. Three particles, proton (say 1), deuteron (say 2) and alpha particle (say 3) have equal momentum. They are projected in a uniform magnetic field such that their velocity and magnetic field are perpendicular. Then the ratio $F_1 : F_2 : F_3$ of the magnetic forces acting on them, and the ratio $v_1 : v_2 : v_3$ of their speeds are:
(a) $2:1:1, 4:2:1$ (b) $2:2:1, 4:2:1$
(c) $4:2:1, 2:1:1$ (d) $4:1:1, 2:2:1$

30. If the ratio of the intensity of two coherent light sources is $2x$, then the value of $\frac{I_{max} - I_{min}}{I_{max} + I_{min}}$ is:
(a) $\frac{2\sqrt{2x}}{2x+1}$ (b) $\frac{\sqrt{2x}}{2x+1}$
(c) $\frac{2\sqrt{2x}}{2x-1}$ (d) $\frac{2x}{2x+1}$

31. The figure shows a solid sphere rolling without slipping. The maximum length that the sphere can travel up the incline is:

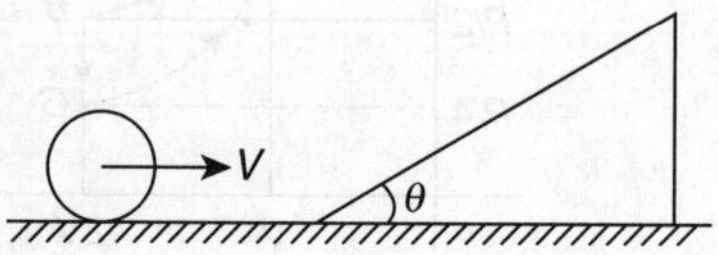

(a) $\frac{7v^2}{10g\sin\theta}$ (b) $\frac{10v^2}{7g\sin\theta}$
(c) $\frac{5v^2}{7g\sin\theta}$ (d) $\frac{7v^2}{5g\sin\theta}$

32. Consider the following two statements regarding a simple microscope:
Statement I: The angular size of the image is the same as the angular size of the object.
Statement II: Magnification is achieved as the object can be kept closer than 25 cm and hence it subtends a greater angle.
The correct option from the following is:
(a) Statement I is true but Statement II is false
(b) Statement I is false but Statement II is true
(c) Both statements are true and Statement II is the correct explanation for Statement I
(d) Both statements are true but Statement II is not the correct explanation for Statement I

33. Sunlight is diffracted through a circular aperture of diameter 0.1 μm. If the diameter is slightly increased, then:
(a) Size of circular fringe will increase, intensity will decrease.
(b) Size of circular fringe will decrease, intensity will increase.
(c) Size of circular fringe will increase, intensity will increase.
(d) Size of circular fringe will decrease, intensity will decrease.

34. If e = electronic charge, ε_0 = permittivity of free space, h = Planck's constant, c = speed of light, then the dimension of $\frac{1}{4\pi\varepsilon_0}\frac{e^2}{hc}$ is:
(a) $[M^1L^1T^{-2}C^2]$ (b) $[M^2L^2T^{-3}C^2]$
(c) $[M^1L^1T^{-2}C^2]$ (d) Dimensionless

35. In a given AC series circuit containing elements R, L and C and source rms voltage = 220 V, it is known that when L alone is removed or if C alone is removed, the phase difference between the current and the voltage remains 45°. If $R = 110\ \Omega$, then the rms value of the current in the L-C-R circuit is:

(a) 2 A (b) 2.5 A
(c) 1 A (d) 1.5 A

36. In the photoelectric effect of a certain metal, the stopping potential is 0.71 V if the wavelength of the incident radiation is 491 nm. Now the stopping potential is shown to be 1.43 V; therefore, the wavelength of the incident radiation is:

(a) 390 nm (b) 382 nm
(c) 275 nm (d) 392 nm

37. An electron enters a capacitor with kinetic energy K_1 at angle α with one plate, and comes out with kinetic energy K_2 at angle β with the other plate. Then the ratio $\frac{K_1}{K_2}$ is:

(a) $\frac{\cos^2\beta}{\cos^2\alpha}$ (b) $\frac{\cos^2\alpha}{\cos^2\beta}$

(c) $\frac{\sin^2\alpha}{\sin^2\beta}$ (d) $\frac{\sin^2\beta}{\sin^2\alpha}$

38. A gas follows the thermodynamic process $PV^{1/2}$ = constant, as shown in the figure. If $V_2 = 2V_1$, then the value of $\frac{T_2}{T_1}$ is:

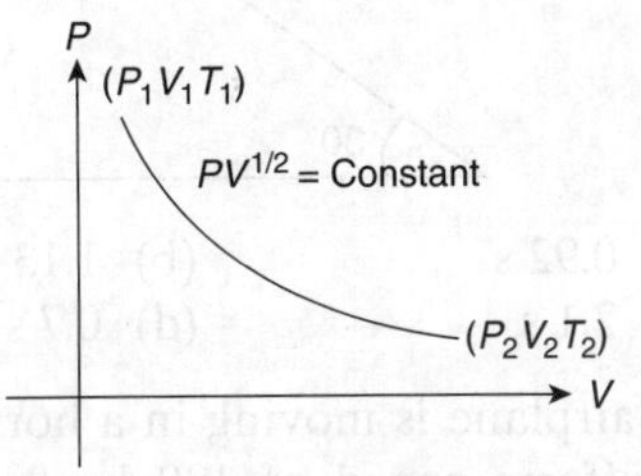

(a) $\frac{1}{\sqrt{2}}$ (b) $\sqrt{2}$

(c) $\sqrt{3}$ (d) $\frac{1}{\sqrt{3}}$

39. For the given logic gates circuit, the correct truth table is:

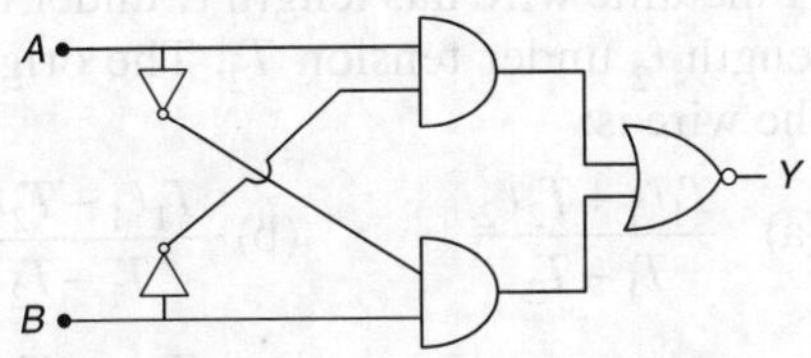

(a)

A	B	Y
0	0	1
1	0	0
0	1	0
1	1	1

(b)

A	B	Y
0	0	0
1	0	1
0	1	0
1	1	0

(c)

A	B	Y
0	0	0
1	0	0
0	1	0
1	1	1

(d)

A	B	Y
0	0	0
1	0	1
0	1	1
1	1	1

40. The equivalent resistance between AB is:

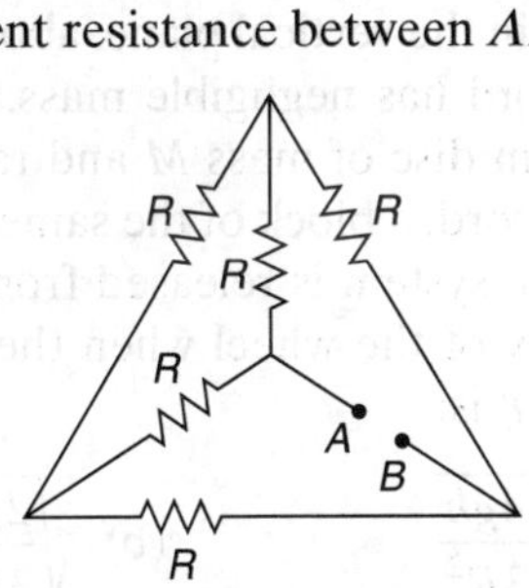

(a) $3R$ (b) $\frac{R}{2}$
(c) $2R$ (d) R

41. A uniform sphere and a uniform ring of the same mass M and same radius R are separated by $\sqrt{8}R$ distance. The gravitational force between them is:

(a) $\frac{\sqrt{2}}{3}\frac{GM^2}{R^2}$ (b) $\frac{\sqrt{8}}{3}\frac{GM^2}{R^2}$

(c) $\frac{\sqrt{8}}{27}\frac{GM^2}{R^2}$ (d) $\frac{\sqrt{2}}{27}\frac{GM^2}{R^2}$

42. If λ_1 represents the wavelength of the 3rd line of the Lyman series, and λ_2 represents the wavelength of the 1st line of the Paschen series in the Hydrogen spectrum, then the ratio $\frac{\lambda_1}{\lambda_2}$ is:

(a) $\frac{7}{135}$ (b) $\frac{5}{133}$

(c) $\frac{6}{135}$ (d) $\frac{9}{135}$

43. A 2-kg object is placed on a frictionless surface in the xy-plane. If a force $\vec{F} = (20\ N)\hat{i} + (10\ N)\hat{j}$ acts on the object, then its displacement along the x-axis in the first 10 seconds is:

(a) 500 m (b) 300 m
(c) 400 m (d) 200 m

44. A particle thrown in air follows the trajectory $y = \alpha x - \beta x^2$ where α and β are constants, and x and y are positions along the horizontal and the vertical, respectively. Its angle of projection and maximum height are:

(a) $\tan^{-1}(\alpha), \dfrac{4\alpha^2}{\beta}$ (b) $\tan^{-1}(\alpha), \dfrac{\alpha^2}{4\beta}$

(c) $\tan^{-1}(\beta), \dfrac{\beta^2}{4\alpha}$ (d) $\tan^{-1}(\beta), \dfrac{\beta}{4\alpha}$

45. A cord is wrapped around a wheel which is free to rotate in the vertical plane, about a horizontal axis. The cord has negligible mass, and the wheel is a uniform disc of mass M and radius R. At the end of the cord, a block of the same mass M is attached and the system is released from rest. The angular velocity of the wheel when the block descends by height h is:

(a) $\sqrt{\dfrac{4gh}{3R^2}}$ (b) $\sqrt{\dfrac{2gh}{3R^2}}$

(c) $\sqrt{\dfrac{3gh}{2R^2}}$ (d) $\sqrt{\dfrac{3gh}{4R^2}}$

46. An H-atom is free to move and its electron is in state $n = 5$. If the electron jumps from $n = 5$ to $n = 1$, the recoil speed of the atom is: (Take speed of light $c = 3\times10^8$ m/s, mass of Hydrogen atom $m_H = 1.6\times10^{-27}$ kg)

(a) 4.35 m/s (b) 1.2 m/s
(c) 13.06 m/s (d) 0.435 m/s

47. If $\lambda = \dfrac{C}{V}$ where C is capacitance and V is voltage, then the dimension of λ is:

(a) $[M^{-3}L^{-3}T^7A^3]$ (b) $[M^{-2}L^{-4}T^7A^3]$

(c) $[M^{-1}L^{-2}T^7A^{-3}]$ (d) $[M^3L^2T^7A^{-3}]$

48. Activity of a sample is A at time t_1 and $\dfrac{A}{5}$ at time t_2. Then the average life of the sample is:

(a) $\dfrac{t_2 - t_1}{\ln 5}$ (b) $\dfrac{t_2 - t_1}{2\ln 5}$

(c) $\dfrac{t_2 + t_1}{\ln 5}$ (d) $\dfrac{t_2 + t_1}{2\ln 5}$

49. For the given R-L-C circuit (see figure), the peak current and resonance frequencies are:

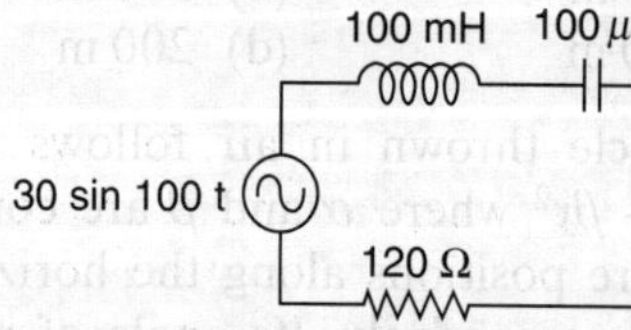

(a) 2 A, 10 Hz (b) 0.2 A, 5 Hz
(c) 2 A, 5 Hz (d) 0.2 A, 10 Hz

50. Two blocks A and B of the same mass M are connected by a spring and kept on a smooth horizontal surface. A constant force F is applied on B, as shown in the figure. At some instant, B is moving with acceleration a directed opposite to the direction of F. The acceleration of A at this instant is:

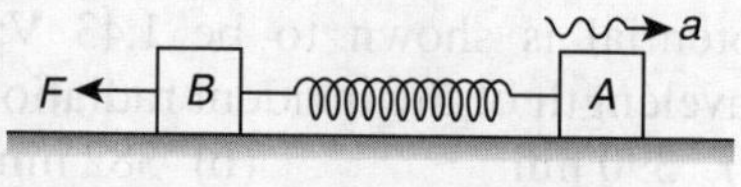

(a) $\dfrac{F + Ma}{M}$ (b) $\dfrac{F - Ma}{M}$

(c) $\dfrac{M}{F + Ma}$ (d) $\dfrac{M}{F - Ma}$

51. The block shown in the figure has mass 1 kg and carries charge 5 mC. A uniform electric field of magnitude 200 N/C exists along the horizontal. The coefficient of friction between the block and the incline is 0.2. The block is released from rest from a height of 1 m above the base of the incline. The time taken by the block to reach the base of the incline is: (Take g = 10 m/s²)

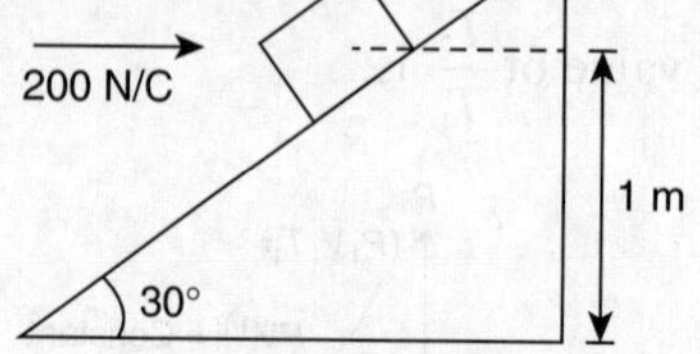

(a) 0.92 s (b) 1.13 s
(c) 2.1 s (d) 0.7 s

52. An airplane is moving in a horizontal plane with a uniform speed of 180 km/h. Its wing span is 10 m. At the position of the airplane, the Earth's magnetic field has magnitude $B = 2.5 \times 10^{-4}$ T and the angle of dip is 60°. The emf induced between its wing span is:

(a) 108 mV (b) 66 mV
(c) 50 mV (d) 80 mV

53. A metallic wire has length ℓ_1 under tension T_1 and length ℓ_2 under tension T_2. The original length of the wire is:

(a) $\dfrac{T_1\ell_1 + T_2\ell_2}{T_1 - T_2}$ (b) $\dfrac{T_1\ell_1 - T_2\ell_2}{T_1 - T_2}$

(c) $\dfrac{\ell_1 + \ell_2}{2}$ (d) $\dfrac{T_1\ell_2 - T_2\ell_1}{T_1 - T_2}$

54. A resistor of length ℓ is stretched by 25%. Assuming no change in its volume, the % change in its resistance is:

(a) 56% (b) 50%

(c) 60% (d) 40%

55. If the internal energy of an ideal gas is given by $U = 3PV + 4$ where P and V are pressure and volume, respectively, then the gas is:

(a) Monoatomic

(b) Diatomic

(c) Polyatomic

(d) Monoatomic or diatomic

56.

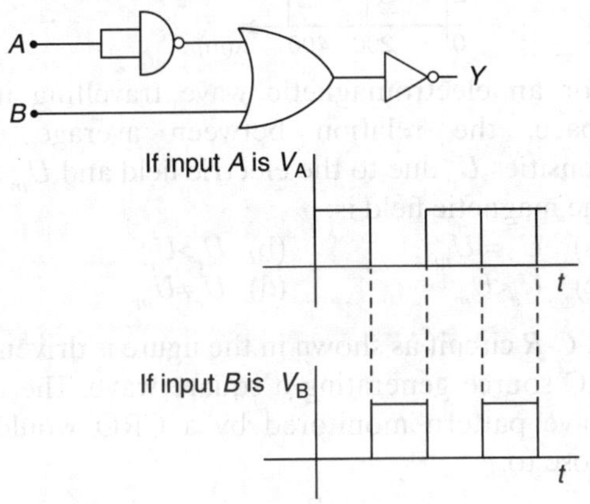

Then the correct output is:

(a)

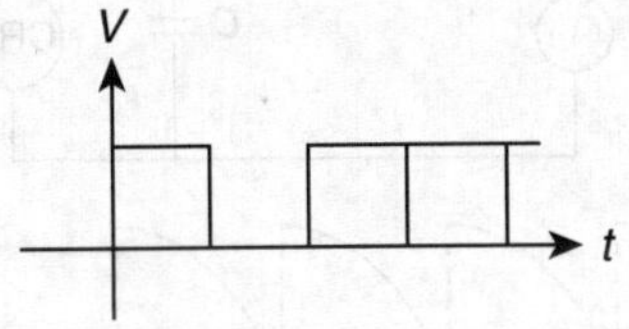

(b)

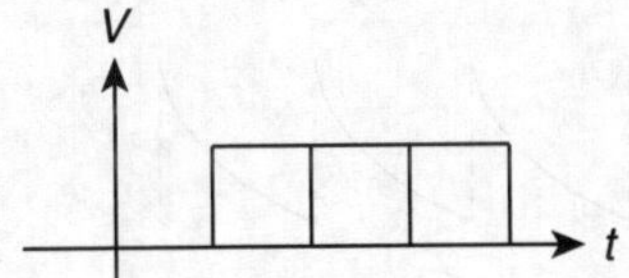

(c)

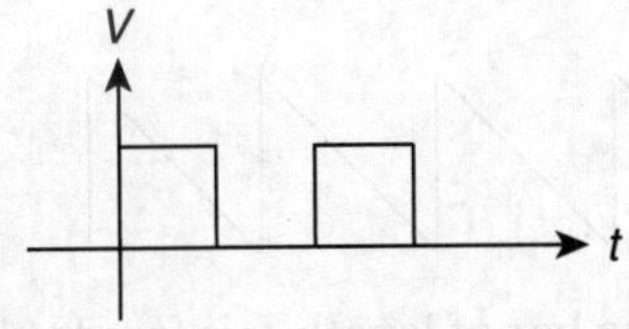

(d)

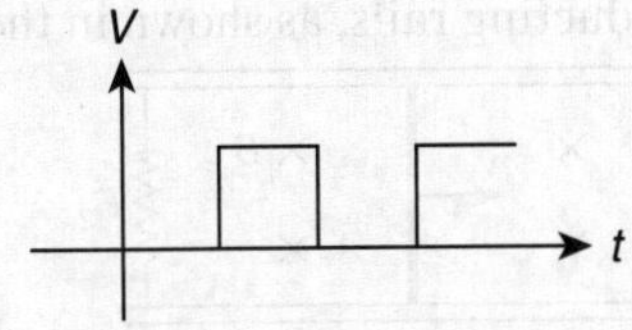

57. One main scale division of a Vernier caliper equals a cm. If n divisions of the Vernier scale coincides with n–1 divisions of the main scale, then the least count (mm) of the Vernier caliper is:

(a) $\dfrac{10na}{(n-1)}$ (b) $\dfrac{10a}{(n-1)}$

(c) $\left(\dfrac{n-1}{10n}\right)a$ (d) $\dfrac{10a}{n}$

58. For changing the capacitance of a given parallel plate capacitor, a dielectric material of dielectric constant k is used, which has the same area as the plates of the capacitor. The thickness of the dielectric slab is $\dfrac{3}{4}d$, where d is the separation between the plates of the parallel plate capacitor. The new capacitance C in terms of original capacitance C_0 is given by the relation:

(a) $C = \dfrac{3+k}{4k}C_0$ (b) $C = \dfrac{4+k}{3}C_0$

(c) $C = \dfrac{4k}{k+3}C_0$ (d) $C = \dfrac{4}{3+k}C_0$

59. The pressure acting on a submarine is 3×10^5 Pa at a certain depth. If the depth is doubled, the percentage increase in the pressure acting on the submarine would be: (Take atmospheric pressure $= 1 \times 10^5$ Pa, density of water $= 10^3$ kg$\cdot$m^{-3}, and $g = 10$ m$\cdot$s^{-2})

(a) $\dfrac{200}{3}\%$ (b) $\dfrac{200}{5}\%$

(c) $\dfrac{5}{200}\%$ (d) $\dfrac{3}{200}\%$

60. A plane electromagnetic wave of frequency 500 MHz is travelling in vacuum along the +ve y-direction. At a particular point in space and time, $\vec{B} = (8.0\times10^{-8}\,\text{T})\hat{k}$. The electric field at this point is:
(Take speed of light $= 3 \times 10^8$ ms^{-1})

(a) $\vec{E} = -(24\,\text{V/m})\hat{i}$ (b) $\vec{E} = (24\,\text{V/m})\hat{i}$

(c) $\vec{E} = -(26\,\text{V/m})\hat{i}$ (d) $\vec{E} = (26\,\text{V/m})\hat{i}$

61. Four masses of m each are placed at the corners of a square of length l, as shown in the figure. The moment of inertia of the system about an axis passing through A and parallel to DB is:

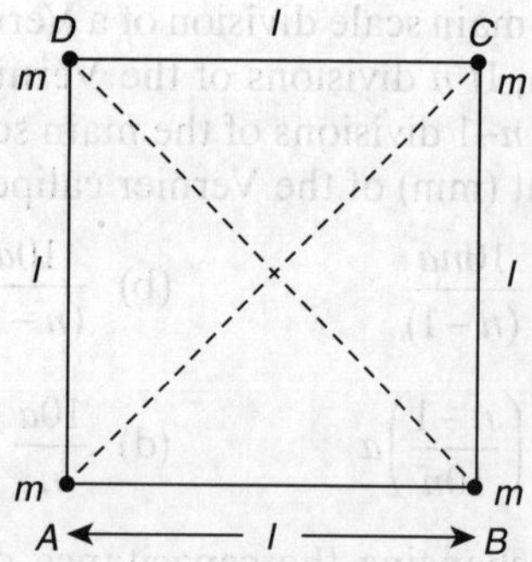

(a) ml^2 (b) $2\,ml^2$
(c) $3\,ml^2$ (d) $\sqrt{3}ml^2$

62. A simple pendulum suspended to the roof of a lift has time-period T when the lift is stationary. If the lift moves upwards with acceleration $g/2$, the time-period of the pendulum will be:

(a) $\sqrt{3}T$ (b) $\dfrac{T}{\sqrt{3}}$

(c) $\sqrt{\dfrac{3}{2}}T$ (d) $\sqrt{\dfrac{2}{3}}T$

63. The velocity-displacement graph describing the motion of a bicycle is shown in the figure.

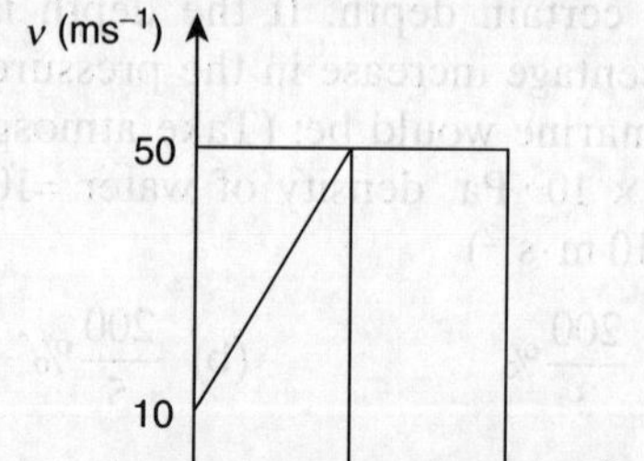

The acceleration-displacement graph of the bicycle's motion is best described by:

(a) 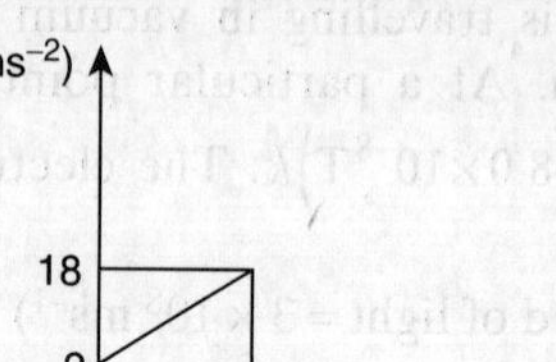

(b) 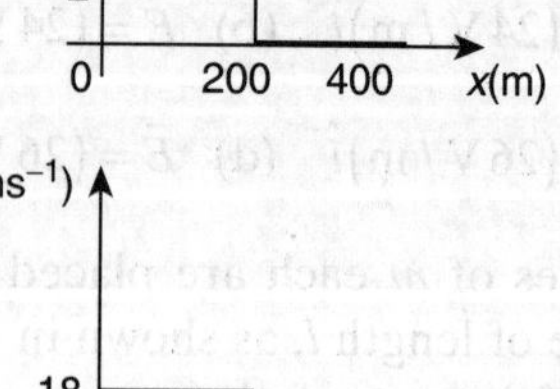

(c) 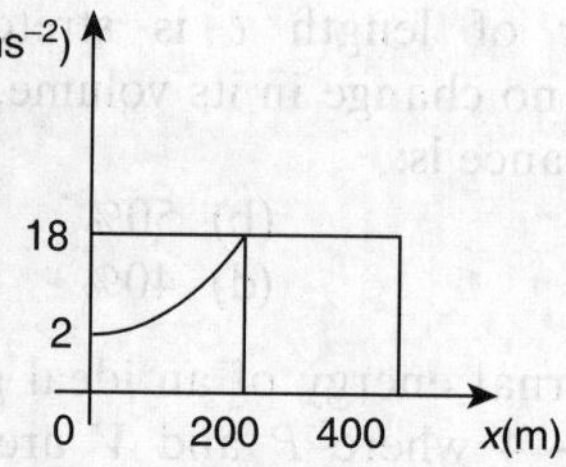

(d) 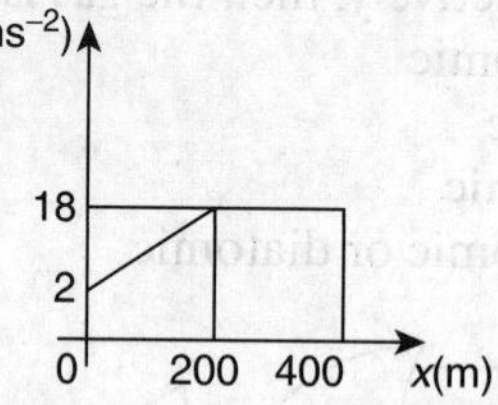

64. For an electromagnetic wave travelling in free space, the relation between average energy densities U_e due to the electric field and U_m due to the magnetic field is:

(a) $U_e = U_m$ (b) $U_e > U_m$
(c) $U_e < U_m$ (d) $U_e \neq U_m$

65. A *C-R* circuit as shown in the figure is driven by an AC source generating a square wave. The output wave pattern monitored by a CRO would look close to:

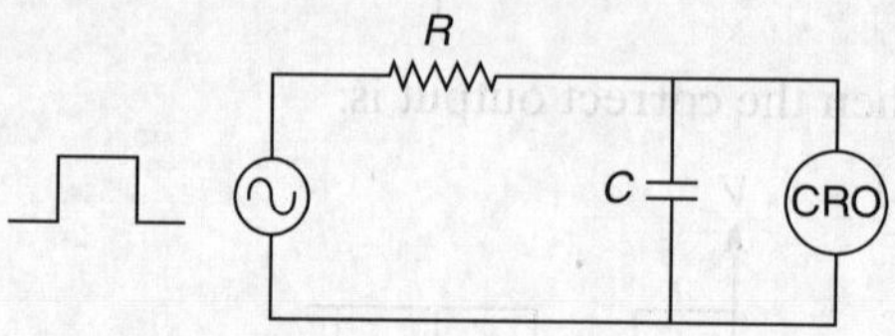

(a) 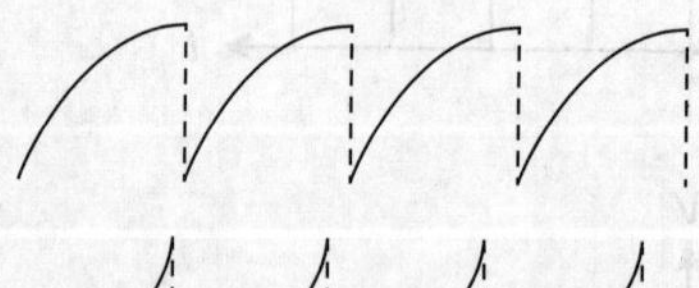

(b) 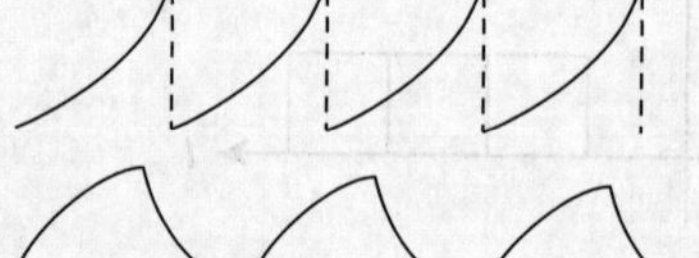

(c) 

(d) 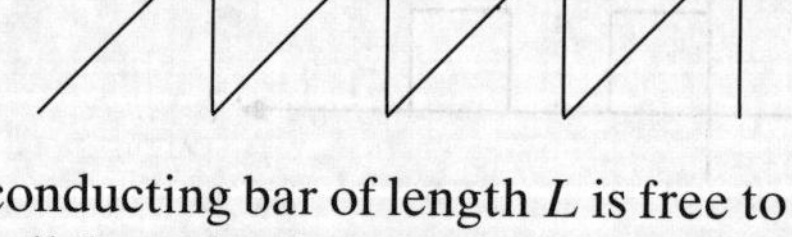

66. A conducting bar of length L is free to slide on two parallel conducting rails, as shown in the figure

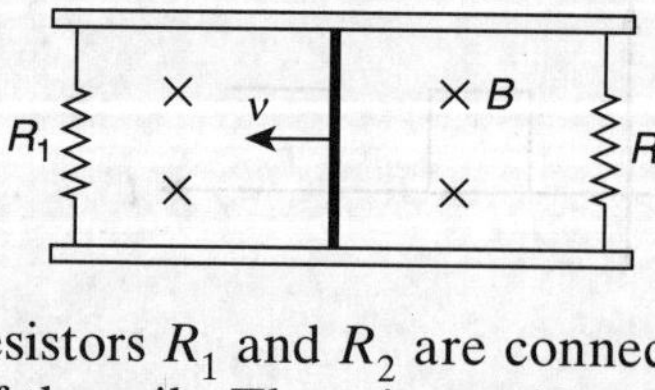

Two resistors R_1 and R_2 are connected across the ends of the rails. There is a uniform magnetic field

of strength B pointing into the page. An external agent pulls the bar to the left at a constant speed v. The correct statement about the directions of induced currents I_1 and I_2 flowing through R_1 and R_2, respectively, is:

(a) Both I_1 and I_2 are in the anticlockwise direction
(b) Both I_1 and I_2 are in the clockwise direction
(c) I_1 is in the clockwise direction and I_2 is in the anticlockwise direction
(d) I_1 is in the anticlockwise direction and I_2 is in the clockwise direction

67. The following logic gates circuit is equivalent to:

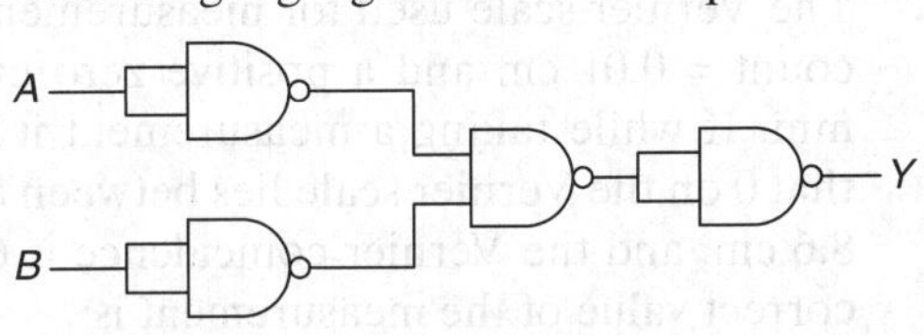

(a) NOR Gate (b) OR Gate
(c) AND Gate (d) NAND Gate

68. A large block of wood of mass $M = 5.99$ kg is hanging from two long massless cords (see figure). A bullet of mass $m = 10$ g is fired into the block and it gets embedded in the block. The (block + bullet) then swing upwards, their centre of mass rising to a maximum vertical height of $h = 9.8$ cm. The speed of the bullet just before collision is: (Take $g = 10$ m/s^2)

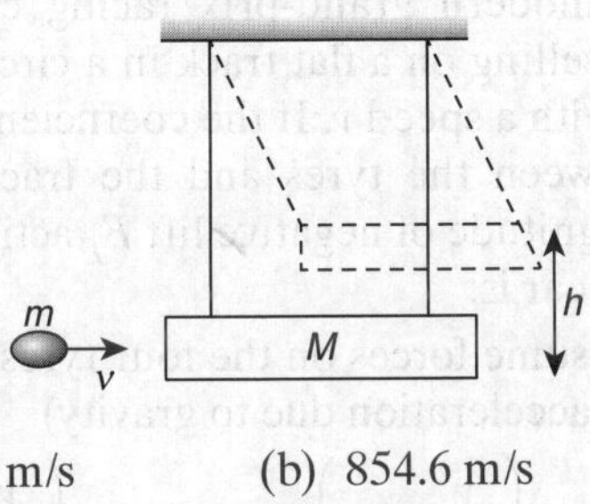

(a) 862.4 m/s (b) 854.6 m/s
(c) 848.5 m/s (d) 830.7 m/s

69. Water flowing out from a tap of radius 0.5 cm has viscosity 10^{-3} Pa·s. If flow rate is increased from 0.18 litre/min to 0.48 litre/min, the nature of flow will change from: (Take density of water = 10^3 kg/m^3)

(a) Unsteady to Steady flow
(b) Remain as Steady flow
(c) Remain as Turbulent flow
(d) Steady flow to Unsteady flow

70. An electron and a proton are accelerated through the same potential difference of 100 V. The ratio of their de Broglie wavelengths is: (Take $m_p : m_e = 1840 : 1$)

(a) 1840 : 1 (b) $(1840)^2 : 1$
(c) 920 : 1 (d) 43 : 1

71. For the given circuit, comment on the type of transformer used:

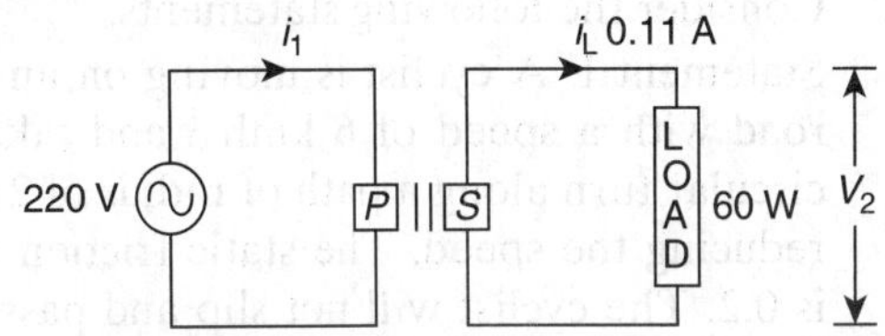

(a) Auxiliary transformer
(b) Auto transformer
(c) Step-up transformer
(d) Step-down transformer

72. The half-life of Au^{198} is 2.7 days. The activity of 1.50 mg of Au^{198} is: (Take $N_A = 6 \times 10^{23}$ mol^{-1} and Ci = 3.2×10^{15} dis/day)

(a) 240 Ci (b) 360 Ci
(c) 540 Ci (d) 680 Ci

73. In order to determine the Young's Modulus of a wire of radius 0.2 cm (measured using a scale of least count = 0.001 cm) and length 1 m (measured using a scale of least count = 1 mm), a weight of mass 1 kg (measured using a scale of least count = 1 g) was hanged to get an elongation of 0.5 cm (measured using a scale of least count 0.001 cm). The fractional error in the calculation of Young's Modulus determined by this experiment is:

(a) 0.14% (b) 0.9%
(c) 9% (d) 1.4%

74. A bimetallic strip consists of metals A and B. It is mounted rigidly, as shown. Metal A has higher coefficient of expansion compared to that of metal B. When the bimetallic strip is placed in a cold bath (see figure), it will:

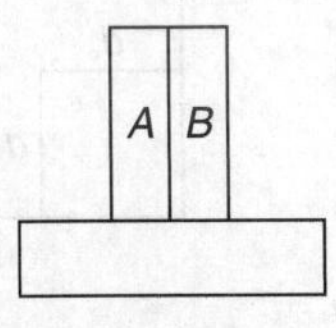

(a) Bend towards the right
(b) Not bend but shrink
(c) Neither bend nor shrink
(d) Bend towards the left

75. A balloon is ascending with an acceleration of 0.2 m/s^2. When the balloon is very high above the ground, two stones are dropped from it at an interval of 2 s. The distance between the two stones 1.5 s after the second stone is dropped is: (take $g = 9.8$ m/s^2)

(a) 50 m (b) 40 m
(c) 30 m (d) 20 m

76. Consider the following statements:
Statement I: A cyclist is moving on an unbanked road with a speed of 6 kmh^{-1} and takes a sharp circular turn along a path of radius of 2 m without reducing the speed. The static friction coefficient is 0.2. The cyclist will not slip and pass the curve ($g = 10$ m/s^2)
Statement II: If the road is banked at an angle of 45°, the cyclist can cross the curve of radius 2 m with the speed of 18 kmh^{-1} without slipping ($g = 10$ m/s^2)
In the light of the above statements, choose the correct answer from the options given below:

(a) Statement I is false and Statement II is true
(b) Statement I is true and Statement II is false
(c) Both Statement I and Statement II are false
(d) Both Statement I and Statement II are true

77. Two antennas mounted on identical towers are separated from each other by a distance of 45 km. The minimum height of the towers for transmission to be possible is:
(Take radius of earth = 6400 km)

(a) 19.77 m (b) 39.55 m
(c) 79.1 m (d) 158.2 m

78. The magnetic field in a region is given by $\vec{B} = B_0\left(\frac{x}{a}\right)\hat{k}$. A square loop of side d is placed with its edges along the x- and y-axes (see figure). The loop is moved with a constant velocity $\vec{v} = v_0\hat{i}$. The emf induced in the loop is:

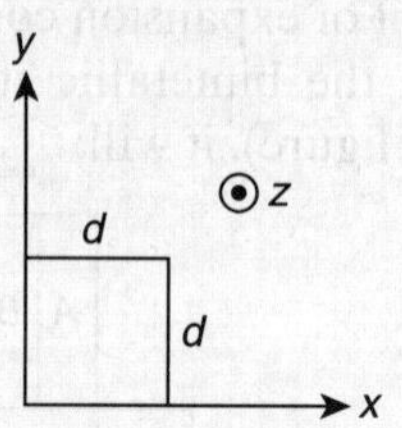

(a) $\frac{B_0 v_0^2 d}{2a}$ (b) $\frac{B_0 v_0 d}{2a}$
(c) $\frac{B_0 v_0 d^2}{a}$ (d) $\frac{B_0 v_0 d^2}{2a}$

79. The time interval between 33% decay and 67% decay of a radioactive sample of half-life 20 minutes is:

(a) 60 min (b) 20 min
(c) 40 min (d) 13 min

80. A polyatomic ideal gas has two vibrational modes. The value of the adiabatic exponent γ is:

(a) 1.10 (2) 1.20
(c) 1.25 (4) 1.30

81. Two identical metal wires of thermal conductivities K_1 and K_2 are connected in series. The effective thermal conductivity of the combination is:

(a) $\frac{2K_1K_2}{K_1+K_2}$ (b) $\frac{K_1+K_2}{2K_1K_2}$
(c) $\frac{K_1+K_2}{K_1K_2}$ (d) $\frac{K_1K_2}{K_1+K_2}$

82. The Vernier scale used for measurement has least count = 0.01 cm and a positive zero error of 0.2 mm. If while taking a measurement it was noted that 0 on the Vernier scale lies between 8.5 cm and 8.6 cm, and the Vernier coincidence is 6, then the correct value of the measurement is:

(a) 8.36 cm (b) 8.54 cm
(c) 8.58 cm (d) 8.56 cm

83. An AC current is given by $I = I_1\sin(\omega t) + I_2\cos(\omega t)$. A hot wire ammeter will give a reading equal to:

(a) $\sqrt{\frac{I_1^2 - I_2^2}{2}}$ (b) $\sqrt{\frac{I_1^2 + I_2^2}{2}}$
(c) $\frac{I_1+I_2}{\sqrt{2}}$ (d) $\frac{I_1+I_2}{2\sqrt{2}}$

84. A modern grand-prix racing car of mass m is travelling on a flat track in a circular arc of radius R with a speed v. If the coefficient of static friction between the tyres and the track is μ_s, then the magnitude of negative lift F_L acting downwards on the car is:
(Assume forces on the four tyres are identical and g = acceleration due to gravity)

(a) $m\left(\frac{v^2}{\mu_s R} + g\right)$ (b) $m\left(\frac{v^2}{\mu_s R} - g\right)$
(c) $m\left(g - \frac{v^2}{\mu_s R}\right)$ (d) mg

85. A car accelerates from rest at a constant rate α for some time after which it decelerates at a constant rate β to come to rest. If the total time elapsed is t seconds, the total distance travelled is:

(a) $\frac{4\alpha\beta}{(\alpha+\beta)}t^2$ (b) $\frac{2\alpha\beta}{(\alpha+\beta)}t^2$
(c) $\frac{\alpha\beta}{2(\alpha+\beta)}t^2$ (d) $\frac{\alpha\beta}{4(\alpha+\beta)}t^2$

86. A solenoid of 1000 turns/metre has a core with relative permeability 500. Insulated windings of the solenoid carry an electric current of 5 A. The magnetic flux density produced by the solenoid is: (Take permeability of free space = $4\pi \times 10^{-7}$ H/m)
(a) π T (b) $2 \times 10^{-3}\pi$ T
(c) $\frac{\pi}{5}T$ (d) $10^{-4}\pi$ T

87. A Carnot's engine working between 400 K and 800 K has a work output of 1200 J/cycle. The amount of heat energy supplied to the engine from the source in each cycle is:
(a) 3200 J (b) 1800 J
(c) 1600 J (d) 2400 J

88. The thickness at the centre of a plano-convex lens is 3 mm and the diameter is 6 cm. If the speed of light in the material of the lens is 2×10^8 m/s, then the focal length of the lens is:
(a) 0.30 cm (b) 15 cm
(c) 1.5 cm (d) 30 cm

89. A boy is rolling a 0.5-kg ball on the frictionless floor with a speed of 20 ms^{-1}. The ball gets deflected by an obstacle on the way. After deflection, it moves with 5% of its initial kinetic energy. What is the speed of the ball now?
(a) 19.0 ms^{-1} (b) 4.47 ms^{-1}
(c) 14.41 ms^{-1} (d) 1.00 ms^{-1}

90. The level of the single ionized carbon which has the same energy as the ground state energy of a Hydrogen atom is:
(a) 1 (b) 6
(c) 4 (d) 8

91. Two ideal polyatomic gases at temperatures T_1 and T_2 are mixed so that there is no loss of energy. If f_1, n_1 and f_2, n_2 are the degrees of freedom, and number of moles of the first and second gas, respectively, the equilibrium temperature of the mixture is:
(a) $\frac{n_1T_1 + n_2T_2}{n_1f_1 + n_2f_2}$ (b) $\frac{n_1f_1T_1 + n_2f_2T_2}{n_1f_1 + n_2f_2}$
(c) $\frac{n_1f_1T_1 + n_2f_2T_2}{f_1 + f_2}$ (d) $\frac{n_1T_1 + n_2T_2}{f_1 + f_2}$

92. An object is located 2 km beneath the surface of the water. If the fractional compression $\frac{\Delta V}{V}$ is 1.36%, the ratio of hydraulic stress to the corresponding hydraulic strain is:
(Take density of water = 1000 kg/m^3, g = 9.8 m/s^2)
(a) 1.96×10^7 N/m^2 (b) 1.44×10^7 N/m^2
(c) 2.26×10^9 N/m^2 (d) 1.44×10^9 N/m^2

93. A geostationary satellite orbiting around the Earth has a height of 11R above the Earth's surface, R being the radius of the Earth. The time-period of another satellite at a height of 2R from the Earths's surface is: (Take Earth's time-period of rotation = 24 hours.)
(a) $6\sqrt{2}$ hrs (b) $\frac{6}{\sqrt{2}}$ hrs
(c) 3 hrs (d) $3\sqrt{2}$ hrs

94. A sound wave of frequency 245 Hz travels with the speed of 300 ms^{-1} along the positive x-axis. Each point of the wave moves to and fro through a distance of 6 cm. The function representing the travelling wave is:
(a) $y(x,t) = 0.06\sin(5.1x - 1.5 \times 10^3 t)$
(b) $y(x,t) = 0.03\sin(5.1x - 0.2 \times 10^3 t)$
(c) $y(x,t) = 0.06\sin(0.8x - 0.5 \times 10^3 t)$
(d) $y(x,t) = 0.03\sin(5.1x - 1.5 \times 10^3 t)$

95. Which one is the correct option for the two different thermodynamic processes:
(a)
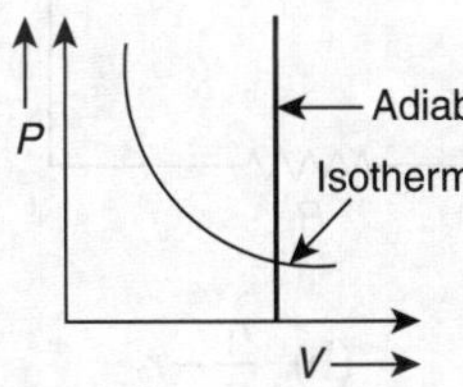

(b)
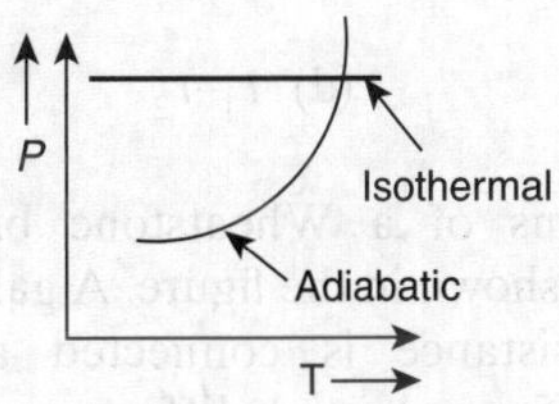

(c)
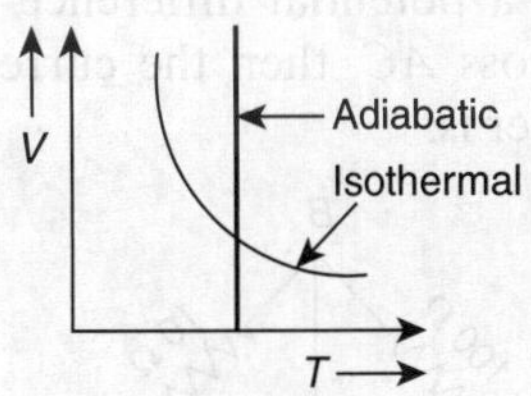

(d)
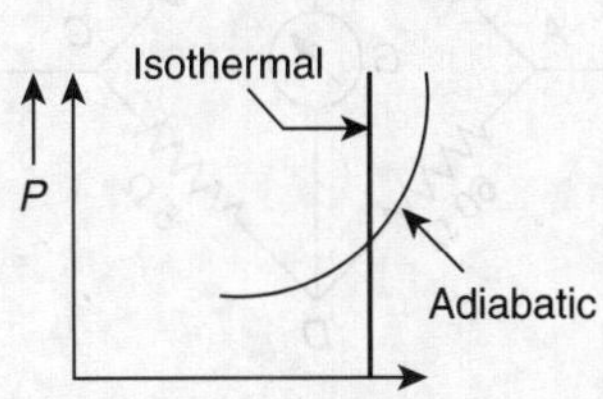

(a) (c) and (a) (2) (c) and (d)
(c) (a) only (4) (b) and (c)

96. The velocity of a particle is $v = v_0 + gt + Ft^2$. Its position is $x = 0$ at $t = 0$, then its displacement after time $t = 1$ is:

(a) $v_0 + g + F$ (b) $v_0 + \frac{g}{2} + \frac{F}{3}$

(c) $v_0 + \frac{g}{2} + F$ (d) $v_0 + 2g + 3F$

97. A carrier signal $C(t) = 25 \sin (2.512 \times 10^{10}t)$ is amplitude modulated by a message signal $M(t) = 5 \sin (1.57 \times 10^8 t)$ and transmitted through an antenna. The bandwidth of the modulated signal is:

(a) 8 GHz (b) 2 GHz
(c) 100 MHz (d) 50 MHz

98. Two cells of emf 2ξ and ξ with internal resistance r_1 and r_2 are connected in series to an external resistor R (see figure).The value of R at which the potential difference across the terminals of the first cell becomes zero is:

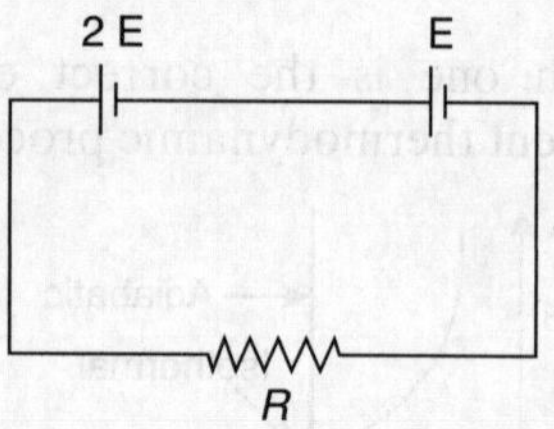

(a) $r_1 + r_2$ (b) $\frac{r_1}{2} - r_2$

(c) $\frac{r_1}{2} + r_2$ (d) $r_1 - r_2$

99. The four arms of a Wheatstone bridge have resistances as shown in the figure. A galvanometer of 15 Ω resistance is connected across BD (see figure). If a potential difference of 10 V is maintained across AC, then the current through the galvanometer is:

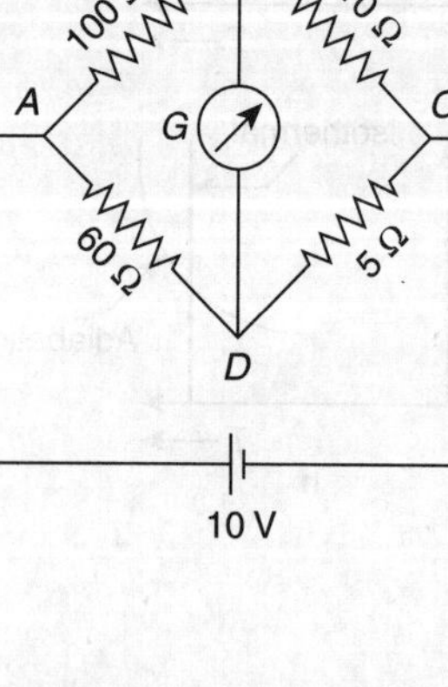

(a) 2.44 μA (b) 2.44 mA
(c) 4.87 μA (d) 4.87 mA

100. Two identical blocks A and B, each of mass m resting on the smooth horizontal floor, are connected by a light spring of spring constant k. A third block C of same mass m moving with a speed v along the line joining A and B collides with A. The maximum compression in the spring is:

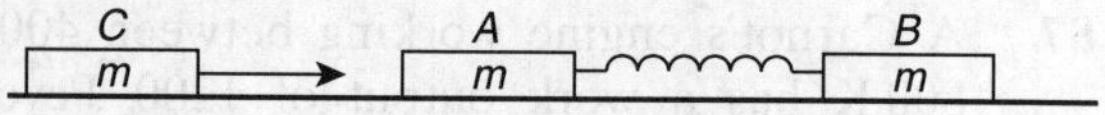

(a) $v\sqrt{\frac{m}{2k}}$ (b) $v\sqrt{\frac{m}{k}}$

(c) $v\sqrt{\frac{3m}{2k}}$ (d) $v\sqrt{\frac{2m}{3k}}$

101. A uniform sphere of mass 2 kg and radius 0.5 m rolling (without slipping) with an initial speed of 1 m/s goes up an inclined plane which makes an angle of 30° with the horizontal plane. The time taken by the sphere to go up and come down to the starting point is:

(a) 0.60 s (b) 0.52 s
(c) 0.57 s (d) 0.80 s

102. The correct relation between α (ratio of collector current to emitter current) and β (ratio of collector current to base current) of a transistor is:

(a) $\beta = \frac{\alpha}{1+\alpha}$ (b) $\alpha = \frac{\beta}{1-\alpha}$

(c) $\beta = \frac{1}{1-\alpha}$ (d) $\alpha = \frac{\beta}{1+\beta}$

103. In a series L-C-R circuit, the inductive reactance is X_L=10 Ω and the capacitive reactance is X_C=4 Ω. The resistance in the circuit is R=6 Ω. The power factor of the circuit is:

(a) $\frac{1}{2}$ (b) $\frac{1}{2\sqrt{2}}$

(c) $\frac{1}{\sqrt{2}}$ (d) $\frac{\sqrt{3}}{2}$

104. The angular momentum of a planet of mass M moving around the sun in an elliptical orbit is L. The magnitude of the areal velocity of the planet is:

(a) $\frac{4L}{M}$ (b) $\frac{L}{M}$

(c) $\frac{2L}{M}$ (d) $\frac{L}{2M}$

105. A solid cylinder of mass m is wrapped with an inextensible light string and is placed on a rough inclined plane, as shown in the figure. If the coefficient of friction is $\mu = 0.4$, the frictional force acting between the cylinder and the inclined plane is:

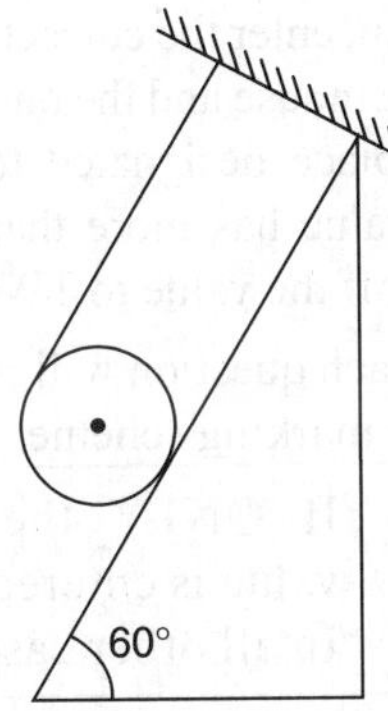

(a) $\frac{7}{2}$mg (b) $5mg$

(c) $\frac{\text{mg}}{5}$ (d) 0

106. The speed of electrons in a scanning electron microscope is 1×10^7 m/s. If protons having the same speed were used instead of electrons, then the resolving power of the scanning proton microscope would change by a factor of: (Take $m_p : m_e = 1840 : 1$)

(a) 1837 (b) $\frac{1}{1840}$

(c) $\sqrt{1840}$ (d) $\frac{1}{\sqrt{1840}}$

107. A very long cylindrical-shaped galaxy has length L and radius $R(R \ll L)$ and has uniformly distributed mass. A star outside the galaxy is revolving in a circular orbit around the galaxy in a plane perpendicular to the length of the galaxy. If the radius of the orbit is R and the time-period of revolution is T, then:

(a) $T \propto r^{1/2}$ (b) $T \propto r$

(c) $T \propto r^{3/2}$ (d) $T \propto r^2$

108. Statement I: As temperature increases, resistivity of a metal increases whereas that of a semiconductor decreases.

Statement II: As temperature increases, lattice vibration in a metal increases whereas in a semiconductor more electrons are now available for conduction.

(a) Statement I is true and Statement II is false
(b) Statement I is false and Statement II is true
(c) Both Statements are true and Statement II is the correct explanation for Statement I
(d) Both Statements are true but Statement II is not the correct explanation for Statement I

109. A charge q is placed at one corner of a cube, as shown in the figure. The electric flux through the shaded surface is:

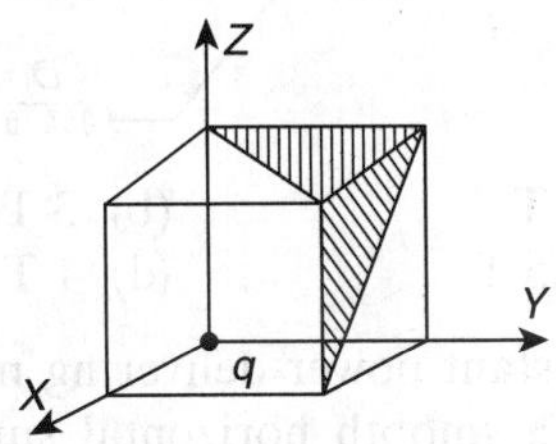

(a) $\frac{q}{4\varepsilon_0}$ (b) $\frac{q}{8\varepsilon_0}$

(c) $\frac{q}{24\varepsilon_0}$ (d) $\frac{q}{48\varepsilon_0}$

110. A radioactive sample disintegrates via two independent decay processes having half-lives T_1 and T_2. The effective half-life of the nuclei is:

(a) $T_1 + T_2$ (b) $|T_1 - T_2|$

(c) $\frac{T_1T_2}{|T_1 - T_2|}$ (d) $\frac{T_1T_2}{T_1 + T_2}$

111. Three rays of light, namely, R (red), G (green) and B (blue) are incident on the face LM of an isosceles right-angled prism LMN (see figure). The refractive indices of the prism for the three colours are 1.27, 1.42 and 1.49, respectively. The rays that will emerge out of the face LN are:

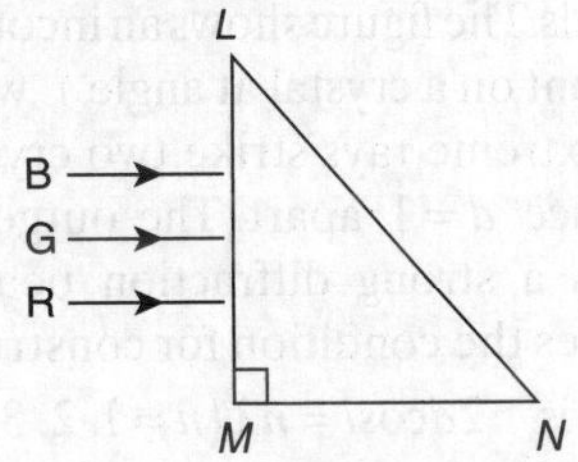

(a) R, G and B (b) R and G
(c) R only (d) None of them

112. In Millikan's oil-drop experiment, an oil drop of radius 2 mm and density 3 g/cm^3 is held stationary under a constant electric field of intensity 3.55×105 V/m. If the oil drop possesses $1.73 \times 10^{\alpha}$ number of surplus electrons, then the value of α is: (Take $g = 9.81$ m/s^2, $e = 1.6 \times 10^{-19}$ C)

(a) 9 (b) 10
(c) 11 (d) 12

113. Four identical solenoids A, B, C, D are connected as shown in the figure. If the magnetic field at the centre of solenoid A is 3 T, then the magnetic field at the centre of solenoid C is:

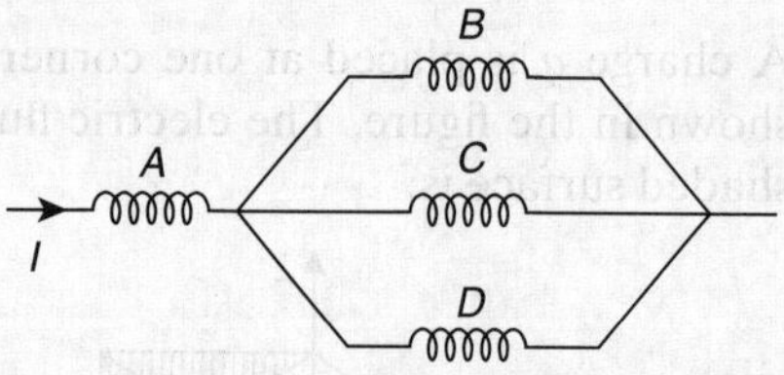

(a) 6 T (b) 3 T
(c) 1.5 T (d) 1 T

114. A constant power delivering machine tows a box along a smooth horizontal surface. If the initial velocity of the box is zero, then the distance travelled by the block in time t is proportional to:
(a) $t^{2/3}$ (b) $t^{3/2}$
(c) $t^{1/2}$ (d) t

115. An AC source rated 220 V, 50 Hz is connected to a resistor. The time taken by the current to change from its peak value to rms value is:
(a) 2.5 ms (b) 25 ms
(c) 1.25 ms (d) 12.5 ms

116. An NPN transistor operates as a common emitter amplifier with a power gain of 106. If the input circuit resistance is 100 Ω and the output load resistance is 10 kΩ, then the current gain β is:
(a) 500 (b) 200
(c) 100 (d) 50

117. The wave property of electrons implies that they will show diffraction effects. Davisson and Germer demonstrated this by diffracting electrons from crystals. The figure shows an incoming electron beam incident on a crystal at angle i with the normal. The two extreme rays strike two crystal planes that are distance $d = 1$ apart. The outgoing electron beam shows a strong diffraction peak only if angle i satisfies the condition for constructive interference, that is, $2d\cos i = n\lambda\,(n = 1, 2, 3, \ldots)$. If electrons accelerated by potential V give a strong diffraction peak for $i = 30°$, then the value of V could be: (Take $h = 6.6\times10^{-34}$ Js, $e = 1.6\times10^{-19}$ C, $m_e = 9.1\times10^{-31}$ kg)

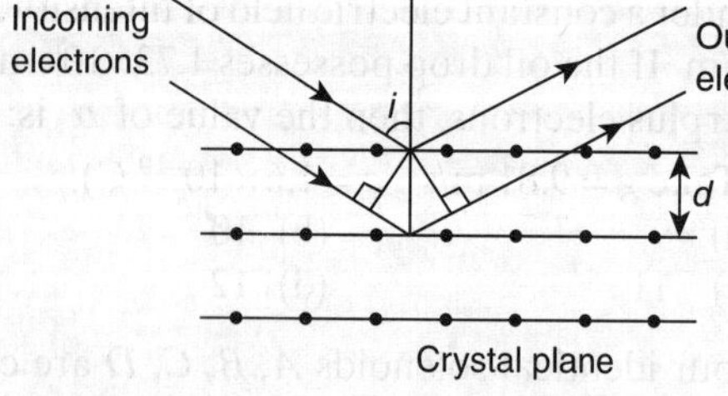

(a) 500 V (b) 500 V
(c) 50 V (d) 10 V

Numerical Value Answer

- The answer to each question is a **NUMERICAL VALUE.**
- For each question, enter the correct numerical value of the answer using the mouse and the on-screen virtual numeric keypad in the place designated to enter the answer. If the numerical value has more than two decimal places, truncate/round-off the value to TWO decimal places.
- The answer to each question will be evaluated according to the following marking scheme:

Full Marks: +4 If ONLY the correct numerical value is entered;
Zero Marks: 0 In all other cases

1. A vertical cross-section of a rough surface is given by $y = \dfrac{x^2}{4\,m^2}$, and the coefficient of friction is 0.5. The maximum height (cm) at which a particle can stay on the surface is equal to______.

2. The figure shows a block being pressed against a rough vertical wall by applying a force normal to the wall. If the coefficient of friction between the block and the wall is $\mu = 0.2$, then the minimum value of the force required to prevent the block from falling is equal to______. (Take $g = 10$ m/s^2)

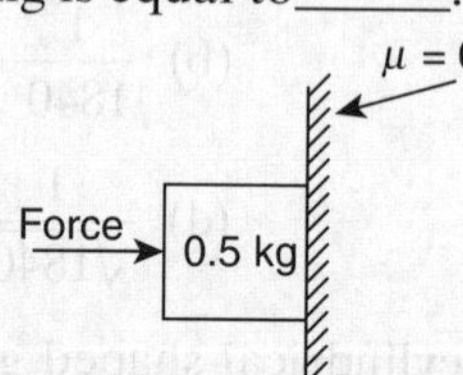

3. A hydraulic lift is fitted with two circular pistons A and B (see figure). A 100-kg mass on piston A can be lifted by a mass m on piston B. If the diameter of piston A is increased by 4 times and that of piston B is decreased by 4 times, then the mass that can be lifted on piston A for the same mass m on piston B is equal to______.

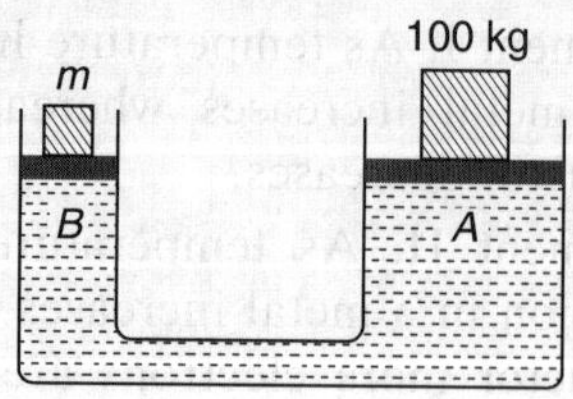

4. An electromagnetic wave is propagating in a medium for which $\mu_r = \varepsilon_r = 2$. If the speed of light in the medium is $x \times 10^7$ m/s, then x is equal to______.

5. The voltage fluctuations for a modulated and a carrier wave are $V_m = 20\text{V}\sin\left(100\pi t + \frac{\pi}{4}\right)$ and $V_c = 80\text{V}\sin\left(10^4\pi t + \frac{\pi}{6}\right)$, respectively. For amplitude modulation wave, the percentage modulation index is equal to______.

6. A point charge $Q = 12\ \mu\text{C}$ is placed at a distance of 6 cm from the centre of a square surface of side 12 cm, as shown in the figure. If the electric flux through the square surface is $x \times 10^3$ V · m, then x is equal to______.

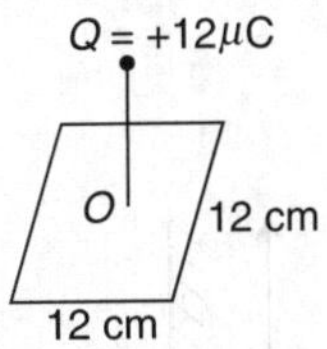

7. A rod of length 2.4 m and mass 6 kg is bent to form a regular hexagon. The moment of inertia (kg · m^2) of the hexagon about an axis perpendicular to the plane of the hexagon and passing through its centre is equal to______.

8. On applying force to a rod along its length, the rod elongates by 0.04 m. Now the length and the diameter of the rod are both doubled, and the same force is applied along its length. If the rod now elongates by $x \times 10^{-2}$ m, then the value of x is equal to______.

9. There is a cylindrical wire of radius 0.5 mm and conductance $5 \times 10^7 \Omega\ \text{m}^{-1}$. If the potential gradient along the length of the cylindrical wire is 10 mV/m, and the current flowing through the cylindrical wire is $\pi\ x^3$ mA, then the value of x is equal to______.

10. In a series LCR circuit at resonance, power consumption in the circuit is 16 W. If the voltage source is of frequency 10^5 rad/s and its rms voltage is 120 V, then the resistance (Ω) of the circuit is equal to______.

11. Two radioactive substances, X and Y, have N_1 and N_2 nuclei initially. The half-life of X is half of the half-life of Y. After a time of three half-lives of Y, the number of nuclei of X and Y become equal. Then the value of $\frac{N_1}{N_2}$ is equal to______.

12. When an object is placed at 10 cm from a convex lens and when it is placed at 20 cm from it, the images obtained are of the same height. Then the focal length of the lens is equal to______.

13. A transmitter circuit is used for transmission of EM waves of wavelength 960 m. If the capacitor used in the circuit has capacitance $C = 2.56\ \mu\text{F}$, and the self-inductance of the inductor coil used in the circuit such that resonance occurs is $L = x \times 10^{-8}$ H, then the value of x is equal to______.

14. In a thermodynamic process, pressure P and volume V are related as $P = kV^3$. If the initial temperature of the gas is 100°C and the final temperature is 300°C, and the work done by the gas in the process is $x(nR)$, then the value of x is equal to______. (n is the number of moles, R is the ideal gas constant)

15. An ideal inductor coil of self-inductance $L = 2$ H is connected to a DC source whose emf varies with time as $\xi = (3\text{V/s})t$. If the circuit is closed at $t = 0$, then the energy (J) stored in the inductor coil at $t = 4$ s is equal to______.

16. A satellite is projected from the surface of the Earth so that it can attain a height of 10R from the surface of the Earth, where R is the radius of the earth. If its speed at the surface of the Earth is $v = \sqrt{\frac{x}{11}}v_{esc}$, then x is equal to______.

17. A stone is dropped from the top of a tower. When it has travelled a distance of 5 m, another stone is dropped from a point 25 m below the top of the tower. If both the stones reach the bottom of the tower simultaneously, then the height of the tower is equal to______. (Take $g = 10$ m/s^2)

18. A particle has the same wavelength and same energy as an X-ray photon of wavelength 10 Å. If the mass of the particle is $\frac{xh}{3}$ where h is Planck's constant, then value of x is equal to______.

19. Two conducting charged bodies of negligible size having charges 2.1 nC and –0.1 nC are brought in contact and then separated by 0.5 m. If the force of interaction between them is $x \times 10^{-9}$ N, then x is equal to______. $\left(\text{Take } \frac{1}{4\pi\epsilon_0} = 9 \times 10^9\ \text{N}\cdot\text{m}^2/\text{C}^2\right)$

20. In a series L-C-R circuit at resonance, the quality factor is 100. If the value of self-inductance is doubled and the resistance is halved, then the new value of the quality factor is equal to______.

21. A 1000-W bulb has optical efficiency 1.2%. The electric field amplitude (V/m) at a distance of 2 m from the bulb is equal to______.
$$\left(\text{Take}\ \frac{1}{4\pi\epsilon_0} = 9\times10^9\ \text{N}\cdot\text{m}^2/\text{C}^2,\ c = 3\times10^8\ \text{m/s}\right)$$

22. Displacement function of a string wave is given by $y = A\sin\{(1\text{m}^{-1})x + (30\text{s}^{-1})t\}$. If the mass per unit length of the wire is 0.325 g/cm, then the tension (N) in the string is equal to______.

23. A non-conducting container consists of two parts A and B having volumes 4.5 litre and 5.5 litre, respectively. Part A is filled with 3 moles of an ideal gas to a pressure of 2 atm, and part B is filled with 4 moles of the same ideal gas to a pressure of 3 atm. If the partition valve is opened, then the common pressure (atm) is equal to______.

24. Gravitational field intensity at points A and C are equal but less than that at point B (see figure). If $OA : AB = x : y$, then the value of x is equal to______. (x and y are in the lowest form)

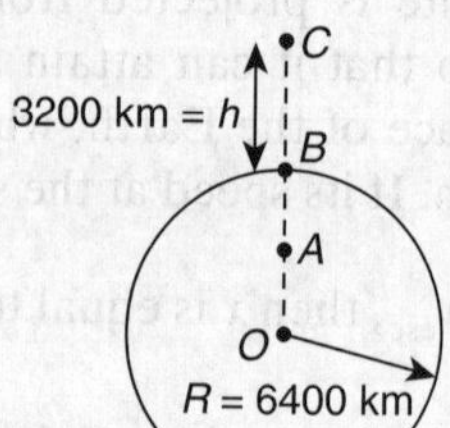

25. The time-period of a simple pendulum is T. In order to cover $\frac{5}{8}$ oscillation starting from its mean position, it takes $\left(\frac{x}{y}\right)T$. Then the value of x is equal to______. (x and y are in the lowest form)

26. The power dissipated across the Zener diode (V_Z = 30 V) in the circuit shown in the figure is equal to______.

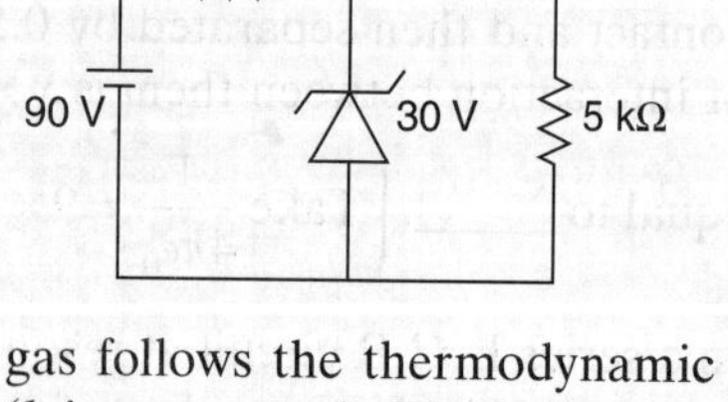

27. An ideal gas follows the thermodynamic process $V = kT^{2/3}$ (k is a constant). When the temperature of the gas is raised by 90°C, the work done by the gas is xR. Then x is equal to______.

28. The work function of a metal is ϕ. Two beams of different intensities, such that the photon energy in one beam is 2ϕ and that in the other beam is $10\ \phi$, are incident on the metal plate. If the ratio of the maximum speed of the photo-electrons emitted in the two cases is $x : y$, then x is equal to______. (x and y are in the lowest form)

29. A person moves parallel to a plane mirror. The figure shows the line of motion of the person. A source of light S is placed midway between the mirror and the line of motion of the person. The maximum distance (cm) over which the person can see the image of S is equal to______.

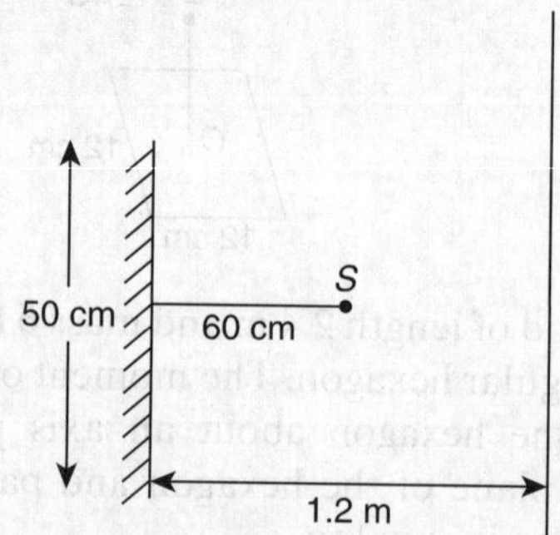

30. Consider a 20-kg uniform circular disk of radius 0.2 m. It is supported at its centre and is at rest initially. The disk is acted upon by a constant force F = 20 N through a light string wrapped around its periphery, as shown in the figure.

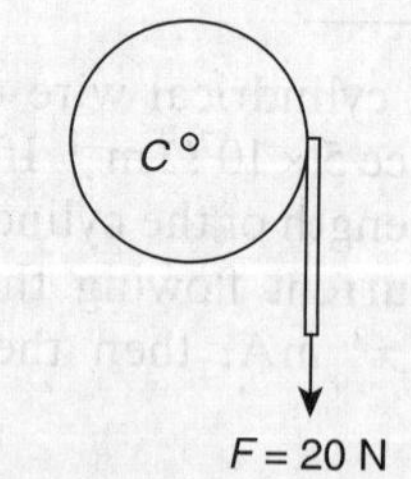

Suppose the disk makes n number of revolutions to attain an angular speed of 50 rad s^{-1}. The value of n is equal to______.

31. In the logic circuit shown in the figure, if inputs A and B are 0 and 1, respectively, then the output at Y is equal to______.

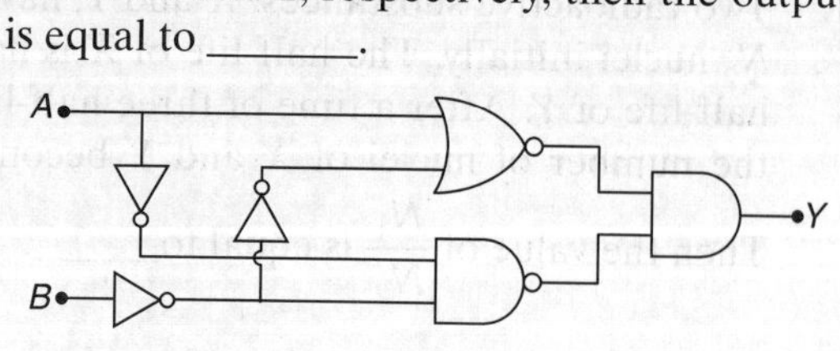

32. The resistance R of a resistor is calculated using the equation $R = \frac{V}{I}$, where V = (50 ± 2) V and I =

(20 ± 0.2) A. If the percentage error in R is $x\%$, then the value of x is equal to ______.

33. A ball of mass 10 kg moving with a velocity $10\sqrt{3}\ \text{ms}^{-1}$ along the x-axis hits another ball of mass 20 kg which is at rest. After collision, the first ball comes to rest and the second one disintegrates into two equal pieces. One of the pieces starts moving along the y-axis at a speed of 10 m/s. The second piece starts moving at a speed of 20 m/s at angle θ with respect to the x-axis. The value of θ (degree) is equal to ______.

34. A force $\vec{F} = (4\text{N})\hat{i} + (3\text{N})\hat{j} + (4\text{N})\hat{k}$ is applied on a particle which lies at the intersection point of $x = 2$ plane and the x-axis. The magnitude of the torque of this force about a point A(2 m, 3 m, 4 m) is equal to ______.

35. If one wants to remove all the mass of the Earth to infinity in order to break it up completely, the amount of energy required is $\frac{x}{5}\frac{GM^2}{R}$. Then x is equal to ______. (M is the mass of the Earth, R is the radius of the Earth, G is the gravitational constant)

36. A deviation of 2° is produced in the yellow ray when prisms of crown and flint glass are achromatically combined. The dispersive powers of the crown and the flint glass prisms are 0.02 and 0.03, respectively. For yellow light, the refractive indices of these glasses are 1.5 and 1.6, respectively. Then the refracting angle (degree) of the crown glass prism is equal to ______.

37. A body of mass 2 kg moves under a force of $\vec{F} = (2\text{N})\hat{i} + (3\text{N})\hat{j} + (5\text{N})\hat{k}$. It starts from rest and is initially at the origin. After $t = 4$ s, its new coordinates are (8 m, b m, 20 m). Then the value of b is equal to ______.

38. A swimmer can swim with velocity of 12 km/h in still water. Water flowing in a river has velocity 6 km/h. The angle (degree) with respect to the direction of flow of river water at which he should swim in order to reach the point on the other bank just opposite his starting point is equal to ______.

39. A closed organ pipe of length L and an open organ pipe of length L' contain gases of densities ρ_1 and ρ_2, respectively. The compressibility of gases is equal in both the pipes. Both the pipes are vibrating in their first overtone with the same frequency. If $L' = \frac{x}{3}L\sqrt{\frac{\rho_1}{\rho_2}}$, then x is equal to ______.

40. For an ideal heat engine, the temperature of the source is 127°C. In order to have 60% efficiency, the temperature (°C) of the sink should be equal to ______.

41. The angular speed of a truck wheel increases from 900 rpm to 2460 rpm in 26 sec. Assuming uniform acceleration, the number of revolutions by the truck engine during this time is equal to ______.

42. The radius (km) to which the present radius of the Earth ($R = 6400$ km) will have to be compressed so that the escape velocity is increased by 10 times is equal to ______.

43. A parallel plate capacitor whose capacitance is C=14 pF is charged by a battery to a potential difference of V = 12 V between its plates. The charging battery is now disconnected and a porcelain slab with dielectric constant k = 7 is inserted between the plates. The slab would oscillate back and forth between the capacitor plates with a constant mechanical energy (pJ) of ______. (Assume no friction)

44. Two blocks of masses $m = 0.5$ kg and $M = 4.5$ kg are arranged on a horizontal frictionless table, shown in the figure. The coefficient of static friction between the two blocks is $\frac{3}{7}$. Then the maximum horizontal force (N) that can be applied on the larger block so that the blocks move together is equal to ______. (Round off to the nearest integer)
(Take $g = 9.8\ \text{m/s}^2$)

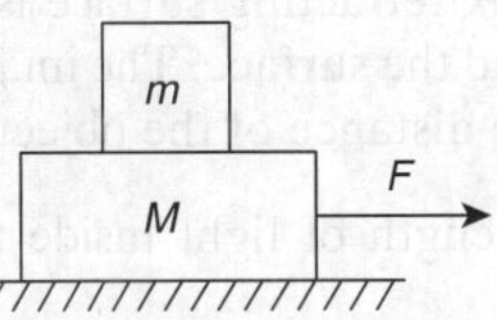

45. Light falling normally on a non-reflecting surface of 30 cm² area exerts an average force of 2.5×10^{-6} N. In a time span of 40 min, if the total energy absorbed per unit area is $x \times 10^8\ \text{J/m}^2$, then x is equal to ______.

46. A body of mass 1 kg rests on a horizontal floor with which it has a coefficient of static friction $\frac{1}{\sqrt{3}}$. It is desired to make the body move by applying a force F. The minimum possible value of F (N) is equal to ______. (Take $g = 10\ \text{m/s}^2$)

47. A boy of mass 4 kg is standing on a piece of wood having mass 5 kg. If the coefficient of friction between the wood and the floor is 0.5, the maximum force that the boy can exert on the rope so that the piece of wood does not move from its place is equal to ______. (Take $g = 10$ m/s^2)

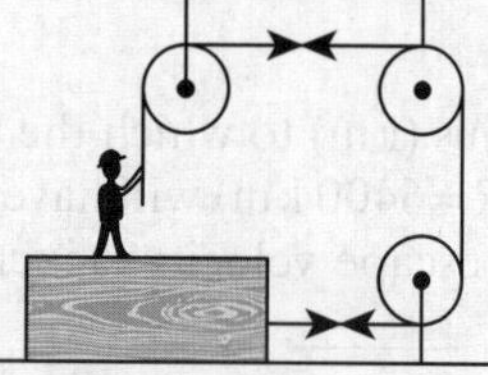

48. A particle of mass m moves in a circular orbit in a central potential field $U(r) = U_0 r^4$. If Bohr's quantization conditions are applied, radii r_n of the permissible orbits are proportional to $n^{1/\alpha}$ $(n = 1, 2, 3, \ldots)$, then α is equal to ______.

49. The figure shows a uniform disc of radius a. If the CM of the quarter disc (the shaded area) is at the position $\left(\dfrac{xa}{3\pi}, \dfrac{xa}{3\pi}\right)$, then x is equal to ______.

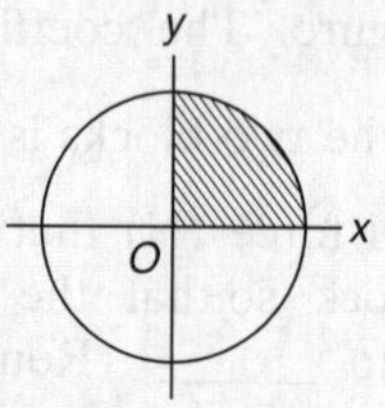

50. The image of an object placed in air formed by a convex refracting surface is at a distance of 10 m behind the surface. The image is real and is at 2/3rd of the distance of the object from the surface. The wavelength of light inside the surface is $\dfrac{2}{3}$ times the wavelength in air. If the radius of the curved surface is $\dfrac{x}{13}$ m, then x is equal to ______.

51. A 2-μF capacitor C_1 is first charged to a potential difference of 10 V using a battery. Then the battery is removed and the capacitor is connected to an uncharged 8-μF capacitor C_2. When steady state is reached, the charge (μC) on C_2 is equal to______.

52. For an EM wave of frequency $f = 9 \times 10^2$ Hz, seawater has permittivity $\varepsilon = 80\varepsilon_0$ and resistivity $\rho = 0.25\ \Omega \cdot$ m. Imagine a parallel plate capacitor immersed in seawater and driven by an alternating voltage source $V(t) = V_0 \sin(2\pi f t)$. If the conduction current density becomes 10^α times the displacement current density after time $= \dfrac{1}{800}$ s, then the value of α is equal to ______.

$\left(\text{Take } \dfrac{1}{4\pi\epsilon_0} = 9 \times 10^9\ \text{N}\cdot\text{m}^2/\text{C}^2\right)$

53. The projectile motion of a particle of mass 5 g is shown in the figure.

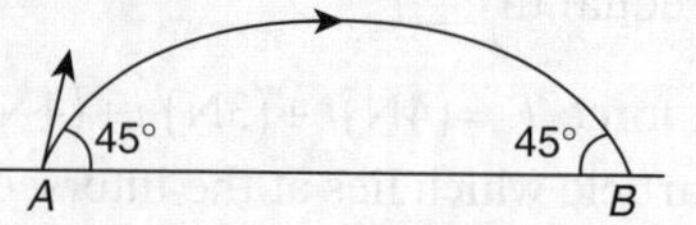

The initial velocity of the particle is $5\sqrt{2}$ m/s and the air resistance is assumed to be negligible. The magnitude of the change in momentum of the projectile between points A and B is $x \times 10^{-2}$ kg·m/s. Then the value of x is equal to ______.

54. The typical output characteristics curve for a transistor working in the common-emitter configuration is shown in the figure.

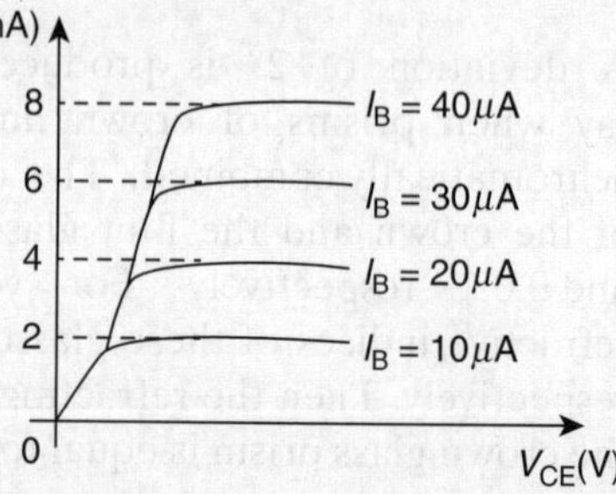

The estimated current gain from the figure is equal to ______.

55. Consider a water tank as shown in the figure. Its cross-sectional area is 0.4 m^2. The tank has an opening B near the bottom whose cross-section area is 1 cm^2. A load of 24 kg is applied on the water at the top when the height of the water level is 40 cm above the bottom, the velocity of water flowing out of the opening B is v m/s. The value of v to the nearest integer is equal to______. (Take g=10 m/s^2)

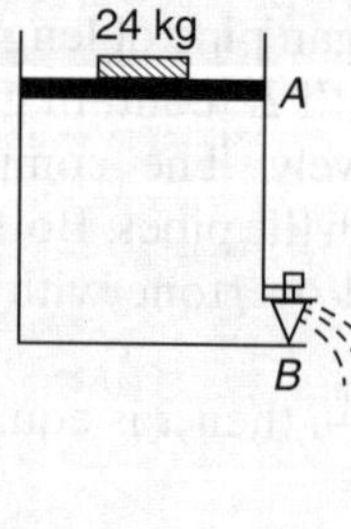

56. A TV transmission antenna is at a height of 20 m. Suppose that the receiving antenna is Case I: at ground level and Case II: at a height of 5 m. If there is an $n\%$ increase in the transmission range in Case II relative to Case I, then the value of n is equal to _____.

57. A galaxy is moving away from the Earth at a speed of 286 km/s. The shift in the wavelength of a red line at 630 nm is $x \times 10^{-10}$ m. Then the value of x to the nearest integer is equal to_____.
(Take $c = 3 \times 10^8$ m/s)

58. The change in the acceleration of the Earth towards the Sun, when the Moon comes from the position of solar eclipse to the exactly opposite side of the Earth, is $a \times 10^{-b}$ m/s^2. Then the value of b is equal to _______.
(Take $G = 6.67 \times 10^{-11}\, \text{N} \cdot \text{m}^2/\text{kg}^2$)

59. Imagine that the electron in a Deuteron atom is replaced by a particle that is 10 times heavier than the electron and has double the charge on an electron. If the ionization energy of this Deuteron atom is xE_H, where E_H is the ionization energy of a Hydrogen atom, then the value of x is equal to _____.

60. A projectile is projected perpendicular to a plane inclined at 37° to the horizontal, as shown in the figure. If the velocity of projection is $u = 20$ m/s, then its range along the incline is equal to ______.

(Take $g = 10$ m/s^2)

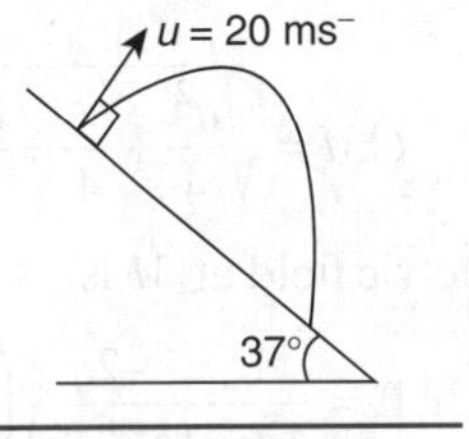

ANSWER KEYS

Only One Correct Option

1. (a)	**2.** (c)	**3.** (c)	**4.** (a)	**5.** (a)	**6.** (a)	**7.** (a)	**8.** (a)	**9.** (b)	**10.** (a)
11. (d)	**12.** (b)	**13.** (b)	**14.** (a)	**15.** (a)	**16.** (a)	**17.** (a)	**18.** (a)	**19.** (a)	**20.** (b)
21. (c)	**22.** (c)	**23.** (a)	**24.** (a)	**25.** (a)	**26.** (c)	**27.** (a)	**28.** (a)	**29.** (a)	**30.** (a)
31. (a)	**32.** (c)	**33.** (b)	**34.** (d)	**35.** (a)	**36.** (b)	**37.** (a)	**38.** (b)	**39.** (a)	**40.** (d)
41. (c)	**42.** (a)	**43.** (a)	**44.** (b)	**45.** (a)	**46.** (a)	**47.** (b)	**48.** (a)	**49.** (a)	**50.** (b)
51. (b)	**52.** (d)	**53.** (d)	**54.** (b)	**55.** (c)	**56.** (c)	**57.** (d)	**58.** (d)	**59.** (a)	**60.** (a)
61. (c)	**62.** (d)	**63.** (a)	**64.** (a)	**65.** (c)	**66.** (c)	**67.** (a)	**68.** (c)	**69.** (d)	**70.** (d)
71. (c)	**72.** (b)	**73.** (d)	**74.** (d)	**75.** (a)	**76.** (d)	**77.** (b)	**78.** (c)	**79.** (b)	**80.** (a)
81. (a)	**82.** (b)	**83.** (b)	**84.** (b)	**85.** (c)	**86.** (a)	**87.** (d)	**88.** (d)	**89.** (b)	**90.** (d)
91. (d)	**92.** (d)	**93.** (d)	**94.** (d)	**95.** (b)	**96.** (b)	**97.** (d)	**98.** (b)	**99.** (c)	**100.** (a)
101. (c)	**102.** (d)	**103.** (c)	**104.** (d)	**105.** (c)	**106.** (a)	**107.** (b)	**108.** (c)	**109.** (c)	**110.** (d)
111. (c)	**112.** (b)	**113.** (d)	**114.** (b)	**115.** (a)	**116.** (c)	**117.** (c)			

Numerical Value Answer

1. 25	**2.** 25	**3.** 25600	**4.** 15	**5.** 25	**6.** 226	**7.** 0.8	**8.** 2	**9.** 5
10. 800	**11.** 8	**12.** 15	**13.** 10	**14.** 50	**15.** 144	**16.** 10	**17.** 45	**18.** 5
19. 36	**20.** 200	**21.** 20	**22.** 29.25	**23.** 2.55	**24.** 4	**25.** 7	**26.** 9	**27.** 60
28. 1	**29.** 150	**30.** 20	**31.** 0	**32.** 5	**33.** 30	**34.** 20	**35.** 3	**36.** 12
37. 12	**38.** 12	**39.** 4	**40.** −113	**41.** 728	**42.** 64	**43.** 864	**44.** 21	**45.** 6
46. 5	**47.** 30	**48.** 30	**49.** 4	**50.** 30	**51.** 16	**52.** 6	**53.** 5	**54.** 200
55. 3	**56.** 50	**57.** 6	**58.** 5	**59.** 640	**60.** 75			

SOLUTIONS

Only One Correct Option

1. (a) Let us replace the point charge $-q$ by two point charges $+q$ and $-2q$. Now, we can see that the field at the centre of the cube is only due to the $-2q$ charge, since the field due to all the $+q$ charges cancel each other.

The centre of the cube is at $M\left(\frac{a}{2},\frac{a}{2},\frac{a}{2}\right)$. The distance

$$OM=\sqrt{\frac{a^2}{4}+\frac{a^2}{4}+\frac{a^2}{4}}=\frac{\sqrt{3}a}{2}$$

The electric field at M is

$$\mathbf{E}=\frac{1}{4\pi\epsilon_0}\frac{-2q}{(3a^2/4)}\left(\frac{\mathbf{OM}}{OM}\right)$$

$$=\frac{-2q}{3\pi\epsilon_0 a^2}\times\frac{2}{\sqrt{3}a}\left(\frac{a}{2}\mathbf{i}+\frac{a}{2}\mathbf{j}+\frac{a}{2}\mathbf{k}\right)$$

$$=\frac{-2q}{3\sqrt{3}\pi\epsilon_0 a^2}(\mathbf{i}+\mathbf{j}+\mathbf{k})$$

2. (c) If $\Delta I_E=4\,\text{mA}$ and $\Delta I_C=3.5\,\text{mA}$, then

$$\Delta I_B=\Delta I_E-\Delta I_C=4\,\text{mA}-3.5\,\text{mA}=0.5\,\text{mA}$$

$$\text{Hence, }\beta=\frac{\Delta I_C}{\Delta I_B}=\frac{3.5\,\text{mA}}{0.5\,\text{mA}}=7.$$

3. (c) We have

$$w_2=3w_1\Rightarrow A_2=3A_1$$

$$\text{Hence, }\frac{I_{\max}}{I_{\min}}=\frac{(A_1+A_2)^2}{(A_1-A_2)^2}=\frac{(1+3)^2}{(1-3)^2}=4$$

4. (a) Before m is placed on M, velocity of M is

$$v=\omega A=\sqrt{\frac{k}{M}}A$$

Immediately after m is placed on M, velocity of the $M+m$ system (by linear momentum conservation principle) is

$$v'=\frac{Mv}{M+m}=\frac{M}{M+m}\sqrt{\frac{k}{M}}A$$

The $M+m$ system now oscillates with angular frequency $\omega'=\sqrt{\frac{k}{M+m}}$. Hence the new oscillation amplitude A' is given by

$$v'=\omega' A'$$

$$\Rightarrow\quad \frac{M}{M+m}\sqrt{\frac{k}{M}}A=\sqrt{\frac{k}{M+m}}A'$$

$$\Rightarrow\quad A'=\sqrt{\frac{M}{M+m}}A$$

5. (a) The gravitational force on the smaller star m is

$$F=\frac{G(2m)m}{d^2}$$

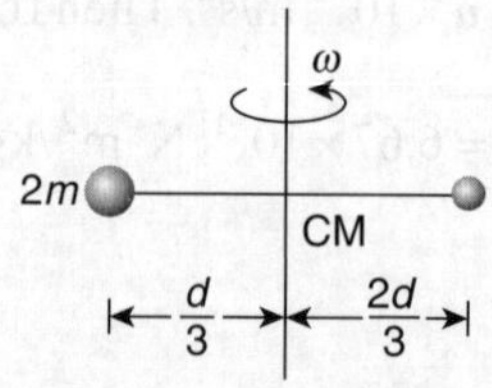

If the stars are rotating about their CM, then the smaller star is rotating in a circle of radius $R=\frac{2d}{3}$ (see figure). If the star system is rotating with an angular velocity ω, then

$$F=m\omega^2 R$$

$$\Rightarrow\quad \frac{G(2m)m}{d^2}=m\omega^2\left(\frac{2d}{3}\right)$$

$$\Rightarrow\quad \omega=\sqrt{\frac{3Gm}{d^3}}$$

Hence, time-period of revolution is $T=2\pi\sqrt{\frac{d^3}{3Gm}}$.

6. (a) Relation between the elastic constants Y,η, and K is given by

$$\frac{3}{Y}=\frac{1}{\eta}+\frac{1}{3K}$$

$$\Rightarrow\quad K=\frac{\eta Y}{9\eta-3Y}$$

7. (a) Current through the circuit is

$$I=\frac{6\,\text{V}-4\,\text{V}}{2\,\Omega+8\,\Omega}=\frac{1}{5}\,\text{A}$$

The current flows in the anti-clockwise direction, that is, from Y to X. Hence, we have

$$V_X+4+\frac{8}{5}=V_Y$$

$$\Rightarrow \quad |V_X - V_Y| = 5.6\text{ V}$$

8. (a) The exponent $\dfrac{x^2}{\alpha kT}$ must be dimensionless. Thus, we have

$$[\alpha] = \left[\frac{x^2}{kT}\right] = \frac{[\text{Length}]^2}{[\text{Energy}]} = \frac{[L^2]}{[ML^2T^{-2}]} = [M^{-1}T^2]$$

The quantity $\alpha\beta^2$ must have the dimension of work. Thus, we have

$$[\beta^2] = \frac{[\text{Work}]}{[\alpha]} = \frac{[ML^2T^{-2}]}{[M^{-1}T^2]} = [M^2L^2T^{-4}]$$

$$\Rightarrow \quad [\beta] = [MLT^{-2}]$$

9. (b) Work done by the gas along the three paths are

$$W_{AB} = P_1(2V_1)\ln 2 = 2nRT\ln 2$$

$$W_{BC} = P_1(V_1 - 2V_1) = -P_1V_1 = -nRT$$

and $\quad W_{CA} = 0$

Hence, total work done by the gas is

$$W = W_{AB} + W_{BC} + W_{CA}$$
$$= nRT(2\ln 2 - 1)$$

10. (a) We have

$$V = a^3$$

$$\Rightarrow \quad \Delta V = 3a^2\Delta a = 3a^2(a\alpha\Delta T) = 3a^3\alpha\Delta T$$

11. (d) When unpolarized light of intensity I_0 passes through a polaroid, the emerging polarized light is of intensity $I_0/2$, irrespective of the orientation of the polaroid axis. Hence, intensity is still 100 lumen.

12. (b)

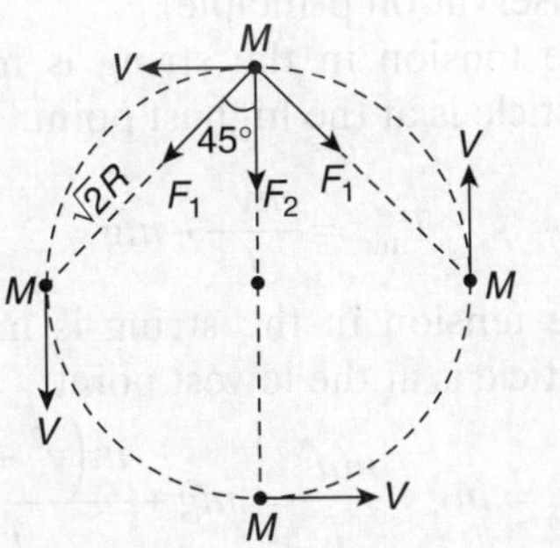

The figure shows the gravitational forces acting on one of the particles. The net force is

$$F = 2(F_1\cos 45°) + F_2$$

$$= \sqrt{2}\frac{GM^2}{(\sqrt{2}R)^2} + \frac{GM^2}{(2R)^2} = \frac{GM^2}{4R^2}(2\sqrt{2}+1)$$

The particle is revolving around O with velocity v. Thus, we have

$$F = M\left(\frac{v^2}{R}\right)$$

$$\Rightarrow \quad \frac{GM^2}{4R^2}(2\sqrt{2}+1) = M\left(\frac{v^2}{R}\right)$$

$$\Rightarrow \quad v = \sqrt{\frac{GM}{4R}(2\sqrt{2}+1)}$$

Putting $M = 1\text{ kg}$ and $R = 1\text{ m}$, we have

$$v = \frac{1}{2}\sqrt{G(2\sqrt{2}+1)}.$$

13. (b) The Zener diode is heavily doped to get a narrow depletion region, and hence a low break-down voltage in reverse bias.

14. (a) The instantaneous acceleration of the body is

$$a = -\frac{\alpha x^2}{m}$$

$$\Rightarrow \quad v\frac{dv}{dx} = -\frac{\alpha x^2}{m}$$

The position s where the velocity reduces to zero is given by

$$\int_{v_0}^{0} v\,dv = -\frac{\alpha}{m}\int_0^s x^2\,dx$$

$$\Rightarrow \quad \frac{v_0^2}{2} = \frac{\alpha s^2}{3m}$$

$$\Rightarrow \quad s = \left(\frac{3mv_0^2}{2\alpha}\right)^{1/3}$$

15. (a) Consider the block to be displaced by an amount x from its equilibrium position. Both springs exert force in the same direction as one spring pushes and the other spring pulls. So the restoring force on the block is $F_{\text{res}} = 2kx$. The instantaneous acceleration of the block is

$$a = -\left(\frac{2k}{m}\right)x$$

Hence, the frequency of oscillation is

$$f = \frac{1}{2\pi}\sqrt{\frac{2k}{m}}$$

16. (a)

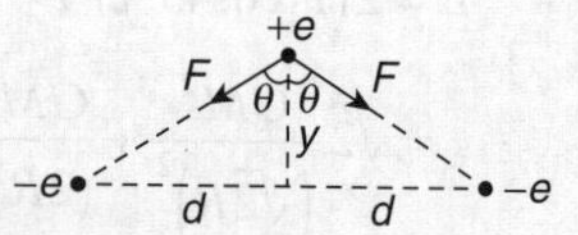

The figure shows the forces acting on the proton when it is displaced by an amount y from its equilibrium position. The restoring force on the proton is

$$F_{res} = 2(F\cos\theta) = \frac{2e^2}{4\pi\epsilon_0(d^2+y^2)} \times \frac{y}{\sqrt{d^2+y^2}}$$

$$= \frac{e^2 y}{2\pi\epsilon_0(d^2+y^2)^{3/2}} = \frac{e^2 y}{2\pi\epsilon_0 d^3} \; [y \ll d]$$

The instantaneous acceleration of the block is

$$a = -\left(\frac{e^2}{2\pi\epsilon_0 m d^3}\right) y$$

Hence, the angular frequency of oscillation is

$$\omega = \sqrt{\frac{e^2}{2\pi\epsilon_0 m d^3}}$$

17. (a) Work done by the gas along the three paths is

$$W_{AB} = PV\ln 2 = RT\ln 2$$

$$W_{BC} = 0$$

and $$W_{CA} = \frac{PV - \left(\frac{P}{4}\right)(2V)}{1-\gamma} = \frac{PV}{2(1-\gamma)} = -\frac{RT}{2(\gamma-1)}$$

Hence, total work done by the gas is

$$W = W_{AB} + W_{BC} + W_{CA}$$

$$= RT\left(\ln 2 - \frac{1}{2(\gamma-1)}\right)$$

18. (a) In SHM, the relation between velocity and displacement is

$$v = \pm\omega\sqrt{A^2 - x^2}$$

$$\Rightarrow \frac{v^2}{(\omega A)^2} + \frac{x^2}{A^2} = 1$$

Hence, the $v-x$ curve will be an ellipse.

19. (a) For H-like atoms, the permissible orbit radii and velocity of the electrons are

$$r = \left(\frac{n^2}{Z}\right) r_0 \text{ and } v = \left(\frac{Z}{n}\right) v_0.$$

Then the permissible values of force F, frequency f and kinetic energy K are

$$F = \frac{mv^2}{r} \propto \frac{Z^2}{n^2} \times \frac{Z}{n^2} = \frac{Z^3}{n^4}$$

$$f = \frac{2\pi r}{v} \propto \frac{n^2}{Z} \times \frac{n}{Z} = \frac{n^3}{Z^2}$$

and $$K = \frac{1}{2}mv^2 \propto \frac{Z^2}{n^2}$$

20. (b) Let l be the length of the train. Then the acceleration a is given by

$$v^2 = u^2 + 2al \Rightarrow a = \frac{v^2 - u^2}{2l}$$

Thus, the velocity of the train when its middle point crosses point P is given by

$$v'^2 = u^2 + 2a\left(\frac{l}{2}\right) = u^2 + \frac{v^2 - u^2}{2} = \frac{v^2 + u^2}{2}$$

$$\Rightarrow \quad v' = \sqrt{\frac{v^2 + u^2}{2}}$$

21. (c) The least count is $\text{LC} = \frac{1}{100}$ mm and the zero error is $e = +0.08$ mm.

The measured reading of the diameter is

$$1\text{ mm} + 72\left(\frac{1}{100}\text{ mm}\right) = 1.72\text{ mm}$$

The correct reading of the diameter is

$$1.72\text{ mm} - 0.08\text{ mm} = 1.64\text{ mm}$$

Hence, radius of the wire = 0.82 mm

22. (c) The velocity of the particle is least at the highest point of the circular trajectory. Let v be the velocity at the highest point. Then velocity at the lowest point is $u = \sqrt{v^2 + 2g(2l)}$ (using energy conservation principle).

The tension in the string is minimum when the particle is at the highest point:

$$T_{min} = \frac{mv^2}{l} - mg$$

The tension in the string is maximum when the particle is at the lowest point:

$$T_{max} = mg + \frac{mu^2}{l} = mg + \frac{m(v^2 + 4gl)}{l} = 5mg + \frac{mv^2}{l}$$

Now using the given condition $T_{max} : T_{min} = 5:1$, we have

$$5mg + \frac{mv^2}{l} = 5\left(\frac{mv^2}{l} - mg\right)$$

$$\Rightarrow \quad \frac{4mv^2}{l} = 10mg \text{ gives} = \sqrt{\frac{5}{2}gl}$$

23. (a) At $t = 0$, the inductor behaves like an infinite resistance path. No current flows through the inductor branch. The equivalent circuit at $t = 0$ is shown below:

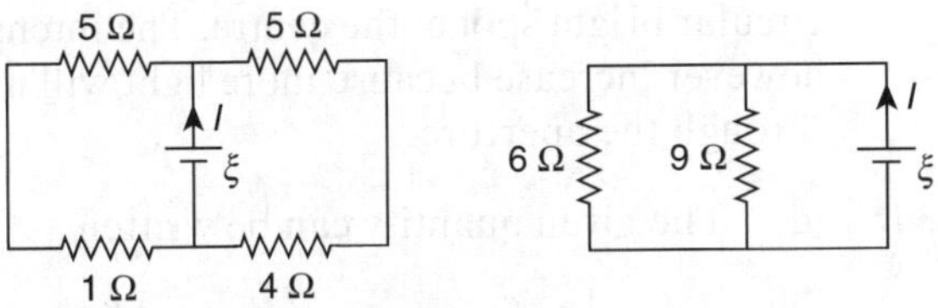

$$\text{Hence, } I(0) = \frac{\xi}{\frac{9 \times 6}{15}} = \frac{5\xi}{18}$$

At $t = \infty$, the inductor behaves like a zero resistance path. The equivalent circuit at $t = \infty$ is shown below:

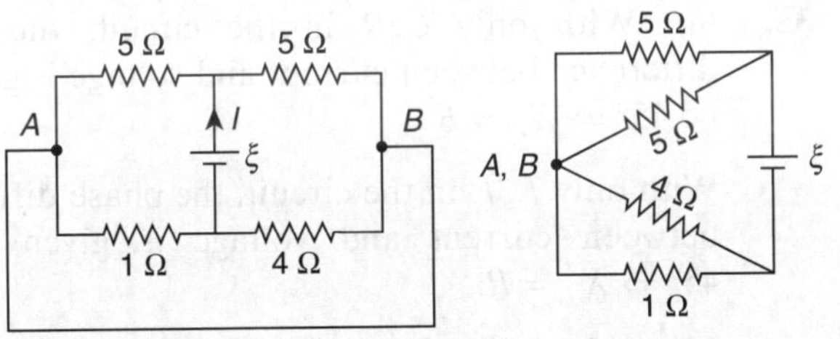

$$\text{Hence, } I(\infty) = \frac{\xi}{\frac{5}{2} + \frac{4}{5}} = \frac{10\xi}{33}$$

24. (a) Only diode D_1 will allow current flow, so current through the cell is

$$I = \frac{5 - 0.7}{10}\text{A} = 0.43 \text{ A}$$

25. (a) For the given gas, we have

$$c_V = \frac{R}{1.4 - 1} = \frac{5}{2}R \text{ and } c_p = \frac{7}{2}R$$

Let the number of moles be μ. Considering a temperature change dT, we have

$$dU = \mu c_V dT = \mu\left(\frac{5}{2}R\right)dT = \frac{5}{2}\mu R dT,$$

$$dQ = \mu c_P dT = \mu\left(\frac{7}{2}R\right)dT = \frac{7}{2}\mu R dT,$$

and $\quad dW = PdV = \mu R dT$

Hence, $dU : dQ : dW = 5 : 7 : 2.$

26. (c) Area vectors representing the yz-plane and the xz-plane, respectively, are

$$\mathbf{A}_1 = \left(0.2 \text{ m}^2\right)\mathbf{i} \text{ and } \mathbf{A}_2 = \left(0.3 \text{ m}^2\right)\mathbf{j}$$

The electric flux cutting these two planes are

$$\phi_{P_1} = \mathbf{E}_1 \cdot \mathbf{A}_1 = \left(\frac{3}{5}E_0\right)(0.2)$$

and $\quad \phi_{P_2} = \mathbf{E}_2 \cdot \mathbf{A}_2 = \left(\frac{4}{5}E_0\right)(0.3)$

$$\text{Hence, } \frac{\phi_{P_1}}{\phi_{P_2}} = \frac{3 \times 0.2}{4 \times 0.3} = 0.5$$

27. (a) Effective length of the resonating air column is $L + 0.3D = L + 1.8$ cm. First resonance occurs when

$$L + 1.8 \text{ cm} = \frac{\lambda}{4} = \frac{v}{4f}$$

$$\Rightarrow \quad L = \frac{336 \times 504}{4 \times 504}\text{cm} - 1.8 \text{ cm} = 14.86 \text{ cm}.$$

28. (a) The voltage drop across the resistor $R = 600\Omega$ is given to be 15 V. Therefore current through the circuit is

$$I = \frac{15}{600}\text{A} = 0.25 \text{ A}$$

The voltage drop across the inductor is given to be 20 V. Thus, we have

$$I(\omega L) = 20$$

$$\Rightarrow \quad L = \frac{20}{I\omega} = \frac{20}{0.25 \times 100}\text{H} = 0.8 \text{ H}$$

The voltage drop across the capacitor is given to be 10 V. Thus, we have

$$I\left(\frac{1}{\omega C}\right) = 10$$

$$\Rightarrow \quad C = \frac{I}{10\omega} = \frac{0.25}{10 \times 100}\text{F} = 250 \,\mu\text{F}$$

29. (a) For a particle moving with momentum p, its velocity is given by

$$v = \frac{p}{m} \propto \frac{1}{m} \text{ [If } p \text{ is same].}$$

The magnetic force on moving charged particles is given by

$$F = qvB = q\left(\frac{p}{m}\right)B \propto \frac{q}{m} \text{ [If } p, B \text{ are the same].}$$

Hence, we have

$$F_1 : F_2 : F_3 = \frac{e}{m} : \frac{e}{2m} : \frac{2e}{4m} = 2:1:1$$

and $\quad v_1 : v_2 : v_3 = \frac{1}{m} : \frac{1}{2m} : \frac{1}{4m} = 4:2:1$

30. (a) Let the intensities of the light coming from the two sources be I_1, I_2. It is given that $\frac{I_1}{I_2} = 2x \Rightarrow I_1 = (2x)I_2$. Then, we have

$$\frac{I_{\max}}{I_{min}} = \frac{\left(\sqrt{I_1}+\sqrt{I_2}\right)^2}{\left(\sqrt{I_1}-\sqrt{I_2}\right)^2} = \frac{\left(\sqrt{2x}+1\right)^2}{\left(\sqrt{2x}-1\right)^2}$$

Hence, we have

$$\frac{I_{\max}-I_{min}}{I_{\max}+I_{min}} = \frac{\left(\sqrt{2x}+1\right)^2-\left(\sqrt{2x}-1\right)^2}{\left(\sqrt{2x}+1\right)^2+\left(\sqrt{2x}-1\right)^2}$$

$$= \frac{4\sqrt{2x}}{2(2x+1)} = \frac{2\sqrt{2x}}{2x+1}$$

31. (a) Let l be the length travelled by the sphere up the incline. Using mechanical energy conservation principle, we have

$$Mgl\sin\theta = \frac{1}{2}Mv^2 + \frac{1}{2}\left(\frac{2}{5}MR^2\right)\left(\frac{v}{R}\right)^2$$

$$\Rightarrow \quad Mgl\sin\theta = \frac{7}{10}Mv^2$$

$$\Rightarrow \quad l = \frac{7Mv^2}{10g\sin\theta}$$

32. (c)

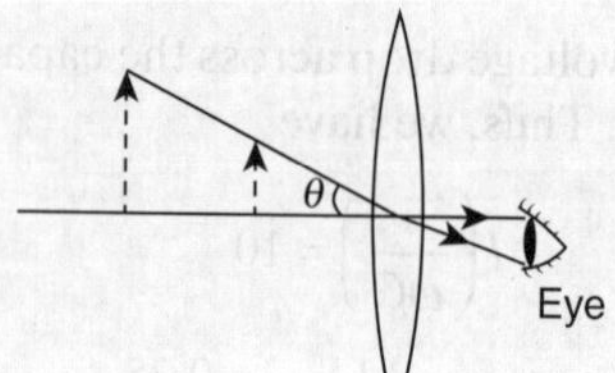

For a normal human eye, the minimum distance of distinct vision is 25 cm from the eye. Therefore for an object of linear size h, its greatest angular size at the eye is $\alpha = \frac{h}{25\text{ cm}}$.

In a simple microscope, the object is kept at a distance less than or equal to the focal length of the convex lens. The angular size θ of the image is the same as that of the object (see figure) but now the angle subtended is greater as it is closer to the eye. If the object is kept, say at the focus, then $\theta = \frac{h}{f}$ and we get a magnification $= \frac{\theta}{\alpha} = \frac{25\text{ cm}}{f}$.

Hence, option (c) is the correct option.

33. (b) The angular position of the first dark ring is given by

$$\sin\theta = \frac{1.22\lambda}{D}\text{ rad/s} = \frac{5\pi}{3}\text{ rad/s}$$

Increasing the diameter D decreases the size of the circular bright spot at the centre. The intensity will however increase because more light will now pass through the aperture.

34. (d) The given quantity can be written as

$$\frac{1}{4\pi\epsilon_0}\frac{e}{hc} = \frac{e}{4\pi\epsilon_0\lambda^2}\frac{\lambda^2}{hc} = \frac{e}{4\pi\epsilon_0\lambda^2}\frac{\lambda}{hc/\lambda}$$

Hence, we have

$$\left[\frac{1}{4\pi\epsilon_0}\frac{e}{hc}\right] = [\text{Force}]\times\frac{[\text{Length}]}{[\text{Energy}]} = \text{Dimensionless}.$$

35. (a) With only C, R in the circuit, the phase difference between current and voltage is given to be $45° \Rightarrow X_C = R$.

With only L, R in the circuit, the phase difference between current and voltage is given to be $45° \Rightarrow X_L = R$.

Thus, for the given circuit, $X_C = X_L = R$. So, when all three are connected in series, the circuit impedance is

$$Z = \sqrt{(X_C - X_L)^2 + R^2} = R$$

Hence, the rms current through the circuit is

$$I_{\text{rms}} = \frac{V_{\text{rms}}}{R} = \frac{220}{110}\text{ A} = 2\text{ A}$$

36. (b) For the photo-electronic emission experiment, we have

$$eV_S = \frac{hc}{\lambda} - \phi$$

$$\Rightarrow \quad 0.71\text{ eV} = \frac{1240}{491}\text{eV} - \phi$$

$$\Rightarrow \quad \phi = 1.82\text{ eV}$$

When stopping potential is shown to be 1.43 V, we have

$$1.43\text{ eV} = \frac{1240\text{ eV}\cdot\text{nm}}{\lambda} - 1.82\text{ eV}$$

$$\Rightarrow \quad \lambda = \frac{1240}{3.25}\text{ nm} = 382\text{ nm}$$

37. (a) There is no force on the electron along the direction parallel to the plates. So, the velocity component along the parallel to the plates remains the same. Thus, we have

$$v_1\cos\alpha = v_2\cos\beta$$

$$\Rightarrow \quad \frac{v_1}{v_2} = \frac{\cos\beta}{\cos\alpha}$$

Hence, we have

$$\frac{K_1}{K_2} = \frac{v_1^2}{v_2^2} = \frac{\cos^2\beta}{\cos^2\alpha}$$

38. (b) The process $PV^{1/2}$ = constant can also be expressed as

$$\left(\frac{T}{V}\right)V^{1/2} = \text{constant}$$

$$\Rightarrow \quad \frac{T}{\sqrt{V}} = \text{constant}$$

$$\Rightarrow \quad T \propto \sqrt{V}$$

Hence, we have

$$\frac{T_2}{T_1} = \frac{\sqrt{V_2}}{\sqrt{V_1}} = \sqrt{2}$$

39. (a) For the given circuit, we have

$$Y = \overline{A\bar{B} + \bar{A}B}$$

$$\Rightarrow \quad Y = \overline{A\bar{B}} \cdot \overline{\bar{A}B}$$

$$\Rightarrow \quad Y = (\bar{A} + B)(A + \bar{B})$$

$$\Rightarrow \quad Y = \bar{A}A + \bar{A}\bar{B} + AB + B\bar{B}$$

$$\Rightarrow \quad Y = \bar{A}\bar{B} + AB$$

Now the truth table can be easily generated.

40. (d) The equivalent circuit is shown below:

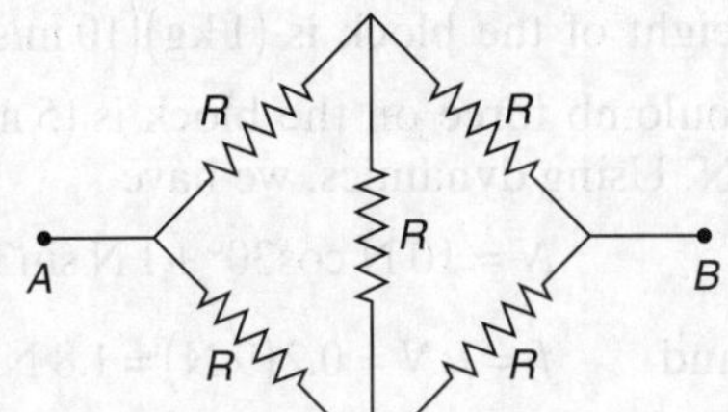

This is a balanced Wheatstone's network. Hence, we have

$$R_{AB} = R$$

41. (c)

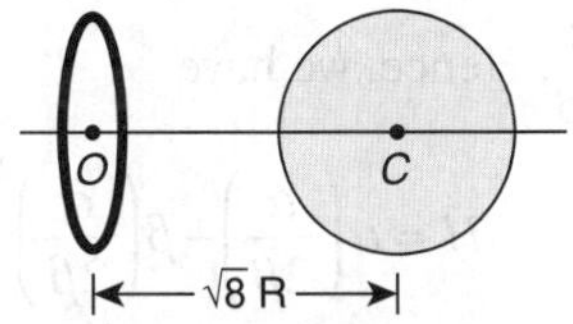

The sphere can be treated as a point mass M kept at its centre C (see figure). The gravitational field intensity at position C due to the ring is

$$g = \frac{GM(\sqrt{8}R)}{\left(R^2 + 8R^2\right)^{3/2}} = \frac{\sqrt{8}}{27}\frac{GM}{R^2}$$

The gravitational force between the ring and the sphere is the same as that between the ring and the point mass M kept at C. Hence, the required force is

$$F = Mg = \frac{\sqrt{8}}{27}\frac{GM^2}{R^2}$$

42. (a) We have

$$\frac{1}{\lambda_1} = R\left(\frac{1}{1^2} - \frac{1}{4^2}\right) = \frac{15}{16}R \text{ [3}^{\text{rd}}\text{ Lyman means } 4 \rightarrow 1]$$

and $$\frac{1}{\lambda_2} = R\left(\frac{1}{3^2} - \frac{1}{4^2}\right) = \frac{7}{9\times 16}R \text{ [1}^{\text{st}}\text{ Paschen means } 4 \rightarrow 3]$$

Hence, we have

$$\frac{\lambda_1}{\lambda_2} = \frac{7}{9\times 16} \times \frac{16}{15} = \frac{7}{135}$$

43. (a) The x-component of the force is $F_x = 20$ N. Thus, we have

$$a_x = \frac{20\text{ N}}{2\text{ kg}} = 10\text{ m/s}^2$$

The displacement along the x-axis in time $t = 4$ s is given by

$$\Delta x = u_x t + \frac{1}{2}a_x t^2 = 0 + \frac{1}{2}(10\text{ m/s}^2)(4\text{ s})^2 = 80\text{ m}.$$

44. (b) Differentiating $y = \alpha x - \beta x^2$, we have

$$\frac{dy}{dx} = \alpha - 2\beta x$$

At $x = 0$, slope is α. Hence, angle of projection is $\theta = \tan^{-1}\alpha$.

At the highest point, slope is zero, that is

$$\alpha - 2\beta x = 0 \Rightarrow x = \frac{\alpha}{2\beta}$$

The maximum height H is the value of y for $x = \dfrac{\alpha}{2\beta}$. Hence, we have

$$H = \alpha\left(\frac{\alpha}{2\beta}\right) - \beta\left(\frac{\alpha}{2\beta}\right)^2 = \frac{\alpha^2}{4\beta}$$

45. (a) Using mechanical energy conservation principle, we have

$$Mgh = \frac{1}{2}Mv^2 + \frac{1}{2}I\omega^2$$

$$\Rightarrow \quad Mgh = \frac{1}{2}M(R\omega)^2 + \frac{1}{2}\left(\frac{1}{2}MR^2\right)\omega^2$$

$$\Rightarrow \quad Mgh = \frac{3}{4}MR^2\omega^2$$

$$\Rightarrow \quad \omega = \sqrt{\frac{4gh}{3R^2}}$$

46. (a) Energy of the emitted photon is

$$\Delta E = 13.6\text{ eV}\left(\frac{1}{1^2} - \frac{1}{5^2}\right) = 13.06\text{ eV}$$

Thus, the momentum of the emitted photon is

$$p = \frac{\Delta E}{c}$$

The Hydrogen atom recoils with the same momentum p. Hence, its recoil velocity is

$$v = \frac{p}{m_H} = \frac{\Delta E}{cm_H} = \frac{13.06\times1.6\times10^{-19}}{(3\times10^8)(1.6\times10^{-27})} = 4.35\text{ m/s}$$

47. (b) The given quantity can be written as

$$\frac{C}{V} = \frac{Q}{V^2} = \frac{Q}{(W/Q)^2} = \frac{Q^3}{W^2}$$

Hence, we have

$$\left[\frac{C}{V}\right] = \frac{[\text{AT}]^3}{[\text{ML}^2\text{T}^{-2}]^2} = [\text{M}^{-2}\text{L}^{-4}\text{T}^7\text{A}^3]$$

48. (a) We have

$$A_0e^{-\lambda t_1} = A \text{ and } A_0e^{-\lambda t_2} = \frac{A}{5}$$

Dividing the above two equations, we have

$$e^{\lambda(t_2-t_1)} = 5$$

$$\Rightarrow \quad \lambda = \frac{\ln 5}{t_2 - t_1}$$

Hence, we have

$$T_{\text{av}} = \frac{1}{\lambda} = \frac{t_2 - t_1}{\ln 5}$$

49. (a) For the given circuit, we have

$$X_C = \frac{1}{\omega C} = \frac{1}{100(100\times10^{-6})}\Omega = 100\ \Omega,$$

$$X_L = \omega L = 100(100\times10^{-3})\Omega = 10\Omega$$

Thus, the circuit impedance is

$$Z = \sqrt{(X_C - X_L)^2 + R^2}$$

$$= \sqrt{(100-10)^2 + 120^2}\ \Omega = 150\ \Omega$$

Hence, the peak current in the circuit is

$$I_{\text{peak}} = \frac{V_{\text{peak}}}{Z} = \frac{30}{150}\text{ A} = 0.2\text{ A}$$

And the resonance frequency of the circuit is

$$f_{\text{res}} = \frac{1}{2\pi\sqrt{LC}} = \frac{1}{2\pi\sqrt{10^{-1}\times10^{-4}}}\text{ Hz} = 50\text{ Hz}$$

50. (b)

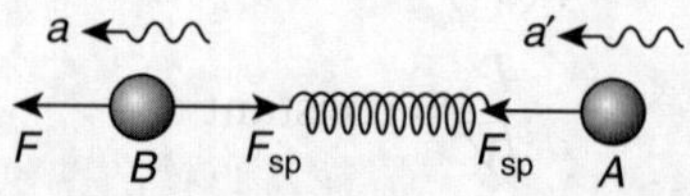

The figure shows the forces acting on the two bodies at some instant. Using dynamics, we have

$$F - F_{\text{sp}} = Ma \text{ and } F_{\text{sp}} = Ma'$$

Adding the above two equations, we have

$$F = Ma + Ma'$$

$$\Rightarrow \quad a' = \frac{F - Ma}{M}$$

51. (b)

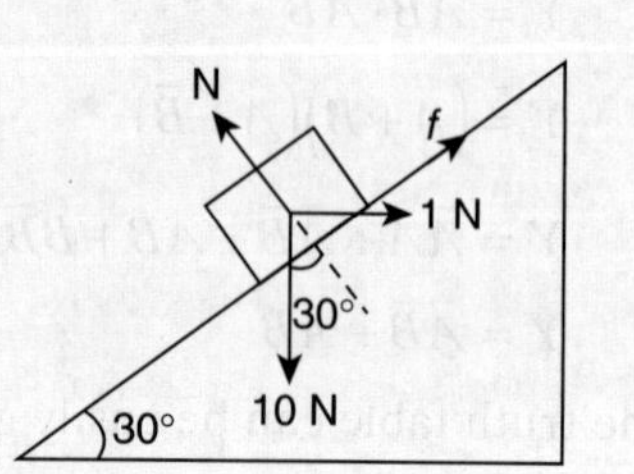

The figure shows the forces acting on the block. The weight of the block is $(1\text{ kg})(10\text{ m/s}^2) = 10\text{ N}$. The Coulomb force on the block is $(5\text{ mC})(200\text{ N/C}) = 1\text{ N}$. Using dynamics, we have

$$N = 10\text{ N}\cos30° + 1\text{ N}\sin30° = 9\text{ N}$$

and $\quad f = \mu N = 0.2(9\text{ N}) = 1.8\text{ N}$

The net force down the incline is

$$F = 10\text{ N}\sin30° - 1\text{ N}\cos30° - f$$

$$= 5\text{ N} - 0.87\text{ N} - 1.8\text{ N} = 2.33\text{ N}$$

Thus, the block moves down the incline with acceleration

$$a = \frac{2.33\ \text{N}}{1\ \text{kg}} = 2.33\ \text{m/s}^2$$

The block travels a distance $s = \dfrac{1\ \text{m}}{\sin 30°} = 2$ m down the incline. The time τ taken to travel this distance is given by

$$\tau = \sqrt{\frac{2s}{a}} = \sqrt{\frac{2\times 2}{2.33}} = 1.31\ \text{s}$$

52. (d) The induced emf, is given by

$$\xi = \mathbf{v}\times\mathbf{B}\cdot\mathbf{l} = vlB\sin 60°$$

$$= \left(180\times\frac{5}{18}\right)\left(10\times 2.5\times 10^{-4}\times\frac{\sqrt{3}}{2}\right)\text{V} = 108\ \text{mV}$$

53. (d) Let l be the natural length of the wire. Then, we have

$$T_1 = AY\left(\frac{l_1 - l}{l}\right) \quad (1)$$

and $$T_2 = AY\left(\frac{l_2 - l}{l}\right) \quad (2)$$

Dividing equation (1) by equation (2), we have

$$\frac{T_1}{T_2} = \frac{l_1 - l}{l_2 - l}$$

$$\Rightarrow \quad l = \frac{T_1 l_2 - T_2 l_1}{T_1 - T_2}$$

54. (b) Let l be the natural length and A be the cross-section area of the wire. Then the new length is $1.25l$ and since the volume is still the same, the new cross-section area is $\dfrac{A}{1.25}$. Thus, the new resistance is

$$R' = \frac{\rho(1.25l)}{A/1.25} = (1.25)^2\frac{\rho l}{A} = 1.5625R$$

Hence, percentage change in resistance is

$$\frac{\Delta R}{R} = \frac{1.5625R - R}{R}\times 100\% = 56.25\%.$$

55. (c) The internal energy of gas, is given by $U = f\left(\dfrac{1}{2}PV\right)$. Equating it with the given expression for internal energy, we have

$$f\left(\frac{1}{2}PV\right) = 3PV + 4$$

$$\Rightarrow \quad f = 6 + \frac{8}{PV} > 6$$

Hence, the gas is polyatomic.

56. (c) For the given circuit, we have

$$Y = \overline{\overline{A\bar{A}} + B}$$

$$\Rightarrow \quad Y = \overline{\bar{A} + B}$$

$$\Rightarrow \quad Y = A\bar{B}$$

Now the output can be easily generated.

57. (d) Given 1MSD = a cm. Let 1VSD = b cm. Then, we have

$$(n-1)a = nb$$

$$\Rightarrow \quad b = \left(1 - \frac{1}{n}\right)a$$

Hence, we have

$$\text{LC} = 1\text{MSD} - 1\text{VSD}$$

$$= (a-b)\text{cm} = \frac{10a}{n}\text{mm}.$$

58. (d) The capacitor can be considered to be made up of two capacitors in series. One air-filled capacitor having capacitance

$$C_1 = \frac{\epsilon_0 A}{d/4} = 4C_0$$

And another dielectric-filled capacitor having capacitance

$$C_2 = k\frac{\epsilon_0 A}{3d/4} = \frac{4k}{3}C_0$$

The combined capacitance C is given by

$$\frac{1}{C} = \frac{1}{C_1} + \frac{1}{C_2}$$

$$\Rightarrow \quad \frac{1}{C} = \frac{1}{4C_0} + \frac{3}{4kC_0} = \frac{k+3}{4kC_0}$$

$$\Rightarrow \quad C = \frac{4k}{k+3}C_0$$

59. (a) The pressure on the submarine is the sum of the atmospheric pressure and the water pressure depending on the depth. At the initial depth, we have

$$P_{\text{sub}} = P_{\text{atm}} + P_{\text{water}}$$

$$\Rightarrow \quad 3\times 10^5\ \text{Pa} = 1\times 10^5\ \text{Pa} + P_{\text{water}}$$

$$\Rightarrow \quad P_{\text{water}} = 2\times 10^5\ \text{Pa}$$

At double depth, the water pressure is doubled. Thus, the pressure on the submarine is

$$P'_{sub} = P_{atm} + P'_{water}$$
$$= 1\times10^5 \text{ Pa} + 4\times10^5 \text{ Pa}$$
$$= 5\times10^5 \text{ Pa}$$

Hence, we have

$$\frac{\Delta P_{sub}}{P_{sub}} = \frac{5\times10^5 - 3\times10^5}{3\times10^5}\times100\% = \frac{200}{3}\%.$$

60. (a) The magnitude of the electric field is
$$E = Bc = (8\times10^{-8})(3\times10^{8})\text{ V/m} = 24\text{ V/m}$$

The direction of $\mathbf{E}\times\mathbf{B}$ must be along the direction of wave propagation. In this question, $\mathbf{B}$ is along z-direction and wave propagation is along y-direction. Thus, $\mathbf{E}$ must be along –ve x-direction.

Hence, $\mathbf{E} = -(24\text{ V/m})\hat{i}$.

61. (c)

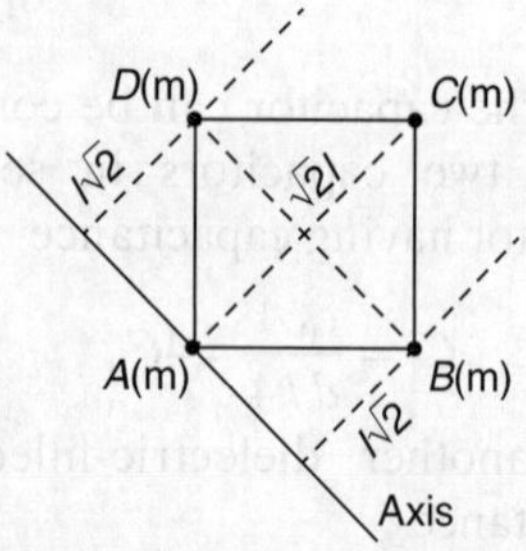

The required moment of inertia (see figure) is

$$I = m(\sqrt{2}l)^2 + 2m\left(\frac{l}{\sqrt{2}}\right)^2 = 3ml^2$$

62. (d) The effective gravity experienced inside the lift is

$$g_{\text{eff}} = g + \frac{g}{2} = \frac{3g}{2}$$

Hence, the new time-period is

$$T' = 2\pi\sqrt{\frac{l}{3g/2}} = \sqrt{\frac{2}{3}}T$$

63. (a) The given $v-x$ graph can be represented by the function

$$v = \begin{cases} 1+\frac{1}{5}x, & 0 \le x < 200 \\ 50, & 200 \le x \le 400 \end{cases}$$

Hence, the acceleration is given by

$$a = v\frac{dv}{dx} = \begin{cases} \frac{1}{5}\left(1+\frac{1}{5}x\right), & 0 < x < 200 \\ 0, & 200 < x < 400 \end{cases}$$

64. (a) The average energy densities due the electric field and the magnetic field are

$$u_E = \frac{1}{2}\epsilon_0 E_0^2 \text{ and } u_B = \frac{B_0^2}{2\mu_0}$$

where E_0 and B_0 are the peak values of the oscillating electric and magnetic fields, respectively. The peak values are related as

$$E_0 = cB_0 = \frac{B_0}{\sqrt{\mu_0\epsilon_0}}$$

Thus, we have

$$u_E = \frac{1}{2}\epsilon_0\left(\frac{B_0}{\sqrt{\mu_0\epsilon_0}}\right)^2 = \frac{B_0^2}{2\mu_0}$$

Hence, $u_E = u_B$.

65. (c) The source voltage is some constant value, say V_0 for one half-cycle, and zero for the other half-cycle. When the source voltage is V_0, the capacitor gets charged, and its voltage grows gradually. When source voltage becomes zero, the capacitor starts discharging, and its voltage falls gradually.

66. (c)

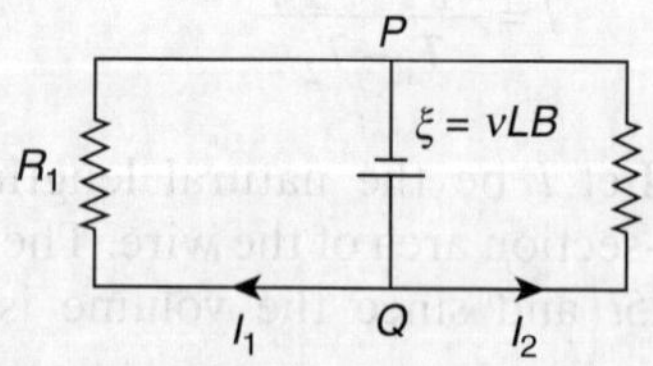

The sliding wire PQ will behave as a source of emf $\xi = vLB$ (see figure). The direction of the emf is along the direction of $\mathbf{v}\times\mathbf{B}$, that is, in the direction PQ. Hence, the currents I_1 and I_2 will flow as shown in the figure.

67. (a) For the given circuit, we have

$$Y = \overline{\overline{\overline{A}}\,\overline{B}} = \overline{A}\,\overline{B} = \overline{A+B}$$

Hence, it is a NOR gate.

68. (c) Let u be the velocity of the bullet. After collision, the velocity of the block plus bullet system is (using linear momentum conservation principle)

$$v = \frac{mu}{m+M} = \frac{0.1u}{0.1+5.9} = \frac{u}{600}$$

Now using mechanical energy conservation principle, we have

$$\frac{1}{2}(M+m)v^2 = (M+m)gh$$

$$\Rightarrow \quad \left(\frac{u}{600}\right)^2 = 2gh$$

$$\Rightarrow \quad u = 600\sqrt{2gh} = 600\sqrt{20\times 0.1} \text{ m/s} = 848 \text{ m/s}$$

69. (d) The Reynold's number is given by

$$R = \frac{\rho v D}{\eta} = \frac{\rho D}{\eta}\frac{Q}{\pi D^2/4} = \frac{4\rho Q}{\pi\eta D}$$

$$\Rightarrow \quad R = \frac{4\times 10^3}{\pi(10^{-3})(1.0\times 10^{-2})}Q = \frac{4\times 10^8}{\pi}Q$$

The value of R for the two given flows are

$$R_1 = \frac{4\times 10^8}{\pi}\times\frac{0.18\times 10^{-3}}{60} = \frac{1200}{\pi} < 1000$$

and $$R_2 = \frac{4\times 10^8}{\pi}\times\frac{0.48\times 10^{-3}}{60} = \frac{3200}{\pi} > 1000$$

Hence, flow changes from steady to unsteady.

70. (d) When particle carrying charge q is accelerated through a potential V, it acquires a kinetic energy $K = qV$. The de Broglie wavelength is given by

$$\lambda = \frac{h}{p} = \frac{h}{\sqrt{2mK}} = \frac{h}{\sqrt{2mqV}}$$

$$\Rightarrow \quad \lambda \propto \frac{1}{\sqrt{m}} \text{ [if } q, V \text{ are the same]}$$

Hence, we have

$$\frac{\lambda_e}{\lambda_p} = \sqrt{\frac{m_p}{m_e}} = \sqrt{1840} \approx 43$$

71. (c) The input voltage is given to be $V_{\text{in}} = 220$ V. The output power and current are given to be $P_{\text{out}} = 60$ W and $I_{\text{out}} = 0.11$ A, respectively. Thus, the output voltage is

$$V_{\text{out}} = \frac{P_{\text{out}}}{I_{\text{out}}} = \frac{60}{0.11} \text{ V} = 545 \text{ V}$$

Since the output voltage is greater than the input voltage, this is a step-up transformer.

Note. An auto transformer has only one winding and multiple tapping points. An auxiliary transformer has two secondary windings.

72. (b) The molar mass of Au^{198} is $M = 198$ g/mol. The number of nuclei in $m = 1.5$ mg of Au^{198} is

$$N = \frac{mN_A}{M} = \frac{(1.5\times 10^{-3})(6\times 10^{23})}{198} = 4.5\times 10^{18}$$

The decay constant of Au^{198} is

$$\lambda = \frac{\ln 2}{T_{\text{half}}} = \frac{0.693}{2.7}\text{day}^{-1}$$

Hence, the activity of the sample is

$$A = \lambda N = \frac{0.693(4.5\times 10^{18})}{2.7}\text{day}^{-1}$$

$$= \frac{0.693(4.5\times 10^{18})}{2.7(3.2\times 10^{15})}\text{Ci} = 360 \text{ Ci}$$

73. (d) Young's modulus is given by

$$Y = \frac{Mg/\pi R^2}{e/L} = \pi g M R^{-2} L e^{-1}$$

Thus, we have

$$\frac{\Delta Y}{Y} = \frac{\Delta M}{M} - 2\frac{\Delta R}{R} + \frac{\Delta L}{L} - \frac{\Delta e}{R}$$

Hence, the maximum error in Y is

$$\frac{\Delta Y}{Y} = \frac{10^{-3}}{1} + 2\left(\frac{0.001}{0.2}\right) + \frac{10^{-3}}{1} + \frac{0.001}{0.5}$$

$$= \frac{1}{1000} + \frac{10}{1000} + \frac{1}{1000} + \frac{2}{1000} = \frac{14}{1000} = 1.4\%.$$

74. (d) For same temperature change, metal strip A will contract more than metal strip B. Hence, the bimetallic strip will bend towards the left.

75. (a) Let us attach our reference frame with the balloon. As seen from this reference frame, both stones will have zero initial velocity when they are released from the balloon, and both stones will fall with a downward acceleration $9.8 \text{ m/s}^2 + 0.2 \text{ m/s}^2 = 10 \text{ m/s}^2$. The first stone has fallen for 3.5 s whereas the second stone has fallen for 1.5 s. Hence, the distance between them is

$$s = \frac{1}{2}(10 \text{ m/s}^2)(3.5 \text{ s})^2 - \frac{1}{2}(10 \text{ m/s}^2)(1.5 \text{ s})^2 = 50 \text{ m}.$$

76. (d) For an unbanked road, motion without slipping is possible if

$$v^2 \le \mu g R \tag{1}$$

From the given data in statement I, we have

$$v^2 = \left(6 \times \frac{5}{18}\right)^2 = 2.78\ \text{m}^2/\text{s}^2$$

and $\mu g R = 0.2 \times 10 \times 2 = 4\ \text{m}^2/\text{s}^2$

The values satisfy inequality (1), so the cyclist will not slip along the curve. Hence, statement I is correct.

For a banked road, motion without slipping is possible if

$$\left(\frac{\tan\theta - \mu}{1 + \mu\tan\theta}\right) gR \le v^2 \le \left(\frac{\tan\theta + \mu}{1 - \mu\tan\theta}\right) gR \qquad (2)$$

From the given data in statement II, we have

$$v^2 = \left(18 \times \frac{5}{18}\right)^2 = 25\ \text{m}^2/\text{s}^2,$$

$$\left(\frac{\tan\theta - \mu}{1 + \mu\tan\theta}\right) gR = \left(\frac{1 - 0.2}{1 + 0.2}\right) 10 \times 2 = 13.33\ \text{m}^2/\text{s}^2$$

and $\left(\dfrac{\tan\theta + \mu}{1 - \mu\tan\theta}\right) gR = \left(\dfrac{1 + 0.2}{1 - 0.2}\right) 10 \times 2 = 30\ \text{m}^2/\text{s}^2$

The values satisfy inequality (2), so the cyclist will not slip along the banked curve. Hence, statement II is correct.

77. (b)

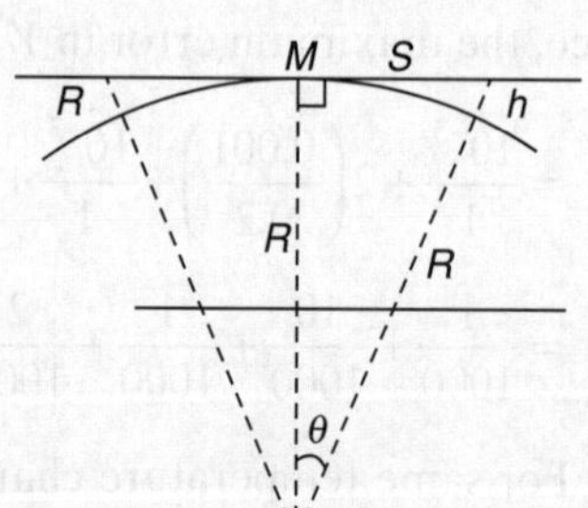

The figure shows two towers of the minimum possible height h so that they can communicate. The line joining the topmost point of the towers just touches the Earth's surface at M. The distance between M and any one tower is

$$s = \frac{1}{2} \times 45\ \text{km} = 22.5\ \text{km}$$

The lines drawn along the lengths of the towers intersect at the centre C of the Earth. Thus, we have

$$(R + h)^2 = R^2 + s^2$$

$$\Rightarrow \quad h = \left(R^2 + s^2\right)^{1/2} - R = R\left[\left(1 + \frac{s^2}{R^2}\right)^{1/2} - 1\right]$$

$$= R\left[1 + \frac{s^2}{2R^2} - 1\right] = \frac{s^2}{2R} = \frac{\left(22.5 \times 10^3\right)^2}{2\left(6400 \times 10^3\right)^2} = 39.55\ \text{m}.$$

The values satisfy inequality (1), so the cyclist will not slip along the curve.

78. (c)

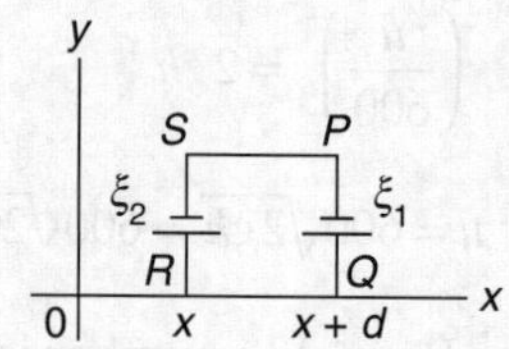

The figure shows the square loop at some arbitrary position. Emf induced due to motion is given by $\mathbf{v} \times \mathbf{B} \cdot \mathbf{L}$. In this question $\mathbf{v} \times \mathbf{B} = -(vB)\hat{j}$.

Thus, no emf is induced along the branches QR and SP since their lengths are along the $\hat{i}$ direction. The emf induced along the branches PQ and RS are along directions shown in the figure. Their values are

$$\xi_1 = v_0 B_0 \left(\frac{x + d}{a}\right) d \text{ and } \xi_2 = v_0 B_0 \left(\frac{x}{a}\right) d$$

The net emf induced in the loop is

$$\xi = \xi_1 - \xi_2 = v_0 B_0 \left(\frac{x + d}{a} - \frac{x}{a}\right) d = \frac{v_0 B_0 d^2}{a}$$

79. (b) Let N_0 be the initial number of nuclei. Now 33% decay means $0.67N_0$ left, and 67% decay means $0.33N_0$. We have to find the time elapsed between $0.67N_0$ and $0.33N_0$ decay.

Let us choose the initial time as the instant when the number of nuclei is $0.67N_0$. Then the time τ when the number reduces to $0.33N_0$, is given by

$$0.33N_0 = 0.67N_0 2^{\frac{-\tau}{T_{1/2}}}$$

$$\Rightarrow \quad 2^{\frac{\tau}{T_{1/2}}} = \frac{0.67}{0.33} = 2$$

$$\Rightarrow \quad \tau = T_{1/2} = 20\ \text{min}.$$

Alternative. Since $0.33N_0 = \frac{1}{2}(0.67N_0)$, the time interval equals one half-life, that is, 20 min.

80. (a) The total degree of freedom of the given polyatomic gas is

$$f = 3\ \text{trans} + 3\ \text{rot} + 2\ \text{vib} = 8\ \text{total}.$$

Thus, the constant volume molar heat capacity is

$$c_V = f\left(\frac{1}{2}R\right) = 4R,$$

And the constant pressure molar heat capacity is

$$c_P = c_P + R = 5R.$$

Hence, we have

$$\gamma = \frac{c_P}{c_V} = \frac{5}{4} = 1.25$$

81. (a) Let L be the length and A be the cross-section area of the wires. The series combination of these wires has a total thermal resistance of

$$R = \frac{L}{K_1 A} + \frac{L}{K_2 A} = \frac{(K_1 + K_2)L}{K_1 K_2 A}$$

Let the series combination of the two wires be replaced by one single wire of length $2L$ and cross-section area A and thermal conductivity K, such that this single wire has the same resistance R. Hence, we have

$$\frac{2L}{KA} = \frac{(K_1 + K_2)L}{K_1 K_2 A}$$

$$\Rightarrow \quad K = \frac{2K_1 K_2}{K_1 + K_2}$$

82. (b) We have

Measured reading $= 8.5\text{ cm} + 6(0.01\text{ cm}) = 8.56\text{ cm}$

Correct reading $= 8.56\text{ cm} - 0.02\text{ cm} = 8.54\text{ cm}$

83. (b) The given function representing current can be written as

$$I = \sqrt{I_1^2 + I_2^2}\sin(\omega t + \phi) \text{ where } \tan\phi = \frac{I_2}{I_1}$$

The hot wire ammeter gives the rms reading, that is

$$I_{\text{rms}} = \frac{I_{\text{peak}}}{\sqrt{2}} = \sqrt{\frac{I_1^2 + I_2^2}{2}}$$

84. (b) Racing cars are designed such that the air pushes the car in the downward direction, and hence the term negative lift. This increases the normal contact force between the road and the tyres. Thus, we have

$$N = mg + F_L \qquad (1)$$

From dynamics along the centripetal direction, we have

$$\mu N = \frac{mv^2}{R} \qquad (2)$$

Eliminating N from equations (1) and (2), we have

$$\mu(mg + F_L) = \frac{mv^2}{R}$$

$$\Rightarrow \quad F_L = m\left(\frac{v^2}{\mu R} - g\right)$$

85. (c) Let v be the peak velocity attained by the car. Then the total time of motion and the total distance travelled by the car are

$$\tau = \frac{v}{\alpha} + \frac{v}{\beta} = \left(\frac{1}{\alpha} + \frac{1}{\beta}\right)v \qquad (1)$$

$$\text{and} \quad s = \frac{v^2}{2\alpha} + \frac{v^2}{2\beta} = \left(\frac{1}{\alpha} + \frac{1}{\beta}\right)\frac{v^2}{2} \qquad (2)$$

From v from equations (1) and (2), we have

$$s = \frac{1}{2}\left(\frac{1}{\alpha} + \frac{1}{\beta}\right) \times \frac{\tau^2}{\left(\frac{1}{\alpha} + \frac{1}{\beta}\right)^2} = \frac{\tau^2}{2\left(\frac{1}{\alpha} + \frac{1}{\beta}\right)} = \frac{\alpha\beta\tau^2}{2(\alpha + \beta)}$$

86. (a) The magnetic flux density inside the solenoid is given by

$$B = \mu_r \mu_0 nI$$
$$= 500(4\pi \times 10^{-7})(1000 \times 5)\text{T} = \pi\text{T}$$

87. (d) The efficiency of a Carnot cycle is given by

$$\eta = 1 - \frac{T_{\text{sink}}}{T_{\text{source}}} = 1 - \frac{400}{800} = 0.5$$

Now, we have

$$\eta = \frac{W}{Q}$$

$$\Rightarrow \quad Q = \frac{W}{\eta} = \frac{1200}{0.5}\text{ J} = 2400\text{ J}$$

88. (d)

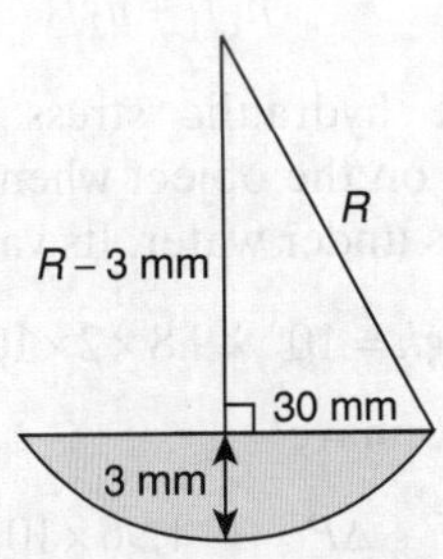

Let R be the radius of curvature of the convex surface of the lens (see figure). Then, we have

$$R^2 = (R-3)^2 + 30^2$$

$$\Rightarrow \quad 6R = 909 \text{ gives } R = 15.15\text{ cm}$$

The refractive index of the lens is

$$\mu = \frac{c_{\text{free space}}}{c_{\text{lens}}} = \frac{3\times10^8}{2\times10^8} = 1.5$$

Hence the focal length of the lens, is given by

$$\frac{1}{f} = (\mu-1)\frac{1}{R} = \frac{1.5-1}{15.15 \text{ cm}} = \frac{1}{30.30 \text{ cm}}$$

$\Rightarrow f = 30.30$ cm.

89. (b) The initial kinetic energy of the rolling ball is

$$K = \frac{1}{2}Mv^2 + \frac{1}{2}\left(\frac{2}{5}MR^2\right)\frac{v^2}{R^2} = \frac{7}{10}Mv^2$$

The kinetic energy after collision is

$$\frac{1}{20}K = \frac{7}{200}Mv^2$$

If v' is the velocity of the ball after collision, then

$$\frac{7}{200}Mv^2 = \frac{7}{10}Mv'^2$$

$$\Rightarrow \quad v' = \frac{v}{\sqrt{20}} = \frac{20}{\sqrt{20}}\frac{\text{m}}{\text{s}} = 4.47 \text{ m/s}$$

90. (d) The ground state energy level of the H atom is –13.6 eV. Energy level for the single electron C atom is given by

$$E_C = -\frac{13.6 \text{ eV}\times6^2}{n^2} \quad \text{[Atomic number of C atom is 6]}$$

Hence, $E_C = -13.6$ eV when $n = 6$.

91. (d) Let T be the equilibrium temperature. Then using energy conservation principle, we have

$$\left(n_1\frac{f_1R}{2} + n_2\frac{f_2R}{2}\right)T = \left(n_1\frac{f_1R}{2}\right)T_1 + \left(n_2\frac{f_2R}{2}\right) = T_2$$

$$\Rightarrow \quad T = \frac{n_1f_1T_1 + n_2f_2T_2}{n_1f_1 + n_2f_2}$$

92. (d) The hydraulic stress is the difference in pressure on the object when it was in air and now when it is under water. Its value is

$$\Delta P = \rho gh = 10^3\times9.8\times2\times10^3 = 1.96\times10^7 \text{ N/m}^2$$

Hence, we have

$$\frac{\Delta P}{\Delta V/V} = \frac{1.96\times10^7}{1.36\times10^{-2}} = 1.44\times10^9 \text{ N/m}^2$$

93. (d) For a satellite revolving around a planet in a circle of radius R, with a time-period T of revolution, we have $T \propto R^{3/2}$. A geostationary satellite has the same period as the Earth's period of rotation, that is, 24 hours.
Hence, we have

$$\frac{T}{24 \text{ hrs}} = \frac{(3R)^{3/7}}{(12R)^{3/7}}$$

$$\Rightarrow \quad T = \frac{24 \text{ hrs}}{8} = 3 \text{ hours}$$

94. (d) The angular frequency ω and the wave-number k are

$$\omega = 2\pi f = 2\pi\times245 \text{ s}^{-1} = 1.54\times10^3 \text{ s}^{-1}$$

and $k = \dfrac{\omega}{v} = \dfrac{1.54\times10^3}{300}\text{m}^{-1} = 5.1 \text{ m}^{-1}$

The oscillation amplitude is $A = \dfrac{6 \text{ cm}}{2} = 0.03$ m.
Now that the wave is travelling along the +ve direction of the x-axis, its wave function is

$$y(x,t) = 0.03\sin\left(5.1x - 1.54\times10^3t\right)$$

95. (b) An adiabatic process can be represented by any one of the following three relations:

$$PV^\gamma = \text{const} \Rightarrow P \propto \frac{1}{V^\gamma} \quad (1)$$

$$TV^{\gamma-1} = \text{const} \Rightarrow V \propto \frac{1}{T^{\gamma-1}} \quad (2)$$

and $$\frac{T^\gamma}{P^{\gamma-1}} = \text{const} \Rightarrow P \propto T^{\frac{\gamma}{\gamma-1}} \quad (3)$$

From relation (1), we see that P decreases as V increases $\Rightarrow P-V$ graph should be a decreasing graph.
From relation (2), we see that V decreases as T increases $\Rightarrow V-T$ graph should be a decreasing graph.
From relation (3), we see that P increases as T increases $\Rightarrow P-T$ graph should be an increasing graph.
Hence, graphs (iii) and (iv) are the correct graphs.

96. (b) The position of the particle as a function of time is given by

$$\int_0^x dx = \int_0^t \left(v_0 + gt + Ft^2\right)dt$$

$$\Rightarrow \quad x = v_0t + \frac{1}{2}gt^2 + \frac{1}{3}Ft^3$$

Hence, displacement after $t = 1$ s is

$$\Delta x = x(1) - x(0) = v_0 + \frac{g}{2} + \frac{F}{3}$$

97. (d) The bandwidth of the modulated signal is given by

$$\text{Bandwidth} = 2f_m = 2\left(\frac{1.57\times 10^8 \text{ Hz}}{2\pi}\right) = 50 \text{ MHz}.$$

98. (b) The current through the circuit is

$$I = \frac{3\xi}{r_1 + r_2 + R}$$

The terminal voltage across the first cell is given to be zero. Hence, we have $2\xi - Ir_1 = 0$.

$$\Rightarrow \quad 2\xi = \frac{3r_1\xi}{r_1 + r_2 + R}$$

$$\Rightarrow \quad 2(r_1 + r_2 + R) = 3r_1$$

$$\Rightarrow \quad R = \frac{1}{2}r_1 - r_2$$

99. (c)

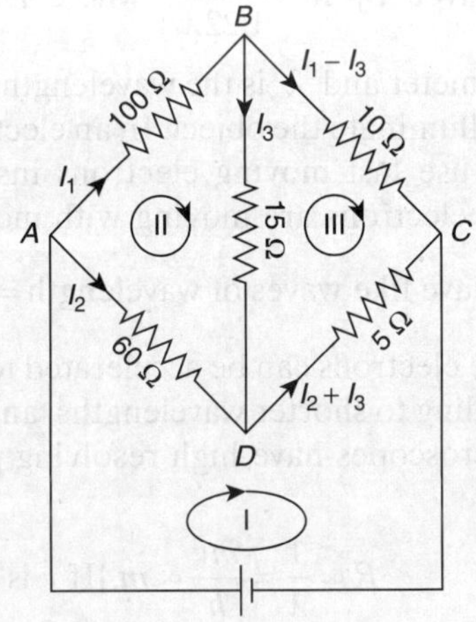

The figure shows the assumed current distribution through the circuit. Let us write the loop equations along the three loops shown in the figure.

Loop I:

$$60I_2 + 5(I_2 + I_3) = 10$$

$$\Rightarrow \quad 13I_2 + I_3 = 2 \qquad (1)$$

Loop II:

$$100I_1 + 15I_3 = 60I_2$$

$$\Rightarrow \quad 20I_1 + 3I_3 = 12I_2 \qquad (2)$$

Loop III:

$$15I_3 + 5(I_2 + I_3) = 10(I_1 - I_3)$$

$$\Rightarrow \quad I_2 + 6I_3 = 2I_1 \qquad (3)$$

Multiplying equation (1) by 3 and then subtracting equation (2), we have

$$39I_2 - 20I_1 = 6 - 12I_2$$

$$\Rightarrow \quad 51I_2 - 20I_1 = 6 \qquad (4)$$

Multiplying equation (2) by 2 and then subtracting equation (3), we have

$$40I_1 - I_2 = 24I_2 - 2I_1$$

$$\Rightarrow \quad 42I_1 = 25I_2 \qquad (5)$$

Solving equations (4) and (5), we have

$$\left(51 - \frac{20\times 25}{42}\right)I_2 = 6$$

$$\Rightarrow \quad I_2 = \frac{6\times 42}{51\times 42 - 20\times 25}\text{A} = \frac{126}{821}\text{A}$$

Putting the value of I_2 in equations (1), we have

$$\Rightarrow \quad I_3 = 2 - 13I_2 = \frac{2\times 821 - 13\times 126}{821}\text{A}$$

$$= \frac{4}{821}\text{A} = 4.87 \text{ mA}$$

100. (a) Immediately after the collision, block C comes to rest and block A starts moving with velocity v. Now the motion of the block A plus block B system is a combination of oscillation plus translation.

At instants when the spring is at its maximum compressed state, the two blocks A and B are moving with the same velocity $v/2$ (from momentum conservation principle). If the maximum compression in the spring is x, then using mechanical energy conservation principle, we have

$$\frac{1}{2}kx^2 + 2\times\frac{1}{2}m\left(\frac{v}{2}\right)^2 = \frac{1}{2}mv^2$$

$$\Rightarrow \quad \frac{1}{2}kx^2 = \frac{1}{4}mv^2 \text{ gives } = v\sqrt{\frac{m}{2k}}$$

101. (c) Acceleration of the sphere is directed down the incline and its magnitude is given by

$$a = \frac{g\sin\theta}{1 + \dfrac{I}{MR^2}} = \frac{g\sin 30°}{1 + \dfrac{2}{5}} = \frac{5g}{14}$$

The total time taken by the sphere to go up and come down is

$$\tau = \frac{2u}{a} = \frac{28\times1}{5\times9.8}\text{s} = 0.57\text{ s}$$

102. (d) For a transistor, we have

$$\alpha = \frac{\Delta I_C}{\Delta I_E} \text{ and } \beta = \frac{\Delta I_C}{\Delta I_B}$$

Also, we know that $\Delta I_E = \Delta I_C + \Delta I_B$. Hence, we have

$$\alpha = \frac{\Delta I_C}{\Delta I_E} = \frac{\Delta I_C}{\Delta I_C + \Delta I_B} = \frac{\beta\Delta I_B}{\beta\Delta I_B + \Delta I_B}$$

$$\Rightarrow \quad \alpha = \frac{\beta}{\beta+1}$$

103. (c) For a series LCR circuit, we have

$$\text{Power factor} = \frac{R}{Z} = \frac{R}{\sqrt{(X_C - X_L)^2 + R^2}}$$

$$= \frac{6}{\sqrt{(4-10)^2 + 6^2}} = \frac{1}{\sqrt{2}}$$

104. (d) At any instant, let r be the distance of the planet from the Sun. In the next time interval dt, suppose the planet moves by an angle $d\theta$, then the area swept out by the planet is

$$dA = \frac{1}{2}r^2 d\theta$$

Hence, the areal velocity is

$$\frac{dA}{dt} = \frac{1}{2}r^2\frac{d\theta}{dt} = \frac{1}{2}r^2\omega = \frac{Mr^2\omega}{2M} = \frac{L}{2M}$$

105. (c)

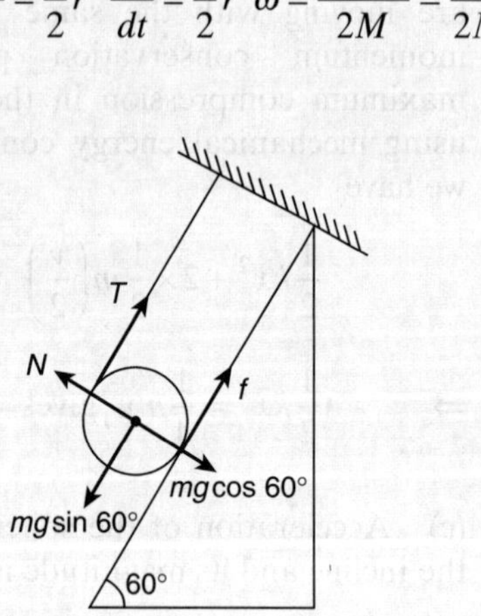

The figure shows the forces acting on the cylinder. The friction force has a limiting value given by

$$f_{\text{lim}} = \mu N = 0.4(mg\cos 60°) = \frac{1}{5}mg$$

The question does not say whether the cylinder is moving or in equilibrium. Suppose it is in equilibrium. Then, we have

$$T + f = mg\sin 60° \text{ [Force down the incline = 0]}$$

and $\quad T - f = 0$ [Torque about CM = 0]

Subtracting the above two equations gives the friction force needed for equilibrium as $f = \frac{1}{2}mg\sin 60° = \frac{\sqrt{3}}{4}mg$. Since this value of f is greater than f_{lim}, this means that the cylinder cannot be in equilibrium.

The cylinder will therefore roll down the incline with slipping, and hence the friction force will be at its limiting value $\frac{1}{5}mg$.

106. (a) The resolving power of an optical instrument is given by $R = \frac{D}{1.22\lambda}$, where D is the aperture diameter and λ is the wavelength of the light used to illuminate the object. In an electron microscope, we use fast moving electrons instead of light. If the electrons are moving with momentum p, they behave like waves of wavelength $= \frac{h}{p}$.

The electrons can be accelerated to large momenta leading to shorter wavelengths, and hence electron microscopes have high resolving power. Thus, we have

$$R \propto \frac{1}{\lambda} = \frac{mv}{h} \propto m \text{ [If } v \text{ is the same]}$$

Hence, $\frac{R_p}{R_e} = \frac{m_p}{m_e} = 1840.$

107. (b) At a perpendicular distance R from the galaxy, the gravitational intensity g is given by $g \propto \frac{1}{R}$ (just like electric field due to an infinitely long line charge). So the force on the revolving star is given by $\propto \frac{1}{R}$. If ω be the angular velocity of the star, then

$$m\omega^2 R \propto \frac{1}{R} \Rightarrow \omega \propto \frac{1}{R}$$

Hence, we have

$$T = \frac{2\pi}{\omega} \propto R$$

108. (c) In a metal, the number of electrons available for conduction does not change much with change in temperature. On the other hand, a rise in temperature increases the vibration of the ions present in the lattice structure of the metal, which inhibits the flow of free electrons. Thus, the conductivity decreases or resistivity increases.
In semi-conductors, a rise in temperature increases the availability of free electrons, as more and more electrons acquire the energy to jump from the valence band to the conduction band. Thus, the conductivity increases or resistivity decreases.

109. (c) The coordinate-axes divide the space into eight regions (four above the *xy*-plane and four below the *xy*-plane). The cube is placed in one of those eight regions. So the total flux through the cube is $\frac{q}{8\varepsilon_0}$.
The three surfaces of the cube which lie in the *xy*-, *yz*- and *xz*- planes, have zero electric flux through them since the electric field lines lie in these planes. The electric flux through the other three surfaces is equal in value as these surfaces are similarly placed with respect to the charge *q*. The electric flux through each of the other three surfaces is $\frac{q}{24\varepsilon_0}$.
Then the flux through each of the shaded areas on the top and the side surfaces of the cube is $\frac{q}{48\varepsilon_0}$.
Hence, the total flux through the shaded area is

$$2\left(\frac{q}{48\varepsilon_0}\right) = \frac{q}{24\varepsilon_0}$$

110. (d) Let λ_1 and λ_2 be the decay constants of the two decay processes. Then the sample activity at any instant is given by

$$\frac{dN}{dt} = -(\lambda_1 + \lambda_2)N$$

Thus, the effective decay constant is $\lambda_1 + \lambda_2$, and hence the effective half-life is

$$T = \frac{\ln 2}{\lambda_1 + \lambda_2} = \frac{\ln 2}{\frac{\ln 2}{T_1} + \frac{\ln 2}{T_2}} = \frac{T_1 T_2}{T_1 + T_2}$$

111. (c) All the rays will fall on surface *LN* with angle of incidence 45°. A ray will emerge out of the surface *LN* if its angle of incidence is less than its critical angle, that is

$$45° < C$$

$$\Rightarrow \quad \sin 45° < \sin C$$

$$\Rightarrow \quad \frac{1}{\sqrt{2}} < \frac{1}{\mu}$$

$$\Rightarrow \quad \mu < \sqrt{2} = 1.414$$

Hence, only the red (*R*) ray will emerge from the surface *LN*. For the other two rays, the refractive index is greater than 1.414 *S*, so they will suffer total internal reflection and will emerge out of the surface *MN*.

112. (b) Let *n* be the number of surplus electrons. Then, we have

$$neE = \rho\left(\frac{4}{3}\pi r^3\right)g$$

$$\Rightarrow \quad n = \frac{4\pi}{3} \times \frac{\rho r^3}{eE} = \frac{4\pi}{3} \times \frac{3000(2\times10^{-3})^3}{(1.6\times10^{-19})(3.55\times10^5)}$$

$$= 1.73\times10^{10}$$

Hence, $\alpha = 10$

113. (d) The solenoids *B*, *C*, *D* will always have the same potential difference since they are parallel $\Rightarrow$ same $L\frac{di}{dt} \Rightarrow$ same $\frac{di}{dt}$ since *L* is the same. This means that current will grow at the same rate in the solenoids *B*, *C*, *D*. Since initial current is the same (zero) in all of them and the current growth rate is the same, the current will always be the same in them.
Thus, if the current through solenoid *A* is *I* , then the currents through each of the three solenoids *B*, *C*, *D* will be *I* /3. Since the magnetic field inside a solenoid is proportional to the current, if the magnetic field inside solenoid *A* is 3 T, then the magnetic field inside each of the three solenoids *B*, *C*, *D* will be $\frac{1}{3}(3\text{ T}) = 1\text{ T}$.

114. (b) Constant power means

$$Fv = \text{constant}$$

$$\Rightarrow \quad \left(m\frac{dv}{dt}\right)v = \text{constant}$$

$$\Rightarrow \int_0^v v\,dv = \alpha \int_0^t dt \quad [\alpha = \text{constant}]$$

$$\Rightarrow \quad v^2 = 2\alpha t$$

$$\Rightarrow \quad v = \sqrt{2\alpha t}$$

Hence, the distance travelled in time is given by

$$s = \sqrt{2\alpha}\int_0^t \sqrt{t}\,dt = \frac{2}{3}\sqrt{2\alpha}\, t^{3/2} \propto t^{3/2}$$

115. (a) The current through the resistor can be represented as $I(t) = I_0 \cos(100\pi t)$, where I_0 is the peak current. We have chosen the function such that the current is at its peak value at time $t = 0$. Now, the time $t = \tau$ at which the current drops to its rms value $I_0/\sqrt{2}$ is given by

$$\Rightarrow \quad I_0 \cos(100\pi\tau) = \frac{I_0}{\sqrt{2}}$$

$$\Rightarrow \quad 100\pi\tau = \frac{\pi}{4}$$

$$\Rightarrow \quad \tau = \frac{1}{400}\,\text{s} = 25\text{ ms}$$

116. (c) In the common emitter configuration, the base is the input and the collector is the output (load). The input power is $I_B^2(100\,\Omega)$ and the output power is $I_C^2(10\text{ k}\Omega)$. It is given that

$$\frac{I_C^2(10\text{ k}\Omega)}{I_B^2(100\,\Omega)} = 10^6$$

$$\Rightarrow \quad \frac{I_C^2}{I_B^2} = 10^4$$

$$\Rightarrow \quad \frac{I_C}{I_B} = 100$$

Hence, the current gain $\beta = 10$.

117. (c) The de Broglie wavelength of an electron accelerated by potential V is

$$\lambda = \frac{h}{p} = \frac{h}{\sqrt{2m_e eV}}$$

Now using the given condition $2d\cos i = n\lambda$, we have

$$2d\cos i = \frac{nh}{\sqrt{2m_e eV}}$$

$$\Rightarrow \quad V = \frac{n^2h^2}{8m_e ed^2\cos^2 i}$$

$$\Rightarrow \quad V = \frac{n^2\left(6.6\times10^{-34}\right)^2}{8\left(9.1\times10^{-31}\right)\left(1.6\times10^{-19}\right)\left(10^{-10}\right)^2(3/4)}\text{ V}$$

$$\Rightarrow \quad V = n^2\left(\frac{6.6^2\times100}{6\times9.1\times1.6}\text{ V}\right) \approx n^2(50\text{ V})$$

Numerical Value Answer

1.

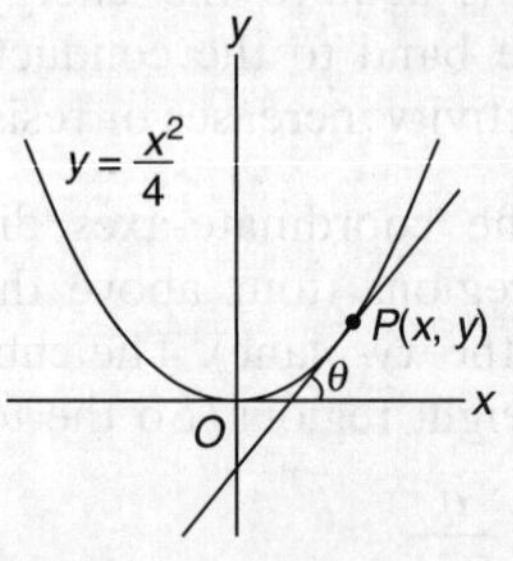

For a particle to rest in equilibrium at point $P(x, y)$ (see figure), we have

$$\mu \ge \tan\theta = \frac{dy}{dx} = \frac{1}{2}x$$

$$\Rightarrow \quad x \le 2\mu = 1 \; [\mu = 0.5\text{, given}]$$

$$\Rightarrow \quad 2\sqrt{y} \le 1$$

$$\Rightarrow \quad y \le \frac{1}{4}\text{ m} = 25\text{ cm.}$$

2.

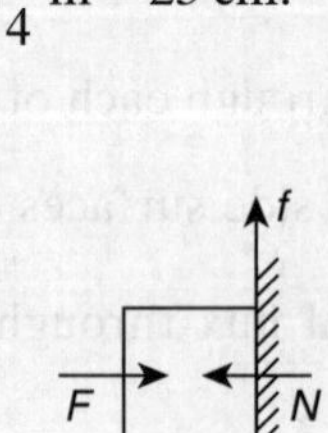

The figure shows the forces acting on the block. Using dynamics, we have

$$N = F \text{ and } f = mg$$

We know that $f \le \mu N$. Thus, we have

$$\Rightarrow \quad mg \le \mu F$$

$$\Rightarrow \quad F \ge \frac{mg}{\mu} = \frac{0.5\times10}{0.2}\text{ N} = 25\text{ N.}$$

3. Let the cross-section areas of piston A and piston B be A_1, A_2, respectively.
In the first case

$$\frac{100}{A_1} = \frac{m}{A_2} \quad (1)$$

In the second case

$$\frac{M}{16A_1} = \frac{m}{A_2/16} \quad (2)$$

Dividing equation (1) by equation (2), we have

$$\frac{100\times 16}{M} = \frac{1}{16} \text{ gives } M = 25600 \text{ kg.}$$

4. Velocity of an EM wave depends on the magnetic permeability $(\mu = \mu_r\mu_0)$ and the electric permittivity $(\epsilon = \epsilon_r\epsilon_0)$ of the medium as

$$v = \frac{1}{\sqrt{\mu\epsilon}} = \frac{1}{\sqrt{(2\mu_0)(2\epsilon_0)}} = \frac{c}{2} = 15\times 10^7 \text{ m/s.}$$

Hence, $x = 15$.

5. Percentage modulation index is given by

$$m = \frac{A_m}{A_c}\times 100\% = \frac{20}{80}\times 100\% = \times 25\%$$

6. The square surface is a part of a cube of side 12 cm with the charge Q at the center. Hence, the electric flux through the square surface is

$$\phi = \frac{Q}{6\epsilon_0} = \frac{12\times 10^{-6}}{6}\times\left(36\pi\times 10^9\right)$$

$$= 226\times 10^3 \text{ N}\cdot\text{m}^2/\text{C}$$

Hence, $x = 226$.

7. (0.8)

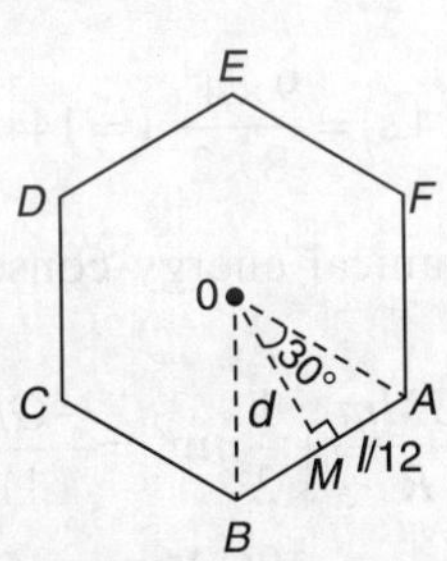

Each portion of the hexagon is of length $l/6$ and mass $m/6$. The perpendicular distance of each portion from the centre of the hexagon (see figure) is

$$d = \frac{l}{12}\cot 30° = \frac{l}{4\sqrt{3}}$$

The MI of any one portion, say AB, about a perpendicular axis through O is

$$I_{AB} = \frac{1}{12}\left(\frac{m}{6}\right)\left(\frac{l}{6}\right)^2 + \left(\frac{m}{6}\right)d^2$$

[Parallel-Axis Theorem]

$$= \frac{1}{12}\left(\frac{m}{6}\right)\left(\frac{l}{6}\right)^2 + \left(\frac{m}{6}\right)\left(\frac{l}{4\sqrt{3}}\right)^2$$

$$= \left(\frac{1}{36\times 72} + \frac{1}{6\times 48}\right)ml^2 = \frac{5}{24\times 54}ml^2$$

Hence, the total MI of the hexagon is

$$I = 6I_{AB} = \frac{5}{24\times 9}ml^2$$

Putting $m = 6$ kg and $l = 2.4$ m, we have

$$I = \frac{5}{24\times 9}\left(9\times 2.4^2\right)\text{kg}\cdot\text{m}^2 = 0.8 \text{ kg}\cdot\text{m}^2$$

8. The elongation in the rod is given by

$$\Delta L = \frac{FL}{AY} \propto \frac{L}{A} \text{ [If } F \text{ is same]}$$

Thus, we have

$$\Delta L = \frac{FL}{AY} \propto \frac{L}{A} \text{ [If } F \text{ is same]}$$

$$\Rightarrow \quad \frac{\Delta L}{0.04 \text{ m}} = \frac{2L/4A}{L/A} = \frac{1}{2}$$

$$\Rightarrow \quad \Delta L = 0.02 \text{ m} = 2\times 10^{-2} \text{ m}$$

Hence, $x = 2$.

9. The current through the wire is

$$I = J\left(\pi r^2\right) = (\sigma E)\left(\pi r^2\right)$$

$$= \left(5\times 10^7\right)\left(10\times 10^{-3}\right)\times\pi\left(0.5\times 10^{-3}\right)^2 \text{ A}$$

$$= 125\pi \text{ mA}$$

Hence, $x = 5$.

10. In a series resonance LCR circuit, the circuit impedance at resonance is $Z = R$ and the power factor is $\cos\phi = \frac{R}{Z} = 1$. Hence, power consumption is

$$P = \frac{V_{\text{rms}}^2}{Z}\cos\phi = \frac{V_{\text{rms}}^2}{R}$$

$$\Rightarrow \quad R = \frac{V_{\text{rms}}^2}{P} = \frac{120^2}{16}\Omega = 800\ \Omega.$$

11. Let T_x and T_y be the half-lives of the nuclei X and Y, respectively. Given $T_x = \frac{1}{2}T_y$. So let $T_x = T$ and $T_y = 2T$. Then, we have

$$N_x(y) = N_1 2^{\frac{-t}{T}} \text{ and } N_y(y) = N_2 2^{\frac{-t}{2T}}$$

After time $t = 3T_y = 6T$, we have

$$N_x(6T) = N_1 2^{-6} \text{ and } N_y(6T) = N_2 2^{-3}$$

It is given that they are equal. Hence, we have

$$N_1 2^{-6} = N_2 2^{-3}$$

$$\Rightarrow \quad \frac{N_1}{N_2} = 8$$

12. Using the lens formula, we have

$$\frac{1}{v} - \frac{1}{u} = \frac{1}{f}$$

$$\Rightarrow \quad \frac{u}{v} - 1 = \frac{u}{f}$$

$$\Rightarrow \quad \frac{1}{m} = 1 + \frac{u}{f}$$

It is given that the image size is same, which means $|m|$ is the same for $u = -10$ cm and $u = -20$ cm. Thus, we have

$$1 + \frac{-10}{f} = -\left(1 + \frac{-20}{f}\right)$$

$$\Rightarrow \quad \frac{30}{f} = 2 \text{ gives } f = +15 \text{ cm}$$

13. For resonance in a series LCR circuit, we have

$$f = \frac{1}{2\pi\sqrt{LC}}$$

$$\Rightarrow \quad \frac{c}{\lambda} = \frac{1}{2\pi\sqrt{LC}}$$

$$\Rightarrow L = \frac{\lambda^2}{4\pi^2 c^2 C} = \frac{960^2}{4\pi^2 (3\times 10^8)^2 (2.56\times 10^{-6})} \text{H}$$

Putting the values, we have

$$L = \frac{960^2}{4\pi^2 (3\times 10^8)^2 (2.56\times 10^{-6})} \text{H} = 10\times 10^{-8} \text{ H.}$$

Hence, $x = 10$.

14. Work done by gas during the process PV^n = constant is given by

$$W = \frac{\Delta(PV)}{1-n} = \frac{\mu R \Delta T}{1-n}$$

Putting the values, we have

$$W = \frac{\mu R(200)}{1-(-3)} = 50\mu R$$

Hence, $x = 50$.

15.

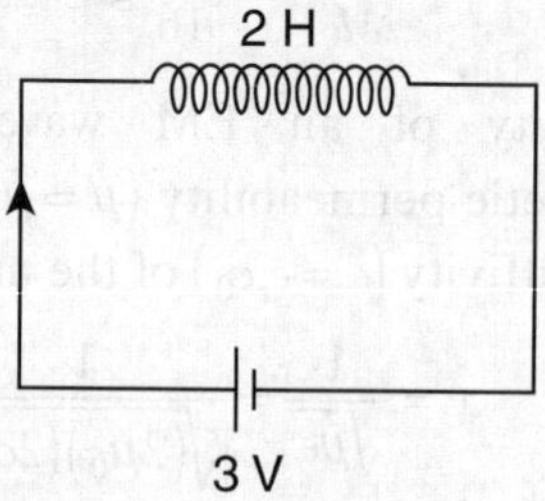

If i denotes the instantaneous current (see figure), then we have

$$L\frac{di}{dt} = 3t$$

$$\Rightarrow \quad \int_0^i di = \frac{3}{L}\int_0^t t\,dt$$

$$\Rightarrow \quad i(t) = \frac{3}{2L}t^2$$

Thus, the energy stored in the inductor at time t is

$$U(t) = \frac{1}{2}Li^2 = \frac{1}{2}L\left(\frac{3}{2L}t^2\right)^2 = \frac{9}{8L}t^4.$$

Hence, energy stored in the inductor at time $t = 4$ s is

$$U(4\text{ s}) = \frac{9\times 4^4}{8\times 2} \text{J} = 144 \text{ J.}$$

16. Using mechanical energy conservation principle, we have

$$\frac{-GMm}{R} + \frac{1}{2}mv^2 = \frac{-GMm}{11R}$$

$$\Rightarrow \quad \frac{1}{2}mv^2 = \frac{10GMm}{11R}$$

$$\Rightarrow \quad v = \sqrt{\frac{20GM}{11R}} = \sqrt{\frac{10}{11}}v_{esc}$$

Hence, $x = 10$.

17. At the instant the 2nd particle is released, the 1st particle is moving with velocity $\sqrt{2g(5\text{ m})} = 10$ m/s and it has moved for time $\sqrt{\frac{2(5\text{ m})}{g}} = 1$ s.

At this instant, the relative distance between the two particles is $s_{\text{rel}} = 25\text{ m} - 5\text{ m} = 20$ m, the relative velocity is $v_{\text{rel}} = 10$ m/s, and the relative acceleration is $a_{\text{rel}} = 0$.

The two particles will meet after time

$$\Rightarrow \quad \frac{s_{\text{rel}}}{v_{\text{rel}}} = \frac{20}{10}\text{s} = 2\text{ s}.$$

Thus, the total time of travel by the 1st particle before it reaches the ground is 1 s + 2 s = 3 s. Hence, height of the tower is

$$\Rightarrow \quad H = \frac{1}{2}g(3\text{ s})^2 = 45\text{ m}.$$

18. Let m be the mass and p be the linear momentum of the particle. Then according to the question, we have

$$\frac{hc}{\lambda} = \frac{p^2}{2m} \text{ and } \lambda = \frac{h}{p}$$

Eliminating p from the above equations, we have

$$\frac{hc}{\lambda} = \frac{\left(\frac{h}{\lambda}\right)^2}{2m}$$

$$\Rightarrow \quad m = \frac{h}{2c\lambda} = \frac{h}{2(3\times10^8)(10\times10^{-10})} = \frac{5h}{3}$$

Hence, $x = 5$.

19. After the charged particles are brought into contact, they acquire equal charges

$$q = \frac{(2.1\text{ nC}) + (-0.1\text{ nC})}{2} = 1\text{ nC}.$$

Then the Coulomb force between them is

$$F = \frac{q^2}{4\pi\epsilon_0 d^2} = \frac{(9\times10^9)(10^{-9})^2}{(0.5)^2}\text{N} = 36\times10^{-9}\text{ N}$$

Hence, $x = 36$.

20. The quality factor of a series resonant LCR is given by

$$Q = \frac{X_L}{R} = \frac{\omega L}{R} = \frac{L}{R\sqrt{LC}} \propto \frac{\sqrt{L}}{R} \text{ [If } C \text{ is the same]}$$

Hence, we have

$$\frac{Q'}{Q} = \frac{\sqrt{2L}}{R/2} \times \frac{R}{\sqrt{L}} = 2\sqrt{2}$$

$$\Rightarrow \quad Q' = 2\sqrt{2}Q = 200\sqrt{2}$$

Hence, $x = 200$.

21. The power of light coming out from the bulb is

$$P = 1.2\% \times 1000\text{ W} = 12\text{ W}$$

The intensity at distance $r = 2$ m is

$$I' = \frac{P}{4\pi r^2} = \frac{12\text{ W}}{4\pi(2^2)} = \frac{3}{4\pi}\text{W}$$

If E_0 is the electric field amplitude at distance $r = 2$ m, then

$$\left(\frac{1}{2}\epsilon_0 E_0^2\right)c = I'$$

$$\Rightarrow \quad E_0 = \sqrt{\frac{2I'}{\epsilon_0 c}} = \sqrt{\frac{6}{4\pi\epsilon_0 c}}$$

$$= \sqrt{\frac{6(9\times10^9)}{3\times10^8}}\text{V/m} = 3\sqrt{20}\text{V/m}$$

Hence, $x = 20$.

22. The velocity of wave propagation is

$$v = \frac{\omega}{k} = 30\text{ m/s}$$

Hence the tension F in the string is given by

$$v = \sqrt{\frac{F}{\mu}}$$

$$\Rightarrow \quad F = \mu v^2 = (0.325\times10^{-1})\times30^2\text{ N} = 29.25\text{ N}.$$

23. The internal energy of gas is given by

$$U = f\left(\frac{1}{2}PV\right)$$

In the given process, the internal energy of the gas remains conserved. Hence, we have

$$\frac{f}{2}(2\times4.5) + \frac{f}{2}(3\times5.5) = \frac{f}{2}(P\times10)$$

$$\Rightarrow \qquad P = \frac{9 + 16.5}{10} \text{ atm} = 2.55 \text{ atm}.$$

24. Let g_0 be the gravitational intensity at B. Then

$$g_C = g_0 \frac{R^2}{(R+h)^2} = g_0 \left(\frac{6400}{6400 + 3200} \right)^2 = \frac{4}{9} g_0$$

and $g_A = g_0 \left(\frac{OA}{R} \right)$.

It is given that $g_A = g_C$. Thus, we have

$$\left(\frac{OA}{R} \right) g_0 = \frac{4}{9} g_0 \text{ gives } OA = \frac{4}{9} R$$

Then $AB = R - OA = \frac{5}{9} R$, and $\frac{OA}{AB} = \frac{4}{5}$. Hence, $x = 4$.

25. If θ_0 is the angular amplitude of the pendulum, then the pendulum covers angle $4\theta_0$ in one oscillation. In the $\frac{5}{8}$th oscillation, it covers angle

$\frac{5}{8}(4\theta_0) = \frac{5\theta_0}{2} = 2\theta_0 + \frac{\theta_0}{2}$.

The angle $2\theta_0$ is covered in time $T/2$. After that, the pendulum is back to its mean position. To find the time taken to move a further angle $\theta_0/2$, let us the write the function representing the angular position of the pendulum as a function of time, which is

$$\theta(t) = \theta_0 \sin\left(\frac{2\pi}{T} t \right)$$

Thus, the time τ in which the pendulum covers angle $\theta_0/2$ from its mean position is given by

$$\theta_0 \sin\left(\frac{2\pi}{T} \tau \right) = \frac{\theta_0}{2}$$

$$\Rightarrow \qquad \frac{2\pi}{T} \tau = \frac{\pi}{6} \text{ gives } \tau = \frac{T}{12}$$

Thus, the required time is $\frac{T}{2} + \frac{T}{12} = \frac{7T}{12}$. Hence, $x = 7$.

26.

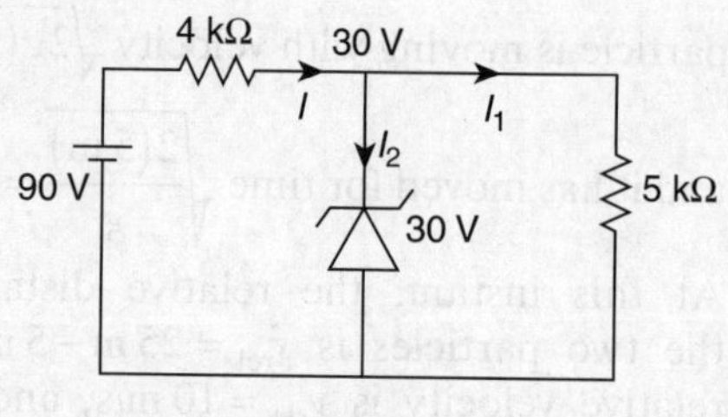

The Zener diode (see figure) maintains a constant PD equal to $V_Z = 30$ V across the 5 kΩ resistor. So current through the resistor is

$$I_1 = \frac{30 \text{ V}}{5 \text{ k}\Omega} = 6 \text{ mA}.$$

The current through the cell is

$$I = \frac{90 \text{ V} - 30 \text{ V}}{4 \text{ k}\Omega} = 15 \text{ mA}.$$

Thus, current through the diode is

$$I_2 = I - I_1 = 15 \text{ mA} - 6 \text{ mA} = 9 \text{ mA}.$$

The power dissipated across the diode is

$$P = V_Z I_2 = 30 \times 9 \text{ mW} = 27 \times 10^{-2} \text{ W}.$$

Hence, $x = 27$.

27. The given process $V = kT^{2/3}$ can also be written as

$$V^{3/2} = kT$$

$$\Rightarrow \qquad V^{3/2} = k(PV)$$

$$\Rightarrow \qquad PV^{-1/2} = 1/k \text{ (constant)}$$

For the process PV^n = constant, work done by the gas is given by $W = \frac{\mu R \Delta T}{1-n}$. In this question, $n = -1/2$ and $\mu = 1, \Delta T = 90°\text{C}$. Thus, we have

$$W = \frac{R(90°\text{C})}{1 + \frac{1}{2}} = 60R.$$

Hence, $x = 60$.

28. The maximum kinetic energies of the photo-electrons emitted in the two cases are

$$K_1 = hf_1 - \phi \text{ and } K_2 = hf_2 - \phi$$

It is given that $hf_1 = 2\phi$ and $hf_2 = 10\phi$. Thus, we have

$$\frac{K_1}{K_2} = \frac{2\phi - \phi}{10\phi - \phi} = \frac{1}{9}$$

$$\Rightarrow \quad \frac{v_1^2}{v_2^2} = \frac{1}{9}$$

$$\Rightarrow \quad \frac{v_1}{v_2} = \frac{1}{3}$$

Hence, $x = 1$.

29.

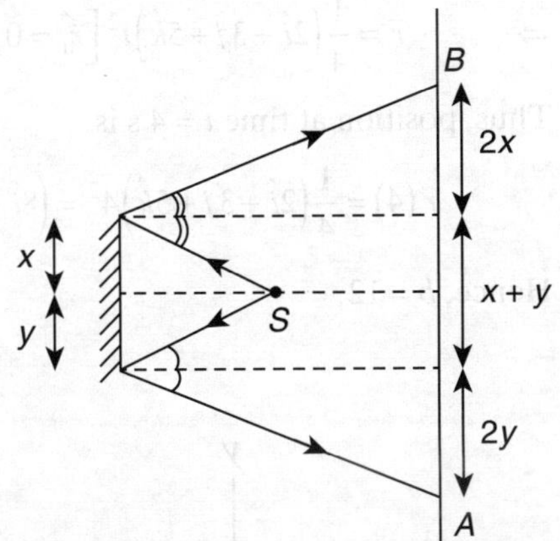

The figure shows a point source of light S placed at some arbitrary distance x from one edge and distance y from the other edge of the mirror. The maximum distance over which the man can see the image of S in the mirror is

$$AB = 3(x+y) = 3(50\text{ cm}) = 150\text{ cm}.$$

30. The disk rotates with angular acceleration given by

$$\alpha = \frac{FR}{\frac{1}{2}MR^2} = \frac{2F}{MR} = \frac{2\times 20}{20\times 0.2}\text{ rad/s}^2 = 10\text{ rad/s}^2$$

The angular velocity ω of the disc as a function of its angular displacement $\Delta\theta$ is given by

$$\omega^2 = \omega_0^2 + 2\alpha\Delta\theta$$

Putting the given values, we have

$$50^2 = 0 + 20\Delta\theta \text{ gives } \Delta\theta = 125\text{ rad}$$

Hence, the number of revolutions is

$$n = \frac{125}{2\pi} = 20\text{ rev.}$$

31.

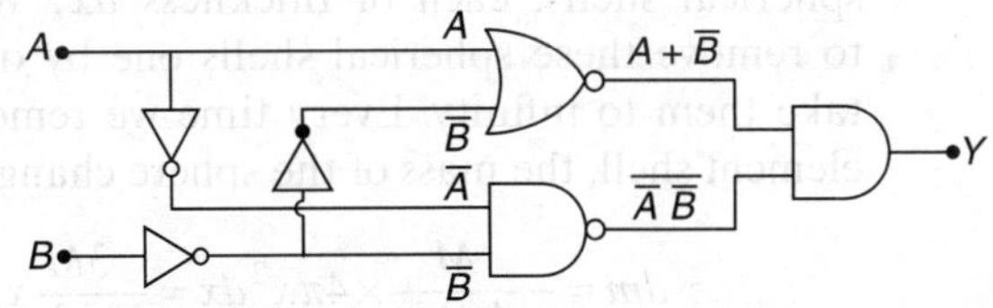

For the given circuit (see figure), we have

$$Y = \left(A+\overline{B}\right)\left(\overline{\overline{A}\,\overline{B}}\right)$$

$$\Rightarrow \quad Y = \left(\overline{A+B}\right)\left(A+B\right)$$

$$\Rightarrow \quad Y = 0 \text{ for all values of } A, B$$

32. For the relation $R = VI^{-1}$, we have

$$\frac{\Delta R}{R} = \frac{\Delta V}{V} - \frac{\Delta I}{I}$$

Hence, the maximum error in R is

$$\frac{\Delta R}{R} = \frac{2}{50} + \frac{0.2}{20} = \frac{5}{100} = 5\%.$$

Hence, $x = 5$.

33. In the absence of external force on the two-ball system, its linear momentum must be conserved. Before collision, the linear momentum is zero along the y-axis; it should remain zero even after collision. Thus, we have

$$10(20\text{ m/s}\sin\theta) = (10\text{ kg})(10\text{ m/s})$$

$$\Rightarrow \quad \sin\theta = \frac{1}{2}$$

Hence, $\theta = 30°$.

34. The point of application of the force $\vec{F}$ is $P(2, 0, 0)$. The position vector of point $P(2, 0, 0)$ with respect to point $A(2, 3, 4)$ is

$$\overrightarrow{AP} = 0\hat{i} - 3\hat{j} - 4\hat{k}$$

Thus, torque of force $\vec{F}$ about point A is

$$\vec{\tau} = \overrightarrow{AP}\times\vec{F} = \begin{vmatrix} \hat{i} & \hat{j} & \hat{k} \\ 0 & -3 & -4 \\ 4 & 3 & 4 \end{vmatrix} = -16\hat{j} + 12\hat{k}$$

Hence, the magnitude of the torque is

$$\tau = \sqrt{16^2 + 12^2}\text{ Nm} = 20\text{ Nm}.$$

35. Let us sub-divide the Earth into thin concentric spherical shells, each of thickness dx. We have to remove these spherical shells one by one, and take them to infinity. Every time we remove one element shell, the mass of the sphere changes by

$$dm = -\frac{M}{\frac{4}{3}\pi R^3} \times 4\pi x^2 dx = -\frac{3M}{R^3} x^2 dx.$$

At any instant when the radius of the sphere is x, its mass is $M' = \frac{M}{\frac{4}{3}\pi R^3} \times \frac{4}{3}\pi x^3 = \frac{Mx^3}{R^3}$, and the gravitational of its surface is

$$V = \frac{GM'}{x} = \frac{GM}{R^3} x^2$$

The work done in removing an element shell of thickness dx and taking it to infinity is given by

$$dW = -V dm = -\left(\frac{GM}{R^3} x^2\right)\left(\frac{3M}{R^3} x^2 dx\right)$$

Thus, the total work done in removing the entire mass of the sphere is

$$W = \frac{3GM^2}{R^6} \int_R^0 x^4 dx = \frac{3GM^2}{5R}$$

Hence, $x = 3$.

36. Let us call the crown and the flint glass prisms as prism 1 and prism 2, respectively. For achromatic combination, we have

$$A_1\omega_1(\mu_{1y} - 1) = A_2\omega_2(\mu_{2y} - 1)$$

$$\Rightarrow \quad 0.02(1.5 - 1)A_1 = 0.03(1.6 - 1)A_2$$

$$\Rightarrow \quad 5A_1 = 9A_2 \qquad (1)$$

The deviation of yellow light is given to be 2°. Thus, we have

$$|A_1(\mu_{1y} - 1) - A_2(\mu_{1y} - 1)| = 2$$

$$\Rightarrow \quad |A_1(1.5 - 1) - A_2(1.6 - 1)| = 2$$

$$\Rightarrow \quad |5A_1 - 6A_2| = 20 \qquad (2)$$

Solving equations (1) and (2), we have

$$A_2 = \frac{20}{3} \text{ and } A_2 = 12.$$

37. The particle moves with acceleration

$$\vec{a} = \frac{\vec{F}}{m} = \frac{1}{2}(2\hat{i} + 3\hat{j} + 5\hat{k}) = 1\hat{i} + \frac{3}{2}\hat{j} + \frac{5}{2}\hat{k}$$

For constant acceleration motion, the relation between position and time is given by

$$\vec{r} = \vec{r_0} + \vec{u}t + \frac{1}{2}\vec{a}t^2$$

$$\Rightarrow \quad \vec{r} = \frac{1}{4}(2\hat{i} + 3\hat{j} + 5\hat{k})t^2 \left[\vec{r_0} = 0, \vec{u} = 0, \text{given}\right]$$

Thus, position at time $t = 4$ s is

$$\vec{r}(4) = \frac{1}{4}(2\hat{i} + 3\hat{j} + 5\hat{k})4^2 = (8\hat{i} + 12\hat{j} + 20\hat{k})v.$$

Hence, $b = 12$.

38.

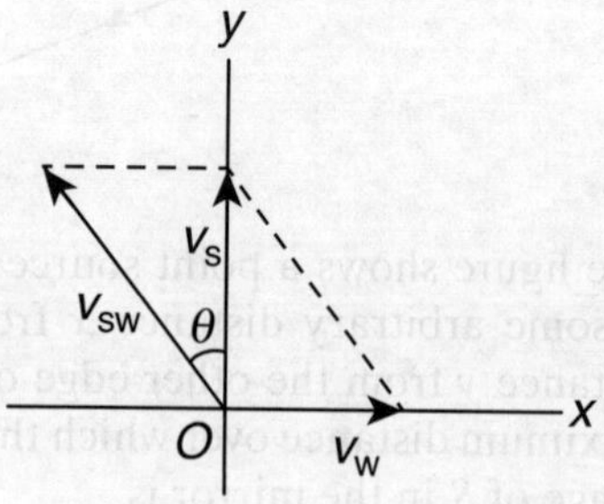

Let $\overrightarrow{v_{sw}}$ denote the velocity of the swimmer with respect to water, v_w denote the velocity of water, and $\overrightarrow{v_s}$ denote the absolute velocity of the swimmer. Then $v_s = v_{sw} + v_w$.

Let us choose the x-axis along $\overrightarrow{v_w}$ (see figure). Let $\overrightarrow{v_{sw}}$ be at angle θ to the y-axis as shown in the figure. Now, according to the question, $\overrightarrow{v_s}$ must be along the y-axis. This is possible if

$$v_{sw}\sin\theta = v_w$$

$$\Rightarrow \quad 12\sin\theta = 6 \text{ gives } \theta = 30°$$

Hence, the angle that $\overrightarrow{v_{sw}}$ should make with the +ve x-axis is $\theta = 90° + 30° = 120°$.

39. The oscillation frequencies in the two pipes are

$$f_1 = \frac{3}{4L}\sqrt{\frac{B}{\rho_1}} \text{ and } f_2 = \frac{2}{2L'}\sqrt{\frac{B}{\rho_2}}$$

where L' is the length of the open pipe.

Equating the two frequencies, we have

$$\vec{r} = \vec{r_0} + \vec{u}t + \frac{1}{2}\vec{a}t^2$$

$$\frac{3}{4L}\sqrt{\frac{B}{\rho_1}} = \frac{2}{2L'}\sqrt{\frac{B}{\rho_2}}$$

$$\Rightarrow \quad L' = \frac{4}{3}\sqrt{\frac{\rho_1}{\rho_2}}L.$$

Hence, $x = 4$.

40. The efficiency of an ideal heat engine is given by

$$\eta = 1 - \frac{T_{sink}}{T_{source}}$$

$$\Rightarrow \quad T_{sink} = (1-\eta)T_{source}$$

$$= (1-0.6)400 \text{ K} = 160 \text{ K} = -113 \text{ °C}.$$

Hence, $x = -113$.

41. The angular displacement is given by

$$\Delta\theta = \left(\frac{\omega_2 + \omega_1}{2}\right)\Delta t$$

$$= \frac{2460+900}{60} \times 26 = 728 \text{ rev}$$

42. The escape velocity from the Earth is given by

$$v_e = \sqrt{\frac{2GM}{R}}$$

$$\Rightarrow \quad v_e \propto \frac{1}{\sqrt{R}} \text{ [If } M \text{ is same]}$$

Hence, we have

$$\frac{10v_e}{v_e} = \sqrt{\frac{R}{R'}}$$

$$\Rightarrow \quad R' = \frac{R}{100} = \frac{6400 \text{ km}}{100} = 64 \text{ km}$$

43. When the dielectric is brought near the plates, polarized charges appear on its surface, and it experiences an attractive force by the charges on the capacitor plates. As the dielectric moves inside the capacitor, its kinetic energy increases and the electric potential energy of the capacitor decreases. But the total mechanical energy remains conserved since friction is absent.

The electric potential energy of the capacitor when the dielectric is completely outside and when it is completely inside the capacitor are

$$U_{max} = \frac{Q^2}{2C} \text{ and } U_{min} = \frac{Q^2}{2(7C)}$$

The difference between the two potential energy values is the energy available for oscillation of the dielectric. Hence, the required mechanical energy is

$$E = U_{max} - U_{max} = \frac{3Q^2}{7C} = \frac{3}{7}CV^2$$

$$= \frac{3}{7}(14\times10^{-12})\times12^2 = 864 \text{ pJ}$$

44. The block m gets its acceleration from the friction force between the two blocks. The limiting value of this friction force is $f_{lim} = \mu mg$. Thus, the maximum possible acceleration for m is

$$a_{max} = \frac{f_{lim}}{m} = \mu g$$

Thus, μg is the maximum acceleration with which the two blocks can move together without slipping. Hence, using dynamics on the two-block system, we have

$$F = (M+m)\mu g = 5\times\frac{3}{7}\times9.8 \text{ N} = 21.2 \text{ N}$$

45. We have

$$P_{rad} = \frac{I}{c}$$

$$\Rightarrow \quad I = cP_{rad} = (3\times10^8)\left(\frac{2.5\times10^{-6}}{30\times10^{-4}}\right)\text{W/cm}^2$$

$$= 2.5\times10^5 \text{ W/m}^2$$

Thus, the energy absorbed per unit area in 40 min is

$$E = (2.5\times10^5 \text{ W/m}^2)(40\times60 \text{ s}) = 6\times10^8 \text{ J/m}^2$$

Hence, $x = 6$.

46.

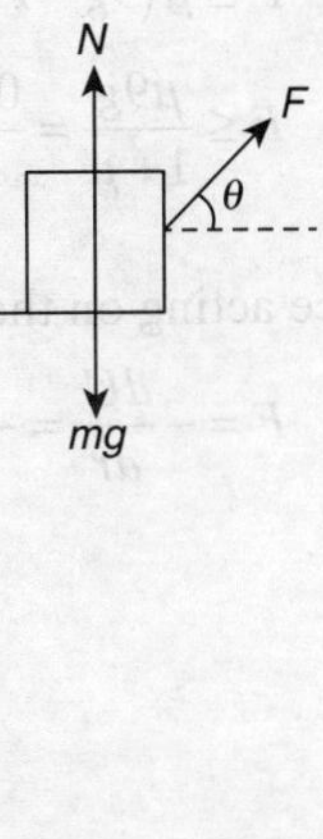

Suppose we are just able to move the block by applying force F at angle θ on the block (see figure). Using dynamics, we have

$$F\sin\theta + N = mg \quad (1)$$

and $$F\cos\theta = \mu N \quad (2)$$

Eliminating N from equations (1) and (2), we have

$$F\cos\theta = \mu(F\sin\theta - mg)$$

$$\Rightarrow \quad F = \frac{\mu mg}{\cos\theta + \mu\sin\theta}$$

$$\Rightarrow \quad F = \frac{\mu mg}{\sqrt{1+\mu^2}\cos(\theta - \phi)}$$

where $\phi = \tan^{-1}(\mu)$

We see that the value of F is minimum when $\theta = \phi$, and the minimum value is

$$F_{\min} = \frac{\mu mg}{\sqrt{1+\mu^2}} = \frac{10}{\sqrt{3}\sqrt{1+\frac{1}{3}}}\text{N} = 5\,\text{N}.$$

47.

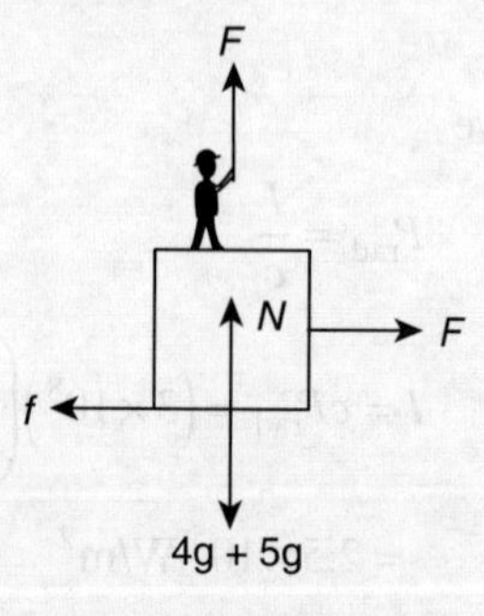

The figure shows the forces acting on the block plus man system. If the system is not moving, then we have

$$F + N = 9g \quad (1)$$

and $$F = f \quad (2)$$

Now using the inequality $f \le \mu N$, we have

$$F \le \mu(9g - F)$$

$$\Rightarrow \quad F \le \frac{\mu 9g}{1+\mu} = \frac{0.5\times 90}{1+0.5}\text{N} = 30\text{ N}$$

48. The force acting on the particle is given by

$$F = -\frac{dU}{dr} = -4U_0 r^3$$

Thus, for a particle moving with velocity v in a circular orbit of radius v, we have

$$4U_0 r^3 = \frac{mv^2}{r} \Rightarrow v \propto r^2 \quad (1)$$

Assuming Bohr's quantization, we have

$$mvr = n\frac{h}{2\pi} \Rightarrow vr \propto n \quad (2)$$

where $n = 1, 2, \ldots$

Eliminating v from equations (1) and (2), we have

$$r^3 \propto n \Rightarrow r \propto n^{1/3}.$$

Hence, $\alpha = 3$.

49.

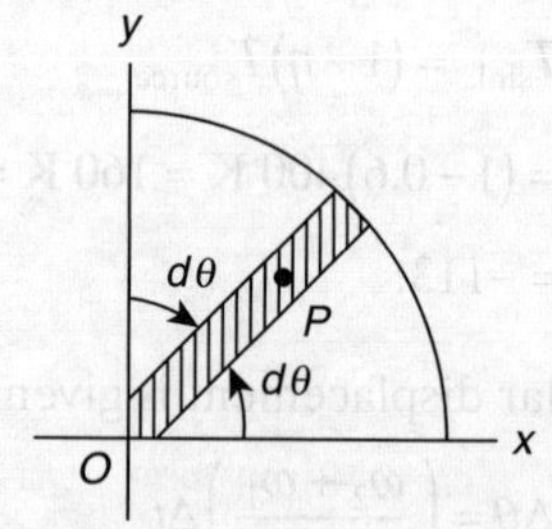

Let us sub-divide the quarter disc into thin sectors, each subtending angle $d\theta$ at the centre O of the disc. The figure shows one such element sector at angular position θ from the x-axis. Let σ be the surface area density of the disc. Then the mass of this element sector is

$$dm = \sigma\left(\frac{1}{2}a^2 d\theta\right)$$

The CM of this element sector is located at point P such that $OP = \frac{2a}{3}$. The coordinates of point P are $\left(\frac{2a}{3}\cos\theta, \frac{2a}{3}\sin\theta\right)$. Thus the coordinates of the CM of the quarter disc are given by

$$x_{\text{cm}} = \frac{\int \frac{2a}{3}\cos\theta\, dm}{\int dm} = \frac{\frac{1}{3}\sigma a^3 \int_0^{\pi/2}\cos\theta\, d\theta}{\sigma\left(\frac{\pi a^3}{4}\right)} = \frac{4a}{3\pi}$$

From symmetry, we can see that $y_{\text{cm}} = x_{\text{cm}} = \frac{4a}{3\pi}$.

Hence, $\alpha = 4$.

50.

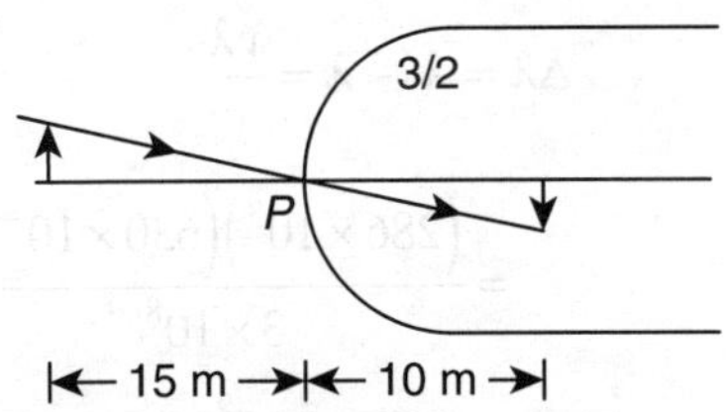

The image distance is 10 m, object distance is 15 m (see figure). The refractive index of the medium is given by

$$\mu = \frac{\lambda_{\text{free space}}}{\lambda_{\text{medium}}} = \frac{1}{2/3} = 1.5$$

Now using refraction formula, we have

$$\frac{1.5}{+10\text{ m}} - \frac{1}{-15\text{ m}} = \frac{1.5-1}{+R}$$

$$\Rightarrow \quad \frac{65}{300\text{ m}} = \frac{1}{2R} \text{ gives } R = \frac{30}{13}\text{ m}.$$

Hence, $\alpha = 30$.

51. Initial charge on capacitor C_1 is

$$q = (2\,..\text{F})(10\text{ V}) = 20\ \mu\text{C}.$$

Now when it is connected to capacitor C_1, the charge q now distributes on both the capacitors such that the PD across the two capacitors is the same. If q_1, q_2 are the charges on capacitors C_1, C_2, respectively, then we have

$$\frac{q_1}{C_1} = \frac{q_2}{C_2} \Rightarrow \frac{q_1}{1} = \frac{q_2}{4}$$

and $\quad q_1 + q_2 = q.$

Hence, we have

$$q_1 = \frac{q}{5} = 4\ \mu\text{C and } q_2 = \frac{4q}{5} = 16\ \mu\text{C}.$$

52. Let A be the plate area and d be the distance between the plates of the capacitor. Then the resistance and the capacitance of the capacitor are

$$R = \frac{\rho d}{A} \text{ and } C = \frac{80\epsilon_0 A}{d}$$

At any instant, the conduction and the displacement current densities are given by

$$j_C = \frac{V/R}{A} = \frac{1}{\rho d} V_0 \sin(2\pi f t)$$

and

$$j_D = 80\epsilon_0 \frac{dE}{dt} = \frac{80\epsilon_0}{d}\frac{d(V)}{dt} = \frac{80\epsilon_0}{d} 2\pi f V_0 \cos(2\pi f t).$$

Thus, we have

$$\frac{j_C}{j_D} = \frac{1}{160\pi\epsilon_0 \rho f}\tan(2\pi f t)$$

$$= \frac{9\times10^9}{40\times0.25\times900}\tan(1800\pi t) = 10^6 \tan(1800\pi t)$$

At time $t = \frac{1}{800}$ s, we have

$$\frac{j_C}{j_D} = 10^6 \tan\left(\frac{9\pi}{4}\right) = 10^6.$$

Hence, $\alpha = 6$.

53. The speed of the projectile at the point of landing is the same as its speed at the point of projection, that is, $v = 5\sqrt{2}$ m/s. Thus, the initial and final momenta of the projectile are

$$\vec{p_1} = mv(\cos45°\hat{x} + \sin45°\hat{y})$$

and $\quad \vec{p_2} = mv(\cos45°\hat{x} - \sin45°\hat{y})$

The change in momentum is given by

$$\Delta\vec{p} = \vec{p_2} - \vec{p_1} = -2mv\sin45°\hat{y}$$

Thus, we have

$$|\Delta\vec{p}| = \sqrt{2}\times5\times10^{-3}\times5\sqrt{2}\text{ kg}\cdot\text{m/s}$$

$$= 5\times10^{-2}\text{ kg}\cdot\text{m/s}$$

Hence, $x = 5$.

54. For a transistor, the current gain is given by

$$\beta = \frac{\Delta I_C}{\Delta I_B}$$

From the graph, we can see that when the base current is changed in steps of 20 μA, the collector currents changes in steps of 2 mA. Hence, we have

$$\beta = \frac{2\text{ mA}}{20\ \mu\text{A}} = 200.$$

55. Let P_0 be the atmospheric pressure. Then the pressure at the opening point B is $P_B = P_0$. At the topmost point A of the water level, the pressure is

$P_A = P_0 + \frac{Mg}{S}$ (M is the load and S is the cross-section area of the water tank).

The velocity of water at point A can be neglected because of the large cross-section area of the water tank compared to the opening point B. Now applying Bernoulli's principle between points A and B, we have

$$P_0 + \frac{1}{2}\rho v^2 = P_0 + \frac{Mg}{S} + \rho g h$$

$$\Rightarrow \quad v^2 = 2gh + \frac{2Mg}{\rho S}$$

$$\Rightarrow \quad v = \sqrt{20\times 0.4 + \frac{2\times 240}{10^3 \times 0.4}} \text{ m/s} \approx 3 \text{ m/s}.$$

56. The figure shows transmitting tower A and receiving tower B. Their respective heights above the ground are H and h. The line joining the tip of the towers touches the Earth's surface at point M. This is the farthest distance the two towers can be positioned for communication to be possible. Thus, the range of communication is

$$s = AM + MB$$

$$= \sqrt{(R+H)^2 - R^2} + \sqrt{(R+h)^2 - R^2}$$

$$= \sqrt{2RH + H^2} + \sqrt{2Rh + h^2}$$

$$= \sqrt{2RH} + \sqrt{2Rh} \; [H, h \ll R]$$

The range depends on the height of the receiving tower. When $h = 0$, the range is $s_1 = \sqrt{2RH}$. When $h = h$, the range is $s_2 = \sqrt{2RH} + \sqrt{2Rh}$. Thus, we have

$$\frac{s_2 - s_1}{s_1} = \frac{\sqrt{2Rh}}{\sqrt{2RH}} = \frac{\sqrt{h}}{\sqrt{H}} = \frac{\sqrt{5}}{\sqrt{20}} = \frac{1}{2} = 50\%$$

Hence, $n = 50$.

57. In this question, the observer is at rest and the light source (star) is moving away from the observer with speed $v = 286\times 10^3$ m/s. Using Doppler's formula, we have

$$f' = \left(\frac{c}{c+v}\right) f$$

$$\Rightarrow \quad \frac{c}{\lambda'} = \left(\frac{c}{c+v}\right)\frac{c}{\lambda}$$

$$\Rightarrow \quad \lambda' = \left(\frac{c+v}{c}\right)\lambda.$$

Thus, the shift in the wavelength is

$$\Delta\lambda = \lambda' - \lambda = \frac{v\lambda}{c}$$

$$= \frac{(286\times 10^3)(630\times 10^{-9})}{3\times 10^8} \text{ m}$$

$$= \frac{2.86\times 6.30}{3} \times 10^{-10} \text{ m} \approx 6\times 10^{-10} \text{ m}.$$

Hence, $x = 6$.

58. Let F_S and F_M denote the magnitude of the gravitational pull of the Sun and the Moon, on Earth. In the solar eclipse position, the net pull on the Earth towards the Sun is $F_S + F_M$. When the Moon is exactly on the opposite side, the net pull on Earth towards the Sun is $F_S - F_M$. So between these two positions of the Moon, there is a net change of $2F_M$ in the gravitational pull on the Earth. Hence, the change in Earth's acceleration towards the Sun is given by

$$\Delta a = \frac{2F_M}{M_E} = \frac{2GM_M}{R^2}$$

$$= \frac{2(6.67\times 10^{-11})(7.36\times 10^{22})}{(3.8\times 10^8)^2} \text{ m/s}^2$$

$$= 6.8\times 10^{-5} \text{ m/s}^2$$

Hence, $b = 5$.

59. The ionization energy for a Hydrogen-like atom is given by

$$E = Z^2(chR) = Z^2\left(\frac{me^4}{8\epsilon_0^2 h^2}\right)$$

We see that $E \propto Z^2 me^4$. For the given Deuteron atom, Z is two times that of the Hydrogen atom. The mass and the charge of the revolving particle are, respectively, ten times and two times that of an electron. Thus, we have

$$E = (2^2 \times 10 \times 2^4) E_H = 640$$

Hence, $x = 640$.

60. Let us choose our x-axis along the incline, the y-axis along the perpendicular to the incline, and the point of projection as the origin. Then the acceleration of the projectile along the x- and the y-axis are

$$a_x = g\sin 37° = \frac{3}{5}\left(10 \text{ m/s}^2\right) = 6 \text{ m/s}^2$$

and $$a_y = -g\cos 37° = -\frac{4}{5}\left(10 \text{ m/s}^2\right) = -8 \text{ m/s}^2$$

The initial velocity of the projectile along the x- and the y-axis are

$$u_x = 0 \quad \text{and } u_y = u = 20 \text{ m/s}.$$

Using kinematics along the y-axis, we get the total time of flight of the projectile as

$$T = \frac{2u_y}{|a_y|} = \frac{2 \times 20}{8} \text{ s} = 5 \text{ s}.$$

Now, using kinematics along the x-axis, we get the range of flight of the projectile along the incline as

$$R = u_x T + \frac{1}{2} a_x T^2 = \frac{1}{2}\left(6 \times 5^2\right) \text{m} = 75 \text{ m}.$$

Appendix B: Previous Years' JEE Advanced Questions and Solutions

QUESTIONS

Only One Correct Option

- Each question has **FOUR** options. **ONLY ONE** of these four options is the correct answer.
- For each question, choose the option corresponding to the correct answer.
- The answer to each question will be evaluated according to the following marking scheme:

Full Marks: +3	If ONLY the correct option is chosen;
Zero Marks: 0	If none of the options is chosen (i.e. the question is unanswered);
Negative Marks: –1	In all other cases

1. A football of radius R is kept on a hole of radius r ($r<R$) made on a plank kept horizontally. One end of the plank is now lifted so that it gets tilted, making an angle θ from the horizontal, as shown in the figure below. The maximum value of θ so that the football does not start rolling down the plank satisfies (figure is schematic and not drawn to scale):

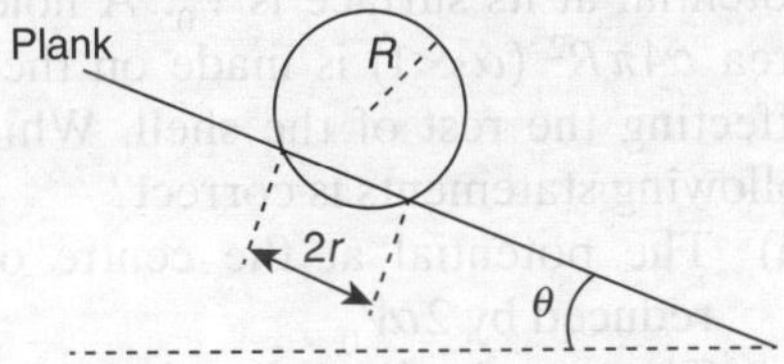

(a) $\sin\theta = \dfrac{r}{R}$ (b) $\tan\theta = \dfrac{r}{R}$

(c) $\sin\theta = \dfrac{r}{2R}$ (d) $\cos\theta = \dfrac{r}{2R}$

2. A light disc made of aluminium (a non-magnetic material) is kept horizontally and is free to rotate about its axis, as shown in the figure. A strong magnet is held vertically at a point above the disc away from its axis. On revolving the magnet about the axis of the disc, the disc will (figure is schematic and not drawn to scale):

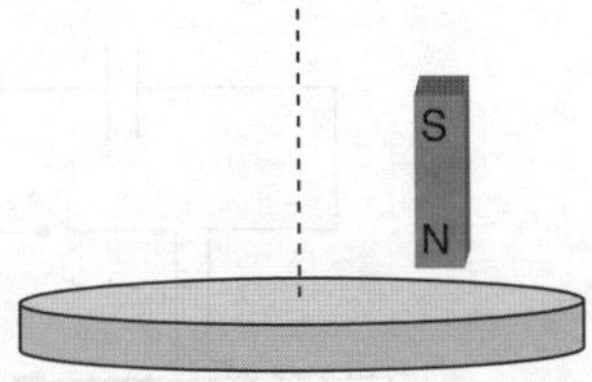

(a) Rotate in the direction opposite to the direction of the magnet's motion

(b) Rotate in the same direction as the direction of the magnet's motion

(c) Not rotate and its temperature will remain unchanged

(d) Not rotate but its temperature will slowly rise

3. A small roller of diameter 20 cm has an axle of diameter 10 cm (see figure below on the left). It is on a horizontal floor and a meter scale is positioned horizontally on its axle with one edge of the scale on top of the axle (see figure on the right). The scale is now pushed slowly on the axle so that it moves without slipping on the axle, and the roller starts rolling without slipping. After the roller has moved 50 cm, the position of the scale will look like (figures are schematic and not drawn to scale):

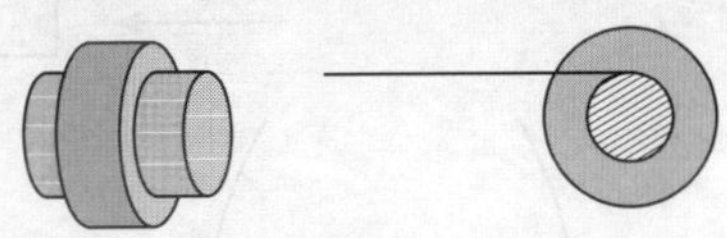

(a)
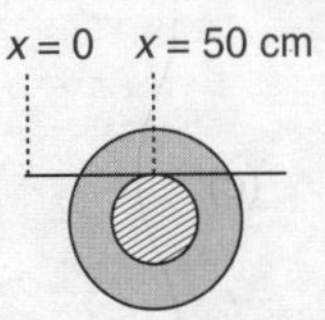

(b)
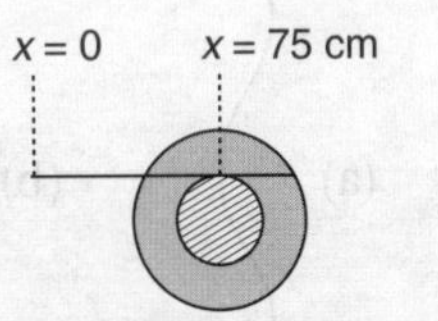

(c)
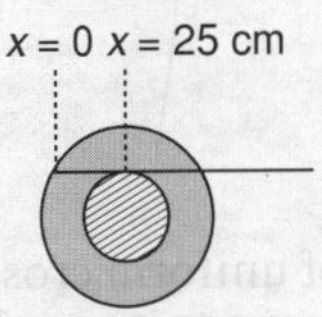

(d)
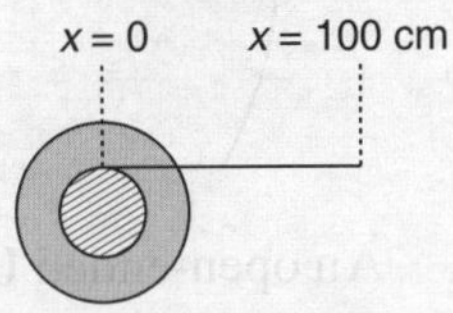

4. A circular coil of radius R and N turns has negligible resistance. As shown in the schematic figure, its two ends are connected to two wires and it is hanging by those wires with its plane being vertical. The wires are connected to a capacitor with charge Q through a switch. The coil is in a horizontal uniform magnetic field B_0 parallel to the plane of the coil. When the switch is closed, the capacitor gets discharged through the coil in a very short time. By the time the capacitor is discharged fully, the magnitude of the angular momentum gained by the coil will be (assume that the discharge time is so short that the coil has hardly rotated during this time):

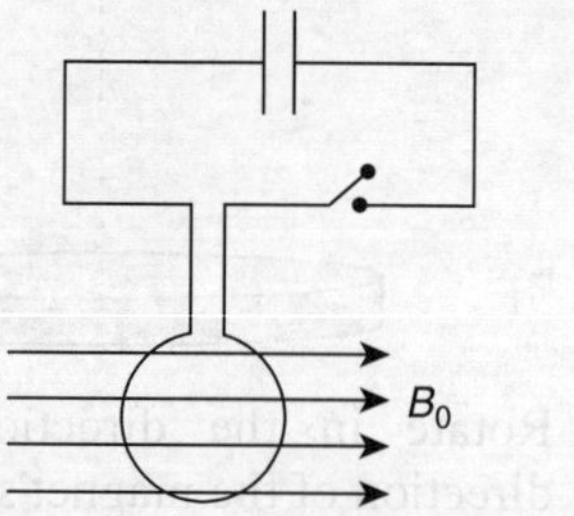

(a) $\frac{\pi}{2}NQB_0R^2$ (b) πNQB_0R^2

(c) $2\pi NQB_0R^2$ (d) $4\pi NQB_0R^2$

5. A parallel beam of light strikes a piece of transparent glass having cross-section as shown in the figure below. The correct shape of the emergent wavefront will be (figures are schematic and not drawn to scale):

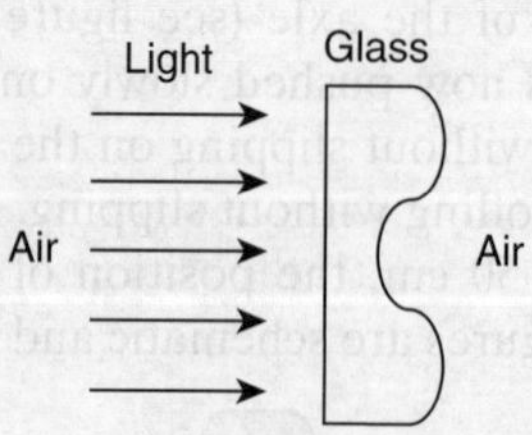

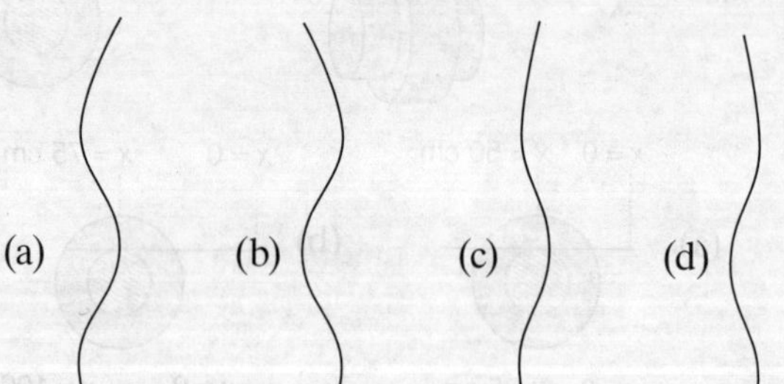

6. An open-ended U-tube of uniform cross-sectional area contains water (density 10^3kg m^{-3}). Initially the water level stands at 0.29 m from the bottom in each arm. Kerosene oil (a water-immiscible liquid) of density 800 kg m^{-3} is added to the left arm until its length is 0.1 m, as shown in the schematic figure below. The ratio $\left(\frac{h_1}{h_2}\right)$ of the heights of the liquid in the two arms is:

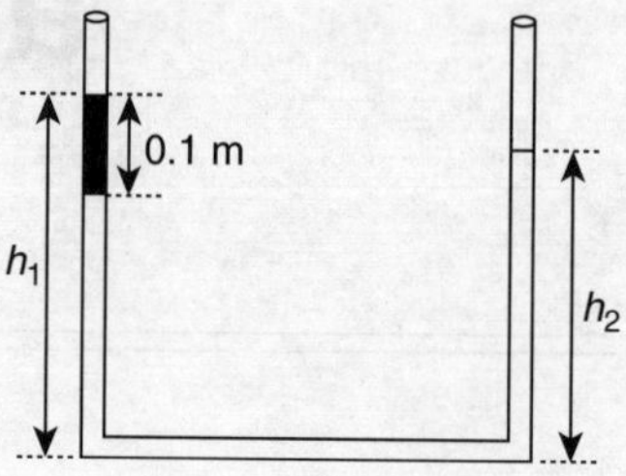

(a) $\frac{15}{14}$ (b) $\frac{35}{33}$

(c) $\frac{7}{6}$ (d) $\frac{5}{4}$

7. Consider a spherical gaseous cloud of mass density $\rho(r)$ in free space, where r is the radial distance from its centre. The gaseous cloud is made up of particles of equal mass m moving in circular orbits about the common centre with the same kinetic energy K. The force acting on the particles is their mutual gravitational force. If $\rho(r)$ is constant in time, the particle number density $n(r) = \rho(r)/m$ is: [G is the universal gravitational constant]

(a) $\frac{K}{2\pi r^2 m^2 G}$ (b) $\frac{K}{\pi r^2 m^2 G}$

(c) $\frac{3K}{\pi r^2 m^2 G}$ (d) $\frac{k}{6\pi r^2 m^2 G}$

8. A thin spherical insulating shell of radius R carries a uniformly distributed charge such that the potential at its surface is V_0. A hole with a small area $\alpha 4\pi R^2$ (α<<1) is made on the shell without affecting the rest of the shell. Which one of the following statements is correct?

(a) The potential at the centre of the shell is reduced by $2\alpha V_0$

(b) The magnitude of electric field at the centre of the shell is reduced by $\frac{\alpha V_0}{2R}$

(c) The ratio of the potential at the centre of the shell to that of the point at $\frac{1}{2}R$ from centre towards the hole will be $\frac{1-\alpha}{1-2\alpha}$

(d) The magnitude of the electric field at a point located on a line passing through the hole and shell's centre, on a distance $2R$ from the centre of the spherical shell, will be reduced by $\frac{\alpha V_0}{2R}$

9. A current carrying wire heats a metal rod. The wire provides a constant power (P) to the rod. The metal rod is enclosed in an insulated container. It is observed that the temperature (T) in the metal rod changes with time (t) as

$$T(t) = T_0(1+\beta t^{\frac{1}{4}}),$$

where β is a constant with appropriate dimension while T_0 is a constant with dimension of temperature. The heat capacity of the metal is:

(a) $\dfrac{4P(T(t)-T_0)^3}{\beta^4 T_0^4}$ (b) $\dfrac{4P(T(t)-T_0)^4}{\beta^4 T_0^5}$

(c) $\dfrac{4P(T(t)-T_0)^2}{\beta^4 T_0^3}$ (d) $\dfrac{4P(T(t)-T_0)}{\beta^4 T_0^2}$

10. In a radioactive sample, ${}^{40}_{19}K$ nuclei either decay into stable ${}^{40}_{20}Ca$ nuclei with decay constant 4.5×10^{-10} per year or into stable ${}^{40}_{18}Ar$ nuclei with decay constant 0.5×10^{-10} per year. Given that in this sample all the stable ${}^{40}_{20}Ca$ and ${}^{40}_{18}Ar$ nuclei are produced by the ${}^{40}_{19}K$ nuclei only. In time $t \times 10^9$ years, if the ratio of the sum of stable ${}^{40}_{20}Ca$ and ${}^{40}_{18}Ar$ nuclei to the radioactive ${}^{40}_{19}K$ nuclei is 99, the value of t will be: [Given: In 10 = 2.3]

(a) 1.15 (b) 9.2

(c) 2.3 (d) 4.6

One or More Correct Options

- Each question has **FOUR** options. **ONE OR MORE THAN ONE** of these four options(s) is(are) correct answer(s).
- For each question, choose the option(s) corresponding to (all) the correct answer(s).
- The answer to each question will be evaluated according to the following marking scheme:

Full Marks: +4	If only (all) the correct option(s) is(are) chosen
Partial Marks: +3	If all the four options are correct but ONLY three options are chosen
Partial Marks: +2	If three or more options are correct but ONLY two options are chosen, both of which are correct
Partial Marks: +1	If two or more options are correct but ONLY one option is chosen and it is a correct option
Zero Marks: 0	If none of the options is chosen (i.e. the question is unanswered)
Negative Marks: –2	In all other cases

1. A particle of mass m moves in circular orbits with potential energy $U(r) = \alpha r$, where α is a positive constant and r is its distance from the origin. Its energies are calculated using the Bohr model. If the radius of the particle's orbit is denoted by R and its speed and energy are denoted by v and E, respectively, then for the nth orbit (h is Planck's constant):

(a) $R \propto n^{1/3}$ and $v \propto n^{2/3}$

(b) $R \propto n^{2/3}$ and $v \propto n^{1/3}$

(c) $E = \dfrac{3}{2}\left(\dfrac{n^2h^2\alpha^2}{4\pi^2 m}\right)^{1/3}$

(d) $E = 2\left(\dfrac{n^2h^2\alpha^2}{4\pi^2 m}\right)^{1/3}$

2. The filament of a light bulb has surface area 64 mm^2. The filament can be considered as a black body at temperature 2500 K emitting radiation like a point source when viewed from far. At night, the light bulb is observed from a distance of 100 m. Assume the pupil of the eyes of the observer to be circular with radius 3 mm. Then (take Stefan–Boltzmann constant = 5.67×10^{-8} Wm^{-2}K^{-4}, Wien's displacement constant = 2.90×10^{-3} m-K, Planck's constant = 6.63×10^{-34}Js, speed of light in vacuum = 3.00×10^8 ms^{-1}):

(a) The power radiated by the filament is in the range 642 W to 645 W

(b) The radiated power entering into one eye of the observer is in the range 3.15×10^{-8} W to 3.25×10^{-8} W

(c) The wavelength corresponding to the maximum intensity of light is 1160 nm

(d) Taking the average wavelength of emitted radiation to be 1740 nm, the total number of photons entering per second into one eye of the observer is in the range 2.75×10^{11} to 2.85×10^{11}

3. Sometimes, it is convenient to construct a system of units so that all quantities can be expressed in terms of only one physical quantity. In one such system, dimensions of different quantities are given in terms of a quantity X as follows: [position] = [X^α]; [speed] = [X^β]; [acceleration] =[X^p]; [linear momentum] = [X^q]; [force] = [X^r]. Then:

(a) $\alpha + p = 2\beta$ (b) $p + q - r = \beta$

(c) $p - q + r = \alpha$ (d) $p + q + r = \beta$

4. A uniform electric field $\vec{E} = -400\sqrt{3}\hat{y}$ NC^{-1} is applied on a region. A charged particle of mass m carrying positive charge q is projected in this region with an initial speed of $2\sqrt{100 \times 10^6}$ ms^{-1}. This particle is aimed to hit a target T, which is 5 m away from its entry point into the field, as shown schematically in the figure. Take $\frac{q}{m} = 10^{10}$ Ckg^{-1}. Then:

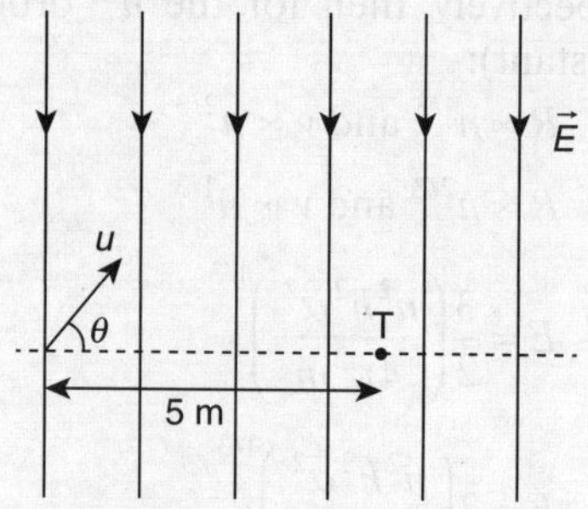

(a) The particle will hit T if projected at an angle of 45° from the horizontal

(b) The particle will hit T if projected either at an angle of 30° or 60° from the horizontal

(c) The time taken by the particle to hit T could be $\sqrt{\frac{5}{6}}$ μs as well as $\sqrt{\frac{5}{2}}$ μs

(d) The time taken by the particle to hit T is $\sqrt{\frac{5}{3}}$ μs

5. Shown in the figure is a semicircular metallic strip that has thickness t and resistivity ρ. Its inner radius is R_1 and outer radius is R_2. If a voltage V_0 is applied between its two ends, a current I flows in it. In addition, it is observed that a transverse voltage ΔV develops between its inner and outer surfaces due to purely kinetic effects of moving electrons (ignore any role of the magnetic field due to the current). Then (figure is schematic and not drawn to scale):

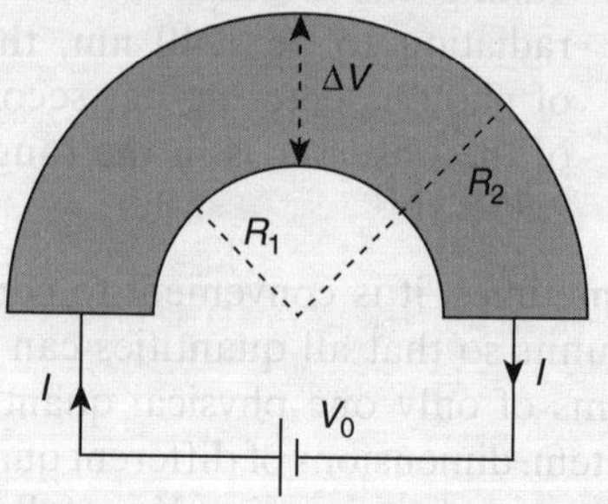

(a) $I = \frac{V_0 t}{\pi\rho} \ln\left(\frac{R_2}{R_1}\right)$

(b) The outer surface is at a higher voltage than the inner surface

(c) The outer surface is at a lower voltage than the inner surface

(d) $\Delta V \propto I^2$

6. As shown schematically in the figure, two vessels contain water solutions (at temperature T) of potassium permanganate ($KMnO_4$) of different concentrations n_1 and n_2 ($n_1 > n_2$) molecules per unit volume with $\Delta n = (n_1 - n_2) \ll n_1$. When they are connected by a tube of small length l and cross-sectional area S, $KMnO_4$ starts to diffuse from the left to the right vessel through the tube. Consider the collection of molecules to behave as dilute ideal gases and the difference in their partial pressure in the two vessels causing the diffusion. The speed v of the molecules is limited by the viscous force $-\beta v$ on each molecule, where β is a constant. Neglecting all terms of the order $(\Delta n)^2$, which of the following is/are correct? (k_B is the Boltzmann constant)

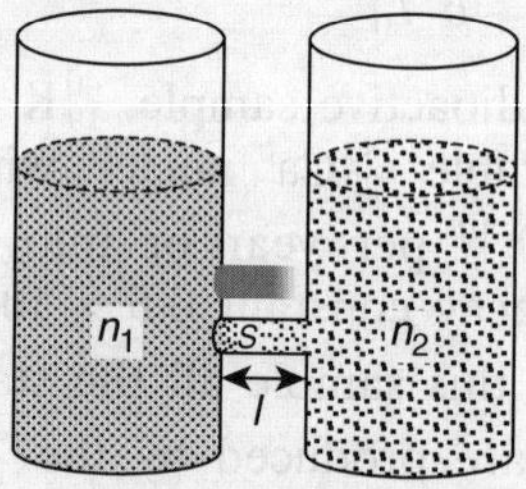

(a) The force causing the molecules to move across the tube is $\Delta n k_B T S$

(b) Force balance implies $n_1 \beta v l = \Delta n k_B T$

(c) Total number of molecules going across the tube per second is $\left(\frac{\Delta n}{l}\right)\left(\frac{k_B T}{\beta}\right)S$

(d) The rate of molecules getting transferred through the tube does not change with time

7. A beaker of radius r is filled with water $\left(\text{refractive index } \frac{4}{3}\right)$ up to a height H, as shown in the figure on the left. The beaker is kept on a horizontal table rotating at angular speed ω. This makes the water surface curved so that the difference in the height of water level at the centre and at the circumference of the beaker is h ($h \ll H$, $h \ll r$), as shown in the figure on the right. Take this surface to be approximately spherical with a radius of curvature R. Which of the following is/are correct? (g is the acceleration due to gravity)

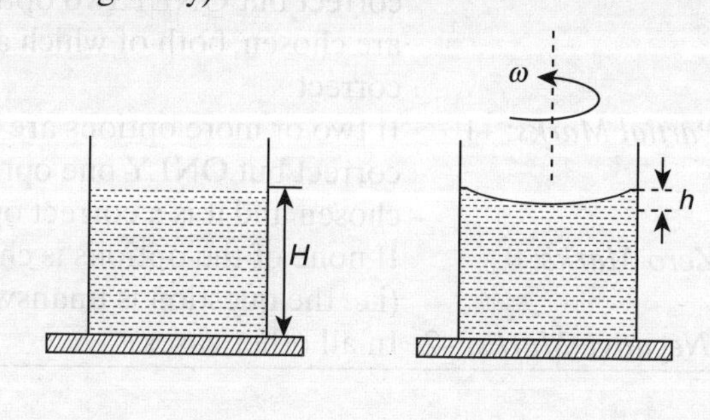

(a) $R = \dfrac{h^2 + r^2}{2h}$

(b) $R = \dfrac{3r^2}{2h}$

(c) Apparent depth of the bottom of the beaker is close to $\dfrac{3H}{2}\left(1 + \dfrac{\omega^2 H}{2g}\right)^{-1}$

(d) Apparent depth of the bottom of the beaker is close to $\dfrac{3H}{4}\left(1 + \dfrac{\omega^2 H}{4g}\right)^{-1}$

8. A student skates up a ramp that makes an angle of 30° with the horizontal. He/She starts (as shown in the figure) at the bottom of the ramp with speed v_0 and wants to turn around over a semicircular path xyz of radius R during which he/she reaches a maximum height h (at point y) from the ground, as shown in the figure. Assume that the energy loss is negligible and the force required for this turn at the highest point is provided by his/her weight only. Then (g is the acceleration due to gravity):

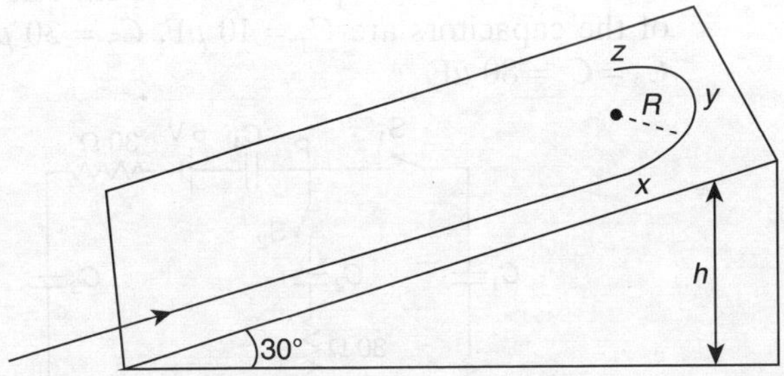

(a) $v_0^2 - 2gh = \dfrac{1}{2}gR$

(b) $v_0^2 - 2gh = \dfrac{\sqrt{3}}{2}gR$

(c) The centripetal force required at points x and z is zero

(d) The centripetal force required is maximum at points x and z

9. A rod of mass m and length L, pivoted at one of its ends, is hanging vertically. A bullet of the same mass moving at speed v strikes the rod horizontally at a distance x from its pivoted end and gets embedded in it. The combined system now rotates with angular speed ω about the pivot. The maximum angular speed ω_M is achieved for $x = x_M$. Then:

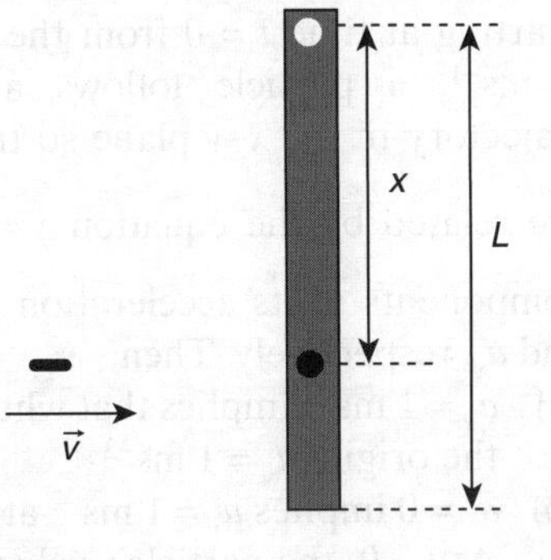

(a) $\omega = \dfrac{3vx}{L^2 + 3x^2}$ (b) $\omega = \dfrac{12vx}{L^2 + 12x^2}$

(c) $x_M = \dfrac{L}{\sqrt{3}}$ (d) $\omega_M = \dfrac{v}{2L}\sqrt{3}$

10. In an X-ray tube, electrons emitted from a filament (cathode) carrying current I hit a target (anode) at a distance d from the cathode. The target is kept at a potential V higher than the cathode resulting in emission of continuous and characteristic X-rays. If the filament current I is decreased to $\dfrac{I}{2}$, the potential difference V is increased to $2V$, and the separation distance d is reduced to $\dfrac{d}{2}$, then:

(a) The cut-off wavelength will reduce to half, and the wavelengths of the characteristic X-rays will remain the same

(b) The cut-off wavelength as well as the wavelengths of the characteristic X-rays will remain the same

(c) The cut-off wavelength will reduce to half, and the intensities of all the X-rays will decrease

(d) The cut-off wavelength will become two times larger, and the intensity of all the X-rays will decrease

11. Two identical non-conducting solid spheres of the same mass and charge are suspended in air from a common point by two non-conducting, massless strings of the same length. At equilibrium, the angle between the strings is α. The spheres are now immersed in a dielectric liquid of density 800 kg m^{-3} and dielectric constant 21. If the angle between the strings remains the same after the immersion, then:

(a) The electric force between the spheres remains unchanged

(b) The electric force between the spheres reduces

(c) The mass density of the spheres is 840 kg m^{-3}

(d) The tension in the strings holding the spheres remains unchanged

12. Starting at time $t = 0$ from the origin with speed $1\ \text{ms}^{-1}$, a particle follows a two-dimensional trajectory in the x–y plane so that its coordinates are related by the equation $y = \frac{x^2}{2}$. The x and y components of its acceleration are denoted by a_x and a_y, respectively. Then:

(a) $a_x = 1\ \text{ms}^{-2}$ implies that when the particle is at the origin, $a_y = 1\ \text{ms}^{-2}$
(b) $a_x = 0$ implies $a_y = 1\ \text{ms}^{-2}$ at all times
(c) At $t = 0$, the particle's velocity points in the x direction
(d) $a_x = 0$ implies that at $t = 1$ s, the angle between the particle's velocity and the x axis is 45°

13. A cylindrical capillary tube of radius 0.2 mm is made by joining two capillaries T1 and T2 of different materials having water contact angles of 0° and 60°, respectively. The capillary tube is dipped vertically in water in two different configurations, case I and II, as shown in the figure. Which of the following option(s) is(are) correct? [Surface tension of water = 0.075 N/m, density of water = 1000 kg/m³, take g = 10 m/s²]

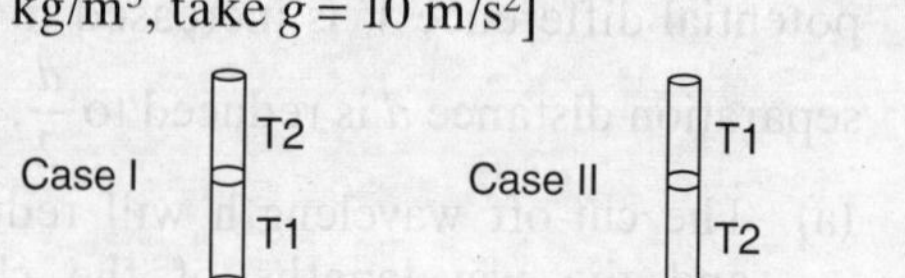

(a) The correction in the height of the water column raised in the tube, due to the weight of the water contained in the meniscus, will be different for both cases.
(b) For case II, if the capillary joint is 5 cm above the water surface, the height of the water column raised in the tube will be 3.75 cm. (Neglect the weight of the water in the meniscus)
(c) For case I, if the joint is kept at 8 cm above the water surface, the height of the water column in the tube will be 7.5 cm. (Neglect the weight of the water in the meniscus)
(d) For case I, if the capillary joint is 5 cm above the water surface, the height of the water column raised in the tube will be more than 8.75 cm. (Neglect the weight of the water in the meniscus)

14. A conducting wire of parabolic shape, initially $y = x^2$, is moving with velocity $\vec{V} = v_0\hat{i}$ in a non-uniform magnetic field $\vec{B} = B_0\left(1+\left(\frac{y}{L}\right)^{\beta}\right)\hat{k}$, as shown in the figure. If V_0, B_0, L and β are positive constants and $\Delta\phi$ is the potential difference developed between the ends of the wire, then the correct statement(s) is/are:

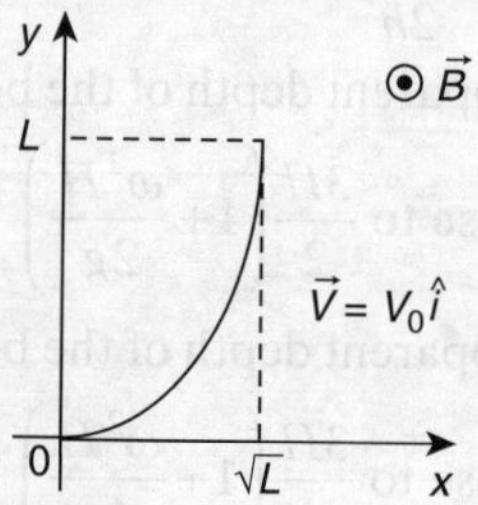

(a) $|\Delta\phi| = \frac{1}{2}B_0V_0L$ for $\beta = 0$
(b) $|\Delta\phi| = \frac{4}{3}B_0V_0L$ for $\beta = 2$
(c) $|\Delta\phi|$ remains the same if the parabolic wire is replaced by a straight wire, $y = x$ initially, of length $\sqrt{2}L$
(d) $|\Delta\phi|$ is proportional to the length of the wire projected on the y-axis

15. In the circuit shown, initially there is no charge on capacitors and keys S_1 and S_2 are open. The values of the capacitors are $C_1 = 10\ \mu F$, $C_2 = 30\ \mu F$ and $C_3 = C_4 = 80\ \mu F$.

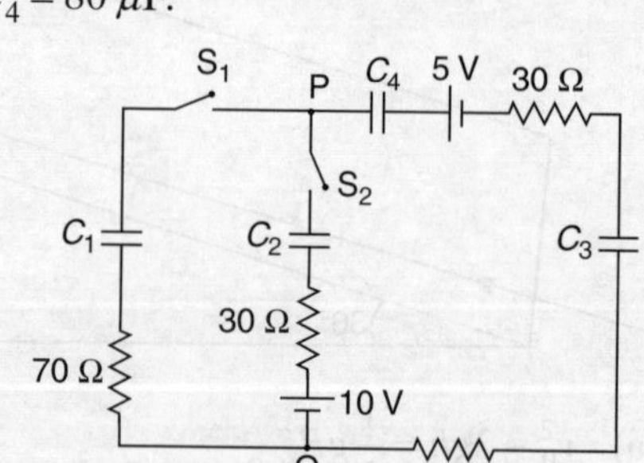

Which of the statement(s) is/are correct?

(a) At time $t = 0$, the key S_1 is closed, the instantaneous current in the closed circuit will be 25 mA.
(b) If key S_1 is kept closed for long time such that the capacitors are fully charged, the voltage across the capacitor C_1 will be 4 V.
(c) The key S_1 is kept closed for a long time such that the capacitors are fully charged. Now key S_2 is closed. At this time, the instantaneous current across the 30 Ω resistor (between points P and Q) will be 0.2 A (round-off to the first decimal place).
(d) If key S_1 is kept closed for a long time such that the capacitors are fully charged, the voltage difference between points P and Q will be 10 V.

16. A charged shell of radius R carries a total charge Q. Given Φ as the flux of the electric field through a closed cylindrical surface of height h, radius r and with its centre the same as that of the shell. Here, the centre of the cylinder is a point on the axis of the cylinder that is equidistant from its top and bottom surfaces. Which of the following option(s) is/are correct? [ϵ_0 is the permittivity of free space]

(a) If $h > 2R$ and $r > R$, then $\Phi = Q/\epsilon_0$
(b) If $h < 8R/5$ and $r = 3R/5$, then $\Phi = 0$
(c) If $h > 2R$ and $r = 3R/5$, then $\Phi = Q/5\epsilon_0$
(d) If $h > 2R$ and $r = 4R/5$, then $\Phi = Q/5\epsilon_0$

17. One mole of a monatomic ideal gas goes through a thermodynamic cycle, as shown in the volume versus temperature (V–T) diagram. The correct statement(s) is/are: [R is the gas constant]

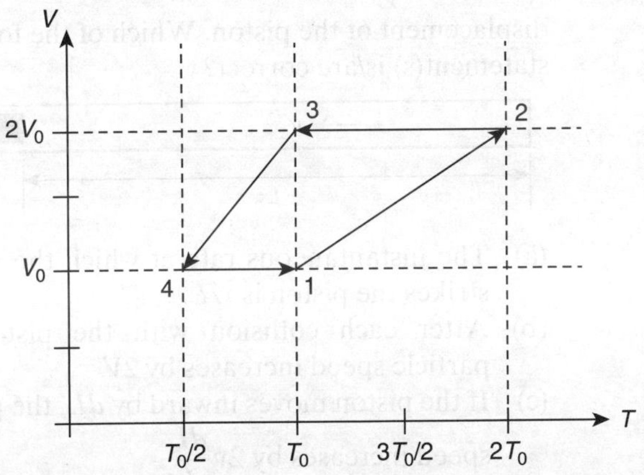

(a) Work done in this thermodynamic cycle ($1 \to 2 \to 3 \to 4 \to 1$) is $|W| = \frac{1}{2}RT_0$
(b) The above thermodynamic cycle exhibits only isochoric and adiabatic processes
(c) The ratio of heat transfer during processes $1 \to 2$ and $2 \to 3$ is $\left|\frac{Q_{1\to2}}{Q_{2\to3}}\right| = \frac{5}{3}$
(d) The ratio of heat transfer during processes $1 \to 2$ and $3 \to 4$ is $\left|\frac{Q_{1\to2}}{Q_{3\to4}}\right| = \frac{1}{2}$

18. A thin convex lens is made of two materials with refractive indices n_1 and n_2, as shown in the figure. The radii of curvature of the left and right spherical surfaces are equal. f is the focal length of the lens when $n_1 = n_2 = n$. The focal length is $f + \Delta f$ when $n_1 = n$ and $n_2 = n + \Delta n$. Assuming $\Delta n \ll (n-1)$ and $1 < n < 2$, the correct statement(s) is/are:

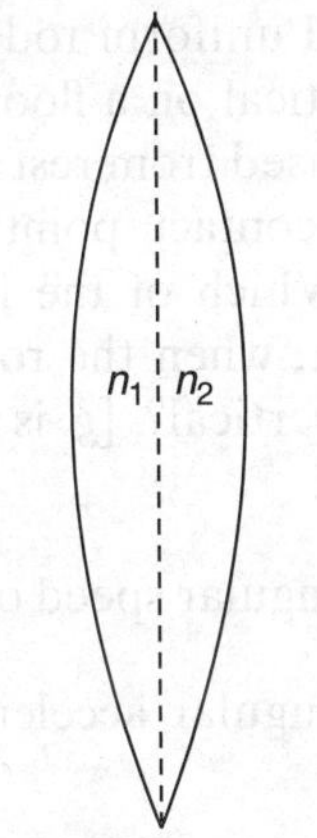

(a) $\left|\frac{\Delta f}{f}\right| < \left|\frac{\Delta n}{n}\right|$
(b) For $n = 1.5$, $\Delta n = 10^{-3}$ and $f = 20$ cm, the value of $|\Delta f|$ will be 0.02 cm (round-off to the second decimal place)
(c) If $\frac{\Delta n}{n} < 0$, then $\frac{\Delta f}{f} > 0$
(d) The relation between $\frac{\Delta f}{f}$ and $\frac{\Delta n}{n}$ remains unchanged if both the convex surfaces are replaced by concave surfaces of the same radius of curvature

19. Let us consider a system of units in which mass and angular momentum are dimensionless. If length has a dimension of L, which of the following statement(s) is/are correct?

(a) The dimension of linear momentum is L^{1}
(b) The dimension of energy is L^{-2}
(c) The dimension of force is L^{-3}
(d) The dimension of power is L^{-5}

20. Two identical moving coil galvanometers have 10 Ω resistance and full-scale deflection at 2 μA current. One of them is converted into a voltmeter of 100-mV, full-scale reading and the other into an ammeter of 1-mA, full-scale current using appropriate resistors. These are then used to measure the voltage and current in the Ohm's law experiment with R = 1000 Ω resistor by using an ideal cell. Which of the following statement(s) is/are correct?

(a) The resistance of the voltmeter will be 100 $k\Omega$
(b) The resistance of the ammeter will be 0.02 Ω (round-off to the second decimal place)
(c) The measured value of R will be 978 Ω $< R <$ 982 Ω
(d) If the ideal cell is replaced by a cell having internal resistance of 5Ω, then the measured value of R will be more than 1000 Ω

21. A thin and uniform rod of mass M and length L is held vertical on a floor with large friction. The rod is released from rest so that it falls by rotating about its contact point with the floor without slipping. Which of the following statement(s) is/are correct, when the rod makes an angle of 60° with the vertical? [g is the acceleration due to gravity]

(a) The angular speed of the rod will be $\sqrt{\dfrac{3g}{2L}}$

(b) The angular acceleration of the rod will be $\dfrac{2g}{L}$

(c) The radial acceleration of the rod's centre of mass will be $\dfrac{3g}{4}$

(d) The normal reaction force from the floor on the rod will be $\dfrac{Mg}{16}$

22. A block of mass $2M$ is attached to a massless spring with spring constant k. This block is connected to two other blocks of masses M and $2M$ using two massless pulleys and strings. The accelerations of the blocks are a_1, a_2 and a_3, as shown in the figure. The system is released from rest with the spring in its unstretched state. The maximum extension of the spring is x_0. Which of the following option(s) is/are correct? [g is the acceleration due to gravity. Neglect friction]

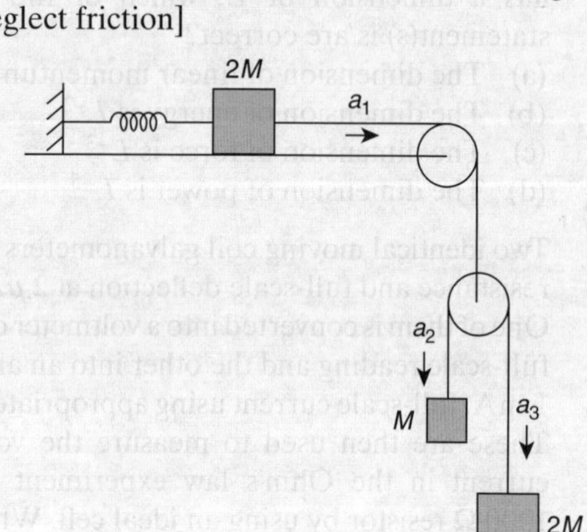

(a) $x_0 = \dfrac{4Mg}{k}$

(b) When the spring achieves an extension of $\dfrac{x_0}{2}$ for the first time, the speed of the block connected to the spring is $8g\sqrt{\dfrac{M}{42k}}$

(c) At an extension of $\dfrac{x_0}{4}$ of the spring, the magnitude of acceleration of the block connected to the springs is $\dfrac{2g}{7}$

(d) $a_2 - a_1 = a_1 - a_3$

23. A small particle of mass m moving inside a heavy, hollow and straight tube along the tube axis undergoes elastic collision at two ends. The tube has no friction and it is closed at one end by a flat surface while the other end is fitted with a heavy movable flat piston, as shown in the figure. When the distance of the piston from the closed end is $L = L_0$, the particle speed is $v = v_0$. The piston is moved inward at a very low speed V such that $V << \dfrac{dL}{L} v_0$, where dL is the infinitesimal displacement of the piston. Which of the following statement(s) is/are correct?

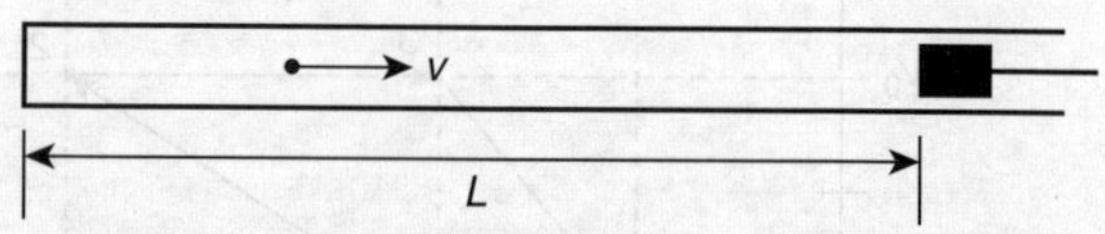

(a) The instantaneous rate at which the particle strikes the piston is v/L.

(b) After each collision with the piston, the particle speed increases by $2V$.

(c) If the piston moves inward by dL, the particle speed increases by $2v\dfrac{dL}{L}$.

(d) The particle's kinetic energy increases by a factor of 4 when the piston is moved inward from L_0 to $\dfrac{1}{2}L_0$.

24. An electric dipole with dipole moment $\dfrac{p_0}{\sqrt{2}}(\hat{i} + \hat{j})$ is held fixed at the origin O in the presence of a uniform electric field of magnitude E_0. If the potential is constant on a circle of radius R centred at the origin as shown in the figure, the correct statement(s) is/are: (ε_0 is the permittivity of free space; $R >>$ dipole size)

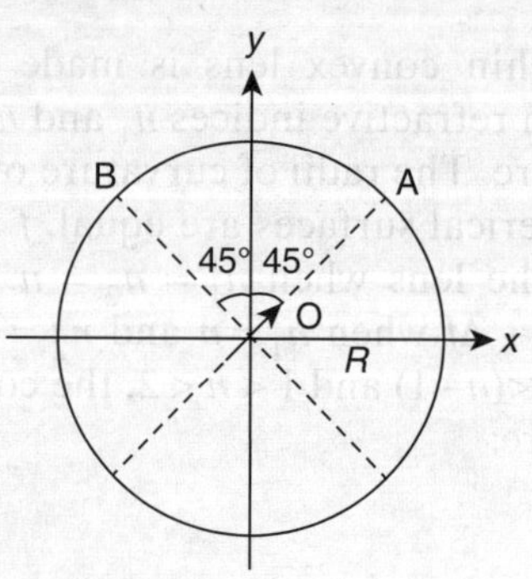

(a) $R = \left(\dfrac{p_0}{4\pi\varepsilon_0 E_0}\right)^{1/3}$

(b) Total electric field at point A is $\vec{E}_A = \sqrt{2}E_0(\hat{i} + \hat{j})$

(c) Total electric field at point B is $\vec{E}_B = 0$

(d) The magnitude of the total electric field on any two points of the circle will be the same

25. A mixture of ideal gas containing 5 moles of monatomic gas and 1 mole of rigid diatomic gas is initially at pressure P_0, volume V_0 and temperature T_0. If the gas mixture is adiabatically compressed to a volume $V_0/4$, then the correct statement(s) is/are: (Given $2^{1.2} = 2.3$; $2^{3.2} = 9.2$; R is gas constant)

(a) The work $|W|$ done during the process is $13RT_0$

(b) The total kinetic energy of the gas mixture after compression is between $18RT_0$ and $19RT_0$

(c) The final pressure of the gas mixture after compression is between $9P_0$ and $10P_0$

(d) The adiabatic constant of the gas mixture is 1.6

26. Three glass cylinders of equal height $H = 30$ cm and same refractive index $n = 1.5$ are placed on a horizontal surface, as shown in the figure. Cylinder I has a flat top, cylinder II has a convex top and cylinder III has a concave top. The radii of curvature of the two curved tops are the same ($R = 3$ m). If H_1, H_2 and H_3 are the apparent depths of a point X on the bottom of the three cylinders, respectively, the correct statement(s) is/are:

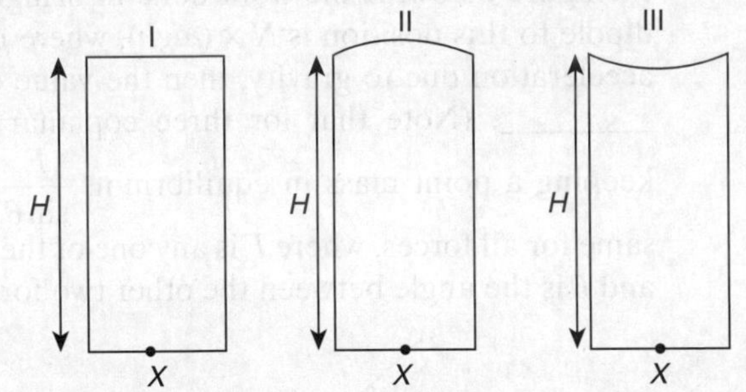

(a) $H_2 > H_1$

(b) $H_3 > H_1$

(c) $H_2 > H_3$

(d) $0.8 \text{ cm} < |H_2 - H_1| < 0.9 \text{ cm}$

27. In a Young's double-slit experiment, the slit separation d is 0.3 mm and the screen distance D is 1 m. A parallel beam of light of wavelength 600 nm is incident on the slits at angle α, as shown in the figure. On the screen, the point O is equidistant from the slits and distance PO is 11.0 mm. Which of the following statement(s) is/are correct?

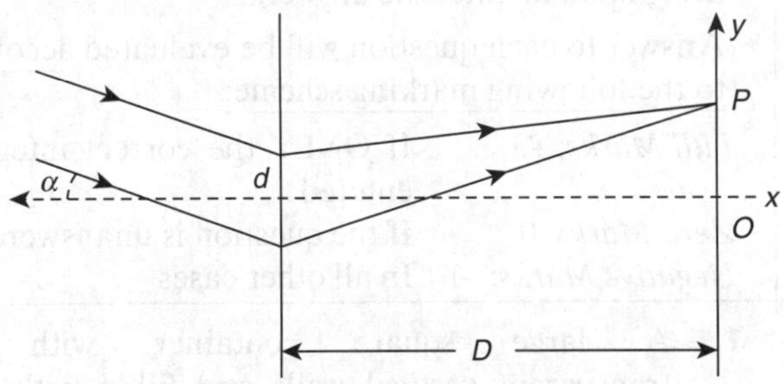

(a) For $\alpha = \dfrac{0.36}{\pi}$ degree, there will be destructive interference at point O.

(b) For $\alpha = 0$, there will be constructive interference at point P.

(c) For $\alpha = \dfrac{0.36}{\pi}$ degree, there will be destructive interference at point P.

(d) Fringe spacing depends on α.

28. A free hydrogen atom absorbing a photon of wavelength λ_a gets excited from state $n = 1$ to state $n = 4$. Immediately after that, the electron jumps to the $n = m$ state by emitting a photon of wavelength λ_e. Let the change in momentum of atom due to the absorption and the emission be Δp_a and Δp_e, respectively. If $\lambda_a / \lambda_e = \dfrac{1}{5}$, which of the option(s) is/are correct? [Use $hc = 1242$ eV nm; 1 nm $= 10^{-9}$ m, h and c are Planck's constant and speed of light, respectively]

(a) $m = 2$

(b) $\lambda_e = 418\,\text{nm}$

(c) $\Delta p_a / \Delta p_e = \dfrac{1}{2}$

(d) The ratio of kinetic energy of the electron in the state $n = m$ to the state $n = 1$ is $\dfrac{1}{4}$

Single Digit Answer

- The answer to each question is a **SINGLE DIGIT INTEGER** ranging from 0 TO 9, **BOTH INCLUSIVE.**
- For each question, enter the correct integer corresponding to the answer using the mouse and the on-screen virtual numeric keypad in the place designated to enter the answer.
- Answer to each question will be evaluated according to the following marking scheme:

Full Marks: +3	If ONLY the correct integer is entered
Zero Marks: 0	If the question is unanswered
Negative Marks: –1	In all other cases

1. A large square container with thin transparent vertical walls and filled with water $\left(\text{refractive index } \frac{4}{3}\right)$ is kept on a horizontal table. A student holds a thin straight wire vertically inside the water 12 cm from one of its corners, as shown schematically in the figure. Looking at the wire from this corner, another student sees two images of the wire, located symmetrically on each side of the line of sight, as shown. The separation (in cm) between these images is ______.

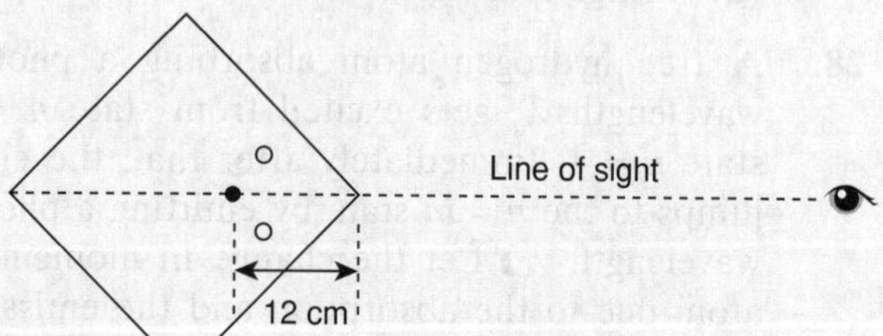

2. A train with cross-sectional area S_t is moving with speed v_t inside a long tunnel of cross-sectional area $S_0(S_0 = 4S_t)$. Assume that almost all the air (density r) in front of the train flows back between its sides and the walls of the tunnel. Also, the air flow with respect to the train is steady and laminar. Take the ambient pressure and that inside the train to be P_0. If the pressure in the region between the sides of the train and the tunnel walls is P, then $P_0 - P = \frac{7}{2N}\rho v_t^2$. The value of N is ______.

3. Two large circular discs separated by a distance of 0.01 m are connected to a battery through a switch, as shown in the figure. Charged oil drops of density 900 kg/m^3 are released through a tiny hole at the centre of the top disc. Once some oil drops achieve terminal velocity, the switch is closed to apply a voltage of 200 V across the discs. As a result, an oil drop of radius 8×10^{-7} m stops moving vertically and floats between the discs. The number of electrons present in this oil drop is ______. (Neglect the buoyancy force, take acceleration due to gravity = 10 m/s^2 and charge on an electron $(e) = 1.6 \times 10^{-19}$ C)

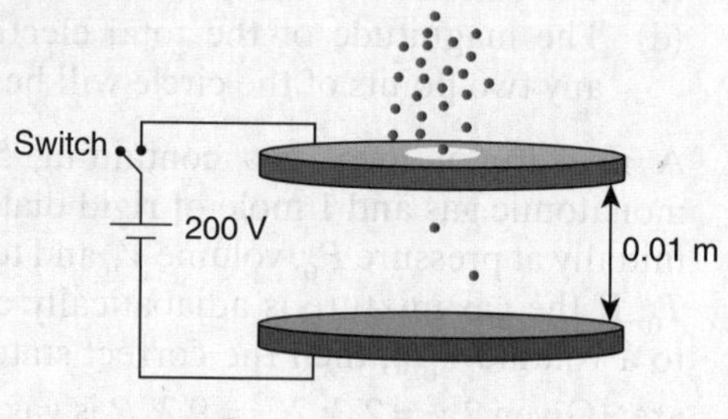

4. A hot air balloon is carrying some passengers and a few sandbags of mass 1 kg each so that its total mass is 480 kg. Its effective volume giving the balloon its buoyancy is V. The balloon is floating at an equilibrium height of 100 m. When N number of sandbags are thrown out, the balloon rises to a new equilibrium height close to 150 m with its volume V remaining unchanged. If the variation of the density of air with height h from the ground is $(h) = \rho_0 e^{-\frac{h}{h_0}}$, where $\rho_0 = 1.25$ kg/m^3 and $h_0 =$ 6000 m, the value of N is ______.

5. A point charge q of mass m is suspended vertically by a string of length l. A point dipole of dipole moment $\vec{p}$ is now brought towards q from infinity so that the charge moves away. The final equilibrium position of the system including the direction of the dipole, the angles and distances is shown in the figure below. If the work done in bringing the dipole to this position is $N \times (mgh)$, where g is the acceleration due to gravity, then the value of N is ______. (Note that for three coplanar forces keeping a point mass in equilibrium, $\frac{F}{\sin\theta}$ is the same for all forces, where F is any one of the forces and θ is the angle between the other two forces).

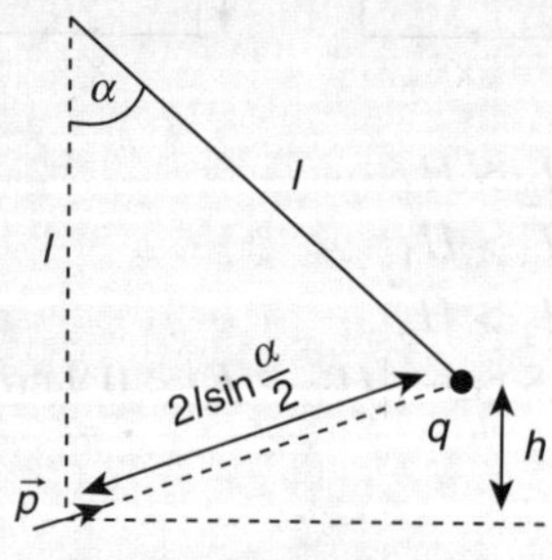

6. A thermally isolated cylindrical closed vessel of height 8 m is kept vertically. It is divided into two equal parts by a diathermic (perfect thermal conductor) frictionless partition of mass 8.3 kg. Thus, the partition is held initially at a distance of 4 m from the top, as shown in the schematic figure below. Each of the two parts of the vessel contains 0.1 mole of an ideal gas at temperature 300 K. The partition is now released and moves without any gas leaking from one part of the vessel to the other. Throughout the process, the temperature is maintained at 300 K. When equilibrium is reached, the distance of the partition from the top (in m) will be ______ (take the acceleration due to gravity = 10 m/s^2 and the universal gas constant = 8.3 J/mol·K).

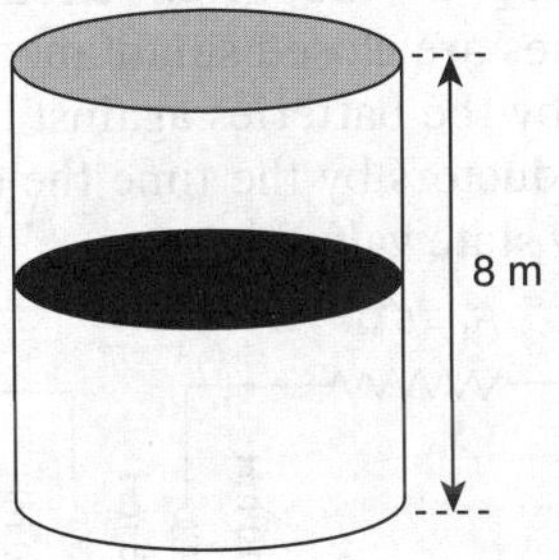

Numerical Value Answer

- The answer to each question is a **NUMERICAL VALUE.**
- For each question, enter the correct numerical value of the answer using the mouse and the on-screen virtual numeric keypad in the place designated to enter the answer. If the numerical value has more than two decimal places, truncate/round-off the value to TWO decimal places.
- The answer to each question will be evaluated according to the following marking scheme:

Full Marks: +4	If ONLY the correct numerical value is entered
Zero Marks: 0	In all other cases

1. Put a uniform meter scale horizontally on your extended index fingers with the left one at 0.00 cm and the right one at 90.00 cm. When you attempt to move both the fingers slowly towards the centre, initially only the left finger slips with respect to the scale and the right finger does not. After some distance, the left finger stops and the right one starts slipping. Then the right finger stops at a distance x_R from the centre (50.00 cm) of the scale and the left one starts slipping again. This happens because of the difference in the frictional forces on the two fingers. If the coefficients of static and dynamic friction between the fingers and the scale are 0.40 and 0.32, respectively, the value of x_R (in cm) is ______.

2. When water is filled carefully in a glass, one can fill it to a height h above the rim of the glass due to the surface tension of water. To calculate h just before water starts flowing, model the shape of the water above the rim as a disc of thickness h having semicircular edges, as shown schematically in the figure. When the pressure of water at the bottom of this disc exceeds what can be withstood due to the surface tension, the water surface breaks near the rim and water starts flowing from there. If the density of water, its surface tension and the acceleration due to gravity are 10^3kg m^{-3}, 0.07 Nm^{-1} and 10 ms^{-2}, respectively, the value of h (in mm) is ______.

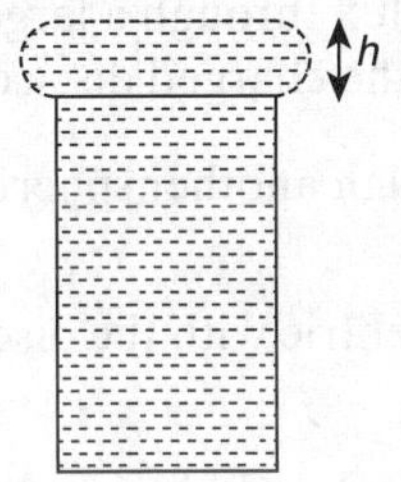

3. One end of a spring of negligible unstretched length and spring constant k is fixed at the origin (0,0). A point particle of mass m carrying a positive charge q is attached at its other end. The entire system is kept on a smooth horizontal surface. When a point dipole $\vec{p}$ pointing towards the charge q is fixed at the origin, the spring is stretched to a length l and attains a new equilibrium position (see figure below). If the point mass is now displaced slightly by $\Delta l \ll l$ from its equilibrium position and released, it is found to oscillate at frequency $\frac{1}{\delta}\sqrt{\frac{k}{m}}$. The value of δ is ______.

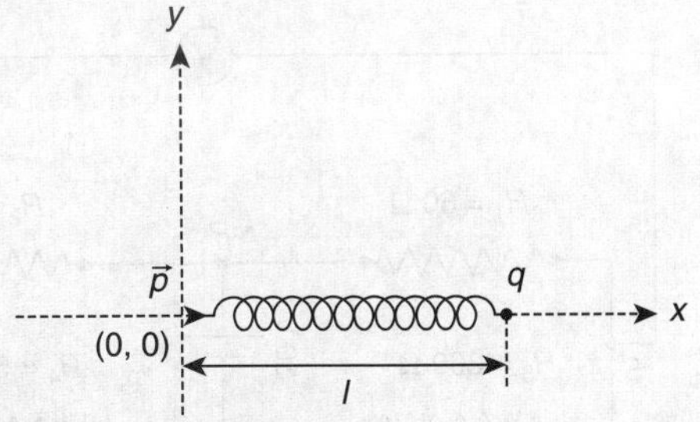

4. Consider one mole of helium gas enclosed in a container at initial pressure P_1 and volume V_1. It expands isothermally to volume $4V_1$. After this, the gas expands adiabatically and its volume becomes $32V_1$. The work done by the gas during isothermal and adiabatic expansion processes are W_{iso} and W_{adia}, respectively. If the ratio $\frac{W_{iso}}{W_{adia}} = f \ln 2$, then f is ______.

5. A stationary tuning fork is in resonance with an air column in a pipe. If the tuning fork is moved with a speed of 2 ms^{-1} in front of the open end of the pipe and parallel to it, the length of the pipe should be changed for the resonance to occur with the moving tuning fork. If the speed of sound in air is 320 ms^{-1}, the smallest value of the percentage change required in the length of the pipe is ______.

6. A circular disc of radius R carries surface charge density $\sigma(r) = \sigma_0\left(1 - \frac{r}{R}\right)$, where σ_0 is a constant and r is the distance from the centre of the disc. Electric flux through a large spherical surface that encloses the charged disc completely is ϕ_0. Electric flux through another spherical surface of radius $\frac{R}{4}$ and concentric with the disc is ϕ. Then the ratio $\frac{\phi_0}{\phi}$ is ______.

7. A spherical bubble inside water has radius R. Take the pressure inside the bubble and the water pressure to be p_0. The bubble now gets compressed radially in an adiabatic manner so that its radius becomes $(R–a)$. For $a << R$, the magnitude of the work done in the process is given by $(4\pi p_0 a R^2)X$, where X is a constant and $\gamma = C_p/C_V = 41/30$. The value of X is______.

8. In the balanced condition, the values of the resistances of the four arms of a Wheatstone bridge are shown in the figure below. The resistance R_3 has temperature coefficient 0.0004°C^{-1}. If the temperature of R_3 is increased by 100°C, the voltage developed between S and T will be ______ volts.

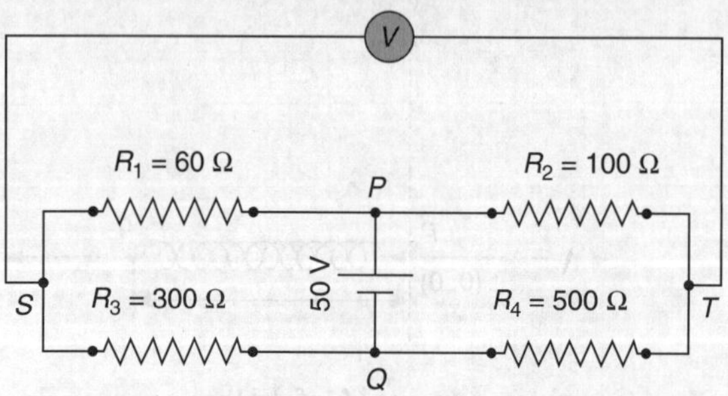

9. Two capacitors with capacitance values C_1 = 2000 ± 10 pF and C_2 = 3000 ± 15 pF are connected in series. The voltage applied across this combination is V = 5.00 ± 0.02 V. The percentage error in the calculation of the energy stored in this combination of capacitors is ______.

10. A cubical solid aluminium (bulk modulus $= -V\frac{dP}{dV}$ = 70 GPa) block has an edge length of 1 m on the surface of the Earth. It is kept on the floor of a 5-km-deep ocean. Taking the average density of water and the acceleration due to gravity to be 10^3 kg m^{-3} and 10 ms^{-2}, respectively, the change in the edge length of the block in mm is ______.

11. The inductors of two LR circuits are placed next to each other, as shown in the figure. The values of the self-inductance of the inductors, resistances, mutual-inductance and applied voltages are specified in the given circuit. After both the switches are closed simultaneously, the total work done by the batteries against the induced EMF in the inductors by the time the currents reach their steady state values is ______ mJ.

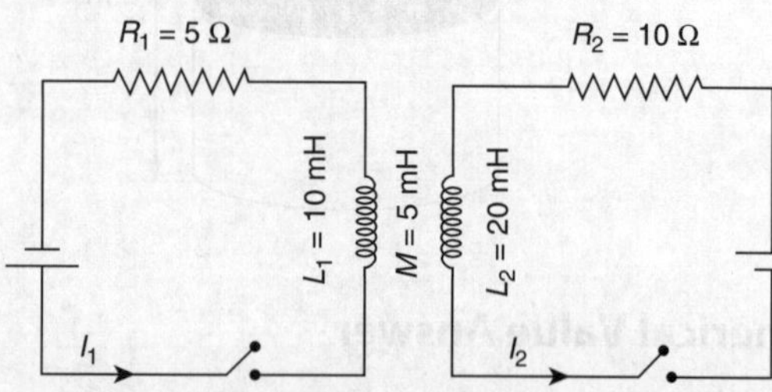

12. A container with 1 kg of water in it is kept in sunlight, which causes the water to get warmer than the surroundings. The average energy per unit time per unit area received due to the sunlight is 700 Wm^{-2} and it is absorbed by the water over an effective area of 0.05 m^2. Assuming that the heat loss from the water to the surroundings is governed by Newton's law of cooling, the difference (in °C) in the temperature of water and the surroundings after a long time will be ______. (Ignore the effect of the container, and take constant for Newton's law of cooling = 0.001 s^{-1}, heat capacity of water = 4200 J kg^{-1} K^{-1})

13. A particle is moved along a path AB-BC-CD-DE-EF-FA, as shown in the figure, in the presence of a force $\vec{F} = (\alpha y\hat{i} + 2\alpha x\hat{j})N$, where x and y are in metres and $\alpha = -1$ Nm^{-1}. The work done on the particle by this force $\vec{F}$ will be ___ joules.

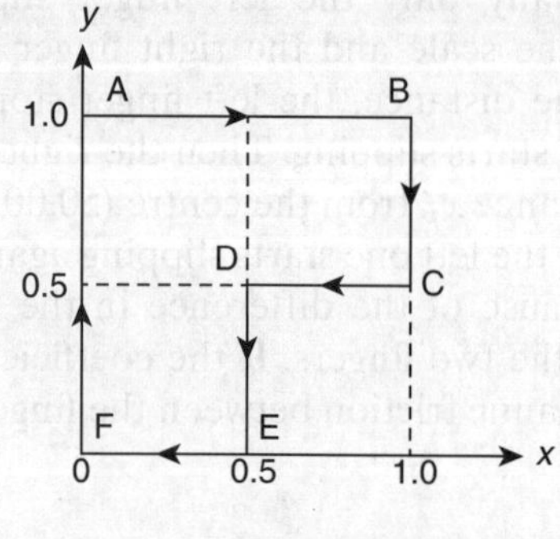

14. A block of weight 100 N is suspended by copper and steel wires of the same cross-sectional area 0.5 cm^2 and length $\sqrt{3}$ m and 1 m, respectively. Their other ends are fixed on a ceiling, as shown in the figure. The angles subtended by the copper and steel wires with the ceiling are 30° and 60°, respectively. If the elongation in the copper wire is (Δl_c) and the elongation in the steel wire is (Δl_s), then the ratio is ______. [Young's modulus for copper and steel are 1×10^{11} N/m^2 and 2×10^{11} N/m^2, respectively]

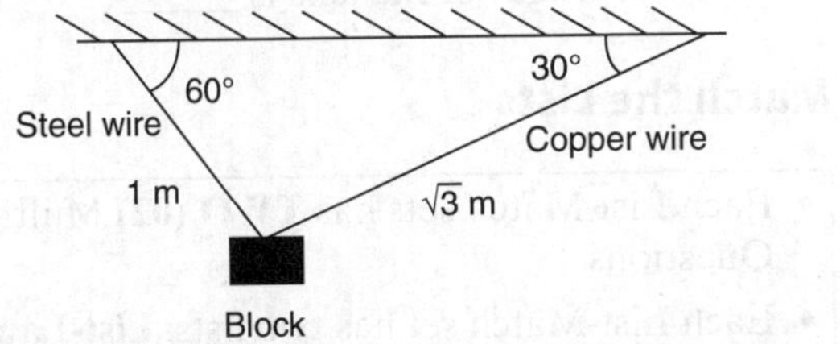

15. A train S_1, moving with a uniform velocity of 108 km/h, approaches another train S_2 standing on a platform. An observer O moves with a uniform velocity of 36 km/h towards S_2, as shown in the figure. Both the trains are blowing whistles of the same frequency of 120 Hz. When O is 600 m away from S_2 and the distance between S_1 and S_2 is 800 m, the number of beats heard by O is ___. [Speed of the sound = 330 m/s]

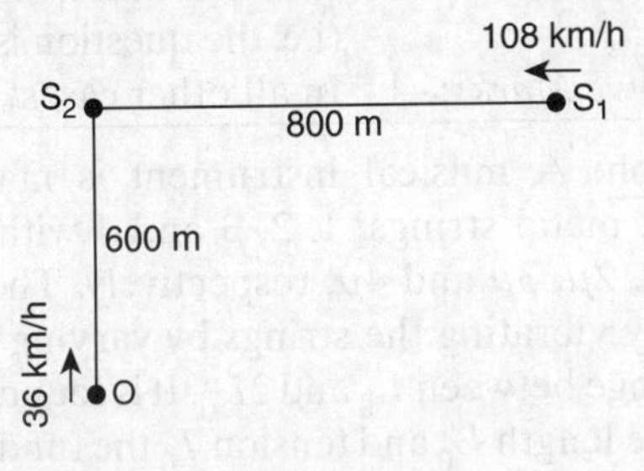

16. A parallel plate capacitor of capacitance C has spacing d between two plates having area A. The region between the plates is filled with N dielectric layers, parallel to its plates, each with thickness $\delta = \frac{d}{N}$. The dielectric constant of the mth layer is $K_m = K\left(1+\frac{m}{N}\right)$. For every large N (> 10^3), the capacitance C is $\alpha\left(\frac{K \epsilon_0 A}{d \ln 2}\right)$. The value of α will be ___. [ϵ_0 is the permittivity of free space]

17. A liquid at 30°C is poured very slowly into a calorimeter that is at a temperature of 110°C. The boiling temperature of the liquid is 80°C. It is found that the first 5 g of the liquid completely evaporates. After pouring another 80 g of the liquid, the equilibrium temperature is found to be 50°C. The ratio of the latent heat of the liquid to its specific heat will be ___°C. [Neglect the heat exchange with the surroundings]

18. A planar structure of length L and width W is made up of two different optical media of refractive indices $n_1 = 1.5$ and $n_2 = 1.44$, as shown in the figure. If $L \gg W$, a ray entering from end AB will emerge from end CD only if the total internal reflection condition is met inside the structure. For $L = 9.6$ m, if the incident angle θ is varied, the maximum time taken by a ray to exit the plane CD is $t \times 10^{-9}$ s, where t is ___. [Speed of light $c = 3 \times 10^8$ m/s]

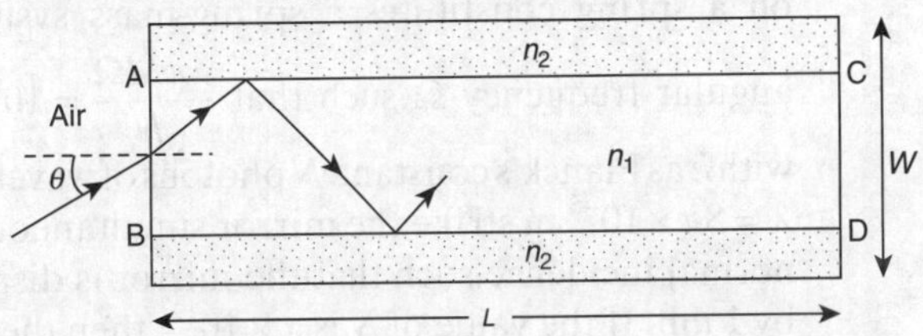

19. A ball is thrown from the ground at an angle of θ with the horizontal and with an initial speed of u_0. For the resulting projectile motion, the magnitude of the average velocity of the ball up to the point when it hits the ground for the first time is V_1. After hitting the ground, the ball rebounds at the same angle θ but with a reduced speed of u_0/α. Its motion continues for a long time, as shown in the figure. If the magnitude of the average velocity of the ball for the entire duration of motion is $0.8\ V_1$, the value of α is ___.

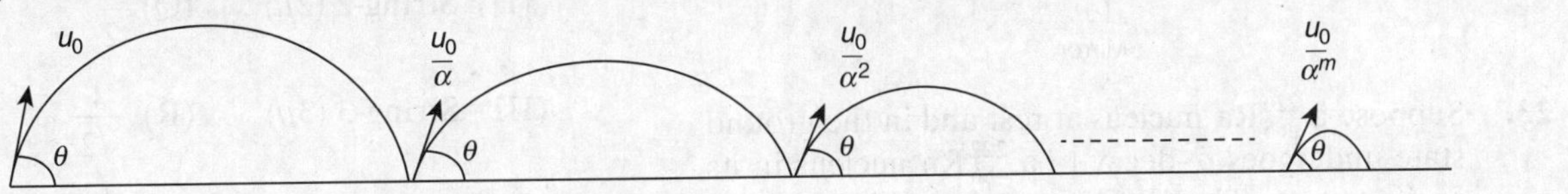

20. A 10-cm-long perfectly conducting wire PQ is moving with a velocity of 1 cm/s on a pair of horizontal rails of zero resistance. One side of the rails is connected to an inductor L = 1 mH and resistance $R = 1\ \Omega$, as shown in the figure. The horizontal rails L and R lie in the same plane with a uniform magnetic field B = 1 T perpendicular to the plane. If the key S is closed at a certain instant, the current in the circuit after 1 millisecond is $x \times 10^{-3}$ A, where the value of x is ______. [Assume that the velocity of wire PQ remains constant (1 cm/s) after key S is closed. Given: $e^{-1} = 0.37$, where e is the base of the natural logarithm]

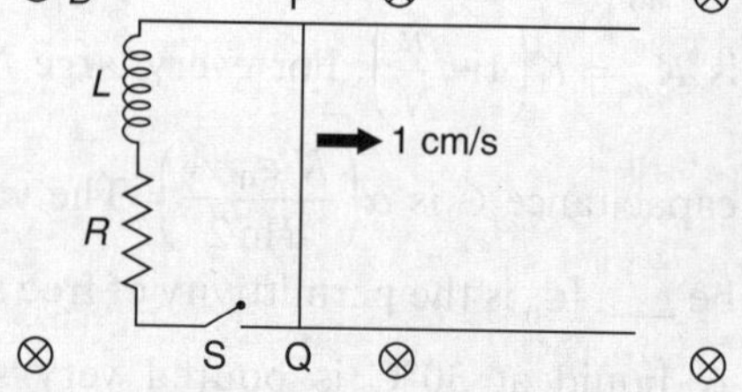

21. A monochromatic light is incident from air on a refracting surface of a prism of angle 75° and refractive index $n_0 = \sqrt{3}$. The other refracting surface of the prism is coated with a thin film of material of refractive index n, as shown in the figure. The light suffers total internal reflection at the coated prism surface for an incidence angle of $\theta \leq 60°$. The maximum value of n^2 is ______.

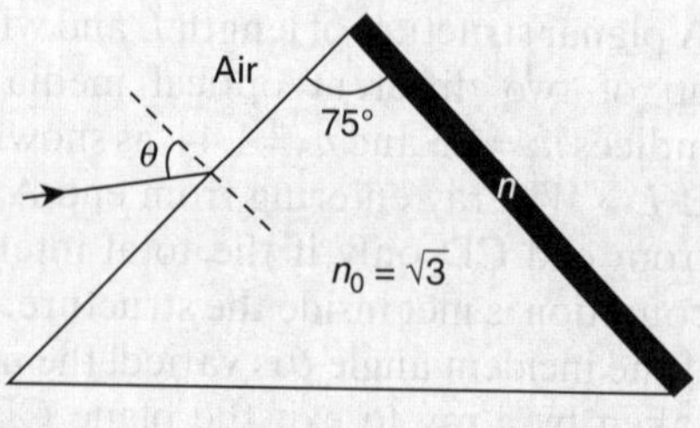

22. A perfectly reflecting mirror of mass M mounted on a spring constitutes a spring-mass system of angular frequency Ω such that $\frac{4\pi M\Omega}{h} = 10^{24}\ \text{m}^{-2}$ with h as Planck's constant. N photons of wavelength $\lambda = 8\pi \times 10^{-6}$ m strike the mirror simultaneously at normal incidence such that the mirror is displaced by 1 μm. If the value of N is $x \times 10^{12}$, then the value of x is ______. [Consider the spring as massless]

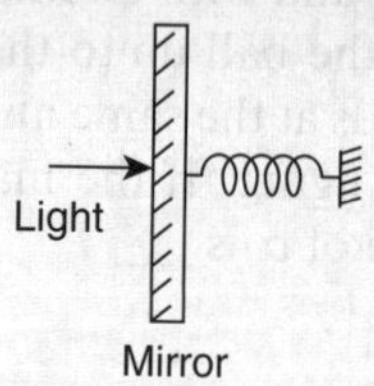

23. Suppose a $^{226}_{88}$Ra nucleus at rest and in the ground state undergoes α-decay to a $^{222}_{86}$Rn nucleus in its excited state. The kinetic energy of the emitted α particle is found to be 4.44 MeV. The $^{222}_{86}$Rn nucleus then goes to its ground state by γ-decay. The energy of the emitted γ photon is ______ keV. [Given: atomic mass of $^{226}_{88}$Ra = 226.005 u, atomic mass of $^{222}_{86}$Rn = 222.000 u, atomic mass of α particle = 4.000 u, 1 u = 931 MeV/c^2, c is the speed of the light]

24. An optical bench has a 1.5-m-long scale having four equal divisions in each cm. While measuring the focal length of a convex lens, the lens is kept at the 75 cm mark of the scale and the object pin is kept at the 45 cm mark. The image of the object pin on the other side of the lens overlaps with the image pin that is kept at the 135 cm mark. In this experiment, the percentage error in the measurement of the focal length of the lens is ______.

Match the Lists

- Each List-Match sets has **TWO (02)** Multiple Choice Questions.
- Each List-Match set has two lists: **List-I** and **List-II**.
- **FOUR** options are given in each Multiple Choice Question based on **List-I** and **List-II** and **ONLY ONE** of these four options satisfies the condition asked in the Multiple Choice Question.
- The answer to each question will be evaluated according to the following marking scheme:

Full Marks: +3	If ONLY the correct option is chosen;
Zero Marks: 0	If none of the options is chosen (i.e. the question is unanswered);
Negative Marks: –1	In all other cases

Paragraph: A musical instrument is made up of four different metal strings, 1, 2, 3 and 4 with mass per unit length μ, 2μ, 3μ and 4μ, respectively. The instrument is played by vibrating the strings by varying the free length in the range between L_0 and $2L_0$. It is found that in string-1 (μ) at free length L_0 and tension T_0 the fundamental mode, the frequency is f_0.

List I gives the above four strings while List II lists the magnitude of some quantity.

List I	List II
(I) String-1 (μ)	(P) 1
(II) String-2 (2μ)	(Q) $\frac{1}{2}$
(III) String-3 (3μ)	(R) $\frac{1}{\sqrt{2}}$
(IV) String-4 (4μ)	(S) $\frac{1}{\sqrt{3}}$
	(T) $\frac{3}{16}$
	(U) $\frac{1}{16}$

Answer Q.1 and Q.2 by appropriately matching the lists based on the information given in the paragraph.

1. If the tension in each string is T_0, the correct match for the highest fundamental frequency in f_0 units will be:
   (a) I → P, II → Q, III → T, IV → S
   (b) I → P, II → R, III → S, IV → Q
   (c) I → Q, II → S, III → R, IV → P
   (d) I → Q, II → P, III → R, IV → T

2. The length of the strings 1, 2, 3 and 4 are kept fixed at L_0, $\frac{3L_0}{2}$, $\frac{5L_0}{4}$, and $\frac{7L_0}{4}$, respectively. Strings 1, 2, 3, and 4 are vibrated at their 1st, 3rd, 5th and 14th harmonics, respectively, such that all the strings have the same frequency. The correct match for the tension in the four strings in the units of T_0 will be:
   (a) I → P, II → R, III → T, IV → U
   (b) I → P, II → Q, III → T, IV → U
   (c) I → P, II → Q, III → R, IV → T
   (d) I → T, II → Q, III → R, IV → U

Paragraph: In a thermodynamic process on an ideal monatomic gas, the infinitesimal heat absorbed by the gas is given by $T\Delta X$, where T is the temperature of the system and ΔX is the infinitesimal change in a thermodynamic quantity X of the system. For a mole of monatomic ideal gas $X = \frac{3}{2}R\ln\left(\frac{T}{T_A}\right) + R\ln\left(\frac{V}{V_A}\right)$. Here, R is the gas constant, V is the volume of the gas, T_A and V_A are constants.

List I below gives some quantities involved in a process and List II gives some possible values of these quantities.

List I	List II
(I) Work done by the system in process 1 → 2 → 3	(P) $\frac{1}{3}RT_0 \ln 2$
(II) Change in internal energy in process 1 → 2 → 3	(Q) $\frac{1}{3}RT_0$
(III) Heat absorbed by the system in process 1 → 2 → 3	(R) RT_0
(IV) Heat absorbed by the system in process 1 → 2	(S) $\frac{4}{3}RT_0$
	(T) $\frac{1}{3}RT_0(3+\ln 2)$
	(U) $\frac{5}{6}RT_0$

Answer Q.3 and Q.4 by appropriately matching the lists based on the information given in the paragraph.

3. If the process carried out on one mole of monatomic ideal gas is as shown in the figure in the PV diagram with $P_0V_0 = \frac{1}{3}RT_0$, the correct match is:

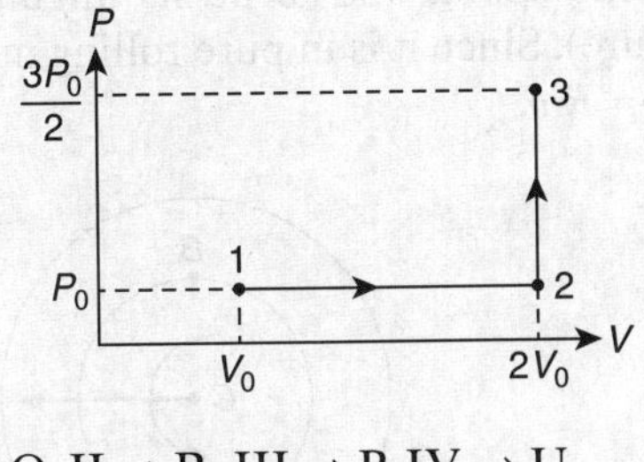

   (a) I → Q, II → R, III → P, IV → U
   (b) I → Q, II → R, III → S, IV → U
   (c) I → S, II → R, III → Q, IV → T
   (d) I → Q, II → S, III → R, IV → U

4. If the process on one mole of monatomic ideal gas is as shown in the TV diagram with $P_0V_0 = \frac{1}{3}RT_0$, the correct match is:

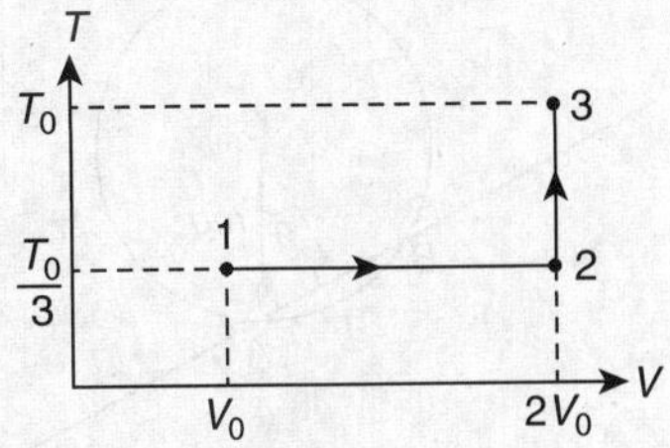

   (a) I → P, II → R, III → T, IV → S
   (b) I → P, II → T, III → Q, IV → T
   (c) I → P, II → R, III → T, IV → P
   (d) I → S, II → T, III → Q, IV → U

ANSWER KEYS

Only One Correct Option

1. (a) **2.** (b) **3.** (c) **4.** (b) **5.** (c) **6.** (b) **7.** (a) **8.** (c) **9.** (a) **10.** (b)

One or More Correct Options

1. (b),(c) **2.** (b),(c),(d) **3.** (a),(b) **4.** (b),(c) **5.** (a),(c),(d) **6.** (a),(b),(c)
7. (a),(d) **8.** (a),(d) **9.** (a),(c),(d) **10.** (b),(c) **11.** (b),(c) **12.** (a),(b),(c),(d)
13. (a),(b),(c) **14.** (b),(c),(d) **15.** (b),(c) **16.** (a),(b) **17.** (a),(c) **18.** (b),(c),(d)
19. (a),(b),(c) **20.** (b),(c) **21.** (a),(c),(d) **22.** (a),(c),(d) **23.** (b),(d) **24.** (a),(c)
25. (a),(c),(d) **26.** (a),(c) **27.** (c) **28.** (a),(d)

Single Digit Answer

1. 3 **2.** 9 **3.** 6 **4.** 4 **5.** 2 **6.** 6

Numerical Value Answer

1. 25.6 **2.** 5.30 **3.** 3.14 **4.** 1.78 **5.** 0.63 **6.** 6.4 **7.** 1 **8.** 0.27 **9.** 1.3 **10.** 0.24
11. 55 **12.** 8.33 **13.** 0.75 **14.** 2 **15.** 5.78 **16.** 1 **17.** 270 **18.** 5 **19.** 4 **20.** 0.63
21. 1.5 **22.** 1 **23.** 130 **24.** 0.69

Match the Lists

1. (b) **2.** (b) **3.** (b) **4.** (c)

SOLUTIONS

Only One Correct Option

1. (a) The football will be stable as long as the line of action of mg lies within the support region (AB).

The figure shows the situation when mg just passes through point A. Hence $\sin\theta = \frac{r}{R}$.

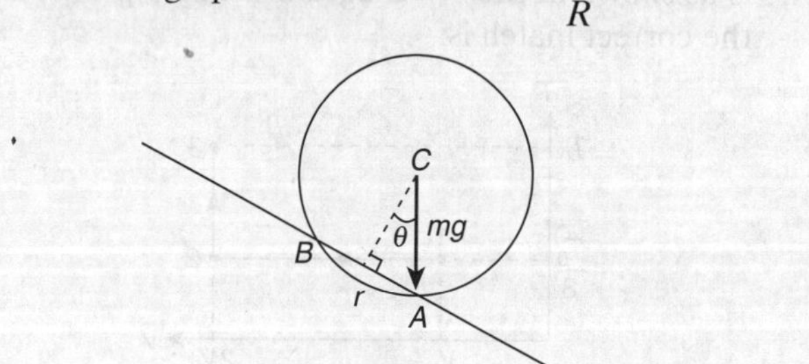

2. (b) The moving magnet will induce EMF in the aluminum disc. This will give rise to circular current loops just below the magnet. The direction of these current loops will be such that the top surface of the dice behaves like the south pole of a magnet so as to attract the north pole of the bar magnet and oppose its motion.

In reaction, the bar magnet will attract the induced south pole on the disc surface. Hence, the disc will follow the bar magnet and rotate in the same direction as the bar magnet.

3. (c) Let v_C be the velocity of the centre of mass of the spool, and ω be its angular velocity (see figure). Since it is in pure rolling motion, $v_A = 0 \Rightarrow v_C = R\omega$.

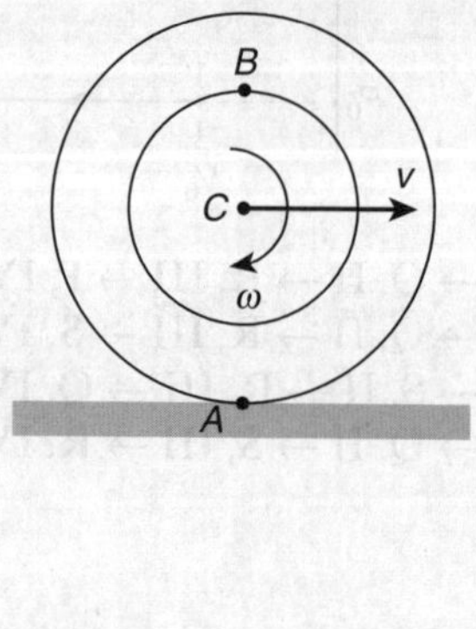

Then

$$v_B = v_C + r\omega = v_C\left(1+\frac{r}{R}\right)$$

$$= v_C\left(1+\frac{5\text{ cm}}{10\text{ cm}}\right) = \frac{3}{2}v_C$$

The distances moved by points C and B over a given time will be in the ratio of their velocities. Hence, if point C moves by 50 cm, point B will move by $\frac{3}{2}(50\text{ cm}) = 75$ cm. Hence, the scale which is in contact with point B and is moving without slipping on it will also move by 75 cm.

4. (b) Let us suppose that the capacitor discharges in a short time t. Then the average current through the coil is $I = \frac{Q}{\Delta t}$. During the time t, the coil behaves like a magnetic pole of moment $\mu = I(N\pi R^2) = \frac{\pi NQR^2}{\Delta t}$. The μ vector is directed out of the plane of the figure, that is perpendicular to the given **B** vector. So the coil experiences a torque of magnitude $\tau = \mu B_0 \sin 90° = \frac{\pi NQB_0R^2}{\Delta t}$.

Hence, the angular momentum gained by the coil is $\Delta L = \tau t = \pi NQB_0R^2$.

5. (c) Light will travel faster in region B (air) than in regions A (glass) or C (glass). Hence, the waves will cover greater distances in region B than in regions A or C.

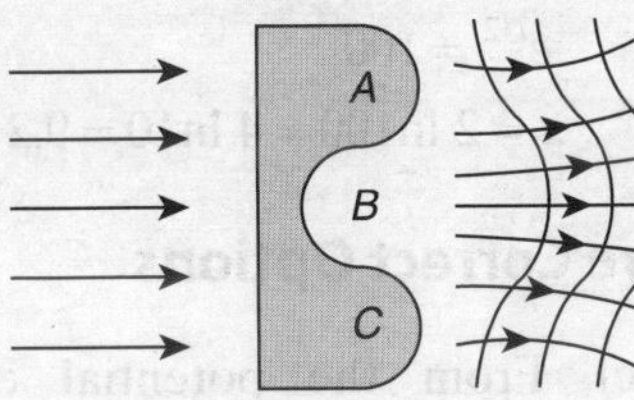

6. (b) Equating the pressures at points A and B (see figure), we have

$$(800\text{ kg/m}^3)g(0.1\text{ cm}) = (100\text{ kg/m}^3)gy$$

$$\Rightarrow \quad y = 0.08\text{ cm}$$

The total length of water column is given to be $2(0.29\text{ cm}) = 0.58$ cm. Thus, we have

$$2h + y = 0.58\text{ cm}$$

$$\Rightarrow \quad h = \frac{0.58-0.08}{2}\text{ cm} = 0.25\text{ cm}$$

Hence, we have

$$\frac{h_1}{h_2} = \frac{h+0.01\text{ cm}}{h+y} = \frac{0.25+0.1}{0.25+0.08} = \frac{35}{33}$$

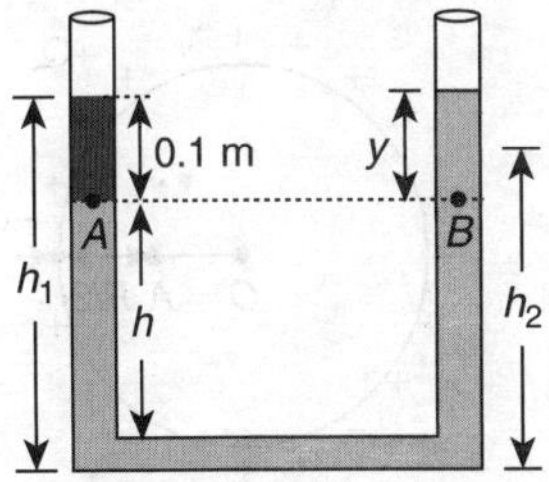

7. (a) The gravitational intensity at distance r from the centre of the gaseous cloud is given by

$$g(r) = \frac{GM}{r^2},$$

where M is the mass inside the spherical region of radius r

$$\Rightarrow \quad g(r) = \frac{G}{r^2}\int_0^r \rho(r)4\pi r^2 dr$$

For a particle moving with velocity in a circular orbit of radius r, we have

$$g(r) = \frac{v^2}{r} = \frac{2K}{mr},$$

where K is the kinetic energy

Equating the two equations, we have

$$\frac{G}{r^2}\int_0^r \rho(r)4\pi r^2 dr = \frac{2K}{mr}$$

$$\Rightarrow \quad \int_0^r \rho(r)r^2 dr = \frac{Kr}{2\pi Gm}$$

Now, differentiating both sides with respect to r, we have

$$\rho(r)r^2 = \frac{K}{2\pi Gm}$$

$$\Rightarrow \rho(r) = \frac{K}{2\pi Gmr^2}$$

Hence, the particle number density is

$$n(r) = \frac{\rho(r)}{m} = \frac{K}{2\pi Gm^2r^2}$$

8. (c) If Q is the total charge on the sphere, then the charge on the surface area $\alpha(4\pi R^2)$ will be αQ. The potential at the surface is given to be V_0. Thus, we have

$$V_0 = \frac{Q}{4\pi\epsilon_0 R} \Rightarrow Q = (4\pi\epsilon_0 R)V_0 \qquad \ldots(1)$$

Now the sphere with a hole can be considered as a complete sphere having uniformly distributed charge Q, and a point charge $-\alpha Q$ at the position of the hole (see figure).

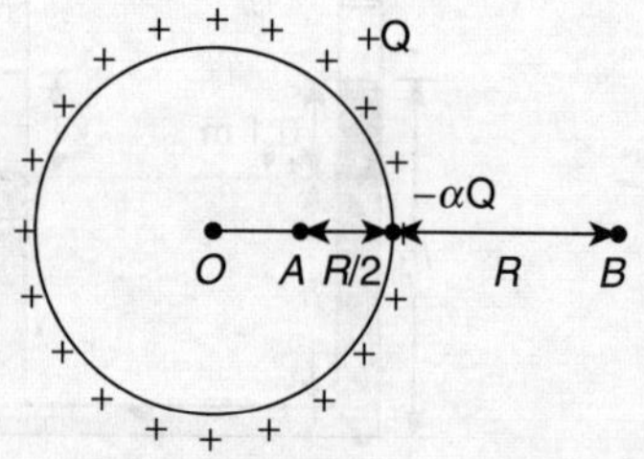

(a) The potential at the centre now becomes

$$V_C = V_0 + \frac{-\alpha Q}{4\pi\epsilon_0 R} = V_0 - \alpha V_0$$

[Using equation (1)]

Thus, the voltage at the centre reduces by $\alpha V_0 \Rightarrow$ Option (a) is incorrect.

(b) Initially the electric field at the centre was zero. Now it becomes

$$E_C = \frac{-\alpha Q}{4\pi\epsilon_0 R^2} = \frac{-\alpha V_0}{R}$$

[Using equation (1)]

Thus, the electric field magnitude at the centre changes by $\frac{\alpha V_0}{R}$

$\Rightarrow$ Option (b) is incorrect.

(c) The potential at point A is

$$V_A = V_0 + \frac{-\alpha Q}{4\pi\epsilon_0\left(\frac{R}{2}\right)} = (1-2\alpha)V_0$$

[Using equation (1)]

Thus, the ratio $\frac{V_C}{V_A} = \frac{1-\alpha}{1-2\alpha}$

$\Rightarrow$ Option (c) is correct.

(d) Initially the electric field at point B was $E_0 = \frac{Q}{4\pi\epsilon_0 (2R)^2}$. The electric field at point B now becomes

$$E_C = E_0 + \frac{-\alpha Q}{4\pi\epsilon_0 R^2} = E_0 - \frac{\alpha V_0}{R}$$

Thus, the electric field magnitude at point B reduces by $\frac{\alpha V_0}{R} \Rightarrow$ Option (d) is incorrect.

9. (a) If C is the heat capacity of the wire, then we have

$$P = C\frac{dT}{dt}$$

From the given relation $T(t) = T_0\left(1+\beta t^{1/4}\right)$, we have

$$\frac{dT}{dt} = T_0\beta\left(\frac{1}{4}t^{-3/4}\right) = \frac{1}{4}T_0\beta\left(\frac{T-T_0}{\beta}\right)^{-3}$$

$$= \frac{1}{4}T_0\beta\left(\frac{T-T_0}{\beta T_0}\right)^{-3} = \frac{\beta^4 T_0{}^4}{4(T-T_0)^3}$$

Hence, we have

$$P = C\frac{T_0{}^4}{4(T-T_0)^3}$$

$$\Rightarrow \quad C = \frac{4P(T-T_0)^3}{T_0{}^4}$$

10. (b) The decay constants of the two nuclei $^{40}_{20}\text{Ca}$ and $^{40}_{18}\text{Ar}$ are given to be $\lambda_1 = 4.5\times10^{-10}$ per year and $\lambda_2 = 0.5\times10^{-10}$ per year. If N is the number of $^{40}_{19}\text{K}$ nuclei at any instant, then we have

$$\frac{dN}{dt} = -(\lambda_1+\lambda_2)N = -\left(5\times10^{-10}\text{ per year}\right)N$$

If N_0 is the initial number of $^{40}_{19}\text{K}$ nuclei, then solving the above differential equation, we have

$$N = N_0 e^{-(0.5\times10^{-10}\text{ per year})t}$$

From the given condition, only 1% of the $^{40}_{19}\text{K}$ nuclei remains after time $t\times10^9$ years. Thus, we have

$$\frac{1}{100}N_0 = N_0 e^{-(5\times10^{-10}\text{ per year})(t\times10^9\text{ years})}$$

$$\Rightarrow \quad e^{t/2} = 100$$

$$\Rightarrow \quad t = 2\ln100 = 4\ln10 = 9.2$$

One or More Correct Options

1. (b), (c) From the potential energy function $U(r) = r$, we can find the force acting on the particle as $F(r) = -\frac{dU}{dr} = -\alpha$

The magnitude of the force is constant equal to α. The –ve sign suggests that the force is directed radically inward.

Now, if the particle is moving with speed v in a circular orbit of radius R, then we have

$$m\frac{v^2}{R} = \alpha \quad \text{...(1)}$$

and $$mvR = n\frac{h}{2\pi} \quad \text{...(2)}$$

Multiplying the two equation, we have

$$m^2v^3 = \frac{n\alpha h}{2\pi} \Rightarrow v = \left(\frac{n\alpha h}{2\pi m^2}\right)^{1/3} \Rightarrow v \propto n^{1/3}$$

Inserting the value of v in equation (1), we have

$$R = \frac{mv^2}{\alpha} = \frac{m}{\alpha}\left(\frac{n\alpha h}{2\pi m^2}\right)^{2/3} \Rightarrow R\alpha n^{2/3}$$

Energy of the particle is

$$E = KE + PE$$

$$\Rightarrow \quad E = \frac{1}{2}mv^2 + \alpha R$$

$$\Rightarrow \quad E = \frac{1}{2}mv^2 + mv^2 = \frac{3}{2}mv^2$$

$$\Rightarrow \quad E = \frac{3}{2}m\left(\frac{n\alpha h}{2\pi m^2}\right)^{2/3} = \frac{3}{2}\left(\frac{n^2\alpha^2 h^2}{4\pi^2 m}\right)^{1/3}$$

$$\Rightarrow \quad E\alpha n^{2/3}$$

2. (b), (c), (d) Emissive power of the light bulb is

$$P = \sigma AT^4 = (5.67 \times 10^{-8})\ (64 \times 10^{-6})\ (2500)^4\ \text{W} = 141.75\ \text{W}$$

At a distance of 100 m from the bulb, its intensity is $= \dfrac{P}{4\pi(100\ \text{m})^2}$. Hence, the power entering into one eye is

$$P_{\text{eye}} = \frac{P}{4\pi(100\ \text{m})^2} \times \pi(3\ \text{mm})^2$$

$$= \frac{(3\times10^{-3})^2}{4(100)^2} \times 141.75\ \text{W} = 3.2\times10^{-8}\ \text{W}$$

The most intense wavelength is

$$\lambda_m = \frac{b}{T} = \frac{2.90\times10^{-3}}{2500}\ \text{m} = 11.6\times10^{-7}\ \text{m} = 1160\ \text{nm}$$

If the average wavelength of the spectrum is 1740 mm, then the energy carried by each photon is

$$E = \frac{hc}{\lambda} = \frac{(6.63\times10^{-34})(3\times10^{8})}{1740\times10^{-9}}\ \text{J} = 1.14\times10^{-19}\ \text{J}$$

Hence, the number of photons entering per second into one eye is

$$n = \frac{P_{\text{eye}}}{E} = \frac{3.2\times10^{-8}}{1.14\times10^{-19}}\ \text{photons/second}$$

$$= 2.80\times10^{11}\ \text{photons/second}$$

3. (a), (b) We have

$$[\text{Time}] = \frac{[\text{Position}]}{[\text{Speed}]} = \left[X^{\alpha-\beta}\right]$$

and

$$[\text{Time}] = \frac{[\text{Speed}]}{[\text{Acceleration}]} = \left[X^{\beta-p}\right]$$

Equating the two, we have

$$\alpha - \beta = \beta - p \Rightarrow \alpha + p = 2\beta$$

Similarly, we have

$$[\text{Mass}] = \frac{[\text{Force}]}{[\text{Acceleration}]} = \left[X^{r-p}\right]$$

and

$$[\text{Mass}] = \frac{[\text{Momentum}]}{[\text{Speed}]} = \left[X^{q-\beta}\right]$$

Equating the two, we have $\gamma - p = q - \beta \Rightarrow p + q - \gamma = \beta$

4. (b), (c) Force on the charged particle is $-(qE)\mathbf{j}$. Hence, acceleration is only along the y axis

$$a_y = -\frac{qE}{m} = -4\sqrt{3}\times10^{12}\ \text{m/s}^2$$

The charged particle will move in a parabolic path (see figure). The range of the projectile is given by

$$R = \frac{u^2\sin(2\theta)}{|a_y|}$$

$$\Rightarrow \quad \sin(2\theta) = \frac{R|a_y|}{u^2} = \frac{5(4\sqrt{3}\times10^{12})}{(2\sqrt{10}\times10^{6})^2} = \frac{\sqrt{3}}{2}$$

$$\Rightarrow \quad 2\theta = 60°, 120° \Rightarrow \theta = 30°, 60°$$

The time of flight is given by

$$T = \frac{2u\sin\theta}{|a_y|} = \frac{5(2\sqrt{10}\times10^{6})\sin\theta}{4\sqrt{2}\times10^{12}}\ \text{ms}$$

$$= \frac{\sqrt{10}\sin\theta}{3}\ \text{ms} = \begin{cases}\sqrt{\dfrac{5}{6}}\ \text{ms for } \theta = 30°\\ \sqrt{\dfrac{5}{2}}\ \text{ms for } \theta = 60°\end{cases}$$

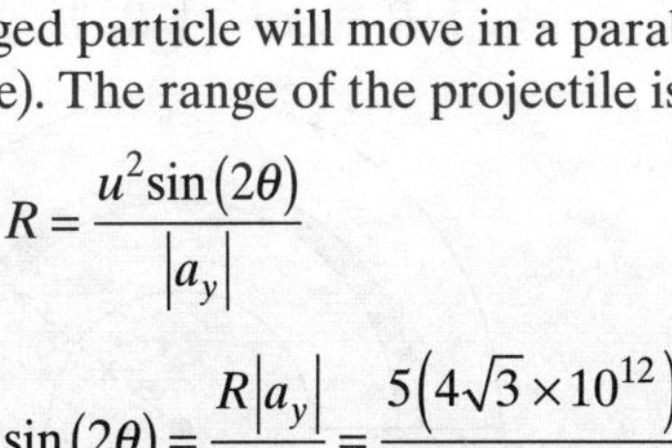

5. (a), (c), (d) We need to find the resistance of the metallic strip. Let us sub-divide the strip into thin semi-circular strips, each of width dx. The figure shows one such element strip of radius x. The length of this element strip is πx and its cross-section area is tdx. The resistance of this element strip is

$$dR = \frac{\rho(\pi x)}{tdx}$$

Now, all the element strips from $x = R_1$ to $x = R_2$ are connected in parallel. Hence, the total resistance R is given by

$$\frac{1}{R} = \int \frac{1}{dR} = \frac{t}{\pi\rho}\int_{R_1}^{R_2} \frac{1}{x}dx = \frac{t}{\pi\rho}\ln\left(\frac{R_2}{R_1}\right)$$

$$\Rightarrow \quad R = \frac{\pi\rho}{t\ln\left(\frac{R_2}{R_1}\right)}$$

Hence, current through the metal strip is

$$I = \frac{V_0}{R} = \frac{V_0 t}{\pi\rho}\ln\left(\frac{R_2}{R_1}\right)$$

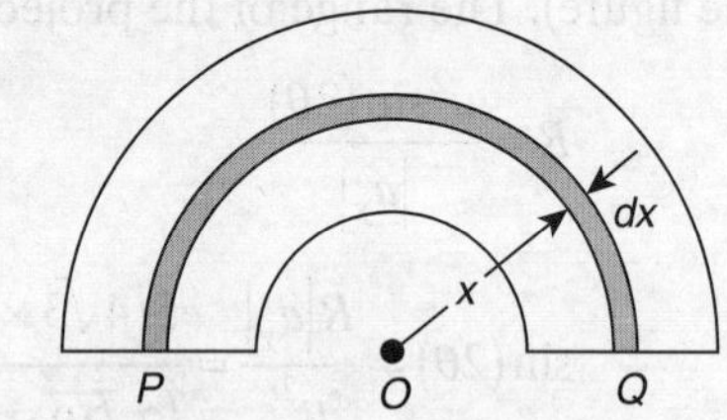

Let us imagine the metallic strip to be made of the semi-circular wires of radii verging from R_1 to R_2. Each wire will carry a fraction of the total current I. For example, the current flowing through the wire of radius x is

$$dI = \frac{V_0}{dR} = \frac{V_0 t}{\pi\rho}\frac{dx}{x} = \frac{I}{\ln\left(\frac{R_2}{R_1}\right)}\frac{dx}{x} = f(x)I$$

Here, $f(x)$ is a fraction and its value decreases with increasing x. Now, consider a particle carrying charge e and drifting with velocity v along the circular path of radius x (see figure). This changed particle experiences a magnetic field due to the other current caring wires. The net magnetic field will be directed out of the plane of the figure, so the Ampere force on the particle is directed radially inward. This will cause accumulation of positive changes on the inner surface, until a point where no more accumulation will be possible because of Coulomb repulsion. A transverse voltage will develop, with the inner side at a higher voltage. To find this transverse voltage, we need to find the force on the charge, which is $F = evB$.

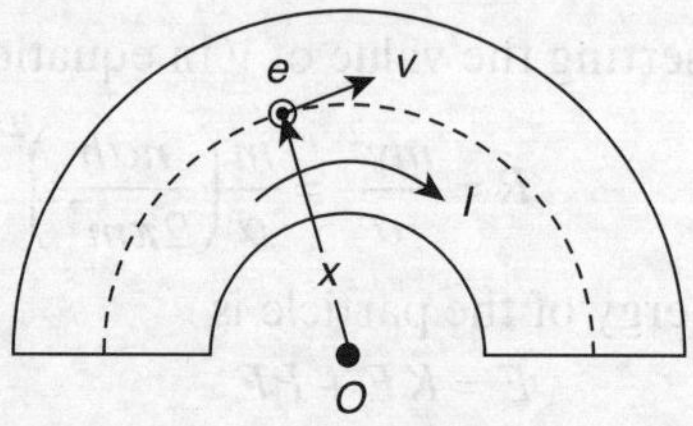

The transverse potential difference is given by

$$\Delta V = \int_{R_1}^{R_2} \frac{F}{e}dx = \int_{R_1}^{R_2} vB\,dx$$

Now, the magnetic field B and the drift velocity v are both proportional to I. Hence, we have $V \propto I^2$.

6. (a), (b), (c) From the ideal gas equation, we have

$$P = \frac{Nk_BT}{V} = nk_BT$$

Here, n is the number of gas molecules per unit volume. The force facing on the molecules at the diffusion partition is due to the pressure difference. Hence, we have

$$F = (\Delta p)S = (nk_BT)S$$

The total number of molecules in the connecting pipe is $n_1(Sl)$. If the limiting speed of the molecules is, say v, then the total friction force is

$$f = n_1(Sl)\beta v$$

Force balancing occurs when pushing force F is balanced by friction force f. That is, when

$$n_1(Sl)\beta v = (nk_BT)S$$

$$\Rightarrow \quad n_1\beta vl = nk_BT \qquad \ldots(1)$$

The number of molecules crossing per second is

$$n_{\text{crossing}} = n_1 vS = \frac{(nk_BT)S}{\beta l}$$

[Inserting the value of v from Eq. (1)]

7. (a), (d) The figure shows the ray diagram of light coming from a point O on the bottom of the cylinder. After refraction at the curved surface, the image is formed at point I. Point L is the centre of the approximately spherical liquid surface. Then from ALM, we have

$$(R - h)^2 + r^2 = R^2$$

$$\Rightarrow \quad h^2 - 2hR + r^2 = 0$$

$$\Rightarrow \quad R = \frac{h^2 + r^2}{2h} \qquad \ldots(1)$$

Consider a point B in the liquid, at depth h below point A and distance r from point P. The pressures at points A and P are equal to the atmospheric pressure, say p_0. The pressure at point B can be written as $p_0 + \rho gh$ or $p_0 + \frac{1}{2}\rho\omega^2 r^2$. Equating the two, we have

$$p_0 + \rho gh = p_0 + \frac{1}{2}\rho\omega^2 r^2$$

$$\Rightarrow \quad gh = \frac{1}{2}\omega^2 r^2 \quad \ldots(2)$$

From Eq. (1), we have

$$R = \frac{r^2}{2h} \quad \text{[for small } h\text{]}$$

$$\Rightarrow \quad r^2 = 2hR$$

Putting this result in Eq. (2), we have

$$R = \frac{g}{\omega^2}$$

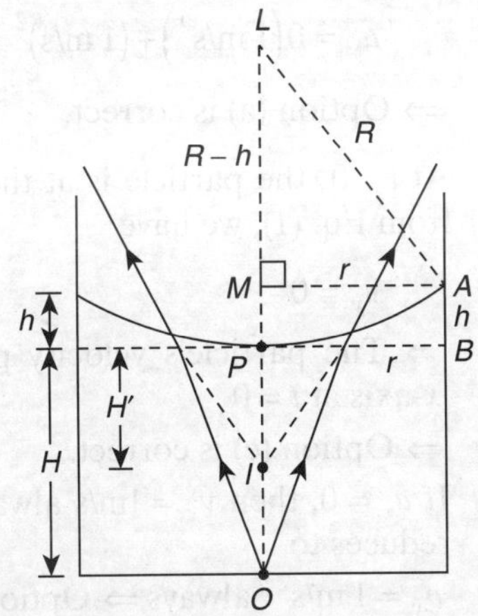

The distance of the object point O from the pole P is given to be H. Let H' be the distance of the image point from the pole. Now, using retraction formula, we have

$$\frac{1}{(-H')} - \frac{\mu}{(-H)} = \frac{1-\mu}{(+R)}$$

$$\Rightarrow \quad \frac{-1}{H'} + \frac{4}{3H} = \frac{-1}{3R}$$

$$\Rightarrow \quad \frac{1}{H'} = \frac{4}{3H} + \frac{\omega^2}{3g}$$

$$\Rightarrow \quad \frac{1}{H'} = \frac{4}{3H}\left(1 + \frac{\omega^2 H}{4g}\right)$$

$$\Rightarrow \quad H' = \frac{3H}{4}\left(1 + \frac{\omega^2 H}{4g}\right)^{-1}$$

8. (a), (d) Using mechanical energy conservation principle between the bottom of the incline and the highest point y, we have

$$\frac{1}{2}mv_y^2 + mgh = \frac{1}{2}mv_0^2$$

$$\Rightarrow \quad v_y^2 = v_0^2 - 2gh \quad \ldots(1)$$

At point y, the component of mg along the incline provides the necessary centripetal force for motion along the circular path. Thus, we have

$$mg\sin(30°) = m\left(\frac{v_y^2}{R}\right)$$

$$\Rightarrow \quad v_y^2 = \frac{1}{2}gR \quad \ldots(2)$$

From Equations (1) and (2), we have

$$v_0^2 - 2gh = \frac{1}{2}gR$$

Centripetal force is required all along the circular path, even at points x and z. The required centripetal force at any point equals $m\left(\frac{v^2}{R}\right)$, where v is the speed. Since v is greatest at points x and z, required centripetal force is also greatest at these points.

9. (a), (c), (d) Let ω be the angular speed of the rod + bullet system, immediately after collision. In the absence of any external torque on the system about the pivot, we can use angular momentum conservation principle. Thus, we have

$$mvx = \left(mx^2 + \frac{1}{3}mL^2\right)\omega$$

$$\Rightarrow \quad \omega = \frac{3vx}{L^2 + 3x^2}$$

The value of ω is maximum where $\frac{d\omega}{dx} = 0$. That is, where

$$3v\left[\frac{(L^2 + 3x^2) - x(6x)}{(L^2 + 3x^2)^2}\right] = 0$$

$$\Rightarrow \quad L^2 - 3x^2 = 0 \Rightarrow x = \frac{L}{\sqrt{3}}$$

Inserting this value of x, we get the maximum value of ω as

$$\omega_M = \frac{3v\left(\frac{L}{\sqrt{3}}\right)}{L^2 + L^2} = \frac{\sqrt{3}v}{2L}$$

10. (b), (c) The cut-off wavelength depends on the voltage as

$$\lambda_{\text{cut-off}} = \frac{hc}{eV}$$

So if the voltage is doubled, the cut-off wavelength will be halved.

The wavelength is characteristic of the target metal. It has got nothing to do with the applied voltage.

Reducing the filament current will decrease the number of electrons striking the target, which will result in a lesser number of X-ray photon-emission. In other words, the intensity of the X-rays will reduce.

11. (b), (c) The figure shows the forces acting on the sphere when it is in air, and when it is immersed in liquid. When in air, F is the Coulomb force, ρVg is the weight, where ρ. is the density of the sphere and T is the tension in the sting. For equilibrium, we have

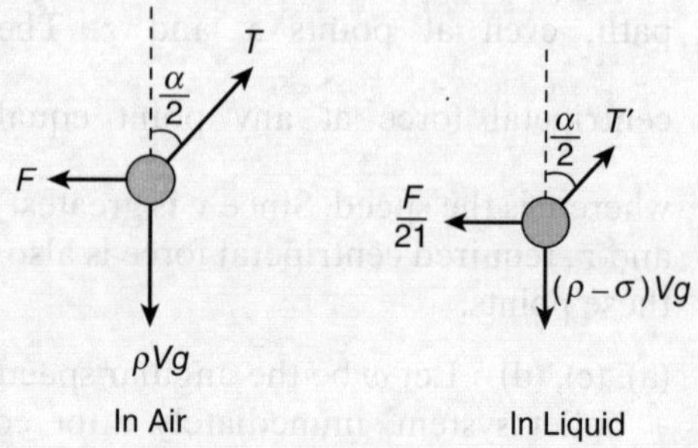

$$T\sin(\alpha/2) = F \text{ and } T\cos(\alpha/2) = \rho Vg$$

$$\Rightarrow \quad \tan(\alpha/2) = \frac{F}{\rho Vg} \quad \text{...(1)}$$

When in liquid, the Coulomb force reduces to $F/21$, the effective weight reduces to $(\rho-\sigma)Vg$, where σ is the density of the liquid, and T' is the tension is the sting. For equilibrium, we have

$$T'\sin(\alpha/2) = F/21$$

and $$T'\cos(\alpha/2) = (\rho-\sigma)Vg$$

$$\Rightarrow \quad \tan(/2) = \frac{F}{21(\rho-\sigma)Vg} \quad \text{...(2)}$$

From the above equations, we have

$$\frac{F}{\rho Vg} = \frac{F}{21(\rho-\sigma)Vg}$$

$$\Rightarrow \quad \rho = 21(\rho-\sigma)$$

$$\Rightarrow \quad \rho = \frac{21}{20}\sigma = \frac{21}{20}(800 \text{ kg/m}^3) = 840 \text{ kg/m}^3$$

Note that if we divide the equations $T\sin(\alpha/2) = F$ and $T'\sin(/2) = F/21$, we get $T' = T/21$. Thus, tension in the string is reduced by a factor 21, when immersed in the liquid.

12. (a), (b), (c), (d) Differentiating the given equation $y = \frac{1}{2}x^2$ with respect to time, we have

$$\frac{dy}{dt} = x\frac{dx}{dt} \Rightarrow v_y = xv_x \quad \text{...(1)}$$

Differentiating again with respect to time, we have

$$\frac{d^2y}{dt^2} = x\frac{d^2y}{dt^2} + \left(\frac{dx}{dt}\right)^2 \Rightarrow a_y = xa_x + v_x^2 \quad \text{...(2)}$$

(a) If $a_x = 1 \text{ m/s}^2$, then Eq. (2) reduces to $a_y = x(1 \text{ m/s}^2) + v_x^2$.

At origin $v_x = 1$ m/s (given). Hence, at the origin

$$a_y = 0(1 \text{ m/s}^2) + (1 \text{ m/s})^2 = 1 \text{ m/s}^2$$

$\Rightarrow$ Option (a) is correct.

(c) At $t = 0$, the particle is at the origin. Hence, from Eq. (1), we have

$$v_y = 0$$

$\Rightarrow$ The particle's velocity points along the x-axis at $t = 0$

$\Rightarrow$ Option (c) is correct.

(b) If $a_x = 0$, then $v_x = 1$m/s always. Eq. (2) then reduces to

$a_y = 1 \text{ m/s}^2$ always $\Rightarrow$ Option (b) is correct.

(d) If $a_x = 0$, then we have already seen that $a_y = 1 \text{ m/s}^2$ always. The value of v_y after $t = 1$ s is $v_y = 0 + (1 \text{ m/s}^2)(1 \text{ m/s}) = 1$ m/s. Now since $v_y = v_y = 1$ m/s, the particle's velocity at $t = 1$ s makes an angle of 45° with the x-axis $\Rightarrow$ Option (d) is correct.

13. (a), (b), (c) The height to which liquid rises in a capillary tube is given by

$$h = \frac{2S\cos\theta}{\rho gr} + \frac{V}{\pi r^2}\left[\begin{matrix}V \text{ is the volume} \\ \text{above the meniscus}\end{matrix}\right]$$

(a) Since V is different for different contact angles θ, the corrections will be different in the two cases $\Rightarrow$ Option (a) is correct.

If we neglect the correction, then we have

$$h = \frac{2(0.075)\cos\theta}{10^3 \times 10 \times (0.2 \times 10^{-3})}\ \text{m}$$

$$= (0.075\ \text{m})\cos\theta = \begin{cases} 7.5\ \text{cm}, & \theta = 0° (T_1) \\ 3.75\ \text{cm}, & \theta = 60° (T_2) \end{cases}$$

(b) In case II, the available height of tube (T_2) is 5 cm whereas it can support water to a height $h = 3.75$ cm. So the water will rise to a height of 3.75 cm $\Rightarrow$ Option (b) is correct.

(c) In case I, the available height of tube (T_1) is 8 cm whereas it can support water to a height $h = 7.5$ cm. So the water will rise to a height of 7.5 cm $\Rightarrow$ Option (c) is correct.

(d) In case I, if the available height of tube (T_1) is 5 cm whereas it can support water to $h = 7.5$ cm, then the available height is insufficient. So water will rise to the available height 5 cm and the meniscus will flatten to adjust the contact angle θ such that

$$5\ \text{cm} = \frac{2S\cos\theta}{\rho g r} \Rightarrow \text{Option (d) is incorrect.}$$

14. (b), (c), (d)

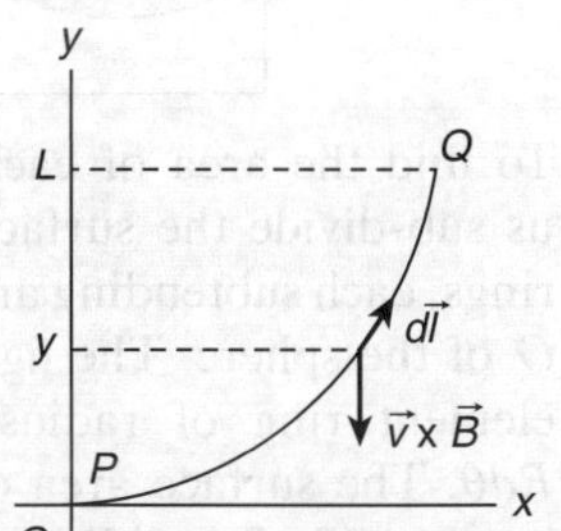

Let us sub-divide the parabolic wire PQ into small elements. The figure shows one such element denoted by $d\mathbf{l}$ at position y above the x-axis. The emf induced across this element wire is

$$d\phi = (\mathbf{v} \times \mathbf{B}) \cdot d\mathbf{l} = \left(v_0 \mathbf{i} \times B_0 \left(1 + \frac{y^\beta}{L^\beta} \right) \mathbf{k} \right) \cdot (dx\mathbf{i} + dy\mathbf{j})$$

$$= -v_0 B_0 \left(1 + \frac{y^\beta}{L^\beta} \right) \mathbf{j} \cdot (dx\mathbf{i} + dy\mathbf{j})$$

$$= -v_0 B_0 \left(1 + \frac{y^\beta}{L^\beta} \right) dy$$

Hence, the total emf across the wire PQ is

$$\Delta\phi = -v_0 B_0 \int_0^L \left(1 + \frac{y^\beta}{L^\beta} \right) dy = -v_0 B_0 \left| y + \frac{y^{\beta+1}}{(\beta+1)L^\beta} \right|_0^L$$

$$= -v_0 B_0 \left(L + \frac{L}{\beta+1} \right) = -\left(\frac{\beta+2}{\beta+1} \right) v_0 B_0 L$$

The –ve sign shows that end Q will be at a lower potential than end P.

(a) For $\beta = 0$, we have

$$|\Delta\phi| = \left(\frac{0+2}{0+1} \right) v_0 B_0 L = 2 v_0 B_0 L v$$

$\Rightarrow$ Option (a) is incorrect.

(b) For $\beta = 2$, we have

$$|\Delta\phi| = \left(\frac{2+2}{2+1} \right) v_0 B_0 L = \frac{4}{3} v_0 B_0 L$$

$\Rightarrow$ Option (b) is correct.

(c) The value of $|\Delta\phi|$ depends only on the projection of the wire on the y-axis. Irrespective of the shape of the wire, as long as its projection on the y-axis lies between $y = 0$ and $y = L$, the value of $|\Delta\phi|$ will remain the same. A wire of length $\sqrt{2}L$ lying along $y = x$ does satisfy this condition $\Rightarrow$ Option (c) is correct.

(d) From the result derived for $\Delta\phi$, we can see that $|\Delta\phi| \propto L$, where L is the projection length of the wire on the y-axis $\Rightarrow$ Option (d) is correct.

15. (b), (c) With switch S_2 open and switch S_1 closed, the circuit is a simple $C-R$ circuit with resistance $R = 30\ \Omega + 70\ \Omega = 100\ \Omega$ and capacitance

$$\frac{1}{C} = \frac{1}{80\ \mu\text{F}} + \frac{1}{80\ \mu\text{F}} + \frac{1}{10\ \mu\text{F}} \Rightarrow C = 8\ \mu\text{F}$$

(a) The instantaneous current in the circuit will be

$$I_0 = \frac{5\ \text{V}}{100\ \Omega} = 50\ \text{mA}$$

$\Rightarrow$ Option (a) is incorrect.

(b) At steady state, the charge on the capacitors (all capacitors will have the same charge since they are in series) will be $Q_0 = (5\ \text{V})(8\ \mu\text{F}) = 40\ \mu\text{C}$. The PD across capacitor $C_1 = 10\ \mu\text{F}$ will be

$$V_1 = \frac{40\ \mu\text{C}}{10\ \mu\text{F}} = 4\ \text{V}$$

$\Rightarrow$ Option (b) is correct.

(c) At the instant when switch S_2 is closed, the PD between points P and Q is $V_P - V_Q = V_1 = 4$ V. Let I be the instantaneous current from Q towards P. Then we have

$$V_Q + 10\ \text{V} - I(30\ \Omega) = V_P$$

$$\Rightarrow I = \frac{(10\ \text{V}) - (V_P - V_Q)}{30\ \Omega} = \frac{10-4}{30}\ \text{A} = 0.2\ \text{A}$$

$\Rightarrow$ Option (c) is correct.

(d) At steady state, let the charge distribution be as shown in the figure. The capacitors $C_3 = 80\ \mu F$ and $C_4 = 80\ \mu F$ have been replaced by one single capacitor of capacitance $40\ \mu F$. The resistances have been omitted from the figure because at steady state there is no current in the circuit. Writing the equations for the outer loop and the left loop, we have

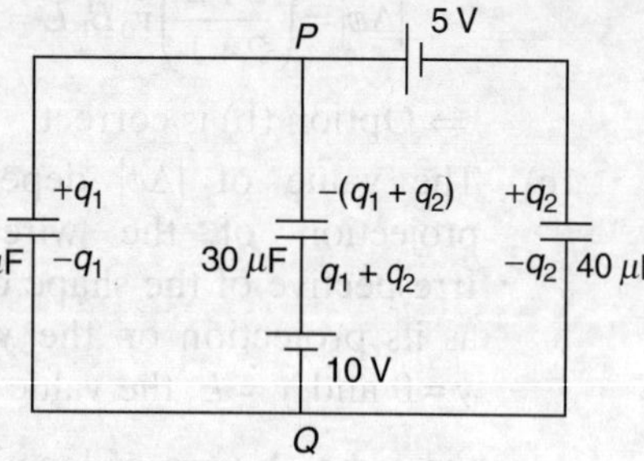

$$5\ \text{V} - \frac{q_1}{10\ \mu F} + \frac{q_2}{40\ \mu F} = 0$$

$$\Rightarrow \quad 4q_1 - q_2 = 200\ \mu C \qquad \ldots(1)$$

and $$10\ \text{V} - \frac{q_1 + q_2}{30\ \mu F} - \frac{q_1}{10\ \mu F} = 0$$

$$\Rightarrow \quad 4q_1 + q_2 = 300\ \mu C \qquad \ldots(2)$$

Solving the above equations gives $q_1 = 62.5\ \mu C$ and $q_2 = 50\ \mu C$. Hence, the PD across points P and Q is

$$V_{PQ} = \frac{q_1}{10\ \mu F} = 6.25\ \text{V}$$

$\Rightarrow$ Option (d) is incorrect.

16. (a), (b)

(a) In this case, the charged sphere lies entirely inside the cylinder. Hence, the electric flux through the cylindrical surface is

$$\phi = \frac{Q}{\epsilon_0} \Rightarrow \text{Option (a) is correct.}$$

(b) If $\left(\frac{h}{2}\right)^2 + r^2 \le R^2$, then the cylinder will lie inside the sphere (see figure).

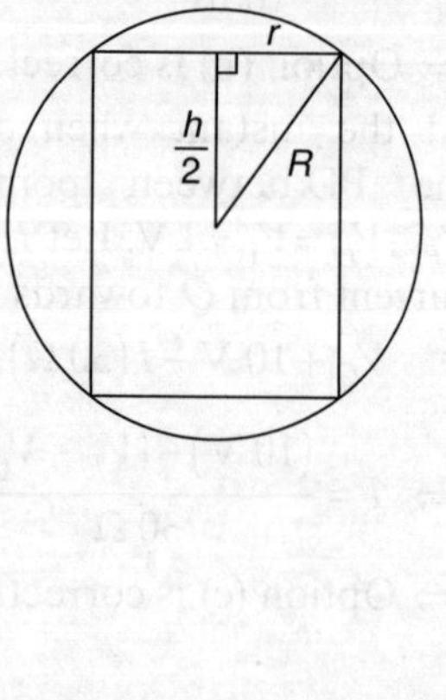

In this case, the cylinder lies entirely inside the charged sphere since

$$\left(\frac{h}{2}\right)^2 + r^2 = \left(\frac{4R}{5}\right)^2 + \left(\frac{3R}{5}\right)^2 = R^2$$

Hence, the electric flux through the cylindrical surface is $\phi = 0 \Rightarrow$ Option (b) is correct.

In both options (c) and (d), only a portion of the sphere lies inside the cylinder (see figure). To find the electric flux through the cylindrical surface, we first need to find the surface area of the portion of the sphere enclosed within the cylinder. Each enclosed half subtends angle 2α, where $\sin\alpha = \frac{r}{R}$.

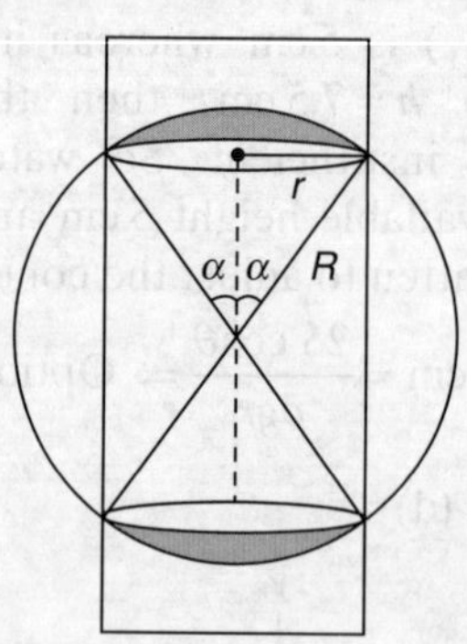

To find the area of each enclosed half, let us sub-divide the surface into thin circular rings, each subtending angle $d\theta$ at the centre O of the sphere. The figure shows one such element ring of radius $R\sin\theta$ and width $Rd\theta$. The surface area of this element ring is $dA = (2\pi R\sin\theta)Rd\theta$. Hence, the total surface area of one enclosed half is

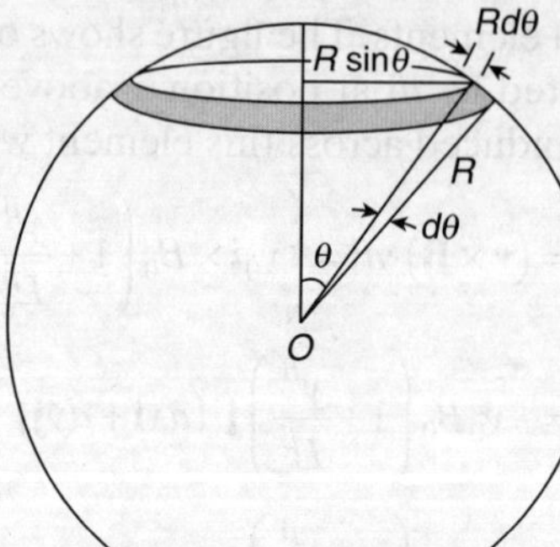

$$A = \int_0^{\alpha} (2\pi R\sin\theta)\, Rd\theta = 2\pi R^2(1 - \cos\alpha),$$

where $\sin\alpha = \frac{r}{R}$

Now, the total charge enclosed by the cylinder is

$$Q_{\text{encl}} = \left(\frac{2A}{4\pi R^2}\right)Q = (1-\cos\alpha)Q$$
$$= \left(1-\sqrt{1-\frac{r^2}{R^2}}\right)Q$$

Hence, the electric flux through the cylindrical surface is

$$\phi = \frac{Q_{\text{encl}}}{\epsilon_0} = \frac{Q}{\epsilon_0}\left(1-\sqrt{1-\frac{r^2}{R^2}}\right)$$

(c) Putting $r = 3R/5$, we have $\phi = \frac{3Q}{5\epsilon_0} \Rightarrow$ Option (c) is incorrect.

(d) Putting $r = 4R/5$, we have $\phi = \frac{4Q}{5\epsilon_0} \Rightarrow$ Option (d) is incorrect.

17. (a), (c) The equation representing line joining point1 (T_0, V_0) and point2 $(2T_0, 2V_0)$ is

$$V - V_0 = \left(\frac{2V_0 - V_0}{2T_0 - T_0}\right)(T - T_0) = \left(\frac{V_0}{T_0}\right)(T - T_0)$$

$$\Rightarrow \quad V - V_0 = \left(\frac{V_0}{T_0}\right)T - V_0$$

$$\Rightarrow \quad V = \left(\frac{V_0}{T_0}\right)T \qquad \ldots(1)$$

This represents an isobaric process. The pressure all along this path is

$$P_{1\to2} = \frac{\mu RT}{V} = \frac{RT_0}{V_0} \quad [\mu = 1 \text{ given}]$$

The equation representing line joining point3 $(T_0, 2V_0)$ and point4 $(T_0/2, V_0)$ is

$$V - 2V_0 = \left(\frac{2V_0 - V_0}{T_0 - T_0/2}\right)(T - T_0) = \left(\frac{2V_0}{T_0}\right)(T - T_0)$$

$$\Rightarrow V - 2V_0 = \left(\frac{2V_0}{T_0}\right)T - 2V_0$$

$$\Rightarrow V = \left(\frac{2V_0}{T_0}\right)T \qquad \ldots(2)$$

This also represents an isobaric process. The pressure all along this path is

$$P_{3\to4} = \frac{\mu RT}{V} = \frac{RT_0}{2V_0} \quad [\mu = 1 \text{ given}]$$

(a) The work done by the gas for the various processes are

$$W_{1\to2} = P_{1\to2}\Delta V = \frac{RT_0}{V_0}(2V_0 - V_0) = RT_0$$

$$W_{2\to3} = 0 = W_{4\to1} \quad \text{[Both are isochoric processes]}$$

and $$W_{3\to4} = P_{3\to4}\Delta V = \frac{RT_0}{2V_0}(V_0 - 2V_0)$$
$$= -\frac{1}{2}RT_0$$

Hence, $$W_{\text{cycle}} = (RT_0) + \left(-\frac{1}{2}RT_0\right) = \frac{1}{2}RT_0$$

$\Rightarrow$ Option (a) is correct.

(b) The given thermodynamic process consists only of isochoric and isobaric processes $\Rightarrow$ Option (b) is incorrect.

(c), (d) The heat transfer for the various processes are

$$Q_{1\to2} = \mu c_P \Delta T = \frac{5}{2}R(2T_0 - T_0) = \frac{5}{2}RT_0$$

$$Q_{2\to3} = \mu c_V \Delta T = \frac{3}{2}R(T_0 - 2T_0) = -\frac{3}{2}RT_0$$

and $$Q_{3\to4} = \mu c_P \Delta T = \frac{5}{2}R(T_0/2 - T_0) = -\frac{5}{4}RT_0$$

Hence, we have

$$\left|\frac{Q_{1\to2}}{Q_{2\to3}}\right| = \frac{5}{3} \Rightarrow \text{Option (c) is correct.}$$

and $$\left|\frac{Q_{1\to2}}{Q_{4\to4}}\right| = \frac{1}{2} \Rightarrow \text{Option (d) is incorrect.}$$

18. (b), (c), (d) Let r be the radius of curvature of the two convex surfaces of the lens. The lens can be treated as a combination of two plano-convex lenses of focal length given by

$$\frac{1}{f_1} = (n_1 - 1)\frac{1}{r} \text{ and } \frac{1}{f_2} = (n_2 - 1)\frac{1}{r}$$

The combined focal length is given by

$$\frac{1}{f_{\text{com}}} = \frac{1}{f_1} + \frac{1}{f_2} = \frac{n_1 + n_2 - 2}{r}$$

It is given that $f_{\text{com}} = f$ when $n_1 = n_2 = n$ and $f_{\text{com}} = f + \Delta f$ when $n_1 = n, n_2 = n + \Delta n$. Thus, we have

$$\frac{1}{f} = \frac{2n-2}{r} \qquad \ldots(1)$$

and $$\frac{1}{f+\Delta f} = \frac{2n-2+\Delta n}{r} \qquad \ldots(2)$$

Subtracting the two equations, we have

$$\frac{1}{f}-\frac{1}{f+\Delta f}=-\frac{\Delta n}{r}$$

$$\Rightarrow \quad \frac{\Delta f}{f(f+\Delta f)}=-\frac{\Delta n}{r}$$

$$\Rightarrow \quad \frac{\Delta f}{f}=-\frac{\Delta n(f+\Delta f)}{r}$$

$$\Rightarrow \quad \frac{\Delta f}{f}=-\frac{\Delta n}{2n-2+\Delta n} \text{ [Using equation (2)]}$$

$$\Rightarrow \quad \frac{\Delta f}{f}=-\frac{\Delta n}{2(n-1)} \qquad \ldots(3)$$

[Since $\Delta n \ll n$]

(a) Let us write equation (3) as

$$\left|\frac{\Delta f}{f}\right|=\frac{\Delta n}{n}\times\frac{n}{2(n-1)}=$$

Now we need to check which is greater, n or $2(n-1)$. To do so, let us check the value of

$$n-2(n-1)=2-n>0 \text{ [Since } n<2 \text{ given]}$$

$$\Rightarrow n>2(n-1)$$

$$\Rightarrow \frac{n}{2(n-1)}>1$$

$$\Rightarrow \left|\frac{\Delta f}{f}\right|>\frac{\Delta n}{n} \Rightarrow \text{Option (a) is incorrect.}$$

(b) Putting the given values in equation (1), we have

$$|\Delta f|=\frac{f\Delta n}{2(n-1)}=\frac{(20\text{ cm})10^{-3}}{2(1.5-1)}=0.02\text{ cm}$$

$\Rightarrow$ Option (b) is correct.

(c) The negative sign in equation (3) indicates that Δf and Δn are of opposite signs. In other words, when one increases, the other decreases $\Rightarrow$ Option (c) is correct.

(d) From equation (3), we can see that the relation between $\frac{\Delta f}{f}$ and $\frac{\Delta n}{n}$ is independent of the value of $r \Rightarrow$ Option (d) is correct.

19. (a), (b), (c)

(a) $$[\text{Linear momentum}]=\frac{[\text{Angular momentum}]}{[\text{Moment arm}]}$$

$\Rightarrow$ Option (a) is correct.

(b) $$[\text{Energy}]=\frac{\left[(\text{Linear momentum})^2\right]}{[\text{Mass}]}=\left[L^{-2}\right]$$

$\Rightarrow$ Option (b) is correct.

(c) $$[\text{Force}]=\frac{[\text{Energy}]}{[\text{Distance}]}=\left[L^{-3}\right]$$

$\Rightarrow$ Option (c) is incorrect.

(d) $$[\text{Power}]=[\text{Force}][\text{Velocity}]$$

$$=[\text{Force}]\times\frac{[\text{Linear momentum}]}{[\text{Mass}]}$$

$$=\left[L^{-4}\right]$$

$\Rightarrow$ Option (d) is incorrect.

20. (b), (c)

(a) Voltmeters need to have a large resistance. Let R_1 be a resistance connected in series with the galvanometer to convert it into the required voltmeter (see figure). When full-scale deflection current 2 μA flows through the voltmeter, the voltmeter scale should measure a voltage of 100 mV. Thus, we have

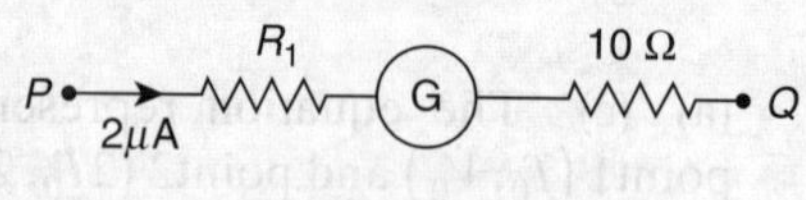

Voltmeter

$$2\,\mu\text{A}(R_1+10\,\Omega)=100\text{ mV}$$

$$\Rightarrow R_1=50000\,\Omega-10\,\Omega=49990\,\Omega\approx 50\,k\Omega$$

$\Rightarrow$ Option (a) is incorrect.

(b) Ammeters need to have a small resistance. Let R_2 be a resistance connected in parallel with the galvanometer to convert it into the required ammeter (see figure). When 1 mA flows through the ammeter, only 2 μA flows through the galvanometer and the remaining current 1 mA – 2 μA = 1000 μA – 2 μA = 998 μA flows through the parallel resistor. Thus, we have

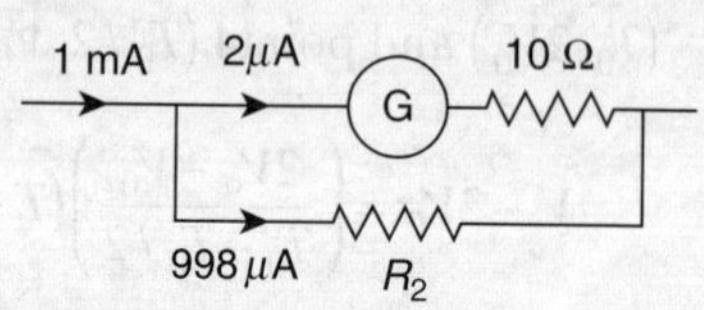

Ammeter

$$(2\,\mu\text{A})(10\,\Omega)=(998\,\mu\text{A})R_2$$

$$\Rightarrow R_2=\frac{20}{998}\,\Omega\approx 20\text{ m}\Omega$$

$\Rightarrow$ Option (b) is correct.

(c) The figure shows the arrangement for the Ohm's law experiment. The voltmeter and the ammeter have resistances $R_1=50\text{ k}\Omega$ and $R_2=20\text{ m}\Omega$, respectively. Let I_1, I_2 be the currents through the voltmeter and the resistance $R=1000\,\Omega$. Then, we have

$$I_1(1\,\text{k}\Omega) = I_2(50\,\text{k}\Omega) \Rightarrow I_1 = 50I_2$$

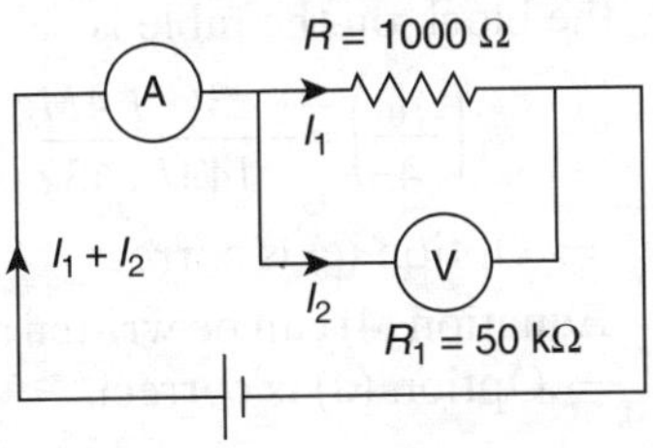

Ohm's law experiment

Now, the voltmeter reads voltage equal $I_2(50\,\text{k}\Omega)$, and the ammeter reads current equal $I_1 + I_2 = 51I_2$. Hence, the measured resistance is

$$R_{\text{measured}} = \frac{I_2(50\,\text{k}\Omega)}{51I_2} = \frac{50}{51}(1\,\text{k}\Omega) = 980.4\,\Omega$$

$\Rightarrow$ Option (c) is correct.

(d) The emf or the internal resistance of the cell has no implication on the measured value of R, which in this case will still be equal to $980.4\,\Omega \Rightarrow$ Option (d) is incorrect.

21. (a), (c), (d)

(a) The figure shows the forces acting on the rod when it is crossing angular position θ from the vertical. If ω is the instantaneous angular velocity of the rod, then from the mechanical energy conservation principle, we have

$$\frac{1}{2}\left(\frac{ML^2}{3}\right)\omega^2 = Mg\frac{L}{2}(1-\cos\theta)$$

$$\Rightarrow \omega^2 = \frac{3g}{L}(1-\cos\theta) \quad \text{...(1)}$$

At $\theta = 60°$, $\omega = \sqrt{\frac{3g}{2L}} \Rightarrow$ Option (a) is correct.

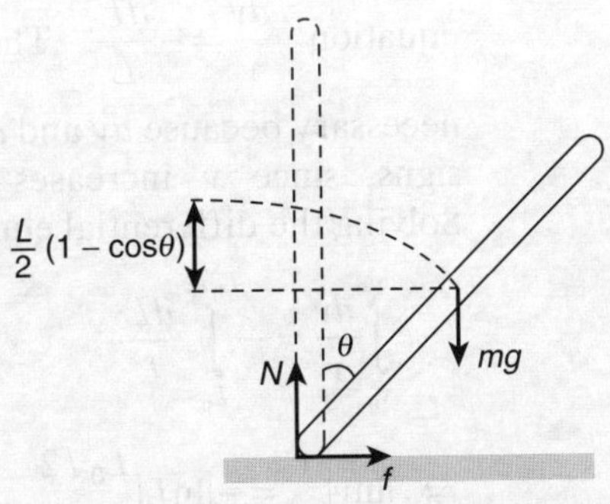

(b) Differentiating equation (1) with respect to θ, we have

$$2\omega\frac{d\omega}{d\theta} = \frac{3g}{L}\sin\theta$$

$$\Rightarrow \alpha = \frac{3g}{2L}\sin\theta \quad \text{...(2)}$$

At $\theta = 60°$, $\alpha = \frac{3\sqrt{3}g}{4L} \Rightarrow$ Option (b) is incorrect.

(c) The centre of mass of the rod is moving in a circular path of radius $L/2$. Thus, the centre of mass has a radial and a tangential acceleration component (see figure) given by

$$a_r = \omega^2\frac{L}{2} = \frac{3g}{2}(1-\cos\theta) \text{ and}$$

$$a_t = \alpha\frac{L}{2} = \frac{3g}{4}\sin\theta$$

At $\theta = 60°$, $a_r = \frac{3g}{4} \Rightarrow$ Option (c) is correct.

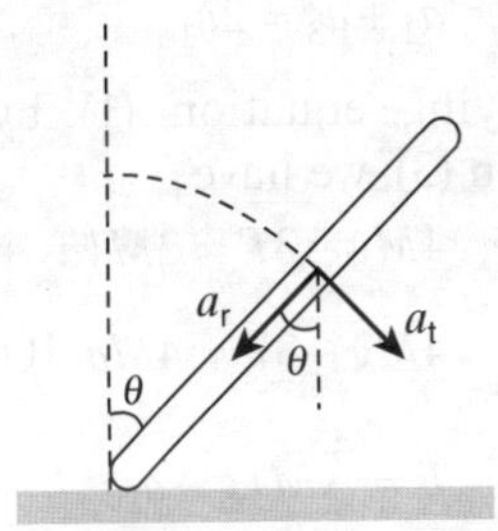

(d) The vertical component of the acceleration of the centre of mass of the rod is

$$a_v = a_r\cos\theta + a_t\sin\theta$$

$$= \frac{3g}{2}(1-\cos\theta)\cos\theta + \frac{3g}{4}\sin^2\theta$$

At $\theta = 60°$, $a_v = \frac{3g}{8} + \frac{9g}{16} = \frac{15g}{16}$.

Using dynamics along the vertical, we have

$$Mg - N = Ma_v$$

$$\Rightarrow N = Mg - \frac{15}{16}Mg - \frac{1}{16}Mg$$

$\Rightarrow$ Option (d) is correct.

22. (a), (c), (d)

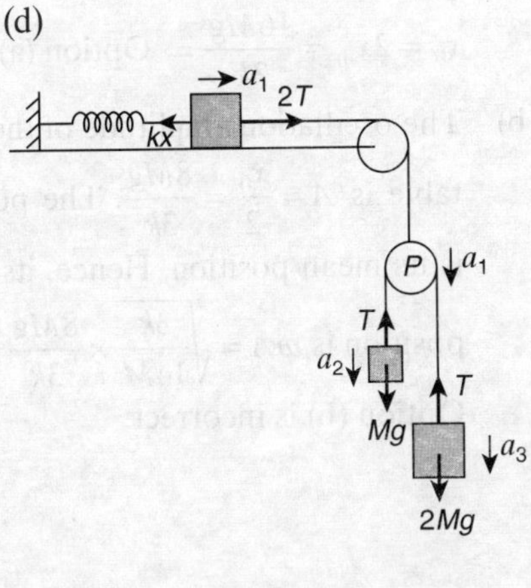

The figure shows the forces acting on the three blocks. The tensions in the two strings are T and $2T$ and x is the elongation in the spring at any instant. Using dynamics, we have

$$2T - kx = 2Ma_1 \quad \ldots(1)$$

$$Mg - T = Ma_2 \quad \ldots(2)$$

and $$2Mg - T = 2Ma_3 \quad \ldots(3)$$

We have one more equation. With respect to pulley P, the accelerations of the two hanging blocks are $a_2 - a_1$ and $a_3 - a_1$ in the vertically downward direction. These accelerations must have the same magnitude and opposite directions because as seen from pulley P, if one block appears to be moving down, the other will appear to be moving up. Hence, we have

$$a_2 - a_1 = -(a_3 - a_1)$$

$$\Rightarrow \quad a_2 + a_3 = 2a_1 \quad \ldots(4)$$

Multiplying equation (1) by 2 and adding to equation (3), we have

$$4Mg - 3T = 2M(a_2 + a_3)$$

$$\Rightarrow \quad 4Mg - 3T = 4Ma_1 \text{ [Using equation (4)]}$$

$$\Rightarrow \quad T = \frac{4}{3}M(g - a_1)$$

Putting the above result in equation (1), we have

$$\frac{8}{3}M(g - a_1) - kx = 2Ma_1$$

$$\Rightarrow \quad \frac{14}{3}Ma_1 = \frac{8}{3}Mg - kx = -k\left(x - \frac{8Mg}{3k}\right)$$

$$\Rightarrow \quad a_1 = -\frac{3k}{14M}\left(x - \frac{8Mg}{3k}\right)$$

The above equation shows that the block on the table executes SHM with angular frequency $\omega = \sqrt{\frac{3k}{14M}}$ about the mean position $x_m = \frac{8Mg}{3k}$

(a) The maximum elongation in the spring is $x_0 = 2x_m = \frac{16Mg}{3k} \Rightarrow$ Option (a) is correct.

(b) The oscillation amplitude of the block on the table is $A = \frac{x_0}{2} = \frac{8Mg}{3k}$. The position $x = \frac{x_0}{2}$ is its mean position. Hence, its speed at this position is $\omega A = \sqrt{\frac{3k}{14M}} \times \frac{8Mg}{3k} = 8g\sqrt{\frac{M}{14k}} \Rightarrow$ Option (b) is incorrect.

(c) At position $x = \frac{x_0}{4} = \frac{4Mg}{3k}$, the acceleration of the block on the table is

$$a_1\left(\frac{x_0}{4}\right) = -\frac{3k}{14M}\left(\frac{4Mg}{3k} - \frac{8Mg}{3k}\right) = \frac{2}{7}g$$

$\Rightarrow$ Option (c) is correct.

(d) Equation (4) can be written as $a_2 - a_1 = a_1 - a_3$ $\Rightarrow$ Option (d) is correct.

23. (b), (d)

(a) At any instant when the velocity of the particle is v and the length of the tube is L, the time between two successive collisions between the particle and the piston is $T = \frac{2L}{v}$. The collision frequency or the rate of collision is $f = \frac{1}{T} = \frac{v}{2L} \Rightarrow$ Option (a) is incorrect.

(b) Let v and v' be the velocities of the particle before and after collision with the piston. Since the collision is elastic, we have

$$v + V = v' - V$$

$$\Rightarrow \quad v' = v + 2V$$

Hence, we see that the velocity of the particle increases by $2V$ after each collision with the piston $\Rightarrow$ Option (b) is correct.

(c) In moving distance dL, the piston takes time $dt = dL / V$. Within this time, the number of collisions between the particle and the piston equals $= \frac{v}{2L} \times \frac{dL}{V} = \frac{vdL}{2LV}$. The change in velocity of the particle in so many collisions will be $dv = 2V \times \frac{vdL}{2LV} = v\frac{dL}{L} \Rightarrow$ Option (c) is incorrect.

(d) From the above, we have the differential equation $\frac{dv}{v} = -\frac{dL}{L}$. The minus sign is necessary because dv and dL are of opposite signs, since v increases as L decreases. Solving the differential equation, we have

$$\int_{v_0}^{v} \frac{dv}{v} = -\int_{L_0}^{L_0/2} \frac{dL}{L}$$

$$\Rightarrow \quad |\ln v|_{v_0}^{v} = -|\ln L|_{L_0}^{L_0/2}$$

$$\Rightarrow \quad \ln\left(\frac{v}{v_0}\right) = \ln 2$$

$\Rightarrow v = 2v_0$

Since velocity of the particle has doubled, its kinetic energy will increase by a factor of four ⇒ Option (d) is correct.

24. (a), (c)

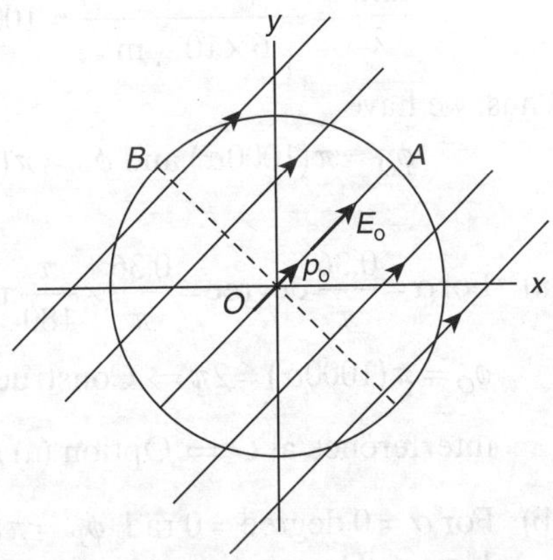

(a) The electric potential due to the dipole varies along the circumference. It is greatest equal to $\dfrac{p_0}{4\pi\epsilon_0 R^2}$ at point A, and least equal to 0 at point B. If we want to have a uniform potential all along the circumference, then the uniform electric field will have to be directed such that the potential due to this field is smallest at point A and greatest at point B. This will be possible if the electric field is directed along the dipole vector (see figure).

If we take the potential due to the uniform electric field to be V_0 at the centre O of the circle, then the potential equals $V_0 - RE_0$ at point A, and V_0 at point B. Thus, the combined potentials at points A and B are, respectively

$$V_A = V_0 - RE_0 + \frac{p_0}{4\pi\epsilon_0 R^2} \text{ and } V_B = V_0$$

Equating the two, we have

$$V_0 - RE_0 + \frac{p_0}{4\pi\epsilon_0 R^2} = V_0$$

$$\Rightarrow 4\pi\epsilon_0 R^3 E_0 = p_0$$

$$\Rightarrow R = \left(\frac{p_0}{4\pi\epsilon_0 E_0}\right)^{1/3}$$

⇒ Option (a) is correct.

(b) The total electric field at point A is

$$E_0 + \frac{2p_0}{4\pi\epsilon_0 R^3} = E_0 + 2E_0 = 3E_0$$

⇒ Option (b) is incorrect.

(c) The total electric field at point B is

E_0 along $(\mathbf{i}+\mathbf{j})$ direction $+\dfrac{p_0}{4\pi\epsilon_0 R^3}$ along $-(\mathbf{i}+\mathbf{j})$ direction

⇒ E_0 along $(\mathbf{i}+\mathbf{j})$ direction $+E_0$ along $-(\mathbf{i}+\mathbf{j})$ direction $= 0$ ⇒ Option (c) is correct.

(d) The electric field due to the dipole is different at different points along the circle ⇒ Option (d) is incorrect.

25. (a), (c), (d)

(a) The adiabatic exponent of the gas mixture is

$$\gamma = \frac{5\left(\dfrac{5R}{2}\right)+1\left(\dfrac{7R}{2}\right)}{5\left(\dfrac{3R}{2}\right)+1\left(\dfrac{5R}{2}\right)} = \frac{32}{20} = 1.6$$

The pressure of the compressed gas is given by

$$P\left(\frac{V_0}{4}\right)^{\gamma} = P_0 V_0^{\gamma} = \frac{32}{20} = 1.6$$

$$\Rightarrow P = 4^{1.6} P_0 = 2^{3.2} P_0 = 9.2 P_0$$

Hence, work done by the gas is

$$W = \frac{\Delta(PV)}{\gamma - 1} = \frac{(9.2P_0)\left(\dfrac{V_0}{4}\right) - P_0 V_0}{1.6 - 1}$$

$$= -\frac{1.3}{0.6} P_0 V_0 = -\frac{13}{6}(6RT_0) = -13RT_0$$

⇒ Option (a) is correct.

(b) The temperature of the compressed gas is given by

$$T = \frac{(9.2P_0)\left(\dfrac{V_0}{4}\right)}{\mu R} = 2.3\frac{P_0 V_0}{\mu R} = 2.3T_0$$

The total kinetic energy or the internal energy of the gas after compression is

$$U = \mu c_V T = \frac{6R(2.3T_0)}{1.6 - 1} = 23RT_0$$

⇒ Option (b) is incorrect.

(c) We have already calculated the final pressure as $9.2P_0$ ⇒ Option (c) is correct.

(d) We have already calculated the adiabatic exponent of the gas mixture as $\gamma = 1.6 \Rightarrow$ Option (d) is correct.

26. (a), (c) In case I, the depth of the image is given by

$$H_1 = \frac{H}{n} = \frac{30\text{ cm}}{1.5} = 20\text{ cm}$$

In case II, the depth of the image is given by

$$\frac{1}{(-H_2)} - \frac{n}{(-H)} = \frac{1-n}{(-R)}$$

$$\Rightarrow \quad \frac{1}{H_2} = \frac{n}{H} - \frac{n-1}{R} = \frac{1.5}{30\text{ cm}} - \frac{1.5-1}{300\text{ cm}}$$

$$= \frac{1}{20\text{ cm}} - \frac{1}{600\text{ cm}} = \frac{29}{600\text{ cm}}$$

$$\Rightarrow \quad H_2 = \frac{600\text{ cm}}{29} = 20.70\text{ cm}$$

In case III, the depth of the image is given by

$$\frac{1}{(-H_3)} - \frac{n}{(-H)} = \frac{1-n}{(+R)}$$

$$\Rightarrow \quad \frac{1}{H_2} = \frac{n}{H} + \frac{n-1}{R} = \frac{1.5}{30\text{ cm}} + \frac{1.5-1}{300\text{ cm}}$$

$$= \frac{1}{20\text{ cm}} + \frac{1}{600\text{ cm}} = \frac{31}{600\text{ cm}}$$

$$\Rightarrow \quad H_2 = \frac{600\text{ cm}}{31} = 19.35\text{ cm}$$

(a) We see that $H_2 > H_1 \Rightarrow$ Option (a) is correct.
(b) We see that $H_3 < H_1 \Rightarrow$ Option (b) is incorrect.
(c) We see that $H_2 > H_3 \Rightarrow$ Option (c) is correct.
(d) We see that $|H_2 - H_1| = 0.65\text{ cm} \Rightarrow$ Option (d) is incorrect.

27. (c)

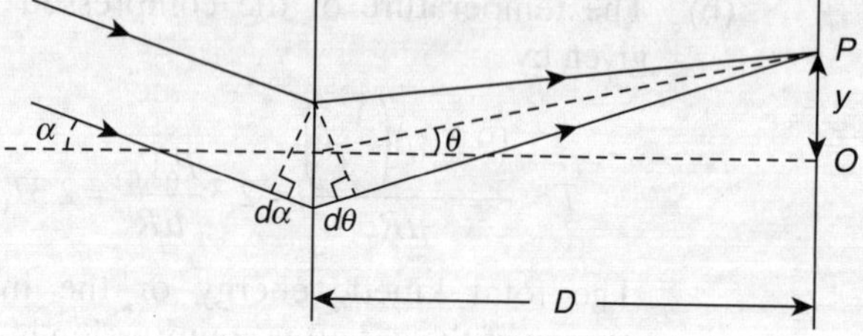

The angular position of point P with respect to the slits (see figure) is $\theta = \frac{y}{D} = \frac{11\text{ mm}}{1\text{ m}} = \frac{11}{1000}$.

The path differences between the two rays arriving at O and at P are respectively

$$\Delta_O = d(\alpha) \text{ and } \Delta_P = d(\alpha + \theta)$$

The phase differences between the two rays arriving at O and at P are respectively

$$\phi_O = \frac{2\pi d}{\lambda}(\alpha) \text{ and } \phi_P = \frac{2\pi d}{\lambda}(\alpha + \theta)$$

Putting the values, we have

$$\frac{2\pi d}{\lambda} = \frac{2\pi(3\times 10^{-4}\text{ m})}{6\times 10^{-7}\text{ m}} = 1000\pi$$

Thus, we have

$$\phi_O = \pi(1000\alpha) \text{ and } \phi_P = \pi(1000\alpha + 11)$$

(a) For $\alpha = \frac{0.36}{\pi}\text{degree} = \frac{0.36}{\pi} \times \frac{\pi}{180}\text{ rad} = \frac{2}{1000}\text{ rad}$,

$\phi_O = \pi(1000\alpha) = 2\pi \Rightarrow$ Constructive interference at $O \Rightarrow$ Option (a) is incorrect.

(b) For $\alpha = 0$ degree $= 0$ rad, $\phi_P = \pi(1000\alpha + 11) = 11\pi \Rightarrow$ Destructive interference at $P \Rightarrow$ Option (b) is incorrect.

(c) For $\alpha = \frac{0.36}{\pi}\text{degree} = \frac{0.36}{\pi} \times \frac{\pi}{180}\text{ rad} = \frac{2}{1000}\text{ rad}$,

$\phi_P = \pi(1000\alpha + 11) = 13\pi \Rightarrow$ Destructive interference at $P \Rightarrow$ Option (c) is correct.

(d) Fringe spacing is given by $\beta = \frac{\lambda D}{d} \Rightarrow$ It has nothing to with $\alpha \Rightarrow$ Option (d) is incorrect.

28. (a), (d)

(a) The wavelengths of the absorbed and emitted photons are, respectively

$$\frac{1}{\lambda_a} = R\left(\frac{1}{1^2} - \frac{1}{4^2}\right) = \frac{15}{16}R \text{ and}$$

$$\frac{1}{\lambda_e} = R\left(\frac{1}{m^2} - \frac{1}{4^2}\right)$$

Using the condition $\frac{\lambda_a}{\lambda_e} = \frac{1}{5} \Rightarrow \frac{5}{\lambda_e} = \frac{1}{\lambda_a}$, we have

$$5R\left(\frac{1}{m^2} - \frac{1}{16}\right) = \frac{15}{16}R$$

$$\Rightarrow \frac{1}{m^2} = \frac{1}{16} + \frac{3}{16} \text{ gives } m = 2$$

$\Rightarrow$ Option (a) is correct.

(b) The wavelength of the emitted photons is given by

$$\frac{1}{\lambda_e} = R\left(\frac{1}{2^2} - \frac{1}{4^2}\right) = \frac{3R}{16}$$

$$\Rightarrow \quad \lambda_e = \frac{16}{3\left(1.1\times10^7 \text{ m}^{-1}\right)} = 485 \text{ nm}$$

$\Rightarrow$ Option (b) is incorrect.

(c) The momentum carried by the absorbed and emitted photons are, respectively, $\frac{h}{\lambda_a}$ and $\frac{h}{\lambda_e}$.

The change in momentum of the atom during photon absorption or emission equals the momentum of the absorbed or the emitted photon, respectively. Hence, we have

$$\frac{\Delta p_a}{\Delta p_e} = \frac{h/\lambda_a}{h/\lambda_e} = \frac{\lambda_e}{\lambda_a} = 5$$

$\Rightarrow$ Option (c) is incorrect.

(d) The kinetic energy K of the orbiting electron depends on the state n of the atom, as $(n) \propto \frac{1}{n^2}$. Hence, we have

$$\frac{K(2)}{K(1)} = \frac{1/2^2}{1/1^2} = \frac{1}{4}$$

$\Rightarrow$ Option (d) is correct.

Single Digit Answer

1. Light from source S forms image A after refracting at plane surface LM and another image B after refracting at plane surface MN (see figure).

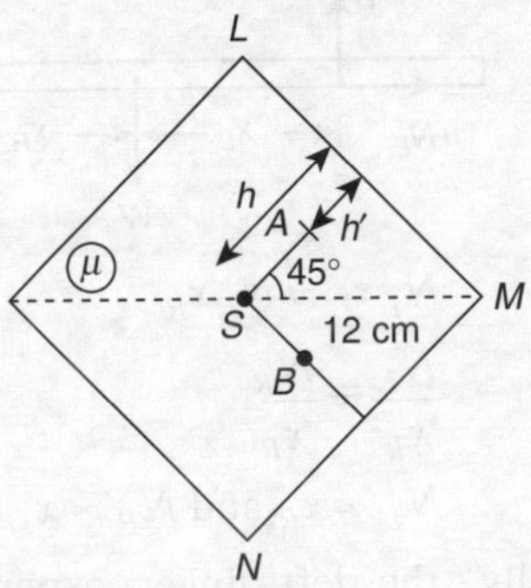

The distance of S from surface LM is $h = 12$ cm cos (45°) $= 6\sqrt{2}$ cm, and the distance of image point A from surface LM is $h' = \frac{h}{\mu} = \frac{6\sqrt{2} \text{ cm}}{4/3} = \frac{9}{\sqrt{2}}$ cm.

The image point B is also at the same distance from the surface MN. Hence, the distance between the image points A, B is

$$AB = 2\times SA \sin(45°) = 2(h - h')\sin(45°)$$

$$= 2\left(6\sqrt{2} - \frac{9}{\sqrt{2}}\right)\frac{1}{\sqrt{2}} \text{ cm} = 3 \text{ cm}$$

2. The figure shows two points on a streamline, point (1) is far away from the train while point (2) is near the train. The air velocity relative to the train is v_t at point (1), and say v at point (2). Using mass continuity, we have

$$v_t(4S_t) = v(4S_t - S_t)$$

$$\Rightarrow \quad v = \frac{4}{3}v_t$$

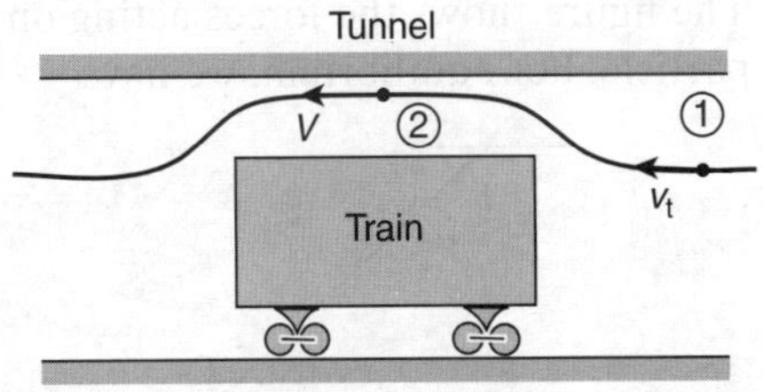

The pressure at point (1) is P_o, and say P at point (2). Using Bernoulli's principle, we have

$$P + \frac{1}{2}\rho v^2 = P_0 + \frac{1}{2}\rho v_t^2$$

Inserting the value of v, we have

$$P_0 - P = \frac{1}{2}\rho\left(\frac{16}{9}v_t^2 - v_t^2\right) = \frac{7}{18}\rho v_t^2$$

Hence, $N = 9$.

3. The electric field between the discs is $= \frac{V}{d}$. If n is the number of electrons on each drop, then

$$\rho\left(\frac{4}{3}\pi r^3\right)g = ne\left(\frac{V}{d}\right)$$

$$\Rightarrow \quad n = \frac{4\pi}{3}\frac{\rho r^3 gd}{eV}$$

$$= \frac{4\pi}{3}\times\frac{900\times\left(8\times10^{-7}\right)^3\times10\times0.01}{1.6\times10^{-19}\times200} = 6$$

4. The weight of the balloon + passengers + sandbags is balanced by the force of buoyancy. If V is the volume of the balloon, then we have

$$480g = \rho(100\text{m})Vg \qquad \ldots(1)$$

and $\quad (480 - N)g = \rho(150\text{m})Vg \qquad \ldots(2)$

Dividing the two equations, we have

$$\frac{480-N}{480} = \frac{\rho(150\text{m})}{\rho(100\text{m})} = \frac{\rho_0 e^{\frac{-150}{6000}}}{\rho_0 e^{\frac{-100}{6000}}}$$

$$\Rightarrow \quad \frac{480-N}{480} = e^{\frac{-50}{6000}}$$

$$\Rightarrow \quad N = 480\left[1 - e^{\frac{-1}{120}}\right]$$

$$\Rightarrow \quad N = 480 \times \frac{1}{120} = 4 \text{ } [e^x = 1 + x \text{ for small } x]$$

5. The elective field due to a dipole at distance d along its axis has magnitude $E = \frac{2Kp}{d^3}$, where $K = \frac{1}{4\pi\varepsilon_0}$.

The figure shows the forces acting on the changed particle. For equilibrium, we have

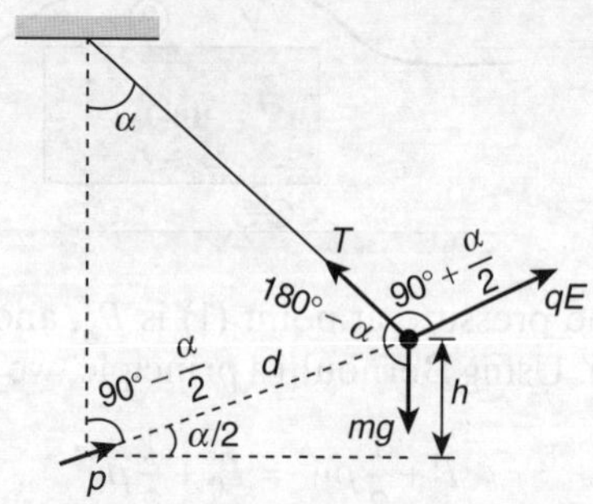

$$\frac{qE}{\sin(180° - \alpha)} = \frac{mg}{\sin(900° + \alpha/2)}$$

$$\Rightarrow \quad \frac{qE}{\sin(\alpha)} = \frac{mg}{\cos(\alpha/2)}$$

$$\Rightarrow \quad qE = 2mg\sin(\alpha/2)$$

$$\Rightarrow \quad \frac{2Kpq}{d^3} = 2mg\left(\frac{h}{d}\right)$$

$$\Rightarrow \quad \frac{Kpq}{d^2} = mgh \qquad \text{...(1)}$$

The electric potential due to a dipole at distance d along its axis is $E = \frac{Kp}{d^2}$. Now using the Work–Energy Theorem, we have

$$W = \Delta PE_{gr} + \Delta PE_{elec}$$

$$\Rightarrow \quad W = mgh + qV$$

$$\Rightarrow \quad W = mgh + \frac{Kpq}{d^2}$$

$$\Rightarrow \quad W = mgh + mgh \text{ [from Eq. (1)]}$$

$$\Rightarrow \quad W = 2mgh$$

Hence $N = 2$.

6. Let P_1 and P_2 be the respective pressures in the top and bottom chambers, at equilibrium. The figure shows the forces acting on the piston. If A is the cross-section area of the piston, then

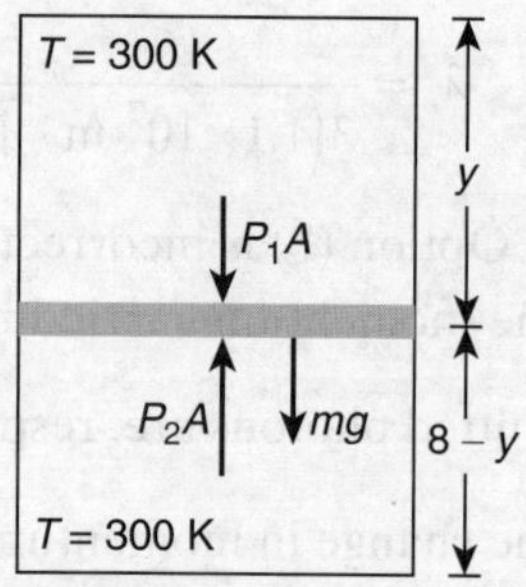

$$P_2A = P_1A + \text{mg}$$

$$\Rightarrow \quad P_2 - P_1 = \frac{mg}{A}$$

$$\Rightarrow \quad \frac{\mu RT}{A(8-y)} - \frac{\mu RT}{Ay} = \frac{mg}{A}$$

$$\Rightarrow \quad \frac{1}{8-y} - \frac{1}{y} = \frac{mg}{\mu RT} = \frac{8.3 \times 10}{0.1 \times 8.3 \times 300}$$

$$\Rightarrow \quad \frac{2y-8}{8y-y^2} = \frac{1}{3}$$

$$\Rightarrow \quad y^2 - 2y - 2y = 0$$

$$\Rightarrow \quad y = 6 \text{ [neglecting the −ve solution]}$$

Numerical Value Answer

1. The figure shows the forces acting on the scale at any instant. For rotational equilibrium, we have

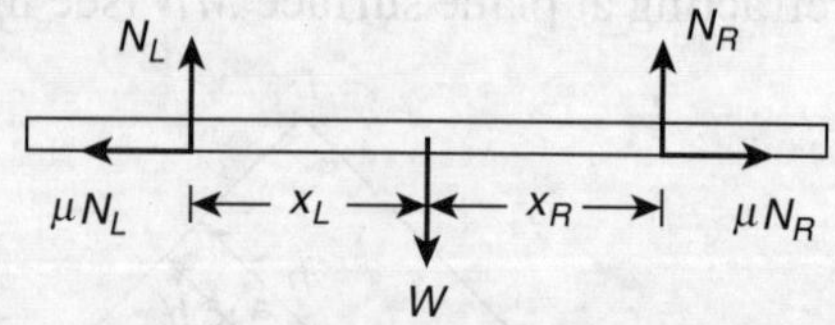

$$N_L x_L = N_R x_R$$

$$\Rightarrow \quad \frac{N_L}{x_L} = \frac{N_R}{x_R}$$

$$\Rightarrow \quad N_L \propto x_R \text{ and } N_R \propto x_L$$

Initially, the left finger experiences a smaller friction force than the right finger, and hence starts moving first. First stop of the moving left finger occurs when

$$0.32\, N_L = 0.40\, N_R$$

$$\Rightarrow \quad 0.32\, x_R = 0.40\, x_L$$

$$\Rightarrow \quad x_L = \frac{0.32}{0.40}x_R = \frac{32}{40}(40 \text{ cm}) = 32 \text{ cm}$$

Now the right finger moves and stops when

$$0.40|\, N_L = 0.32\, N_R$$

$$\Rightarrow \quad 0.40\, x_R = 0.32\, x_L$$

$$\Rightarrow \quad x_R = \frac{0.32}{0.40}x_L = \frac{32}{40}(32 \text{ cm}) = 25.6 \text{ cm}$$

2. If the pressures on two sides of a liquid surface are different, then the liquid surface becomes curved. If the radii of the surface in two mutually perpendicular directions are r_1, r_2 and ΔP is the pressure difference, then we have the result $\Delta P = \frac{S}{r_1} + \frac{S}{r_2}$, where S is the surface tension of the liquid.

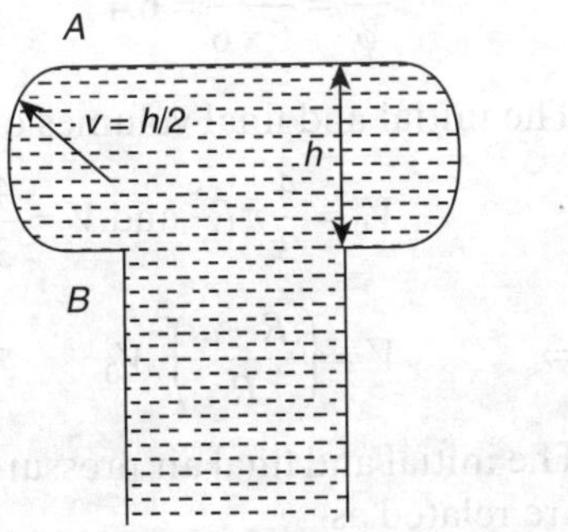

For the liquid surface shown in the figure, the outside pressure is P_0(atmospheric pressure). The inside pressure varies from 0 at the highest point A to $P_0 + \rho gh$ at the lowest point B. So the average pressure on the inside is

$$P = \frac{P_0 + P_0 + \rho gh}{2} = P_0 + \frac{1}{2}\rho gh$$

The pressure difference is

$$\Delta P = P - P_0 = \frac{1}{2}\rho gh$$

The radii of the liquid surface are $r = \frac{h}{2}$ in one direction and ∞ in the perpendicular direction. Hence, we have

$$\Delta P = \frac{S}{r} + \frac{S}{\infty}$$

$$\Rightarrow \quad \frac{1}{2}\rho gh = \frac{S}{h/2}$$

$$\Rightarrow \quad h = \sqrt{\frac{4S}{\rho g}} = \sqrt{\frac{4 \times 0.07}{10^3 \times 10}} = 5.30 \text{ mm}$$

3. The electric field due to a dipole at distance d along its axis has magnitude $E = \frac{2p}{4\pi\epsilon_0 d^3}$, where p is the dipole moment. So when the charged particle is in equilibrium, we have

$$q\left(\frac{2p}{4\pi\epsilon_0 l^3}\right) = kl \quad \ldots(1)$$

Now, when the charged particle is at a portion x from its equilibrium position, the restring force is

$$F_{\text{res}} = k(l+x) - \frac{2pq}{4\pi\epsilon_0 (l+x)^3}$$

$$= k(l+x) - \frac{kl^4}{(l+x)^3} \quad \text{[Using Eq. (1)]}$$

$$= k(l+x) - kl\left(1+\frac{x}{l}\right)^{-3}$$

$$= k(l+x) - kl\left(1-\frac{3x}{l}\right)$$

$$[(1+x)^n = 1+nx \text{ for small } x]$$

$$= 4kx$$

The instantaneous acceleration is

$$a = \frac{F_{\text{res}}}{m} = \frac{4k}{m}x$$

Hence, oscillation frequency is $= \frac{1}{2\pi}\sqrt{\frac{4k}{m}} = \frac{1}{\pi}\sqrt{\frac{k}{m}}$

4.

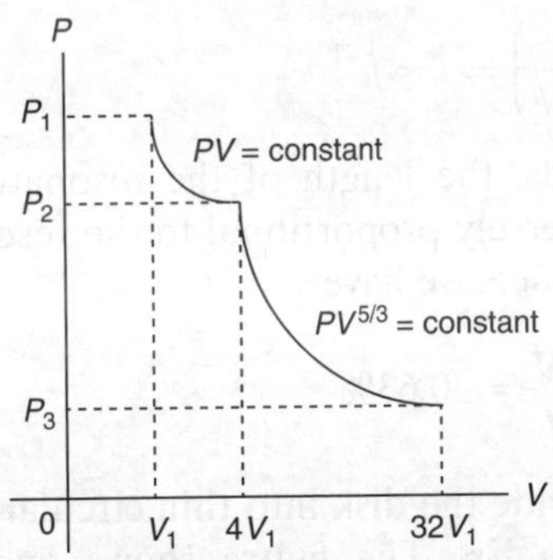

The figure shows the PV diagram of the process. At the end of the isothermal expansion, the pressure P_2 is given by

$$P_2(4V) = P_1V_1 \Rightarrow P_2 = \frac{P_1}{4}$$

At the end of the adiabatic expansion, the pressure P_3 is given by

$$P_3(32V_1)^{5/3} = \frac{P_1}{4}(4V_1)^{5/3} \Rightarrow P_3 = \frac{P_1}{128}$$

Now, we have

$$W_{\text{isothermal}} = \mu RT \ln\left(\frac{V_2}{V_1}\right)$$

$$= P_1V_1 \ln\left(\frac{4V_1}{V_1}\right) = 2P_1V_1 \ln 2$$

and $W_{\text{adiabatic}} = -\frac{\Delta(PV)}{\gamma - 1}$

$$= -\frac{\left(\frac{P_1}{128}\right)(32V_1) - \left(\frac{P_1}{4}\right)(4V_1)}{\gamma - 1}$$

$$= \frac{9}{8}P_1V_1$$

Hence, we have

$$\frac{W_{\text{isothermal}}}{W_{\text{adiabatic}}} = \frac{2P_1V_1\ln 2}{\frac{9}{8}P_1V_1} = \frac{16}{9}\ln 2 = 1.78\ln 2$$

5. If the tuning fork approaches the pipe, the frequency received by the air in the pipe is

$$f' = \left(\frac{320}{320-2}\right)f = \left(1-\frac{2}{320}\right)^{-1} f = \left(1+\frac{1}{160}\right)f$$

$$\Rightarrow \quad f' - f = \left(\frac{1}{160}\right)f$$

$$\Rightarrow \quad \frac{\Delta f}{f} = \frac{100}{160}\% = 0.63\%$$

If the tuning fork would have moved away from the pipe, even then, the percentage change in frequency would have been the same but for a minus sign.

Now for resonance, we have

$$f = n\left(\frac{v}{2l}\right) \Rightarrow l \propto f^{-1}$$

In other words, the length of the resonating air column is inversely proportional to the resonance frequency. Hence, we have

$$\frac{\Delta l}{l} = -\frac{\Delta f}{f} = -0.63\%$$

6. Let us sub-divide the disk into thin circular rings, each of width dx. The figure shows one such element ring of radius x. The charge is this element ring is

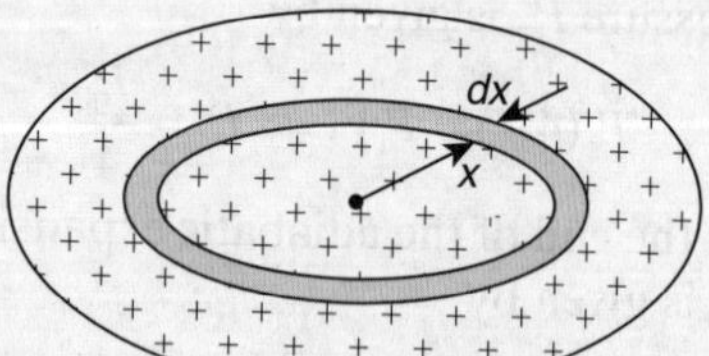

$$dq = (2\pi x dx)\sigma(x) = 2\pi\sigma_0\left(1-\frac{x}{R}\right)xdx$$

$$= 2\pi\sigma_0\left(x-\frac{x^2}{R}\right)dx$$

Thus, we have

$$\epsilon_0\phi_0 = 2\pi\sigma_0\int_0^R\left(x-\frac{x^2}{R}\right)dx$$

$$= 2\pi\sigma_0\left|\frac{x^2}{2}-\frac{x^3}{3R}\right|_0^R = 2\pi\sigma_0\left(\frac{R^2}{6}\right)$$

and

$$\epsilon_0\phi = 2\pi\sigma_0\int_0^{R/4}\left(x-\frac{x^2}{R}\right)dx$$

$$= 2\pi\sigma_0\left|\frac{x^2}{2}-\frac{x^3}{3R}\right|_0^{R/4} = 2\pi\sigma_0\left(\frac{5R^2}{192}\right)$$

Hence, we have

$$\frac{\phi_0}{\phi} = \frac{192}{5\times 6} = 6.4$$

7. The initial and final volumes of the bubble are

$$V_0 = \frac{4}{3}\pi R^3 \text{ and } V = \frac{4}{3}\pi(R-a)^3$$

$$\Rightarrow \quad V = \left(\frac{R-a}{R}\right)^3 V_0$$

The initial and final air pressures inside the bubble are related as

$$PV^{\gamma} = P_0V_0^{\gamma}$$

$$\Rightarrow \quad P = \left(\frac{V_0}{V}\right)^{\gamma} P_0$$

$$\Rightarrow \quad P = \left(\frac{R-a}{R}\right)^{-3\gamma} P_0$$

Work done by the air inside the bubble is

$$W = -\frac{\Delta(PV)}{\gamma-1} = -\frac{PV-P_0V_0}{\gamma-1}$$

$$= \frac{1}{\gamma-1}\left[P_0V_0\left(\frac{R-a}{R}\right)^{3-3\gamma} - P_0V_0\right]$$

$$= -\frac{P_0V_0}{\gamma-1}\left[\left(1-\frac{a}{R}\right)^{3-3\gamma} - 1\right]$$

$$= -\frac{P_0V_0}{\gamma-1}\left[(3\gamma-3)\frac{a}{R}\right]$$

$$[(1+x)^n = 1+nx \text{ for small } x]$$

$$= -\frac{3a}{R}P_0V_0.$$

Now, inserting $V_0 = \frac{4}{3}\pi R^3$, we get the magnitude of the work as

$$W = \frac{3a}{R}P_0 \times \frac{4}{3}\pi R^3 = 4\pi P_0 a R^2$$

Hence $X = 1$.

8. After the temperature is increased, the resistance R_3 becomes

$$R = (1 + 0.0004 \times 100)\, 300\ \Omega$$
$$= 1.04 \times 300\ \Omega = 312\ \Omega$$

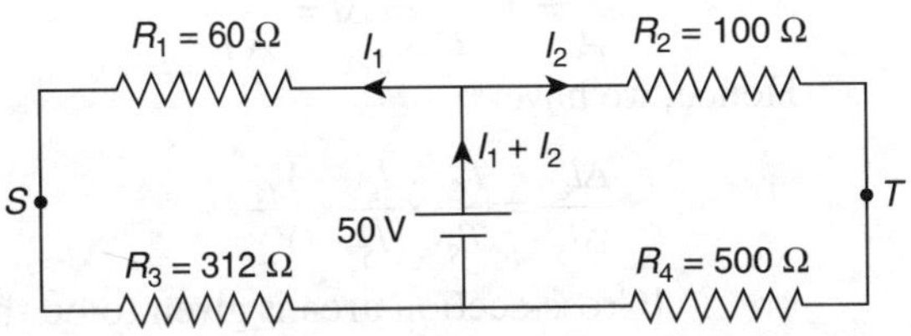

The figure shows the current distribution. Their values are

$$I_1 = \frac{50\ \text{V}}{60 + 312} = \frac{50}{372}\ \text{A}$$

and $$I_2 = \frac{50\ \text{V}}{100 + 500} = \frac{50}{600}\ \text{A}$$

The potential difference between points S and T are

$$V_{ST} = |I_1 R_1 - I_2 R_2|$$
$$= \left| \frac{50}{372} \times 60 - \frac{50}{600} \times 100 \right| \text{V} = 0.27\ \text{V}$$

9. The equivalent capacitance for series combination is given by

$$\frac{1}{C} = \frac{1}{C_1} + \frac{1}{C_2}.$$

Inserting $C_1 = 2000$ pF, $C_2 = 3000$ pF gives $C = 1200$ pF. Taking the differential of the above equation, we have

$$\frac{\Delta C}{C^2} = \frac{\Delta C_1}{C_1^2} + \frac{\Delta C_2}{C_2^2}$$

$$\Rightarrow \quad \frac{\Delta C}{C} = \left[\frac{\Delta C_1}{C_1^2} + \frac{\Delta C_2}{C_2^2} \right] C$$

Inserting the values, we have

$$\frac{\Delta C}{C} = \left[\frac{10}{2000^2} + \frac{15}{3000^2} \right] 1200$$
$$= \left(\frac{5}{2} + \frac{5}{3} \right) \frac{12}{100} = \frac{25}{6} \times 12\% = 0.5\%$$

Energy shored in the capacitors is given by $E = \frac{1}{2} CV^2$. The percentage error in the calculation of energy is given by

$$\frac{\Delta E}{E} = \frac{\Delta C}{C} + 2\frac{\Delta V}{V} = 0.5\% + 2\left(\frac{0.02}{5} \right)$$
$$= 0.5\% + 0.8\% = 1.3\%$$

10. The change in pressure is

$$P = \rho g h = 103 \times 10 \times 5000\ \text{Pa} = 5 \times 10^7\ \text{Pa}$$

The fractional change in volume is

$$\frac{\Delta V}{V} = -\frac{\Delta P}{B} = -\frac{5 \times 10^7}{70 \times 10^9} = -\frac{5}{7000}$$

The volume of the cube is given by $V = a^3$. Hence, we have

$$\frac{\Delta V}{V} = 3\frac{\Delta a}{a}$$

$$\Rightarrow \quad \Delta a = \left(\frac{\Delta V}{V} \right) \frac{a}{3}$$
$$= -\frac{5}{7000} \times \frac{1000\ \text{mm}}{3} = -0.24\ \text{mm}$$

11. At steady state, the currents in the left and right circuits are, respectively

$$I_1 = \frac{5\ \text{V}}{5} = 1\ \text{A and } I_2 = \frac{20\ \text{V}}{10} = 2\ \text{A}$$

Total work done by the batteries is

$$W_{\text{batt}} = \frac{1}{2} L_1 I_1^2 + \frac{1}{2} L_1 I_1^2 + M I_1 I_2$$
$$= \frac{1}{2}(10\ \text{mH})(1\ \text{A})^2 + \frac{1}{2}(20\ \text{mH})(2\ \text{A})^2$$
$$+ (5\ \text{mH})(1\ \text{A})(2\ \text{A})$$
$$= 5\ \text{mJ} + 40\ \text{mJ} + 10\ \text{mJ} = 55\ \text{mJ}$$

12. The rate at which energy is absorbed by the water

$$P = (700\ \text{W/m}^2)(0.05\ \text{m}^2) = 35\ \text{J/s}$$

This will cause a rise in temperature at the rate

$$\frac{dT}{dt} = \frac{P}{ms}$$

On the other hand, radiation will cause a decrease in temperature at the rate

$$\frac{dT}{dt} = c\Delta T, \text{[Newton's law of cooling]}$$

where ΔT is the temperature of water above the surrounding temperature.

After a long time, when the water reaches equilibrium, we have

$$c\Delta T = \frac{P}{ms}$$

$$\Rightarrow \quad \Delta T = \frac{P}{cms} = \frac{35}{0.001 \times 1 \times 4200} = 8.33\ ^\circ\text{C}$$

13. The force acting on the particle is given to be $\mathbf{F} = -y\mathbf{i} - 2x\mathbf{j}$. Let us sub-divide the path into small displacement vectors $d\mathbf{r} = dx\mathbf{i} + dy\mathbf{j}$. The expression for work done by the force $\mathbf{F}$ from any one point, say P, to another point, say Q, is given by

$$W = \int_P^Q \mathbf{F}\cdot d\mathbf{r} = -\int_P^Q (ydx + 2xdy)$$

Now, we have to perform the above integral separately for all the different paths.

For path AB, we have $y = 1$ and $dy = 0$. Hence

$$W_{AB} = -\int_0^1 1dx = -1\text{ J}$$

For path BC, we have $x = 1$ and $dx = 0$. Hence

$$W_{BC} = -\int_1^{0.5} 2dy = -2(0.5 - 1)\text{ J} = 1\text{ J}$$

For path CD, we have $y = 0.5$ and $dy = 0$. Hence

$$W_{CD} = -\int_1^{0.5} 0.5dx = -0.5(0.5 - 1)\text{ J} = 0.25\text{ J}$$

For path DE, we have $x = 0.5$ and $dx = 0$. Hence

$$W_{DE} = -\int_{0.5}^{0} 1dy = -1(0 - 0.5)\text{ J} = 0.5\text{ J}$$

For path EF, we have $y = 0$ and $dy = 0$. Hence

$$W_{EF} = 0\text{ J}$$

For path FA, we have $x = 0$ and $dx = 0$. Hence

$$W_{FA} = 0\text{ J}$$

Hence, we have

$$W_{\text{cycle}} = (-1 + 1 + 0.25 + 0.5 + 0 + 0)\text{ J} = 0.75\text{ J}$$

14. The figure shows the force acting on the block. Let T_C and T_S be the tensions in the copper and steel wires, respectively. Then, for equilibrium, we have

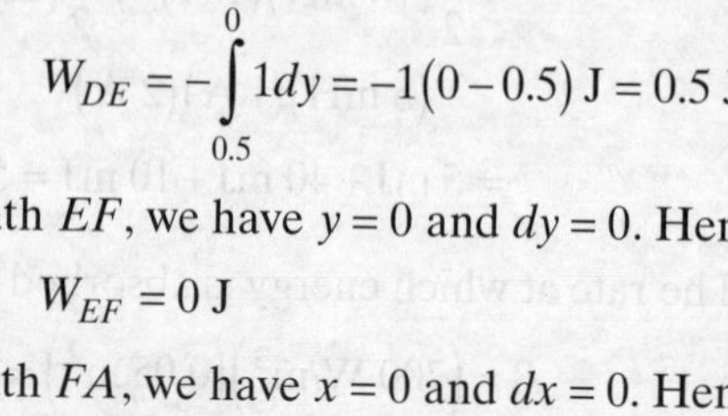

$$\frac{T_C}{\sin(90° + 60°)} = \frac{T_S}{\sin(90° + 30°)}$$

$$\Rightarrow \quad \frac{T_C}{\cos(60°)} = \frac{T_S}{\cos(30°)}$$

$$\Rightarrow \quad \frac{T_C}{1} = \frac{T_S}{\sqrt{3}}$$

Now, the tension and elongation in a wire are related as

$$\frac{T}{A} = Y\frac{\Delta l}{l} \Rightarrow \Delta l = \frac{Tl}{AY}$$

Hence, we have

$$\frac{\Delta l_C}{\Delta l_S} = \frac{T_C}{T_S} \times \frac{l_C}{l_S} \times \frac{Y_C}{Y_C}$$

[Cross-section area is given to be the same]

$$\Rightarrow \quad \frac{\Delta l_C}{\Delta l_S} = \frac{1}{\sqrt{3}} \times \sqrt{3} \times 2 = 2$$

15.

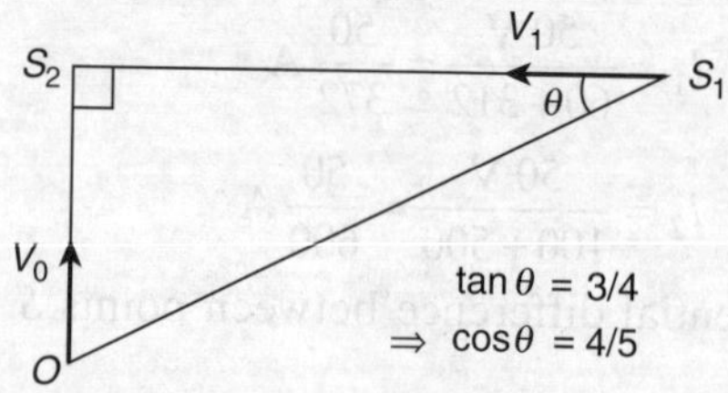

The velocities of the source S_1 and the observer O in SI units are, respectively, $v_1 = 108 \times \frac{5}{18}$ m/s = 30 m/s and $v_0 = 36 \times \frac{5}{18}$ m/s = 10 m/s. The frequencies received by the observer from sources S_1 and S_2 are, respectively

$$f_1 = \left(\frac{v}{v - v_1\cos,}\right)f = \left(\frac{320}{320 - 30 \times \frac{4}{5}}\right)120\text{ Hz}$$

$$= \left(\frac{55}{51}\right)120\text{ Hz}$$

and $$f_2 = \left(\frac{v + v_0}{v}\right)f = \left(\frac{330 + 10}{330}\right)120\text{ Hz}$$

$$= \left(\frac{34}{33}\right)120\text{ Hz}$$

Hence, the beat frequency heard by the observer is

$$|f_1 - f_2| = \left(\frac{55}{51} - \frac{34}{33}\right)120\text{ Hz}$$

$$= \frac{81 \times 120}{51 \times 33}\text{ Hz} = 5.78\text{ Hz}$$

16. The capacitance of the mth layer is

$$dC_m = K_m\left(\frac{\epsilon_0 A}{\delta}\right) = \left(\frac{\epsilon_0 A}{d/N}\right)K\left(1 + \frac{m}{N}\right)$$

$$= \frac{K\epsilon_0 AN}{d}\left(1 + \frac{m}{N}\right)$$

Since all the dielectric layers are in series, the equivalent capacitance is given by

$$\frac{1}{C}=\sum_{m=1}^{N}\frac{1}{dC_m}=\frac{d}{K\epsilon_0 A}\times\frac{1}{N}\sum_{m=1}^{N}\frac{1}{1+\frac{m}{N}}$$

For large N, the above sum reduces to

$$\frac{1}{C}=\frac{d}{K\epsilon_0 A}\int_0^1\left(\frac{1}{1+x}\right)dx$$

$$=\frac{d}{K\epsilon_0 A}\left|\ln|1+x|\right|_0^1=\frac{d\ln 2}{K\epsilon_0 A}$$

$$\Rightarrow \quad C=\frac{K\epsilon_0 A}{d\ln 2}$$

Hence $\alpha=1$.

17. Let s, L be the specific heat capacity and latent heat of vaporization of the liquid, and let S be the heat capacity of the calorimeter.

The first 5 g completely evaporates and thereafter no liquid evaporates. This means that the temperature of the calorimeter has fallen to the boiling temperature of 80 °C of the liquid. Equating the energy absorbed by the 5 g liquid with the energy released by the calorimeter, we have

$$5\text{ g}\left[s(80°\text{C}-30°\text{C})+L\right]=S(110°\text{C}-80°\text{C})$$

$$\Rightarrow \quad 5\text{ g}(50s+L)=30S \qquad \ldots(1)$$

Equating the energy absorbed by the next 80 g liquid with the energy released by the calorimeter, we have

$$80\text{ g}\left[s(50°\text{C}-30°\text{C})\right]=S(80°\text{C}-50°\text{C})$$

$$\Rightarrow \quad 80\text{ g}(20s)=30S \qquad \ldots(2)$$

From equations (1) and (2), we have

$$5(50s+L)=80(20s)$$

$$\Rightarrow \quad 50s+L=320s$$

$$\Rightarrow \quad 270s-L$$

$$\Rightarrow \quad \frac{L}{s}=270$$

18.

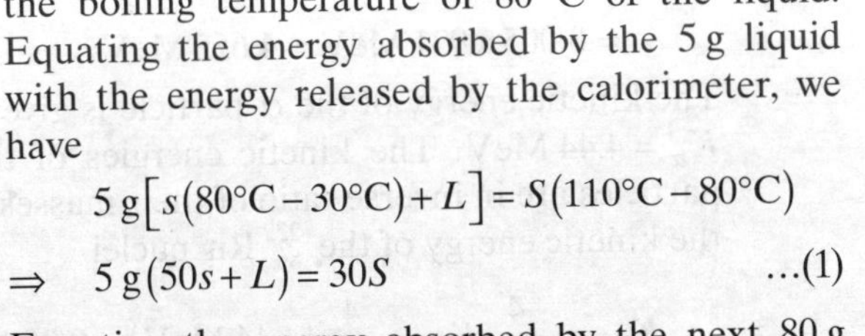

To find the maximum time taken by a light ray to travel through the structure, we need to find the longest path that light would follow inside the structure. Distance travelled by light will be longest when angle α (see figure) is smallest, that is, just greater than the critical angle. Thus, for the longest distance path $\sin\alpha=\frac{n_2}{n_1}$. In that case, the total distance travelled by the light is

$$S=\sum s=\sum\frac{p}{\sin\alpha}=\frac{n_1}{n_2}\sum p=\frac{n_1}{n_2}L$$

Inside the structure, light travels with speed c/n_1. Hence, the maximum time taken by a light ray to travel through the structure is

$$T=\frac{S}{c/n_1}=\frac{n_1}{c}\times\frac{n_1 L}{n_2}=\frac{1.5^2\,(9.6)}{1.44\left(3\times10^8\right)}\text{s}=5\times10^{-9}\text{ s}$$

Hence $t=5$.

19. Let $R_1, R_2, R_3, \ldots$ be the successive ranges (distance between projection and landing), and $T_1, T_2, T_3, \ldots$ be the successive flight times (time between projection and landing).

The total displacement of the projectile is

$$R=R_1+R_2+R_3+\ldots\infty \text{ terms}$$

$$=\frac{u_0^2\sin(2\theta)}{g}+\frac{u_0^2\sin(2\theta)}{\alpha^2 g}+\frac{u_0^2\sin(2\theta)}{\alpha^4 g}+\ldots\infty \text{ terms}$$

$$=R_1\left[1+\frac{1}{\alpha^2}+\frac{1}{\alpha^4}+\ldots\infty\text{ terms}\right]$$

$$=R_1\left(\frac{1}{1-\frac{1}{\alpha^2}}\right)=R_1\left(\frac{\alpha^2}{\alpha^2-1}\right)$$

The total flight time of the projectile is

$$T=T_1+T_2+T_3+\ldots\infty\text{ terms}$$

$$=\frac{2u_0\sin\theta}{g}+\frac{2u_0\sin\theta}{-g}+\frac{2u_0\sin\theta}{\alpha^2 g}+\ldots\infty\text{ terms}$$

$$=T_1\left[1+\frac{1}{\alpha}+\frac{1}{\alpha^2}+\ldots\infty\text{ terms}\right]$$

$$=T_1\left(\frac{1}{1-\frac{1}{\alpha}}\right)=T_1\left(\frac{\alpha}{\alpha-1}\right)$$

The average velocity of the projectile is

$$V=\frac{R}{T}=\frac{R_1}{T_1}\left(\frac{\alpha^2}{\alpha^2-1}\right)\left(\frac{\alpha-1}{\alpha}\right)=V_1\left(\frac{\alpha}{\alpha+1}\right)$$

According to the question, we have

$$\frac{\alpha}{\alpha+1}=0.8 \text{ gives } \alpha=4$$

20. The moving rod produces a steady emf of value

$$\xi=vlB=(1\text{ cm/s})(10\text{ cm})(1\text{ T})=10^{-3}\text{ V}=1\text{ mV}$$

The circuit is an $L-R$ circuit with time constant

$$\tau=\frac{L}{R}=\frac{1\text{ mH}}{1\,\Omega}=1\text{ ms}$$

and a steady state current

$$I_0=\frac{\xi}{R}=\frac{1\text{ mV}}{1\,\Omega}=1\text{ mA}$$

The current through the circuit is given by

$$I(t)=I_0\left[1-e^{-t/\tau}\right]=1\text{ mA}\left[1-e^{-t(\text{ms})^{-1}}\right]$$

The current through the circuit at time $t=1$ ms is

$$I(1\text{ ms})=1\text{ mA}\left[1-e^{-1}\right]=1\text{ mA}[1-0.37]=0.63\text{ mA}$$

21.

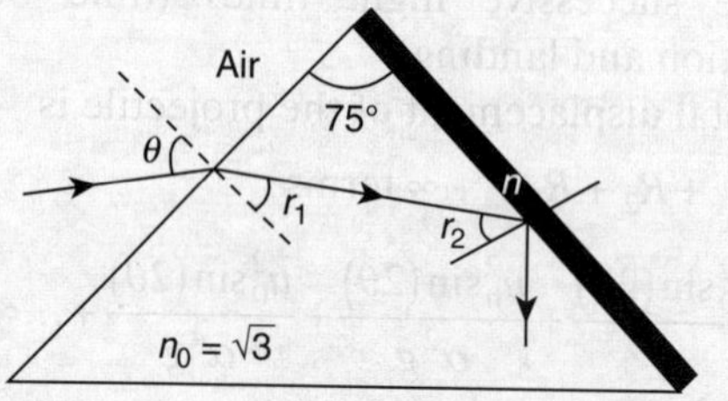

Let r_1, r_2 be the refraction angles inside the prism (see figure). Then we have.

$$\sin\theta=\sqrt{3}\sin r_1 \quad \text{[From Snell's law]} \quad \ldots(1)$$

and $$r_1+r_2=75° \quad \text{[From geometry]} \quad \ldots(2)$$

It is given that $\theta \le 60°$. Thus, we have

$$\sin\theta \le \sin 60°$$

$\Rightarrow$ $\sqrt{3}\sin r_1 \le \sqrt{3}/2$ [Using equation (1)]

$\Rightarrow$ $\sin r_1 \le 1/2$

$\Rightarrow$ $r_1 \le 30°$

$\Rightarrow$ $75°-r_2 \le 30°$ [Using equation (2)]

$\Rightarrow$ $r_2 \ge 45°$

Therefore, for total internal reflection to occur at the second refracting surface of the prism, for all values of $\theta \le 60°$, the critical angle $C=\sin^{-1}\left(\frac{n}{\sqrt{3}}\right)$ must be less than 45°. Thus, we have

$$\frac{n}{\sqrt{3}} \le \sin 45°$$

$\Rightarrow$ $n \le \sqrt{3}/\sqrt{3}$

$\Rightarrow$ $n^2 \le 1.5$

22. Each photon carries momentum equal to h/λ. When it rebounds elastically from the mirror surface, it transfers a momentum $2h/\lambda$ to the mirror. For N photons colliding with the mirror, the total momentum transferred to the mirror is

$$p=N\left(\frac{2h}{\lambda}\right)$$

The velocity acquired by the mirror is $v=\frac{p}{M}=\frac{2Nh}{\lambda M}$.

The displacement amplitude is given to be A and the angular frequency of the spring-mirror system is given to be Ω. Then the peak velocity v of the system equals ΩA. Thus, we have

$$\frac{2Nh}{\lambda M}=\Omega A$$

$$\Rightarrow \quad N=\frac{M\Omega}{2h}\times\lambda A=\frac{10^{24}}{8\pi}\times(8\pi\times10^{-6})(10^{-6})$$

$$=1\times10^{12}$$

Hence, $x=1$

23. The energy released in the reaction is

$$Q=[226.005-(222.000+4.000)]931\text{ MeV}$$
$$=0.005\times931\text{ MeV}=4.655\text{ MeV}$$

The kinetic energy of the α particle is given to be $K_\alpha=4.44$ MeV. The kinetic energies of the two particles are in inverse ratio of their masses. Thus, the kinetic energy of the $^{222}_{86}$Rn nuclei

$$K_{\text{Rn}}=\frac{4}{222}K_\alpha=\frac{4}{222}(4.44\text{ MeV})=0.08\text{ MeV}$$

The energy available for excitation of the $^{222}_{86}$Rn nuclei is

$$E_{\text{exc}}=Q-(K_\alpha+K_{\text{Rn}})$$
$$=4.655\text{ MeV}-(4.44\text{ MeV}+0.08\text{ MeV})$$
$$=0.130\text{ MeV}$$

Hence, the energy of the gamma photon released by the excited $^{222}_{86}$Rn nuclei is 0.130 MeV = 130 keV.

24. The least count of the measuring scale is $\frac{1}{4}$ cm = 0.25 cm. Thus, the measured values of the object and the image positions are, respectively, $u=-30\text{ cm}\pm0.25\text{ cm}$ and $v=60\text{ cm}\pm0.25\text{ cm}$. The focal length of the lens is given by

$$\frac{1}{f}=\frac{1}{v}-\frac{1}{u}$$

Putting $u=-30$ cm, $v=60$ cm gives $f=20$ cm. Taking the differential of the above equation, we have

$$\frac{\Delta f}{f^2} = \frac{\Delta v}{v^2} - \frac{\Delta u}{u^2}$$

$$\Rightarrow \quad \frac{\Delta f}{f} = \left[\frac{\Delta v}{v^2} + \frac{-\Delta u}{u^2}\right] f$$

Hence, the maximum percentage error in determining the focal length is

$$\frac{\Delta f}{f} = \left[\frac{0.25}{60^2} + \frac{0.25}{30^2}\right] 20$$

$$= \left(\frac{1}{36} + \frac{1}{9}\right)\frac{5}{100} = \frac{5}{36} \times 5\% = 0.69\%$$

Match the Lists

1. (b) The fundamental frequency of a string fixed at both ends is given by $f = \frac{1}{2L}\sqrt{\frac{T}{\mu}}$. In the given question, all the strings are under the same tension T_0, and their lengths can be varied between L_0 and $2L_0$. However, we need to find the highest fundamental frequency, which will occur when the length is kept shortest. So, in determining the highest fundamental frequency, all the strings have to be of the same length L_0.
Hence, the highest fundamental frequencies of strings 1, 2, 3 and 4 are, respectively

$$f_1 = \frac{1}{2L_0}\sqrt{\frac{T_0}{\mu}} = f_0 \text{ (string 1)}$$

$$f_2 = \frac{1}{2L_0}\sqrt{\frac{T_0}{2\mu}} = \frac{1}{\sqrt{2}} f_0 \text{ (string 2)}$$

$$f_3 = \frac{1}{2L_0}\sqrt{\frac{T_0}{3\mu}} = \frac{1}{\sqrt{3}} f_0 \text{ (string 3)}$$

$$f_4 = \frac{1}{2L_0}\sqrt{\frac{T_0}{4\mu}} = \frac{1}{2} f_0 \text{ (string 4)}$$

2. (b) The natural frequencies of a string fixed at both ends are given by $f = \frac{n}{2L}\sqrt{\frac{T}{\mu}}$. Then the tension in the string is given by $f = \frac{4f\mu L^2}{n^2}$.
In the given question. All the strings are vibrating with the same frequency $f_0 = \frac{1}{2L_0}\sqrt{\frac{T_0}{\mu}}$ but in different harmonics. Hence, the tensions in the strings 1, 2, 3 and 4 are, respectively

$$T_1 = \frac{4f_0\mu L_0^2}{1^2} = T_0 \text{ (string 1)}$$

$$T_2 = \frac{4f_0(2\mu)}{3^2}\frac{9L_0^2}{4} = \frac{1}{2}T_0 \text{ (string 2)}$$

$$T_3 = \frac{4f_0(3\mu)}{5^2}\frac{25L_0^2}{16} = \frac{3}{16}T_0 \text{ (string 3)}$$

$$T_4 = \frac{4f_0(4\mu)}{14^2}\frac{49L_0^2}{16} = \frac{1}{16}T_0 \text{ (string 4)}$$

3. (b) The question defines a thermodynamic quantity $X = \frac{3}{2}R\ln\left(\frac{T}{T_A}\right) + R\ln\left(\frac{V}{V_A}\right)$ for one mole of a monoatomic ideal gas. If write this quantity as $X = \frac{3}{2}R\ln T + R\ln V + \text{constant}$, and then take its differential, then we have

$$\Delta X = \frac{3}{2}R\frac{\Delta T}{T} + R\frac{\Delta V}{V}$$

Now the question says that infinitesimal heat absorbed is given by $\Delta Q = T\Delta X$. Thus, we have

$$\Delta Q = \frac{3}{2}R\Delta T + \frac{RT}{V}\Delta V$$

$$\Rightarrow \quad \Delta Q = c_V\Delta T + P\Delta V \quad \text{[For one mole of the monoatomic gas]}$$

$$\Rightarrow \quad \Delta Q = \Delta U + \Delta W$$

Here, the question tells us how to calculate the heat absorbed by the gas. However, it is not new information because it is simply the first law of thermodynamics. So this information in the question is irrelevant.

It is given that $P_0V_0 = \frac{1}{3}RT_0$. The temperatures at the states 1, 2 and 3 are, respectively

$$T_1 = \frac{P_0V_0}{R} = \frac{1}{3}T_0 \text{ (state 1)},$$

$$T_2 = \frac{P_0(2V_0)}{R} = \frac{2}{3}T_0 \text{ (state 2)}$$

$$T_3 = \frac{\left(\frac{3P_0}{2}\right)(2V_0)}{R} = T_0 \text{ (state 3)}$$

Thus, we have

$$W_{123} = P_0(2V_0 - V_0) = P_0V_0 = \frac{1}{3}RT_0$$

$$\Delta U_{123} = \frac{3}{2}R\left(T_0 - \frac{1}{3}T_0\right) = RT_0$$

$$Q_{123} = RT_0 + \frac{1}{3}RT_0 = \frac{4}{3}RT_0$$

$$Q_{12} = \frac{3}{2}R\left(\frac{2}{3}T_0 - \frac{1}{3}T_0\right) + P_0(2V_0 - V_0)$$

$$= \frac{1}{2}RT_0 + \frac{1}{3}RT_0 = \frac{5}{6}RT_0$$

4. (c) It is given that $P_0V_0 = \frac{1}{3}RT_0$. The pressures at states 1, 2 and 3 are, respectively

$$P_1 = \frac{R\left(\frac{T_0}{3}\right)}{V_0} = P_0 \text{ (state 1)}$$

$$P_2 = \frac{R\left(\frac{T_0}{3}\right)}{2V_0} = \frac{1}{2}P_0 \text{ (state 2)}$$

$$P_3 = \frac{RT_0}{2V_0} = \frac{3}{2}P_0 \text{ (state 3)}$$

Thus, we have

$$W_{123} = R\frac{T_0}{3}\ln\left(\frac{2V_0}{V_0}\right) = \frac{1}{3}RT_0\ln 2$$

$$\Delta U_{123} = \frac{3}{2}R\left(T_0 - \frac{1}{3}T_0\right) = RT_0$$

$$Q_{123} = RT_0 + \frac{1}{3}RT_0\ln 2 = \frac{1}{3}RT_0(3 + \ln 2)$$

$$Q_{12} = \frac{3}{2}R\left(\frac{1}{3}T_0 - \frac{1}{3}T_0\right) + R\frac{T_0}{3}\ln\left(\frac{2V_0}{V_0}\right)$$

$$= \frac{1}{3}RT_0\ln 2$$